LEND ME
YOUR EARS

OTHER BOOKS BY WILLIAM SAFIRE

LEND ME YOUR EARS

GREAT SPEECHES IN HISTORY

Updated and Expanded

Selected and Introduced by

WILLIAM SAFIRE

W. W. NORTON & COMPANY

New York • London

Copyright © 2004, 1997, 1992 by The Cobbett Corporation

All rights reserved
Printed in the United States of America

For information about permission to reproduce selections from this book, write to
Permissions, W. W. Norton & Company, Inc., 500 Fifth Avenue, New York, NY 10110

Manufacturing by LSC Communications, Crawfordsville, IN
Production manager: Andrew Marasia

Library of Congress Cataloging-in-Publication Data
Lend me your ears : great speeches in history / selected and introduced by William Safire.
p. cm.
"Updated and expanded."
Includes index.
ISBN 0-393-05931-6
1. Speeches, addresses, etc. I. Safire, William, 1929–
PN6122.L4 2004
808.85—dc22
2004013625

W. W. Norton & Company, Inc., 500 Fifth Avenue, New York, N.Y. 10110
www.wwnorton.com

W. W. Norton & Company Ltd., 15 Carlisle Street, London W1D 3BS

8 9 0

CONTENTS

III. Tributes and Eulogies

IV. Debates and Argumentation

V. Trials

VI. Gallows and Farewell Speeches

VII. Sermons

VIII. Inspirational Speeches

IX. Lectures and Instructive Speeches

X. Speeches of Social Responsibility

XI. Media Speeches

XII. Political Speeches

XIII. Commencement Speeches

XIV. Undelivered Speeches

Preface

A CURATOR AT the National Archives in Washington called one day and invited me over to take a look at a new exhibit before it opened. The archivist said there was an item in its "American Originals" presentation that would surely intrigue me.

So I went. There in the rotunda was the usual stuff: an early copy of the Magna Carta and one of the few copies of the Emancipation Proclamation in Lincoln's handwriting. Over on the side were some interesting curiosities: the canceled check for $7.2 million that purchased Alaska from Russia, along with John Wayne's World War II application to go to work for the OSS, our nascent spy agency.

But what grabbed my attention was a two-page typescript displayed in a glass case next to Lincoln's work. It was a memo from me when I was a White House speechwriter, dated July 18, 1969, when everyone was excited about our incipient landing on the moon. The subject line read "In the Event of Moon Disaster." It included a draft of a short speech that President Nixon would have made if the astronauts of *Apollo XI* were stranded on the moon and had to "close down communication" lest the peoples of the world would have to agonize with them as they starved to death. The somber speech was never delivered, of course—the moon shot initiated in the Kennedy era was a triumph for the United States and "all mankind"—but it had been filed away, forgotten for three decades until a reporter found it while digging around in the archives. The document has become one of the odd artifacts of that historic day, a sobering reminder of the risk the crew ran (and tragedy did strike a space shuttle crew years later). I include it at the end of the updated edition of this anthology in a new section of "undelivered speeches," along with quite different addresses drafted by or for Presidents Kennedy and Clinton that they did not use.

What struck me, peering down through the unbreakable glass into the case containing my treasured curiosity, was this question: When did a speech become a speech—when it was drafted or when it was given? The answer came just as quickly: Words on a page do not a speech make. Nor is a script a play, nor a screenplay a movie. What makes a draft speech a real speech is the speaking of it; but without that articulation, without the strong presence of the deliverer, without the audience to be aroused or moved, all you have is a polemic on a page. A speech is an event.

I looked to my right, at the larger glass case with the guard standing next to it. The document in it was no speech, either, and was not even much of an inspirational piece of writing; one eminent historian said its words had "all the moral fervor of a bill of lading." Lincoln, the greatest presidential speechwriter of all, chose to put his proclamation in sere, legalistic language because no fanfare was needed for such a monumental change of national direction. The stunning extension of human freedom, not to mention the largest seizure of property in history, was thunderbolt enough.

What if there had been television and streaming media and the Internet back in 1863? The wartime president could not have avoided presenting his unprecedented executive act of emancipation in a speech to the divided nation. If you are interested in speechwriting as an art form or in speech viewing as an actively involved member of an audience, take a crack at drafting such a speech. Your purpose is to rally your war-weary North to a greater cause than Union, which is wearing thin, and to stop antislavery Europe from trading with the South; at the same time, you do not want to trigger a bloody slave rebellion or lose border states or preclude peace negotiations with Confederate leaders. Your policy decision, after much private agonizing, had been made: to free the slaves in all states in rebellion, but not to free those in the slaveholding border states that did not secede. Now explain that in a speech to the nation in a way that advances all your morale-building, military, diplomatic, and moral goals.

Standing in that rotunda with its incongruous juxtaposition of writings on display, and turning that imaginary assignment over in my mind, this recovered speechwriter confronted the larger question, one of special interest to the reader hefting this volume: What is the single most important element in turning a speech into a memorable event? Is a "great" speech created by the dramatic occasion, or the persuasive style of the orator, or the eloquence of the words themselves?

Here's the answer:

The astute reader will note that the previous declarative sentence ends with a colon. The purpose of a colon is to signal a dramatic pause and point to what's coming next. And yet, nothing but this interruption follows "Here's the answer:" (it is not because I do not have an answer).

The even more astute reader will readily grasp the writerly manipulation under way. This is the preface to the third edition of an anthology of great speeches. Its primary purpose, like that of the book it introduces, is to instruct and inspire, largely by example, those interested in speech-making, speechwriting, and speech listening. (A secondary purpose is to provide a doorstop-sized reference for students of history and politics who want to examine primary sources beyond quotation-book snippets, which is probably why it has a wider readership than any of my language books or novels.)

The best way to begin an informal speech that does not deal with a crisis or tragedy is to tell a little story. If the anecdote is amusing, fine—that wakes up or relaxes an audience, whichever is required—but most attempts at humor from the lectern by noncomedians lay an egg. More reliable is a story about something poignant or instructive that has happened to you—neither funny nor tragic—and that connects to the theme of your speech. It gets personal without "getting personal."

In these introductory words, the visit to the Archives about the moon-shot draft speech was such an opening. They led quickly to the point about a speech being an event rather than a script and set up the imaginary Lincoln speech proclaiming emancipation. From there it was an easy transition to internal dialogue asking about the relative importance of occasion, presentation, and content. If this were a speech (and it's not—I used that device in the intro to the first edition, which follows this preface) we would be six or seven minutes along the way, and you'd want the answer to the relative-importance question.

Now here's my answer: "Great" speeches are made on occasions of emotional turmoil. The occasion can be a political victory or concession speech, a eulogy of a beloved figure, a summation at a murder trial or political show trial; it can be a prime minister's rallying a nation threatened by invasion or a president's consoling a nation after a disaster.

The next most important element in the formation of a speech deemed great is the forum. This can be a joint session of Congress or a national convention, an academic ceremony or a testimonial dinner, a battlefield or a deck of an aircraft carrier, a pulpit or a gallows or a grave. Such moments and such places cry out for momentous addresses and imbue efforts toward them with solemnity or at least seriousness. The newsworthy setting adds respect for the words just as the tradition-filled hall's dramatic echoes lend gravitas to the speaker's message.

Of course, content and its phrasing take advantage of occasion and forum to put a speech over the top in the making of history or the creation of a reputation. There is a caveat: Such a spotlight and its demanding audience call all the more attention to a weak speech or a bumbling speaker. New York Mayor John Lindsay strode on the national scene in a speech to Washington's Gridiron Club, where the tradition is for gentle, often self-mocking humor, followed by a short, serious conclusion; he told a series of off-color jokes and was no longer taken seriously on the national scene. Arkansas Governor Bill Clinton gave a tedious speech to bored Democratic conventioneers in 1988 and the only applause came when he said, "And in conclusion." (He was later taken seriously; his uplifting speech to Memphis ministers is collected here.)

But the moment and the milieu sharply focus the mind. Winston Churchill's speech after the military disaster that led to the evacuation of the British Army from Europe at Dunkirk—which he skillfully characterized as "a miracle of deliverance" even as he had to acknowledge a military disaster—is a great speech because it combined the elements of occasion, forum, and delivery of content. Not only was it an elegantly phrased explanation of the defeat culminating in a ringing "we shall fight on the beaches" peroration, not only was the prime minister's deep-throated delivery forcefully defiant in a hushed Parliament, and broadcast to the world, but the overriding reason was the historic occasion: at that moment tyranny was on the verge of victory, and democracy's main weapon was Churchill's rallying voice.

I will return to that tripod theme. But first let me tell you some of what I've discovered about speechifying during the years of gathering up and analyzing these addresses, ancient and modern.

Let me come clean about the possibility of textual error. When it comes to the accuracy of the report of some great speeches, it ain't necessarily so. Did Patrick Henry really deliver the speech in 1775 as you see it here? No written text exists; the inflammatory speech may have been wholly ad-libbed with no notes. Without a contemporaneous newspaper report at hand, we must rely on a biographer's account written forty years afterward. The only evidence that the inflammatory patriot's most famous exhortation is genuine comes from a motto on a flag of the Virginia militia that served under him: "Liberty or Death." I know not what course other anthologists may take, but as for me, I'll take whatever recollected text we have with a grain of salt.

The same applies to Oliver Cromwell's expression of displeasure to the English Parliament, concluding with the ultimate dismissal: "Depart, I say: and let us have done with you. In the name of God—go!" Not until two centuries after Cromwell's death did the historian Thomas Carlyle assemble bits and pieces of what the Lord Protector's contemporaries said he said into a half-quoted, half-narrated account. I include it here as the best approximation of what the regicidal spurner of a crown said that memorable day, but we should not assume—as many histories and quotation books do—the words attributed to him are from a transcript of Cromwell's dispersal of a legislature.

A similar simulation can happen here, and did recently. General George Patton's powerful exhortation, laced with pungent profanity, to American troops before D-Day—so forcefully delivered by the actor George C. Scott in the movie entitled *Patton*—is used to great effect by motivation gurus in and out of the military. But that was a fine scriptwriter's version of what Patton said just before the Normandy invasion. Other versions of the general's go-get-'em rouser can be found in the published *Patton Papers* and on the Internet. Evidently the controversial leader gave roughly the same speech several times to different groups of soldiers, and some took notes. No recording was made. I laid out all the accounts I could find, spoke to the editor of the *Patton Papers*, and, conjuring the ghost of Carlyle, assembled a good approximation of long excerpts from the salty, savage, inspiring pep talk by "Old Blood and Guts." But don't take a patchwork quilt for a blanket.

Now to a more general review: What about the technique of speechwriting and speechmaking—how is it changing, and why? (And in today's speeches and introductions, are we overusing the technique of internal dialogue?)

Major addresses—talks running forty minutes or more, laying out a comprehensive point of view, report, program, critique, case, or vision—have in recent years been going out of style. Happily for those who like a full meal of oratory, as well as for those who like the sound of their own voices, we still have exceptions to this squeezing down of oratory at quadrennial national political conventions and frequently in the U.S. Senate. But from commencement ceremonies to eulogies, from lectures to sermons, brevity is now considered the soul of wisdom as much as wit.

Speech doctors are performing major surgery. Sentences are shortening. (By a lot.) On television, time is money, and you'd better get your point across in a hurry or the channel-cruising viewer with the clicker at the ready will wipe your face from the screen. On the stump, the ripsnorting harangues of yesteryear are being replaced by instant coffee-klatches in primary season and air-kissing "drop-bys" at October fund-raisers. (When television news does cover a candidate's stump speaking, it is usually to show a reporter standing in front summarizing the muffled message in less than a half minute.) In lecture halls and garden clubs, nervous moderators ask speakers to hold their prepared remarks to twenty minutes and allow a half hour for Q. and A. At testimonial dinners, after-dinner speakers are warned that the audience is filled with overfed people who have been dragooned into attending and are worried about their baby-sitters at home. In the United States, though speech has never been freer, it has also never been shorter.

This does not presage the end of the formal, meat-and-potatoes spellbinder. As the more recent entries in this collection show, sustained eloquence is not dead. Whatever revolutionary changes may occur in the media of transmission and reception, I believe that human beings will continue to seek leadership or instruction through the speaking voice of another person who presents a position in an organized and persuasive fashion.

Certain elements of classic oratory are sure to remain: salutations, for example—from FDR's warm "My friends" to Napoleon's "Soldiers!" to Lenin's "Comrades"—will begin speeches, though the traditional "My countrymen" that used to open presidential inaugural addresses has now become "My fellow Americans," which more directly encompasses women, or the slightly less inclusive "My fellow citizens." (Unfortunately, the story of FDR addressing the Daughters of the American Revolution as "My fellow immigrants" is apocryphal. My favorite is the catchy opener by Demosthenes in his classic oration "On the Crown," directed at his accuser, Aeschines, an acolyte of Philip of Macedon: "Accursed scribbler!")

But there is no denying the trends in the new millennium toward brevity, toward personal interchange, toward visual aids (including a Big Brotherly image of a speaker's face on a huge screen alongside him), and toward conflict. President Bill Clinton's sermon-speech in a Memphis church is an example included herein of modern old-fashioned oratory, seen in person by hundreds. Another speech following his grand jury testimony—both the mild draft reported to have been prepared for him and the more defiant speech he gave—was short, pointed, and seen on television by tens of millions.

Because those who stage public presentations want large audiences, and because most members of those audiences want a show, the pressure is on to provide direct, personal conflict. In politics, debates between candidates delivering short speeches draw more attention than thoughtful or passionate (scorned as "set") speeches by stand-alone candidates about the issues being debated. The clash is the thing; the retort and riposte (exemplified by the Bentsen-Quayle debate herein) gets the play, as the return is watched more closely than the serve.

In the same way, the confrontational interview is more exciting and draws a more rapt audience than the thought-provoking conversation. In lecture halls across the United States, where celebrated guest speakers in every field draw substantial fees for an hour on stage (and I'm the last one to knock that), the trend has not only been toward setting aside half the time to answer questions from the floor, but toward the interview-speech, where the speaker's views are drawn out by the interviewer, thereby breaking up the presentation into easily chewable bites. The old suspension bridge between speaker and listener is shortened to an attention span.

A hybrid form of prepared address is coming into vogue to overcome the dismay of audiences that begin to fidget as soon as the person on the podium puts on spectacles and begins to read. That is the quasi-extemporaneous "building block" speech. In this presentation, the idea is to appear to be ad-libbing while not rambling off on tangents. The speaker maintains eye contact with the audience in a room that has not been darkened. He has before him a single, large index card with a dozen or so "talking points" on it. Each point is a building block—a subtheme illustrated by an anecdote or well-rehearsed riff—that can be assembled into a coherent talk. Some can be left out if time is short; fresh, topical blocks can be inserted to make the speech seem genuinely off-the-cuff. (That expression comes from notes surreptitiously made on a shirt cuff, perhaps by a student cheating on a test or by the progenitor of this technique.) For verisimilitude, the speaker will pause occasionally, seem to think about what he will say next, emit a few uhs and ahs, and plunge ahead toward the prepared peroration that has been fairly well committed to memory. I saw Charles de Gaulle do this at a state dinner in Paris to an audience of Americans who believed he was saying whatever came into his head. (The game was given away by an interpreter who had a written translation ready.)

Wait a minute. Before we indulge in longing for the good old days of Lincoln shouting out words he had written by candlelight to a throng that could hardly hear him, or decry the decline of the splendid oration, let us not forget (or, as Ronald Reagan would have said in his resolutely upbeat style, let us always remember) the past legions of stupefying orators. I have a leather-bound set of *Modern Eloquence* stuffing my bookshelf that every antiquarian bookseller is eager to push out the door. Though cheap enough, it was no bargain; I went through all twelve volumes, page by dreary page, and have inflicted none of its sustained somnolence on the reader of this collection.

Is there a future for truly modern eloquence? (We know the future is secure for internal dialogue.) Yes, but it will have to adapt to the new needs of the audience—more likely to be one person than a thousand—as driven by new methods of transmission. Radio, pioneered by Theodore Roosevelt (why didn't they use the invention to record the "speech that saved his life," as anthologized herein?), was used by his cousin Franklin to speak to millions in a person-to-person style, in contrast to declaiming to thousands, as Teddy did, in an orator-to-multitude style. Television made possible both the intimate, informal but teleprompted speech from a Queen Anne chair, with a wall of fake books in the background (they can have my *Modern Eloquence* set), and the use of a cheering crowd as backdrop to an eyeball contact with the viewer at home.

The convergence of television and computer screen, Internet and Outernet, may make possible interactive communication with tomorrow's speaker and an audience adept at video games. This would turn a formerly passive listener into a kind of participant in the speaker's remarks, deconstructing his text to fit the listener's preference or to reflect his anger. From a speaker's or speechwriter's viewpoint, the possibility of instantaneous worldwide or community-wide reaction by responding clickers would enable him to measure a speech's impact second by second and to adjust it on the fly to make a more favorable impression—unless the speaker preferred to pose as an iconoclast choosing rational persuasion rather than emotional manipulation. O brave new world, that might have such speeches in it.

I used to be a writer. Now my son, a Web site analyst, calls me a "content provider." "That's cool," as Lincoln wrote long before cool was cool. I believe that when the moment is critical, and when the forum or mode of communication is dramatic, then the content of what is said and the way it is spoken will result in what future generations will judge to be "a great speech." The novelist and prime minister Benjamin Disraeli said, "With words we govern men." (Three quotations in a single paragraph? There's a hard-and-fast speechwriting rule forbidding that. "I hate quotations," said Ralph Waldo Emerson. "Tell me what *you* know." That makes four; as long as we know the rules, we can break them.)

Do not begin by mining the gold in this book's speeches for nuggets, sound bites, or sight nibbles. Instead, place yourself in the moments they were spoken, in the places where the orator stood, and then read them, silently or aloud, for their content. That's why these speeches are complete or their excerpts are long. Although more than a few of these presentations of ideas are considered immortal, they were spoken by mortals to move other mortals. I like to think this method of making minds meet has a shining future.

An Introductory Address

FRIENDS, READERS, STUDENTS OF RHETORIC, WOULD-BE ORATORS: LEND ME YOUR EARS.

Please understand—that is only a metaphor. "Your ears" is a figure of speech; all I seek is your attention to speeches by historic figures.

That little rhetorical antithesis—figure of speech, speech by figures—is known as a contrapuntal turnaround. Lincoln used the device in switching the cynical "might makes right" to the moral "right makes might"; John Kennedy did the same with never negotiating out of fear, but never fearing to negotiate. That's the way some phrasemakers do their thing—we contrapunt and pray—to provide a speech with some quotable nugget. Since the 1970s, as speeches were recorded on tape, they have been known as sound bites.

But, sound bites and zingers, aphorisms and epigrams, are for quotation anthologists. The study of one-liners is engaging if you like the smorgasbord or quick review, but here we offer the meat and potatoes of oratory—oral communication in context, human persuasion in action.

To stir the blood of patriots, we have Daniel Webster reminding us of the meaning of sacrifice at Bunker Hill; we have Judge Learned Hand transcending superpatriotism on "I Am an American Day"; we have Douglas MacArthur calling West Point cadets to "duty, honor, country."

To sound the clarion of war, we have the virgin queen, Elizabeth I, defying the Spanish Armada; we have Patrick Henry (or Judge St. George Tucker, who may have coined the phrase in retrospect) crying, "Give me liberty, or give me death"; we have Winston Churchill, in Britain's finest hour, calling for "blood, toil, tears, and sweat."

To honor the memory of our illustrious dead, we have Henry Lee's tribute to the man who was "first in war, first in peace"; and we have John F. Kennedy using his eulogy at the funeral of poet Robert Frost to pay tribute to the arts in America.

To recall the clash of hot debate, we have Cicero lashing into Catiline; we have Stephen Douglas's reply to Lincoln, and portions of the first televised confrontation between presidential candidates.

To watch the accused reach heights of defiance against injustice, we have Irish rebel Robert Emmet warning his sentencers, "Let no man write my epitaph"; we have Gandhi of India professing his religious faith in a secular court; we have dissident Anatoly Shcharansky expressing his contempt of his Communist judges.

To see how powerful figures best take their leave, we hear Socrates before taking the hemlock; we hear abolitionist John Brown foreseeing the blood of civil war; we hear the simple good-bye of first baseman Lou Gehrig at Yankee Stadium; we hear Dwight Eisenhower startle his old friends with a warning about a "military-industrial complex."

To stir our soul, we listen to Jesus' Sermon on the Mount; Lincoln's curious sermon at his second inaugural; Rabbi Louis Finkelstein at the White House; and Billy Graham preaching the gospel.

To enrich and uplift our spirit, we have Louis Pasteur on education; Mark Twain on stage fright; Senator Everett Dirksen on his beloved marigolds; William Faulkner on how mankind will not merely endure but prevail. We have Secretary of State Dean Acheson present at the creation of the Cold War and Boris Yeltsin at its effective end.

Nor is that all; we are not limited to political figures. To stretch the mind, we have Edgar Allan Poe explaining the poetic principle; Frank Lloyd Wright on the flight of the floo floo bird through the backward-looking world of architecture.

But what of the burning issue of social justice? To stir our conscience, we have Lord Byron on the rights of labor; populist Huey Long and his "Every Man a King"; Margaret Chase Smith on the conscience of a senator; and Czech dissident become president Václav Havel on improvement politics as "the art of the impossible."

We dare not neglect the media. Here you will find a calculated cacophony, from Newton Minow's warning of a "vast wasteland" to Spiro Agnew's blast at the "instant analysts"; from Norman Mailer and Salman Rushdie on the rejection of intimidation to an extemporaneous rumination by Daniel Schorr on the ambiguities of news suppression.

And now to the mother's milk of this anthologist, the political speech. Here is Demosthenes showing how to mount a defense by savaging his attacker; Edmund Burke on conciliation with America; FDR's first inaugural, Truman's stump speech, Goldwater on vice and virtue, Khrushchev's secret speech on Stalin's cult of personality, Nixon's "silent majority," Barbara Jordan at the Watergate hearings, Reagan on the "evil empire," Bush's "thousand points of light," as well as Judge Soggy Sweat's drily damp evocation of fence straddling in his "if by whisky" speech.

We will conclude on a note of hope, with the advice of leaders to students at commencement. Woodrow Wilson inspires the midshipmen, and editor William Allen White challenges the generation about to fight a world war; Art Buchwald kids them, Mario Cuomo instructs their parents, and Lane Kirkland warns them, in the words of his favorite western villain, "life ain't going to be like anything you ever heard of before."

That survey of contents is an appetizer for our feast of oratory. But before plunging in, you will want to know what turns an everyday expression of views into more than a respectable address—into a "great speech."

Ambassador Robert Strauss likes to start his addresses this way: "Before I begin this speech," he says, "I have something to say." Before beginning the instructive part of this introduction (composed in a style to make it possible for the reader to declaim in a stentorian tone), I want to make a point: there are secrets to speechwriting and speechmaking that you can learn and use. Dip into this book often enough, and you will get the hang of them. Here is how to acquire eloquence by osmosis: close the door, or go out in the woods with only a dog as an audience, and read these speeches aloud. Even the dog will profit, especially from Senator Vest's tear-jerking but immortal "tribute to a dog."

Now to my theme: the ten steps to a great speech. One of the criteria in selecting the speeches herein is shapeliness. Most people associate shapeliness with the female form or masculine physique, but those of us in the rhetorics dodge—students or practitioners of persuasion—think of shapeliness as necessary forensic form, the configuring contours of communication.

That's because a great speech—even a good speech—must have a structure, some thematic anatomy. "Tell 'em what you're going to tell 'em; then tell 'em; then tell 'em what you told 'em." That simple organizing principle is the primary adage of speechmaking. That old saying, you note, is packaged in perfect oratorical style; the imperative mood, the force of a command, the parallel structure that invites a rhythm in delivery. None of that pompous "The well-crafted speech should begin with an introductory survey of content to come and conclude with a summary of main points." At meetings of the Judson Welliver Society, the association of former White House speechwriters, you can hear a low buzz in the room between after-dinner toasts. It is the distinguished membership murmuring the mantra, "Tell them what you're going to tell them; then tell them; then tell them what you told them." We know whereof we speak. Take it from the fast-shuffling old pros: graceful organization—shapeliness—is the second step to a great speech.

(Wait a minute; what was the first step? That was "Shake hands with your audience." I did that with the Bob Strauss line. Make the first step a quickstep; get your smile, then get to work.)

A skeleton needs life. Beyond structure is pulse. A good speech has a beat, a changing rhythm, a sense of movement that gets the audience tapping its mind's foot. (If the mind can have an eye, it can have a foot; every metaphor can be extended.) If there is one technique that orators down the ages have agreed to use, it's anaphora, the repeated beginning. Here's Demosthenes: "When they brought . . . suits against me—when they menaced—when they promised—when they set these miscreants like wild beasts upon me. . . ." Here's Jesus: "Blessed are the poor in spirit. . . . Blessed are the meek. . . . Blessed are the peacemakers. . . ." Here's JFK: "Let both sides explore. . . . Let both sides seek. . . . Let both sides unite. . . ." Don't knock this obvious parallelism: It sings. It excites. It works.

What else makes a great speech? Occasion. There comes a dramatic moment in the life of a person or a party or a nation that cries out for the uplift and release of a speech. Someone is called upon to articulate the hope, pride, or grief of all. The speaker becomes the cynosure, the brilliant object of guidance; he or she is all alone out there on the cusp, and the world stops to look and listen. That instant access to fame gives the edge to an inaugural address, or to a speech on some state occasion or award ceremony; the occasion, by being invested with solemnity or importance, boosts the speech itself. Some great occasions are frittered away with pedestrian addresses, as in Jimmy Carter's inaugural or in Nelson Mandela's speech thanking the dais upon his release from a lifetime ordeal in a South African prison; neither is included here. But other memorable occasions are made immortal by the words said at them: Lincoln's poem at Gettysburg is worth close analysis, not simply recitation by rote; and Martin Luther King's "I have a dream today" is worth rereading in its entirety, and not just taken in sound bites on anniversaries.

An idea closely related to occasion is "forum," from the Roman place of speechifying. When I was writing speeches in the White House, I had a perfect forum: the Oval Office, which is now a permanent television set. Using this setting, a president must explain rather than declaim; the technique of televised speechmaking is to speak to an audience of one. That calls for a conversational tone, even though the conversation is a monologue, and a seriousness of expression; not even Ronald Reagan, the most adept television speaker, smiled much in the course of a speech from his desk. It also calls for a short, intense speech, twenty minutes tops; tuning out, mental or physical, becomes rampant as attention spans shorten. When the speaker wants to exhort or solemnify, or add a sense of occasion to the forum, or cover a lot more than one subject, he takes the cameras out on location. That's when we see the State of the Union address making a prop of Congress, or a "convention speech" outlining a vision of America. On these occasions, the speaker must decide whether to speak to the people in the hall or to look at the camera and try to reach the people at home; I've always felt that a great-hall speech should be directed to the people on the scene, leaving the viewer at home with the sense of being an onlooker once removed; the recipient takes in the speech as an event to be observed and feels not like the specific target of the speaker but like an extension of a vast audience. One-on-one sells; one-on-a-million thrills.

To the handshake, shape, pulse, and occasion or forum, add the fifth step: focus. A "great" speech need not start out great and stay great all the way through to a great finish. It should first engage the interest, and allow a dip for the audience to get comfortable as the speaker works his way into the theme; then it should build toward its key moment well ahead of the peroration. Here is how political economist John Stuart Mill defined the art of the orator: "Everything important to his purpose was said at the exact moment when he had brought the minds of his audience into the state most fitted to receive it."

Note the word "purpose." A speech should be made for a good reason. No worthy speech was ever made to sound off, to feed the speaker's ego, to flatter or intimidate the crowd. Fidel Castro makes that kind of speech, running to seven hours long, and no rhetorical ramble of that sort is honored by inclusion here. Why not? Because a great speech is made for a high purpose—to inspire, to ennoble, to instruct, to rally, to lead.

What about quotation in a speech? In the past, orators occasionally studded their rhetoric with references to ancient Greeks, but now quotation seems to be a must. Usually it is tossed in to show a little erudition, a crutch when a speech is limping along and needs a touch of class. I did that a moment ago with John Stuart Mill; his point about preparing the audience for the message is apt, but it doesn't sing; I should have stolen his idea and phrased it more forcefully. If I'd felt I had to use a direct quotation, I should have found a dramatic context. Richard Nixon, closeted in a small room off the Oval Office, used to tell his speechwriters, "Never give me a naked quote. Put it in a little story." He was right. Try this: John Stuart Mill loved a woman for twenty years, but she was married; only when her husband died did the philosopher have the chance to marry the widow who had been his lifelong inspiration. Harriet Mill helped teach her inarticulate new husband the art of oratory. They worked together on his masterpiece, *On Liberty*, but she died before it was published; the heartbroken philosopher dedicated it to the woman he had waited for, loved, and lost, and in an article about oratory, he must have remembered what she told him: "Everything important to his purpose. . . ." There you have a little story, a utilitarian trick to put a little flesh on the bones of quotation.

Are all the speeches herein "great" speeches—thrilling, profound orations delivered on momentous occasions? Of course not. Some are merely famous speeches. Mark Twain on speechmaking is humor on wry. Kissinger on isolationism won't knock your emotional socks off; in fact, any speech by a living politician is hard to categorize as "great" until the speaker is elevated to iconhood, dispatched down to Gehenna, or dead. Some of the speeches herein were chosen because they are representative of an era or a style, or instructive to modern orators: Malcolm X's incendiary words are not "great" in the sense of being timeless or majestic, but they contain a persuasive passion.

On the other hand, not every great speech is a good speech. What Harry Truman's stump speech lacks in depth and shape, it makes up for in zest. What Jonathan Edwards's sermon lacks in grace, it delivers in hellfire. In this anthology, the ultimate criterion in what makes a speech great is whether I think it's great. Do not be shocked by that subjectivism: oratory is an art, not a science, and a great rhetorician may choose to grab, slug, inspire, provoke, or tickle. Whatever tone the orator chooses, if he wants to make a memorable speech, he should make a phrase.

Phrasemaking is easy. Suppose you want to enliven a speech about the division of a continent. Think of a metaphor about division; how about the asbestos sheet that is lowered onto the stage to separate the audience from fire backstage? It's called an iron curtain. Go ahead, the metaphor may be trite, but give it a shot. And you can use it derivatively: if you're writing about China, boost the analogy to a bamboo curtain, or, in a rousing speech to an underwear convention, a lace curtain. If you're unwilling to let a simile be your umbrella, there's always alliteration: "not nostrums but normalcy" (a catchier word, by the way, than "normality") or the "nattering nabobs of negativism." If you're really stuck, put "new" in front of any grand noun, and capitalize the phrase: it worked with "nationalism," "freedom," "deal" "frontier," and "world order," and it can work for you.

To the mix of welcome, structure, pulse, forum, focus, phrase, and purpose, add this single most important ingredient: theme. In the end, you must answer in a word or sentence the question of the person who couldn't be there: What was the speech about? Churchill, in the radio talk that coined a phrase that was transmuted into "blood, sweat, and tears," made a speech about sacrifice. He was the one who faced a sloppy dessert and said, "Take away this pudding: it has no theme," The speech you are reading now is about how to judge a great speech. I have that theme clear in my mind; if you do not discern that as my theme, this is not much of a speech.

Delivered by Demosthenes, however, even this modest effort would seem like a great speech. In a story perhaps apocryphal, his countryman Pericles, who also had a reputation as an orator, made this admiring comparison: "When Pericles speaks, the people say, 'How well he speaks.' But when Demosthenes speaks, the people say, 'Let us march!'" Ronald Reagan's delivery could lift a bad speech up by the scruff of its neck, shake it, and make it sing. Contrariwise, the best-written speech can fall on its face if poorly delivered. There is the old chestnut about the Texan striding along Fifty-seventh Street in Manhattan who asked a stranger, "Tell me, partner, how do I get to Carnegie Hall?" and the stranger replied, "Practice, practice." Delivery is the final step to eloquence; it requires practice, discipline, drill, and you can be your own personal trainer. You develop the self-confidence that puts an audience at ease, or sits them up; your eye is in contact with the people, not the page; your joy in your job is contagious.

Woodrow Wilson was originally a political-science professor, and his lecture delivery matched his stilted writing. But Wilson labored to overcome the professorial style. His earliest writing was about orators and their oratory. He founded the debating society at Princeton and added debate coaching to his teaching; he declaimed in the woods; he set out to defeat his natural inclinations to aloofness and reserve. Ultimately, as he got better at it, the future president gained confidence in himself and wrote to his fiancée, "I enjoy it because it sets my mind—all my faculties—aglow; and I suppose that this very excitement gives my manner an appearance of confidence and self-command which arrests the attention. However that may be, I feel a sort of transformation—and it's hard to go to sleep afterwards." Later, in an essay on the oratory of William Pitt the Elder, Wilson wrote, "Passion is the pith of eloquence."

And on delivery, caveat stentor: when preparing a speech, beware of undeliverable words. "Undeliverable" is one such tripword; it may look easy enough on the page, and it may be easy to pronounce in the mind when read silently, but when the moment comes to push it past your lips, such a word invites a stumble. And if you practice a tripword out loud, and put a check mark over it in your text, you will be all the more sure to stumble. As a young speechwriter, I drafted remarks for New York City's official greeter, whose assignment was to welcome Syngman Rhee of South Korea. I referred to the visiting president's "indomitable will"; the greeter, a bumbling former ambassador, knew he would say something like "indomatabubble" and asked for a synonym. When I gave him "indefatigable," he fired me on the spot; somebody else had to slip him "steadfast." In retrospect, I now see I was intransigent. (That's my penance: in reading this aloud, I will surely stumble over "intransigent.") Embrace the thin word; eschew the fat.

Beware, too, of words that may vaguely trouble your listeners. A moment ago, I quoted Wilson saying, "Passion is the pith of eloquence." I know what "pith" means—"nub, core, quintessence"—and so do you. But I would never stand in front of an audience and say "pith"; it sounds like a vulgar word being spoken with a lisp. Nobody would criticize you for it, but you as the speaker or speechwriter are responsible for preventing those little internal winces in the minds of your listeners. They distract attention from the message you want to get across. While we are on the subject of troubling vocabulary, observe how the great speeches steer clear of forty-dollar words. Big words, or terms chosen for their strangeness—I almost said "unfamiliarity"—are a sign of pretension. What do you do when you have a delicious word, one with a little poetry in it, that is just the right word for the meaning—but you know it will sail over the head of your audience? You can use it, just as FDR used "infamy," and thereby stretch the vocabulary of your listeners. But it is best if you subtly define it in passing, as if you were adding emphasis—as I did a moment ago, with "cynosure, the brilliant object of guidance." Who knows that a cynosure is a constellation in the heavens that sailors steered by, even among those who use the cliché "cynosure of all eyes"? Who will know what "deltoids" are, when I refer to them in a moment? The speaker will; if he subtly helps his audience, nobody should notice the medicine go down.

I admit that what you have in your hands is a heavy book. Intellectually weighty, too, but the meaning I have in mind is "hefty"—2.4 pounds, to be exact—nothing to slip into pocket or purse on your way to a speech doctor's office. "This I freely assert," said the verb-conscious Franklin Roosevelt, "and I hope my friends in the press do not change that to 'admit.'" The weight of this book is a boon to both mental and physical health. I once received a thick anthology from Sidney Perelman, the great humorist—it was called *The Most of S. J. Perelman*—and the inscription read, "To William Safire, together with a small jar of antiphlogiston to rub on his deltoids, should you read this compendium in bed." That sent me to the dictionary: "the deltoids" are the book-holding muscles of the shoulder and Antiphlogiston was the name of a soothing ointment that was rubbed out by Ben-Gay. I pick up Perelman's big book now and then; lifting it gives me a lift, as I hope this volume will do for you. (It would have been lighter but for the stream of speeches brought in by my chief of research,

Jeffrey McQuain, and my editorial aide, Ann Elise Rubin; thanks, too, to Jeanne Smith of the Library of Congress, and to Professor Janet Coryell for hard-to-find speeches by women, and to Gerald Howard and Emma Lewis from W. W. Norton, the intrepid publishers. We have just saved a page of acknowledgments.)

You are now an abnormally sophisticated audience. You know the tricks of the speech trade, some of the devices of the phrasemaker and speechwriter, and you expect the speaker now to summarize—to tell 'em what he told 'em.

Sorry; there's a secret eleventh step: cross 'em up now and then. This is, after all, a speech meant to be read, not spoken; the metaphoric listener is really a reader who can skip back as no real listener easily can. You, dear speech reader, are lending not your ears but your eyes, which are much more perceptive and analytic organs. After receiving the moral directions summarized on the tablets he brought down from Mount Sinai, Moses spoke to the people of Israel—but nowhere is it written that he found a need to summarize the Ten Commandments.

What every audience needs, however, is a sense of completion; what the speaker needs is a way out on a high note. That's a necessary ingredient to shapeliness. That calls for a peroration.

A peroration, my friends, is a devastating defense against the dread disease of dribbling-off. It should start with a quiet, declarative sentence; it should build in a series of semicolons; it should employ the puissance of parallelism; it should make the farthest rafter reverberate with the action and passion of our time, and—throwing aside all rules of short sentences or self-quotation—it should reach into the hearts and souls of a transfixed humankind to say, "This—this!—is the end of the best damned speech you've ever had the good fortune to experience." (Sustained applause, punctuated by "Bravo!" "Let us march!" and "You tell 'em, Buster!"—followed by some smart-aleck pundit wrinkling his nose and wondering aloud, "But what did he really say?")

I

MEMORIALS
AND
PATRIOTIC
SPEECHES

Pericles Extols the Glory
That Is Greece at the
Funeral of Its Fallen Sons

*"THOSE . . . have the greatest souls, who, most acutely sensible of the miseries of war
and the sweets of peace, are not hence in the least deterred from facing danger."*

PERICLES was a cautious general, a stern imperialist, an ardent patron
of the arts, and a radical politician. Although he was born an aristocrat
around the turn of the fifth century B.C., his "graces of persuasion," in
Cicero's phrase, did much to curb the power of the aristocracy and extend
democracy to the citizens of the city-state of Athens. For example, he
pressed successfully for the payment of fees to jurors and, later, to public
officials—which made it possible for a poor man to hold public office.

Fewer than forty thousand males made up the polity of Athens, and all
were members of the Assembly. It chose by lot the Council of Five
Hundred, fifty from each tribe, to manage its affairs, and elected juries of a
hundred to a thousand men to decide cases. This was before lawyers came
on the scene; each man was his own pleader, and a citizen required a
mastery of the art of oratory to gain or defeat justice. Pericles was reputed
to be one of the most eloquent at these meetings of the democratic legislature, exceeded only by fourth-century Greek orator Demosthenes.

"Reputed" is a necessary qualifier because we have no text of these
Greek speeches. The reputation of Pericles rests on the writings of historian Thucydides, in his *History of the Peloponnesian War.* "With reference to
the speeches in this history," the chronicler wrote candidly, ". . . some I
heard myself, others I got from various quarters; it was in all cases difficult to carry them word for word in one's memory, so my habit has been
to make my speakers say what was in my opinion demanded of them by
the various occasions, of course adhering as closely as possible to what
they really said."

Fortunately, Thucydides was a friend of Pericles and was probably
present at the delivery of this oration. Here, then, are portions of a translation of one historian's recollection of what the orator Pericles said at

the funeral of soldiers killed in the first year of the war. Athens was soon to be destroyed; the purpose of this speech (like that of Lincoln's Gettysburg Address over two millennia later) was to use the occasion of a eulogy for the fallen to examine the cause for which they fell.

□   □   □

Many of those who have spoken before me on these occasions have commended the author of that law which we now are obeying for having instituted an oration to the honor of those who sacrifice their lives in fighting for their country. For my part, I think it sufficient for men who have proved their virtue in action, by action to be honored for it—by such as you see the public gratitude now performing about this funeral; and that the virtues of many ought not to be endangered by the management of any one person when their credit must precariously depend on his oration, which may be good and may be bad. . . .

We are happy in a form of government which cannot envy the laws of our neighbors—for it hath served as a model to others, but is original at Athens. And this our form, as committed not to the few but to the whole body of the people, is called a democracy. How different soever in a private capacity, we all enjoy the same general equality our laws are fitted to preserve; and superior honors just as we excel. The public administration is not confined to a particular family but is attainable only by merit. Poverty is not a hindrance, since whoever is able to serve his country meets with no obstacle to preferment from his first obscurity. The offices of the state we go through without obstructions from one another, and live together in the mutual endearments of private life without suspicions, not angry with a neighbor for following the bent of his own humor, nor putting on that countenance of discontent which pains though it cannot punish—so that in private life we converse without diffidence or damage, while we dare not on any account offend against the public, through the reverence we bear to the magistrates and the laws, chiefly to those enacted for redress of the injured, and to those unwritten. a breach of which is thought a disgrace.

Our laws have further provided for the mind most frequent intermissions of care by the appointment of public recreations and sacrifices throughout the year, elegantly performed with a peculiar pomp, the daily delight of which is a charm that puts melancholy to flight. The grandeur of this our Athens causeth the produce of the whole earth to be imported here, by which we reap a familiar enjoyment, not more of the delicacies of our own growth than of those of other nations.

In the affairs of war we excel those of our enemies, who adhere to methods opposite to our own. For we lay open Athens to general resort, nor ever drive any stranger from us whom either improvement or curiosity hath brought amongst us, lest any enemy should hurt us by seeing what is never concealed. We place not so great a confidence in the preparatives and artifices of war as in the native warmth of our souls impelling us to action. In point of education the youth of some peoples are inured, by a course of laborious exercise, to support toil and exercise like men, but we, notwithstanding our easy and elegant way of life, face all the dangers of war as intrepidly as they. . . .

In our manner of living we show an elegance tempered with frugality, and we cultivate philosophy without enervating the mind. We display our wealth in the season of beneficence, and not in the vanity of discourse. A confession of poverty is disgrace to no man; no effort to avoid it is disgrace indeed. There is visible in the same persons an attention to their own private concerns and those of the public; and in others engaged in the labors of life there is a competent skill in the affairs of government. For we are the only people who think him that does not meddle in state affairs not indolent but good for nothing. And yet we pass the soundest judgments and are quick at catching the right apprehensions of things, not thinking that words are prejudicial to actions, but rather the not being duly prepared by previous debate before we are obliged to proceed to execution. Herein consists our distinguishing excellence, that in the hour of action we show the greatest courage, and yet debate beforehand the expediency of our measures. The courage of others is the result of ignorance; deliberation makes them cowards. And those undoubtedly must be owned to have the greatest souls, who, most acutely sensible of the miseries of war and the sweets of peace, are not hence in the least deterred from facing danger.

In acts of beneficence, further, we differ from the many. We preserve friends not by receiving, but by conferring, obligations. For he who does a kindness hath the advantage over him who, by the law of gratitude, becomes a debtor to his benefactor. The person obliged is compelled to act the more insipid part, conscious that a return of kindness is merely a payment and not an obligation. And we alone are splendidly beneficent to others, not so much from interested motives as for the credit of pure liberality. I shall sum up what yet remains by only adding that our Athens in general is the school of Greece, and that every single Athenian amongst us is excellently formed, by his personal qualification, for all the various scenes of active life, acting with a most graceful demeanor and a most ready habit of dispatch.

That I have not on this occasion made use of a pomp of words, but the truth of facts, that height to which by such a conduct this state hath risen, is an undeniable proof. For we are now the only people of the world who are found by experience to be greater than in report. . . .

In the just defense of such a state, these victims of their own valor, scorning the ruin threatened to it, have valiantly fought and bravely died. And every one of those who survive is ready, I am persuaded, to sacrifice life in such a cause. And for this reason have I enlarged so much on national points, to give the clearest proof that in the present war we have more at stake than men whose public advantages are not so valuable, and to illustrate, by actual evidence, how great a commendation is due to them who are now my subject, and the greatest part of which they have already received. For the encomiums with which I have celebrated the state have been earned for it by the bravery of these and of men like these. And such compliments might be thought too high and exaggerated if passed on any Greeks but them alone.

The fatal period to which these gallant souls are now reduced is the surest evidence of their merit—an evidence begun in their lives and completed in their deaths. For it is a debt of justice to pay superior honors to men who have devoted their lives in fighting for their country, though inferior to others in every virtue but that of valor. Their last service effaceth all former demerits—it extends to the public; their private demeanors reached only to a few. Yet not one of these was at all induced to shrink from danger, through fondness of those delights which the peaceful affluent life bestows—not one was the less lavish of his life, through that flattering hope attendance upon want, that poverty at length might be exchanged for affluence. One passion there was in their minds much stronger than these—the desire of vengeance on their enemies. Regarding this as the most honorable prize of dangers, they boldly rushed towards the mark to glut revenge and then to satisfy those secondary passions. The uncertain event they had already secured in hope; what their eyes showed plainly must be done they trusted their own valor to accomplish, thinking it more glorious to defend themselves and die in the attempt than to yield and live. From the reproach of cowardice, indeed, they fled, but presented their bodies to the shock of battle; when, insensible of fear, but triumphing in hope, in the doubtful charge they instantly dropped—and thus discharged the duty which brave men owed to their country.

As for you, who now survive them, it is your business to pray for a better fate, but to think it your duty also to preserve the same spirit and warmth of courage against your enemies; not judging of the expediency of this from a mere harangue—where any man indulging a flow of words may tell you what you yourselves know as well as he, how many advantages there are in fighting valiantly against your enemies—but, rather, making the daily-increasing grandeur of this community the object of your thoughts and growing quite enamored of it. And when it really appears great to your apprehensions, think again that this grandeur was acquired by brave and valiant men, by men who knew their duty, and in the moments of action were sensible of shame—who, whenever their attempts were unsuccessful, thought it no dishonor for their country to stand in need of anything their valor could do for it, and so made it the most glorious present. Bestowing thus their lives on the public, they have every one received a praise that will never decay, a sepulcher that will always be most illustrious—not that in which their bones lie moldering, but that in which their fame is preserved, to be on every occasion, when honor is the employ of either word or act, eternally remembered.

For the whole earth is the sepulcher of illustrious men; nor is it the inscription on the columns in their native land alone that shows their merit, but the memorial of them, better than all inscriptions in every foreign nation, reposited more durably in universal remembrance than on their own tombs. From this very moment, emulating these noble patterns, placing your happiness in liberty, and liberty in valor, be prepared to encounter all the dangers of war. For to be lavish of life is not so noble in those whom misfortunes have reduced to misery and despair, as in men who hazard the loss of a comfortable subsistence and the enjoyment of all the blessings this world affords by an unsuccessful enterprise. Adversity, after a series of ease and affluence, sinks deeper into the heart of a man of spirit than the stroke of death insensibly received in the vigor of life and public hope.

For this reason, the parents of those who are now gone, whoever of them may be attending here, I do not bewail—I shall rather comfort. . . . I know it in truth a difficult task to fix comfort in those breasts which will have frequent remembrances, in seeing the happiness of others, of what they once themselves enjoyed. And sorrow flows not from the absence of those good things we have never yet experienced but from the loss of those to which we have been accustomed. . . . But you, whose age is already far advanced, compute the greater share of happiness your longer time hath afforded for so much gain, persuaded in yourselves the remainder will be but short, and enlighten that space by the glory gained by these. It is greatness of soul alone that never grows old, nor is it wealth that delights in the latter stage of life, as some give out, so much as honor.

To you, the sons and brothers of the deceased, whatever number of you are here, a field of hardy contention is opened. For him who no longer is, everyone is ready to commend, so that to whatever height you push your deserts, you will scarce ever be thought to equal, but to be somewhat inferior to these. Envy will exert itself against a competitor while life remains; but when death stops the competition, affection will applaud without restraint.

If after this it be expected from me to say anything to you who are now reduced to a state of widowhood, about female virtue, I shall express it all in one short admonition: it is your greatest glory not to be deficient in the virtue peculiar to your sex, and to give men as little handle as possible to talk of your behavior, whether well or ill.

I have now discharged the province allotted me by the laws, and said what I thought most pertinent to this assembly. Our departed friends have by facts been already honored. Their children from this day till they arrive at manhood shall be educated at the public expense of the state which hath appointed so beneficial a meed for these and all future relics of the public contests. For wherever the greatest rewards are proposed for virtue, there the best of patriots are ever to be found. Now let everyone respectively indulge in becoming grief for his departed friends, and then retire. ■

Roman Empress
Theodora Refuses to Flee

"THE royal purple is the noblest shroud."

BYZANTINE OR EASTERN ROMAN EMPEROR JUSTINIAN, on
January 18 of the year 532, was certain he was about to be overthrown
by rebel leader Hypatius and killed. A fast galley waited at the palace's
private harbor to take him and Empress Theodora to safety in Thrace. His
timorous advisers persuaded him that the rebellion could not be stopped
and that the way out for the imperial couple was flight. As the panicky
leader made for the door, the indomitable empress rose from her throne
and delivered a brief speech that kept her husband from taking flight and
led to the slaughter of the rebels.

□   □   □

My lords, the present occasion is too serious to allow me to follow
the convention that a woman should not speak in a man's council. Those whose interests are threatened by extreme danger should think
only of the wisest course of action, not of conventions.

In my opinion, flight is not the right course, even if it should bring us
to safety. It is impossible for a person, having been born into this world,
not to die; but for one who has reigned it is intolerable to be a fugitive.
May I never be deprived of this purple robe, and may I never see the day
when those who meet me do not call me empress.

If you wish to save yourself, my lord, there is no difficulty. We are rich;
over there is the sea, and yonder are the ships. Yet reflect for a moment
whether, when you have once escaped to a place of security, you would
not gladly exchange such safety for death. As for me, I agree with the
adage that the royal purple is the noblest shroud. ∎

Founding Father
Gouverneur Morris Defines
National Greatness

"It is in the national spirit . . . I anticipate the day when to command respect in the remotest regions it will be sufficient to say, 'I am an American.'"

GOUVERNEUR (that was his first name; he was a New York congressman, never a governor) Morris was among the most conservative of the nation's founders, at first opposing separation from England. Once the Revolution was under way, however, he responded to Lord North's appeal for reconciliation by making independence a prerequisite for peace. This strong stand, along with his advocacy of religious tolerance and the abolition of slavery, cost Morris political support in New York; rejected by the voters, he moved to Pennsylvania and aligned himself with financier Robert Morris (no kin) and a group of men around George Washington who later became Federalists—supporters, with Alexander Hamilton, of a central bank and strong central government, opposed by the Jeffersonians. He is the father of dollars and cents: his ideas on decimal coinage became the basis of U.S. currency.

Although the proceedings were secret, what we know of the Constitutional Convention of 1787 suggests that Gouverneur Morris had more to say than anybody else, speaking against slavery and for life tenure for the president. Chosen to be a member of the committee on style and management, he was primarily responsible for the literary form of the U.S. Constitution. However, "We, the people" was not his philosophy; his antidemocratic mind-set troubled the French radicals when he represented America in Paris, and they asked for his recall. By 1800, when he made this speech about greatness in a nation, he was serving in the U.S. Senate, a stanch Federalist standing against the incoming tide of Jeffersonian democracy.

□   □   □

Had it been permitted to consult my wishes on this day, I should have selected a theme more suited to my talents or rather have shrouded their weakness in the veil of silence. For I feel but too well that in venturing to discuss the subject of national greatness I must fall short of the ideas in your minds and disappoint your expectations. Instead of irradiating with the light of genius, I must take the more humble course of investigation and begin by inquiring what is national greatness.

Does it consist in numbers, wealth, or extent of territory? Certainly not. Swollen with the pride inspired by such circumstances, the Persians addressed their master as the Great King, but Darius felt in repeated discomfiture the superiority of a great nation led by Alexander. We see in our day a prince who may boast that the sun never sets on his domain, yet his authority superseded in his ports and insulted in his capital, it would seem as if his territory were extended around the globe only to display before all the world his ignominious condition. Such is the state of that proud monarchy which once menaced the liberties of Europe. But who trembles now at the name of Spain? There is none so abject. Nay, should there exist a government in which fear is the incurable disease, no paroxysm would be excited by the menace of Spain. To the wise a word is sufficient, and therefore it will be needless before this audience to prove that a nation small like Greece may rise to the heights of national greatness while littleness shall mark every public act of a numerous people. And equally needless must it be to express what you cannot but feel: that in proportion to the high esteem, respect, and admiration with which we view the splendor of Greece in the day of her glory is our profound contempt for those who presiding over a powerful people shall tamely submit to the multiplied repetition of indignities from all who through interest or for sport may plunder and insult them. These are feelings so natural that to disguise them would be vain, to suppress them impossible. I could indeed, were I to indulge a licentious imagination, suppose a number of men who without national spirit or sentiment shall presume to call themselves a nation—I can suppose a herd of piddling huckstering individuals base and insensible. . . .

Let us pause. Perhaps there never was a society of men so completely void of virtue. But between them and the brave band at Thermopylae gradations are infinite.

Perhaps it may be asked if genius and excellence in the arts constitute national greatness. To this question the answer must be given with caution and not without some modification. The ages of Pericles, of Augustus, and of Louis XIV were indeed ages of splendor. They were unquestionably the evidence, but I must venture to believe they were the result, not the cause of national greatness. A nation truly great cannot but excel in arts as well as in arms. And as a great mind stamps with its own impression the most common arts, so national greatness will show itself alike in the councils of policy, in the works of genius, in monuments of magnificence and deeds of glory. All these are the fruits, but they are not the tree.

Here I anticipate the general and the generous question: Does it not consist in liberty? That liberty is a kind and fostering nurse of greatness will be cheerfully and cordially admitted, but as we have seen national greatness where there was no freedom, so we have seen free nations where baseness rather than greatness constituted the national character. The intrepidity of the Swiss troops is generally known and acknowledged. In a contest for freedom with the duke of Burgundy the nation was great and covered itself with glory, but, alas, how changed, how fallen when distributing stipendiary aid to hostile hosts. Their valor was arrayed against itself, and brothers fell by the swords of brothers. They became at length the proverbial examples of mercenary disposition. And then neither liberty no[r] discipline nor courage rescued Helvetian fame from the charge of baseness.

Thus, then, we have seen that a people may be numerous, powerful, wealthy, free, brave, and inured to war without being great, and by reflecting on the reason why a combination of those qualities and circumstances will not alone suffice. We are close to the true source and principle of national greatness.

It is in the national spirit. It is in that high, haughty, generous, and noble spirit which prizes glory more than wealth and holds honor dearer than life. It is that spirit, the inspiring soul of heroes, which raises men above the level of humanity. It is present with us when we read the story of ancient Rome. It [s]wells our bosoms at the view of her gigantic deeds and makes us feel that we must ever be irresistible while human nature shall remain unchanged. I have called it a high, haughty, generous, and noble spirit. It is high—elevated above all low and vulgar considerations. It is haughty—despising whatever is little and mean, whether in character, council, or conduct. It is generous—granting freely to the weak and to the indigent protection and support. It is noble—dreading shame and dishonor as the greatest evil, esteeming fame and glory beyond all things human.

When this spirit prevails, the government, whatever its form, will be wise and energetic because such government alone will be borne by such men. And such a government, seeking the true interest of those over whom they preside, will find it in the establishment of a national character becoming the spirit by which the nation is inspired. Foreign powers will then know that to withhold a due respect and deference is dangerous, that wrongs may be forgiven but that insults will be avenged. As a necessary result every member of the society bears with him everywhere full protection, and when he appears his firm and manly port mark him of a superior order in the race of man. The dignity of sentiment which he has inhaled with his native air gives to his manner an ease superior to the politeness of courts and a grace unrivaled by the majesty of kings.

These are blessings which march in the train of national greatness and come on the pinions of youthful hope. I anticipate the day when to command respect in the remotest regions it will be sufficient to say, "I am an American." Our flag shall then wave in glory over the ocean and our commerce feel no restraint but what our own government may impose. Happy, thrice happy day. Thank God, to reach this envied state we need only to will. Yes, my countrymen, our destiny depends on our will. But if we would stand high on the record of time, that will must be inflexible. ∎

Daniel Webster Speaks at the Dedication of the Bunker Hill Monument

"LET our age be the age of improvement."

AS A LAWYER practicing before John Marshall's Supreme Court, Daniel Webster earned the sobriquet Expounder of the Constitution. From the Webster brief in *McCulloch v. Maryland,* Marshall selected "An unlimited power to tax involves, necessarily, the power to destroy"; he edited the phrase to "the power to tax is the power to destroy" in his decision to deny states the right to tax the new federal bank. This ruling effectively established the supremacy of national over state power.

Webster was unafraid to use the same word twice in a single sentence: the double use of "power" in that famous apothegm is similar to the repetition of "age" in the key line of his seminal Bunker Hill Monument address.

On June 17, 1825, while a member of the House of Representatives from Massachusetts, Webster spoke at the laying of the cornerstone of that monument, at Charlestown, near Boston. In four years, the ardent nationalist would be elected to the Senate, where his eloquence placed him in the senatorial firmament along with Henry Clay and John Calhoun; Webster's reply to Senator Hayne (see p. 283) made the case for union and against a state's claim to the power of nullifying national laws.

At Bunker Hill, where the British forces had won a Pyrrhic victory, Webster's theme was the meaning to the world of the American Revolution. In a message later taken up by Lincoln, the representative from Massachusetts held that the American experiment in popular government was crucial to the hopes for freedom around the world and that "the last hopes of mankind, therefore, rest with us." The tone of the speech is thoughtful and historical; the exhortation in the peroration, with its six sentences beginning with "let," is neither grandiloquent nor shrill. In saying at the start, "We see before us a probable train of great events," Webster set the stage for a speech in plain words that offered Americans one of their earliest glimpses of a worldview and an understanding of the new nation's global significance. It is curious that the rising nationalist should have made the most famous internationalist speech of his day.

□   □   □

. . . We are among the sepulchers of our fathers. We are on ground distinguished by their valor, their constancy, and the shedding of their blood. We are here, not to fix an uncertain date in our annals, nor to draw into notice an obscure and unknown spot. If our humble purpose had never been conceived, if we ourselves had never been born, the seventeenth of June, 1775, would have been a day on which all subsequent history would have poured its light, and the eminence where we stand, a point of attraction to the eyes of successive generations. But we are Americans. We live in what may be called the early age of this great continent; and we know that our posterity, through all time, are here to suffer and enjoy the allotments of humanity. We see before us a probable train of great events; we know that our own fortunes have been happily cast; and it is natural, therefore, that we should be moved by the contemplation of occurrences which have guided our destiny before many of us were born, and settled the condition in which we should pass that portion of our existence which God allows to men on earth. . . .

The great event, in the history of the continent, which we are now met here to commemorate—that prodigy of modern times, at once the wonder and the blessing of the world—is the American Revolution. In a day of extraordinary prosperity and happiness, of high national honor, distinction, and power, we are brought together, in this place, by our love of country, by our admiration of exalted character, by our gratitude for signal services and patriotic devotion . . .

The great wheel of political revolution began to move in America. Here its rotation was guarded, regular, and safe. Transferred to the other continent, from unfortunate but natural causes, it received an irregular and violent impulse; it whirled along with a fearful celerity, till at length, like the chariot wheels in the races of antiquity, it took fire from the rapidity of its own motion and blazed onward, spreading conflagration and terror around. . . .

When Louis XIV said, "I am the state," he expressed the essence of the doctrine of unlimited power. By the rules of that system, the people are disconnected from the state; they are its subjects; it is their lord. These ideas, founded in the love of power, and long supported by the excess and the abuse of it, are yielding in our age to other opinions; and the civilized world seems at last to be proceeding to the conviction of that fundamental and manifest truth, that the powers of government are but a trust, and that they cannot be lawfully exercised but for the good of the community. . . .

We may hope that the growing influence of enlightened sentiments will promote the permanent peace of the world. Wars, to maintain family alliances, to uphold or to cast down dynasties, to regulate successions to thrones, which have occupied so much room in the history of modern times, if not less likely to happen at all, will be less likely to become general and involve many nations, as the great principle shall be more and more established, that the interest of the world is peace, and its first great statute, that every nation possesses the power of establishing a government for itself. But public opinion has attained also an influence over governments which do not admit the popular principle into their organization. A necessary respect for the judgment of the world operates, in some measure, as a control over the most unlimited forms of authority. . . . Let us thank God that we live in an age when something has influence besides the bayonet, and when the sternest authority does not venture to encounter the scorching power of public reproach. . . .

When the Battle of Bunker Hill was fought, the existence of South America was scarcely felt in the civilized world. The thirteen little colonies of North America habitually called themselves the "continent." Borne down by colonial subjugation, monopoly, and bigotry, these vast regions of the South were hardly visible above the horizon. But in our day there hath been, as it were, a new creation. The Southern Hemisphere emerges from the sea. Its lofty mountains begin to lift themselves into the light of heaven; its broad and fertile plains stretch out in beauty to the eye of civilized man, and at the mighty being of the voice of political liberty the waters of darkness retire.

And now let us indulge an honest exultation in the conviction of the benefit which the example of our country has produced and is likely to produce on human freedom and human happiness. And let us endeavor to comprehend in all its magnitude and to feel in all its importance the part assigned to us in the great drama of human affairs. We are placed at the head of the system of representative and popular governments. Thus far our example shows that such governments are compatible, not only with respectability and power, but with repose, with peace, with security of personal rights, with good laws and a just administration.

We are not propagandists. Wherever other systems are preferred, either as being thought better in themselves or as better suited to existing conditions, we leave the preference to be enjoyed. Our history hitherto proves, however, that the popular form is practicable and that, with wisdom and knowledge, men may govern themselves; and the duty incumbent on us is to preserve the consistency of this cheering example and take care that nothing may weaken its authority with the world. If in our case the representative system ultimately fail, popular governments must be pronounced impossible. No combination of circumstances more favorable to the experiment can ever be expected to occur. The last hopes of mankind, therefore, rest with us; and if it should be proclaimed that our example had become an argument against the experiment, the knell of popular liberty would be sounded throughout the earth.

These are incitements to duty; but they are not suggestions of doubt. Our history and our condition, all that is gone before us and all that surrounds us, authorize the belief that popular governments, though subject to occasional variations, perhaps not always for the better in form, may yet in their general character be as durable and permanent as other systems. We know, indeed, that in our country any other is impossible. The principle of free governments adheres to the American soil. It is bedded in it—immovable as its mountains.

And let the sacred obligations which have devolved on this generation and on us sink deep into our hearts. Those are daily dropping from among us who established our liberty and our government. The great trust now descends to new hands. Let us apply ourselves to that which is presented to us as our appropriate object. We can win no laurels in a war for independence. Earlier and worthier hands have gathered them all. Nor are there places for us by the side of Solon, and Alfred, and other founders of states. Our fathers have filled them. But there remains to us a great duty of defense and preservation; and there is opened to us also a noble pursuit to which the spirit of the times strongly invites us.

Our proper business is improvement. Let our age be the age of improvement. In a day of peace let us advance the arts of peace and the works of peace. Let us develop the resources of our land, call forth its powers, build up its institutions, promote all its great interests, and see whether we also, in our day and generation, may not perform something worthy to be remembered. Let us cultivate a true spirit of union and harmony. In pursuing the great objects which our condition points out to us, let us act under a settled conviction, and a habitual feeling that these twenty-four states are one country. Let our conceptions be enlarged to the circle of our duties. Let us extend our ideas over the whole of the vast field in which we are called to act. Let our object be our country, our whole country, and nothing but our country. And by the blessing of God may that country itself become a vast and splendid monument, not of oppression and terror, but of wisdom, of peace, and of liberty, upon which the world may gaze with admiration, forever. ■

Lecturer
Frances Wright Speaks
on Independence Day

"PATRIOTISM, in the exclusive meaning, is surely not made for America."

SCOTTISH-BORN FRANCES WRIGHT was the first woman to gain fame giving public lectures in America, and more than once she was nearly mobbed for this audacity.

After her first visit to the United States, Frances Wright produced *Views of Society and Manners in America*, an 1821 book in favor of American life. She returned to America in 1824 and this time stayed for good—the good being social reform, including the founding of Nashoba, a colony for free blacks in Tennessee. Although that venture failed, she continued writing and lecturing to promote abolition as well as universal education and equal rights for women.

She lived for a time in New Harmony, Indiana, the cooperative colony founded by Robert Owen, the Welsh social reformer. At New Harmony, she delivered her Independence Day address on July 4, 1828. Her definitions of "patriotism" and America as "the favored scene of human improvement" emphasize the liberal views that permeated her lectures on marriage and religion as well as on social reform.

With parallel structure that begins with "It is for Americans," Frances Wright forcefully uses anaphora, the repetition of a phrase, in six consecutive sentences to tell Americans what "it is for them" to do to celebrate and extend their independence.

□ □ □

. . . Our hearts should expand on this day, which calls to memory the conquest achieved by knowledge over ignorance, willing cooperation over blind obedience, opinion over prejudice, new ways over old ways—when, fifty-two years ago, America declared her national independence, and associated it with her republic federation. Reasonable is it to rejoice on this day, and useful to reflect thereon; so that we rejoice for the real, and not any imaginary, good; and reflect on the positive advantages obtained, and on those which it is ours farther to acquire.

Dating, as we justly may, a new era in the history of man from the Fourth of July, 1776, it would be well—that is, it would be useful—if on each anniversary we examined the progress made by our species in just knowledge and just practice. Each Fourth of July would then stand as a tidemark in the flood of time by which to ascertain the advance of the human intellect, by which to note the rise and fall of each successive error, the discovery of each important truth, the gradual melioration in our public institutions, social arrangements, and, above all, in our moral feelings and mental views. . . .

In continental Europe, of late years, the words "patriotism" and "patriot" have been used in a more enlarged sense than it is usual here to attribute to them, or than is attached to them in Great Britain. Since the political struggles of France, Italy, Spain, and Greece, the word "patriotism" has been employed, throughout continental Europe, to express a love of the public good; a preference for the interests of the many to those of the few; a desire for the emancipation of the human race from the thrall of despotism, religious and civil: in short, "patriotism" there is used rather to express the interest felt in the human race in general than that felt for any country, or inhabitants of a country, in particular. And "patriot," in like manner, is employed to signify a lover of human liberty and human improvement rather than a mere lover of the country in which he lives, or the tribe to which he belongs.

Used in this sense, patriotism is a virtue, and a patriot a virtuous man. With such an interpretation, a patriot is a useful member of society, capable of enlarging all minds and bettering all hearts with which he comes in contact; a useful member of the human family, capable of establishing fundamental principles and of merging his own interests, those of his associates, and those of his nation in the interests of the human race. Laurels and statues are vain things, and mischievous as they are childish; but could we imagine them of use, on *such* a patriot alone could they be with any reason bestowed. . . .

If such a patriotism as we have last considered should seem likely to obtain in any country, it should be certainly in this. In this which is truly the home of all nations and in the veins of whose citizens flows the blood of every people on the globe. Patriotism, in the exclusive meaning, is surely not made for America. Mischievous everywhere, it were here both mischievous and absurd. The very origin of the people is opposed to it. The institutions, in their principle, militate against it. The day we are celebrating protests against it.

It is for Americans, more especially, to nourish a nobler sentiment, one more consistent with their origin, and more conducive to their future improvement. It is for them more especially to know why they love their country; and to *feel* that they love it, not because it *is* their country, but because it is the palladium of human liberty—the favored scene of human improvement. It is for them, more especially, to examine their institutions; and to *feel* that they honor them because they are based on just principles. It is for them, more especially, to examine their institutions, because they have the means of improving them; to examine their laws, because at will they can alter them. It is for them to lay aside luxury whose wealth is in industry; idle parade whose strength is in knowledge; ambitious distinctions whose principle is equality. It is for them not to rest, satisfied with words, who can seize upon things; and to remember that equality means, not the mere equality of political rights, however valuable, but equality of instruction and equality in virtue; and that liberty means, not the mere voting at elections, but the free and fearless exercise of the mental faculties and that self-possession which springs out of well-reasoned opinions and consistent practice. It is for them to honor principles rather than men—to commemorate events rather than days; when they rejoice, to know for what they rejoice, and to rejoice only for what has brought and what brings peace and happiness to men.

The event we commemorate this day has procured much of both, and shall procure in the onward course of human improvement more than we can now conceive of. For this—for the good obtained and yet in store for our race—let us rejoice! But let us rejoice as men, not as children—as human beings rather than as Americans—as reasoning beings, not as ignorants. So shall we rejoice to good purpose and in good feeling; so shall we improve the victory once on this day achieved, until all mankind hold with us the Jubilee of Independence. ■

Lincoln Rededicates the
Union at Gettysburg

". . . A new birth of freedom . . ."

"I SHALL BE GLAD," wrote orator Edward Everett to the president a day after the dedication of the cemetery at Gettysburg, "if I could flatter myself that I came as near to the central idea of the occasion in two hours as you did in two minutes." Lincoln replied, "In our respective parts yesterday, you could not have been excused to make a short address, nor I a long one. . . ."

The back-of-the-envelope legend is strictly a legend; this carefully composed speech was not written on the way to the event. Noah Brooks, Lincoln's favorite reporter, stated that some days before the November 19, 1863, dedication, he saw Lincoln in Washington and that the president told him his Gettysburg remarks were "written, 'but not finished.'"

In an early draft, according to historian J. G. Randall, "It is for us, the living, to stand here" was changed to ". . . to be dedicated here." After the speech was delivered, Lincoln made further revisions in the copy to be distributed to the Associated Press; it included "under God," which he had added on the podium; perhaps he recalled Treasury Secretary Chase's admonition to add a reference to the Deity to the Emancipation Proclamation, issued at the start of 1863.

The 266-word address opens with "Four score and seven," adding a note of biblical solemnity to the number 87. It concludes with a succession of parallel phrases that may have been inspired by abolitionist preacher Theodore Parker, who in 1850 wrote, "This [American] idea, demands . . . a democracy, that is, a government of all the people, by all the people, for all the people. . . ."

The speech can be read as a poem based on the metaphor of birth, death, and rebirth—with its subtle evocation of the resurrection of Christ—and focused on the theme of the nation's rededication to the principle of freedom,

Four images of birth are embedded in its opening sentence: the nation was *"conceived* in liberty"; *"brought forth,"* or born, "by our *fathers"*; with all men *"created* equal." This birth is followed by images of death—*"final resting place,"* "who *gave their lives,"* "brave men, living and *dead,"* "these honored *dead"*—and by verbs of religious purification—*"consecrate . . . hallow."*

After the nation's symbolic birth and death comes resurrection: out of the scene of death, "this nation, under God, shall have a *new birth* of freedom" and thus *"not perish,"* but be immortal.

The central word, as Lincoln's emendation of his early draft illustrates, is "dedicate"—used five times in the short speech, its meaning rooted in consecration, making the secular sacred by pledging it to God. The first two dedications are to the Declaration of Independence's ideal—"that all men are created equal." The third dedication centers on the purpose of the occasion at Gettysburg's bloody battleground, "to dedicate a portion of that field, as a final resting place." The fourth and fifth are rededications to the ideals of the reborn nation: "to the unfinished work" and "to the great task remaining before us."

Birth of a nation and its ideal; its symbolic death and purification in civil war; its rebirth in freedom with "increased devotion to that cause"— a profound and timeless idea, poetically presented in metaphor and a reverent tone, rolling toward its conclusion of immortality with a succession of four "that" clauses that lend themselves to rhythmic delivery—no wonder this is recognized so widely as the best short speech since the Sermon on the Mount.

□   □   □

Four score and seven years ago our fathers brought forth on this continent, a new nation, conceived in liberty, and dedicated to the proposition that all men are created equal.

Now we are engaged in a great civil war, testing whether that nation, or any nation so conceived and so dedicated, can long endure. We are met on a great battlefield of that war. We have come to dedicate a portion of that field, as a final resting place for those who here gave their lives that that nation might live. It is altogether fitting and proper that we should do this.

But, in a larger sense, we cannot dedicate—we cannot consecrate—we cannot hallow—this ground. The brave men, living and dead, who struggled here, have consecrated it, far above our poor power to add or detract. The world will little note, nor long remember, what we say here, but it can never forget what they did here. It is for us the living, rather, to be dedicated here to the unfinished work which they who fought here have thus far so nobly advanced. It is rather for us to be here dedicated to the great task remaining before us—that from these honored dead we take increased devotion to that cause for which they gave the last full measure of devotion—that we here highly resolve that these dead shall not have died in vain—that this nation, under God, shall have a new birth of freedom—and that government of the people, by the people, for the people, shall not perish from the earth.

Mark Twain Celebrates the Fourth of July

"THE . . . Fourth of July is not perfect as it stands. See what it costs us every year. . . ."

AMERICAN HUMORIST MARK TWAIN was in London on July 4, 1899, and was asked to deliver one of the speeches at the Fourth of July dinner given there by the American society. After a series of speakers that included Joseph Hodges Choate, America's new ambassador to Great Britain, Twain delivered his address, "The Day We Celebrate."

Typical of Twain's anecdotal style, this speech veered dangerously far afield from the stated topic of Independence Day. Differences in etiquette and language began his address, as he raised the usage question of "an historical" that has continued to be linguistically controversial throughout the twentieth century. With little pretense of transitions, Twain moved from his story of the clergyman's hat to an assessment of the financial and physical dangers of the Fourth of July, a day that sparks "the old war spirit."

Eight years later on July 4, when Twain addressed the same society, he embellished his assessment with a tall tale. On Independence Day, he said, one of his uncles had "opened his mouth to hurrah, and a rocket went down his throat. . . . It blew up and scattered him all over the forty-five states, and—really, now, this is true—I know about it myself—twenty-four hours after that it was raining buttons, recognizable as his, on the Atlantic seaboard."

□   □   □

I noticed in Ambassador Choate's speech that he said, "You may be Americans or Englishmen, but you cannot be both at the same time." You responded by applause.

Consider the effect of a short residence here. I find the ambassador rises first to speak to a toast, followed by a senator, and I come third. What a subtle tribute that to monarchial influence of the country when you place rank above respectability!

I was born modest, and if I had not been things like this would force it upon me. I understand it quite well. I am here to see that between them they do justice to the day we celebrate, and in case they do not I must do it myself. But I notice they have considered this day merely from one side—its sentimental, patriotic, poetic side. But it has another side. It has a commercial, a business side that needs reforming. It has a historical side.

I do not say "an" historical side, because I am speaking the American language. I do not see why our cousins should continue to say "an" hospital, "an" historical fact, "an" horse. It seems to me the Congress of Women, now in session, should look to it. I think "an" is having a little too much to do with it. It comes of habit, which accounts for many things.

Yesterday, for example, I was at a luncheon party. At the end of the party a great dignitary of the English Established Church went away half an hour before anybody else and carried off my hat. Now, that was an innocent act on his part. He went out first and, of course, had the choice of hats. As a rule, I try to get out first myself. But I hold that it was an innocent, unconscious act, due, perhaps, to heredity. He was thinking about ecclesiastical matters, and when a man is in that condition of mind he will take anybody's hat. The result was that the whole afternoon I was under the influence of his clerical hat and could not tell a lie. Of course, he was hard at it.

It is a compliment to both of us. His hat fitted me exactly; my hat fitted him exactly. So I judge I was born to rise to high dignity in the church somehow or other, but I do not know what he was born for. That is an illustration of the influence of habit, and it is perceptible here when they say "an" hospital, "an" European, "an" historical.

The business aspect of the Fourth of July is not perfect as it stands. See what it costs us every year with loss of life, the crippling of thousands with its fireworks, and the burning down of property. It is not only sacred to patriotism and universal freedom but to the surgeon, the undertaker, the insurance offices—and they are working it for all it is worth.

I am pleased to see that we have a cessation of war for the time. This coming from me, a soldier, you will appreciate. I was a soldier in the southern war for two weeks, and when gentlemen get up to speak of the great deeds our army and navy have recently done, why, it goes all through me and fires up the old war spirit. I had in my first engagement three horses shot under me. The next ones went over my head, the next hit me in the back. Then I retired to meet an engagement.

I thank you, gentlemen, for making even a slight reference to the war profession, in which I distinguished myself, short as my career was. ■

President Calvin Coolidge Affirms His Faith in Massachusetts

"HAVE faith in Massachusetts."

"IT APPEARED to me in January, 1914," wrote Coolidge in his 1929 autobiography, "that a spirit of radicalism prevailed which unless checked was likely to prove very destructive. . . . What was needed was a restoration of confidence in our own institutions and in each other, on which economic progress might rest."

In taking the chair of the Massachusetts senate, the Vermonter who would become the thirtieth president made what he described as "a short address, which [he] had carefully prepared, appealing to the conservative spirit of the people." The speech was widely remarked in Republican circles; it was circulated at the party's national convention in Chicago in 1920, and helped get him on the Harding ticket.

"Keep Cool with Coolidge" was the slogan he ran on in 1924, having succeeded Harding; the reputation for taciturnity was a source of both admiration and scorn. Dorothy Parker declared him "weaned on a pickle," and although President Reagan hung the Coolidge portrait in the Cabinet Room, his reputation today is that of an inarticulate sourpuss. Few of those who put him down, however, could write the sort of direct, powerful prose in the address that launched his national career, and which is printed here in its entirety.

The sentences are short and declarative. The argument marches steadily to its conclusion. The paragraph that begins, "Do the day's work . . . ," is as punchy and sensible as any delivered by a U.S. politician. French philosopher Buffon wrote, "The style is the man himself," meaning that the expression reveals the person, and nowhere is that more true than in this exposition of limited government by a man who limited what he had to say to what he thought strictly necessary.

□   □   □

I thank you—with gratitude for the high honor given, with appreciation for the solemn obligations assumed—I thank you.

This commonwealth is one. We are all members of one body. The welfare of the weakest and the welfare of the most powerful are inseparably bound together. Industry cannot flourish if labor languish. Transportation cannot prosper if manufactures decline. The general welfare cannot be provided for in any one act, but it is well to remember that the benefit of one is the benefit of all, and the neglect of one is the neglect of all. The suspension of one man's dividends is the suspension of another man's pay envelope.

Men do not make laws. They do but discover them. Laws must be justified by something more than the will of the majority. They must rest on the eternal foundation of righteousness. That state is most fortunate in its form of government which has the aptest instruments for the discovery of laws. The latest, most modern, and nearest perfect system that statesmanship has devised is representative government. Its weakness is the weakness of us imperfect human beings who administer it. Its strength is that even such administration secures to the people more blessings than any other system ever produced. No nation has discarded it and retained liberty. Representative government must be preserved.

Courts are established, not to determine the popularity of a cause, but to adjudicate and enforce rights. No litigant should be required to submit his case to the hazard and expense of a political campaign. No judge should be required to seek or receive political rewards. The courts of Massachusetts are known and honored wherever men love justice. Let their glory suffer no diminution at our hands. The electorate and judiciary cannot combine. A hearing means a hearing. When the trial of causes goes outside the courtroom, Anglo-Saxon constitutional government ends.

The people cannot look to legislation generally for success. Industry, thrift, character, are not conferred by act or resolve. Government cannot relieve from toil. It can provide no substitute for the rewards of service. It can, of course, care for the defective and recognize distinguished merit. The normal just care for themselves. Self-government means self-support.

Man is born into the universe with a personality that is his own. He has a right that is founded upon the constitution of the universe to have property that is his own. Ultimately, property rights and personal rights are the same thing. The one cannot be preserved if the other be violated. Each man is entitled to his rights and the rewards of his service, be they never so large or never so small.

History reveals no civilized people among whom there were not a highly educated class, and large aggregations of wealth, represented usually by the clergy and the nobility. Inspiration has always come from above. Diffusion of learning has come down from the university to the common school—the kindergarten is last. No one would now expect to aid the common school by abolishing higher education.

It may be that the diffusion of wealth works in an analogous way. As the little red schoolhouse is builded in the college, it may be that the fostering and protection of large aggregations of wealth are the only foundation on which to build the prosperity of the whole people. Large profits mean large payrolls. But profits must be the result of service performed. In no land are there so many and such large aggregations of wealth as here; in no land do they perform larger service; in no land will the work of a day bring so large a reward in material and spiritual welfare.

Have faith in Massachusetts. In some unimportant detail some other states may surpass her, but in the general results, there is no place on earth where the people secure, in a larger measure, the blessings of organized government, and nowhere can those functions more properly be termed self-government.

Do the day's work. If it be to protect the rights of the weak, whoever objects, do it. If it be to help a powerful corporation better to serve the people, whatever the opposition, do that. Expect to be called a standpatter, but don't be a standpatter. Expect to be called a demagogue, but don't be a demagogue. Don't hesitate to be as revolutionary as science. Don't hesitate to be as reactionary as the multiplication table. Don't expect to build up the weak by pulling down the strong. Don't hurry to legislate. Give administration a chance to catch up with legislation.

We need a broader, firmer, deeper faith in the people—a faith that men desire to do right, that the commonwealth is founded upon a righteousness which will endure, a reconstructed faith that the final approval of the people is given not to demagogues, slavishly pandering to their selfishness, merchandising with the clamor of the hour, but to statesmen, ministering to their welfare, representing their deep, silent, abiding convictions.

Statutes must appeal to more than material welfare. Wages won't satisfy, be they never so large. Nor houses; nor lands; nor coupons, though they fall thick as the leaves of autumn. Man has a spiritual nature. Touch it, and it must respond as the magnet responds to the pole. To that, not to selfishness, let the laws of the commonwealth appeal. Recognize the immortal worth and dignity of man. Let the laws of Massachusetts proclaim to her humblest citizen, performing the most menial task, the recognition of his manhood, the recognition that all men are peers, the humblest with the most exalted, the recognition that all work is glorified. Such is the path to equality before the law. Such is the foundation of liberty under the law. Such is the sublime revelation of man's relation to man—democracy. ■

Interior Secretary Harold Ickes Lashes Isolationists and Defeatists

"DESTROY a whole generation of those who have known how to walk with heads erect in God's free air, and the next generation will rise against the oppressors and restore freedom."

HAROLD ICKES was a Chicago lawyer and newspaper reporter with a flair for plain speaking and an instinct for the killing phrase. He styled himself a "curmudgeon"; when he resigned from Harry Truman's cabinet over the selection of a Truman friend to be undersecretary of the navy, he entered political phrasemaking immortality with "I am against government by crony."

As Franklin Roosevelt's secretary of the interior, the outspoken Ickes was point man attacking the New Deal's detractors. As World War II began, he took on Senator Burton K. Wheeler and members of the America First Committee, getting out in front of FDR in castigating the isolationists. In 1940, poet Anne Morrow Lindbergh, like her husband, Charles, impressed by Germany's power, wrote a long essay titled "The Wave of the Future," which many readers took as an apologia for fascism. In his May 18, 1941, "I Am an American Day" speech on the Central Park Mall in New York City, Ickes made the case for intervention and chose as his villain "the wavers of the future." The sentences are short, declarative, punchy, answering simple self-directed questions: "Do you know why? Because we cannot live in the world alone. . . ." The accusations admit no pussyfooting: "I tell you that this is a cold-blooded lie." It is a classic of rock-'em, sock-'em political oratory with an undercurrent of idealism.

□   □   □

I want to ask a few simple questions. And then I shall answer them.

What has happened to our vaunted idealism? Why have some of us been behaving like scared chickens? Where is the million-throated, democratic voice of America?

For years it has been dinned into us that we are a weak nation; that we are an inefficient people; that we are simple-minded. For years we have been told that we are beaten, decayed, and that no part of the world belongs to us any longer.

Some amongst us have fallen for this carefully pickled tripe. Some amongst us have fallen for this calculated poison. Some amongst us have begun to preach that the "wave of the future" has passed over us and left us a wet, dead fish.

They shout—from public platforms, in printed pages, through the microphones—that it is futile to oppose the "wave of the future." They cry that we Americans, we free Americans nourished on Magna Carta and the Declaration of Independence, hold moth-eaten ideas. They exclaim that there is no room for free men in the world any more and that only the slaves will inherit the earth. America—the America of Washington and Jefferson and Lincoln and Walt Whitman—they say, is waiting for the undertaker and all the hopes and aspirations that have gone into the making of America are dead too.

However, my fellow citizens, this is not the real point of the story. The real point—the shameful point—is that many of us are listening to them and some of us almost believe them.

I say that it is time for the great American people to raise its voice and cry out in mighty triumph what it is to be an American. And why it is that only Americans, with the aid of our brave allies—yes, let's call them "allies"—the British, can and will build the only future worth having. I mean a future, not of concentration camps, not of physical torture and mental straitjackets, not of sawdust bread or of sawdust Caesars—I mean a future when free men will live free lives in dignity and in security.

This tide of the future, the democratic future, is ours. It is ours if we show ourselves worthy of our culture and of our heritage.

But make no mistake about it; the tide of the democratic future is not like the ocean tide—regular, relentless, and inevitable. Nothing in human affairs is mechanical or inevitable. Nor are Americans mechanical. They are very human indeed.

What constitutes an American? Not color nor race nor religion. Not the pedigree of his family nor the place of his birth. Not the coincidence of his citizenship. Not his social status nor his bank account. Not his trade nor his profession. An American is one who loves justice and believes in the dignity of man. An American is one who will fight for his freedom and that of his neighbor. An American is one who will sacrifice property, ease, and security in order that he and his children may retain the rights of free men. An American is one in whose heart is engraved the immortal second sentence of the Declaration of Independence.

Americans have always known how to fight for their rights and their way of life. Americans are not afraid to fight. They fight joyously in a just cause.

We Americans know that freedom, like peace, is indivisible. We cannot retain our liberty if three-fourths of the world is enslaved. Brutality, injustice, and slavery, if practiced as dictators would have them, universally and systematically, in the long run would destroy us as surely as a fire raging in our nearby neighbor's house would burn ours if we didn't help to put out his.

If we are to retain our own freedom, we must do everything within our power to aid Britain. We must also do everything to restore to the conquered peoples their freedom. This means the Germans too.

Such a program, if you stop to think, is selfishness on our part. It is the sort of enlightened selfishness that makes the wheels of history go around. It is the sort of enlightened selfishness that wins victories.

Do you know why? Because we cannot live in the world alone, without friends and without allies. If Britain should be defeated, then the totalitarian undertaker will prepare to hang crepe on the door of our own independence.

Perhaps you wonder how this could come about? Perhaps you have heard "them"—the wavers of the future—cry, with calculated malice, that even if Britain were defeated we could live alone and defend ourselves single-handed, even against the whole world.

I tell you that this is a cold-blooded lie.

We would be alone in the world, facing an unscrupulous military-economic bloc that would dominate all of Europe, all of Africa, most of Asia, and perhaps even Russia and South America. Even to do that, we would have to spend most of our national income on tanks and guns and planes and ships. Nor would this be all. We would have to live perpetually as an armed camp, maintaining a huge standing army, a gigantic air force, two vast navies. And we could not do this without endangering our freedom, our democracy, our way of life. . . .

We should be clear on this point. What is convulsing the world today is not merely another old-fashioned war. It is a counterrevolution against our ideas and ideals, against our sense of justice and our human values.

Three systems today compete for world domination. Communism, fascism, and democracy are struggling for social-economic-political world control. As the conflict sharpens, it becomes clear that the other two, fascism and communism, are merging into one. They have one common enemy, democracy. They have one common goal, the destruction of democracy.

This is why this war is not an ordinary war. It is not a conflict for markets or territories. It is a desperate struggle for the possession of the souls of men. . . .

No, liberty never dies. The Genghis Khans come and go. The Attilas come and go. The Hitlers flash and sputter out. But freedom endures.

Destroy a whole generation of those who have known how to walk with heads erect in God's free air, and the next generation will rise against the oppressors and restore freedom. Today in Europe, the Nazi Attila may gloat that he has destroyed democracy. He is wrong. In small farmhouses all over Central Europe, in the shops of Germany and Italy, on the docks of Holland and Belgium, freedom still lives in the hearts of men. It will endure like a hardy tree gone into the wintertime, awaiting the spring.

And, like spring, spreading from the South into Scandinavia, the democratic revolution will come. And men with democratic hearts will experience comradeship across artificial boundaries.

These men and women, hundreds of millions of them, now in bondage or threatened with slavery, are our comrades and our allies. They are only waiting for our leadership and our encouragement, for the spark that we can supply.

These hundreds of millions of liberty-loving people, now oppressed, constitute the greatest sixth column in history. They have the will to destroy the Nazi gangsters. . . .

We will help brave England drive back the hordes from hell who besiege her, and then we will join for the destruction of savage and bloodthirsty dictators everywhere. But we must be firm and decisive. We must know our will and make it felt. And we must hurry. ■

Judge Learned Hand Evokes the Spirit of Liberty

"THE spirit of liberty is the spirit which is not too sure that it is right. . . ."

THE INFLUENTIAL JURIST with the unlikely but appropriate name Learned Hand served as presiding judge of the Second Circuit Court of Appeals from 1939 to 1951, and as senior judge for a decade after. Though never appointed to the Supreme Court, he was able, through his two thousand decisions, to uphold the liberty of the individual and to show that the written and the spoken word did not need the most august forum to have an impact on the law.

Toward the end of World War II, Judge Hand spoke at an "I Am an American Day" ceremony in New York City's Central Park. Instead of a rousing, patriotic address, he delivered a thoughtful credo that profoundly moved the audience; when his "Spirit of Liberty" speech was widely reprinted, the judge took care to add a footnote crediting historian H. G. Wells for a thought on which he bottomed the line about how Jesus "taught mankind a lesson it has never learned, but has never quite forgotten"; the Wells phrasing was "whose pitiless and difficult doctrine of self-abandonment and self-forgetfulness we can neither disregard nor yet bring ourselves to obey." Such scrupulous attribution of an idea is rare, but it was characteristic of Judge Hand, who was careful about not stealing anything.

The following year, on May 20, 1945, he spoke again at the same occasion. The two talks fit together nicely in reverse order, and I've taken the liberty of so arranging them; the 1944 section begins, "We have gathered here to affirm a faith. . . ."

□ □ □

We meet once more to attest our loyalty, and pledge our allegiance. . . . As we renew our mutual fealty, it is fitting that we should pause, and seek to take account of the meaning of our cost and suffering. Was not the issue this: whether mankind should be divided between those who command and those who serve; between those who use others at their will and those who must submit; whether the measure of a man's power to shape his own destiny should be the force at his disposal? Our nation was founded upon an answer to those questions, and we have fought this war to make good that answer. For ourselves and for the present, we are safe; our immediate peril is past. But for how long are we safe, and how far have we removed our peril? If our nation could not itself exist half slave and half free, are we sure that it can exist in a world half slave and half free? Is the same conflict less irrepressible when worldwide than it was eighty years ago when it was only nationwide? Right knows no boundaries, and justice no frontiers; the brotherhood of man is not a domestic institution.

No, our job will not end with the sound of the guns. Even in our own interest we must have an eye to the interests of others; a nation which lives only to itself will in the end perish; false to the faith, it will shrivel and pass to that oblivion which is its proper receptacle. We may not stop until we have done our part to fashion a world in which there shall be some share of fellowship; which shall be better than a den of thieves. Let us not disguise the difficulties; and, above all, let us not content ourselves with noble aspirations, counsels of perfection, and self-righteous advice to others. We shall need the wisdom of the serpent; we shall have to be content with short steps; we shall be obliged to give and take: we shall face the strongest passions of mankind—our own not the least; and in the end we shall have fabricated an imperfect instrument. But we shall not have wholly failed; we shall have gone forward, if we bring to our task a pure and chastened spirit, patience, understanding, sympathy, forbearance, generosity, fortitude, and, above all, an inflexible determination. The history of man has just begun: in the aeons which lie before him lie limitless hope or limitless despair. The choice is his; the present choice is ours: it is worth the trial. . . .

We have gathered here to affirm a faith, a faith in a common purpose, a common conviction, a common devotion. Some of us have chosen America as the land of our adoption; the rest have come from those who did the same. For this reason we have some right to consider ourselves a picked group, a group of those who had the courage to break from the past and brave the dangers and the loneliness of a strange land. What was the object that nerved us, or those who went before us, to this choice? We sought liberty—freedom from oppression, freedom from want, freedom to be ourselves. This we then sought; this we now believe that we are by way of winning. What do we mean when we say that first of all we seek liberty? I often wonder whether we do not rest our hopes too much upon constitutions, upon laws, and upon courts. These are false hopes; believe me, these are false hopes. Liberty lies in the hearts of men and women; when it dies there, no constitution, no law, no court can save it; no constitution, no law, no court can even do much to help it. While it lies there, it needs no constitution, no law, no court to save it. And what is this liberty which must lie in the hearts of men and women? It is not the ruthless, the unbridled will; it is not freedom to do as one likes. That is the denial of liberty, and leads straight to its overthrow. A society in which men recognize no check upon their freedom soon becomes a society where freedom is the possession of only a savage few—as we have learned to our sorrow.

What, then, is the spirit of liberty? I cannot define it; I can only tell you my own faith. The spirit of liberty is the spirit which is not too sure that it is right; the spirit of liberty is the spirit which seeks to understand the minds of other men and women; the spirit of liberty is the spirit which weighs their interests alongside its own without bias; the spirit of liberty remembers that not even a sparrow falls to earth unheeded; the spirit of liberty is the spirit of him who, near two thousand years ago, taught mankind that lesson it has never learned, but has never quite forgotten—that there may be a kingdom where the least shall be heard and considered side by side with the greatest. And now in that spirit, that spirit of an America which has never been, and which may never be—nay, which never will be except as the conscience and courage of Americans create it—yet in the spirit of that America which lies hidden in some form in the aspirations of us all; in the spirit of that America for which our young men are at this moment fighting and dying; in that spirit of liberty and of America so prosperous, and safe, and contented, we shall have failed to grasp its meaning, and shall have been truant to its promise, except as we strive to make it a signal, a beacon, a standard, to which the best hopes of mankind will ever turn. In confidence that you share that belief, I now ask you to raise your hands and repeat with me this pledge:

I pledge allegiance to the flag of the United States of America, and to the Republic for which it stands—one nation, indivisible, with liberty and justice for all. ■

Underground Fighter Menachem Begin Pledges His Group's Allegiance to the Newborn State of Israel

"QUICKLY! Quickly! Our nation has no time! Bring in hundreds of thousands. . . .
We are now in the midst of a war for survival; and our tomorrow and theirs depend
on the quickest concentration of our nation's exiles."

MENACHEM BEGIN, a Polish-born Holocaust survivor, served as head of Israel's main opposition party until 1977, when he became prime minister; he shared the Nobel Peace Prize in 1978 with President Anwar el-Sadat of Egypt as a result of their peace accords. At the White House ceremony with President Carter on March 26, 1979, Begin began to speak in his customary formal style: "The ancient Jewish people gave the New World a vision of eternal peace, of universal disarmament, of abolishing the teaching and learning of war." He used both the Hebrew and the Arabic words for peace: "No more war, no more bloodshed, no more bereavement. Peace unto you. *Shalom, salaam*, forever." Finally, he offered a prayer of thanksgiving, which he "learned as a child in the home of father and mother, who do not exist anymore, because they were among the six million people—men, women and children—who sanctified the Lord's name with their sacred blood, which reddened the rivers of Europe from the Rhine to the Danube, from the Bug to the Volga, because—only because—they were born Jews; and because they didn't have a country of their own, or a valiant Jewish army to defend them. And because nobody, nobody, came to their rescue, although they cried out 'Save us! Save us!' *de profundis*, from the depths of the pit and agony."

He called that treaty-signing day "the third greatest day" in his life. He said the second was in 1967, when Israeli soldiers turned back a Jordanian attack and unified Jerusalem. The first was the day in 1948 on which Israel became a state.

In his youth, the head of the Irgun Zvai Leumi was a fiery speaker. The emblem of the Irgun was a raised right arm grasping a bayoneted rifle, with the legend "Only Thus"; the point was that only through military uprising could Jews achieve their homeland.

On May 14, 1948—Begin's "greatest day"—the less militant Jewish leaders in the Haganah dared to proclaim a provisional Hebrew government. The next night, as Arab forces prepared for attack, Begin went to the secret radio station of the Irgun in Tel Aviv. He wrote later, "I felt no stage-fright. I was among my friends, in 'my house,' in the radio station from which the voice of Revolt and Freedom had for years gone forth to every town and village in our land. But the solemnity of the hour over-awed me. . . . My comrades told me that almost every Jewish home with a radio had listened in to my address, and I was thankful that my words had helped to hearten the people."

□   □   □

After many years of underground warfare, years of persecution and moral and physical suffering, the rebels against the oppressor stand before you, with a blessing of thanks on their lips and a prayer in their hearts. The blessing is the age-old blessing with which our fathers and our forefathers have always greeted holy days. It was with this blessing that they used to taste any fruit for the first time in the season. Today is truly a holiday, a holy day, and a new fruit is visible before our very eyes. The Hebrew revolt of 1944–48 has been blessed with success—the first Hebrew revolt since the Hasmonean insurrection that has ended in victory. The rule of oppression in our country has been beaten, uprooted; it has crumbled and been dispersed. The state of Israel has arisen in bloody battle. The highway for the mass return to Zion has been cast up.

The foundation has been laid—but only the foundation—for true independence. One phase of the battle for freedom, for the return of the whole people of Israel to its homeland, for the restoration of the whole land of Israel to its God-covenanted owners, has ended. But only one phase. . . .

The state of Israel has arisen. And it has arisen "Only Thus": through blood, through fire, with an outstretched hand and a mighty arm, with sufferings and with sacrifices. It could not have been otherwise. And yet, even before our state is able to set up its normal national institutions, it is compelled to fight—or to continue to fight satanic enemies and blood-thirsty mercenaries, on land, in the air, and on the sea. In these circumstances, the warning sounded by the philosopher-president Thomas Masaryk to the Czechoslovak nation when it attained its freedom, after three hundred years of slavery, has a special significance for us.

In 1918, when Masaryk stepped out onto the Wilson railway station in Prague, he warned his cheering countrymen, "It is difficult to set up a state; it is even more difficult to keep it going." In truth, it has been difficult for us to set up our state. Tens of generations, and millions of wanderers, from one land of massacre to another, were needed; it was necessary that there be exile, burning at the stake and torture in the dungeons; we had to suffer agonizing disillusionments; we needed the warnings—though they often went unheeded—of prophets and of seers; we needed the sweat and toil of generations of pioneers and builders; we had to have an uprising of rebels to crush the enemy; we had to have the gallows, the banishments beyond seas, the prisons, and the cages in the deserts—all this was necessary that we might reach the present stage where six hundred thousand Jews are in the homeland, where the direct rule of oppression has been driven out, and Hebrew independence declared in part at least of the country, the whole of which is ours.

It has been difficult to create our state. But it will be still more difficult to keep it going. We are surrounded by enemies who long for our destruction. And that same oppressor, who has been defeated by us directly, is trying indirectly to make us surrender with the aid of mercenaries from the south, the north, and the east. Our one-day-old state is set up in the midst of the flames of battle. And the first pillar of our state must therefore be victory, total victory, in the war which is raging all over the country. For this victory, without which we shall have neither freedom nor life, we need arms—weapons of all sorts, in order to strike the enemies, in order to disperse the invaders, in order to free the entire length and breadth of the country from its would-be destroyers.

But in addition to these arms, each and every one of us has need of another weapon, a spiritual weapon, the weapon of unflinching endurance in face of attacks from the air; in face of grievous casualties; in face of local disasters and temporary defeats; unflinching resistance to threats and cajolery. If, within the coming days and weeks, we can put on this whole armor of an undying nation in resurrection, we shall in the meantime receive the blessed arms with which to drive off the enemy and bring freedom and peace to our nation and country.

But, even after emerging victorious from this campaign—and victorious we shall be—we shall still have to exert superhuman efforts in order to remain independent, in order to free our country. First of all it will be necessary to increase and strengthen the fighting arm of Israel, without which there can be no freedom and no survival for our homeland. . . .

We shall need a wise foreign policy in order to free our country and maintain our state. We must turn our declaration of independence into a reality. And we must grasp this fact: that so long as even one British or any other foreign soldier treads the soil of our country, our sovereign independence remains nothing but an aspiration, an aspiration for whose fulfillment we must be ready to fight not only on the battlefront but also in the international arena. Secondly, we must establish and maintain the principle of reciprocity in our relations with the nations of the world. There must be no self-denigration. There must be no surrender, and no favoritism. There must be reciprocity. Enmity for enmity. Aid for aid. Friendship must be repaid with friendship. . . .

We must foster friendship and understanding between us and every nation, great or small, strong or weak, near or far, which recognizes our independence, which aids our national regeneration, and which is interested, even as we are, in international justice and peace among nations.

Of no less importance is our internal policy. The first pillar of this policy is the return to Zion. Ships! For heaven's sake, let us have ships! Let us not be poisoned with inertia. Let us not talk empty words about absorptive capacity. Let us not make restrictions for the sake of so-called order. Quickly! Quickly! Our nation has no time! Bring in hundreds of thousands. . . . We are now in the midst of a war for survival; and our tomorrow and theirs depend on the quickest concentration of our nation's exiles.

And within our homeland: justice must be the supreme ruler, the ruler over all rulers. There must be no tyranny. The ministers and officials must be the servants of the nation and not their masters. There must be no exploitation. There must be no man within our country—be he citizen or foreigner—compelled to go hungry, to want for a roof over his head, or to lack elementary education. "Remember, ye were strangers in the land of Egypt"—this supreme rule must continually light our way in our relations with the strangers within our gates. "Righteousness, Righteousness shalt thou pursue!" Righteousness must be the guiding principle in our relations amongst ourselves. . . .

The Irgun Zvai Leumi is leaving the underground inside the boundaries of the Hebrew independent state. We went underground, we *arose* in the underground under the rule of oppression, in order to strike at oppression and to overthrow it. And right well have we struck. Now, for the time being, we have Hebrew rule in part of our homeland. And as in this part there will be Hebrew law—and that is the only rightful law in this country—there is no need for a Hebrew underground. In the state of Israel we shall be soldiers and builders. And we shall respect its government, for it is our government. . . .

The state of Israel has arisen, but we must remember that our country is not yet liberated. The battle continues, and you see now that the words of your Irgun fighters were not vain words: it is Hebrew arms which decide the boundaries of the Hebrew state. So it is now in this battle; so it will be in the future. Our God-given country is a unity. The attempt to dissect it is not only a crime but a blasphemy and an abortion. Whoever does not recognize our natural right to our entire homeland, does not recognize our right to any part of it. And we shall never forgo this natural right. We shall continue to foster the aspiration of full independence.

Citizens of the Hebrew state, soldiers of Israel, we are in the midst of battles. Difficult days lie ahead of us. . . . We cannot buy peace from our enemies with appeasement. There is only one kind of "peace" that can be bought—the peace of the graveyard, the peace of Treblinki. Be brave of spirit and ready for more trials. We shall withstand them. The Lord of Hosts will help us; he will sustain the bravery of the Hebrew youth, the bravery of the Hebrew mothers who, like Hannah, offer their sons on the altar of God.

And you, brothers of our fighting family, do you remember how we started? With what we started? You were alone and persecuted, rejected, despised, and numbered with the transgressors. But you fought on with deep faith and did not retreat; you were tortured but you did not surrender; you were cast into prison but you did not yield; you were exiled from your country but your spirit was not crushed; you were driven to the gallows but went forth with a song. You have written a glorious page in history. . . . You will not recall past grievances; you will ask for no reward.

But for the time being let us think of the battle, for only the outcome of the battle will decide our fate and future. We shall go on our way into battle, soldiers of the Lord of Hosts, inspired by the spirit of our ancient heroes, from the conquerors of Canaan to the Rebels of Judah. We shall be accompanied by the spirit of those who revived our nation, Zeev Benjamin Herzl, Max Nordau, Joseph Trumpeldor, and the father of resurrected Hebrew heroism, Zeev Jabotinsky. We shall be accompanied by the spirit of David Raziel, greatest of the Hebrew commanders of our day; and by Dov Gruner, one of the greatest of Hebrew soldiers. We shall be accompanied into battle by the spirit of the heroes of the gallows, the conquerors of death. And we shall be accompanied by the spirit of millions of our martyrs, our ancestors tortured and burned for their faith, our murdered fathers and butchered mothers, our murdered brothers and strangled children. And in this battle we shall break the enemy and bring salvation to our people, tried in the furnace of persecution, thirsting only for freedom, for righteousness, and for justice. ■

Democratic Candidate Adlai Stevenson Defines the Nature of Patriotism

"MEN who have offered their lives for their country know that patriotism is not the fear of something; it is the love of something."

"THE ORDEAL of the twentieth century—the bloodiest, most turbulent era of the Christian age—is far from over," Governor Adlai Stevenson of Illinois told the Democratic National Convention that selected him as standard-bearer in 1952. ". . . Let's face it. Let's talk sense to the American people. Let's tell them the truth, that there are no gains without pains."

"Sense" was a favorite word of the man for whom the epithet "egghead" was coined. Four years later, in his second unsuccessful campaign against Dwight Eisenhower, he said, "If I were to attempt to put my political philosophy tonight into a single phrase, it would be this: Trust the people. Trust their good sense. . . ."

In 1952, after the Truman administration had been labeled "the mess in Washington," Stevenson had to run against "communism, corruption, and Korea." Thanks to the effectiveness of charges of "twenty years of treason" in high places by Republican senator Joseph McCarthy, Democrats were on the defensive. Stevenson had to confront this corrosive theme directly; he put on his veteran's cap and addressed the American Legion Convention in New York's Madison Square Garden on August 27 on "the nature of patriotism."

□   □   □

. . . I have no claim, as many of you do, to the honored title of old soldier. Nor have I risen to high rank in the armed services. The fact that a great general and I are competing candidates for the presidency will not diminish my warm respect for his military achievements. Nor will that respect keep me from using every honest effort to defeat him in November! . . .

We talk a great deal about patriotism. What do we mean by "patriotism" in the context of our times? I venture to suggest that what we mean is a sense of national responsibility which will enable America to remain master of her power—to walk with it in serenity and wisdom, with self-respect and the respect of all mankind; a patriotism that puts country ahead of self; a patriotism which is not short, frenzied outbursts of emotion, but the tranquil and steady dedication of a lifetime. The dedication of a lifetime—these are words that are easy to utter, but this is a mighty assignment. For it is often easier to fight for principles than to live up to them.

Patriotism, I have said, means putting country before self. This is no abstract phrase, and unhappily, we find some things in American life today of which we cannot be proud.

Consider the groups who seek to identify their special interests with the general welfare. I find it sobering to think that their pressures might one day be focused on me. I have resisted them before, and I hope the Almighty will give me the strength to do so again and again. And I should tell you—my fellow Legionnaires—as I would tell all other organized groups, that I intend to resist pressures from veterans, too, if I think their demands are excessive or in conflict with the public interest, which must always be the paramount interest.

Let me suggest, incidentally, that we are rapidly becoming a nation of veterans. If we were all to claim a special reward for our service, beyond that to which specific disability or sacrifice has created a just claim, who would be left to pay the bill? After all, we are Americans first and veterans second, and the best maxim for any administration is still Jefferson's: "Equal rights for all, special privileges for none."

True patriotism, it seems to me, is based on tolerance and a large measure of humility.

There are men among us who use "patriotism" as a club for attacking other Americans. What can we say for the self-styled patriot who thinks that a Negro, a Jew, a Catholic, or a Japanese-American is less an American than he? That betrays the deepest article of our faith, the belief in individual liberty and equality which has always been the heart and soul of the American idea.

What can we say for the man who proclaims himself a patriot—and then for political or personal reasons attacks the patriotism of faithful public servants? I give you, as a shocking example, the attacks which have been made on the loyalty and the motives of our great wartime chief of staff, General Marshall. To me this is the type of "patriotism" which is, in Dr. Johnson's phrase, "the last refuge of scoundrels."

The anatomy of patriotism is complex. But surely intolerance and public irresponsibility cannot be cloaked in the shining armor of rectitude and righteousness. Nor can the denial of the right to hold ideas that are different—the freedom of man to think as he pleases. To strike freedom of the mind with the fist of patriotism is an old and ugly subtlety.

And the freedom of the mind, my friends, has served America well. The vigor of our political life, our capacity for change, our cultural, scientific, and industrial achievements, all derive from free inquiry, from the free mind—from the imagination, resourcefulness, and daring of men who are not afraid of new ideas. Most all of us favor free enterprise for business. Let us also favor free enterprise for the mind. For, in the last analysis, we would fight to the death to protect it. Why is it, then, that we are sometimes slow to detect, or are indifferent to, the dangers that beset it?

Many of the threats to our cherished freedoms in these anxious, troubled times arise, it seems to me, from a healthy apprehension about the Communist menace within our country. Communism is abhorrent. It is strangulation of the individual; it is death for the soul. Americans who have surrendered to this misbegotten idol have surrendered their right to our trust. And there can be no secure place for them in our public life.

Yet, as I have said before, we must take care not to burn down the barn to kill the rats. All of us, and especially patriotic organizations of enormous influence like the American Legion, must be vigilant in protecting our birthright from its too zealous friends while protecting it from its evil enemies.

The tragedy of our day is the climate of fear in which we live, and fear breeds repression. Too often sinister threats to the Bill of Rights, to freedom of the mind, are concealed under the patriotic cloak of anticommunism.

I could add, from my own experience, that it is never necessary to call a man a Communist to make political capital. Those of us who have undertaken to practice the ancient but imperfect art of government will always make enough mistakes to keep our critics well supplied with standard ammunition. There is no need for poison gas. . . .

Let me now, in my concluding words, inquire with you how we may affirm our patriotism in the troubled yet hopeful years that are ahead.

The central concern of the American Legion—the ideal which holds it together—the vitality which animates it—is patriotism. And those voices which we have heard most clearly and which are best remembered in our public life have always had the accent of patriotism.

It was always accounted a virtue in a man to love his country. With us it is now something more than a virtue. It is a necessity, a condition of survival. When an American says that he loves his country, he means not only that he loves the New England hills, the prairies glistening in the sun, the wide and rising plains, the great mountains, and the sea. He means that he loves an inner air, an inner light in which freedom lives and in which a man can draw the breath of self-respect.

Men who have offered their lives for their country know that patriotism is not the *fear* of something; it is the *love* of something. Patriotism with us is not the hatred of Russia; it is the love of this Republic and of the ideal of liberty of man and mind in which it was born, and to which this Republic is dedicated.

With this patriotism—patriotism in its large and wholesome meaning—America can master its power and turn it to the noble cause of peace. We can maintain military power without militarism; political power without oppression; and moral power without compulsion or complacency.

The road we travel is long, but at the end lies the grail of peace. And in the valley of peace we see the faint outlines of a new world, fertile and strong. It is odd that one of the keys to abundance should have been handed to civilization on a platter of destruction. But the power of the atom to work evil gives only the merest hint of its power for good.

I believe that man stands on the eve of his greatest day. I know, too, that that day is not a gift but a prize—that we shall not reach it until we have won it.

Legionnaires are united by memories of war. Therefore, no group is more devoted to peace. I say to you now that there is work to be done, that the difficulties and dangers that beset our path at home and abroad are incalculable. There is sweat and sacrifice; there is much of patience and quiet persistence in our horoscope. Perhaps the goal is not even for us to see in our lifetime.

But we are embarked on a great adventure. Let us proclaim our faith in the future of man. Of good heart and good cheer, faithful to ourselves and our traditions, we can lift the cause of freedom, the cause of free men, so high no power on earth can tear it down. We can pluck this flower, safety, from this nettle, danger. Living, speaking, like men—like Americans—we can lead the way to our rendezvous in a happy, peaceful world. ■

General Douglas MacArthur Reminds West Point Cadets of Duty, Honor, Country

"YOUR mission remains fixed, determined, inviolable. It is to win our wars. . . When I cross the river, my last conscious thoughts will be of the corps, and the corps, and the corps."

DOUGLAS MACARTHUR'S record as a cadet at West Point has served as a criterion for generations; after World War I, he returned to serve as commandant of the military academy; he went on to command all Allied forces in the Far East in World War II, and UN forces in Korea until he was fired by President Truman (see "Old Soldiers Never Die" speech, p. 425); and he returned to West Point on May 12, 1962, to deliver his most memorable address. He spoke as a soldier of one era to the soldiers of another to remind them of the values that undergird the profession of arms.

He took as his text "Duty, Honor, Country" from the legend on the West Point coat of arms, a motto adopted in 1898, one year before he entered the academy. Instead of dealing with each word, making that the organizing principle of his speech, MacArthur unified them as a trinity of patriotism. After an ostentatious bit of humility ("Unhappily, I possess neither that eloquence of diction, that poetry of imagination. . ."), perhaps patterned on Lincoln's "the world will little note, nor long remember what we say here," the general pointed to all the valuable qualities that a dedication to the three created. From there, he pointed to the sufferings of the soldier who persevered to victory under the single "password" of duty, honor, country. From that look back, he then took a long look ahead, to "a conflict between a united human race and the sinister forces of some other planetary galaxy," theme of a thousand television movies to come. Having established that sense of timelessness to the need for the military profession, the speaker reasserted the values that keep it outside the realm of politics—a poignant point to be made by a general who wanted to be president.

The language is poetic. Evoking the ghosts of the military dead, he dresses them in the colors of their wars: the "olive drab" of World War II, the "brown khaki" of World War I, "the blue and gray" of the Civil War. He uses surprising metaphors: "a thirsty ear," the "mournful mutter of the battlefields," and the curious "My days of old have vanished—tone and tints." (The once-strong sound of fighting and once-vivid color of war?)

□   □   □

No human being could fail to be deeply moved by such a tribute as this, coming from a profession I have served so long and a people I have loved so well. It fills me with an emotion I cannot express. But this award is not intended primarily for a personality, but to symbolize a great moral code—the code of conduct and chivalry of those who guard this beloved land of culture and ancient descent.

"Duty," "honor," "country"—those three hallowed words reverently dictate what you want to be, what you can be, what you will be. They are your rallying point to build courage when courage seems to fail, to regain faith when there seems to be little cause for faith, to create hope when hope becomes forlorn.

Unhappily, I possess neither that eloquence of diction, that poetry of imagination, nor that brilliance of metaphor to tell you all that they mean.

The unbelievers will say they are but words, but a slogan, but a flamboyant phrase. Every pedant, every demagogue, every cynic, every hypocrite, every troublemaker, and, I am sorry to say, some others of an entirely different character, will try to downgrade them even to the extent of mockery and ridicule.

But these are some of the things they build. They build your basic character. They mold you for your future roles as the custodians of the nation's defense. They make you strong enough to know when you are weak, and brave enough to face yourself when you are afraid.

They teach you to be proud and unbending in honest failure, but humble and gentle in success; not to substitute words for action; not to seek the path of comfort, but to face the stress and spur of difficulty and challenge; to learn to stand up in the storm, but to have compassion on those who fall; to master yourself before you seek to master others; to have a heart that is clean, a goal that is high; to learn to laugh, yet never forget how to weep; to reach into the future, yet never neglect the past; to be serious, yet never take yourself too seriously; to be modest so that you will remember the simplicity of true greatness; the open mind of true wisdom, the meekness of true strength.

They give you a temperate will, a quality of imagination, a vigor of the emotions, a freshness of the deep springs of life, a temperamental predominance of courage over timidity, an appetite for adventure over love of ease.

They create in your heart the sense of wonder, the unfailing hope of what next, and the joy and inspiration of life. They teach you in this way to be an officer and a gentleman.

And what sort of soldiers are those you are to lead? Are they reliable? Are they brave? Are they capable of victory?

Their story is known to all of you. It is the story of the American man-at-arms. My estimate of him was formed on the battlefields many, many years ago, and has never changed. I regarded him then, as I regard him now, as one of the world's noblest figures—not only as one of the finest military characters, but also as one of the most stainless.

His name and fame are the birthright of every American citizen. In his youth and strength, his love and loyalty, he gave all that mortality can give. He needs no eulogy from me, or from any other man. He has written his own history and written it in red on his enemy's breast.

In twenty campaigns, on a hundred battlefields, around a thousand campfires, I have witnessed that enduring fortitude, that patriotic self-abnegation, and that invincible determination which have carved his statue in the hearts of his people.

From one end of the world to the other, he has drained deep the chalice of courage. As I listened to those songs in memory's eye, I could see those staggering columns of the First World War, bending under soggy packs on many a weary march, from dripping dusk to drizzling dawn, slogging ankle deep through mire of shell-pocked roads; to form grimly for the attack, blue-lipped, covered with sludge and mud, chilled by the wind and rain, driving home to their objective, and for many, to the judgment seat of God.

I do not know the dignity of their birth, but I do know the glory of their death. They died unquestioning, uncomplaining, with faith in their hearts, and on their lips the hope that we would go on to victory.

Always for them: duty, honor, country. Always their blood, and sweat, and tears, as they saw the way and the light. And twenty years after, on the other side of the globe, against the filth of dirty foxholes, the stench of ghostly trenches, the slime of dripping dugouts, those boiling suns of the relentless heat, those torrential rains of devastating storms, the loneliness and utter desolation of jungle trails, the bitterness of long separation of those they loved and cherished, the deadly pestilence of tropic disease, the horror of stricken areas of war.

Their resolute and determined defense, their swift and sure attack, their indomitable purpose, their complete and decisive victory—always victory, always through the bloody haze of their last reverberating shot, the vision of gaunt, ghastly men, reverently following your password of duty, honor, country.

You now face a new world, a world of change. The thrust into outer space of the satellite spheres and missiles marks a beginning of another epoch in the long story of mankind. In the five or more billions of years the scientists tell us it has taken to form the earth, in the three or more billion years of development of the human race, there has never been a more abrupt or staggering evolution.

We deal now, not with things of this world alone, but with the illimitable distances and yet unfathomed mysteries of the universe. We are reaching out for a new and boundless frontier. We speak in strange terms of harnessing the cosmic energy, of making winds and tides work for us . . . of the primary target in war, no longer limited to the armed forces of an enemy, but instead to include his civil population; of ultimate conflict between a united human race and the sinister forces of some other planetary galaxy; such dreams and fantasies as to make life the most exciting of all times.

And through all this welter of change and development your mission remains fixed, determined, inviolable. It is to win our wars. Everything else in your professional career is but corollary to this vital dedication. All other public purpose, all other public projects, all other public needs, great or small, will find others for their accomplishments; but you are the ones who are trained to fight.

Yours is the profession of arms, the will to win, the sure knowledge that in war there is no substitute for victory, that if you lose, the nation will be destroyed, that the very obsession of your public service must be duty, honor, country.

Others will debate the controversial issues, national and international, which divide men's minds. But serene, calm, aloof, you stand as the nation's war guardians, as its lifeguards from the raging tides of international conflict, as its gladiators in the arena of battle. For a century and a half you have defended, guarded, and protected its hallowed traditions of liberty and freedom, of right and justice.

Let civilian voices argue the merits or demerits of our processes of government: whether our strength is being sapped by deficit financing indulged in too long, by federal paternalism grown too mighty, by power groups grown too arrogant, by politics grown too corrupt, by crime grown too rampant, by morals grown too low, by taxes grown too high, by extremists grown too violent; whether our personal liberties are as firm and complete as they should be.

These great national problems are not for your professional participation or military solution. Your guidepost stands out like a tenfold beacon in the night: duty, honor, country.

You are the lever which binds together the entire fabric of our national system of defense. From your ranks come the great captains who hold the nation's destiny in their hands the moment the war tocsin sounds.

The long gray line has never failed us. Were you to do so, a million ghosts in olive drab, in brown khaki, in blue and gray, would rise from their white crosses, thundering those magic words: duty, honor, country.

This does not mean that you are warmongers. On the contrary, the soldier above all other people prays for peace, for he must suffer and bear the deepest wounds and scars of war. But always in our ears ring the ominous words of Plato, that wisest of all philosophers: "Only the dead have seen the end of war."

The shadows are lengthening for me. The twilight is here. My days of old have vanished—tone and tints. They have gone glimmering through the dreams of things that were. Their memory is one of wondrous beauty, watered by tears and coaxed and caressed by the smiles of yesterday. I listen, then, but with thirsty ear, for the witching melody of faint bugles blowing reveille, of far drums beating the long roll.

In my dreams I hear again the crash of guns, the rattle of musketry, the strange, mournful mutter of the battlefield. But in the evening of my memory I come back to West Point. Always there echoes and re-echoes: duty, honor, country.

Today marks my final roll call with you. But I want you to know that when I cross the river, my last conscious thoughts will be of the corps, and the corps, and the corps.

I bid you farewell.

■ ■ ■

II

WAR
AND
REVOLUTION
SPEECHES

Catiline the Conspirator Turns and Fights

"Those who are most afraid are always in most danger; but courage is equivalent to a rampart."

CATILINE is a name synonymous with conspiracy. The Roman politician and general plotted, schemed, and maneuvered to take power from consul Cicero, who—using facts gained from Catiline's mistress—defamed him before the Senate (the first of Cicero's famous orations against Catiline is on p. 257). Catiline took those of his followers who escaped execution and raced for Gaul, but was cornered at Pistoria, more than two hundred miles north of Rome. He had the choice of fighting and dying or surrendering and dying. In January of 62 B.C., he spoke to his band of sure losers in a way that informed his doomed conspiracy with a nobility in the face of defeat. He was killed in the battle that followed.

The words are those of historian Sallust, who reconstructed the speech from what Catiline was reported to have said, much as a later historian did with Patrick Henry's oration. The opening paragraph, pure flattery, is quite untrue, but offers the sort of compliment an audience facing death likes to receive; the observation, near the close, that necessity "makes even cowards brave" is painfully true.

□   □   □

I am well aware, soldiers, that words cannot inspire courage and that a spiritless army cannot be rendered active, or a timid army valiant, by the speech of its commander. Whatever courage is in the heart of a man, whether from nature or from habit, so much will be shown by him in the field; and on him whom neither glory nor danger can move, exhortation is bestowed in vain, for the terror in his breast stops his ears.

I have called you together, however, to give you a few instructions, and to explain to you, at the same time, my reasons for the course which I have adopted. You all know, soldiers, how severe a penalty the inactivity and cowardice of Lentulus has brought upon himself and us; and how, while waiting for reinforcements from the city, I was unable to

march into Gaul. In what situation our affairs now are, you all understand as well as myself. Two armies of the enemy, one on the side of
Rome, and the other on that of Gaul, oppose our progress; while the
want of corn, and of other necessaries, prevents us from remaining,
however strongly we may desire to remain, in our present position.
Whithersoever we would go, we must open a passage with our swords.

I conjure you, therefore, to maintain a brave and resolute spirit and to
remember, when you advance to battle, that on your own right hands
depend riches, honor, and glory, with the enjoyment of your liberty and
of your country. If we conquer, all will be safe; we shall have provisions
in abundance, and the colonies and corporate towns will open their gates
to us. But if we lose the victory through want of courage, those same
places will turn against us, for neither place nor friend will protect him
whom his arms have not protected. Besides, soldiers, the same exigency
does not press upon our adversaries as presses upon us; we fight for our
country, for our liberty, for our life; they contend for what but little concerns them, the power of a small party. Attack them, therefore, with so
much the greater confidence, and call to mind your achievements of old.

We might, with the utmost ignominy, have passed the rest of our days
in exile. Some of you, after losing your property, might have waited at
Rome for assistance from others. But because such a life, to men of spirit,
was disgusting and unendurable, you resolved upon your present course.
If you wish to quit it, you must exert all your resolution, for none but
conquerors have exchanged war for peace. To hope for safety in flight,
when you have turned away from the enemy the arms by which the
body is defended, is indeed madness. In battle, those who are most afraid
are always in most danger; but courage is equivalent to a rampart.

When I contemplate you, soldiers, and when I consider your past
exploits, a strong hope of victory animates me. Your spirit, your age,
your valor, give me confidence—to say nothing of necessity, which
makes even cowards brave. To prevent the numbers of the enemy from
surrounding us, our confined situation is sufficient. But should fortune
be unjust to your valor, take care not to lose your lives unavenged; take
care not to be taken and butchered like cattle, rather than fighting like
men, to leave to your enemies a bloody and mournful victory. ∎

Pope Urban II Launches the First Crusade

"DIEU li volt—God wills it!"

ELECTED POPE IN 1088, Urban waited three years until the antipope was ejected before entering Rome. Europe was a maelstrom of warring feudal barons, lawless nobles, and Norman buccaneers. The new pope came up with the way to channel their energies into what he thought would be both diverting and constructive: the recovery of the Holy Land, which was then in the hands of unbelievers. He proposed to start a war—a holy war, or crusade—to tame the threatening Turks on their home ground, to open the Eastern Mediterranean to Italian commerce, and to make possible the adventurous penitentiary pilgrimages that would recruit new adherents to the Church.

At Clermont in November 1095, to an audience of thousands who had pitched their tents in open fields, the French pope stood on a platform to deliver what historian Will Durant called "the most influential speech in medieval history." He summoned Christendom to a crusade, sanctified by God, against the common enemy. He promised them that their families and property would be protected while they were on the crusade, and if they died for God's glory, all their sins would be remitted and Heaven would await their souls. "God wills it!" he shouted in Latin, and the crowd roared back, "God wills it!"

What was willed by Urban II turned out to be a slaughter. After the first wave of twenty thousand disorganized rabble failed, the nobles took over and defeated the Turks at Antioch, driving across Asia Minor to lay siege to Jerusalem, demanding unconditional surrender. After forty days, the small Muslim force gave in. An eyewitness priest, Raymond of Agiles, wrote delightedly, "Wonderful things were to be seen. Numbers of the Saracens were beheaded . . . or forced to jump from the towers; others were tortured for several days and then burned . . . one rode about everywhere amid the corpses of men and horses." All seventy thousand Muslim residents of Jerusalem were butchered; Jews were herded into their synagogue and burned alive.

The first of the nine crusades that would turn Asia Minor into a field of blood and death over two centuries had begun. The national monarchies of Europe were unified and strengthened, the ports of Italy prospered, the native Christians were oppressed by the European rulers, and the seeds of religious hatred were firmly planted.

□   □   □

O race of Franks! race beloved and chosen by God! . . .
   From the confines of Jerusalem and from Constantinople a grievous report has gone forth that an accursed race, wholly alienated from God, has violently invaded the lands of these Christians, and has depopulated them by pillage and fire. They have led away a part of the captives into their own country, and a part they have killed by cruel tortures. They destroy the altars, after having defiled them with their uncleanliness. The kingdom of the Greeks is now dismembered by them, and has been deprived of territory so vast in extent that it could not be traversed in two months' time.

   On whom, then, rests the labor of avenging these wrongs, and of recovering this territory, if not upon you—you upon whom, above all others, God has conferred remarkable glory in arms, great bravery, and strength to humble the heads of those who resist you? Let the deeds of your ancestors encourage you—the glory and grandeur of Charlemagne and your other monarchs. Let the Holy Sepulcher of Our Lord and Saviour, now held by unclean nations, arouse you, and the holy places that are now stained with pollution. . . . Let none of your possessions keep you back, nor anxiety for your family affairs. For this land which you now inhabit, shut in on all sides by the sea and the mountain peaks, is too narrow for your large population; it scarcely furnishes food enough for its cultivators. Hence it is that you murder and devour one another, that you wage wars, and that many among you perish in civil strife.

   Let hatred, therefore, depart from among you; let your quarrels end. Enter upon the road to the Holy Sepulcher; wrest that land from a wicked race, and subject it to yourselves. Jerusalem is a land fruitful above all others, a paradise of delights. That royal city, situated at the center of the earth, implores you to come to her aid. Undertake this journey eagerly for the remission of your sins, and be assured of the reward of imperishable glory in the Kingdom of Heaven.

   Dieu li volt—"God wills it!" ■

Queen Elizabeth Inveighs against the Spanish Armada

"I know I have but the body of a weak and feeble woman; but I have the heart of a king. . . ."

VAIN, MISERLY, AND FICKLE, the spinster queen commanded the affection of her subjects by virtue of her courage and her identification with the nation's fate. One of her many rejected suitors, Philip II of Spain, in 1588 assembled what was called the "Invincible Armada" of tall ships to invade England, thereby to assert Catholic power against the center of Protestantism. Elizabeth I, despite the danger of a cross-Channel invasion, went with a small army to visit the troops in Tilbury. Her ostentatious unconcern for personal security while in the midst of the English people was expressed in a strong "Let tyrants fear"; as her soldiers knelt, she affirmed her faith in a "famous victory."

□   □   □

My loving people, we have been persuaded by some, that are careful of our safety, to take heed how we commit ourselves to armed multitudes, for fear of treachery; but I assure you, I do not desire to live to distrust my faithful and loving people. Let tyrants fear; I have always so behaved myself that, under God, I have placed my chiefest strength and safeguard in the loyal hearts and good will of my subjects. And therefore I am come amongst you at this time, not as for my recreation or sport, but being resolved, in the midst and heat of the battle, to live or die amongst you all; to lay down, for my God, and for my kingdom, and for my people, my honor and my blood, even the dust. I know I have but the body of a weak and feeble woman; but I have the heart of a king, and of a king of England, too; and think foul scorn that Parma or Spain, or any prince of Europe, should dare to invade the borders of my realms: to which, rather than any dishonor should grow by me, I myself will take up arms; I myself will be your general, judge, and rewarder of every one of your virtues in the field. I know already, by your forwardness, that you have deserved rewards and crowns; and we do assure you, on the word of a prince, they shall be duly paid you. In the mean my lieutenant general shall be in my stead, than whom never prince commanded a more noble and worthy subject; not doubting by your obedience to my general, by your concord in the camp, and by your valor in the field, we shall shortly have a famous victory over the enemies of my God, of my kingdom, and of my people. ■

Patrick Henry Ignites the American Revolution

"Is life so dear, or peace so sweet, as to be purchased at the price of chains and slavery? Forbid it, Almighty God! I know not what course others may take; but as for me, give me liberty, or give me death!"

ON MARCH 23, 1775—the same day that Edmund Burke was urging conciliation with America in London's House of Commons—a thirty-eight-year-old self-taught lawyer named Patrick Henry rose in St. John's Church in Richmond, Virginia, where 122 of the colony's delegates were meeting. The church's windows were open on the fine spring day to let a crowd gather outside listen to the deliberations of the British colony's representatives. Henry handed a series of resolutions to the clerk, who read them out, concluding, "Resolved therefore, That this Colony be immediately put into a posture of defence; and that [blank] be a Committee to prepare a plan for the embodying, arming, and disciplining such a number of men as may be sufficient for that purpose." As the proposer, Henry would have been the first called upon to speak for his resolutions, although the initial lines of his reported speech refer graciously to colleagues who differed with him; perhaps he alluded to what they had said the day before.

He spoke without notes; at least, none have ever been found. His speech began in a quiet smolder and ended ablaze with passion. A Baptist clergyman present wrote of the orator's crescendo, "The tendons of his neck stood out white and rigid, like whipcords. His voice rose louder and louder, until the walls of the building and all within them seemed to shake and rock in its tremendous vibrations. Finally his pale face and glaring eyes became terrible to look upon. Men leaned forward in their seats with the heads strained forward, their faces pale and their eyes glaring like the speaker's. . . . When he sat down, I felt sick with excitement." No applause; no known reply; Richard Henry Lee seconded the resolutions; Thomas Jefferson and Thomas Nelson were reported to have spoken in favor. The vote was called for and taken; the resolutions carried by a narrow margin of five, and the American Revolution in the largest colony was under way.

With "This is no time for ceremony," the speaker goes right to the heart of the matter: "freedom or slavery." His rhetorical approach is one of loaded question and scathing reply. Q.: "Are fleets and armies necessary to a work of love and reconciliation?" A.: "These are the implements of war and subjugation. . . ." Q.: "Shall we try argument?" A.: "Sir, we have been trying that for the last ten years."

The past pleas to the crown are listed in an active parallel construction: "We have petitioned; we have remonstrated; we have supplicated. . . ." The answers are recounted in parallel also, but in the passive, leaving George III out of it: "Our petitions have been slighted; our remonstrances have produced additional violence and insult; our supplications have been disregarded. . . ."

When Henry says, "An appeal to arms and the God of Hosts is all that is left us," on top of his earlier refusal to commit "an act of disloyalty towards the majesty of heaven," he is directly referring to a euphemism put forward a century before: English philosopher John Locke, in advancing the courageous idea that man had natural, God-given rights, was presuming to say that these superseded the divine right of kings, but—to save his life—couched his justification for revolution to unseat an unjust monarch in the phrase "an appeal to heaven." This idea undergirded the philosophy Jefferson expressed later in the Declaration of Independence, and the religious image was used by the fiery Henry in calling for what he never named: revolution.

He then knocks down the arguments used against the revolutionaries. "They tell us, sir, that we are weak. . . ." He answers that time is not on the colonists' side, that the king will grow stronger, but that "the battle . . .

is not to the strong alone; it is to the vigilant, the active, the brave." The men gathered in the church could fairly hear echoes of Ecclesiastes 9:11: "The race is not to the swift, nor the battle to the strong. . . ." And then he adds the crusher: there is no real choice when the alternatives are fighting for liberty or submission to slavery. "The war is inevitable," he concludes, but not in despair, "—and let it come!"

In the peroration, he flays his audience with rhetorical questions, three short and then one long, setting up his answer choosing death rather than slavery. Note the breath, or beat, provided by "I know not what course others may take"; it enables the orator to deliver the punch line with such added force that it echoes down through history,

One small question: Is this what Patrick Henry really said? We know he spoke that day; we know he made a powerful impact with his speech; but we do not know if the speech that has come down to us is the speech he gave. No notes; no manuscript then or later; no contemporaneous account. The first publication of the speech, in 1816, came forty-one years after the Richmond convention, taken from William Wirt's then forthcoming biography of Patrick Henry, who died in 1799. Evidence that the final line was accurate comes from the slogan on the flag of the militia that subsequently served under him: "Liberty or Death." (One rebel wag noted he preferred a less severe "Liberty or Be Crippled.")

In a doctoral dissertation on the authenticity of the Wirt transcript, Stephen T. Olsen—using traditional methods of historical research as well as computer analysis of texts—argues that sometime between 1805 and 1815 biographer Wirt elicited a reconstituted transcript from a friend, federal judge St. George Tucker, who claimed to have been a spectator in the church when Henry delivered his speech. Other scholarship may refute this one day, but until then, my own judgment is that Patrick Henry made a rousing speech that day that did conclude with the line about liberty or death; that a generation later, to respond to the wishes of his friend writing a biography of the patriot, Judge Tucker recalled what he could and made up the rest. If that is so, Judge Tucker belongs among the ranks of history's best ghostwriters. Here is the Henry/Tucker/Wirt transcript in full:

□ □ □

Mr. President:

No man thinks more highly than I do of the patriotism, as well as abilities, of the very worthy gentlemen who have just addressed the House. But different men often see the same subject in different lights; and, therefore, I hope that it will not be thought disrespectful to those gentlemen, if, entertaining as I do opinions of a character very opposite to theirs, I shall speak forth my sentiments freely and without reserve. This is no time for ceremony. The question before the House is one of awful moment to this country. For my own part I consider it as nothing less than a question of freedom or slavery; and in proportion to the magnitude of the subject ought to be the freedom of the debate. It is only in this way that we can hope to arrive at truth, and fulfill the great responsibility which we hold to God and our country. Should I keep back my opinions at such a time, through fear of giving offense, I should consider myself as guilty of treason towards my country, and of an act of disloyalty towards the majesty of heaven, which I revere above all earthly kings.

Mr. President, it is natural to man to indulge in the illusions of hope. We are apt to shut our eyes against a painful truth, and listen to the song of that siren, till she transforms us into beasts. Is this the part of wise men, engaged in a great and arduous struggle for liberty? Are we disposed to be of the number of those who, having eyes, see not, and having ears, hear not, the things which so nearly concern their temporal salvation? For my part, whatever anguish of spirit it may cost, I am willing to know the whole truth—to know the worst and to provide for it.

I have but one lamp by which my feet are guided; and that is the lamp of experience. I know of no way of judging of the future but by the past. And judging by the past, I wish to know what there has been in the conduct of the British ministry for the last ten years, to justify those hopes with which gentlemen have been pleased to solace themselves and the House? Is it that insidious smile with which our petition has been lately received? Trust it not, sir; it will prove a snare to your feet. Suffer not yourselves to be betrayed with a kiss.

Ask yourselves how this gracious reception of our petition comports with these warlike preparations which cover our waters and darken our land. Are fleets and armies necessary to a work of love and reconciliation? Have we shown ourselves so unwilling to be reconciled that force must be called in to win back our love? Let us not deceive ourselves, sir. These are the implements of war and subjugation—the last arguments to which kings resort. I ask gentlemen, sir, what means this martial array, if its purpose be not to force us to submission? Can gentlemen assign any other possible motives for it? Has Great Britain any enemy, in this quarter of the world, to call for all this accumulation of navies and armies? No, sir, she has none. They are meant for us; they can be meant for no other. They are sent over to bind and rivet upon us those chains which the British ministry have been so long forging.

And what have we to oppose to them? Shall we try argument? Sir, we have been trying that for the last ten years. Have we anything new to offer on the subject? Nothing. We have held the subject up in every light of which it is capable; but it has been all in vain. Shall we resort to entreaty and humble supplication? What terms shall we find which have not been already exhausted? Let us not, I beseech you, sir, deceive ourselves longer.

Sir, we have done everything that could be done to avert the storm which is now coming on. We have petitioned; we have remonstrated; we have supplicated; we have prostrated ourselves before the throne, and have implored its interposition to arrest the tyrannical hands of the ministry and Parliament. Our petitions have been slighted; our remonstrances have produced additional violence and insult; our supplications have been disregarded; and we have been spurned, with contempt, from the foot of the throne. In vain, after these things, may we indulge the fond hope of peace and reconciliation. There is no longer any room for hope.

If we wish to be free—if we mean to preserve inviolate those inestimable privileges for which we have been so long contending—if we mean not basely to abandon the noble struggle in which we have been so long engaged, and which we have pledged ourselves never to abandon until the glorious object of our contest shall be obtained, we must fight! I repeat it, sir, we must fight! An appeal to arms and to the God of Hosts is all that is left us!

They tell us, sir, that we are weak—unable to cope with so formidable an adversary. But when shall we be stronger? Will it be the next week, or the next year? Will it be when we are totally disarmed, and when a British guard shall be stationed in every house? Shall we gather strength by irresolution and inaction? Shall we acquire the means of effectual resistance, by lying supinely on our backs, and hugging the delusive phantom of hope, until our enemies shall have bound us hand and foot?

Sir, we are not weak, if we make a proper use of the means which the God of nature hath placed in our power. Three millions of people, armed in the holy cause of liberty, and in such a country as that which we possess, are invincible by any force which our enemy can send against us. Besides, sir, we shall not fight our battles alone. There is a just God who presides over the destinies of nations, and who will raise up friends to fight our battles for us. The battle, sir, is not to the strong alone; it is to the vigilant, the active, the brave. Besides, sir, we have no election. If we were base enough to desire it, it is now too late to retire from the contest. There is no retreat but in submission and slavery! Our chains are forged! Their clanking may be heard on the plains of Boston! The war is inevitable—and let it come! I repeat it, sir, let it come!

It is in vain, sir, to extenuate the matter. Gentlemen may cry, "Peace! Peace!"—but there is no peace. The war is actually begun! The next gale that sweeps from the north will bring to our ears the clash of resounding arms! Our brethren are already in the field! Why stand we here idle? What is it that gentlemen wish? What would they have? Is life so dear, or peace so sweet, as to be purchased at the price of chains and slavery? Forbid it, Almighty God! I know not what course others may take; but as for me, give me liberty, or give me death! ■

An Indian Chief Pledges Help

"Only point out to me where your enemies keep. . . ."

THIS BRIEF PLEDGE of assistance was delivered to the Massachusetts congress by an American Indian, in 1775, as hostilities began in the colonies. *The Columbian Orator*, published in 1810, did not identify the speaker other than as a member of the Stockbridge tribe. Note the dignity of the simple, declarative prose; the early indication of the value to armies of what came to be known as unconventional warfare; and the ominous innocence at the end.

□   □   □

Brothers !
You remember, when you first came over the great waters, I was great and you were little—very small. I then took you in for a friend, and kept you under my arms, so that no one might injure you. Since that time we have ever been true friends: there has never been any quarrel between us. But now our conditions are changed. You are become great and tall. You reach to the clouds. You are seen all round the world. I am become small—very little. I am not so high as your knee. Now you take care of me; and I look to you for protection.

Brothers! I am sorry to hear of this great quarrel between you and old England. It appears that blood must soon be shed to end this quarrel. We never till this day understood the foundation of this quarrel between you and the country you came from. Brothers! Whenever I see your blood running, you will soon find me about you to revenge my brothers' blood. Although I am low and very small, I will grip hold of your enemy's heel, that he cannot run so fast, and so light, as if he had nothing at his heels.

Brothers! You know I am not so wise as you are; therefore I ask your advice in what I am now going to say. I have been thinking, before you come to action, to take a run to the westward and feel the mind of my Indian brethren, the Six Nations, and know how they stand—whether they are on your side or for your enemies. If I find they are against you, I will try to turn their minds. I think they will listen to me, for they have always looked this way for advice, concerning all important news that comes from the rising sun. If they hearken to me, you will not be afraid of any danger from behind you. However their minds are affected, you shall soon know by me. Now I think I can do you more service in this way than by marching off immediately to Boston and staying there. It may be a great while before blood runs. Now, as I said, you are wiser than I; I leave this for your consideration, whether I come down immediately or wait till I hear some blood is spilled.

Brothers! I would not have you think by this that we are falling back from our engagements. We are ready to do anything for your relief, and shall be guided by your counsel.

Brothers! One thing I ask of you, if you send for me to fight: that you will let me fight in my own Indian way. I am not used to fight English fashion; therefore you must not expect I can train like your men. Only point out to me where your enemies keep, and that is all I shall want to know. ■

General Washington Talks His Officers Out of Insurrection

"GENTLEMEN, you will permit me to put on my spectacles, for I have not only grown gray but almost blind in the service of my country."

THE MOST DANGEROUS MOMENT in the life of the young American republic came on March 15, 1783, when officers of the revolutionary army gathered in Newburgh, New York, to discuss insurrection against what was considered to be perfidious congressional rule. Word had come from Philadelphia to the officers that the United States government was broke and that the army would not be paid. Alexander Hamilton sent warning from New York City to General Washington that, if the war continued, the army would soon have to live off the land, and that army officers might not be recompensed for all owed them when peace came. A cabal of officers behind General Horatio Gates, Washington's deputy, was intent on seeking justice—that is, putting military pressure on the state capitals to pay up. That would surely have been seen as insurrection by the states, with bloodshed to follow; the issue was civilian versus military control of the new government. If the army could hold up the legislatures, no matter how just its cause, the nature of the Republic would be irrevocably changed.

In a vaulted hall called the Temple, used as a church and dancing academy, General Washington unexpectedly showed up at the meeting. He faced a gathering of officers who felt he did not represent their interests; these leaders were angry, resentful, and not happy to see him. His speech was not well received—until the end, when he used a device of reading a letter, and captured his audience with an emotional and impromptu remark.

□   □   □

Gentlemen: By an anonymous summons, an attempt has been made to convene you together; how inconsistent with the rules of propriety, how unmilitary, and how subversive of all order and discipline, let the good sense of the army decide. . . .

Thus much, gentlemen, I have thought it incumbent on me to observe to you, to show upon what principles I opposed the irregular and hasty meeting which was proposed to have been held on Tuesday last: and not because I wanted a disposition to give you every opportunity consistent with your own honor, and the dignity of the army, to make known your grievances. If my conduct heretofore has not evinced to you that I have been a faithful friend to the army, my declaration of it at this time would be equally unavailing and improper. But as I was among the first who embarked in the cause of our common country. As I have never left your side one moment, but when called from you on public duty. As I have been the constant companion and witness of your distresses, and not among the last to feel and acknowledge your merits. As I have ever considered my own military reputation as inseparably connected with that of the army. As my heart has ever expanded with joy, when I have heard its praises, and my indignation has arisen, when the mouth of detraction has been opened against it, it can *scarcely be supposed*, at this late stage of the war, that I am indifferent to its interests.

But how are they to be promoted? The way is plain, says the anonymous addresser. If war continues, remove into the unsettled country, there establish yourselves, and leave an ungrateful country to defend itself. But who are they to defend? Our wives, our children, our farms, and other property which we leave behind us. Or, in this state of hostile separation, are we to take the two first (the latter cannot be removed) to perish in a wilderness, with hunger, cold, and nakedness? If peace takes place, never sheathe your swords, says he, until you have obtained full and ample justice; this dreadful alternative, of either deserting our country in the extremest hour of her distress or turning our arms against it (which is the apparent object, unless Congress can be compelled into instant compliance), has something so shocking in it that humanity revolts at the idea. My God! What can this writer have in view, by recommending such measures? Can he be a friend to the army? Can he be a friend to this country? Rather, is he not an insidious foe? Some emissary, perhaps, from New York, plotting the ruin of both, by sowing the seeds of discord and separation between the civil and military powers of the continent? And what a compliment does he pay to our understandings when he recommends measures in either alternative, impracticable in their nature? . . .

I cannot, in justice to my own belief, and what I have great reason to conceive is the intention of Congress, conclude this address, without giving it as my decided opinion, that that honorable body entertain exalted sentiments of the services of the army; and, from a full conviction of its merits and sufferings, will do it complete justice. That their endeavors to discover and establish funds for this purpose have been unwearied, and will not cease till they have succeeded, I have not a doubt. But, like all other large bodies, where there is a variety of different interests to reconcile, their deliberations are slow. Why, then, should we distrust them? And, in consequence of that distrust, adopt measures which may cast a shade over that glory which has been so justly acquired; and tarnish the reputation of an army which is celebrated through all Europe, for its fortitude and patriotism? And for what is this done? To bring the object we seek nearer? No! most certainly, in my opinion, it will cast it at a greater distance.

For myself (and I take no merit in giving the assurance, being induced to it from principles of gratitude, veracity, and justice), a grateful sense of the confidence you have ever placed in me, a recollection of the cheerful assistance and prompt obedience I have experienced from you, under every vicissitude of fortune, and the sincere affection I feel for an army I have so long had the honor to command will oblige me to declare, in this public and solemn manner, that, in the attainment of complete justice for all your toils and dangers, and in the gratification of every wish, so far as may be done consistently with the great duty I owe my country and those powers we are bound to respect, you may freely command my services to the utmost of my abilities.

While I give you these assurances, and pledge myself in the most unequivocal manner to exert whatever ability I am possessed of in your favor, let me entreat you, gentlemen, on your part, not to take any measures which, viewed in the calm light of reason, will lessen the dignity and sully the glory you have hitherto maintained; let me request you to rely on the plighted faith of your country, and place a full confidence in the purity of the intentions of Congress; that, previous to your dissolution as an army, they will cause all your accounts to be fairly liquidated, as directed in their resolutions, which were published to you two days ago, and that they will adopt the most effectual measures in their power to render ample justice to you, for your faithful and meritorious services. And let me conjure you, in the name of our common country, as you value your own sacred honor, as you respect the rights of humanity, and as you regard the military and national character of America, to express your utmost horror and detestation of the man who wishes, under any specious pretenses, to overturn the liberties of our country, and who wickedly attempts to open the floodgates of civil discord and deluge our rising empire in blood.

By thus determining and thus acting, you will pursue the plain and

direct road to the attainment of your wishes. You will defeat the insidious designs of our enemies, who are compelled to resort from open force
to secret artifice. You will give one more distinguished proof of unexampled patriotism and patient virtue, rising superior to the pressure of the
most complicated sufferings. And you will, by the dignity of your conduct, afford occasion for posterity to say, when speaking of the glorious
example you have exhibited to mankind, "Had this day been wanting,
the world had never seen the last stage of perfection to which human
nature is capable of attaining."

□   □   □

AT THE CONCLUSION of his speech, which he read from pages of his
own clear writing, Washington looked at his sullen audience and drew a
letter from his pocket. It was from a member of Congress, he said,
explaining the straits the country was in and what that body was
attempting to do to pay the debts of the war. He squinted at the writing
in the letter and could not go on. The audience of officers stirred in their
seats, wondering what was wrong with their commander. Washington
then groped in his waistcoat pocket and drew out an item that only his
intimates, and very few in that audience, had seen him use. They were
stunned to see him required to put on a pair of glasses to read the
crabbed writing.

"Gentlemen," he apologized, "you will permit me to put on my spectacles, for I have not only grown gray but almost blind in the service of my
country."

Biographer James Thomas Flexner writes, "This simple statement
achieved what all Washington's rhetoric and all his arguments had been
unable to achieve. The officers were instantly in tears, and, from behind
the shining drops, their eyes looked with love at the commander who
had led them all so far and long. Washington quietly finished reading the
congressman's letter. He knew the battle was won, and avoiding, with his
instinctive sense of the dramatic, any anticlimax, he walked out of the
hall. . . ."

Did he plan to use his infirmity to wring their hearts that way? Was his
remark, so felicitously and poignantly phrased, totally spontaneous?
We'll never know, but the officers then voted to ask Washington to forward their request to Congress, the granting of which would "prevent
any further machinations of designing men." ■

Richard Price,
an English Cleric,
Hails the Revolutions

"TREMBLE, all ye oppressors of the world!"

RICHARD PRICE, a nonconformist English clergyman, wrote pamphlets on ethical, political, and economic subjects, inveighed against the oppression of American colonists, and supported the tide of revolution that swept across the end of the eighteenth century. His radical sermon "On the Love of Our Country" was preached to a Protestant Dissenters' society on November 4, 1789; supporting political upheaval in France, it seemed to associate the nonconformist split from the Church of England a century earlier (the Glorious Revolution of 1688–89) with the ideals of the French Revolution, and was the "red rag" that drew the parliamentarian Edmund Burke—who saw anarchy and atheism on the march in Europe—into the conservative forefront.

The peroration beginning with the exclamatory "What an eventful period is this!" is a classic because it rivets the audience by addressing discrete, contrasting groups. The penultimate paragraph is addressed directly to the "friends of freedom" and begins with the imperative "Be encouraged"; the final paragraph is addressed to the "oppressors" and directs them to "tremble." In this way, the orator divides the world into good and bad, right and wrong, and thrusts upon his listeners his unmistakable stand.

□   □   □

We are met to thank God for that event in this country to which the name of *the Revolution* has been given; and which, for more than a century, it has been usual for the friends of freedom, and more especially Protestant Dissenters, under the title of the Revolution Society, to celebrate with expressions of joy and exultation. My highly valued and excellent friend who addressed you on this occasion last year has given you an interesting account of the principal circumstances that attended this event, and of the reasons we have for rejoicing in it. By a bloodless victory, the fetters which despotism had been long preparing for us were broken; the rights of the people were asserted, a tyrant expelled, and a sovereign of our own choice appointed in his room. Security was given to our property, and our consciences were emancipated. The bounds of free inquiry were enlarged; the volume in which are the words of eternal life was laid more open to our examination; and that era of light and liberty was introduced among us by which we have been made an example to other kingdoms and became the instructors of the world. Had it not been for this deliverance, the probability is that, instead of being thus distinguished, we should now have been a base people, groaning under the infamy and misery of popery and slavery. Let us, therefore, offer thanksgivings to God, the author of all our blessings.

. . . We have particular reason, as Protestant Dissenters, to rejoice on this occasion. It was at this time we were rescued from persecution, and obtained the liberty of worshiping God in the manner we think most acceptable to him. It was then our meetinghouses were opened, our worship was taken under the protection of the law, and the principles of toleration gained a triumph. We have, therefore, on this occasion, peculiar reasons for thanksgiving. But let us remember that we ought not to satisfy ourselves with thanksgivings. Our gratitude, if genuine, will be accompanied with endeavors to give stability to the deliverance our country has obtained, and to extend and improve the happiness with which the Revolution has blessed us. Let us, in particular, take care not to forget the principles of the Revolution. This society has, very properly, in its reports, held out these principles, as an instruction to the public. I will only take notice of the three following:

First: the right to liberty of conscience in religious matters.

Secondly: the right to resist power when abused. And,

Thirdly: the right to choose our own governors; to cashier them for misconduct; and to frame a government for ourselves.

On these three principles, and more especially the last, was the Revolution founded. Were it not true that liberty of conscience is a sacred right; that power abused justifies resistance; and that civil authority is a delegation from the people—were not, I say, all this true, the Revolution would have been not an *assertion* but an *invasion* of rights; not a *revolution* but a *rebellion.* Cherish in your breasts this conviction, and act under its influence; detecting the odious doctrines which, had they been acted upon in this country, would have left us at this time wretched slaves—doctrines which imply that God made mankind to be oppressed and plundered, and which are no less a blasphemy against him than an insult on common sense. . . .

You may reasonably expect that I should now close this address to you. But I cannot yet dismiss you. I must not conclude without recalling, particularly, to your recollection a consideration to which I have more than once alluded, and which, probably, your thoughts have been all along anticipating—a consideration with which my mind is impressed more than I can express. I mean, the consideration of the favorableness of the present times to all exertions in the cause of public liberty.

What an eventful period is this! I am thankful that I have lived to it; and I could almost say, "Lord, now lettest thou thy servant depart in peace, for mine eyes have seen thy salvation." I have lived to see a diffusion of knowledge which has undermined superstition and error—I have lived to see the rights of men better understood than ever; and nations panting for liberty which seemed to have lost the idea of it. I have lived to see thirty millions of people, indignant and resolute, spurning at slavery, and demanding liberty with an irresistible voice; their king led in triumph, and an arbitrary monarch surrendering himself to his subjects. After sharing in the benefits of one revolution, I have been spared to be a witness to two other revolutions, both glorious. And now, methinks, I see the ardor for liberty catching and spreading; a general amendment beginning in human affairs; the dominion of priests giving way to the dominion of reason and conscience.

Be encouraged, all ye friends of freedom and writers in its defense! The times are auspicious. Your labors have not been in vain. Behold kingdoms, admonished by you, starting from sleep, breaking their fetters, and claiming justice from their oppressors! Behold, the light you have struck out, after setting America free, reflected to France, and there kindled into a blaze that lays despotism in ashes and warms and illuminates Europe!

Tremble, all ye oppressors of the world! Take warning all ye supporters of slavish governments and slavish hierarchies! Call no more (absurdly and wickedly) *reformation* innovation. You cannot now hold the world in darkness. Struggle no longer against increasing light and liberality. Restore to mankind their rights, and consent to the correction of abuses, before they and you are destroyed together. ∎

Revolutionist
Georges-Jacques Danton
Demands Death for
the Squeamish

"To conquer we have need to dare, to dare again, always to dare!"

PARISIAN LAWYER Georges-Jacques Danton was a tyrant in revolutionary clothing. He established himself as a patriot by helping lead the storming of the Tuileries in August 1792 to overthrow the Bourbon monarchy, but his passionate oratory and merciless zeal were directed more to the acquisition of power than to the dream of democracy. He professed not to care for popularity: "Let France be free, though my name be cursed." A few weeks after the success of the Revolution, and almost two years before the Reign of Terror, which led to his own execution on the guillotine, Danton made this speech on the defense of the new republic, already threatened by invading Prussians and Austrians. Though it is remembered for the line enshrining audacity, Danton's rallying call to the sans-culottes to defend the republic contained a proposal of the most draconian penalty for dissent.

□   □   □

It seems a satisfaction for the ministers of a free people to announce to them that their country will be saved, All are stirred, all are enthused, all burn to enter the combat.

You know that Verdun is not yet in the power of our enemies and that its garrison swears to immolate the first who breathes a proposition of surrender.

One portion of our people will guard our frontiers, another will dig and arm the entrenchments, the third with pikes will defend the interior of our cities, Paris will second these great efforts. The commissioners of the Commune will solemnly proclaim to the citizens the invitation to arm and march to the defense of the country. At such a moment you can proclaim that the capital deserves the esteem of all France. At such a moment this

National Assembly becomes a veritable committee of war. We ask that you concur with us in directing this sublime movement of the people, by naming commissioners to second and assist all these great measures. We ask that anyone refusing to give personal service or to furnish arms shall meet the punishment of death. We ask that proper instructions be given to the citizens to direct their movements. We ask that carriers be sent to all the departments to notify them of the decrees that you proclaim here. The tocsin we shall sound is not the alarm signal of danger; it orders the charge on the enemies of France. To conquer we have need to dare, to dare again, always to dare! And France will be saved!

(Pour les vaincre, il nous faut de l'audace; encore de l'audace, toujours de l'audace; et la France est sauvée.) ■

Napoleon Exhorts His Troops against France's Enemies

"LET them tremble!"

AFTER MAKING A REPUTATION for ferocity by giving a crowd of Parisian rioters what he called "a whiff of grapeshot"—and killing one hundred—Napoleon Bonaparte made his bid for power in 1796. He sold the French regime on a plan for an Italian campaign, married Josephine, and set out at the head of a ragtag French army.

He understood, as few commanders did, the need to take care of the essential needs of his men; "An army marches on its stomach" is a remark attributed to him, as well as "The first virtue in a soldier is endurance of fatigue; courage is only the second virtue." He determined to keep his men fed by living off the land in Italy, to rest them when possible, and to instill in them his own sense of destiny.

All his addresses to his troops began with the salutation "Soldiers!" He put pride in the word and, in crediting "his" army with triumphs, had no need to credit himself. In his oratory, he employed the internal dialogue ("Shall it be said of us . . . ?") and the visionary quotation to promise fame ("Your fellow citizens, pointing you out, shall say, 'There goes one who . . .'"). Winston Churchill would use the same history-conscious construction in his predictive quotation "This was their finest hour."

□   □   □

Soldiers: you are precipitated like a torrent from the heights of the Apennines; you have overthrown and dispersed all that dared to oppose your march. Piedmont, rescued from Austrian tyranny, is left to its natural sentiments of regard and friendship to the French. Milan is yours; and the republican standard is displayed throughout all Lombardy. The dukes of Parma and Modern a are indebted for their political existence only to your generosity.

The army, which so proudly menaced you, has had no other barrier than its dissolution to oppose your invincible courage. The Po, the Tessin, the Adds, could not retard you a single day. The vaunted bulwarks of Italy were insufficient. You swept them with the same rapidity that you did the Apennines. Those successes have carried joy into the bosom of your country. Your representatives decreed a festival dedicated to your victories, and to be celebrated throughout all the communes of the republic. Now your fathers, your mothers, your wives, and your sisters will rejoice in your success, and take pride in their relation to you.

Yes, soldiers, you have done much; but more still remains for you to do. Shall it be said of us, that we know how to conquer but not to profit by our victories? Shall posterity reproach us with having found a Capua in Lombardy? But already I see you fly to arms. You are fatigued with an inactive repose. You lament the days that are lost to your glory! Well, then, let us proceed; we have other forced marches to make, other enemies to subdue, more laurels to acquire, and more injuries to avenge.

Let those who have unsheathed the daggers of civil war in France, who have basely assassinated our ministers, who have burnt our ships at Toulon—let them tremble! The knell of vengeance has already tolled!

But to quiet the apprehensions of the people, we declare ourselves the friends of all, and particularly of those who are the descendants of Brutus, of Scipio, and those other great men whom we have taken for our models.

To reestablish the capital, to replace the statues of those heroes who have rendered it immortal, to rouse the Roman people entranced in so many ages of slavery—this shall be the fruit of your victories. It will be an epoch for the admiration of posterity; you will enjoy the immortal glory of changing the aspect of affairs in the finest part of Europe. The free people of France, not regardless of moderation, shall accord to Europe a glorious peace; but it will indemnify itself for the sacrifices of every kind which it has been making for six years past. You will again be restored to your firesides and homes; and your fellow citizens, pointing you out, shall say, "There goes one who belonged to the army of Italy!" ■

Garibaldi Prepares Italy's Guerrillas for Battle

"THE slave shall show at last to his free brothers a sharpened sword forged from the links of his fetters."

GIUSEPPE GARIBALDI was among the first to understand how irregular troops—guerrillas, as they later came to be called—could wear down and defeat regular armies. He learned his profession as patriot and soldier under revolutionary leader Mazzini, and was condemned to death after the unsuccessful insurrection of 1832. Garibaldi escaped to South America and sharpened his command skills leading guerrillas in Brazil and Argentina; using that experience, he returned to Italy in 1859 to rout the Austrians for the Piedmont government. At the head of his thousand Redshirts, he seized Sicily and—after serving as dictator of half of what is now Italy for a couple of months—turned his nearly united nation over to King Victor Emmanuel II. Garibaldi is remembered as the unifier of the Italian nation; he might be more familiar to Americans had he taken up Abraham Lincoln's offer of a command in our Civil War.

This speech loses flavor in the translation, not only between languages, but from spoken exhortation to written word. But the unifier's call beyond his troops to Italian women—"Cast away all the cowards from your embraces; they will give you only cowards for children"—has a ring that leaps off the page.

□   □   □

We must now consider the period which is just drawing to a close as almost the last stage of our national resurrection, and prepare ourselves to finish worthily the marvelous design of the elect of twenty generations, the completion of which Providence has reserved for this fortunate age.

Yes, young men, Italy owes to you an undertaking which has merited the applause of the universe. You have conquered and you will conquer still, because you are prepared for the tactics that decide the fate of battles. You are not unworthy of the men who entered the ranks of a Macedonian phalanx, and who contended not in vain with the proud conquerors of Asia. To this wonderful page in our country's history another more glorious still will be added, and the slave shall show at last to his free brothers a sharpened sword forged from the links of his fetters.

To arms, then, all of you! all of you! And the oppressors and the mighty shall disappear like dust. You, too, women, cast away all the cowards from your embraces; they will give you only cowards for children, and you who are the daughters of the land of beauty must bear children who are noble and brave. Let timid doctrinaires depart from among us to carry their servility and their miserable fears elsewhere. This people is its own master. It wishes to be the brother of other peoples, but to look on the insolent with a proud glance, not to grovel before them imploring its own freedom. It will no longer follow in the trail of men whose hearts are foul. No! No! No!

Providence has presented Italy with Victor Emmanuel. Every Italian should rally round him. By the side of Victor Emmanuel every quarrel should be forgotten, all rancor depart. Once more I repeat my battle cry: "To arms, all—all of you!" If March 1861 does not find one million of Italians in arms, then alas for liberty, alas for the life of Italy. Ah, no, far be from me a thought which I loathe like poison. March of 1861, or if need be February, will find us all at our post—Italians of Calatafimi, Palermo, Ancona, the Volturno, Castelfidardo. and Isernia, and with us every man of this land who is not a coward or a slave. Let all of us rally round the glorious hero of Palestro and give the last blow to the crumbling edifice of tyranny. Receive, then, my gallant young volunteers, at the honored conclusion of ten battles, one word of farewell from me.

I utter this word with deepest affection and from the very bottom of my heart. Today I am obliged to retire, but for a few days only. The hour of battle will find me with you again, by the side of the champions of Italian liberty. Let those only return to their homes who are called by the imperative duties which they owe to their families, and those who by their glorious wounds have deserved the credit of their country. These, indeed, will serve Italy in their homes by their counsel, by the very aspect of the scars which adorn their youthful brows. Apart from these, let all others remain to guard our glorious banners. We shall meet again before long to march together to the redemption of our brothers who are still slaves of the stranger. We shall meet again before long to march to new triumphs. ∎

Jefferson Davis Takes His Leave of the U.S. Senate

"I carry with me no hostile remembrance."

THIS WAS THE MOST CIVIL SPEECH that ever prefigured a civil war. Jefferson Davis, senator from Mississippi, was a champion of southern rights and an advocate of the extension of slavery into the territories, but he was not one of the firebrand secessionists. After the election of Lincoln, when his state declared its intention to secede from the Union, Davis had no choice but to bid farewell to the Senate, which he did on January 21, 1861. He was soon elected president of the Confederate States of America.

Though his oratory never had the sonority or evocativeness of Lincoln's, and his words were derided as cold and sere and legalistic in the North, Davis showed a simplicity, dignity, and sense of sadness in his farewell to the Senate that echoed years later in the second, "malice toward none" inaugural address of his adversary.

□　□　□

I rise, Mr. President, for the purpose of announcing to the Senate that I have satisfactory evidence that the state of Mississippi, by a solemn ordinance of her people in convention assembled, has declared her separation from the United States. Under these circumstances. of course, my functions are terminated here. It has seemed to me proper, however, that I should appear in the Senate to announce that fact to my associates, and I will say but very little more. The occasion does not invite me to go into argument, and my physical condition would not permit me to do so if it were otherwise; and yet it seems to become me to say something on the part of the state I here represent, on an occasion so solemn as this.

It is known to senators who have served with me here that I have for many years advocated. as an essential attribute of state sovereignty, the right of a state to secede from the Union. Therefore, if I had not believed there was justifiable cause; if I had thought that Mississippi was acting without sufficient provocation, or without an existing necessity, I should still, under my theory of the government, because of my allegiance to the state of which I am a citizen, have been bound by her action. I, however, may be permitted to say that I do think that she has justifiable cause, and I approve of her act. I conferred with her people before that act was taken, counseled them then that, if the state of things which they apprehended should exist when the convention met, they should take the action which they have now adopted.

I hope none who hear me will confound this expression of mine with the advocacy of the right of a state to remain in the Union, and to disregard its constitutional obligations by the nullification of the law. Such is not my theory. Nullification and secession, so often confounded, are indeed antagonistic principles. Nullification is a remedy which it is sought to apply within the Union, and against the agent of the states. It is only to be justified when the agent has violated his constitutional obligation, and a state, assuming to judge for itself, denies the right of the agent thus to act, and appeals to the other states of the Union for a decision; but when the states themselves, and when the people of the states, have so acted as to convince us that they will not regard our constitutional rights, then, and then for the first time, arises the doctrine of secession in its practical application.

A great man who now reposes with his fathers, and who has been often arraigned for a want of fealty to the Union, advocated the doctrine of nullification, because it preserved the Union. It was because of his deep-seated attachment to the Union, his determination to find some remedy for existing ills short of a severance of the ties which bound South Carolina to the other states, that Mr. Calhoun advocated the doctrine of nullification, which he proclaimed to be peaceful, to be within the limits of state power, not to disturb the Union, but only to be a means of bringing the agent before the tribunal of the states for their judgment.

Secession belongs to a different class of remedies. It is to be justified upon the basis that the states are sovereign. There was a time when none denied it. I hope the time may come again, when a better comprehension of the theory of our government, and the inalienable rights of the people of the states, will prevent anyone from denying that each state is a sovereign, and thus may reclaim the grants which it has made to any agent whomsoever.

I therefore say I concur in the action of the people of Mississippi, believing it to be necessary and proper, and should have been bound by their action if my belief had been otherwise; and this brings me to the important point which I wish on this last occasion to present to the Senate. It is by this confounding of nullification and secession that the name of the great man whose ashes now mingle with his mother earth has been invoked to justify coercion against a seceded state. The phrase "to execute the laws" was an expression which General Jackson applied to the case of a state refusing to obey the laws while yet a member of the Union. That is not the case which is now presented. The laws are to be executed over the United States, and upon the people of the United States. They have no relation to any foreign country. It is a perversion of terms, at least it is a great misapprehension of the case, which cites that expression for application to a state which has withdrawn from the Union. You may make war on a foreign state. If it be the purpose of gentlemen. they may make war against a state which has withdrawn from the Union; but there are no laws of the United States to be executed within the limits of a seceded state. A state finding herself in the condition in which Mississippi has judged she is, in which her safety requires that she should provide for the maintenance of her rights out of the Union, surrenders all the benefits (and they are known to be many), deprives herself of the advantages (they are known to be great), severs all the ties of affection (and they are close and enduring) which have bound her to the Union; and thus divesting herself of every benefit, taking upon herself every burden, she claims to be exempt from any power to execute the laws of the United States within her limits.

I well remember an occasion when Massachusetts was arraigned before the bar of the Senate, and when then the doctrine of coercion was rife and to be applied against her because of the rescue of a fugitive slave in Boston. My opinion then was the same that it is now. Not in a spirit of egotism, but to show that I am not influenced in my opinion because the case is my own, I refer to that time and that occasion as containing the opinion which I then entertained, and on which my present conduct is based. I then said, if Massachusetts, following her through a stated line of conduct, chooses to take the last step which separates her from the Union, it is her right to go, and I will neither vote one dollar nor one man to coerce her back, but will say to her, Godspeed, in memory of the kind associations which once existed between her and the other states.

It has been a conviction of pressing necessity; it has been a belief that we are to be deprived in the Union of the rights which our fathers bequeathed to us, which has brought Mississippi into her present decision. She has heard proclaimed the theory that all men are created free and equal, and this made the basis of an attack upon her social institutions; and the sacred Declaration of Independence has been invoked to maintain the position of the equality of the races. That Declaration of Independence is to be construed by the circumstances and purposes for which it was made. The communities were declaring their independence; the people of those communities were asserting that no man was born—to use the language of Mr. Jefferson—booted and spurred to ride over the rest of mankind; that men were created equal—meaning the men of the political community; that there was no divine right to rule; that no man inherited the right to govern; that there were no classes by which power and place descended to families, but that all stations were equally within the grasp of each member of the body politic. These were the great principles they announced; these were the purposes for which they made their declaration; these were the end to which their enunciation was directed. They have no reference to the slave; else, how happened it that among the items of arraignment made against George III was that he endeavored to do just what the North had been endeavoring of late to do—to stir up insurrection among our slaves? Had the Declaration announced that the Negroes were free and equal, how was the prince to be arraigned for stirring up insurrection among them? And how was this to be enumerated among the high crimes which caused the colonies to sever their connection with the mother country? When our Constitution was formed, the same idea was rendered more palpable, for there we find provision made for that very class of persons as property; they were not put upon the footing of equality with white men—not even upon that of paupers and convicts; but, so far as representation was concerned, were discriminated against as a lower caste, only to be represented in the numerical proportion of three-fifths.

Then, senators, we recur to the compact which binds us together; we recur to the principles upon which our government was founded; and when you deny them, and when you deny to us the right to withdraw from a government which, thus perverted, threatens to be destructive of our rights, we but tread in the path of our fathers when we proclaim our independence, and take the hazard. This is done not in hostility to others, not to injure any section of the country, not even for our own pecuniary benefit; but from the high and solemn motive of defending and protecting the rights we inherited, and which it is our sacred duty to transmit unshorn to our children.

I find in myself, perhaps, a type of the general feeling of my constituents toward yours. I am sure I feel no hostility to you, senators from the North. I am sure there is not one of you, whatever sharp discussion there may have been between us, to whom I cannot now say, in the presence of my God, I wish you well; and such, I am sure, is the feeling of the people whom I represent toward those whom you represent. I therefore feel that I but express their desire when I say I hope, and they hope, for peaceful relations with you, though we must part. They may be mutually beneficial to us in the future, as they have been in the past, if you so will it. The reverse may bring disaster on every portion of the country; and if you will have it thus, we will invoke the God of our fathers, who delivered them from the power of the lion, to protect us from the ravages of the bear; and thus, putting our trust in God, and in our own firm hearts and strong arms, we will vindicate the right as best we may.

In the course of my service here, associated at different times with a great variety of senators, I see now around me some with whom I have served long; there have been points of collision; but whatever of offense there has been to me, I leave here; I carry with me no hostile remembrance. Whatever offense I have given which has not been redressed, or for which satisfaction has not been demanded, I have, senators, in this hour of our parting, to offer you my apology for any pain which, in heat of discussion, I have inflicted. I go hence unencumbered of the remembrance of any injury received, and having discharged the duty of making the only reparation in my power for any injury offered.

Mr. President and senators, having made the announcement which the occasion seemed to me to require, it only remains for me to bid you a final adieu. ■

Chief Joseph Surrenders

"From where the sun now stands I will fight no more forever."

CHIEF JOSEPH OF THE NEZ PERCE, known to his people as Thunder Traveling to the Loftier Mountain Heights, with bullet holes riddling his robes, surrendered to the U.S. Army in 1877. His words were interpreted by a scout and taken down by an artist for *Harper's Weekly,* and come up at the reader from the depths of defeat.

□   □   □

Tell General Howard I know his heart. What he told me before, I have it in my heart. I am tired of fighting. Our chiefs are killed; Looking-Glass is dead, Ta-Hool-Hool-Shute is dead. The old men are all dead. It is the young men who say yes or no. He who led on the young men is dead. It is cold, and we have no blankets; the little children are freezing to death. My people, some of them, have run away to the hills, and have no blankets, no food. No one knows where they are—perhaps freezing to death. I want to have time to look for my children, and see how many of them I can find. Maybe I shall find them among the dead. Hear me, my chiefs! I am tired; my heart is sick and sad. From where the sun now stands I will fight no more forever. ■

President Woodrow Wilson Presents an Ideal to the War Congress

"THE world must be made safe for democracy."

WHEN THE UNITED STATES prepared to enter the First World War (known at the time as the Great War), President Woodrow Wilson called Congress into session on April 2, 1917, and denounced German submarine attacks on commerce as "a war against all nations." Within four days after making the speech, Wilson approved Congress's official declaration of war against Germany.

Wilson's style was professorial but inspiring. In even, measured phrases, Wilson's words point to principle, not selfish interests, as the motive for war. He envisions that principle as the rallying point for all Americans; in fact, his most frequent sentence starter is the collective pronoun "we" in outlining the country's intentions both to Congress and to the world. Wilson's final sentence underscores his moral certainty of America's course ("God helping her, she can do no other"), with its direct allusion to Martin Luther's moral stance in his speech to the Diet of Worms: "Here I stand; God helping me, I can do no other."

Regarding this speech's best-known line, the American historian James Harvey Robinson commented two decades after Wilson's call for war, "With supreme irony, the war to 'make the world safe for democracy' ended by leaving democracy more unsafe in the world than at any time since the collapse of the revolutions of 1848." For a time, his international idealism was derided, as was his arrogant attitude toward the Congress that helped defeat American participation in the League of Nations, but by the end of the twentieth century, Wilson's crusade for the self-determination of nations had gained moral acceptance and political momentum.

□   □   □

Gentlemen of the Congress: I have called the Congress into extraordinary session because there are serious, very serious, choices of policy to be made, and made immediately, which it was neither right nor constitutionally permissible that I should assume the responsibility of making.

On the third of February last I officially laid before you the extraordinary announcement of the imperial German government that on and after the first day of February it was its purpose to put aside all restraints of law or of humanity and use its submarines to sink every vessel that sought to approach either the ports of Great Britain and Ireland or the western coasts of Europe or any of the ports controlled by the enemies of Germany within the Mediterranean. That had seemed to be the object of the German submarine warfare earlier in the war, but since April of last year the imperial government had somewhat restrained the commanders of its undersea craft in conformity with its promise then given to us that passenger boats should not be sunk and that due warning would be given to all other vessels which its submarines might seek to destroy, when no resistance was offered or escape attempted, and care taken that their crews were given at least a fair chance to save their lives in their open boats. The precautions taken were meager and haphazard enough, as was proved in distressing instance after instance in the progress of the cruel and unmanly business, but a certain degree of restraint was observed. The new policy has swept every restriction aside. Vessels of every kind, whatever their flag, their character, their cargo, their destination, their errand, have been ruthlessly sent to the bottom without warning and without thought of help or mercy for those on board, the vessels of friendly neutrals along with those of belligerents. Even hospital ships and ships carrying relief to the sorely bereaved and stricken people of Belgium, though the latter were provided with safe conduct through the proscribed areas by the German government itself and were distinguished by unmistakable marks of identity, have been sunk with the same reckless lack of compassion or of principle.

I was for a little while unable to believe that such things would in fact be done by any government that had hitherto subscribed to the humane practices of civilized nations. International law had its origin in the attempt to set up some law which would be respected and observed upon the seas, where no nation had right of dominion and where lay the free highways of the world. By painful stage after stage has that law been built up, with meager enough results, indeed, after all was accomplished that could be accomplished, but always with a clear view, at least, of what the heart and conscience of mankind demanded. This minimum of right the German government has swept aside under the plea of retaliation and necessity and because it had no weapons which it could use at sea except these which it is impossible to employ as it is employing them without throwing to the winds all scruples of humanity or of respect for the understandings that were supposed to underlie the intercourse of the world. I am not now thinking of the loss of property involved, immense and serious as that is, but only of the wanton and wholesale destruction of the lives of noncombatants, men, women, and children, engaged in pursuits which have always, even in the darkest periods of modern history, been deemed innocent and legitimate. Property can be paid for; the lives of peaceful and innocent people cannot be. The present German submarine warfare against commerce is a warfare against mankind.

It is a war against all nations. American ships have been sunk, American lives taken, in ways which it has stirred us very deeply to learn of, but the ships and people of other neutral and friendly nations have been sunk and overwhelmed in the waters in the same way. There has been no discrimination. The challenge is to all mankind. Each nation must decide for itself how it will meet it. The choice we make for ourselves must be made with a moderation of counsel and a temperateness of judgment befitting our character and our motives as a nation. We must put excited feeling away. Our motive will not be revenge or the vic-

torious assertion of the physical might of the nation, but only the vindication of right, of human right, of which we are only a single champion.

When I addressed the Congress on the twenty-sixth of February last, I
thought that it would suffice to assert our neutral rights with arms, our
right to use the seas against unlawful interference, our right to keep our
people safe against unlawful violence. But armed neutrality, it now
appears, is impracticable. Because submarines are in effect outlaws when
used as the German submarines have been used against merchant shipping, it is impossible to defend ships against their attacks as the law of
nations has assumed that merchantmen would defend themselves
against privateers or cruisers, visible craft giving chase upon the open
sea. It is common prudence in such circumstances, grim necessity indeed,
to endeavor to destroy them before they have shown their own intention. They must be dealt with upon sight, if dealt with at all. The German
government denies the right of neutrals to use arms at all within the
areas of the sea which it has proscribed, even in the defense of rights
which no modern publicist has ever before questioned their right to
defend. The intimation is conveyed that the armed guards which we
have placed on our merchant ships will be treated as beyond the pale of
law and subject to be dealt with as pirates would be. Armed neutrality is
ineffectual enough at best; in such circumstances and in the face of such
pretensions it is worse than ineffectual; it is likely only to produce what it
was meant to prevent; it is practically certain to draw us into the war
without either the rights or the effectiveness of belligerents. There is one
choice we cannot make, we are incapable of making: we will not choose
the path of submission and suffer the most sacred rights of our nation
and our people to be ignored or violated. The wrongs against which we
now array ourselves are no common wrongs; they cut to the very roots
of human life.

With a profound sense of the solemn and even tragical character of the
step I am taking and of the grave responsibilities which it involves, but in
unhesitating obedience to what I deem my constitutional duty, I advise
that the Congress declare the recent course of the imperial German government to be in fact nothing less than war against the government and
people of the United States; that it formally accept the status of belligerent which has thus been thrust upon it; and that it take immediate steps
not only to put the country in a more thorough state of defense but also
to exert all its power and employ all its resources to bring the government of the German Empire to terms and end the war.

What this will involve is clear. It will involve the utmost practicable
cooperation in counsel and action with the governments now at war

with Germany and, as incident to that, the extension to those governments of the most liberal financial credits, in order that our resources may so far as possible be added to theirs. It will involve the organization and mobilization of all the material resources of the country to supply the materials of war and serve the incidental needs of the nation in the most abundant and yet the most economical and efficient way possible. It will involve the immediate full equipment of the navy in all respects, but particularly in supplying it with the best means of dealing with the enemy's submarines. It will involve the immediate addition to the armed forces of the United States already provided for by law in case of war of at least five hundred thousand men, who should, in my opinion, be chosen upon the principle of universal liability to service, and also the authorization of subsequent additional increments of equal force so soon as they may be needed and can be handled in training. It will involve also, of course, the granting of adequate credits to the government, sustained, I hope, so far as they can equitably be sustained by the present generation, by well-conceived taxation.

I say sustained so far as may be equitable by taxation because it seems to me that it would be most unwise to base the credits which will now be necessary entirely on money borrowed. It is our duty, I most respectfully urge, to protect our people so far as we may against the very serious hardships and evils which would be likely to arise out of the inflation which would be produced by vast loans.

In carrying out the measures by which these things are to be accomplished, we should keep constantly in mind the wisdom of interfering as little as possible in our own preparation and in the equipment of our own military forces with the duty—for it will be a very practical duty—of supplying the nations already at war with Germany with the materials which they can obtain only from us or by our assistance. They are in the field, and we should help them in every way to be effective there.

I shall take the liberty of suggesting, through the several executive departments of the government, for the consideration of your committees, measures for the accomplishment of the several objects I have mentioned. I hope that it will be your pleasure to deal with them as having been framed after very careful thought by the branch of the government upon which the responsibility of conducting the war and safeguarding the nation will most directly fall.

While we do these things, these deeply momentous things, let us be very clear, and make very clear to all the world, what our motives and our objects are. My own thought has not been driven from its habitual and normal course by the unhappy events of the last two months, and I do not believe that the thought of the nation has been altered or clouded by them. I have exactly the same things in mind now that I had in mind when I addressed the Senate on the twenty-second of January last; the same that I had in mind when I addressed the Congress on the third of February and on the twenty-sixth of February. Our object now, as then, is to vindicate the principles of peace and justice in the life of the world as against selfish and autocratic power and to set up amongst the really free and self-governed peoples of the world such a concert of purpose and of action as will henceforth ensure the observance of those principles. Neutrality is no longer feasible or desirable where the peace of the world is involved and the freedom of its peoples, and the menace to that peace and freedom lies in the existence of autocratic governments backed by organized force which is controlled wholly by their will, not by the will of their people. We have seen the last of neutrality in such circumstances. We are at the beginning of an age in which it will be insisted that the same standards of conduct and of responsibility for wrong done shall be observed among nations and their governments that are observed among the individual citizens of civilized states.

We have no quarrel with the German people. We have no feeling toward them but one of sympathy and friendship. It was not upon their impulse that their government acted in entering this war. It was not with their previous knowledge or approval. It was a war determined upon as wars used to be determined upon in the old, unhappy days when peoples were nowhere consulted by their rulers and wars were provoked and waged in the interest of dynasties or of little groups of ambitious men who were accustomed to use their fellow men as pawns and tools. Self-governed nations do not fill their neighbor states with spies or set the course of intrigue to bring about some critical posture of affairs which will give them an opportunity to strike and make conquest. Such designs can be successfully worked out only under cover and where no one has the right to ask questions. Cunningly contrived plans of deception or aggression, carried, it may be, from generation to generation, can be worked out and kept from the light only within the privacy of courts or behind the carefully guarded confidences of a narrow and privileged class. They are happily impossible where public opinion commands and insists upon full information concerning all the nation's affairs.

A steadfast concert for peace can never be maintained except by a partnership of democratic nations. No autocratic government could be trusted to keep faith within it or observe its covenants. It must be a league of honor, a partnership of opinion. Intrigue would eat its vitals away; the plottings of inner circles who could plan what they would and render account to no one would be a corruption seated at its very heart. Only free peoples can hold their purpose and their honor steady to a common end and prefer the interests of mankind to any narrow interest of their own.

Does not every American feel that assurance has been added to our hope for the future peace of the world by the wonderful and heartening things that have been happening within the last few weeks in Russia? Russia was known by those who knew it best to have been always in fact democratic at heart, in all the vital habits of her thought, in all the intimate relationships of her people that spoke their natural instinct, their habitual attitude toward life. The autocracy that crowned the summit of her political structure, long as it had stood and terrible as was the reality of its power, was not in fact Russian in origin, character, or purpose; and now it has been shaken off, and the great, generous Russian people have been added in all their native majesty and might to the forces that are fighting for freedom in the world, for justice, and for peace. Here is a fit partner for a league of honor.

One of the things that has served to convince us that the Prussian autocracy was not and could never be our friend is that from the very outset of the present war it has filled our unsuspecting communities and even our offices of government with spies and set criminal intrigues everywhere afoot against our national unity of counsel, our peace within and without, our industries, and our commerce. Indeed, it is now evident that its spies were here even before the war began; and it is unhappily not a matter of conjecture but a fact proved in our courts of justice that the intrigues which have more than once come perilously near to disturbing the peace and dislocating the industries of the country have been carried on at the instigation, with the support, and even under the personal direction of official agents of the imperial government accredited to the government of the United States. Even in checking these things and trying to extirpate them, we have sought to put the most generous interpretation possible upon them because we knew that their source lay, not in any hostile feeling or purpose of the German people toward us (who were no doubt as ignorant of them as we ourselves were), but only in the selfish designs of a government that did what it pleased and told its people nothing. But they have played their part in serving to convince us at last that that government entertains no real friendship for us and means to act against our peace and security at its convenience. That it means to stir up enemies against us at our very doors the intercepted note to the German minister at Mexico City is eloquent evidence.

We are accepting this challenge of hostile purpose because we know that in such a government, following such methods, we can never have a friend; and that in the presence of its organized power, always lying in wait to accomplish we know not what purpose, there can be no assured security for the democratic governments of the world. We are now about to accept gage of battle with this natural foe to liberty and shall, if necessary, spend the whole force of the nation to check and nullify its pretensions and its power. We are glad, now that we see the facts with no veil of false pretense about them, to fight thus for the ultimate peace of the world and for the liberation of its peoples, the German peoples included: for the rights of nations great and small and the privilege of men everywhere to choose their way of life and of obedience. *The world must be made safe for democracy.* Its peace must be planted upon the tested foundations of political liberty. We have no selfish ends to serve. We desire no conquest, no dominion. We seek no indemnities for ourselves, no material compensation for the sacrifices we shall freely make. We are but one of the champions of the rights of mankind. We shall be satisfied when those rights have been made as secure as the faith and the freedom of nations can make them.

Just because we fight without rancor and without selfish object, seeking nothing for ourselves but what we shall wish to share with all free peoples, we shall, I feel confident, conduct our operations as belligerents without passion and ourselves observe with proud punctilio the principles of right and of fair play we profess to be fighting for.

I have said nothing of the governments allied with the imperial government of Germany because they have not made war upon us or challenged us to defend our right and our honor. The Austro-Hungarian government has, indeed, avowed its unqualified endorsement and acceptance of the reckless and lawless submarine warfare adopted now without disguise by the imperial German government, and it has therefore not been possible for this government to receive Count Tarnowski, the ambassador recently accredited to this government by the imperial and royal government of Austria-Hungary; but that government has not actually engaged in warfare against citizens of the United States on the seas, and I take the liberty, for the present at least, of postponing a discussion of our relations with the authorities at Vienna. We enter this war only where we are clearly forced into it because there are no other means of defending our rights.

It will be all the easier for us to conduct ourselves as belligerents in a high spirit of right and fairness because we act without animus, not in enmity towards a people or with the desire to bring any injury or disadvantage upon them but only in armed opposition to an irresponsible government which has thrown aside all considerations of humanity and of right and is running amuck. We are, let me say again, the sincere friends of the German people, and shall desire nothing so much as the early reestablishment of intimate relations of mutual advantage between us—however hard it may be for them, for the time being, to believe that this is spoken from our hearts. We have borne with their present government through all these bitter months because of that friendship—exercising a patience and forbearance which would otherwise have been impossible. We shall, happily, still have an opportunity to prove that friendship in our daily attitude and actions towards the millions of men and women of German birth and native sympathy who live amongst us and share our life, and we shall be proud to prove it towards all who are in fact loyal to their neighbors and to the government in the hour of test. They are, most of them, as true and loyal Americans as if they had never known any other fealty or allegiance. They will be prompt to stand with us in rebuking and restraining the few who may be of a different mind and purpose. If there should be disloyalty, it will be dealt with with a firm hand of stern repression; but, if it lifts its head at all, it will lift it only here and there and without countenance except from a lawless and malignant few.

It is a distressing and oppressive duty, gentlemen of the Congress, which I have performed in thus addressing you. There are, it may be, many months of fiery trial and sacrifice ahead of us. It is a fearful thing to lead this great peaceful people into war, into the most terrible and disastrous of all wars, civilization itself seeming to be in the balance. But the right is more precious than peace, and we shall fight for the things which we have always carried nearest our hearts—for democracy, for the right of those who submit to authority to have a voice in their own governments, for the rights and liberties of small nations, for a universal dominion of right by such a concert of free peoples as shall bring peace and safety to all nations and make the world itself at last free. To such a task we can dedicate our lives and our fortunes, everything that we are and everything that we have, with the pride of those who know that the day has come when America is privileged to spend her blood and her might for the principles that gave her birth and happiness and the peace which she has treasured. God helping her, she can do no other. ■

Lenin Defends Proletarian Dictatorship

"HISTORY teaches that no oppressed class has ever come into power, and cannot come into power, without passing through a period of dictatorship."

FROM RUSSIAN REVOLUTIONIST TO SOVIET PREMIER, Vladimir Ilyich Lenin worked for the social upheaval outlined in his 1917 *State and Revolution:* "The substitution of the proletarian for the bourgeois state is impossible without a violent revolution."

After the October Revolution of 1917, Lenin led his Bolshevik party to power and. as chairman of the Communist party, ruled from then until his death in 1924. A powerful orator, he delivered the following speech before the 1919 Communist International Congress.

Denying the efficacy of "democracy in general," Lenin upholds the "proletariat," a term borrowed from the Latin *proletarius,* for any member of the lowest class in ancient Roman society. By drawing a distinction between "dictatorship in general" and "dictatorship of the proletariat," Lenin redefines a number of terms, with sarcastic reference to "equality" and "freedom" in capitalist usage. The movement from bourgeois rule to proletarian dictatorship, according to Lenin, will lead to "democratism by the toiling classes."

Later, Lenin derided "the saying that Russia is a prison of nations," but the internal and external empire he built was pockmarked by the gulag archipelago, or network of prison camps. Economic strains and a yearning for freedom broke it into its historical component parts seven decades after the supposedly temporary, but in fact unending, period of dictatorship. In this speech, the disciplined revolutionist makes the case that the end of socialism justifies the means of dictatorship; it was later shown that the means become the ends.

□   □   □

The growth of the revolutionary movement of the proletariat in all countries has called forth convulsive efforts of the bourgeoisie, and its agents in workmen's organizations, to find ideal political arguments in defense of the rule of the exploiters. Among these arguments stands out particularly condemnation of dictatorship and defense of democracy. The falseness and hypocrisy of such an argument, which has been repeated in thousands of forms in the capitalist press and at the conference of the yellow International in February 1919, Berne, are evident to all who have not wished to betray the fundamental principle of socialism.

First of all, this argument is used with certain interpretations of "democracy in general" and "dictatorship in general" without raising the point as to which class one has in mind. Such a statement of the question, leaving out of consideration the question of class as though it were a general national matter, is direct mockery of the fundamental doctrine of socialism, namely, the doctrine of class struggle, which the socialists who have gone over to the side of the bourgeoisie recognize when they talk, but forget when they act. For in no civilized capitalist country does there exist "democracy in general" but there exists only bourgeois democracy, and one is speaking not of "dictatorship in general" but of dictatorship of the oppressed classes, that is, of the proletariat with respect to the oppressors and exploiters, that is, the bourgeoisie, in order to overcome the resistance which the exploiters make in their struggle to preserve their rule.

History teaches that no oppressed class has ever come into power, and cannot come into power, without passing through a period of dictatorship, that is, the conquest of power and the forcible suppression of the most desperate and mad resistance which does not hesitate to resort to any crimes, such has always been shown by the exploiters. The bourgeoisie, whose rule is now defended by the socialists who speak against "dictatorship in general" and who espouse the cause of "democracy in general" has won power in the progressive countries at the price of a series of uprisings, civil wars, forcible suppression of kings, feudal lords, and slave owners, and of their attempts at restoration. The socialists of all countries in their books and pamphlets, in the resolutions of their congresses, in their propaganda speeches, have explained to the people thousands and millions of times the class character of these bourgeois revolutions, and of this bourgeois dictatorship. Therefore the present defense of bourgeois democracy in the form of speeches about "democracy in general" and the present wails and shouts against the dictatorship of the proletariat in the form of wails about "dictatorship in general" are a direct mockery of socialism, and represent in fact going over to the bourgeoisie and denying the right of the proletariat to its own proletariat revolution, and a defense of bourgeois reformism, precisely at the historic moment when bourgeois reformism is collapsing the world over, and when the war has created a revolutionary situation.

All socialists who explain the class character of bourgeois civilization, or bourgeois democracy, of bourgeois parliamentarism, express the thought which Marx and Engels expressed with the most scientific exactness when they said that the most democratic bourgeois republic is nothing more than a machine for the suppression of the working class by the bourgeoisie, for the suppression of the mass of the toilers by a handful of capitalists. There is not a single revolutionist, not a single Marxist of all those who are now shouting against dictatorship and for democracy, who would not have sworn before the workmen that he recognizes this fundamental truth of socialism. And now, when the revolutionary proletariat begins to act and move for the destruction of this machinery of oppression, and to win the proletarian dictatorship, these traitors to socialism report the situation as though the bourgeoisie were giving the laborers pure democracy, as though the bourgeoisie were abandoning resistance and were ready to submit to the majority of the toilers, as though there were no state machinery for the suppression of labor by capital in a democratic republic.

Workmen know very well that "freedom of meetings," even in the most democratic bourgeois republic is an empty phrase, for the rich have all the best public and private buildings at their disposal, and also sufficient leisure time for meetings and for protection of these meetings by the bourgeois apparatus of authority. The proletarians of the city and of the village, and the poor peasants, that is, the overwhelming majority of the population, have none of these three things. So long as the situation is such, "equality," that is, "pure democracy," is sheer fraud.

The capitalists have always called "freedom" the freedom to make money for the rich, and the freedom to die of hunger for workmen. The capitalists call "freedom" the freedom of the rich, freedom to buy up the press, to use wealth, to manufacture and support so-called public opinion. The defenders of "pure democracy" again in actual fact turn out to be the defenders of the most dirty and corrupt system of the rule of the rich over the means of education of the masses. They deceive the people by attractive, fine-sounding, beautiful but absolutely false phrases, trying to dissuade the masses from the concrete historic task of freeing the press from the capitalists who have gotten control of it. Actual freedom and equality will exist only in the order established by the Communists, in which it will be impossible to become rich at the expense of another, where it will be impossible either directly or indirectly to subject the press to the power of money, where there will be no obstacle to prevent any toiler from enjoying and actually realizing the equal right to the use of public printing presses and of the public fund of paper.

Dictatorship of the proletariat resembles dictatorship of other classes in that it was called forth by the need to suppress the forcible resistance of a class that was losing its political rulership. But that which definitely distinguishes a dictatorship of the proletariat from a dictatorship of other classes, from a dictatorship of the bourgeoisie in all the civilized capitalist countries, is that the dictatorship of the landlords and of the bourgeoisie was the forcible suppression of the resistance of the overwhelming majority of the population, namely, the toilers. On the other hand, the dictatorship of the proletariat is the forcible suppression of the resistance of the exploiters, that is, of an insignificant minority of the population— of landlords and capitalists.

It therefore follows that a dictatorship of the proletariat must necessarily carry with it not only changes in the form and institutions of democracy, speaking in general terms, but specifically such a change as would secure an extension such as has never been seen in the history of the world of the actual use of democratism by the toiling classes. ∎

Mussolini Justifies His Invasion of Ethiopia

"To acts of war, we shall answer with acts of war."

IL DUCE (THE LEADER) was the title assumed by Benito Mussolini, Italy's Fascist dictator from 1922 to 1943. At first cool to Hitler, he joined his fellow dictator as France was falling to German arms. ("The hand that held the dagger," said FDR, "has struck it into the back of its neighbor.") When the Allies invaded Sicily in World War II, Mussolini was removed from power and placed under arrest, but he was rescued by the Germans. After an unsuccessful attempt to reorganize his government in 1945, he was shot while trying to escape to Germany in the guise of a German soldier.

At the height of his power, however, Mussolini gave forceful speeches to his Fascist followers. (The term "Fascist" comes from the Italian *fascio,* which means "group, bundle"; the most frequent line of defense for the corporate state of fascism was the 1930s expression "But you must admit that Mussolini made the trains run on time.") He had a way with metaphor, exclaiming in 1934, "We have buried the putrid corpse of liberty." The following speech, broadcast on October 2, 1933, announced the invasion of Ethiopia.

Using metonymy, Mussolini begins by addressing the "Blackshirts of revolution," referring to the paramilitary Fascist force that helped him seize power in the 1922 march on Rome. His nationalistic appeals, often exclamatory ("Italy! Italy! entirely and universally Fascist!"), lead to the anaphora of the closing sentences: "It is the cry of Italy. . . . It is the cry of justice and of victory."

□   □   □

command

Blackshirts of revolution, men and women of all Italy, Italians all over the world, beyond the mountains, beyond the seas, listen. A solemn hour is about to strike in the history of the country. Twenty million Italians are at this moment gathered in the squares of all Italy. It is the greatest demonstration that human history records. Twenty millions, one heart alone, one will alone, one decision. *emphrases himself*
This manifestation signifies that the tie between Italy and fascism is perfect, absolute, unalterable. Only brains softened by puerile illusions, by sheer ignorance, can think differently, because they do not know what exactly is the Fascist Italy of 1935.

For many months the wheel of destiny and of the impulse of our calm determination moves toward the goal. In these last hours the rhythm has increased and nothing can stop it now.

It is not only an army marching towards its goal, but it is forty-four million Italians marching in unity behind this army. Because the blackest of injustices is being attempted against them, that of taking from them their place in the sun. When in 1915 Italy threw in her fate with that of the Allies, how many cries of admiration, how many promises were heard? But after the common victory, which cost Italy six hundred thousand dead, four hundred thousand lost, one million wounded, when peace was being discussed around the table only the crumbs of a rich colonial booty were left for us to pick up. For thirteen years we have been patient while the circle tightened around us at the hands of those who wish to suffocate us.

We have been patient with Ethiopia for forty years. It is enough now.

The League of Nations, instead of recognizing the rights of Italy, dares talk of sanctions, but until there is proof of the contrary, I refuse to believe that the authentic people of France will join in supporting sanctions against Italy. Six hundred thousand dead whose devotion was so heroic that the enemy commander justly admired them—those fallen would now turn in their graves.

And until there is proof to the contrary, I refuse to believe that the authentic people of Britain will want to spill blood and send Europe into a catastrophe for the sake of a barbarian country, unworthy of ranking among civilized nations. Nevertheless, we cannot afford to overlook the possible developments of tomorrow.

To economic sanctions, we shall answer with our discipline, our spirit of sacrifice, our obedience. To military sanctions, we shall answer with military measures. To acts of war, we shall answer with acts of war.

A people worthy of their past and their name cannot and never will take a different stand. Let me repeat, in the most categorical manner, that the sacred pledge which I make at this moment, before all the Italians gathered together today, is that I shall do everything in my power to prevent a colonial conflict from taking on the aspect and weight of a European war.

This conflict may be attractive to certain minds which hope to avenge their disintegrated temples through this new catastrophe. Never, as at this historical hour, have the people of Italy revealed such force of character, and it is against this people to which mankind owes its greatest conquest, this people of heroes, of poets and saints, of navigators, of colonizers, that the world dares threaten sanctions.

Italy! Italy! entirely and universally Fascist! The Italy of the blackshirt revolution, rise to your feet; let the cry of your determination rise to the skies and reach our soldiers in East Africa. Let it be a comfort to those who are about to fight. Let it be an encouragement to our friends and a warning to our enemies. It is the cry of Italy which goes beyond the mountains and the seas out into the great world. It is the cry of justice and of victory. ■

Hitler Declares
Germany's Intentions

"THE world would then see, as quick as lightning, to what extent this Reich, people, party, and these armed forces are fanatically inspired with one spirit, one will."

"STRENGTH LIES NOT IN DEFENSE BUT IN ATTACK," wrote Adolf Hitler in *Mein Kampf* ("My Battle"), translated into English in 1933. The assault strategy was applied to the content of his oratory: "The great masses of the people . . . will more easily fall victims to a big lie than to a small one."

In his rise from the rank of a World War I corporal to that of dictator of Nazi Germany, Austrian-born Hitler used attacks based on violent anti-Semitism and totalitarian tactics to murder his opponents and support the aims of his "Third Reich," or third German empire. In the twelve years that followed his seizing of power in 1933, Der Führer (the Leader) was responsible for the mass murder of millions of Jews and other innocents. Shortly after his suicide in 1945, Germany announced an unconditional surrender to end the Second World War.

Hitler's speeches often lacked the strength of coherence, but with slashing racism and the powerful imagery of nationalism, he was able to delight and control crowds resentful of the reminders of past defeat—what he derided as "the death sentence of Versailles." On February 20, 1938, the chancellor addressed the Reichstag, formed during the Second Reich as the lower chamber of Germany's federal parliament; in this speech, Hitler speaks repeatedly of German strength and indicates his dark intentions toward Europe. The inimical language includes a warning based on an Ibsen phrase ("Whoever disturbs this mission is the enemy of the people"), and Hitler rounds out his Reich rhetoric with parallel structure, seeking divine intervention to bless "our work, our deeds, our foresight, our resolve."

□   □   □

... We have seen that a certain portion of the foreign press inundated the new Reich with a virtual flood of lies and calumnies. It was a remarkable mixture of arrogance and deplorable ignorance which led them to act as the judges of a people who should be presented as models to these democratic apostles.

The best proof for showing up these lies is success. For if we had acted during these five years like the democratic world citizens of Soviet Russia, that is, like those of the Jewish race, we would not have succeeded in making out of a Germany which was in the deepest material collapse a country of material order. For this very reason we claim the right to surround our work with that protection which renders it impossible for criminal elements or for the insane to disturb it.

Whoever disturbs this mission is the enemy of the people, whether he pursues his aim as a Bolshevist democrat, a revolutionary terrorist, or a reactionary dreamer. In such a time of necessity those who act in the name of God are not those who, citing Bible quotations, wander idly about the country and spend the day partly doing nothing and partly criticizing the work of others; but those whose prayers take the highest form of uniting man with his God, that is, the form of work.

I had a right to turn against every one who, instead of helping, thought his mission was to criticize our work. Foreign nations contributed nothing apart from this spirit, for their rejection was tinged by hate or a spirit of knowing better than we know.

It was the ABC of our creed to find help in our own strength. The standard of living of the nation is the outcome of its total production; in other words, the value of every wage and salary corresponds to the volume of goods produced as a result of the work performed. This is a very unpopular doctrine in a time resounding with cries such as "higher wages and less work."

Next to the United States, Germany today has become the greatest steel country in the world. I could give many more examples. They are documentary proof of the work such as our people never before achieved. To these successes will be added in a few years the gigantic results of the Four-Year Plan. Is it not a joke of history when those very countries which themselves have only crises think they can criticize us and give us advice?

We have given the German nation that weapon of steel which presents a wall at our frontiers against the intentions of the malicious international press campaign.

At the conclusion of the next decade the German people will bear in mind the success of their efficiency and will be filled with a supreme pride. One of these achievements is the construction of a national leadership which is as far removed from parliamentary democracy as it is from military dictatorship.

If ever international agitation or poisoning of opinion should attempt to rupture the peace of the Reich, then steel and iron would take the German people and German homesteads under their protection. The world would then see, as quick as lightning, to what extent this Reich, people, party, and these armed forces are fanatically inspired with one spirit, one will.

If Great Britain should suddenly dissolve today and England become dependent solely on her own territory, then the people there would, perhaps, have more understanding of the seriousness of the economic tasks which confront us. If a nation which commands no gold reserves, no foreign exchange—not because National Socialism reigns but because a parliamentary, democratic state was exploited for fifteen years by a world hungry after loot—in other words, if a nation which must feed 140 people to the square kilometer and has no colonies, if a nation which lacks numerous raw materials and is not willing to live an illusory life through credits, reduces the number of its unemployed in five years to nil and improves its standard of living, then all those should remain silent who, despite great economic advantages, scarcely succeed in solving their own unemployment problems.

The claim for German colonial possessions, therefore, will be voiced from year to year with increasing vigor. These possessions, which Germany did not take away from other countries and which today are practically of no value to these powers, are indispensable for our own people.

I should like to refute here the hope that such claims can be averted by granting credits. Above all, we do not wish for naive assurances that we shall be permitted to buy what we need. We reject such statements once and for all.

You will not expect me to discuss in detail the individual international plans which appear to arouse the varied interests of the various governments. They are too uncertain and they lack the clarity necessary for me to be able to express myself on these questions. Above all, however, take note of my deep-seated distrust of all so-called conferences which may provide interesting hours of conversation for those taking part in them, but generally lead to the disappointment of hopeful mankind.

I cannot allow our natural claims to be coupled with political business. Recently rumors have been cropping up, rumors that Germany was about to revise her opinion concerning her return to the League of Nations. I should like again to declare that in 1919 the peace treaty was forced upon some countries. This treaty brought in its train far-reaching inroads upon the lives of the peoples involved. The rape of national and economic destinies and of the communal lives of the nations took place under a cloud of moralizing phrases which, perhaps, tended to salve the uneasy conscience of those who instituted the affair.

After the revision of the map of the world and of territorial and racial spheres, which was as thorough as it was fundamental, had been effected by means of force, a League of Nations was founded whose task it was to crystallize these crazy, unreasonable proceedings and to coordinate its results into an everlasting and unalterable basis of life.

I notice very often that English politicians would be glad to give back to us our colonies if they were not so disturbed by the thought of the wrong and violence which would thus be done to the native inhabitants.

All those colonial empires have not come into being through plebiscites. They are today naturally integral parts of the states in question and form, as such, part of that world order which always has been designated to us, especially by democratic policies, as the "world order of right."

That right the League of Nations now has been ordered to protect. I cannot understand why a nation which itself has been robbed by force should join such illustrious company, and I cannot permit the conclusion to be drawn that we should not be prepared to fight for the principles of justice just because we are not in the League of Nations. On the contrary, we do not belong to the League of Nations, because we believe that it is not an institution of justice but an institution for defending the interests of Versailles.

A number of material considerations must, however, be added.

First, we left the League of Nations because—loyal to its origin and obligations—it refused us the right to equal armament and just as equal security.

Second, we will never reenter it, because we do not intend to allow ourselves to be used anywhere in the world by a majority vote of the League of Nations for the defense of an injustice.

Third, we believe we will please all those nations who are misled by misfortune to rely on and trust the League of Nations as a factor of genuine help. We should have regarded it as more correct, for instance, in the case of the Ethiopian war, for the League to have shown more understanding for vital Italian needs and less disposition to help the Ethiopians with promises. This would, perhaps, have enabled a more simple and reasonable solution for the whole problem.

Fourth, on no account will we allow the German nation to become entangled in conflicts in which the nation itself is not interested. We are not willing to stand up for the territorial or economic interests of others without the slightest benefits to Germans being visible. Moreover, we ourselves do not expect such support from others. Germany is determined to impose upon herself wise moderation in her interests and demands. But if German interests should be seriously at stake we shall not expect to receive support from the League of Nations but we shall assume the right from the beginning to shoulder our task ourselves.

Fifth, we do not intend to allow our attitude to be determined in the future by any international institution which, while excluding official recognition of indisputable facts, resembles less the acts of a man of considered judgment than the habits of a certain type of large bird. The interests of nations in so far as their existence or nonexistence are ultimately concerned are stronger than formalistic considerations. For in the year 2038 it is possible that new states may have arisen or others disappeared without this new state of affairs having been registered at Geneva.

Germany will not take part in such unreasonable proceedings by being a member of the League of Nations.

With one country alone have we scorned to enter into relations. That state is Soviet Russia. We see in bolshevism more now than before the incarnation of human destructive forces. We do not blame the Russian people as such for this gruesome ideology of destruction. We know it is a small Jewish intellectual group which led a great nation into this position of madness. If this doctrine would confine itself territorially to Russia maybe one could put up with it. Alas, Jewish international bolshevism attempts to hollow out the nations of the world from its Soviet center.

As I have more than once stated, Germany has in Europe no more territorial demands to make of France. With the return of the Saar we trust the period of Franco-German territorial differences is finally closed.

Germany also has no quarrel with England apart from her colonial wishes. However, there is no cause for any conceivable conflict. The only thing that has poisoned and thus injured the common life of these two countries is the utterly unendurable press campaign which in these two countries has existed under the motto "freedom of personal opinion."

The British government desires the limitation of armaments or the prohibition of bombing. I myself proposed this some time ago. However, I also suggested at the time that the most important thing was to prevent the poisoning of the world's public opinion by infamous press articles. That which strengthened our sympathy with Italy, if this were possible, is the fact that in that country state policy and press policy tread the same road.

There are more than ten million Germans in states adjoining Germany which before 1866 were joined to the bulk of the German nation by a national link. Until 1918 they fought in the Great War shoulder to shoulder with the German soldiers of the Reich. Against their own free will they were prevented by peace treaties from uniting with the Reich.

This was painful enough, but there must be no doubt about one thing: political separation from the Reich may not lead to deprivation of rights, that is the general rights of racial self-determination which were solemnly promised to us in Wilson's Fourteen Points as a condition for the armistice. We cannot disregard it just because this is a case concerning Germans.

In the long run it is unbearable for a world power, conscious of herself, to know there are citizens at her side who are constantly being inflicted with the severest sufferings for their sympathy or unity with the total nation, its faith and philosophy.

We will know there can scarcely be a frontier line in Europe which satisfies all. It should be all the more important to avoid the torture of national minorities in order not to add to the suffering of political separation, the suffering of persecution on account of their belonging to a certain people.

That it is possible to find ways leading to the lessening of tension has been proved. But he who tries to prevent by force such lessening of tension through creating an equilibrium in Europe will someday inevitably conjure up force among the nations themselves. It cannot be denied that Germany herself, as long as she was powerless and defenseless, was compelled to tolerate many of these continual persecutions of the German people on our frontier.

But just as England stands up for her interests all over the globe, present-day Germany will know how to guard its more restricted interests. To these interests of the German Reich belong also the protection of those German peoples who are not in a position to secure along our frontiers their political and philosophical freedom by their own efforts.

I may say that since the League of Nations has abandoned its continuous attempts at disturbance in Danzig and since the advent of the new commissioner this most dangerous place for European peace has entirely lost its menace.

Poland respects the national conditions in the free city of Danzig and Germany respects Polish rights.

Now I turn to Austria. It is not only the same people but above all a long communal history and culture which bind together the Reich and Austria.

Difficulties which emerged in the carrying out of the agreement of July 11, 1936, made essential an attempt to remove misunderstandings and obstacles to final reconciliation. It is clear that whether we wished it or not an intolerable position might have developed that would have contained the seeds of catastrophe. It does not lie in the power of man to stop the rolling stone of fate which through neglect or lack of wisdom has been set moving.

I am happy to say that these ideas correspond with the viewpoint of the Austrian chancellor, whom I invited to visit me. The underlying intention was to bring about a détente in our relations which would guarantee to National Socialist sympathizers in Austria within the limits of the law the same rights enjoyed by other citizens.

In connection with it there was to be an act of conciliation in the form of a general amnesty and better understanding between the two states through closer and friendlier relations in the various spheres of cultural, political, and economic cooperation. All this is a development within the framework of the treaty of July 11.

I wish to pay tribute to the Austrian chancellor for his efforts to find together with me a way which is just as much in the interests of both countries as in that of the entire German people, whose sons we all are regardless of where we came from. I believe we have thus made a contribution to European peace.

Our satisfactory relations with other countries are known to all. Above all is to be mentioned our cooperation with those two great powers which, like Germany, have recognized bolshevism as a world danger and are therefore determined to resist the Comintern with a common defense. It is my earnest wish to see this cooperation with Italy and Japan more and more extended.

The German people is no warlike nation. It is a soldierly one which means it does not want a war but does not fear it. It loves peace, but it also loves its honor and freedom.

The new Reich shall belong to no class, no profession, but to the German people. It shall help the people find an easier road in this world. It shall help them in making their lot a happier one. Party, state, armed forces, economics are institutions and functions which can only be estimated as a means toward an end. They will be judged by history according to the services they render toward this goal. Their purpose, however, is to serve the people.

I now pray to God that he will bless in the years to come our work, our deeds, our foresight, our resolve; that the almighty may protect us from both arrogance and cowardly servility, that he may help us find the right way which he has laid down for the German people and that he may always give us courage to do the right thing and never to falter or weaken before any power or any danger.

Long live Germany and the German people! ■

Winston Churchill Braces Britons to Their Task

"I have nothing to offer but blood, toil, tears, and sweat."

WHEN WINSTON CHURCHILL addressed Parliament on May 13, 1940, he had just been appointed prime minister, a position that he held from 1940 to 1945 and again from 1951 until his retirement in 1955. His Conservative party sought to ready England for defense in the face of Nazi aggression, and Churchill rallied his country after succeeding Neville Chamberlain, a prime minister who thought he had achieved "peace for our time," in the appeasement of Hitler at Munich in 1938.

Churchill delivered speeches eminently suited for quoting, their memorable phrases ranging from "their finest hour" to "iron curtain." But no orator can guarantee that his prose will survive the editing of history: this 1940 speech about "blood, toil, tears, and sweat" is now often identified by the altered quotation "blood, sweat, and tears." (The editing is apt; "toil" and "sweat" are redundant.) Curiously, common usage prefers to begin sequential phrases with "blood": Otto von Bismarck's warlike 1862 *Eisen und Blut* was also switched around to "blood and iron."

The German threat, memorably described by Churchill as "a monstrous tyranny never surpassed in the dark and lamentable catalogue of human crime," is the foremost concern of the new prime minister. Addressing the House of Commons, he uses repetition and alliteration ("many, many months of struggle and suffering") to pound home the period of stress and sacrifice ahead. Through answers to his countrymen's questions ("You ask, what is our policy?" and "You ask, what is our aim?"), Churchill outlines his intentions for England during the onset of World War II.

□   □   □

On Friday evening last I received from His Majesty the mission to form a new administration.

It was the evident will of Parliament and the nation that this should be conceived on the broadest possible basis and that it should include all parties.

I have already completed the most important part of this task. A war cabinet has been formed of five members, representing, with the Labour, Opposition, and Liberals, the unity of the nation.

It was necessary that this should be done in one single day on account of the extreme urgency and rigor of events. Other key positions were filled yesterday. I am submitting a further list to the king tonight. I hope to complete the appointment of principal ministers during tomorrow.

The appointment of other ministers usually takes a little longer. I trust when Parliament meets again this part of my task will be completed and that the administration will be complete in all respects.

I considered it in the public interest to suggest to the Speaker that the House should be summoned today. At the end of today's proceedings, the adjournment of the House will be proposed until May 21 with provision for earlier meeting if need be. Business for that will be notified to MPs at the earliest opportunity.

I now invite the House by a resolution to record its approval of the steps taken and declare its confidence in the new government. The resolution:

"That this House welcomes the formation of a government representing the united and inflexible resolve of the nation to prosecute the war with Germany to a victorious conclusion."

To form an administration of this scale and complexity is a serious undertaking in itself. But we are in the preliminary phase of one of the greatest battles in history. We are in action at many other points—in Norway and in Holland—and we have to be prepared in the

Mediterranean. The air battle is continuing, and many preparations have to be made here at home.

In this crisis I think I may be pardoned if I do not address the House at any length today, and I hope that any of my friends and colleagues or former colleagues who are affected by the political reconstruction will make all allowances for any lack of ceremony with which it has been necessary to act.

I say to the House as I said to ministers who have joined this government, I have nothing to offer but blood, toil, tears, and sweat. We have before us an ordeal of the most grievous kind. We have before us many, many months of struggle and suffering.

You ask, what is our policy? I say it is to wage war by land, sea, and air. War with all our might and with all the strength God has given us, and to wage war against a monstrous tyranny never surpassed in the dark and lamentable catalogue of human crime. That is our policy.

You ask, what is our aim? I can answer in one word. It is victory. Victory at all costs—victory in spite of all terrors—victory, however long and hard the road may be, for without victory there is no survival.

Let that be realized. No survival for the British Empire, no survival for all that the British Empire has stood for, no survival for the urge, the impulse of the ages, that mankind shall move forward toward his goal.

I take up my task in buoyancy and hope. I feel sure that our cause will not be suffered to fail among men.

I feel entitled at this juncture, at this time, to claim the aid of all and to say, "Come then, let us go forward together with our united strength." ■

Churchill Rallies the British People after the "Miracle of Deliverance" at Dunkirk

"We shall not flag or fail . . . We shall fight on the beaches . . . we shall fight in the fields and in the streets . . . we shall never surrender."

THE EVACUATION OF 340,000 BRITISH SOLDIERS from the beaches of Dunkirk on the continent of Europe, with 40,000 left behind to be taken prisoner by the Nazi forces, was called by Churchill "a miracle of deliverance," as if it were a kind of allied victory. But the retreat to the beaches and across the English Channel on May 26 and 27, 1940, was—as British Prime Minister Winston Churchill was reported to have said privately afterward—"the greatest military defeat for many centuries."

He spoke to the House of Commons on June 4, as directional signs were being taken down at crossroads throughout Britain in anticipation of Hitler's invasion. Three weeks before, he had delivered his speech offering nothing but "blood, toil, tears, and sweat" (see p. 143) but showing "buoyancy and hope" and concluding with a ringing "let us go forward together with our united strength." That was before Allied forces suffered a crushing defeat and the real possibility of the landing of German troops swept the country. Now a longer speech in a more somber mood was required, containing a report more detailed in its military analysis, and with some silver lining seen in the war cloud.

After reviewing the tactical defenses put up by the British, French, and Belgian "armies of the north," he reported how "the German eruption swept like a sharp scythe" around them. By showing how "the whole root and core and brain of the British Army . . . seemed about to perish or be led into an ignominious and starving captivity," he accentuated the worst case possible, which made the successful retreat a "miracle of deliverance" for which Britain should be grateful. His repetition of the biblical word "deliverance" was the cue to the press to refer to "the miracle of Dunkirk." By emphasizing the scope of the losses that were not suffered, the new prime minister lessened the impact of the defeat that took place.

Churchill was careful not to destroy his credibility by overtly minimizing the defeat that drove the British from the Continent and would be followed in three weeks by the surrender of France. "We must be very careful not to assign to this deliverance the attributes of a victory. Wars are not won by evacuations." Then came his crucial and upbeat *but*: "But there is a victory inside this deliverance . . . gained by the air force." Only after paying tribute to the few thousand young airmen who beat back the Luftwaffe in this engagement, and calling their future defense of the realm an unprecedented "opportunity for youth," did Churchill admit that the past week had been "a colossal military disaster."

The "We shall not flag or fail" peroration is as inspiring as any written in the twentieth century. He first sounds a note of defiance, "whatever the cost may be," then uses "we shall fight" seven times, culminating in "we shall never surrender." As a participant in World War I and as an historian, Churchill was surely familiar with the French leader Georges Clemenceau's defiant formulation in 1918, translated as "I shall fight in front of Paris, within Paris, behind Paris." Consciously or not, Churchill echoed that theme and improved on its rhythm in his unforgettable "We shall fight on the beaches . . . we shall fight in the fields and in the streets . . . we shall never surrender." (This may be apocryphal, but in the roar of cheering and applause that followed in the House of Commons, he added in an aside to a colleague, "And we'll fight them with the butt ends of broken beer bottles, because that's bloody well all we've got!")

Most orators would have ended on that high never-surrender note. But what makes Churchill's peroration especially powerful is its double change of pace and mood at the end: first solemnly recognizing the terrible consequences of failure with Britons "subjugated and starving," then ameliorating this depressing prospect with an expression of confidence that the New World—that is, the United States—supported by surviving British seapower, would "step forth to the rescue and the liberation of the old."

□   □   □

. . . When a week ago today I asked the House to fix this afternoon for the occasion of a statement, I feared it would be my hard lot to announce from this box the greatest military disaster of our long history.

I thought, and there were good judges who agreed with me, that perhaps 20,000 or 30,000 men might be reembarked, but it certainly seemed that the whole French First Army and the whole British Expeditionary Force, north of the Amiens-Abbeville gap would be broken up in open field or else have to capitulate for lack of food and ammunition.

These were the hard and heavy tidings for which I called on the House and nation to prepare themselves a week ago. The whole root and core and brain of the British Army, on which and around which we were to build, and are to build, the great British armies in the later years of the war, seemed due to perish upon the field or to be led into an ignominious and starving captivity. . . .

The surrender of the Belgian Army compelled the British Army at the shortest notice to cover a flank to the sea of more than thirty miles' length which otherwise would have been cut off. In doing this and closing this flank, contact was lost inevitably between the British and two of three corps forming the First French Army, who were then further from the coast than we were. It seemed impossible that large numbers of Allied troops could reach the coast. The enemy attacked on all sides in great strength and fierceness, and their main power, air force, was thrown into the battle. . . . For four or five days the intense struggle raged. All armored divisions, or what was left of them, together with great masses of German infantry and artillery, hurled themselves on the ever-narrowing and contracting appendix within which the British and French armies fought.

Meanwhile the Royal Navy, with the willing help of countless merchant seamen and a host of volunteers, strained every nerve and every effort and every craft to embark the British and Allied troops. Over 220 light warships and more than 650 other vessels were engaged. They had to approach this difficult coast, often in adverse weather, under almost ceaseless hail of bombs and increasing concentration of artillery fire. Nor were the seas themselves free from mines and torpedoes.

It was in conditions such as these that our men carried on with little or no rest for days and nights, moving troops across dangerous waters and bringing with them always the men whom they had rescued. The numbers they brought back are the measure of their devotion and their courage. Hospital ships, which were plainly marked, were the special target for Nazi bombs, but the men and women aboard them never faltered in their duty.

Meanwhile the Royal Air Force, which had already been intervening in the battle so far as its range would allow it to go from home bases, now used a part of its main metropolitan fighter strength to strike at German bombers. . . . The struggle was protracted and fierce. Suddenly the scene has cleared, the crash and thunder has momentarily, but only for the moment, died away. . . . A miracle of deliverance . . . is manifest to us all. The enemy was hurled back by the retreating British and French troops. He was so roughly handled that he dared not molest their departure seriously. The Royal Air Force decisively defeated the main strength of the German Air Force and inflicted on them a loss of at least four to one. And the navy, using nearly 1,000 ships of all kinds, carried over 335,000 men, French and British, from the jaws of death back to their native land and to the tasks which lie immediately before them.

We must be very careful not to assign to this deliverance attributes of a victory. Wars are not won by evacuations. But there was a victory inside this deliverance which must be noted. . . . Can you conceive of a greater objective for the power of Germany in the air than to make all evacuations from these beaches impossible and to sink all of the ships, numbering almost 1,000? Could there have been an incentive of greater military importance and significance to the whole purpose of the war?

They tried hard and were beaten back. They were frustrated in their task; we have got the armies away. . . . I will pay my tribute to these young airmen. The great French Army was very largely . . . cast back and disturbed by the onrush of a few thousands of armored vehicles. May it not be that the cause of civilization itself will be defended by the skill and devotion of a few thousand airmen?

There never has been, I suppose, in all the history of the world such opportunity for youth. The Knights of the Round Table and Crusaders have fallen back into distant days, not only distant but prosaic; but these young men are going forth every morning, going forth holding in their hands an instrument of colossal shattering power, of whom it may be said that "every morn brought forth a noble chance and every chance brought forth a noble deed." These young men deserve our gratitude, as all brave men who in so many ways and so many occasions are ready and will continue to be ready to give their life and their all to their native land. . . .

Nevertheless, our thankfulness at the escape of our army with so many men, and the thankfulness of their loved ones, who passed through an agonizing week, must not blind us to the fact that what happened in France and Belgium is a colossal military disaster. . . .

We are told that Hitler has plans for invading the British Isles. This has often been thought of before. When Napoleon lay at Boulogne for a year with his flat-bottomed boats and his Grand Army, someone told him, "There are bitter weeds in England." There are certainly a great many more of them since the British Expeditionary Force returned. . . .

We have found it necessary to take measures of increasing stringency, not only against enemy aliens and suspicious characters of other nationalities but also against British subjects who may become a danger or a nuisance should the war be transported to the United Kingdom. I know there are a great many people affected by the orders which we have made who are passionate enemies of Nazi Germany. I am very sorry for them, but we cannot, under the present circumstances, draw all the distinctions we should like to do. If parachute landings were attempted and fierce fighting attendant on them followed, those unfortunate people would be far better out of the way for their own sake as well as ours.

There is, however, another class for which I feel not the slightest sympathy. Parliament has given us powers to put down fifth column activities with a strong hand, and we shall use those powers subject to the supervision and correction of the House without the slightest hesitation until we are satisfied, and more than satisfied, that this malignancy in our midst has been effectively stamped out.

Turning once again to the question of invasion, there has, I will observe, never been a period in all those long centuries of which we boast when an absolute guarantee against invasion, still less against serious raids, could have been given to our people. In the days of Napoleon the same wind which might have carried his transports across the Channel might have driven away the blockading fleet. There is always the chance, and it is that chance which has excited and befouled the imaginations of many Continental tyrants.

Many are the tales that are told. We are assured that novel methods will be adopted, and when we see the originality of malice, the ingenuity of aggression, which our enemy displays, we may certainly prepare ourselves for every kind of novel stratagem and every kind of brutal and treacherous maneuver. I think no idea is so outlandish that it should not be considered and viewed with a watchful, but at the same time steady, eye. . . .

We shall prove ourselves once again able to defend our island home, ride out the storm of war, outlive the menace of tyranny, if necessary for years, if necessary alone. At any rate, that is what we are going to try to do. That is the resolve of His Majesty's government, every man of them. That is the will of Parliament and the nation. The British Empire and the French Republic, linked together in their cause and their need, will defend to the death their native soils, aiding each other like good comrades to the utmost of their strength, even though a large tract of Europe and many old and famous states have fallen or may fall into the grip of the Gestapo and all the odious apparatus of Nazi rule.

We shall not flag nor fail. We shall go on to the end. We shall fight in France, we shall fight on the seas and oceans, we shall fight with growing confidence and growing strength in the air, we shall defend our island, whatever the cost may be, we shall fight on the beaches, we shall fight on the landing grounds, we shall fight in the fields and in the streets, we shall fight in the hills; we shall never surrender. And even if, which I do not for a moment believe, this island or a large part of it were subjugated and starving, then our Empire beyond the seas, armed and guarded by the British Fleet, will carry on the struggle, until, in God's good time, the New World, with all its power and might, sets forth to the liberation and rescue of the old. ■

Stalin Commands the Soviet Peoples to Scorch the Earth Being Taken by Hitler's Troops

"To the enemy must not be left a single engine, a single railway car, not a single pound of grain or a gallon of fuel."

CAN AN EVIL LEADER make a good speech? Of course; an example is Joseph Stalin's stirring broadcast on July 3, 1941, as German troops blitzed across lightly defended Soviet borders in an invasion that began on June 22.

Stalin had signed a nonaggression pact with Hitler in 1939, annexed the Baltic states in a Molotov-Ribbentrop agreement, and invaded Finland. But his paranoid purges of the high command of the Red Army left his own forces poorly led, and—after Khrushchev's "secret speech"

(p. 964)—dismantled the cult of personality and revealed Stalin's excesses—it became known that the dictator had been surprised and immobilized for days after the Nazi invasion.

He felt called upon to explain why he had signed a nonaggression treaty with the men he now called "fiends and cannibals," but after this diplomatic defensiveness, he turned to war. Ruthlessness against his own people was the order of the day: he castigated "whimperers and cowards" and equated rumormongers with enemy parachutists; few of his listeners doubted that what he called being "haled before a military tribunal" meant being summarily shot. Nevertheless, millions of Ukrainians welcomed Hitler's troops at first as liberators from Stalin's repression.

What the West heard, however, was his order that "grain and fuel which cannot be withdrawn must without fail be destroyed"; this was characterized as the "scorched-earth policy," a term first used in the Sino-Japanese war during the 1930s.

□   □   □

Comrades! Citizens! Brothers and sisters! Men of our army and navy! I am addressing you, my friends!

The perfidious military attack on our fatherland, begun on June 22 by Hitler's Germany, is continuing.

In spite of heroic resistance of the Red Army, and although the enemy's finest divisions and finest air force units have already been smashed and have met their doom on the field of battle, the enemy continues to push forward, hurling fresh forces into the attack.

Hitler's troops have succeeded in capturing Lithuania, a considerable part of Latvia, the western part of Byelorussia, and a part of the western Ukraine.

The Fascist air force is extending the range of operations of its bombers and is bombing Murmansk, Orsha, Mogilev, Smolensk, Kiev, Odessa, and Sevastopol.

A grave danger hangs over our country.

How could it have happened that our glorious Red Army surrendered a number of our cities and districts to the Fascist armies?

Is it really true that German Fascist troops are invincible, as is ceaselessly trumpeted by boastful Fascist propagandists? Of course not!

History shows that there are no invincible armies, and never have been. Napoleon's army was considered invincible, but it was beaten successively by Russian, English, and German armies. Kaiser Wilhelm's German army in the period of the first imperialist war was also considered invincible, but it was beaten several times by Russian and Anglo-French forces, and was finally smashed by Anglo-French forces.

The same must be said of Hitler's German Fascist army today. This army has not yet met with serious resistance on the continent of Europe. Only on our territory has it met serious resistance, and if as a result of this resistance the finest divisions of Hitler's German Fascist army have been defeated by our Red Army, it means that this army, too, can be smashed and will be smashed as were the armies of Napoleon and Wilhelm.

As to part of our territory having nevertheless been seized by German Fascist troops, this is chiefly due to the fact that the war of Fascist Germany on the USSR began under conditions favorable for German forces and unfavorable for Soviet forces.

The fact of the matter is that troops of Germany, as a country at war, were already fully mobilized, and 170 divisions hurled by Germany against the USSR and brought up to the Soviet frontiers were in a state of complete readiness, only awaiting the signal to move into action, whereas Soviet troops had little time to effect mobilization and move up to the frontiers.

Of no little importance in this respect is the fact that Fascist Germany suddenly and treacherously violated the nonaggression pact she concluded in 1939 with the USSR, disregarding the fact that she would be regarded as an aggressor by the whole world. Naturally, our peace-loving country, not wishing to take the initiative of breaking the pact, could not resort to perfidy.

It may be asked, How could the Soviet Government have consented to conclude a nonaggression pact with such treacherous fiends as Hitler and Ribbentrop? Was not this an error on the part of the Soviet government? Of course not!

Nonaggression pacts are pacts of peace between two states. It was such a pact that Germany proposed to us in 1939. Could the Soviet government have declined such a proposal? I think that not a single peace-loving state could decline a peace treaty with a neighboring state even though the latter was headed by such fiends and cannibals as Hitler and Ribbentrop. . . .

What is required to put an end to the danger hovering over our country, and what measures must be taken to smash the enemy?

Above all, it is essential that our people, the Soviet people, should understand the full immensity of the danger that threatens our country and abandon all complacency, all heedlessness, all those moods of peaceful, constructive work which were so natural before the war but which are fatal today, when war has fundamentally changed everything.

The enemy is cruel and implacable. He is out to seize our lands watered with our sweat, to seize our grain and soil secured by our labor.

He is out to restore the rule of landlords, to restore czarism, to destroy national culture and the national state existence of Russians, Ukrainians, Byelorussians, Lithuanians, Letts, Estonians, Uzbeks, Tartars, Moldavians, Georgians, Armenians, Azerbaijanians, and the other free peoples of the Soviet Union, to Germanize them, to convert them into slaves of German princes and barons.

Thus the issue is one of life or death for the Soviet state, for the peoples of the USSR: the issue is whether peoples of the Soviet Union shall remain free or fall into slavery.

The Soviet people must realize this and abandon all heedlessness; they must mobilize themselves and reorganize all their work on new, wartime lines, when there can be no mercy to the enemy.

Further, there must be no room in our ranks for whimperers and cowards, for panicmongers and deserters; our people must know no fear in the fight and must selflessly join our patriotic war of liberation, our war against the Fascist enslavers. . . .

The peoples of the Soviet Union must rise against the enemy and defend their rights and their land. The Red Army, Red Navy, and all citizens of the Soviet Union must defend every inch of Soviet soil, must fight to the last drop of blood for our towns and villages, must display the daring initiative and intelligence that are inherent in our people.

We must organize all-round assistance to the Red Army, ensure powerful reinforcements for its ranks and supply of everything it requires; we must organize rapid transport of troops and military freight and extensive aid to the wounded.

We must strengthen the Red Army's rear, subordinating all our work to this cause; all our industries must be got to work with greater intensity to produce more rifles, machine guns, artillery, bullets, shells, airplanes; we must organize the guarding of factories, power stations, telephonic and telegraphic communications, and arrange effective air raid precautions in all localities.

We must wage a ruthless fight against all disorganizers of the rear, deserters, panicmongers, rumormongers, exterminate spies, diversionists, enemy parachutists, rendering rapid aid in all this to our destroyer battalions. We must bear in mind that the enemy is crafty, unscrupulous, experienced in deception and dissemination of false rumors.

We must reckon with all this and not fall victim to provocation. All who by their panicmongering and cowardice hinder the work of defense, no matter who they are, must be immediately haled before a military tribunal.

In case of a forced retreat of Red Army units, all rolling stock must be evacuated; to the enemy must not be left a single engine, a single railway car, not a single pound of grain or a gallon of fuel.

Collective farmers must drive off all their cattle and turn over their grain to the safekeeping of state authorities for transportation to the rear. All valuable property including nonferrous metals, grain, and fuel which cannot be withdrawn must without fail be destroyed.

In areas occupied by the enemy, guerrilla units, mounted and foot, must be formed; diversionist groups must be organized to combat enemy troops, to foment guerrilla warfare everywhere, to blow up bridges, roads, damage telephone and telegraph lines, and to set fire to forests, stores, and transports.

In occupied regions conditions must be made unbearable for the enemy and all his accomplices. They must be hounded and annihilated at every step and all their measures frustrated. . . .

Comrades, our forces are numberless. The overweening enemy will soon learn this to his cost. Side by side with the Red Army and Navy thousands of workers, collective farmers, and intellectuals are rising to fight the enemy aggressor. The masses of our people will rise up in their millions. The working people of Moscow and Leningrad already have commenced to form vast popular levies in support of the Red Army.

Such popular levies must be raised in every city which is in danger of an enemy invasion; all working people must be roused to defend our freedom, our honor, our country—in our patriotic war against German fascism. . . .

All our forces for the support of our heroic Red Army and our glorious Red Navy!

All the forces of the people—for the demolition of the enemy!

Forward, to our victory! ■

President Franklin D. Roosevelt Asks Congress to Declare War on Japan

"YESTERDAY, December 7, 1941—a date which will live in infamy. . . ."

FDR drafted this brief, formal speech to the Congress himself, relying on his speechwriters at the time, Robert E. Sherwood and Samuel I. Rosenman, to work on a longer radio speech to the American people the following night. The use of a date to start, similar to Lincoln's Gettysburg reference to a number of years, showed solemn deference to the historic nature of the occasion. In Roosevelt's first draft, the opening line read, ". . . a date which will live in world history, the United States was simultaneously and deliberately attacked"; he crossed out "world history" and inserted the less familiar but much stronger "infamy" and crossed out "simultaneously" to substitute "suddenly," again a stronger word. His adviser Harry Hopkins suggested the addition of some reference to the Deity (as Salmon Chase suggested to Lincoln, reviewing a draft of the Emancipation Proclamation), and FDR inserted the sentence "So help us God."

The salutation contains an error. The vice-president of the United States, when he sits in the Senate as its president, is properly addressed by the president of the United States as "Mr. President," not as "Mr. Vice President." And grammarians would prefer "a date *that* will live in infamy," but it was a tense moment in a busy time.

□ □ □

Mr. Vice-President, Mr. Speaker, members of the Senate and the House of Representatives:

Yesterday, December 7, 1941—a date which will live in infamy—the United States of America was suddenly and deliberately attacked by naval and air forces of the empire of Japan.

The United States was at peace with that nation and, at the solicitation of Japan, was still in conversation with its government and its emperor looking toward the maintenance of peace in the Pacific.

Indeed, one hour after Japanese air squadrons had commenced bombing in the American island of Oahu the Japanese ambassador to the United States and his colleague delivered to our secretary of state a formal reply to a recent American message. And, while this reply stated that it seemed useless to continue the existing diplomatic negotiations, it contained no threat or hint of war or of armed attack.

It will be recorded that the distance of Hawaii from Japan makes it obvious that the attack was deliberately planned many days or even weeks ago. During the intervening time the Japanese government has deliberately sought to deceive the United States by false statements and expressions of hope for continued peace.

The attack yesterday on the Hawaiian Islands has caused severe damage to American naval and military forces. I regret to tell you that very many American lives have been lost. In addition, American ships have been reported torpedoed on the high seas between San Francisco and Honolulu.

Yesterday the Japanese government also launched an attack against Malaya.

Last night Japanese forces attacked Hong Kong.

Last night Japanese forces attacked Guam.

Last night Japanese forces attacked the Philippine Islands.

Last night the Japanese attacked Wake Island.

And this morning the Japanese attacked Midway Island.

Japan has therefore undertaken a surprise offensive extending throughout the Pacific area. The facts of yesterday and today speak for themselves. The people of the United States have already formed their opinions and well understand the implications to the very life and safety of our nation.

As commander in chief of the army and navy I have directed that all measures be taken for our defense, that always will our whole nation remember the character of the onslaught against us.

No matter how long it may take us to overcome this premeditated invasion, the American people, in their righteous might, will win through to absolute victory.

I believe that I interpret the will of the Congress and of the people when I assert that we will not only defend ourselves to the uttermost but will make it very certain that this form of treachery shall never again endanger us.

Hostilities exist. There is no blinking at the fact that our people, our territory, and our interests are in grave danger.

With confidence in our armed forces, with the unbounding determination of our people, we will gain the inevitable triumph. So help us God.

I ask that the Congress declare that since the unprovoked and dastardly attack by Japan on Sunday, December 7, 1941, a state of war has existed between the United States and the Japanese Empire. ■

General Montgomery Takes Command and Draws the Line at El Alamein

"HERE we will stand and fight; there will be no further withdrawal. . . . If we can't stay here alive, then let us stay here dead."

THE BRITISH EIGHTH ARMY, whose troops called themselves "the Desert Rats," were being driven out of North Africa in the summer of 1942 by the German forces under the inspired command of General Erwin Rommel. The British troops were dispirited; the officers demoralized; the defensive war was being lost.

On August 13, 1942, the new commander, Lieutenant General Bernard Law Montgomery—"Monty" he was called—gathered his officer corps in Cairo, pointed to a place on the map and stated, "The defense of Egypt lies here at Alamein. . . ." The general was sure of himself; he spoke in declarative sentences; he used "I" frequently. "I don't want any doubters in this party." The purpose of the speech was to instill confidence, and he made his point by pointing to it: "The great point to remember is that we are going to finish with this chap Rommel once and for all."

The staccato style and supremely confident tone of this speech could be emulated by any newly appointed CEO hired to turn around a failing company. It is bombastic, arrogant, but not profane. In this last his oratory differed from that of American Lieutenant General George S. Patton, who would exhort his soldiers in this way: "You can thank God," said "Old Blood and Guts," "that twenty years from now when you're sitting by the fireside with your grandson on your knee, and he asks you what you did in the war, you won't have to shift him to the other knee, cough, and say, 'I shoveled shit in Louisiana.'"

The Montgomery style, in both military tactics and rhetoric, was less earthy and more carefully prepared than Patton's. He uses slang: in promising "to hit Rommel and his army for six," he employed a Briticism for "to vanquish."

At El Alamein, Monty launched his counteroffensive after pounding the enemy with the heaviest artillery barrage in military history; his victory was one of the turning points of World War II. Two years later, in a message to his troops before the Allied invasion in Normandy, he expressed himself in a sentence with Churchillian sweep: "To us is given the honor of striking a blow for freedom which will live in history, and in the better days that lie ahead men will speak with pride of our doings."

□   □   □

I want first of all to introduce myself to you. You do not know me. I do not know you. But we have got to work together; therefore we must understand each other, and we must have confidence each in the other. I have only been here a few hours. But from what I have seen and heard since I arrived I am prepared to say, here and now, that I have confidence in you. We will then work together as a team; and together we will gain the confidence of this great army and go forward to final victory in Africa.

I believe that one of the first duties of a commander is to create what I call "atmosphere," and in that atmosphere his staff, subordinate commanders, and troops will live and work and fight.

I do not like the general atmosphere I find here. It is an atmosphere of doubt, of looking back to select the next place to which to withdraw, of loss of confidence in our ability to defeat Rommel, of desperate defense measures by reserves in preparing positions in Cairo and the Delta.

All that must cease.

Let us have a new atmosphere.

The defense of Egypt lies here at Alamein and on the Ruweisat Ridge. What is the use of digging trenches in the Delta? It is quite useless; if we lose this position we lose Egypt; all the fighting troops now in the Delta must come here at once, and will. *Here* we will stand and fight; there will be no further withdrawal. I have ordered that all plans and instructions dealing with further withdrawal are to be burned, and at once. We will stand and fight *here*.

If we can't stay here alive, then let us stay here dead.

I want to impress on everyone that the bad times are over. Fresh divisions from the UK are now arriving in Egypt, together with ample reinforcements for our present divisions. We have three hundred to four hundred new Sherman tanks coming and these are actually being unloaded at Suez *now*. Our mandate from the prime minister is to destroy the Axis forces in North Africa; I have seen it, written on half a sheet of notepaper. And it will be done. If anyone here thinks it can't be done, let him go at once; I don't want any doubters in this party. It can be done, and it will be done: beyond any possibility of doubt.

Now I understand that Rommel is expected to attack at any moment. Excellent. Let him attack.

I would sooner it didn't come for a week, just give me time to sort things out. If we have two weeks to prepare we will be sitting pretty; Rommel can attack as soon as he likes after that, and I hope he does.

Meanwhile, we ourselves will start to plan a great offensive; it will be the beginning of a campaign which will hit Rommel and his army for six right out of Africa.

But first we must create a reserve corps, mobile and strong in armor, which we will train *out of the line*. Rommel has always had such a force in his Africa Corps, which is never used to hold the line but which is always in reserve, available for striking blows. Therein has been his great strength. We will create such a corps ourselves, a British Panzer Corps; it will consist of two armored divisions and one motorized division; I gave orders yesterday for it to begin to form, back in the Delta.

I have no intention of launching our great attack until we are completely ready; there will be pressure from many quarters to attack soon; *I will not attack until we are ready,* and you can rest assured on that point.

Meanwhile, if Rommel attacks while we are preparing, let him do so with pleasure; we will merely continue with our own preparations and *we* will attack when *we* are ready, and not before.

I want to tell you that I always work on the Chief of Staff system. I have nominated Brigadier de Guingand as Chief of Staff Eighth Army. I will issue orders through him. Whatever he says will be taken as coming from me and will be acted on *at once*. I understand there has been a great deal of "bellyaching" out here. By bellyaching I mean inventing poor reasons for *not* doing what one has been told to do.

All this is to stop at once.

I will tolerate no bellyaching.

If anyone objects to doing what he is told, then he can get out of it: and at once. I want that made very clear right down through the Eighth Army.

I have little more to say just at present. And some of you may think it is quite enough and may wonder if I am mad.

I assure you I am quite sane.

I understand there are people who often think I am slightly mad; so often that I now regard it as rather a compliment.

All I have to say to that is that if I am slightly mad, there are a large number of people I could name who are raving lunatics!

What I have done is to get over to you the "atmosphere" in which we will now work and fight; you must see that that atmosphere permeates right through the Eighth Army to the most junior private soldier. All the soldiers must know what is wanted; when they see it coming to pass there will be a surge of confidence throughout the army.

I ask you to give me your confidence and to have faith that what I have said will come to pass.

There is much work to be done.

The orders I have given about no further withdrawal will mean a complete change in the layout of our dispositions; also, we must begin to prepare for our great offensive.

The first thing to do is to move our HQ to a decent place where we can live in reasonable comfort and where the army staff can all be together and side by side with the HQ of the Desert Air Force. This is a frightful place here, depressing, unhealthy, and a rendezvous for every fly in Africa; we shall do no good work here. Let us get over there by the sea where it is fresh and healthy. If officers are to do good work they must have decent messes, and be comfortable. So off we go on the new line.

The Chief of Staff will be issuing orders on many points very shortly, and I am always available to be consulted by the senior officers of the staff. The great point to remember is that we are going to finish with this chap Rommel once and for all. It will be quite easy. There is no doubt about it.

He is definitely a nuisance. Therefore we will hit him a crack and finish with him. ■

Senator Eugene McCarthy Crystallizes Dissent by Denouncing the War in Vietnam

"THE war in Vietnam. . . . A war of questionable legality and questionable constitutionality. A war which is diplomatically indefensible. . . . A war which is not defensible even in military terms. . . . Finally, it is a war which is morally wrong."

BY 1967, a substantial minority had turned against the U.S. involvement in the war between North and South Vietnam. The dissenters awaited a responsible political voice to transform the dissent into a movement. It came from a Minnesota Democrat, Eugene McCarthy, whose challenge in the following year's Democratic primaries caused President Lyndon Johnson to step down.

McCarthy had been the nominator of Adlai Stevenson in 1960, after his two defeats. "Do not reject this man," he begged the convention, which did. The Minnesota poet-senator evoked the memory of Stevenson as well as of John Kennedy in a speech on December 2, 1967, to the Conference of Concerned Democrats, organized to oppose the war. Stevenson was the metaphoric horn (the biblical trumpet not uncertain) and Kennedy the drum that caused the people to march. McCarthy was brushed aside by Robert Kennedy after Johnson's retirement, and was defeated at the convention by Hubert Humphrey after Kennedy's assassination; he retired from the Senate in 1970. He is remembered for identifying the "joyless spirit" of part of America in 1967–68 and enabling it to turn a sitting president out of power.

□　□　□

In 1952, in this city of Chicago, the Democratic party nominated as its candidate for the presidency Adlai Stevenson.

His promise to his party and to the people of the country then was that he would talk sense to them. . . .

Under the presidency of John F. Kennedy his ideas were revived in new language and in a new spirit. To the clear sound of the horn was added the beat of a steady and certain drum.

John Kennedy set free the spirit of America. The honest optimism was released. Quiet courage and civility became the mark of American government, and new programs of promise and of dedication were presented: the Peace Corps, the Alliance for Progress, the promise of equal rights for all Americans—and not just the promise but the beginning of the achievement of that promise.

All the world looked to the United States with new hope, for here was youth and confidence and an openness to the future. Here was a country not being held by the dead hand of the past, nor frightened by the violent hand of the future which was grasping at the world.

This was the spirit of 1963.

What is the spirit of 1967? What is the mood of America and of the world toward America today?

It is a joyless spirit—a mood of frustration, of anxiety, of uncertainty.

In place of the enthusiasm of the Peace Corps among the young people of America, we have protests and demonstrations.

In place of the enthusiasm of the Alliance for Progress, we have distrust and disappointment.

Instead of the language of promise and of hope, we have in politics today a new vocabulary in which the critical word is "war": war on poverty, war on ignorance, war on crime, war on pollution. None of these problems can be solved by war but only by persistent, dedicated, and thoughtful attention.

But we do have one war which is properly called a war—the war in Vietnam, which is central to all of the problems of America.

A war of questionable legality and questionable constitutionality.

A war which is diplomatically indefensible; the first war in this century in which the United States, which at its founding made an appeal to the decent opinion of mankind in the Declaration of Independence, finds itself without the support of the decent opinion of mankind.

A war which cannot be defended in the context of the judgment of history. It is being presented in the context of an historical judgment of an era which is past. Munich appears to be the starting point of history for the secretary of state and for those who attempt to support his policies. What is necessary is a realization that the United States is a part of the movement of history itself; that it cannot stand apart, attempting to control the world by imposing covenants and treaties and by violent military intervention; that our role is not to police the planet but to use military strength with restraint and within limits, while at the same time we make available to the world the great power of our economy, of our knowledge, and of our good will.

A war which is not defensible even in military terms, which runs contrary to the advice of our greatest generals—Eisenhower, Ridgway, Bradley, and MacArthur—all of whom admonished us against becoming involved in a land war in Asia. Events have proved them right, as estimate after estimate as to the time of success and the military commitment necessary to success has had to be revised—always upward: more troops, more extensive bombing, a widening and intensification of the war. Extension and intensification have been the rule, and projection after projection of success have been proved wrong.

With the escalation of our military commitment has come a parallel of overleaping of objectives: from protecting South Vietnam, to nation building in South Vietnam, to protecting all of Southeast Asia, and ultimately to suggesting that the safety and security of the United States itself is at stake.

Finally, it is a war which is morally wrong. The most recent statement of objectives cannot be accepted as an honest judgment as to why we are in Vietnam. It has become increasingly difficult to justify the methods we are using and the instruments of war which we are using as we have moved from limited targets and somewhat restricted weapons to greater variety and more destructive instruments of war, and also have extended the area of operations almost to the heart of North Vietnam.

Even assuming that both objectives and methods can be defended, the war cannot stand the test of proportion and of prudent judgment. It is no longer possible to prove that the good that may come with what is called victory, or projected as victory, is proportionate to the loss of life and property and to other disorders that follow from this war. . . .

Beyond all of these considerations, two further judgments must be passed: a judgment of individual conscience, and another in the broader context of the movement of history itself.

The problem of individual conscience is, I think, set most clearly before us in the words of Charles Péguy in writing about the Dreyfus case: "a single injustice, a single crime, a single illegality, if it is officially recorded, . . . will bring about the loss of one's honor, the dishonor of a whole people."

And the broader historical judgment as suggested by Arnold Toynbee in his comments on Rome's war with Carthage: "Nemesis is a potent goddess. . . . War posthumously avenges the dead on the survivors, and the vanquished on the victors. The nemesis of war is intrinsic. It did not need the invention of the atomic weapon to make this apparent. It was illustrated more than two thousand years before our time, by Hannibal's legacy to Rome." Hannibal gained a "posthumous victory over Rome. Although he failed to defeat the great nation militarily because of the magnitude of her military manpower and solidity of the structure of the Roman Commonwealth, he did succeed in inflicting grievous wounds on the Commonwealth's body social and economic. They were so grievous that they festered into the revolution that was precipitated by Tiberius Gracchus and that did not cease till it was arrested by Augustus a hundred years later. . . . This revolution," Toynbee said, "was the nemesis of Rome's superficially triumphant career of military conquest," and ended, of course, the Republic and substituted for it the spirit of the dictators and of the Caesars.

Those of us who are gathered here tonight are not advocating peace at any price. We are willing to pay a high price for peace—for an honorable, rational, and political solution to this war, a solution which will enhance our world position, which will permit us to give the necessary attention to our other commitments abroad, both military and nonmilitary, and leave us with both human and physical resources and with moral energy to deal effectively with the pressing domestic problems of the United States itself.

I see little evidence that the administration has set any limits on the price which it will pay for a military victory which becomes less and less sure and more hollow and empty in promise.

The scriptural promise of the good life is one in which the old men see visions and the young men dream dreams. In the context of this war and all of its implications, the young men of America do not dream dreams, but many live in the nightmare of moral anxiety, of concern and great apprehension; and the old men, instead of visions which they can offer to the young, are projecting, in the language of the secretary of state, a specter of one billion Chinese threatening the peace and safety of the world—a frightening and intimidating future.

The message from the administration today is a message of apprehension, a message of fear, yes—even a message of fear of fear.

This is not the real spirit of America. I do not believe that it is. This is a time to test the mood and spirit:

To offer in place of doubt—trust.

In place of expediency—right judgment.

In place of ghettos, let us have neighborhoods and communities.

In place of incredibility—integrity.

In place of murmuring, let us have clear speech; let us again hear America singing.

In place of disunity, let us have dedication of purpose.

In place of near despair, let us have hope.

This is the promise of greatness which was seated for us by Adlai Stevenson and which was brought to form and positive action in the words and actions of John Kennedy.

Let us pick up again these lost strands and weave them again into the fabric of America.

Let us sort out the music from the sounds and again respond to the trumpet and the steady drum. ■

Prime Minister Margaret Thatcher Acts to Defend the Falkland Islands

"LET us, then, draw together in the name, not of jingoism, but of justice."

BRITAIN'S FIRST FEMALE PRIME MINISTER, and the person who served longest (1979–90) in 10 Downing Street in the twentieth century, Margaret Thatcher made her mark as an unswerving conservative ("This lady's not for turning," she said, in a play on "The lady's not for burning") and as an unapologetic nationalist. Asked to select her three most memorable speeches, she chose a 1988 speech in Bruges setting out her views on the European community; a 1984 speech to a Conservative party conference at Brighton following an IRA bomb attack; and a speech on May 26, 1982, to a Conservative Women's conference in the early stages of the campaign to liberate the Falkland

Islands after their invasion by Argentina, which long called them the Malvinas and considered them Argentine. That Falklands speech is the one reprinted almost in its entirety here because it best reflects the Thatcher style: modified Churchillian, resolute but not ringing, stubborn but sensible. Her concluding words are based on the final lines of Shakespeare's *King John*.

☐   ☐   ☐

. . . In a series of measured and progressive steps, over the past weeks, our forces have tightened their grip of the Falkland Islands. They have retaken South Georgia. Gradually they have denied fresh supplies to the Argentine garrison.

Finally, by the successful amphibious landing at San Carlos Bay in the early hours of Friday morning, they have placed themselves in a position to retake the islands and reverse the illegal Argentine invasion.

By the skill of our pilots, our sailors, and those manning the Rapier missile batteries onshore, they have inflicted heavy losses on the Argentine air force—over fifty fixed-wing aircraft have been destroyed.

There have, of course, been tragic losses. You will have heard of the further attacks on our task force. HMS *Coventry* came under repeated air attack yesterday evening and later sank. One of our merchant marine ships, the *Atlantic Conveyor*, supporting the task force, was also damaged and had to be abandoned. We do not yet know the number of casualties, but our hearts go out to all those who had men in these ships.

Despite these grievous losses, our resolve is not weakened. . . .

It was eight weeks ago today that information reached us that the Argentine fleet was sailing towards the Falklands.

Eight thousand miles away. . . . At that stage there were only two ways of trying to stop it—through President Reagan, whose appeal to Argentina was rebuffed, and the United Nations, whose plea was also rejected.

There were those who said we should have accepted the Argentine invasion as a fait accompli. But whenever the rule of force as distinct from the rule of law is seen to succeed, the world moves a step closer to anarchy.

The older generation in this country and generations before them have made sacrifices so that we could be a free society and belong to a community of nations which seeks to resolve disputes by civilized means.

Today it falls to us to bear the same responsibility.

What has happened since that day, eight weeks ago, is a matter of history—the history of a nation which rose instinctively to the needs of the occasion.

For decades, the peoples of those islands had enjoyed peace—with freedom, with justice, with democracy.

That peace was shattered by a wanton act of armed aggression by Argentina in blatant violation of international law. And everything that has happened since has stemmed from that invasion by the military dictatorship of Argentina.

We want that peace restored. But we want it with the same freedom, justice, and democracy that the islanders previously enjoyed.

For seven weeks we sought a peaceful solution by diplomatic means— through the good offices of our close friend and ally the United States; through the unremitting efforts of the secretary-general of the United Nations. . . . We worked tirelessly for a peaceful solution. But when there is no response of substance from the other side, there comes a point when it is no longer possible to trust the good faith of those with whom one is negotiating.

Playing for time is not working for a peaceful solution. Wasting time is not *willing* a peaceful solution. It is simply leaving the aggressor with the fruits of his aggression.

It would be a betrayal of our fighting men and of the islanders if *we* continued merely to talk, when talk alone was getting nowhere.

And so, seven weeks to the day after the invasion, we moved to recover by force what was taken from us by force. It cannot be said too often: we are the victims; they are the aggressors.

As always, we came to military action reluctantly.

But when territory which has been British for almost 150 years is seized and occupied; when not only British land but British citizens are in the power of an aggressor—then we have to restore our rights and the rights of the Falkland Islanders.

There have been a handful of questioning voices raised here at home. I would like to answer them. It has been suggested that the size of the Falkland Islands and the comparatively small number of its inhabitants— some eighteen hundred men, women, and children—should somehow affect our reaction to what has happened to them.

To those—not many—who speak lightly of a few islanders beyond the seas and who ask the question "Are they worth fighting for?" let me say this: right and wrong are not measured by a head count of those to whom that wrong has been done. That would not be principle but expediency.

And the Falklanders, remember, are not strangers. They are our own people. As the prime minister of New Zealand, Bob Muldoon, put it in his usual straightforward way, "With the Falkland Islanders, it is family."

When their land was invaded and their homes were overrun, they naturally turned to us for help, and we, their fellow citizens, eight thousand miles away in our much larger island, could not and did not beg to be excused.

We sent our men and our ships with all speed, hoping against hope that we would not have to use them in battle but prepared to do so if all attempts at a peaceful solution failed. When those attempts failed, we could not sail by on the other side.

And let me add this. If we, the British, were to shrug our shoulders at what has happened in the South Atlantic and acquiesce in the illegal seizure of those faraway islands, it would be a clear signal to those with similar designs on the territory of others to follow in the footsteps of aggression.

Surely we, of all people, have learned the lesson of history: that to appease an aggressor is to invite aggression elsewhere, and on an ever-increasing scale.

Other voices—again only a few—have accused us of clinging to colonialism or even imperialism. Let me remind those who advance that argument that the British have a record second to none of leading colony after colony to freedom and independence. We cling not to colonialism but self-determination.

Still others—again only a few—say we must not put at risk our investments and interests in Latin America; that trade and commerce are too important to us to put in jeopardy some of the valuable markets of the world.

But what would the islanders, under the heel of the invader, say to that?

What kind of people would we be if, enjoying the birthright of freedom ourselves, we abandoned British citizens for the sake of commercial gain?

Now we are present in strength on the Falkland Islands.

Our purpose is to repossess them. We shall carry on until that purpose is accomplished.

When the invader has left, there will be much to do—rebuilding, restoring homes and farms, and, above all, renewing the confidence of the people in their future.

Their wishes will need time to crystallize and, of course, will depend in some measure on what we and others are prepared to do to develop the untapped resources and safeguard the islands' future.

Madam Chairman, our cause is just.

It is the cause of freedom and the rule of law.

It is the cause of support for the weak against aggression by the strong.

Let us, then, draw together in the name, not of jingoism, but of justice.

And let our nation, as it has so often in the past, remind itself—and the world:

> Nought shall make us rue,
> If England to herself do rest but true. ■

Israel's Yitzhak Rabin Shakes Hands with His Lifelong Enemy

"We who have fought against you, the Palestinians—we say to you today, in a loud and a clear voice: enough of blood and tears. Enough!"

THE LAWN OF THE WHITE HOUSE in Washington was the scene of the signing of a peace agreement, secretly negotiated in Oslo, between the government of Israel and the Palestine Liberation Organization. President Bill Clinton introduced Prime Minister Rabin and PLO Chairman Yasir Arafat with a biblical allusion: "We must realize the prophecy of Isaiah, that the cry of violence shall no more be heard in your land, nor wrack nor ruin within your borders."

Rabin made a momentary show of reluctance to shake the former terrorist's hand, then did so. The former general's short speech, drafted by his veteran spokesman Eitan Haber, hewed to the style of a plain soldier. The audience on the lawn, including this anthologist, noted the strength modified by pain in the delivery. Rabin spoke directly to his former enemies, addressing them not as "Palestinian Arabs" but giving them the status of a people: "Let me say to you, the Palestinians . . ." He was also speaking to his own people, many of whom were ambivalent about or opposed to the ultimate direction of the "peace process." As a soldier turned peacemaker, he evoked the Book of Ecclesiastes 3:1–8 to dramatize the reason for his new direction: "To everything there is a season . . . A time to love and a time to hate, a time of war and a time of peace."

Especially powerful to the Jews listening to him on the lawn and around the world on September 13, 1993, was his conclusion, spoken in Hebrew. What he described as "words taken from the prayer recited by Jews daily" were from the Kaddish, which are also spoken in a Mourners' Kaddish at graveside and repeated by the bereaved in remembrance of the dead. The prayer makes no mention of death; rather, it affirms faith in God even in the midst of death. As the speaker buried the past, his choice of Hebrew words remembered its bloodshed.

After Prime Minister Rabin's assassination by an Israeli fanatic two years after this speech, the memory of that prayer was especially poignant, and all television obituaries included his exhortation "Enough!"

□   □   □

President of the United States, your excellencies, ladies and gentlemen: This signing of the Israeli-Palestinian declaration of principle here today—it's not so easy—neither for myself as a soldier in Israel's war nor for the people of Israel, not to the Jewish people in the diaspora, who are watching us now with great hope mixed with apprehension. It is certainly not easy for the families of the victims of the war's violence, terror, whose pain will never heal, for the many thousands who defended our lives in their own and have even sacrificed their lives for our own. For them this ceremony has come too late.

Today on the eve of an opportunity, opportunity for peace and perhaps end of violence and war, we remember each and every one of them with everlasting love. We have come from Jerusalem, the ancient and eternal capital of the Jewish people. We have come from an anguished and grieving land. We have come from a people, a home, a family that has not known a single year, not a single month, in which mothers have not wept for their sons. We have come to try and put an end to the hostilities so that our children, our children's children, will no longer experience the painful cost of war: violence and terror. We have come to secure their lives and to ease the soul and the painful memories of the past—to hope and pray for peace.

Let me say to you, the Palestinians, we are destined to live together on the same soil in the same land. We, the soldiers who have returned from battles stained with blood; we who have seen our relatives and friends killed before our eyes; we who have attended their funerals and cannot look in the eyes of their parents; we who have come from a land where parents bury their children; we who have fought against you, the Palestinians—we say to you today, in a loud and a clear voice: enough of blood and tears. Enough!

We have no desire for revenge. We harbor no hatred towards you. We, like you, are people—people who want to build a home. To plant a tree. To love—live side by side with you. In dignity. In empathy. As human beings. As free men. We are today giving peace a chance—and saying to you and saying again to you: enough. Let us pray that a day will come when we all will say farewell to the arms. We wish to open a new chapter in the sad book of our lives together—a chapter of mutual recognition, of good neighborliness, of mutual respect, of understanding. We hope to embark on a new era in the history of the Middle East. Today here in Washington at the White House, we will begin a new reckoning in the relations between peoples, between parents tired of war, between children who will not know war.

President of the United States, ladies and gentlemen, our inner strength, our high moral values, have been the right for thousands of years, from the book of the books. In one of which, we read: "To everything there is a season and a time to every purpose under heaven: a time to be born and a time to die . . . a time to kill and a time to heal . . . a time to weep and a time to laugh . . . a time to love and a time to hate, a time of war and a time of peace." Ladies and gentlemen, the time for peace has come.

In two days the Jewish people will celebrate the beginning of a new year. I believe, I hope, I pray that the new year will bring a message of redemption for all peoples—a good year for you, for all of you; a good year Israelis and Palestinians; a good year for all the peoples of the Middle East; a good year for our American friends who so want peace and are helping to achieve it.

For presidents and members of previous administrations, especially for you, President Clinton, and your staff, for all citizens of the world, may peace come to all your homes. In the Jewish tradition it is customary to conclude our prayers with the word *Amen*. With your permission, men of peace, I shall conclude with the words taken from the prayer recited by Jews daily, and whoever of you who volunteer, I would ask the entire audience to join me in saying Amen. [Speaking in Hebrew.] May He who brings peace to His universe bring peace to us and to all Israel. Amen.

■   ■   ■

III

TRIBUTES
AND
EULOGIES

Mark Antony Urges Mourners to Vengeance over the Body of Julius Caesar

"If you have tears, prepare to shed them now. . . . This was the most unkindest cut of all"

IF WE CAN ACCEPT Thucydides' recollected account of the funeral oration of Pericles, we can stretch further from accuracy to accept William Shakespeare's version, in his play *Julius Caesar*, of a speech by Mark Antony referred to by historians Plutarch and Dion Cassius.

The technique of the speaker is to seem to agree with what has been said before—in this case by Brutus, tool and front of the conspirators, who had told the crowd of Caesar, "As he was ambitious, I slew him." But the dramatist plants the seeds of doubt by acting against the words, at first subtly imputing dishonor while appearing to concede honor in the previous speaker, and later savaging him with increasing sarcasm overlaying "honorable."

The speaker poses (falsely, as the playwright shows the audience) as "a plain blunt man" without "the power of speech to stir men's blood," who can "only speak right on." Of course, the murdered man's friend speaks obliquely, pulling from his listeners the mutinous calls he professes not to make himself, closing with an egregious bribe. This mostly fictional speech about a factual conqueror is a playwright's lesson in how politicians can manipulate mobs.

□   □   □

> ANTONY. Friends, Romans, countrymen, lend me your ears;
> I come to bury Caesar, not to praise him.
> The evil that men do lives after them;
> The good is oft interred with their bones;
> So let it be with Caesar. The noble Brutus
> Hath told you Caesar was ambitious:

If it were so, it was a grievous fault,
And grievously hath Caesar answer'd it.
Here, under leave of Brutus and the rest,—
For Brutus is an honorable man;
So are they all, all honorable men;
Come I to speak in Caesar's funeral.
He was my friend, faithful and just to me:
But Brutus says he was ambitious;
And Brutus is an honorable man.
He hath brought many captives home to Rome,
Whose ransoms did the general coffers fill:
Did this in Caesar seem ambitious?
When that the poor have cried, Caesar hath wept:
Ambition should be made of sterner stuff:
Yet Brutus says he was ambitious;
And Brutus is an honorable man.
You all did see that on the Lupercal
I thrice presented him a kingly crown,
Which he did thrice refuse: was this ambition?
Yet Brutus says he was ambitious;
And, sure, he is an honorable man.
I speak not to disprove what Brutus spoke,
But here I am to speak what I do know.
You all did love him once, not without cause:
What cause withholds you then to mourn for him?
O judgment, thou are fled to brutish beasts,
And men have lost their reason. Bear with me;
My heart is in the coffin there with Caesar,
And I must pause till it come back to me.

FIRST CITIZEN. Methinks there is much reason in his sayings.

SECOND CITIZEN. If you consider rightly of the matter, Caesar has had great wrong.

THIRD CITIZEN. Has he, masters?
  I fear there will a worse come in his place.

FOURTH CITIZEN. Mark'd ye his words? He would not take the crown;
  Therefore 'tis certain he was not ambitious.

FIRST CITIZEN. If it be found so, some will dear abide it.

SECOND CITIZEN. Poor soul! his eyes are red as fire with weeping.

THIRD CITIZEN. There's not a nobler man in Rome than Antony.

FOURTH CITIZEN. Now mark him, he begins again to speak.

ANTONY. But yesterday the word of Caesar might
    Have stood against the world: now lies he there,
    And none so poor to do him reverence.
    O masters, if I were disposed to stir
    Your hearts and minds to mutiny and rage,
    I should do Brutus wrong and Cassius wrong
    Who, you all know, are honorable men.
    I will not do them wrong; I rather choose
    To wrong the dead, to wrong myself and you,
    Than I will wrong such honorable men.
    But here's a parchment with the seal of Caesar;
    I found it in his closet; 'tis his will:
    Let but the commons hear this testament—
    Which pardon me, I do not mean to read—
    And they would go and kiss dead Caesar's wounds
    And dip their napkins in his sacred blood,
    Yea, beg a hair of him for memory,
    And, dying, mention it within their wills,
    Bequeathing it as a rich legacy
    Unto their issue.
FOURTH CITIZEN. We'll hear the will; read it, Mark Antony.
ALL. The will, the will! we will hear Caesar's will.
ANTONY. Have patience, gentle friends, I must not read it;
    It is not meet you know how Caesar loved you.
    You are not wood, you are not stones, but men;
    And, being men, hearing the will of Caesar,
    It will inflame you, it will make you mad:
    'Tis good you know not that you are his heirs;
    For if you should, O, what would come of it.
FOURTH CITIZEN. Read the will; we'll hear it, Antony;
    You shall read us the will, Caesar's will.
ANTONY. Will you be patient? will you stay awhile?
    I have o'ershot myself to tell you of it:
    I fear I wrong the honorable men
    Whose daggers have stabb'd Caesar; I do fear it.
FOURTH CITIZEN. They were traitors: honorable men!
ALL. The will! the testament!
SECOND CITIZEN. They were villains, murderers: the will! read
the will.
ANTONY. You will compel me then to read the will?
    Then make a ring about the corpse of Caesar,

    And let me show you him that made the will.
    Shall I descend? and will you give me leave?
ALL. Come down.
SECOND CITIZEN. Descend. [*He comes down from the pulpit.*]
THIRD CITIZEN. You shall have leave.
FOURTH CITIZEN. A ring; stand round.
FIRST CITIZEN. Stand from the hearse, stand from the body.
SECOND CITIZEN. Room for Antony, most noble Antony.
ANTONY. Nay, press not so upon me; stand far off.
ALL. Stand back. Room. Bear back.
ANTONY. If you have tears, prepare to shed them now.
    You all do know this mantle: I remember
    The first time ever Caesar put it on;
    'Twas on a summer's evening, in his tent,
    That day he overcame the Nervii:
    Look, in this place ran Cassius' dagger through:
    See what a rent the envious Casca made:
    Through this the well-belov'd Brutus stabb'd;
    And as he pluck'd his cursed steel away,
    Mark how the blood of Caesar follow'd it,
    As rushing out of doors, to be resolved
    If Brutus so unkindly knock'd, or no:
    For Brutus, as you know, was Caesar's angel:
    Judge, O you gods, how dearly Caesar loved him.
    This was the most unkindest cut of all;
    For when the noble Caesar saw him stab,
    Ingratitude, more strong than traitors' arms,
    Quite vanquish'd him: then burst his mighty heart;
    And, in his mantle muffling up his face,
    Even at the base of Pompey's statue,
    Which all the while ran blood, great Caesar fell.
    O, what a fall was there, my countrymen!
    Then I, and you, and all of us fell down,
    Whilst bloody treason flourish'd over us.
    O, now you weep, and I perceive you feel
    The dint of pity: these are gracious drops.
    Kind souls, what weep you when you but behold
    Our Caesar's vesture wounded? Look you here,
    Here is himself, marr'd, as you see, with traitors.
FIRST CITIZEN. O piteous spectacle!
SECOND CITIZEN. O noble Caesar!

THIRD CITIZEN. O woeful day!

FOURTH CITIZEN. O traitors, villains!

FIRST CITIZEN. O most bloody sight!

SECOND CITIZEN. We will be revenged.

ALL. Revenge! About! Seek! Burn! Fire!
     Kill! Slay! Let not a traitor live!

ANTONY. Stay, countrymen.

FIRST CITIZEN. Peace there! hear the noble Antony.

SECOND CITIZEN. We'll hear him, we'll follow him, we'll die
with him.

ANTONY. Good friends, sweet friends, let me not stir you up
     To such a sudden flood of mutiny.
     They that have done this deed are honorable;
     What private griefs they have, alas, I know not,
     That made them do it; they are wise and honorable,
     And will, no doubt, with reasons answer you.
     I come not, friends, to steal away your hearts: I am no orator, as
     Brutus is;
     But, as you know me all, a plain blunt man,
     That love my friend; and that they know full well
     That gave me public leave to speak of him:
     For I have neither wit, nor words, nor worth,
     Action, nor utterance, nor the power of speech,
     To stir men's blood: I only speak right on;
     I tell you that which you yourselves do know;
     Show you sweet Caesar's wounds, poor poor dumb mouths,
     And bid them speak for me: but were I Brutus,
     And Brutus Antony, there were an Antony
     Would ruffle up your spirits, and put a tongue
     In every wound of Caesar, that should move
     The stones of Rome to rise and mutiny.

ALL. We'll mutiny.

FIRST CITIZEN. We'll burn the house of Brutus.

THIRD CITIZEN. Away, then! come, seek the conspirators.

ANTONY. Yet hear me, countrymen; yet hear me speak.

ALL. Peace, ho! Hear Antony. Most noble Antony!

ANTONY. Why, friends, you go to do you know not what:
     Wherein hath Caesar thus deserved your loves?
     Alas, you know not; I must tell you then:
     You have forgot the will I told you of.

ALL. Most true: the will! Let's stay and hear the will.

ANTONY. Here is the will, and under Caesar's seal.
　To every Roman citizen he gives,
　To every several man, seventy-five drachmas.
SECOND CITIZEN. Most noble Caesar! we'll revenge his death.
THIRD CITIZEN. O royal Caesar!
ANTONY. Hear me with patience.
ALL. Peace, ho!
ANTONY. Moreover, he hath left you all his walks,
　His private arbors and new-planted orchards,
　On this side Tiber; he hath left them you,
　And to your heirs for ever; common pleasures,
　To walk abroad and recreate yourselves.
　Here was a Caesar! when comes such another?
FIRST CITIZEN. Never, never. Come, away, away!
　We'll burn his body in the holy place,
　And with the brands fire the traitors' houses.
　Take up the body.
SECOND CITIZEN. Go fetch fire.
THIRD CITIZEN. Pluck down benches.
FOURTH CITIZEN. Pluck down forms, windows, anything.
　[*Exeunt Citizens with the body.*]
ANTONY. Now let it work. Mischief, thou art afoot,
　Take thou what course thou wilt. ■

Edmund Burke Laments the Death of Marie Antoinette

"THE age of chivalry is gone. . . ."

PICTURED AS SPOILED AND FRIVOLOUS, Marie Antoinette never said the most famous words attributed to her. When told that the French people had no bread to eat, she supposedly replied, "Let them eat cake" ("Qu'ils mangent de la brioche"). Rousseau, however, had already recorded that "thoughtless saying of a great princess" in his *Confessions,* in 1767, years before Marie Antoinette's arrival in France.

Dissatisfaction of the common people and a sense of royal indifference to their plight fomented the French Revolution. King Louis XVI was executed for treason in early 1793, and his queen, Marie Antoinette, was sent to the guillotine later that same year.

Edmund Burke, the great English orator and conservative parliamentarian, had vigorously opposed the French Revolution as an unnecessary evil. Burke mourned the loss of Marie Antoinette and delivered a glowing tribute to her, remembering his vision of her twenty years before her execution. This drew the accusation of "foppery" from a friend who favored the Revolution, and Burke adamantly defended his words:

"Am I obliged to prove judicially the virtues of those I see suffering every kind of wrong? . . . I tell you again that the recollection of the manner in which I saw the queen of France in 1774 and the contrast between that brilliancy, splendor, and beauty, with the prostrate homage of a nation to her, and the abominable scene of 1789, which I was describing, did draw tears from me and wetted the paper. Those tears came again into my eyes almost as often as I looked at the description. They may again. You do not believe this fact nor that these are my real feelings, but that the whole is affected or, as you express it, 'downright foppery.' My friend, I tell you it is truth and that it is true and will be true when you and I are no more, and will exist as long as men with their natural feelings shall exist."

Was that last line in the mind of the *New York Evening Sun* editorialist who wrote the Santa-Claus-lives editorial to "Dear Virginia"? Probably not; it is one of those long thoughts expressed in a widely used but memorable construction.

□   □   □

It is now sixteen or seventeen years since I saw the queen of France, then the dauphiness, at Versailles; and surely never lighted on this orb, which she hardly seemed to touch, a more delightful vision. I saw her just above the horizon, decorating and cheering the elevated sphere she had just begun to move in, glittering like the morning star full of life and splendor and joy. O, what a revolution! and what a heart must I have, to contemplate without emotion that elevation and that fall! Little did I dream, when she added titles of veneration to those of enthusiastic, distant, respectful love, that she should ever be obliged to carry the sharp antidote against disgrace concealed in that bosom; little did I dream that I should have lived to see such disasters fallen upon her, in a nation of gallant men, in a nation of men of honor, and of cavaliers! I thought ten thousand swords must have leaped from their scabbards, to avenge even a look that threatened her with insult.

But the age of chivalry is gone; that of sophisters, economists, and calculators has succeeded, and the glory of Europe is extinguished forever. Never, never more, shall we behold that generous loyalty to rank and sex, that proud submission, that dignified obedience, that subordination of the heart, which kept alive, even in servitude itself, the spirit of an exalted freedom! The unbought grace of life, the cheap defense of nations, the nurse of manly sentiment and heroic enterprise is gone. It is gone, that sensibility of principle, that chastity of honor, which felt a stain like a wound, which inspired courage whilst it mitigated ferocity, which ennobled whatever it touched, and under which vice itself lost half its evil, by losing all its grossness. ■

Henry Lee Remembers George Washington

"FIRST in war—first in peace—and first in the hearts of his countrymen. . . ."

THE DEATH OF GEORGE WASHINGTON in 1799 elicited a memorable tribute from Henry Lee. Lee, the father of Confederate military leader Robert E. Lee, was himself a Virginia officer whose revolutionary-war exploits and quick movements lent him the nickname Light-Horse Harry.

Henry Lee's funeral oration for Washington includes lists of reverential modifiers ("pious, just, humane") and archaic language ("Methinks I see his august image"). The dramatic device of attributing a speech to the deceased will appear again in Daniel Webster's eulogy for John Adams. Lee's tribute is remembered, however, almost exclusively for the elegant opening line ("First in war—first in peace—and first in the hearts of his countrymen") that has a horse's-hoofbeats rhythm and encapsulates in three short phrases the record and reputation of the first president of the United States.

□   □   □

First in war—first in peace—and first in the hearts of his countrymen, he was second to none in the humble and endearing scenes of private life; pious, just, humane, temperate, and sincere; uniform, dignified, and commanding, his example was as edifying to all around him as were the effects of that example lasting.

To his equals he was condescending, to his inferiors kind, and to the dear object of his affections exemplarily tender; correct throughout, vice shuddered in his presence, and virtue always felt his fostering hand; the purity of his private character gave effulgence to his public virtues.

His last scene comported with the whole tenor of his life—although in extreme pain, not a sigh, not a groan escaped him; and with undisturbed serenity he closed his well-spent life. Such was the man America has lost—such was the man for whom our nation mourns.

Methinks I see his august image, and I hear falling from his venerable lips these deep-sinking words:

"Cease, sons of America, lamenting our separation; go on, and confirm by your wisdom the fruits of our joint councils, joint efforts, and common dangers; reverence religion, diffuse knowledge throughout your land, patronize the arts and sciences; let liberty and order be inseparable companions. Control party spirit, the bane of free governments; observe good faith to, and cultivate peace with, all nations, shut up every avenue to foreign influence, contract rather than extend national connection, rely on ourselves only: be Americans in thought, word, and deed—thus will you give immortality to that union which was the constant object of my terrestrial labors; thus will you preserve undisturbed to the latest posterity the felicity of a people to me most dear, and thus will you supply (if my happiness is now aught to you) the only vacancy in the round of pure bliss high heaven bestows." ■

Daniel Webster Puts a Speech in the Mouth of John Adams

"SINK or swim, live or die, survive or perish, I give my hand and my heart to this vote."

ON JULY 4, 1826, the fiftieth anniversary of the adoption of the Declaration of Independence, John Adams died. His last words: "Thomas Jefferson still surv——." But Jefferson did not survive; by coincidence, he also died that same day. (His last words were "This is the Fourth?" Maybe it's a good idea that we have stopped recording "last words.")

At a double memorial service for these framers, the great orator of the day, Representative Daniel Webster, spoke in Boston's Faneuil Hall. In the style of the ancient historians, he included in his address a speech that might have been given by John Adams. In his grandiloquent but moving manner, Webster set the scene with a supposed speech by John Hancock dissenting from the Declaration as "unseasonable and ill-judged," warning of the day "when we ourselves, given up by an exhausted, a misled people, shall have expiated our rashness and atoned for our presumption on the scaffold."

Said Webster, "It was for Mr. Adams to reply to arguments like these. We know his opinions, we know his character. He would commence with his accustomed directness and earnestness." Then Webster delivered his speech within a speech; it is sometimes mistakenly taken to be Adams's own words, but Adams would have writhed listening to it because Adams's style was much more brisk and businesslike ("May none but honest and wise men ever rule under this roof"). Here was the first retrospective ghostwriting for one of America's founders.

□   □   □

"Sink or swim, live or die, survive or perish, I give my hand and my heart to this vote. It is true, indeed, that in the beginning we aimed not at independence. But there's a divinity which shapes our ends. The injustice of England has driven us to arms; and, blinded to her own interest for our good, she has obstinately persisted, till independence is now within our grasp. We have but to reach forth to it, and it is ours.

"Why, then, should we defer the Declaration? Is any man so weak as now to hope for a reconciliation with England, which shall leave either safety to the country and its liberties, or safety to his own life and his own honor? Are not you, sir, who sit in that chair—is not he, our venerable colleague near you—are you not both already the proscribed and predestined objects of punishment and of vengeance? Cut off from all hope of royal clemency, what are you, what can you be, while the power of England remains, but outlaws? If we postpone independence, do we mean to carry on, or to give up, the war? Do we mean to submit to the measures of Parliament, Boston Port Bill and all? Do we mean to submit, and consent that we ourselves shall be ground to powder, and our country and its rights trodden down in the dust? I know we do not mean to submit. We never shall submit. Do we intend to violate that most solemn obligation ever entered into by men—that plighting, before God, of our sacred honor to Washington, when, putting him forth to incur the dangers of war, as well as the political hazards of the times, we promised to adhere to him, in every extremity, with our fortunes and our lives? I know there is not a man here who would not rather see a general conflagration sweep over the land, or an earthquake sink it, than one jot or tittle of that plighted faith fall to the ground.

"For myself, having twelve months ago in this place moved you that George Washington be appointed commander of the forces, raised or to be raised, for defense of American liberty, may my right hand forget her cunning, and my tongue cleave to the roof of my mouth, if I hesitate or waiver in the support I give him. The war, then, must go on. We must fight it through. And, if the war must go on, why put off longer the Declaration of Independence? That measure will strengthen us. It will give us character abroad. The nations will then treat with us, which they never can do while we acknowledge ourselves subjects in arms against our sovereign. Nay, I maintain that England herself will sooner treat for peace with us on the footing of independence than consent, by repealing her acts, to acknowledge that her whole conduct toward us has been a course of injustice and oppression. Her pride will be less wounded by submitting to that course of things which now predestinates our independence than by yielding the points in controversy to her rebellious subjects. The former she would regard as the result of fortune; the latter she would feel as her own deep disgrace. Why, then—why, then, sir, do we not, as soon as possible, change this from a civil to a national war? And since we must fight it through, why not put ourselves in a state to enjoy all the benefits of victory, if we gain the victory?

"If we fail, it can be no worse for us. But we shall not fail. The cause will raise up armies; the cause will create navies. The people—the people, if we are true to them, will carry us, and will carry themselves, gloriously through this struggle. I care not how fickle other people have been found. I know the people of these colonies, and I know that resistance to British aggression is deep and settled in their hearts and cannot be eradicated. Every colony, indeed, has expressed its willingness to follow, if we but take the lead. Sir, the Declaration will inspire the people with increased courage. Instead of a long and bloody war for restoration of privileges, for redress of grievances, for chartered immunities, held under a British king, set before them the glorious object of entire independence, and it will breathe into them anew the breath of life. Read this Declaration at the head of the army; every sword will be drawn from its scabbard, and the solemn vow uttered to maintain it, or to perish on the bed of honor. Publish it from the pulpit; religion will approve it, and the love of religious liberty will cling round it, resolved to stand with it, or fall with it. Send it to the public halls; proclaim it there; let them hear it who heard the first roar of the enemy's cannon; let them see it who saw their brothers and their sons fall on the field of Bunker Hill, and in the streets of Lexington and Concord, and the very walls will cry out in its support.

"Sir, I know the uncertainty of human affairs, but I see, I see clearly, through this day's business. You and I, indeed, may rue it. We may not live to the time when this Declaration shall be made good. We may die; die, colonists; die, slaves; die, it may be, ignominiously and on the scaffold. Be it so. Be it so. If it be the pleasure of heaven that my country shall require the poor offering of my life, the victim shall be ready at the appointed hour of sacrifice, come when that hour may. But while I do live, let me have a country, or at least the hope of a country, and that a free country.

"But, whatever may be our fate, be assured, be assured, that this Declaration will stand. It may cost treasure, and it may cost blood; but it will stand, and it will richly compensate for both. Through the thick gloom of the present I see the brightness of the future as the sun in heaven. We shall make this a glorious, an immortal day. When we are in our graves, our children will honor it. They will celebrate it with thanksgiving, with festivity, with bonfires, and illuminations. On its annual return they will shed tears, copious, gushing tears, not of subjection and slavery, not of agony and distress, but of exultation, of gratitude, and of joy. Sir, before God, I believe the hour has come. My judgment approves this measure, and my whole heart is in it. All that I have, and all that I am, and all that I hope, in this life, I am now ready here to stake upon it; and I leave off as I began, that, live or die, survive or perish, I am for the Declaration. It is my living sentiment, and, by the blessing of God, it shall be my dying sentiment; independence now, and independence forever." ■

Senator George Graham Vest Offers a Tribute to the Dog

"WHEN all other friends desert, he remains."

GEORGE GRAHAM VEST, a member of the Confederate Congress during the Civil War, served as U.S. senator from Missouri from 1879 to 1903. He was a leading debater, inveighed at length against the "menace" of Mormonism, and could claim as his hometown the oxymoronic Sweet Springs in Saline County, Missouri.

He is remembered for a speech he made as a young lawyer in Georgetown, Missouri, and repeated hundreds of times around the country throughout his life. He was representing a plaintiff who sued a neighbor for the killing of his dog. He paid little attention to his own client's charges, or to the testimony of the defendant; instead, he waited for his turn to address the jury and won the case unfairly by wringing its heart with an emotional evocation of the fidelity of dogs in general.

It is a great short speech. The logician may dismiss it as the rankest sentimentalism, and the cool intellectual may object to its shameless tear-jerking, but the rhetorician is prepared to lick the orator's hand.

The theme is fidelity. The first paragraph, with its half dozen uses of "may," sets forth the conditional nature of human affection, preparing for the coming contrast; the second paragraph slams home the unconditional faithfulness of the dog. (He focuses on the male dog because "he" is more personal than "it" or "they"; in my own experience, the bitch is more faithful.) The final paragraph is hearts and flowers—"the violin," as newsmagazine writers call lyrical thematic essays—but despite Vest's clichés about "the last scene of all" and "the cold ground," the picture of fidelity at the graveside induces a lump in the throat of the listener every time. If there has ever been a good dog in your life, read this with a handkerchief handy; your eyes will begin to well up at "He will kiss the hand that has no food to offer. . . ."

☐   ☐   ☐

G entlemen of the jury:
     The best friend a man has in the world may turn against him and become his enemy. His son or daughter that he has reared with loving care may prove ungrateful. Those who are nearest and dearest to us, those whom we trust with our happiness and our good name may become traitors to their faith. The money that a man has, he may lose. It flies away from him, perhaps when he needs it most. A man's reputation may be sacrificed in a moment of ill-considered action. The people who are prone to fall on their knees to do us honor when success is with us may be the first to throw the stone of malice when failure settles its cloud upon our heads.

The one absolutely unselfish friend that man can have in this selfish world, the one that never deserts him, the one that never proves ungrateful or treacherous is his dog. A man's dog stands by him in prosperity and in poverty, in health and in sickness. He will sleep on the cold ground, where the wintry winds blow and the snow drives fiercely, if only he may be near his master's side. He will kiss the hand that has no food to offer; he will lick the wounds and sores that come in encounter with the roughness of the world. He guards the sleep of his pauper master as if he were a prince. When all other friends desert, he remains. When riches take wings, and reputation falls to pieces, he is as constant in his love as the sun in its journey through the heavens.

If fortune drives the master forth an outcast in the world, friendless and homeless, the faithful dog asks no higher privilege than that of accompanying him, to guard him against danger, to fight against his enemies. And when the last scene of all comes, and death takes his master in its embrace and his body is laid away in the cold ground, no matter if all other friends pursue their way, there by the graveside will the noble dog be found, his head between his paws, his eyes sad, but open in alert watchfulness, faithful and true even in death. ∎

Ralph Waldo Emerson Commemorates the Centennial of Robert Burns

"HE had that secret of genius to draw from the bottom of society the strength of its speech . . . filtered of all offense through his beauty."

RALPH WALDO EMERSON, American philosopher and minor poet, recognized the major poetic talent in Scotsman Robert Burns. Although the "low" speech of Burns, writing in the Scottish vernacular, kept his reputation from rising to the level of a Keats, Shelley, or Tennyson, Emerson saw in him a "poet of the poor" and "of the middle class" who could transform "a patois unintelligible to all but natives" into "a Doric dialect of fame."

In his eulogy, Emerson first established his subject's political significance to his audience in Boston, on January 25, 1859: "Burns, the poet of the middle class, represents in the mind of men today that great uprising of the middle class against the armed and privileged minorities. . . ." He proceeded to touch on Burns's importance to poetry—"artless words, better than art"—and then evoked his poetry in a poetic peroration.

□   □   □

. . . I heartily feel the singular claims of the occasion. At the first announcement, from I know not whence, that the twenty-fifth of January was the hundredth anniversary of the birth of Robert Burns, a sudden consent warned the great English race, in all its kingdoms, colonies, and states, all over the world, to keep the festival. We are here to hold our parliament with love and poesy, as men were wont to do in the Middle Ages. Those famous parliaments might or might not have had more stateliness, and better singers than we—though that is yet to be known—but they could not have better reason.

I can only explain this singular unanimity in a race which rarely acts together—but rather after their watchword, each for himself—by the fact that Robert Burns, the poet of the middle class, represents in the mind of men today that great uprising of the middle class against the armed and privileged minorities—that uprising which worked politically in the American and French revolutions, and which, not in governments so much as in education and in social order, has changed the face of the world. In order for this destiny, his birth, breeding, and fortune were low. His organic sentiment was absolute independence, and resting, as it should, on a life of labor.

No man existed who could look down on him. They that looked into his eyes saw that they might look down on the sky as easily: His muse and teaching was common sense, joyful, aggressive, irresistible. Not Latimer, nor Luther, struck more telling blows against false theology than did this brave singer. The Confession of Augsburg, the Declaration of Independence, the French Rights of Man, and the "Marseillaise" are not more weighty documents in the history of freedom than the songs of Burns. His satire has lost none of its edge. His musical arrows yet sing through the air. He is so substantially a reformer, and I find his grand, plain sense in close chain with the greatest masters—Rabelais, Shakespeare in comedy, Cervantes, and Butler. He is an exceptional genius. The people who care nothing for literature and poetry care for Burns. It was indifferent—they thought who saw him—whether he wrote verse or not; he could have done anything else as well.

Yet how true a poet is he! And the poet, too, of poor men, of hodden-gray, and the Guernsey-coat, and the blouse. He has given voice to all the experiences of common life; he has endeared the farmhouse and cottages, patches and poverty, beans and barley; ale the poor man's wine; hardship, the fear of debt, the dear society of weans and wife, of brothers and sisters, proud of each other, knowing so few, and finding amends for want and obscurity in books and thought. What a love of nature! And—shall I say?— of middle-class nature. Not great, like Goethe, in the stars, or like Byron, on the ocean, or Moore, in the luxurious East, but in the homely landscape which the poor see around them—bleak leagues of pasture and stubble, ice, and sleet, and rain, and snow-choked brooks; birds, hares, field mice, thistles, and heather, which he daily knew. How many "Bonny Doons," and "John Anderson My Joes," and "Auld Lang Synes," all around the earth, have his verses been applied to! And his love songs still woo and melt the youths and maids; the farm work, the country holiday, the fishing cobble, are still his debtors today.

And, as he was thus the poet of the poor, anxious, cheerful, working humanity, so had he the language of low life. He grew up in a rural district, speaking a patois unintelligible to all but natives, and he has made that Lowland Scotch a Doric dialect of fame. It is the only example in history of a language made classic by the genius of a single man. But more than this. He had that secret of genius to draw from the bottom of society the strength of its speech, and astonish the ears of the polite with these artless words, better than art, and filtered of all offense through his beauty. It seemed odious to Luther that the devil should have all the best tunes; he would bring them into the churches; and Burns knew how to take from fairs and gypsies, blacksmiths and drovers, the speech of the market and street, and clothe it with melody.

But I am detaining you too long. The memory of Burns— I am afraid heaven and earth have taken too good care of it to leave us anything to say. The west winds are murmuring it. Open the windows behind you, and hearken for the incoming tide, what the waves say of it. The doves, perching always on the eaves of the Stone Chapel opposite, may know something about it. Every home in broad Scotland keeps his fame bright. The memory of Burns—every man's and boy's, and girl's head carries snatches of his songs, and can say them by heart, and, what is strangest of all, never learned them from a book, but from mouth to mouth. The wind whispers them, the birds whistle them, the corn, barley, and bulrushes hoarsely rustle them; nay, the music boxes at Geneva are framed and toothed to play them; the hand organs of the Savoyards in all cities repeat them, and the chimes of bells ring them in the spires. They are the property and the solace of mankind. ■

Frederick Douglass Cuts through the Lincoln Myth to Consider the Man

"He knew the American people better than they knew themselves, and his truth was based upon this knowledge."

WHEN POLICE TRIED to prevent former slave Frederick Douglass from attending the inaugural reception in 1865, President Lincoln went to the door and said, "Here comes my friend Douglass." Later, Douglass was to observe, "In all my interviews with Mr. Lincoln I was impressed with his entire freedom from popular prejudice against the colored race."

The tall, articulate Douglass was the leading black abolitionist for the generation preceding the Civil War. A fugitive slave himself. he used his lecture fees to aid others; he raised money for John Brown, though he opposed that fiery abolitionist's Harpers Ferry raid; during the war, he recruited Negroes for the Union Army. The leading spokesman for what later became known as the black community often had to repress his emotions and bite his tongue, although—in a passage once quoted by Clarence Thomas—he cried, "Oh! Had I the ability and could I reach the nation's ear, I would today put out a fiery stream of biting ridicule . . . and stem reproach. . . . We need the storm, the whirlwind and the earthquake."

In 1876, Douglass was asked to speak at the dedication of the Freedmen's Monument in Washington, D.C., in a ceremony attended by President U. S. Grant and all the capital's notables. The sculptor had expressed a familiar theme: the Great Emancipator standing over a kneeling black, who was gazing at him in gratitude. Douglass chose not to give the usual Lincoln encomium, to join the line of those creating the Lincoln myth. He gave an assessment that shocked the Republicans present, who were trying to forget their 1860 priority of union over abolition; speaking to the whites present as *you* and the blacks as *we*, he dared point out that Lincoln was not "either our man or our model. . . . He was preeminently the white man's president. . . ." Douglass's speech reads well today; he was one of the lone observers in a century that followed who saw Lincoln without tears—as a man and politician, not as a martyred saint.

□   □   □

. . . Fellow citizens, in what we have said and done today, and in what we may say and do hereafter, we disclaim everything like arrogance and assumption. We claim for ourselves no superior devotion to the character, history, and memory of the illustrious name whose monument we have here dedicated today. We fully comprehend the relation of Abraham Lincoln both to ourselves and to the white people of the United States. Truth is proper and beautiful at all times and in all places, and it is never more proper and beautiful in any case than when speaking of a great public man whose example is likely to be commended for honor and imitation long after his departure to the solemn shades, the silent continents of eternity. It must be admitted, truth compels me to admit, even here in the presence of the monument we have erected to his memory, Abraham Lincoln was not, in the fullest sense of the word, either our man or our model. In his interests, in his associations, in his habits of thought, and in his prejudices, he was a white man.

He was preeminently the white man's president, entirely devoted to the welfare of white men. He was ready and willing at any time during the first years of his administration to deny, postpone, and sacrifice the rights of humanity in the colored people to promote the welfare of the white people of this country. In all his education and feeling he was an American of the Americans. He came into the presidential chair upon one principle alone, namely, opposition to the extension of slavery. His arguments in furtherance of this policy had their motive and mainspring in his patriotic devotion to the interests of his own race. To protect, defend, and perpetuate slavery in the states where it existed Abraham Lincoln was not less ready than any other president to draw the sword of the nation. He was ready to execute all the supposed constitutional guarantees of the United States Constitution in favor of the slave system anywhere inside the slave states. He was willing to pursue, recapture, and send back the fugitive slave to his master, and to suppress a slave rising for liberty, though his guilty master were already in arms against the government. The race to which we belong were not the special objects of his consideration. Knowing this, I concede to you, my white fellow citizens, a preeminence in this worship at once full and supreme. First, midst, and last, you and yours were the objects of his deepest affection and his most earnest solicitude. You are the children of Abraham

Lincoln. We are at best only his stepchildren—children by adoption, children by force of circumstances and necessity. To you it especially belongs to sound his praises, to preserve and perpetuate his memory, to multiply his statues, to hang his pictures high upon your walls, and commend his example, for to you he was a great and glorious friend and benefactor. Instead of supplanting you at this altar, we would exhort you to build high his monuments; let them be of the most costly material, of the most cunning workmanship; let their forms be symmetrical, beautiful, and perfect; let their bases be upon solid rocks, and their summits lean against the unchanging blue, overhanging sky, and let them endure forever! But while in the abundance of your wealth, and in the fullness of your just and patriotic devotion, you do all this, we entreat you to despise not the humble offering we this day unveil to view; for while Abraham Lincoln saved for you a country, he delivered us from a bondage, according to Jefferson, one hour of which was worse than ages of the oppression your fathers rose in rebellion to oppose.

Fellow citizens, ours is no newborn zeal and devotion—merely a thing of this moment. The name of Abraham Lincoln was near and dear to our hearts in the darkest and most perilous hours of the Republic. We were no more ashamed of him when shrouded in clouds of darkness, of doubt, and defeat than when we saw him crowned with victory, honor, and glory. Our faith in him was often taxed and strained to the uttermost, but it never failed. When he tarried long in the mountain; when he strangely told us that we were the cause of the war; when he still more strangely told us to leave the land in which we were born; when he refused to employ our arms in defense of the Union; when, after accepting our services as colored soldiers, he refused to retaliate our murder and torture as colored prisoners; when he told us he would save the Union if he could with slavery; when he revoked the Proclamation of Emancipation of General Fremont; when he refused to remove the popular commander of the Army of the Potomac, in the days of its inaction and defeat, who was more zealous in his efforts to protect slavery than to suppress rebellion; when we saw all this, and more, we were at times grieved, stunned, and greatly bewildered; but our hearts believed while they ached and bled. Nor was this, even at that time, a blind and unreasoning superstition. Despite the mist and haze that surrounded him; despite the tumult, the hurry, and confusion of the hour, we were able to take a comprehensive view of Abraham Lincoln, and to make reasonable allowance for the circumstances of his position. . . .

Though he loved Caesar less than Rome, though the Union was more to him than our freedom or our future, under his wise and beneficent rule we saw ourselves gradually lifted from the depths of slavery to the heights of liberty and manhood; under his wise and beneficent rule, and by measures approved and vigorously pressed by him, we saw that the handwriting of ages, in the form of prejudice and proscription, was rapidly fading away from the face of our whole country; under his rule, and in due time, about as soon after all as the country could tolerate the strange spectacle, we saw our brave sons and brothers laying off the rags of bondage, and being clothed all over in the blue uniforms of the soldiers of the United States; under his rule we saw two hundred thousand of our dark and dusky people responding to the call of Abraham Lincoln, and with muskets on their shoulders, and eagles on their buttons, timing their high footsteps to liberty and union under the national flag; under his rule we saw the independence of the black republic of Haiti, the special object of slaveholding aversion and horror, fully recognized, and her minister, a colored gentleman, duly received here in the city of Washington; under his rule we saw the internal slave trade, which so long disgraced the nation, abolished, and slavery abolished in the District of Columbia; under his rule we saw for the first time the law enforced against the foreign slave trade, and the first slave trader hanged like any other pirate or murderer; under his rule, assisted by the greatest captain of our age, and his inspiration, we saw the Confederate States, based upon the idea that our race must be slaves, and slaves forever, battered to pieces and scattered to the four winds; under his rule, and in the fullness of time, we saw Abraham Lincoln, after giving the slaveholders three months' grace in which to save their hateful slave system, penning the immortal paper, which, though special in its language, was general in its principles and effect, making slavery forever impossible in the United States. Though we waited long, we saw all this and more. . . .

I have said that President Lincoln was a white man, and shared the prejudices common to his countrymen towards the colored race. Looking back to his times and to the condition of his country, we are compelled to admit that this unfriendly feeling on his part may be safely set down as one element of his wonderful success in organizing the loyal American people for the tremendous conflict before them, and bringing them safely through that conflict. His great mission was to accomplish two things: first, to save his country from dismemberment and ruin; and second, to free his country from the great crime of slavery. To do one or the other, or both, he must have the earnest sympathy and the powerful cooperation of his loyal fellow countrymen. Without this primary and essential condition to success his efforts must have been vain and utterly fruitless. Had he put the abolition of slavery before the salvation of the Union, he would have inevitably driven from him a powerful class of the American people and rendered resistance to rebellion impossible. Viewed from the genuine abolition ground, Mr. Lincoln seemed tardy, cold, dull, and indifferent; but measuring him by the sentiment of his country, a sentiment he was bound as a statesman to consult, he was swift, zealous, radical, and determined.

Though Mr. Lincoln shared the prejudices of his white fellow countrymen against the Negro, it is hardly necessary to say that in his heart of hearts he loathed and hated slavery. The man who could say, "Fondly do we hope, fervently do we pray, that this mighty scourge of war shall soon pass away, yet if God wills it continue till all the wealth piled by two hundred years of bondage shall have been wasted, and each drop of blood drawn by the lash shall have been paid for by one drawn by the sword, the judgments of the Lord are true and righteous altogether," gives all needed proof of his feeling on the subject of slavery. He was willing, while the South was loyal, that it should have its pound of flesh, because he thought that it was so nominated in the bond; but farther than this no earthly power could make him go.

Fellow citizens, whatever else in this world may be partial, unjust, and uncertain, time, time! is impartial, just, and certain in its action. In the realm of mind, as well as in the realm of matter, it is a great worker, and often works wonders. The honest and comprehensive statesman, clearly discerning the needs of his country, and earnestly endeavoring to do his whole duty, though covered and blistered with reproaches, may safely leave his course to the silent judgment of time. Few great public men have ever been the victims of fiercer denunciation than Abraham Lincoln was during his administration. He was often wounded in the house of his friends. Reproaches came thick and fast upon him from within and from without, and from opposite quarters. He was assailed by abolitionists; he was assailed by slaveholders; he was assailed by the men who were for peace at any price; he was assailed by those who were for a more vigorous prosecution of the war; he was assailed for not making the war an abolition war; and he was most bitterly assailed for making the war an abolition war.

But now behold the change: the judgment of the present hour, that taking him for all in all, measuring the tremendous magnitude of the work before him, considering the necessary means to ends, and surveying the end from the beginning, infinite wisdom has seldom sent any man into the world better fitted for his mission than Abraham Lincoln. . . .

Upon his inauguration as president of the United States, an office, even where assumed under the most favorable conditions, fitted to tax and strain the largest abilities, Abraham Lincoln was met by a tremendous crisis. He was called upon not merely to administer the government but to decide, in the face of terrible odds, the fate of the Republic.

A formidable rebellion rose in his path before him; the Union was already practically dissolved; his country was torn and rent asunder at the center. Hostile armies were already organized against the Republic, armed with the munitions of war which the Republic had provided for its own defense. The tremendous question for him to decide was whether his country should survive the crisis and flourish, or be dismembered and perish. His predecessor in office had already decided the question in favor of national dismemberment, by denying to it the right of self-defense and self-preservation—a right which belongs to the meanest insect.

Happily for the country, happily for you and for me, the judgment of James Buchanan, the patrician, was not the judgment of Abraham Lincoln, the plebeian. He brought his strong common sense, sharpened in the school of adversity, to bear upon the question. He did not hesitate, he did not doubt, he did not falter; but at once resolved that at whatever peril, at whatever cost, the union of the states should be preserved. A patriot himself, his faith was strong and unwavering in the patriotism of his countrymen. Timid men said before Mr. Lincoln's inauguration, that we had seen the last president of the United States. A voice in influential quarters said, "Let the Union slide." Some said that a Union maintained by the sword was worthless. Others said a rebellion of eight million cannot be suppressed; but in the midst of all this tumult and timidity, and against all this, Abraham Lincoln was clear in his duty, and had an oath in heaven. He calmly and bravely heard the voice of doubt and fear all around him; but he had an oath in heaven, and there was not power enough on the earth to make this honest boatman, backwoodsman, and broad-handed splitter of rails evade or violate that sacred oath. He had not been schooled in the ethics of slavery; his plain life had favored his love of truth. He had not been taught that treason and perjury were the proof of honor and honesty. His moral training was against his saying one thing when he meant another. The trust which Abraham Lincoln had in himself and in the people was surprising and grand, but it was also enlightened and well founded. He knew the American people better than they knew themselves, and his truth was based upon this knowledge. . . .

Fellow citizens, I end, as I began, with congratulations. We have done a good work for our race today. In doing honor to the memory of our friend and liberator, we have been doing highest honors to ourselves and those who come after us; we have been fastening ourselves to a name and fame imperishable and immortal; we have also been defending ourselves from a blighting scandal. When now it shall be said that the colored man is soulless, that he has no appreciation of benefits or benefactors; when the foul reproach of ingratitude is hurled at us, and it is attempted to scourge us beyond the range of human brotherhood, we may calmly point to the monument we have this day erected to the memory of Abraham Lincoln. ∎

Humanist Robert Green Ingersoll Speaks at His Brother's Grave

"LIFE is a narrow vale between the cold and barren peaks of two eternities. We strive in vain to look beyond the heights."

COLORFUL AND CONTROVERSIAL, Robert Green Ingersoll became known as the "great agnostic" and was among the most popular of nineteenth-century American orators. His speaking style proved potent with audiences, even though his antireligious views were galling to the pious, and his creed was easily expressed in simple declarative statements: "Happiness is the only good. The time to be happy is now. The place to be happy is here. The way to be happy is to make others so." That humanistic creed became central to Ingersoll's agnosticism, his certainty that God is unknowable. The peak of his political oratory came at the nomination of James Blaine of Maine for president, a portion of which is on p. 204, in the introduction to Blaine's eulogy for President James Garfield.

Robert Ingersoll's beloved brother, Clark, who had been his law partner and had also served in Congress, died in 1879. Ingersoll delivered an emotional eulogy beside his brother's grave. In that oration, he made use of the first part of the creed, adding such balanced phrases as "reason the only torch, justice the only worship, humanity the only religion, and love the only priest."

Ingersoll's eloquent expressions of grief are both heartfelt and carefully crafted. Parallelism ("brother, husband, father, friend") and rhyme ("tears and fears") combine to add force to his words, building to the eulogy's emotional climax, the knowledge that "speech cannot contain our love."

□   □   □

My friends:
I am going to do that which the dead oft promised he would do for me.

The loved and loving brother, husband, father, friend died where manhood's morning almost touches noon, and while the shadows still were falling toward the west.

He had not passed on life's highway the stone that marks the highest point, but, being weary for a moment, he lay down by the wayside and, using his burden for a pillow, fell into that dreamless sleep that kisses down his eyelids still. While yet in love with life and raptured with the world, he passed to silence and pathetic dust.

Yet, after all, it may be best, just in the happiest, sunniest hour of all the voyage, while eager winds are kissing every sail, to dash against the unseen rock, and in an instant hear the billows roar above a sunken ship. For, whether in midsea or 'mong the breakers of the farther shore, a wreck at last must mark the end of each and all. And every life, no matter if its hour is rich with love and every moment jeweled with joy, will, at its close, become a tragedy as sad and deep and dark as can be woven of the warp and woof of mystery and death.

This brave and tender man in every storm of life was oak and rock, but in the sunshine he was vine and flower. He was the friend of all heroic souls. He climbed the heights and left all superstitions far below, while on his forehead fell the golden dawning of the grander day.

He loved the beautiful, and was with color, form, and music touched to tears. He sided with the weak, and with a willing hand gave alms; with loyal heart and with purest hands he faithfully discharged all public trusts.

He was a worshiper of liberty, a friend of the oppressed. A thousand times I have heard him quote these words: "For justice all places, a temple, and all seasons, summer." He believed that happiness was the only good, reason the only torch, justice the only worship, humanity the only religion, and love the only priest. He added to the sum of human joy; and were everyone to whom he did some loving service to bring a blossom to his grave, he would sleep tonight beneath a wilderness of flowers.

Life is a narrow vale between the cold and barren peaks of two eternities. We strive in vain to look beyond the heights. We cry aloud, and the only answer is the echo of our wailing cry. From the voiceless lips of the unreplying dead there comes no word; but in the night of death hope sees a star, and listening love can hear the rustle of a wing.

He who sleeps here, when dying, mistaking the approach of death for the return of health, whispered with his latest breath, "I am better now." Let us believe, in spite of doubts and dogmas, and tears and fears, that these dear words are true of all the countless dead.

And now to you who have been chosen, from among the many men he loved, to do the last sad office for the dead, we give this sacred dust. Speech cannot contain our love. There was, there is, no greater, stronger, manlier man. ■

James Blaine of Maine Eulogizes Assassinated President Garfield

"Great in life, he was surpassingly great in death."

ON FEBRUARY 27, 1882, six months after the death of President James A. Garfield, a eulogy was delivered in the House of Representatives by James Gillespie Blaine, the slain president's secretary of state. Blaine, a noted orator who had previously served as Speaker of the House and U. S. senator, provided a lengthy and memorable tribute to our twentieth president.

Blaine became known as "the plumed knight" when nominated in 1876 as the Republican candidate for president. The sobriquet came from the rousing nomination speech by Robert Green Ingersoll of Illinois:

"Like an armed warrior, like a plumed knight, James G. Blaine marched down the halls of the American Congress and threw his shining lance full and fair against the brazen foreheads of the defamers of his country and the maligners of his honor. For the Republicans to desert this gallant leader now is as though an army should desert their general upon the field of battle. . . .

"Gentlemen of the convention, in the name of the great Republic, the only republic that ever existed upon this earth; in the name of all her defenders and of all her supporters; in the name of all her soldiers living; in the name of all her soldiers dead upon the field of battle; and in the name of those who perished in the skeleton clutch of famine at Andersonville and Libby, whose sufferings he so vividly remembers, Illinois—Illinois nominates for the next president of this country that prince of parliamentarians, that leader of leaders, James G. Blaine!"

In his own speech, Blaine uses a straightforward oratorical style, often likened to that of Henry Clay. Through balanced phrases ("Great in life, . . . great in death") and parallel structure ("With unfaltering front . . . With unfailing tenderness . . ."), he provides a stirring portrait of President Garfield that ennobles this victim of assassination.

□   □   □

For the second time in this generation the great departments of the government of the United States are assembled in the Hall of Representatives, to do honor to the memory of a murdered president. Lincoln fell at the close of a mighty struggle, in which the passions of men had been deeply stirred. The tragic termination of his great life added but another to the lengthened succession of horrors which had marked so many lintels with the blood of the firstborn. Garfield was slain in a day of peace, when brother had been reconciled to brother, and when anger and hate had been banished from the land. . . .

Great in life, he was surpassingly great in death. For no cause in the very frenzy of wantonness and wickedness, by the red hand of murder, he was thrust from the full tide of this world's interest, from its hopes, its aspirations, its victories, into the visible presence of death—and he did not quail.

Not alone for one short moment in which, stunned and dazed, he could give up life, hardly aware of its relinquishment, but through days of deadly languor, through weeks of agony, that was not less agony because silently borne, with clear sight and calm courage he looked into his open grave. What blight and ruin met his anguished eyes, whose lips may tell—what brilliant, broken plans, what baffled, high ambitions, what sundering of strong, warm, manhood's friendship, what bitter rending of sweet household ties! Behind him a proud, expectant nation, a great host of sustaining friends, a cherished and happy mother, wearing the full, rich honors of her early toil and tears; the wife of his youth, whose whole life lay in his; the little boys not yet emerged from childhood's day of frolic; the fair young daughter; the sturdy sons just springing into closest companionship, claiming every day and every day rewarding a father's love and care; and in his heart the eager, rejoicing power to meet all demands. And his soul was not shaken.

His countrymen were thrilled with instant, profound, and universal sympathy. Masterful in his mortal weakness, he became the center of a nation's love, enshrined in the prayers of a world. But all the love and all the sympathy could not share with him his suffering. He trod the winepress alone. With unfaltering front he faced death. With unfailing tenderness he took leave of life. Above the demoniac hiss of the assassin's bullet he heard the voice of God. With simple resignation he bowed to the divine decree.

As the end drew near, his early craving for the sea returned. The stately mansion of power had been to him the wearisome hospital of pain, and he begged to be taken from his prison walls, from its oppressive, stifling air, from its homelessness and its hopelessness. Gently, silently, the love of a great people bore the pale sufferer to the longed-for healing of the sea, to live or to die, as God should will, within sight of the heaving billows, within sound of its manifold voices.

With a wan, fevered face, tenderly lifted to the cooling breeze, he looked out wistfully upon the ocean's changing wonders; on its far sails; on its restless waves, rolling shoreward to break and die beneath the noonday sun; on the red clouds of evening, arching low to the horizon; on the serene and shining pathway of the star. Let us think that his dying eyes read a mystic meaning which only the rapt and parting soul may know. Let us believe that in the silence of the receding world he heard the great waves breaking on a further shore and felt already upon his wasted brow the breath of the eternal morning. ■

Jane Addams Praises George Washington

"The lessons of great men are lost unless they reinforce upon our minds the highest demands which we make upon ourselves. . . ."

A PACIFIST and early activist in social service, Jane Addams is best remembered for her humanitarian efforts in helping to found Hull House. That settlement house, a welfare center in Chicago, opened in 1889, and her 1910 book, *Twenty Years at Hull House,* proved an important document in the history of social reform. Its central point: "Private beneficence is totally inadequate to deal with the vast numbers of the city's disinherited." In 1931, she was awarded the Nobel Peace Prize.

On February 23, 1903, Jane Addams was invited to give an address at the Union League Club in Chicago. Ostensibly a celebration of George Washington's birthday, the speech moved beyond a remembrance of "Washington, the man" to outline the values and priorities necessary for Washington's America in the twentieth century.

Refusing to advocate warmongering or materialism, Jane Addams argues for "the life of a larger cause" and the need for "public-spirited men and women, with a thoroughly aroused conscience." Through a barrage of rhetorical questions, she points out political and social corruption, particularly the absence of labor laws and of "like opportunity" (later to be known as "equal opportunity"). The peroration is particularly forceful, in moving the audience "forward in the direction of their highest ideals," a standard to which the wise and honest can repair.

□   □   □

We meet together upon these birthdays of our great men, not only to review their lives but to revive and cherish our own patriotism. This matter is a difficult task. In the first place, we are prone to think that by merely reciting these great deeds we get a reflected glory, and that the future is secure to us because the past has been so fine.

In the second place, we are apt to think that we inherit the fine qualities of those great men, simply because we have had a common descent and are living in the same territory.

As for the latter, we know full well that the patriotism of common descent is the mere patriotism of the clan—the early patriotism of the tribe. We know that the possession of a like territory is merely an advance upon that, and that both of them are unworthy to be the patriotism of a great cosmopolitan nation whose patriotism must be large enough to obliterate racial distinction and to forget that there are such things as surveyor's lines. Then when we come to the study of great men it is easy to think only of their great deeds, and not to think enough of their spirit. What is a great man who has made his mark upon history? Every time, if we think far enough, he is a man who has looked through the confusion of the moment and has seen the moral issue involved; he is a man who has refused to have his sense of justice distorted; he has listened to his conscience until conscience becomes a trumpet call to like-minded men, so that they gather about him and together, with mutual purpose and mutual aid, they make a new period in history.

Let us assume for a moment that if we are going to make this day of advantage to us, we will have to take this definition of a great man. We will have to appeal to the present as well as to the past. We will have to rouse our national consciences as well as our national pride, and we will all have to remember that it lies with the young people of this nation whether or not it is going to go on to a finish in any wise worthy of its beginning.

If we go back to George Washington and ask what he would be doing were he bearing our burdens now, and facing our problems at this moment, we would, of course, have to study his life bit by bit—his life as a soldier, as a statesman, and as a simple Virginia planter.

First, as a soldier. What is it that we admire about the soldier? It certainly is not that he goes into battle; what we admire about the soldier is that he has the power of losing his own life for the life of a larger cause; that he holds his personal suffering of no account; that he flings down in the gage of battle his all and says, "I will stand or fall with this cause." That, it seems to me, is the glorious thing we most admire, and if we are going to preserve that same spirit of the soldier, we will have to found a similar spirit in the civil life of the people, the same pride in civil warfare, the spirit of courage, and the spirit of self-surrender which lies back of this.

If we look out upon our national perspective, do we not see certainly one great menace which calls for patriotism? We see all around us a spirit of materialism—an undue emphasis put upon material possessions; an inordinate desire to win wealth; an inordinate fear of losing wealth; an inordinate desire to please those who are the possessors of wealth. Now, let us say, if we feel that this is a menace, that with all our power, with all the spirit of a soldier, we will arouse high-minded youth of this country against this spirit of materialism. We will say today that we will not count the opening of markets the one great field which our nation is concerned in, but that when our flag flies anywhere it shall fly for righteousness as well as for increased commercial prosperity; that we will see to it that no sin of commercial robbery shall be committed where it floats; that we shall see to it that nothing in our commercial history will not bear the most careful scrutiny and investigation; that we will restore commercial life, however complicated, to such honor and simple honesty as George Washington expressed in his business dealings.

Let us take, for a moment, George Washington as a statesman. What was it he did, during those days when they were framing a constitution, when they were meeting together night after night, and trying to adjust the rights and privileges of every class in the community? What was it that sustained him during all those days, all those weeks, during all those months and years? It was the belief that they were founding a nation on the axiom that all men are created free and equal. What would George Washington say if he found that among us there were causes constantly operating against that equality? If he knew that any child which is thrust prematurely into industry has no chance in life with children who are preserved from that pain and sorrow; if he knew that every insanitary street, and every insanitary house, cripples a man so that he has no health and no vigor with which to carry on his life labor; if he knew that all about us are forces making against skill, making against the best manhood and womanhood, what would he say? He would say that if the spirit of equality means anything, it means like opportunity, and if we once lose like opportunity we lose the only chance we have toward equality throughout the nation.

Let us take George Washington as a citizen. What did he do when he retired from office, because he was afraid holding office any longer might bring a wrong to himself and harm to his beloved nation? We say that he went back to his plantation on the Potomac. What were his thoughts during the all too short days that he lived there? He thought of many possibilities, but, looking out over his country, did he fear that there should rise up a crowd of men who held office, not for their country's good, but for their own good? Would he not have foreboded evil if he had known that among us were groups and hordes of professional politicians, who, without any blinking or without any pretense that they did otherwise, apportioned the spoils of office, and considered an independent man as a mere intruder, as a mere outsider; if he had seen that the original meaning of office-holding and the function of government had become indifferent to us, that we were not using our foresight and our conscience in order to find out this great wrong which was sapping the foundations of self-government? He would tell us that anything which makes for better civic service, which makes for a merit system, which makes for fitness for office, is the only thing which will tell against this wrong, and that this course is the wisest patriotism. What did he write in his last correspondence? He wrote that he felt very unhappy on the subject of slavery, that there was, to his mind, a great menace in the holding of slaves. We know that he neither bought nor sold slaves himself, and that he freed his own slaves in his will. That was a century ago. A man who a century ago could do that, would he, do you think, be indifferent now to the great questions of social maladjustment which we feel all around us? His letters breathe a yearning for a better condition for the slaves as the letters of all great men among us breathe a yearning for the better condition of the unskilled and underpaid. A wise patriotism, which will take hold of these questions by careful legal enactment, by constant and vigorous enforcement, because of the belief that if the meanest man in the Republic is deprived of his rights, then every man in the Republic is deprived of his rights, is the only patriotism by which public-spirited men and women, with a thoroughly aroused conscience, can worthily serve this Republic. Let us say again that the lessons of great men are lost unless they reinforce upon our minds the highest demands which we make upon ourselves; that they are lost unless they drive our sluggish wills forward in the direction of their highest ideals. ■

Rabbi Stephen S. Wise Offers a Tribute to Lincoln

"THERE could be no poorer way of honoring the memory of Lincoln than to assume, as we sometimes do, that the race of Lincolns has perished from the earth, and that we shall never look upon his like again."

STEPHEN SAMUEL WISE, the American Jewish visionary, was asked in 1914 to give a Lincoln's Birthday address at Springfield, Illinois. Below is a portion of that speech, delivered February 12, 1914.

The Zionist leader and rabbi who founded the Free Synagogue of New York in 1907, Wise became widely recognized for his oratorical power. His sermons, attracting large audiences to Carnegie Hall, focused on American and Jewish concerns, particularly issues that would lead Wise into world politics. In 1936, he became the founder of the World Jewish Congress, an outspoken organization in the fight against Hitler and nazism.

In contemplating Abraham Lincoln, Wise enumerates the qualities that set apart this leader from other "servants of the Republic." Paraphrasing Hamlet's tribute to his dead father, Wise warns against the assumption "that we shall never look upon his like again." This is the line in Shakespeare's *Hamlet*—"He was a man, take him for all in all, I shall not look upon his like again"—that has been used so often in eulogies that it has become a cliché. Instead, Rabbi Wise offers the example of Lincoln as the model for all Americans and leaders.

□   □   □

We dwell in times of great perplexity and are beset by far-reaching problems of social, industrial, and political import. We shall not greatly err if upon every occasion we consult the genius of Abraham Lincoln. We shall not falter nor swerve from the path of national right-eousness if we live by the moral genius of the great American commoner.

Instead of following Lincoln, we too often strive to make it appear that he is following us. Instead of emulating him, we too often venture to appropriate him. Instead of sitting at his feet as his disciples, and humbly heeding the echoes of his lips, we attribute to him our own petty slogans. The truth is that Lincoln belongs to no party today, though in his time he stood well and firmly within party ranks. His spirit ought today to inform all parties. He was a partisan second, an American first, as he is the first of Americans. Men and measures must not claim him for their own. He remains the standard by which to measure men. His views are not bind-ing upon us, but his point of view will always be our inspiration. He would not be blindly followed who was open-minded and open-visioned. He did not solve all the problems of the future, but he did solve the problem of his own age. Ours is not to claim his name for our stan-dards but his aim as our standard.

Lincoln is become for us the test of human worth, and we honor men in the measure in which they approach the absolute standard of Abraham Lincoln. Other men may resemble and approach him; he remains the standard whereby all other men are measured and appraised. . . .

Such a standard is Lincoln become for us, save that we dare not hope that any American may serve his country better than did Lincoln. However covetous of honor for our country we may be, we cherish no higher hope for the land we love than that the servants of the Republic in all time may rise to the stature of Abraham Lincoln.

In his lifetime Lincoln was maligned and traduced, but detraction dur-ing a man's lifetime affords no test of his life's value nor offers any fore-cast of history's verdict. It would almost seem as if the glory of immortality were anticipated in the life of the great by detraction and denial whilst yet they lived. When a Lincoln-like man arises, let us recognize and fitly honor him. There could be no poorer way of honoring the memory of Lincoln than to assume, as we sometimes do, that the race of Lincolns has perished from the earth, and that we shall never look upon his like again. One way to ensure the passing of the Lincolns is to assume that another Lincoln can nevermore arise. Would we find Lincoln today, we must not seek him in the guise of a rail-splitter, nor as a wielder of the backwoodsman's ax, but as a mighty smiter of wrong in high places and low.

Not very long ago I chanced upon a rarely beautiful custom in the city of Florence. It was the day of the martyrdom "of a prophet sent by God." A multitude stood before the spot where he was done to death—his hands miraculously uplifted in blessing in the very moment of torture and death—and every man brought a rose petal in token of reverence and gratitude to the martyred soul. This day every American citizen, every American man and woman and child has in spirit brought a petal to the grave of Lincoln, who sleeps tonight beneath a wilderness of love tokens from men of all faiths and tongues and races and backgrounds— who are become one and indivisible in their love and honor for the memory of Abraham Lincoln.

I have sometimes thought that the noblest tribute paid to the memory of Lincoln was the word of Phillips Brooks in Westminster Abbey when, pointing out that the test of the world to every nation was "Show us your man," he declared that America names Lincoln. But the first word spoken after the death of Lincoln is truest and best—the word of Secretary of War Stanton, standing by the side of that scene of peace— "Now he belongs to the ages." It was verdict and prophecy alike, for Lincoln is not America's, he is the world's; he belongs not to our age, but to the ages; and yet, though he belongs to all time and to all peoples, he is our own, for he was an American. ■

Will Rogers Eulogizes Woodrow Wilson

"THE world lost a friend."

WHEN WOODROW WILSON DIED on February 23, 1924, solemn eulogies and serious orations followed in abundance. Great American humorist Will Rogers, however, chose to pay tribute in his own way, which called for a lighter vein.

With a humanizing eulogy drawn from his personal experience of President Wilson, Rogers offers a glimpse of the man's greatness outside of the White House, in the everyday setting of a theater. In "Wilson Could Laugh at a Joke on Himself," the humorist recounts his first occasion to perform before our twenty-eighth president.

The eulogy's narrative structure is typical of the storytelling technique that Rogers used to great comic effect. In this case, though, the jokes are secondary to the purpose of illustrating one of President Wilson's most memorable qualities: the ability to laugh at himself.

□   □   □

Some of the most glowing and deserving tributes ever paid to the memory of an American have been paid in the last few days to our past president, Woodrow Wilson. They have been paid by learned men of this and all nations who knew what to say, and how to express their feelings. They spoke of their close association and personal contact with him. Now I want to add my little mite, even though it be of no importance. . . .

The Friars Club of New York, one of the biggest theatrical social clubs in New York, had decided to make a whirlwind tour of the principal cities of the East, all in one week. We played a different city every night. We made a one-night stand out of Chicago and New York. We were billed for Baltimore, but not for Washington. President Wilson came over from Washington to see the performance. It was the first time in theatrical history that the president of the United States came over to Baltimore, just to see a comedy show.

It was just at the time that we were having our little set-to with Mexico, and when we were at the height of our note-exchanging career with Germany and Austria.

The house was packed with the elite of Baltimore. The show was going great. It was a collection of clever skits, written mostly by our stage's greatest man, George M. Cohan, and even down to the minor bits was played by stars with big reputations. I was the least-known member of the entire aggregation, doing my little specialty with a rope, and telling jokes on national affairs, just a very ordinary little vaudeville act, by chance sandwiched in among this great array.

Finally a warden knocked at my dressing room door, and said, "You die in five minutes for kidding your country." They just literally shoved me out on the stage.

Now, by a stroke of what I call good fortune (for I will keep them always), I have a copy of the entire act that I did for President Wilson on the five times I worked for him. My first remark in Baltimore was "I am kinder nervous here tonight." Now, that is not an especially bright remark, and I don't hope to go down in history on the strength of it, but it was so apparent to the audience that I was speaking the truth that they laughed heartily at it. After all, we all love honesty,

Then I said, "I shouldn't be nervous, for this is really my second presidential appearance. The first time was when William Jennings Bryan spoke in our town once, and I was to follow his speech and do my little roping act." Well you all know that Bryan never made the White House, even though he was the Democratic candidate three times, but I heard them laughing, so I took a sly glance at the president's box, and sure enough he was laughing just as big as anyone. So I went on, "As I say, I was to follow him, but he spoke so long that it was so dark when he finished, they couldn't see my roping." That went over great, so I said, "I wonder what ever become of him?" That was all right, it got over, but still I had made no direct reference to the president.

Now, General Pershing was in Mexico at the time, and there was a lot in the papers for and against the invasion into Mexican territory to capture Pancho Villa, after he had raided an American town.

I said, "I see where they have captured Villa. Yes, they got him in the morning editions, and then the afternoon ones let him get away." Now everybody in the house before they would laugh looked at the president, to see how he was going to take it. Well, he started laughing, and they all followed suit.

"Villa raided Columbus, New Mexico. We had a man on guard that night at the post. But to show you how crooked this Villa is, he sneaked up on the opposite side. We chased him over the line five miles, but run into a lot of government red tape, and had to come back. There is some talk of getting a machine gun, if we can borrow one. The one we have now they are using to train our army with in Plattsburg. If we go to war, we will just about have to go to the trouble of getting another gun."

Now, mind you, the president was being criticized on all sides for lack of preparations, yet he sat there and led that entire audience in laughing at the gags on himself.

At that time there was talk of forming an army of two hundred thousand men. So I said, "We are going to have an army of two hundred thousand men. Henry Ford makes three hundred thousand cars every year. I think, Mr. President, we ought to at least have a man to every car. I see where they got Villa hemmed in between the Atlantic and Pacific. Now all we got to do is to stop up both ends. Pershing located him at a town called Los Quas Ka Jasbo. Now all we got to do is to locate Los Quas Ka Jasbo. . . ."

After various other ones on Mexico, I started in on European affairs, which at that time was long before we entered the war. "We are facing another crisis tonight, but our president here has had so many of them lately that he can just lay right down and sleep beside one of those things." Then I pulled the one which he afterwards repeated to various friends as the best one told on him: "President Wilson is getting along fine now to what he was a few months ago. Do you realize, people, that at one time in our negotiations with Germany he was five notes behind?"

How he did laugh at that! Well, due to him being a good fellow and setting a real example, I had the proudest and most successful night I ever had on the stage. I had lots of gags on other subjects, but the ones on him were the heartiest laughs with him; and so it was on all other occasions I played for him. He come backstage at intermission, and chatted and shook hands with all.

What he stood for and died for will be strived after for years. It will take time, for with all our boasted advancement and civilization, it's hard to stamp out selfishness and greed. For after all, nations are nothing but individuals, and you can't even stop brothers from fighting sometimes. But he helped it along a lot and what a wonderful cause to have laid down your life for! The world lost a friend. The theater lost its greatest supporter. And I lost the most distinguished person who ever laughed at my little nonsensical jokes. I looked forward to playing for him every year.

Now I have only to look on it as my greatest memory. ■

Prime Minister
Stanley Baldwin
Toasts a
Lexicographer

"I wonder if you realize, living in a haunt of learning, how much secret curiosity in the work of dictionaries exists among those whom some would call our common people."

THIS IS AN EXAMPLE of a mildly humorous and quite graceful toast by a layman to a group of specialists.

Stanley Baldwin, on June 6, 1928, was prime minister of England. He would later become known for his firmness in opposing the marriage of King Edward VIII to the divorced Wallis Simpson, and his lack of foresight as the threat of Hitler arose in Europe. At the time of this address in Goldsmiths' Hall in London, his purpose was to "do justice to the merits" of William Craigie, the foremost lexicographer of his day, in charge of bringing up to date the monumental Oxford English Dictionary with a four-volume supplement.

From rising under a mock "feeling of oppression and depression" at the seeming weightiness of his toast to concluding with an apt quotation of Samuel Johnson (who defined *lexicographer* in his great, early dictionary as "a harmless drudge"), Baldwin showed how a statesman can shape a toast with gentle humor and infuse erudition with rhetorical warmth.

Note the use of internal dialogue: "When I ask myself in what mood we are gathered here tonight . . ." He makes his quotation set up his simple peroration with "It is in that spirit" and gives a sense of form to his remarks by introducing his conclusion with "I end as I began." The word men gathered must have been charmed by the politician's skilled use of words.

☐   ☐   ☐

I have spoken at many dinners—I have never been allowed to dine without speaking—but I have never risen under such a feeling of oppression and depression as I do tonight, partly by the weight of learning in this room and partly by the weight of the toast which I have to propose.

I am expected in a few words to do justice to the merits of Professor Craigie and his coeditor and the staff, of 15,000 pages of literature, of 400,000 words, of 2,000,000 quotations, and 178 miles of type. Sir, not even Gladstone in the plenitude of his power and with the pomp of his polysyllables could have done justice to that subject in anything less than a rectorial address; my task is to put what I have to say on one of his postcards, and with all my well-known love of monosyllables I cannot do it. But perhaps before I begin I may make a confession about the Dictionary. I have not read it. But if ever a work was destined for eternity that is it, because no sooner have we, like myself, the second generation of subscribers, drawn our last check, had it cashed, and seen it honored, and had the last volume delivered, than we are told that supplements are about to begin; and Oxford, with that sure touch of the modern generation, is appealing to us to buy this new book because there is going to be a little article in it on appendicitis, and, by an obvious association of ideas, the panel doctor is not to be omitted. Indeed, we see here that all the words with a shady past are going to be added to the words of a more than doubtful future.

Professor Craigie has indeed stood by and helped to rock the cradle of our tongue, and has listened to the alliterative babbling of our ancestors in the nursery. He has watched that tongue through the ages, in its birth, its marriages, and its deaths, and in its associations with foreign countries, and he has brought it up to the time when it is, as we have known it for long, the most efficient instrument that has ever been used by man. I have not much acquaintance myself with tongues, . . . but those whose powers of comparison exceed mine—and they are many—assure me that English yields place to no tongue in its power of expressing human thought, except to the tongue of ancient Greece alone. Whoever told me that I think must have been a relation of the Greek scholar in *The Squirrel Inn*, who was so convinced that Greek would be the one surviving tongue in the days to come, outliving English, that he started by translating Dickens's novels into Greek in the hope that future generations would be able to enjoy them even as he did, and you will also remember the results of the retranslations which caused him to abandon that effort still in its infancy.

What was the genesis of this great work? It was this: it was the desire to record and to safeguard and to establish for all time the manifold riches of the English tongue. It was that desire that led a small group of men to lay the foundations of that structure whose completion we are celebrating tonight. It is half a century now since Dr. Murray had his first interview with the Delegates of the Clarendon Press. That year is not without interest to me, for it was just about that time that the words "Prime Minister" began to creep into regular official use. . . .

When I ask myself in what mood we are gathered together tonight I do not think I can express it better than it was expressed by the young man of Christ Church who, if reported truly by Bolingbroke, was overheard in his prayers acknowledging the Divine goodness in furnishing the world with makers of dictionaries. In the self-denying, lifelong labors of a succession of great scholars from Dean Trench to the present day, we remember perhaps above all others, Dr. Murray, Henry Bradley, Professor Craigie, and Dr. Onions. We remember with them the subeditors, the voluntary readers, the assistants, the pressmen, and the compositors, and, under and above and around and behind all, the ancient and beneficent University of Oxford. These men whom we celebrate tonight, and for whom Professor Craigie will speak, have defined, they have pronounced, and they have illustrated all the words in our language. They have uncovered their origins; they have dissolved their metaphors; they have unwrapped and exposed mummies; and they have laid bare in their work the soul of England and the mind of our people for a score of generations—our great people in all aspects of life, in their labor, in their worship, in their play, in their pride, and in their prejudice; our people sublime and sometimes ridiculous; our people in their prose and in their poetry, and every aspiration and idea and feeling that has clothed the living word and made it into the written symbol. That is very nearly literally true. It is quite true if we include with the Oxford Dictionary those priceless six volumes of Wright's Dialect Dictionary, which is also published by the Oxford University Press.

Long may it be before the rich gift of our people for vivid word-making is sterilized by what for the want of a better word—and if there be a better Professor Craigie will tell me—we call today, education. I wonder if you realize, living in a haunt of learning, how much secret curiosity in the work of dictionaries exists among those whom some would call our common people.

I had occasion to make some observations lately at a dinner of mariners, and I threw out the suggestion that, before the old sailing ships were forgotten, it would be well if someone would compile a dictionary of such idiomatic phrases and turns of speech and language as were used before the mast in the old sailing-ship days. And driving down two days later from Baker Street to Downing Street—a fairly prosaic voyage—my taxi driver said to me when I dismounted: "Excuse me, sir, but when is that dictionary of—er—marine—er—slang coming out?" I realized for the first time that I had been broadcast, and I said: "Well I don't know, but I don't suppose it could teach you anything." To which he replied: "Well, I'm not sure, but I should like to see it." And there spoke the love of learning.

Your work, Sir, has been achieved by the highest form of cooperative private enterprise, and except for the gift which I am happy to think this great Company [of Goldsmiths] made to Oxford the whole of the great and necessary expense has been borne by Oxford. I wish I could think that the government had had something to do with it. We had a little, through the post office. We carried millions of slips, and only lost one packet. Give us credit at least for that.

Unrivaled in completeness and unapproachable in authority is the Oxford Dictionary; as near infallibility, indeed, as we can hope to get this side of Rome, and I have every respect for you in this, that no human frailty tempers your verdict; threats of libel have not haunted your staff as nearly always haunted earlier lexicographers; and above all, in your sacred pages, from the first to the last, is found no pun such as may be found in all of the earlier editions of the great Liddell and Scott. . . .

Now I may make another confidence to you. You all remember how Betteridge in *The Moonstone* used Robinson Crusoe as his *Sors Virgiliana*. I have been using the Oxford Dictionary, and I began by trying potluck at the word "Cabinet," and I read that "Cabinet councils are a remedy worse than the disease." Then this morning—and you will see the appositeness of this in a moment—I held a cabinet from which some of my most prominent colleagues were absent, including, I may add, the Home Secretary. I opened my Oxford Dictionary, and what did I read? Under the head "Cabinet" this: "Today the Duke was forced to go to the races while the Cabinet was held." Then, trying to frame the policy for that great party of which I happen to be the leader for the moment, I looked to see what Professor Craigie and his friends say on the word "Conservative." I have here a perfect guide to my conduct through the years: "Like a great English statesman, he was constitutionally conservative, but he had the tact to perceive the conditions under which, in critical times, conservatism is possible." Then I am going to use this at the next election: "Let no one presume to identify Conservatism with reaction." This I have kept from all my friends, but I will tell you tonight in confidence: "We find girls naturally timid, prone to dependence, but born conservatives."[1] I wish my critics would read this book! I confess that one glance at "Politician" was enough: "1592, the Devil was so famous a politician that hell, which at the beginning was but an obscure village, is now become a huge city." That day, as Francesca said, "I read no farther." I made a few observations some time ago at the Literary Fund dinner about a book, and in a few hours it was sold out and had to be reprinted. I hope to compensate for the rather lengthy speech I am making tonight by achieving a similar result for the Oxford Press.

Now I have only one or two more words to add. Lord Oxford once said that if he were cast on a desert island, and could only choose one author for company, he would have the forty volumes of Balzac. I choose the Dictionary every time. Like Ezekiel in the valley of dry bones, I should pray for the four winds to breathe upon those words, that they might emerge and stand upon their feet an exceeding great army. Our histories, our novels, our poems, our plays—they are all in this one book. I could live with your Dictionary, Professor Craigie. I choose it, and I think that my choice would be justified. It is a work of endless fascination. It is true that I have not read it—perhaps I never shall—but that does not mean that I do not often go to it.

Let me remind you of those words which Dr. Johnson used in his famous Preface about translators in his time which I think are apt today: "If the changes that we fear be thus irresistible . . . it remains that we retard what we cannot repel; that we palliate what we cannot cure. Life may be lengthened by care, though death cannot be ultimately defeated; tongues, like Governments, have a natural tendency to degeneration; we have long preserved our constitution; let us make some struggle for our language."

It is in that spirit of devotion to our language as the great and noble instrument of our national life and literature that the editors and the staff of the Oxford Dictionary have labored. They have labored so well that, so far from lowering the high standard with which the work began, they have sought to raise it as the work advanced. They have given us of their best. There can be no worldly recompense. ∎

---

[1] Alluding to the Franchise Act of 1928.

George Bernard Shaw
Salutes His Friend
Albert Einstein

"THE heavenly bodies go in curves because that is the natural way for them to go, and so the whole Newtonian universe crumpled up and was succeeded by the Einstein universe."

DUBLIN-BORN BRITISH DRAMATIST George Bernard Shaw admired upsetters of applecarts, an activity he engaged in both as socialist essayist and as author of *Pygmalion* and *Mrs. Warren's Profession.* Shaw and Einstein met in 1921; Shaw looked on physicist Albert Einstein, twenty-six years his junior, as the man who annihilated the scientific establishment's tidy Newtonian world.

"We ought to have declared war on Germany," Shaw said, "the moment Hitler's police stole Einstein's violin." At the Savoy Hotel in London on October 28, 1930, Shaw spoke at a dinner honoring the scientist and raising funds for indigent European Jews. In a brief toast, he gave other laymen an inkling of the meaning of Einstein's work.

□   □   □

Napoleon and other great men were makers of empires, but these eight men whom I am about to mention were makers of universes, and their hands were not stained with the blood of their fellow men. I go back twenty-five hundred years, and how many can I count in that period? I can count them on the fingers of my two hands.

Pythagoras, Ptolemy, Kepler, Copernicus, Aristotle, Galileo, Newton, and Einstein—and I still have two fingers left vacant.

Even among those eight men I must make a distinction. I have called them makers of the universe, but some of them were only repairers. Newton made a universe which lasted for three hundred years. Einstein has made a universe, which I suppose you want me to say will never stop, but I don't know how long it will last.

These great men, they have been the makers of one side of humanity, which has two sides. We call the one side religion, and we call the other science. Religion is always right. Religion protects us against that great problem which we all must face. Science is always wrong; it is the very artifice of men. Science can never solve one problem without raising ten more problems.

What have all of those great men been doing? Each in turn claimed the other was wrong, and now you are expecting me to say that Einstein proved that Newton was wrong. But you forget that when science reached Newton, science came up against that extraordinary Englishman. That had never happened to it before.

Newton lent a power so extraordinary that if I was speaking fifteen years ago, as I am old enough to have done, I would have said that he had the greatest mind that ever man was endowed with. Combine the light of that wonderful mind with credulity, with superstition. He knew his people; he knew his language; he knew his own folk; he knew a lot of things; he knew that an honest bargain was a square deal and an honest man was one who gave a square deal.

He knew his universe; he knew that it consisted of heavenly bodies that were in motion, and he also knew the one thing you cannot do to anything whatsoever is to make it move in a straight line. In other words, motion will not go in a straight line.

Mere fact will never stop an Englishman. Newton invented a straight line, and that was the law of gravitation, and when he had invented this, he had created a universe which was wonderful in itself. When applying his wonderful genius, when he had completed a book of that universe, what sort of book was it? It was a book which told you the station of all the heavenly bodies. It showed the rate at which they were traveling; it showed the exact hour at which they would arrive at such and such a point to make an eclipse. It was not a magical marvelous thing; it was a matter-of-fact thing.

For three hundred years we believed in that Newtonian universe as I suppose no system has been believed in before. I know I was educated in it and was brought up to believe in it firmly. Then a young professor came along. He said a lot of things, and we called him a blasphemer. He claimed Newton's theory of the apple was wrong.

He said, "Newton did not know what happened to the apple, and I can prove this when the next eclipse comes."

We said, "The next thing you will be doing is questioning the law of gravitation."

The young professor said, "No, I mean no harm to the law of gravitation, but for my part, I can go without it."

"What do you mean, go without it?"

He said, "I can tell you about that afterward."

The world is not a rectilinear world: It is a curvilinear world. The heavenly bodies go in curves because that is the natural way for them to go, and so the whole Newtonian universe crumpled up and was succeeded by the Einstein universe. Here in England, he is a wonderful man.

This man is not challenging the fact of science; he is challenging the action of science. Not only is he challenging the action of science, but the action of science has surrendered to his challenge.

Now, ladies and gentlemen, are you ready for the toast? I drink to the greatest of our contemporaries, Einstein. ■

India's Prime Minister Jawaharlal Nehru Delivers the Eulogy for Gandhi

"In ages to come, centuries and maybe millennia after us, people will think of this generation when this man of God trod on earth. . . . Let us be worthy of him."

KNOWN TO HIS LOYAL Indian followers as the Mahatma (variously translated as "Great Soul" or "Teacher"), Mohandas K. Gandhi spent his lifetime perfecting the techniques of nonviolence and "fasts unto death" to achieve political goals. In 1948, however, he was shot to death by a Hindu extremist who held him responsible for the 1947 partition of India into the nations of India and Pakistan, a partition that Gandhi himself had fought without success.

In the aftermath of Gandhi's assassination, Jawaharlal Nehru, the prime minister of India, stood before the Constituent Assembly in New Delhi to offer a stirring tribute to the dead leader, who had been his life-long friend. Although their vision of India was not the same—the Mahatma hoped for an agrarian society, Nehru for an industrial nation—the two were united in opposition to British rule.

Nehru's eulogy for Gandhi, delivered on February 2, 1948, makes extended use of poetic language ("A glory has departed") and repetition ("All we know is that there was a glory and that it is no more; all we know is that for the moment there is darkness"). In describing the sadness that pervades India at Gandhi's passing, Nehru acknowledges the widespread feeling of loss and honestly admits, "I do not know when we shall be able to get rid of it." He does, however, offer the consolation of Gandhi's enlighten-ment; throughout the eulogy, in fact, he stresses the imagery of light and darkness to illuminate the loss of "this man of divine fire."

□   □   □

. . . A glory has departed and the sun that warmed and brightened our lives has set, and we shiver in the cold and dark. Yet he would not have us feel this way. After all, that glory that we saw for all these years, that man with the divine fire, changed us also—and such as we are, we have been molded by him during these years; and out of that divine fire many of us also took a small spark which strengthened and made us work to some extent on the lines that he fashioned. And so if we praise him, our words seem rather small, and if we praise him, to some extent we also praise ourselves. Great men and eminent men have monuments in bronze and marble set up for them, but this man of divine fire man-aged in his lifetime to become enshrined in millions and millions of hearts so that all of us became somewhat of the stuff that he was made of, though to an infinitely lesser degree. He spread out in this way all over India, not in palaces only, or in select places or in assemblies, but in every hamlet and hut of the lowly and those who suffer. He lives in the hearts of millions and he will live for immemorial ages.

What, then, can we say about him except to feel humble on this occa-sion? To praise him we are not worthy—to praise him whom we could not follow adequately and sufficiently. It is almost doing him an injustice just to pass him by with words when he demanded work and labor and sacrifice from us; in a large measure he made this country, during the last thirty years or more, attain to heights of sacrifice which in that particular domain have never been equaled elsewhere. He succeeded in that. Yet ultimately things happened which no doubt made him suffer tremendously, though his tender face never lost its smile and he never spoke a harsh word to anyone. Yet, he must have suffered—suffered for the failing of this generation whom he had trained, suffered because we went away from the path that he had shown us. And ultimately the hand of a child of his—for he, after all, is as much a child of his as any other Indian—the hand of a child of his struck him down.

Long ages afterwards history will judge of this period that we have passed through. It will judge of the successes and the failures—we are too near it to be proper judges and to understand what has happened and what has not happened. All we know is that there was a glory and that it is no more; all we know is that for the moment there is darkness, not so dark certainly, because when we look into our hearts we still find the living flame which he lighted there. And if those living flames exist, there will not be darkness in this land, and we shall be able, with our effort, remembering him and following his path, to illumine this land again, small as we are, but still with the fire that he instilled into us.

He was perhaps the greatest symbol of the India of the past, and may I say, of the India of the future, that we could have had. We stand on this perilous edge of the present, between that past and the future to be, and we face all manner of perils. And the greatest peril is sometimes the lack of faith which comes to us, the sense of frustration that comes to us, the sinking of the heart and of the spirit that comes to us when we see ideals go overboard, when we see the great things that we talked about somehow pass into empty words, and life taking a different course. Yet, I do believe that perhaps this period will pass soon enough.

He has gone, and all over India there is a feeling of having been left desolate and forlorn. All of us sense that feeling, and I do not know when we shall be able to get rid of it. And yet together with that feeling there is also a feeling of proud thankfulness that it has been given to us of this generation to be associated with this mighty person. In ages to come, centuries and maybe millennia after us, people will think of this generation when this man of God trod on earth, and will think of us who, however small, could also follow his path and tread the holy ground where his feet had been. Let us be worthy of him. ∎

John F. Kennedy, in Praise of Robert Frost, Celebrates the Arts in America

"I look forward to an America which commands respect throughout the world not only for its strength but for its civilization as well."

LESS THAN A MONTH BEFORE HIS ASSASSINATION, President John F. Kennedy spoke at Amherst College, in Massachusetts, on October 27, 1963, to praise American poet Robert Frost. The poet, a striking figure with windblown hair at the inauguration of our thirty-fifth president, had died in January 1963, and the tribute that Kennedy paid him became a memorable statement on the value of the arts in American society. Quotations from the president's speech, in fact, may be found carved in his Washington memorial, the Kennedy Center.

President Kennedy's speech for this formal occasion emphasized poetry ("he knew the midnight as well as the high noon") and balance ("A nation reveals itself not only by the men it produces but also by the men it honors, the men it remembers"). He freely cited Frost's poetry, and he also quoted poet Archibald MacLeish, who attended the ceremony honoring Frost.

Particularly effective is Kennedy's use of a favored construction of speechwriters. His anaphora in beginning a series of sentences with "I look forward" dates back at least to 1876, in the repeated "I see a world" clauses that were used by Robert Green Ingersoll.

□   □   □

. . . This day, devoted to the memory of Robert Frost, offers an opportunity for reflection which is prized by politicians as well as by others and even by poets. For Robert Frost was one of the granite figures of our time in America. He was supremely two things—an artist and an American.

A nation reveals itself not only by the men it produces but also by the men it honors, the men it remembers.

In America our heroes have customarily run to men of large accomplishments. But today this college and country honors a man whose contribution was not to our size but to our spirit; not to our political beliefs but to our insight; not to our self-esteem but to our self-comprehension.

In honoring Robert Frost, we therefore can pay honor to the deepest sources of our national strength. That strength takes many forms, and the most obvious forms are not always the most significant.

The men who create power make an indispensable contribution to the nation's greatness. But the men who question power make a contribution just as indispensable, especially when that questioning is disinterested.

For they determine whether we use power or power uses us. Our national strength matters; but the spirit which informs and controls our strength matters just as much. This was the special significance of Robert Frost.

He brought an unsparing instinct for reality to bear on the platitudes and pieties of society. His sense of the human tragedy fortified him against self-deception and easy consolation.

"I have been," he wrote, "one acquainted with the night."

And because he knew the midnight as well as the high noon, because he understood the ordeal as well as the triumph of the human spirit, he gave his age strength with which to overcome despair.

At bottom he held a deep faith in the spirit of man. And it's hardly an accident that Robert Frost coupled poetry and power. For he saw poetry as the means of saving power from itself.

When power leads man toward arrogance, poetry reminds him of his limitations. When power narrows the areas of man's concern, poetry reminds him of the richness and diversity of his existence. When power corrupts, poetry cleanses.

For art establishes the basic human truths which must serve as the touchstones of our judgment. The artist, however faithful to his personal vision of reality, becomes the last champion of the individual mind and sensibility against an intrusive society and an officious state.

The great artist is thus a solitary figure. He has, as Frost said, "a lover's quarrel with the world." In pursuing his perceptions of reality, he must often sail against the currents of his time. This is not a popular role.

If Robert Frost was much honored during his lifetime, it was because a good many preferred to ignore his darker truths.

Yet in retrospect we see how the artist's fidelity has strengthened the fiber of our national life. If sometimes our great artists have been the most critical of our society, it is because their sensitivity and their concern for justice, which must motivate any true artist, makes him aware that our nation falls short of its highest potential.

I see little of more importance to the future of our country and our civilization than full recognition of the place of the artist. If art is to nourish the roots of our culture, society must set the artist free to follow his vision wherever it takes him.

We must never forget that art is not a form of propaganda; it is a form of truth. And as Mr. MacLeish once remarked of poets, "There is nothing worse for our trade than to be in style."

In free society, art is not a weapon and it does not belong to the sphere of polemics and ideology. Artists are not engineers of the soul.

It may be different elsewhere. But democratic society—in it—the highest duty of the writer, the composer, the artist is to remain true to himself and to let the chips fall where they may.

In serving his vision of the truth, the artist best serves his nation. And the nation which disdains the mission of art invites the fate of Robert Frost's hired man—"the fate of having nothing to look backward to with pride and nothing to look forward to with hope."

I look forward to a great future for America—a future in which our country will match its military strength with our moral restraint, its wealth with our wisdom, its power with our purpose.

I look forward to an America which will not be afraid of grace and beauty, which will protect the beauty of our national environment, which will preserve the great old American houses and squares and parks of our national past and which will build handsome and balanced cities for our future.

I look forward to an America which will reward achievement in the arts as we reward achievement in business or statecraft.

I look forward to an America which will steadily raise the standards of artistic accomplishment and which will steadily enlarge cultural opportunities for all of our citizens.

And I look forward to an America which commands respect throughout the world not only for its strength but for its civilization as well.

And I look forward to a world which will be safe not only for democracy and diversity but also for personal distinction.

Robert Frost was often skeptical about projects for human improvement. Yet I do not think he would disdain this hope.

As he wrote during the uncertain days of the Second War:

> Take human nature altogether since time began . . .
> And it must be a little more in favor of man,

Say a fraction of one percent at the very least . . .
Our hold on the planet wouldn't have so increased.

Because of Mr. Frost's life and work, because of the life and work of this college, our hold on this planet has increased. ■

Senator Robert F. Kennedy Speaks after the Assassination of Reverend Martin Luther King, Jr.

"LET us dedicate ourselves to what the Greeks wrote so many years ago: to tame the savageness of man and to make gentle the life of this world."

WHILE CAMPAIGNING IN INDIANAPOLIS for the Democratic nomination for president, Senator Robert F. Kennedy was told of the assassination on April 4, 1968, of the nation's preeminent black leader, Reverend Martin Luther King, Jr. The senator, scheduled to speak to a black audience that night, was warned by police that the crowd would be furious and might be dangerous; however, with a shield of personal courage and the memory of the loss of his own brother to an assassin's bullet, he went and broke the news to the crowd.

As attorney general, Robert Kennedy had approved the FBI wiretapping of Dr. King, which led to even more intimate surveillance by state and local police; this action may have been in the back of his mind as he shared his shock and sorrow with a stunned audience. His statement "It is not the end of violence" was prescient; Robert Kennedy was gunned down in California three months later.

□   □   □

I have bad news for you, for all of our fellow citizens, and people who love peace all over the world, and that is that Martin Luther King was shot and killed tonight.

Martin Luther King dedicated his life to love and to justice for his fellow human beings, and he died because of that effort.

In this difficult day, in this difficult time for the United States, it is perhaps well to ask what kind of a nation we are and what direction we want to move in. For those of you who are black—considering the evidence there evidently is that there were white people who were responsible—you can be filled with bitterness, with hatred, and a desire for revenge. We can move in that direction as a country, in great polarization—black people amongst black, white people amongst white, filled with hatred toward one another.

Or we can make an effort, as Martin Luther King did, to understand and to comprehend, and to replace that violence, that stain of bloodshed that has spread across our land, with an effort to understand with compassion and love.

For those of you who are black and are tempted to be filled with hatred and distrust at the injustice of such an act, against all white people, I can only say that I feel in my own heart the same kind of feeling. I had a member of my family killed, but he was killed by a white man. But we have to make an effort in the United States, we have to make an effort to understand, to go beyond these rather difficult times.

My favorite poet was Aeschylus. He wrote, "In our sleep, pain which cannot forget falls drop by drop upon the heart until, in our own despair, against our will, comes wisdom through the awful grace of God."

What we need in the United States is not division; what we need in the United States is not hatred; what we need in the United States is not violence or lawlessness but love and wisdom, and compassion toward one another, and a feeling of justice towards those who still suffer within our country, whether they be white or they be black.

So I shall ask you tonight to return home, to say a prayer for the family of Martin Luther King, that's true, but more importantly to say a prayer for our own country, which all of us love—a prayer for understanding and that compassion of which I spoke.

We can do well in this country. We will have difficult times. We've had difficult times in the past. We will have difficult times in the future. It is not the end of violence; it is not the end of lawlessness; it is not the end of disorder.

But the vast majority of white people and the vast majority of black people in this country want to live together, want to improve the quality of our life, and want justice for all human beings who abide in our land.

Let us dedicate ourselves to what the Greeks wrote so many years ago: to tame the savageness of man and to make gentle the life of this world.

Let us dedicate ourselves to that, and say a prayer for our country and for our people. ■

Electronic Journalist
Eric Sevareid Remembers
Rocket Scientist
Wernher von Braun

"WITHOUT this man, Hitler would not have held out as long as he did; without him, Americans would not have got to the moon as soon as they did."

HOW DO YOU ASSESS a man's life when that man has been a force for both good and bad? An assessment is not a eulogy; you set forth both and hope one can illuminate the other.

When German-born rocket engineer Wernher von Braun died on June 16, 1977, CBS newsman Eric Sevareid provided a memorable depiction of the man. Aired the following day, Sevareid's commentary celebrates the accomplishments of von Braun as a scientist and pioneer in developing spacecraft; at the same time, however, it acknowledges the darker aspects of von Braun's work in helping Hitler develop weapons of mass destruction.

Through contrasting words and images, Sevareid develops a thoughtful analysis of von Braun's contributions. The journalist depicts the scientist in seven short paragraphs, with language that is at times practical ("Counting up the moral balance sheet"), at times lyrical ("There's always a dream to begin with, and the dream is always benign").

What emerges is a complex vision of von Braun, celebrated in the ultimate juxtaposition of "outer space" and "inner man."

Eric Sevareid died in July 1992.

□   □   □

A generation ago, the Allied military, using the old-fashioned airplane, did their best to kill the German, his associates, and their new-fashioned rockets which were killing the people in London. Yesterday. Wernher von Braun, American citizen, died peacefully in George Washington's hometown of Alexandria, Virginia.

Without this man, Hitler would not have held out as long as he did; without him, Americans would not have got to the moon as soon as they did.

Counting up the moral balance sheet for this man's life would be a difficult exercise. The same could be said for the Wright brothers. Perhaps the exercise is meaningless. Airplanes would have come anyway from someone, somewhere, and so would modern rockets. And what was done with these instruments would have been equally beyond the control of the individuals who first made them work.

There's always a dream to begin with, and the dream is always benign. Charles Lindbergh, as a young man, saw the airplane not only as an instrument to liberate man from the plodding earth but as a force for peacefully uniting the human race through faster communication and the common adventure. Now its benefits are measured against its role in returning warfare to the savagery of the Middle Ages, burning whole cities with their occupants.

And rockets are now the easiest instrument for sending the ultimate atomic weapon against any spot on the globe. They've also put men into space; and von Braun, like Lindbergh with the upper atmosphere, saw goodness in that. He said once, when men manning an orbital station can view our planet as a planet among planets, on that day fratricidal war will be banished from the star on which we live.

Lindbergh was wrong about aircraft in the atmosphere; there's no reason to believe that von Braun was right about spacecraft in space.

Everything in space, von Braun said, obeys the laws of physics. If you know these laws and obey them, space will treat you kindly. The difficulty is that man brings the laws of his own nature into space. The issue is how man treats man. The problem does not lie in outer space, but where it's always been: on terra firma in inner man. ∎

President Richard M. Nixon Defines "Politician" in Eulogizing Senator Everett Dirksen

"As he could persuade, he could be persuaded."

A PERSONAL NOTE from the anthologist: as a Nixon White House speechwriter, I turned out a speech for Senate Minority Leader Everett McKinley Dirksen, hailing the first hundred days of the Nixon administration. In it, I had the senator saying, "We finally have a firm hand on the rudder of the Ship of State." He passed on to me this comment from a constituent: "If there's a firm hand on the rudder, then somebody's drowning and nobody's minding the tiller."

I felt guilty about that mixed-up metaphor, and when the Illinois senator with the mellifluous voice and carefully tousled hair died, I volunteered to write the eulogy President Nixon was to deliver in the Capitol Rotunda on September 9, 1969. Mr. Nixon returned my first draft, a respectable but commonplace effort with the comment "Ev was a politician, in the best sense. Show here what that word meant to him." I drafted a passage defining the Dirksen idea of an honorable politician, which the president edited and used as the centerpiece of his tribute. Mr. Nixon added his own Sophoclean closing, which he has used for many years in most of his tributes and memorials.

The reference to Dirksen's love of the marigold had to do with his annual attempt to have it named our national flower; that oratorical interlude in Senate business is on p. 565.

□   □   □

When Daniel Webster died more than a century ago, a man who differed strongly with him on many public issues rose in Congress to say this in eulogy, "Our great men are the common property of the country."

Everett Dirksen, of Illinois, was and is the "common property" of all the fifty states.

Senator Dirksen belonged to all of us because he always put his country first. He was an outspoken partisan, he was an individualist of the first rank, but he put his nation before himself and before his party. . . .

Through four presidencies, through the adult life of most Americans living today, Everett Dirksen has had a hand in shaping almost every important law that affects our lives.

Everett Dirksen was a politician in the finest sense of that much abused word. If he were here, I think he might put it this way:

A politician knows that more important than the bill that is proposed is the law that is passed.

A politician knows that his friends are not always his allies, and that his adversaries are not his enemies.

A politician knows how to make the process of democracy work, and loves the intricate workings of the democratic system.

A politician knows not only how to count votes, but how to make his vote count.

A politician knows that his words are his weapons, but that his word is his bond.

A politician knows that only if he leaves room for discussion and room for concession can he gain room for maneuver.

A politician knows that the best way to be a winner is to make the other side feel it does not have to be a loser.

And a politician—in the Dirksen tradition—knows both the name of the game and the rules of the game, and he seeks his ends through the time-honored democratic means.

By being that kind of politician, this "Man of the Minority" earned the respect and affection of the majority. And by the special way he gave leadership to legislation, he added grace and elegance and courtliness to the word "politician."

That is how he became the leader of a minority, and one of the leaders of our nation. And that is why, when the Senate worked its way, Everett Dirksen so often worked his way. . . .

Some will remember his voice—that unforgettable voice—that rolled as deep and majestically as the river that defines the western border of the state of Illinois he loved so well. Others will remember the unfailing—often self-deprecating—sense of humor, which proved that a man of serious purpose need never take himself too seriously.

Others will remember the mastery of language, the gift of oratory that placed him in a class with Bryan and Churchill, showing, as only he would put it, that "the oil can is mightier than the sword."

But as we do honor to his memory, let us never forget the single quality that made him unique, the quality that made him powerful made him beloved: the quality of character.

Everett Dirksen cultivated an appearance that made him seem old-fashioned, an incarnation of a bygone year. But that quality of character is as modern as a Saturn 5.

As he could persuade, he could be persuaded. His respect for other points of view lent weight to his own point of view. He was not afraid to change his position if he were persuaded that he had been wrong. That tolerance and sympathy were elements of his character, and that character gained him the affection and esteem of millions of his fellow Americans.

We shall always remember Everett Dirksen in the terms he used to describe his beloved marigolds: hardy, vivid, exuberant, colorful—and uniquely American.

To his family, his staff, and his legion of friends who knew and loved Everett Dirksen, I would like to add a personal word.

There are memorable moments we will never know again—those eloquent speeches, the incomparable anecdotes, those wonderfully happy birthday parties.

But he, least of all, would want this to be a sad occasion. With his dramatic sense of history, I can hear him now speaking of the glory of this moment.

As a man of politics, he knew both victory and defeat.

As a student of philosophy, he knew the triumph of and the tragedy and the misery of life.

And as a student of history, he knew that some men achieve greatness, others are not recognized for their greatness until after their death. Only a privileged few live to hear the favorable verdict of history on their careers.

Two thousand years ago the poet Sophocles wrote, "One must wait until the evening to see how splendid the day has been."

We who were privileged to be his friends can take comfort in the fact that Everett Dirksen—in the rich evening of his life, his leadership unchallenged, his mind clear, his great voice still powerful across the land—could look back upon his life and say, "The day has indeed been splendid." ■

President Jimmy Carter Salutes His Good Friend Hubert H. Humphrey

"I'LL always remember Senator Humphrey sitting there . . . with brownie all over his face."

"ELOQUENCE" IS not a word associated with President Carter. After his inaugural address, he walked instead of riding in his parade, triggering the assessment from this quarter that the whole day's work was pedestrian. Yet his "the" speech—the one that he made and remade throughout his campaign to the nomination—touched a chord with many in that post-

Watergate period. "All I want is the same thing you want," he told the California State Senate in May of 1976. "To have a nation with a government that is as good and honest and decent and competent and compassionate and as filled with love as are the American people."

He delivered set speeches stiffly, smiling at the wrong moments, but could come across warmly in recounting anecdotes. On December 2, 1977, President Carter appeared before a large Washington dinner raising funds for Hubert Humphrey's institute at the University of Minnesota. He told a few personal stories about his relationship with the guest of honor; the low-key, self-deprecating humor went over well and the three episodes about Humphrey's brief and sometimes unknowing relationship with three members of the Carter family—especially because of the mental pictures evoked—make a lasting impression.

□   □   □

He is a man who has touched my life and that of my family, as I'm sure he's touched almost everyone here, in a strange and very delightful way. And I'm going to tell you just a few brief instances that occurred, actually, long before I had any dreams of coming to Washington myself.

The first time I heard about Senator Humphrey was when I was in the navy, and he made a famous speech at the Democratic National Convention. He was quite well known in Georgia. I don't think anyone else has kept more Georgia politicians from seeing the end of a Democratic convention than Senator Humphrey has, because it got so that every time he walked in, they walked out and came back home.

So, in 1964, when he became the vice-presidential candidate, in Georgia, it wasn't a very popular thing to be for the Johnson-Humphrey slate. My mother, Lillian, ran the Sumter County Johnson-Humphrey headquarters. And I could always tell when my mother was coming down the road, because she was in a brand-new automobile with the windows broken out, the radio antenna tied in a knot, and the car painted with soap.

In that campaign, Hubert and Muriel came down to south Georgia to Moultrie for a Democratic rally. And because of my mother's loyalty, she was given the honor of picking up Muriel at the airport. And Rosalynn and my mother and Muriel and my sister Gloria went down to Moultrie to attend the rally. Senator Humphrey made a speech, and they had a women's reception for Muriel. And they were riding around that south Georgia town getting ready for the reception. Everybody in town was very excited. And as Muriel approached the site, she said, "Are any black women invited to the reception?"

For a long time no one spoke, and finally my sister said, "I don't know." She knew quite well that they weren't. And Muriel said, "I'm not going in." So, they stopped the car, and my sister Gloria went inside to check and let the hostess know that Muriel was not coming to the reception. But in a few minutes, Gloria came back and said, "Mrs. Humphrey, it's okay." So, she went in and, sure enough, there were several black ladies there at the reception. And Muriel never knew until now that the maids just took off their aprons for the occasion. But that was the first integrated reception in south Georgia, Muriel, and you are responsible for it.

Ten or eleven years ago, when I was not in political office at all, Senator Humphrey was vice-president. He had been to Europe on a long, tedious, very successful trip. And he came down to Atlanta, Georgia, to visit in the home of a friend named Marvin Shube. And I was invited there to meet him, which was a great honor for me. I have never yet met a Democratic president, and he was the only Democratic vice-president I had ever met. And I stood there knowing that he was very weary because he had just returned from Europe. But he answered the eager questions of those Georgia friends until quite late in the morning, about two o'clock. And he was very well briefed, because when I walked in the room, he said, "Young man, I understand that your mother is in the Peace Corps in India."

And I said, "Yes, sir, that's right." He said, "Well I've been very interested in the Peace Corps. The idea originally came from me, and I've been proud to see it put into effect." He said, "Where's your mother?" And I said, "She's near Bombay." He said, "How's she getting along?" I said, "Well she's quite lonely, sir. She's been there about six months, and she's not seen anybody, even the Peace Corps officials. She's in a little town called Vikhroli."

About a month later, I got a letter from my mother. She was in her room one evening, and the head of the Peace Corps in India had driven up to the little town of Vikhroli. He came in and asked my mother if she needed anything. She said, no, she was getting along quite well, but she would like to go over to Bombay. He said, "Well, can I take you in shopping, Mrs. Carter?" She said, "Yes, I'd like that." So, they went in, and he bought her a very fine supper and brought her back to Vikhroli. When he got out, he handed her a fifth of very good bourbon. And he turned around to get in the car to leave, and he finally turned back to her and said, "By the way, Miss Lillian, who in the hell are you, anyway?" And that's a true story. It was not until later that my mother knew who she was. She was a friend of Hubert Humphrey.

And, of course, the next time he crossed my path was in 1968 when he was our nominee for president. And all of us in this room went through that year of tragedy together when he was not elected to be the leader of our country. And I think he felt then an urging to be loyal to his president and, unfortunately, many people were not that loyal to him. And his loss was our nation's even greater loss in 1968.

The next time I saw him was when I was governor. He came to our home in 1972. All the candidates just happened to stop by to see me that year, and my daughter, Amy, was about four years old. And most of the ones who would come into the mansion—she stayed away from them, having an early aversion to politicians. But when Senator Humphrey came in, she loved him instantly.

And I'll never forget sitting in the front presidential suite of the Georgia governor's mansion, a very beautiful room, trying to talk to Senator Humphrey. Amy came in eating a soft brownie, and she climbed up on his lap without any timidity at all. In a very natural way, he put his arm around her as though she was his own grandchild. And I'll always remember Senator Humphrey sitting there talking to me about politics and about the campaign, smiling often, with brownie all over his face. And each time he frowned, brownie crumbs fell to the floor. And Amy loved him then and has loved him ever since. But I think she recognized in him the qualities that have aroused the love of so many people.

And then, of course, last year all I could hear everywhere I went when I said, "Would you help me become president?" almost invariably they would say, "Well, my first preference is Hubert Humphrey. If he doesn't run, I'll support you." And there again, I learned on a nationwide basis the relationship between Senator Humphrey and the people of this country.

But I think the most deep impression I have of my good friend Hubert Humphrey is since I've been president. I've seen him in the Oval Office early in the morning. I've seen him in meetings with other congressional leaders. I've called him on the phone when I was in trouble. I've gotten his quiet and private and sound advice. And I've come to recognize that all the attributes that I love about America are resident in him. And I'm proud to be the president of a nation that loves a man like Hubert Humphrey and is loved so deeply by him. ■

Senator Daniel P. Moynihan Spoofs Abstractionist Art at a Dedication Ceremony

"AESTHETIC transubstantiation . . . at once elusive yet ineluctable. . . ."

PAT MOYNIHAN, academic turned White House domestic adviser and later senator from New York, made his mark as a supporter of the dignity of ethnicity and the creator of family assistance programs. He also had an off-beat sense of humor, which led him to the sponsorship of the thirty-two-letter "floccinaucinihilipilificationism" (meaning "the action of estimating as worthless") as "the longest word in the English language."

At the Hirshhorn Museum and Sculpture Garden, in the nation's capital on July 19, 1978, he was asked for dedicatory remarks on the receipt of the massive sculpture *Isis* by the artist Mark di Suvero. The hard-to-ignore work is apparently the impression of the severed brow of a Grimsby trawler, appropriately given to the nation by the Institute of Scrap Iron and Steel. The senator's dedication was both succinct and mouth filling.

□   □   □

As chairman of the board of the Hirshhorn Museum and Sculpture Garden it falls to me to accept this splendid gift from the Institute of Scrap Iron and Steel, and I recall that on the occasion that Margaret Fuller declared, "I accept the universe," Carlyle remarked that she had better.

Isis achieves an aesthetic transubstantiation of that which is at once elusive yet ineluctable in the modern sensibility.

Transcending socialist realism with an unequaled abstractionist range, Mr. di Suvero brings to the theme of recycling both the hard-edge reality of the modern world and the transcendent fecundity of the universe itself; a lasting assertion both of the fleetingness of the living, and the permanence of life; a consummation before which we stand in consistorial witness.

It will be with us a long time. ∎

Actor-Director Orson Welles Eulogizes Another Hollywood Legend, Darryl F. Zanuck

"IF I committed some abominable crime, and if all the police in the world were after me . . . there was one man and only one man I could come to. . . . He would not have made a speech about the good of the industry. . . . He would not have been mealymouthed or put me aside. He would have hid me under the bed."

ORSON WELLES IS REMEMBERED as the star and director of *Citizen Kane*, considered by many the greatest movie ever made, and as the radio producer and actor who, on Halloween eve, panicked a huge audience with his all-too-realistic broadcast of an invasion of Earth by Martians. European audiences hailed his portrayal of the racketeer Harry Lime in *The Third Man*, but his later years were spent fighting for financing and acting in lesser roles. In a moment of bitterness, he said that his business was "about 2 percent moviemaking and 98 percent hustling."

Darryl F. Zanuck is remembered as the legendary movie producer who began in the silent era with *Rin Tin Tin*, headed production of the first talkie, *The Jazz Singer*, launched Twentieth Century–Fox in the thirties, winning Oscars for *Gentlemen's Agreement*, *All About Eve*, and, after a six-year series of flops, an Oscar nomination for *The Longest Day*. He was an eccentric and often tyrannical boss; the title of his biography is *Don't Say Yes Until I Finish Talking*. After saving his studio from the disastrous budgetary overruns of *Cleopatra*, he fired his son for financial mismanagement and was himself forced from power a decade before his death.

Welles, a writer as well as a star, delivered this eulogy of Zanuck on December 27, 1979, at the Westwood United Methodist Church in Los Angeles, in the voice that first scared and thrilled radio audiences as "The Shadow" in the 1930s. It begins with a gripping anecdote about Winston Churchill's funeral, for which Churchill wrote the script: in England, noted the film director in his industry's lingo, "they give you the final cut."

The eulogy is notable for what it leaves out. Welles does not recount the movies Zanuck produced or the stars he worked with, as did the obituaries. He dispenses with the deceased's harsh reputation in a few lines: "Darryl didn't sign on to be the recreation director of a summer camp. Of course he was tough. . . . But unlike many of the others, he was never cruel." He closes on the quality of friendship and personal loyalty in adversity, which both men had and suffered. Unlike many of Zanuck's self-protective corporate peers, testified his friend Welles in a conclusion of seven short, declarative sentences, "He would have hid me under the bed."

□   □   □

At Winston Churchill's funeral, there was a moment when the coffin was to be carried out of Westminster Abbey and onto a barge for a trip up the Thames River. A special group of pallbearers from the various military services in Great Britain was selected for this. One, a sailor, broke his ankle carrying the coffin down the stone steps of the Abbey. For a moment it seemed that the coffin would drop to the ground, but it was safely carried onto the barge.

Afterward, officials said to the sailor, "How did you manage to go on?" And the sailor said, "I would have carried him all over London."

That's the way I feel about my friend Darryl Zanuck.

Churchill wrote the script for his own funeral. Lord Mountbatten recently did the same thing in England—in England, if you're going to have a state funeral, they let you do that. They give you what amounts to a final cut. We don't have state funerals in our movie community, but if we did, Darryl would certainly have been given one—and he would have produced it. And what a show that would have been. Virginia and Dick have reminded me that Darryl himself would not wish this occasion to be too lugubrious. That's true. I'm pretty sure that if he was the producer in charge of this occasion, Darryl would have wished for us all to leave this gathering with lightened spirits. The trouble is that I'm the wrong man for that job—I can't find anything cheerful to say about the loss of my friend.

To understand the special nature of his contribution, we must understand the full meaning of the word "producer" in Darryl's day. In the Golden Age of Hollywood, it meant something quite different than it does now. There were producers assigned to each movie, and then there was the man in charge of all the movies. In Darryl's day that was a lot of movies—forty, fifty, sixty, seventy feature pictures a year. He was one of the legendary tycoons presiding over production.

The whole point about Darryl was that he did not just preside. He did so very much more than preside. Of all the big-boss producers, Darryl was unquestionably the man with the greatest gifts—true personal, professional, and artistic gifts for the filmmaking process itself. He began as a writer and in a sense he never stopped functioning as a writer. Others may have matched him as a star maker, but with all of Darryl's flair for the magic personalities, his first commitment was always to the story. For Darryl that was what it was to make a film: to tell a story.

God bless him for that. With half a hundred and more stories to tell every dozen months, this great storyteller was, of necessity, an editor and a great editor. There never was an editor in our business to touch him.

Every great career is a roller coaster and Darryl had his disasters. He knew eclipse. He knew comebacks and triumphs. It was a giant roller coaster. And then there were studio politics, and that's the roughest game there is. But has anybody—anybody—ever claimed that Darryl Zanuck advanced himself by dirty tricks? Or by leaving behind him the usual trail of bloody corpses? Of course, there were some aching egos and some bruised temperaments. If you're in charge of a regiment of artists, some of your commands are going to hurt. Some of your decisions are bound to seem arbitrary, but Darryl didn't sign on to be the recreation director of a summer camp. Of course he was tough. That was his job. But unlike many of the others, he was never cruel. Never vindictive. He wasn't—and what a rare thing it is to say in the competitive game of ours, he was a man totally devoid of malice. But he was great with irony. Great sense of humor, even about himself; of which of the others can we say that?

I always knew that if I did something really outrageous, that if I committed some abominable crime, and if all the police in the world were after me, there was one man and only one man I could come to, and that was Darryl. He would not have made a speech about the good of the industry or the good of his studio. He would not have been mealy-mouthed or put me aside. He would have hid me under the bed. Very simply, he was a friend. I don't mean just my friend. I mean that friendship was something he was very good at.

And that is why it is so very hard to say good-bye to him. ∎

Secretary Jack Kemp, Saluting Winston Churchill, Applies the Munich Analogy to Kuwait

"THE Western democracies did nothing to stop Mussolini in Abyssinia; . . . then Hitler took the Rhineland . . . , then Prague, then Poland, and Pearl Harbor. . . . We know what will follow if the world does nothing to reverse Saddam Hussein's aggression in Kuwait. Saudi Arabia will be next. . . ."

FORMER PRO FOOTBALL QUARTERBACK, New York congressman, and first Bush Administration housing secretary, Jack Kemp is an ardent supply-side economist, a believer in "empowerment" for the poor through home ownership, and a hard-line activist in foreign affairs.

His speaking style is akin to Hubert Humphrey's—passionate, uplifting, anecdotal, and often verbose. (Senator Humphrey used to say, "I'm like the little boy who learned how to spell 'banana' and never knew when to stop.") Kemp is an unabashed ideologue: this quality has the oratorical disadvantage of the hard sell, but the advantage of clarity and intensity; he leaves no audience ambivalent.

Chosen to be Bob Dole's running mate on the Republican ticket in 1996, Kemp eschewed the usual attack role of the vice-presidential nominee and dismayed some partisans by "staying Kemp"—with the ebullient, upbeat style and sunny message of inclusion that was his trademark.

Though best known for his extemporaneous, rambling, too-detailed style, Kemp has occasionally submitted to oratorical discipline. In the prepared speech accepting the Winston Churchill Award of the Claremont Institute, in Los Angeles, on November 30, 1990, Kemp's purpose was to turn the occasion toward a case for armed intervention in the Persian Gulf. Opponents of the Bush buildup to war to push Iraq out of Kuwait were using the Vietnam quagmire analogy; Kemp used the tribute to Churchill to press home the Munich analogy, of the need to stop forcibly rather than appease an aggressor.

One technique to note here is the dramatic setup of a quotation. Instead of a dull "As Churchill said," Kemp says, "Listen to his words as war threatened. . . ."

□   □   □

Ilove the Churchill story they tell about the reporter who was once kind enough to let a rising young politician named Winston Churchill preview an upcoming article about his recent speech. At the end of a long quotation from Churchill's remarks, the newsman had written the word "cheers" to describe the audience's reaction. Churchill scratched it out. The reporter was amazed by what he thought was an unusual display of modesty, until Churchill wrote instead, "loud and prolonged applause."

So if there are any reporters in the room tonight, I'd like to have a word with you after the speech. . . .

This thrilling era of global change—of peaceful democratic revolutions following the sudden collapse of Soviet totalitarianism labeled by President Bush the "Revolution of 1989"—was anticipated by Churchill over four decades ago.

But more than that, I believe his postwar leadership helped lay the foundation for the policies of deterrence and strength that culminated in today's historic events. . . .

Far from being a "warmonger," Churchill was in fact the earliest advocate of "peace through strength." He spent ten lonely years determined to inform the British people about the growing threat of Nazi rearmament and aggression and repeatedly challenged the government's policies of appeasement and weakness.

He openly disputed the government's figures on the balance between British and German military strength.

He insistently demanded the creation of a ministry to supply munitions.

He bluntly asked whether Britain was doing all it could to defend democracy.

"We must recognize that we have a great treasure to guard," Churchill said two years before Munich. "The inheritance in our possession represents the prolonged achievement of the centuries. . . . There is not one of our simple uncounted rights today for which better men than we are have not died on the scaffold or the battlefield. We have not only a great treasure; we have a great cause."

The tragedy of Munich marked the turning point for Great Britain and for Winston Churchill's political future.

The policies of weakness and appeasement followed by Ramsay MacDonald, Stanley Baldwin, and Neville Chamberlain failed.

The Nazis marched through Czechoslovakia, Poland, Scandinavia, the Low Countries, and rolled through France to the very gates of Paris in just forty days. Malevolent eyes turned on Britain.

In this dark hour, a desperate Britain summoned Churchill to lead the nation into war. The Wilderness Years were over. The battle of France had ended. The Battle of Britain had begun.

Now in charge of the entire scene, Churchill recorded that he "slept soundly and had no need for cheering dreams."

"I felt as if I were walking with Destiny," he said, "and that all my past life had been but a preparation for this hour and for this trial. . . . I was sure I would not fail."

Three weeks into Churchill's government—while British forces were evacuating at Dunkirk—Mussolini offered to mediate between Britain and Germany. Germany would get France and the Continent; Britain would get independence—to be assured by Hitler.

Many in the war cabinet favored opening talks. They believed Britain could win better terms before the attack that was sure to come. Churchill was vehemently opposed.

When the meeting was opened to the entire cabinet, Churchill gave an impassioned speech. His wrath grew with every word, words that poured forth relentlessly, hurled down like thunderbolts.

"Nations which went down fighting rose again," he told his ministers, "but those which surrender tamely are finished."

The stunned cabinet erupted in applause.

In a few minutes of powerful reasoning, Churchill turned uncertainty into resolve, apprehension into determination, fear into hope—and, with it, a near defeat into an eventual triumph.

Ladies and gentlemen, *that* is what great leadership is all about! . . .

Listen to his words as war threatened to engulf the British Isles and fear had displaced hope. Sir Winston said, "These are not dark days: these are great days—the greatest days our country has ever lived; and we must all thank God that we have been allowed, each of us according to our stations, to play a part in making these days memorable in the history of our race."

What was it that ultimately sustained him over six long decades of public life in triumph and in tragedy—in the first World Crisis, following the Dardanelles, throughout the Wilderness Years, during the War Years, after his defeat in 1945?

President Kennedy talked of his courage; Field Marshal Montgomery spoke of his domination; President Eisenhower said it was his defiance;

Lord Beaverbrook mentioned his ambition; President Reagan credited his optimism; Clement Attlee called it luck.

Yes, all these attributes marked the essential character of Winston Churchill. But in the end, I believe the anchor of his being was a profound faith in the overpowering force of ideas. Not just any ideas—Churchill's was a deeply held commitment to freedom and democracy, ideas which ennoble the long story of Britain, ideas extending from the Magna Carta to the birth of America's declaration "that all men are created equal," ideas which he believed were an eternal promise to transform the world for men and women everywhere.

From statesmen of Churchill's rank, lessons can be learned that apply to nearly every political situation. What can we learn from him in our new post–Cold War era?

There is a debate raging on the right, where most interesting debates now take place: How involved should the U.S. be in the world now that the Soviet empire is shrinking and aggression is waning? What should our stance be in a post–Cold War world that is unipolar rather than bipolar or multipolar?

Some want to turn inward since there are no great threats to our national security. Some say, "Come home, America!"

Others believe we must continue an activist, forward-based strategy of spreading the global democratic imperative of freedom and opportunity for all; and that spreading democracy and entrepreneurial capitalism is a *moral* as well as a political necessity. . . .

Only a few months ago, probably about as many people had heard of Kuwait, or knew where it is on a map, as had heard in 1935 of Abyssinia or knew where it was. Churchill, still out of power, saw Mussolini moving into Abyssinia. With typical foresight, he asked, "Who is to say what will come of it in a year, or two, or three . . . with Germany arming at breakneck speed, England lost in a pacifist dream, France corrupt and torn by dissension, America remote and indifferent . . . ?"

The Western democracies did nothing to stop Mussolini in Abyssinia; Ethiopia fell; then Hitler took the Rhineland; the *Anschluss* followed—then the Sudetenland, then Prague, then Poland, and Pearl Harbor. The world, supposedly liberated from global threats only twenty years before, once again plunged into war.

I believe President Reagan, President Bush, Prime Minister Thatcher, and others in the West learned Churchill's lesson. We know what will follow if the world does nothing to reverse Saddam Hussein's aggression in Kuwait. Saudi Arabia will be next, and the United Arab Emirates, Oman, Jordan, and then the only democracy of the Middle East, Israel.

With Hussein asserting hegemony over all the Persian Gulf, the world might be at war yet a third time.

In the early 1930s, Hitler and Mussolini were far more dangerous than the clownish dictators portrayed by Charlie Chaplin. And . . . Saddam Hussein is far more than a two-bit tyrant or Third World expansionist.

He is armed with chemical weapons. He has already waged a ten-year war of aggression that cost one million lives. He will have nuclear weapons in the not too distant future. Not only must we stop Hussein—we must break his sword!

Those who think that conservatism only meant anticommunism only know half the story. America must do more than just stand *against* something. America's mission is to stand *for* something, to be that "city on a hill," as President Reagan said.

When the American colonies broke away from Britain, Jefferson, Adams, and the founders published the immortal Declaration of Independence. Isn't it remarkable that they did not begin with what they were against? The Declaration's story begins by stating what America is *for*: we are *for* the idea that all men are created equal. We are *for* the natural rights of all human beings. We are *for* government by consent of the governed.

America's mission to the world did not end when communism ended. Our mission is ongoing. It was recognized by Sir Winston in his "Iron Curtain" speech, inscribed in the very words on this wonderful award. Our mission is to continue to tell the world that we are *for* the freedom and human rights of all men and women, for all time—and to do everything we can to transform the ancient dream and hope of freedom into a democratic reality everywhere! And with God's help, we will. ■

President Boris Yeltsin
of Russia Eulogizes Victims
# of Communism's Final
Power Play

"FORGIVE me, your president, that I could not defend, could not save your sons. . ."

SOMETIMES AN OCCASION MAKES A SPEECH. Boris Yeltsin, long treated by Western leaders and media as a buffoon for his heckling of Mikhail Gorbachev's "half-measures" of reform, surged to prominence atop a tank resisting a coup attempt by Communist hard-liners. During that abortive military-KGB putsch in August of 1991, three young Russians were killed in the popular resistance; to capitalize on the emotion of the moment, and to rally opinion to pulverize the still-entrenched Communist apparat, a state funeral was held and nationally telecast; religious leaders conducted services, further identifying the reformers with the pre-Communist culture (including prayers in rarely heard Hebrew, because one of the dead heroes, Ilya Krichevsky, was a Jew).

Gorbachev, on that August 24, announced to the crowd that he had decreed that the three dead men would be declared heroes of the Soviet Union, a central entity he was eager to save, and referred to the coup plotters only with "They won't be pardoned." Yeltsin spoke ten times of Russia, and used a powerful figure of speech to describe the fallen-out coup leaders: "like cockroaches in a bottle, trying to eat each other." Gorbachev began his speech, "Dear Muscovites!" Yeltsin began more somberly and personally:

□   □   □

Dear relatives and loved ones of Dmitri Komar, Vladimir Usov, and Ilya Krichevsky, dear fellow countrymen and Muscovites:

Today many millions of Muscovites, the whole of Russia, are parting with our heroes, with our defenders, with our saviors. Of course, we are not parting with their names forever, because from now on their names are sacred names for Russia, for all the people of our long-suffering Russia.

When television and radio reported about the coup on Monday, the hearts of millions and millions of mothers and fathers trembled most of all because they were scared for their children. Because it was young people, it was our children, who more than anyone else rushed to defend Russia's honor, its freedom, its independence, and its democracy, to defend its parliament.

Yes, from now on, this square, on which a battle raged for three days, on which tens of thousands of Muscovites kept vigil, will be called the Square of Free Russia.

The enemy is cruel and, of course, bloodthirsty, especially when he knows that if he loses no one will take him in. All the participants, all the main participants of the putsch, are arrested. Criminal proceedings have been started against them, and I am sure that they will be made to answer for everything.

But even today, how cynical the words of arrested [the former head of the KGB, Vladimir A.] Kryuchkov sound, the man who yesterday said that if he could do it over again he would have started a little faster and more energetically, and that the most important thing was to behead Russia.

This entire plot, and we must understand this very clearly, was aimed in the first place against Russia, its parliament, its government, its president. But all of Russia stood up to its defense: Moscow, Leningrad, the Urals, the Far East, the Kuzbass, practically all regions of the republic, although there were some regions which immediately put up banners and slogans expressing loyalty to the Extraordinary Committee. These officials already have been dismissed from their posts. And the prosecutor's office is considering their cases.

But we cannot resurrect those who died at the walls of our White House. We pay tribute to their courage, those who have become Heroes of the Soviet Union in death. I bow down to the mothers and fathers of Dmitri, Volodya, and Ilya, and I express to them my deep condolences, and to all their relatives and loved ones. Forgive me, your president, that I could not defend, could not save your sons.

In this day of Russia's national mourning, we, of course, need to strengthen our unity to energetically act further. We have cleared ourselves a path. Our deceased heroes have helped us to do so. This is a difficult day for us, a hard day. But it could have been even worse, because the enemies are already like cockroaches in a bottle, trying to eat each other. They are pointing fingers at each other, asking who played a more important role in the plot, revealing to each other the lists of people they wanted to kill first, second, third, fourth.

Only the first twelve victims in these lists were designated to be killed at 6 P.M. on August 19 during the storming of the House of Soviets. So it was not in vain the Muscovites were here, defending the honor of Russia.

It was a difficult loss, and the memory of it will be with us forever. For that reason, our heroes, sleep peacefully and let the earth be soft for you. ■

Senate Leader Robert Dole Remembers Richard Nixon as "One of Us"

"I believe the second half of the twentieth century will be known as the Age of Nixon."

BADLY WOUNDED AS AN ARMY LIEUTENANT in World War II, Bob Dole rose from years in a hospital bed to become a Kansas congressman, Republican national chairman, Senate majority leader, and three-time candidate for national office.

Over the years, his speaking style changed: Dole was known in the sixties for a mordant wit, which sometimes backfired: at the start of the Nixon campaign of 1972, he referred to the Committee to Reelect the President by its acronym CREEP, an innocuous crack that gained a sinister second meaning after the stealthy Watergate break-in. In a 1976 debate with Walter Mondale, Dole as Republican vice-presidential nominee struck viewers as an embittered man with his denunciation of "Democrat wars," and in the aftermath of a primary loss in New Hampshire to George Bush in 1988, the defeated candidate lashed back with an admonition to Bush to "stop lying about my record." That became known as "the old Dole."

In the nineties, he blunted the edge of bitterness and usually adopted a more relaxed, somewhat less partisan demeanor. When the Republicans took control of Congress in 1994, the pragmatic Dole presented a contrast to the fiery Speaker Newt Gingrich. His speaking style as well as the substance of his speeches was more attuned to the Senate than the stump: policy-laden, detailed, argumentative with overtones of reasonableness, passion-free, sometimes persuasive, but not especially memorable. His best speeches, including his 1996 farewell to the Senate, lay ahead.

His acceptance address at the 1996 Republican convention in San Diego, drafted by the novelist Mark Helprin, began with a reference to "plain speaking"—in contrast to the soaring rhetoric of his opponent, President Clinton—but contained such felicitous phrases as "the gracious compensations of age" and "Let me be the bridge to a time of tranquillity, faith, and confidence in action." That bridge metaphor was taken up by Mr. Clinton and turned against Dole, as the President contrasted the seventy-three-year-old challenger's "bridge to the past" with his own "bridge to the twenty-first century." Almost as if in anticipation of that counterattack, Dole wrote the headline to his own coverage by pronouncing himself at the end "the most optimistic man in America."

His speaking style on the stump, however, was staccato, repeating words and phrases for emphasis, and sometimes lamely ending a series of points with "whatever." Skillful in talk-show appearances, his campaign oratory came across as strident and unfocused; on occasion, however, he would attack ethical lapses with a theme that reverberated later, as in "Where's the outrage?"

At moments of high drama throughout his career, the seemingly stoic Dole allowed his emotion to show through. His eulogy at the funeral of Richard Nixon on April 27, 1994, brought to the surface a deep emotion at the loss of a friend and mentor. The setting was the Nixon Library and birthplace in Yorba Linda, California; four thousand diehard Nixon supporters and family members were in attendance, along with all of America's living presidents and first ladies. (President Gerald Ford began his eulogy with "Mr. President, Mr. President, Mr. President, Mr. President . . .")

Dole began with, and in the end reprised, the theme of Nixon as "one of us" (the title of liberal columnist Tom Wicker's surprisingly admiring biography of Nixon). The end of each of four sentences naming some example of his us-ness was punctuated effectively with "How American." In defining Nixon's "silent majority," Dole described his own political lodestar: "Like them, he valued accomplishment more than ideology."

Delivering a eulogy to a loved one or a close friend is the greatest strain in oratory, as anyone who has done it knows. Halfway through the final paragraph, Dole began to break down and sobbed his way through the last sentence. Appearing on television with the anthologist a half-hour later, Dole—known more for sarcasm than for sentiment—was slightly, not greatly, embarrassed by the loss of control at the end that had underscored his sincerity: "Just couldn't make it through. Almost did."

□   □   □

I believe the second half of the twentieth century will be known as the Age of Nixon. Why was he the most durable public figure of our time? Not because he gave the most eloquent speeches, but because he provided the most effective leadership. Not because he won every battle, but because he always embodied the deepest feelings of the people he led.

One of his biographers said that Richard Nixon was one of us, and so he was. He was a boy who heard the train whistle in the night and dreamed of all the distant places that lay at the end of the track. How American.

He was the grocer's son who got ahead by working harder and longer than everyone else. How American.

He was a student who met expenses by doing research at the law library for thirty-five cents an hour while sharing a rundown farmhouse without water or electricity. How American.

He was the husband and father who said that the best memorial to his wife was her children. How American.

To tens of millions of his countrymen, Richard Nixon was an American hero. A hero who shared and honored their belief in working hard, worshiping God, loving their families, and saluting the flag. He called them the silent majority. Like them, he valued accomplishment more than ideology. They wanted their government to do the decent thing, but not to bankrupt them in the process. They wanted his protection in a dangerous world, but they also wanted creative statesmanship in achieving a genuine peace with honor. These were the people from whom he had come and who have come to Yorba Linda these past few days by the tens of thousands, no longer silent in their grief.

The American people love a fighter, and in Dick Nixon they found a gallant one. In her marvelous biography of her mother, Julie recalls an occasion where Pat Nixon expressed amazement at her husband's ability to persevere in the face of criticism, to which the president replied, "I just get up every morning to confound my enemies." It was what Richard

Nixon did after he got up every morning that not just confounded his enemies but turned them into admirers.

It is true that no one knew the world better than Richard Nixon, and as a result, the man who was born in a house his father built would go on to become this century's greatest architect of peace.

But we should also not underestimate President Nixon's domestic achievements, for it was Richard Nixon who ended the draft, strengthened environmental and nutritional programs, and committed the government to a war on cancer. He leap-frogged the conventional wisdom to propose revolutionary solutions to health care and welfare reform, anticipating by a full generation the debates now raging on Capitol Hill.

I remember the last time I saw him, at a luncheon held at the Capitol honoring the twenty-fifth anniversary of his first inaugural. Without a note, President Nixon stood and delivered a compelling speech, capturing the global scene as only he could, and sharing his vision of America's future. When it was over, he was surrounded by Democrats and Republicans alike, each wanting just one more word of Nixonian counsel, one more insight into world affairs.

Afterward the president rested in my office before leaving the Capitol, only he got very little rest. For the office was filled with young Hill staffers, members of the Capitol police, and many, many others, all hoping to shake his hand, get an autograph, or simply convey their special feelings for a man who was truly one of us.

Today our grief is shared by millions of people the world over, but it is also mingled with intense pride in a great patriot who never gave up and who never gave in. To know the secret of Richard Nixon's relationship with the American people, you need only to listen to his words: "You must never be satisfied with success," he told us, "and you should never be discouraged by failure. Failure can be sad, but the greatest sadness is not to try and fail, but to fail to try. In the end what matters is that you have always lived life to the hilt."

Strong, brave, unafraid of controversy, unyielding in his convictions, living every day of his life to the hilt, the largest figure of our time whose influence will be timeless. That was Richard Nixon. How American. May God bless Richard Nixon and may God bless the United States.

■   ■   ■

IV

DEBATES
AND
ARGUMENTATION

Cicero Rails against Catiline and His Conspiracies

"You are not, O Catiline, one whom either shame can recall from infamy, or fear from danger, or reason from madness."

MARCUS TULLIUS CICERO, renowned Roman statesman and orator, is said to have praised Greek historian Thucydides with the observation that "he almost equals the number of his words by the number of his thoughts."

Cicero himself recognized the power of words. Born in 106 B.C., he used his oratorical abilities to raise his social position, serving first as a lawyer and then as a politician. After winning a Roman consulship at the age of forty-three, he became aware of a "conspiracy" by Roman politician Catiline and thwarted Catiline's attempt to have him assassinated. Two days later, Cicero rose to address the Roman Senate in the first of his four orations against Catiline, using facts gained from a scorned mistress.

With a series of seven probing questions, Cicero began the denunciation of his adversary for scheming against the state. He repeatedly used parallel structure ("the enemies of good men, the foes of the Republic, the robbers of Italy") and direct address to move from the focus of his attack ("O Catiline") to those whom he wished to persuade ("O conscript fathers"), leading to the divine apostrophe "O Jupiter" at the speech's conclusion.

In December of 63 B.C., the Roman Senate debated the fate of the conspirators, with Julius Caesar moderately advocating their imprisonment and Cicero and Cato the Younger sternly seeking their execution. The summary judgment carried the day, though Cicero was later exiled for abusing the law; Catiline, who refused to surrender for his execution, was killed on the battlefield the next year, following his forceful speech to rally the troops (see p. 91).

□   □   □

When, O Catiline, do you mean to cease abusing our patience? How long is that madness of yours still to mock us? When is there to be an end of that unbridled audacity of yours, swaggering about as it does now? Do not the mighty guards placed on the Palatine Hill—do not the watches posted throughout the city—does not the alarm of the people, and the union of all good men—does not the precaution taken of assembling the Senate in this most defensible place—do not the looks and countenances of this venerable body here present, have any effect upon you? Do you not feel that your plans are detected? Do you not see that your conspiracy is already arrested and rendered powerless by the knowledge which everyone here possesses of it? What is there that you did last night, what the night before—where is it that you were—who was there that you summoned to meet you—what design was there which was adopted by you, with which you think that any one of us is unacquainted?

Shame on the age and on its principles! The Senate is aware of these things; the consul sees them; and yet this man lives. Lives! aye, he comes even into the Senate. He takes a part in the public deliberations; he is watching and marking down and checking off for slaughter every individual among us. And we, gallant men that we are, think that we are doing our duty to the Republic if we keep out of the way of his frenzied attacks.

You ought, O Catiline, long ago to have been led to execution by command of the counsel. That destruction which you have been long plotting against us ought to have already fallen on your own head. . . .

I wish, O conscript fathers, to be merciful; I wish not to appear negligent amid such danger to the state; but I do now accuse myself of remissness and culpable inactivity. A camp is pitched in Italy, at the entrance of Etruria, in hostility to the Republic; the number of the enemy increases every day; and yet the general of that camp, the leader of those enemies, we see within the walls—aye, and even in the senate—planning every day some internal injury to the Republic. If, O Catiline, I should now order you to be arrested, to be put to death, I should, I suppose, have to fear lest all good men should say that I had acted tardily, rather than that any one should affirm that I acted cruelly. But yet this, which ought to have been done long since, I have good reason for not doing as yet; I will put you to death, then, when there shall be not one person possible to be found so wicked, so abandoned, so like yourself, as not to allow that it has been rightly done. As long as one person exists who can dare to defend you, you shall live; but you shall live as you do now, surrounded by my many and trusted guards, so that you shall not be able to stir one finger against the Republic; many eyes and ears shall still observe and watch you as they have hitherto done, though you shall not perceive them.

For what is there, O Catiline, that you can still expect, if night is not able to veil your nefarious meetings in darkness, and if private houses cannot conceal the voice of your conspiracy within their walls—if everything is seen and displayed? Change your mind: trust me: forget the slaughter and conflagration you are meditating. You are hemmed in on all sides; all your plans are clearer than the day to us; let me remind you of them. Do you recollect that on the twenty-first of October I said in the Senate, that on a certain day, which was to be the twenty-seventh of October, C. Manilius, the satellite and servant of your audacity, would be in arms? Was I mistaken, Catiline, not only in so important, so atrocious, so incredible a fact but, what is much more remarkable, in the very day? I said also in the Senate that you had fixed the massacre of the nobles for the twenty-eighth of October, when many chief men of the Senate had left Rome, not so much for the sake of saving themselves as of checking your designs. Can you deny that on that very day you were so hemmed in by my guards and my vigilance that you were unable to stir one finger against the Republic; when you said that you would be content with the flight of the rest, and the slaughter of us who remained? What? When you made sure that you would be able to seize Praeneste on the first of November by a nocturnal attack, did you not find that that colony was fortified by my order, by my garrison, by my watchfulness and care? You do nothing, you plan nothing, think of nothing which I not only do not hear but which I do not see and know every particular of.

Listen while I speak of the night before. You shall now see that I watch far more actively for the safety than you do for the destruction of the Republic. I say that you came the night before (I will say nothing obscurely) into the scythe dealers' street, to the house of Marcus Lecca; that many of your accomplices in the same insanity and wickedness came there, too. Do you dare to deny it? Why are you silent? I will prove it if you do deny it; for I see here in the senate some men who were there with you.

O ye immortal gods, where on earth are we? in what city are we living? what constitution is ours? There are here—here in our body, O conscript fathers, in this the most holy and dignified assembly of the whole world— men who meditate my death, and the death of all of us, and the destruction of this city, and of the whole world. I, the consul, see them; I ask them their opinion about the Republic, and I do not yet attack, even by words, those who ought to be put to death by the sword. . . .

You are summoning to destruction and devastation the temples of the immortal gods, the houses of the city, the lives of all the citizens; in short, all Italy. Wherefore, since I do not yet venture to do that which is the best thing, and which belongs to my office and to the discipline of our ancestors, I will do that which is more merciful if we regard its rigor, and more expedient for the state. For if I order you to be put to death, the rest of the conspirators will still remain in the Republic; if, as I have long been exhorting you, you depart, your companions, these worthless dregs of the Republic, will be drawn off from the city too. What is the matter, Catiline? Do you hesitate to do that when I order you which you were already doing of your own accord? The consul orders an enemy to depart from the city. Do you ask me, are you to go into banishment? I do not order it; but if you consult me, I advise it.

For what is there, O Catiline, that can now afford you any pleasure in this city? For there is no one in it, except that band of profligate conspirators of yours, who does not fear you—no one who does not hate you. What brand of domestic baseness is not stamped upon your life? What disgraceful circumstance is wanting to your infamy in your private affairs? From what licentiousness have your eyes, from what atrocity have your hands, from what iniquity has your whole body ever abstained? Is there one youth, when you have once entangled him in the temptations of your corruption, to whom you have not held out a sword for audacious crime, or a torch for licentious wickedness?

What? When lately by the death of your former wife you had made your house empty and ready for a new bridal, did you not even add another incredible wickedness to this wickedness? But I pass that over, and willingly allow it to be buried in silence, that so horrible a crime may not be seen to have existed in this city, and not to have been chastised. I pass over the ruin of your fortune, which you know is hanging over you against the ides of the very next month; I come to those things which relate not to the infamy of your private vices, not to your domestic difficulties and baseness, but to the welfare of the Republic and to the lives and safety of us all. . . .

If your parents feared and hated you, and if you could by no means pacify them, you would, I think, depart somewhere out of their sight. Now your country, which is the common parent of all of us, hates and fears you, and has no other opinion of you than that you are meditating parricide in her case; and will you feel neither awe of her authority, nor deference for her judgment, nor fear of her power?

And she, O Catiline, thus pleads with you, and after a manner silently speaks to you: There has now for many years been no crime committed but by you; no atrocity has taken place without you; you alone unpunished and unquestioned have murdered the citizens, have harassed and plundered the allies; you alone have had power not only to neglect all laws and investigations but to overthrow and break through them. Your former actions, though they ought not to have been borne, yet I did bear as well as I could; but now that I should be wholly occupied with fear of you alone, that at every sound I should dread Catiline, that no design should seem possible to be entertained against me which does not proceed from your wickedness, this is no longer endurable. Depart, then, and deliver me from this fear; that, if it be a just one, I may not be destroyed; if an imaginary one, that at least I may at last cease to fear.

If, as I have said, your country were thus to address you, ought she not to obtain her request, even if she were not able to enforce it? What shall I say of your having given yourself into custody? What of your having said, for the sake of avoiding suspicion, that you were willing to dwell in the house of Marcus Lepidus? And when you were not received by him, you dared even to come to me, and begged me to keep you in my house; and when you had received answer from me that I could not possibly be safe in the same house with you, when I considered myself in great danger as long as we were in the same city, you came to Quintus Metellus, the praetor, and being rejected by him, you passed on to your associate, that most excellent man Marcus Marcellus, who would be, I suppose you thought, most diligent in guarding you, most sagacious in suspecting you, and most bold in punishing you; but how far can we think that man ought to be from bonds and imprisonment who has already judged himself deserving of being given into custody?

Since, then, this is the case, do you hesitate, O Catiline, if you cannot remain here with tranquillity, to depart to some distant land, and to trust your life, saved from just and deserved punishment, to flight and solitude? Make a motion, say you, to the Senate (for that is what you demand), and if this body votes that you ought to go into banishment, you say that you will obey. I will not make such a motion, it is contrary to my principles, and yet I will let you see what these men think of you. Begone from the city, O Catiline, deliver the Republic from fear; depart into banishment, if that is the word you are waiting for. What now, O Catiline? Do you not perceive, do you not see the silence of these men? They permit it, they say nothing; why wait you for the authority of their words, when you see their wishes in their silence? . . .

And yet, why am I speaking? That anything may change your purpose? That you may ever amend your life? That you may meditate flight or think of voluntary banishment? I wish the gods may give you such a mind; though I see, if alarmed at my words you bring your mind to go into banishment, what a storm of unpopularity hangs over me, if not at present, while the memory of your wickedness is fresh, at all events hereafter. But it is worthwhile to incur that, as long as that is but a private misfortune of my own, and is unconnected with the dangers of the Republic. But we cannot expect that you should be concerned at your own vices, that you should fear the penalties of the laws, or that you should yield to the necessities of the Republic, for you are not, O Catiline, one whom either shame can recall from infamy, or fear from danger, or reason from madness.

Wherefore, as I have said before, go forth, and if you wish to make me, your enemy as you call me, unpopular, go straight into banishment. I shall scarcely be able to endure all that will be said if you do so; I shall scarcely be able to support my load of unpopularity if you do go into banishment at the command of the consul; but if you wish to serve my credit and reputation, go forth with your ill-omened band of profligates; betake yourself to Manlius, rouse up the abandoned citizens, separate yourselves from the good ones, wage war against your country, exult in your impious banditti, so that you may not seem to have been driven out by me and gone to strangers, but to have gone invited to your friends. . . .

Now that I may remove and avert, O conscript fathers, any in the least reasonable complaint from myself, listen, I beseech you, carefully to what I say, and lay it up in your inmost hearts and minds. In truth, if my country, which is far dearer to me than my life—if all Italy—if the whole Republic were to address me, Marcus Tullius, what are you doing? Will you permit that man to depart whom you have ascertained to be an enemy? Whom you see ready to become the general of the war? Whom you know to be expected in the camp of the enemy as their chief, the author of all this wickedness, the head of the conspiracy, the instigator of the slaves and abandoned citizens, so that he shall seem not driven out of the city by you, but let loose by you against the city? Will you not order him to be thrown into prison, to be hurried off to execution, to be put to death with the most prompt severity? What hinders you? Is it the customs of our ancestors? But even private men have often in this Republic slain mischievous citizens. Is it the laws which have been passed about the punishment of Roman citizens? But in this city those who have rebelled against the Republic have never had the rights of citizens. Do you fear odium with posterity? You are showing fine gratitude to the Roman people which has raised you, a man known only by your own actions, of no ancestral renown, through all the degrees of honor at so early an age to the very highest office, if from fear of unpopularity or of any danger you neglect the safety of your fellow citizens. But if you have a fear of unpopularity, is that arising from the imputation of vigor and boldness, or that arising from that of inactivity and indecision most to be feared? When Italy is laid waste by war, when cities are attacked and houses in flames, do you not think that you will be then consumed by a perfect conflagration of hatred? . . .

If this man alone were put to death, I know that this disease of the Republic would be only checked for a while, not eradicated forever. But if he banishes himself, and takes with him all his friends, and collects at one point all the ruined men from every quarter, then not only will this full-grown plague of the Republic be extinguished and eradicated, but also the root and seed of all future evils.

We have now for a long time, O conscript fathers, lived among these dangers and machinations of conspiracy; but somehow or other, the ripeness of all wickedness, and of this long-standing madness and audacity, has come to a head at the time of my consulship. But if this man alone is removed from this piratical crew, we may appear, perhaps, for a short time relieved from fear and anxiety, but the danger will settle down and lie hid in the veins and bowels of the Republic. As it often happens that men afflicted with a severe disease, when they are tortured with heat and fever, if they drink cold water seem at first to be relieved, but afterwards suffer more and more severely; so this disease which is in the Republic, if relieved by the punishment of this man, will only get worse and worse, as the rest will be still alive.

Wherefore, O conscript fathers, let the worthless begone—let them separate themselves from the good—let them collect in one place—let them, as I have often said before, be separated from us by a wall; let them cease to plot against the consul in his own house—to surround the tribunal of the city praetor—to besiege the Senate house with swords—to prepare brands and torches to burn the city; let it, in short, be written on the brow of every citizen what are his sentiments about the Republic. I promise you this, O conscript fathers, that there shall be so much diligence in us the consuls, so much authority in you, so much virtue in the Roman knights, so much unanimity in all good men, that you shall see everything made plain and manifest by the departure of Catiline—everything checked and punished.

With these omens, O Catiline, begone to your impious and nefarious war, to the great safety of the Republic, to your own misfortune and injury, and to the destruction of those who have joined themselves to you in every wickedness and atrocity. Then do you, O Jupiter, who were consecrated by Romulus with the same auspices as this city, whom we rightly call the stay of this city and empire, repel this man and his companions from your altars and from the other temples—from the houses and walls of the city— from the lives and fortunes of all the citizens; and overwhelm all the enemies of good men, the foes of the Republic, the robbers of Italy, men bound together by a treaty and infamous alliance of crimes, dead and alive, with eternal punishments. ■

Lord General Oliver Cromwell Orders the "Rump Parliament" Out of the House

"DEPART, I say; and let us have done with you. In the name of God—go!"

IN THE ENGLISH CIVIL WARS of the seventeenth century, with religious "Roundheads" fighting the royalists behind the absolutist Charles Stuart, a Puritan member of Parliament from Cambridge named Oliver Cromwell emerged as a military leader of genius. His forces defeated the royalists, and Cromwell, in an act remembered as regicide, signed the death warrant that brought about the execution of Charles I in 1649.

Cromwell and his New Model Army purged the Parliament of many of the members he considered disloyal to him, governing with the remainder (called the "Rump Parliament"). But even this reduced group, supposedly an interim legislature, resisted the leader of the Puritan Commonwealth. On April 26, 1653, its members started to pass an act that would perpetuate their power. Cromwell saw this as a threat to his control, and took a company of musketeers with him into the House.

We do not know exactly what he said that day because on January 7, 1659, a year after his death, in an act of historical vandalism, Parliament ordered the official version of his speech expunged from the record. (Two years later, after the Restoration of the monarchy, King Charles II had Cromwell's remains disinterred from Westminster Abbey and his head placed on a pike atop the Hall throughout the king's reign.) A century after that, when the Lord Protector, or dictator, was no longer so widely hated, free-speech advocates who wanted to castigate Parliament for its sedition persecution of the outspoken John Wilkes came up with a spurious version of the Cromwell speech. Here it is; the "shining bauble" referred to at the end was the parliamentary mace, symbol of authority:

"It is high time for me to put an end to your sitting in this place, which you have dishonored by your contempt of all virtue, and defiled by your practice of every vice; ye are a factious crew, and enemies to all good government; ye are a pack of mercenary wretches, and would like Esau sell your country for a mess of pottage, and like Judas betray your God for a few pieces of money; is there a single virtue now remaining amongst you? Is there one vice you do not possess? Ye have no more religion than my horse; gold is your God; which of you have not barter'd your conscience for bribes? Is there a man amongst you that has the least care for the good of the Commonwealth? Ye sordid prostitutes have you not defil'd this sacred place, and turn'd the Lord's temple into a den of thieves, by your immoral principles and wicked practices?

"Ye are grown intolerably odious to the whole nation; you who were deputed here by the people to get grievances redress'd, are yourselves become the greatest grievance. Your country therefore calls upon me to cleanse this Augean stable, by putting a final period to your iniquitous proceedings in this House; and which by God's help, and the strength he has given me, I am now come to do; I command ye therefore, upon the peril of your lives, to depart immediately out of this place; go, get you out! Make haste! Ye venal slaves be gone! Go! Take away that shining bauble there, and lock up the doors. In the name of God, go!"

Close, perhaps, but not wholly authentic. A century after that, the famed English historian Thomas Carlyle pored over three contemporary sources to get as close as he could to what Cromwell actually said. "Combining these originals," he wrote in 1845, "we have, after various perusals and collations and considerations, obtained the following authentic, moderately conceivable account."

Here is Carlyle's reconstruction in the form of narrative studded with direct quotation. The Lord General was Cromwell; he had not yet promoted himself to Lord Protector. Note the report of Cromwell's "clapping on his hat," the angry general's calculated insult to parliamentary rule. With his company of armed soldiers outside the hall at the ready, the general takes his seat.

□   □   □

Whereupon the Lord General sat still, for about a quarter of an hour longer. But now the question being put, That this Bill do now pass, he beckons again to Harrison, says, "This is the time; I must do it!"—and so rose up, put off his hat, and spake. At the first, and for a good while, he spake to the commendation of the Parliament for their pains and care of the public good; but afterwards he changed his style, told them of their injustice, delays of justice, self-interest, and other faults—rising higher and higher, into a very aggravated style indeed. An honorable Member, Sir Peter Wentworth by name, not known to my readers, and by me better known than trusted, rises to order, as we phrase it; says, "It is a strange language this; unusual within the walls of Parliament this! And from a trusted servant too; and one whom we have so highly honored; and one"—"Come, come!" exclaims my Lord General in a very high key, "we have had enough of this,"—and in fact my Lord General now blazing all up into clear conflagration, exclaims, "I will put an end to your prating," and steps forth into the floor of the House, and clapping on his hat, and occasionally stamping the floor with his feet, begins a discourse: . . .

"It is not fit that you should sit here any longer! You have sat too long here for any good you have been doing lately. You shall now give place to better men!—Call them in!" adds he briefly, to Harrison, in word of command: and some twenty or thirty grim musketeers enter, with bullets and their snaphances; grimly prompt for orders. . . .

"You call yourselves a Parliament," continues my Lord General in clear blaze of conflagration: "You are no Parliament: I say you are no Parliament! Some of you are drunkards," and his eye flashes on poor Mr. Chaloner, an official man of some value, addicted to the bottle; "some of you are—" and he glares into Harry Marten, and the poor Sir Peter who rose to order, lewd livers both; "living in open contempt of God's Commandments. Following your own greedy appetites, and the Devil's Commandments."

"Corrupt unjust persons; scandalous to the profession of the Gospel; how can you be a Parliament for God's People? Depart, I say; and let us have done with you. In the name of God—go!" ■

A Youthful William Pitt the Elder Debates the Merits of Age

"I will not sit unconcerned while my liberty is invaded, nor look in silence upon public robbery."

IN **1741,** a limit of thirty-five shillings a month was proposed for the wages of sailors, and the discussion of this proposition led the elder William Pitt to demonstrate his eloquence in debate. Born in 1708, Pitt eventually served as prime minister and was known as the Great Commoner. The year that he turned thirty-three, however, his reputation as a debater was secured with his response to the accusation of what he called "the atrocious crime of being a young man."

The speech to which Pitt was replying has been variously attributed to Sir Robert Walpole, prime minister of England from 1721 to 1742, and to his third son, Horace (originally Horatio), statesman and writer. Samuel Johnson's original edition of *Parliamentary Debates,* the source of the debate's text, credits Horatio Walpole, although he was born in 1717, almost ten years after the elder Pitt.

William Pitt's impassioned answer weighs first the difference between age and experience and then the proper language for debate. Through the repeated use of the correlative conjunctions "neither" and "nor," he balances his ideas in parallel structure and turns the attack from "youth" to "age, which always brings one privilege, that of being insolent and supercilious without punishment."

□   □   □

Sir, I was unwilling to interrupt the course of this debate while it was carried on with calmness and decency, by men who do not suffer the ardor of opposition to cloud their reason, or transport them to such expressions as the dignity of this assembly does not admit.

I have hitherto deferred to answer the gentleman who declaimed against the bill with such fluency of rhetoric and such vehemence of gesture, who charged the advocates for the expedients now proposed with having no regard to any interest but their own, and with making laws only to consume paper, and threatened them with the defection of their adherents and the loss of their influence upon this new discovery of their folly and their ignorance. Nor, sir, do I now answer him for any other purpose than to remind him how little the clamors of rage and petulancy of invectives contribute to the purposes for which this assembly is called together; how little the discovery of truth is promoted and the security of the nation established by pompous diction and theatrical emotions.

Formidable sounds and furious declamations, confident assertions and lofty periods, may affect the young and inexperienced, and, perhaps, the gentleman may have contracted his habits of oratory by conversing more with those of his own age than with such as have had more opportunities of acquiring knowledge and more successful methods of communicating their sentiments. If the heat of his temper, sir, would suffer him to attend to those whose age and long acquaintance with business give them an indisputable right to deference and superiority, he would learn, in time, to reason rather than declaim and to prefer justness of argument, and an accurate knowledge of facts, to sounding epithets and splendid superlatives, which may disturb the imagination for a moment, but leave no lasting impression on the mind.

He will learn, sir, that to accuse and prove are very different, and that reproaches unsupported by evidence affect only the character of him that utters them. Excursions of fancy and flights of oratory are, indeed, pardonable in young men, but in no other; and it would surely contribute more, even to the purpose for which some gentlemen appear to speak, that of depreciating the conduct of the administration, to prove the inconveniences and injustice of this bill, than barely to assert them, with whatever magnificence of language or appearance of zeal, honesty, or compassion.

[PITT:] Sir, the atrocious crime of being a young man, which the honorable gentleman has with such spirit and decency charged upon me, I shall neither attempt to palliate nor deny, but content myself with wishing that I may be one of those whose follies may cease with their youth, and not of that number who are ignorant in spite of experience. Whether youth can be imputed to any man as a reproach, I will not, sir, assume the province of determining; but surely age may become justly contemptible, if the opportunities which it brings have passed away without improvement, and vice appears to prevail when the passions have subsided. The wretch that, after having seen the consequences of a thousand errors, continues still to blunder, and whose age has only added obstinacy to stupidity, is surely the object of either abhorrence or contempt, and deserves not that his gray head should secure him from insults. Much more, sir, is he to be abhorred who, as he has advanced in age, has receded from virtue, and becomes more wicked with less temptation; who prostitutes himself for money which he cannot enjoy, and spends the remains of his life in the ruin of his country. But youth, sir, is not my only crime; I have been accused of acting a theatrical part. A theatrical part may either imply some peculiarities of gesture or a dissimulation of my real sentiments and an adoption of the opinions and language of another man.

In the first sense, sir, the charge is too trifling to be confuted, and deserves only to be mentioned that it may be despised. I am at liberty, like every other man, to use my own language; and though I may, perhaps, have some ambition to please this gentleman, I shall not lay myself under any restraint, nor very solicitously copy his diction or his mien, however matured by age or modeled by experience. If any man shall by charging me with theatrical behavior imply that I utter any sentiments but my own, I shall treat him as a calumniator and a villain; nor shall any protection shelter from the treatment which he deserves. I shall, on such an occasion, without scruple, trample upon all those forms with which wealth and dignity entrench themselves, nor shall anything but age restrain my resentment; age, which always brings one privilege, that of being insolent and supercilious without punishment. But with regard, sir, to those whom I have offended, I am of the opinion that if I had acted a borrowed part, I should have avoided their censure; the heat that offended them is the ardor of conviction, and that zeal for the service of my country which neither hope nor fear shall influence me to suppress. I will not sit unconcerned while my liberty is invaded, nor look in silence upon public robbery. . . . ■

William Pitt the Younger and Charles Fox Disagree on Napoleon's Offers of Peace

"I see no reason to believe that the present usurpation will be more permanent than any other despotism. . . ."

NAPOLEON BONAPARTE, whose oratorical salutation was unsurpassed ("Soldiers!"), ruled France from the overthrow of the French Directory in 1799 until the restoration of the Bourbons in 1814. As ruler, he posed a strong military threat to England, already debilitated by failures in Continental warfare and a rising debt. In late 1799, however, Napoleon proposed peace to George III of England, an offer that swiftly became a topic of parliamentary debate.

On February 3, 1800, William Pitt the Younger, then prime minister, presented an eloquent appeal in the House of Commons for refusing Napoleon's offer. His arguments make extensive use of parallel structure ("I never thought it, I never hoped it, I never wished it"), and that parallelism is particularly forceful in a series of "if" clauses that speculate on a stabilization of the French government.

Immediately following Pitt's rejection of Napoleon's proposal came the response by Charles James Fox, British orator and statesman. A proponent of liberal reform and an enthusiastic supporter of the French Revolution, Fox was known for his genial temperament and his ability in debating. His extemporaneous reply to Pitt in the House of Commons ranks among the best of debate rhetoric, particularly in its point-by-point refutation of the opposing view.

Fox's response, though measured and insightful, failed to sway the House of Commons, which voted almost four to one against accepting Napoleon's offer. Pitt's position was victorious in the debate, but within two years England had signed the 1802 Treaty of Amiens, accepting less favorable terms for its peace with France.

□　□　□

. . .Through all the stages of the Revolution military force has governed; public opinion has scarcely been heard. But still I consider this as only an exception from a general truth; I still believe that in every civilized country (not enslaved by a Jacobin faction) public opinion is the only sure support of any government: I believe this with the more satisfaction from a conviction that if this contest is happily terminated, the established governments of Europe will stand upon that rock firmer than ever; and whatever may be the defects of any particular constitution, those who live under it will prefer its continuance to the experiment of changes which may plunge them into the unfathomable abyss of revolution, or extricate them from it, only to expose them to the terrors of military despotism. And to apply this to France, I see no reason to believe that the present usurpation will be more permanent than any other despotism, which has been established by the same means, and with the same defiance of public opinion.

What, then, is the inference I draw from all that I have now stated? Is it that we will in no case treat with Bonaparte? I say no such thing. But I say, as has been said in the answer returned to the French note, that we ought to wait for *experience, and the evidence of facts,* before we are convinced that such a treaty is admissible. The circumstances I have stated would well justify us if we should be slow in being convinced; but on a question of peace and war, everything depends upon degree and upon comparison.

If, on the one hand, there should be an appearance that the policy of France is at length guided by different maxims from those which have hitherto prevailed; if we should hereafter see signs of stability in the government, which are not now to be traced; if the progress of the allied army should not call forth such a spirit in France as to make it probable that the act of the country itself will destroy the system now prevailing; if the danger, the difficulty, the risk of continuing the contest, should increase, while the hope of complete ultimate success should be diminished; all these, in their due place, are considerations which, with myself and (I can answer for it) with every one of my colleagues, will have their just weight. But at present these considerations all operate one way; at present there is nothing from which we can presage a favorable disposition to change in the French councils: there is the greatest reason to rely on powerful cooperation from our allies; there are the strongest marks of a disposition in the interior of France to active resistance against this new tyranny; and there is every ground to believe, on reviewing our situation and that of the enemy, that if we are ultimately disappointed of that complete success which we are at present entitled to hope, the continuance of the contest, instead of making our situation comparatively worse, will have made it comparatively better.

If, then, I am asked how long are we to persevere in the war, I can only say that no period can be accurately assigned beforehand. Considering the importance of obtaining complete security for the objects for which we contend, we ought not to be discouraged too soon: but on the other hand, considering the importance of not impairing and exhausting the radical strength of the country, there are limits beyond which we ought not to persist, and which we can determine only by estimating and comparing fairly, from time to time, the degree of security to be obtained by treaty, and the risk and disadvantage of continuing the contest.

But, sir, there are some gentlemen in the House who seem to consider it already certain that the ultimate success to which I am looking is unattainable: they suppose us contending only for the restoration of the French monarchy, which they believe to be impracticable and deny to be desirable for this country. We have been asked in the course of this debate, Do you think you can impose monarchy upon France against the will of the nation? I never thought it, I never hoped it, I never wished it: I have thought, I have hoped, I have wished, that the time might come when the effect of the arms of the allies might so far overpower the military force which keeps France in bondage as to give vent and scope to the thoughts and actions of its inhabitants.

We have, indeed, already seen abundant proof of what is the disposition of a large part of the country; we have seen almost through the whole of the Revolution the western provinces of France deluged with the blood of its inhabitants, obstinately contending for their ancient laws and religion. We have recently seen, in the revival of that war, a fresh instance of the zeal which still animates those countries, in the same cause. These efforts (I state it distinctly, and there are those near me who can bear witness to the truth of the assertion) were not produced by any instigation from hence; they were the effects of a rooted sentiment prevailing through all those provinces, forced into action by the Law of the Hostages and the other tyrannical measures of the Directory, at the moment when we were endeavoring to discourage so hazardous an enterprise. . . .

On the question, sir, how far the restoration of the French monarchy, if practicable, is desirable, I shall not think it necessary to say much. Can it be supposed to be indifferent to us or to the world whether the throne of France is to be filled by a prince of the house of Bourbon or by him whose principles and conduct I have endeavored to develop? Is it nothing, with a view to influence and example, whether the fortune of this last adventurer in the lottery of revolutions shall appear to be permanent? Is it nothing whether a system shall be sanctioned which confirms by one of its fundamental articles that general transfer of property from its ancient and lawful possessors which holds out one of the most terrible examples of national injustice, and which has furnished the great source of revolutionary finance and revolutionary strength against all the powers of Europe?

In the exhausted and impoverished state of France it seems for a time impossible that any system but that of robbery and confiscation, anything but the continued torture which can be applied only by the engines of the Revolution, can extort from its ruined inhabitants more than the means of supporting in peace the yearly expenditure of its government. Suppose, then, the heir of the house of Bourbon reinstated on the throne; he will have sufficient occupation in endeavoring, if possible, to heal the wounds and gradually to repair the losses of ten years of civil convulsion—to reanimate the drooping commerce, to rekindle the industry to replace the capital, and to revive the manufactures of the country.

Under such circumstances there must probably be a considerable interval before such a monarch, whatever may be his views, can possess the power which can make him formidable to Europe; but while the system of the Revolution continues the case is quite different. It is true indeed that even the gigantic and unnatural means by which that Revolution has been supported are so far impaired, the influence of its principles and the terror of its arms so far weakened, and its power of action so much contracted that against the embodied force of Europe, prosecuting a vigorous war, we may justly hope that the remnant and wreck of this system cannot long oppose an effectual resistance. . . .

[FOX:] . . . What! at the end of seven years of the most burdensome and the most calamitous struggle that this country was ever engaged in, are we again to be amused with notions of finance and calculations of the exhausted resources of the enemy as a ground of confidence and of hope? Gracious God! Were we not told, five years ago, that France was not only on the brink but that she was actually in the gulf of bankruptcy? Were we not told, as an unanswerable argument against treating, that she could not hold out another campaign—that nothing but peace could save her—that she wanted only time to recruit her exhausted finances—that to grant her repose was to grant her the means of again molesting this country, and that we had nothing to do but persevere for a short time in order to save ourselves forever from the consequences of her ambition and her Jacobinism? What! after having gone on from year to year upon assurances like these, and after having seen the repeated refutations of every prediction, are we again to be seriously told that we have the same prospect of success on the same identical grounds? And without any other argument or security, are we invited, at this new era of the war, to carry it on upon principles which, if adopted, may make it eternal? If the right honorable gentleman shall succeed in prevailing on Parliament and the country to adopt the principles which he has advanced this night, I see no possible termination to the contest. No man can see an end to it. . . .

Sir, what is the question this night? We are called upon to support ministers in refusing a frank, candid, and respectful offer of negotiation and to countenance them in continuing the war. Now, I would put the question in another way. Suppose ministers have been inclined to adopt the line of conduct which they pursued in 1796 and 1797, and that tonight, instead of a question on a war address, it had been an address to His Majesty to thank him for accepting the overture and for opening a negotiation to treat for peace: I ask the gentlemen opposite—I appeal to the whole 558 representatives of the people—to lay their hands upon their hearts, and to say whether they would not have cordially voted for such an address. Would they, or would they not? Yes, sir, if the address had breathed a spirit of peace, your benches would have resounded with rejoicings and with praises of a measure that was likely to bring back the blessings of tranquility. On the present occasion, then, I ask for the vote of none but of those who, in the secret confession of their conscience, admit, at this instant while they hear me, that they would have cheerfully and heartily voted with the minister for an address directly the reverse of this. If every such gentleman were to vote with me, I should be this night in the greatest majority that ever I had the honor to vote with in this House.

Sir, we have heard tonight a great many most acrimonious invectives against Bonaparte, against the whole course of his conduct, and against the unprincipled manner in which he seized upon the reins of government. I will not make his defense—I think all this sort of invective, which is used only to inflame the passions of this House and of the country, exceeding ill timed and very impolitic—but I say I will not make his defense. I am not sufficiently in possession of materials upon which to form an opinion on the character and conduct of this extraordinary man. Upon his arrival in France he found the government in a very unsettled state, and the whole affairs of the republic deranged, crippled, and involved. He thought it necessary to reform the government; and he did reform it, just in the way in which a military man may be expected to carry on a reform—he seized on the whole authority to himself. It will not be expected from me that I should either approve or apologize for such an act. I am certainly not for reforming governments by such expedients; but how this House can be so violently indignant at the idea of military despotism is, I own, a little singular, when I see the composure with which they can observe it nearer home; nay, when I see them regard it as a frame of government most peculiarly suited to the exercise of free opinion on a subject the most important of any that can engage the attention of a people. Was it not the system that was so happily and so advantageously established of late all over Ireland; and which, even now, the government may, at its pleasure, proclaim over the whole of that kingdom? Are not the persons and property of the people left in many districts at this moment to the entire will of military commanders? And is not this held out as peculiarly proper and advantageous at a time when the people of Ireland are free, and with unbiased judgment, to discuss the most interesting question of a legislative union? Notwithstanding the existence of martial law, so far do we think Ireland from being enslaved that we think it precisely the period and the circumstances under which she may best declare her free opinion! Now really, sir, I cannot think that gentlemen who talk in this way about Ireland can, with a good grace, rail at military despotism in France.

But, it seems, "Bonaparte has broken his oaths. He has violated his oath of fidelity to the constitution of the year 3." Sir, I am not one of those who think that any such oaths ought ever to be exacted. They are seldom or ever of any effect; and I am not for sporting with a thing so sacred as an oath. I think it would be good to lay aside all such oaths. Whoever heard that, in revolutions, the oath of fidelity to the former government was ever regarded; or even when violated that it was imputed to the persons as a crime? In times of revolution, men who take up arms are called rebels—if they fail, they are adjudged to be traitors. But who ever heard before of their being perjured? On the restoration of Charles II, those who had taken up arms for the Commonwealth were stigmatized as rebels and traitors, but not as men forsworn. Was the earl of Devonshire charged with being perjured on account of the allegiance he had sworn to the house of Stuart and the part he took in those struggles which preceded and brought about the Revolution? The violation of oaths of allegiance was never imputed to the people of England, and will never be imputed to any people. But who brings up the question of oaths? He who strives to make twenty-four millions of persons violate the oaths they have taken to their present constitution, and who desires to reestablish the house of Bourbon by such violation of their vows. I put it so, sir, because, if the question of oaths be of the least consequence, it is equal on both sides. He who desires the whole people of France to perjure themselves, and who hopes for success in his project only upon their doing so, surely cannot make it a charge against Bonaparte that he has done the same.

"Ah! but Bonaparte has declared it as his opinion that the two governments of Great Britain and of France cannot exist together. After the Treaty of Campo Formio he sent two confidential persons, Berthier and Monge, to the Directory to say so in his name." Well, and what is there in this absurd and puerile assertion, if it was ever made? Has not the right honorable gentleman, in this House, said the same thing? In this, at least, they resemble one another. They have both made use of this assertion; and I believe that these two illustrious persons are the only two on earth who think it. But let us turn the tables. We ought to put ourselves at times in the place of the enemy, if we are desirous of really examining with candor and fairness the dispute between us. How may they not interpret the speeches of ministers and their friends in both houses of the British Parliament? If we are to be told of the idle speech of Berthier and Monge, may they not also bring up speeches in which it has not been merely hinted, but broadly asserted, that "the two constitutions of England and France could not exist together"? May not these offenses and charges be reciprocated without end? Are we ever to go on in this miserable squabble about words? Are we still, as we happen to be successful on the one side or other, to bring up these impotent accusations, insults, and provocations against each other; and only when we are beaten and unfortunate to think of treating? Oh! pity the condition of man, gracious God! and save us from such a system of malevolence, in which all our old and venerated prejudices are to be done away, and by which we are to be taught to consider war as the natural state of man, and peace but as a dangerous and difficult extremity.

Sir, this temper must be corrected. It is a diabolical spirit and would lead to interminable war. Our history is full of instances that where we have overlooked a proffered occasion to treat, we have uniformly suffered by delay. At what time did we ever profit by obstinately persevering in war? We accepted at Ryswick the terms we had refused five years before, and the same peace which was concluded at Utrecht might have been obtained at Gertruydenberg. And as to security from the future machinations or ambition of the French, I ask you what security you ever had or could have. Did the different treaties made with Louis XIV serve to tie up his hands, to restrain his ambition, or to stifle his restless spirit? At what period could you safely repose in the honor, forbearance, and moderation of the French government? Was there ever an idea of refusing to treat because the peace might be afterwards insecure? The peace of 1763 was not accompanied with securities; and it was no sooner made than the French court began, as usual, its intrigues. And what security did the right honorable gentleman exact at the peace of 1783, in which he was engaged? Were we rendered secure by that peace? The right honorable gentleman knows well that soon after that peace the French formed a plan, in conjunction with the Dutch, of attacking our Indian possessions, of raising up the native powers against us, and of driving us out of India; as the French are desirous of doing now—only with this difference, that the cabinet of France entered into this project in a moment of profound peace, and when they conceived us to be lulled into perfect security. After making the peace of 1783, the right honorable gentleman and his friends went out, and I, among others, came into office. Suppose, sir, that we had taken up the jealousy upon which the right honorable gentleman now acts, and had refused to ratify the peace which he had made. Suppose that we had said, "No; France is acting a perfidious part—we see no security for England in this treaty—they want only a respite, in order to attack us again in an important part of our dominions; and we ought not to confirm the treaty." I ask, would the right honorable gentleman have supported us in this refusal? I say that upon his reasoning he ought; but I put it fairly to him, would he have supported us in refusing to ratify the treaty upon such a pretense? He certainly ought not, and I am sure he would not, but the course of reasoning which he now assumes would have justified his taking such a ground. On the contrary, I am persuaded that he would have said, "This is a refinement upon jealousy. Security! You have security, the only security that you can ever expect to get. It is the present interest of France to make peace. She will keep it if it be her interest: she will break it if it be her interest; such is the state of nations; and you have nothing but your own vigilance for your security."

"It is not the interest of Bonaparte," it seems, "sincerely to enter into a negotiation, or, if he should even make peace, sincerely to keep it." But how are we to decide upon his sincerity? By refusing to treat with him? Surely, if we mean to discover his sincerity, we ought to hear the propositions which he desires to make. "But peace would be unfriendly to his system of military despotism." Sir, I hear a great deal about the short-lived nature of military despotism. I wish the history of the world would bear gentlemen out in this description of military despotism. Was not the government erected by Augustus Caesar a military despotism? and yet it endured for six hundred or seven hundred years. Military despotism, unfortunately, is too likely in its nature to be permanent, and it is not true that it depends on the life of the first usurper. Though half the Roman emperors were murdered, yet the military despotism went on; and so it would be, I fear, in France. If Bonaparte should disappear from the scene, to make room, perhaps, for a Berthier, or any other general, what difference would that make in the quality of French despotism or in our relation to the country? We may as safely treat with a Bonaparte or with any of his successors, be they who they may, as we could with a Louis XVI, a Louis XVII, or a Louis XVIII. There is no difference but in the name. Where the power essentially resides, thither we ought to go for peace.

But, sir, if we are to reason on the fact, I should think that it is the interest of Bonaparte to make peace. A lover of military glory, as that general must necessarily be, may he not think that his measure of glory is full—that it may be tarnished by a reverse of fortune, and can hardly be increased by any new laurels? He must feel that, in the situation to which he is now raised, he can no longer depend on his own fortune, his own genius, and his own talents for a continuance of his success; he must be under the necessity of employing other generals, whose misconduct or incapacity might endanger his power, or whose triumphs even might affect the interest which he holds in the opinion of the French. Peace, then, would secure to him what he has achieved, and fix the inconstancy of fortune. But this will not be his only motive. He must see that France also requires a respite—a breathing interval to recruit her wasted strength. To procure her this respite would be, perhaps, the attainment of more solid glory, as well as the means of acquiring more solid power, than anything which he can hope to gain from arms and from the proudest triumphs. May he not then be zealous to gain this fame, the only species of fame, perhaps, that is worth acquiring? Nay, granting that his soul may still burn with the thirst of military exploits, is it not likely that he is earnestly disposed to yield to the feelings of the French people, and to consolidate his power by consulting their interests? I have a right to argue in this way, when suppositions of his insincerity are reasoned upon on the other side. Sir, these aspersions are, in truth, always idle and even mischievous. I have been too long accustomed to hear imputations and calumnies thrown out upon great and honorable characters to be much influenced by them.

My learned friend has paid this night a most just, deserved, and honorable tribute of applause to the memory of that great and unparalleled character who has been so recently lost to the world. I must, like him, beg leave to dwell a moment on the venerable George Washington, though I know that it is impossible for me to bestow anything like adequate praise on a character which gave us, more than any other human being, the example of a perfect man; yet, good, great, and unexampled as General Washington was, I can remember the time when he was not better spoken of in this House than Bonaparte is now. The right honorable gentleman who opened this debate may remember in what terms of disdain, of virulence, and even of contempt General Washington was spoken of by gentlemen on that side of the House. Does he not recollect with what marks of indignation any member was stigmatized as an enemy to his country who mentioned with common respect the name of General Washington? If a negotiation had then been proposed to be opened with that great man, what would have been said? "Would you treat with a rebel, a traitor! What an example would you not give by such an act!" I do not know whether the right honorable gentleman may not yet possess some of his old prejudices on the subject. I hope not. I hope by this time we are all convinced that a republican government like that of America may exist without danger or injury to social order or to established monarchies. They have happily shown that they can maintain the relations of peace and amity with other states: they have shown, too, that they are alive to the feelings of honor; but they do not lose sight of plain good sense and discretion. They have not refused to negotiate with the French, and they have accordingly the hopes of a speedy termination of every difference. We cry up their conduct, but we do not imitate it. At the beginning of the struggle we were told that the French were setting up a set of wild and impracticable theories, and that we ought not to be misled by them—we could not grapple with theories. Now we are told that we must not treat, because, out of the lottery, Bonaparte has drawn such a prize as military despotism. Is military despotism a theory? One would think that this is one of the practical things which ministers might understand, and to which they would have no particular objection. But what is our present conduct founded on but a theory, and that a most wild and ridiculous theory? What are we fighting for? Not for a principle; not for security; not for conquest even; but merely for an experiment and a speculation, to discover whether a gentleman at Paris may not turn out a better man than we now take him to be. . . .

Sir, I wish the atrocities of which we hear so much, and which I abhor as much as any man, were indeed unexampled. I fear that they do not belong exclusively to the French. When the right honorable gentleman speaks of the extraordinary successes of the last campaign, he does not mention the horrors by which some of those successes were accompanied. Naples, for instance, has been, among others, what is called "delivered"; and yet, if I am rightly informed, it has been stained and polluted by murders so ferocious, and by cruelties of every kind so abhorrent, that the heart shudders at the recital. It has been said, not only that the miserable victims of the rage and brutality of the fanatics were savagely murdered but that, in many instances, their flesh was eaten and devoured by the cannibals who are the advocates and the instruments of social order! Nay, England is not totally exempt from reproach, if the rumors which are circulated be true. I will mention a fact to give ministers the opportunity, if it be false, of wiping away the stain that it must otherwise fix on the British name. It is said that a party of the republican inhabitants of Naples took shelter in the fortress of the Castel de Uova. They were besieged by a detachment from the royal army, to whom they refused to surrender; but demanded that a British officer should be brought forward, and to him they capitulated. They made terms with him under the sanction of the British name. It was agreed that their persons and property should be safe, and that they should be conveyed to Toulon. They were accordingly put on board a vessel; but before they sailed their property was confiscated, numbers of them taken out, thrown into dungeons, and some of them, I understand, notwithstanding the British guarantee, actually executed.

Where then, sir, is this war, which on every side is pregnant with such horrors, to be carried? Where is it to stop? Not till you establish the house of Bourbon! And this you cherish the hope of doing, because you have had a successful campaign. Why, sir, before this you have had a successful campaign. The situation of the allies, with all they have gained, is surely not to be compared now to what it was when you had taken Valenciennes, Quesnoy, Condé, etc., which induced some gentlemen in this House to prepare themselves for a march to Paris. With all that you have gained, you surely will not say that the prospect is brighter now than it was then. What have you gained but the recovery of a part of what you before lost? One campaign is successful to you—another to them; and in this way, animated by the vindictive passions of revenge, hatred, and rancor, which are infinitely more flagitious even than those of ambition and the thirst of power, you may go on forever, as, with such black incentives, I see no end to human misery. And all this without an intelligible motive, all this because you may gain a better peace a year or two hence! So that we are called upon to go on merely as a speculation. We must keep Bonaparte for some time longer at war as a state of probation. Gracious God, sir, is war a state of probation? Is peace a rash system? Is it dangerous for nations to live in amity with each other? Is your vigilance, your policy, your common powers of observation, to be extinguished by putting an end to the horrors of war? Cannot this state of probation be as well undergone without adding to the catalogue of human sufferings? "But we must pause!" What! must the bowels of Great Britain be torn out—her best blood be spilt—her treasure wasted—that you may make an experiment? Put yourselves—oh! that you would put yourselves—in the field of battle, and learn to judge of the sort of horrors that you excite. In former wars a man might at least have some feeling, some interest, that served to balance in his mind the impressions which a scene of carnage and of death must inflict. If a man had been present at the Battle of Blenheim, for instance, and had inquired the motive of the battle, there was not a soldier engaged who could not have satisfied his curiosity, and even perhaps allayed his feelings—they were fighting to repress the uncontrolled ambition of the *grand monarque*. But if a man were present now at a field of slaughter, and were to inquire for what they were fighting—"Fighting!" would be the answer; "they are not fighting, they are pausing." "Why is that man expiring? Why is that other writhing with agony? What means this implacable fury?" The answer must be "You are quite wrong, sir; you deceive yourself—they are not fighting—do not disturb them—they are merely pausing!—this man is not expiring with agony—that man is not dead—he is only pausing! Lord help you, sir! they are not angry with one another; they have now no cause of quarrel—but their country thinks that there should be a pause. All that you see, sir, is nothing like fighting—there is no harm, nor cruelty, nor bloodshed in it whatever—it is nothing more than *a political pause!*—it is merely to try an experiment—to see whether Bonaparte will not behave himself better than heretofore; and in the meantime we have agreed to a pause, in pure friendship!" And is this the way, sir, that you are to show yourselves the advocates of order? You take up a system calculated to uncivilize the world, to destroy order, to trample on religion, to stifle in the heart, not merely the generosity of noble sentiment, but the affections of social nature; and in the prosecution of this system you spread terror and devastation all around you.

Sir, I have done. I have told you my opinion. I think you ought to have given a civil, clear, and explicit answer to the overture which was fairly and handsomely made you. If you were desirous that the negotiation should have included all your allies, as the means of bringing about a general peace, you should have told Bonaparte so; but I believe you were afraid of his agreeing to the proposal. You took that method before. "Ay, but," you say, "the people were anxious for peace in 1797." I say they are friends to peace now; and I am confident that you will one day own it. Believe me, they are friends to peace; although, by the laws which you have made restraining the expression of the sense of the people, public opinion cannot now be heard as loudly and unequivocally as heretofore.

But I will not go into the internal state of this country. It is too afflicting to the heart to see the strides which have been made by means of, and under the miserable pretext of, this war against liberty of every kind, both of speech and of writing; and to observe in another kingdom the rapid approaches to that military despotism which we affect to make an argument against peace. I know, sir, that public opinion, if it could be collected, would be for peace as much now as in 1797, and I know that it is only by public opinion—not by a sense of their duty—not by the inclination of their minds—that ministers will be brought, if ever, to give us peace. I conclude, sir, with repeating what I said before; I ask for no gentleman's vote who would have reprobated the compliance of ministers with the proposition of the French government; I ask for no gentleman's support tonight who would have voted against ministers, if they had come down and proposed to enter into a negotiation with the French; but I have a right to ask—I know that, in honor, in consistency, in conscience, I have a right to expect the vote of every gentleman who would have voted with ministers in an address to His Majesty diametrically opposite to the motion of this night. ■

Senator Daniel Webster Backs the Union in His Reply to Senator Hayne

"I have not allowed myself, sir, to look beyond the Union to see what might lie hidden in the dark recess behind."

IN **1829,** Samuel Foot proposed in the U.S. Senate what became known as the Foot resolution, an inquiry into the limiting of the sale of public land. Senator Robert Young Hayne of South Carolina, a staunch advocate of states' rights, fought this resolution (and its attempt by New England's business interests to limit western expansion) by affirming the doctrine of nullification, the ability of each state to declare "null and void" any federal law that infringed upon the state's sovereignty.

Daniel Webster, senator from Massachusetts, listened carefully to Hayne's argument and then, with minimal time for preparation, delivered one of the most forceful rebuttals in the history of American debate. Considerably abridged here, Webster's lengthy argument on January 26, 1830, moved far beyond the Foot resolution to make his case for a strong Union.

Beginning with the analogy of a sailor driven off course in a storm, Webster forces the argument back to the specific resolution. With rhetorical questions and humor, he points the debate to what "the real question" between Hayne and him is, arguing against a regionalism that would divide the Union. Webster's use of anaphora in successive clauses that start with "It is to that Union" or "God grant that" lends unity to his rhythmic call for "Liberty and Union, now and forever, one and inseparable!"

□   □   □

M r. President:
When the mariner has been tossed for many days, in thick weather, and on an unknown sea, he naturally avails himself of the first pause in the storm, the earliest glance of the sun, to take his latitude and ascertain how far the elements have driven him from his true course. Let us imitate this prudence and, before we float further on the waves of this debate, refer to the point from which we departed, that we may at

least be able to conjecture where we now are. I ask for the reading of the resolution.

The secretary read the resolution, as follows:

> Resolved, That the Committee on Public Lands be instructed to inquire and report the quantity of public lands remaining unsold within each State and Territory, and whether it be expedient to limit, for a certain period, the sales of the public lands to such lands only as have heretofore been offered for sale. and are now subject to entry at the minimum price. And, also, whether the office of Surveyor General, and some of the land offices, may not be abolished without detriment to the public interest; or whether it be expedient to adopt measures to hasten the sales and extend more rapidly the surveys of the public lands.

We have thus heard, sir, what the resolution is, which is actually before us for consideration; and it will readily occur to everyone that it is almost the only subject about which something has not been said in the speech, running through two days, by which the Senate has been now entertained by the gentleman from South Carolina. Every topic in the wide range of our public affairs, whether past or present—everything, general or local, whether belonging to national politics or party politics, seems to have attracted more or less of the honorable member's attention, save only the resolution before the Senate. He has spoken of everything but the public lands. They have escaped his notice. To that subject, in all his excursions, he has not paid even the cold respect of a passing glance.

When this debate, sir, was to be resumed on Thursday morning, it so happened that it would have been convenient for me to be elsewhere. The honorable member, however, did not incline to put off the discussion to another day. He had a shot, he said, to return, and he wished to discharge it. That shot, sir, which it was kind thus to inform us was coming, that we might stand out of the way, or prepare ourselves to fall before it and die with decency, has now been received. Under all advantages, and with expectation awakened by the tone which preceded it, it has been discharged and has spent its force. It may become me to say no more of its effect than that if nobody is found, after all, either killed or wounded by it, it is not the first time, in the history of human affairs, that the vigor and success of the war have not quite come up to the lofty and sounding phrase of the manifesto.

The gentleman, sir, in declining to postpone the debate, told the Senate, with the emphasis of his hand upon his heart, that there was something rankling here, which he wished to relieve.

[Mr. Hayne rose and disclaimed having used the word "rankling."]

It would not, Mr. President, be safe for the honorable member to appeal to those around him upon the question whether he did, in fact, make use of that word. But he may have been unconscious of it. At any rate, it is enough that he disclaims it. But still, with or without the use of that particular word, he had yet something here, he said, of which he wished to rid himself by an immediate reply. In this respect, sir, I have a great advantage over the honorable gentleman. There is nothing here, sir, which gives me the slightest uneasiness; neither fear, nor anger, nor that which is sometimes more troublesome than either,—the consciousness of having been in the wrong. There is nothing, either originating here or now received here by the gentleman's shot. Nothing original, for I had not the slightest feeling of disrespect or unkindness towards the honorable member. Some passages, it is true, had occurred since our acquaintance in this body, which I could have wished might have been otherwise; but I had used philosophy and forgotten them. When the honorable member rose, in his first speech, I paid him the respect of attentive listening; and when he sat down, though surprised and, I must say, even astonished at some of his opinions, nothing was further from my intention than to commence any personal warfare: and through the whole of the few remarks I made in answer, I avoided, studiously and carefully, everything which I thought possible to be construed into disrespect. And, sir, while there is thus nothing originating here which I wished at any time or now wish to discharge, I must repeat, also, that nothing has been received here which rankles or in any way gives me annoyance. I will not accuse the honorable member of violating the rules of civilized war—I will not say that he poisoned his arrows. But whether his shafts were or were not dipped in that which would have caused rankling, if they had reached, there was not, as it happened, quite strength enough in the bow to bring them to their mark. If he wishes now to gather up those shafts, he must look for them elsewhere; they will not be found fixed and quivering in the object at which they were aimed. . . .

I need not repeat at large the general topics of the honorable gentleman's speech. When he said yesterday that he did not attack the eastern states, he certainly must have forgotten, not only particular remarks, but the whole drift and tenor of his speech; unless he means by not attacking that he did not commence hostilities—but that another had preceded him in the attack. He, in the first place, disapproved of the whole course of the government, for forty years, in regard to its dispositions of the public land; and then turning northward and eastward, and fancying he had found a cause for alleged narrowness and niggardliness in the "accursed policy" of the tariff, to which he represented the people of New England as wedded, he went on for a full hour with remarks, the whole scope of which was to exhibit the results of this policy, in feelings and in measures unfavorable to the West. I thought his opinions unfounded and erroneous as to the general course of the government, and ventured to reply to them.

The gentleman had remarked on the analogy of other cases, and quoted the conduct of European governments towards their own subjects, settling on this continent, as a point to show that we had been harsh and rigid in selling, when we should have given the public lands to settlers without price. I thought the honorable member had suffered his judgment to be betrayed by a false analogy—that he was struck with an appearance of resemblance where there was no real similitude. I think so still. The first settlers of North America were enterprising spirits, engaged in private adventure or fleeing from tyranny at home. When arrived here they were forgotten by the mother country, or remembered only to be oppressed. Carried away again by the appearance of analogy, or struck with the eloquence of the passage, the honorable member yesterday observed that the conduct of government towards the western emigrants, or my representation of it, brought to his mind a celebrated speech in the British Parliament. It was, sir, the speech of Colonel Barre. On the question of the Stamp Act, or tea tax, I forget which, Colonel Barre had heard a member on the treasury bench argue that the people of the United States, being British colonists, planted by the maternal care, nourished by the indulgence, and protected by the arms of England, would not grudge their mite to relieve the mother country from the heavy burden under which she groaned. The language of Colonel Barre, in reply to this, was: They planted by your care? Your oppression planted them in America. They fled from your tyranny, and grew by your neglect of them. So soon as you began to care for them, you showed your care by sending persons to spy out their liberties, misrepresent their character, prey upon them, and eat out their substance.

And how does the honorable gentleman mean to maintain that language like this is applicable to the conduct of the government of the United States towards the western emigrants, or to any representation given by me of that conduct? Were the settlers in the West driven thither by our oppression? Have they flourished only by our neglect of them? Has the government done nothing but to prey upon them and eat out their substance? Sir, this fervid eloquence of the British speaker, just when and where it was uttered, and fit to remain an exercise for the schools, is not a little out of place when it is brought thence to be applied here to the conduct of our own country towards her own citizens. From America to England, it may be true; from Americans to their own government it would be strange language. Let us leave it to be recited and declaimed by our boys against a foreign nation—not introduce it here, to recite and declaim ourselves against our own.

But I come to the point of the alleged contradiction. In my remarks on Wednesday I contended that we could not give away gratuitously all the public lands; that we held them in trust; that the government had solemnly pledged itself to dispose of them as a common fund for the common benefit, and to sell and settle them as its discretion should dictate. Now, sir, what contradiction does the gentleman find to this sentiment, in the speech of 1825? He quotes me as having then said that we ought not to hug these lands as a very great treasure. Very well, sir, supposing me to be accurately reported in that expression, what is the contradiction? I have not now said that we should hug these lands as a favorite source of pecuniary income. No such thing. It is not my view. What I have said, and what I do say, is that they are a common fund—to be disposed of for the common benefit—to be sold at low prices for the accommodation of settlers, keeping the object of settling the lands as much in view as that of raising money from them. This I say now, and this I have always said. Is this hugging them as a favorite treasure? Is there no difference between hugging and hoarding this fund, on the one hand, as a great treasure and, on the other, of disposing of it at low prices, placing the proceeds in the general treasury of the Union? My opinion is that as much is to be made of the land as fairly and reasonably may be, selling it all the while at such rates as to give the fullest effect to settlement. This is not giving it all away to the states, as the gentleman would propose; nor is it hugging the fund closely and tenaciously, as a favorite treasure; but it is, in my judgment, a just and wise policy, perfectly according with all the various duties which rest on government. So much for my contradiction. And what is it? Where is the ground for the gentleman's triumph? What inconsistency in word or doctrine has he been able to detect? Sir, if this be a sample of that discomfiture with which the honorable gentleman threatened me, commend me to the word "discomfiture" for the rest of my life.

But, after all, this is not the point of the debate, and I must now bring the gentleman back to what is the point.

The real question between me and him is, Has the doctrine been advanced at the South or the East that the population of the West should be retarded, or at least need not be hastened, on account of its effect to drain off the people from the Atlantic states? Is this doctrine, as has been alleged, of eastern origin? That is the question. Has the gentleman found anything by which he can make good his accusation? I submit to the Senate that he has entirely failed; and as far as this debate has shown, the only person who has advanced such sentiments is a gentleman from South Carolina, and a friend to the honorable member himself. The honorable gentleman has given no answer to this; there is none which can be given. The simple fact, while it requires no comment to enforce it, defies all argument to refute it. I could refer to the speeches of another southern gentleman, in years before, of the same general character, and to the same effect, as that which has been quoted; but I will not consume the time of the Senate by the reading of them.

So then, sir, New England is guiltless of the policy of retarding western population, and of all envy and jealousy of the growth of the new states. Whatever there be of that policy in the country, no part of it is hers. If it has a local habitation, the honorable member has probably seen, by this time, where to look for it; and if it now has received a name, he has himself christened it.

We approach, at length, sir, to a more important part of the honorable gentleman's observations. Since it does not accord with my views of justice and policy to give away the public lands altogether, as mere matter of gratuity, I am asked by the honorable gentleman on what ground it is that I consent to vote them away in particular instances. How, he inquires, do I reconcile with these professed sentiments my support of measures appropriating portions of the lands to particular roads, particular canals, particular rivers, and particular institutions of education in the West? This leads, sir, to the real and wide difference, in political opinion, between the honorable gentleman and myself. On my part, I look upon all these objects as connected with the common good, fairly embraced in its object and its terms; he, on the contrary, deems them all, if good at all, only local good. This is our difference. The interrogatory which he proceeded to put at once explains this difference. "What interest," asks he, "has South Carolina in a canal in Ohio?" Sir, this very question is full of significance. It develops the gentleman's whole political system; and its answer expounds mine. Here we differ. I look upon a road over the Allegheny, a canal round the falls of the Ohio, or a canal or railway from the Atlantic to the western waters, as being an object large and extensive enough to be fairly said to be for the common benefit. The gentleman thinks otherwise, and this is the key to open his construction of the powers of the government. He may well ask, What interest has South Carolina in a canal in Ohio? On his system, it is true, she has no interest.

On that system, Ohio and Carolina are different governments and different countries: connected here, it is true, by some slight and ill-defined bond of union, but, in all main respects, separate and diverse. On that system, Carolina has no more interest in a canal in Ohio than in Mexico. The gentleman, therefore, only follows out his own principles; he does no more than arrive at the natural conclusions of his own doctrines; he only announces the true results of that creed, which he has adopted himself, and would persuade others to adopt, when he thus declares that South Carolina has no interest in a public work in Ohio. Sir, we narrow-minded people of New England do not reason thus. Our notion of things is entirely different. We look upon the states, not as separated, but as united. We love to dwell on that union, and on the mutual happiness which it has so much promoted, and the common renown which it has so greatly contributed to acquire. In our contemplation, Carolina and Ohio are parts of the same country—states, united under the same general government, having interests, common, associated, intermingled. In whatever is within the proper sphere of the constitutional power of this government, we look upon the states as one. We do not impose geographical limits to our patriotic feeling or regard; we do not follow rivers and mountains, and lines of latitude, to find boundaries beyond which public improvements do not benefit us. We who come here as agents and representatives of these narrow-minded and selfish men of New England consider ourselves as bound to regard, with an equal eye, the good of the whole, in whatever is within our power of legislation. Sir, if a railroad or canal, beginning in South Carolina and ending in South Carolina, appeared to me to be of national importance and national magnitude, believing, as I do, that the power of government extends to the encouragement of works of that description, if I were to stand up here, and ask, What interest has Massachusetts in a railroad in South Carolina? I should not be willing to face my constituents. These same narrow-minded men would tell me that they had sent me to act for the whole country, and that one who possessed too little comprehension, either of intellect or feeling, one who was not large enough, both in mind and in heart, to embrace the whole, was not fit to be entrusted with the interest of any part. Sir, I do not desire to enlarge the powers of the government by unjustifiable construction, nor to exercise any not within a fair interpretation. But when it is believed that a power does exist, then it is, in my judgment, to be exercised for the general benefit of the whole. So far as respects the exercise of such a power, the states are one. It was the very object of the Constitution to create unity of interests to the extent of the powers of the general government. In war and peace we are one; in commerce, one; because the authority of the general government reaches to war and peace and to the regulation of commerce. I have never seen any more difficulty in erecting lighthouses on the lakes than on the ocean; in improving the harbors of inland seas than if they were within the ebb and flow of the tide; or of removing obstructions in the vast streams of the west more than in any work to facilitate commerce on the Atlantic coast. If there be any power for one, there is power also for the other; and they are all and equally for the common good of the country.

There are other objects apparently more local, or the benefit of which is less general, towards which, nevertheless, I have concurred with others to give aid, by donations of land. It is proposed to construct a road, in or through one of the new states, in which this government possesses large quantities of land. Have the United States no right or, as a great and untaxed proprietor, are they under no obligation to contribute to an object thus calculated to promote the common good of all the proprietors, themselves included? And even with respect to education, which is the extreme case, let the question be considered. In the first place, as we have seen, it was made matter of compact with these states, that they should do their part to promote education. In the next place, our whole system of land laws proceeds on the idea that education is for the common good, because, in every division, a certain portion is uniformly reserved and appropriated for the use of schools. And, finally, have not these new states singularly strong claims, founded on the ground already stated, that the government is a great untaxed proprietor, in the ownership of the soil? It is a consideration of great importance that, probably, there is in no part of the country, or of the world, so great call for the means of education as in those new states—owing to the vast numbers of persons within those ages in which education and instruction are usually received, if received at all. This is the natural consequence of recency of settlement and rapid increase. The census of these states shows how great a proportion of the whole population occupies the classes between infancy and manhood. These are the wide fields, and here is the deep and quick soil for the seeds of knowledge and virtue; and this is the favored season, the very springtime for sowing them. Let them be disseminated without stint. Let them be scattered with a bountiful broadcast. Whatever the government can fairly do towards these objects, in my opinion, ought to be done.

These, sir, are the grounds succinctly stated on which my votes for grants of lands for particular objects rest; while I maintain, at the same time, that it is all a common fund for the common benefit. And reasons like these, I presume, have influenced the votes of other gentlemen from New England! Those who have a different view of the powers of the government, of course, come to different conclusions on these as on other questions. . . .

Mr. President, the honorable gentleman would be in a dilemma like that of another great general. He would have a knot before him which he could not untie. He must cut it with his sword. He must say to his followers, Defend yourselves with your bayonets; and this is war—civil war.

Direct collision, therefore, between force and force is the unavoidable result of that remedy for the revision of unconstitutional laws which the gentleman contends for. It must happen in the very first case to which it is applied. Is not this the plain result? To resist, by force, the execution of a law generally is treason. Can the courts of the United States take notice of the indulgence of a state to commit treason? The common saying that a state cannot commit treason herself is nothing to the purpose. Can she authorize others to do it? If John Fries had produced an act of Pennsylvania annulling the law of Congress, would it have helped his case? Talk about it as we will, these doctrines go the length of revolution. They are incompatible with any peaceable administration of the government. They lead directly to disunion and civil commotion; and, therefore, it is, that at their commencement, when they are first found to be maintained by respectable men and in a tangible form, I enter my public protest against them all.

The honorable gentleman argues that if this government be the sole judge of the extent of its own powers, whether that right of judging be in Congress or the Supreme Court, it equally subverts state sovereignty. This the gentleman sees, or thinks he sees, although he cannot perceive how the right of judging, in this matter, if left to the exercise of state legislatures, has any tendency to subvert the government of the Union. The gentleman's opinion may be that the right ought not to have been lodged with the general government; he may like better such a Constitution, as we should have under the right of state interference; but I ask him to meet me on the plain matter of fact; I ask him to meet me on the Constitution itself; I ask him if the power is not found there—clearly and visibly found there.

But, sir, what is this danger, and what the grounds of it? Let it be remembered that the Constitution of the United States is not unalterable. It is to continue in its present form no longer than the people who established it shall choose to continue it. If they shall become convinced that they have made an injudicious or inexpedient partition and distribution of power, between the state governments and the general government, they can alter that distribution at will.

If anything be found in the national Constitution, either by original provision or subsequent interpretation, which ought not to be in it, the people know how to get rid of it. If any construction be established, unacceptable to them, so as to become, practically, a part of the Constitution, they will amend it, at their own sovereign pleasure: but while the people choose to maintain it as it is, while they are satisfied with it and refuse to change it, who has given, or who can give, to the state legislatures a right to alter it, either by interference, construction, or otherwise? Gentlemen do not seem to recollect that the people have any power to do anything for themselves; they imagine there is no safety for them any longer than they are under the close guardianship of the state legislatures. Sir, the people have not trusted their safety, in regard to the general constitution, to these hands. They have required other security and taken other bonds. They have chosen to trust themselves, first, to the plain words of the instrument and to such construction as the government itself, in doubtful cases, should put on its own powers, under their oaths of office and subject to their responsibility to them; just as the people of a state trust their own state governments with a similar power. Secondly, they have reposed their trust in the efficacy of frequent elections, and in their own power to remove their own servants and agents, whenever they see cause. Thirdly, they have reposed trust in the judicial power, which, in order that it might be trustworthy, they have made as respectable, as disinterested, and as independent as was practicable. Fourthly, they have seen fit to rely, in case of necessity or high expediency, on their known and admitted power to alter or amend the Constitution, peaceably and quietly, whenever experience shall point out defects or imperfections. And, finally, the people of the United States have, at no time, in no way, directly or indirectly, authorized any state legislature to construe or interpret their high instrument of government—much less to interfere, by their own power, to arrest its course and operation.

If, sir, the people, in these respects, had done otherwise than they have done, their Constitution could neither have been preserved nor would it have been worth preserving. And, if its plain provisions shall now be disregarded, and these new doctrines interpolated in it, it will become as feeble and helpless a being as its enemies, whether early or more recent, could possibly desire. It will exist in every state, but as a poor dependent on state permission. It must borrow leave to be, and it will be no longer than state pleasure or state discretion sees fit to grant the indulgence and to prolong its poor existence.

But, sir, although there are fears, there are hopes also. The people have preserved this, their own chosen Constitution, for forty years and have seen their happiness, prosperity, and renown grow with its growth, and strengthen with its strength. They are now, generally, strongly attached to it. Overthrown by direct assault, it cannot be; evaded, undermined, nullified, it will not be, if we, and those who shall succeed us here, as agents and representatives of the people, shall conscientiously and vigilantly discharge the two great branches of our public trust—faithfully to preserve and wisely to administer it.

Mr. President, I have thus stated the reasons of my dissent to the doctrines which have been advanced and maintained. I am conscious of having detained you and the Senate much too long. I was drawn into the debate with no previous deliberation such as is suited to the discussion of so grave and important a subject. But it is a subject of which my heart is full, and I have not been willing to suppress the utterance of its spontaneous sentiments. I cannot, even now, persuade myself to relinquish it without expressing once more my deep conviction that since it respects nothing less than the Union of the states, it is of most vital and essential importance to the public happiness. I profess, sir, in my career, hitherto, to have kept steadily in view the prosperity and honor of the whole country, and the preservation of our federal Union. It is to that Union we owe our safety at home and our consideration and dignity abroad. It is to that Union that we are chiefly indebted for whatever makes us most proud of our country. That Union we reached only by the discipline of our virtues in the severe school of adversity. It had its origin in the necessities of disordered finance, prostrate commerce, and ruined credit. Under its benign influence, these great interests immediately awoke as from the dead and sprang forth with newness of life. Every year of its duration has teemed with fresh proofs of its utility and its blessings; and, although our territory has stretched out wider and wider, and our population spread further and further, they have not outrun its protection or its benefits. It has been to us all a copious fountain of national, social, and personal happiness. I have not allowed myself, sir, to look beyond the Union to see what might lie hidden in the dark recess behind. I have not coolly weighed the chances of preserving liberty when the bonds that unite us together shall be broken asunder. I have not accustomed myself to hang over the precipice of disunion to see whether, with my short sight, I can fathom the depth of the abyss below; nor could I regard him as a safe counselor in the affairs of this government, whose thoughts should be mainly bent on considering not how the Union should be best preserved but how tolerable might be the condition of the people when it shall be broken up and destroyed. While the Union lasts we have high, exciting, gratifying prospects spread out before us, for us and our children. Beyond that I seek not to penetrate the veil. God grant that in my day, at least, that curtain may not rise. God grant that, on my vision, never may be opened what lies behind. When my eyes shall be turned to behold, for the last time, the sun in heaven, may I not see him shining on the broken and dishonored fragments of a once glorious Union; on states dissevered, discordant, belligerent; on a land rent with civil feuds, or drenched, it may be, in fraternal blood! Let their last feeble and lingering glance rather behold the gorgeous ensign of the Republic, now known and honored throughout the earth, still full high advanced, its arms and trophies streaming in their original luster, not a stripe erased or polluted, nor a single star obscured, bearing for its motto no such miserable interrogatory as "What is all this worth?" nor those other words of delusion and folly "Liberty first and union afterwards"; but everywhere, spread all over in characters of living light, blazing on all its ample folds, as they float over the sea and over the land, and in every wind under the whole heavens, that other sentiment, dear to every true American heart—Liberty and Union, now and forever, one and inseparable! ■

Senator John C. Calhoun Fights the Expunging of His Criticism of President Andrew Jackson

"You are going to violate the Constitution, and you get rid of the infamy by a falsehood."

THE **"EXPUNGING RESOLUTION"** of 1837, an attempt to erase criticism of a president, became the focus of a particularly bitter debate in the U.S. Senate.

President Andrew Jackson, first elected in 1828, had energetically opposed the Bank of the United States, which he perceived as a threat to his policies. While campaigning in 1832 for a second term, the popular president vetoed the recharter of the bank; once reelected, he tried to limit the bank's effectiveness by transferring its funds to local banks (called "pet banks" by his opponents). The Senate, in turn, passed a resolution to condemn the president's actions against the bank. When Jackson protested that resolution, his friends in the Senate sought to have the resolution expunged from the official record.

John C. Calhoun, who had given up the vice-presidency under Jackson to be elected senator from South Carolina, became an outspoken critic of Jackson's administration. One of the original "war hawks" in 1812, and ultimately the leading voice for states' rights against a powerful union, Calhoun fought Jackson's plan to remove government funds from the Bank of the United States; he inveighed against what came to be alliterated as "the cohesive power of public plunder," and the South Carolinian was even more adamant about the need to preserve the Senate's criticism of the president's actions.

In the January 1837 debate on the expunging resolution, Calhoun skillfully uses repetition in numerous references to "the Constitution" and, with skepticism about Jackson's popularity, "the voice of the people." By answering questions that he poses himself, Calhoun makes a constitutional case for maintaining the record of criticism. Even though he recognizes the certainty of the outcome ("But why do I waste my breath?"), Calhoun is at his most eloquent in registering his opposition to a resolution that was soon carried.

□   □   □

The gentleman from Virginia [Mr. Rives] says that the argument in favor of this expunging resolution has not been answered. Sir, there are some questions so plain that they cannot be argued. Nothing can make them more plain; and this is one. No one not blinded by party zeal can possibly be insensible that the measure proposed is a violation of the Constitution. The Constitution requires the Senate to keep a journal; this resolution goes to expunge the journal. If you may expunge a part, you may expunge the whole; and if it is expunged, how is it kept? The Constitution says the journal shall be kept; this resolution says it shall be destroyed. It does the very thing which the Constitution declares shall not be done. That is the argument, the whole argument. There is none other. Talk of precedents? and precedents drawn from a foreign country? They don't apply. No, sir. This is to be done, not in consequence of argument, but in spite of argument. I understand the case. I know perfectly well the gentlemen have no liberty to vote otherwise. They are coerced by an exterior power. They try, indeed, to comfort their conscience by saying that it is the will of the people, and the voice of the people. It is no such thing. We all know how these legislative returns have been obtained. It is by dictation from the White House. The president himself, with that vast mass of patronage which he wields, and the thousand expectations he is able to hold up, has obtained these votes of the state legislatures; and this, forsooth, is said to be the voice of the people. The voice of the people! Sir, can we forget the scene which was exhibited in this chamber when that expunging resolution was first introduced here? Have we forgotten the universal giving way of conscience, so that the senator from Missouri was left alone? I see before me senators who could not swallow that resolution; and has its nature changed since then? Is it any more constitutional now than it was then? Not at all. But executive power has interposed. Talk to me of the voice of the people! No, sir. It is the combination of patronage and power to coerce this body into a gross and palpable violation of the Constitution. Some individuals, I perceive, think to escape through the particular form in which this act is to be perpetrated. They tell us that the resolution on your records is not to be expunged, but is only to be endorsed "Expunged." Really, sir, I do not know how to argue against such contemptible sophistry. The occasion is too solemn for an argument of this sort. You are going to violate the Constitution, and you get rid of the infamy by a falsehood. You yourselves say that the resolution is expunged by your order. Yet you say it is not expunged. You put your act in express words. You record it, and then turn round and deny it.

But what is the motive? What is the pretext for this enormity? Why, gentlemen tell us the Senate has two distinct consciences—a legislative conscience and a judicial conscience. As a legislative body we have decided that the president has violated the Constitution. But gentlemen tell us that this is an impeachable offense; and, as we may be called to try it in our judicial capacity, we have no right to express the opinion. I need not show how inconsistent such a position is with the eternal, imprescriptible right of freedom of speech, and how utterly inconsistent it is with precedents drawn from the history of our British ancestors, where the same liberty of speech has for centuries been enjoyed. There is a shorter and more direct argument in reply. Gentlemen who take that position cannot, according to their own showing, vote for this resolution; for if it is unconstitutional for us to record a resolution of condemnation, because we may afterwards be called to try the case in a judicial capacity, then it is equally unconstitutional for us to record a resolution of acquittal. If it is unconstitutional for the Senate to declare before a trial that the president has violated the Constitution, it is equally unconstitutional to declare before a trial that he has not violated the Constitution. The same principle is involved in both. Yet, in the very face of this principle, gentlemen are here going to condemn their own act.

But why do I waste my breath? I know it is all utterly vain. The day is gone; night approaches, and night is suitable to the dark deed we meditate. There is a sort of destiny in this thing. The act must be performed; and it is an act which will tell on the political history of this country forever. Other preceding violations of the Constitution (and they have been many and great) filled my bosom with indignation, but this fills it only with grief. Others were done in the heat of partisanship. Power was, as it were, compelled to support itself by seizing upon new instruments of influence and patronage; and there were ambitious and able men to direct the process. Such was the removal of the deposits. which the president seized upon by a new and unprecedented act of arbitrary power—an act which gave him ample means of rewarding friends and punishing enemies. Something may, perhaps, be pardoned to him in this matter, on the old apology of tyrants—the plea of necessity. But here there can be no such apology. Here no necessity can so much as be pretended. This act originates in pure, unmixed, personal idolatry. It is the melancholy evidence of a broken spirit, ready to bow at the feet of power. The former act was such a one as might have been perpetrated in the days of Pompey or Caesar; but an act like this could never have been consummated by a Roman Senate until the times of Caligula and Nero. ■

Abolitionist Charles Sumner Excoriates Two Senate Colleagues on the Issue of "Bloody Kansas"

"THE noisome, squat, and nameless animal to which I now refer is not a proper model for an American senator."

AN UNCOMPROMISING FOE OF SLAVERY, Charles Sumner of Massachusetts took the floor of the U.S. Senate on May 20, 1856, to decry "the crime against Kansas." Violence over the slavery issue had escalated in the Kansas territory, and the heated debate in Congress reached its peak when Senator Sumner began his denunciation of Senator Stephen Douglas of Illinois and the absent Senator Andrew Pickens Butler of South Carolina.

After the first part of Sumner's tirade, Senator Lewis Cass of Michigan showed his disgust at the vituperation: "I have listened with equal regret and surprise to the speech of the honorable senator from Massachusetts— such a speech, the most un-American and unpatriotic that ever grated on the ears of the members of this high body, as I hope never to hear again, here or elsewhere."

Through literary allusion and indirect name-calling, the "black Republican" Sumner heaped invective on the proslavery forces in Congress. Stephen Douglas, "the Little Giant," responded to Sumner's attack for the Democrats, and before it was over, Senator James Murray Mason of Virginia had also been drawn into the verbal combat.

When the violent words stopped, violent actions soon followed. Shortly after his speech, Sumner was attacked in the Senate chamber by Congressman Preston Brooks, the nephew of Senator Butler. Brooks assaulted Sumner with a cane, whipping him repeatedly, and it took Sumner more than three years to recover from the brutal attack.

□ □ □

[SUMNER:] Before entering upon the argument, I must say something of a general character, particularly in response to what has fallen from senators who have raised themselves to eminence on this floor in championship of human wrongs. I mean the senator from South Carolina [Mr. Butler], and the senator from Illinois [Mr. Douglas], who, though unlike as Don Quixote and Sancho Panza, yet, like this couple, sally forth together in the same adventure. I regret much to miss the elder senator from his seat; but the cause, against which he has run atilt, with such activity of animosity, demands that the opportunity of exposing him should not be lost; and it is for the cause that I speak. The senator from South Carolina has read many books of chivalry, and believes himself a chivalrous knight, with sentiments of honor and courage. Of course, he has chosen a mistress to whom he has made his vows, and who, though ugly to others, is always lovely to him; though polluted in the sight of the world, is chaste in his sight—I mean the harlot Slavery. For her, his tongue is always profuse in words. Let her be impeached in character, or any proposition made to shut her out from the extension of her wantonness, and no extravagance of manner or hardihood of assertion is then too great for this senator. The frenzy of Don Quixote, in behalf of his wench, Dulcinea del Toboso, is all surpassed. The asserted rights of slavery, which shock equality of all kinds, are cloaked by a fantastic claim of equality. If the slave states cannot enjoy what, in mockery of the great fathers of the Republic, he misnames equality under the Constitution—in other words, the full power in the national territories to compel fellow men to unpaid toil, to separate husband and wife, and to sell little children at the auction block—then, sir, the chivalric senator will conduct the state of South Carolina out of the Union! Heroic knight! Exalted senator! A second Moses come for a second exodus!

But not content with this poor menace, which we have been twice told was "measured," the senator, in the unrestrained chivalry of his nature, has undertaken to apply opprobrious words to those who differ from him on this floor. He calls them "sectional and fanatical"; and opposition to the usurpation in Kansas he denounces as "an uncalculating fanaticism." To be sure, these charges lack all grace of originality, and all sentiment of truth; but the adventurous senator does not hesitate. He is the uncompromising, unblushing representative on this floor of a flagrant sectionalism, which now domineers over the Republic, and yet with a ludicrous ignorance of his own position—unable to see himself as others see him— or with an effrontery which even his white head ought not to protect from rebuke, he applies to those here who resist his sectionalism the very epithet which designates himself. The men who strive to bring back the government to its original policy, when freedom and not slavery was sectional, he arraigns as sectional. This will not do. It involves too great a perversion of terms. I tell that senator that it is to himself, and to the "organization" of which he is the "committed advocate," that this epithet belongs. I now fasten it upon them. . . .

As the Senator from South Carolina is the Don Quixote, the Senator from Illinois [Mr. Douglas] is the Squire of slavery, its very Sancho Panza, ready to do all its humiliating offices. . . .

[DOUGLAS:] I shall not detain the Senate by a detailed reply to the speech of the senator from Massachusetts. Indeed, I should not deem it necessary to say one word, but for the personalities in which he has indulged, evincing a depth of malignity that issued from every sentence, making it a matter of self-respect with me to repel the assaults which have been made. . . .

The charge is made against the body of which we are members. It is not a charge made in the heat of debate. It is not made as a retort growing out of excited controversy. If it were of that nature, I could make much allowance for it. I can pay great deference to the frailties and the impulses of an honorable man, when indignant at what he considers to be a wrong. If the senator, betraying that he was susceptible of just indignation, had been goaded, provoked, and aggravated on the spur of the moment into the utterance of harsh things, and then had apologized for them in his cooler hours, I could respect him much more than if he had never made such a departure from the rules of the Senate, because it would show that he had a heart to appreciate what is due among brother senators and gentlemen. But, sir, it happens to be well known—it has been the subject of conversation for weeks, that the senator from Massachusetts has had his speech written, printed, committed to memory, practiced every night before the glass with a Negro boy to hold the candle and watch the gestures, and has been thus annoying boarders in adjoining rooms until they were forced to quit the house. It was rumored that he read parts of it to friends and they repeated in all the saloons and places of amusement in the city what he was going to say. The libels and gross insults we have heard today have been conned over, written with cool, deliberate malignity, repeated from night to night in order to catch the appropriate grace, and then he came here to spit forth that malignity upon men who differ from him—for that is their offense! . . .

Why these attacks on individuals by name, and two-thirds of the Senate collectively? Is it the object to drive men here to dissolve social relations with political opponents? Is it to turn the Senate into a beer garden, where senators cannot associate on terms which ought to prevail between gentlemen? These attacks are heaped upon me by man after man. When I repel them, it is intimated that I show some feeling on the subject. Sir, God grant that when I denounce an act of infamy I shall do it with feeling, and do it under the sudden impulses of feeling, instead of sitting up at night writing out my denunciation of a man whom I hate, copying it, having it printed, punctuating the proof sheets, and repeating it before the glass, in order to give refinement to insult, which is only pardonable when it is the outburst of a just indignation. . . .

[SUMNER:] Mr. President, to the senator from Illinois, I should willingly leave the privilege of the common scold—the last word; but I will not leave to him, in any discussion with me, the last argument, or the last semblance of it. He has crowned the audacity of this debate by venturing to rise here and calumniate me. He said that I came here, took an oath to support the Constitution, and yet determined not to support a particular clause in that Constitution. To that statement I give, to his face, the flattest denial. . . .

The senator has gone on to infuse into his speech the venom which has been sweltering for months—aye, for years; and he has alleged facts that are entirely without foundation, in order to heap upon me some personal obloquy. I will not go into the details which have flowed out so naturally from his tongue. I only brand them to his face as false. I say also to that senator, and I wish him to bear it in mind, that no person with the upright form of man—[Here the speaker hesitated.]

[DOUGLAS:] Say it!

[SUMNER:] I will say it! No person with the upright form of man can be allowed without the violation of all decency to switch out from his tongue the perpetual stench of offensive personality. Sir, this is not a proper weapon of debate, at least, on this floor! The noisome, squat, and nameless animal to which I now refer is not a proper model for an American senator. Will the senator from Illinois take notice!

[DOUGLAS:] I will, and therefore will not imitate you, sir.

[SUMNER:] I did not hear the senator.

[DOUGLAS:] I said, if that be the case, I would certainly never imitate you in that capacity, recognizing the force of the illustration.

[SUMNER:] Mr. President, again the senator has switched his tongue, and again he fills the chamber with its offensive odor.

I pass from the senator from Illinois. There is still another, the senator from Virginia, who is now also in my eye. That senator said nothing of argument, and there is therefore nothing of that for response. I simply say to him that hard words are not argument, frowns not reasons; nor do scowls belong to the proper arsenals of parliamentary debate. The senator has not forgotten that on a former occasion I did something to exhibit on this floor the plantation manners he displayed. I will not do any more now!

[MASON:] Manners of which the senator is unconscious.

[DOUGLAS:] I am not going to pursue this subject further. I will only say that a man who has been branded by me in the Senate, and convicted by the Senate of falsehood, cannot use language requiring reply, and therefore I have nothing more to say. ■

Senator Stephen Douglas Differs with Lincoln on the "Popular Sovereignty" Decision on Slavery

"LEAVE the people free to do as they please. . . ."

SEEKING REELECTION AS SENATOR FROM ILLINOIS in 1858, Stephen Douglas—"the Little Giant," five feet tall and barrel-chested—accepted Abraham Lincoln's challenge to a series of debates. The intellectual and rhetorical clash that followed is unmatched in American political history for its force, length, undiminished focus of audience attention, and ultimate significance. Douglas won the gerrymandered senatorial campaign but alienated enough southern Democratic voters to undermine his presidential hopes in 1860; Lincoln, in winning a popular majority but losing the legislative vote for the Senate, made himself known nationally, positioning himself to win the Republican nomination and the presidency.

Douglas's program was "popular sovereignty," a phrase now expressed as "local option," which in his Kansas-Nebraska Act of 1854 divided northern Democrats and helped lead to the formation of the Republican party. On the slavery issue, "pop sov" meant allowing the residents of territories to express their wishes on slavery before those territories became states of the Union. Lincoln took the contrary position, opposing the extension of slavery, which did not evolve to one in favor of its abolition until 1862.

This extract from their joint debate at Freeport, Illinois, on June 17, 1858, gives a flavor of Douglas's style, which includes the use of homely metaphor within a forensic structure. His criticism of Frederick Douglass as a Lincoln supporter was a racist effort to appeal to southern Democrats who thought Douglas was not proslavery enough.

□   □   □

. . . Can the people of the territory in any lawful way, against the wishes of any citizen of the United States, exclude slavery from their limits prior to the formation of a state constitution? I answer emphatically, as Mr. Lincoln has heard me answer a hundred times from every stump in Illinois, that in my opinion the people of a territory can, by lawful means, exclude slavery from their limits prior to the formation of a state constitution. Mr. Lincoln knew that I had answered that question over and over again. He heard me argue the Nebraska Bill on that principle all over the state in 1854, in 1855, and in 1856, and he has no excuse for pretending to be in doubt as to my position on that question. It matters not what way the Supreme Court may hereafter decide as to the abstract question whether slavery may or may not go into a territory under the Constitution; the people have the lawful means to introduce it or exclude it as they please, for the reason that slavery cannot exist a day or an hour anywhere, unless it is supported by local police regulations. Those police regulations can only be established by the local legislature; and if the people are opposed to slavery, they will elect representatives to that body who will by unfriendly legislation effectually prevent the introduction of it into their midst. If, on the contrary, they are for it, their legislation will favor its extension. Hence, no matter what the decision of the Supreme Court may be on that abstract question, still the right of the people to make a slave territory or a free territory is perfect and complete under the Nebraska Bill. I hope Mr. Lincoln deems my answer satisfactory on that point. . . .

The third question which Mr. Lincoln presented is "If the Supreme Court of the United States shall decide that a state of this Union cannot exclude slavery from its own limits, will I submit to it?" I am amazed that Lincoln should ask such a question. "A schoolboy knows better." Yes, a schoolboy does know better. Mr. Lincoln's object is to cast an imputation upon the Supreme Court. He knows that there never was but one man in America, claiming any degree of intelligence or decency, who ever for a moment pretended such a thing. It is true that the *Washington Union,* in an article published on the seventeenth of last December, did put forth that doctrine, and I denounced the article on the floor of the Senate in a speech which Mr. Lincoln now pretends was against the president. The *Union* had claimed that slavery had a right to go into the free states, and that any provisions in the Constitution or laws of the free states to the contrary were null and void. I denounced it in the Senate, as I said before, and I was the first man who did. Lincoln's friends Trumbull and Seward and Hale and Wilson and the whole black Republican side of the Senate were silent. They left it to me to denounce it. And what was the reply made to me on that occasion? Mr. Toombs, of Georgia, got up and undertook to lecture me on the ground that I ought not to have deemed the article worthy of notice and ought not to have replied to it; that there was not one man, woman, or child south of the Potomac, in any slave state, who did not repudiate any such pretension. Mr. Lincoln knows that that reply was made on the spot, and yet now he asks this question. He might as well ask me, "Suppose Mr. Lincoln should steal a horse, would you sanction it?" and it would be as genteel in me to ask him, in the event he stole a horse, what ought to be done with him. He casts an imputation upon the Supreme Court of the United States by supposing that they would violate the Constitution of the United States. I tell him that such a thing is not possible. It would be an act of moral treason that no man on the bench could ever descend to. Mr. Lincoln himself would never in his partisan feelings so far forget what was right as to be guilty of such an act.

The fourth question of Mr. Lincoln is "Are you in favor of acquiring additional territory, in disregard as to how such acquisition may affect the Union on the slavery question?" This question is very ingeniously and cunningly put.

The black Republican creed lays it down expressly, that under no circumstances shall we acquire any more territory unless slavery is first prohibited in the country. I ask Mr. Lincoln whether he is in favor of that proposition. Are you [addressing Mr. Lincoln] opposed to the acquisition of any more territory, under any circumstances, unless slavery is prohibited in it? That he does not like to answer. When I ask him whether he stands up to that article in the platform of his party he turns, Yankee fashion, and, without answering it, asks me whether I am in favor of acquiring territory without regard to how it may affect the Union on the slavery question. I answer that whenever it becomes necessary, in our growth and progress, to acquire more territory, that I am in favor of it, without reference to the question of slavery; and when we have acquired it, I will leave the people free to do as they please, either to make it slave or free territory, as they prefer. . . .

I tell you, increase and multiply and expand is the law of this nation's existence. You cannot limit this great Republic by mere boundary lines, saying, "Thus far shalt thou go, and no further." Any one of you gentlemen might as well say to a son twelve years old that he is big enough, and must not grow any larger, and in order to prevent his growth put a hoop around him to keep him to his present size. What would be the result? Either the hoop must burst and be rent asunder, or the child must die. So it would be with this great nation. With our natural increase, growing with a rapidity unknown in any other part of the globe, with the tide of emigration that is fleeing from despotism in the Old World to seek refuge in our own, there is a constant torrent pouring into this country that requires more land, more territory upon which to settle; and just as fast as our interests and our destiny require additional territory in the North, in the South, or on the islands of the ocean, I am for it, and when we acquire it, will leave the people, according to the Nebraska Bill, free to do as they please on the subject of slavery and every other question.

I trust now that Mr. Lincoln will deem himself answered on his four points. He racked his brain so much in devising these four questions that he exhausted himself, and had not strength enough to invent the others. As soon as he is able to hold a council with his advisers Lovejoy, Farnsworth, and Fred Douglass, he will frame and propound others. You black Republicans who say good, I have no doubt, think that they are all good men. I have reason to recollect that some people in this country think that Fred Douglass is a very good man. The last time I came here to make a speech, while talking from the stand to you, people of Freeport, as I am doing today, I saw a carriage, and a magnificent one it was, drive up and take a position on the outside of the crowd; a beautiful young lady was sitting on the box seat, whilst Fred Douglass and her mother reclined inside and the owner of the carriage acted as driver. I saw this in your own town. All I have to say of it is this, that if you black Republicans think that the Negro ought to be on a social equality with your wives and daughters, and ride in a carriage with your wife, whilst you drive the team, you have a perfect right to do so. I am told that one of Fred Douglass's kinsmen, another rich black Negro, is now traveling in this part of the state making speeches for his friend Lincoln as the champion of black men. All I have to say on that subject is that those of you who believe that the Negro is your equal and ought to be on an equality with you socially, politically, and legally have a right to entertain these opinions and, of course, will vote for Mr. Lincoln. ■

John Cabell Breckinridge Disputes Colonel E. D. Baker's Charge of Treason

"I infinitely prefer to see a peaceful separation of these states, than to see endless, aimless, devastating war, at the end of which I see the grave of public liberty and personal freedom."

"PERHAPS THE MOST dramatic scene that ever took place in the Senate Chamber—old or new—," wrote John Forney in his 1873 *Anecdotes of Public Men*, "was that between [John Cabell] Breckinridge and Colonel E. D. Baker of Oregon on the 1st of August, 1861."

Breckinridge, vice-president of the United States under James Buchanan, had run for president in 1860 and lost to Lincoln, but the popular young Kentuckian was returned to the Senate. He sought a compromise between North and South, remaining in the Senate after the southern states seceded, a lonely voice earning the enmity of Union defenders. So long as he dissented "in his place"—as representative of a loyal border state, in the Senate Chamber—his criticism of Lincoln's repression of civil liberties in the name of preserving the nation could not be prosecuted as a crime.

Edwin Baker had served in the Black Hawk War and the Illinois state legislature with Lincoln; he was one of the president's closest friends and the namesake of Lincoln's firstborn. Baker served with distinction in the Mexican war, at one point with both U. S. Grant and R. E. Lee as his subordinates; he donned his uniform again as the Civil War began, and—in boots and riding crop—entered the Senate that day to clash with Breckinridge, whom he knew and liked. James Blaine of Maine later wrote, "In the history of the Senate, no more thrilling speech was ever delivered" than Ned Baker's.

Baker, whose slashing oratory was heightened by a series of accusing questions, was to fall at Ball's Bluff; Breckinridge was to serve as a Confederate general in charge of Kentucky's "Orphan Brigade"—troops of rebels from a state loyal to the Union—and in the war's final stages as Confederate secretary of war.

Their words, spoken without notes, were transcribed and published in the *Congressional Globe* of August 2; to lend clarity and dramatic impact, I have broken up the mostly uninterrupted speeches into refutations of each other's main points. The "Tarpeian Rock" interrupting voice was incorrectly presumed by Breckinridge to be Charles Sumner of Massachusetts; the senator who recalled the execution ground for Roman traitors was William Pitt Fessenden of Maine. The debate was occasioned by proposals to establish martial law and to punish sedition, actions that Baker thought necessary to silence agitation capable of weakening the Union war effort and that Breckinridge thought undermined the principle of liberty they sought to defend.

□   □   □

[BRECKINRIDGE:] I am quite aware that all I say is received with a sneer of incredulity in this body. But let the future determine who was right and who was wrong. We are making our record here; I, my humble one, amid the aversion of nearly all who surround me. I have forgotten what an approving voice sounds like, and am surrounded by scowls. . . .

What is this bill but vesting first in the discretion of the president, to be by him detailed to a subaltern military commander, the authority to enter the commonwealth of Kentucky, to abolish the state, to abolish the judiciary, and to substitute just such rules as that military commander may choose. This bill contains provisions conferring authority which never was exercised in the worst days of Rome, by the worst of her dictators.

I have wondered why this bill was introduced. Possibly to prevent the expression of that reaction which is now evidently going on in the public mind against these procedures so fatal to constitutional liberty. The army may be used, perhaps, to collect the enormous direct taxes to come to finance the war.

Mr. President, gentlemen here talk about the Union as if it was an end instead of a means. Take care that in pursuing one idea you do not destroy not only the Constitution of your country, but sever what remains of the federal Union.

[BAKER:] A question.

[BRECKINRIDGE:] I prefer no interruptions. The senator from California will have the floor later.

[BAKER:] Oregon.

[BRECKINRIDGE:] The senator seems to have charge of the whole Pacific coast. . . . Oregon, then. I desire the country to know this fact: that it is openly avowed upon this floor that the Constitution is put aside in a struggle like this. You are acting just as if there were two nations upon this continent. one arrayed against the other; some twenty million on one side, and some twelve million on the other as to whom the Constitution is naught, and the rules of war alone apply.

The "war power," whatever that means, applies to external enemies only. I do not believe it applies to any of our political communities bound by the Constitution in this association. Nor do I believe that the founders ever contemplated the preservation of the Union of these states by one half the states warring on the other half.

Mr. President, we are on the wrong tack; we have been from the beginning. The people begin to see it. Here we have been hurling gallant fellows on to death, and the blood of Americans has been shed—for what? To carry out principles that three-fourths of them abhor; for the principles of despotism contained in this bill before us.

Nothing but ruin, utter ruin, to the North and South, to the East and West, will follow the prosecution of this contest. You may look forward to innumerable armies. You may look forward to raising and borrowing vast treasures for the purpose of ravaging and desolating this continent. At the end, we will be just where we are now. Or if you are gloriously victorious, and succeed in ravaging the South, what will you do with it? Can you not see what is so plain to the world, that what you insist on seeing as a mere faction is a whole people, wanting to go its own way?

To accomplish your purpose, it will be necessary to subjugate, to conquer, aye, to *exterminate*—nearly ten million people! Does anybody here not know that? Does anyone here hope vainly for conquest without carnage?

Let us pause while there is still time for men of good will to draw back from hatred and bloodshed. Let the Congress of the United States respond here and now to the feeling, rising all over this land, in favor of peace.

[BAKER:] A few words as to the senator's predictions. The senator from Kentucky stands up here in a manly way, in opposition to what he sees as the overwhelming sentiment of the Senate, and utters reproof, malediction, and prediction combined. Well, sir, it is not every prediction that is prophecy.

What would have been thought, if in another capitol, in another republic, in a yet more martial age, a senator as grave, not more eloquent or dignified than the senator from Kentucky, yet with the Roman purple flowing over his shoulders, had risen in his place, surrounded by all the illustrations of Roman glory, and declared that advancing Hannibal was just and that Carthage ought to be dealt with in terms of peace?

What would have been thought if, after the battle of Cannae, a senator there had risen in his place and denounced every levy of the Roman people, every expenditure of its treasures, and every appeal to the old glories?

[VOICE:] He would have been hurled from the Tarpeian Rock!

[BAKER:] Yes, a colleague more learned than I says that the speaker of such words would have been hurled from the Tarpeian Rock. It is a grand commentary on the American Constitution that we permit such words as spoken by the senator from Kentucky to be uttered here and now.

But I ask the senator, what, save to send aid and comfort to the enemy, do these predictions of his amount to? Every word thus uttered falls as a note of inspiration upon every Confederate ear. Every sound thus spoken is a word—and from his lips a mighty word—of kindling and triumph to a foe that determines to advance. . . .

For me, amid temporary defeat, disaster, disgrace, it seems that my duty calls me to utter another word, and that word is "war." Bold, sudden, forward, determined war, according to the laws of war, by armies and by military commanders clothed with full power, advancing with all the past glories of the Republic urging them on to conquest.

I do not stop to consider whether it is "subjugation" or not. The senator animadverts to my use of "subjugation." Why play on words? We propose to subjugate rebellion into loyalty; we propose to subjugate insurrection into peace; we propose to subjugate Confederate anarchy into constitutional Union liberty. . . .

And when we subjugate South Carolina, what will we do? We shall compel its obedience to the Constitution of the United States; that is all. The senator knows that we propose no more. I yield for his reply.

[BRECKINRIDGE:] By whose indulgence am I speaking? Not by any man's indulgence, I am speaking by the guarantees of that Constitution which seems to be here now so little respected. . . .

When the senator asked what would have been done with a Roman senator who had uttered such words as mine, a certain senator on this floor,—whose courage has much risen of late, replied in audible tones, "He would have been hurled from the Tarpeian Rock." Sir, if ever we find an American Tarpeian Rock, and a suitable victim is to be selected, the people will turn, not to me, but to that senator who has been the chief author of the public misfortunes.

Let him remember, too, that while in ancient Rome the defenders of the public liberty were sometimes torn to pieces by the people, yet their memories were cherished in grateful remembrance; while to be hurled from the Tarpeian Rock was ever the fate of usurpers and tyrants. . . . I reply with just indignation at such an insult offered on the floor of the Senate Chamber to a senator who is speaking in his place. . . .

War is separation. War is disunion, eternal and final disunion. We have separation now; it is only made worse by war, and war will extinguish all those sentiments of common interest and feeling which might lead to a political reunion founded upon consent and upon a conviction of its advantages.

Let this war go on, however, you will see further separation. Let this war go on, and the people of the West see the beautiful features of the old Confederacy beaten out of shape by the brutalizing hand of war, and they will turn aside in disgust from the sickening spectacle and become a separate nation.

[BAKER:] The Pacific states will be true to the Union to the last of her blood and her treasure. . . .

I confess, Mr. President, that I would not have predicted three weeks ago the disasters which have overtaken our arms. But I ask the senator from Kentucky, will he tell me it is our duty to stay here, within fifteen miles of the enemy seeking to advance upon us every hour, and talk about nice questions of constitutional construction? Are we to stop and talk about rising sentiment against the war in the North? Are we to predict evil and flinch from what we predict? Is it not the manly part to go on as we have begun, to raise money, to levy armies, to prepare to advance?

To talk to us about stopping is idle; we will never stop. Will the senator yield to rebellion? Will he shrink from armed insurrection? Will his state justify it? Shall we send a flag of truce? What would he have us do? Or would he conduct the war so feebly, that the whole world would smile at us in derision? What would he have us do? Those speeches of his, sown broadcast over the land, what clear distinct meaning have they? Are they not meant for disorganization in our very midst? Are they not intended to dull our weapons? Are they not intended to destroy our zeal? Are they not intended to animate our enemies? Sir—are they not words of brilliant, polished *treason*?

[BRECKINRIDGE:] The senator asks me, "What would you have us do?" I have already indicated what I would have us do. I would have us stop the war.

We can do it. There is none of that inexorable necessity to continue this war which the senator seems to suppose. I do not hold that constitutional liberty on this continent is bound up in this fratricidal, devastating, horrible contest. Upon the contrary, I fear it will find its grave in it. . . .

The senator is mistaken in supposing that we can reunite these states by war. He is mistaken in supposing that if twenty million on one side subjugate twelve million on the other side, that you can restore constitutional government as our fathers made it. . . . Sir, I would prefer to see these states all reunited upon true constitutional principles to any other object that could be offered me in life. But I infinitely prefer to see a peaceful separation of these states, than to see endless, aimless, devastating war, at the end of which I see the grave of public liberty and personal freedom.

[BAKER:] The senator is right about the devastation ahead. There will be privation; there will be loss of luxury; there will be graves reeking with blood, watered with tears. When that is said, all is said. If we have the country, the whole country, the Union, the Constitution, free government—with these there will return all the blessings of a well-ordered civilization. The path of the whole country will be one of greatness and peace such as would have been ours today, if it had not been for the treason for which the senator from Kentucky too often seeks to apologize.

[BRECKINRIDGE:] You say that the opinions I express are but brilliant treason. Mr. President, if I am speaking treason, I am not aware of it. I am speaking what I believe to be for the good of my country. If I am speaking treason, I am speaking it *in my place* in the Senate. . . . If my opinions do not reflect the judgment of the people I represent, I am not a man to cling to the emoluments of public life. If the commonwealth of Kentucky, instead of attempting to mediate as a neutral in this struggle, shall throw her energies into the strife on the side of what I believe to be a war of subjugation and annihilation, then she shall take her course. I am her son and will share her destiny, but she will be represented by some other man on the floor of this Senate. ∎

Henry Cabot Lodge
Speaks on the League of Nations

"Let us beware how we palter with our independence."

THIS SPEECH, READ ON AUGUST 12, 1919, to the U. S. Senate during the "great debate" on postwar foreign policy, made the case against Woodrow Wilson's campaign for the United States to join the League of Nations. Internationalists have long remembered this stand of the "irreconcilables" as the supreme example of misguided isolationism.

Lodge was Senate majority leader and chairman of the Foreign Relations Committee; he detested Wilson personally, but took a middle position on the League, which the U.S. president had proposed at the Versailles conference. He argued that the Senate should accept it with a key reservation: that the Congress had to remain central in any commitment as important as war.

Lodge's view, not Wilson's, prevailed; the United States was not about to surrender that much of its sovereignty to a world body, and a policy of selective intervention with senatorial participation remained bipartisan doctrine throughout the twentieth century. His grandson, Massachusetts senator Henry Cabot Lodge, Jr., an internationalist who later became our ambassador to the UN, in 1953 resolutely defended the much maligned Lodge reservation as one that "simply preserved the power of Congress—a power which is jealously guarded today, which is completely safeguarded both in the United Nations Charter and the Atlantic Pact, and which President Wilson was unwilling categorically to express at that time."

The essence of the speech is expressed in a single verb: "Let us beware how we *palter* with our independence." "Palter," perhaps rooted in a Germanic word for "rag," means "deal frivolously"; it has a more solemn tone than "fiddle around." The use of an archaic or unfamiliar word at a critical moment is rhetorically effective; Franklin Roosevelt used the same technique in referring to Pearl Harbor Day as one that would live in "infamy" rather than "history." A defensive note is struck in Lodge's speech by a speaker aware of the appeal of Wilsonian idealism and the bitter charges of isolation and selfishness being made against opponents of the League. Note how he closes with a serious, low-key effort to overcome Wilson's "monopoly of idealism."

□   □   □

Iobject in the strongest possible way to having the United States agree, directly or indirectly, to be controlled by a league which may at any time, and perfectly lawfully and in accordance with the terms of the covenant, be drawn in to deal with internal conflicts in other countries, no matter what those conflicts may be. We should never permit the United States to be involved in any internal conflict in another country, except by the will of her people expressed through the Congress which represents them. . . .

Those of us, Mr. President, who are either wholly opposed to the League or who are trying to preserve the independence and the safety of the United States by changing the terms of the League, and who are endeavoring to make the League, if we are to be a member of it, less certain to promote war instead of peace have been reproached with selfishness in our outlook and with a desire to keep our country in a state of isolation. So far as the question of isolation goes, it is impossible to isolate the United States. I well remember the time, twenty years ago, when eminent senators and other distinguished gentlemen who were opposing the Philippines and shrieking about imperialism sneered at the statement made by some of us, that the United States had become a world power. I think no one now would question that the Spanish war marked the entrance of the United States into world affairs to a degree which had never obtained before. It was both an inevitable and an irrevocable step, and our entrance into the war with Germany certainly showed once and for all that the United States was not unmindful of its world responsibilities.

We may set aside all this empty talk about isolation. Nobody expects to isolate the United States or to make it a hermit nation, which is a sheer absurdity. But there is a wide difference between taking a suitable part and bearing a due responsibility in world affairs and plunging the United States into every controversy and conflict on the face of the globe. By meddling in all the differences which may arise among any portion or fragment of humankind, we simply fritter away our influence and injure ourselves to no good purpose. We shall be of far more value to the world and its peace by occupying, so far as possible, the situation which we have occupied for the last twenty years and by adhering to the policy of Washington and Hamilton, of Jefferson and Monroe, under which we have risen to our present greatness and prosperity. . . .

It has been reiterated here on this floor, and reiterated to the point of weariness, that in every treaty there is some sacrifice of sovereignty. That is not a universal truth by any means, but it is true of some treaties and it is a platitude which does not require reiteration. The question and the only question before us here is how much of our sovereignty we are justified in sacrificing. In what I have already said about other nations putting us into war I have covered one point of sovereignty which ought never to be yielded—the power to send American soldiers and sailors everywhere, which ought never to be taken from the American people or impaired in the slightest degree. Let us beware how we palter with our independence. . . .

Contrast the United States with any country on the face of the earth today, and ask yourself whether the situation of the United States is not the best to be found. I will go as far as anyone in world service, but the first step to world service is the maintenance of the United States. You may call me selfish if you will, conservative or reactionary, or use any other harsh adjective you see fit to apply, but an American I was born, an American I have remained all my life. I can never be anything else but an American, and I must think of the United States first, and when I think of the United States first in an arrangement like this I am thinking of what is best for the world, for if the United States fails, the best hopes of mankind fail with it. I have never had but one allegiance—I cannot divide it now. I have loved but one flag, and I cannot share that devotion and give affection to the mongrel banner invented for a league. Internationalism, illustrated by the Bolshevik and by the men to whom all countries are alike provided they can make money out of them, is to me repulsive. National I must remain, and in that way I, like all other Americans, can render the amplest service to the world. The United States is the world's best hope, but if you fetter her in the interests and quarrels of other nations, if you tangle her in the intrigues of Europe, you will destroy her power for good and endanger her very existence. Leave her to march freely through the centuries to come as in the years that have gone. Strong, generous, and confident, she has nobly served mankind. Beware how you trifle with your marvelous inheritance, this great land of ordered liberty, for if we stumble and fall, freedom and civilization everywhere will go down in ruin.

We are told that we shall "break the heart of the world" if we do not take this League just as it stands. I fear that the hearts of the vast majority of mankind would beat on strongly and steadily and without any quickening if the League were to perish altogether. If it should be effectively and beneficiently changed, the people who would lie awake in sorrow for a single night could be easily gathered in one not very large room, but those who would draw a long breath of relief would reach to millions.

We hear much of visions, and I trust we shall continue to have visions and dream dreams of a fairer future for the race. But visions are one thing and visionaries are another, and the mechanical appliances of the rhetorician designed to give a picture of a present which does not exist and of a future which no man can predict are as unreal and short-lived as the steam or canvas clouds, the angels suspended on wires, and the artificial lights of the stage. They pass with the moment of effect and are shabby and tawdry in the daylight. Let us at least be real. Washington's entire honesty of mind and his fearless look into the face of all facts are qualities which can never go out of fashion and which we should all do well to imitate. . . .

No doubt many excellent and patriotic people see a coming fulfillment of noble ideals in the words "league for peace." We all respect and share these aspirations and desires, but some of us see no hope, but rather defeat, for them in this murky covenant. For we, too, have our ideals, even if we differ from those who have tried to establish a monopoly of idealism. Our first ideal is our country, and we see her in the future, as in the past, giving service to all her people and to the world. Our ideal of the future is that she should continue to render that service of her own free will. She has great problems of her own to solve, very grim and perilous problems, and a right solution, if we can attain to it, would largely benefit mankind. We would have our country strong to resist a peril from the West, as she has flung back the German menace from the East. We would not have our politics distracted and embittered by the dissensions of other lands. We would not have our country's vigor exhausted, or her moral force abated, by everlasting meddling and muddling in every quarrel, great and small, which afflicts the world. Our ideal is to make her ever stronger and better and finer, because in that way alone, as we believe, can she be of the greatest service to the world's peace and to the welfare of mankind. ■

Emperor Haile Selassie of Ethiopia Appeals to the League of Nations to Stop Aggression

"GOD and history will remember your judgment."

ON JUNE 30, 1936, only six years after becoming "Haile Selassie I, King of Kings of Ethiopia, Lion of Judah, Elect of God," a slight black man in a black cape appeared before the League of Nations in Geneva, the first head of state to appeal for the rescue of his nation from the wave of aggression about to engulf the world. A generation later, he returned to the successor organization, the United Nations, to recall, "I spoke then both to and for the conscience of the world. My words went unheeded, but history testifies to the accuracy of the warning that I gave in 1936."

□   □   □

I, Haile Selassie I, emperor of Ethiopia, am here today to claim that justice which is due to my people, and the assistance promised to them eight months ago, when fifty nations asserted that an aggression had been committed in violation of international treaties.

There is no precedent for a head of state himself speaking in this assembly. But there is also no precedent for a people being victim of such injustice and being at present threatened by abandonment to its aggressors. Also, there has never before been an example of any government proceeding to the systematic extermination of a nation by barbarous means, in violation of the most solemn promises made to all the nations of the earth that there should be no resort to a war of conquest, and that there should not be used against innocent human beings the terrible poison of harmful gases. It is to defend a people struggling for its age-old independence that the head of the Ethiopian Empire has come to Geneva to fulfill this supreme duty, after having himself fought at the head of his armies.

I pray Almighty God that he may spare nations the terrible sufferings that have just been inflicted on my people, and of which the chiefs who accompany me here have been the horrified witnesses.

It is my duty to inform the governments assembled in Geneva, responsible as they are for the lives of millions of men, women, and children, of the deadly peril which threatens them, by describing to them the fate which has been suffered by Ethiopia.

It is not only upon warriors that the Italian government has made war. It has above all attacked populations far removed from hostilities, in order to terrorize and exterminate them.

At the beginning, towards the end of 1935, Italian aircraft hurled upon my armies bombs of tear gas. Their effects were but slight. The soldiers learned to scatter, waiting until the wind had rapidly dispersed the poisonous gases.

The Italian aircraft then resorted to mustard gas. Barrels of liquid were hurled upon armed groups. But this means also was not effective; the liquid only affected a few soldiers, and barrels upon the ground were themselves a warning to troops and to the population of the danger.

It was at the time when the operations for the encircling of Makale were taking place that the Italian command, fearing a rout, followed the procedure which it is now my duty to denounce to the world. Special sprayers were installed on board aircraft so that they could vaporize, over vast areas of territory, a fine, death-dealing rain. Groups of nine, fifteen, eighteen aircraft followed one another so that the fog issuing from them formed a continuous sheet. It was thus that, as from the end of January 1936, soldiers, women, children, cattle, rivers, lakes, and pastures were drenched continually with this deadly rain. In order to kill off systematically all living creatures, in order the more surely to poison waters and pastures, the Italian command made its aircraft pass over and over again. That was its chief method of warfare.

The very refinement of barbarism consisted in carrying ravage and terror into the most densely populated parts of the territory—the points farthest removed from the scene of hostilities. The object was to scatter fear and death over a great part of the Ethiopian territory.

These fearful tactics succeeded. Men and animals succumbed. The deadly rain that fell from the aircraft made all those whom it touched fly shrieking with pain. All those who drank the poisoned water or ate the infected food also succumbed in dreadful suffering. In tens of thousands the victims of the Italian mustard gas fell. It is in order to denounce to the civilized world the tortures inflicted upon the Ethiopian people that I resolved to come to Geneva. . . .

In October 1935, the fifty-two nations who are listening to me today gave me an assurance that the aggressor would not triumph, that the resources of the Covenant would be employed in order to ensure the reign of right and the failure of violence.

I ask the fifty-two nations not to forget today the policy upon which they embarked eight months ago, and in faith of which I directed the resistance of my people against the aggressor whom they had denounced to the world. Despite the inferiority of my weapons, the complete lack of aircraft, artillery, munitions, hospital services, my confidence in the League was absolute. I thought it to be impossible that fifty-two nations, including the most powerful in the world, should be successfully opposed by a single aggressor. Counting on the faith due to treaties, I had made no preparation for war, and that is the case with certain small countries in Europe. . . .

War then took place in the atrocious conditions which I have laid before the assembly. In that unequal struggle between a government commanding more than forty-two million inhabitants, having at its disposal financial, industrial, and technical means which enabled it to create unlimited quantities of the most death-dealing weapons, and, on the other hand, a small people of twelve million inhabitants, without arms, without resources, having on its side only the justice of its own cause and the promise of the League of Nations. What real assistance was given to Ethiopia by the fifty-two nations who had declared the Rome government guilty of a breach of the Covenant and had undertaken to prevent the triumph of the aggressor? Has each of the member states, as it was its duty to do in virtue of its signature appended to Article 16 of the Covenant, considered the aggressor as having committed an act of war personally directed against itself? I had placed all my hopes in the execution of these undertakings. My confidence had been confirmed by the repeated declaration made in the council to the effect that aggression must not be rewarded and that force would be compelled to bow before right.

In December 1935, the council made it quite clear that its feelings were in harmony with those of hundreds of millions of people who, in all parts of the world, had protested against the proposal to dismember Ethiopia. It was constantly repeated that there was not merely a conflict between the Italian government and Ethiopia but also a conflict between the Italian government and the League of Nations, and that is why I personally refused all proposals to my personal advantage made to me by the Italian government if only I would betray my people and the Covenant of the League of Nations. I was defending the cause of all small peoples who are threatened with aggression.

What have become of the promises made to me? As long ago as October 1935, I noted with grief, but without surprise, that three powers considered their undertakings under the Covenant as absolutely of no value. Their connections with Italy impelled Italian aggression. On the contrary, it was a profound disappointment to me to learn the attitude of a certain government which, whilst ever protesting its scrupulous attachment to the Covenant, has tirelessly used all its efforts to prevent its observance. As soon as any measure which was likely to be effective was proposed, various pretexts were devised in order to postpone even consideration of that measure. Did the secret agreements of January 1935 provide for this tireless obstruction? The Ethiopian government never expected other governments to shed their soldiers' blood to defend the Covenant when their own immediate personal interests were not at stake. Ethiopian warriors asked only for means to defend themselves. On many occasions, I have asked for financial assistance for the purchase of arms. That assistance has been constantly refused me. What, then, in practice, is the meaning of Article 16 and of collective security?

Apart from the Kingdom of the Lord there is not on this earth any nation that is superior to any other. Should it happen that a strong government finds it may, with impunity, destroy a weak people, then the hour strikes for that weak people to appeal to the League of Nations to give its judgment in all freedom. God and history will remember your judgment. . . .

Representatives of the world, I have come to discharge in your midst the most painful of the duties of the head of a state. What reply shall I have to take back to my people? ■

Candidates Nixon and Kennedy Meet in the First Televised Presidential Debate

KENNEDY: "I think it's time America started moving again."
NIXON: "I know what it means to be poor."

THESE WERE NOT CLASSIC DEBATES, in the Lincoln-Douglas tradition, with each man challenging, contradicting, rebutting the other. The four Kennedy-Nixon joint appearances on television were panel shows, the principals separated by journalist-interviewers, the presentations limited to short summaries of previously stated positions. Yet they performed the function of a modern debate, allowing an audience to size up two candidates under the same pressure at the same moment and to reach a judgment on which person seemed more trustworthy or in presidential command.

The reaction of the radio audience was that Nixon "won"; his voice was more resonant and reassuring, his debating points more clearly made. The reaction of the wider and more important television audience to the first debate was that Kennedy "won"—he appeared vigorous, tanned, and confident while Nixon looked pale, worried, and sweaty. For years afterward, Nixon would ruefully joke about the importance of makeup men, as if that were what had made all the difference; in fact, it was the surprise that the lesser-known Kennedy could hold his own in debate with Eisenhower's famed vice-president that energized the Kennedy campaign and ultimately enabled him to win in the closest "squeaker" in U.S. presidential history.

The Q. and A. is not especially useful to students of speechmaking; the opening and closing statements of both candidates, however, are presented here as good capsule presentations of themes by men working from notes inside their heads. The moderator was Howard K. Smith.

□   □   □

The candidates need no introduction. The Republican candidate, Vice-President Richard M. Nixon, and the Democratic candidate, Senator John F. Kennedy.

According to rules set by the candidates themselves, each man shall make an opening statement of approximately eight minutes' duration and a closing statement of approximately three minutes' duration.

In between, the candidates will answer or comment upon answers to questions put by a panel of correspondents.

In this, the first discussion in a series of four joint appearances, the subject matter, it has been agreed, will be restricted to internal or domestic American matters.

And now, for the first opening statement by Senator John F. Kennedy.

[KENNEDY:] Mr. Smith, Mr. Nixon.

In the election of 1860, Abraham Lincoln said the question was whether this nation could exist half slave or half free.

In the election of 1960, and with the world around us, the question is whether the world will exist half slave or half free, whether it will move in the direction of freedom, in the direction of the road that we are taking, or whether it will move in the direction of slavery.

I think it will depend in great measure upon what we do here in the United States, on the kind of society that we build, on the kind of strength that we maintain.

We discuss tonight domestic issues, but I would not want that to be— any implication to be given that this does not involve directly our struggle with Mr. Khrushchev for survival.

Mr. Khrushchev is in New York, and he maintains the Communist offensive throughout the world because of the productive power of the Soviet Union itself.

The Chinese Communists have always had a large population, but they are important and dangerous now because they are mounting a major effort within their own country; the kind of country we have here, the kind of society we have, the kind of strength we build in the United States, will be the defense of freedom.

If we do well here, if we meet our obligations, if we are moving ahead, then I think freedom will be secure around the world. If we fail, then freedom fails.

Therefore, I think the question before the American people is, Are we doing as much as we can do? Are we as strong as we should be? Are we as strong as we must be if we are going to maintain our independence, and if we're going to maintain and hold out the hand of friendship to those who look to us for assistance, to those who look to us for survival? I should make it very clear that I do not think we're doing enough, that I am not satisfied as an American with the progress that we are making.

This is a great country, but I think it could be a greater country; and this is a powerful country, but I think it could be a more powerful country.

I'm not satisfied to have 50 percent of our steel mill capacity unused.

I'm not satisfied when the United States had last year the lowest rate of economic growth of any major industrialized society in the world—because economic growth means strength and vitality. It means we're able to sustain our defenses. It means we're able to meet our commitments abroad.

I'm not satisfied, when we have over nine billion dollars worth of food, some of it rotting even though there is a hungry world and even though four million Americans wait every month for a food package from the government which averages five cents a day per individual.

I saw cases in West Virginia, here in the United States, where children took home part of their school lunch in order to feed their families, because I don't think we are meeting our obligations toward these Americans.

I'm not satisfied when the Soviet Union is turning out twice as many scientists and engineers as we are.

I'm not satisfied when many of our teachers are inadequately paid or when our children go to school on part-time shifts. I think we should have an educational system second to none.

I'm not satisfied when I see men like Jimmy Hoffa, in charge of the largest union in the United States, still free.

I'm not satisfied when we are failing to develop the natural resources of the United States to the fullest. Here in the United States, which developed the Tennessee Valley and which built the Grand Coulee and the other dams in the northwest United States, at the present rate of hydropower production—and that is the hallmark of an industrialized society—the Soviet Union by 1975 will be producing more power than we are.

These are all the things, I think, in this country that can make our society strong or can mean that it stands still.

I'm not satisfied until every American enjoys his full constitutional rights. If a Negro baby is born, and this is true also of Puerto Ricans and Mexicans in some of our cities, he has about one-half as much chance to get through high school as a white baby. He has one-third as much chance to get through college as a white student. He has about a third as much chance to be a professional man, and about half as much chance to own a house. He has about four times as much chance that he'll be out of work in his life as the white baby. I think we can do better. I don't want the talents of any American to go to waste.

I know that there are those who say that we want to turn everything over to the government. I don't at all. I want the individuals to meet their responsibilities and I want the states to meet their responsibilities. But I think there is also a national responsibility.

The argument has been used against every piece of social legislation in the last twenty-five years. The people of the United States individually could not have developed the Tennessee Valley. Collectively, they could have.

A cotton farmer in Georgia or a peanut farmer or a dairy farmer in Wisconsin or Minnesota—he cannot protect himself against the forces of supply and demand in the marketplace, but working together in effective governmental programs, he can do so.

Seventeen million Americans who live over sixty-five on an average Social Security check of about seventy-eight dollars a month—they're not able to sustain themselves individually, but they can sustain themselves through the Social Security system.

I don't believe in big government, but I believe in effective government action, and I think that's the only way that the United States is going to maintain its freedom; it's the only way that we're going to move ahead. I think we can do a better job. I think we're going to have to do a better job if we are going to meet the responsibilities which time and events have placed upon us.

We cannot turn the job over to anyone else. If the United States fails, then the whole cause of freedom fails, and I think it depends in great measure on what we do here in this country.

The reason Franklin Roosevelt was a good neighbor in Latin America was because he was a good neighbor in the United States, because they felt that the American society was moving again. I want us to recapture that image. I want people in Latin America and Africa and Asia to start to look to America to see how we're doing things, to wonder what the president of the United States is doing, and not to look at Khrushchev or look at the Chinese Communists. That is the obligation upon our generation.

In 1933 Franklin Roosevelt said in his inaugural that this generation of Americans has a "rendezvous with destiny." I think our generation of Americans has the same "rendezvous." The question now is, Can freedom be maintained under the most severe attack it has ever known? I think it can be, and I think in the final analysis it depends upon what we do here. I think it's time America started moving again.

[SMITH:] And now the opening statement by Vice-President Richard M. Nixon.

[NIXON:] Mr. Smith, Senator Kennedy.

The things that Senator Kennedy has said, many of us can agree with. There is no question but that we cannot discuss our internal affairs in the United States without recognizing that they have a tremendous bearing on our international position. There is no question but that this nation cannot stand still, because we are in a deadly competition, a competition not only with the men in the Kremlin but the men in Peking. We're ahead in this competition, as Senator Kennedy, I think, has implied. But when you're in a race, the only way to stay ahead is to move ahead, and I subscribe completely to the spirit that Senator Kennedy has expressed tonight, the spirit that the United States should move ahead.

Where, then, do we disagree?

I think we disagree on the implication of his remarks tonight and on the statements that he has made on many occasions during his campaign to the effect that the United States has been standing still.

We heard tonight, for example, the statement made that our growth and national product last year was the lowest of any industrial nation in the world.

Now, last year, of course, was 1958. That happened to be a recession year, but when we look at the growth of GNP this year—a year of recovery—we find that it is 6.9 percent and one of the highest in the world today. More about that later.

Looking then to this problem of how the United States should move ahead and where the United States is moving, I think it is well that we take the advice of a very famous campaigner: "Let's look at the record."

Is the United States standing still?

Is it true that this administration, as Senator Kennedy has charged, has been an administration of retreat, of defeat, of stagnation?

Is it true that as far as this country is concerned in the field of electric power, and all of the fields that he has mentioned, we have not been moving ahead?

Well, we have a comparison that we can make. We have the record of the Truman administration of seven and a half years, and the seven and a half years of the Eisenhower administration.

When we compare these two records in the areas that Senator Kennedy has discussed tonight, I think we find that America has been moving ahead.

Let's take schools. We have built more schools in these last seven and a half years than we built in the previous seven and a half, for that matter in the previous twenty years.

Let's take hydroelectric power. We have developed more hydroelectric power in these seven and a half years than was developed in any previous administration in history.

Let us take hospitals. We find that more have been built in this administration than in the previous administration. The same is true of highways.

Let's put it in terms that all of us can understand.

We often hear gross national product discussed, and in that respect may I say that when we compare the growth in this administration with that of the previous administration, that then there was a total growth of 11 percent over seven years; in this administration there has been a total growth of 19 percent over seven years.

That shows that there has been more growth in this administration than in its predecessor. But let's not put it there; let's put it in terms of the average family.

What has happened to you?

We find that your wages have gone up five times as much in the Eisenhower administration as they did in the Truman administration.

What about the prices you pay?

We find that the prices you pay went up five times as much in the Truman administration as they did in the Eisenhower administration.

What's the net result of this?

This means that the average family income went up 15 percent in the Eisenhower years as against 2 percent in the Truman years.

Now, this is not standing still, but good as this record is, may I emphasize it isn't enough.

A record is never something to stand on; it's something to build on, and in building on this record I believe that we have the secret for progress.

We know the way to progress, and I think first of all our own record proves that we know the way.

Senator Kennedy has suggested that he believes he knows the way.

I respect the sincerity with he—which he makes that suggestion, but on the other hand when we look at the various programs that he offers, they do not seem to be new. They seem to be simply retreads of the programs of the Truman administration which preceded him, and I would suggest that during the course of the evening he might indicate those areas in which his programs are new, where they will mean more progress than we had then.

What kind of programs are we for?

We are for programs that will expand educational opportunities, that will give to all Americans their equal chance for education, for all of the things which are necessary and dear to the hearts of our people.

We are for programs in addition which will see that our medical care for the aged is much better handled than it is at the present time.

Here again may I indicate that Senator Kennedy and I are not in disagreement as to the aim. We both want to help the old people. We want to see that they do have adequate medical care. The question is the means.

I think that the means that I advocate will reach that goal better than the means that he advocates.

I could give better examples, but for whatever it is, whether it's in the field of housing or health or medical care or schools or the development of electric power, we have programs which we believe will move America, move her forward and build on the wonderful record that we have made over these past seven and a half years.

Now, when we look at these programs, might I suggest that in evaluating them we often have a tendency to say that the test of a program is how much you are spending. I will concede that in all of the areas to which I have referred, Senator Kennedy would have the federal government spend more than I would have it spend.

I costed out the cost of the Democratic platform. It runs a minimum of $13.2 billion a year more than we are presently spending to a maximum of $18 billion a year more than we are presently spending.

Now, the Republican platform will cost more, too. It will cost a minimum of $4 billion a year more, a maximum of $4.9 billion a year more than we are presently spending.

Now, does this mean that his program is better than ours?

Not at all, because it isn't a question of how much the federal government spends. It isn't a question of which government does the most. It's a question of which administration does the right things, and in our case I do believe that our programs will stimulate the creative energies of 180 million free Americans.

I believe the programs that Senator Kennedy advocates will have a tendency to stifle those creative energies.

I believe, in other words, that his programs would lead to the stagnation of the motive power that we need in this country to get progress.

The final point that I would like to make is this: Senator Kennedy has suggested in his speeches that we lack compassion for the poor, for the old, and for others that are unfortunate.

Let us understand throughout this campaign that his motives and mine are sincere. I know what it means to be poor. I know what it means to see people who are unemployed.

I know Senator Kennedy feels as deeply about these problems as I do, but our disagreement is not about the goals for America but only about the means to reach those goals . . .

[SMITH:] Three minutes and twenty seconds for each candidate, Vice-President Nixon, will you make the first summation?

[NIXON:] Thank you, Mr. Smith.

Senator Kennedy, first of all I think it is well to put in perspective where we really do stand with regard to the Soviet Union in this whole matter of growth.

The Soviet Union has been moving faster than we have, but the reason for that is obvious. They start from a much lower base.

Although they have been moving faster in growth than we have, we find for example today that their total gross national product is only 44 percent of our total gross national product. That's the same percentage that it was twenty years ago; and as far as the absolute gap is concerned, we find that the United States is even further ahead than it was twenty years ago.

Is this any reason for complacency?

Not at all, because these are determined men, they are fanatical men, and we have to get the very most out of our economy.

I agree with Senator Kennedy completely on that score.

Where we disagree is in the means that we would use to get the most out of our economy.

I respectfully submit that Senator Kennedy too often would rely too much on the federal government on what it would do to solve our problems, to stimulate growth.

I believe that when we examine the Democratic platform, when we examine the proposals that he has discussed tonight, when we compare them with the proposals that I have made, that these proposals that he makes would not result in greater growth for this country than would be the case if we followed the programs that I have advocated.

There are many of the points that he has made that I would like to comment upon; the one in the field of health is worth mentioning.

Our health program, the one that Senator Javits and other Republican senators as well as I supported, is one that provides for all people over sixty-five who want health insurance—the opportunity to have it if they want it. It provides a choice of having either government insurance or private insurance, but it compels nobody to have insurance who does not want it.

His program under Social Security would require everybody who had Social Security to take government health insurance whether he wanted it or not, and it would not cover several million people who are not covered by Social Security at all.

Here is one place where I think that our program does a better job than his.

The other point that I would make is this: this downgrading of how much things cost, I think many of our people will understand better when they look at what happened when during the Truman administration, when the government was spending more than it took in.

We found savings over a lifetime eaten up by inflation. We found the people who could least afford it, people on retired incomes, people on fixed incomes, we found them unable to meet their bills at the end of the month.

It is essential that a man who is president of this country certainly stand for every program that will mean growth, and I stand for programs that mean growth and progress.

But it is also essential that he not allow a dollar spent that could be better spent by the people themselves.

[SMITH:] Senator Kennedy, your conclusion.

[KENNEDY:] The point was made by Mr. Nixon that the Soviet production is only 44 percent of ours. I must say that 44 percent in that Soviet country is causing us a good deal of trouble tonight. I want to make sure that it stays in that relationship. I don't want to see the day when it's 60 percent of ours and 70 and 75 and 80 and 90 percent of ours, with all the force and power that it could bring to bear in order to cause our destruction.

Secondly, the vice-president mentioned medical care for the aged. Our program was an amendment to the Kerr bill; the Kerr bill provided assistance to all those who are not on Social Security. I think it's a very clear contrast.

In 1935 when the Social Security Act was written, 94 out of 95 Republicans voted against it. Mr. Landon ran in 1936 to repeal it.

In August of 1960 when we tried to get it again, this time for medical care, we received the support of one Republican in the Senate on this occasion.

Thirdly, I think the question before the American people is, as they look at this country, and as they look at the world around them, the goals are the same for all Americans; the means are at question; the means are at issue.

If you feel that everything that is being done now is satisfactory, that the relative power and prestige and strength of the United States is increasing in relation to that of the Communists, that we are gaining more security, that we are achieving everything as a nation that we should achieve, that we are achieving a better life for our citizens and greater strength, then I agree. I think you should vote for Mr. Nixon.

But if you feel that we have to move again in the sixties, that the function of the president is to set before the people the unfinished business of our society, as Franklin Roosevelt did in the thirties, the agenda for our people, what we must do as a society to meet our needs in this country and protect our security and help the cause of freedom—as I said at the beginning, the question before us all that faces all Republicans and all Democrats is, Can freedom in the next generation conquer, or are the Communists going to be successful? That's the great issue.

And if we meet our responsibilities, I think freedom will conquer. If we fail—if we fail to move ahead, if we fail to develop sufficient military and economic and social strength here in this country, then I think that the tide could begin to run against us, and I don't want historians ten years from now to say these were the years when the tide ran out for the United States. I want them to say these were the years when the tide came in, these were the years when the United States started to move again. That's the question before the American people, and only you can decide what you want, what you want this country to be, what you want to do with the future.

I think we're ready to move. And it is to that great task, if we are successful, that we will address ourselves. ■

Senators Dan Quayle and Lloyd Bentsen Clash on Qualifications for the Presidency

"SENATOR, I served with Jack Kennedy. I knew Jack Kennedy. Jack Kennedy was a friend of mine. Senator, you're no Jack Kennedy."

J. DANFORTH QUAYLE, forty-one, second-term senator from Indiana, was Vice-President George H. W. Bush's surprise choice for a running mate on the Republican ticket in 1988. Lloyd Bentsen, sixty-seven, fourth-term senator from Texas (who defeated Bush for a Senate seat in 1970), was the choice of the Democratic candidate, Governor Michael Dukakis of Massachusetts.

The fall campaign began with Dukakis-Bentsen in the lead, but Bush-Quayle quickly caught up and surged ahead. By early October, the Dukakis camp was relying heavily on the assertion that its vice-presidential candidate was better qualified for the presidency than the young man who was chosen by George Bush and who was unprepared at first for the savage onslaught of the media,

On October 6, 1988, Bentsen and Quayle met in a panel debate moderated by Judy Woodruff of PBS. Senator Quayle looked young up against the veteran Bentsen, who was determined to exploit the Republican's relative inexperience. The youthful Republican was not above taking an adept pop at the older man: when the sound system had some difficulty, Senator Bentsen said to a panelist, "John, we can't hear you," and Senator Quayle volunteered, "I can hear you okay." The panel of reporters helped Mr. Bentsen by concentrating on the subject of personal preparedness, and—when Senator Quayle mentioned he had as much experience in the Congress as former President John F. Kennedy did when he sought the presidency, Senator Bentsen delivered with the most effective single punch in the history of televised presidential debates. The four simple declarative sentences, each with "Jack Kennedy" in them, built to a stunning rhetorical climax that charged effrontery in evoking the name of a Democratic icon. Quayle could say only that the shot was "uncalled for"; he could not then point out that he had been comparing experience before running for president and that his opponent had escalated his remark to a comparison with the martyred president in his totality.

This moment was Mr. Bentsen's high point and Mr. Quayle's low point in life; the issue of vice-presidential experience was seen to be minor, and Bush-Quayle went on to defeat Dukakis-Bentsen in a landslide.

□   □   □

[QUAYLE:] The question goes to whether I am qualified to be vice-president, and in the case of a tragedy whether I'm qualified to be president. Qualifications for the office of vice-president or president are not age alone. You must look at accomplishments, and you must look at experience. I have more experience than others that have sought the office of vice-president. Let's look at qualifications, and let's look at the three biggest issues that are going to be confronting America in the next presidency.

Those three issues are national security and arms control, jobs and education, and the federal budget deficit. On each one of those issues I have more experience than does the governor of Massachusetts. In national security and arms control, you have to understand the relationship between a ballistic missile, a warhead, what throw weight, what megatonnage is. You better understand about telemetry and acryption, and you better understand that you have to negotiate from a position of strength. These are important issues because we want to have more arms control and arms reductions.

In the areas of jobs and education, I wrote the Job Training Partnership Act—a bipartisan bill, a bill that has trained and employed over three million economically disadvantaged youths and adults in this country.

On the area of the federal budget deficit, I have worked eight years on the Senate Budget Committee, and I wish that the Congress would give us the line item veto to help deal with that.

And if qualifications alone are going to be the issue in this campaign, George Bush has more qualifications than Michael Dukakis and Lloyd Bentsen combined. . . .

[BENTSEN:] This debate tonight is not about the qualifications for the vice-presidency. The debate is whether or not Dan Quayle and Lloyd Bentsen are qualified to be president of the United States. Because, Judy, just as you have said, that has happened too often in the past. And if that tragedy should occur, we have to step in there without any margin for error, without time for preparation, to take over the responsibility for the biggest job in the world, that of running this great country of ours—to take over the awesome responsibility for commanding the nuclear weaponry that this country has.

Now, the debate tonight is a debate about the presidency itself and a presidential decision that has to be made by you. The stakes could not be higher. . . .

[Q:] Senator Quayle, I want to take you back, if I can, to the question Judy asked you about some of the apprehensions people may feel about your being a heartbeat away from the presidency.

And let us assume, if we can, for the sake of this question that you become vice-president and the president is incapacitated for one reason or another and you have to take the reins of power. When that moment came, what would be the first steps that you'd take, and why?

[QUAYLE:] First I'd—first I'd say a prayer for myself and for the country that I'm about to lead. And then I would assemble his people and talk. And I think this question keeps going back to the qualifications and what kind of a vice-president and, in this hypothetical situation, if I had to assume the responsibilities of president what I would be.

And as I have said, age alone—although I can tell you after the experience of these last few weeks in the campaign, I've added ten years to my age—age alone is not the only qualification. You've got to look at experience, and you've got to look at accomplishments. And can you make a difference?

Have I made a difference in the United States Senate, where I've served for eight years? Yes, I have. Have I made a difference in the Congress that I've served for twelve years? Yes, I have.

As I said before, looking at the issue of qualifications—and I am delighted that it comes up, because on the three most important challenges facing America—arms control and national security; jobs and education, and budget deficit—I have more experience and accomplishments than does the governor of Massachusetts.

I have been in the Congress, and I've worked on these issues. And believe me, when you look at arms control and trying to deal with the Soviet Union, you cannot come at it from a naive position. You have to understand the Soviet Union; you have to understand how they will respond. Sitting on that Senate Armed Services Committee for eight years has given me the experience to deal with the Soviet Union and how we can move forward.

That is just one of the troubling issues that's going to be facing this nation. And I'm prepared. . . .

[Q:] Senator, I want to take you back to the question that I asked you earlier about what would happen if you were to take over in an emergency, and what you would do first and why. You said you'd say a prayer, and you said something about a meeting. What would you do next?

[QUAYLE:] I don't believe that it's proper for me to get into the specifics of a hypothetical situation like that. The situation is that if I was called upon to serve as the president of this country or the responsibilities of the president of this country, would I be capable and qualified to do that. And I have tried to list the qualifications of twelve years in the United States Congress. I have served in the Congress for twelve years. I have served in the Congress, and served eight years on the Senate Arms Services Committee. I have traveled a number of times. I've been to Geneva many times to meet with our negotiators as we're hammering out the INF treaty. I've met with the Western political leaders: Margaret Thatcher, Chancellor Kohl. I know them. They know me. I know what it takes to lead this country forward. And if that situation arises, yes, I will be prepared and I'll be prepared to lead this country if that happens.

[BENTSEN:] Once again, I think what we're looking at here is someone that can step in at the presidency level at the moment if that tragedy would occur.

And if that's the case, again, you have to look at maturity of judgment. And you have to look at breadth of experience. You have to see what kind of leadership roles that person has played in his life before that crisis struck him.

And if you do that type of thing, then you'll arrive at a judgment that I think would be a wise one. And I hope that would mean that you'd say, We're going to vote for Mike Dukakis and Lloyd Bentsen. . . .

[QUAYLE:] Three times that I have had this question, and I'll try to answer it again for you as clearly as I can, because the question you're asking is what kind of qualifications does Dan Quayle have to be president. What kind of qualifications do I have, and what would I do in this kind of a situation? And what would I do in this situation?

I would make sure that the people in the cabinet and the people and advisers to the president are called in, and I'll talk to them and I'll work with them. And I will know them on a firsthand basis, because as vice-president I'll sit on the National Security Council. And I'll know them on a firsthand basis because I'm going to be coordinating the drug effort. I'll know them on a firsthand basis because Vice-President George Bush is going to re-create the space council, and I'll be in charge of that, I will have day-to-day activities with all the people in government.

And then, if that unfortunate situation happens, if that situation, which would be very tragic, happens, I will be prepared to carry out the responsibilities of the presidency of the United States of America. And I will be prepared to do that, I will be prepared not only because of my service in the Congress but because of my ability to communicate and to lead. It is not just age—it's accomplishments, it's experience. I have far more experience than many others that sought the office of vice-president of this country. I have as much experience in the Congress as Jack Kennedy did when he sought the presidency. I will be prepared to deal with the people in the Bush administration if that unfortunate event would ever occur.

[QUAYLE:] Senator, I served with Jack Kennedy. I knew Jack Kennedy. Jack Kennedy was a friend of mine. Senator, you're no Jack Kennedy.

What has to be done in a situation like that is to call in the joint—

[QUAYLE:] That was really uncalled for, Senator.

[BENTSEN:] You're the one that was making the comparison, Senator. And I'm one who knew him well. And frankly I think you're so far apart in the objectives you choose for your country that I did not think the comparison was well taken. . . .

[QUAYLE:] Tonight has been a very important evening. You have been able to see Dan Quayle as I really am, and how George Bush and I want to lead this country into the future. Thank you, America, for listening, and thank you for your fairness. Now, you will have a choice to make on election day; you will have a choice of whether America is going to choose the road of Michael Dukakis or the road of George Bush, as we march toward the twenty-first century.

The road of Michael Dukakis comes down to this: bigger government, higher taxes. They've always believed in higher taxes; they always have and they always will. Cuts in national defense. Back to the old economics of high interest rates, high inflation and the old politics of high unemployment.

Now, the road of George Bush is the road to the future, and it comes down to this: an America second to none, with visions of greatness, economic expansion, tough laws, tough judges, strong values, respect for the flag and our institutions. George Bush will lead us to the twenty-first century, a century that will be of hope and peace. Ronald Reagan and George Bush saved America from decline; we changed America. Michael Dukakis fought us every step of the way.

It's not that they're not sympathetic; it's simply that they will take America backwards. George Bush has the experience, and with me the future. A future committed to our family, a future committed to the freedom.

Thank you. Good night, and God bless you.

[BENTSEN:] In just thirty-four days America will elect new leadership for our country. It's a most important decision, because there is no bigger job than governing this great country of ours and leading it into its future.

Mike Dukakis and Lloyd Bentsen offer you experience, tempered, capable leadership to meet those challenges of the future. Our opposition says lower your sights, rest on your laurels.

Mike Dukakis and Lloyd Bentsen think America can do better; that America can't just coast into the future, clinging to the past. This race is too close. The competition is too tough, and the stakes are too high.

Michael Dukakis and Lloyd Bentsen think America must move into that future united in a commitment to make this country of ours the most powerful, the most prosperous nation in the world.

As Americans we honor our past, and we should. But our children are going to live in the future. And Mike Dukakis says the best of America is yet to come. But that won't happen taking care of our economy, just putting it on automatic pilot. It won't happen by accident. It's going to take leadership, and it's going to take courage and the commitment and a contribution by all of us to do that.

I have worked for the betterment of our country both in war and peace, as a bomber pilot, as one who has been a businessman and a United States senator, working to make this nation the fairest and the strongest and the most powerful in the world.

Help us bring America to a new era of greatness. The debate has been ours, but the decision is yours. God bless you.

■ ■ ■

V

TRIALS

Job Pleads the Record of a Good Life against God's Inexplicable Punishment

"LET me but call a witness in my defense! Let the Almighty state his case against me!"

THE BOOK OF JOB is replete with legal metaphors. God and Satan have made a bet about the purity of motive in mankind's worship; Satan is given the power to torture a blameless man to see if he will crack and curse God. When unjustly afflicted Job wishes that his "adversary had written a book" (in the King James translation), he is calling for a written list of charges against himself, an indictment he can answer in court. He seeks justice by bringing the Almighty before some kind of tribunal, with an intercessor or vindicator to represent him (and to restrain God, with whom Job wants to argue).

The legend of Job is as ancient as any in our culture, and served as the basis of a poet-rabbi's book written about five or six centuries before the birth of Christ. The book was written to confront the doctrine of divine retribution, which did not seem to be working: all too often, the wicked prospered while the good died young. The author rejected the prevailing notion that human suffering was evidence of sin and put forward the more comforting argument that God's ways were beyond mankind's ken. On the way to that discovery, however, the justifiably angry Job insists on a fair trial. Here, in the Oxford New English Bible translation, is his summary of his case:

□　□　□

> If I could only go back to the old days,
> to the time when God was watching over me,
> when his lamp shone above my head,
> and by its light I walked through the darkness!
> If I could be as in the days of my prime,
> when God protected my home,
> while the Almighty was still there at my side,

and my servants stood round me,
while my path flowed with milk,
and the rocks streamed oil!
If I went through the gate out of the town
to take my seat in the public square,
young men saw me and kept out of sight;
old men rose to their feet,
men in authority broke off their talk
and put their hands to their lips;
the voices of the nobles died away,
and every man held his tongue.
They listened to me expectantly
and waited in silence for my opinion.
When I had spoken, no one spoke again;
my words fell gently on them;
they waited for them as for rain
and drank them in like showers in spring.
When I smiled on them, they took heart;
when my face lit up, they lost their gloomy looks.
I presided over them, planning their course,
like a king encamped with his troops.

                         Whoever heard of me spoke in my favor,
and those who saw me bore witness to my merit,
how I saved the poor man when he called for help
and the orphan who had no protector.
The man threatened with ruin blessed me,
and I made the widow's heart sing for joy.
I put on righteousness as a garment and it clothed me;
justice, like a cloak or a turban, wrapped me round.
I was eyes to the blind
and feet to the lame;
I was a father to the needy,
and I took up the stranger's cause.
I broke the fangs of the miscreant
and rescued the prey from his teeth.
I thought, "I shall die with my powers unimpaired
and my days uncounted as the grains of sand,
with my roots spreading out to the water
and the dew lying on my branches,
with the bow always new in my grasp
and the arrow ever ready to my hand."

But now I am laughed to scorn
by men of a younger generation,
men whose fathers I would have disdained
to put with the dogs who kept my flock. . . .
Now I have become the target of their taunts,
my name is a byword among them.
They loathe me, they shrink from me,
they dare to spit in my face.
They run wild and savage me;
at sight of me they throw off all restraint.
On my right flank they attack in a mob;
they raise their siege ramps against me,
they tear down my crumbling defenses to my undoing,
and scramble up against me unhindered;
they burst in through the gaping breach;
at the moment of the crash they come rolling in.
Terror upon terror overwhelms me,
it sweeps away my resolution like the wind,
and my hope of victory vanishes like a cloud.
So now my soul is in turmoil within me,
and misery has me daily in its grip.
By night pain pierces my very bones,
and there is ceaseless throbbing in my veins;
my garments are all bespattered with my phlegm,
which chokes me like the collar of a shirt.
God himself has flung me down in the mud,
no better than dust or ashes.

I call for thy help, but thou dost not answer;
I stand up to plead, but thou sittest aloof;
thou hast turned cruelly against me
and with thy strong hand pursuest me in hatred;
thou dost snatch me up and set me astride the wind,
and the tempest tosses me up and down.
I know that thou wilt hand me over to death,
to the place appointed for all mortal men.
Yet no beggar held out his hand
but was relieved by me in his distress.
Did I not weep for the man whose life was hard?
Did not my heart grieve for the poor?
Evil has come though I expected good;
I looked for light but there came darkness.

My bowels are in ferment and know no peace;
days of misery stretch out before me.
I go about dejected and friendless;
I rise in the assembly, only to appeal for help.
The wolf is now my brother,
the owls of the desert have become my companions. . . .

        What is the lot prescribed by God above,
the reward from the Almighty on high?
Is not ruin prescribed for the miscreant
and calamity for the wrongdoer?
Yet does not God himself see my ways
and count my every step?

        I swear I have had no dealings with falsehood
and have not embarked on a course of deceit.
I have come to terms with my eyes,
never to take notice of a girl.
Let God weigh me in the scales of justice,
and he will know that I am innocent!
If my steps have wandered from the way,
if my heart has followed my eyes,
or any dirt stuck to my hands,
may another eat what I sow,
and may my crops be pulled up by the roots!
If my heart has been enticed by a woman
or I have lain in wait at my neighbor's door,
may my wife be another man's slave,
and may other men enjoy her. . . .
If I have withheld their needs from the poor
or let the widow's eye grow dim with tears,
if I have eaten my crust alone,
and the orphan has not shared it with me—
the orphan who from boyhood honored me like a father,
whom I guided from the day of his birth—
if I have seen anyone perish for lack of clothing,
or a poor man with nothing to cover him,
if his body had no cause to bless me,
because he was not kept warm with a fleece from my flock,
if I have raised my hand against the innocent,
knowing that men would side with me in court,
then may my shoulder blade be torn from my shoulder.

my arm be wrenched out of its socket!
But the terror of God was heavy upon me,
and for fear of his majesty I could do none of these things.
If I have put my faith in gold
and my trust in the gold of Nubia,
if I have rejoiced in my great wealth
and in the increase of riches;
if I ever looked on the sun in splendor
or the moon moving in her glory,
and was led astray in my secret heart
and raised my hand in homage;
this would have been an offense before the law,
for I should have been unfaithful to God on high.
If my land has cried out in reproach at me,
and its furrows have joined in weeping,
if I have eaten its produce without payment
and have disappointed my creditors,
may thistles spring up instead of wheat,
and weeds instead of barley!

       Have I rejoiced at the ruin of the man that hated me
or been filled with malice when trouble overtook him,
even though I did not allow my tongue to sin
by demanding his life with a curse?
Have the men of my household never said,
"Let none of us speak ill of him!
No stranger has spent the night in the street"?
For I have kept open house for the traveler.
Have I ever concealed my misdeeds as men do,
keeping my guilt to myself,
because I feared the gossip of the town
or dreaded the scorn of my fellow citizens?

       Let me but call a witness in my defense!
Let the Almighty state his case against me!
If my accuser had written out his indictment,
I would not keep silence and remain indoors.
No! I would flaunt it on my shoulder
and wear it like a crown on my head;
I would plead the whole record of my life
and present that in court as my defense. ■

Martin Luther Addresses
the Diet of Worms

"HERE I stand; I cannot do otherwise."

EXCOMMUNICATED BY POPE LEO X but still vocal and determined, Martin Luther was not to be deterred from facing his critics at the Diet of Worms, an imperial deliberative body. He maintained that defiance afterward: "If I had heard that as many devils would set on me in Worms as there are tiles on the roofs, I should nonetheless have ridden there."

Luther's 1517 posting of ninety-five theses that questioned church doctrine had angered the Catholic authorities. Unswayed by a condemnation from Rome and driven to burn a papal bull in 1520, the German founder of Protestantism was tried the following year by a secular tribunal at the diet and then condemned for heresy by Emperor Charles V.

At his trial. Luther uses both simile ("as clear as noonday") and Scripture, quoting from both the Old and the New Testament in refusing to retract his writings that were deemed heretical. By addressing himself specifically to the charges brought against him, Luther reiterates his own positions against popery and provides the emperor with "a simple, clear, and direct answer"—that he cannot "speak against his conscience."

Added to the first printed copies of the speech was the German statement "Hier steh' ich, ich kann nicht anders," a quotation that can be found today on the Worms monument to Luther. This remark, which has been translated as "I stand here and can say no more," is more forcefully rendered at the end of the translation given below.

□   □   □

Most Serene Emperor, and you illustrious princes and gracious lords: I this day appear before you in all humility, according to your command, and I implore Your Majesty and your august highnesses, by the mercies of God, to listen with favor to the defense of a cause which I am well assured is just and right. I ask pardon, if by reason of my ignorance, I am wanting in the manners that befit a court; for I have not been brought up in kings' palaces, but in the seclusion of a cloister.

Two questions were yesterday put to me by His Imperial Majesty; the first, whether I was the author of the books whose titles were read; the second, whether I wished to revoke or defend the doctrine I have taught. I answered the first, and I adhere to that answer.

As to the second, I have composed writings on very different subjects. In some I have discussed faith and good works, in a spirit at once so pure, clear, and Christian that even my adversaries themselves, far from finding anything to censure, confess that these writings are profitable, and deserve to be perused by devout persons. The pope's bull, violent as it is, acknowledges this. What, then, should I be doing if I were now to retract these writings? Wretched man! I alone, of all men living, should be abandoning truths approved by the unanimous voice of friends and enemies, and opposing doctrines that the whole world glories in confessing!

I have composed, secondly, certain works against popery, wherein I have attacked such as by false doctrines, irregular lives, and scandalous examples afflict the Christian world, and ruin the bodies and souls of men. And is not this confirmed by the grief of all who fear God? Is it not manifest that the laws and human doctrines of the popes entangle, vex, and distress the consciences of the faithful. while the crying and endless extortions of Rome engulf the property and wealth of Christendom, and more particularly of this illustrious nation?

If I were to revoke what I have written on that subject, what should I do . . . but strengthen this tyranny, and open a wider door to so many and flagrant impieties? Bearing down all resistance with fresh fury, we should behold these proud men swell, foam, and rage more than ever! And not merely would the yoke which now weighs down Christians be made more grinding by my retraction—it would thereby become, so to speak, lawful—for, by my retraction, it would receive confirmation from Your Most Serene Majesty, and all the states of the empire. Great God! I should thus be like to an infamous cloak, used to hide and cover over every kind of malice and tyranny.

In the third and last place, I have written some books against private individuals, who had undertaken to defend the tyranny of Rome by destroying faith. I freely confess that I may have attacked such persons with more violence than was consistent with my profession as an ecclesiastic: I do not think of myself as a saint; but neither can I retract these books, because I should, by so doing, sanction the impieties of my opponents, and they would thence take occasion to crush God's people with still more cruelty.

Yet, as I am a mere man, and not God, I will defend myself after the example of Jesus Christ, who said, "If I have spoken evil, bear witness against me" (John 18:23). How much more should I, who am but dust and ashes, and so prone to error, desire that every one should bring forward what he can against my doctrine.

Therefore, Most Serene Emperor, and you illustrious princes, and all, whether high or low, who hear me, I implore you by the mercies of God to prove to me by the writings of the prophets and apostles that I am in error. As soon as I shall be convinced, I will instantly retract all my errors, and will myself be the first to seize my writings and commit them to the flames.

What I have just said I think will clearly show that I have well considered and weighed the dangers to which I am exposing myself; but far from being dismayed by them, I rejoice exceedingly to see the Gospel this day, as of old, a cause of disturbance and disagreement. It is the character and destiny of God's word. "I came not to send peace unto the earth, but a sword," said Jesus Christ. God is wonderful and awful in his counsels. Let us have a care, lest in our endeavors to arrest discords, we be bound to fight against the holy word of God and bring down upon our heads a frightful deluge of inextricable dangers, present disaster, and everlasting desolations. . . . Let us have a care lest the reign of the young and noble prince, the emperor Charles, on whom, next to God, we build so many hopes, should not only commence, but continue and terminate its course under the most fatal auspices. I might cite examples drawn from the oracles of God. I might speak of pharaohs, of kings of Babylon, or of Israel, who were never more contributing to their own ruin that when, by measures in appearances most prudent, they thought to establish their authority! "God removeth the mountains and they know not" (Job 9:5).

In speaking thus, I do not suppose that such noble princes have need of my poor judgment; but I wish to acquit myself of a duty that Germany has a right to expect from her children. And so commending myself to Your August Majesty, and your most serene highnesses, I beseech you in all humility, not to permit the hatred of my enemies to rain upon me an indignation I have not deserved.

Since Your Most Serene Majesty and Your High Mightinesses require of me a simple, clear, and direct answer, I will give one, and it is this: I cannot submit my faith either to the pope or to the council, because it is as clear as noonday that they have fallen into error and even into glaring inconsistency with themselves. If, then, I am not convinced by proof from Holy Scripture, or by cogent reasons, if I am not satisfied by the very text I have cited, and if my judgment is not in this way brought into subjection to God's word, I neither can nor will retract anything; for it cannot be right for a Christian to speak against his conscience. Here I stand; I cannot do otherwise. God help me. Amen. ■

Sir Thomas More Defends Himself against Charges of Treason

"IF this oath of yours . . . be true, then pray I that I may never see God in the face. . . ."

SCHOLAR AND STATESMAN, author of *Utopia,* and martyr, Sir Thomas More proved himself, as one contemporary called him, "a man for all seasons." (This famous designation for a man of conscience first appeared in the early sixteenth century, when educator Robert Whittington composed a passage for students to translate from English into Latin.)

One of Henry VIII's most trusted advisers, Thomas More succeeded Cardinal Wolsey as lord chancellor of England, even though More had disapproved of the dissolution of the king's first marriage. Less acceptable to Henry, however, was More's refusal to deny papal supremacy, and the stubborn cleric was committed to the Tower of London. Charges of treason, at first difficult to prove, were justified when Lord Rich, the solicitor general, testified of a private conversation in which More supposedly denied Henry's right to be called "supreme head" of the Church of England.

In his defense speech, reported in detail by his son-in-law William Roper, More argues against the credibility of Lord Rich's assertions, denying revelation of "the secrets of my conscience." Referring to saints of the New Testament (Peter, Paul, and Stephen), he insists upon the rights of the Catholic Church ("the See of Rome") and calls "temporal" powers "insufficient to charge any Christian man."

Although he accused Lord Rich of perjury, More was still found guilty of treason. On July 7, 1535, Sir Thomas More was beheaded; four centuries later, he was canonized by the Catholic Church.

□　□　□

If I were a man, my lords, that did not regard an oath, I need not, as it is well known, in this place, at this time, nor in this case to stand as an accused person. And if this oath of yours, Master Rich, be true, then pray

I that I may never see God in the face, which I would not say, were it otherwise to win the whole world.

In good faith, Master Rich, I am sorrier for your perjury than for mine own peril, and you shall understand that neither I nor any man else to my knowledge ever took you to be a man of such credit in any matter of importance I or any other would at any time vouchsafe to communicate with you. And I, as you know, of no small while have been acquainted with you and your conversation, who have known you from your youth hitherto, for we long dwelled together in one parish. Whereas yourself can tell (I am sorry you compel me to say) you were esteemed very light of tongue, a great dicer, and of no commendable fame. And so in your house at the Temple, where hath been your chief bringing up, were you likewise accounted. Can it therefore seem likely to your honorable lordships, that I would, in so weighty a cause, so unadvisedly overshoot myself as to trust Master Rich, a man of men always reputed for one of little truth, as your lordships have heard, so far above my sovereign lord the king, or any of his noble counselors, that I would unto him utter the secrets of my conscience touching the king's supremacy, the special point and only mark at my hands so long sought for?

A thing which I never did, nor ever would, after the statute thereof made, reveal unto the King's Highness himself or to any of his honorable counselors, as it is not unknown to your honors, at sundry and several times, sent from His Grace's own person unto the Tower unto me for none other purpose. Can this in your judgment, my lords, seem likely to be true? And if I had so done, indeed, my lords, as Master Rich hath sworn, seeing it was spoken but in familiar, secret talk, nothing affirming, and only in putting of cases, without other displeasant circumstances, it cannot justly be taken to be spoken maliciously; and where there is no malice there can be no offense. And over this I can never think, my lords, that so many worthy bishops, so many noble personages, and many other worshipful, virtuous, wise, and well-learned men as at the making of that law were in Parliament assembled, ever meant to have any man punished by death in whom there could be found no malice, taking *malitia pro malevolentia*: for if *malitia* be generally taken for sin, no man is there that can excuse himself. *Quia si dixerimus quod peccatum non habemus, nosmetipsos seducimus, et veritas in nobis non est.* [If we say we have no sin, we deceive ourselves and the truth is not in us.] And only this word "maliciously" is in the statute material, as this term "forcibly" is in the statute of forcible entries, by which statute if a man enter peaceably, and put not his adversary out "forcibly," it is no offense, but if he put him out "forcibly," then by that statute it is an offense, and so shall be punished by this term "forcibly."

Besides this, the manifold goodness of the King's Highness himself, that hath been so many ways my singular good lord and gracious sovereign, and that hath so dearly loved and trusted me, even at my first coming into his noble service, with the dignity of his honorable privy council, vouchsafing to admit me, and to offices of great credit and worship most liberally advanced me; and finally with the weighty room of His Grace's higher chancellor, the like whereof he never did to temporal man before, next to his own royal person the highest office in this whole realm, so far above my qualities or merits and meet therefore of his own incomparable benignity honored and exalted me, by the space of twenty years or more, showing his continual favors towards me, and (until, at mine own poor suit it pleased His Highness, giving me license with His Majesty's favor to bestow the residue of my life wholly for the provision of my soul in the service of God. and of his special goodness thereof to discharge and unburden me) most benignly heaped honors continually more and more upon me; all this His Highness's goodness, I say, so long thus bountifully extended towards me, were in my mind, my lords, matter sufficient to convince this slanderous surmise by this man so wrongfully imagined against me. . . .

Forasmuch, my lord, as this indictment is grounded upon an act of Parliament directly oppugnant to the laws of God and his holy church, the supreme government of which, or of any part thereof, may no temporal prince presume by any law to take upon him, as rightfully belonging to the See of Rome, a spiritual preeminence by the mouth of our Savior himself, personally present upon the earth, to Saint Peter and his successors, bishops of the same see, by special prerogative granted; it is therefore in law amongst Christian men, insufficient to charge any Christian man. . . .

More have I not to say, my lords, but that like as the blessed apostle Saint Paul, as we read in the Acts of the Apostles, was present and consented to the death of Saint Stephen, and kept their clothes that stoned him to death, and yet be they now both twain holy saints in heaven, and shall continue there friends forever: so I verily trust and shall therefore right heartily pray, that though your lordships have now in earth been judges to my condemnation, we may yet hereafter in heaven merrily all meet together to our everlasting salvation. ■

Robert Emmet Demands
That Posterity Be the Judge
of His Irish Patriotism

"LET no man dare, when I am dead, to charge me with dishonor. . . . Let no man write my epitaph. . . ."

AS A STUDENT AT TRINITY COLLEGE, poet Thomas Moore was playing the melody "Let Erin Remember" on the piano, and later recalled Robert Emmet exclaiming passionately, "Oh, that I were at the head of twenty thousand men marching to that air!"

Emmet protested the inclusion of questions about his political views at the college and withdrew from the school. He joined the United Irishmen, a group seeking support from France in a rebellion against English rule of Ireland. He traveled to Paris and, in 1802, met Napoleon, who assured him that a French invasion of England would take place the following year. As the time approached, the idealistic Emmet, twenty-five, in a green-and-white uniform, led a band of eighty men, mostly drunken brawlers, toward Dublin Castle. But treachery, bungling, and murderous violence marred the plan, and Emmet was driven into hiding. While trying to persuade the daughter of another Irish patriot, John Philpot Curran, to flee with him to America, Emmet was apprehended. His trial was a farce, with his lawyer in the secret pay of the prosecution. Emmet's reputation as an Irish patriot was made in his impromptu protest to the court on September 29, 1803, against his sentence as a traitor.

The judges cut him off whenever his speech dipped too deeply into contempt, but he refused to be silenced, using the interruptions as openings to new lines of attack. Emmet spoke to history, to demand a later accounting of his actions and the court's justice, asking the tribunal only "the charity of its silence" as a future age was born to judge him. The repeated "let" construction has never been better used; the final three paragraphs are as gripping as perorations get.

□   □   □

My lords:
What have I to say why sentence of death should not be pronounced on me according to law? I have nothing to say that can alter your predetermination, nor that it will become me to say with any view to the mitigation of that sentence which you are here to pronounce, and I must abide by. But I have that to say which interests me more than life, and which you have labored (as was necessarily your office in the present circumstances of this oppressed country) to destroy. I have much to say why my reputation should be rescued from the load of false accusation and calumny which has been heaped upon it. I do not imagine that, seated where you are, your minds can be so free from impurity as to receive the least impression from what I am going to utter—I have no hopes that I can anchor my character in the breast of a court constituted and trammeled as this is—I only wish, and it is the utmost I expect, that your lordships may suffer it to float down your memories untainted by the foul breath of prejudice, until it finds some more hospitable harbor to shelter it from the storm by which it is at present buffeted.

Was I only to suffer death after being adjudged guilty by *your* tribunal, I should bow in silence and meet the fate that awaits me without a murmur; but the sentence of law which delivers my body to the executioner will, through the ministry of that law, labor in its own vindication to consign my character to obloquy—for there must be guilt somewhere: whether in the sentence of the court or in the catastrophe, posterity must determine. A man in my situation, my lords, has not only to encounter the difficulties of fortune, and the force of power over minds which it has corrupted or subjugated, but the difficulties of established prejudice: the man dies, but his memory lives. That mine may not perish, that it may live in the respect of my countrymen, I seize upon this opportunity to vindicate myself from some of the charges alleged against me. When my spirit shall be wafted to a more friendly port; when my shade shall have joined the bands of those martyred heroes who have shed their blood on the scaffold and in the field, in defense of their country and of virtue, this is my hope: I wish that my memory and name may animate those who survive me, while I look down with complacency on the destruction of that perfidious government which upholds its domination by blasphemy of the Most High—which displays its power over man as over the beasts of the forest—which sets man upon his brother, and lifts his hand in the name of God against the throat of his fellow who believes or doubts a little more or a little less than the government standard—a government which is steeled to barbarity by the cries of the orphans and the tears of the widows which it has made. [Interruption by the court.]

I appeal to the immaculate God—I swear by the throne of heaven, before which I must shortly appear—by the blood of the murdered patriots who have gone before me—that my conduct has been through all this peril and all my purposes governed only by the convictions which I have uttered, and by no other view than that of their cure, and the emancipation of my country from the superinhuman oppression under which she has so long and too patiently travailed; and that I confidently and assuredly hope that, wild and chimerical as it may appear, there is still union and strength in Ireland to accomplish this noble enterprise. Of this I speak with the confidence of intimate knowledge, and with the consolation that appertains to that confidence. Think not, my lords, I say this for the petty gratification of giving you a transitory uneasiness; a man who never yet raised his voice to assert a lie will not hazard his character with posterity by asserting a falsehood on a subject so important to his country, and on an occasion like this. Yes, my lords, a man who does not wish to have his epitaph written until his country is liberated will not leave a weapon in the power of envy, nor a pretense to impeach the probity which he means to preserve even in the grave to which tyranny consigns him. [Interruption by the court.]

Again I say, that what I have spoken was not intended for your lordship, whose situation I commiserate rather than envy—my expressions were for my countrymen; if there is a true Irishman present, let my last words cheer him in the hour of his affliction. [Interruption by the court.]

I have always understood it to be the duty of a judge, when a prisoner has been convicted, to pronounce the sentence of the law; I have also understood that judges sometimes think it their duty to hear with patience and to speak with humanity, to exhort the victim of the laws, and to offer with tender benignity his opinions of the motives by which he was actuated in the crime, of which he had been adjudged guilty: that a judge has thought it his duty so to have done, I have no doubt—but where is the boasted freedom of your institutions, where is the vaunted impartiality, clemency, and mildness of your courts of justice, if an unfortunate prisoner, whom your policy, and not pure justice, is about to deliver into the hands of the executioner, is not suffered to explain his motives sincerely and truly, and to vindicate the principles by which he was actuated?

My lords, it may be a part of the system of angry justice, to bow a man's mind by humiliation to the purposed ignominy of the scaffold; but worse to me than the purposed shame, or the scaffold's terrors, would be the shame of such unfounded imputations as have been laid against me in this court: you, my lord [Lord Norbury], are a judge, I am the supposed culprit; I am a man, you are a man also; by a revolution of power, we might change places, though we never could change characters; if I stand at the bar of this court and dare not vindicate my character, what a farce is your justice? If I stand at this bar and dare not vindicate my character, how dare you calumniate it? Does the sentence of death which your unhallowed policy inflicts on my body also condemn my tongue to silence and my reputation to reproach? Your executioner may abridge the period of my existence, but while I exist I shall not forbear to vindicate my character and motives from your aspersions; and as a man to whom fame is dearer than life, I will make the last use of that life in doing justice to that reputation which is to live after me, and which is the only legacy I can leave to those I honor and love, and for whom I am proud to perish. As men, my lord, we must appear at the great day at one common tribunal, and it will then remain for the searcher of all hearts to show a collective universe who was engaged in the most virtuous actions, or actuated by the purest motives—my country's oppressors or— [Interruption by the court.]

My lord, will a dying man be denied the legal privilege of exculpating himself, in the eyes of the community, of an undeserved reproach thrown upon him during his trial, by charging him with ambition and attempting to cast away, for a paltry consideration, the liberties of his country? Why did your lordship insult me? or rather why insult justice, in demanding of me why sentence of death should not be pronounced? I know, my lord, that form prescribes that you should ask the question; the form also presumes a right of answering. This no doubt may be dispensed with—and so might the whole ceremony of trial, since sentence was already pronounced at the castle, before your jury was impaneled; your lordships are but the priests of the oracle, and I submit; but I insist on the whole of the forms.

I am charged with being an emissary of France! An emissary of France! And for what end? It is alleged that I wished to sell the independence of my country! And for what end? Was this the object of my ambition? And is this the mode by which a tribunal of justice reconciles contradictions? No, I am no emissary; and my ambition was to hold a place among the deliverers of my country—not in power, nor in profit, but in the glory of the achievement! . . .

Connection with France was indeed intended, but only as far as mutual interest would sanction or require. Were they to assume any authority inconsistent with the purest independence, it would be the signal for their destruction; we sought aid, and we sought it, as we had assurances we should obtain it—as auxiliaries in war and allies in peace. . . .

I wished to procure for my country the guarantee which Washington procured for America. To procure an aid, which, by its example, would be as important as its valor, disciplined, gallant, pregnant with science and experience; which would perceive the good and polish the rough points of our character. They would come to us as strangers and leave us as friends, after sharing in our perils and elevating our destiny. These were my objects—not to receive new taskmasters but to expel old tyrants; these were my views, and these only became Irishmen. It was for these ends I sought aid from France; because France, even as an enemy, could not be more implacable than the enemy already in the bosom of my country. [Interruption by the court.]

I have been charged with that importance in the efforts to emancipate my country, as to be considered the *keystone* of the combination of Irishmen; or, as Your Lordship expressed it, "the life and blood of conspiracy." You do me honor overmuch. You have given to the subaltern all the credit of a superior. There are men engaged in this *conspiracy,* who are not only superior to me but even to your own conceptions of yourself, my lord; men, before the splendor of whose genius and virtues, I should bow with respectful deference, and who would think themselves dishonored to be called your friend—who would not disgrace themselves by shaking your bloodstained hand—[Interruption by the court.]

What, my lord, shall you tell me, on the passage to that scaffold, which that tyranny, of which you are only the intermediary executioner, has erected for my murder, that I am accountable for all the blood that has and will be shed in this struggle of the oppressed against the oppressor?— shall you tell me this—and must I be so very a slave as not to repel it?

I do not fear to approach the omnipotent Judge, to answer for the conduct of my whole life; and am I to be appalled and falsified by a mere remnant of mortality here? By you, too, who, if it were possible to collect all the innocent blood that you have shed in your unhallowed ministry, in one great reservoir, Your Lordship might swim in it. [Interruption by the court.]

Let no man dare, when I am dead, to charge me with dishonor; let no man attaint my memory by believing that I could have engaged in any cause but that of my country's liberty and independence, or that I could have become the pliant minion of power in the oppression or the miseries of my countrymen. The proclamation of the provisional government speaks for our views; no inference can be tortured from it to countenance barbarity or debasement at home, or subjection, humiliation, or treachery from abroad; I would not have submitted to a foreign oppressor for the same reason that I would resist the foreign and domestic oppressor; in the dignity of freedom I would have fought upon the threshold of my country, and its enemy should enter only by passing over my lifeless corpse. Am I, who lived but for my country, and who have subjected myself to the dangers of the jealous and watchful oppressor, and the bondage of the grave, only to give my countrymen their rights, and my country her independence, and am I to be loaded with calumny and not suffered to resent or repel it—no, God forbid!

If the spirits of the illustrious dead participate in the concerns and cares of those who are dear to them in this transitory life—oh, ever dear and venerated shade of my departed father, look down with scrutiny upon the conduct of your suffering son; and see if I have even for a moment deviated from those principles of morality and patriotism which it was your care to instil into my youthful mind, and for which I am now to offer up my life!

My lords, you are impatient for the sacrifice—the blood which you seek is not congealed by the artificial terrors which surround your victim; it circulates warmly and unruffled, through the channels which God created for noble purposes, but which you are bent to destroy, for purposes so grievous, that they cry to heaven. Be yet patient! I have but a few words more to say. I am going to my cold and silent grave: my lamp of life is nearly extinguished: my race is run: the grave opens to receive me, and I sink into its bosom! I have but one request to ask at my departure from this world—it is the charity of its silence! Let no man write my epitaph: for as no man who knows my motives dare now vindicate them, let not prejudice or ignorance asperse them. Let them and me repose in obscurity and peace, and my tomb remain uninscribed, until other times, and other men, can do justice to my character; when my country takes her place among the nations of the earth, then, and not till then, let my epitaph be written. I have done. ■

Novelist Emile Zola Turns His Libel Defense into an Appeal to Free Falsely Convicted Dreyfus

"DREYFUS is innocent. I swear it! I stake my life on it. . . ."

THE NOTORIOUS DREYFUS AFFAIR, which sharply divided France's political scene in the late nineteenth century, revolved around the 1895 conviction of Captain Alfred Dreyfus, a Jew who had been accused of passing French military secrets to the Germans. Among those sympathetic with the plight of Dreyfus was liberal French novelist Emile Zola. In 1898, Zola published a fiery letter, *"J'accuse,"* accusing the authorities of having framed Dreyfus.

Brought to trial on libel charges for this letter, Zola used his appeal to the jury as a forum for demanding a new trial for Dreyfus. His appeal for Dreyfus was made in a Paris courtroom on February 22, 1898; Zola, who disdained to defend his own actions, was found guilty of libel. That verdict was soon overturned, but before a second trial could begin, Zola moved to England to avoid further prosecution. The novelist's purpose, however, was fulfilled: a subsequent reopening of the Dreyfus case led to the exoneration of the military officer.

Zola prefaces his statement by addressing the jury directly as "you, you, the loftiest, the most direct emanation of French justice." His appeal for Dreyfus, though, contains no flattery, and the only sentiment is reserved for the France that he believes to be in jeopardy; through a series of rhetorical questions, he wonders aloud, "Are we still the most noble, the most fraternal, the most generous of nations?" Zola's appeal culminates in the parallel structure by which he swears (five "by" phrases that begin, "By my forty years of work, by the authority that this toil may have given me") and in the vision of ultimate vindication.

□   □   □

. . . You have heard the witnesses; you are about to hear my counsel, who will tell you the true story, the story that maddens everybody and that everybody knows. I am, therefore, at my ease. You have the truth at last, and it will do its work. M. Méline thought to dictate your decision by entrusting to you the honor of the army. And it is in the name of the honor of the army that I too appeal to your justice. . . .

You know the legend, which has grown up: Dreyfus was condemned justly and legally by seven infallible officers, whom it is impossible even to suspect of a blunder without insulting the whole army. Dreyfus expiates in merited torments his abominable crime, and as he is a Jew, a Jewish syndicate is formed, an international *sans patrie* syndicate disposing of hundreds of millions, the object of which is to save the traitor at any price, even by the most shameless intrigues. And thereupon this syndicate began to heap crime on crime, buying consciences, precipitating France into a disastrous tumult, resolved on selling her to the enemy, willing even to drive all Europe into a general war rather than renounce its terrible plan.

It is very simple, nay childish, if not imbecile. But it is with this poisoned bread that the unclean press has been nourishing our poor people now for months. And it is not surprising if we are witnessing a dangerous crisis; for when folly and lies are thus sown broadcast, you necessarily reap insanity.

Gentlemen, I would not insult you by supposing that you have yourselves been duped by this nursery tale. I know you; I know who you are. You are the heart and the reason of Paris, of my great Paris, where I was born, which I love with an infinite tenderness, which I have been studying and writing of now for forty years. And I know likewise what is now passing in your brains; for, before coming to sit here as defendant, I sat there on the bench where you are now. You represent there the average opinion; you try to illustrate prudence and justice in the mass. Soon I shall be in thought with you in the room where you deliberate, and I am convinced that your effort will be to safeguard your interests as citizens, which are, of course, the interests of the whole nation. You may make a mistake, but you will do so in the thought that while securing your own weal you are securing the weal of all.

I see you at your homes at evening under the lamp; I hear you talk with your friends; I accompany you into your factories and shops. You are all workers—some tradesmen, others manufacturers, some professional men; and your very legitimate anxiety is the deplorable state into which business has fallen. Everywhere the present crisis threatens to become a disaster. The receipts fall off; transactions become more and more difficult.

So that the idea which you have brought here, the thought which I read in your countenances, is that there has been enough of this and that it must be ended. You have not gone the length of saying, like many, "What matters it that an innocent man is at the Ile du Diable? Is the interest of a single man worth this disturbing a great country?" But you say, nevertheless, that the agitation, which we are carrying on, we who hunger for truth and justice, costs too dearly! And if you condemn me, gentlemen, it is that thought which will be at the bottom of your verdict. You desire tranquillity for your homes, you wish for the revival of business, and you may think that by punishing me you will stop a campaign which is injurious to the interests of France.

Well, gentlemen, if that is your idea, you are entirely mistaken. Do me the honor of believing that I am not defending my liberty. By punishing me you would only magnify me. Whoever suffers for truth and justice becomes august and sacred. Look at me. Have I the look of a hireling, of a liar, and a traitor? Why should I be playing a part? I have behind me neither political ambition nor sectarian passion. I am a free writer, who has given his life to labor; who tomorrow will go back to the ranks and resume his interrupted task. . . .

Do you not understand now that what the nation is dying of is the darkness in which there is such an obstinate determination to leave her? The blunders of those in authority are being heaped upon those of others; one lie necessitates another, so that the mass is becoming formidable. A judicial blunder was committed, and then to hide it, it has been necessary to commit every day fresh crimes against good sense and equity! The condemnation of an innocent man has involved the acquittal of a guilty man, and now today you are asked in turn to condemn me because I have cried out in my anguish on beholding our country embarked on this terrible course. Condemn me, then! But it will be one more error added to the others—a fault the burden of which you will hear in history. And my condemnation, instead of restoring the peace for which you long, and which we all of us desire, will be only a fresh seed of passion and disorder. The cup, I tell you, is full; do not make it run over!

Why do you not judge justly the terrible crisis through which the country is passing? They say that we are the authors of the scandal, that we who are lovers of truth and justice are leading the nation astray and urging it to violence. Surely this is a mockery! . . .

The Dreyfus case, gentlemen, has now become a very small affair. It is lost in view of the formidable questions to which it has given rise. There is no longer a Dreyfus case. The question now is whether France is still the France of the rights of man, the France which gave freedom to the world, and ought to give it justice. Are we still the most noble, the most fraternal, the most generous of nations? Shall we preserve our reputation in Europe for justice and humanity? Are not all the victories that we have won called in question? Open your eyes, and understand that, to be in such confusion, the French soul must have been stirred to its depths in face of a terrible danger. A nation cannot be thus moved without imperiling its moral existence. This is an exceptionally serious hour; the safety of the nation is at stake.

When you have understood that, gentlemen, you will feel that but one remedy is possible—to tell the truth, to do justice. Anything that keeps back the light, anything that adds darkness to darkness, will only prolong and aggravate the crisis. The duty of good citizens, of all who feel it to be imperatively necessary to put an end to this matter, is to demand broad daylight. . . .

Alas! gentlemen, like so many others, you expect the thunderbolt to descend from heaven in proof of the innocence of Dreyfus. Truth does not come thus. It requires research and knowledge. We know well where the truth is, or where it might be found. But we dream of that only in the recesses of our souls, and we feel patriotic anguish lest we expose ourselves to the danger of having this proof some day cast in our face after having involved the honor of the army in a falsehood. I wish also to declare positively that, though, in the official notice of our list of witnesses, we included certain embassadors, we had decided in advance not to call them. Our boldness has provoked smiles. But I do not think that there was any real smiling in our foreign office, for there they must have understood! We intended to say to those who know the whole truth that we also know it. This truth is gossiped about at the embassies; tomorrow it will be known to all, and, if it is now impossible for us to seek it where it is concealed by official red tape, the government which is not ignorant—the government which is convinced as we are—of the innocence of Dreyfus, will be able, whenever it likes and without risk, to find witnesses who will demonstrate everything.

Dreyfus is innocent. I swear it! I stake my life on it—my honor! At this solemn moment, in the presence of this tribunal which is the representative of human justice, before you, gentlemen, who are the very incarnation of the country, before the whole of France, before the whole world, I swear that Dreyfus is innocent. By my forty years of work, by the authority that this toil may have given me, I swear that Dreyfus is innocent. By all I have now, by the name I have made for myself, by my works which have helped for the expansion of French literature, I swear that Dreyfus is innocent. May all that melt away, may my works perish if

Dreyfus be not innocent! He is innocent. All seems against me—the two chambers, the civil authority, the most widely circulated journals, the public opinion which they have poisoned. And I have for me only an ideal of truth and justice. But I am quite calm; I shall conquer. I was determined that my country should not remain the victim of lies and injustice. I may be condemned here. The day will come when France will thank me for having helped to save her honor. ∎

Antiwar Dissident Eugene V. Debs Addresses the Court before Sentencing

"I can see the dawn of the better day for humanity. The people are awakening. In due time they will and must come to their own."

LABOR LEADER AND SOCIALIST, Eugene V. Debs organized the American Railway Union and served as its president until the Pullman strike of 1894. Debs, in prison after violating an injunction in that strike, became an ardent believer in socialism. He was a socialist candidate for president five times, including the 1920 election, during which he was again imprisoned.

Vehemently opposed to America's participation in the First World War, Debs was arrested in 1918 and convicted for violating the Espionage Act. Before receiving his sentence on September 14, 1918, he delivered his most eloquent speech to the court. The judge, however, was unmoved by the passionate words and sentenced Debs to ten years in prison. (President Warren Harding commuted that sentence three years later, and Debs was released.)

He had previously shown his affinity for parallel structure: "While there is a lower class, I am in it; while there is a criminal element, I am of it; and while there is a soul in prison, I am not free"—thus Debs quotes himself in his opening paragraph. In this speech, Debs asks nothing for himself ("I ask no mercy and I plead for no immunity"), reminding listeners instead of those who have no platform to speak: "I am thinking this morning of the men in the mills and factories. . . . I am thinking of the women . . . of the little children." His allusion to "the remorseless grasp of Mammon" (the New Testament's symbol for the worship of greed and immorality) leads to the condemning of our society, in which "gold is god." That condemnation, made all the more forceful by alliteration, joins with other alliterative expressions (including "common cause" and "waiting, watching, and working") to emphasize his plea for socialism.

□   □   □

Your Honor, years ago I recognized my kinship with all living beings, and I made up my mind that I was not one bit better than the meanest on earth. I said then, and I say now, that while there is a lower class, I am in it; while there is a criminal element, I am of it; and while there is a soul in prison, I am not free.

I listened to all that was said in this court in support and justification of this prosecution, but my mind remains unchanged. I look upon the Espionage Law as a despotic enactment in flagrant conflict with democratic principles and with the spirit of free institutions. . . .

Your Honor, I have stated in this court that I am opposed to the social system in which we live, that I believe in a fundamental change—but if possible by peaceable and orderly means. . . .

Standing here this morning, I recall my boyhood. At fourteen I went to work in a railroad shop; at sixteen I was firing a freight engine on a railroad. I remember all the hardships and privations of that earlier day, and from that time until now my heart has been with the working class. I could have been in Congress long ago. I have preferred to go to prison. . . .

I am thinking this morning of the men in the mills and factories; of the men in the mines and on the railroads. I am thinking of the women who for a paltry wage are compelled to work out their barren lives; of the little children who in this system are robbed of their childhood and in their tender years are seized in the remorseless grasp of Mammon and forced into the industrial dungeons, there to feed the monster machines while they themselves are being starved and stunted, body and soul. I see them dwarfed and diseased and their little lives broken and blasted because in this high noon of our twentieth-century Christian civilization money is still so much more important than the flesh and blood of childhood. In very truth gold is god today and rules with pitiless sway in the affairs of men.

In this country—the most favored beneath the bending skies—we have vast areas of the richest and most fertile soil, material resources in inexhaustible abundance, the most marvelous productive machinery on earth, and millions of eager workers ready to apply their labor to that machinery to produce in abundance for every man, woman, and child— and if there are still vast numbers of our people who are the victims of poverty and whose lives are an unceasing struggle all the way from youth to old age, until at last death comes to their rescue and stills their aching hearts and lulls these hapless victims to dreamless sleep, it is not the fault of the Almighty: it cannot be charged to nature, but it is due entirely to the outgrown social system in which we live, that ought to be abolished not only in the interest of the toiling masses but in the higher interest of all humanity. . . .

I believe, Your Honor, in common with all socialists, that this nation ought to own and control its own industries. I believe, as all socialists do, that all things that are jointly needed and used ought to be jointly owned— that industry, the basis of our social life, instead of being the private property of the few and operated for their enrichment, ought to be the common property of all, democratically administered in the interest of all. . . .

I am opposing a social order in which it is possible for one man who does absolutely nothing that is useful to amass a fortune of hundreds of millions of dollars, while millions of men and women who work all the days of their lives secure barely enough for a wretched existence.

This order of things cannot always endure. I have registered my protest against it. I recognize the feebleness of my effort, but fortunately I am not alone. There are multiplied thousands of others who, like myself, have come to realize that before we may truly enjoy the blessings of civilized life, we must reorganize society upon a mutual and cooperative basis; and to this end we have organized a great economic and political movement that spreads over the face of all the earth.

There are today upwards of sixty millions of socialists, loyal, devoted adherents to this cause, regardless of nationality, race, creed, color, or sex. They are all making common cause. They are spreading with tireless energy the propaganda of the new social order. They are waiting, watching, and working hopefully through all the hours of the day and the night. They are still in a minority. But they have learned how to be patient and to bide their time. They feel—they know, indeed—that the time is coming, in spite of all opposition, all persecution, when this emancipating gospel will spread among all the peoples, and when this minority will become the triumphant majority and, sweeping into power, inaugurate the greatest social and economic change in history.

In that day we shall have the universal commonwealth—the harmonious cooperation of every nation with every other nation on earth. . . .

Your Honor, I ask no mercy and I plead for no immunity. I realize that finally the right must prevail. I never so clearly comprehended as now the great struggle between the powers of greed and exploitation on the one hand and upon the other the rising hosts of industrial freedom and social justice.

I can see the dawn of the better day for humanity. The people are awakening. In due time they will and must come to their own. . . .

I am now prepared to receive your sentence. ■

Gandhi Defends His Beliefs

"I know that I was playing with fire. I ran the risk, and if I was set free, I would still do the same."

SATYAGRAHA, OR NONVIOLENT RESISTANCE, marked the political path of Mohandas K. Gandhi, India's spiritual leader. Until his assassination in 1948, Gandhi worked to achieve political goals through methods of nonviolence and noncooperation. By means of fasts and boycotts, he guided his followers to India's independence from British rule.

In promoting satyagraha, however, Gandhi was arrested in 1922 and charged with sedition for his articles in the magazine *Young India*. On March 23, at the end of his trial, he was permitted to address the court before sentencing. A packed Indian courtroom listened to Gandhi's remarks and to the judge's sentence of six years in prison.

In his preliminary remarks, Gandhi accepts full responsibility for his actions, asserting, "Nonviolence is the first article of my faith. . . . But I had to make my choice." His reading of the prepared statement, chronicling his resistance efforts, also shows his understanding of the consequences ("Nonviolence implies voluntary submission to the penalty for noncooperation with evil"). Pervading the speech is parallel structure ("as a man and as an Indian I had no rights"), which adds force to the moving statement of Gandhi's beliefs.

□   □   □

Before I read this statement, I would like to state that I entirely endorse the learned advocate general's remarks in connection with my humble self. I think that he was entirely fair to me in all the statements that he has made, because it is very true, and I have no desire whatsoever to conceal from this court the fact that to preach disaffection toward the existing system of government has become almost a passion with me; and the learned advocate general is also entirely in the right when he says that my preaching of disaffection did not commence with my connection with *Young India*, but that it commenced much earlier; and in the statement that I am about to read, it will be my painful duty to admit before this court that it commenced much earlier than the period stated by the advocate general. It is the most painful duty with me, but I have to discharge that duty knowing the responsibility that rests upon my shoulders, and I wish to endorse all the blame that the learned advocate general has thrown on my shoulders, in connection with the Bombay occurrences, Madras occurrences, and the Chauri Chaura occurrences. Thinking over these deeply and sleeping over them night after night, it is impossible for me to dissociate myself from the diabolical crimes of Chauri Chaura or the mad outrages of Bombay. He is quite right when he says that as a man of responsibility, a man having received a fair share of education, having had a fair share of experience of this world, I should have known the consequences of every one of my acts. I know that I was playing with fire. I ran the risk, and if I was set free, I would still do the same. I have felt it this morning that I would have failed in my duty, if I did not say what I said here just now.

I wanted to avoid violence, I want to avoid violence. Nonviolence is the first article of my faith. It is also the last article of my creed. But I had to make my choice. I had either to submit to a system which I considered had done an irreparable harm to my country, or incur the risk of the mad fury of my people bursting forth, when they understood the truth from my lips. I know that my people have sometimes gone mad. I am deeply sorry for it, and I am therefore here to submit not to a light penalty but to the highest penalty. I do not ask for mercy. I do not plead any extenuating act. I am here, therefore, to invite and cheerfully submit to the highest penalty that can be inflicted upon me for what in law is a deliberate crime and what appears to me to be the highest duty of a citizen. The only course open to you, the judge, is, as I am just going to say in my statement, either to resign your post or inflict on me the severest penalty, if you believe that the system and law you are assisting to administer are good for the people. I do not expect that kind of conversation, but by the time I have finished with my statement, you will perhaps have a glimpse of what is raging within my breast to run this maddest risk which a sane man can run.

I owe it perhaps to the Indian public and to the public in England to placate which this prosecution is mainly taken up that I should explain why from a staunch loyalist and cooperator I have become an uncompromising disaffectionist and non-cooperator. To the court too I should say why I plead guilty to the charge of promoting disaffection toward the government established by law in India.

My public life began in 1893 in South Africa in troubled weather. My first contact with British authority in that country was not of a happy character. I discovered that as a man and as an Indian I had no rights. More correctly, I discovered that I had no rights as a man because I was an Indian.

But I was not baffled. I thought that this treatment of Indians was an excrescence upon a system that was intrinsically and mainly good. I gave the government my voluntary and hearty cooperation, criticizing it freely where I felt it was faulty but never wishing its destruction.

Consequently, when the existence of the empire was threatened in 1899 by the Boer challenge, I offered my services to it, raised a volunteer ambulance corps, and served at several actions that took place for the relief of Ladysmith. Similarly in 1906, at the time of the Zulu revolt, I raised a stretcher-bearer party and served till the end of the "rebellion." On both these occasions I received medals and was even mentioned in dispatches. For my work in South Africa I was given by Lord Hardinge a Kaiser-i-Hind Gold Medal. When the war broke out in 1914 between

England and Germany, I raised a volunteer ambulance corps in London consisting of the then resident Indians in London, chiefly students. Its work was acknowledged by the authorities to be valuable. Lastly, in India, when a special appeal was made at the War Conference in Delhi in 1918 by Lord Chelmsford for recruits, I struggled at the cost of my health to raise a corps in Kheda, and the response was being made when the hostilities ceased and orders were received that no more recruits were wanted. In all these efforts at service I was actuated by the belief that it was possible by such services to gain a status of full equality in the empire for my countrymen.

The first shock came in the shape of the Rowlatt Act, a law designed to rob the people of all real freedom. I felt called upon to lead an intensive agitation against it. Then followed the Punjab horrors beginning with the massacre at Jallianwala Bagh and culminating in crawling orders, public floggings, and other indescribable humiliations. I discovered too that the plighted word of the prime minister to the Mussulmans of India regarding the integrity of Turkey and the holy places of Islam was not likely to be fulfilled. But in spite of the forebodings and the grave warnings of friends, at the Amritsar Congress in 1919, I fought for cooperation and working with the Montagu-Chelmsford reforms, hoping that the prime minister would redeem his promise to the Indian Mussulmans, that the Punjab wound would be healed, and that the reforms, inadequate and unsatisfactory though they were, marked a new era of hope in the life of India.

But all that hope was shattered. The Khilafat promise was not to be redeemed. The Punjab crime was whitewashed, and most culprits went not only unpunished but remained in service and in some cases continued to draw pensions from the Indian revenue, and in some cases were even rewarded. I saw too that not only did the reforms not mark a change of heart, but they were only a method of further draining India of her wealth and of prolonging her servitude.

I came reluctantly to the conclusion that the British connection had made India more helpless than she ever was before, politically and economically. A disarmed India has no power of resistance against any aggressor if she wanted to engage in an armed conflict with him. So much is this the case that some of our best men consider that India must take generations before she can achieve the dominion status. She has become so poor that she has little power of resisting famines. Before the British advent, India spun and wove in her millions of cottages just the supplement she needed for adding to her meager agricultural resources. This cottage industry, so vital for India's existence, has been ruined by incredibly heartless and inhuman processes as described by English witnesses. Little do town dwellers know how the semistarved masses of India are slowly sinking to lifelessness. Little do they know that their miserable comfort represents the brokerage they get for the work they do for the foreign exploiter, that the profits and the brokerage are sucked from the masses. Little do they realize that the government established by law in British India is carried on for this exploitation of the masses. No sophistry, no jugglery in figures can explain away the evidence that the skeletons in many villages present to the naked eye. I have no doubt whatsoever that both England and the town dwellers of India will have to answer, if there is a God above, for this crime against humanity which is perhaps unequaled in history. The law itself in this country has been used to serve the foreign exploiter. My unbiased examination of the Punjab Martial Law cases has led me to believe that at least 95 percent of convictions were wholly bad. My experience of political cases in India leads me to the conclusion that in nine out of every ten the condemned men were totally innocent. Their crime consisted in the love of their country. In ninety-nine cases out of a hundred justice has been denied to Indians as against Europeans in the courts of India. This is not an exaggerated picture. It is the experience of almost every Indian who has had anything to do with such cases. In my opinion, the administration of the law is thus prostituted consciously or unconsciously for the benefit of the exploiter.

The greatest misfortune is that Englishmen and their Indian associates in the administration of the country do not know that they are engaged in the crime I have attempted to describe. I am satisfied that many Englishmen and Indian officials honestly believe that they are administering one of the best systems devised in the world and that India is making steady though slow progress. They do not know that a subtle but effective system of terrorism and an organized display of force, on the one hand, and the deprivation of all powers of retaliation or self-defense, on the other, have emasculated the people and induced in them the habit of simulation. This awful habit has added to the ignorance and the self-deception of the administrators. Section 124-A, under which I am happily charged, is perhaps the prince among the political sections of the Indian Penal Code designed to suppress the liberty of the citizen. Affection cannot be manufactured or regulated by law. If one has an affection for a person or system, one should be free to give the fullest expression to his disaffection, so long as he does not contemplate, promote, or incite to violence. But the section under which Mr. Banker [a colleague in nonviolence] and I are charged is one under which mere promotion of disaffection is a crime. I have studied some of the cases tried under it, and I know that some of the most loved of India's patriots have been convicted under it. I consider it a privilege, therefore, to be charged under that section. I have endeavored to give in their briefest outline the reasons for my disaffection. I have no personal ill will against any single administrator; much less can I have any disaffection toward the king's person. But I hold it to be a virtue to be disaffected toward a government which in its totality has done more harm to India than any previous system. India is less manly under the British rule than she ever was before. Holding such a belief, I consider it to be a sin to have affection for the system. And it has been a precious privilege for me to be able to write what I have in the various articles, tendered in evidence against me.

In fact, I believe that I have rendered a service to India and England by showing in non-cooperation the way out of the unnatural state in which both are living. In my humble opinion, non-cooperation with evil is as much a duty as is cooperation with good. But in the past, non-cooperation has been deliberately expressed in violence to the evildoer. I am endeavoring to show to my countrymen that violent non-cooperation only multiplies evil and that as evil can only be sustained by violence, withdrawal of support of evil requires complete abstention from violence. Nonviolence implies voluntary submission to the penalty for non-cooperation with evil. I am here, therefore, to invite and submit cheerfully to the highest penalty that can be inflicted upon me for what in law is a deliberate crime and what appears to me to be the highest duty of a citizen. The only course open to you, the judge, is either to resign your post, and thus dissociate yourself from evil if you feel that the law you are called upon to administer is an evil and that in reality I am innocent, or to inflict on me the severest penalty if you believe that the system and the law you are assisting to administer are good for the people of this country and that my activity is therefore injurious to the public weal. ■

Defense Lawyer Clarence Darrow Answers a Supporter of Capital Punishment

"IT is a question of how you feel, that is all. . . . If you love the thought of somebody being killed, why, you are for it. If you hate the thought of somebody being killed, you are against it."

SELF-ASSURED ON HIS FEET, skilled in the art of debating, Clarence Seward Darrow gained fame first as a labor lawyer and then as a defense attorney. In the early twentieth century, he defended clients throughout the country and established himself as the preeminent trial lawyer of his time.

In the controversial 1925 Scopes "monkey trial," Darrow achieved worldwide renown defending a Tennessee teacher of biology for espousing Darwin's evolution theory rather than creationism; the prosecutor, William Jennings Bryan—see his "Cross of Gold" speech on p. 922—won a conviction and fine in a decision later overturned by a higher court. Darrow also defended Eugene V. Debs during the 1894 Pullman strike and in 1924 saved convicted murderers Leopold and Loeb from the death sentence by pioneering the insanity plea.

Championing the "common man," pledged to fight for the underdog, Darrow took a public stand against capital punishment. He debated the issue with Alfred J. Talley, a New York City judge, and the speech that follows was taken from his remarks in that debate on October 27, 1924.

Exhibiting his skills as a trial lawyer, Darrow laced his argument with commonsense observations and humorous aphorisms ("Statistics are a pleasant indoor sport—not so good as crossword puzzles"). Throughout the discussion, however, is the interplay of sarcasm and disgust ("an afternoon's pleasure to kill a Negro") in expressing his repugnance. With a series of rhetorical questions (beginning with "But why not do a good job of it?"), he suggests his own version of Jonathan Swift's satiric "modest proposal"—brutal measures to equal what he considers the brutal inhumanity of capital punishment. In his lifetime in the law, Darrow defended a hundred clients charged with murder; not one was sentenced to death.

□ □ □

I hope I will not be obliged to spend too much time on my friend's address. I don't think I shall need to.

First, I deny his statement that every man's heart tells him it is wrong to kill. I think every man's heart desires killing. Personally, I never killed anybody that I know of. But I have had a great deal of satisfaction now and then reading obituary notices, and I used to delight, with the rest of my 100 percent patriotic friends, when I saw ten or fifteen thousand Germans being killed in a day.

Everybody loves killing. Some of them think it is too mussy for them. Every human being that believes in capital punishment loves killing, and the only reason they believe in capital punishment is because they get a kick out of it. Nobody kills anyone for love, unless they get over it temporarily or otherwise. But they kill the one they hate. And before you can get a trial to hang somebody or electrocute him, you must first hate him and then get a satisfaction over his death.

There is no emotion in any human being that is not in every single human being. The degree is different, that is all. And the degree is not always different in different people. It depends likewise on circumstances, on time, and on place.

I shall not follow my friend into the labyrinth of statistics. Statistics are a pleasant indoor sport—not so good as crossword puzzles—and they prove nothing to any sensible person who is familiar with statistics.

I might just observe, in passing, that in all of these states where the mortality by homicide is great, they have capital punishment and always have had it. A logical man, when he found out that the death rate increased under capital punishment, would suggest some other way of dealing with it.

I undertake to say—and you can look them up yourselves, for I haven't time to bother with it (and there is nothing that lies like statistics)—I will guarantee to take any set of statistics and take a little time to it and prove they mean directly the opposite for what is claimed. But I will undertake to say that you can show by statistics that the states in which there was no capital punishment have a very much smaller percentage of homicides.

I know it is true. That doesn't prove anything, because, as a rule, they are states with a less diverse population, without as many large cities, without as much mixtures of all sorts of elements, which go to add to the general gaiety—and homicide is a product of that. There is no sort of question but what those states in the United States where there is no capital punishment have a lower percentage than the others. But that doesn't prove the question. It is a question that cannot be proven one way or the other by statistics. It rests upon things, upon feelings and emotions and arguments much deeper than statistics.

The death rate in Memphis and in some other southern cities is high from homicide. Why? Well, it is an afternoon's pleasure to kill a Negro— that is about all. Everybody knows it.

The death rate recently in the United States and all over the world has increased. Why? The same thing has happened that has happened in every country in the world since time began. A great war always increases death rates.

We teach people to kill, and the state is the one that teaches them. If a state wishes that its citizens respect human life, then the state should stop killing. It can be done in no other way, and it will perhaps not be fully done that way. There are infinite reasons for killing. There are infinite circumstances under which there are more or less deaths. It never did depend and never can depend upon the severity of the punishment.

He talks about the United States being a lawless country. Well, the people somehow prefer it. There is such a thing as a people being too servile to law. You may take China with her caste system and much of Europe, which has much more caste than we. It may be full of homicides, but there is less bread and there is less fun; there is less opportunity for the poor. In any new country, homicide is more frequent than in an old country, because there is a higher degree of equality. It is always true wherever you go. And in the older countries, as a general rule, there are fewer homicides because nobody ever thinks of getting out of his class; nobody ever dreams of such a thing.

But let's see what there is in this argument. He says, "Everybody who kills, dreads hanging." Well, he has had experiences as a lawyer on both sides. I have had experience on one side. I know that everybody who is taken into court on a murder charge desires to live, and they do not want to be hanged or electrocuted. Even a thing as alluring as being cooked with electricity doesn't appeal to them.

But that hasn't anything to do with it. What was the state of mind when the homicide was committed? The state of mind is one thing when a homicide is committed and another thing weeks or months afterward, when every reason for committing it is gone. There is no comparison between it. There never can be any comparison between it.

We might ask why people kill. I don't want to dispute with him about the right of the state to kill people. Of course, they have got a right to kill them. That is about all we do. The great industry of the world for four long years was killing. They have got a right to kill, of course. That is, they have got the power. And you have got a right to do what you get away with. The words "power" and "right," so far as this is concerned, mean exactly the same thing. So nobody who has any knowledge of philosophy would pretend to say that the state had not the right to kill.

But why not do a good job of it? If you want to get rid of killings by hanging people or electrocuting them because these are so terrible, why not make a punishment that is terrible? This isn't so much. It lasts but a short time. There is no physical torture in it. Why not boil them in oil, as they used to do? Why not burn them at the stake? Why not sew them into a bag with serpents and throw them out to sea? Why not take them out on the sand and let them be eaten by ants? Why not break every bone in their body on the rack, as has been done for such serious offenses as heresy and witchcraft?

Those were the good old days in which the judge should have held court. Glorious days, when you could kill them by the million because they worshiped God in a different way from that which the state provided, or when you could kill old women for witchcraft! There might be some sense in it if you could kill young ones, but not old ones. Those were the glorious days of capital punishment. And there wasn't a judge or a preacher who didn't think that the life of the state depended upon their right to hang old women for witchcraft and to persecute others for worshiping God in the wrong way.

Why, our capital punishment isn't worth talking about, so far as its being a preventive is concerned. It isn't worth discussing. Why not call back from the dead and barbarous past the hundred and sixty or seventy-odd crimes that were punishable by death in England? Why not once more reenact the blue laws of our own country and kill people right? Why not resort to all the tortures that the world has always resorted to to keep men in the straight and narrow path? Why reduce it to a paltry question of murder?

Everybody in this world has some pet aversion to something, and on account of that pet aversion they would like to hang somebody. If the prohibitionists made the law, they would be in favor of hanging you for taking a drink, or certainly for bootlegging, because to them that is the most heinous crime there is.

Some men slay or murder. Why? As a matter of fact, murder as murder is very rare; and the people, who commit it, as a rule, are of a much higher type than others. You may go to any penitentiary and, as a rule, those who have been convicted of murder become the trusties; whereas, if you are punishing somebody as a sneak thief or a counterfeiter or a confidence man, they never get over it—never.

Now, I don't know how injustice is administered in New York. I just know about Chicago. But I am glad to learn from the gentleman that if a man is so poor in New York that he can't hire a lawyer, that he has a first-class lawyer appointed to defend him—a first-class lawyer appointed to defend him. Don't take a chance and go out and kill anybody on the statement made by my friend.

I suppose anybody can go out and kill somebody and ask to have my friend Sam Untermyer appointed. There never was such a thing. Here and there, a good lawyer may have defended people for nothing. But no court ever interferes with a good lawyer's business by calling him in and compelling him to give his time. They have been lawyers too recently themselves to ever work a trick like that on a lawyer. As a rule, it is the poor and the weak and the friendless who furnish the victims of the law.

Let me take another statement of my friend. He said, "Oh, we don't hang anybody if they kill when they are angry; it is only when they act premeditatedly." Yes, I have been in courts and heard judges instruct people on this premeditated act. It is only when they act under their judgment and with due consideration. He would also say that if a man is moved by anger, but if he doesn't strike the deadly blow until such time as reason and judgment has a chance to possess him, even if it is a second—how many times have I heard judges say, "Even if it is a second?" What does any judge know about premeditation? What does anybody know about it? How many people are there in this world that can premeditate on anything? I will strike out the "pre" and say how many people are there that can meditate?

How long does it take the angry man for his passions to cool when he is in the presence of the thing that angers him? There never was a premeditated murder in any sense of psychology or of science. There are planned murders—planned, yes—but back of every murder and back of every human act are sufficient causes that move the human machine beyond their control.

The other view is an outworn, outlawed, unscientific theory of the metaphysicians. Does anybody ever act in this world without a motive? Did they ever act without a sufficient motive? And who am I to say that John Smith premeditated? I might premeditate a good deal quicker than

John Smith did. My judgment might have a chance to act quicker than John Smith's judgment had a chance to act.

We have heard talk of justice. Is there anybody who knows what justice is? No one on earth can measure out justice. Can you look at any man and say what he deserves—whether he deserves hanging by the neck until dead or life in prison or thirty days in prison or a medal? The human mind is blind to all who seek to look in at it and to most of us that look out from it. Justice is something that man knows little about. He may know something about charity and understanding and mercy, and he should cling to these as far as he can.

Now, let me see if I am right about my statement that no man believes in hanging, except for a kick or revenge. How about my friend Judge Talley, here. He criticizes the state of New York because a prisoner may be shown moving pictures. What do you think about it—those of you who think? What do you feel about it—those of you who have passed the hyena age? I know what they think. What do you think about shutting up a man in a penitentiary for twenty years, in a cell four feet wide and seven feet long—twenty years, mind!—and complaining because he had a chance now and then to go out and see a moving picture—go out of his cell?

A body of people who feels that way could never get rid of capital punishment. If you really felt it, you would feel like the Indian who used the tomahawk on his enemy and who burned him and embalmed his face with the ashes.

But what is punishment about anyway? I put a man in prison for the purpose of getting rid of him and for such example as there might be. Is it up to you to torture him while he is there? Supposing you provided that every man who went to prison should be compelled to wear a nail half an inch long in his shoe. I suppose some of you would do it. I don't know whether the judge would or not, from what he said.

Is there any reason for torturing someone who happens to be in prison? Is there any reason why an actor or even an actress might not go there and sing? There is no objection to a preacher going there. Why not give him a little pleasure?

And they really get food there—what do you know about that? Now, when I heard him tell about what wonderful food they get—dietary food— did you ever know anybody that liked dietary food? I suppose the constitution of the state of New York contains the ordinary provision against cruel and inhuman punishment, and yet you send them up there and feed them on dietary food.

And you can take your meals out! Now, some of you might not have noticed that I walked over and asked the warden about it. The reason I did that is because I am stopping over here at the Belmont, and I didn't know but I'd rather go up and board with him.

Now, this is what I find out: that those who have gained consideration by good conduct over a considerable period—one year—they may spend three dollars a week for board. I pay more than that over here. They ought to pass some law in New York to prevent the inmates getting dyspepsia. And for those who attain the second class, they may spend a dollar and a half a week. And for those below the second class, nothing can come from outside—nothing. A pure matter of prison discipline!

Why, I wonder if the judge ever took pains to go up there. I will tell you. I have had some experience with people that know them pretty well. I never saw a man who wanted to go to prison, even to see the movies. I never saw a man in my life who didn't want to get out.

I wonder what you would have. Of course, I live in Chicago, where people are fairly human—I don't know, maybe I don't understand the New York people. What would you have? Suppose you could tell yourselves how a person was to be treated while in prison—and it doesn't require a great amount of imagination. Most people can think of some relative or some friends who are there. If you can't, most of you can think of a good many that ought to be there. How would you have them treated—something worse than being shut up in a cell, four by seven, and given light work—like being a judge or practicing law—something worse than dietary food?

I will tell you. There is just one thing in all this question. It is a question of how you feel, that is all. It is all inside of you. If you love the thought of somebody being killed, why, you are for it. If you hate the thought of somebody being killed, you are against it.

Let me just take a little brief review of what has happened in this world. They used to hang people on the crossways and on a high hill, so that everybody would be awed into goodness by the sight. They have tortured them in every way that the brain of man could conceive. They have provided every torture known or that could be imagined for one who believed differently from his fellowman—and still the belief persisted. They have maimed and scarred and starved and killed human beings since man began penning his fellowman. Why? Because we hate him. And what has added to it is that they have done it under the false ideal of self-righteousness.

I have heard parents punish their children and tell their children it hurt the parent more than it did the child. I don't believe it. I have tried it both ways, and I don't believe it. I know better.

Gradually, the world has been lopping off these punishments. Why?

Because we have grown a little more sensitive, a little more imaginative, a little kindlier, that is all.

Why not reenact the code of Blackstone's day? Why, the judges were all for it—every one of them—and the only way we got rid of those laws was because juries were too humane to obey the courts.

That is the only way we got rid of punishing old women, of hanging old women in New England—because, in spite of all the courts, the juries would no longer convict them for a crime that never existed. And in that way they have cut down the crimes in England for punishment by death from one hundred and seventy to two. What is going to happen if we get rid of them? Is the world coming to an end? The earth has been here ages and ages before man came. It will be here ages and ages after he disappears, and the amount of people you hang won't make the slightest difference with it.

Now, why am I opposed to capital punishment? It is too horrible a thing for a state to undertake. We are told by my friend, "Oh, the killer does it; why shouldn't the state?" I would hate to live in a state that I didn't think was better than a murderer.

But I told you the real reason. The people of the state kill a man because he killed someone else—that is all—without the slightest logic, without the slightest application to life, simply from anger, nothing else!

I am against it because I believe it is inhuman, because I believe that as the hearts of men have softened they have gradually gotten rid of brutal punishment, because I believe that it will only be a few years until it will be banished forever from every civilized country—even New York—because I believe that it has no effect whatever to stop murder.

Now, let's make that simple and see. Where do the murders come from? I would say the second-largest class of what we call murders grows out of domestic relations. They follow those deep and profound feelings that are at the basis of life—and the feelings which give the greatest joy are susceptible of the greatest pain when they go ariot.

Can you imagine a woman following a man around with a pistol to kill him that would stop if you said, "Oh, you will be hanged!" Nothing doing—not if the world was coming to an end! Can you imagine a man doing it? Not at all. They think of it afterwards, but not before.

They come from acts like burglary and robbery. A man goes out to rob or to burglarize. Somebody catches him or stops him or recognizes him, and he kills to save himself. Do you suppose there was ever a burglar or robber since the world began who would not kill to save himself? Is there anybody who wouldn't? It doesn't make any difference who. Wouldn't he take a chance shooting? Anyone would do it. Why, my friend himself said he would kill in self-defense. That is what they do. If you are going to stop them, you ought to hang them for robbery—which would be a good plan—and then, of course, if one started out to rob, he would kill the victim before he robbed him.

There isn't, I submit, a single admissible argument in favor of capital punishment. Nature loves life. We believe that life should be protected and preserved. The thing that keeps one from killing is the emotion they have against it; and the greater the sanctity that the state pays to life, the greater the feeling of sanctity the individual has for life.

There is nothing in the history of the world that ever cheapened human life like our great war; next to that, the indiscriminate killing of men by the states.

My friend says a man must be proven guilty first. Does anybody know whether anybody is guilty? There is a great deal implied in that. For me to do something or for you to do something is one thing; for some other man to do something quite another. To know what one deserves, requires infinite study, which no one can give to it. No one can determine the condition of the brain that did the act. It is out of the question.

All people are products of two things, and two things only—their heredity and their environment. And they act in exact accord with the heredity which they took from all the past, and for which they are in no wise responsible, and the environment, which reaches out to the farthest limit of all life that can influence them. We all act from the same way. And it ought to teach us to be charitable and kindly and understanding of our fellowman. ■

Cuban Rebel Fidel Castro Defies His Captors and Predicts That History Will Absolve Him

"My voice will not be stilled—it will rise from my breast even when I feel most alone, and my heart will give it all the fire that callous cowards deny it."

DRESSED IN BUSINESS SUIT and tie at a luncheon in the Fifth Avenue home of a prominent New York publisher, Cuba's President Fidel Castro—permitted in the United States to attend a United Nations ceremony—spoke with charm and vivacity to the elite of the media world. One of the world's few remaining totalitarian leaders said he understood the politics of the American embargo against his country because he had been a successful politician all his life, having first run for office in college.

An anti-Communist columnist (the anthologist) interrupted the flow of his talk with a question: "If you're such a great politician, why have you been afraid to hold an election in Cuba for the past thirty-seven years?" Castro drew himself to military attention and icily replied: "I am not afraid, but we do not have presidential elections in our country." He compared his own selection to that of the pope, elected by a ballot of cardinals.

At the time the following speech was made, Castro was an embryonic military-political leader. On July 26, 1953, his armed attack on the Moncada Barracks in Santiago de Cuba had failed; 122 codefendants were tried in the Palace of Justice, but Castro's trial took place in a small hospital in relative secrecy. His speech from the dock on October 16, 1953, little reported at the time, achieved the level of official scripture after his two-year incarceration, his release and sojourn in Mexico, his return to the Sierra Maestra mountains in Oriente province, and his toppling of Fulgencio Batista's dictatorial regime in 1959.

Though he would later be famous for his self-indulgent seven-hour harangues, the young Castro, a lawyer turned revolutionary, was able to keep his gift of passionate presentation within bounds. His speech to the court is studded with terrifying images—"They crushed their testicles and they tore out their eyes. But no one yielded"—but he also can begin paragraphs, or new departures in a speech, with quietly declarative short sentences ("In every society there are men of base instincts"). He evokes the names of the heroes of his country; "the Apostle" referred to here is José Martí, the poet and Cuban patriot who led the struggle for independence from Spain in the last part of the nineteenth century. Martí lived for a time in New York City and was an occasional contributor to the *New York Sun*. The centennial of his birth in 1953 was overlooked in Cuba; Castro, who wished to associate himself with the revolutionary hero, made a point of it.

□   □   □

Honorable Judges: If there is in your hearts a vestige of love for your country, love for humanity, love for justice, listen carefully. I know that I will be silenced for many years; I know that the regime will try to suppress the truth by all possible means; I know that there will be a conspiracy to bury me in oblivion. But my voice will not be stilled—it will rise from my breast even when I feel most alone, and my heart will give it all the fire that callous cowards deny it. . . .

From a shack in the mountains on Monday, July the twenty-seventh, I listened to the dictator's voice on the air while there were still eighteen of our men in arms against the government. Those who have never experienced similar moments will never know that kind of bitterness and indignation. While the long cherished hopes of freeing our people lay in ruins about us we heard those crushed hopes gloated over by a tyrant more vicious, more arrogant, than ever. The endless stream of lies and slanders, poured forth in his crude, odious, repulsive language, may only be compared to the endless stream of clean young blood which had flowed since the previous night—with his knowledge, consent, complicity and approval—being spilled by the most inhuman gang of assassins it is possible to imagine.

To have believed him for a single moment would have sufficed to fill a man of conscience with remorse and shame for the rest of his life. At that time I could not even hope to brand his miserable forehead with the mark of truth, which condemns him for the rest of his days and for all time to come. Already a circle of more than a thousand men, armed with weapons more powerful than ours and with peremptory orders to bring in our bodies, was closing in around us. . . .

Moncada Barracks were turned into a workshop of torture and death.

Some shameful individuals turned their uniforms into butchers' aprons. The walls were splattered with blood. The bullets embedded in the walls were encrusted with singed bits of skin, brains and human hair, the grisly reminders of rifle shots fired full in the face. The grass around the barracks was dark and sticky with human blood. The criminal hands that are guiding the destiny of Cuba had written for the prisoners at the entrance of that den of death the very inscription of Hell: "Forsake all hope."

They did not even attempt to cover appearances. They did not bother in the least to conceal what they were doing. They thought they had deceived the people with their lies and they ended up deceiving themselves. They felt themselves lords and masters of the universe, with power over life and death. So the fear they had experienced upon our attack at daybreak was dissipated in a feast of corpses, in a drunken orgy of blood. . . .

Dante divided his *Inferno* into nine circles. He put the criminals in the seventh, the thieves in the eighth, and the traitors in the ninth. Difficult dilemma the devils will be faced with, when they try to find an adequate spot for this man's soul—if this man has a soul. The man who instigated the atrocious acts in Santiago de Cuba doesn't even have a heart.

In every society there are men of base instincts. The sadists, brutes, conveyors of all the ancestral atavisms go about in the guise of human beings, but they are monsters, only more or less restrained by discipline and social habit. If they are offered a drink from a river of blood, they will not be satisfied until they drink the river dry. All these men needed was the order. At their hands the best and noblest Cubans perished: the most valiant, the most honest, the most idealistic. The tyrant called them mercenaries. There they were dying as heroes at the hands of men who collect a salary from the republic and who, with the arms the republic gave them to defend her, serve the interests of a clique and murder her best citizens.

Throughout their torturing of our comrades, the army offered them the chance to save their lives by betraying their ideology and falsely declaring that Prío had given them money. When they indignantly rejected that proposition, the army continued with its horrible tortures. They crushed their testicles and they tore out their eyes. But no one yielded. No complaint was heard nor a favor asked. Even when they had been deprived of their virile organs, our men were still a thousand times more men than all their tormentors together. Photographs, which do not lie, show the bodies torn to pieces. Other methods were used. Frustrated by the valor of the men, they tried to break the spirit of our women. With a bleeding human eye in their hands, a sergeant and several other men went to the cell where our comrades Melba Hernández and Haydée Santamaría were held. Addressing the latter, and showing her the eye, they said: "This eye belonged to your brother. If you will not tell us what he refused to say, we will tear out the other." She, who loved her valiant brother above all things, replied full of dignity: "If you tore out an eye and he did not speak, much less will I." Later they came back and burned their arms with lit cigarettes until at last, filled with spite, they told the young Haydée Santamaría: "You no longer have a fiancé because we have killed him too." But, still imperturbable, she answered: "He is not dead, because to die for one's country is to live forever." Never had the heroism and the dignity of Cuban womanhood reached such heights. . . .

We are Cubans and to be Cuban implies a duty; not to fulfill that duty is a crime, is treason. We are proud of the history of our country; we learned it in school and have grown up hearing of freedom, justice and human rights. We were taught to venerate the glorious example of our heroes and martyrs. Céspedes, Agramonte, Maceo, Gómez, and Martí were the first names engraved in our minds. We were taught that the Titan once said that liberty is not begged for but won with the blade of a machete. We were taught that for the guidance of Cuba's free citizens, the Apostle wrote in his book *The Golden Age:* "The man who abides by unjust laws and permits any man to trample and mistreat the country in which he was born is not an honourable man. . . . In the world there must be a certain degree of honour just as there must be a certain amount of light. When there are many men without honour, there are always others who bear in themselves the honour of many men. These are the men who rebel with great force against those who steal the people's freedom, that is to say, against those who steal human honour itself. In those men thousands more are contained, an entire people is contained, human dignity is contained. . . ." We were taught that the tenth of October and the twenty-fourth of February are glorious anniversaries of national rejoicing because they mark days on which Cubans rebelled against the yoke of infamous tyranny. We were taught to cherish and defend the beloved flag of the lone star, and to sing every afternoon the verses of our national anthem: "To live in chains is to live in disgrace and in opprobrium" and "To die for one's homeland is to live forever!" All this we learned and will never forget, even though today in our land there is murder and prison for the men who practice the ideas taught to them since the cradle. We were born in a free country that our parents bequeathed to us and the island will sink into the sea before we consent to be slaves of anyone.

It seemed that the Apostle would die during his centennial. It seemed that his memory would be extinguished forever. So great was the affront! But he is alive; he has not died. His people are rebellious. His people are worthy. His people are faithful to his memory. There are Cubans who have fallen defending his doctrines. There are young men who in magnificent selflessness came to die beside his tomb, giving their blood and their lives so that he could keep on living in the heart of his nation. Cuba, what would have become of you had you let your Apostle die?

I come to the close of my defense plea but I will not end it as lawyers usually do, asking that the accused be freed. I cannot ask freedom for myself while my comrades are already suffering in the ignominious prison of the Isle of Pines. Send me there to join them and to share their fate. It is understandable that honest men should be dead or in prison in a republic where the president is a criminal and a thief. . . .

I know that imprisonment will be harder for me than it has ever been for anyone, filled with cowardly threats and hideous cruelty. But I do not fear prison, as I do not fear the fury of the miserable tyrant who took the lives of seventy of my comrades. Condemn me. It does not matter. History will absolve me. ■

Soviet Dissident Anatoly Shcharansky Defies His Judges before Sentencing

"To you I have nothing to say."

FREEDOM FOR SOVIET JEWRY was the cause taken up by computer scientist Anatoly Shcharansky (now Natan Sharansky) in the mid-1970s. The best- known "refusenik"—denied permission to emigrate and persecuted for having tried—was arrested in 1978, at the age of thirty, and sentenced to thirteen years in prison and labor camp for "treason, espionage, and anti-Soviet agitation." For eight years, his wife, Avital, visited newspaper columnists and human-rights organizations and haunted summit conferences to focus attention on his imprisonment and his cause of free emigration. When he was freed, in what Soviet officials insisted was an exchange of spies, the conclusion of his statement to the court on July 14, 1978—as drawn from notes taken by his brother, Leonid—was widely reprinted. Its drama is partly in the starkness of the choice he made to suffer rather than to turn informer, partly in its rhetorical attitude: he addressed his speech to the people in the courtroom and the world press present, and at the end turned and expressed his contempt at the Soviet legal system with a seven-word dismissal.

☐   ☐   ☐

In March and April, during interrogation, the chief investigators warned me that in the position I have taken during investigation, and held to here in court, I would be threatened with execution by a firing squad, or at least with fifteen years. If I agreed to cooperate with the investigation for the purpose of destroying the Jewish emigration movement, they promised me freedom and a quick reunion with my wife.

Five years ago, I submitted my application for exit to Israel. Now I am further than ever from my dream. It would seem to be cause for regret. But it is absolutely the other way around. I am happy. I am happy that I lived honorably, at peace with my conscience. I never compromised my soul, even under the threat of death.

I am happy that I helped people. I am proud that I knew and worked with such honorable, brave, and courageous people as Sakharov, Orlov, Ginzburg, who are carrying on the traditions of the Russian intelligentsia. I am fortunate to have been witness to the process of the liberation of Jews of the USSR.

I hope that the absurd accusation against me and the entire Jewish emigration movement will not hinder the liberation of my people. My near ones and friends know how I wanted to exchange activity in the emigration movement for a life with my wife, Avital, in Israel.

For more than two thousand years the Jewish people, my people, have been dispersed. But wherever they are, wherever Jews are found, every year they have repeated, "Next year in Jerusalem." Now, when I am further than ever from my people, from Avital, facing many arduous years of imprisonment, I say, turning to my people, my Avital, "Next year in Jerusalem."

Now I turn to you, the court, who were required to confirm a predetermined sentence: To you I have nothing to say. ■

Defense Attorney Johnnie Cochran Wins Acquittal for the Accused Killer O. J. Simpson

"IF it doesn't fit, you must acquit."

AN ESTIMATED **95** MILLION TELEVISION VIEWERS watched the slow police chase of a Bronco vehicle that led to the arrest of a famous former football player and television personality. The 1995 criminal trial of Orenthal James Simpson for the murders of his wife, Nicole, and Ronald Goldman lasted 133 days, transfixing much of the nation and—through saturation coverage of the courtroom drama on live television—became a world event, often decried as a "media circus."

One of the trial's many dramatic moments came when the prosecution, led by Marcia Clark, demanded that the defendant try on the gloves worn by the killer. When O. J. Simpson had to struggle to get his fingers into them, that showed them to be too tight, and he delightedly exclaimed that they did not fit. (The prosecution lamely suggested that the gloves had shrunk after being bloodstained.) His lead attorney, Johnnie Cochran, then used a rhyming imperative repeatedly in his summation to the jury, equating the glove with all other anomalies in the prosecution's case, charging a scandalous frame-up by publicity-driven police: "If it doesn't fit, you must acquit." He characterized the seemingly damning evidence alliteratively as "contaminated, compromised, and ultimately corrupted." In his summation, Cochran repeated this theme, putting on a knit cap that was supposedly planned for use by his client: "It's no disguise. It makes no sense. It doesn't fit. If it doesn't fit, you must acquit."

The trial divided the nation along racial lines. Because Simpson, Cochran, and much of the jury were African-Americans, Cochran seemed to assume the role of a black preacher, especially in his rhyme and biblical citations. In a powerful summation, he began by quoting Frederick Douglass, the former slave who became a social reformer and the first black American political hero, on equal rights, which he said was of special interest "with a jury such as this." He recalled that one of the detectives testifying for the prosecution, Mark Fuhrman, lied when he claimed never to have used the word "nigger," thereby imputing the motive of racism to a key prosecution witness. Cochran drove that point home by returning to Douglass near the end, "for there are still the Mark Fuhrmans in this world, in this country, who hate and are yet embraced by people in power. . . . But you and I . . . must continue to fight to expose hate and genocidal racism. . . ."

He posed a list of fifteen questions for the prosecution to answer. Prosecutor Clark took up the challenge and answered them forcefully in her final summation that followed, evidently not to the jury's satisfaction. When the verdict of "not guilty" came in on October 3, 1995, after only four hours of deliberation, television pictures showed groups of black viewers elated and cheering while white viewers were stunned and silent, dramatizing the polarization of attitudes this case caused in the nation. Afterward, Cochran co-counsel Robert Shapiro condemned the Cochran summation for "not only playing the race card, but playing it from the bottom of the deck."

True or not, the skilled lawyer's argument (and this excerpt includes only his summary of the details he presented to jurors) certainly helped establish the "reasonable doubt" that calls for acquittal. Two years after being freed, Simpson was tried on civil charges of having been responsible for wrongful death, where the standard of proof is lower and incarceration not a penalty. Simpson lost that case and was heavily fined.

▢   ▢   ▢

At the outset, let me join with the others in thanking you for the service that you've rendered. You are truly a marvelous jury, the longest serving jury in Los Angeles County, perhaps the most patient and healthy jury we've ever seen. I hope that your health and your good health continues. . . .

You are empowered to do justice. You are empowered to ensure that this great system of ours works.

Listen for a moment, will you, please. One of my favorite people in history is the great Frederick Douglass. He said shortly after the slaves were freed, quote, "In a composite nation like ours as before the law, there should be no rich, no poor, no high, no low, no white, no black, but common country, common citizenship, equal rights and a common destiny."

This marvelous statement was made more than a hundred years ago. It's an ideal worth striving for and one that we still strive for. We haven't reached this goal yet, but certainly in this great country of ours, we're trying. With a jury such as this, we hope we can do that in this particular case. . . .

A good efficient, competent, noncorrupt police department will carefully set about the business of investigating homicides. They won't rush to judgment. They won't be bound by an obsession to win at all costs. They will set about trying to apprehend the killer or killers and trying to protect the innocent from suspicion.

In this case, the victims' families had an absolute right to demand exactly just that in this case. But it was clear, unfortunately, that in this case there was another agenda. From the very first orders issued by the LAPD so-called brass, they were more concerned with their own images, the publicity that might be generated from this case, than they were in doing professional police work. That's why this case has become such a hallmark, and that's why Mr. Simpson is the one on trial.

But your verdict in this case will go far beyond the walls of Department 103, because your verdict talks about justice in America and it talks about the police and whether they're above the law and it looks at the police perhaps as though they haven't been looked at very recently. Remember, I told you this is not for the naïve, the faint of heart, or the timid.

So it seems to us that the evidence shows that professional police work took a backseat right at the beginning. Untrained officers trampled—remember, I used the word in opening statement—they traipsed through the evidence. . . .

I was thinking last night about this case and their theory and how it didn't make sense and how it didn't fit and how something is wrong. It occurred to me how they were going to come here, stand up here and tell you how O. J. Simpson was going to disguise himself. He was going to put on a knit cap and some dark clothes, and he was going to get in his white Bronco, this recognizable person, and go over and kill his wife. That's what they want you to believe. That's how silly their argument is.

And I said to myself, maybe I can demonstrate this graphically. Let me show you something. This is a knit cap. Let me put this knit cap on. [Puts on cap.] You have seen me for a year. If I put this knit cap on, who am I? Still I'm Johnnie Cochran with a knit cap. And if you looked at O. J. Simpson over there—and he has a rather large head—O. J. Simpson in a knit cap from two blocks away is still O. J. Simpson. It's no disguise. It's no disguise. It makes no sense. It doesn't fit. If it doesn't fit, you must acquit. . . .

I hope that during this phase of my argument I have demonstrated to you that this really is a case about a rush to judgment, an obsession to win, at all costs, a willingness to distort, twist, theorize in any fashion to try to get you to vote guilty in this case where it is not warranted. These metaphors about an ocean of evidence or a mountain of evidence are little more than a tiny, tiny stream, if at all, that points equally toward innocence, that any mountain has long ago been reduced to little more than a molehill under an avalanche of lies and complexity and conspiracy.

This is what we've shown you. And so as great as America is, we have not yet reached the point where there is equality in rights or equality of opportunity.

I started off talking to you a little bit about Frederick Douglass and what he said more than a hundred years ago, for there are still the Mark Fuhrmans in this world, in this country, who hate and are yet embraced by people in power. But you and I, fighting for freedom and ideals and for justice for all, must continue to fight to expose hate and genocidal racism and these tendencies. We then become the guardians of the Constitution. . . .

This case is a tragedy for everybody, for certainly the victims and their families, for the Simpson family—and they are victims, too, because they lost the ex–daughter-in-law—for the defendant. He has been in custody since June of 1994 for a crime that he didn't commit. Someone has taken these children's mother. I certainly hope that your decision doesn't take their father. . . .

I may never have an opportunity again to speak to you, certainly not in this setting. . . . In times like these we often turn to the Bible for some answers. . . . I happen to really like the book of Proverbs and in Proverbs it talks a lot about false witnesses. It says that a false witness shall not be unpunished and he that speaketh lies shall not escape.

That meant a lot to me in this case because there was Mark Fuhrman acting like a choirboy, making you believe he was the best witness that walked in here, generally applauded for his wonderful performance. It turns out he was the biggest liar in this courtroom during this process, for the Bible had already told us the answer, that a false witness shall not be unpunished and he that speaketh lies shall not escape. In that same book it tells us that a faithful witness will not lie but a false witness will utter lies. Finally, in Proverbs it says that he that speaketh the truth showeth the forthrightfulness but a false witness shows deceit.

So when we are talking about truth, we are talking about truth and lies and conspiracies and cover-ups. I always think about one of my favorite poems, which I think is so very appropriate for this case. You know when things are at the darkest there is always light the next day. In your life, in all of our lives, you have the capacity to transform Mr. O. J.

Simpson's dark yesterday into bright tomorrow. You have that capacity. You have that power in your hands. And James Russell Lowell said it best about wrong and evil. He said that truth forever on the scaffold, wrong forever on the throne, yet that scaffold sways the future and beyond the dim unknown standeth God within the shadows, keeping watch above his own.

You walk with that every day, you carry that with you and things will come to you and you will be able to reveal people who come to you in uniforms and high positions who lie and are corrupt. That is what happened in this case and so the truth is now out. It is now up to you. We are going to pass this baton to you soon.

You will do the right thing. You have made a commitment for justice. You will do the right thing. I will someday go on to other cases, no doubt as will Miss Clark and Mr. Darden. Judge Ito will try another case someday, I hope, but this is O. J. Simpson's one day in court.

By your decision you control his very life in your hands. Treat it carefully. Treat it fairly. Be fair. Don't be part of this continuing cover-up. Do the right thing, remembering that "If it doesn't fit, you must acquit." That if these messengers have lied to you, you can't trust their message. That this has been a search for truth. That no matter how bad it looks, if truth is out there on a scaffold and wrong is in here on the throne, when that scaffold sways, in the future and beyond the dim unknown standeth the same God for all people keeping watch above his own.

He watches all of us and he will watch you in your decision. Thank you for your attention. God bless you.

■　■　■

VI

GALLOWS
AND
FAREWELL
SPEECHES

Socrates, Condemned to Death, Addresses His Judges

"It is now time to depart—for me to die, for you to live. But which of us is going to a better state is unknown to everyone but God."

WISE, PRINCIPLED, GOOD-NATURED even in the face of death, Greek philosopher Socrates lived his philosophy of seeking virtue in self-knowledge.

Son of an Athenian sculptor, Socrates eschewed other employment to be a public teacher, using questions to elicit dialectical truths. Falling into disfavor with the ruling powers of Athens, however, he was arrested and tried, ostensibly for two stated charges: "firstly, of denying the gods recognized by the state and introducing new divinities; and, secondly, of corrupting the young." Found guilty in a trial clouded by political issues, he refused to compromise his principles by seeking a lighter sentence and was condemned to death in 399 B.C.

Perhaps most remarkable about his address to the judges is his evenness of temper, evinced by a gentle humor and spirit of teaching that belie any fear of impending death. With an expert use of direct address ("O Athenians" and "O my judges") and allusions to historical figures "who have died by an unjust sentence," he leads his listeners into a philosophical contemplation of death and the desire for good.

The peroration, or dramatic conclusion to the speech, summarizes his central point, "that to a good man nothing is evil, neither while living nor when dead."

□ □ □

That I should not be grieved, O Athenians, at what has happened—namely, that you have condemned me—as well many other circumstances concur in bringing to pass; and, moreover, this, that what has happened has not happened contrary to my expectation; but I much rather wonder at the number of votes on either side. For I did not expect that I should be condemned by so small a number, but by a large majority; but now, as it seems, if only three more votes had changed sides, I should have been acquitted. . . .

For the sake of no long space of time, O Athenians, you will incur the character and reproach at the hands of those who wish to defame the city, of having put that wise man Socrates to death. For those who wish to defame you will assert that I am wise, though I am not. If, then, you had waited for a short time, this would have happened of its own accord; for observe my age, that it is far advanced in life and near death. But I say this not to you all but to those only who have condemned me to die. And I say this, too, to the same persons. Perhaps you think, O Athenians, that I have been convicted through the want of arguments, by which I might have persuaded you, had I thought it right to do and say anything, so that I might escape punishment. Far otherwise: I have been convicted through want indeed, yet not of arguments but of audacity and impudence, and of the inclination to say such things to you as would have been most agreeable for you to hear, had I lamented and bewailed and done and said many other things unworthy of me, as I affirm, but such as you are accustomed to hear from others. But neither did I then think that I ought, for the sake of avoiding danger, to do anything unworthy of a freeman, nor do I now repent of having so defended myself; but I should much rather choose to die, having so defended myself, than to live in that way. For neither in a trial nor in battle is it right that I or anyone else should employ every possible means whereby he may avoid death; for in battle it is frequently evident that a man might escape death by laying down his arms and throwing himself on the mercy of his pursuers. And there are many other devices in every danger, by which to avoid death, if a man dares to do and say everything. But this is not difficult, O Athenians, to escape death; but it is much more difficult to avoid depravity, for it runs swifter than death. And now I, being slow and aged, am overtaken by the slower of the two; but my accusers, being strong and active, have been overtaken by the swifter, wickedness. And now I depart, condemned by you to death; but they condemned by truth, as guilty of iniquity and injustice: and I abide my sentence, and so do they. These things, perhaps, ought so to be, and I think that they are for the best. . . .

I say, then, to you, O Athenians, who have condemned me to death, that immediately after my death a punishment will overtake you far more severe, by Jupiter! than that which you have inflicted on me. For you have done this, thinking you should be freed from the necessity of giving an account of your lives. The very contrary, however, as I affirm, will happen to you. Your accusers will be more numerous, whom I have now restrained, though you did not perceive it; and they will be more severe, inasmuch as they are younger, and you will be more indignant. For if you think that by putting men to death you will restrain anyone from upbraiding you because you do not live well, you are much mistaken; for this method of escape is neither possible nor honorable; but that other is most honorable and most easy, not to put a check upon others, but for a man to take heed to himself how he may be most perfect. Having predicted thus much to those of you who have condemned me, I take my leave of you. . . .

To die is one of two things: for either the dead may be annihilated and have no sensation of anything whatever, or, as it is said, there are a certain change and passage of the soul from one place to another. And if it is a privation of all sensation—as it were, a sleep in which the sleeper has no dream—death would be a wonderful gain. For I think that if anyone, having selected a night in which he slept so soundly as not to have had a dream, and having compared this night with all the other nights and days of his life, should be required, on consideration, to say how many days and nights he had passed better and more pleasantly than this night throughout his life, I think that not only a private person but even the great king himself would find them easy to number, in comparison with other days and nights.

If, therefore, death is a thing of this kind, I say it is a gain; for thus all futurity appears to be nothing more than one night. But if, on the other hand, death is a removal from hence to another place, and what is said be true, that all the dead are there, what greater blessing can there be than this, my judges? For if, on arriving at Hades, released from these who pretend to be judges, one shall find those who are true judges and who are said to judge there, Minos and Rhadamanthus, Aeacus and Triptolemus, and such others of the demigods as were just during their own lives, would this be a sad removal? At what price would you not estimate a conference with Orpheus and Musaeus, Hesiod and Homer? I, indeed, should be willing to die often, if this be true. For to me the sojourn there would be admirable, when I should meet with Palamedes, and Ajax, son of Telamon, and any other of the ancients who have died by an unjust sentence. The comparing my sufferings with theirs would, I think, be no unpleasing occupation. But the greatest pleasure would be to spend my time in questioning and examining the people there as I have done those here, and discovering who among them is wise, and who fancies himself to be so, but is not. At what price, my judges, would not anyone estimate the opportunity of questioning him who led that mighty army against Troy, or Ulysses, or Sisyphus, or ten thousand others whom one might mention, both men and women—with whom to converse and associate, and to question them, would be an inconceivable happiness? Surely for that judges there do not condemn to death; for in other respects those who live there are more happy than those who are here, and are henceforth immortal, if, at least, what is said to be true.

You, therefore, O my judges, ought to entertain good hopes with respect to death, and to meditate on this one truth, that to a good man nothing is evil, neither while living nor when dead, nor are his concerns neglected by the gods. And what has befallen me is not the effect of chance; but this is clear to me, that now to die and be freed from my cares is better for me. On this account the warning in no way turned me aside; and I bear no resentment toward those who condemned me, or against my accusers, although they did not condemn and accuse me with this intention, but thinking to injure me: in this they deserve to be blamed.

Thus much, however, I beg of them. Punish my sons when they grow up, O judges, paining them, as I have pained you, if they appear to you to care for riches or anything else before virtue; and if they think themselves to be something when they are nothing, reproach them as I have done you, for not attending to what they ought, and for conceiving themselves to be something when they are worth nothing. If ye do this, both I and my sons shall have met with just treatment at your hands.

But it is now time to depart—for me to die, for you to live. But which of us is going to a better state is unknown to everyone but God. ∎

Charles I and, Later, His Regicide Speak from the Scaffold

"HURT not the ax that may hurt me."

THE UPHEAVAL OF THE ENGLISH MONARCHY during the seventeenth century led inevitably to civil war, retributions, and bloodshed.

More than two decades after James VI of Scotland became James I of England, the king died. His second son survived him and in 1625 ascended to the throne as King Charles I. A ruler more interested in the privileges of kingship and the reign of the Stuarts than in governance of the people, Charles I became embroiled in confrontations with Parliament that evolved into armed conflict. Oliver Cromwell, general and statesman, led the Roundheads—Parliament's army, their hair cropped short to set them apart from the Cavaliers—to victory, and Charles I was condemned to death.

His beheading, on January 30,1649, followed a royal address from the scaffold in Whitehall. In this final speech, Charles I professes his faith, with New Testament overtones of charity and forgiveness for those who will execute him. The speech's emphasis on endings is underscored by the king's use of epistrophe, particularly in the repetition of the word "due" in "God will never prosper you, until you give God his due, the king his due . . . , and the people their due."

The turbulence between 1649 and 1660, a period that became known as the interregnum ("between kings"), ended when Charles I's eldest son was called from Paris to assume the English throne as Charles II. Among the many regicides arrested in 1660 for the king's death eleven years earlier, Thomas Harrison became the first put to death.

Speaking in measured phrases, expressing no remorse for Charles I's death, Harrison explains the palsy that makes some scoffers think he is "afraid to die." With Christian humility that pervades his self-references as "poor worm" and "nothing creature," he expresses his final thoughts with professions of joy and willingness to face death. The parallel structure found in most of his sentences ("by God I have leaped over a wall, by God I have run through a troop, and by my God I will go through this death") shows the evenness of temperament—though not the royal generosity—with which Harrison faced the executioner.

□   □   □

I shall be very little heard of anybody here; I shall therefore speak a word unto you here; indeed I could hold my peace very well, if I did not think that holding my peace would make some men think that I did submit to the guilt, as well as to the punishment; but I think it is my duty to God first and then to my country for to clear myself both as an honest man and a good king and a good Christian. I shall begin first with my innocency. In troth I think it not very needful for me to insist long upon this, for all the world knows that I never did begin a war with the two houses of Parliament, and I call God to witness, to whom I must shortly make my account, that I never did intend for to encroach upon their privileges; they began upon me, it is the militia, they began upon, they contest that the militia was mine, but they thought it fit for to have it from me; and to be short, if anybody will look to the dates of the commissions, of their commissions and mine, and likewise to the declarations, will see clearly that they began these unhappy troubles, not I; so that as the guilt of these enormous crimes that are laid against me, I hope in God that God will clear me of it, I will not, I am in charity; God forbid that I should lay it upon the two houes of Parliament; there is no necessity of either, I hope they are free of this guilt, for I do believe that ill instruments between them and me has been the chief cause of all this bloodshed; so that by way of speaking, as I find myself clear of this, I hope (and pray God) that they may too: yet for all this, God forbid that I should be so ill a Christian as not to say that God's judgments are just upon me: many times he does pay justice by an unjust sentence, that is ordinary; I will only say this, that an unjust sentence that I suffered for to take effect is punished now, by an unjust sentence upon me; that is, so far I have said, to show you that I am an innocent man.

Now for to show you that I am a good Christian: I hope there is a good man that will bear me witness, that I have forgiven all the world; even those in particular that have been the chief causes of my death; who they are, God knows, I do not desire to know, I pray God forgive them. But this is not all; my charity must go farther, I wish that they may repent, for indeed they have committed a great sin in that particular; I pray God with Saint Stephen that they may take the right way to the peace of the kingdom, for my charity commands me not only to forgive particular men, but my charity commands me to endeavor to the last gasp the peace of the kingdom: so, sirs, I do with all my soul, and I do hope (there is some here will carry it further) that they may endeavor the peace of the kingdom. Now, sirs, I must show you both how you are out of the way and will put you in a way; first, you are out of the way, for certainly all the way you ever had yet as I could find by anything is in the way of conquest; certainly this is an ill way, for conquest, sir, in my opinion is never just, except there be a good just cause, either for the matter of wrong or just title, and then if you go beyond it, the first quarrel that you have to it, that makes it unjust at the end, that was just as first: But if it be only matter of conquest, then it is a great robbery; as a pirate said to Alexander, that he was the great robber, he was but a petty robber; and so, sir, I do think the way that you are in, is much out of the way. Now, sir, for to put you in the way, believe it you will never do right, nor God will never prosper you, until you give God his due, the king his due (that is, my successor), and the people their due; I am as much for them as any of you; you must give God his due by regulating rightly his church according to his Scripture which is now out of order: for to set you in a way particularly now I cannot, but only this, a national synod freely called, freely debating among themselves, must settle this, when that every opinion is freely and clearly heard.

For the king, indeed I will not . . . [At this point a gentleman touched the ax, and the king said, "Hurt not the ax that may hurt me."] For the king: the laws of the land will clearly instruct you for that; therefore, because it concerns my own particular, I only give you a touch of it.

For the people. And truly I desire their liberty and freedom, as much as anybody whomsoever; but I must tell you that their liberty and their freedom consists in having of government those laws by which their life and their goods may be most their own. It is not for having share in government, sir, that is nothing pertaining to them. A subject and a sovereign are clean different things; and therefore, until they do that, I mean, that you do put the people in that liberty as I say, certainly they will never enjoy themselves.

Sirs, it was for this that now I am come here: if I would have given way to an arbitrary way, for to have all laws changed according to the power of the sword, I needed not to have come here; and therefore, I tell you (and I pray God it be not laid to your charge) that I am the martyr of the people.

In troth, sirs, I shall not hold you much longer; for I will only say this to you, that in truth I could have desired some little time longer, because that I would have put this I have said in a little more order, and a little better digested, than I have done; and therefore I hope you will excuse me.

I have delivered my conscience, I pray God, that you do take those courses that are best for the kingdom, and your own salvation.

[Doctor Juxon: Will Your Majesty (though it may be very well known Your Majesty's affections to religion, yet it may be expected that you should) say somewhat to the world's satisfaction.]

I thank you very heartily, my lord, for that; I had almost forgotten it. In troth, sirs, my conscience in religion, I think, is very well known to the world; and therefore I declare before you all that I die a Christian according to the profession of the church of England, as I found it left me by my father; and this honest man [pointing to Dr. Juxon] will witness it. Sirs, excuse me for this same. I have a good cause, and I have a gracious God; I will say no more. I go from a corruptible to an incorruptible crown, where no disturbance can be, no disturbance in the world.

□   □   □

Gentlemen, I did not expect to have spoken a word to you at this time; but seeing there is a silence commanded, I will speak something of the work God had in hand in our days. Many of you have been witnesses of the finger of God, that hath been seen amongst us of late years, in the deliverance of his people from their oppressors, and in bringing to judgment those that were guilty of the precious blood of the dear servants of the Lord. And how God did witness thereto by many wonderful and evident testimonies, as it were immediately from heaven, insomuch that many of our enemies—who were persons of no mean quality—were forced to confess that God was with us; and if God did but stand neuter, they should not value us; and, therefore, seeing the finger of God hath been pleading this cause, I shall not need to speak much to it; in which work I, with others, was engaged; for the which I do from my soul bless the name of God, who out of the exceeding riches of his grace accounted me worthy to be instrumental in so glorious a work. And though I am wrongfully charged with murder and bloodshed, yet I must tell you I have kept a good conscience both toward God and toward man. I never had malice against any man, neither did I act maliciously toward any person, but as I judged them to be enemies to God and his people; and the Lord is my witness that I have done what I did out of the sincerity of my heart to the Lord. I bless God I have no guilt upon my conscience, but the spirit of God beareth witness that my actions are acceptable to the Lord, through Jesus Christ; though I have been compassed about with manifold infirmities, failings, and imperfections in my holiest duties, but in this I have comfort and consolation, that I have peace with God, and do see all my sins washed away in the blood of my dear Savior. And I do declare as before the Lord that I should not be guilty wittingly, nor willingly, of the blood of the meanest man—no, not for ten thousand worlds, much less of the blood of such as I am charged with.

I have again and again besought the Lord with tears to make known his will and mind unto me concerning it, and to this day he hath rather confirmed me in the justice of it, and therefore I leave it to him, and to him I commit my ways; but some that were eminent in the work did wickedly turn aside themselves, and to set up their nests on high, which caused great dishonor to the name of God and the profession they had made. And the Lord knows I could have suffered more than this, rather than have fallen in with them in that iniquity, though I was offered what I would if I would have joined with them; my aim in all my proceedings was the glory of God, and the good of his people, and the welfare of the whole commonwealth.

Gentlemen, by reason of some scoffing that I do hear, I judge that some do think I am afraid to die, by the shaking I have in my hands and knees; I tell you no, but it is by reason of much blood I have lost in the wars, and many wounds I have received in my body, which caused this shaking and weakness in my nerves; I have had it this twelve years; I speak this to the praise and glory of God; he hath carried me above the fear of death; and I value not my life, because I go to my Father, and am assured I shall take it up again.

Gentlemen, take notice that for being instrumental in that cause and interest of the Son of God, which hath been pleaded amongst us and which God hath witnessed to my appeals and wonderful victories, I am brought to this place to suffer death this day; and if I had ten thousand lives, I could freely and cheerfully lay them down all, to witness to this matter.

Oh, what am I, poor worm, that I should be accounted worthy to suffer anything for the sake of my Lord and Savior Jesus Christ! I have gone joyfully and willingly, many a time, to lay down my life upon the account of Christ, but never with so much joy and freedom as at this time; I do not lay down my life by constraint, but willingly, for if I had been minded to have run away, I might have had many opportunities; but being so clear in the thing, I durst not turn my back, nor step a foot out of the way, by reason I had been engaged in the service of so glorious and great a God. However men presume to call it by hard names, yet I believe, ere it be long, the Lord will make it known from heaven that there was more of God in it than men are now aware of.

I do desire as from my own soul that they and everyone may fear the Lord, that they may consider their latter end, and so it may be well with them; and even for the worst of those that have been most malicious against me, from my soul, I would forgive them all so far as anything concerns me; and so far as it concerns the cause and glory of God, I leave it for him to plead; and as for the cause of God, I am willing to justify it by my sufferings, according to the good pleasure of his will. I have been this morning, before I came hither, so hurried up and down stairs (the meaning whereof I knew not) that my spirits are almost spent; therefore, you may not expect much from me.

Oh, the greatness of the love of God to such a poor, vile, and nothing creature as I am! What am I, that Jesus Christ should shed his heart's blood for me, that I might be happy to all eternity, that I might be made a son of God, and an heir of heaven! Oh, that Christ should undergo so great sufferings and reproaches for me! And should not I be willing to lay down my life, and suffer reproaches for him that hath so loved me; blessed be the name of God that I have a life to lose upon so glorious and so honorable an account.

I have one word more to the Lord's people that desire to serve him with an upright heart; let them not think hardly of any of the good ways of God for all this; for I have been near this seven years a suffering person, and have found the way of God to be a perfect way, his word a tried word, a buckler to them that trust in him, and will make known his glorious arm in the sight of all nations. And though we may suffer hard things, yet he hath a gracious end, and will make a good end for his own glory and the good of his people; therefore be cheerful in the Lord your God, hold fast that which you have and be not afraid of suffering, for God will make hard and bitter things sweet and easy to all that trust in him; keep close to the good confession you have made of Jesus Christ, and look to the recompense of reward; be not discouraged by reason of the cloud that now is upon you, for the sun will shine, and God will give a testimony unto what he hath been doing, in a short time.

And now I desire to commit my concernments into the hands of my Lord and Savior Jesus Christ, he that hath delivered himself for the chief of sinners; he that came into the world, was made flesh, and was crucified; that hath loved me and washed me from my sins in his own blood, and is risen again, sitting at the right hand of God, making intercession for me.

And as for me, Oh! who am I, poor, base, vile worm, that God should deal thus by me? For this will make me come the sooner into his glory, and to inherit the kingdom and that crown prepared for me. Oh, I have served a good Lord and Master, which hath helped me from my beginning to this day, and hath carried me through many difficulties, trials, straits, and temptations, and hath always been a very present help in time of trouble; he hath covered my head many times in the day of battle; by God I have leaped over a wall, by God I have run through a troop, and by my God I will go through this death, and he will make it easy to me, Now into thy hands, O Lord Jesus, I commit my spirit! ■

Rebel Richard Rumbold, on the Gallows, Attacks Booted and Spurred Privilege

"I am sure there was no man born marked of God above another; for none comes into the world with a saddle on his back, neither any booted and spurred to ride him. . . ."

AT THE MARKET CROSS IN EDINBURGH, rebel Richard Rumbold came to the gallows in June of 1685, after the failure of the Monmouth rebellion. Having supported Cromwell, Rumbold was among the Puritan leaders to be executed following the restoration of the Stuarts, specifically for his actions against the monarchy. The republican sentiments of his final words, however, continued to make an impression almost a century later, in the rhetoric of the American Revolution.

Particularly forceful in this gallows speech is Rumbold's attack on "booted and spurred" privilege, a phrase that came to suggest the "man on horseback" imagery of dictatorship. Through rhetorical questions and biblical allusions (to the destruction that occurs in stories of Adam and

Eve, Noah, and Nimrod), he emphasizes his view of "a deluded generation, veiled with ignorance." Rumbold's commentary on his generation,
with "popery and slavery be riding in upon them," sets up the horseback
imagery of his most memorable phrase.

□   □   □

It is for all men that come into the world once to die; and after death
the judgment! And since death is a debt that all of us must pay, it is but
a matter of small moment what way it be done. Seeing the Lord is
pleased in this manner to take me to himself, I confess, something hard
to flesh and blood, yet blessed be his name, who hath made me not only
willing but thankful for his honoring me to lay down the life he gave, for
his name; in which, were every hair in this head and beard of mine a life,
I should joyfully sacrifice them for it, as I do this. Providence having
brought me hither, I think it most necessary to clear myself of some
aspersions laid on my name; and, first, that I should have had so horrid an
intention of destroying the king and his brother. . . . It was also laid to my
charge that I was antimonarchical. It was ever my thoughts that kingly
government was the best of all where justly executed; I mean, such as it
was by our ancient laws—that is, a king, and a legal, free-chosen
Parliament—the king having, as I conceive, power enough to make him
great; the people also as much property as to make them happy; they
being, as it were, contracted to one another! And who will deny me that
this was not the justly constituted government of our nation? How
absurd is it, then, for men of sense to maintain that though the one party
of his contract breaketh all conditions, the other should be obliged to
perform their part? No, this error is contrary to the law of God, the law of
nations, and the law of reason. But as pride hath been the bait the devil
hath caught most by ever since the creation, so it continues to this day
with us. Pride caused our first parents to fall from the blessed state
wherein they were created—they aiming to be higher and wiser than
God allowed, which brought an everlasting curse on them and their posterity. It was pride caused God to drown the old world. And it was
Nimrod's pride in building Babel that caused that heavy curse of division
of tongues to be spread among us, as it is at this day, one of the greatest
afflictions the church of God groaneth under, that there should be so
many divisions during their pilgrimage here; but this is their comfort that
the day draweth near where, as there is but one shepherd, there shall be
but one sheepfold. It was, therefore, in the defense of this party, in their
just rights and liberties, against popery and slavery—

[Being here interrupted by drum beating, he said that they need not trouble themselves, for he should say no more of his mind on that subject, since they were so disingenuous as to interrupt a dying man. He then continued:]

I die this day in the defense of the ancient laws and liberties of these nations; and though God, for reasons best known to himself, hath not seen it fit to honor us, as to make us the instruments for the deliverance of his people, yet as I have lived, so I die in the faith that he will speedily arise for the deliverance of his church and people. And I desire of all you to prepare for this with speed. I may say this is a deluded generation, veiled with ignorance, that though popery and slavery be riding in upon them, do not perceive it; though I am sure there was no man born marked of God above another; for none comes into the world with a saddle on his back, neither any booted and spurred to ride him; not but that I am well satisfied that God hath wisely ordered different stations for men in the world, as I have already said; kings having as much power as to make them great and the people as much property as to make them happy. And to conclude, I shall only add my wishes for the salvation of all men who were created for that end. ■

Revolutionist Robespierre Delivers His Final Speech

"SHALL we say that all is well? Shall we continue to praise by force of habit or practice that which is wrong? We would ruin the country."

"INCORRUPTIBLE" was the contemporary description applied to Maximilien-François-Marie-Isidore de Robespierre, controversial leader of the French Revolution. With a concern more for championing "virtue" than for maintaining political friendships or meeting the material needs of the people, he fell out of favor as quickly as he had ascended to power. In the same way that the Reign of Terror had executed any and all political opponents, so Robespierre himself was not able to escape a death sentence.

On July 26, 1794, he addressed the National Convention to deny charges made against him and to seek another purge of his enemies. The next morning, however, the Convention ordered his arrest, and he was guillotined the following day.

In the July 26 address, his final speech, Robespierre speaks directly to "Frenchmen" and "my people." He delineates the powers of virtue and vice that have commingled in the Revolution and, with a series of rhetorical questions, refuses to allow his sense of virtue to give way to vice. That refusal to compromise, and the memory of his implacable bloodiness, led inevitably to Robespierre's execution at the age of thirty-six.

□   □   □

When I see the mass of vices the torrent of the Revolution has rolled pell-mell with the civic virtues, I have sometimes trembled for fear of becoming tainted in the eyes of posterity by the impure vicinage of those perverse men who mingled in the ranks of the sincere defenders of humanity; but the overthrow of the rival factions has, as it were, emancipated all the vices; they believed that the only question for them was to make division of the country as a booty rather than make her free and prosperous. I am thankful that the fury that animates them against everything that opposes itself to their projects has traced the line of demarcation between them and all right-minded people; but if the Verres and the Catilines of France believe themselves already far enough advanced in the career of crime to expose on the rostrum the head of their accuser, I also have but now promised to my fellow citizens a testament formidable to the oppressors of the people, and I bequeath to them from this moment opprobrium and death!

I conceive that it is easy for the league of the tyrants of the world to overwhelm a man; but I also know what are the duties of one who can die in defending the cause of humanity. I have seen in history all defenders of liberty overcome by ill fortune or by calumny; but soon their oppressors and their assassins also met their death. The good and the bad, the tyrants and the friends of liberty, disappear from the earth, but under different conditions. Frenchmen, do not allow your enemies to degrade your souls and to unnerve your virtues by a baleful heresy! No, Chaumette, no, Fouchet, death is not an unending sleep. Citizens, efface from the tombstones this impious maxim which throws a funeral crape upon all nature and flings insults upon death. Rather engrave that: "Death is the beginning of immortality!" My people, remember that if in the republic justice does not reign with absolute sway, and if this word does not signify love of equality and of country, then liberty is but a vain phrase! O people, you who are feared—whom one flatters! you who are despised; you who are acknowledged sovereign, and are ever being treated as a slave—remember that wherever justice does not reign, it is the passions of the magistrates that reign instead, and that the people have changed their chains and not their destinies!

Remember that there exists in your bosom a league of knaves struggling against public virtue, and that it has a greater influence than yourselves upon your own affairs—a league that dreads you and flatters you in the mass, but proscribes you in detail in the person of all good citizens!

Also recall that, instead of sacrificing this handful of knaves for your happiness, your enemies wish to sacrifice you to this handful of knaves—authors of all our evils and the only obstacles to public prosperity!

Know, then, that any man who will rise to defend public right and public morals will be overwhelmed with outrage and proscribed by the knaves! Know, also, that every friend of liberty will ever be placed between duty and calumny; that those who cannot be accused of treason will be accused of ambition; that the influence of uprightness and principles will be compared to tyranny and the violence of factions; that your confidence and your esteem will become certificates of proscription for all your friends; that the cries of oppressed patriotism will be called cries of sedition; and that, as they do not dare to attack you in mass, you will be proscribed in detail in the person of all good citizens, until the ambitious shall have organized their tyranny. Such is the empire of the tyrants armed against us. Such is the influence of their league with corrupt men, ever inclined to serve them.

Thus the unprincipled wretches impose upon us law to force us to betray the people, under penalty of being called dictators! Shall we subscribe to this law? No! Let us defend the people at the risk of becoming their victims! Let them hasten to the scaffold by the path of crime and we by that of virtue. Shall we say that all is well? Shall we continue to praise by force of habit or practice that which is wrong? We would ruin the country. Shall we reveal hidden abuses? Shall we denounce traitors? We shall be told that we are unsettling the constituted authorities, that we are endeavoring to acquire personal influence at their cost. What are we to do? Our duty! What objection can be made to him who wishes to tell the truth and who consents to die for it? Let us then say that there exists a conspiracy against public liberty; that it owes its strength to a criminal coalition that is intriguing even in the bosom of the Convention; that this coalition has accomplices in the Committee of General Safety and in the offices of this committee, which they control; that the enemies of the republic have opposed this committee to the Committee of Public Safety and have thus constituted two governments; that members of the Committee of Public Safety have entered into this scheme of mischief; that the coalition thus formed tries to ruin all patriots and the fatherland.

What is the remedy for this evil? Punish the traitors, renew the offices of the Committee of General Safety, weed out this committee itself, and subordinate it to the Committee of Public Safety; weed out the Committee of Public Safety also, constitute the unity of the government under the supreme authority of the National Convention, which is the center and the judge, and thus crush all factions by the weight of national authority, in order to erect upon their ruins the power of justice and of liberty. Such are my principles. If it be impossible to support them without being taken for an ambitious one, I shall conclude that principles are proscribed and that tyranny reigns among us, but not that I should remain silent! For what can be objected to a man who is in the right and knows how to die for his country?

I was created to battle against crime, not to govern it. The time has not come when upright men may serve their country with impunity! The defenders of liberty will be but outlaws so long as a horde of knaves shall rule! ■

President George Washington Delivers His Farewell

"Observe good faith and justice towards all nations. Cultivate peace and harmony with all."

THE FIRST PRESIDENT OF THE UNITED STATES served two terms before he decided to retire from public life. Although George Washington had tried to keep partisan politics out of his administration, the growing struggle between Federalists and Jeffersonians precluded such neutrality, and there was to be no third term for the "Father of Our Country" (from the use by Henry Knox, his secretary of war, of the phrase "the Father of your Country" in a 1787 letter to Washington).

On September 17, 1796, as he neared the end of his second term, Washington delivered his Farewell Address. The president, though an underrated politician, was not a great orator; the speech was largely intended for reading, and its text soon appeared in newspapers for the general public.

In addition to his decision not to seek reelection, Washington's address includes warnings against party dissension and "the alternate domination of one faction over another, . . . itself a frightful despotism." Just as Thomas Jefferson in his first inaugural address, five years later, would warn of "entangling alliances," Washington warns about "the insidious wiles of foreign influence" and seeks harmony with all nations, intimate ties with none.

Washington's words are marked by maxim ("honesty is always the best policy") and allusion. When he alludes to the unity of states as "the palladium of your political safety and prosperity," he refers to the ancient Greek statue of the goddess Pallas Athena; the safety of the ancient city of Troy depended upon the safekeeping of that statue, and Washington skillfully uses the allusion to give the same sense of urgency to the necessity of valuing union for the sake of self-preservation. He extends to himself as well as to his fellow citizens a benediction of "the benign influence of good laws under a free government."

□   □   □

Friends, and fellow citizens: The period for a new election of a citizen, to administer the executive government of the United States, being not far distant, and the time actually arrived when your thoughts must be employed in designating the person who is to be clothed with that important trust, it appears to me proper, especially as it may conduce to a more distinct expression of the public voice, that I should now apprise you of the resolution I have formed, to decline being considered among the number of those out of whom a choice is to be made.

I beg you, at the same time, to do me the justice to be assured that this resolution has not been taken without a strict regard to all the considerations appertaining to the relation which binds a dutiful citizen to his country, and that, in withdrawing the tender of service which silence in my situation might imply, I am influenced by no diminution of zeal for your future interest, no deficiency of grateful respect for your past kindness; but am supported by a full conviction that the step is compatible with both.

The acceptance of and continuance hitherto in the office to which your suffrages have twice called me have been a uniform sacrifice of inclination to the opinion of duty, and to a deference for what appeared to be your desire. I constantly hoped that it would have been much earlier in my power, consistently with motives which I was not at liberty to disregard, to return to that retirement from which I had been reluctantly drawn. The strength of my inclination to do this, previous to the last election, had even led to the preparation of an address to declare it to you; but mature reflection on the then perplexed and critical posture of our affairs with foreign nations, and the unanimous advice of persons entitled to my confidence, impelled me to abandon the idea.

I rejoice that the state of your concerns, external as well as internal, no longer renders the pursuit of inclination incompatible with the sentiment of duty or propriety, and am persuaded whatever partiality may be retained for my services, that in the present circumstances of our country, you will not disapprove my determination to retire. . . .

In looking forward to the moment, which is intended to terminate the career of my public life, my feelings do not permit me to suspend the deep acknowledgment of that debt of gratitude which I owe to my beloved country, for the many honors it has conferred upon me; still more for the steadfast confidence with which it has supported me. . . .

Here, perhaps, I ought to stop. But a solicitude for your welfare, which cannot end but with my life, and the apprehension of danger, natural to that solicitude, urge me on an occasion like the present to offer to your solemn contemplation, and to recommend to your frequent review, some sentiments which are the result of much reflection, of no inconsiderable observation, and which appear to me all important to the permanency of your felicity as a people. These will be offered to you with the more freedom, as you can only see in them the disinterested warnings of a parting friend, who can possibly have no personal motive to bias his counsel. Nor can I forget, as an encouragement to it, your indulgent reception of my sentiments on a former and not dissimilar occasion.

Interwoven as is the love of liberty with every ligament of your hearts, no recommendation of mine is necessary to fortify or confirm the attachment.

The unity of government which constitutes you one people is also now dear to you. It is justly so; for it is a main pillar in the edifice of your real independence, the support of your tranquillity at home, your peace abroad, of your safety, of your prosperity, of that very liberty which you so highly prize. But as it is easy to foresee that from different causes and from different quarters, much pains will be taken, many artifices employed, to weaken in your minds the conviction of this truth; as this is the point in your political fortress against which the batteries of internal and external enemies will be most constantly and actively (though often covertly and insidiously) directed, it is of infinite moment that you should properly estimate the immense value of your national union to your collective and individual happiness; that you should cherish a cordial, habitual, and immovable attachment to it; accustoming yourselves to think and speak of it as of the palladium of your political safety and prosperity; watching for its preservation with jealous anxiety; discountenancing whatever may suggest even a suspicion that it can in any event be abandoned; and indignantly frowning upon the first dawning of every attempt to alienate any portion of our country from the rest, or to enfeeble the sacred ties which now link together the various parts.

For this you have every inducement of sympathy and interest. Citizens by birth or choice, of a common country, that country has a right to concentrate your affections. The name of American, which belongs to you, in your national capacity, must always exalt the just pride of patriotism, more than any appellation derived from local discriminations. With slight shades of difference, you have the same religion, manners, habits, and political principles. You have in a common cause fought and triumphed together. The independence and liberty you possess are the work of joint councils and joint efforts, of common dangers, sufferings. and successes.

But these considerations, however powerfully they address themselves to your sensibility, are greatly outweighed by those which apply more immediately to your interest. Here every portion of our country finds the most commanding motives for carefully guarding and preserving the union of the whole.

The North, in an unrestrained intercourse with the South, protected by the equal laws of a common government, finds in the productions of the latter great additional resources of maritime and commercial enterprise and precious materials of manufacturing industry. The South, in the same intercourse, benefiting by the agency of the North, sees its agriculture grow and its commerce expand. Turning partly into its own channels the seamen of the North, it finds its particular navigation envigorated; and while it contributes, in different ways, to nourish and increase the general mass of the national navigation, it looks forward to the protection of a maritime strength, to which itself is unequally adapted. The East, in a like intercourse with the West, already finds and, in the progressive improvement of interior communications, by land and water, will more and more find a valuable vent for the commodities which it brings from abroad, or manufactures at home. The West derives from the East supplies requisite to its growth and comfort, and what is perhaps of still greater consequence, it must of necessity owe the *secure* enjoyment of indispensable *outlets* for its own productions to the weight, influence, and the future maritime strength of the Atlantic side of the union, directed by an indissoluble community of interest as *one nation.* Any other tenure by which the West can hold this essential advantage, whether derived from its own separate strength or from an apostate and unnatural connection with any foreign power, must be intrinsically precarious.

While, then, every part of our country thus feels an immediate and particular interest in union, all the parts combined cannot fail to find in the united mass of means and efforts greater strength, greater resource, proportionably greater security from external danger, a less frequent interruption of their peace by foreign nations; and, what is of inestimable value, they must derive from union an exemption from those broils and wars between themselves, which so frequently afflict neighboring countries not tied together by the same government—which their own rivalships alone would be sufficient to produce, but which opposite foreign alliances, attachments, and intrigues would stimulate and embitter. Hence likewise they will avoid the necessity of those overgrown military establishments which under any form of government are inauspicious to liberty, and which are to be regarded as particularly hostile to republican liberty: in this sense it is that your union ought to be considered as a main prop of your liberty, and that the love of the one ought to endear to you the preservation of the other.

These considerations speak a persuasive language to every reflecting and virtuous mind, and exhibit the continuance of the Union as a primary object of patriotic desire. Is there a doubt, whether a common government can embrace so large a sphere? Let experience solve it. To listen to mere speculation in such a case were criminal. We are authorized to hope that a proper organization of the whole, with the auxiliary agency of governments for the respective subdivisions, will afford a happy issue to the experiment. 'Tis well worth a fair and full experiment. . . .

All obstructions to the execution of the laws, all combinations and associations, under whatever plausible character, with the real design to direct, control, counteract, or awe the regular deliberation and action of the constituted authorities, are destructive of this fundamental principle and of fatal tendency. They serve to organize faction, to give it an artificial and extraordinary force; to put in the place of the delegated will of the nation, the will of a party, often a small but artful and enterprising minority of the community; and, according to the alternate triumphs of different parties, to make the public administration the mirror of the ill-concerted and incongruous projects of faction, rather than the organ of consistent and wholesome plans digested by common councils and modified by mutual interests. However combinations or associations of the above description may now and then answer popular ends, they are likely, in the course of time and things, to become potent engines, by which cunning, ambitious, and unprincipled men will be enabled to subvert the power of the people, and to usurp for themselves the reins of government—destroying afterwards the very engines which have lifted them to unjust dominion. . . .

I have already intimated to you the danger of parties in the state, with particular reference to the founding of them on geographical discriminations. Let me now take a more comprehensive view, and warn you in the most solemn manner against the baneful effects of the spirit of party, generally.

This spirit, unfortunately, is inseparable from our nature, having its root in the strongest passions of the human mind. It exists under different shapes in all governments, more or less stifled, controlled, or repressed; but in those of the popular form it is seen in its greatest rankness and is truly their worst enemy.

The alternate domination of one faction over another, sharpened by the spirit of revenge natural to party dissension, which in different ages and countries has perpetrated the most horrid enormities, is itself a

frightful despotism. But this leads at length to a more formal and permanent despotism. The disorders and miseries which result gradually incline
the minds of men to seek security and repose in the absolute power of an
individual: and sooner or later the chief of some prevailing faction more
able or more fortunate than his competitors, turns this disposition to the
purposes of his own elevation, on the ruins of public liberty. . . .

There is an opinion that parties in free countries are useful checks
upon the administration of the government and serve to keep alive the
spirit of liberty. This within certain limits is probably true, and in governments of a monarchical cast patriotism may look with indulgence, if not
with favor, upon the spirit of party. But in those of the popular character,
in governments purely elective, it is a spirit not to be encouraged. . . .

Of all the dispositions and habits which lead to political prosperity, religion and morality are indispensable supports. In vain would that man
claim the tribute of patriotism who should labor to subvert these great
pillars of human happiness, these firmest props of the duties of men and
citizens. The mere politician, equally with the pious man, ought to
respect and to cherish them. A volume could not trace all their connections with private and public felicity. Let it simply be asked where is the
security for property, for reputation, for life, if the sense of religious obligation *desert* the oaths which are the instruments of investigation in
courts of justice? And let us with caution indulge the supposition that
morality can be maintained without religion. Whatever may be conceded
to the influence of refined education on minds of peculiar structure, reason and experience both forbid us to expect that national morality can
prevail in exclusion of religious principle.

'Tis substantially true that virtue or morality is a necessary spring of popular government. The rule indeed extends with more or less force to every
species of free government. Who that is a sincere friend to it can look with
indifference upon attempts to shake the foundations of the fabric?

Promote, then, as an object of primary importance, institutions for the
general diffusion of knowledge. In proportion as the structure of a government gives force to public opinion, it is essential that public opinion
should be enlightened.

As a very important source of strength and security, cherish public
credit. One method of preserving it is to use it as sparingly as possible:
avoiding occasions of expense by cultivating peace, but remembering
also that timely disbursements to prepare for danger frequently prevent
much greater disbursements to repel it; avoiding likewise the accumulation of debt, not only by shunning occasions of expense but by vigorous
exertions in time of peace to discharge the debts which unavoidable wars

may have occasioned, not ungenerously throwing upon posterity the burden which we ourselves ought to bear. The execution of these maxims belongs to your representatives, but it is necessary that public opinion should cooperate. To facilitate to them the performance of their duty, it is essential that you should practically bear in mind that towards the payment of debts there must be revenue; that to have revenue there must be taxes; that no taxes can be devised which are not more or less inconvenient and unpleasant. . . .

Observe good faith and justice towards all nations. Cultivate peace and harmony with all. Religion and morality enjoin this conduct; and can it be that good policy does not equally enjoin it? It will be worthy of a free, enlightened, and, at no distant period, a great nation to give to mankind the magnanimous and too novel example of a people always guided by an exalted justice and benevolence. Who can doubt that in the course of time and things the fruits of such a plan would richly repay any temporary advantages which might be lost by a steady adherence to it? Can it be, that Providence has not connected the permanent felicity of a nation with its virtue? The experiment, at least, is recommended by every sentiment which ennobles human nature. Alas! is it rendered impossible by its vices?

In the execution of such a plan nothing is more essential than that permanent, inveterate antipathies against particular nations and passionate attachments for others should be excluded, and that in place of them just and amicable feelings towards all should be cultivated. The nation which indulges towards another an habitual hatred, or an habitual fondness, is in some degree a slave. It is a slave to its animosity or to its affection, either of which is sufficient to lead it astray from its duty and its interest. Antipathy in one nation against another disposes each more readily to offer insult and injury, to lay hold of slight causes of umbrage, and to be haughty and intractable, when accidental or trifling occasions of dispute occur. Hence frequent collisions, obstinate, envenomed, and bloody contests. The nation prompted by ill will and resentment sometimes impels to war the government, contrary to the best calculations of policy. The government sometimes participates in the national propensity, and adopts through passion what reason would reject; at other times, it makes the animosity of the nation subservient to projects of hostility instigated by pride, ambition, and other sinister and pernicious motives. The peace often, sometimes perhaps the liberty, of nations has been the victim.

So likewise, a passionate attachment of one nation for another produces a variety of evils. Sympathy for the favorite nation, facilitating the illusion of an imaginary common interest, in cases where no real common interest exists, and infusing into one the enmities of the other, betrays the former into a participation in the quarrels and wars of the latter, without adequate inducement or justification. It leads also to concessions to the favorite nation of privileges denied to others, which is apt doubly to injure the nation making the concessions; by unnecessarily parting with what ought to have been retained; and by exciting jealousy, ill will, and a disposition to retaliate, in the parties from whom equal privileges are withheld. And it gives to ambitious, corrupted, or deluded citizens (who devote themselves to the favorite nation) facility to betray or sacrifice the interests of their own country, without odium, sometimes even with popularity. . . . Against the insidious wiles of foreign influence (I conjure you to believe me, fellow citizens), the jealousy of a free people ought to be *constantly* awake, since history and experience prove that foreign influence is one of the most baneful foes of republican government. But that jealousy to be useful must be impartial; else it becomes the instrument of the very influence to be avoided, instead of a defense against it. . . .

'Tis our true policy to steer clear of permanent alliances, with any portion of the foreign world. So far, I mean, as we are now at liberty to do it, for let me not be understood as capable of patronizing infidelity to existing engagements (I hold the maxim no less applicable to public than to private affairs, that honesty is always the best policy). I repeat it, therefore, let those engagements be observed in their genuine sense. But, in my opinion, it is unnecessary and would be unwise to extend them.

Taking care always to keep ourselves, by suitable establishments, on a respectably defensive posture, we may safely trust to temporary alliances for extraordinary emergencies.

Harmony, liberal intercourse with all nations, are recommended by policy, humanity, and interest. But even our commercial policy should hold an equal and impartial hand: neither seeking nor granting exclusive favors or preferences; consulting the natural course of things; diffusing and diversifying by gentle means the streams of commerce, but forcing nothing; establishing with powers so disposed; in order to give to trade a stable course, to define the rights of our merchants, and to enable the government to support them; conventional rules of intercourse, the best that present circumstances and mutual opinion will permit, but temporary, and liable to be from time to time abandoned or varied, as experience and circumstances shall dictate; constantly keeping in view, that 'tis folly in one nation to look for disinterested favors from another; that it must pay with a portion of its independence for whatever it may accept under that character; that by such acceptance, it may place itself in the condition of having given equivalents for nominal favors and yet of being reproached with ingratitude for not giving more. There can be no greater error than to expect, or calculate upon, real favors from nation to nation. 'Tis an illusion which experience must cure, which a just pride ought to discard.

In offering to you, my countrymen, these counsels of an old and affectionate friend, I dare not hope they will make the strong and lasting impression I could wish, that they will control the usual current of the passions, or prevent our nation from running the course which has hitherto marked the destiny of nations. But if I may even flatter myself that they may be productive of some partial benefit, some occasional good; that they may now and then recur to moderate the fury of party spirit, to warn against the mischiefs of foreign intrigue, to guard against the impostures of pretended patriotism; this hope will be a full recompense for the solicitude for your welfare, by which they have been dictated. . . .

Though in reviewing the incidents of my administration, I am unconscious of intentional error, I am nevertheless too sensible of my defects not to think it probable that I may have committed many errors. Whatever they may be, I fervently beseech the Almighty to avert or mitigate the evils to which they may tend. I shall also carry with me the hope that my country will never cease to view them with indulgence, and that after forty-five years of my life dedicated to its service, with an upright zeal, the faults of incompetent abilities will be consigned to oblivion, as myself must soon be to the mansions of rest.

Relying on its kindness in this as in other things, and actuated by that fervent love towards it which is so natural to a man who views in it the native soil of himself and his progenitors for several generations, I anticipate with pleasing expectation that retreat, in which I promise myself to realize, without alloy, the sweet enjoyment of partaking, in the midst of my fellow citizens, the benign influence of good laws under a free government, the ever favorite object of my heart, and the happy reward, as I trust, of our mutual cares, labors, and dangers. ■

John Brown Has a Few Words to Say about His Death Sentence

"Now, if it is deemed necessary that I should . . . mingle my blood further with the blood of my children and with the blood of millions in this slave country whose rights are disregarded by wicked, cruel, and unjust enactments, I say let it be done."

JOHN BROWN WAS A KILLER WITH A CAUSE. In the clashes in Kansas between Free Soilers and proslavery partisans (called border ruffians), "Osawatamie Brown" led a party that killed five men in the name of abolition.

Eastern liberals, including Ralph Waldo Emerson and Henry David Thoreau, admired this man of action, who set himself up in 1858 as "commander in chief" of a nebulous army to seize power and property from slaveholders; he gained fame as a rebel in a raid in Missouri to free a group of slaves, whom he took to Canada and freedom.

Brown rented a farmhouse in Maryland, fifty-five miles north of the nation's capital, in 1859; his plan was to strike across the Potomac River at the arsenal in Harpers Ferry, Virginia. With a band of thirteen whites and five blacks, Brown seized the town, killing several citizens, including a free Negro; he let news of the raid go forth in the hope of raising an army of insurrection. Federal troops under the command of Colonel Robert E. Lee and Lieutenant J. E. B. Stuart arrived and demanded his surrender; Brown and his band, including two of his sons, holed themselves up in the firehouse and chose a suicidal fight. Seven of Brown's men, his sons among them, were killed; the rebels took the lives of ten of the U.S. troops.

To what end? Abraham Lincoln at the Cooper Union a few months later dismissed Brown as a monomaniac whose insurrection "ends in little else than his own execution," but abolitionist orator Wendell Phillips believed that emancipation began at Harpers Ferry. Southerners used him as evidence of the North's intent to seize their property by force and violence, but most northerners—who did not like slavery but did not favor its abolition in the South—saw him as fanatic if not insane. He was mythologized in song, to the tune of the "Battle Hymn of the

Republic," sung by Union soldiers in the coming war: "John Brown's body lies a-mouldering in the grave, but his soul is marching on."

In prison and on trial. Brown felt the attention of the nation on himself and his cause, and comported himself with dignity. On November 2, 1859, following his conviction and sentence of death, he made these extemporaneous remarks, printed here in their entirety. The powerful evocation of the Christian message would have gained even greater force without the last three, self-serving paragraphs, ending on "I say let it be done," but excess was in his nature.

□   □   □

I have, may it please the court, a few words to say.

In the first place, I deny everything but what I have all along admitted: of a design on my part to free slaves. I intended certainly to have made a clean thing of that matter, as I did last winter, when I went into Missouri and there took slaves without the snapping of a gun on either side, moving them through the country, and finally leaving them in Canada. I designed to have done the same thing again on a larger scale. That was all I intended. I never did intend murder, or treason, or the destruction of property, or to excite or incite slaves to rebellion, or to make insurrection.

I have another objection, and that is that it is unjust that I should suffer such a penalty. Had I interfered in the manner which I admit, and which I admit has been fairly proved—for I admire the truthfulness and candor of the greater portion of the witnesses who have testified in this case—had I so interfered in behalf of the rich, the powerful, the intelligent, the so-called great, or in behalf of any of their friends, either father, mother, brother, sister, wife, or children, or any of that class, and suffered and sacrificed what I have in this interference, it would have been all right. Every man in this court would have deemed it an act worthy of reward rather than punishment.

This court acknowledges, too, as I suppose, the validity of the law of God. I see a book kissed, which I suppose to be the Bible, or at least the New Testament, which teaches me that all things whatsoever I would that men should do to me, I should do even so to them. It teaches me, further, to remember them that are in bonds as bound with them. I endeavored to act up to the instruction. I say I am yet too young to understand that God is any respecter of persons. I believe that to have interfered as I have done, as I have always freely admitted I have done, in behalf of his despised poor, I did not wrong but right. Now, if it is deemed necessary that I should forfeit my life for the furtherance of the ends of justice, and mingle my blood further with the blood of my children and with the blood of millions in this slave country whose rights are disregarded by wicked, cruel and unjust enactments, I say let it be done.

Let me say one word further. I feel entirely satisfied with the treatment I have received on my trial. Considering all the circumstances, it has been more generous than I expected. But I feel no consciousness of guilt. I have stated from the first what was my intention, and what was not. I never had any design against the liberty of any person, nor any disposition to commit treason or incite slaves to rebel or make any general insurrection. I never encouraged any man to do so, but always discouraged any idea of that kind.

Let me say, also, in regard to the statements made by some of those who were connected with me, I hear it has been stated by some of them that I have induced them to join me. But the contrary is true. I do not say this to injure them, but as regretting their weakness. Not one but joined me of his own accord, and the greater part at his own expense. A number of them I never saw, and never had a word of conversation with, till the day they came to me, and that was for the purpose I have stated.

Now I have done. ■

King Edward VIII
Abdicates His Throne

"I have found it impossible to carry the heavy burden of responsibility. . . without the help and support of the woman I love."

FOR KING EDWARD VIII to marry Wallis Simpson, a divorcée, he was required by the religious and political establishment to abdicate the British throne. On December 11, 1936, the former king, now the duke of Windsor, spoke to an international audience from Windsor Castle in the radio broadcast of his farewell address.

Although Winston Churchill is often credited with writing the farewell, the duke of Windsor denied such reports and said that Churchill added only a few phrases to the speech that he himself wrote. This is probably true, although his friend and aide Walter Monckton surely had a hand in the drafting. Lord Beaverbrook called it "a triumph of natural and sincere eloquence," but Lady Ravensdale considered it "hot-making and melodramatic." The abdicating king's mother, Queen Mary, wrote bitterly of "the failure of my Son in not carrying on the duties and responsibilities of the Sovereign of our great Empire," and many commoners in Britain felt he had "let down the side" by putting love before duty; Albert Julius, a jeweler in Piccadilly, a generation later traced the decline of British moral and political power to that day. But Churchill, in bidding farewell to the ex-monarch after the speech, quoted poet Andrew Marvell's ode on the beheading of Charles I: "He nothing common did or mean / Upon that memorable scene."

Succeeded by his brother, George VI, the duke of Windsor was introduced on the broadcast by his brother's instructions as "His Royal Highness Prince Edward." Legend has it that Edward VIII's reference to "radio" rather than "wireless" was responsible for making the older term obsolete, but the address itself contains neither word. In America, radio listeners in the early-morning hours were moved by the brave-sounding words over the crackling signal; the anthologist, then six, learned of the impact a speech could have as he listened with his mother, who cried at the royal reference to "the woman I love."

□ □ □

At long last I am able to say a few words of my own. I have never wanted to withhold anything, but until now it has not been constitutionally possible for me to speak.

A few hours ago I discharged my last duty as king and emperor, and now that I have been succeeded by my brother, the duke of York, my first words must be to declare my allegiance to him. This I do with all my heart.

You all know the reasons which have impelled me to renounce the throne. But I want you to understand that in making up my mind I did not forget the country or the empire, which, as prince of Wales and lately as king, I have for twenty-five years tried to serve.

But you must believe me when I tell you that I have found it impossible to carry the heavy burden of responsibility and to discharge my duties as king as I would wish to do without the help and support of the woman I love.

And I want you to know that the decision I have made has been mine and mine alone. This was a thing I had to judge entirely for myself. The other person most nearly concerned has tried up to the last to persuade me to take a different course.

I have made this, the most serious decision of my life, only upon the single thought of what would, in the end, be best for all.

This decision has been made less difficult to me by the sure knowledge that my brother, with his long training in the public affairs of this country and with his fine qualities, will be able to take my place forthwith without interruption or injury to the life and progress of the empire. And he has one matchless blessing, enjoyed by so many of you, and not bestowed on me—a happy home with his wife and children.

During these hard days I have been comforted by Her Majesty my mother and by my family. The ministers of the crown and, in particular, Mr. Baldwin, the prime minister, have always treated me with full consideration. There has never been any constitutional difference between me and them, and between me and Parliament. Bred in the constitutional tradition by my father, I should never have allowed any such issue to arise.

Ever since I was prince of Wales, and later on when I occupied the throne, I have been treated with the greatest kindness by all classes of the people wherever I have lived or journeyed throughout the empire. For that I am very grateful.

I now quit altogether public affairs, and I lay down my burden. It may be some time before I return to my native land, but I shall always follow the fortunes of the British race and empire with profound interest, and if at any time in the future I can be found of service to His Majesty in a private station, I shall not fail.

And now, we all have a new king. I wish him and you, his people, happiness and prosperity with all my heart. God bless you all! God save the king! ∎

Yankee Great
Lou Gehrig Bids Farewell
to Baseball

"I consider myself the luckiest man on the face of the earth."

ON JULY 4, 1939, LOU GEHRIG STOOD before a crowd of more than sixty thousand fans in Yankee Stadium to bid farewell to a game in which he'd become legendary. Within two years of that tearful speech, the baseball great was dead of a paralyzing disease that still bears his name.

In spite of the fatal ailment, however, the "Iron Horse" heroically spoke in 1939 of his great fortune in teammates and family. As first baseman of the New York Yankees, Gehrig had played 2,130 consecutive games, a major-league record; with a career batting average of .340, he became known as the Pride of the Yankees.

The emotion of his farewell speech wells up in this direct address to his fans, particularly in the repeated assertion of "Sure, I'm lucky."

□   □   □

Fans, for the past two weeks you have been reading about a bad break I got. Yet today I consider myself the luckiest man on the face of the earth. I have been in ballparks for seventeen years and have never received anything but kindness and encouragement from you fans.

Look at these grand men. Which of you wouldn't consider it the highlight of his career just to associate with them for even one day?

Sure, I'm lucky. Who wouldn't consider it an honor to have known Jacob Ruppert; also the builder of baseball's greatest empire, Ed Barrow; to have spent six years with that wonderful little fellow Miller Huggins; then to have spent the next nine years with that outstanding leader, that smart student of psychology—the best manager in baseball today—Joe McCarthy!

Sure, I'm lucky. When the New York Giants, a team you would give your right arm to beat, and vice versa, sends you a gift, that's something! When everybody down to the groundskeepers and those boys in white coats remember you with trophies, that's something.

When you have a wonderful mother-in-law who takes sides with you in squabbles against her own daughter, that's something. When you have a father and mother who work all their lives so that you can have an education and build your body, it's a blessing! When you have a wife who has been a tower of strength and shown more courage than you dreamed existed, that's the finest I know.

So I close in saying that I might have had a tough break; but I have an awful lot to live for! ■

General Douglas MacArthur Moves Congress with "Old Soldiers Never Die"

"In war there can be no substitute for victory."

AS A SOLDIER, the man who had served in World War II as supreme commander of the Allied powers in the Far East, and later as commander of the UN forces in Korea, was aloof, magisterial, decisive, and brilliant; as a speaker, the man who transfixed a joint meeting of Congress after being fired for insubordination by Harry Truman was purposeful, serious, disingenuous about his nonpartisanship, and in the end devastatingly sentimental.

The MacArthur style was usually unabashedly florid. After taking the Japanese surrender aboard the USS *Missouri* on September 2, 1945, he condemned war in these terms: "If we will not devise some greater and more equitable system, Armageddon will be at our door. The problem basically is theological and involves a spiritual recrudescence and improvement of human character that will synchronize with our almost matchless advances. . . of the past two thousand years." Only Douglas MacArthur would write and say a mouthfilling, unfamiliar word like "recrudescence" instead of "revival" (and, in fact, the sense of "breaking out afresh" is rooted in the return of a rash and is unsuited for association with spirituality). On another occasion, in his "duty, honor, country" address at West Point in 1962 (see p. 83), he showed himself to be the master of the high style of formal hortatory oratory.

His "Old soldiers never die" speech, as it came to be known, is different: the tone is subdued, the cadences thoughtful. the vision strategic. Its voice is not martial but orderly, as arguments are marshaled: "With this brief insight into the surrounding areas, I now turn to the Korean conflict." Though the April 19, 1951, speech about that war—called "conflict"—is remembered for its tear-jerking peroration, it reads decades later like a sober exposition of a view of warfare that holds up well against the ambiguities of Vietnam.

□   □   □

Istand on this rostrum with a sense of deep humility and great pride— humility in the wake of those great American architects of our history who have stood here before me, pride in the reflection that this forum of legislative debate represents human liberty in the purest form yet devised.

Here are centered the hopes and aspirations and faiths of the entire human race.

I do not stand here as advocate for any partisan cause, for the issues are fundamental and reach quite beyond the realm of partisan consideration. They must be resolved on the highest plane of national interest if our course is to prove sound and our future protected.

I trust, therefore, that you will do me the justice of receiving that which I have to say as solely expressing the considered viewpoint of a fellow American.

I address you with neither rancor nor bitterness in the fading twilight of life, with but one purpose in mind: to serve my country.

The issues are global, and so interlocked that to consider the problems of one sector oblivious to those of another is but to court disaster for the whole. While Asia is commonly referred to as the gateway to Europe, it is no less true that Europe is the gateway to Asia, and the broad influence of the one cannot fail to have its impact upon the other. There are those who claim our strength is inadequate to protect on both fronts, that we cannot divide our effort. I can think of no greater expression of defeatism.

If a potential enemy can divide his strength on two fronts, it is for us to counter his effort. The Communist threat is a global one. Its successful advance in one sector threatens the destruction of every other sector. You cannot appease or otherwise surrender to communism in Asia without simultaneously undermining our efforts to halt its advance in Europe.

Beyond pointing out these general truisms, I shall confine my discussion to the general areas of Asia.

Before one may objectively assess the situation now existing there, he must comprehend something of Asia's past and the revolutionary changes which have marked her course up to the present. Long exploited by the so-called colonial powers, with little opportunity to achieve any degree of social justice, individual dignity, or a higher standard of life such as guided our own noble administration of the Philippines, the peoples of Asia found their opportunity in the war just past to throw off the shackles of colonialism and now see the dawn of new opportunity, and heretofore unfelt dignity, and the self-respect of political freedom.

Mustering half of the earth's population, and 60 percent of its natural resources, these peoples are rapidly consolidating a new force, both moral and material, with which to raise the living standard and erect adaptations of the design of modern progress to their own distinct cultural environments.

Whether one adheres to the concept of colonization or not, this is the direction of Asian progress and it may not be stopped. It is a corollary to the shift of the world economic frontiers as the whole epicenter of world affairs rotates back toward the area whence it started.

In this situation, it becomes vital that our own country orient its policies in consonance with this basic evolutionary condition rather than pursue a course blind to the reality that the colonial era is now past and the Asian peoples covet the right to shape their own free destiny. What they seek now is friendly guidance, understanding, and support, not imperious direction; the dignity of equality, not the shame of subjugation.

Their prewar standard of life, pitifully low, is infinitely lower now in the devastation left in war's wake. World ideologies play little part in Asian thinking and are little understood.

What the people strive for is the opportunity for a little more food in their stomachs, a little better clothing on their backs, a little firmer roof over their heads, and the realization of a normal nationalist urge for political freedom.

These political-social conditions have but an indirect bearing upon our own national security, but do form a backdrop to contemporary planning which must be thoughtfully considered if we are to avoid the pitfalls of unrealism.

Of more direct and immediate bearing upon our national security are the changes wrought in the strategic potential of the Pacific Ocean in the course of the past war.

Prior thereto the western strategic frontier of the United States lay on the littoral line of the Americas, with an exposed island salient extending out through Hawaii, Midway, and Guam to the Philippines. That salient proved not an outpost of strength but an avenue of weakness along which the enemy could and did attack. The Pacific was a potential area of advance for any predatory force intent upon striking at the bordering land areas.

All this was changed by our Pacific victory. Our strategic frontier then shifted to embrace the entire Pacific Ocean, which became a vast moat to protect us as long as we held it. Indeed, it acts as a protective shield for all of the Americas and all free lands of the Pacific Ocean area. We control it to the shores of Asia by a chain of islands extending in an arc from the Aleutians to the Marianas, held by us and our free allies.

From this island chain we can dominate with sea and air power every Asiatic port from Vladivostok to Singapore—with sea and air power, every port, as I said, from Vladivostok to Singapore—and prevent any hostile movement into the Pacific.

Any predatory attack from Asia must be an amphibious effort. No amphibious force can be successful without control of the sea lanes and the air over those lanes in its avenue of advance. With naval and air supremacy and modest ground elements to defend bases, any major attack from continental Asia toward us or our friends of the Pacific would be doomed to failure.

Under such conditions, the Pacific no longer represents menacing avenues of approach for a prospective invader. It assumes, instead, the friendly aspect of a peaceful lake. . . .

The Japanese people since the war have undergone the greatest reformation recorded in modern history. With a commendable will, eagerness to learn, and marked capacity to understand, they have from the ashes left in war's wake erected in Japan an edifice dedicated to the primacy of individual liberty and personal dignity, and in the ensuing process there has been created a truly representative government committed to the advance of political morality, freedom of economic enterprise, and social justice.

Politically, economically, and socially Japan is now abreast of many free nations of the earth and will not again fail the universal trust. That it may be counted upon to wield a profoundly beneficial influence over the course of events in Asia is attested by the magnificent manner in which the Japanese people have met the recent challenge of war, unrest, and confusion surrounding them from the outside and checked communism within their own frontiers without the slightest slackening in their forward progress.

I sent all four of our occupation divisions to the Korean battlefront without the slightest qualms as to the effect of the resulting power vacuum upon Japan. The results fully justified my faith. . . .

With this brief insight into the surrounding areas, I now turn to the Korean conflict.

While I was not consulted prior to the president's decision to intervene in support of the Republic of Korea, that decision, from a military standpoint, proved a sound one. As I say, a brief and sound one, as we hurled back the invader and decimated his forces. Our victory was complete, and our objectives within reach when Red China intervened with numerically superior ground forces.

This created a new war and an entirely new situation, a situation not contemplated when our forces were committed against the North Korean invaders—a situation which called for new decisions in the diplomatic sphere to permit the realistic adjustment of military strategy. Such decisions have not been forthcoming.

While no man in his right mind would advocate sending our ground forces into continental China, and such was never given a thought, the new situation did urgently demand a drastic revision of strategic planning if our political aim was to defeat this new enemy as we had defeated the old.

Apart from the military need, as I saw it, to neutralize the sanctuary protection given the enemy north of the Yalu, I felt that military necessity in the conduct of the war made necessary (1) the intensification of our economic blockade against China; (2) the imposition of a naval blockade against the China coast; (3) removal of restrictions on air reconnaissance of China's coastal areas and of Manchuria; (4) removal of restrictions on the forces of the Republic of China on Formosa, with logistical support to contribute to their effective operation against the Chinese mainland.

For entertaining these views, all professionally designed to support our forces in Korea and to bring hostilities to an end with the least possible delay and at a saving of countless American and Allied lives, I have been severely criticized in lay circles, principally abroad, despite my understanding that from a military standpoint the above views have been fully shared in the past by practically every military leader concerned with the Korean campaign, including our own Joint Chiefs of Staff.

I called for reinforcements. but was informed that reinforcements were not available. I made clear that if not permitted to destroy the enemy built-up bases north of the Yalu, if not permitted to utilize the friendly Chinese force of some 600,000 men on Formosa. if not permitted to blockade the China coast to prevent the Chinese Reds from getting succor from without, and if there were to be no hope of major reinforcements, the position of the command from the military standpoint forbade victory.

We could hold in Korea by constant maneuver and at an approximate area where our supply-line advantages were in balance with the supply-line disadvantages of the enemy, but we could hope at best for only an indecisive campaign with its terrible and constant attrition upon our forces if the enemy utilized its full military potential.

I have constantly called for the new political decisions essential to a solution.

Efforts have been made to distort my position. It has been said in effect that I was a warmonger. Nothing could be further from the truth.

I know war as few other men now living know it, and nothing to me—nothing to me—is more revolting. I have long advocated its complete abolition, as its very destructiveness on both friend and foe has rendered it useless as a means of settling international disputes. . . .

But once war is forced upon us, there is no other alternative than to apply every available means to bring it to a swift end. War's very object is victory, not prolonged indecision.

In war there can be no substitute for victory.

There are some who for varying reasons would appease Red China. They are blind to history's clear lesson, for history teaches with unmistakable emphasis that appeasement but begets new and bloodier war. It points to no single instance where the end has justified that means, where appeasement has led to more than a sham peace. Like blackmail, it lays the basis for new and successively greater demands until, as in blackmail, violence becomes the only other alternative. Why, my soldiers asked of me, surrender military advantages to an enemy in the field? I could not answer.

Some may say to avoid spread of the conflict into an all-out war with China. Others, to avoid Soviet intervention. Neither explanation seems valid, for China is already engaging with the maximum power it can commit, and the Soviet will not necessarily mesh its actions with our moves. Like a cobra, any new enemy will more likely strike whenever it feels that the relativity in military or other potential is in its favor on a worldwide basis.

The tragedy of Korea is further heightened by the fact that its military action is confined to its territorial limits. It condemns that nation, which it is our purpose to save, to suffer the devastating impact of full naval and air bombardment while the enemy's sanctuaries are fully protected from such attack and devastation.

Of the nations of the world Korea alone, up to now, is the sole one which has risked its all against communism. The magnificence of the courage and fortitude of the Korean people defies description. They have chosen to risk death rather than slavery. Their last words to me were "Don't scuttle the Pacific."

I have just left your fighting sons in Korea. They have met all tests there, and I can report to you without reservation that they are splendid in every way. It was my constant effort to preserve them and end this savage conflict honorably and with the least loss of time and a minimum sacrifice of life. Its growing bloodshed has caused me the deepest anguish and anxiety. Those gallant men will remain often in my thoughts and in my prayers always.

I am closing my fifty-two years of military service. When I joined the army, even before the turn of the century, it was the fulfillment of all of my boyish hopes and dreams. The world has turned over many times since I took the oath on the plain at West Point, and the hopes and dreams have long since vanished, but I still remember the refrain of one of the most popular barrack ballads of that day which proclaimed most proudly that old soldiers never die; they just fade away. And, like the old soldier of that ballad, I now close my military career and just fade away, an old soldier who tried to do his duty as God gave him the light to see that duty. Good-bye. ■

President Dwight D. Eisenhower Takes His Leave with a Surprising Theme

"WE must guard against the acquisition of unwarranted influence, whether sought or unsought, by the military-industrial complex."

AT THE END OF HIS SECOND PRESIDENTIAL TERM, Dwight David Eisenhower surprised the nation with his farewell address on January 17, 1961. A man who rose to the top of the vast U. S. military establishment, and a political leader with most of his personal friends in industry, Eisenhower chose in his last speech to warn about the dangers of military-industrial power.

Eisenhower's biographers note that a month before the address, *Saturday Review* editor Norman Cousins called the president with the suggestion of this farewell address, "a great, sweeping document" to review his administration and discuss the country's future,

The primary focus of his address, however, was on the Cold War and the "permanent armaments industry" needed for the national defense. Credit for the catchphrase "military-industrial complex" goes to his speechwriters Malcolm Moos and Ralph Williams. When reporters asked about it a few days later, the departing president said he was thinking not of a willful abuse of power but of "an almost insidious penetration of our own minds that the only thing this country is engaged in is weaponry and missiles." He added, "And I tell you we can't afford that."

With biblical allusion to swords and plowshares, Eisenhower introduces the theme of a military-industrial threat, necessitating careful regulation by "an alert and knowledgeable citizenry." The long series of parallel clauses in the closing prayer includes a return to this idea: "that those who have freedom will understand, also, its heavy responsibilities,"

Pundit Walter Lippmann, who had become critical of Eisenhower in the president's second term, called this farewell "in the great tradition. Washington made the theme of his Farewell Address a warning against allowing the influence of foreign governments to invade our political life. That was then the menace to the civilian power. Now Eisenhower, speaking from his experience and looking ahead, is concerned with a contemporary threat to the supremacy of the civilian power."

□   □   □

This evening I come to you with a message of leave-taking and farewell, and to share a few final thoughts with you, my countrymen. . .

We now stand ten years past the midpoint of a century that has witnessed four major wars among great nations—three of these involved our own country.

Despite these holocausts America is today the strongest, the most influential, and most productive nation in the world. Understandably proud of this preeminence, we yet realize that America's leadership and prestige depend, not merely upon our unmatched material progress, riches, and military strength, but on how we use our power in the interests of world peace and human betterment.

A vital element in keeping the peace is our military establishment. Our arms must be mighty, ready for instant action, so that no potential aggressor may be tempted to risk his own destruction.

Our military organization today bears little relation to that known by any of my predecessors in peacetime—or, indeed, by the fighting men of World War II or Korea.

Until the latest of our world conflicts, the United States had no armaments industry. American makers of plowshares could, with time and as required, make swords as well.

But we can no longer risk emergency improvisation of national defense. We have been compelled to create a permanent armaments industry of vast proportions. Added to this, three and a half million men and women are directly engaged in the defense establishment. We annually spend on military security alone more than the net income of all United States corporations.

Now, this conjunction of an immense military establishment and a large arms industry is new in the American experience. The total influence—economic, political, even spiritual—is felt in every city, every state house, every office of the federal government. We recognize the imperative need for this development. Yet we must not fail to comprehend its grave implications. Our toil, resources, and livelihood are all involved; so is the very structure of our society.

In the councils of government, we must guard against the acquisition of unwarranted influence, whether sought or unsought, by the military-industrial complex. The potential for the disastrous rise of misplaced power exists and will persist.

We must never let the weight of this combination endanger our liberties or democratic processes. We should take nothing for granted. Only an alert and knowledgeable citizenry can compel the proper meshing of the huge industrial and military machinery of defense with our peaceful methods and goals, so that security and liberty may prosper together.

Akin to and largely responsible for the sweeping changes in our industrial-military posture has been the technological revolution during recent decades.

In this revolution research has become central. It also becomes more formalized, complex, and costly. A steadily increasing share is conducted for, by, or at the direction of the federal government.

Today the solitary inventor, tinkering in his shop, has been overshadowed by task forces of scientists, in laboratories and testing fields. In the same fashion, the free university, historically the fountainhead of free ideas and scientific discovery, has experienced a revolution in the conduct of research. Partly because of the huge costs involved, a government contract becomes virtually a substitute for intellectual curiosity.

For every old blackboard there are now hundreds of new electronic computers.

Another factor in maintaining balance involves the element of time. As we peer into society's future, we—you and I, and our government—must avoid the impulse to live only for today, plundering, for our own ease and convenience, the precious resources of tomorrow.

We cannot mortgage the material assets of our grandchildren without risking the loss also of their political and spiritual heritage. We want democracy to survive for all generations to come, not to become the insolvent phantom of tomorrow.

Such a confederation must be one of equals. The weakest must come to the conference table with the same confidence as do we, protected as we are by our moral economic, and military strength. That table, though scarred by many past frustrations, cannot be abandoned for the certain agony of the battlefield.

Disarmament, with mutual honor and confidence, is a continuing imperative. Together we must learn how to compose differences—not with arms but with intellect and decent purpose. Because this need is so sharp and apparent, I confess that I lay down my official responsibilities in this field with a definite sense of disappointment. As one who has witnessed the horror and the lingering sadness of war, as one who knows that another war could utterly destroy this civilization which has been so slowly and painfully built over thousands of years, I wish I could say tonight that a lasting peace is in sight.

Happily, I can say that war has been avoided. Steady progress toward our ultimate goal has been made. But so much remains to be done. As a private citizen, I shall never cease to do what little I can to help the world advance along that road.

So, in this, my last "good night" to you as your president, I thank you for the many opportunities you have given me for public service in war and in peace. I trust that, in that service, you find some things worthy. As for the rest of it, I know you will find ways to improve performance in the future.

To all the peoples of the world, I once more give expression to America's prayerful and continuing aspiration:

We pray that peoples of all faiths, all races, all nations, may have their great human needs satisfied; that those now denied opportunity shall come to enjoy it to the full; that all who yearn for freedom may experience its spiritual blessings; that those who have freedom will understand, also, its heavy responsibilities; that all who are insensitive to the needs of others will learn charity; that the scourges of poverty, disease, and ignorance will be made to disappear from the earth; and that in the goodness of time, all peoples will come to live together in a peace guaranteed by the binding force of mutual respect and love.

Now, on Friday noon, I am to become a private citizen. I am proud to do so. I look forward to it.

Thank you, and good night. ∎

President Lyndon B. Johnson Halts the Bombing in Vietnam and Drops His Own Political Bomb

"I shall not seek, and I will not accept, the nomination of my party for another term as your president."

DEPRESSED BY DEPRESSING POLLS, dismayed by the hatred of protesters shouting, "Hey, Hey, LBJ, how many kids did you kill today?," and facing divisive primary challenges from Senators Eugene McCarthy and Robert Kennedy, President Johnson chose to step down in the most dramatic way possible: with a surprise announcement at the end of a prime-time speech about the Vietnam War on March 31, 1968.

Sixteen years before, Harry Truman—another accidental Democratic president nearing the end of his first elected term, also buffeted by a stalemated Asian war, compounded by the "mess in Washington"—

announced he would "not accept a renomination." Johnson's farewell was more stunning, primarily because it was a major television event in which each viewer felt he took part. The surprise came at the end of a well-crafted but unrelenting recitation of the history of the nation's involvement in an unpopular war, including a plaintive repetition of John F. Kennedy's inaugural promise "to pay any price, bear any burden, meet any hardship, support any friend, oppose any foe, to assure the survival and the success of liberty."

The immediate reaction in millions of living rooms was "Did he say what I think he said?" When the news had sunk in, the viewer was left with a taste of history in his mouth.

□   □   □

Good evening, my fellow Americans.
Tonight I want to speak to you of peace in Vietnam and Southeast Asia.

No other question so preoccupies our people. No other dream so absorbs the 250 million human beings who live in that part of the world. No other goal motivates American policy in Southeast Asia.

For years, representatives of our government and others have traveled the world—seeking to find a basis for peace talks.

Since last September, they have carried the offer that I made public at San Antonio.

That offer was this: that the United States would stop its bombardment of North Vietnam when that would lead promptly to productive discussions—and that we would assume that North Vietnam would not take military advantage of our restraint.

Hanoi denounced this offer, both privately and publicly. Even while the search for peace was going on, North Vietnam rushed their preparations for a savage assault on the people, the government, and the allies of South Vietnam.

Their attack—during the Tet holidays—failed to achieve its principal objectives.

It did not collapse the elected government of South Vietnam or shatter its army—as the Communists had hoped.

It did not produce a "general uprising" among the people of the cities as they had predicted.

The Communists were unable to maintain control of any of the more than thirty cities that they attacked. And they took very heavy casualties.

But they did compel the South Vietnamese and their allies to move certain forces from the countryside, into the cities.

They caused widespread disruption and suffering. Their attacks, and the battles that followed, made refugees of half a million human beings. The Communists may renew their attack any day.

They are, it appears, trying to make 1968 the year of decision in South Vietnam—the year that brings, if not final victory or defeat, at least a turning point in the struggle.

This much is clear: if they do mount another round of heavy attacks, they will not succeed in destroying the fighting power of South Vietnam and its allies.

But tragically, this is also clear: many men—on both sides of the struggle—will be lost. A nation that has already suffered twenty years of warfare will suffer once again. Armies on both sides will take new casualties. And the war will go on.

There is no need for this to be so.

There is no need to delay the talks that could bring an end to this long and this bloody war.

Tonight, I renew the offer I made last August—to stop the bombardment of North Vietnam. We ask that talks begin promptly, that they be serious talks on the substance of peace. We assume that during those talks Hanoi will not take advantage of our restraint.

We are prepared to move immediately toward peace through negotiations.

So, tonight, in the hope that this action will lead to early talks, I am taking the first step to deescalate the conflict. We are reducing—substantially reducing—the present level of hostilities.

And we are doing so unilaterally, and at once. Tonight, I have ordered our aircraft and our naval vessels to make no attacks on North Vietnam, except in the area north of the Demilitarized Zone where the continuing enemy buildup directly threatens allied forward positions and where the movements of their troops and supplies are clearly related to that threat.

The area in which we are stopping our attacks includes almost 90 percent of North Vietnam's population, and most of its territory. Thus there will be no attacks around the principal populated areas, or in the food-producing areas of North Vietnam.

Even this very limited bombing of the North could come to an early end—if our restraint is matched by restraint in Hanoi. But I cannot in good conscience stop all bombing so long as to do so would immediately and directly endanger the lives of our men and our allies. Whether a complete bombing halt becomes possible in the future will be determined by events.

Our purpose in this action is to bring about a reduction in the level of violence that now exists.

It is to save the lives of brave men—and to save the lives of innocent women and children. It is to permit the contending forces to move closer to a political settlement. . . .

I call upon President Ho Chi Minh to respond positively, and favorably, to this new step toward peace.

But if peace does not come now through negotiations, it will come when Hanoi understands that our common resolve is unshakable, and our common strength is invincible.

Tonight, we and the other allied nations are contributing 600,000 fighting men to assist 700,000 South Vietnamese troops in defending their little country.

Our presence there has always rested on this basic belief: the main burden of preserving their freedom must be carried out by them—by the South Vietnamese themselves.

We and our allies can only help to provide a shield—behind which the people of South Vietnam can survive and can grow and develop. On their efforts—on their determination and resourcefulness—the outcome will ultimately depend.

That small, beleaguered nation has suffered terrible punishment for more than twenty years.

I pay tribute once again tonight to the great courage and endurance of its people. South Vietnam supports armed forces tonight of almost 700,000 men—and I call your attention to the fact that that is the equivalent of more than 10 million in our own population. Its people maintain their firm determination to be free of domination by the North.

There has been substantial progress, I think, in building a durable government during these last three years. The South Vietnam of 1965 could not have survived the enemy's Tet offensive of 1968. The elected government of South Vietnam survived that attack—and is rapidly repairing the devastation that it wrought.

The South Vietnamese know that further efforts are going to be required: to expand their own armed forces; to move back into the countryside as quickly as possible to increase their taxes; to select the very best men that they have for civilian and military responsibility; to achieve a new unity within their constitutional government; and to include in the national effort all of those groups who wish to preserve South Vietnam's control over its own destiny.

Last week President Thieu ordered the mobilization of 135,000 additional South Vietnamese. He plans to reach—as soon as possible—a total military strength of more than 800,000 men. . . .

We applaud this evidence of determination on the part of South Vietnam. Our first priority will be to support their effort.

We shall accelerate the reequipment of South Vietnam's armed forces—in order to meet the enemy's increased firepower. This will enable them progressively to undertake a larger share of combat operations against the Communist invaders. . . .

Now let me give you my estimate of the chances for peace: the peace that will one day stop the bloodshed in South Vietnam; that all the Vietnamese people will be permitted to rebuild and develop their land; that will permit us to turn more fully to our own tasks here at home.

I cannot promise that the initiative that I have announced tonight will be completely successful in achieving peace any more than the thirty others that we have undertaken and agreed to in recent years.

But it is our fervent hope that North Vietnam, after years of fighting that has left the issue unresolved, will now cease its efforts to achieve a military victory and will join with us in moving toward the peace table.

And there may come a time when South Vietnamese—on both sides—are able to work out a way to settle their own differences by free political choice rather than by war.

As Hanoi considers its course, it should be in no doubt of our intentions. It must not miscalculate the pressures within our democracy in this election year.

We have no intention of widening this war.

But the United States will never accept a fake solution to this long and arduous struggle and call it peace.

No one can foretell the precise terms of an eventual settlement.

Our objective in South Vietnam has never been the annihilation of the enemy. It has been to bring about a recognition in Hanoi that its objective—taking over the South by force—could not be achieved.

We think that peace can be based on the Geneva accords of 1954—under political conditions that permit the South Vietnamese—all the South Vietnamese—to chart their course free of any outside domination or interference, from us or from anyone else.

So tonight I reaffirm the pledge that we made at Manila—that we are prepared to withdraw our forces from South Vietnam as the other side withdraws its forces to the North, stops the infiltration, and the level of violence thus subsides.

Our goal of peace and self-determination in Vietnam is directly related to the future of all of Southeast Asia—where much has happened to inspire confidence during the past ten years. We have done all that we knew how to do to contribute and to help build that confidence. . . .

One day, my fellow citizens, there will be peace in Southeast Asia.

It will come because the people of Southeast Asia want it—those whose armies are at war tonight, and those who, though threatened, have thus far been spared.

Peace will come because Asians were willing to work for it—and to sacrifice for it—and to die by the thousands for it.

But let it never be forgotten: peace will come also because America sent her sons to help secure it.

It has not been easy—far from it. During the past four and a half years, it has been my fate and my responsibility to be commander in chief. I have lived—daily and nightly—with the cost of this war. I know the pain that it has inflicted. I know perhaps better than anyone the misgivings that it has aroused.

Throughout this entire, long period, I have been sustained by a single principle: that what we are doing now, in Vietnam, is vital not only to the security of Southeast Asia, but it is vital to the security of every American.

Surely we have treaties which we must respect. Surely we have commitments that we are going to keep. Resolutions of the Congress testify to the need to resist aggression in the world and in Southeast Asia.

But the heart of our involvement in South Vietnam—under three presidents, three separate administrations—has always been America's own security. . . .

I believe that a peaceful Asia is far nearer to reality, because of what America has done in Vietnam. I believe that the men who endure the dangers of battle—fighting there for us tonight—are helping the entire world avoid far greater conflicts, far wider wars, far more destruction, than this one.

The peace that will bring them home someday will come. Tonight I have offered the first in what I hope will be a series of mutual moves toward peace.

I pray that it will not be rejected by the leaders of North Vietnam. I pray that they will accept it as a means by which the sacrifices of their own people may be ended. And I ask your help and your support, my fellow citizens, for this effort to reach across the battlefield toward an early peace.

Finally, my fellow Americans, let me say this:

Of those to whom much is given, much is asked. I cannot say and no man could say that no more will be asked of us.

Yet, I believe that now, no less than when the decade began, this generation of Americans is willing to pay any price, bear any burden, meet any hardship, support any friend, oppose any foe, to assure the survival and the success of liberty.

Since those words were spoken by John F. Kennedy, the people of America have kept that compact with mankind's noblest cause.

And we shall continue to keep it.

Yet, I believe that we must always be mindful of this one thing, whatever the trials and the tests ahead. The ultimate strength of our country and our cause will lie not in powerful weapons or infinite resources or boundless wealth, but will lie in the unity of our people.

This, I believe very deeply.

Throughout my entire public career I have followed the personal philosophy that I am a free man, an American, a public servant, and a member of my party, in that order always and only.

For thirty-seven years in the service of our nation, first as a congressman, as a senator, and as vice-president and now as your president, I have put the unity of the people first. I have put it ahead of any divisive partisanship.

And in these times as in times before, it is true that a house divided against itself by the spirit of faction, of party, of region, of religion, of race, is a house that cannot stand.

There is division in the American house now. There is divisiveness among us all tonight. And holding the trust that is mine, as president of all the people, I cannot disregard the peril to the progress of the American people and the hope and the prospect of peace for all peoples.

So, I would ask all Americans, whatever their personal interests or concern, to guard against divisiveness and all its ugly consequences.

Fifty-two months and ten days ago, in a moment of tragedy and trauma, the duties of this office fell upon me. I asked then for your help and God's that we might continue America on its course, binding up our wounds, healing our history, moving forward in new unity, to clear the American agenda and to keep the American commitment for all of our people.

United we have kept that commitment. United we have enlarged that commitment.

Through all time to come, I think, America will be a stronger nation, a more just society, and a land of greater opportunity and fulfillment because of what we have all done together in these years of unparalleled achievement.

Our reward will come in the life of freedom, peace, and hope that our children will enjoy through ages ahead.

What we won when all of our people united just must not now be lost in suspicion, distrust, selfishness, and politics among any of our people.

Believing this as I do, I have concluded that I should not permit the presidency to become involved in the partisan divisions that are developing in this political year.

With America's sons in the fields far away, with America's future under challenge right here at home, with our hopes and the world's hopes for peace in the balance every day, I do not believe that I should devote an hour or a day of my time to any personal partisan causes or to any duties other than the awesome duties of this office—the presidency of your country.

Accordingly, I shall not seek, and I will not accept, the nomination of my party for another term as your president.

But let men everywhere know, however, that a strong, a confident, and a vigilant America stands ready tonight to seek an honorable peace—and stands ready tonight to defend an honored cause—whatever the price, whatever the burden, whatever the sacrifices that duty may require.

Thank you for listening.

Good night, and God bless all of you. ■

Speaker of the House
James Wright Resigns
as "Propitiation"
for Ill Will

*"I*T *is grievously hurtful to our society when vilification becomes an accepted form of political debate, when negative campaigning becomes a full-time occupation, when members of each party become self-appointed vigilantes. . . ."*

DEMOCRAT JAMES WRIGHT came to the House of Representatives from Fort Worth, Texas, in 1954; after serving as Tip O'Neill's lieutenant as party whip, he became Speaker of the House in 1987. Only two years later, he was embroiled in controversy over a series of ethical lapses that might have resulted in a minor rebuke but for an atmosphere of rancor in the House, rectitude in the media, and resentment among the voting public at the scope of unpunished political involvement in the savings-and-loan scandal. The House ethics committee found "reason to believe" that Speaker Wright had violated its rules of conduct sixty-nine times, the violations ranging from scheming to evade limits on outside income in a book-publishing venture to taking improper gifts from a constituent.

On May 31, 1989, speaking to a full House with packed galleries, working from notes and text, Jim Wright first offered a detailed defense of the ethics charges leveled at him, which was not persuasive to most, but then touched a chord with a speech about "a frenzy of feeding on other people's reputation"—the metaphor taken from sharks in a furious orgy of eating.

□   □   □

Mr. Speaker, for thirty-four years I have had the great privilege to be a member of this institution, the people's house, and I shall forever be grateful for that wondrous privilege.

I never cease to be thankful to the people of the Twelfth District of Texas for their friendship and their understanding and their partiality toward me. Eighteen times they have voted to permit me the grand privilege of representing them here in this repository of the democratic principles.

Only a few days ago, even in the face of harsh news accounts and bitter criticisms, they indicated in a poll taken by the leading newspaper in the district that 78 percent of them approved of my services, and that includes 73 percent of the Republicans in my district. And I'm very proud of that.

And you, my colleagues, Democrats and Republicans, I owe a great deal to you. You have given me the greatest gift within your power to give. To be the Speaker of the United States House of Representatives is the grandest opportunity that can come to any lawmaker anywhere in the Western world. And I would be deeply remiss if I didn't express my sincere appreciation to you for that opportunity. I hope that I have reflected credit upon the people of my district who know me best, perhaps, and upon the people of this House who, next to them, would know me best. . . .

I love this institution. I want to assure each of you that under no circumstances, having spent more than half my life here—this House being my home—would I ever knowingly or intentionally do or say anything to violate its rules or detract from its standards. All of us are prone to human error.

The Speaker of the House is in fact the chief enforcer of the rules of the House, and it's really a wonderful thing that any member of the House may at his will bring questions against any other member. And under our rules that has to be looked into. And I have no quarrel with that nor any criticism of people who serve on the Committee on Standards. It's a thankless job, and we have to have such a committee.

For over a year—well, just about a year—I have ached to tell my side of the story. That to which I have to respond keeps changing, but today silence is no longer tolerable, nor for the good of the House is it even desirable. So without any rancor and without any bitterness, without any hard feelings toward anybody, I thank you for indulging me because I answer to you and to the American people for my honor, my reputation, and all the things that I've tried to stand for all these years. . . .

Having gone through this agonizing experience for about a year now—I mean, almost every day there's a new story and a newspaper leak without any chance for me to know what's coming next—no chance for me to go to the committee and answer it and say, "Hey, wait a minute, that's not correct."

Maybe the committee, which is currently required to sit as a kind of grand jury and a petit jury both, ought to have a different composition rather than those who issue the statement of alleged violations being the same people who have to judge them. I think it clearly is difficult to expect members who have a publicly announced reason to believe there's a violation to reverse their position at a hearing stage and dismiss charges against a member.

Maybe, once a report of alleged violations is issued, the committee rules ought to allow the member to respond expeditiously and that to deny a member their opportunity to deny quickly can cause serious political injury. It's unfair. Once alleged violations are announced, the committee ought to just immediately release to the member all the evidence that it could have to indicate that that's happened.

In my case, for example, the committee has yet to release any witness testimony or documents that it obtained during the investigation.

Why hide the evidence? What's there to hide? This ought not to be the kind of proceeding in which strategic maneuvering be allowed to override the fundament relations of fair play. . . .

It is intolerably hurtful to our government that qualified members of the executive and legislative branches are resigning because of the ambiguities and the confusion surrounding the ethics laws and because of their own consequent vulnerability to personal attack. That's a shame. It's happening.

And it is grievously hurtful to our society when vilification becomes an accepted form of political debate, when negative campaigning becomes a full-time occupation, when members of each party become self-appointed vigilantes carrying out personal vendettas against members of the other party. In God's name, that's not what this institution is supposed to be all about.

When vengeance becomes more desirable than vindication, harsh personal attacks on one another's motives, one another's character, drown out the quiet logic of serious debate on important issues, things that we ought to be involved ourselves in. Surely, that's unworthy of our institution, unworthy of our American political process.

All of us in both political parties must resolve to bring this period of mindless cannibalism to an end. There's been enough of it.

I pray to God that we will do that, and restore the spirit that always existed in this House. When I first came here all those years ago, in 1955, this was a place where a man's word was his bond, and his honor and the truth of what he said to you were assumed—you didn't have to prove it.

I remember one time Cleve Bailey of West Virginia, in a moment of impassioned concern over a tariff bill, jumped up and made an objection to the fact that Chet Holifield had voted—in those days we shouted our answers to the votes and Holifield back there in the back—and Bailey said, "I object to the gentleman from California's vote being counted. He came down and voted late." He said, "He was not in the chamber when his name was called and therefore is not entitled to vote." It was a close vote.

Speaker Rayburn grew red as a tomato, and I thought he was going to break the gavel when he hammered. He said, "The chair always takes the word of a member."

And then, because I was sitting over here behind Cleve Bailey, I heard other members come and say, "Cleve, you're wrong. Chet was back there behind the rail. I was standing by him when he answered, and his answer just wasn't heard." And others said, "You shouldn't have said that." And Cleve Bailey, crusty old West Virginian, came down here and abjectly—literally with tears in his eyes—apologized for having questioned the word of a member. And we need that.

If I made mistakes—oh, boy, how many! I made a lot of mistakes; mistakes in judgment, oh yes, a lot of them. I'll make some more.

Recently—let me just comment on this briefly because it's such a sensational thing and injury's been done to me in this particular moment because of it. John, John Mack—many of you remember him, know him. I think a lot of you like him, respect him.

I helped John one time in his life when he was about nineteen years old, twenty. I didn't know him, never had met him. I didn't know the nature of the crime he had been convicted of, I knew only that John Mack was a young man whom my daughter had known in high school. My daughter was married to his brother, incidentally—that's how she knew about John. And she mentioned it to me. All I knew was that he'd been convicted of assault and that he'd served twenty-seven months in a Fairfax County jail.

Contrary to what's been published, I did not interfere with the court, I didn't suggest anything to the court, I didn't have anything to do with his sentencing. I really didn't—didn't know, and didn't inquire. Maybe that's bad judgment. I didn't inquire as to the exact nature of the crime. The sheriff's office in Fairfax County called and asked me if I would know of any job that I could help this young man get. They wanted to parole him; they said he's been a model rehabilitated prisoner. And I gave him a job as a file clerk, you know, $9,000 a year.

After that he really blossomed and grew and developed, and those of you who know him can't conceive, as I never could conceive when finally, just two years ago, I read in the newspaper the precise nature of that crime. It just didn't fit his character. He married and had two beautiful children, wonderfully responsible, and I think became a very fine person.

Now, was that bad judgment? Yes, maybe so. It doesn't have anything to do with the rules, but it's got all mixed up with it. And I don't think, though, that it's bad judgment to try to give a young man a second chance.

Maybe I should have known more about it, but in this case I think—I think he has turned out well. and I don't believe that America really stands for the idea that a person should ever, forever, be condemned, and I think maybe he ought to have a second chance. And that's what I thought in the case of John Mack and, good judgment or bad, I mean, that's it. And I believe in giving somebody a second chance.

Have I contributed unwittingly to this manic idea of a frenzy of feeding on other people's reputation? Have I—have I caused a lot of this stuff? Maybe I have—God, I hope I haven't, but maybe I have. Have I been too partisan? Too insistent? Too abrasive? Too determined to have my way? Perhaps. Maybe so. If I've offended anybody in the other party, I'm sorry. I never meant to—would not have done so intentionally. I've always tried to treat all of our colleagues, Democrats and Republicans, with respect.

Are there things I'd do differently if I had them to do over again? Oh, boy! How many may I name for you!

Well, I'll tell you what, I'm going to make you a proposition: Let me give you back this job you gave to me as a propitiation for all of this season of bad will that has grown up among us. Give it back to you. I will resign as Speaker of the House effective upon the election of my successor. And I'll ask that we call a caucus on the Democratic side for next Tuesday to choose a successor.

I don't want to be a party to tearing up the institution; I love it. Tell you the truth, this year it has been very difficult for me to offer the kind of moral leadership that the organization needs, because every time I've tried to talk about the needs of the country, about the needs for affordable homes—Jack Kemp's idea and the idea developing here.

Every time I've tried to talk about the need for a minimum wage, tried to talk about the need for day care centers, embracing ideas on both sides of the aisle, the media have not been interested in that. They wanted to ask about petty personal finances.

You need—you need somebody else, someone to give you that back. We'll have the caucus on Tuesday. And then I will offer to resign from the House sometime before the end of June. Let that be a total payment for the anger and hostility we feel toward each other. Let's not try to get even with each other. Republicans, please don't get it in your heads you need to *get* somebody else because of John Tower. Democrats, please don't feel that you need to *get* somebody on the other side because of me. We ought to be more mature than that.

Let's restore to this institution the rightful priorities of what's good for this country, and let's all work together to try to achieve them. The nation has important business, and it can't afford these distractions, and that's why I offer to resign.

I've enjoyed these years in Congress. I am grateful for all of you who have taught me things and been patient with me. Horace Greeley had a quote that Harry Truman used to like—and fame is a vapor, popularity an accident, riches take wings, those who cheer today may curse tomorrow, only one thing endures: character.

I'm not a bitter man—I'm not going to be. I'm a lucky man. God has given me the privilege of serving in this, the greatest institution on earth, for a great many years. And I'm grateful to the people of my district in Texas, I'm grateful to you, my colleagues, all of you.

God bless this institution. God bless the United States.

■　■　■

VII

SERMONS

The Buddha Urges
a Turning Away
from Craving in
His "Fire Sermon"

"AND with what are these on fire? With the fire of passion, say I, with the fire of hatred, with the fire of infatuation . . ."

THE BUDDHA IS A TITLE—The Enlightened One, or The Awakened One—given a prince named Siddhartha Gautama, born about the year 563 B.C. in a kingdom on the border of what today is Nepal and India. At twenty-nine he became an ascetic, then searched for a "middle way" between the hedonist's self-indulgence and the ascetic's self-mortification. Seated cross-legged under a banyan tree, he achieved what Buddhists call the great Enlightenment: the central truths are that mankind's life is filled with suffering; it is caused by craving; and there is freedom from such craving that is called the state of Nirvana, a cool and liberating detachment.

To a gathering of one thousand ascetics in the region of Uruvela, the Buddha delivered a *sutra*, or discourse, known as the "Fire Sermon." It is one of the basic scriptures of one of the world's great religions, driven by a drumbeat of repetition of key words and the evocation of all the senses.

Modern Westerners became more familiar with this particular sermon of the Buddha's when its title was used to head Section III of T. S. Eliot's "The Waste Land," one of the seminal poems of the twentieth century, its metaphor a landscape of moral bleakness and its final word *burning*. The Buddha's message in this 2,500-year-old speech is both more positive and intellectually accessible.

□　□　□

All things, O priests, are on fire. And what, O priests, are all these things which are on fire?

The eye, O priests, is on fire; forms are on fire; eye-consciousness is on fire; impressions received by the eye are on fire; and whatever sensation, pleasant, unpleasant, or indifferent, originates in dependence on impressions received by the eye, that also is on fire.

And with what are these on fire?

With the fire of passion, say I, with the fire of hatred, with the fire of infatuation; with birth, old age, death, sorrow, lamentation, misery, grief, and despair are they on fire.

The ear is on fire; sounds are on fire; . . . the nose is on fire; odors are on fire; . . . the tongue is on fire; tastes are on fire; . . . the body is on fire; things tangible are on fire; . . . the mind is on fire; ideas are on fire; . . . mind-consciousness is on fire; impressions received by the mind are on fire; and whatever sensation, pleasant, unpleasant, or indifferent, originates in dependence on impressions received by the mind, that also is on fire.

And with what are these on fire?

With the fire of passion, say I, with the fire of hatred, with the fire of infatuation; with birth, old age, death, sorrow, lamentation, misery, grief, and despair are they on fire.

Perceiving this, O priests, the learned and noble disciple conceives an aversion for the eye, conceives an aversion for forms, conceives an aversion for eye-consciousness, conceives an aversion for the impressions received by the eye; and whatever sensation, pleasant, unpleasant, or indifferent, originates in dependence on impressions received by the eye, for that also he conceives an aversion. Conceives an aversion for the ear, conceives an aversion for sounds, . . . conceives an aversion for the nose, conceives an aversion for odors, . . . conceives an aversion for the tongue, conceives an aversion for tastes, . . . conceives an aversion for the body, conceives an aversion for things tangible, . . . conceives an aversion for the mind, conceives an aversion for ideas, conceives an aversion for mind-consciousness, conceives an aversion for the impressions received by the mind; and whatever sensation, pleasant, unpleasant, or indifferent, originates in dependence on impressions received by the mind, for this also he conceives an aversion. And in conceiving this aversion, he becomes divested of passion, and by the absence of passion he becomes free, and when he is free he becomes aware that he is free; and he knows that rebirth is exhausted, that he has lived the holy life, that he has done what it behooved him to do, and that he is no more for this world. . . . ■

Jesus of Nazareth Delivers the Sermon on the Mount

"JUDGE not, that ye be not judged."

PREACHED IN THE THIRD DECADE OF THE FIRST CENTURY A.D., the Sermon on the Mount remains the single most important discourse on Christian law and living. It was delivered by Jesus of Nazareth, a Jewish teacher whom Christians recognize as Jesus Christ, the Messiah and Son of God. The Greek *Christos* literally means "anointed," and *Christ* was originally a title, not a proper name.

Recounted in the Gospel of Matthew, the first book of the New Testament, the Sermon on the Mount was delivered to Jesus' disciples and the multitude. The sermon reinterprets the laws of the Old Testament in light of Christian doctrine and contains two of the central statements of Christian ethics. First, the Beatitudes express a promise of blessings to come; these sayings take the rhetorical form of anaphora, repeating the opening words "Blessed are. . . ." Also invoked in the sermon is the Lord's Prayer, an apostrophe directed to "Our Father, which art in heaven."

Among the many figures of speech used in the Sermon on the Mount, foremost is metaphor. Listeners are identified as "the salt of the earth" and "the light of the world," the latter image introducing what has become the frequently revived image of "a city that is set on a hill." The elegant and slightly archaic English of the King James Version supports the sermon's extended use of parallel structure ("Ask, and it shall be given you; seek, and ye shall find; knock, and it shall be opened unto you") and of antithesis ("Judge not, that ye be not judged").

□   □   □

Blessed are the poor in spirit: for theirs is the kingdom of heaven. Blessed are they that mourn: for they shall be comforted.

Blessed are the meek: for they shall inherit the earth.

Blessed are they which do hunger and thirst after righteousness: for they shall be filled.

Blessed are the merciful: for they shall obtain mercy.

Blessed are the pure in heart: for they shall see God.

Blessed are the peacemakers: for they shall be called the children of God.

Blessed are they which are persecuted for righteousness' sake: for theirs is the kingdom of heaven.

Blessed are ye, when men shall revile you, and persecute you, and shall say all manner of evil against you falsely, for my sake.

Rejoice, and be exceeding glad: for great is your reward in heaven: for so persecuted they the prophets which were before you.

Ye are the salt of the earth: but if the salt have lost his savor, wherewith shall it be salted? It is thenceforth good for nothing, but to be cast out, and to be trodden under foot of men.

Ye are the light of the world. A city that is set on a hill cannot be hid.

Neither do men light a candle, and put it under a bushel, but on a candlestick; and it giveth light unto all that are in the house.

Let your light so shine before men, that they may see your good works, and glorify your Father which is in heaven.

Think not that I am come to destroy the law, or the prophets: I am not come to destroy, but to fulfill.

For verily I say unto you, "Till heaven and earth pass, one jot or one tittle shall in no wise pass from the law, till all be fulfilled."

Whosoever therefore shall break one of these least commandments, and shall teach men so, he shall be called the least in the kingdom of heaven: but whosoever shall do and teach them, the same shall be called great in the kingdom of heaven.

For I say unto you, "Except your righteousness shall exceed the righteousness of the scribes and Pharisees, ye shall in no case enter into the kingdom of heaven."

Ye have heard that it was said by them of old time, "Thou shalt not kill"; and whosoever shall kill shall be in danger of the judgment.

But I say unto you, "Whosoever is angry with his brother without a cause shall be in danger of the judgment: and whosoever shall say to his brother, 'Raca,' shall be in danger of the council: but whosoever shall say, 'Thou fool,' shall be in danger of hellfire."

Therefore if thou bring thy gift to the altar, and there rememberest that thy brother hath ought against thee; leave there thy gift before the altar, and go thy way; first be reconciled to thy brother, and then come and offer thy gift.

Agree with thine adversary quickly, while thou art in the way with him; lest at any time the adversary deliver thee to the judge, and the judge deliver thee to the officer, and thou be cast into prison. Verily I say unto thee, "Thou shalt by no means come out thence, till thou has paid the uttermost farthing."

Ye have heard that it was said by them of old time, "Thou shalt not commit adultery." But I say unto you, "Whosoever looketh on a woman to lust after her hath committed adultery with her already in his heart. And if thy right eye offend thee, pluck it out, and cast it from thee: for it is profitable for thee that one of thy members should perish, and not that thy whole body should be cast into hell. And if thy right hand offend thee, cut it off, and cast it from thee: for it is profitable for thee that one of thy members should perish, and not that thy whole body should be cast into hell."

It hath been said, "Whosoever shall put away his wife, let him give her a writing of divorcement." But I say unto you, "Whosoever shall put away his wife, saving for the cause of fornication, causeth her to commit adultery: and whosoever shall marry her that is divorced committeth adultery."

Again, ye have heard that it hath been said by them of old time, "Thou shalt not forswear thyself, but shalt perform unto the Lord thine oaths."

But I say unto you, "Swear not at all; neither by heaven; for it is God's throne: nor by the earth; for it is his footstool: neither by Jerusalem; for it is the city of the great King. Neither shalt thou swear by thy head, because thou canst not make one hair white or black. But let your communication be, 'Yea, yea'; 'Nay, nay': for whatsoever is more than these cometh of evil."

Ye have heard that it hath been said, "An eye for an eye, and a tooth for a tooth." But I say unto you, "Resist not evil: but whosoever shall smite thee on thy right cheek, turn to him the other also. And if any man will sue thee at the law, and take away thy coat, let him have thy cloak also. And whosoever shall compel thee to go a mile, go with him twain. Give to him that asketh thee, and from him that would borrow of thee turn not thou away."

Ye have heard that it hath been said, "Thou shalt love thy neighbor, and hate thine enemy." But I say unto you, "Love your enemies, bless them that curse you, do good to them that hate you, and pray for them which despitefully use you, and persecute you; that ye may be the children of your Father which is in heaven: for he maketh his sun to rise on the evil and on the good, and sendeth rain on the just and on the unjust." For if ye love them which love you, what reward have ye? Do not even the publicans the same? And if ye salute your brethren only, what do ye more than others? Do not even the publicans so? Be ye therefore perfect, even as your Father which is in heaven is perfect.

Take heed that ye do not your alms before men, to be seen of them: otherwise ye have no reward of your Father which is in heaven. Therefore when thou doest thine alms, do not sound a trumpet before thee, as the hypocrites do in the synagogues and in the streets, that they may have glory of men. Verily I say unto you, "They have their reward." But when thou doest alms, let not thy left hand know what thy right hand doeth: that thine alms may be in secret: and thy Father which seeth in secret himself shall reward thee openly.

And when thou prayest. thou shalt not be as the hypocrites are: for they love to pray standing in the synagogues and in the corners of the streets, that they may be seen of men. Verily I say unto you, "They have their reward." But thou, when thou prayest, enter into thy closet, and when thou has shut thy door, pray to thy Father which is in secret; and thy Father which seeth in secret shall reward thee openly. But when ye pray, use not vain repetitions, as the heathen do: for they think that they shall be heard for their much speaking. Be not ye therefore like unto them: for your Father knoweth what things ye have need of, before ye ask him. After this manner therefore pray ye:

Our Father which art in heaven,
Hallowed be thy name.
Thy kingdom come.
Thy will be done in earth, as it is in heaven.
Give us this day our daily bread.
And forgive us our debts, as we forgive our debtors.
And lead us not into temptation, but deliver us from evil: For thine is the kingdom, and the power, and the glory, for ever. Amen.

For if ye forgive men their trespasses, your heavenly Father will also forgive you: but if ye forgive not men their trespasses, neither will your Father forgive your trespasses.

Moreover when ye fast, be not, as the hypocrites, of a sad countenance: for they disfigure their faces, that they may appear unto men to fast. Verily I say unto you, "They have their reward." But thou, when thou fastest, anoint thine head, and wash thy face; that thou appear not unto men to fast. but unto thy Father which is in secret: and thy Father, which seeth in secret shall reward thee openly.

Lay not up for yourselves treasures upon earth, where moth and rust doth corrupt, and where thieves break through and steal: But lay up for yourselves treasures in heaven, where neither moth nor rust doth corrupt, and where thieves do not break through nor steal. For where your treasure is, there will your heart be also.

The light of the body is the eye: if therefore thine eye be single, thy whole body shall be full of light. But if thine eye be evil, thy whole body shall be full of darkness. If therefore the light that is in thee be darkness, how great is that darkness!

No man can serve two masters: for either he will hate the one, and love the other; or else he will hold to the one, and despise the other. Ye cannot serve God and Mammon.

Therefore I say unto you, "Take no thought for your life, what ye shall eat, or what ye shall drink; nor yet for your body, what ye shall put on." Is not the life more than meat, and the body than raiment? Behold the fowls of the air: for they sow not, neither do they reap, nor gather into barns; yet your heavenly Father feedeth them. Are ye not much better than they? Which of you by taking thought can add one cubit unto his stature?

And why take ye thought for raiment? Consider the lilies of the field, how they grow; they toil not, neither do they spin: and yet I say unto you that even Solomon in all his glory was not arrayed like one of these.

Wherefore, if God so clothe the grass of the field, which today is, and tomorrow is cast into the oven, shall he not much more clothe you, O ye of little faith?

Therefore take no thought, saying, "What shall we eat?" or, "What shall we drink?" or, "Wherewithal shall we be clothed?" (For after all these things do the Gentiles seek): for your heavenly Father knoweth that ye have need of all these things. But seek ye first the kingdom of God, and his righteousness; and all these things shall be added unto you.

Take therefore no thought for the morrow: for the morrow shall take thought for the things of itself. Sufficient unto the day is the evil thereof.

Judge not, that ye be not judged. For with what judgment ye judge, ye shall be judged: and with what measure ye mete, it shall be measured to you again. And why beholdest thou the mote that is in thy brother's eye, but considerest not the beam that is in thine own eye?

Or how wilt thou say to thy brother, "Let me pull out the mote out of thine eye"; and, behold, a beam is in thine own eye? Thou hypocrite, first cast out the beam out of thine own eye; and then shalt thou see clearly to cast out the mote out of thy brother's eye.

Give not that which is holy unto the dogs, neither cast ye your pearls before swine, lest they trample them under their feet, and turn again and rend you.

Ask, and it shall be given you; seek, and ye shall find; knock, and it shall be opened unto you: For every one that asketh receiveth; and he that seeketh findeth; and to him that knocketh it shall be opened.

Or what man is there of you, whom if his son ask bread, will he give him a stone? Or if he ask a fish, will he give him a serpent? If ye then, being evil, know how to give good gifts unto your children, how much more shall your Father which is in heaven give good things to them that ask him? Therefore all things whatsoever ye would that men should do to you, do ye even so to them: for this is the law and the prophets.

Enter ye in at the strait gate: for wide is the gate, and broad is the way, that leadeth to destruction, and many there be which go in thereat: because strait is the gate, and narrow is the way, which leadeth unto life, and few there be that find it.

Beware of false prophets, which come to you in sheep's clothing, but inwardly they are ravening wolves. Ye shall know them by their fruits. Do men gather grapes of thorns, or figs of thistles?

Even so every good tree bringeth forth good fruit; but a corrupt tree bringeth forth evil fruit. A good tree cannot bring forth evil fruit, neither can a corrupt tree bring forth good fruit. Every tree that bringeth not forth good fruit is hewn down, and cast into the fire. Wherefore by their fruits ye shall know them.

Not every one that saith unto me, "Lord, Lord," shall enter into the kingdom of heaven; but he that doeth the will of my Father which is in heaven. Many will say to me in that day, "Lord, Lord, have we not prophesied in thy name? And in thy name have cast out devils? And in thy name done many wonderful works?" And then will I profess unto them, "I never knew you: depart from me, ye that work iniquity."

Therefore whosoever heareth these sayings of mine, and doeth them, I will liken him unto a wise man, which built his house upon a rock; and the rain descended, and the floods came and the winds blew, and beat upon that house; and it fell not: for it was founded upon a rock. And every one that heareth these sayings of mine, and doeth them not, shall be likened unto a foolish man, which built his house upon the sand: and the rain descended, and the floods came, and the winds blew, and beat upon that house; and it fell: and great was the fall of it. ∎

Saint Francis Preaches to the Birds

"THEREFORE, my little sisters, beware of the sin of ingratitude. . . ."

BAPTIZED AS JOHN IN 1182, this saint became known as Francis of Assisi from his nickname of Francesco, "the Frenchman." Although he was born in Assisi, a town in central Italy, his mother's family was of French descent, and he knew some French as well as Latin.

When he was twenty-three, Francis sought a military career. He intended to join an army supporting the pope's cause in southeastern Italy, but he became ill at Spoleto and never reached the fighting. While ill, he received a "heavenly visitation," a voice in a dream asking him, "Why do you desert the Lord for his vassal?"

After serving as a repairer of run-down churches and a nurse of lepers, Francis started a religious order dedicated to a strict renunciation of the material values of this world and a literal adherence to the Christian Gospel. His followers numbered only eleven in 1209, but his joyous preaching and asceticism increased the numbers a decade later to more than five thousand. This was the ebullient message attributed to him: "Lord, make me an instrument of your peace. Where there is hatred, let me sow love; where there is injury, pardon; where there is doubt, faith; where there is despair, hope; where there is darkness, light; and where there is sadness, joy."

The faith of Francis in the brotherhood of men and nature led him to preach the Gospel, or "good news," to all of God's creatures, great and small. In this sermon, his personification of birds as "my little sisters" introduces the evidence of God's love for them and, by extension, argues the need for a human posture of gratefulness toward the Creator.

☐ ☐ ☐

My little sisters, the birds, much bounden are ye unto God, your creator, and always in every place ought ye to praise him, for that he hath given you liberty to fly about everywhere, and hath also given you double and triple raiment; moreover he preserved your seed in the ark of Noah, that your race might not perish out of the world; still more are ye beholden to him for the element of the air which he hath appointed for you; beyond all this, ye sow not, neither do you reap; and God feedeth you, and giveth you the streams and fountains for your drink; the mountains and the valleys for your refuge and the high trees whereon to make your nests; and because ye know not how to spin or sew, God clotheth you, you and your children; wherefore your Creator loveth you much, seeing that he hath bestowed on you so many benefits; and therefore, my little sisters, beware of the sin of ingratitude, and study always to give praises unto God. ■

John Wyclif Gives the Sixth Sunday Gospel after Easter

"ALL men should beware . . . the fiend. . . ."

THE "MORNING STAR OF THE REFORMATION," John Wyclif (or Wycliffe) may now be best known for having translated the Bible into English; his translation was the basis for religious instruction for over two centuries, until the King James Version. (He is also known to phrase detectives as the coiner, or at least the first user in print, of "by hook or by crook," in one of his controversial tracts. Tenants of manors were allowed to take as much firewood as could be cut with a crook, or loose timber that could be pulled from the tree by a hook; Wyclif used the phrase to mean "one way or the other," as we do today.)

As a religious reformer and doctor of theology, however, he gained renown in his time for his preaching, despite what were considered heretical notions about the need for the reform of papal authority, ideas expressed both in his writings and in his lectures. When his controversial theses were denounced by Oxford University in 1381, Wyclif added to the controversy by choosing to appeal not to the pope but to the king.

Many of the radical views that informed his preaching may be glimpsed in his remarks on the Gospel for the sixth Sunday after Easter. In this sermon, Wyclif questions papal control and favors an untraditional doctrinal position—that the Holy Ghost is not of God alone but of the Father and the Son.

The formal style, complicated for us by obsolete or archaic words such as "sclaundred" (offended) and "cautelies" (craftiness or trickery), lends solemnity to Wyclif's argument. With quotations from Jesus interspersed throughout the message, Wyclif carefully couches his controversial position in what "say some men." The message against the pope, however, comes across clearly, ending with exhortations to condemn false priests and to beware the fiend or devil, the personification of evil.

□   □   □

Christ telleth his disciples of coming of the Comforter, the which is the Holy Ghost, and what life they shall after lead. And each man should con here this lore, for then he may be soul's leech, and wit, by signs of his life, whether his soul be sick or whole.

Lord! if a physician learneth diligently his signs, in veins, in pulse, and other things, whether a man's body be whole; how much more should he know such signs that tell help of man's soul, and how he hath him to God. Although such things be privy and pass worldly wit of men, natheless, the Holy Ghost telleth men some of such signs, and maketh them more certain than man can judge a bodily health. And, for we should kindly desire for to know the soul's state, therefore the Holy Ghost, that teacheth us to know these signs, is cleped a comforter, passing other comforters. And as a man's soul is better than the body, and endless good passeth temporal good, so this knowing of the soul passeth other man's cunning.

Christ saith thus to his disciples, "When this comforter shall come that I shall send you of the Father, Ghost of truth that cometh forth of him, he shall also bear witness of me; and ye shall also bear witness, for ye be with me always from the beginning of my preaching." But here may Greeks be moved to trow that the Holy Ghost cometh not forth but of the

Father and not of Christ that is his Son; for the one saith Christ and in this Gospel leaveth the other.

And it seemeth to some men, if this were truth that should be trowed, God would lightly tell this truth as he telleth other that we trow; and else it were presumption to charge the church with this truth, since neither authority of God, nor reason, teacheth that this is so; and all belief needful to men is told them in the law of God. Here me thinketh that Latins sinned somewhat in this point, for many other points are now more needful to the church; as it were more needful to wit whether all the church hang in the power of the pope, as it is said commonly, and whether men that shall be saved be needed here to shrive them to priests, and thus of many decrees that the pope hath lightly ordained. But me thinketh that it is so that this Ghost cometh both of the Father and of the Son, and these persons be one cause of him; and me thinketh, to no intent should Christ say, he sendeth his Ghost, or that this Ghost is his, but if this Ghost come of him.

And to this that Greeks say, that Christ leaveth this word, certainly so doth he many other for certain cause, and yet we trow them; as Christ saith that his lore is not his, for it is principally of his Father; and yet we trow that it is his, but the will is in his Father. So we believe that the will by which the Father loveth the Son cometh of wit that is in the Son, but principally of God's power. And in this word Christ teacheth us to do algates worship to God.

And thus these Greeks may not prove that we trow false in this belief, or that Christ left this truth, without cause to tell it thus: for by this that Christ saith, the Holy Ghost came of his Father, and leaveth thus the coming of him, He stoppeth the pride of the Church and teacheth men to worship God. But when he saith that he sendeth the Holy Ghost to his disciples, and all that his Father hath is his, he teacheth clearly that this Ghost cometh of him; and otherwise should Christ not speak.

And thus Latins are to blame, for they leave needful truth, and deepen them in other truth, that is now not so needful. And thus say some men that the bishop of Rome, that they clepe head of the church and thereto pope and Christ's vicar, doth more harm to the Church of Christ than doth vicar of Thomas in India, or vicar of Paul in Greece, or the sultan of Babylon. For the root of which he came, that is doing of the church and the haying of the emperor, is not full holy ground, but envenomed with sin. But this venom first was little, and hid by the cautelies of the fiend, but now is grown too much and too hard to amend. So it is that each apostle was obedient to each other, as Peter obeysed unto Paul when he reproved him; and thus think some men that they should obeyse to the pope, but no more than Christ biddeth, no more than to other priests, but if he teach better Christ's will and more profit to men; and so of all his ordinance, but if it be grounded in God's law, set no more price thereby than by law of the emperor. Men should say much in this matter, and other men should do in deed; but men would hold them heretics, as the fiend's limbs did Christ. And so thick are his members that whoso holdeth with Christ's law, he shall be shent many ways and algates with lies.

And this telleth Christ before unto his Apostles, to make them strong and arm them against such persecutions. "These things," saith he, "I spake to you, that ye be not sclaundred." He is sclaundred that is let by word or deed, so that his right will fall down from his wit; and so if a man be pursued and suffer it patiently, he is not sclaundred, although men sin against him.

The first pursuit against Christ shall be of false priests, not alone letting the members of Christ to rule the people in churches, as curates should do, but putting them out of church as cursed men or heretics. And therefore saith Christ that they shall make you "without synagogues." But yet shall more woodness come after this, for they procure the people, both more and less, to kill Christ's disciples for hope of great meed. And hereto Christ saith certainly of this matter, "That hour is come that each man that killeth thus good men, shall judge him to do God meedful obedience." And to this end procure friars Antichrist disciples, that well nigh it is thus now among Christian men. Some men are summoned to Rome and there put in prison, and some are cried as heretics among the common people; and over this, as men say, friars kill their own brethren, and procure men of the world to kill men that say them truth. And one dread letteth them that they start not to more woodness, for they defend that it is lawful and meedful, priests for to fight in cause that they feign God's; and so if their party be stronger than seculars, they may move these priests to fight against these gentlemen. And as they have robbed them of temporal goods, so they will deprive them of the sword as unable, and say that such fighting should best fall to priests. Thus had priests this sword before Christ came, and they drowned so far out of religion of God that they had killed Christ, head of holy church.

All men should beware of the cautelies of the fiend, for he sleepeth not, casting false wiles, and all these do the fiend's limbs; "for they know not the Father and his Son" by properties of them. The fiend blindeth them so in worldly purpose, that they know not strength of God nor wisdom of his bidding; for faith faileth unto them that they look not afar, but thing that is nigh their eye, as beasts without reason. "All this hath Christ spoke to his disciples that when time cometh of them, they should have mind that he hath said them these perils to come." And the Holy Ghost moveth ever some men to study God's law and have mind of this wit; and so love of God's law and sad savour therein is token to men that they are God's children, but yet of their end are uncertain. ■

Religious Scourge Savonarola Demands Repentance from the Citizens of Florence

"To thy tongue say, 'Speak no more evil.'"

THE FIERY WORDS OF GIROLAMO SAVONAROLA, the most forceful of Italy's religious reformers in the fifteenth century, led to a "bonfire of the vanities." In those public conflagrations of 1497, devoted followers of Savonarola burned items considered immoral and representative of the gaudy excesses of life in Florence; books, masks, and other "vanities" (trivial or frivolous objects) fueled the religious flames as Savonarola exhorted his listeners to repent and find forgiveness in a new austerity.

Savonarola had begun his formal religious training in the most severe of Dominican orders. Sent to Florence, the cultural center that became the cradle of the Renaissance, he sought to reform what he considered the moral corruption of both church and state. Prophesying divine wrath, Savonarola used biblical allusions and straightforward, unadorned words to denounce the Medici and convey the inevitability of purging that he expected divine wrath to bring.

After charging the pope with having achieved his election through simony, or the corrupt sale of preferments, he was excommunicated in 1497, and a year later he was tried for heresy, with severe cross-examination and torture that supposedly extorted from him a confession of false prophecy. Savonarola was hanged and then burned at the stake.

In his May 12, 1496, sermon on the Feast of the Ascension, Savonarola excoriated the vices and wickedness that he saw everywhere. Especially forceful are the parallel passages that conclude the sermon, as Savonarola instructs followers on addressing their eyes, ears, tongues, and hands as ways to preach to themselves.

□   □   □

In everything am I oppressed; even the spiritual power is against me with Peter's mighty key. Narrow is my path and full of trouble; like Balaam's ass, I must throw myself on the ground and cry, "See, here I am; I am ready to die for the truth." But when Balaam beat his fallen beast, it said to him, "What have I done to thee?" So I say to you, "Come here and tell me: what have I done to you? Why do you beat me? I have spoken the truth to you; I have warned you to choose a virtuous life; I have led many souls to Christ." But you answer, "Thou hast spoken evil of us, therefore thou shouldst suffer the stripes thou deservest." But I named no one; I only blamed your vices in general. If you have sinned, be angry with yourselves, not with me. I name none of you, but if the sins I have mentioned are without question yours, then they and not I make you known.

As the smitten beast asked Balaam, so I ask you, "Tell me, am I not your ass? And do you not know that I have been obedient to you up to this very moment, that I have even done what my superiors have commanded, and have always behaved myself peaceably?" You know this, and because I am now so entirely different, you may well believe that a great cause drives me to it. Many knew me as I was at first; if I remained so I could have had as much honor as I wanted. I lived six years among you, and now I speak otherwise; nevertheless I announce to you the truth that is well known. You see in what sorrows and what opposition I must now live, and I can say with Jeremiah, "O my mother, that thou hast borne me a man of strife and contention to the whole earth!" But where is a father or a mother that can say I have led their son into sin;

one that can say I have ruined her husband or his wife? Everybody knows my manner of life; therefore it is right for you to believe that I speak the truth which everybody knows. You think that it is impossible for a man to do what the faith I have preached tells him to do: with God it would be easy for you.

The ass alone saw the angel; the others did not, so open your eyes. Thank God, many have them open. You have seen many learned men whom you thought wise, and they have withstood our cause: now they believe; many noted masters who were hard and proud against us: now humility casts them down. You have also seen many women turn from their vanity to simplicity; vicious youths who are now improved and conduct themselves in a new way. Many, indeed, have received this doctrine with humility. That doctrine has stood firm, no matter how attacked with the intention of showing that it was a doctrine opposed to Christ. God does that to manifest his wisdom, to show how it finally overcomes all other wisdom. And he is willing that his servants be spoken against that they may show their patience and humility, and for the sake of his love not be afraid of martyrdom.

O ye men and women, I bid you to this truth; let those who are in captivity contradict you as much as they will, God will come and oppose their pride. Ye proud, however, if you do not turn about and become better, then will the sword and the pestilence fall upon you; with famine and war will Italy be turned upside down. I foretell you this because I am sure of it: if I were not, I would not mention it. Open your eyes as Balaam opened his eyes when the angel said to him, "Had it not been for thine ass, I would have slain thee." So I say to you, ye captives, "Had it not been for the good and their preaching, it would have been woe unto you." Balaam said, "If this way is not good, I will return." You say likewise, you would turn back to God, if your way is not good. And to the angel you say as Balaam said, "What wilt thou that we should do?" The angel answers thee as he answered Balaam, "Thou shalt not curse this people, but shalt say what I put in thy mouth." But in thy mouth he puts the warning that thou shouldst do good, convince one another of the divine truth, and bear evil manfully. For it is the life of a Christian to do good and to bear wrong and to continue steadfast unto death, and this is the Gospel, which we, according to the text of the Gospel for today, shall preach in all the world.

"What wilt thou have of us, brother?" you ask. I desire that you serve Christ with zeal and not with sloth and indifference. I desire that you do not mourn, but in thankfulness raise your hands to heaven, whenever your brother or your son enters the service of Christ. The time is come when Christ will work not only in you but through you and in others; whoever hears, let him say, "Come, brother." Let one draw the other. Turn about, thou who thinkest that thou art of a superior mind and therefore canst not accept the faith. If I could only explain this whole Gospel to thee word for word, I would then scourge thy forehead and prove to thee that the faith could not be false and that Christ is thy God who is enthroned in heaven, and waits for thee. Or dost thou believe? Where are thy works? Why dost thou delay about them?

Hear this: There was once a monk who spoke to a distinguished man about the faith and got him to answer why he did not believe. He answered thus: "You yourself do not believe, for if you believed you would show other works." Therefore, to you also I say, If you believe, where are your works? Your faith is something everyone knows, for everyone knows that Christ was put to death by the Jews, and that everywhere men pray to him. The whole world knows that his glory has not been spread by force and weapons but by poor fishermen. O wise man, do you think the poor fishermen were not clever enough for this? Where they worked, there they made hearts better; where they could not work, there men remained bad; and therefore was the faith true and from God. The signs which the Lord had promised followed their teaching: in his name they drove out the devil; they spoke in new tongues; if they drank any deadly drink, they received therefrom no harm. Even if these wonders had not occurred, there would have been the wonder of wonders, that poor fishermen without any miracle could accomplish so great a work as the faith. It came from God, and so is Christ true and Christ is thy God, who is in heaven and awaits thee.

You say you believe the Gospel. but you do not believe me. But the purer anything is, so much the nearer it stands to its end and purpose. The Christian life purifies the heart and places it very near to the truth. To the Christian life will I lead you, if you would have the knowledge of the truth. If I had wished to deceive you, why should I have given you as the chief of my gifts the means of discovering my fraud? I would be verily a fool to try to impose upon you with a falsehood which you would soon detect; only because I offered you the truth, did I call you. Come here, I fear you not; the closer you examine, the clearer the truth will become to you.

There are some, however, who are ashamed of the cross of Jesus Christ, and say, "If we should believe that, we should be despised everywhere, especially by the wisest." But if you would know the truth, look only on the lives of those who would have to cry woe on their unbelief if they should be measured by deeds. If you are ashamed of the cross, the

Lord was not ashamed to bear that cross for you, and to die on that cross for you. Be not ashamed of his service and of the defense of the truth. Look at the servants of the devil who are not ashamed in the open places, in the palaces, and everywhere to speak evil and to revile us. Bear then a little shame only for your Lord; for whoever follows him will, according to our Gospel, in his name drive out the devil; that is, he will drive out his sins and lead a virtuous life; he will drive out serpents; he will throw out the lazy who come into the houses, and say evil things under the pretense of righteousness, and so are like poisonous serpents. You will see how children can withstand them with the truth of God and drive them away. If a believer drinks anything deadly it will not hurt him: this deadly drink is the false doctrines of the lazy, from whom, as you contend with them, a little comes also to you. But he who stands unharmed in the faith, cries to you, "See that you do good; seek God's glory, not your own." He that does that is of the truth, and remains unharmed. The Lord says further of the faithful, "They shall lay their hands on the sick and shall heal them." The hands are the works, and the good lay such hands on the weak that they may support them when they totter. Do I not teach you according to the Gospel? Why do you hesitate and go not into the service of the Lord? Do you ask me still what you ought to do? I will, in conclusion, tell you.

Look to Christ, and you will find that all he says concerns faith. Ask the Apostle; he speaks of nothing else than of faith. If you have the ground of all, if you have faith, you will always do what is good. Without faith man always falls into sin. You must seek faith in order to be good, or else your faith will become false. Christ commanded his disciples to preach the Gospel to all the world, and your wise men call a man a little world, a microcosm. So then, preach to yourself, O man, woman, and child. Three parts the world has in you also. Preach first of all to your knowledge, and say to it, "If you draw near this truth, you will have much faith; wherefore do you hesitate to use it?" To your will, say, "Thou seest that everything passes away; therefore love not the world, love Christ." Thereupon turn to the second part of your world, and say to it, "Be thankful, O my memory, for the mercies God has shown thee, that thou thinkest not of the things of this world but of the mercy of thy creation, and thy redemption through the blood of the Son of God." Then go to the third part, to thy imagination, and proclaim to it, "Set nothing before my eyes but my death, bring nothing before me but the Crucified, embrace him, fly to him." Then go through all the cities of thy world, and preach to them.

First say to thine eyes, "Look not on vanity." To thy ears say, "Listen not to the words of the lazy, but only to the words of Jesus." To thy tongue say, "Speak no more evil." For thy tongue is as a great rock that rolls from the summit of a mountain, and at first falls slowly, then ever faster and more furiously. It begins with gentle murmuring, then it utters small sins, and then greater, until it finally breaks forth in open blasphemy. To thy palate say, "It is necessary that we do a little penance." In all thy senses be clean, and turn to the Lord, for he it is who will give you correction and purity. To thy hands say, "Do good and give alms"; and let thy feet go in the good way.

Our reformation has begun in the Spirit of God, if you take it to heart that each one has to preach to himself. Then will we in the name of Jesus drive out the devils of temptation. Yes, call upon Jesus as often as temptation approaches: call upon him a hundred times and believe firmly, and the temptation will depart. Then will we speak with new tongues; we will speak with God. We shall drive away serpents; the enticement of the senses are these serpents. If we drink anything deadly, it will not hurt us; if anger and lust arise in us, at the name of Jesus they will have to give way. We shall lay our hands upon the sick and heal them; with good deeds shall we strengthen the weak soul. If thou feelest thy weakness, flee to God, and he will strengthen; therefore he is thy only refuge. He is thy Savior and thy Lord, who went into the heavens to prepare a place for thee, and to wait thee there. What do you intend to do? Go and follow Jesus, who is praised from everlasting to everlasting. Amen. ■

John Calvin Preaches on Suffering Persecution

"A hundred thousand deaths would not suffice for a small portion of our misdeeds!"

A STERN MORAL CODE IS THE BASIS OF CALVINISM, the eponymous term for the doctrines espoused by John Calvin and his followers. The French-born leader of the Protestant Reformation in the sixteenth century supported ideas of predestination (salvation or damnation of souls foreordained by God), the controlling power of grace, and the supreme authority of the Scriptures.

Such rigor in religious thought, however, was not widely welcomed, and Calvin was essentially banished from Paris in 1533 and from Geneva in 1538. He was called back to Geneva in 1541, and that city became the center of his labors to establish a rigid moral discipline and to spread the faith. Strictly enforced laws against drunkenness, gambling, and even disrespectful singing and dancing caused the opposition to Calvin to grow.

Among Calvin's most significant sermons is his message on suffering persecution. Recalling the words of the apostle Paul ("We are called and appointed to suffer"), Calvin argues against values based in worldly pleasures. Instead, he upholds, through a series of rhetorical questions and parallel phrases ("no toil, no pain, no trouble"), the necessity of enduring earthly persecutions and trials to be deserving of God's grace.

☐   ☐   ☐

The apostle says, "Let us go forth from the city after the Lord Jesus, bearing his reproach." In the first place he reminds us, although the swords should not be drawn over us nor the fires kindled to burn us, that we cannot be truly united to the Son of God while we are rooted in this world. Wherefore, a Christian, even in repose, must always have one foot lifted to march to battle, and not only so, but he must have his affections withdrawn from the world although his body is dwelling in it. Grant that this at first sight seems to us hard; still, we must be satisfied with the words of Saint Paul "We are called and appointed to suffer." As if he had said, Such is our condition as Christians; this is the road by which we must go if we would follow Christ.

Meanwhile, to solace our infirmity and mitigate the vexation and sorrow which persecution might cause us, a good reward is held forth: in suffering for the cause of God, we are walking step by step after the Son of God and have him for our guide. Were it simply said that to be Christians we must pass through all the insults of the world boldly, to meet death at all times and in whatever way God may be pleased to appoint, we might apparently have some pretext for replying, It is a strange road to go at a peradventure. But when we are commanded to follow the Lord Jesus, his guidance is too good and honorable to be refused.

Are we so delicate as to be unwilling to endure anything? Then we must renounce the grace of God by which he has called us to the hope of salvation. For there are two things which cannot be separated—to be members of Christ, and to be tried by many afflictions. We certainly ought to prize such a conformity to the Son of God much more than we do. It is true that in the world's judgment there is disgrace in suffering for the Gospel. But since we know that unbelievers are blind, ought we not to have better eyes than they? It is ignominy to suffer from those who occupy the seat of justice, but Saint Paul shows us by his example that we have to glory in scourgings for Jesus Christ, as marks by which God recognizes us and avows us for his own. And we know what Saint Luke narrates of Peter and John; namely, that they rejoiced to have been "counted worthy to suffer infamy and reproach for the name of the Lord Jesus."

Ignominy and dignity are two opposites: so says the world, which. being infatuated, judges against all reason, and in this way converts the glory of God into dishonor. But, on our part, let us not refuse to be vilified as concerns the world, in order to be honored before God and his angels. We see what pains the ambitious take to receive the commands of a king, and what a boast they make of it. The Son of God presents his commands to us, and everyone stands back! Tell me, pray, whether in so doing are we worthy of having anything in common with him? There is nothing here to attract our sensual nature, but such, notwithstanding, are the true escutcheons of nobility in the heavens. Imprisonment, exile, evil report, imply in men's imagination whatever is to be vituperated; but what hinders us from viewing things as God judges and declares them, save our unbelief? Wherefore let the name of the Son of God have all the weight with us which it deserves, that we may learn to count it honor when he stamps his marks upon us. If we act otherwise, our ingratitude is insupportable.

Were God to deal with us according to our deserts, would he not have just cause to chastise us daily in a thousand ways? Nay, more, a hundred thousand deaths would not suffice for a small portion of our misdeeds! Now, if in his infinite goodness he puts all our faults under his foot and abolishes them and, instead of punishing us according to our demerit, devises an admirable means to convert our afflictions into honor and a special privilege, inasmuch as through them we are taken into partnership with his Son, must it not be said, when we disdain such a happy state, that we have indeed made little progress in Christian doctrine?

It were easy indeed for God to crown us at once without requiring us to sustain any combats; but as it is his pleasure that until the end of the world Christ shall reign in the midst of his enemies, so it is also his pleasure that we, being placed in the midst of them, shall suffer their oppression and violence till he deliver us. I know, indeed, that the flesh kicks when it is to be brought to this point, but still the will of God must have the mastery. If we feel some repugnance in ourselves it need not surprise us; for it is only too natural for us to shun the cross. Still, let us not fail to surmount it, knowing that God accepts our obedience, provided we bring all our feelings and wishes into captivity and make them subject to him.

In ancient times vast numbers of people, to obtain a simple crown of leaves, refused no toil, no pain, no trouble; nay, it even cost them nothing to die, and yet every one of them fought for a peradventure, not knowing whether he was to gain or lose the prize. God holds forth to us the immortal crown by which we may become partakers of his glory. He does not mean us to fight a haphazard, but all of us have a promise of the prize for which we strive. Have we any cause, then, to decline the struggle? Do we think it has been said in vain, "If we die with Jesus Christ we shall also live with him?" Our triumph is prepared, and yet we do all we can to shun the combat. ■

Calvinist Jonathan Edwards Promises Hellfire and Damnation to the Sinful

"O sinner, consider the fearful danger you are in. . . ."

THE GREAT AWAKENING sparked a revival of religious fervor throughout New England in 1740, after a dormant period in American religion. Lasting several years, the Great Awakening was marked by fanaticism in religious activity, with shrieking and violent trembling during religious services and direct personal visions of God and Satan.

Jonathan Edwards was the most powerful of the preachers of this movement. A forceful Calvinist, he drew word pictures of the torments of hell to attack materialism and earthly sin. Although a biographer once described his voice as "feeble," the impact of his words could not be denied: "It was a kind of moral inquisition; and sinners were put upon argumentative racks, and beneath screws, and, with an awful revolution of the great truth in hand, evenly and steadily screwed down and crushed."

"Sinners in the Hands of an Angry God" is the best-known of the sermons to come out of Puritan New England. Preached at Enfield, Connecticut, on July 8, 1741, this sermon was based on Deuteronomy 32:35 ("To me belongeth vengeance, and recompense; their foot shall slide in due time: for the day of their calamity is at hand, and the things that shall come upon them make haste").

Central to this sermon is his comparison of the sinner to a spider, hanging "by a slender thread" and being dangled over the pit of hell. Edwards uses the initial repetition of anaphora to warn of the coming destruction: "nothing to lay hold of to save yourself, nothing to keep off the flames of wrath, nothing of your own, nothing that you have ever done, nothing that you can do. . . ." His reliance on retribution theology, and his unconcern with the more sophisticated "wisdom" literature of Job and Ecclesiastes, is underscored by the concluding analogy between New England and the biblical city of Sodom.

□   □   □

The God that holds you over the pit of hell much as one holds a spider or some loathsome insect over the fire abhors you, and is dreadfully provoked; his wrath towards you burns like fire; he looks upon you as worthy of nothing else but to be cast into the fire; he is of purer eyes than to bear you in his sight; you are ten thousand times as abominable in his eyes as the most hateful and venomous serpent is in ours. You have offended him infinitely more than ever a stubborn rebel did his prince, and yet it is nothing but his hand that holds you from falling into the fire every moment; it is abscribed to nothing else that you did not go to hell the last night that you were suffered to awake again in this world, after you closed your eyes to sleep; and there is no other reason to be given why you have not dropped into hell since you arose in the morning, but that God's hand has held you up; there is no other reason to be given why you have not gone to hell, since you have sat here in the house of God provoking his pure eye by your sinful. wicked manner of attending his solemn worship; yea, there is nothing else that is to be given as a reason why you do not this very moment drop down into hell.

O sinner, consider the fearful danger you are in; it is a great furnace of wrath, a wide and bottomless pit, full of the fire of wrath that you are held over in the hands of that God whose wrath is provoked and incensed as much against you as against many of the damned in hell; you hang by a slender thread, with the flames of divine wrath flashing about it, and ready every moment to singe it and burn it asunder, and you have no interest in any mediator, and nothing to lay hold of to save yourself, nothing to keep off the flames of wrath, nothing of your own, nothing that you have ever done, nothing that you can do to induce God to spare you one moment. . . .

It would be dreadful to suffer this fierceness and wrath of Almighty God one moment; but you must suffer it to all eternity: there will be no end to this exquisite, horrible misery: when you look forward, you shall see along forever a boundless duration before you, which will swallow up your thoughts, and amaze your soul; and you will absolutely despair of ever having any deliverance, any end, any mitigation, any rest at all; you will know certainly that you must wear out long ages, millions of millions of ages in wrestling and conflicting with this almighty, merciless vengeance; and then when you have so done, when so many ages have actually been spent by you in this manner, you will know that all is but a point to what remains, so that your punishment will indeed be infinite.

Oh, who can express what the state of a soul in such circumstances is! All that we can possibly say about it gives but a very feeble, faint representation of it; it is inexpressible and inconceivable: for "who knows the power of God's anger!"

How dreadful is the state of those that are daily and hourly in danger of this great wrath and infinite misery! But this is the dismal case of every soul in this congregation that has not been born again, however moral and strict, sober and religious, they may otherwise be. Oh, that you would consider it, whether you be young or old! There is reason to think that there are many in this congregation now hearing this discourse that will actually be the subjects of this very misery to all eternity. We know not who they are, or in what seats they sit, or what thoughts they now have—it may be they are now at ease, and hear all these things without much disturbance, and are now flattering themselves that they are not the persons, promising themselves that they shall escape. If we knew that there was one person, and but one, in the whole congregation, that was to be the subject of this misery, what an awful thing it would be to think of! If we knew who it was, what an awful sight it would be to see such a person! How might all the rest of the congregation lift up a lamentable and bitter cry over him! But, alas, instead of one, how many is it likely will remember this discourse in hell! And it would be a wonder, if some that are now present should not be in hell in a very short time, before this year is out. And it would be no wonder if some persons that now sit here in some seats of this meetinghouse, in health, and quiet and secure, should be there before tomorrow morning! . . .

Therefore let everyone that is out of Christ now awake and fly from the wrath to come. The wrath of Almighty God is now undoubtedly hanging over a great part of this congregation. Let everyone fly out of Sodom. "Haste and escape for your lives, look not behind you, escape to the mountain, lest ye be consumed." ∎

Methodist John Wesley Asserts "Free Grace" to Deny the Implacability of Fate

"GOD is not divided against himself."

BEFORE BECOMING THE FATHER of Methodism, John Wesley was ordained a deacon at the age of twenty-two and a priest at twenty-five in the Church of England. It was not until he was thirty-four, however, at a religious society in Aldersgate Street, London, that he experienced the famous conversion in which he felt his "heart strangely warmed": "I felt I did trust in Christ, Christ alone, for salvation, and an assurance was given me that he had given away my sins."

That assurance led Wesley to pursue his evangelism with unparalleled enthusiasm in "field preaching," taking the message outside the churches and onto the fields and highways. By one accounting, Wesley preached more than forty thousand sermons and traveled farther than 200,000 miles on horseback; statues of him today at Methodist institutions often show him on a horse.

In what may be his greatest sermon, Wesley questioned the entire doctrine of predestination. On a field near Bristol, England, on April 29, 1739, he preached against this notion and sought to replace it with the concept of "free grace," the love of God that is "free in all, and free for all."

Wesley uses ancient images ("weeping crocodile tears") and scriptural references to press the logic of his argument, enumerating and linking each step of the thought process that led him to deny predestination. For instance, the simple repetition of the adjective "uncomfortable" draws together the third and fourth points of the sermon, just as the anaphora of "It does not depend on . . ." introduces a listing of the many conditions previously held to be the sources of God's grace.

□   □   □

He, that spared not his own Son, but delivered him up for us all, how shall he not with him also freely give us all things?

—Romans 8:32

How freely does God love the world! While we were yet sinners, "Christ died for the ungodly." While we were "dead in sin," God "spared not his own Son, but delivered him up for us all." And how freely with him does he "give us all things!" Verily, *free grace* is all in all!

The grace or love of God, whence cometh our salvation, is *free in all*, and *free for all*.

First: it is free *in all* to whom it is given. It does not depend on any power or merit in man; no, not in any degree, neither in whole, not in part. It does not in any wise depend either on the good works or righteousness of the receiver—not on anything he has done or anything he is. It does not depend on his endeavors. It does not depend on his good tempers, or good desires, or good purposes and intentions; for all these flow from the free grace of God; they are the streams only, not the fountain. They are the fruits of free grace, and not the root. They are not the cause but the effects of it. Whatsoever good is in man, or is done by man, God is the author and doer of it. Thus is his grace free in all; that is, no way depending on any power or merit in man, but on God alone, who freely gave us his own Son, and "with him freely giveth us all things,"

But is it free *for all* as well as *in all*? To this some have answered, "No, it is free only for those whom God hath ordained to life; and they are but a little flock. The greater part of mankind God hath ordained to death; and it is not free for them. Them God hateth; and therefore, before they were born, decreed they should die eternally. And this he absolutely decreed; because so was his good pleasure; because it was his sovereign will. Accordingly, they are born for this, to be destroyed body and soul in hell. And they grow up under the irrevocable curse of God, without any possibility of redemption; for what grace God gives he gives only for this, to increase, not prevent, their damnation." . . .

But if this be so, then is all preaching vain. It is needless to them that are elected; for they, whether with preaching or without, will infallibly be saved. Therefore, the end of preaching, to save souls, is void with regard to them. And it is useless to them that are not elected, for they cannot possibly be saved. They, whether with preaching or without, will infallibly be damned. The end of preaching is therefore void with regard to them likewise; so that in either case our preaching is vain, as your hearing is also vain.

This, then, is a plain proof that the doctrine of predestination is not a doctrine of God, because it makes void the ordinance of God: and God is not divided against himself. A second is that it directly tends to destroy that holiness which is the end of all the ordinances of God. . . .

Thirdly, this doctrine tends to destroy the comfort of religion, the happiness of Christianity. This is evident as to all those who believe themselves to be reprobated, or who only suspect or fear it. All the great and precious promises are lost to them; they afford them no ray of comfort: for they are not the elect of God: therefore, they have neither lot nor portion in them. This is an effectual bar to their finding any comfort or happiness, even in that religion whose ways are designed to be "ways of pleasantness, and all her paths peace.". . .

Again: how uncomfortable a thought is this, that thousands and millions of men, without any preceding offense or fault of theirs, were unchangeably doomed to everlasting burnings! How peculiarly uncomfortable must it be to those who have put on Christ! To those who, being filled with bowels of mercy, tenderness, and compassion, could even "wish themselves accursed for their brethren's sake"!

Fourthly: this uncomfortable doctrine directly tends to destroy our zeal for good works. And this it does, first, as it naturally tends (according to what was observed before) to destroy our love to the greater part of mankind, namely, the evil and unthankful. For whatever lessens our love must so far lessen our desire to do them good. . . .

But, fifthly, this doctrine not only tends to destroy Christian holiness, happiness, and good works, but hath also a direct and manifest tendency to overthrow the whole Christian revelation. . . .

You represent him as mocking his helpless creatures by offering what he never intends to give. You describe him as saying one thing and meaning another; as pretending the love which he had not. Him, in "whose mouth was no guile," you make full of deceit, void of common sincerity—then especially, when, drawing nigh the city, he wept over it and said, "O Jerusalem, Jerusalem, thou that killest the prophets, and stonest them that are sent unto thee, how oft *would I* have gathered thy children together—and *ye would not.*" Now, if you say, *they would,* but *he would not,* you represent him (which who could hear?) as weeping crocodile tears: weeping over the prey which himself had doomed to destruction ! . . .

This is the blasphemy clearly contained in *the horrible decree* of predestination! And here I fix my foot. On this I join issue with every assertor of it. You represent God as worse than the devil—more false, more cruel, more unjust. . . .

Oh, hear ye this, ye that forget God! Ye cannot charge your death upon him! "Have I any pleasure at all that the wicked should die? saith the Lord God" (Ezekiel 18:23, etc.). "Repent, and turn yourselves from all your transgressions; so iniquity shall not be your ruin. Cast away from you all your transgressions, whereby ye have transgressed. . . for why will ye die, O house of Israel? For I have no pleasure in the death of him that dieth, saith the Lord God: wherefore turn yourselves, and live ye." "As I live, saith the Lord God, I have no pleasure in the death of the wicked. . . . Turn ye, turn ye from your evil ways; for why will ye die, O house of Israel?" ■

Clergyman John Witherspoon Couples Religion with Politics

"WHOEVER is an avowed enemy to God, I scruple not to call him an enemy to his country."

THE ONLY CLERGYMAN to sign the declaration of independence, Reverend John Witherspoon was a Scottish Presbyterian who in 1768 came to America to serve as president of the College of New-Jersey, now known as Princeton. Within a decade of his arrival, however, he was as actively involved in the political struggles of the colonies as in education.

In May 1776, Witherspoon caused controversy in preaching "The

Dominion of Providence over the Passions of Men" in Princeton. This stern sermon, which was his first to discuss politics, preceded by a month his election to the Continental Congress and signaled the outspokenness of his political stance. When he was told that America was not ripe for independence, Witherspoon was said to have answered, "In my judgment, sir, we are not only ripe but rotting."

Witherspoon's sermon uses various rhetorical devices in urging that liberty is a religious as well as a political issue. Among these devices are the rhetorical question ("Would any man who could prevent it give up his estate, person, and family to the disposal of his neighbor. . . ?") and parrhesia, or apologizing for what follows ("Pardon me, my brethren, for insisting so much upon this"). The sermon concludes with what may be considered his central theme—"that in America true religion and civil liberty may be inseparable."

□   □   □

There is not a greater evidence either of the reality or the power of religion than a firm belief of God's universal presence, and a constant attention to the influence and operation of his Providence. It is by this means that the Christian may be said, in the emphatical Scripture language, "to walk with God, and to endure as seeing him who is invisible."

The doctrine of divine Providence is very full and complete in the sacred oracles. It extends not only to things which we may think of great moment, and therefore worthy of notice, but to things the most indifferent and inconsiderable; "Are not two sparrows sold for a farthing," says our Lord, "and one of them falleth not to the ground without your heavenly Father"; nay, "the very hairs of your head are all numbered." It extends not only to things beneficial and salutary, or to the direction and assistance of those who are the servants of the living God, but to things seemingly most hurtful and destructive, and to persons the most refractory and disobedient. He overrules all his creatures, and all their actions.

Thus we are told that "fire, hail, snow, vapor, and stormy wind, fulfill his word," in the course of nature; and even so the most impetuous and disorderly passions of men, that are under no restraint from themselves, are yet perfectly subject to the dominion of Jehovah. They carry his commission, they obey his orders, they are limited and restrained by his authority, and they conspire with everything else in promoting his glory. There is the greater need to take notice of this, that men are not generally sufficiently aware of the distinction between the law of God and his purpose; they are apt to suppose that as the temper of the sinner is contrary to the one, so the outrages of the sinner are able to defeat the other; than which nothing can be more false. The truth is plainly asserted and nobly expressed by the psalmist in the text "Surely the wrath of man shall praise thee; the remainder of wrath shalt thou restrain."

This psalm was evidently composed as a song of praise for some signal victory obtained. . . .

I am sensible, my brethren, that the time and occasion of this psalm may seem to be in one respect ill suited to the interesting circumstances of this country at present. It was composed after the victory was obtained; whereas we are now but putting on the harness and entering upon an important contest, the length of which it is impossible to foresee. and the issue of which it will perhaps be thought presumption to foretell. . . .

The truth, then, asserted in this text, which I propose to illustrate and improve, is that all the disorderly passions of men, whether exposing the innocent to private injury, or whether they are the arrows of divine judgment in public calamity, shall, in the end, be to the praise of God: or, to apply it more particularly to the present state of the American colonies, and the plague of war, the ambition of mistaken princes, the cunning and cruelty of oppressive and corrupt ministers, and even the inhumanity of brutal soldiers, however dreadful, shall finally promote the glory of God, and in the meantime, while the storm continues, his mercy and kindness shall appear in prescribing bounds to their rage and fury.

In discoursing on this subject, it is my intention, through the assistance of divine grace,

- □ I. To point out to you in some particulars, how the wrath of man praises God.
- □ II. To apply these principles to our present situation, by inferences of truth for your instruction and comfort, and by suitable exhortations to duty in the important crisis.

In the first place, I am to point out to you in some particulars, how the wrath of man praises God. I say in some instances, because it is far from being in my power either to mention or explain the whole. There is an unsearchable depth in the divine counsels, which it is impossible for us to penetrate. It is the duty of every good man to place the most unlimited confidence in divine wisdom, and to believe that those measures of Providence that are most unintelligible to him are yet planned with the same skill, and directed to the same great purposes, as others, the reason and tendency of which he can explain in the clearest manner. But where revelation and experience enables us to discover the wisdom, equity, or mercy of divine Providence, nothing can be more delightful or profitable to a serious mind, and therefore I beg your attention to the following remarks.

In the first place, the wrath of man praises God, as it is an example and illustration of divine truth, and clearly points out the corruption of our nature, which is the foundation stone of the doctrine of redemption. Nothing can be more absolutely necessary to true religion than a clear and full conviction of the sinfulness of our nature and state. Without this there can be neither repentance in the sinner nor humility in the believer. Without this all that is said in Scripture of the wisdom and mercy of God in providing a Savior, is without force and without meaning. . . .

It would be a criminal inattention not to observe the singular interposition of Providence hitherto, in behalf of the American colonies. It is, however, impossible for me, in a single discourse, as well as improper at this time, to go through every step of our past transactions. I must therefore content myself with a few remarks. How many discoveries have been made of the designs of enemies in Britain and among ourselves, in a manner as unexpected to us as to them, and in such season as to prevent their effect? What surprising success has attended our encounters in almost every instance? Has not the boasted discipline of regular and veteran soldiers been turned into confusion and dismay, before the new and maiden courage of freemen, in defense of their property and right? In what great mercy has blood been spared on the side of this injured country?

Some important victories in the South have been gained with so little loss that enemies will probably think it has been dissembled; as many, even of ourselves thought, till time rendered it undeniable. But these were comparatively of small moment. The signal advantage we have gained by the evacuation of Boston, and the shameful flight of the army and navy of Britain, was brought about without the loss of a man. To all this we may add that the counsels of our enemies have been visibly confounded, so that I believe that I may say with truth that there is hardly any step which they have taken, but it has operated strongly against themselves, and been more in our favor than if they had followed a contrary course.

While we give praise to God, the supreme disposer of all events, for his interposition in our behalf, let us guard against the dangerous error of trusting in, or boasting of, an arm of flesh. I could earnestly wish that while our arms are crowned with success, we might content ourselves with a modest ascription of it to the power of the Highest. It has given me great uneasiness to read some ostentatious, vaunting expressions in our newspapers, though happily I think, much restrained of late. Let us not return to them again.

If I am not mistaken, not only the holy Scriptures in general, and the truths of the glorious Gospel in particular, but the whole course of Providence, seem intended to abase the pride of man and lay the vainglorious in the dust. How many instances does history furnish us with, of those who, after exulting over and despising their enemies, were signally and shamefully defeated. The truth is, I believe, the remark may be applied universally, and we may say that through the whole frame of nature, and the whole system of human life, that which promises most performs the least. The flowers of finest color seldom have the sweetest fragrance. The trees of quickest growth or fairest form are seldom of the greatest value or duration. Deep waters move with least noise. Men who think most are seldom talkative. And I think it holds as much in war as in anything that every boaster is a coward.

Pardon me, my brethren, for insisting so much upon this, which may seem but an immaterial circumstance. It is in my opinion of very great moment. I look upon ostentation and confidence to be a sort of outrage upon Providence, and when it becomes general and infuses itself into the spirit of a people, it is a forerunner of destruction. . . .

You shall not, my brethren, hear from me in the pulpit what you have never heard from me in conversation, I mean railing at the king personally, or even his ministers and the Parliament, and people of Britain, as so many barbarous savages. Many of their actions have probably been worse than their intentions. That they should desire unlimited dominion, if they can obtain or preserve it, is neither new nor wonderful. I do not refuse submission to their unjust claims, because they are corrupt or profligate, although probably many of them are so, but because they are men, and therefore liable to all the selfish bias inseparable from human nature. I call this claim unjust, of making laws to bind us in all cases whatsoever, because they are separated from us, independent of us, and have an interest in opposing us.

Would any man who could prevent it give up his estate, person, and family to the disposal of his neighbor, although he had liberty to choose the wisest and the best master? Surely not. This is the true and proper hinge of the controversy between Great Britain and America. . . .

If your principles are pure—the meaning of this is, if your present opposition to the claims of the British ministry does not arise from a seditious and turbulent spirit, or a wanton contempt of legal authority; from a blind and factious attachment to particular persons or parties; or from a selfish rapacious disposition, and a desire to turn public confusion to private profit—but from a concern for the interest of your country, and the safety of yourselves and your posterity. On this subject I cannot help observing that though it would be a miracle if there were not many selfish persons among us, and discoveries now and then made of mean and interested transactions, yet they have been comparatively inconsiderable both in number and effect. In general, there has been so great a degree of public spirit that we have much more reason to be thankful for its vigor and prevalence than to wonder at the few appearances of dishonesty or disaffection. It would be very uncandid to ascribe the universal ardor that has prevailed among all ranks of men, and the spirited exertions in the most distant colonies, to anything else than public spirit. Nor was there ever perhaps in history so general a commotion from which religious differences have been so entirely excluded. . . .

What follows from this? That he is the best friend to American liberty who is most sincere and active in promoting true and undefiled religion, and who sets himself with the greatest firmness to bear down profanity and immorality of every kind. Whoever is an avowed enemy to God, I scruple not to call him an enemy to his country. Do not suppose, my brethren, that I mean to recommend a furious and angry zeal for the circumstantials of religion, or the contentions of one sect with another about their peculiar distinctions. I do not wish you to oppose anybody's religion, but everybody's wickedness. Perhaps there are few surer marks of the reality of religion than when a man feels himself more joined in spirit to a true holy person of a different denomination than to an irregular liver of his own. It is therefore your duty in this important and critical season to exert yourselves, everyone in his proper sphere, to stem the tide of prevailing vice, to promote the knowledge of God, the reverence of his name and worship, and obedience to his laws.

Perhaps you will ask what it is that you are called to do for this purpose farther than your own personal duty. I answer this itself when taken in its proper extent is not a little. The nature and obligation of visible religion is, I am afraid, little understood and less attended to. . . .

Upon the whole, I beseech you to make a wise improvement of the present threatening aspect of public affairs, and to remember that your duty to God, to your country, to your families, and to yourselves is the same. True religion is nothing else but an inward temper and outward conduct suited to your state and circumstances in Providence at any time. And as peace with God, and conformity to him, adds to the sweetness of created comforts while we possess them, so in times of difficulty and trial, it is in the man of piety and inward principle that we may expect to find the uncorrupted patriot, the useful citizen, and the invincible soldier. God grant that in America true religion and civil liberty may be inseparable, and that the unjust attempts to destroy the one may in the issue tend to the support and establishment of both. ■

Chief Red Jacket Rejects a Change of Religion

"You say that you are right and we are lost. How do we know this to be true?"

AN EARLY DEFENDER OF THE RIGHTS OF AMERICAN INDIANS, the chief of the Seneca tribe was born in 1758 and given the Indian name of Otetiani. When he became chief, his title was Sagoyewatha. But his lasting identification, the colorful name of Red Jacket, came from the bright red coat given him by the British when he supported their side during the American Revolution.

Red Jacket did, however, come to earn the respect and friendship of George Washington. The Indian leader eventually sought peace with the U.S. government and even influenced his followers to support the United States against Britain in the War of 1812, despite his lifelong struggle to maintain native traditions against the introduction of white customs.

In proud and impassioned words, this spokesman for his people's indigenous culture frequently opposed attempts to bring European values and ideas to his tribe. When Christian missionaries sought to baptize his followers in 1805, Red Jacket rose to speak out against efforts to convert the tribe. His moving appeal gains its effect from rhetorical questions ("How shall we know when to believe, being so often deceived by the white people?") and anaphora, particularly forceful in repeatedly addressing the missionary as "Brother," perhaps ironically, and in the refuting of everything that follows "You say. . . ."

□   □   □

Friend and Brother, it was the will of the Great Spirit that we should meet together this day. . . .

Brother, this council fire was kindled by you. It was at your request that we came together at this time. We have listened with attention to what you have said. You requested us to speak our minds freely. This gives us great joy; for we now consider that we stand upright before you and can speak what we think. All have heard your voice, and all speak to you now as one man. Our minds are agreed. . . .

Brother, listen to what we say.

There was a time when our forefathers owned this great island. Their seats extended from the rising to the setting sun. The Great Spirit had made it for the use of Indians. He had created the buffalo, the deer, and other animals for food. He had made the bear and the beaver. Their skins served us for clothing. He had scattered them over the country and taught us how to take them. He had caused the earth to produce corn for bread. All this he had done for his red children because he loved them. If we had some disputes about our hunting ground, they were generally settled without the shedding of much blood.

But an evil day came upon us. Your forefathers crossed the great water and landed on this island. Their numbers were small. They found friends and not enemies. They told us they had fled from their own country for fear of wicked men and had come here to enjoy their religion. They asked for a small seat. We took pity on them, granted their request, and they sat down among us. We gave them corn and meat; they gave us poison in return.

Brother, our seats were once large and yours were small. You have now become a great people, and we have scarcely a place left to spread our blankets. You have got our country, but are not satisfied; you want to force your religion upon us.

Brother, continue to listen.

You say that you are sent to instruct us how to worship the Great Spirit agreeably to his mind; and, if we do not take hold of the religion which you white people teach, we shall be unhappy hereafter. You say that you are right and we are lost. How do we know this to be true?

We understand that your religion is written in a book. If it was intended for us, as well as you, why has not the Great Spirit given to us, and not only to us, but why did he not give to our forefathers the knowledge of that book, with the means of understanding it rightly. We only know what you tell us about it. How shall we know when to believe, being so often deceived by the white people?

Brother, you say there is but one way to worship and serve the Great Spirit. If there is but one religion, why do you white people differ so much about it? Why do not all agree, as you can all read the book?

Brother, we do not understand these things. We are told that your religion was given to your forefathers and has been handed down from father to son. We also have a religion which was given to our forefathers and has been handed down to us, their children. We worship in that way. It teaches us to be thankful for all the favors we receive, to love each other, and to be united. We never quarrel about religion. . . .

Brother, we do not wish to destroy your religion or take it from you. We only want to enjoy our own. ■

Bishop James Madison Speaks on Divine Providence toward America

"DOTH the morning of America break forth refulgent with unclouded glory?"

WHEN RONALD REAGAN claimed it was "morning in America," he was unconsciously drawing on the work of Bishop James Madison, whose cousin James Madison became our fourth president. Bishop Madison was ordained an Anglican priest in 1775 and consecrated the first bishop of Virginia for the Episcopal church in 1790. His eclectic interests, including science and philosophy, also led him to serve as president of the College of William and Mary from 1777 until his death in 1812.

When George Washington in 1795 proclaimed a day of national thanksgiving, Bishop Madison preached a sermon, published later that year under the title *Manifestation of the Beneficence of Divine Providence towards America: A Discourse, Delivered on Thursday the 19th of February, 1795, Being the Day Recommended by the President of the United States, for General Thanksgiving and Prayer.*

The bishop's sermon, interspersed with quotations from Psalms and John Milton's *Paradise Lost* and ending with a prayer of gratitude, argues for "rational religion," which is "not that of fanatics or inquisitors," to form the basis of virtuous behavior. Although the speech's opening makes use of what we now consider a weak adjective ("interesting"), Bishop Madison shrewdly uses the direct address of "Brethren" and "Fellow citizens" to link the notions of church and state. Employing structural balance of parallel clauses and infinitive phrases, he builds his argument for virtue not so much as its own reward but as the common ground of religion and government.

□   □   □

Only fear the lord, and serve him; for consider how great things he hath done for you.

—I Samuel 12:24

Brethren, there are few situations more interesting to the human race than that which the people of America this day presents.

The temples of the living God are everywhere, throughout this rising empire, this day, crowded, I trust, with worshipers, whose hearts, impressed with a just and lively sense of the great things, which he hath done for them, pour forth, in unison, the grateful tribute of praise and thanksgiving. Yes, this day, brethren, "the voice of rejoicing and salvation is in the tabernacles of the righteous"; and with reason, for the history of nations doth not exhibit a people who ever had more cause to offer up to the great author of every good the most fervent expressions of gratitude and thanksgiving.

Let, my brethren, the sons of irreligion, wrapped in their dark and gloomy system of fatality, refuse to open their eyes to the great luminous proofs of providential government, which America displays; let them turn from a light, which their weak vision cannot bear; but let the right-eous, let those who trust in God, who can trace in that good and glorious being the relations of father, friend, and governor, let them with eagle eyes look up to that full blaze of salvation, which he hath vouchsafed to this new world.

Permit me, then, upon this occasion, to turn your attention to those great things which the Lord hath done for us, to those manifold displays of divine Providence, which the history of America exhibits; and let the subject afford an opportunity to revive within us sentiments of lively gratitude, and excite sincere resolutions to fear the Lord, and to serve him—in a word, to increase daily in piety, and in all those noble affec-tions of the soul which dignify the Christian and the patriot.

Who can tell how many ages had been swallowed up in the all-absorbing gulf of time, before the bold navigator first essayed to visit these distant regions of the earth? Who can tell how long this western world had been the habitation of the listless savage, or the wild beasts of the forest? At these questions chronology drops her epochs, as incapable of conducting her to periods so remote, and which have escaped her grasp. The ways of heaven must oft appear to us weak mortals dark and intricate.

But the first suggestion, which here presents itself, is that Providence seems to have thrown a veil over this portion of the globe, in order to conceal it from the eyes of the nations of the East, until the destined period had arrived for the regeneration of mankind, in this New World, after those various other means, which the wisdom of the Almighty had permitted to operate in the Old, had proved ineffectual. In vain had reason, the handmaid of pure religion, long attempted to convince men of the reciprocal duties which equality and fraternity impose. Still there would arise some one,

> "of proud ambitious heart, who, not content
> with fair equality, fraternal state,
> would arrogate dominion undeserved
> over his brethren, and quite dispossess
> concord and law of nature from the earth."

In vain had even thy dispensation of love and peace, blessed Jesus, long essayed to disarm ambition of the ensanguined sword, and to diffuse benevolence, equality, and fraternity among the human race. Millions still groaned under the heavy pressure which tyranny imposed. Yes, even thy gospel of love, of universal fraternity, had been, too often, perverted into the most formidable system of oppression; and mankind, instead of seeing it diffuse the heavenly rays of philanthropy, too frequently beheld it as imposing a yoke to degrade and enslave them. The princes of the earth sought not for the sacred duties which it enjoined; but they sought to render it the sanction of their exterminating vengeance, or their deep-laid systems of usurpation. Is not the history of almost all Europe pregnant with proofs of this calamitous truth? If you can point to some small portion where the religion of the blessed Jesus, untrammeled with political usurpations, was left to operate its happy effects upon the passions and the conduct of men; or where toleration extended wide her arms of mercy to embrace the whole family of Christ, the spot appears like a solitary star, which in the midst of night, beams forth alone, whilst clouds and thick darkness obscure the rest of the innumerable host of heaven. Alas, what avails the voice of reason or religion, when the lust of domination has usurped the soul! At the shrine of this fell demon, the human race was sacrificed by thousands. Nay, too many of the sons of Europe are still bound with cords to the altars of ambition, and there immolated, not only by thousands, but by tens of thousands. . . .

But, brethren, important considerations still demand our attention. Has heaven been thus propitious; are we possessed of all those blessings which flow from governments founded in wisdom, justice, and equality; doth the morning of America break forth refulgent with unclouded glory? Then it behooves us, above all things, to inquire how are these blessings to be preserved? How shall we ensure to her a meridian splendor worthy of such a morning? This inquiry immediately resolves itself into another. What is there in this sublunary state that can attract the smiles of heaven, or ensure political happiness, but virtue? Never was there a mortal so depraved, never was there a conscience so deaf to that internal voice, which always whispers truth, but must acknowledge that virtue only gives a title to hope for the favor of that high and lofty one, who inhabiteth eternity.

Fellow citizens, let virtue, then, I entreat you, be the ruling principle, the polar star, which should influence every sentiment and guide every action, since it alone will conduct us into the haven of felicity. But will you trust, for the diffusion of virtue, to that political morality which a vain philosophy would substitute in the room of those lessons which the heavenly teacher delivered? Shall virtue trickle from the oozy bed of political catechisms, or shall it gush, pure and in full stream, from the rock of our salvation? Ah, brethren, the moment that we drop the idea of a God, the remunerator of virtue but the avenger of iniquity; the moment we abandon that divine system of equality, fraternity, and universal benevolence which the blessed Jesus taught and exemplified; the moment that religion, the pure and undefiled religion, which heaven, in compassion to the infirmity of human reason, vouchsafed to mortals, loses its influence over their hearts—from that fatal moment, farewell to public and private happiness, farewell, a long farewell to virtue, to patriotism, to liberty!

Virtue such as republics and heaven require must have its foundation in the heart; it must penetrate the whole man; it must derive its obligations and its sanctions, not from the changeable ideas of the political moralist, or the caprice of the wisest of human legislators, but from the unchangeable father of the universe, the God of love, whose laws and whose will we are incited to obey by motives, the most powerful that can actuate the human soul. Men must see and feel, that it is God himself, their maker and their judge, who demands obedience to duties which constitute their individual, their social, their eternal happiness. Then, and not till then, will virtue reign triumphant in the hearts of citizens; then will she have her sacrifices in the midst of the deepest obscurity, as well as in the open day, in the most private and secret retirements, as well as upon the house tops. . . .

Fellow citizens, it is an easy task, for those who may have the honor of addressing an American audience this day, to point out the excellencies of our civil governments, to shew their superior aptitude for the promo-

tion of political happiness, to evince that obedience to laws constitutionally enacted is the only means of preserving liberty, and that every
expression of the public will is obligatory upon every citizen; to prove,
that representative republics, instead of being the prolific parents of anarchy and confusion, are, on the contrary, of all the forms of government
under which men have yet associated, either through compulsion or
choice, the most promotive of private and public happiness, the most
susceptible of that energy which is equally capable of curbing the licentiousness of the multitude or of frustrating the wicked designs of the
ambitious; it is easy for them to shew that virtue is the vital principle of a
republic, that unless a magnanimous spirit of patriotism animates every
breast, unless a sincere and ardent love for justice, for temperance, for
prudence, for fortitude, in short, for all those qualities which dignify
human nature, pervades, enlivens, invigorates the whole mass of citizens, these fair superstructures of political wisdom must soon crumble
into dust. Certainly, my brethren, it is a fundamental maxim that virtue
is the soul of a republic.

But, zealous for the prosperity of my country, I will repeat, and in
these days it is of infinite moment to insist, that without religion—I
mean *rational religion,* the religion which our Savior himself delivered,
not that of fanatics or inquisitors—chimeras and shadows are substantial
things compared with that virtue, which those who reject the authority
of religion would recommend to our practice. Ye, then, who love your
country, if you expect or wish that real virtue and social happiness
should be preserved among us or that genuine patriotism and a dignified
obedience to law, instead of that spirit of disorganizing anarchy, and
those false and hollow pretenses to patriotism, which are so pregnant
with contentions, insurrections, and misery, should be the distinguishing
characteristics of Americans; or that the same almighty arm which hath
hitherto protected your country, and conducted her to this day of glory,
should still continue to shield and defend her, remember that your first
and last duty is "to fear the Lord and to serve him"; remember that in the
same proportion as irreligion advances, virtue retires; remember that in
her stead will succeed factions, ever ready to prostitute public good to the
most nefarious private ends, whilst unbounded licentiousness and a total
disregard to the sacred names of liberty and of patriotism will here once
more realize that fatal catastrophe which so many free states have
already experienced. Remember, the law of the Almighty is, they shall
expire, with their expiring virtue.

God of all nature! Father of the human spirit. preserve these prosperous,
these happy republics from so dreadful a calamity. May thy gracious

Providence, which hath hitherto nurtured, protected, and conducted them to this day of praise and thanksgiving, ever be the supreme object of their regard. May the blessings already received, inspire every heart with just sentiments of gratitude, and with the inflexible resolution to perform those duties which become us as Christians and as citizens. May peace and happiness, truth and justice, order and freedom, religion and piety, ever proclaim thy praises, thy providential goodness, thy love to man, not only in this land of liberty but wherever the human race is found. Amen. ■

Lincoln, in His Second Inaugural, Seeks to Heal the Spiritual Wounds of War

"WITH malice toward none, with charity for all, with firmness in the right as God gives us to see the right, let us strive on to finish the work we are in . . . to do all which may achieve and cherish a just and lasting peace among ourselves and with all nations."

ON MARCH 4, 1865, the Civil War was thirty-seven days from its end. Lincoln, having incorporated the abstract cause of preserving the Union and majority rule into the more rallying cause of human freedom, used his second inaugural to preach a sermon looking past the war's bitterness to a time of what he felt had to be reconciliation and reconstruction.

He raises a Joban question in this most religiously philosophical of inaugural addresses: Why did God put this nation through such terrible punishment? Could God have a different purpose from that supposed to be right by man? Lincoln's suggested answer: God's purpose is part of some unknown and unknowable design; "the Almighty has his own purposes." He cites the Gospel according to Saint Matthew (18:7), quoting Jesus' warning of fearsome retribution to those who harm his believing children: "Woe unto the world because of offenses! for it must needs be that offenses come; but woe to that man by whom the offense cometh!" Lincoln reasons that the offense, or temptation to sin, to the innocent children was slavery, and that the people of both North and South were those by whom that offense of slavery came; therefore, Lincoln asks rhetorically, are we to question God's justice? No; even if that justice means that "every drop of blood drawn with the lash shall be paid by another drawn with the sword," we must accept the justice hailed in the Psalm of David (19:9); "the judgments of the Lord are true and righteous altogether."

Lincoln (unlike Job) bids his countrymen accept the punishment as evidence that great offense was committed and for expiation thereof, which gives them "firmness in the right as God gives us to see the right"—which is only a limited and imperfect vision, but which includes God's justice in "a just and lasting peace." Lincoln's final, unifying touch is to say this peace comes not *between* the warring regions but *among* ourselves, as American individuals, and, looking beyond civil war, "with all nations."

Lincoln wrote later of his second inaugural and its theme of the inscrutability of God's seeming injustice, "I expect it to wear as well as, perhaps better than, any thing I have produced; but I believe it is not immediately popular. Men are not flattered by being shown that there has been a difference of purpose between the Almighty and them. To deny it, however, in this case, is to deny that there is a God governing the world."

□   □   □

Fellow Countrymen:

At this second appearing to take the oath of the presidential office there is less occasion for an extended address than there was at the first. Then a statement, somewhat in detail, of a course to be pursued seemed fitting and proper. Now, at the expiration of four years, during which public declarations have been constantly called forth on every point and phase of the great contest which still absorbs the attention and engrosses the energies of the nation, little that is new could be presented. The progress of our arms, upon which all else chiefly depends, is as well known to the public as to myself, and it is, I trust, reasonably satisfactory and encouraging to all. With high hope for the future, no prediction in regard to it is ventured.

On the occasion corresponding to this four years ago all thoughts were anxiously directed to an impending civil war. All dreaded it; all sought to avert it. While the inaugural address was being delivered from this place, devoted altogether to *saving* the Union without war, insurgent agents were in the city seeking to *destroy* it without war—seeking to dissolve the Union and divide effects by negotiation. Both parties deprecated war, but one of them would *make* war rather than let the nation survive, and the other would *accept* war rather than let it perish, and the war came.

One-eighth of the whole population were colored slaves, not distributed generally over the Union, but localized in the southern part of it. These slaves constituted a peculiar and powerful interest. All knew that this interest was somehow the cause of war. To strengthen, perpetuate, and extend this interest was the object for which the insurgents would rend the Union even by war, while the government claimed no right to do more than to restrict the territorial enlargement of it. Neither party expected for the war the magnitude or the duration which it has already attained. Neither anticipated that the *cause* of the conflict might cease with or even before the conflict itself should cease. Each looked for an easier triumph. and a result less fundamental and astounding. Both read the same Bible and pray to the same God, and each invokes his aid against the other. It may seem strange that any men should dare to ask a just God's assistance in wringing their bread from the sweat of other men's faces, but let us judge not, that we be not judged. The prayers of both could not be answered. That of neither has been answered fully. The Almighty has his own purposes. "Woe unto the world because of offenses; for it must needs be that offenses come, but woe to that man by whom the offense cometh." If we shall suppose that American slavery is one of those offenses which, in the providence of God, must needs come, but which, having continued through his appointed time, he now wills to remove, and that he gives to both North and South this terrible war as the woe due to those by whom the offense came, shall we discern therein any departure from those divine attributes which the believers in a living God always ascribe to him? Fondly do we hope, fervently do we pray, that this mighty scourge of war may speedily pass away. Yet, if God wills that it continue until all the wealth piled by the bondsman's two hundred and fifty years of unrequited toil shall be sunk, and until every drop of blood drawn with the lash shall be paid by another drawn with the sword, as was said three thousand years ago, so still it must be said "the judgments of the Lord are true and righteous altogether."

With malice toward none, with charity for all, with firmness in the right as God gives us to see the right, let us strive on to finish the work we are in, to bind up the nation's wounds, to care for him who shall have borne the battle and for his widow and his orphan, to do all which may achieve and cherish a just and lasting peace among ourselves and with all nations. ■

Preacher Henry Ward Beecher Speaks of Visions

"Do not neglect these hours."

HARRIET BEECHER STOWE, whose novel *Uncle Tom's Cabin* inflamed abolitionist sentiments preceding the Civil War, had a brother who provided a similarly strong voice in the struggle for social reform. Henry Ward Beecher's name was used for "Beecher's Bibles"—the nickname for Sharps rifles used to combat the spread of slavery in the Kansas Territory before the Civil War. At an 1856 abolitionist meeting in Connecticut, Beecher argued that a Sharps rifle held a better argument than a Bible for persuading slaveholders, a precursor to Mao Tse-tung's observation that political power came out of the barrel of a gun.

Beecher was among the most popular and controversial of American clergymen in the nineteenth century, because he spoke out on current social issues as well as on religious doctrine, and because he dressed differently and flaunted his unorthodoxy. For almost forty years, he served as pastor of Plymouth Church in Brooklyn, where his weekly sermons drew more than two thousand listeners (they were so popular that ferries from Manhattan were nicknamed Beecher Boats); an 1870s scandal involving charges of adultery led to a sensational trial; he was acquitted, and the notoriety failed to diminish his popularity.

In his January 15, 1866, sermon on visions, Beecher told Plymouth Church in narrative form about the uplifting experience of standing "on a mount of vision." (Note the sermon's start with the indefinite use of "they" to lead the audience into the story.) The same sense of being uplifted occurs early in the sermon with Beecher's reference to "Sabbath mornings that rose upon me with healing in their wings." That last phrase has been used frequently in presidential speeches; Woodrow Wilson used it, and I added it to one of Richard Nixon's speeches. It comes from the biblical book of the prophet Malachi: "But unto you that fear my name shall the Sun of righteousness arise with healing in his wings" (Malachi 4:2).

□   □   □

They come, sometimes, without our knowing what brings them. There is always a cause, but we are not always conscious of it. I have had some Sabbath mornings that rose upon me with healing in their wings, after a troubled week. I can scarcely tell why I was troubled, but the mind's fruit was not sweet. Yet, when the Sabbath morning came, I no sooner looked down upon the bay, and across at my morning signal— the star on Trinity Church, symbolic of the star that hung over the spot where the child Jesus lay—than I felt that it was an elect morning. And when I went into the street, all the trees—if it was summer—were murmuring to me; all the birds were singing to me; the clouds were bearing messages to me; everything was kindred to me. All my soul rejoiced; I do not know why. I had met with no unusual good fortune. I had been moody all the week, perhaps. My heart had said, "I will not pray." I was unprepared for any such experience, so far as my own volition was concerned; but undoubtedly there was some cause operating which was in consonance with the laws of the mind; and when the morning came, with its propitious conjunction of circumstances, these results took place. We do not understand the reason of these hours; and when they come without volition or preparation on our part, they seem more like a sheet let down from heaven than like natural phenomena. I like to think that they are divine inspirations. My reason tells me that they are not, but I like to think that they are. Such poetic illusions help to make truth higher and better. . . .

I never shall forget the half day that I spent on Gorner Grat, in

Switzerland. I was just emerging from that many-formed crystal country (for Switzerland is one vast multiform crystal), and, coming up through the valley of the Rhône, and threading my way along the valley of the Visp, I arrived in the evening at Zermatt, in a perfect intoxication of delight. I lay that night and dreamed of the morning till it broke on me, when we directed our footsteps up the mountain; and after climbing two or three hours, we reached the top of Gorner Grat. It is a barren rock, with snow only here and there in the cracks and crevices; but, oh, what a vision opened upon me as I cast my eyes around the horizon! There stood some fifteen of Europe's grandest mountains. There were Monte Rosa, Lyskamm, Breithorn, Steinbock, Weisshorn, Mischabel, and, most wonderful of all, Matterhorn, that lifts itself up thirteen thousand feet and more and is a square-cut granite rock, standing like a vast tower in the air, and all of it apparently, from basis to summit, rising right up before you. And there was Gorner Glacier, a great river of ice, always moving, but never seeming to move. Down from the sides of these mountains flowed ten distinct glaciers beside. I swept the horizon and saw at one glance these glorious elevations, on whose tops the sun kindled all the melodies and harmonies of light. I was alone. I disdained company. I was a son of God, and I felt eternity, and God, and glory. And life!—its murmur was like the murmur of the ocean when you hear the beating of the surf against the shore twenty miles away. Life!—it was like the faintest memory of a fading dream. And the influences that had subdued me or warped me—in that royal hour of coronation I lifted them up and asked, in the light of the other sphere, What are ambition, and vanity, and selfishness, and all other worldly passions? Looking down from that altitude, I gained anew a right measure of life. I never have forgotten it, and I never shall forget it till that vision lapses into the eternal one! Thus, too, one may stand on a mount of vision, quite apart from life and its seductive influences, and there fashion again and readjust all his moral measurements.

My dear Christian brethren, if any of you have been accustomed to look upon these hours as mere visionary hours, in the bad sense of *visionary*, I beseech you to review your judgment. How many of them have you lost! Remember that these hours, although they are not meant to be absolute hours of revelation, are hours of exaltation, in which you have clearer faculties, a higher range of thought and feeling, and a better capacity for moral judgment. You have ecstasies of joy then that perhaps you never have at any other time.

Do not neglect these hours. They are hours in which the gates of the celestial city are opened to you; they are hours in which the guiding stars of heaven shine out for you. ■

Evangelist Billy Sunday
Preaches a
Revival Sermon

"I pity anyone who can't laugh. There must be something wrong with their religion or their lives."

WILLIAM ASHLEY ("BILLY") SUNDAY, the most famous preacher of the early twentieth century, began his extraordinary career in another line of work: playing baseball.

After eight years of major-league play, the baseball star decided to pursue a religious calling and became an ordained minister. In revival meetings around the country, with a tent overhead and sawdust underfoot, Billy Sunday—that was his real name—attracted an audience estimated at a hundred million.

Sunday's typical revival sermon shows his idiomatic language and common-man approach to sermonizing. With direct address and humorous imagery ("a face so long you could eat oatmeal out of the end of a gas pipe"), Sunday testifies to the conversions he has witnessed, a method aimed to bring more converts "to the front."

□　□　□

The trouble with many men is that they have got just enough religion to make them miserable. If there is not joy in religion, you have got a leak in your religion. Some haven't religion enough to pay their debts. Would that I might have a hook and for every debt that you left unpaid I might jerk off a piece of clothing. If I did some of you fellows would have not anything on but a celluloid collar and a pair of socks.

Some of you have not got religion enough to have family prayer. Some of you haven't got religion enough to take the beer bottles out of your cellar and throw them in the alley. You haven't got religion enough to tell the proprietor of the red light, "No, you can't rent my house after the first of June"; to tell the saloonkeeper, "You can't have my house when the lease runs out"; and I want to tell you that the man who rents his property to a saloonkeeper is as low-down as the saloonkeeper. The trouble with you is that you are so taken up with business, with politics, with making money, with your lodges, and each and every one is so dependent on the other, that you are scared to death to come out and live clean-cut for God Almighty.

The matter with a lot of you people is that your religion is not complete. Why, I am almost afraid to make some folks laugh for fear that I will be arrested for breaking a costly piece of antique bric-a-brac.

To see some people you would think that the essential of orthodox Christianity is to have a face so long you could eat oatmeal out of the end of a gas pipe. Sister, that is not religion; I want to tell you that the smiling, happy, sunny-faced religion will win more people to Jesus Christ than the miserable old, grim-faced kind will in ten years.

I pity anyone who can't laugh. There must be something wrong with their religion or their lives. The devil can't laugh.

I have seen women come down the aisle by the thousands, men who drank whisky enough to sink a ship. I see fallen women come to the front by scores and hundreds, and I have seen them go away cleansed by the power of God.

I saw a woman that for twenty-seven years had been proprietor of a disorderly house, and I saw her come down the aisle, close her doors, turn the girls out of her house, to live for God. I saw enough converted in one town where there were four disorderly houses to close their doors; they were empty; the girls have all fled home to their mothers.

Out in Iowa a fellow came to me and spread a napkin on the platform—a napkin as big as a tablecloth. He said, "I want a lot of shavings and sawdust."

"What for?"

"I'll tell you: I want enough to make a sofa pillow. Right here is where I knelt down and was converted, and my wife and four children, and my neighbors. I would like to have enough to make a sofa pillow to have something in the house to help me talk to God. I don't want to forget God, or that I was saved. Can you give me enough?"

I said, "Yes indeed, and if you want to make a mattress, all right, take it; and if you want enough of that tent to make a pair of breeches for all the boys, why take your scissors and cut it right out, if it will help you to keep your mind on God."

That is why I like to have people come down to the front and publicly acknowledge God. I like to have a man have a definite experience in religion—something to remember. ■

Bishop Fulton John Sheen
Makes a Wartime Plea

"PEACE is not a passive but an active virtue. Our Lord never said, 'Blessed are the peaceful,' but 'Blessed are the peacemakers.'"

WITH AN OPTIMISTIC OUTLOOK and the power of radio broadcasting, Fulton John Sheen spread the message of Roman Catholicism. An intensely persuasive thinker and speaker, he gained fame as the priest who helped convert such well-known writers as Heywood Broun and Clare Boothe Luce to Catholicism. The longtime teacher of the philosophy of religion at Catholic University reached his largest audience through radio and television sermons in the 1940s and 1950s. At a time when comedian Milton Berle ("Uncle Miltie") dominated early network television, Fulton Sheen's piercing eyes and homely sermons gained him the counterpoint title of "Uncle Fultie," which he accepted with a smile; it demonstrated his reach through the new medium. He continued propagating the word until his death, as an archbishop, in 1979.

"The Cross and the Double Cross," below, was part of a sermon on his radio show, "The Catholic Hour," on April 6, 1941. Addressing himself to the menace of another world war, Bishop Sheen pointed to the image of the swastika as the "double cross," a parody of the German emblem from Charlie Chaplin's 1940 film, *The Great Dictator*.

To Bishop Sheen, however, the image of the double cross represents far more than a military threat; it is any movement away from Christian faith. He offers words on war from Mussolini and von Moltke, but then he counters with New Testament passages, including the Beatitudes ("Blessed are the peacemakers"), to emphasize that "the hope of the world is in the Cross of Christ." His forceful conclusion about "America's power of regeneration" relies heavily on Christian imagery; the Resurrection on Easter, Bishop Sheen explains, comes only after the death of Jesus on Good Friday.

□   □   □

There is no such thing as living without a cross. We are free only to choose between crosses. Will it be the Cross of Christ which redeems us from our sins, or will it be the double cross, the swastika, the hammer and sickle, the fasces?

Why are we a troubled nation today? Why do we live in fear—we who define freedom as the right to do whatever we pleased; we who have no altars in our churches, no discipline in our schools, and no sacrifices in our lives? We fear because our false freedom and license and apostasy from God have caught up with us, as they did with the prodigal. We would not accept the yoke of Christ; so now we must tremble at the yoke of Caesar. We willed to be free from God; now we must face the danger of being enslaved to a citizen of the foreign country. In seeking to live without the Cross, we got a cross—not one of Christ's making or our own, but the devil's!

The basic spirit of the modern world for the last century has been a determination to escape the Cross. But has the world escaped Calvary? What did Finland, Estonia, Latvia, Poland, China, Czechoslovakia, Albania, Austria, France, and other nations get within the past two years but a cross? What is England fearing today but a cross? What do we fear today, but a cross? What does the world fear, but a diabolically cruel tortured cross made of guns, hammers, sickles, and bombs—the thing that started out to be a cross and then double-crossed itself because it has double-crossed the world?

And that threat throws us into a terrific dilemma. Can we meet that double cross without the Cross? Can a democracy of ease and comfort overcome a system built on sacrifices? Can a nation which permits the breakup of the family by divorce defeat a nation which forcefully bends the family to the nation? Can they who for seven years tightened their belts, gave up butter for guns, endured every conceivable limitation, be conquered by ease and comfort? Dr. Alexis Carrel was right in saying that in America "a good time has been our national cry. The perfect life as viewed by the average youth or adult is a round of ease or entertainment; of motion pictures, radio programs, parties, alcohol, and sexual excesses. This indolent and undisciplined way of life has sapped our individual vigor and imperiled our democratic form of government. Our race pitifully needs new supplies of discipline, morality, and intelligence."

The rise of militarism and the gospel of force in the modern world is a result of the vacuum created by the abandonment of the Cross. Europe was nourished on Christian virtues; it knew obedience to authority, self-discipline, penance, and the need of redemption. But when it began to starve through the abandonment of the bread of the Father's house, it seized, like the prodigal, on the fodder of militarism and the glorification of fame. Like the empty house of the Gospel, the modern world swept itself clean of the Cross of Christ, but only to be possessed by the devils of the double cross. As Voltaire said, "If man had no God, he would make himself one!" So too, we might add, if man had no Cross, he would make himself one. And he has. Apostate from Calvary, the glorification of military virtues in these states is the feeble compensation for a yoke that is sweet and a burden that is light. As Mussolini said on August 24, 1934, "We are becoming a warlike nation—that is to say, one endowed to a higher degree with virtues of obedience, sacrifice, and dedication to country." This so-called heroic attitude toward life is being invoked in deadly earnest by millions in Germany and Russia, and by all who espouse their cause in other nations. In the days when the Cross lived in the hearts of men, war was considered a calamity, a scourge sent by God; but now in the days of the double cross, it is justified as the noblest of virtues for the sake of the nation as in Italy, the race as in Germany, and the class as in Russia. They believe what von Moltke wrote in 1880: "Without war the world would become swamped in materialism." Imagine! To save us from materialism, we must have war! He is right in saying that to save us from materialism we must have sacrifice. He is wrong in saying it must come from war. But if there is no Cross to inspire it, whence shall it come but from the double cross?

We in America are now faced with the threat of that double cross. To revert to our theme. Our choice is not: Will we or will we not have more discipline, more respect for law, more order, more sacrifice; but, where will we get it? Will we get it from without, or from within? Will it be inspired by Sparta or Calvary? By Valhalla or Gethsemane? By militarism or religion? By the double cross or the Cross? By Caesar or by God?

That is the choice facing America today. The hour of false freedom is past. No longer can we have education without discipline, family life without sacrifice, individual existence without moral responsibility, economics and politics without subservience to the common good. We are now only free to say whence it shall come. We will have a sword. Shall it be only the sword that thrusts outward to cut off the ears of our enemies, or the sword that pierces inward to cut out our own selfish pride? May heaven grant that, unlike the centurion, we pierce not the heart of Christ before we discover his divinity and salvation.

Away with those educators and propagandists who, by telling us we need no Cross, make possible having one forged for us abroad. Away with those who, as we gird ourselves for sacrifice based on love of God and Calvary, sneer, "Come down from the Cross" (Matthew 27:40). That cry has been uttered before on Calvary, as his enemies shouted, "He saved others, himself he cannot save" (Mark 15:31). They were now willing to admit he had saved others; they could well afford to do it, for now he apparently could not save himself.

Of course, he could not save himself. No man can save himself who saves another. The rain cannot save itself, if it is to bud the greenery; the sun cannot save itself if it is to light the world; the seed cannot save itself if it is to make the harvest; a mother cannot save herself if she is to save her child; a soldier cannot save himself if he is to save his country. It was not weakness which made Christ hang on the Cross; it was obedience to the law of sacrifice, of love. For how could he save us if he ever saved himself? Peace he craved; but as Saint Paul says, there is no peace but through the blood of the Cross. Peace we want; but there is none apart from sacrifice. Peace is not a passive but an active virtue. Our Lord never said, "Blessed are the peaceful," but "Blessed are the peacemakers." The Beatitude rests only on those who *make* it out of trial, out of suffering, out of cruelty, even out of sin. God hates peace in those who are destined for war. And we are destined for war—a war against a false freedom which endangered our freedom; a war for the Cross against the double cross; a war to make America once more what it was intended to be from the beginning—a country dedicated to liberty under God; a war of the *militia Christi:* "Having our loins girt about with truth and having on the breastplate of justice. . . the shield of faith. . . the helmet of salvation" (Ephesians 6:10-17). For only those who carry the sword of the spirit have the right and have the power to say to the enemies of the Cross, "Put thy sword back into its scabbard."

The great tragedy is that the torch of sacrifice and truth has been snatched from the hands of those who should hold it, and is borne aloft by the enemies of the Cross. The Pentecostal fires have been stolen from the altar of God and now burn as tongues of fire in those who grind the altars into dust. The fearlessness born of love of God which once challenged the armies of Caesar is now espoused to Caesar. We live in an age of saints in reverse, when apostles who are breathed on by the evil spirit outdare those animated by the Holy Spirit of God. The fires for causes like communism, nazism, and fascism, that burn downwards, are more intense than the fires that burn upwards in the hearts of those who pay only lip service to God. But this passion by which men deliver themselves over to half-truths and idiocies should make us realize what a force would enter history again if there were but a few saints in every nation who could help the world, because they were not enmeshed in it; who would, like their Master on the Cross, not seek to save the world as it is, but to be saved from it; who would demonstrate to those who still have decent hearts, as we believe we have in America, that it is possible to practice sacrifice without turning the world into a vast slaughterhouse. There is no escaping the Cross!

That is why the hope, the real hope of the world, is not in those politicians who, indifferent to divinity, offer Christ and Barabbas to the mob to save their tumbling suffrage. It is not in those economists who would drive Christ from their shores like the Gerasenes, because they feared loss of profit on their swine. It is not in those educators who, like other Pilates, sneer, "What is truth"—then crucify it. The hope of the world is in the crucified in every land; in those bearing the Cross of Christ; in the mothers of Poland who, like other Rachels, mourn for their children; in the wives weeping for their husbands stolen into the servitude of war; in the sons and daughters kissing the cold earth of Siberia as the only one of the things God made that they are left to see; in bleeding feet and toil-worn hands; in persecuted Jews, blood brothers of Christ, of whom God said, "He who curses you, I shall curse"; in the priests in concentration camps who, like Christ, in other Gethsemanes, find a way to offer their own blood in the chalice of their own body.

The hope of the world is in the Cross of Christ borne down the ages in the hearts of suffering men, women, and children, who, if we only knew it, are saving us from the double cross more than our guns and ships.

We in America are now brought face to face with the heritage of a freedom derived from God. The hour has struck when we have to take up a cross. There is no escaping the Cross. Who shall give it to us? Shall it be imposed by chastisement, or shall it be freely accepted by penance? I believe in America's power of regeneration. I believe we can remake ourselves from within in order that we be not remade from without. I believe in the future of America; but I believe in it only as I believe in Easter—after it has passed through Good Friday. ■

Theologian Karl Barth Preaches Deliverance by Faith

"A drowning man cannot pull himself out of the water by his own hair. Neither can you do it. Someone else must rescue you."

SWISS PROTESTANT THEOLOGIAN KARL BARTH (whose name is pronounced to rhyme with "art") has often been compared in theological significance to seventeenth-century reformer John Calvin. Dr. Barth, when asked about his rejection of some Calvinist doctrines such as predestination, replied, "Calvin is in heaven and has had time to ponder where he went wrong. Doubtless he is pleased that I am setting him right."

Barth, who died in 1968, was well acquainted with controversy, in politics as well as in theology. Prior to World War II, he refused to swear personal loyalty to Hitler. Expelled from Germany by Nazi leaders in 1935, he led church opposition to the Third Reich and became a symbol of political resistance to the spread of nazism.

More than a decade after the Second World War, Barth delivered his sermon "He Stands By Us" before a Christmas communion service in 1958.

This sermon indicates the ability of Barth's preaching to hold an audience. Through direct address that includes pointing to the listeners, he informs in parallel structure that Jesus "stands by you, stands by me, and stands by us all." With Scripture lessons and hymn references, he asserts the Christmas message and, through a repetition of "But, now, the good news of Christmas," ties together his argument of redemption by faith.

□   □   □

My dear brothers and sisters, let me get to the main point without delay. Who is he who was born the son of Mary, wrapped in swaddling cloths, and laid in a manger? Who *is* he? I do not ask who he *was*. Christmas is not the birthday celebration of a man who lived long ago, then died and passed away, and whose centennial we solemnly commemorate. True, he once lived and then died—and *how* he died!—but he also rose from the dead; he lives and is present among us now, much closer to each one of us than we are to ourselves. Still, who is he? The answer to this question is the good news of Christmas.

Today let me say simply this: *He who was born in the stable is he who stands by you, stands by me, and stands by us all.* I do not say *one* who stands by you, but *he* who stands by you. For only one, only he who was born on the first Christmas Day, can stand by us in utter unselfishness and with ultimate authority and power.

I would like to state it in very personal terms. *He stands by you—and by you—and by you!* When I point my finger at you, each one must know he is personally addressed. Yes, he stands by *you!* This is what you yearn for, this is what you desire. You cannot live without a fellow human being. You may ask now, "Who is he who really wants to stand by me?" And a further question will immediately rise in your mind: "Is there some one, or perhaps is there no one who is willing and able to stand by me? Perhaps nobody cares? Do all others pass me by like the priest and the Levite in the parable of the good Samaritan? Or have they even turned against me?" When such questions beset you, a great loneliness may have descended upon you, and you felt totally deserted. And then you came very close to saying, "If no one is ready to stand by me, I shall stand by myself!" But this is a great, even the very greatest, error! A drowning man cannot pull himself out of the water by his own hair. Neither can you do it. Someone else must rescue you.

This is the good news of Christmas. He who stands by you and helps you is alive and present! It is he who was born that Christmas Day! Open your eyes, open your ears, open your heart! You may truly see, hear, and experience that he is here, and stands by you as no one else can do! He stands by you, really by you, now and for evermore!

He stands by you without ulterior motive, without thinking of himself. Perhaps you asked yourself a while ago, "Is it really so bad? Does not one or the other of my fellowmen stand by me?" This is quite possible. Yet does there not remain a shadow between him and you, even though he be your very best friend? Perhaps he stands by you as long as he enjoys your company, perhaps expecting that you will reciprocate, perhaps because it makes him feel good. You sense that fundamentally he thinks first of himself; he does not stand by you; he stands only by himself. When this recognition dawns on you, loneliness will again descend on you, only more poignantly.

But, now, the good news of Christmas. He who was born on Christmas Day stands by you, without thinking of himself for one moment. He does not demand anything from you; he demands *you.*

Love caused thine incarnation,
Love brought thee down to me;
Thy thirst for my salvation
Procured my liberty.
O love beyond all telling
That led thee to embrace
In love, all love excelling,
Our lost and fallen race.

He is the one who was born that Christmas morning and became your fellowman par excellence, your neighbor, your friend, your brother. He reaps no benefit from it. He is not concerned with himself. He is concerned only with you.

He stands by you in the fullness of his authority and power. Suppose you do find a fellowman who stands by you in all adversities. But he will never be more than a man, endowed with only human power. He would certainly like to help you, and he does help you to a certain extent. Yet is it not true that a fellowman can only be of little help and ultimately of no help at all? Let us choose an obvious example. Here you sit, and here I stand before you. I sincerely desire to stand by you. You possibly feel it and even believe me. I might succeed in comforting you and cheering you up by telling you about Christmas. But let us be honest. I cannot help you effectively. I cannot put your life in order. I cannot save you. No man can do this for his fellowmen. No one can stand by the others with unlimited authority and power.

But now, the good news of Christmas! He who was born on Christmas Day is not only the son of Mary; he is also the Son of God. If he stands by you, he does so in full power, in the power to help you at any cost, to shield you against each and everyone, above all against your worst enemy, yourself. He stands by you in the power to help you effectively, to carry you, to save you. He is not content to bring you some comfort and good cheer; he is all out to bring you everlasting joy. Only he can bring it, but he really brings it. He stands by you in the power to guide you through this life, and to carry you through death to life eternal. It is he who was born on Christmas Day, your Savior and mine, the Savior of us all, the first son of Mary, the firstborn of all creation, as it is affirmed elsewhere in the Bible. He, "Christ the Savior is born."

But this is not the whole story. We are furthermore told that there was no room in the inn for Joseph and Mary. No room for him who was to be born and who was born. No room for him who stands by us men in unlimited power and utter selfishness. For him there was no room in the inn.

The inn must have been something like a modest or more fashionable hotel, a nice or not so nice house with guest rooms, dining room, and lounges. Today it would also include a large garage! It was certainly a comfortable place to stay and to rest and to eat. In this nice and comfortable inn there happened to be no room for the child about to be born, no room for this new guest. There were too many other and better clients around. Too bad! Too bad indeed for this inn! Now Jesus Christ could not be born there. Now he had to be born in totally different surroundings.

What does this say to our situation? The Savior does not need to be born again. He was born once for all. But he would like to take up quarters among us, by whom he stands so faithfully and so powerfully, whose Savior he is. What about our various inns? The city hall, the casino, the university, or the cathedral could very well be these inns. So could the many private homes and apartments, the restaurants and the stores, of Basel. So could the Bundeshaus in Berne, or the Kremlin in Moscow, or the Vatican in Rome, or the White House in Washington. These are inns where he surely would like to dwell. Why not? All these places, including ours here with its work rooms and cells, are inhabited by people. And people are his main concern. By them and by us all he stands, faithfully and powerfully.

But what if in these inns there is no room left? Because there may be people with better status, better jobs, and better knowledge who have no place for him? Who have no idea that he who wants to enter is the one who stands by them and whom they so desperately need? What if the doors of all these inns remain closed to him, and everything continues in its old beaten path, since he cannot put up quarters among us? Perhaps this holds also for this house or this cell where you dwell? What if he then went on to other places and other people, far away, possibly to Africa or Asia? I am reminded this moment of a dear friend in Japan who was baptized a few weeks ago after having weighed this step for twenty-five years. Now he has come forward and others do the same, far away from here. What if Christ had already passed by our closed inns? What, then, shall we say?

No doubt a Christmas message is also addressed to the inns and their inhabitants. "Behold, I stand at the door and knock; if anyone hears my voice and opens the door, I will come in to him and eat with him, and he with me." Yes, if . . . ! The good news of Christmas raises indeed a serious question in relation to our various inns.

But I do not want to conclude by raising this question. Fortunately, our story makes one more point. The Savior did not find room in the inn. But this did not hinder him from being born elsewhere, and in what surroundings! We hear about a manger. We probably find ourselves in a stable or an open-air feeding spot for animals. Certainly not in a nice and comfortable place where people like to dwell because it looks so cosy and homely, or at least decent. No, it was a place compared to which the cells of this house might well be called luxurious. There were animals right beside, oxen and donkeys, as many painters have represented it. In this gloomy place Jesus Christ was born. Likewise, he died in an even gloomier place. There, in the manger, in the stable next to the animals, it happened that the sky opened above the dark earth, that God became man, to be wholly with us and for us. There it happened that this fellow-man, this neighbor, this friend, this brother was given to us. There it happened. Thanks be to God, the parents and the baby for whom there was no room in the inn found this other spot where this could happen, and indeed did happen.

And, thanks be to God, as we now consider the Savior's coming into our own midst, there are not only the various inns where he stands outside, knocking and asking. There is quite another place where he simply enters, indeed has already secretly entered, and waits until we gladly recognize his presence. What kind of a place in our life is this? Do not suggest some presumably noble, beautiful, or at least decent compartment of your life and work, where you could give the Savior a respectable reception. Not so, my friends! The place where the Savior enters in looks rather like the stable of Bethlehem. It is not beautiful, but quite ugly; not at all cosy, but really frightening; not at all decently human, but right beside the animals. You see, the proud or modest inns, and our behavior as their inhabitants, are but the surface of our lives. Beneath there lurks the depth, even the abyss. Down below, we are, without exception, but each in his own way, only poor beggars, lost sinners, moaning creatures on the threshold of death, only people who have lost their way.

Down there Jesus Christ sets up quarters. Even better, he has already done so! Yes, praise be to God for this dark place, for this manger, for this stable in our lives! There we need him, and there he can use each one of us. There we are ready for him. There he only waits that we see him, recognize him, believe in him, and love him. There he greets us. What else can we do but return his greeting and bid him welcome? Let us not be ashamed that the oxen and donkeys are close by. Precisely there he firmly stands by us all. In this dark place he will have Holy Communion with us. This is what we now shall have with him and with one another. Amen. ■

Rabbi Louis Finkelstein
Delivers a Sermon in
the White House

"'You must leave a little bit to God.'"

CINCINNATI-BORN LOUIS FINKELSTEIN studied for the rabbinate at the Jewish Theological Seminary in New York, taught Hebrew theology and the study of the Talmud, and was elected chancellor of that center of Jewish learning in 1951. Until his death in 1991, he was widely regarded as the preeminent voice of Conservative Judaism in America.

In a 1958 address to a rabbinical assembly, he spoke of a series of conversations that Roman emperor Hadrian had in the year 130 with a Jewish sage named Y'Hoshua Ben Chananyah. "Under Hadrian's rule, Rome had reached the zenith of its power," recounted Dr. Finkelstein. "Yet Y'Hoshua Ben Chananyah, who had keen eyes and was a great sage, foresaw the time, not far off, when this empire would be a great ruin. It couldn't help but be a great ruin, because it was surrounded by enemies and its own citizens did not want to be soldiers. The only way to survive was to take barbarians, as they called them, and train them to be soldiers to hold back the other barbarians, and then it was only a question of time before these barbarians would go over to their brother barbarians and attack Rome, which actually happened within 250 years."

"He was trying to say to the Roman emperor," the rabbi speculated, "that the future peace of the world, the very survival of Roman civilization, depended on a shift in policy—that they had come to the end of what could be done with arms. There was no more land that could be conquered, and all future battles would have to be either stalemates or defeats. Therefore he believed that Rome had to bring to its policy a new idea, the idea of brotherhood with the Parthians and the Saxons and the other tribes.

"Reb Y'Hoshua Ben Chananyah urged the emperor not to arm the barbarians, not to give them technical knowledge which ultimately they would use to destroy Rome, but to give them instead an understanding of what life is all about, which the Jews were trying to spread in the world. . . .

"The emperor could not accept this, because in order to accept it he would have had to change not Roman policy but Roman character. He would have had to persuade the Roman people not to look upon the barbarians as barbarians, but to look upon them as brothers; to give up their own high standard of living in order to lift the so-called barbarians from their savage ways, and that the Romans were unwilling to do. If they could have done it, Rome could have survived to this day." Rabbi Finkelstein then gave the bridge—"We are living in a world in which the white race is a corporate Hadrian"—that carried his argument to the need for education and an end to racial discrimination.

When President Richard Nixon instituted a series of sermons to be delivered on Sunday mornings in the East Room of the White House, some of his aides felt uncomfortable at possible sectarianism as well as a breach between church and state. "Get the top rabbi," he directed; Dr. Finkelstein agreed to come and, on June 29, 1969, delivered this sermon. (According to his nephew David Finn, Dr. Finkelstein added impromptu comments, specifically on the creation of the State of Israel, to his prepared sermon.)

□   □   □

Mr. President, Mrs. Nixon, Mr. Chief Justice, Mrs. Burger, ladies, and gentlemen:

One is frequently asked to define the American way of life, which we struggle so hard to protect and develop. No satisfactory definition describes this way of life to those who have not experienced it. However, there are scenes, distinctive of America, scarcely occurring anywhere else, even in the free world, which may help to make it understood. One is taking place in this room today. Here are gathered leaders of our nation, among others, to pray together, uniting across differences of background and doctrine, before the throne of the Judge of us all. Here the assembly looks to a faith, long subject to disdain, and even persecution, for light to our severely tried generation.

In the face of crisis which seemed insoluble, my great predecessor Solomon Schechter used to say, "You must leave a little bit to God." He did not mean that we are free from responsibility to alleviate human agony. He tried to express in a single aphorism the insight of Rabbi Tarfon, a sage who flourished in Judea toward the end of the first century, and who taught his disciples, "You are not obliged to complete the task (that is, the task of making the world a better dwelling-place), but neither are you free to desist from it." Or, as he put it on another occasion, "Do not flinch from a task which by its nature can never be completed."

How little the mightiest of us can hope to accomplish, and how much we have to leave to God! And how secure we may be that, no matter what follies we may commit, he will ultimately save us from the worst results of our errors! After all, here we are, all sentient human beings, yet all descended from primeval bits of protoplasm, themselves incredibly combined from inanimate bits of protein. Perhaps some three billion years were required for those primeval cells to become thinking men and women; but that is surely a brief span for a bacterium to graduate into manhood.

The primeval cells had no notion of purpose. Neither did the earth-worms, who, in the course of eons, began the adventuresome roads to mammals, primates, and humans, impelled by a force which still eludes our understanding. Heirs to all their strengths and weaknesses, we are their direct descendants, thinking, writing, speaking, speculating, planning, and even from time to time communing with God himself.

Having brought us so far, did this cosmic force desert us, simply because we are sentient human beings, rather than unicellular bacteria and amoebae? Instead, must we not rationally assume that—privileged to think, to have purpose, to work toward goals—the divine power that brought us from such humble origins will continue to guide us, turning our very folly into wisdom?

As men, we alone among animal species have the power to envisage the future and to choose. We can act wisely, and we can also act foolishly. The machinery which constantly saves us from our sins of omission and commission appears most clearly perhaps in the life of society. American history could properly be told in the style of the Book of Judges. Whenever self-induced danger threatened, leaders have been sent to save our country for its intended destiny of service.

Where would we be today, where would be the hope of the free world, where would be the future of civilization, if in the crises at the beginning of the Republic it had lacked the redoubtable figures of Benjamin Franklin, George Washington, Thomas Jefferson, and Alexander Hamilton, to mention only a few? That great tragedy the War between the States arose from many failures of human judgment. But—remarkably—the compassion and wisdom of Abraham Lincoln became available just when they were most essential. Where would the Western world (including our own country) have been today, if Winston Churchill had not, through what seemed at the time mere chance, become the articulate leader of Britain, standing alone between impending barbarism and civilization, guarding us, until we could protect ourselves and others?

Miracles occur not only in historical crises; they are happening every day, all the time, for each of us. Everyone in this room is alive due to uncounted miracles, as commonplace as the rising and setting of the sun.

A student at our seminary once asked whether I really believe in the miracle of the ancient Israelites crossing the Red Sea. (Actually, properly interpreted, Scripture says that they crossed not the Red Sea but a "Sea of Reeds," which may have been a smaller body of water.) As related in Exodus, the story is about as remarkable as the American defeat of the Japanese navy at Midway, a turning point in the Second World War. I might have mentioned this fact. I might also have mentioned the miracle of the American Constitution, a document drawn up by human beings, but which seems to reflect almost divine wisdom, which has guided us for generations and become a model for many other peoples. I might have mentioned the miracle of the Second World War, during which, in 1940, the Allies seemed hopelessly defeated, and yet emerged victorious in 1945. As he was himself a refugee from oppression, who had fled to Jerusalem before coming to the United States, I might have come very near his own experience by mentioning the miracle of the emergence of the state of Israel, an event unique in the annals of mankind.

However, all these answers only occurred to me on my way home from the seminary. My answer to him was different. I said, "I was not present at the crossing of the Red Sea, so that I cannot add to what is recorded. But I certainly believe in miracles; and one of the miracles in which I most firmly believe is that you and I exist, and that despite the fact that our lives are in dire jeopardy momentarily, and would cease if everything depended on our conscious thought." I recommended that he read a book by Walter B. Cannon, professor of physiology at Harvard, called *The Wisdom of the Body*. It is learned and wise; though doubtless since its appearance early in the century, others have superseded some of its facts. Professor Cannon shows what miracles go on at every moment within us; what ingenuity beyond the power of the cleverest engineer enables the eye to see, the ear to hear, the hand to touch, and above all the mind to think. How strange it is that no matter how much liquid we drink, our blood never becomes diluted, but is kept in proper balance! How incredible that the single cell from which each of us developed should carry the potential of every quality destined to appear in us, in its proper season; that the cells multiplying from this original one should have separate functions, one becoming a brain cell, another a red blood corpuscle, a third a bone cell—without confusion or error!

Of course, sometimes the miraculous is obscured. There is much that is imperfect in man's life, both individual and communal. That is what we should expect. Why should it be otherwise? What needs explanation is how much happens to be right, even though the world in each of its parts is far too complex for the wisest of us to comprehend.

Once more, as Solomon Schechter said, "You must leave a little bit to God." He has been; he is; he will be. We must try to do what we can, and are enjoying a great privilege when we do well and find the path of the right. At such times, we are cooperating with God: in the rabbinic phrase, we become his partners. And he is working through us, and with us. Happy is he, who, like Lincoln, is privileged to save his fellows when they are threatened by their own misdeeds, whose life represents an intervention of the divine into human affairs.

The faith that all will be well enables us to be steadfast in peril, and modest in success; to escape foolish hand-wringing and paralysis, as well as thoughtless panic and fear.

Once more, as Schechter said, "You must leave a little bit to God." I hope that it is not presumptuous for me, a guest of the president of the United States, to pray that, looking back at our generation, a future historian may say, as I have said of Lincoln, "In a period of great trials and tribulations, the finger of God pointed to Richard Milhous Nixon, giving him the wisdom and the vision to save the world and civilization, opening the way for our country to realize the good that the twentieth century offered mankind." ■

President Ronald Reagan Inveighs against the Sinfulness of Communism

"I urge you to beware the temptation of pride—the temptation blithely to declare yourselves above it all and label both sides equally at fault, to ignore the facts of history and the aggressive impulses of an evil empire. . . ."

SPEAKING ON MARCH 8, 1983, to the National Association of Evangelists meeting in Orlando, Florida, President Reagan delivered a politically controversial sermon on an undeniably moral topic: the sources of evil in the modern world. The address was drafted by Anthony Dolan and delivered with appropriate evangelistic fervor by the president to a group that agreed with him on such issues as prayer in public schools and limitation on abortion, but tended to accept the Soviet position on nuclear disarmament. Liberal historian Henry Steele Commager called this speech the worst ever given by a president, savage criticism that did not trouble the conservative president or his aides a bit. Although the "evil empire" phrase was derided by accommodationists as extreme and simplistic, it set forth with clarity and force the basic Reagan beliefs before the onset of Gorbachevian *perestroika*, and was recalled with respect at the President's state funeral in 2004. Here is his sermon's conclusion:

□   □   □

During my first press conference as president, in answer to a direct question, I pointed out that, as good Marxist-Leninists, the Soviet leaders have openly and publicly declared that the only morality they recognize is that which will further their cause, which is world revolution.

I think I should point out I was only quoting Lenin, their guiding spirit, who said in 1920 that they repudiate all morality that proceeds from supernatural ideas or ideas that are outside class conceptions; morality is entirely subordinate to the interests of class war; and everything is moral that is necessary for the annihilation of the old exploiting social order and for uniting the proletariat.

I think the refusal of many influential people to accept this elementary fact of Soviet doctrine illustrates a historical reluctance to see totalitarian powers for what they are. We saw this phenomenon in the 1930s; we see it too often today. This does not mean we should isolate ourselves and refuse to seek an understanding with them. . . .

Let us pray for the salvation of all those who live in totalitarian darkness, pray they will discover the joy of knowing God.

But until they do, let us be aware that while they preach the supremacy of the state, declare its omnipotence over individual man, and predict its eventual domination of all peoples of the earth—they are the focus of evil in the modern world.

It was C. S. Lewis who, in his unforgettable *Screwtape Letters*, wrote, "The greatest evil is not now done in those sordid 'dens of crime' that Dickens loved to paint. It is not done even in concentration camps and labor camps. In those we see its final result. But it is conceived and ordered (moved, seconded, carried, and minuted) in clear, carpeted, warmed, and well-lighted offices, by quiet men with white collars and cut fingernails and smooth shaven cheeks who do not need to raise their voice."

Because these "quiet men" do not "raise their voices," because they sometimes speak in soothing tones of brotherhood and peace, because, like other dictators before them, they are always making "their final territorial demand," some would have us accept them at their word and accommodate ourselves to their aggressive impulses.

But, if history teaches anything, it teaches: simple-minded appeasement or wishful thinking about our adversaries is folly—it means the betrayal of our past, the squandering of our freedom.

So I urge you to speak out against those who would place the United States in a position of military and moral inferiority. You know, I have always believed that old Screwtape reserves his best efforts for those of you in the church.

So in your discussions of the nuclear freeze proposals, I urge you to beware the temptation of pride—the temptation blithely to declare yourselves above it all and label both sides equally at fault, to ignore the facts of history and the aggressive impulses of an evil empire, to simply call the arms race a giant misunderstanding and thereby remove yourself from the struggle between right and wrong, good and evil.

I ask you to resist the attempts of those who would have you withhold your support for this administration's efforts to keep America strong and free, while we negotiate real and verifiable reductions in the world's nuclear arsenals and one day, with God's help, their total elimination.

While America's military strength is important, let me add here that I have always maintained that the struggle now going on for the world will never be decided by bombs or rockets, by armies or military might.

The real crisis we face today is a spiritual one; at root, it is a test of moral will and faith.

Whittaker Chambers, the man whose own religious conversion made him a "witness" to one of the terrible traumas of our age, the Hiss-Chambers case, wrote that the crisis of the Western world exists to the degree in which the West is indifferent to God, the degree to which it collaborates in communism's attempt to make man stand alone without God.

For Marxism-Leninism is actually the second-oldest faith, he said, first proclaimed in the Garden of Eden with the words of temptation "Ye shall be as gods." The Western world can answer this challenge, he wrote, "but only provided that its faith in God and the freedom he enjoins is as great as communism's faith in man."

I believe we shall rise to this challenge; I believe that communism is another sad, bizarre chapter in human history whose last pages even now are being written. I believe this because the source of our strength in the quest for human freedom is not material but spiritual, and, because it knows no limitation, it must terrify and ultimately triumph over those who would enslave their fellow man.

For, in the words of Isaiah, "He giveth power to the faint; and to them that have no might he increased strength. But they that wait upon the Lord shall renew their strength; they shall mount up with wings as eagles; they shall run, and not be weary." ■

Billy Graham Preaches about Salvation through Jesus

"YES, man has a terminal disease. It is called sin."

EVANGELIST WILLIAM FRANKLIN GRAHAM, known worldwide as Reverend Billy Graham, lifts his audiences with "I'm not preaching Christ hanging from a cross. I'm preaching a living Christ."

The preacher and friend of presidents who took the gospel behind the Iron Curtain was born in North Carolina in 1918 and was ordained a Southern Baptist church minister in 1939. Since 1949, however, his principal work has been conducting evangelistic crusades in major American cities and around the world.

Of the following sermon, Billy Graham writes the anthologist, "I have preached on the Bible verse found in John 3:16 more than any other sermon during my ministry. One reason is that it contains in a nutshell a miniature Bible—the heart of the Bible's unchanging and relevant message, applicable to all persons in every culture. One Sunday I preached it to a tribe in Africa which had barely heard of the name of Jesus Christ; the following Sunday I preached it at Cambridge University in England, only changing a few of the illustrations."

The version below was preached on September 18, 1984, in Novosibirsk, Siberia. Its effectiveness springs from the mixture of Bible verses and personal anecdotes that illustrate the biblical passages. Other dramatic devices of this sermon include the relating of conversations and a series of questions posed directly to get each listener to consider his or her own relationship with God.

□   □   □

Tonight I am reading from the third chapter of John, verse 16. This is perhaps the best-known verse in all the Bible. My mother taught me this verse when I was a little boy on the farm, and perhaps many of you also learned it when you were younger. For some of you it may be new—but it contains the teaching of the Bible in a nutshell.

"For God so loved the world, that he gave his only begotten Son, that whosoever believeth in him should not perish, but have everlasting life" (John 3:16).

Around the world people ask me one question: "If there is a God of love, why does he allow all of the suffering that goes on in the world? Why doesn't God stop it?" There is so much suffering in the world—disease, poverty, war, hate, loneliness, boredom, and all kinds of other problems. We are told that right now forty small wars are going on in the world. If God loves the human race, why doesn't he stop it? In my country, at least, millions of people are getting depressed; they get discouraged with life. Many end up committing suicide. But God did not intend for the world to be this way, as we see in this verse. So let's look at this verse very closely.

The first phrase says, "For God." It brings us right at the start to the subject of God. Does God exist?

Several years ago I was in Siberia at the famed academic city in Novosibirsk, and we met some of their leading scientists, As we talked, I thought to myself, "I cannot prove the existence of God in one of their laboratories." Yes, we can come close to it from a philosophical point of view. But we cannot prove scientifically that God exists, because God is a spirit, and science can only deal with the physical. But almost everybody believes there is some kind of supreme being. We are born with that belief that there is something—or someone—beyond this life, something in control of this vast universe. Down inside we are born with a yearning for God.

We had a woman in America who was born deaf, and dumb, and blind. Her name was Helen Keller. She could not see; she could not hear; she could not speak. They tried for years to communicate with her. How would you communicate with a person like that? Finally, after much struggle, they communicated with her, and she became a famous and much admired scholar and writer. When they first communicated the word "God" to her, she said, "I knew him, but I did not know his name." Deep in her heart she knew there is God.

Recently I read a statement from a scientific magazine which said that many of our astrophysicists are seldom atheists. Not long ago I was in England, and while I was there one of their most distinguished scientists said, "After working for years on the theories of cosmic beginnings, I have come to a belief there is a God."

What is God like? We may believe something exists out there—but what is God really like? The Bible tells us what God is like, because God has revealed himself to us. What is he like?

First, the Bible teaches that God created the universe. "In the beginning God created the heaven and the earth" (Genesis 1:1), Think of all the millions and billions of stars and planets—we don't even know how many there are. God made them all. He made this earth. He made you. And because he made you, he loves you. You are important to God. If you were the only person in this whole world, Christ would have died for you.

God is not only the Creator of the universe, but the Bible tells us God also is a spirit. He is greater than the created world. The Bible says in John 4:24, "God is a spirit: and they that worship him must worship him in spirit and in truth." God does not have a body like we do. If he had a body like yours or mine, he could not be all over the world at the same time. At this very moment, God is all over the Soviet Union, all over America, all over Latin America, all over Africa, all over the whole world at the same time. He is not bound by a body. He does not have to get on an airplane to go to another part of the world. God is a spirit.

The Bible also says God never changes. Malachi 3:6 says, "For I am the Lord, I change not." The Bible teaches that God is from "everlasting to everlasting" (Psalm 90:2). He is eternal. During all of the thousands of years of changing human history, God has not changed in the slightest. I cannot understand how God could always be. I cannot understand how God will always be—from everlasting to everlasting. That is beyond my poor human mind to conceive, but I believe it. Something inside my heart tells me God is infinite, and the word of God teaches it.

The Bible teaches as well that God is a holy God. In Psalm 145:17 it says, "The Lord is righteous in all his ways, and holy in all his works." That means that God is absolute perfection.

I remember one time my mother taught me a lesson. She usually did her washing on Monday, and she would hang the washing out on the line to dry. One Monday we had a snowstorm, and the snow was beautiful and white. She washed her clothes and hung them out to dry. She thought they were very white and clean. But in comparison to the snow, they were dirty. "That is like our goodness compared to God's perfect holiness," she said. God is absolutely holy; and in comparison to him, all of us have sinned. We all have moral impurities. The Scripture teaches that if we are ever to get to heaven, we have to be as holy and as righteous as God. Now, how will we get this holiness? How will we get this righteousness? We don't have it ourselves. You can't work for it. There's not enough money in the world to buy it. Where do you get it? I'll tell you in just a moment.

The Bible also says that God is a God of judgment. In Hebrews 9:27 it says, "It is appointed unto men once to die, but after this the judgment."

There are three things you cannot escape. When I went to the university, they said there were certain courses I would have to take if I were to graduate. And there are certain things that all of us as a human race cannot escape. First, we cannot escape being born. You have been born, and you cannot be unborn. Second, we cannot escape death. You are going to die. Everybody in this room will be dead in the next hundred years. Death is total in every generation. The third thing you cannot escape is the judgment of God. Jesus said in Matthew, the twelfth chapter, and the thirty-sixth verse, "Every idle word that men shall speak, they shall give account . . . in the day of judgment." In Acts 17:31, the apostle Paul speaking to the intellectuals of Athens said, "[God has] appointed a day, in . . . which he will judge the world." You and I will be at the judgment if we do not know Christ.

The Bible says that God has two sets of books: the book of judgment and the book of life. The moment you are born your name is written in the book of judgment, and all the sins that you commit are in that book. When you receive Christ, all of those sins are wiped out because of what Christ did for you on the cross. God cannot remember your sins any more. Hebrews 10:17 says, "Their sins and iniquities will I remember no more." That is a very wonderful thing God does for you. Then your name is written in the book of life. Which book is your name written in? The book of judgment or the book of life? I would not leave here tonight unless I knew that my name was written in the book of life. You can know it by coming to the cross where Christ, God's only Son, died and shed his blood, and to the resurrection where he was raised from the dead.

Then the Bible says God is love. God says, "I have loved [you] with an everlasting love" (Jeremiah 31:3). This is why God created man. Have you ever asked yourself, "Who am I? Where did I come from? Why am I here? What is the purpose of my life? When I die, where am I going?" Have you ever asked yourself those questions? God created man because God loves us and wants to have a personal relationship with us, and he wants us to love him in return.

God placed man and woman in the Garden of Eden. It was a perfect environment. God said, "We are going to build a wonderful world together—no war, no crime, no divorce, no sickness, no sorrow, no death." But something happened. God had said to man in Genesis 2:17, "But of the tree of the knowledge of good and evil, thou shalt not eat of it: for in the day that thou eatest thereof thou shalt surely die." Man had control of the whole world, and it was a perfect world. He had all the food he could possibly eat. There was no death; God never meant that anybody should die. But God gave man a gift—the gift of freedom of moral choice. Man could serve God if he wanted to, or man could disobey God. If he disobeyed God, he was going to suffer and die. So God tested man, and man failed the test and broke God's law. He rebelled against God, and death had to come because God had said it, and rebellion against our Creator is a terrible thing. If death had not followed, God would have been a liar.

I remember when I was in school many years ago. We thought science could save us. This was before the atomic bomb. We had the idea that technology was going to save the world. So what have science and technology done? They have brought us to the edge of paradise with all the wonderful new things that have been invented—but they also have created terrible weapons of mass destruction that have brought us to the edge of a man-made hell, And man has to make a choice.

Leo Tolstoy, the great Russian writer, wrote *War and Peace*. He was a believer, and that book reminds us of the frightening things we can do to each other. I have read the story of Dostoevsky and how the czarist regimes put him in prison. But someone gave him a New Testament when he went to prison, and he memorized large parts of it. His favorite passage was the fifteenth chapter of Luke, the story of the prodigal son in which Jesus tells how we foolishly run from God and yet how God still loves us and wants to welcome us back and forgive us if we will return to him. You will find the theme of that passage of Scripture all the way through Dostoevsky's novels.

Yes, man has a terminal disease, It is called *sin*. Out of the human heart come the problems of the world. The apostle Paul, writing in 2 Thessalonians 2:7, says, "For the mystery of iniquity [does] already work." In 1 John 3:4 the Bible says, "Sin is the transgression of the law."

Let me tell you something. Billy Graham is a sinner. I have broken God's law. The Bible says that if we break it in one point, we are guilty of all. "For whosoever shall keep the whole law, and yet offend in one point, he is guilty of all" (James 2:10). So what does that mean? That means I must face judgment. I am under condemnation. How can I be saved? It seems impossible. God says I have to be as holy as he is holy, and I have no way of being holy. I am a sinner, and so are you, if you measure yourself against God's goodness.

There was a great French scientist who lived in the seventeenth century by the name of Blaise Pascal. He invented many things that we take for granted today, like the calculator. At the age of fifteen he had already astounded the world with his mathematical ability. But at the age of thirty-one he was very miserable in his heart in spite of his brilliance and his fame. He said, to himself, "There is something else that I need and want in my life." Later he wrote in his diary, "1 found out that I am a sinner before God. I received Jesus Christ into my life by faith." From that moment on, for the rest of his life, Pascal followed in the steps of Christ. He recognized that he was a sinner before God, and he turned to Christ for forgiveness. Christ filled the empty place in his heart.

When I was still a teenager, I received Christ. The Scripture says that he clothed me in a robe of righteousness because of the cross, and when God looks at me, he does not see my sins. He sees the blood of Christ, and we celebrate that blood when we take communion. When we take the fruit of the vine, or we break the bread, we are remembering that death almost two thousand years ago. Why is that death so important? Because in that moment, God laid on Christ the sins of us all. He had never committed sin or broken God's moral law. He never deserved to die. But in those few moments on the cross, Christ did not die just physically; he died spiritually. Your sins and my sins were placed on him and caused him to feel the pangs of hell. He took the hell and the judgment I deserve on that cross. But, thank God, he didn't stay on the cross. He rose from the dead, and he is alive. And the Scripture says that someday he is coming back to establish his eternal kingdom.

I remember some years ago I was preaching in New Zealand, and I was invited to give a lecture at the university in Auckland, the capital of New Zealand. During my lecture I mentioned the word "hell." That night—I had already gone to bed—there came a loud knock at the door. I got up and rubbed the sleep from my eyes, and I went to the door and found a student. He was very angry. He said, "Tonight you talked to us, and you said there is a hell. I don't believe there is a hell or a judgment. You shouldn't talk like that to us." I said, "Come in. Sit down," and he did. We talked for a long time. I said, "Would you admit that there is a 10 percent chance Jesus was right and there is a hell?" He scratched his head, and he thought a minute. He said, "Yes, I would say there is a 10 percent chance, but," he added, "that's not much." I said, "I want to ask you another question. Suppose you go out to the airport, and you are planning to take a plane to Sydney, Australia. You have the ticket, and just as you are ready to get on the plane, they make the announcement 'There is only a 10 percent chance the plane won't make it.' Would you get on the plane?" He said, "No." "And you tell me," I replied, "that you believe there is a 10 percent chance there is a hell, and you are willing to take the eternal risk?" He said "I suppose not." I said, "Then you'll receive Christ." He said no. "Because," he said, "I admit that my problem is not intellectual. My problem is moral. I'm not ready to surrender to Christ.

His moral demands are too high." How tragic it is to turn our backs on God and his salvation!

What did God do? How could man be saved? We live in the mountains in the southern part of America. I was walking there with my younger son one time years ago, and we stepped on an anthill. We looked down and a lot of the ants had been killed, and many of them were hurt. Their little house was destroyed. I said to my son, "Wouldn't it be wonderful if we could go down and tell those ants we are sorry and we care about them, and then help them rebuild their house?" And he said, "Father, we're too big, and they're too little. There's no way we could help them. The only way we could talk with them is if we somehow could become ants and live with them." I wanted to teach him a little lesson, so I said, "One time God—the mighty God of heaven—looked down on this little speck of dust that we call the earth and saw that we were like those little ants crawling around. And God said, 'I want to help them; I want to save them; I want to help them rebuild their lives.' But how could the mighty God of heaven communicate with us? You know what God did? God became a man, and that's who Jesus Christ was. Christ was the God-man who came for the purpose of showing us what God is like, and dying on the cross for our sins."

That is what the verse I read a few minutes ago says God did for us: "For God so loved the world, that he gave his only begotten Son, that whosoever believeth in him should not perish, but have everlasting life" (John 3:16).

Now, what does God require of you and me? He gave his Son—the most personal, costly gift he could give. But what must we do in return? What do you have to do if you are to have your name written in the book of life, have your sins forgiven and have eternal life? Listen carefully.

First, you must repent of your sins. What does repent mean? It means to change—to change your mind, to change your way of living. It means to turn away from sin, and with God's help to live the way God wants you to live. It means that you have become a man or a woman of love. It means that you are willing to live for Christ. The first sermon Jesus ever preached was on the theme of repentance. Peter said in Acts 3:19, "Repent ye therefore, and be converted, that your sins may be blotted out." The apostle Paul said that God "commandeth all men every where to repent" (Acts 17:30). Have you repented? Has your life been changed? Do people know it? Does your wife, does your husband, your father, your mother know it by the way you live?

Second, you must come by faith and trust to Christ as your Savior and

Lord. You cannot understand it all with your mind, but don't let that keep you from Christ. I don't understand light or electricity, but that doesn't keep me from turning on the light switch. The Bible says by wisdom man cannot know God. Our minds are limited, and they have been affected by sin. The Bible says, "Without faith it is impossible to please him" (Hebrews 11:6). John 1:12, promises, "But as many as received him, to them gave he power to become the sons of God, even to them that believe on his name."

Some people say, "I could never receive Christ, because I couldn't live up to what God expects of me." That is like a person saying, "I can never fly on an airplane, because I don't think I have the strength to keep it in the air." Keeping the plane in the air is not the job of the passenger. It's the job of the pilot and the people that work on the plane and the people who designed it and built it.

I heard about a man who had never flown in an airplane. My father, who died about twenty-five years ago, never flew in an airplane. I tried to get him to; but he said, "If God had meant for man to fly, he'd have given him wings." But anyway, this one man finally said, "All right, I'll go up in this airplane." When the plane landed, his son asked him, "How did you like it?" He said, "It was all right, but I never did put my full weight on the seat." That's the way many people approach faith in Christ. When you put your faith in Christ, you make a total commitment to him—you put your full weight on him—and trust him alone for your salvation. The Bible says, "For by grace are ye saved through faith; and . . . not of yourselves: it is the gift of God" (Ephesians 2:8).

What are you going to do? Are you going to open your heart to Christ? The Bible says, "Now is the accepted time; behold, now is the day of salvation" (2 Corinthians 6:2). You may be closer to God at this moment than ever before in your life. You may never be this close again. Tonight is the night to receive him, and to put your whole weight on Christ. If you have a doubt about your relationship with Christ, you can make sure tonight. Some of you belong to the church or attend church. But deep in your heart you have doubts about your relationship to Christ. Whatever your background, come to him by faith and make your commitment to him now. ■

The Exiled Dalai Lama
Espouses a Philosophy of
Compassion

"WHEN the days become longer and there is more sunshine, the grass becomes fresh and, consequently, we feel very happy. On the other hand, in autumn, one leaf falls down and another leaf falls down. These beautiful plants become as if dead and we do not feel very happy. Why? I think it is because deep down our human nature likes construction, and does not like destruction. . . . Therefore, I think that in terms of basic human feeling, violence is not good. Nonviolence is the only way."

TENZIN GYATSO, ENTHRONED as Dalai Lama ("ocean-wide priest") in 1940 at the age of two, is the fourteenth person in a line of leaders of Buddhist Tibet that began in 1641. His Buddhist followers believe he is the divine reincarnation of Bodhisattva Avalokitesvara, ancestor of the Tibetan people. He was driven into exile in 1950 after vainly resisting the Communist Chinese takeover of Tibet (escaping in the disguise of a soldier), and has led a government in exile, headquartered in India, in the generations since.

Though he has addressed world bodies frequently in his crusade to achieve a degree of autonomy for his people, the red-robed "god-king" of an oppressed nation is at his most impressive in a small gathering. And though he once told an interviewer, "I think this lifetime as Dalai Lama is the most difficult of all the Dalai Lamas," the world's best-known monk comes across to an audience as determinedly optimistic, involved, interested, and good-humored.

His lecture accepting the Nobel Peace Prize on December 10, 1989, was a formal presentation of his government's Five-Point Peace Plan, concluding a fairly dry address with a moving prayer "to dispel the misery of the world." That evening in Oslo, however, he spoke again informally, from notes, to a group more interested in his philosophy. His "Nobel Evening Address" is tightly organized, each thought linking to the next, presented in deceptively simple declarative sentences. The passage about smiles—"How to develop smiles?"—walks the listener into the theme of compassion and then to nonviolence, toward a conclusion asserting the power of nonviolence and the weakness of anger and force.

□   □   □

. . . So now, firstly, what is the purpose of life for a human being? I believe that happiness is the purpose of life. Whether or not there is a purpose to the existence of the universe or galaxies, I don't know. In any case, the fact is that we are here on this planet with other human beings. Then, since every human being wants happiness and does not want suffering, it is clear that this desire does not come from training, or from some ideology. It is something natural. Therefore, I consider that the attainment of happiness, peace, and joy is the purpose of life. Therefore, it is very important to investigate what are happiness and satisfaction and what are their causes.

I think that there is a mental factor as well as a physical factor. Both are very important. If we compare these two things, the mental factor is more important, superior to the physical factor. This we can know through our daily life. Since the mental factor is more important, we have to give serious thought to inner qualities.

Then, I believe compassion and love are necessary in order for us to obtain happiness or tranquillity. These mental factors are key. I think they are the basic source. What is compassion? From the Buddhist viewpoint there are different varieties of compassion. The basic meaning of compassion is not just a feeling of closeness, or just a feeling of pity. Rather, I think that with genuine compassion we not only feel the pains and suffering of others but we also have a feeling of determination to overcome that suffering. One aspect of compassion is some kind of determination and responsibility. Therefore, compassion brings us tranquillity and also inner strength. Inner strength is the ultimate source of success.

When we face some problem, a lot depends on the personal attitude toward that problem or tragedy. In some cases, when one faces the difficulty, one loses one's hope and becomes discouraged and then ends up depressed. On the other hand, if one has a certain mental attitude, then tragedy and suffering bring one more energy, more determination.

Usually, I tell our generation we are born during the darkest period in our long history. There is a big challenge. It is very unfortunate. But if there is a challenge then there is an opportunity to face it, an opportunity to demonstrate our will and our determination. So from that viewpoint I think that our generation is fortunate. These things depend on inner qualities, inner strength. Compassion is very gentle, very peaceful, and soft in nature, not harsh. You cannot destroy it easily as it is very powerful. Therefore, compassion is very important and useful.

Then, again, if we look at human nature, love and compassion are the foundation of human existence. According to some scientists, the fetus has feeling in the mother's womb and is affected by the mother's mental state. Then the few weeks after birth are crucial for the enlarging of the brain of the child. During that period, the mother's physical touch is the greatest factor for the healthy development of the brain. This shows that the physical needs some affection to develop properly.

When we are born, our first action is sucking milk from the mother. Of course, the child may not know about compassion and love, but the natural feeling is one of closeness toward the object that gives the milk. If the mother is angry or has ill feeling, the milk may not come fully. This shows that from our first day as human beings the effect of compassion is crucial.

If unpleasant things happen in our daily life, we immediately pay attention to them but do not notice other pleasant things. We experience these as normal or usual. This shows that compassion and affection are part of human nature.

Compassion or love has different levels; some are more mixed than others with desire or attachment. For example, parents' attitudes toward their children contain a mixture of desire and attachment with compassion. The love and compassion between husband and wife—especially at the beginning of marriage when they don't know the deep nature of each other—are on a superficial level. As soon as the attitude of one partner changes, the attitude of the other becomes opposite to what it was. That kind of love and compassion is more of the nature of attachment. Attachment means some kind of feeling of closeness projected by oneself. In reality, the other side may be very negative, but due to one's own mental attachment and projection, it appears as something nice. Furthermore, attachment causes one to exaggerate a small good quality and make it appear 100 percent beautiful or 100 percent positive. As soon as the mental attitudes change, that picture completely changes. Therefore, that kind of love and compassion is, rather, attachment.

Another kind of love and compassion is not based on something appearing beautiful or nice, but based on the fact that the other person, just like oneself, wants happiness and does not want suffering and indeed has every right to be happy and to overcome suffering. On such a basis, we feel a sense of responsibility, a sense of closeness toward that being. That is true compassion. This is because the compassion is based on reason, not just on emotional feeling. As a consequence, it does not matter what the other's attitude is, whether negative or positive. What matters is that it is a human being, a sentient being that has the experience of pain and pleasure. There is no reason not to feel compassion so long as it is a sentient being.

The kinds of compassion at the first level are mixed, interrelated. Some people have the view that some individuals have a very negative, cruel attitude toward others. These kinds of individuals appear to have no compassion in their minds. But I feel that these people do have the seed of compassion. The reason for this is that even these people very much appreciate it when someone else shows them affection. A capacity to appreciate other people's affection means that in their deep mind there is the seed of compassion. . . .

What is my purpose in life, what is my responsibility? Whether I like it or not, I am on this planet, and it is far better to do something for humanity. So you see that compassion is the seed or basis. If we take care to foster compassion, we will see that it brings the other good human qualities. The topic of compassion is not at all religious business; it is very important to know that it is human business, that it is a question of human survival, that it is not a question of human luxury. I might say that religion is a kind of luxury. If you have religion, that is good. But it is clear that even without religion we can manage. However, without these basic human qualities we cannot survive. It is a question of our own peace and mental stability.

Next, let us talk about the human being as a social animal. Even if we do not like other people, we have to live together. Natural law is such that even bees and other animals have to live together in cooperation. I am attracted to bees because I like honey—it is really delicious. Their product is something that we cannot produce, very beautiful, isn't it? I exploit them too much, I think. Even these insects have certain responsibilities, they work together very nicely. They have no constitution, they have no law, no police, nothing, but they work together effectively. This is because of nature. Similarly, each part of a flower is not arranged by humans but by nature. The force of nature is something remarkable. We human beings, we have constitutions, we have law, we have a police force, we have religion, we have many things. But in actual practice, I think that we are behind those small insects. . . .

I will tell you something. I love friends, I want more friends. I love smiles. That is a fact. How to develop smiles? There are a variety of smiles. Some smiles are sarcastic. Some smiles are artificial—diplomatic smiles. These smiles do not produce satisfaction, but rather fear or suspicion. But a genuine smile gives us hope, freshness. If we want a genuine smile, then first we must produce the basis for a smile to come. On every level of human life, compassion is the key thing.

Now, on the question of violence and nonviolence. There are many different levels of violence and nonviolence. On the basis of external action, it is difficult to distinguish whether an action is violent or nonviolent. Basically, it depends on the motivation behind the action. If the motivation is negative, even though the external appearance may be very smooth and gentle, in a deeper sense the action is very violent. On the contrary, harsh actions and words done with a sincere, positive motivation are essentially nonviolent. In other words, violence is a destructive power. Nonviolence is constructive.

When the days become longer and there is more sunshine, the grass becomes fresh and, consequently, we feel very happy. On the other hand, in autumn, one leaf falls down and another leaf falls down. These beautiful plants become as if dead and we do not feel very happy. Why? I think it is because deep down our human nature likes construction, and does not like destruction. Naturally, every action which is destructive is against human nature. Constructiveness is the human way. Therefore, I think that in terms of basic human feeling, violence is not good. Nonviolence is the only way.

Practically speaking, through violence we may achieve something, but at the expense of someone else's welfare. That way, although we may solve one problem, we simultaneously seed a new problem. The best way to solve problems is through human understanding, mutual respect. On one side make some concessions; on the other side take serious consideration about the problem. There may not be complete satisfaction, but something happens. At least future danger is avoided. Nonviolence is very safe.

Before my first visit to Europe in 1973, I had felt the importance of compassion, altruism. On many occasions I expressed the importance of the sense of universal responsibility. Sometimes during this period, some people felt that the Dalai Lama's idea was a bit unrealistic. Unfortunately, in the Western world Gandhian nonviolence is seen as passive resistance more suitable to the East. The Westerners are very active, demanding immediate results, even in the course of daily life. But today the actual situation teaches nonviolence to people. The movement for freedom is nonviolent. These recent events reconfirm to me that nonviolence is much closer to human nature.

Again, if there are sound reasons or bases for the points you demand, then there is no need to use violence. On the other hand, when there is no sound reason that concessions should be made to you but mainly your own desire, then reason cannot work and you have to rely on force. Thus, using force is not a sign of strength but rather a sign of weakness. Even in daily human contact, if we talk seriously, using reasons, there is no need to feel anger. We can argue the points. When we fail to prove with reason, then anger comes. When reason ends, then anger begins. Therefore, anger is a sign of weakness. . . .

We are passing through a most difficult period. I am very encouraged by your warm expression and by the Nobel Peace Prize. I thank you from the depth of my heart.

■ ■ ■

VIII

INSPIRATIONAL SPEECHES

Chemist Louis Pasteur Praises the Rise of Scientific Education

"WORSHIP the spirit of criticism."

LOUIS PASTEUR, French chemist of the nineteenth century who founded the science of microbiology, made the most important discovery in medical history: contagious diseases are transmitted by germs. A champion of rigorous scientific inquiry, he was honored in 1888 with the opening in Paris of the Pasteur Institute.

As the first director of this institute named for him, Pasteur was asked to address his colleagues on November 14, 1888. He was, it is reported, "overcome by his feelings," and his son delivered for him the prepared speech in praise of education, a talk that specifically expressed Pasteur's pride in his country's respect for educational progress ("From village schools to laboratories, everything has been founded or renovated").

Pasteur's speech celebrates the accomplishments of his countrymen while mourning the passage of time, with a series of subordinate "if" clauses to express regrets. The speech begins and ends in patriotic sentiment, marked by a study in contrast of "two contrary laws" ("The one seeks violent conquests; the other, the relief of humanity"). It also contains straightforward advice, always effective in a speech, especially by an acknowledged expert.

The portion of the speech that follows is from René Valery-Radot's *The Life of Pasteur*, translated from the French by Mrs. R. L. Devonshire.

□   □   □

. . . When the day came that, foreseeing the future which would be opened by the discovery of the attenuation of virus, I appealed to my country, so that we should be allowed, through the strength and impulse of private initiative, to build laboratories to be devoted, not only to the prophylactic treatment of hydrophobia, but also to the study of virulent and contagious diseases—on that day again, France gave in handfuls. . . . It is now finished, this great building, of which it might be said that there is not a stone but what is the material sign of a generous thought. All the virtues have subscribed to build this dwelling place for work.

Alas! mine is the bitter grief that I enter it, a man "vanquished by time," deprived of my masters, even of my companions in the struggle, Dumas, Bouley, Paul Bert, and lastly Vulpian, who, after having been with you, my dear Grancher, my counselor at the very first, became the most energetic, the most convinced champion of this method.

However, if I have the sorrow of thinking that they are no more, after having valiantly taken their part in discussions which I have never provoked but have had to endure; if they cannot hear me proclaim all that I owe to their counsels and support; if I feel their absence as deeply as on the morrow of their death, I have at least the consolation of believing that all that we struggled for together will not perish. The collaborators and pupils who are now here share our scientific faith. . . . Keep your early enthusiasm, dear collaborators, but let it ever be regulated by rigorous examinations and tests. Never advance anything which cannot be proved in a simple and decisive fashion.

Worship the spirit of criticism. If reduced to itself, it is not an awakener of ideas or a stimulant to great things, but, without it, everything is fallible; it always has the last word. What I am now asking you, and you will ask of your pupils later on, is what is most difficult to an inventor.

It is indeed a hard task, when you believe you have found an important scientific fact and are feverishly anxious to publish it, to constrain yourself for days, weeks, years sometimes, to fight with yourself, to try and ruin your own experiments and only to proclaim your discovery after having exhausted all contrary hypotheses.

But when, after so many efforts, you have at last arrived at a certainty, your joy is one of the greatest, which can be felt by a human soul, and the thought that you will have contributed to the honor of your country renders that joy still deeper.

If science has no country, the scientist should have one, and ascribe to it the influence which his works may have in this world. . . . Two contrary laws seem to be wrestling with each other nowadays; the one, a law of blood and of death, ever imagining new means of destruction and forcing nations to be constantly ready for the battlefield—the other, a law of peace, work and health, ever evolving new means of delivering man from the scourges which beset him.

The one seeks violent conquests; the other, the relief of humanity. The latter places one human life above any victory; while the former would sacrifice hundreds and thousands of lives to the ambition of one. The law of which we are the instruments seeks, even in the midst of carnage, to cure the sanguinary ills of the law of war; the treatment inspired by our antiseptic methods may preserve thousands of soldiers. Which of those two laws will ultimately prevail, God alone knows. But we may assert that French science will have tried, by obeying the law of humanity, to extend the frontiers of life. ■

Theodore Roosevelt Blasts Ignoble Ease and Advocates the Strenuous Life

"FAR better it is to dare mighty things, to win glorious triumphs, even though checkered by failure, than to take rank with those poor spirits who neither enjoy much nor suffer much, because they live in the gray twilight that knows not victory nor defeat."

ASTHMATIC, NEARSIGHTED, TUTORED AT HOME because he was too sickly a boy to attend school, Theodore Roosevelt in his teens threw himself into bodybuilding and the achievement of what would now be called his "personal best." The word that expresses vigorous exertion is "strenuous"; he chose "The Strenuous Life" as the title of his best-known speech and the collection of his speeches.

This inspirational lecture was delivered on April 10, 1899, the year after he resigned as assistant secretary of the navy in the McKinley administration, gained national fame leading the "Rough Riders" up Kettle Hill in the battle for San Juan, Puerto Rico, and later led the Republicans of New York to victory in his race for governor.

The speech works well because it uses the example of the vigorous person—one who will "wrest triumph from toil and risk"—as a paradigm for a can-do populace in a triumphant nation. He leaves unsaid, but clearly implies, that he is the exemplar of that self-helping nation.

He takes Tennyson's thought "'Tis better to have loved and lost, than never to have loved at all" and transmutes it into politics as "It is hard to fail, but it is worse never to have tried to succeed." In another form on another occasion, Teddy Roosevelt expressed the same idea, beginning, "It is not the critic who counts, not the one who points out how the strong man stumbled or how the doer of deeds might have done them better. The credit belongs to the man who is actually in the arena, whose face is marred with sweat and dust and blood; who strives valiantly; who errs and comes short again and again; who knows the great enthusiasms, the great devotions, and spends himself in a worthy cause; and who, if he fails, at least fails while daring greatly, so that his place shall never be with those cold and timid souls who know neither victory nor defeat."

The publicist John R. ("Tex") McCrary called this quotation to the attention of Dwight Eisenhower, who sent it to friends during the campaign of 1952; after Richard Nixon's 1960 loss to John Kennedy, the defeated Nixon sent the same strenuous sentiments, suitable for framing, to many of his supporters as a credo of potential comeback.

□   □   □

. . . I wish to preach, not the doctrine of ignoble ease, but the doctrine of the strenuous life, the life of toil and effort, of labor and strife; to preach that highest form of success which comes, not to the man who desires mere easy peace, but to the man who does not shrink from danger, from hardship, or from bitter toil, and who out of these wins the splendid ultimate triumph.

A life of slothful ease, a life of that peace which springs merely from lack either of desire or of power to strive after great things, is as little worthy of a nation as of an individual. I ask only that what every self-respecting American demands from himself and from his sons shall be demanded of the American nation as a whole. Who among you would teach your boys that ease, that peace, is to be the first consideration in their eyes—to be the ultimate goal after which they strive? . . . You work yourselves, and you bring up your sons to work. If you are rich and are worth your salt, you will teach your sons that though they may have leisure, it is not to be spent in idleness; for wisely used leisure merely means that those who possess it, being free from the necessity of working for their livelihood, are all the more bound to carry on some kind of non-remunerative work in science, in letters, in art, in exploration, in historical research—work of the type we most need in this country, the successful carrying out of which reflects most honor upon the nation. We do not admire the man of timid peace. We admire the man who embodies victorious effort; the man who never wrongs his neighbor, who is prompt to help a friend, but who has those virile qualities necessary to win in the stem strife of actual life. It is hard to fail, but it is worse never to have tried to succeed. . . .

In the last analysis a healthy state can exist only when the men and women who make it up lead clean, vigorous, healthy lives; when the children are so trained that they shall endeavor, not to shirk difficulties, but to overcome them; not to seek ease, but to know how to wrest triumph from toil and risk. The man must be glad to do a man's work, to dare and endure and to labor; to keep himself, and to keep those dependent upon him. The woman must be the housewife, the helpmeet of the homemaker, the wise and fearless mother of many healthy children. In one of Daudet's powerful and melancholy books he speaks of "the fear of maternity, the haunting terror of the young wife of the present day." When such words can be truthfully written of a nation, that nation is rotten to the heart's core. When men fear work or fear righteous war, when women fear motherhood, they tremble on the brink of doom; and well it is that they should vanish from the earth, where they are fit subjects for the scorn of all men and women who are themselves strong and brave and high-minded.

As it is with the individual so it is with the nation. It is a base untruth to say that happy is the nation that has no history. Thrice happy is the nation that has a glorious history. Far better it is to dare mighty things, to win glorious triumphs, even though checkered by failure, than to take rank with those poor spirits who neither enjoy much nor suffer much, because they live in the gray twilight that knows not victory nor defeat. If in 1861 the men who loved the Union had believed that peace was the end of all things, and war and strife the worst of all things, and had acted up to their belief, we would have saved hundreds of thousands of lives, we would have saved hundreds of millions of dollars. Moreover, besides saving all the blood and treasure we then lavished, we would have prevented the heartbreak of many women, the dissolution of many homes, and we would have spared the country those months of gloom and shame when it seemed as if our armies marched only to defeat. We could have avoided all this suffering simply by shrinking from strife. And if we had thus avoided it, we would have shown that we were weaklings, and that we were unfit to stand among the great nations of the earth. Thank God for the iron in the blood of our fathers, the men who upheld the wisdom of Lincoln, and bore sword or rifle in the armies of Grant! Let us, the children of the men who proved themselves equal to the mighty days, let us, the children of the men who carried the great Civil War to a triumphant conclusion, praise the God of our fathers that the ignoble counsels of peace were rejected; that the suffering and loss, the blackness of sorrow and despair, were unflinchingly faced, and the years of strife endured; for in the end the slave was freed, the Union restored, and the mighty American Republic placed once more as a helmeted queen among nations.

We of this generation do not have to face a task such as that our fathers faced, but we have our tasks, and woe to us if we fail to perform them!. . .

The timid man, the lazy man, the man who distrusts his country, the overcivilized man, who has lost the great fighting, masterful virtues, the ignorant man, and the man of dull mind, whose soul is incapable of feeling the mighty lift that thrills "stern men with empires in their brains"—all these, of course, shrink from seeing the nation undertake its new duties; shrink from seeing us build a navy and an army adequate to our needs; shrink from seeing us do our share of the world's work, by bringing order out of chaos in the great, fair tropic islands from which the valor of our soldiers and sailors has driven the Spanish flag. These are the men who fear the strenuous life, who fear the only national life which is really worth leading. They believe in that cloistered life which saps the hardy virtues in a nation, as it saps them in the individual; or else they are wedded to that base spirit of gain and greed which recognizes in commercialism the be-all and end-all of national life, instead of realizing that, though an indispensable element, it is, after all, but one of the many elements that go to make up true national greatness. No country can long endure if its foundations are not laid deep in the material prosperity which comes from thrift, from business energy and enterprise, from hard, unsparing effort in the fields of industrial activity; but neither was any nation ever yet truly great if it relied upon material prosperity alone. All honor must be paid to the architects of our material prosperity, to the great captains of industry who have built our factories and our railroads, to the strong men who toil for wealth with brain or hand; for great is the debt of the nation to these and their kind. But our debt is yet greater to the men whose highest type is to be found in a statesman like Lincoln, a soldier like Grant. They showed by their lives that they recognized the law of work, the law of strife; they toiled to win a competence for themselves and those dependent upon them; but they recognized that there were yet other and even loftier duties—duties to the nation and duties to the race.

We cannot sit huddled within our own borders and avow ourselves merely an assemblage of well-to-do hucksters who care nothing for what happens beyond. Such a policy would defeat even its own end; for as the nations grow to have ever wider and wider interests, and are brought into closer and closer contact, if we are to hold our own in the struggle for naval and commercial supremacy, we must build up our power without our own borders. We must build the Isthmian canal, and we must grasp the points of vantage which will enable us to have our say in deciding the destiny of the oceans of the East and the West. . . .

The army and the navy are the sword and the shield which this nation must carry if she is to do her duty among the nations of the earth—if she is not to stand merely as the China of the Western Hemisphere. Our proper conduct toward the tropic islands we have wrested from Spain is merely the form which our duty has taken at the moment. Of course, we are bound to handle the affairs of our own household well. We must see that there is civic honesty, civic cleanliness, civic good sense in our home administration of city, state, and nation. We must strive for honesty in office, for honesty toward the creditors of the nation and of the individual; for the widest freedom of individual initiative where possible, and for the wisest control of individual initiative where it is hostile to the welfare of the many. But because we set our own household in order we are not thereby excused from playing our part in the great affairs of the world. A man's first duty is to take his own home, but he is not thereby excused from doing his duty to the state; for if he fails in this second duty it is under the penalty of ceasing to be a freeman. In the same way, while a nation's first duty is within its own borders, it is not thereby absolved from facing its duties in the world as a whole; and if it refuses to do so, it merely forfeits its right to struggle for a place among the peoples that shape the destiny of mankind. . . .

England's rule in India and Egypt has been of great benefit to England, for it has trained up generations of men accustomed to look at the larger and loftier side of public life. It has been of even greater benefit to India and Egypt. And finally, and most of all, it has advanced the cause of civilization. So, if we do our duty aright in the Philippines, we will add to that national renown which is the highest and finest part of national life, will greatly benefit the people of the Philippine Islands, and, above all, we will play our part well in the great work of uplifting mankind. But to do this work, keep ever in mind that we must show in a very high degree the qualities of courage, of honesty, and of good judgment. Resistance must be stamped out. The first and all-important work to be done is to establish the supremacy of our flag. We must put down armed resistance before we can accomplish anything else, and there should be no parleying, no faltering, in dealing with our foe. As for those in our own country who encourage the foe, we can afford contemptuously to disregard them; but it must be remembered that their utterances are not saved from being treasonable merely by the fact that they are despicable.

When once we have put down armed resistance, when once our rule is acknowledged, then an even more difficult task will begin, for then we must see to it that the islands are administered with absolute honesty and with good judgment. If we let the public service of the islands be turned into the prey of the spoils politician, we shall have begun to tread the path which Spain trod to her own destruction. We must send out there only good and able men, chosen for their fitness, and not because of their partisan service, and these men must not only administer impartial justice to the natives and serve their own government with honesty and fidelity, but must show the utmost tact and firmness, remembering that, with such people as those with whom we are to deal, weakness is the greatest of crimes, and that next to weakness comes lack of consideration for their principles and prejudices.

I preach to you, then, my countrymen, that our country calls not for the life of ease but for the life of strenuous endeavor. The twentieth century looms before us big with the fate of many nations. If we stand idly by, if we seek merely swollen, slothful ease and ignoble peace, if we shrink from the hard contests where men must win at hazard of their lives and at the risk of all they hold dear, then the bolder and stronger peoples will pass us by, and will win for themselves the domination of the world. Let us therefore boldly face the life of strife, resolute to do our duty well and manfully; resolute to uphold righteousness by deed and by word; resolute to be both honest and brave, to serve high ideals, yet to use practical methods. Above all, let us shrink from no strife, moral or physical, within or without the nation, provided we are certain that the strife is justified, for it is only through strife, through hard and dangerous endeavor, that we shall ultimately win the goal of true national greatness. ■

Mark Twain Reveals
Stage Fright

"I shall never forget my feelings before the agony left me. . . ."

HE CAME AND WENT WITH HALLEY'S COMET, which appeared in 1835 and 1910. Born Samuel Langhorne Clemens, America's greatest and most embittered humorist took the pseudonym Mark Twain from a term used on the Mississippi River for "two fathoms deep." The author of *Huckleberry Finn* and *The Innocents Abroad,* Twain gained fame not only as a major figure of American literature but also as a first-rate raconteur, able to move as well as amuse his audiences.

With white hair, white mustache, and white suit, Twain took to the stage and entertained his listeners with barbed observations and humorous anecdotes. Among the best of these seemingly impromptu talks is "Mark Twain's First Appearance," delivered after one of his daughters had made her singing debut as a contralto in Norfolk, Connecticut. He attended her recital and then addressed the audience about his own stage debut.

In the speech, given on October 5, 1906, Twain recounts his own first public appearance with a style more folksy than formal. Through a careful use of direct address and asides, interjections and well-timed pauses, Twain's rhetorical techniques combine to lend his words an offhand quality, a sense of familiarity that provokes sympathy as well as laughter.

□   □   □

My heart goes out in sympathy to anyone who is making his first appearance before an audience of human beings. By a direct process of memory I go back forty years, less one month—for I'm older than I look.

I recall the occasion of my first appearance. San Francisco knew me then only as a reporter, and I was to make my bow to San Francisco as a lecturer. I knew that nothing short of compulsion would get me to the theater. So I bound myself by a hard-and-fast contract so that I could not escape. I got to the theater forty-five minutes before the hour set for the lecture. My knees were shaking so that I didn't know whether I could stand up. If there is an awful, horrible malady in the world, it is stage fright—and seasickness. They are a pair. I had stage fright then for the first and last time. I was only seasick once, too. It was on a little ship on which there were two hundred other passengers. I—was—sick. I was so sick that there wasn't any left for those other two hundred passengers.

It was dark and lonely behind the scenes in that theater, and I peeked through the little peek holes they have in theater curtains and looked into the big auditorium. That was dark and empty, too. By and by it lighted up, and the audience began to arrive.

I had got a number of friends of mine, stalwart men, to sprinkle themselves through the audience armed with big clubs. Every time I said anything they could possibly guess I intended to be funny, they were to pound those clubs on the floor. Then there was a kind lady in a box up there, also a good friend of mine, the wife of the governor. She was to watch me intently, and whenever I glanced toward her she was going to deliver a gubernatorial laugh that would lead the whole audience into applause.

At last I began. I had the manuscript tucked under a United States flag in front of me where I could get at it in case of need. But I managed to get started without it. I walked up and down—I was young in those days and needed the exercise—and talked and talked.

Right in the middle of the speech I had placed a gem. I had put in a moving, pathetic part which was to get at the hearts and souls of my hearers. When I delivered it, they did just what I hoped and expected. They sat silent and awed. I had touched them. Then I happened to glance up at the box where the governor's wife was—you know what happened.

Well, after the first agonizing five minutes, my stage fright left me, never to return. I know if I was going to be hanged I could get up and make a good showing, and I intend to. But I shall never forget my feelings before the agony left me, and I got up here to thank you for her for helping my daughter, by your kindness, to live through her first appearance. And I want to thank you for your appreciation of her singing, which is, by the way, hereditary. ■

Branch Rickey Discovers the Quality That Makes a Ballplayer Great

"'HE made his own breaks.'"

AN UNDISTINGUISHED CATCHER for the St. Louis Browns, Branch Rickey reached baseball's Hall of Fame for inventing the minor-league "farm system" to develop young players, and—as general manager of the Brooklyn Dodgers—for breaking the major-league color barrier by signing Jackie Robinson to play in 1947.

He was manager of the St. Louis Cardinals in the early twenties, failed to win a pennant, and was moved upstairs to find his real talents as an off-the-field baseball executive. On November 12, 1926, he made this speech, entitled "The Greatest Single Thing a Man Can Have," to the Executives Club of Chicago. It offers a good example of beginning with an anecdote and closing with its lesson; the movement from the specific to the general and finally to the universal makes an effective speech with a memorable point.

Rickey began by telling of Ty Cobb's baserunning. His Cardinals were playing the Detroit Tigers; it was the eleventh inning, Cobb had drawn a walk, and he made his move to steal second base. . . .

□ □ □

Well, when the ball was finally thrown to second base, it hit in front of the bag and bounced over Levan's head. Cobb came down, touched second base, and angularly went on towards third without a ghost of a chance to make it. The third baseman, knowing the abandonment of that fellow Cobb, and his slide—knowing that, when he set out voluntarily to get an objective, he was willing to pay the price to get it—having this knowledge in his head, had one eye on Cobb's shiny spikes and the other eye on the ball.

I then saw the quickest reflex action I ever saw in my life. That boy Cobb had reflex centers in his heels; he did not have time to telegraph his brain. He slid twelve feet in front of third base; and when the dust had cleared away, the ball had fallen out of the hands of the third baseman and was going over toward the concrete in front of the grandstand—and before we could get that ball, he scored. I saw the crowd tumbling out from every place.

I said to the umpire, "Interference, interference, Tom, at third base. He did not make a slide for the base, but he made a play for the ball."

He paid no attention to me—they have a habit of doing that. I followed him and said, "Tom, listen to me!"

"Mr. Rickey," he said then, "listen to me. Give the boy credit. He made his own breaks."

Oh, I tell you as I went down towards the clubhouse, with the crowd joshing me and guying us, I thought to myself, as I passed the Detroit players, I did not hear a man saying, "See what luck did for us today. Old Billiken was on our side." I heard everybody saying, "He is a great player. He won the game by himself."

As I came to my locker and listened to the remarks about the game, I commenced to ask myself what it was that made a man a distinguished ballplayer. Take two men with equal ability; one of them will always stay in mediocrity and another will distinguish himself in the game. What is the difference?

The more we compress and confine the element of luck—luck has its place in games; it is in the English language; it is in the dictionary, and we ought to keep it there—and put it in a small area, just to that extent do you enlarge the area for the exercise of a man's own functions in controlling his workings, his destinies, and his game.

The more that a man exercises himself and asserts his own influence over his work, the less the part that luck plays. It is true in baseball that the greatest single menace that a man has is a willingness to alibi his own failures; the greatest menace to a man's success in business, I think, sometimes is a perfect willingness to excuse himself for his own mistakes.

What is the greatest single thing in the character of a successful enterprise, in the character of a boy, in the character of a great baseball player? I think it is the desire to be a great baseball player, a desire that dominates him, a desire that is so strong that it does not admit of anything that runs counter to it, a desire to excel that so confines him to a single purpose that nothing else matters.

That thing makes men come in at night, that makes men have good health, that makes men change their bad technique to good technique, that makes capacity and ability in men. That makes a team with 80 percent possibility come from 60 to 70 percent, that makes them approach their possibility; and with a dominant desire to excel, that simply transcends them into a great spiritual force.

The greatest single thing in the qualification of a great player, a great team, or a great man is a desire to reach the objective that admits of no interference anywhere. That is the greatest thing I know about baseball or anything else. ■

Justice Oliver Wendell Holmes Acknowledges a Ninetieth-Birthday Tribute

"To live is to function."

AS A YOUNG UNION OFFICER, Oliver Wendell Holmes told President Lincoln, visiting his battery, to get his head down before it was blown off. In 1902, Theodore Roosevelt appointed the Harvard law professor, then sixty, to the Supreme Court. Justice Holmes emerged from the shadow of his famous father, the Autocrat of the Breakfast Table, to become what biographers called the Yankee from Olympus. Though he wrote only 173 dissents in his thirty years on the Court, their quality earned him the sobriquet the Great Dissenter—a judge whose disagreements with the majority presaged a judicial movement toward free expression and a more liberal reading of the Constitution.

On March 7, 1931, on the occasion of the celebration of his ninetieth birthday, Justice Holmes concluded a radio tribute with this response. The "little finishing canter" is a vivid metaphor; he lived four more years.

□   □   □

In this symposium my part is only to sit in silence. To express one's feelings as the end draws near is too intimate a task.

But I may mention one thought that comes to me as a listener in. The riders in a race do not stop short when they reach the goal. There is a little finishing canter before coming to a standstill. There is time to hear the kind voices of friends and to say to oneself, "The work is done." But just as one says that, the answer comes: "The race is over, but the work never is done while the power to work remains. The canter that brings you to a standstill need not be only coming to rest. It cannot be, while you still live. For to live is to function. That is all there is to living."

And so I end with a line from a Latin poet who uttered the message more than fifteen hundred years ago, "Death plucks my ear and says, Live—I am coming." ■

John D. Rockefeller, Jr., Sets Forth His Family's Creed

"THEY point the way to usefulness and happiness in life, to courage and peace in death."

JDR, JR., as he liked to be called, was the youngest child and only son of the oil baron. After a searing experience in labor relations at Colorado Fuel & Iron in 1914, at which forty workers died, the son of John D. turned from business to philanthropy, and built and supported the Rockefeller Institute for Medical Research, New York's Riverside Church, and Colonial Williamsburg. He helped change the public's image of the name of Rockefeller from predatory to beneficent, which aided the Republican political career of his second son, Nelson; by 1992, a grand-nephew, West Virginia Democratic senator Jay Rockefeller, could say, "You shouldn't have to be a Rockefeller to afford health care."

The following radio speech was aired July 8, 1941; it is carved in granite at the entrance to the Rockefeller Center skating rink. Nelson Rockefeller referred to its last line while campaigning for governor of New York so often that a shorthand reporter took down "brotherhood of man, father-hood of God" with the brief form "bomfog"; that acronym came to mean "pious political rhetoric." The creed itself has the elements of simplicity and timelessness that elevate it above the acronym.

□ □ □

They are the principles on which my wife and I have tried to bring up our family. They are the principles in which my father believed and by which he governed his life. They are the principles, many of them, which I learned at my mother's knee.

They point the way to usefulness and happiness in life, to courage and peace in death.

If they mean to you what they mean to me, they may perhaps be help-ful also to our sons for their guidance and inspiration.

Let me state them:

I believe in the supreme worth of the individual and in his right to life, liberty, and the pursuit of happiness.

I believe that every right implies a responsibility; every opportunity, an obligation; every possession, a duty.

I believe that the law was made for man and not man for the law; that government is the servant of the people and not their master.

I believe in the dignity of labor, whether with head or hand; that the world owes no man a living but that it owes every man an opportunity to make a living.

I believe that thrift is essential to well-ordered living and that economy is a prime requisite of a sound financial structure, whether in government, business, or personal affairs.

I believe that truth and justice are fundamental to an enduring social order.

I believe in the sacredness of a promise, that a man's word should be as good as his bond, that character—not wealth or power or position—is of supreme worth.

I believe that the rendering of useful service is the common duty of mankind and that only in the purifying fire of sacrifice is the dross of selfishness consumed and the greatness of the human soul set free.

I believe in an all-wise and all-loving God, named by whatever name, and that the individual's highest fulfillment, greatest happiness, and widest usefulness are to be found in living in harmony with his will.

I believe that love is the greatest thing in the world; that it alone can overcome hate; that right can and will triumph over might.

These are the principles, however formulated, for which all good men and women throughout the world, irrespective of race or creed, education, social position, or occupation, are standing, and for which many of them are suffering and dying.

These are the principles upon which alone a new world recognizing the brotherhood of man and the fatherhood of God can be established. ■

General Patton Motivates the 3rd Army on the Eve of the Invasion of Europe

"You are not all going to die. . . . The real hero is the man who fights even though he's scared. Some get over their fright in a minute under fire, others take an hour, for some it takes days, but a real man will never let the fear of death overpower his honor, his sense of duty to his country and to his manhood."

GENERAL GEORGE S. PATTON, JR., who proudly bore the sobriquet Old Blood and Guts, led a tank brigade on the Western Front in World War I and, a generation later, led the U.S. 3rd Army's armored division's sweep across France and Germany in World War II. His tanks relieved the surrounded U.S. forces at Bastogne in the crucial December 1944 Battle of the Bulge.

In his diary of May 17 of that year, Patton—in England helping Eisenhower prepare for the invasion—noted, "Made a talk. . . . As in all my talks, I stressed fighting and killing." Martin Blumenson, editor of the 1974 two-volume collection of *The Patton Papers,* wrote that it was about this time "he began to give his famous speech to the troops. Since he spoke extemporaneously, there were several versions. But if the words were always somewhat different, the message was always the same: the necessity to fight, the necessity to kill the enemy viciously, the necessity for everyone, no matter what his job, to do his duty. The officers were usually uncomfortable with the profanity he used. The enlisted men loved it."

For the third edition of this anthology, I sought out Blumenson in late 2003 for an authentic copy of "the" Patton motivational speech. He informed me that no definitive text exists. Reports of the speeches the general was making in that month before D-Day have been collected and patched together over a half century.

The most famous version—expurgated and much shortened—was the one that dramatically opened the 1970 movie *Patton,* starring George C. Scott. (I recall it being played and replayed in the screening room of the Nixon White House.) It began with the line certainly characteristic of

Patton: "Now I want you to remember that no bastard ever won a war by dying for his country. You won it by making the other poor dumb bastard die for his country." That is not in any of the contemporaneous accounts I know about, but surely sounds like Patton. That's the problem with presenting any amalgamated text of what was a series of ad-lib speeches: What was added for effect, or taken out to avoid repetition or skirt obscenity? However, even a patched-together version can reflect much of what he said in many of the words he probably used. Here is my assembly of the several accounts, no more "authentic" than the belated account of the "give me liberty" speech in the eighteenth century by Patrick Henry, but a faithful summary of his message.

The general's reference to the "bilious bastards who write that kind of stuff for the *Saturday Evening Post*" was his angry dismissal of an article about his slapping of an ailing soldier he thought malingering. The subsequent controversy temporarily cost Patton his command.

The anecdote he relates about the gutsy soldier fixing wires atop a telephone pole during a battle in the North African campaign is an example of self-deprecating humor that broke the pace of the intense speech and must have been well received.

In line with the general's sobriquet, the collated address is both bloody and gutsy.

□   □   □

Be seated.

Men, this stuff that some sources sling around about America wanting to stay out of this war, not wanting to fight, is a crock of bullshit. Americans love to fight, traditionally. All real Americans love the sting and clash of battle. Americans love a winner. Americans will not tolerate a loser. Americans despise cowards. Americans play to win. That's why Americans have never lost nor will ever lose a war.

You are not all going to die. Only 2 percent of you right here today would be killed in a major battle. Death must not be feared. Death, in time, comes to all of us. And every man is scared in his first battle. If he says he's not, he's a goddam liar. Some men are cowards but they fight the same as the brave men or they get the hell slammed out of them watching men fight who are just as scared as they are. Remember that the enemy is just as frightened as you are, and probably more so. They are not supermen.

The real hero is the man who fights even though he's scared. Some men get over their fright in a minute under fire, others take an hour, for some it takes days, but a real man will never let his fear of death over-power his honor, his sense of duty to his country and to his manhood.

All through your army careers, you men have bitched about what you call "chickenshit drilling." That, like everything else in this army, has a definite purpose. That purpose is alertness. Alertness must be bred into every soldier. A man must be alert at all times if he expects to stay alive. If you're not alert, sometime, a German son-of-a-bitch is going to sneak up behind you and beat you to death with a sockful of shit! There are four hundred neatly marked graves somewhere in Sicily, all because one man went to sleep on the job. But they are German graves, because we caught the bastard asleep.

An army is a team. It lives, sleeps, eats, and fights as a team. This individual hero stuff is a lot of horseshit. The bilious bastards who write that kind of stuff for the *Saturday Evening Post* don't know any more about real fighting under fire than they know about fucking! We have the finest food, the finest equipment, the best spirit, and the best men in the world. Why, by God, I actually pity those poor sons-of-bitches we're going up against.

My men don't surrender, and I don't want to hear of any soldier under my command being captured unless he has been hit. Even if you are hit, you can still fight back. The kind of man that I want in my command is just like the lieutenant in Libya, who, with a Luger against his chest, jerked off his helmet, swept the gun aside with one hand, and busted the hell out of the Kraut with his helmet. Then he jumped on the gun and went out and killed another German before they knew what the hell was coming off. And, all of that time, this man had a bullet through a lung. There was a real man!

Every single man in this army has a job to do and he must do it. Every man is a vital link in the great chain. What if every truck driver suddenly decided that he didn't like the whine of those shells overhead, turned yellow, and jumped headlong into a ditch? The cowardly bastard could say, "Hell, they won't miss me, just one man in thousands." But, what if every man thought that way? Where in the hell would we be now? What would our country, our loved ones, our homes, even the world, be like? No, goddamnit, Americans don't think like that. Every man does his job, serves the whole. Ordnance men are needed to supply the guns and machinery of war to keep us rolling. Quartermasters are needed to bring up food and clothes because where we are going there isn't a hell of a lot to steal. Every last man on KP has a job to do, even the one who heats our water to keep us from getting the "GI Shits." Each man must not think only of himself, but also of his buddy fighting beside him.

One of the bravest men that I ever saw was a fellow on top of a telegraph pole in the midst of a furious firefight in Tunisia. I stopped and asked what the hell he was doing up there at a time like that. He answered, "Fixing the wire, Sir." I asked, "Isn't that a little unhealthy right about now?" He answered, "Yes, Sir, but the goddamned wire has to be fixed." I asked, "Don't those planes strafing the road bother you?" And he answered, "No, Sir, but you sure as hell do!"

Now, there was a real man. A real soldier. There was a man who devoted all he had to his duty, no matter how seemingly insignificant his duty might appear at the time, no matter how great the odds. And you should have seen those trucks on the road to Tunisia. Those drivers were magnificent. All day and all night they rolled over those son-of-a-bitching roads, never stopping, never faltering from their course, with shells bursting all around them all of the time. We got through on good old American guts. Many of those men drove for over forty consecutive hours. These men weren't combat men, but they were soldiers with a job to do. They did it, and in one hell of a way they did it. They were part of a team. Without team effort, without them, the fight would have been lost. All of the links in the chain pulled together and the chain became unbreakable.

Remember, men, you men don't know I'm here. No mention of that fact is to be made in any letters. The world is not supposed to know what the hell happened to me. I'm not supposed to be commanding this army. I'm not even supposed to be here in England. Let the first bastards to find out be the goddamn Germans. We want to get the hell over there. The quicker we clean up this mess, the quicker we can take a little jaunt against the purple-pissing Japs and clean out their nest, too. Before the goddamn marines get all of the credit.

Sure, we want to go home. We want this war over with. The quickest way to get it over with is to go get the bastards who started it. The quicker they are whipped, the quicker we can go home. The shortest way home is through Berlin and Tokyo. And when we get to Berlin, I am personally going to shoot that paper-hanging son-of-a-bitch Hitler. Just like I'd shoot a snake!

When a man is lying in a shell hole, if he just stays there all day, a German will get to him eventually. The hell with that idea. The hell with taking it. My men don't dig foxholes. I don't want them to. Foxholes only slow up an offensive. Keep moving. And don't give the enemy time to dig one either. We'll win this war, but we'll win it only by fighting and by showing the Germans that we've got more guts than they have; or ever will have.

War is a bloody, killing business. You've got to spill their blood, or they will spill yours. Rip them up the belly. Shoot them in the guts. When shells are hitting all around you and you wipe the dirt off your face and realize that instead of dirt it's the blood and guts of what once was your best friend beside you, you'll know what to do!

I don't want to get any messages saying, "I am holding my position." We are not holding a goddamned thing. Let the Germans do that. We are advancing constantly and we are not interested in holding on to anything, except the enemy's balls. We are going to twist his balls and kick the living shit out of him all of the time. Our basic plan of operation is to advance and to keep on advancing regardless of whether we have to go over, under, or through the enemy.

From time to time there will be some complaints that we are pushing our people too hard. I don't give a good goddamn about such complaints. I believe in the old and sound rule that an ounce of sweat will save a gallon of blood. The harder *we* push, the more Germans we will kill. The more Germans we kill, the fewer of our men will be killed. Pushing means fewer casualties. I want you all to remember that.

There is one great thing that you men will all be able to say after this war is over and you are home once again. You may be thankful that twenty years from now, when you are sitting by the fireplace with your grandson on your knee and he asks you what you did in the great World War II, you won't have to shift him to the other knee, cough, and say, "Well, your granddaddy shoveled shit in Louisiana." No, sir, you can look him straight in the eye and say, "Son, your granddaddy rode with the Great Third Army and a son-of-a-goddamned-bitch named Georgie Patton!"

That is all. ■

Nobel Laureate William Faulkner Charges Writers with the Duty to Help Humanity Prevail

"I decline to accept the end of man. . . . I believe that man will not merely endure: he will prevail."

ONE MINUTE FAULKNER WAS A journeyman literary-type author and romantic poet and the next I guess it was when the Depression began he found a voice in the fictional Yoknapatawpha county of Mississippi, his characters transcending their setting to make their case about the capacity of human beings to endure suffering and emerge ennobled if still in pain

Then he won the Nobel prize for *The Sound and the Fury* and *As I Lay Dying* and the quiet life of the artist in Oxford Miss was over and he became a big name and the stream of consciousness technique was accepted as a proper literary form so long as you didn't use it too much

Then he went to Stockholm and on December 10, 1950, gave a better short speech than most writers write and it proved you didn't have to be a nihilist to be taken seriously you could be affirmative and even optimistic and still be considered gutsy

Remember the key word is prevail it means win but isn't so corny

□   □   □

I feel that this award was not made to me as a man, but to my work—a life's work in the agony and sweat of the human spirit, not for glory and least of all for profit, but to create out of the materials of the human spirit something which did not exist before. So this award is only mine in trust. It will not be difficult to find a dedication for the money part of it commensurate with the purpose and significance of its origin. But I would like to do the same with the acclaim too, by using this moment as a pinnacle from which I might be listened to by the young men and women already dedicated to the same anguish and travail, among whom is already that one who will some day stand here where I am standing.

Our tragedy today is a general and universal physical fear so long sustained by now that we can even bear it. There are no longer problems of the spirit. There is only the question, When will I be blown up? Because of this, the young man or woman writing today has forgotten the problems of the human heart in conflict with itself which alone can make good writing because only that is worth writing about, worth the agony and the sweat.

He must learn them again. He must teach himself that the basest of all things is to be afraid; and, teaching himself that, forget it forever, leaving no room in his workshop for anything but the old verities and truths of the heart, the old universal truths lacking which any story is ephemeral and doomed—love and honor and pity and pride and compassion and sacrifice. Until he does so, he labors under a curse. He writes not of love but of lust, of defeats in which nobody loses anything of value, of victories without hope and, worst of all, without pity or compassion. His griefs grieve on no universal bones, leaving no scars. He writes not of the heart but of the glands.

Until he relearns these things, he will write as though he stood among and watched the end of man. I decline to accept the end of man. It is easy enough to say that man is immortal simply because he will endure: that when the last ding-dong of doom has clanged and faded from the last worthless rock hanging tideless in the last red and dying evening, that even then there will still be one more sound: that of his puny inexhaustible voice, still talking. I refuse to accept this. I believe that man will not merely endure: he will prevail. He is immortal, not because he alone among creatures has an inexhaustible voice, but because he has a soul, a spirit capable of compassion and sacrifice and endurance. The poet's, the writer's, duty is to write about these things. It is his privilege to help man endure by lifting his heart, by reminding him of the courage and honor and hope and pride and compassion and pity and sacrifice which have been the glory of his past. The poet's voice need not merely be the record of man, it can be one of the props, the pillars to help him endure and prevail. ■

President John F. Kennedy Assures West Germany of America's Steadfastness

"ALL free men, wherever they may live, are citizens of Berlin, and, therefore, as a free man, I take pride in the words Ich bin ein Berliner.*"*

SIX WEEKS AFTER THE FAILURE of American-backed rebels at Cuba's Bay of Pigs, President John F. Kennedy met General Secretary Nikita Khrushchev in Vienna and apparently impressed him as indecisive. The Soviet leader first tested him on Berlin, forcing the issue of the Allied power's access to that divided city. Kennedy went on U.S. television to say that he would take the nation to war, if necessary, to defend Berlin. Khrushchev's response was not to risk a war but to erect the Berlin Wall. A year later, in the Cuban missile "eyeball to eyeball" confrontation, Kennedy rebuffed another Communist probe.

By 1963, the youthful American president had established his bona fides as a staunch defender of the West against Communist expansionism. On June 26, 1963, as more than a million Berliners lined the streets to shout "Ken-ned-dee," and with red cloth hanging from the Brandenburg Gate to prevent East Berliners from seeing the reception, he addressed a throng in Rudolf Wilde Platz.

The short, almost shouted speech—implicitly based on John Donne's idea that no man is an island—employs repetition skillfully, both in the "Let them come to Berlin" lines and the *"Ich bin ein Berliner"* theme stated fore and aft.

□   □   □

I am proud to come to this city as the guest of your distinguished mayor, who has symbolized throughout the world the fighting spirit of West Berlin. And I am proud to visit the Federal Republic with your distinguished chancellor, who for so many years has committed Germany to democracy and freedom and progress, and to come here in the company of my fellow American General Clay, who has been in this city during its great moments of crisis and will come again if ever needed.

Two thousand years ago the proudest boast was *Civis Romanus sum.* Today, in the world of freedom, the proudest boast is *Ich bin ein Berliner.*

I appreciate my interpreter translating my German!

There are many people in the world who really don't understand, or say they don't, what is the great issue between the free world and the Communist world. Let them come to Berlin. There are some who say that communism is the wave of the future. Let them come to Berlin. And there are some who say in Europe and elsewhere we can work with the Communists. Let them come to Berlin. And there are even a few who say that it is true that communism is an evil system, but it permits us to make economic progress. *Lass' sie nach Berlin kommen.* Let them come to Berlin.

Freedom has many difficulties and democracy is not perfect, but we have never had to put a wall up to keep our people in, to prevent them from leaving us. I want to say, on behalf of my countrymen, who live many miles away on the other side of the Atlantic, who are far distant from you, that they take the greatest pride that they have been able to share with you, even from a distance, the story of the last eighteen years. I know of no town, no city, that has been besieged for eighteen years that still lives with the vitality and the force, and the hope and the determination of the city of West Berlin. While the wall is the most obvious and vivid demonstration of the failures of the Communist system, for all the world to see, we take no satisfaction in it, for it is, as your mayor has said, an offense not only against history but an offense against humanity, separating families, dividing husbands and wives and brothers and sisters, and dividing a people who wish to be joined together.

What is true of this city is true of Germany—real, lasting peace in Europe can never be assured as long as one German out of four is denied the elementary right of free men, and that is to make a free choice. In eighteen years of peace and good faith, this generation of Germans has earned the right to be free, including the right to unite their families and their nation in lasting peace, with good will to all people. You live in a defended island of freedom, but your life is part of the main. So let me ask you, as I close, to lift your eyes beyond the dangers of today, to the hopes of tomorrow, beyond the freedom merely of this city of Berlin, or your country of Germany, to the advance of freedom everywhere, beyond the wall to the day of peace with justice, beyond yourselves and ourselves to all mankind.

Freedom is indivisible, and when one man is enslaved, all are not free. When all are free, then we can look forward to that day when this city will be joined as one and this country and this great continent of Europe in a peaceful and hopeful globe. When that day finally comes, as it will, the people of West Berlin can take sober satisfaction in the fact that they were in the front lines for almost two decades.

All free men, wherever they may live, are citizens of Berlin, and, therefore, as a free man, I take pride in the words *Ich bin ein Berliner.* ■

Reverend Martin Luther King, Jr., Ennobles the Civil Rights Movement at the Lincoln Memorial

"I have a dream that my four little children will one day live in a nation where they will not be judged by the color of their skin but by the content of their character."

DR. KING WAS THE MOST SIGNIFICANT BLACK LEADER since Frederick Douglass and, like Douglass, owed much of his preeminence to the ability to write with power (as in his 1963 "Letter from a Birmingham Jail") and to speak with passion. A disciple of Mohandas Gandhi's dedication to achieve great change through nonviolent means, the well-educated King—awarded a Ph.D. from Boston University in 1955—came to national attention later that year by leading the Montgomery, Alabama, bus boycott. He was subjected to harassment by racists and wiretapping by the Justice Department, fearful of Communist associations. Dr. King was awarded the Nobel Peace Prize in 1964; having led the "Poor People's

Campaign" and been active in the antiwar movement during the Vietnam War, he was assassinated in 1968.

He had the ability to tailor his speaking style to the audience he faced. In a black church, where listener involvement is active, King the preacher was skilled at evoking and answering the congregation's reactions; in a small meeting of New York attorneys and publicists organized by Theodore Kheel to aid his court defenses, King the activist put forward a low-key, businesslike, cogent summation of his problems,

On August 23, 1963, as a principal speaker at a peaceful march on Washington, D.C. Dr. King spoke from the steps of the Lincoln Memorial. The televised address did more to advance the cause of civil rights than did any other speech or demonstration. He began with a financial metaphor—the bad check drawn by a defaulting system of justice that was uncashable by the Negro. A series of sentences beginning with "now" spoke to the sense of urgency that justice no longer be delayed. A Shakespearean allusion—"this sweltering summer of the Negro's legitimate discontent," based on "now is the winter of our discontent," from *Richard III*—indicated a broad education at work. After raising his voice in a passage about the potential "whirlwind of revolt," he countered with a passage urging restraint on his followers.

The internal question "When will you be satisfied?" was answered by a series beginning "We can never be satisfied as long as" and culminating with a biblical "we will not be satisfied until justice rolls down like waters and righteousness like a mighty stream." This is all before he comes to the passage most often rebroadcast: "I have a dream today. . . ."

In 1876, Robert Ingersoll offered a series of visions—"I see our country filled with happy homes. . . . I see a world without a slave"—and this technique was adopted by FDR's speechwriter Samuel Rosenman in 1940: "I see an America where factory workers are not discarded. . . . I see an America of great cultural and educational opportunity. . . . I see an America devoted to our freedom. . . ." On occasion, a speaker can take the audience to the mountaintop and point to his vision of America. In his unforgettable peroration, Dr. King took the "let freedom ring" phrase from his recitation of the patriotic "My Country, 'Tis of Thee" lyric, took it up to the mountain ranges of five specific states, and capped it with the words from the Negro spiritual, familiar only to the audience at the Mall but soon familiar to all Americans, "Free at last! Free at last! Thank God Almighty, we are free at last!" The speech was worthy of its setting.

□   □   □

I am happy to join with you today in what will go down in history as the greatest demonstration for freedom in the history of our nation.

Five score years ago, a great American, in whose symbolic shadow we stand, signed the Emancipation Proclamation. This momentous decree came as a great beacon light of hope to millions of Negro slaves who had been seared in the flames of withering injustice. It came as a joyous daybreak to end the long night of captivity.

But one hundred years later, we must face the tragic fact that the Negro is still not free. One hundred years later, the life of the Negro is still sadly crippled by the manacles of segregation and the chains of discrimination. One hundred years later, the Negro lives on a lonely island of poverty in the midst of a vast ocean of material prosperity. One hundred years later the Negro is still languishing in the corners of American society and finds himself an exile in his own land. So we have come here today to dramatize an appalling condition.

In a sense we have come to our nation's capital to cash a check. When the architects of our republic wrote the magnificent words of the Constitution and the Declaration of Independence, they were signing a promissory note to which every American was to fall heir. This note was a promise that all men would be guaranteed the unalienable rights of life, liberty, and the pursuit of happiness.

It is obvious today that America has defaulted on this promissory note insofar as her citizens of color are concerned. Instead of honoring this sacred obligation, America has given the Negro people a bad check; a check which has come back marked "insufficient funds." But we refuse to believe that the bank of justice is bankrupt. We refuse to believe that there are insufficient funds in the great vaults of opportunity of this nation. So we have come to cash this check—a check that will give us upon demand the riches of freedom and the security of justice. We have also come to this hallowed spot to remind America of the fierce urgency of *now*. This is no time to engage in the luxury of cooling off or to take the tranquilizing drug of gradualism. *Now* is the time to make real the promises of democracy. *Now* is the time to rise from the dark and desolate valley of segregation to the sunlit path of racial justice. *Now* is the time to open the doors of opportunity to all of God's children. *Now* is the time to lift our nation from the quicksands of racial injustice to the solid rock of brotherhood.

It would be fatal for the nation to overlook the urgency of the moment and to underestimate the determination of the Negro. This sweltering summer of the Negro's legitimate discontent will not pass until there is an invigorating autumn of freedom and equality. Nineteen sixty-three is not an end, but a beginning. Those who hope that the Negro needed to blow off steam and will now be content will have a rude awakening if the nation returns to business as usual. There will be neither rest nor tranquillity in America until the Negro is granted his citizenship rights. The whirlwinds of revolt will continue to shake the foundations of our nation until the bright day of justice emerges.

But there is something that I must say to my people who stand on the warm threshold which leads into the palace of justice. In the process of gaining our rightful place, we must not be guilty of wrongful deeds. Let us not seek to satisfy our thirst for freedom by drinking from the cup of bitterness and hatred. We must forever conduct our struggle on the high plane of dignity and discipline. We must not allow our creative protest to degenerate into physical violence. Again and again we must rise to the majestic heights of meeting physical force with soul force. The marvelous new militancy which has engulfed the Negro community must not lead us to a distrust of all white people, for many of our white brothers, as evidenced by their presence here today, have come to realize that their destiny is tied up with our destiny and their freedom is inextricably bound to our freedom. We cannot walk alone.

And as we talk, we must make the pledge that we shall march ahead. We cannot turn back. There are those who are asking the devotees of civil rights, "When will you be satisfied?" We can never be satisfied as long as the Negro is the victim of the unspeakable horrors of police brutality. We can never be satisfied as long as our bodies, heavy with the fatigue of travel, cannot gain lodging in the motels of the highways and the hotels of the cities. We cannot be satisfied as long as the Negro's basic mobility is from a smaller ghetto to a larger one. We can never be satisfied as long as a Negro in Mississippi cannot vote and a Negro in New York believes he has nothing for which to vote. No, no, we are not satisfied, and we will not be satisfied until justice rolls down like waters and righteousness like a mighty stream.

I am not unmindful that some of you have come here out of great trials and tribulations. Some of you have come fresh from narrow jail cells. Some of you have come from areas where your quest for freedom left you battered by the storms of persecution and staggered by the winds of police brutality. You have been the veterans of creative suffering. Continue to work with the faith that unearned suffering is redemptive.

Go back to Mississippi, go back to Alabama, go back to South Carolina, go back to Georgia, go back to Louisiana, go back to the slums and ghettos of our modern cities, knowing that somehow this situation can and will be changed. Let us not wallow in the valley of despair.

I say to you today, my friends, that in spite of the difficulties and frustrations of the moment I still have a dream. It is a dream deeply rooted in the American dream.

I have a dream that one day this nation will rise up and live out the true meaning of its creed: "We hold these truths to be self-evident; that all men are created equal."

I have a dream that one day on the red hills of Georgia the sons of former slaves and the sons of former slave owners will be able to sit down together at the table of brotherhood.

I have a dream that one day even the state of Mississippi, a desert state sweltering with the heat of injustice and oppression, will be transformed into an oasis of freedom and justice.

I have a dream that my four little children will one day live in a nation where they will not be judged by the color of their skin but by the content of their character.

I have a dream today.

I have a dream that one day the state of Alabama, whose governor's lips are presently dripping with the words of interposition and nullification, will be transformed into a situation where little black boys and black girls will be able to join hands with little white boys and white girls and walk together as sisters and brothers.

I have a dream today.

I have a dream that one day every valley shall be exalted, every hill and mountain shall be made low, the rough places will be made plain, and the crooked places will be made straight, and the glory of the Lord shall be revealed, and all flesh shall see it together.

This is our hope. This is the faith with which I return to the South. With this faith we will be able to hew out of the mountain of despair a stone of hope. With this faith we will be able to transform the jangling discords of our nation into a beautiful symphony of brotherhood. With this faith we will be able to work together, to pray together, to struggle together, to go to jail together, to stand up for freedom together, knowing that we will be free one day.

This will be the day when all of God's children will be able to sing with new meaning "My country, 'tis of thee, sweet land of liberty, of thee I sing. Land where my fathers died, land of the pilgrim's pride, from every mountainside, let freedom ring."

And if America is to be a great nation this must become true. So let freedom ring from the prodigious hilltops of New Hampshire. Let freedom ring from the mighty mountains of New York. Let freedom ring from the heightening Alleghenies of Pennsylvania!

Let freedom ring from the snowcapped Rockies of Colorado!

Let freedom ring from the curvaceous peaks of California!

But not only that; let freedom ring from Stone Mountain of Georgia!

Let freedom ring from Lookout Mountain of Tennessee!

Let freedom ring from every hill and molehill of Mississippi. From every mountainside, let freedom ring.

When we let freedom ring, when we let it ring from every village and every hamlet, from every state and every city, we will be able to speed up that day when all of God's children, black men and white men, Jews and Gentiles, Protestants and Catholics, will be able to join hands and sing in the words of the old Negro spiritual, "Free at last! Free at last! Thank God Almighty, we are free at last!" ∎

Senator Everett Dirksen Extols the Marigold

"IT beguiles the senses and ennobles the spirit of man."

CONSERVATIVE REPUBLICAN DIRKSEN OF ILLINOIS came to national attention denouncing moderate Thomas E. Dewey of New York at a GOP convention for having "led us down the road to defeat." In later years, the senator became more likable, especially to journalists who enjoyed his colorful dramatics in a deep baritone and dubbed him the Wizard of Ooze.

Here is an example of a "little speech" of little legislative import, but touching a chord of symbolism that reverberates long after speeches on weighty matters have lost their zing.

Dirksen periodically submitted a bill to the Senate to establish a national floral symbol, much as the American bald eagle was the animal symbol (over the objection of Benjamin Franklin, who preferred the turkey). Others thought no national flower should be chosen, reflecting the idea of the United States as a bouquet of many states' flowers, but Dirksen vainly plumped for the marigold. This speech was given on April 17, 1967; in 1986, Congress decided to adopt a national floral symbol, and President Reagan signed the bill so designating the rose.

□   □   □

M r. President: On January 8, 1965, I introduced Senate Joint Resolution 19, to designate the American marigold—*Tagetes erecta*—as the national floral emblem of the United States. Today I am introducing the same resolution with the suggestion that it again be referred to the Committee on the Judiciary.

The American flag is not a mere assembly of colors, stripes, and stars but, in fact, truly symbolizes our origin, development, and growth.

The American eagle, king of the skies, is so truly representative of our might and power.

A national floral emblem should represent the virtues of our land and be national in character.

The marigold is a native of North America and can in truth and in fact be called an American flower.

It is national in character, for it grows and thrives in every one of the fifty states of this nation. It conquers the extremes of temperature. It well withstands the summer sun and the evening chill.

Its robustness reflects the hardihood and character of the generations who pioneered and built this land into a great nation. It is not temperamental about fertility. It resists its natural enemies, the insects. It is self-reliant and requires little attention. Its spectacular colors—lemon and orange, rich brown and deep mahogany—befit the imaginative qualities of this nation.

It is as sprightly as the daffodil, as colorful as the rose, as resolute as the zinnia, as delicate as the carnation, as haughty as the chrysanthemum, as aggressive as the petunia, as ubiquitous as the violet, and as stately as the snapdragon.

It beguiles the senses and ennobles the spirit of man. It is the delight of the amateur gardener and a constant challenge to the professional.

Since it is native to America and nowhere else in the world, and common to every state in the Union, I present the American marigold for designation as the national floral emblem of our country. ■

President William Jefferson Clinton Urges Memphis Churchgoers to "Make Our People Whole Again"

"If Martin Luther King . . . were to reappear by my side today . . . what would he say? . . . he would say, I fought to stop white people from being so filled with hate that they would wreak violence on black people. I did not fight for the right of black people to murder other black people with reckless abandon."

AT A RECEPTION in Washington, D.C., in 1994, President Clinton told the anthologist: "I have a copy of your collection of speeches on my night table, and I learn a lot from it." (The President, known to flatter authors frequently in that way, is said to have a night table the size of a football field.) I replied that the next edition would have one of his speeches in it, and he quickly asked, "Which one?" Without the deliberation over the collected works that such a decision deserves, I blurted, "Memphis?" Mr. Clinton nodded approval, adding: "Especially toward the end."

On November 13, 1993, Mr. Clinton flew to Memphis, Tennessee, to make a noontime talk to five thousand ministers, mostly black, at the Convocation of the Mason Temple Church of God in Christ. Because he tended to ignore texts when speaking to audiences he knew, speech-writer Carolyn Curiel prepared only a three-page series of talking points, including highlights of addresses of the Reverend Martin Luther King, Jr.; it was at this church that Dr. King had preached his last sermon before his 1968 assassination.

However, on Air Force One flying to the event, staff members urged the President to stay "on message" to the traveling press corps, devoting some time to his support of the North American Free Trade Agreement. Preprinted signs about NAFTA were set to be held by children during Atlanta appearances. Accordingly, the President cobbled together half a speech that included a review of blacks appointed by his administration, reminders that poor families had been given a tax cut, and five long paragraphs about the job benefits of NAFTA. He delivered it uncomfortably and knew it was received only politely; none of that is included in the text that follows.

But speaking in a Pentecostal church, in front of a white-robed choir, the person in the pulpit is expected to speak as the spirit moves him—which means no prepared text. Working from his terse list of prompts, but "winging it," Mr. Clinton then gave the second half of his speech, which was the most moving long passage of his presidency. Daring to place himself in Dr. King's shoes, he challenged the audience to assume moral responsibility to teach nonviolence to meet "the great crisis of the spirit that is gripping America today."

Clintonian oratory usually runs long. In some cases, as in his 1992 Democratic convention speech, the length seemed self-indulgent; it was as if he recalled his boring 1988 convention speech, in which the only applause came at the words "in conclusion," and was determined to milk his winning convention for all the applause in it. Two other long speeches, however—on religious liberty, made to the James Madison High School in Vienna, Virginia, on July 12, 1995, and on affirmative action made one week later—were thoughtful, persuasive presentations of his views on these most controversial topics. (Clinton credited Ms. Curiel with the affirmative action drafting; Jonathan Prince worked on religious liberty.)

The final portion of his Memphis speech, however, is what Clintonites like to think of as quintessential Clinton: personal, impassioned, anecdotal, self-questioning, colloquial ("bitty"), and—with Bible-quoting Southern Baptist cadences—uplifting. On Ms. Curiel's wall is a picture of audience members, many with hands in chins, in pensive rather than revivalist mood. "This had not been billed as a major speech," she recalled, "but on the way back, we all knew something major had happened."

Just before mounting the pulpit, Mr. Clinton listened to a lone saxophonist play the hymn "Amazing Grace." He heard himself introduced as "Bishop Clinton" and immediately played off that in his opening,

□   □   □

. . . You know, in the last ten months, I've been called a lot of things, but nobody's called me a bishop yet. [*Laughter.*]

When I was about nine years old, my beloved and now departed grandmother, who was a very wise woman, looked at me and she said, "You know, I believe you could be a preacher if you were just a little better boy." [*Laughter.*]

Proverbs says, "A happy heart doeth good like medicine, but a broken spirit dryeth the bone." This is a happy place, and I'm happy to be here. I thank you for your spirit.

By the grace of God and your help, last year I was elected president of this great country. I never dreamed that I would ever have a chance to come to this hallowed place where Martin Luther King gave his last sermon. I ask you to think today about the purpose for which I ran and the purpose for which so many of you worked to put me in this great office. I have worked hard to keep faith with our common efforts: to restore the economy, to reverse the politics of helping only those at the top of our totem pole and not the hard-working middle class or the poor; to bring our people together across racial and regional and political lines, to make a strength out of our diversity instead of letting it tear us apart; to reward work and family and community and try to move us forward into the twenty-first century. I have tried to keep faith. . . .

If Martin Luther King, who said, "Like Moses, I am on the mountaintop, and I can see the promised land, but I'm not going to be able to get there with you, but we will get there"—if he were to reappear by my side today and give us a report card on the last twenty-five years, what would he say? You did a good job, he would say, voting and electing people who formerly were not electable because of the color of their skin. You have more political power, and that is good. You did a good job, he would say, letting people who have the ability to do so live wherever they want to live, go wherever they want to go in this great country. You did a good job, he would say, elevating people of color into the ranks of the United States armed forces to the very top or into the very top of our government. You did a very good job, he would say. He would say, you did a good job creating a black middle class of people who really are doing well, and the middle class is growing more among African-Americans than among non–African-Americans. You did a good job; you did a good job in opening opportunity.

But he would say, I did not live and die to see the American family destroyed. I did not live and die to see thirteen-year-old boys get automatic weapons and gun down nine-year-olds just for the kick of it. I did not live and die to see young people destroy their own lives with drugs and then build fortunes destroying the lives of others. That is not what I came here to do. I fought for freedom, he would say; but not for the freedom of people to kill each other with reckless abandon, not for the freedom of children to have children and the fathers of the children walk away from them and abandon them as if they don't amount to anything. I fought for people to have the right to work but not to have whole communities and people abandoned. This is not what I lived and died for.

My fellow Americans, he would say, I fought to stop white people from being so filled with hate that they would wreak violence on black people. I did not fight for the right of black people to murder other black people with reckless abandon.

The other day the mayor of Baltimore, Kurt Schmoke, a dear friend of mine, told me a story of visiting the family of a young man who had been killed—eighteen years old—on Halloween. He always went out with little bitty kids so they could trick-or-treat safely. And across the street from where they were walking on Halloween, a fourteen-year-old boy gave a thirteen-year-old boy a gun and dared him to shoot the eighteen-year-old boy, and he shot him dead. And the mayor had to visit the family.

In Washington, D.C., where I live, your nation's capital, the symbol of freedom throughout the world, look how that freedom is being exercised. The other night a man came along the street and grabbed a one-year-old child and put the child in his car. The child may have been the child of the man. And two people were after him, and they chased him in the car, and they just kept shooting with reckless abandon, knowing that baby was in the car. And they shot the man dead, and a bullet went through his body into the baby's body, and blew the little bootie off the child's foot.

The other day on the front page of our paper, the nation's capital, are we talking about world peace or world conflict? No, big article on the front page of *The Washington Post* about an eleven-year-old child planning her funeral: "These are the hymns I want sung. This is the dress I want to wear. I know I'm not going to live very long." That is not the freedom, the freedom to die before you're a teenager is not what Martin Luther King lived and died for.

More than thirty-seven thousand people die from gunshot wounds in this country every year. Gunfire is the leading cause of death in young men. And now that we've all gotten so cool that everybody can get a semiautomatic weapon, a person shot now is three times more likely to die than fifteen years ago, because they're likely to have three bullets in them. A hundred and sixty thousand children stay home from school every day because they are scared they will be hurt in their schools.

The other day I was in California at a town meeting, and a handsome young man stood up and said, "Mr. President, my brother and I, we don't belong to gangs. We don't have guns. We don't do drugs. We want to go to school. We want to be professionals. We want to work hard. We want to do well. We want to have families. And we changed our school because the school we were in was so dangerous. So when we showed up to the new school to register, my brother and I were standing in line and somebody ran into the school and started shooting a gun. My brother was shot down standing right in front of me at the safer school." The freedom to do that kind of thing is not what Martin Luther King lived and died for, not what people gathered in this hallowed church for the night before he was assassinated in April of 1968. If you had told anybody who was here in that church on that night that we would abuse our freedom in that way, they would have found it hard to believe. And I tell you, it is our moral duty to turn it around.

And now I think finally we have a chance. Finally, I think, we have a chance. We have a pastor here from New Haven, Connecticut. I was in his church with Reverend Jackson when I was running for president on a snowy day in Connecticut to mourn the death of children who had been killed in that city. And afterward we walked down the street for more than a mile in the snow. Then, the American people were not ready. People would say, "Oh, this is a terrible thing, but what can we do about it?"

Now when we read that foreign visitors come to our shores and are killed at random in our fine state of Florida, when we see our children planning their funerals, when the American people are finally coming to grips with the accumulated weight of crime and violence and the breakdown of family and community and the increase in drugs and the decrease in jobs, I think finally we may be ready to do something about it.

And there is something for each of us to do. There are changes we can make from the outside in; that's the job of the president and the Congress and the governors and the mayors and the social service agencies. And then there's some changes we're going to have to make from the inside out, or the others won't matter. That's what that magnificent song was about, isn't it? Sometimes there are no answers from the outside in; sometimes all the answers have to come from the values and the stirrings and the voices that speak to us from within.

So we are beginning. We are trying to pass a bill to make our people safer, to put another 100,000 police officers on the street, to provide boot camps instead of prisons for young people who can still be rescued, to provide more safety in our schools, to restrict the availability of these awful assault weapons, to pass the Brady Bill and at least require people to have their criminal background checked before they get a gun, and to say, if you're not old enough to vote and you're not old enough to go to war, you ought not to own a handgun, and you ought not to use one unless you're on a target range. . . .

We need this crime bill now. We ought to give it to the American people for Christmas. And we need to move forward on all these other fronts. But I say to you, my fellow Americans, we need some other things as well. I do not believe we can repair the basic fabric of society until people who are willing to work have work. Work organizes life. It gives structure and discipline to life. It gives meaning and self-esteem to people who are parents. It gives a role model to children.

The famous African-American sociologist William Julius Wilson has written a stunning book called *The Truly Disadvantaged* in which he chronicles in breathtaking terms how the inner cities of our country have crumbled as work has disappeared. And we must find away, through public and private sources, to enhance the attractiveness of the American people who live there to get investment there. We cannot, I submit to you, repair the American community and restore the American family until we provide the structure, the values, the discipline, and the reward that work gives.

I read a wonderful speech the other day given at Howard University in a lecture series funded by Bill and Camille Cosby, in which the speaker said, "I grew up in Anacostia years ago. Even then it was all black, and it was a very poor neighborhood. But you know, when I was a child in Anacostia, a 100 percent African-American neighborhood, a very poor neighborhood, we had a crime rate that was lower than the average of the crime rate of our city. Why? Because we had coherent families. We had coherent communities. The people who filled the church on Sunday lived in the same place they went to church. The guy that owned the drugstore lived down the street. The person that owned the grocery store lived in our community. We were whole." And I say to you, we have to make our people whole again.

This church has stood for that. Why do you think you have five million members in this country? Because people know you are filled with the spirit of God to do the right thing in this life by them. So I say to you, we have to make a partnership, all the government agencies, all the business folks; but where there are no families, where there is no order, where there is no hope, where we are reducing the size of our armed services because we have won the cold war, who will be there to give structure, discipline, and love to these children? You must do that. And we must help you. Scripture says, you are the salt of the Earth and the light of the world, that if your light shines before men they will give glory to the Father in heaven. That is what we must do.

That is what we must do. How would we explain it to Martin Luther King if he showed up today and said, yes, we won the Cold War. Yes, the biggest threat that all of us grew up under, communism and nuclear war, communism gone, nuclear war receding. Yes, we developed all these miraculous technologies. Yes, we all have got a VCR in our home; it's interesting. Yes, we get fifty channels on the cable. Yes, without regard to race, if you work hard and play by the rules, you can get into a service academy or a good college, you'll do just great. How would we explain to him all these kids getting killed and killing each other? How would we justify the things that we permit that no other country in the world would permit? How could we explain that we gave people the freedom to succeed, and we created conditions in which millions abuse that freedom to destroy the things that make life worth living and life itself? We cannot.

And so I say to you today, my fellow Americans, you gave me this job, and we're making progress on the things you hired me to do. But unless we deal with the ravages of crime and drugs and violence and unless we recognize that it's due to the breakdown of the family, the community, and the disappearance of jobs, and unless we say some of this cannot be done by government, because we have to reach deep inside to the values, the spirit, the soul, and the truth of human nature, none of the other things we seek to do will ever take us where we need to go.

So in this pulpit, on this day, let me ask all of you in your heart to say: We will honor the life and the work of Martin Luther King. We will honor the meaning of our church. We will, somehow, by God's grace, we will turn this around. We will give these children a future. We will take away their guns and give them books. We will take away their despair and give them hope. We will rebuild the families and the neighborhoods and the communities. We won't make all the work that has gone on here benefit just a few. We will do it together by the grace of God. ■

Broadcaster
Alistair Cooke Sends
a Christmas "Letter
from America"

"If I were compelled at pistol point to choose between the Big Bang and the book of Genesis, I should plump for Genesis: 'And God said—"Let there be light. . . ."And there—was—light.'"

BRITISH-BORN ALISTAIR COOKE was an American for more than sixty years, many of them spent interpreting the United States to Britain (and fifty other countries) through his weekly radio program on BBC, *Letter From America.*

On December 21, 2001, a few months after the Al Qaeda attacks on the World Trade Center and the Pentagon, Cooke devoted his Christmas week broadcast to the varied subjects of the conductor Leonard Bernstein's introduction to Handel's *Messiah*, to the self-styled messianic figure of Osama bin Laden, to the role model of the golf champion Tiger Woods. His writing style is that of an informal essayist, his speaking style that of an intelligent friend. In this short address, Cooke gently weaves together the strands of his observations about his famous human subjects into a conclusion about the spiritual uplift provided by the music's Hallelujah Chorus. The seemingly rambling oral "letter" turns out to have a moving point.

In 2003, still active on the air at age ninety-five, Cooke sent the text of his talk as a Christmas card to friends. Before he died a year later, he sent a note to his friend Jacques Barzun typical of his style of writing as he spoke: "I have two or three months to go. Shush. G'bye."

☐　☐　☐

I am not myself a great collector of old letters but, from time to time, riffling through the chaos of what I dare to call my files, I come on a note from someone I'd long forgotten. And the other morning I fell on a funny, shrewd letter from a shrewd and funny man who has been lost to us for much too long a time, a loss I feel now because in our heyday of pretentious theories in literature, art, music and—help!—architecture, this man was the sanest of critics and a splendid slaughterer of sacred cows in England, whether of the Left or Right, the lowbrow or the high-brow, as Tom Wolfe has been in America: Philip Larkin.

I had the privilege of keeping up a correspondence with him in what, alas, turned out to be the last year or two of his life. We exchanged ideas mostly about poetry, and always about jazz—the word "jazz" being understood as only and always what *we* agreed to like—namely, jazz from the earliest New Orleans days up through, say, the 1940s. And there an end. Our friendship was sealed (as so many are by a shared hate) by the discovery that with the arrival of bebop we both heard the death knell of jazz. Larkin called Thelonius Monk the "elephant on the keyboard."

In this—as it turned out—his last letter, there was a PS. "Another thing I note we have in common: you say you play the *Messiah* right through every Christmas. So do I."

I must not assume, as old people tend to, that a permanent item of their culture passes on to the next and the next generation. Nearly fifty years ago, I had the rare, weird pleasure of introducing the *Messiah* to— Leonard Bernstein! (Please don't ask who is Leonard Bernstein, as indeed one of the greatest living golfers once did ask me.)

Leonard Bernstein came to fame with a national audience, as distinct from the concert audience everywhere, when he appeared first on television. The show was the first ninety-minute show of any kind. It was a collection, collage, or mishmash of music, science, drama, politics, history, anything and everything; and Bernstein was one of our earliest stars, when he was already blazing his way from Boston to Vienna in the works of the nineteenth-century Romantics, the Russians especially. One day a half dozen of us were sitting around tossing ideas and sketching out the Christmas show. It was then I threw in what I thought to be the very hack-neyed but beautiful idea of having Bernstein conduct a short version of the *Messiah*. Bernstein, I remember, looked up—"Handel?" he said with a rising inflection, as he might have been guessing an obscurity. That's the man. "You know something," said Bernstein, "I don't know it."

Well, need I say he came to know it, and I—as one brought up in the nonconformist north of England and, therefore, having known every note of the *Messiah* since the age of five—had the pride of standing before a television audience of 290 stations and introducing the great George Frederic. He was then a pretty old man—fifty-six was beyond the usual span in 1742—not doing well with his concert music or operas, in bad financial trouble, being invited to go to Dublin for a few weeks and for a price compose an oratorio. He lived alone in two rooms in a small house but, once he had this conception of writing the life of Christ not as a chronicle but as a series of spiritual musical themes, he scarcely paused from dawn to midnight. He had his meals pushed under the door. At the end of fifteen days only, during the last twilight, he finished the Hallelujah Chorus, and wrote in his journal: "I felt that the Lord God Almighty had come down and did stand before me."

At the end, Bernstein embraced us all. "What a sublime work!" he said.

One of the oldest musical traditions of New York City is a performance of the *Messiah* given with the instruments of the original scoring, first done here in 1770 in a church which stands, miraculously today, only three blocks from the mountainous rubble and ashes of the Twin Towers. On that twelfth of September, the minister and the choirmaster padded in gas masks through the horrors underfoot and knew that this 230-year-old tradition was bound to be broken. However, three months passed, and the ninety pipes of the old organ were still choked, and the burning smell was everywhere, and though the church has stained glass but no open windows, the ash and the grime and smoke came in through the leading. But last Sunday once more, into an acrid atmosphere, the mighty work came alive again.

It may strike some listeners as odd that of all cities, New York City, which houses 2 million of America's six million Jews, should hold to this by now ancient Christian tradition. But if you knew New York City, as this administration is desperately trying to have it known to the Arab world, you would know this to be most characteristic of the city. Long ago, the most elegant essayist of the twentieth century, E. B. White, wrote, "the admirable thing about New York is not the conflict of the races and religions but the truce they keep."

The word "Messiah" exists in many languages, though it wasn't until the sixteenth century that translators of the Bible chose to fix its spelling with an aitch: M-e-s-s-i-a-h—as sounding more Hebrew. And that's the way it stayed. It meant, as everyone knows, the one who would come and set free the oppressed children of Israel. And ever since, it has been used in general in other languages, to signify the liberator of the oppressed.

Such a self-proclaimed liberator we saw the other evening on that appalling tape of bin Laden. It struck me that one of the tragedies of this war is the fact of his striking good looks: a somber and handsome presence—the fine eyes, an expression almost of tenderness. It was hard from the beginning to appreciate that this man is the latest of a dreaded breed we have known to our rage and sorrow in the twentieth century: Stalin, Hitler, Pol Pot, Saddam Hussein, each of them either ordinary or ugly. And here is a totalitarian fanatic whose majestic presence lends itself at least to the role of Robin Hood, which is how he sees himself and—to many Muslims—as a messianic figure who will deliver the impoverished peoples of Arabia from what some see as the superpower bully of the Western world.

Enough of these morbid musings! There are other, more modest, saviors of the oppressed, and as I settle in for Christmas Eve sipping the twilight wine of Scotland, a young and happier example comes to mind.

Everyone who has followed a sport for long is frequently caught, I believe, between two emotions in watching the stars of the game: horrified awe at the huge monies they earn, and yet relief that they are not paid, as they used to be, at the going rate of plumbers' assistants. We're bound to wonder from time to time what they do with all this loot. And too often the answer is—as one famous golfer put it, "Well, what d'you think? I used to ride the subway. Now I have six cars, a yacht, and a private jet. How *about* that?" Well, the tale I have to tell is quite another story and shines like a good deed in a naughty world.

The final tournament of the season was won by the young man who is without question the best golfer in the world. He had just picked up $2 million from winning this one tournament and was asked if it was true that the money would go to the Tiger Woods Foundation. Yes, it would, he said. His foundation he described simply as a fund with the simple aim of "helping poor children of color make something of themselves." What, asked the breezy interviewer, is your main goal in life? Tiger blinked, as if he'd been talking to a deaf man. "I said—the Foundation—I want to make it global, based in the United States but taking in many, many countries. That's far more important than golf or winning tournaments."

Here is a young man, just twenty-six, who was urged only four years ago by a well-wishing friend, an old man and a ravenous golfer, to stay one more year in college and "enrich" his life. Tiger decided on the contrary to turn pro and sign a first sponsor's contract for $52 million. Since then, new contracts and renewals have poured in like Niagara. And he has grown in maturity as a human being, stayed remarkably modest, and, with his enormous fame, levelheaded. From the start he decided to hand over his fortune to enriching the lives of impoverished colored children across the globe. At Christmas time, it is hard to think of a finer role model, young or old, of any color, any faith, or no faith at all.

As midnight strikes and the holy—or holiday comes in, a very irreligious item leads the news. It seems that among the experts, the expert physicists, there is now grave doubt about the truth, the validity, of the Big Bang theory. Well, how our universe came about—especially who done it—has for long been beyond *me*. I've never trusted the Big Bang theory and won't until someone tells me who triggered it, who struck the match. But if I were compelled at pistol point to choose between the Big Bang and the book of Genesis, I should plump for Genesis: "And God said—'Let there be light. . . .' And there—was—light." And then, bring on the thunder, and lightning, of the Hallelujah Chorus!!!

Merry Christmas! ■

President George W. Bush Envisions the "Age of Liberty"

"SIXTY *years of Western nations excusing and accommodating the lack of freedom in the Middle East did nothing to make us safe—because in the long run, stability cannot be purchased at the expense of liberty.*"

SIX MONTHS AFTER AMERICAN AND BRITISH FORCES liberated Baghdad, the flush of victory had been replaced by the dismayed reaction to the guerrilla warfare being waged by terrorists and die-hard supporters of the ousted Saddam Hussein, who had not yet been captured. Nor had weapons of mass destruction been found, and critics led at the time by Democrat Howard Dean derided claims of a link between Osama bin Laden's Al Qaeda network and Iraq. President George W. Bush found it necessary to counter his critics at home and abroad by placing the second Iraq war in a greater context than "regime change."

At a dinner in Washington, D.C., on November 6, 2003, honoring the twentieth anniversary of the National Endowment for Democracy, he delivered what had become a rarity in recent political rhetoric: a thematic speech.

In articulating what had become, after the attacks of September 11, 2001, the central purpose of his presidency, he evoked three of his predecessors in the twentieth century: Woodrow Wilson, trying to make the world safe for democracy in 1918; Franklin D. Roosevelt, in 1941 giving hope to peoples crushed and endangered by nazism; and Ronald Reagan, in 1982 (derogated at the time, as Bush often is, as a "cowboy") telling the British Parliament that a turning point had been reached in confronting the menace of world communism. "From the Fourteen Points to the Four Freedoms, to the speech at Westminster, America has put our power at the service of principle." (A copyeditor would have changed "our" to "its.") He stated his theme in ten words: "The advance of freedom is the calling of our time."

The speech is structured, like a concerto, on a tripod. It begins with its forceful statement of theme and an optimistic evocation of recent history: "We've witnessed, in little over a generation, the swiftest advance of freedom in the 2,500-year story of democracy. . . . It is no accident that the rise of so many democracies took place in a time when the world's most influential nation was itself a democracy." (He chose the adjective "influential" rather than the customary "powerful" to stress our democratic example. And the formulation "It is no accident" parodies, perhaps unconsciously, the communist cliché "As is well known.")

The second movement turns from the successes of freedom in South Africa, Central America, and a unified Germany to a *tour d'horizon* of the places where restrictions on freedom are an anomaly in an age of liberty: from the assonant "outposts of oppression"—including Cuba, North Korea, and Zimbabwe—to those Palestinian leaders who are "the main obstacles to peace" in the Middle East. That brings him to the challenge to leaders of nations of that turbulent area: "Will they be remembered for resisting reform, or for leading it?"

The transition to the speech's third movement is a startling charge of error in previous U.S. policy toward that area. He faults presidents since FDR—including his father, George H. W. Bush—for not doing more to urge freedom on authoritarian regimes: "Sixty years of Western nations excusing and accommodating the lack of freedom in the Middle East did nothing to make us safe—because in the long run, stability cannot be purchased at the expense of liberty." In thus breaking with the advocates of realpolitik, he associated his policy with that of the Wilsonian idealism so long derided by pragmatic Kissingerians. In that way, he wrapped his controversial decision to overthrow Saddam Hussein in the larger purpose of advancing human freedom everywhere in the "age of liberty." (He first used that phrase in his speech to a joint session of Congress a week after the September 11, 2001, attacks.)

Both the daring and profundity of the speech were a surprise coming from a speaker not known for his eloquence. Because it had not been heralded in advance as a major foreign policy address, the text was not printed in the *New York Times* nor telecast at length on network newscasts, and its impact was delayed. Bush's main speechwriters—Michael Gerson, John McConnell, and Matthew Scully—followed up this speech by drafting an address to the British Parliament two weeks later that developed the freedom theme further. Because of the dramatic setting and delayed reaction to the first speech, the London effort was far more extensively covered. It included a defiant, Churchillian applause line: "We did not charge hundreds of miles into the heart of Iraq and pay a bitter cost of casualties, and liberate 25 million people, only to retreat before a band of thugs and assassins."

However, his earlier, shorter effort in D.C. was seminal and that is why I chose it for this anthology, despite the greater sense of occasion in London. Just as he used a spiritual word in stating his theme—"the *calling* of our time"—Bush invoked, without excessive religiosity, the Deity in his conclusion: "As we meet the terror and violence of the world, we can be certain the author of freedom is not indifferent to the fate of freedom."

□   □   □

The roots of our democracy can be traced to England, and to its Parliament—and so can the roots of this organization. In June of 1982, President Ronald Reagan spoke at Westminster Palace and declared, the turning point had arrived in history. He argued that Soviet communism had failed, precisely because it did not respect its own people—their creativity, their genius, and their rights.

President Reagan said that the day of Soviet tyranny was passing, that freedom had a momentum which would not be halted. He gave this organization its mandate: to add to the momentum of freedom across the world. Your mandate was important twenty years ago; it is equally important today.

A number of critics were dismissive of that speech by the president. According to one editorial of the time, "It seems hard to be a sophisticated European and also an admirer of Ronald Reagan." Some observers on both sides of the Atlantic pronounced the speech simplistic and naïve, and even dangerous. In fact, Ronald Reagan's words were courageous and optimistic and entirely correct.

The great democratic movement President Reagan described was already well under way. In the early 1970s, there were about forty democracies in the world. By the middle of that decade, Portugal and Spain and Greece held free elections. Soon there were new democracies in Latin America, and free institutions were spreading in Korea, in Taiwan, and in East Asia. This very week in 1989, there were protests in East Berlin and in Leipzig. By the end of that year, every communist dictatorship in Central America had collapsed. Within another year, the South African government released Nelson Mandela. Four years later, he was elected president of his country—ascending, like Walesa and Havel, from prisoner of state to head of state.

As the twentieth century ended, there were around 120 democracies in the world—and I can assure you more are on the way. Ronald Reagan would be pleased, and he would not be surprised.

We've witnessed, in little over a generation, the swiftest advance of freedom in the 2,500-year story of democracy. Historians in the future will offer their own explanations for why this happened. Yet we already know some of the reasons they will cite. It is no accident that the rise of so many democracies took place in a time when the world's most influential nation was itself a democracy.

The United States made military and moral commitments in Europe and Asia, which protected free nations from aggression, and created the conditions in which new democracies could flourish. As we provided security for whole nations, we also provided inspiration for oppressed peoples. In prison camps, in banned union meetings, in clandestine churches, men and women knew that the whole world was not sharing their own nightmare. They knew of at least one place—a bright and hopeful land—where freedom was valued and secure. And they prayed that America would not forget them, or forget the mission to promote liberty around the world.

Historians will note that in many nations, the advance of markets and free enterprise helped to create a middle class that was confident enough to demand their own rights. They will point to the role of technology in frustrating censorship and central control—and marvel at the power of instant communications to spread the truth, the news, and courage across borders.

Historians in the future will reflect on an extraordinary, undeniable fact: Over time, free nations grow stronger and dictatorships grow weaker. In the middle of the twentieth century, some imagined that the central planning and social regimentation were a shortcut to national strength. In fact, the prosperity, and social vitality and technological progress of a people, are directly determined by extent of their liberty. Freedom honors and unleashes human creativity—and creativity determines the strength and wealth of nations. Liberty is both the plan of heaven for humanity, and the best hope for progress here on Earth.

The progress of liberty is a powerful trend. Yet, we also know that liberty, if not defended, can be lost. The success of freedom is not determined by some dialectic of history. By definition, the success of freedom rests upon the choices and the courage of free peoples, and upon their willingness to sacrifice. In the trenches of World War I, through a two-front war in the 1940s, the difficult battles of Korea and Vietnam, and in missions of rescue and liberation on nearly every continent, Americans have amply displayed our willingness to sacrifice for liberty.

The sacrifices of Americans have not always been recognized or appreciated, yet they have been worthwhile. Because we and our allies were steadfast, Germany and Japan are democratic nations that no longer threaten the world. A global nuclear standoff with the Soviet Union ended peacefully—as did the Soviet Union. The nations of Europe are moving towards unity, not dividing into armed camps and descending into genocide. Every nation has learned, or should have learned, an important lesson: Freedom is worth fighting for, dying for, and standing for—and the advance of freedom leads to peace.

And now we must apply that lesson in our own time. We've reached another great turning point—and the resolve we show will shape the next stage of the world democratic movement.

Our commitment to democracy is tested in countries like Cuba and Burma and North Korea and Zimbabwe—outposts of oppression in our world. The people in these nations live in captivity, and fear and silence. Yet, these regimes cannot hold back freedom forever—and, one day, from prison camps and prison cells, and from exile, the leaders of new democracies will arrive. Communism, and militarism and rule by the capricious and corrupt, are the relics of a passing era. And we will stand with these oppressed peoples until the day of their freedom finally arrives.

Our commitment to democracy is tested in China. That nation now has a sliver, a fragment of liberty. Yet, China's people will eventually want their liberty pure and whole. China has discovered that economic freedom leads to national wealth. China's leaders will also discover that freedom is indivisible—that social and religious freedom is also essential to national greatness and national dignity. Eventually, men and women who are allowed to control their own wealth will insist on controlling their own lives and their own country.

Our commitment to democracy is also tested in the Middle East, which is my focus today, and must be a focus of American policy for decades to come. In many nations of the Middle East—countries of great strategic importance—democracy has not yet taken root. And the questions arise: Are the peoples of the Middle East somehow beyond the reach of liberty? Are millions of men and women and children condemned by history or culture to live in despotism? Are they alone never to know freedom, and never even to have a choice in the matter? I, for one, do not believe it. I believe every person has the ability and the right to be free.

Some skeptics of democracy assert that the traditions of Islam are inhospitable to the representative government. This "cultural condescension," as Ronald Reagan termed it, has a long history. After the Japanese surrender in 1945, a so-called Japan expert asserted that democracy in that former empire would "never work." Another observer declared the prospects for democracy in post-Hitler Germany are, and I quote, "most uncertain at best"—he made that claim in 1957. Seventy-four years ago, The Sunday London *Times* declared nine-tenths of the population of India to be "illiterates not caring a fig for politics." Yet when Indian democracy was imperiled in the 1970s, the Indian people showed their commitment to liberty in a national referendum that saved their form of government.

Time after time, observers have questioned whether this country, or that people, or this group, are "ready" for democracy—as if freedom were a prize you win for meeting our own Western standards of progress. In fact, the daily work of democracy itself is the path of progress. It teaches cooperation, the free exchange of ideas, and the peaceful resolution of differences. As men and women are showing, from Bangladesh to Botswana, to Mongolia, it is the practice of democracy that makes a nation ready for democracy, and every nation can start on this path.

It should be clear to all that Islam—the faith of one-fifth of humanity—is consistent with democratic rule. Democratic progress is found in many predominantly Muslim countries—in Turkey and Indonesia, and Senegal and Albania, Niger and Sierra Leone. Muslim men and women are good citizens of India and South Africa, of the nations of western Europe, and of the United States of America.

More than half of all the Muslims in the world live in freedom under democratically constituted governments. They succeed in democratic societies, not in spite of their faith, but because of it. A religion that demands individual moral accountability, and encourages the encounter of the individual with God, is fully compatible with the rights and responsibilities of self-government.

Yet there's a great challenge today in the Middle East. In the words of a recent report by Arab scholars, the global wave of democracy has—and I quote—"barely reached the Arab states." They continue: "This freedom deficit undermines human development and is one of the most painful manifestations of lagging political development." The freedom deficit they describe has terrible consequences, of the people of the Middle East and for the world. In many Middle Eastern countries, poverty is deep and it is spreading, women lack rights and are denied schooling. Whole societies remain stagnant while the world moves ahead. These are not the failures of a culture or a religion. These are the failures of political and economic doctrines.

As the colonial era passed away, the Middle East saw the establishment of many military dictatorships. Some rulers adopted the dogmas of socialism, seized total control of political parties and the media and universities. They allied themselves with the Soviet bloc and with international terrorism. Dictators in Iraq and Syria promised the restoration of national honor, a return to ancient glories. They've left instead a legacy of torture, oppression, misery, and ruin.

Other men, and groups of men, have gained influence in the Middle East and beyond through an ideology of theocratic terror. Behind their language of religion is the ambition for absolute political power. Ruling cabals like the Taliban show their version of religious piety in public whippings of women, ruthless suppression of any difference or dissent, and support for terrorists who arm and train to murder the innocent. The Taliban promised religious purity and national pride. Instead, by systematically destroying a proud and working society, they left behind suffering and starvation.

Many Middle Eastern governments now understand that military dictatorship and theocratic rule are a straight, smooth highway to nowhere. But some governments still cling to the old habits of central control. There are governments that still fear and repress independent thought and creativity, and private enterprise—the human qualities that make for strong and successful societies. Even when these nations have vast natural resources, they do not respect or develop their greatest resources—the talent and energy of men and women working and living in freedom.

Instead of dwelling on past wrongs and blaming others, governments in the Middle East need to confront real problems, and serve the true interests of their nations. The good and capable people of the Middle East all deserve responsible leadership. For too long, many people in that region have been victims and subjects—they deserve to be active citizens.

Governments across the Middle East and North Africa are beginning to see the need for change. Morocco has a diverse new parliament; King Mohammed has urged it to extend the rights to women. Here is how His Majesty explained his reforms to parliament: "How can society achieve progress while women, who represent half the nation, see their rights violated and suffer as a result of injustice, violence, and marginalization, notwithstanding the dignity and justice granted to them by our glorious religion?" The king of Morocco is correct: the future of Muslim nations will be better for all with the full participation of women.

In Bahrain last year, citizens elected their own parliament for the first time in nearly three decades. Oman has extended the vote to all adult citizens; Qatar has a new constitution; Yemen has a multiparty political system; Kuwait has a directly elected national assembly; and Jordan held historic elections this summer. Recent surveys in Arab nations reveal broad support for political pluralism, the rule of law, and free speech. These are the stirrings of Middle Eastern democracy, and they carry the promise of greater change to come.

As changes come to the Middle Eastern region, those with power should ask themselves: Will they be remembered for resisting reform, or for leading it? In Iran, the demand for democracy is strong and broad, as we saw last month when thousands gathered to welcome home Shirin Ebadi, the winner of the Nobel Peace Prize. The regime in Tehran must heed the democratic demands of the Iranian people, or lose its last claim to legitimacy.

For the Palestinian people, the only path to independence and dignity and progress is the path of democracy. And the Palestinian leaders who block and undermine democratic reform, and feed hatred and encourage violence, are not leaders at all. They're the main obstacles to peace, and to the success of the Palestinian people.

The Saudi government is taking first steps toward reform, including a plan for gradual introduction of elections. By giving the Saudi people a greater role in their own society, the Saudi government can demonstrate true leadership in the region.

The great and proud nation of Egypt has shown the way toward peace in the Middle East, and now should show the way toward democracy in the Middle East. Champions of democracy in the region understand that democracy is not perfect, it is not the path to utopia, but it's the only path to national success and dignity.

As we watch and encourage reforms in the region, we are mindful that modernization is not the same as Westernization. Representative governments in the Middle East will reflect their own cultures. They will not, and should not, look like us. Democratic nations may be constitutional monarchies, federal republics, or parliamentary systems. And working democracies always need time to develop—as did our own. We've taken a two-hundred-year journey toward inclusion and justice—and this makes us patient and understanding as other nations are at different stages of this journey.

There are, however, essential principles common to every successful society, in every culture. Successful societies limit the power of the state and the power of the military—so that governments respond to the will of the people, and not the will of an elite. Successful societies protect freedom with the consistent and impartial rule of law, instead of selecting applying—selectively applying the law to punish political opponents. Successful societies allow room for healthy civic institutions—for political parties and labor unions and independent newspapers and broadcast media. Successful societies guarantee religious liberty—the right to serve and honor God without fear of persecution. Successful societies privatize their economies, and secure the rights of property. They prohibit and punish official corruption, and invest in the health and education of their people. They recognize the rights of women. And instead of directing hatred and resentment against others, successful societies appeal to the hopes of their own people.

These vital principles are being applied in the nations of Afghanistan and Iraq. With the steady leadership of President Karzai, the people of Afghanistan are building a modern and peaceful government. Next month, five hundred delegates will convene a national assembly in Kabul to approve a new Afghan constitution. The proposed draft would establish a bicameral parliament, set national elections next year, and recognize Afghanistan's Muslim identity, while protecting the rights of all citizens. Afghanistan faces continuing economic and security challenges—it will face those challenges as a free and stable democracy.

In Iraq, the Coalition Provisional Authority and the Iraqi Governing Council are also working together to build a democracy—and after three decades of tyranny, this work is not easy. The former dictator ruled by terror and treachery, and left deeply ingrained habits of fear and distrust. Remnants of his regime, joined by foreign terrorists, continue their battle against order and against civilization. Our coalition is responding to recent attacks with precision raids, guided by intelligence provided by the Iraqis, themselves. And we're working closely with Iraqi citizens as they prepare a constitution, as they move toward free elections and take increasing responsibility for their own affairs. As in the defense of Greece in 1947, and later in the Berlin Airlift, the strength and will of free peoples are now being tested before a watching world. And we will meet this test.

Securing democracy in Iraq is the work of many hands. American and coalition forces are sacrificing for the peace of Iraq and for the security of free nations. Aid workers from many countries are facing danger to help the Iraqi people. The National Endowment for Democracy is promoting women's rights, and training Iraqi journalists, and teaching the skills of political participation. Iraqis, themselves—police and borders guards and local officials—are joining in the work and they are sharing in the sacrifice.

This is a massive and difficult undertaking—it is worth our effort, it is worth our sacrifice, because we know the stakes. The failure of Iraqi democracy would embolden terrorists around the world, increase dangers to the American people, and extinguish the hopes of millions in the region. Iraqi democracy will succeed—and that success will send forth the news, from Damascus to Tehran—that freedom can be the future of every nation. The establishment of a free Iraq at the heart of the Middle East will be a watershed event in the global democratic revolution.

Sixty years of Western nations excusing and accommodating the lack of freedom in the Middle East did nothing to make us safe—because in the long run, stability cannot be purchased at the expense of liberty. As long as the Middle East remains a place where freedom does not flourish, it will remain a place of stagnation, resentment, and violence ready for export. And with the spread of weapons that can bring catastrophic harm to our country and to our friends, it would be reckless to accept the status quo.

Therefore, the United States has adopted a new policy, a forward strategy of freedom in the Middle East. This strategy requires the same persistence and energy and idealism we have shown before. And it will yield the same results. As in Europe, as in Asia, as in every region of the world, the advance of freedom leads to peace.

The advance of freedom is the calling of our time; it is the calling of our country. From the Fourteen Points to the Four Freedoms, to the speech at Westminster, America has put our power at the service of principle. We believe that liberty is the design of nature; we believe that liberty is the direction of history. We believe that human fulfillment and excellence come in the responsible exercise of liberty. And we believe that freedom—the freedom we prize—is not for us alone; it is the right and the capacity of all mankind.

Working for the spread of freedom can be hard. Yet, America has accomplished hard tasks before. Our nation is strong; we're strong of heart. And we're not alone. Freedom is finding allies in every country; freedom finds allies in every culture. And as we meet the terror and violence of the world, we can be certain the author of freedom is not indifferent to the fate of freedom.

With all the tests and all the challenges of our age, this is, above all, the age of liberty. Each of you at this Endowment is fully engaged in the great cause of liberty. And I thank you. May God bless your work. And may God continue to bless America.

■ ■ ■

IX

LECTURES
AND
INSTRUCTIVE
SPEECHES

Philosopher-Poet
Ralph Waldo Emerson
Defines the Duties of
the American Scholar

"FREE should the scholar be—free and brave . . . for fear is a thing which a scholar, by his very function, puts behind him."

RALPH WALDO EMERSON held a prominent position among the greatest of nineteenth-century lecturers and has also been identified as "the greatest mind of New England."

He knew how to craft an aphorism. Quotations from his works stud American literature, from "To be great is to be misunderstood" to "A foolish consistency is the hobgoblin of little minds, adored by little statesmen and philosophers and divines." Consistency was never a burden to him: "Next to the originator of a good sentence is the first quoter of it," he said in 1876, having forgotten his famous remark of 1849: "I hate quotations. Tell me what you know."

When the American essayist and poet was thirty-four years old, he was asked to give the Phi Beta Kappa address at Harvard University. This lecture, "The American Scholar," was delivered on August 31, 1837, and proved popular with his listeners and with the reading public, although his unorthodox views on nature and personal revelation soon led to a break with the Harvard Divinity School. Throughout the lecture, he elevates self-trust and deflates the world's hyperbole ("a popgun is a popgun, though the ancient and honorable of the earth affirm it to be the crack of doom"). The scholarly allusions that Emerson makes are few and are lucidly explained, as in his reference to the eighteenth-century astronomers John Flamsteed and Sir William Herschel; in contradistinction to book learning, he emphasizes the importance of the lessons of nature.

Through a parallel structure of infinitive phrases, Emerson presents the scholar's duties: "to cheer, to raise, and to guide." In fact, the same parallel thought, with a balance in phrases ("Each philosopher, each bard, each actor") as well as in clauses ("It is one light . . ." and "It is one soul . . ."), informs the entire speech.

□   □   □

I hear with joy whatever is beginning to be said of the dignity and necessity of labor to every citizen. There is virtue yet in the hoe and the spade, for learned as well as for unlearned hands. And labor is everywhere welcome; always we are invited to work; only be this limitation observed, that a man shall not for the sake of wider activity sacrifice any opinion to the popular judgments and modes of action.

I have spoken of the education of the scholar by nature, by books, and by action. It remains to say somewhat of his duties.

They are such as become Man Thinking. They may all be comprised in self-trust. The office of the scholar is to cheer, to raise, and to guide men by showing them facts amidst appearances. He plies the slow, unhonored, and unpaid task of observation. Flamsteed and Herschel, in their glazed observatories, may catalogue the stars with the praise of all men, and, the results being splendid and useful, honor is sure. But he, in his private observatory, cataloguing obscure and nebulous stars of the human mind, which as yet no man has thought of as such—watching days and months, sometimes, for a few facts; correcting still his old records—must relinquish display and immediate fame. In the long period of his preparation, he must betray often an ignorance and shiftlessness in popular arts, incurring the disdain of the able who shoulder him aside. Long he must stammer in his speech; often forgo the living for the dead. Worse yet, he must accept—how often!—poverty and solitude. For the ease and pleasure of treading the old road, accepting the fashions, the education, the religion of society, he takes the cross of making his own, and, of course, the self-accusation, the faint heart, the frequent uncertainty and loss of time, which are the nettles and tangling vines in the way of the self-relying and self-directed; and the state of virtual hostility in which he seems to stand to society, and especially to educated society. For all this loss and scorn, what offset? He is to find consolation in exercising the highest functions of human nature. He is one who raises himself from private considerations, and breathes and lives on public and illustrious thoughts. He is the world's eye. He is the world's heart. He is to resist the vulgar prosperity that retrogrades ever to barbarism, by preserving and communicating heroic sentiments, noble biographies, melodious verse, and the conclusions of history. Whatsoever oracles the human heart, in all emergencies, in all solemn hours, has uttered as its commentary on the world of actions—these he shall receive and impart. And whatsoever new verdict reason from her inviolable seat pronounces on the passing men and events of today—this he shall hear and promulgate.

These being his functions, it becomes him to feel all confidence in himself, and to defer never to the popular cry. He, and he only, knows the world. The world of any moment is the merest appearance. Some great decorum, some fetish of a government, some ephemeral trade, or war, or man, is cried up by half mankind and cried down by the other half, as if all depended on this particular up or down. The odds are that the whole question is not worth the poorest thought which the scholar has lost in listening to the controversy. Let him not quit his belief that a popgun is a popgun, though the ancient and honorable of the earth affirm it to be the crack of doom. In silence, in steadiness, in severe abstraction, let him hold by himself; add observation to observation, patient of neglect, patient of reproach; and bide his own time—happy enough, if he can satisfy himself alone, that this day he has seen something truly. Success treads on every right step. For the instinct is sure that prompts him to tell his brother what he thinks. He then learns that, in going down into the secrets of his own mind, he has descended into the secrets of all minds. He learns that he who has mastered any law in his private thoughts is master to that extent of all men whose language he speaks, and of all into whose language his own can be translated. The poet, in utter solitude remembering his spontaneous thoughts and recording them, is found to have recorded that which men in crowded cities find true for them also. The orator distrusts at first the fitness of his frank confessions—his want of knowledge of the persons he addresses—until he finds that he is the complement of his hearers; that they drink his words because he fulfills for them their own nature; the deeper he dives into his privatest, secretest presentiment, to his wonder he finds this is the most acceptable, most public, and universally true. The people delight in it; the better part of every man feels, This is my music, this is myself.

In self-trust, all the virtues are comprehended. Free should the scholar be—free and brave. Free even to the definition of freedom, "without any hindrance that does not arise out of his own constitution." Brave; for fear is a thing which a scholar, by his very function, puts behind him. Fear always springs from ignorance. It is a shame to him if his tranquillity, amid dangerous times, arise from the presumption that, like children and women, his is a protected class; or if he seek a temporary peace by the diversion of his thoughts from politics or vexed questions, hiding his head like an ostrich in the flowering bushes, peeping into microscopes, and turning rhymes, as a boy whistles to keep his courage up. So is the danger to their immense moral capacity, for their acquiescence in a political and social inferiority. They are content to be brushed like flies from the path of a great person, so that justice shall be done by him to that common nature which it is the dearest desire of all to see enlarged and glorified. They sun themselves in the great man's light, and feel it to be their own element. They cast the dignity of man from their downtrod selves upon the shoulders of a hero, and will perish to add one drop of blood to make that great heart beat, those giant sinews combat and conquer. He lives for us and we live in him.

Men such as they are very naturally seek money or power; and power because it is as good as money—the "spoils," so called, "of office." And why not? for they aspire to the highest, and this, in their sleepwalking, they dream is highest. Wake them, and they shall quit the false good and leap to the true, and leave governments to clerks and desks. This revolution is to be wrought by the gradual domestication of the idea of culture. The main enterprise of the world for splendor, for extent, is the upbuilding of a man. Here are the materials strewn along the ground. The private life of one man shall be a more illustrious monarchy—more formidable to its enemy, more sweet and serene in its influence to its friend, than any kingdom in history. For a man, rightly viewed, comprehendeth the particular natures of all men. Each philosopher, each bard, each actor, has only done for me, as by a delegate, what one day I can do for myself. The books which once we valued more than the apple of the eye we have quite exhausted. What is that but saying that we have come up with the point of view which the universal mind took through the eyes of one scribe; we have been that man and have passed on. First, one; then, another; we drain all cisterns, and, waxing greater by all these supplies, we crave a better and more abundant food. The man has never lived that can feed us ever. The human mind cannot be enshrined in a person who shall set a barrier on any one side to this unbounded, unboundable empire. It is one central fire, which, flaming now out of the lips of Etna, lightens the capes of Sicily; and now out of the throat of Vesuvius, illuminates the towers and vineyards of Naples. It is one light which beams out of a thousand stars. It is one soul, which animates all men. ∎

Edgar Allan Poe Presents His Theory of Beauty and Poetry

"THAT pleasure which is at once the most pure, the most elevating, and the most intense is derived, I maintain, from the contemplation of the beautiful."

THE AUTHOR OF "THE RAVEN" AND "THE GOLD BUG" is remembered primarily for the macabre and mysterious elements in his poetry and short stories. But Edgar Allan Poe was also a critic, who sought to explain the literary process in essays such as "The Philosophy of Composition." In the preface to his 1845 collection of poems, he wrote, "With me poetry has been not a purpose, but a passion; and the passions should be held in reverence: they must not—they cannot at will be excited, with an eye to the paltry compensations, or the more paltry commendations, of mankind."

Rarely did Poe, who died in 1849 at the age of forty, present lectures to the public. "The Poetic Principle," however, was an exception. What follows is a portion of that lecture, specifically his designation of "the beautiful" in language.

Having enumerated the three parts of the mind—"pure intellect, taste, and the moral sense"—Poe identifies taste as the "sole arbiter" in poetic creation of beauty. He uses parallel structure in equating beauty "to the fitting, to the appropriate, to the harmonious." On the importance of music in poetry, Poe produces a crescendo of words, at last identifying the goal of "the true artist" as the presenter of "that beauty which is the atmosphere and the real essence of the poem."

□   □   □

With as deep a reverence for the true as ever inspired the bosom of man, I would, nevertheless, limit in some measure its modes of inculcation. I would limit to enforce them. I would not enfeeble them by dissipation. The demands of truth are severe; she has no sympathy with the myrtles. All that which is so indispensable in song is precisely all that with which she has nothing whatever to do. It is but making her a flaunting paradox to wreathe her in gems and flowers. In enforcing a truth we need severity rather than efflorescence of language. We must be simple, precise, terse. We must be cool, calm, unimpassioned. In a word, we must be in that mood, which, as nearly as possible, is the exact converse of the poetical. He must be blind, indeed, who does not perceive the radical and chasmal differences between the truthful and poetical modes of inculcation. He must be theory-mad beyond redemption, who, in spite of these differences, shall still persist in attempting to reconcile the obstinate oils and waters of poetry and truth.

Dividing the world of mind into its three most immediately obvious distinctions, we have the pure intellect, taste, and the moral sense. I place taste in the middle, because it is just this position which in the mind it occupies. It holds intimate relations with either extreme, but from the moral sense is separated by so faint a difference that Aristotle has not hesitated to place some of its operations among the virtues themselves. Nevertheless, we find the offices of the trio marked with a sufficient distinction. Just as the intellect concerns itself with truth, so taste informs us of the beautiful, while the moral sense is regardful of duty. Of this latter, while conscience teaches the obligation, and reason the expediency, taste contents herself with displaying the charms: waging war upon vice solely on the ground of her deformity; her disproportion, her animosity to the fitting, to the appropriate, to the harmonious—in a word to beauty.

An immortal instinct, deep within the spirit of man, is thus plainly a sense of the beautiful. This it is which administers to his delight in the manifold forms and sounds and odors and sentiments amid which he exists; and just as the lily is repeated in the lake, or the eyes of Amaryllis in the mirror, so is the mere oral or written repetition of these forms and sounds and colors and odors and sentiments a duplicate source of delight. But this mere repetition is not poetry. He who shall simply sing, with however glowing enthusiasm, or with however vivid a truth of description, of the sights and sounds and odors and sentiments which greet him in common with all mankind—he, I say, has yet failed to prove his divine title. There is still a something in the distance which he has been unable to attain. We have still a thirst unquenchable, to allay which he has not shown us the crystal springs. This thirst belongs to the immortality of man. It is at once a consequence and an indication of his perennial existence. It is the desire of the moth for the star. It is no mere appreciation of the beauty before us, but a wild effort to reach the beauty above. Inspired by an ecstatic prescience of the glories beyond the grave, we struggle by multiform combinations among the things and thoughts of time to attain a portion of that loveliness whose very elements, perhaps, appertain to eternity alone. And thus when by poetry—or when by music, the most entrancing of the poetic moods—we find ourselves melted into tears, not as the Abbate Gravia supposes through excess of pleasure, but through a certain petulant, impatient sorrow at our inability to grasp now, wholly, here on earth, at once and forever, those divine and rapturous joys, of which through the poem, or through the music, we attain to but brief and indeterminate glimpses.

The struggle to apprehend the supernal loveliness—this struggle, on the part of souls fittingly constituted—has given to the world all that which it (the world) has ever been enabled at once to understand and to feel as poetic.

The poetic sentiment, of course, may develop itself in various modes—in painting, in sculpture, in architecture, in the dance, very especially in music—and very peculiarly, and with a wide field, in the composition of the landscape garden. Our present theme, however, has regard only to its manifestation in words. And here let me speak briefly on the topic of rhythm. Contenting myself with the certainty that music, in its various modes of meter, rhythm, and rhyme, is of so vast a moment in poetry as never to be wisely rejected—is so vitally important an adjunct that he is simply silly who declines its assistance—I will not now pause to maintain its absolute essentiality. It is in music, perhaps, that the soul most nearly attains the great end for which, when inspired by the poetic sentiment, it struggles—the creation of supernal beauty. It may be, indeed, that here this sublime end is, now and then, attained in fact. We are often made to feel, with a shivering delight, that from an earthly harp are stricken notes which cannot have been unfamiliar to the angels. And thus there can be but little doubt that in the union of poetry with music in its popular sense we shall find the wildest field for the poetic development. The old bards and minnesingers had advantages, which we do not possess, and Thomas Moore singing his own songs was, in the most legitimate manner, perfecting them as poems.

To recapitulate, then, I would define, in brief, the poetry of words as the rhythmical creation of beauty. Its sole arbiter is taste. With the intellect or with the conscience, it has only collateral relations; unless, incidentally, it has no concern whatever either with duty or with truth.

A few words, however, in explanation. That pleasure which is at once the most pure, the most elevating, and the most intense is derived, I maintain, from the contemplation of the beautiful. In the contemplation of beauty we alone find it possible to attain that pleasurable elevation, or excitement, of the soul, which we recognize as the poetic sentiment, and which is so easily distinguished from truth, which is the satisfaction of the reason, or from passion, which is the excitement of the heart. I make beauty, therefore—using the word as inclusive of the sublime—I make beauty the province of the poem, simply because it is an obvious rule of art that effects should be made to spring as directly as possible from their causes—no one as yet having been weak enough to deny that the peculiar elevation in question is at least the most readily attainable in the poem. It by no means follows, however, that the incitements of passion, or the precepts of duty, or even the lessons of truth, may not be introduced into a poem, and with advantage; for they may subserve, incidentally, in various ways, the general purposes of the work; but the true artist will always contrive to tone them down in proper subjection to that beauty which is the atmosphere and the real essence of the poem. ■

Mark Twain Stuns the Littery World by Spoofing Emerson, Longfellow, and Holmes to Their Faces

"AND what queer talk they used!"

WHAT DOES A SPEAKER DO when he senses that his audience is offended at what he is saying, or does not get the humor? If a speaker is going to deliver a satirical or parodic speech, he or she must do so with authority; must not flinch at the first reaction; and must save the day with a cheerful, mordant, and, above all, confident delivery.

Mark Twain, a budding author on December 17, 1877, came before a dinner given by the *Atlantic Monthly* honoring poet John Greenleaf Whittier's seventieth birthday. The American literary world was assembled at the Hotel Brunswick in Boston, and Twain's speech was perceived by both the audience and the speaker as a disaster. He explains why in 1906, long after he achieved an eminence greater than that of the men he had spoofed three decades before. Here is an excerpt from his autobiography followed by a transcript of the offending speech in its entirety.

□   □   □

I vaguely remember some of the details of that gathering—dimly I can see a hundred people—no, perhaps fifty—shadowy figures sitting at tables feeding, ghosts now to me, and nameless forevermore. I don't know who they were, but I can very distinctly see, seated at the grand table and facing the rest of us, Mr. Emerson, supernaturally grave, unsmiling; Mr. Whittier, grave, lovely, his beautiful spirit shining out of his face; Mr. Longfellow, with his silken white hair and his benignant face; Dr. Oliver Wendell Holmes, flashing smiles and affection and all good-fellowship everywhere like a rose-diamond whose facets are being turned toward the light first one way and then another—a charming man, and always fascinating, whether he was talking or whether he was sitting still (what *he* would call still, but what would be more or less motion to other people). I can see those figures with entire distinctness across this abyss of time. . . .

Now at that point ends all that was pleasurable about that notable celebration of Mr. Whittier's seventieth birthday—because *I* got up at that point . . . with what I have no doubt I supposed would be the gem of the evening—the gay oration above quoted from the Boston paper. I had written it all out the day before and had perfectly memorized it, and I stood up there at my genial and happy and self-satisfied ease, and began to deliver it. Those majestic guests, that row of venerable and still active volcanoes, listened, as did everybody else in the house, with attentive interest. Well, I delivered myself of—we'll say the first two hundred words of my speech. I was expecting no returns from that part of the speech, but this was not the case as regarded the rest of it. I arrived now at the dialogue: "The old miner said, 'You are the fourth, I'm going to move.' 'The fourth what?' said I. He answered, 'The fourth littery man that has been here in twenty-four hours. I am going to move.' 'Why, you don't tell me,' said I. 'Who were the others?' 'Mr. Longfellow, Mr. Emerson, Mr. Oliver Wendell Holmes, consound the lot—'"

Now, then, the house's *attention* continued, but the expression of interest in the faces turned to a sort of black frost. I wondered what the trouble was. I didn't know. I went on, but with difficulty—I struggled along, and entered upon that miner's fearful description of the bogus Emerson, the bogus Holmes, the bogus Longfellow, always hoping—but with a gradually perishing hope—that somebody would laugh, or that somebody would at least smile, but nobody did. I didn't know enough to give it up and sit down, I was too new to public speaking, and so I went on with this awful performance, and carried it clear through to the end, in front of a body of people who seemed turned to stone with horror. It was the sort of expression their faces would have worn if I had been making these remarks about the Deity and the rest of the Trinity; there is no milder way in which to describe the petrified condition and the ghastly expression of those people.

When I sat down it was with a heart which had long ceased to beat. I shall never be as dead again as I was then. I shall never be as miserable again as I was then. I speak now as one who doesn't know what the condition of things may be in the next world, but in this one I shall never be as wretched again as I was then. [William Dean] Howells, who was near me, tried to say a comforting word, but couldn't get beyond a gasp. There was no use—he understood the whole size of the disaster. He had good intentions, but the words froze before they could get out. It was an atmosphere that would freeze anything. If Benvenuto Cellini's salamander had been in that place he would not have survived to be put into Cellini's autobiography. There was a frightful pause. There was an awful silence, a desolating silence. Then the next man on the list had to get up—there was no help for it. That was Bishop—Bishop had just burst handsomely upon the world with a most acceptable novel, which had appeared in the *Atlantic Monthly,* a place which would make any novel respectable and any author noteworthy. In this case the novel itself was recognized as being, without extraneous help, respectable. Bishop was away up in the public favor, and he was an object of high interest, consequently there was a sort of national expectancy in the air; we may say our American millions were standing, from Maine to Texas and from Alaska to Florida, holding their breath, their lips parted, their hands ready to applaud, when Bishop should get up on that occasion, and for the first time in his life speak in public. It was under these damaging conditions that he got up to "make good," as the vulgar say. I had spoken several times before, and that is the reason why I was able to go on without dying in my tracks, as I ought to have done—but Bishop had had no experience. He was up facing those awful deities—facing those other people, those strangers—facing human beings for the first time in his life, with a speech to utter. No doubt it was well packed away in his memory, no doubt it was fresh and usable, until I had been heard from. I suppose that after that, and under the smothering pall of that dreary silence, it began to waste away and disappear out of his head like the rags breaking from the edge of a fog, and presently there wasn't any fog left. He didn't go on—he didn't last long. It was not many sentences after his first before he began to hesitate, and break, and lose his grip, and totter, and wobble, and at last he slumped down in a limp and mushy pile.

Well, the programme for the occasion was probably not more than one-third finished, but it ended there. Nobody rose. The next man hadn't strength enough to get up, and everybody looked so dazed, so stupefied, paralyzed, it was impossible for anybody to do anything, or even try. Nothing could go on in that strange atmosphere. Howells mournfully, and without words, hitched himself to Bishop and me and supported us out of the room. It was very kind—he was most generous. He towed us tottering away into some room in that building, and we sat down there. I don't know what my remark was now, but I know the nature of it. It was the kind of remark you make when you know that nothing in the world can help your case. But Howells was honest—he had to say the heart-breaking things he did say: that there was no help for this calamity, this shipwreck, this cataclysm; that this was the most disastrous thing that had ever happened in anybody's history—and then he added, "That is, for *you*—and consider what you have done for Bishop. It is bad enough in your case, you deserve to suffer. You have committed this crime, and you deserve to have all you are going to get. But here is an innocent man. Bishop had never done you any harm, and see what you have done to him. He can never hold his head up again. The world can never look upon Bishop as being a live person. He is a corpse."

That is the history of that episode of twenty-eight years ago, which pretty nearly killed me with shame during that first year or two whenever it forced its way into my mind.

□   □   □

Now then, I take that speech up and examine it. As I said, it arrived this morning, from Boston. I have read it twice, and unless I am an idiot, it hasn't a single defect in it from the first word to the last. It is just as good as good can be. It is smart; it is saturated with humor. There isn't a suggestion of coarseness or vulgarity in it anywhere. What could have been the matter with that house? It is amazing, it is incredible, that they didn't shout with laughter, and those deities the loudest of them all. Could the fault have been with me? Did I lose courage when I saw those great men up there whom I was going to describe in such a strange fashion? If that happened, if I showed doubt, that can account for it, for you can't be successfully funny if you show that you are afraid of it. Well, I can't account for it, but if I had those beloved and revered old literary immortals back here now on the platform at Carnegie Hall I would take that same old speech, deliver it, word for word, and melt them till they'd run all over that stage. Oh, the fault must have been with *me*, it is not in the speech at all.

This is an occasion peculiarly meet for the digging up of pleasant reminiscences concerning literary folk; therefore I will drop lightly into history myself. Standing here on the shore of the Atlantic and contemplating certain of its largest literary billows, I am reminded of a thing which happened to me thirteen years ago, when I had just succeeded in stirring up a little Nevadian literary puddle myself, whose spume-flakes were beginning to blow thinly Californiaward. I started an inspection tramp through the southern mines of California. I was callow and conceited, and I resolved to try the virtue of my nom de guerre.

I very soon had an opportunity. I knocked at a miner's lonely log cabin in the foothills of the Sierras just at nightfall. It was snowing at the time. A jaded, melancholy man of fifty, barefooted, opened the door to me. When he heard my nom de guerre he looked more dejected than before. He let me in—pretty reluctantly, I thought—and after the customary bacon and beans, black coffee, and hot whisky, I took a pipe. This sorrowful man had not said three words up to this time. Now he spoke up and said, in the voice of one who is secretly suffering, "You're the fourth—I'm going to move." "The fourth what?" said I. "The fourth littery man that has been here in twenty-four hours—I'm going to move." "You don't tell me!" said I; "who were the others?" "Mr. Longfellow, Mr. Emerson, and Mr. Oliver Wendell Holmes—consound the lot!"

You can easily believe I was interested. I supplicated—three hot whiskys did the rest—and finally the melancholy miner began. Said he:

"They came here just at dark yesterday evening, and I let them in of course. Said they were going to the Yosemite. They were a rough lot, but that's nothing; everybody looks rough that travels afoot. Mr. Emerson was a seedy little bit of a chap, redheaded. Mr. Holmes was as fat as a balloon; he weighed as much as three hundred, and had double chins all the way down to his stomach. Mr. Longfellow was built like a prize-fighter. His head was cropped and bristly, like as if he had a wig made of hairbrushes. His nose lay straight down his face, like a finger with the end joint tilted up. They had been drinking, I could see that.

And what queer talk they used! Mr. Holmes inspected this cabin, then he took me by the buttonhole, and says he:

" 'Through the deep caves of thought
I hear a voice that sings,
Build thee more stately mansions,
O my soul!'

"Says I, 'I can't afford it, Mr. Holmes, and moreover I don't want to.' Blamed if I liked it pretty well, either, coming from a stranger, that way. However, I started to get out my bacon and beans, when Mr. Emerson came and looked on awhile, and then *he* takes me aside by the button-hole and says:

" 'Give me agates for my meat;
Give me cantharids to eat;
From air and ocean bring me foods,
From all zones and altitudes.'

"Says I, 'Mr. Emerson, if you'll excuse me, this ain't no hotel.' You see it sort of riled me—I warn't used to the ways of littery swells. But I went on a-sweating over my work, and next comes Mr. Longfellow and buttonholes me, and interrupts me. Says he:

" 'Honor be to Mudjekeewis!
You shall hear how Pau-Puk-Keewis—'

"But I broke in, and says I, 'Beg your pardon, Mr. Longfellow, if you'll be so kind as to hold your yawp for about five minutes and let me get this grub ready, you'll do me proud.' Well, sir, after they'd filled up I set out the jug. Mr. Holmes looks at it, and then he fires up all of a sudden and yells:

" 'Flash out a stream of blood-red wine!
For I would drink to other days.'

"By George, I was getting kind of worked up. I don't deny it, I was getting kind of worked up. I turns to Mr. Holmes, and says I, 'Looky here, my fat friend, I'm a-running this shanty, and if the court knows herself, you'll take whisky straight or you'll go dry.' Them's the very words I said to him. Now, I don't want to sass such famous littery peo-ple, but you see they kind of forced me. There ain't nothing onreasonable 'bout me; I don't mind a passel of guests a-treadin' on my tail three or four times, but when it comes to *standing* on it it's different, 'and if the court knows herself,' I says, 'you'll take whisky straight or you'll go dry.' Well, between drinks they'd swell around the cabin and strike attitudes and spout; and pretty soon they got out a greasy old deck and went to playing euchre at ten cents a corner—on trust. I began to notice some pretty suspicious things. Mr. Emerson dealt, looked at his hand, shook his head, says:

> " 'I am the doubter and the doubt—'

and ca'mly bunched the hands and went to shuffling for a new layout, Says he:

> " 'They reckon ill who leave me out;
> They know not well the subtle ways I keep.
> I pass and deal *again!*'

Hang'd if he didn't go ahead and do it, too! Oh, he was a cool one! Well, in about a minute things were running pretty tight, but all of a sudden I see by Mr. Emerson's eye he judged he had 'em. He had already corralled two tricks, and each of the others one. So now he kind of lifts a little in his chair and says:

> " 'I tire of globes and aces!—
> Too long the game is played!'

—and down he fetched a right bower. Mr. Longfellow smiles as sweet as pie and says:

> " 'Thanks, thanks to thee, my worthy friend,
> For the lesson thou hast taught.'

—and blamed if he didn't down with *another* right bower! Emerson claps his hand on his bowie, Longfellow claps his on his revolver, and I went under a bunk. There was going to be trouble; but that monstrous Holmes rose up, wobbling his double chins, and says he, 'Order, gentlemen; the first man that draws, I'll lay down on him and smother him!' All quiet on the Potomac, you bet!

"They were pretty how-come-you-so by now, and they begun to blow. Emerson says, 'The nobbiest thing I ever wrote was "Barbara Frietchie."' Says Longfellow, 'It don't begin with my "Biglow Papers."'

Says Holmes, 'My "Thanatopsis" lays over 'em both.' They mighty near ended in a fight. Then they wished they had some more company— and Mr. Emerson pointed to me and says:

> " 'Is yonder squalid peasant all
> That this proud nursery could breed?'

He was a-whetting his bowie on his boot—so I let it pass. Well, sir, next they took it into their heads that they would like some music; so they made me stand up and sing 'When Johnny Comes Marching Home' till I dropped—at thirteen minutes past four this morning. That's what I've been through, my friend. When I woke at seven, they were leaving, thank goodness, and Mr. Longfellow had my only boots on, and his'n under his arm. Says I, 'Hold on, there, Evangeline, what are you going to do with *them?*' He says, 'Going to make tracks with 'em; because:

> " 'Lives of great men all remind us
> We can make our lives sublime;
> And, departing, leave behind us
> Footprints on the sands of time.'

As I said, Mr. Twain, you are the fourth in twenty-four hours—and I'm going to move; I ain't suited to a littery atmosphere."

I said to the miner, "Why, my dear sir, *these* were not the gracious singers to whom we and the world pay loving reverence and homage; these were impostors."

The miner investigated me with a calm eye for a while; then said he, "Ah! impostors, were they? Are *you?*"

I did not pursue the subject, and since then I have not traveled on my nom de guerre enough to hurt. Such was the reminiscence I was moved to contribute, Mr. Chairman. In my enthusiasm I may have exaggerated the details a little, but you will easily forgive me that fault, since I believe it is the first time I have ever deflected from perpendicular fact on an occasion like this. ∎

First Female Member of Parliament, Lady Astor, Expounds on Women in Politics

---

"WE realize that no one sex can govern alone. . . . I can conceive of nothing worse than a man-governed world except a woman-governed world . . ."

NANCY LANGHORNE of Virginia began her political career at the age of fourteen during a visit to the Chicago World's Fair in 1893. When a band struck up the Union song "Marching Through Georgia," she leaped to her feet to yell, "Three cheers for Robert E. Lee!" In recounting this episode to the *New York Herald Tribune*'s John Reagan "Tex" McCrary, Lady Astor noted: "That was the last time I was spanked for a combination of patriotism and cheek."

The southern beauty (her sister married the artist Charles Gibson and was the model for the Gibson Girl) married Waldorf Astor, who owned the *Observer* and served in the House of Commons until he was elevated to the House of Lords as the second Viscount Astor in 1910. Nine years later, his wife was elected to his constituency in Plymouth, and took her place in history as the first woman chosen by the people to serve in the "Mother of Parliaments."

Renowned for her outspokenness, she recalled being told in 1906 by the other American at the Court of St. James's, United States Ambassador Whitelaw Reid, "Modulate your voice, my dear, modulate your voice." She learned to do that, but not her opinions: in the late thirties, her home at Cliveden in Buckinghamshire became the salon for Prime Minister Neville Chamberlain and British isolationists despised as "appeasers" by Winston Churchill. She retired from Parliament in 1945 and died in 1964, remembered for her espousal of women's rights, public education, temperance, and—unfortunately—the appeasement of "the Cliveden set."

This speech, made at Town Hall in New York on April 9, 1922, and put together from newspaper reports, was delivered (presumably in a well-modulated voice) less than three years after she became the first woman M.P. It is notable for its projection of personality and character: the tone is chatty, feisty, common-sensical, and unabashedly opinionated. The account of personal experience in the beginning leads to the didactic middle and exhortative conclusion. "Now, why are we in politics? What is it all about?" she asks rhetorically, and answers, "Something bigger than ourselves. Schopenhauer was wrong . . ."

□   □   □

I know that this welcome has nothing to do with me. Ever since I entered the "Mother of Parliaments" I realized that I ceased to be a person and had become a symbol. The safe thing about being a symbol is this—you realize that you, of yourself, can do nothing, but what you symbolize gives you courage and strength and should give you wisdom. I certainly have been given courage and strength, and I won't say too much about wisdom.

My entrance into the House of Commons was not, as some thought, in the nature of a revolution. It was an evolution. It is rather interesting how it came about. My husband was the one who started me off on this downward path—from the fireside to public life. If I have helped the cause of women he is the one to thank, not me. He is a strange and a remarkable man.

First, it was strange to urge your wife to take up public life, especially as he is a most domesticated man; but the truth is that he is a born social reformer. He has avoided the pitfalls which so many well-to-do men fall into. He doesn't think that you can right wrongs with philanthropy. He realizes that one must go to the bottom of the causes of wrongs and not simply gild them up.

For eleven years, I helped my husband with his work at Plymouth—I found out the wrongs and he tried to right them—and this combination of work was a wonderful and happy combination and I often wish that it was still going on.

However, I am not here to tell you of his work, but it is interesting in so far that it shows you how it came about that I stood for Parliament at all. Unless he had been the kind of a man he was, I don't believe that the first woman member of the oldest Parliament in the world would have come from Plymouth, and that would have been a pity. Plymouth is an ideal port to sail from or to. It has been bidding godspeed to so many voyagers. I felt that I was embarking on a voyage of faith, but when I arrived at my destination some of the honorable members looked upon me more as a pirate than a pilgrim.

A woman in the House of Commons! It was almost enough to have broken up the House. I don't blame them—it was equally hard on the woman as it was on them. A pioneer may be a picturesque figure, but they are often rather lonely ones. I must say for the House of Commons, they bore their shock with dauntless decency. No body of men could have been kinder and fairer to a "pirate" than they were. When you hear people over here trying to run down England, please remember that England was the first large country to give the vote to women and that the men of England welcomed an American-born woman in the House with a fairness and a justice which, at least, this woman never will forget.

The different ones received me in different ways. I shall never forget a Scotch labor leader coming up to me, after I had been in the House a little while, and telling me that I wasn't a bit the sort of woman he thought I would be—"I'll not tell you that, but I know now that you are an ordinary, homely, kindly body," and he has proved it since by often asking my advice on domestic questions.

Then there was an Irish member who said to me, "I don't know what you are going to speak about, but I am here to back you." And the last was from a regular Noah's Ark man, a typical squire type. After two and a half years of never agreeing on any point with him, he remarked to someone that I was a very stupid woman but he must add that I was a "very attractive one," and he feared I was a thoroughly honest social reformer. I might add that being the first woman, I had to take up many causes which no one would call exactly popular. I also had to go up against a prejudice of generations, but I must say their decency has never failed, though my manners must have been somewhat of a trial.

Now I must leave the more personal side and get to what it is all about and why we are here. Women and politics—some women have always been in politics, and have not done badly, either. It was when we had the Lancastrian kings that it was said that the kings were made kings by act of Parliament—they did rule by means of Parliament. Then Henry VIII, that old scalawag, accepted the principles of the Lancastrians to rule by Parliament, but he wanted the principle in an entirely different way. He made Parliament the engine of his will: he pressed or frightened it into doing anything he wished. Under his guidance Parliament defied and crushed all other powers, spiritually and temporally, and he did things which no king or Parliament ever attempted to do—things unheard of and terrible.

Then Elizabeth came along. It is true she scolded her Parliaments for meddling with matters with which, in her opinion, they had no concern, and more than once soundly rated the Speaker of her Commons, but she never carried her quarrels too far, and was able to end her disputes by some clever compromise; in other words, she never let Parliament down, and that is what I don't believe any wise woman will do in spite of the fears of some of the men.

Now, why are we in politics? What is it all about? Something much bigger than ourselves. Schopenhauer was wrong in nearly everything he wrote about women—and he wrote a lot, but he was right in one thing. He said, in speaking of women, "the race is to her more than the individual," and I believe that it is true. I feel somehow we do care about the race as a whole, our very nature makes us take a forward vision; there is no reason why women should look back—mercifully we have no political past; we have all the mistakes of sex legislation with its appalling failures to guide us.

We should know what to avoid, it is no use blaming the men—we made them what they are—and now it is up to us to try and make ourselves—the makers of men—a little more responsible in the future. We realize that no one sex can govern alone. I believe that one of the reasons why civilization has failed so lamentably is that it has had a one-sided government. Don't let us make the mistake of ever allowing that to happen again.

I can conceive of nothing worse than a man-governed world except a woman-governed world—but I can see the combination of the two going forward and making civilization more worthy of the name of civilization based on Christianity, not force. A civilization based on justice and mercy. I feel men have a greater sense of justice and we of mercy. They must borrow our mercy and we must use their justice. We are new brooms; let us see that we sweep the right rooms.

Personally, I feel that every woman should take an active part in local politics. I don't mean by that that every woman should go in for a political career—that, of course, is absurd—but you can take an active part in local government without going in for a political career. You can be certain when casting your vote you are casting it for what seems nearest right—for what seems more likely to help the majority and not bolster up an organized minority. There is a lot to be done in local politics, and it is a fine apprenticeship to central government; it is very practical, and I think that, although practical, it is too near to be attractive. The things that are far away are more apt to catch our eye than the ones which are just under our noses; then, too, they are less disagreeable.

Political development is like all other developments. We must begin with ourselves, our own consciences, and clean out our own hearts before we take on the job of putting others straight. So with politics if we women put our hands to local politics, we begin the foundations. After all, central governments only echo local ones; the politician in Washington, if he is a wise man, will always have one eye on his constituency, making that constituency so clean, so straight, so high in its purpose, that the man from home will not dare to take a small, limited view about any question, be it a national or an international one. You must remember that what women are up against is not what they see, but the unseen forces.

We are up against generations and generations of prejudice. Ever since Eve ate the apple—but I would like to remind you, and all men, why she ate the apple. It was not simply because it was good for food or pleasant to the eyes, it was a tree to be desired to make one wise. "She took of the fruit thereof, and did eat; and she gave also unto her husband with her, and he did eat." We have no record of Adam murmuring against the fruit—of his not doing anything but eat it with docility. In passing, I would like to say that the first time Adam had a chance he laid the blame on woman—however, we will leave Adam.

Ever since woman's consciousness looked beyond the material, men's consciousness has feared her vaguely, he has gone to her for inspiration, he has relied on her for all that is best and most ideal in his life, yet by sheer material force he has limited her. He has, without knowing it, westernized the harem mind of the East. I don't believe he knows it yet so we must break it to him gently. We must go on being his guide, his mother, and his better half. But we must prove to him that we are a necessary half not only in private but in political life.

The best way that we can do that is to show them our ambitions are not personal. Let them see that we desire a better, safer, and a cleaner world for our children and their children and we realize that only by doing our bit by facing unclean things with cleanliness, by facing wrongs with right, by going fearlessly into all things that may be disagreeable, that we will somehow make it a little better world.

I don't know that we are going to do this—I don't say that women will change the world but I do say that they can if they want and I, coming in from the Old World which has seen a devastating war, cannot face the future without this hope—that the women of all countries will do their duty and raise a generation of men and women who will look upon war and all that leads to it with as much horror as we now look upon a cold-blooded murder. All of the women of England want to do away with war.

If we want this new world, we can only get it by striving for it; the real struggle will be within ourselves, to put out of our consciousness, of our hearts, and of our thoughts all that makes for war, hate, envy, greed, pride, force, and material ambition. ■

William Lyon Phelps Praises the Owning of Books

"Books are for use, not for show; you should own no book that you are afraid to mark up. . . ."

SPENDING HIS "INDOOR LIFE" in a room of six thousand books, William Lyon Phelps displayed a love for literature that infused his four decades of teaching at Yale. When he retired, Professor Phelps shared that same love for books with a wider audience, in the following speech that was broadcast on April 6, 1933.

Rarely does the professor lapse into the formal third-person address ("One should have one's own bookshelves"); instead, he uses the second-person "you" to explain conversationally the joy of owning books. By comparing books to friends, he celebrates the democratic nature of literature ("Books are of the people, by the people, for the people").

Professor Phelps has a ready reply for strangers who ask, "Have you read all of these books?" His stock answer is disarming: "Some of them twice." Of course, in the case of antiquarian volumes, his advice to mark them up is an invitation to vandalism; get a reading copy and mark that up.

□   □   □

The habit of reading is one of the greatest resources of mankind; and we enjoy reading books that belong to us much more than if they are borrowed. A borrowed book is like a guest in the house; it must be treated with punctiliousness, with a certain considerate formality. You must see that it sustains no damage; it must not suffer while under your roof. You cannot leave it carelessly, you cannot mark it, you cannot turn down the pages, you cannot use it familiarly. And then, someday, although this is seldom done, you really ought to return it.

But your own books belong to you; you treat them with that affectionate intimacy that annihilates formality. Books are for use, not for show; you should own no book that you are afraid to mark up, or afraid to place on the table, wide open and face down. A good reason for marking favorite passages in books is that this practice enables you to remember more easily the significant sayings, to refer to them quickly, and then in later years, it is like visiting a forest where you once blazed a trail. You have the pleasure of going over the old ground, and recalling both the intellectual scenery and your own earlier self.

Everyone should begin collecting a private library in youth; the instinct of private property, which is fundamental in human beings, can here be cultivated with every advantage and no evils. One should have one's own bookshelves, which should not have doors, glass windows, or keys; they should be free and accessible to the hand as well as to the eye. The best of mural decorations is books; they are more varied in color and appearance than any wallpaper, they are more attractive in design, and they have the prime advantage of being separate personalities, so that if you sit alone in the room in the firelight, you are surrounded with intimate friends. The knowledge that they are there in plain view is both stimulating and refreshing. You do not have to read them all. Most of my indoor life is spent in a room containing six thousand books; and I have a stock answer to the invariable question that comes from strangers. "Have you read all of these books?" "Some of them twice." This reply is both true and unexpected.

There are, of course, no friends like living, breathing, corporeal men and women; my devotion to reading has never made me a recluse. How could it? Books are of the people, by the people, for the people. Literature is the immortal part of history; it is the best and most enduring part of personality. But book friends have this advantage over living friends; you can enjoy the most truly aristocratic society in the world whenever you want it. The great dead are beyond our physical reach, and the great living are usually almost as inaccessible; as for our personal friends and acquaintances, we cannot always see them. Perchance they are asleep, or away on a journey. But in a private library, you can at any moment converse with Socrates or Shakespeare or Carlyle or Dumas or Dickens or Shaw or Barrie or Galsworthy. And there is no doubt that in these books you see these men at their best. They wrote for *you*. They "laid themselves out," they did their ultimate best to entertain you, to make a favorable impression. You are necessary to them as an audience is to an actor; only instead of seeing them masked, you look into their inmost heart of heart. ■

Broadcaster
John Hilton Talks
about Talking

*"To read as if you were talking you must first write as if you were talking.
What you have on the paper in front of you must be talk stuff, not book stuff."*

JOHN HILTON, A BBC BROADCASTER in London before World War II, proved a popular announcer with the radio audience. Instead of reading the prepared text in monotones, Hilton enlivened his words with what he called "calculated spontaneity"—the ability to make reading sound like conversational speaking.

Hilton discussed this ability when he ended a lengthy series of broadcasts with the following lecture on the topic of talking. Hilton's focus in this broadcast, delivered on the BBC on July 1, 1937, is the art of public address, particularly the tricks that allow speakers to sound as if they were thinking out loud. With colloquial expressions ("I must buckle to") and deliberate interjections ("Well, there you are"), he uses an informal tone designed to keep listeners interested. Through the internal dialogue—a conversational device of asking questions and then offering the answers himself—Hilton is able to achieve "calculated spontaneity."

□   □   □

I kept wondering what to say to you in this last talk, and then I had a bright idea. At least I *hope* it's a bright idea. I said to myself. "Suppose you give a talk about giving a talk."—"A talk about giving a talk! How d'you mean?"—"Why, how you set about it, and the tricks of the trade, and so on."—"Yes, that *is* rather an idea," I said to myself. So here goes. . . .

There've been bits in the paper sometimes about my broadcasts. The bits I've always liked best are those that refer to John Hilton "who just comes to the microphone and *talks*. So different from listening to something being *read*." Oh yes, I like that. For, of course, I read every word of every talk. If only I could pull it off every time—but you have to be at the top of your form. Yes, of course, every word's on paper even now—this— what I'm saying to you now—it's all here. Talking! Just as it comes to him! Right out of his head! I hope it sounds so; it's meant to. If it does—well—this is one of my good days.

"Tricks of the trade." Must I really tell you those? All right. The first trick of the trade is that there aren't any tricks. I mean tricks don't come off. That's my experience, anyway. I've tried, in my time, this way and that. I like experiments. I'll try anything once. But the little stunts and try-ons—no good! For me, I mean, of course. I think what listeners can spot more surely than anything else is any trace of falseness. I think you've got to find yourself—the radio rendering of yourself, and then be true to it. Truth, not tricks. For my sort of stuff, I mean, of course.

"But to read as if you were talking! Isn't that a trick?" Oh no, that's an art—or a craft, whichever you like. And in every art or craft there's a technique, a method, a way. What is it here? Well, I suppose each has to find his own; but my notion is that to read as if you were talking you must first write as if you were talking. What you have on the paper in front of you must be talk stuff, not book stuff.

It's, in part, a mere matter of how you put the words down on the paper. That very sentence now, the one you've just heard. It began with "It's in part. . . ." If I'd said to you, "It is, in part," you'd have thought, "He's reading." In speech we say, "It's," not "It is." So I write "I T apostrophe S," and not "It is" on the paper. I know if I wrote, "It is," I should say "It is." . . .

I don't know anything about others, as I say, but my way is to speak my sentences aloud as I write them. In fact, here's my second rule, all pat: "To write as you would talk you must talk while you write." If you were outside my room while I'm writing a talk you'd hear muttering and mumbling and outright declaration from beginning to end. You'd say, "There's somebody in there with a slate loose; he never stops talking to himself." No, I wouldn't be talking to *myself* but to you. . . .

You can scrap, in writing a talk, most of what you've been told all your life was literary good form. You have to; if you want your talk to ring the bell and walk in and sit down by the hearth. You've been told, for instance, that it's bad form to end a sentence with a preposition. It may be, in print. But not in talk. Not in talk. I'm coming to the view that what I call the "prepositional verb" (I'm no grammarian—I invent my own names for those things)—that what I call the prepositional verb is one of the glories of the English language. You start with a simple verb like "to stand"; and with the help of a pocketful of prepositions you get all those lovely changes: to stand up, to stand down, to stand off, to stand in, to stand by, to stand over—and twenty others. We score over the French there. The Germans have it; but they stick their prepositions in front of the verbs. I think our way has much more punch to it. And what bull's-eyes you can score with the prepositional verb if only you'll search for it and, having found it, let the preposition come at the end of the sentence.

You know how odd moments stick in the memory. One stays in mine. I was dealing with retirement pensions. I was tired. Tired to the point of writing that awful jargon that passes for English. I'd written something like "I don't want what I've said to discourage you from pursuing this question further; rather I would wish that my arguments should prove an added stimulus. . . ." At that point I said to myself, "Now, come on, John, pull yourself together. That won't do: what is it you're trying to say?" And I pulled myself together (tired as I was)—I pulled myself together and searched and found it. "I don't want to put you off. I want rather to set you on." That was all. (What torment we have to go through to find what it is we're trying to say and how to say it in simple words.) That was all. Two simple sentences: put you *off*—set you *on*. Each ending with a preposition.

At that point, as I wrote this script, I went for a walk round the houses. Two lads were talking as I passed. One had three dogs on a leash. The other asked, as I went by, "What d'you keep dogs for?" I pricked up my ears at that (for more reasons than one, you know). But I'm always interested in the way people say things. Quite as much as in what they say. "What d'you keep dogs for?" That was his way of asking, "Why do you keep dogs?" It's most people's way. I fancy it's my way, as often as not. In my everyday speech, I mean. But suppose I'm writing a talk, and want to ask a question like that in it. Which form shall I use? Shall I say, "Why," or shall I say, "What for"? The first saves a word, and over the air a word saved in expressing a thought is a kingdom gained. The second not only wastes a word, but the sentence ends in the wrong sort of preposition, the one on which you drop your voice: "What d'you keep *dogs* for?" So you'd say, "Use the first." Yes, but I like what I say to get home; and to get at that lad, mustn't I use *his* form, not the best form? The times I've had to face that question: popular English or good English!

I think I've mostly dodged it. There's an idiom, I believe, lies behind both. Behind both stiff speech and loose talk. I think if you can get back to *that*, the boy on the bike and the girl at the counter and the man at the works and the woman in the home will all feel the speech you're using to be, perhaps not "true to life"—but something better: truer than life. It's a choice of word and a turn of speech that, if only you can get it, reflects the very soul and spirit of our language. It comes down, of course, through Shakespeare and the Authorized Version. But there's nothing old-fashioned, nothing dead and done with about it. It's all alive and kicking. But it keeps to the homely words that belong to the oldest English and to homely turns of speech. That's the way out I've tried to find. Sometimes I've felt I've really found it, and then what a thrill! How often I've tried for it and failed. . . .

I do believe that's all I want to say about the technique of *composing* talk. All I want to say here and now, I mean. It's all I *can* say, anyhow. But about delivering over the air what's composed? Ah, there I think I'd better keep quiet. Each has a way that best suits himself (or herself, of course). Each must find that way: his or her own way. To find it one has to experiment, as I've said. You may even, I think, copy or mimic someone else's style now and again just to see if there's anything in it that fits you. But in the end, you've got to find your own self. Or rather, you've got to find or create a radio version of your real self (all that about being natural's no good, you know. Fine art's never natural, it only looks it. Or sounds it.) You've got to find or create a radio version of yourself, the radio quintessence of yourself, and then write for it, and go to the microphone and act it—with truth and sincerity.

Just two odd things from my own experience on the matter of delivery. My belief is that listeners hear speech, not in a sequence of words—one after the other—but in chunks; and what I try to do, though I may seldom succeed in my good intentions, is to throw out my words in bunches . . . like that . . . and then pause long enough for the listener to take that bunch in. I don't know if that's right for everyone; I don't even know if others would think it right for me; but it's been my theory, and it's what I've aimed at in practice, however often I may have missed the mark.

The other oddment is this. The matter of speed. All over, average speed. Many of you have written to me from time to time: "What you were saying was so exciting. But oh I wish you'd gone slower. I missed some words." Yes, but if I'd gone slower you wouldn't have been excited. You'd have written then and said, "Why were you so solemn? You nearly sent me to sleep!" Oh, I know. . . . You can't have it both ways. When I *have* gone slow it's not been for that. It's been because of my many friends in Wales who have trouble in following too rapid English, however clearly it may be spoken.

Well, there you are. That's my last talk—a talk about giving a talk. It's a sort of—well, I won't say "last will and testament," but at any rate a testament. So now, I leave you for a year or two. I'm going to take things easy for a while—or try to. Then I must buckle to on all sorts of other explorations and enterprises. I know I shall have your good wishes. You have mine. Look after yourselves. Blessings on you. ■

Architect Frank Lloyd Wright Calls Up the Image of "the Floo Floo Bird"

"I know of nothing more silly than to expect 'government' to solve our advanced problems for us. If we have no ideas, how can government have any?"

"EARLY IN LIFE," said the greatest of American architects, "I had to choose between honest arrogance and hypocritical humility. I chose honest arrogance and have seen no occasion to change." Frank Lloyd Wright died in 1959, at the age of ninety-one. During the seven decades of his innovative career, Wright developed a "prairie style" in the design of buildings with long, low horizontal lines and open interiors.

In his autobiography, he wrote, "No house should ever be *on* any hill or on anything. It should be *of* the hill belonging to it, so hill and house could live together each the happier for the other." This central concern of Wright's work was expressed in the title of his 1939 book, *An Organic Architecture*.

In 1938, he addressed a meeting of the Association of Federal Architects. Speaking in the nation's capital, he discussed organic architecture as a field outside of governmental regulation, and added to his reputation for being irascibly opinionated.

In the speech, he derogates America's cultural heritage and doubts the effectiveness of government in advancing American architecture. In addition to the repetition of "now" to introduce his ideas, Wright uses rhetorical questions and the unforgettable illustration of "the floo floo bird" to construct his argument.

□   □   □

. . . The cultural influences in our country are like the floo floo bird. I am referring to the peculiar and especial bird who always flew backward. To keep the wind out of its eyes? No. Just because it didn't give a darn where it was going, but just had to see where it had been. Now, in the floo floo bird you have the true symbol of our government architecture—too, and in consequence, how discredited American culture stands in the present time. All the world knows it to be funny except America. What prevented us and still prevents us from knowing it? Armchair education, let's say.

Now, all this has parallels in history. The Romans were just as incognizant as we of the things of the spirit. They, too, had no culture of their own. England had none of her own, and we, having none, got what we have as a substitute second, third, or fourth hand from them all. Roman culture, for instance, was Greek. The Romans, however, did have great engineers (you have all heard of the arch), but what did the Romans do with their greatest invention—the arch? You know well enough that for centuries they wasted it by pasting a travesty of Greek trabeation over it to conceal the truth of structure, until finally, some vulgar Roman, more "uncultured" than the rest, one day got up and said, "Hell! Take it all away! What's the matter with the arch? It's a genuine, beautiful, and noble thing"; and finally they got it, got the common arch as indigenous architecture.

We, the modern Romans, probably are going to get architecture something like that same way. We are going to have a true architecture of glass, steel, and the forms that gratify our new sense of space. We are going to have it. No Colonial Eden is able, long, to say us nay.

Culture, given time, will catch up and assert itself in spite of reaction. This thing, which we call America, as I have said, goes around the world today. It is chiefly spirit but that spirit is reality. Not by way of government can we find encouragement of any help. No, we can have nothing by way of official government until the thing is at least ten years in the past.

What can government do with an advanced idea? If it is still a controversial idea, and any good idea must be so, can government touch it without its eye on at least the next election? It cannot. I know of nothing more silly than to expect "government" to solve our advanced problems for us. If we have no ideas, how can government have any? ■

Secretary of State
Dean Acheson Explains
Tensions between the
United States and
the Soviet Union

"WE want peace, but not at any price."

AMERICAN DIPLOMAT DEAN ACHESON served as secretary of state
under President Harry Truman, from 1949 to 1953—"present at the creation," as he put it in titling his memoirs, of the policy of the contain-
ment of communism. Acheson supported the forming of the North
Atlantic Treaty Organization and favored military strength as well as foreign aid to curb the expansion of Soviet power.

While secretary of state, Acheson was invited to speak at the
University of California at Berkeley in March 1950. This address, in
abbreviated form below, was part of the Conference on International
Cooperation for World Economic Development.

In this talk Acheson enumerates seven primary points of disagreement
between the United States and the Soviet Union. These points of contention in Soviet-American tension range from the use of military force
to the control of atomic energy. Acheson's approach to these issues is
underscored by the anaphora of "We must not"—an expression that
introduces several clauses. Through the positive reinforcement of the
principles of freedom and justice, Acheson foresees the achievement of
American purpose, borrowing from Lincoln's second inaugural the words
that end this address.

□   □   □

I wish to make a report to you about the tensions between the United
States and the Soviet Union. . . . It is now nearly five years since the end
of hostilities, and the victorious Allies have been unable to define the terms
of peace with the defeated countries. This is a grave, a deeply disturbing

fact. For our part, we do not intend nor wish, in fact we do not know how, to create satellites. Nor can we accept a settlement which would make Germany, Japan, or liberated Austria satellites of the Soviet Union. The experience in Hungary, Romania, and Bulgaria has been one of bitter disappointment and shocking betrayal of the solemn pledges by the wartime Allies. The Soviet leaders joined in the pledge at Tehran that they looked forward "with confidence to the day when all peoples of the world may live free lives, untouched by tyranny, and according to their varying desires and their own consciences." We can accept treaties of peace, which would give reality to this pledge and to the interests of all in security.

With regard to Germany, unification under a government chosen in free elections under international observation is a basic element in an acceptable settlement. With that need recognized and with a will to define the terms of peace, a German treaty could be formulated which, while not pretending to solve all of the complex and bitter problems of the German situation, would, nevertheless, go far toward a relaxation of a set of major tensions.

With regard to Austria, that unhappy country is still under occupation because the Soviet leaders do not want a treaty. The political and economic independence of Austria is being sabotaged by the determination of the Soviets, camouflaged in technicalities, to maintain their forces and special interests in eastern Austria.

With regard to Japan, we feel that the Soviet leaders could recognize the interest which nations other than the members of the Council of Foreign Ministers have in a Japanese peace treaty and could refrain from taking positions and insisting on procedures which block progress toward a treaty.

In the Far East generally, there are many points where the Soviet leaders could, if they chose, relax tensions. They could, for example, permit the United Nations Commission in Korea to carry out its duties by allowing the commission's entry into North Korea and by accepting its report as the basis for a peaceful settlement of that liberated country's problems. They could repatriate Japanese prisoners of war from Siberian camps. They could refrain from subverting the efforts of the newly independent states of Asia and their native leaders to solve their problems in their own way.

With regard to the whole group of countries which we are accustomed to think of as the satellite area, the Soviet leaders could withdraw their military and police force and refrain from using the shadow of that force to keep in power persons or regimes which do not command the confidence of the respective peoples, freely expressed through orderly representative processes. In other words, they could elect to observe, in practice, the declaration to which they set their signatures at Yalta concerning liberated Europe. . . .

This is a question of elementary good faith, and it is vital to a spirit of confidence that other treaties and other agreements will be honored. Nothing would so alter the international climate as the holding of elections in the satellite states in which the true will of the people could be expressed.

The Soviet leaders could drop their policy of obstruction in the United Nations and could instead act as if they believe the United Nations is, as Stalin himself has recently called it, a serious instrumentality for the maintenance of international peace and security. They are simply not acting that way now.

Their policy of walkout and boycott is a policy that undermines the concept of majority decision. Indeed, they seem deliberately to entrench themselves in a minority position in the United Nations. . . .

The Soviet leaders could join us in seeking realistic and effective arrangements for the control of atomic weapons and the limitation of armaments in general. We know that it is not easy for them under their system to contemplate the functioning on their territory of an authority in which people would participate who are not of their political persuasion.

If we have not hesitated to urge that they as well as we accept this requirement, it is because we believe that a spirit of genuine responsibility to mankind is widely present in this world. Many able administrators and scientists could be found to operate such an authority who would be only too happy, regardless of political complexion, to take an elevated and enlightened view of the immense responsibility, which would rest upon them. There are men who would scorn to use their powers for the negative purpose of intrigue and destruction. We believe that an authority could be established which would not be controlled or subject to control by either ourselves or the Soviet Union.

The Kremlin could refrain from using the Communist apparatus controlled by it throughout the world to attempt to overthrow, by subversive means, established governments with which the Soviet government stands in an outward state of friendship and respect. In general, it could desist from, and could cooperate in efforts to prevent, indirect aggression across national frontiers—a mode of conduct which is inconsistent with the spirit and the letter of the United Nations Charter.

The Soviet leaders could cooperate with us to the end that the official representatives of all countries are treated everywhere with decency and respect and that an atmosphere is created in which these representatives could function in a normal and helpful manner, conforming to the accepted codes of diplomacy. . . .

When we now find our representatives treated as criminals, when we see great official propaganda machines reiterating that they are sinister people and that contact with them is pregnant with danger—we cannot believe that such insinuations are advanced in good faith, and we cannot be blind to the obvious implications of such an attitude.

In general, the Soviet leaders could refrain, I think, from systematically distorting to their own peoples the picture of the world outside their borders, and of our country in particular.

We are not suggesting that they become propagandists for any country or system other than their own. But the Soviet leaders know, and the world knows, with what genuine disappointment and concern the people of this country were brought to the realization that the wartime collaboration between the major Allies was not to be the beginning of a happier and freer era in the association between the peoples of the Soviet Union and other peoples.

What are we now to conclude from the morbid fancies which their propaganda exudes of a capitalist encirclement, of a United States craftily and systematically plotting another world war? They know, and the world knows, how foreign is the concept of aggressive war to our philosophy and our political system. They know that we are not asking to be the objects of any insincere and effusive demonstrations of sentimental friendship. But we feel that the Soviet leaders could at least permit access to the Soviet Union of persons and ideas from other countries so that other views might be presented to the Russian people.

These are some of the things which we feel that the Soviet leaders could do, which would permit the rational and peaceful development of the coexistence of their system and ours. They are not things that go to the depths of the moral conflict. They are not things that promise the kingdom of heaven. They have been formulated by us, not as moralists but as servants of government, anxious to get on with the practical problems that lie before us, and to get on with them in a manner consistent with mankind's deep longing for a respite from fear and uncertainty.

Nor have they been formulated as a one-sided bargain. A will to achieve binding, peaceful settlements would be required of all participants. All would have to produce unmistakable evidence of their good faith. All would have to accept agreements in the observance of which all nations could have real confidence.

The United States is ready, as it has been and always will be, to cooperate in genuine efforts to find peaceful settlements. Our attitude is not inflexible, our opinions are not frozen, our positions are not and will not be obstacles to peace. But it takes more than one to cooperate. . . .

So our course of action in the world of hard reality which faces us is not one that is easily charted. It is not one, which this nation can adopt without consideration of the needs and views of other free nations. It is one which requires all the devotion and resolve and wisdom that can be summoned up. . . .

We want peace, but not at any price. We are ready to negotiate, but not at the expense of rousing false hopes which would be dashed by new failures. We are equally determined to support all real efforts for peaceful settlements and to resist aggression.

The times call for a total diplomacy equal to the task of defense against Soviet expansion and to the task of building the kind of world in which our way of life can flourish. We must continue to press ahead with the building of a free world which is strong in its faith and in its material progress. The alternative is to allow the free nations to succumb one by one to the erosive and encroaching processes of Soviet expansion. . . .

We must recognize that our ability to achieve our purposes cannot rest alone on a desire for peace, but that it must be supported by the strength to meet whatever tasks Providence may have in store for us.

We must not make the mistake, in other words, of using Soviet conduct as a standard for our own. Our efforts cannot be merely reactions to the latest moves by the Kremlin. The bipartisan line of American foreign policy has been and must continue to be the constructive task of building, in cooperation with others, the kind of world in which freedom and justice can flourish. We must not be turned aside from this task by the diversionary thrusts of the Soviet Union. And if it is necessary, as it sometimes is, to deal with such a thrust or the threat of one, the effort should be understood as one which, though essential, is outside the main stream of our policy.

Progress is to be gained in the doing of the constructive tasks which give practical affirmation to the principles by which we live.

The success of our efforts rests finally on our faith in ourselves and in the values for which this Republic stands. We will need courage and steadfastness and the cool heads and steady nerves of a citizenry which has always faced the future "with malice toward none; with charity toward all; with firmness in the right, as God gives us to see the right." ■

Senator Henry Jackson Analyzes International Terrorism

"I believe that it is both wrong and foolhardy for any democratic state to consider international terrorism to be 'someone else's' problem."

SENATOR HENRY ("SCOOP") JACKSON, who died in 1983, was a maverick: a liberal on domestic affairs, a hard-liner on defense and foreign affairs. He served as senator from Washington, and as a leader of the Democratic party, for three decades. A conservationist before such a person became known as an environmentalist, and a staunch supporter of Israel. Jackson was twice unsuccessful in the seventies in his bid to become the Democratic candidate for president. He was offered, and turned down, the defense portfolio by President Nixon.

Jackson was not widely praised for his speechmaking; in fact, a 1976 barb about the delivery of the presidential candidate suggested, "If he gave a fireside chat, the fire would go out." On a controversial issue like the handling of terrorism, however, the senator could speak forcefully and authoritatively.

In July 1979, he was invited to address the Conference on International Terrorism, in Jerusalem. The meeting was sponsored by the Jonathan Institute, which was named for Lieutenant Colonel Jonathan Netanyahu, remembered for his courage and death in the 1976 rescue of Israeli hostages at Entebbe.

Among the effective rhetorical devices of his lecture is his tribute to the namesake of the Jonathan Institute with a parallel listing of adjectives ("strong, dedicated, courageous, dependable"). He enumerates five ways to combat terrorists and uses rhetorical questions to concentrate on the moral issue of conducting business with countries that promote or allow terrorism.

☐ ☐ ☐

As we gather here this evening, our thoughts turn to Lieutenant Colonel Jonathan Netanyahu. We recall the quality of his personal character, his inner devotion to the public good, his voluntary performance of the most demanding duties that the defense of democracy entails, and the sacrifice consummated in the heroic rescue at Entebbe. Jonathan's heritage is an unpurchasable treasure of the spirit that moth and rust cannot consume nor thieves break through and steal.

When, in George Bernard Shaw's play, they tell Joan of Arc that they are going to burn her at the stake, she foresees the effect upon the people. "If I go through the fire," she says, "I shall go through it to their hearts for ever and ever." So Jonathan went through the Entebbe fire to our hearts for ever and ever.

I believe that international terrorism is a modern form of warfare against liberal democracies. I believe that the ultimate but seldom stated goal of these terrorists is to destroy the very fabric of democracy. I believe that it is both wrong and foolhardy for any democratic state to consider international terrorism to be "someone else's" problem.

If you believe as I do, then you must join me in wondering why the community of liberal democracies has not banded together more effectively to oppose these international murderers and to loudly and vigorously expose those states, which cynically provide terrorists with comfort and support. One of the great cover-ups of this century is the effort by Western governments, who know better, to muffle the facts about Soviet bloc support for international terrorism.

I'm not talking about individual acts of madmen. I'm talking about highly organized groups with international connections and support who systematically rely on major acts of violence as a political instrument. I'm thinking of the Basque and Puerto Rican terrorists, the European terrorist groups, and the PLO attacks, or threats of attack, against moderate Arab states which might be motivated to support the Egyptian-Israeli peace agreement. I have in mind the PLO attacks against moderate Palestinians— the murder of a moderate leader in the Gaza is a recent brutal example. I am reminded of radical Palestinian terrorist attacks on airliners servicing Israel. I'm thinking of the Palestinian operations in Lebanon and the activities of Turkish terrorists. Such acts of terrorism are part of a broad campaign aimed at the disintegration of democratic societies through undermining the confidence of their citizenry in their governments.

International terrorism is a special problem for democracies. To a totalitarian regime like the Soviet Union, it is mainly a nuisance. The government applies whatever force is needed to liquidate the group and its members; borders are closed to unwanted entry or exit; individual rights are held subservient to "law and order"; publicity can be denied by fiat. The biggest difference between the Soviet Union and such states as Libya, Iraq, and Iran is that these governments are not as efficient—yet.

A democratic government, on the other hand, rests on the consent of the governed. It is responsible for assuring the democratic freedoms of speech, assembly, travel, press, and privacy. These conditions, obviously, facilitate terrorist operations, directed against a particular government or as the battleground for opposing terrorist groups. When the PLO and Iraqi terrorists were at war, they chose to fight it out in Europe, not in the Middle East.

Terrorism is not a new phenomenon. What is new is the international nature of the terrorism. Today's terrorists have modern technology to help them, permitting rapid international communications, travel, and the transfer of monies; they can work with others of like mind across the international borders of the world's free nations.

More important, however, these groups receive extensive support from the Soviet bloc. Most terrorists use Soviet or East European weapons; they have been trained in the Warsaw Pact countries, or in such Middle East countries as South Yemen and the PLO-controlled areas of Lebanon; they generally flee for protection and rest to East Europe or to such countries as Libya. The primary supporters of international terrorism are the Soviet Union and those states which the Soviets support: the Warsaw Pact and the radical Arab camp.

Modern terrorism is a form of "warfare by remote control" waged against free nations or against nondemocratic but moderate states which dare to sympathize with freedom. In this kind of war, the totalitarian regimes see little risk of retribution directed at them.

What can be done?

First, and foremost, liberal democracies must acknowledge that international terrorism is a "collective problem." Everything else follows from this. When one free nation is under attack, the rest must understand that democracy itself is under attack, and behave accordingly. We must be allied in our defense against terrorists. . . .

Let me emphasize two propositions whose truth should be evident to all democracies. To insist that free nations negotiate with terrorist organizations can only strengthen the latter and weaken the former. To crown with statehood a movement based on terrorism would devastate the moral authority that rightly lies behind the effort of free states everywhere to combat terrorism.

Secondly, every free nation must work against Soviet and radical state efforts to define away terrorism. The idea that one person's "terrorist" is another's "freedom fighter" cannot be sanctioned. Freedom fighters or revolutionaries don't blow up buses containing noncombatants; terrorist murderers do. Freedom fighters don't set out to capture and slaughter schoolchildren; terrorist murderers do. Freedom fighters don't assassinate innocent businessmen or hijack and hold hostage innocent men, women, and children; terrorist murderers do. It is a disgrace that democracies would allow the treasured word "freedom" to be associated with the acts of the terrorists.

Third, we must turn the publicity instrument against the terrorists, and we must expose Soviet and other state support of terrorist groups whenever we identify it. When PLO terrorists toss a bomb into a marketplace or murder a holy man or shoot rockets randomly at a village, each and every democracy in the world should stand up to condemn those radical Arab states and the Soviet Union who train, arm, finance, harbor, and encourage them.

When an act of terrorism occurs, and the odds are it will occur in one of the free countries, democracies should unite in sponsoring resolutions in the United Nations condemning the act. Where we have evidence of support for the terrorists by some other state, this support should be censured in the strongest terms. If the Soviet Union, its allies, and the radical Arab and Third World states want to vote against such resolutions, let them. Let's educate the whole world as to who opposes and who tolerates international terrorism.

I am convinced that this will make a difference; I am convinced, for instance, that the exposure of East European support for European terrorism has contributed to the lessening of this support and to the signs of some cooperation to combat terrorism between these countries and the nations of West Europe.

Fourth, liberal democracies must work together to apply sanctions against countries which provide sanctuary to international terrorists. The Bonn Anti-Hijacking Agreement is a good start. It is ironic that the pilots and the airlines, and not our statesmen, provided the leadership which led to this agreement.

We can do more. For instance, is it moral to trade openly and freely with states who use the profits from such trade to finance the murder of innocents? Why should those who conduct remote control warfare against us rest easy that we will contribute to financing our own destruction?

Fifth, within each of our own countries, we must organize to combat terrorism in ways consistent with our democratic principles and with the strong support of our citizens. Israel has long done this. And the nations of Western Europe are moving in this direction. In my country, we are making some progress in organizing federal, state, and local agencies to deal more realistically with terrorist threats. . . .

Now this final word:

In providing for her own defense against terrorism, Israeli courage has inspired those who love freedom around the world. The Entebbe rescue was a classic lesson for all free nations that terrorism can be effectively countered with strength, skill, and determination. These are qualities in short supply in many countries where freedom comes more easily. Indeed, the great need in the world today is for men and women who stand in the tradition of Jonathan Netanyahu—strong, dedicated, courageous, dependable. ■

Broadcaster Alistair Cooke Needles the Jargonauts in Assessing the State of the English Language

"THE time to rinse the mind free of verbal cant cannot begin too early."

ALISTAIR COOKE'S *Letter from America,* which began in 1946, was the longest-running series in the history of broadcasting and was regularly heard in more than fifty nations. His precise phrasing, literate style, and avuncular demeanor became familiar throughout the English-speaking world, and his training in linguistics led him to talk occasionally about the philological tool of his trade.

Born in Manchester, England, he came to America as a correspondent of *The Times* and of *The Guardian* before joining the BBC. His "letter"—a weekly essay in conversational style—did more to explain the United States to Britons than any other form of communication. Later, as television host of Public Broadcasting's *Masterpiece Theater,* he finally became well known to his fellow Americans.

This speech to the English Speaking Union's conference of scholars was given on November 1, 1979, in San Francisco. Mr. Cooke delighted in noting that it was the only address not printed in the scholarly compendium.

Note the flow of the speech, as the speaker moves fluidly from anecdote to example, taking a breath with self-questioning, planting the "area" theme that he reprises at the conclusion. Sentences are effectively stylish, as in the bump-to-an-end conclusion of "That shuts them up, even though I wouldn't know a nucleic acid if it were served to me chilled, with an olive, in a glass." Another speech of his can be found on p. 574.

□   □   □

I apologize for taking out a script. I am in the habit, myself—especially after dinner—of speaking off the cuff or the top of the head, according to which is more available at the time. But this is an occasion with a special hazard. I am facing a pack of linguistic watchdogs who, like the people who review anthologies, are not going to be impressed by a wealth of accurate knowledge (even if I had it) so much as by small omissions and single slips.

As when J. B. Sykes put out, after seven years of lonely labor, his monumental new *Concise Oxford Dictionary* (a small monument but an exquisite one), one London reviewer spent little time applauding the thousands of definitions that are miracles of clarity and exactness. He took up most of his column protesting the secondary definition given to a simple four-letter word that, Sykes said, was a slang term of abuse applied usually to a woman. Not so, said the reviewer, and he went on and on about Sykes's insensitivity to pejorative usage in general and this cutting example in particular. I blush, even in this year of liberation, to pronounce the word. I leave you to rush home, get out your Sykes, and—beginning with the letter A—keep going till you find it.

I am told that the coming seminars will be addressed by experts in Legal English and Black English, in everything from the new Episcopalian liturgy to the new liturgy of copulation. I am honored to be invited to kick off this series of matches between the structuralists and the semanticists and the other fashionable combatants. Fifty years ago, I might have had something special to offer, for it was a time when I sat at the feet of Dr. Richards trying to fathom the Meaning of Meaning, start talking like John Bunyan, or Defoe, or Lincoln, or Art Buchwald. I am thinking rather of the millions of schoolchildren who might yet be saved. Children to whom a television set is, in a literal sense, more impressive than any teacher they hear in a classroom. Who is to train them in the splendid flexibility of English tenses? Who is going to get them used to saying "because" instead of "in view of the fact that"? Who is to warn them that "in terms of" is usually a way of vamping till you're ready to think? Who is to give them warning signals about the whole Grammar of Anxiety, which springs from the chronic fear of being thought uneducated or banal and coins such things as "more importantly," "he invited Mary and I," "when I was first introduced," and "the end result"? Is anybody, in any high school in this country or in Britain, doing—under the lively influence of old Quiller-Couch and the Fowler brothers—what was done to me: giving out every so often a list of vogue words, and buzzwords, and current jargon, which you must translate into simple English and so need never use? If this had happened soon enough, and was a standard routine of early education, we should now have politicians who'd tell us what they have in mind, instead of which "scenarios" they are in the process of "orchestrating."

I have an English friend, the chairman of an advertising firm, who had the luck to go, forty-some years ago, to an English elementary school. Otherwise, he might be considered (as an advertising man) a kind of genius. For he is proof against genteelisms, circumlocutions, and general pomp. A few months ago, he sent a memo to his copywriters. It said:

> On their way across the Atlantic are one or two pernicious buzzwords. The latest have been invented by dramatic critics, but you might be tempted to pick them up and apply them to some product or fashion model. An actor is now said to give a "resonant" performance. The movie critics have just discovered that the chief virtue of every sympathetic actress is that she is "vulnerable." I also caught one of you last week using the most meaningless word in the language—"meaningful." Wake up, beware!

What is the point of sending promising students (what in American we call "very bright" students) running after courses in creative writing when they haven't learned to walk with simple adverbs and prepositions? There is surely no point whatever in setting up a course in the works of S. J. Perelman (which, since he has died, they will soon be doing) for any student who has not acquired considerable sophistication in sensing the emotional tone—what you might call the secret public attitude—of various vocabularies from the Anglo-Saxon Chronicles to *Time*, from Thackeray to Erica Jong.

We are back with the impressionable child, who sits before the tube for several hours a day and gradually ceases to know that the words "early" and "late" are going from the language: Americans are either "ahead of schedule" or "behind schedule." No child today has heard of toothpaste. My grandson, at the age of three, babbled for his dentifrice. Long before he gets false teeth (or "dentures") he'll want some personal notepaper, but he'll have to ask for "personalized" notepaper. At the moment, his teacher tells us, he cannot be said to love football: he is "football-oriented," No American girl with cracked lips is told how to moisten them. She is handed a "moisturizer" by a mother who, no doubt, thinks of herself as nothing so square as a good parent but as a "supportive" or "caring" one, but doesn't care enough to stop her child imbibing from the telly, at a fearful daily rate, words, locutions, solecisms, and absurdities beyond the wit or attention of its teachers ever to correct. Children listen to the evening weather reports. They must be now inured to the fact (which may astonish some of our English visitors) that in the United States there is no longer any thunder, any rain, hail or snow, and no clouds. There is only "thunderstorm activity" and "precipitation activity" and "cloud cover." A television weatherman told me the other evening that precipitation activity was spreading down from the Illinois area through the Kentucky and Tennessee areas into the Mississippi area. Poor Jack Teagarden! If he were alive today, he would have to sing "Stars Fell on the Alabama Area."

"Area" is my all-time nonfavorite: a cloudy word that has blanketed, and hence obliterated, the differences between neighborhood, district, part of town, region, state, field (of study), topic, theme. Airplanes used to stop at the gate. Now they "make a complete stop at the gate area." From which you proceed to the baggage claim area, and on into the New York or Dallas or San Francisco area. I once asked a skittish and amiable stewardess—or "in-flight hostess"—"How is it possible to be approaching the San Francisco area without approaching San Francisco?" She looked alarmed. "Search me," she said. My theory is simple, if revolutionary. There is an area of the United States that was named Illinois. There's another called New York, and yet another called Boston. However much they expand, that is what they should be called. When the time comes, I should be happy if they chiseled on my gravestone: "He killed off area."

I used to think that Americans were much better informed than Britons about medicine. Because they used, with enviable flipness, exact medical terms like deviated septum or congested sinuses, whereas Britons tended to go round grumbling about their catarrh (catarrh in my day covered everything from pneumonia to a brain tumor). I remember becoming so ashamed of my lumpish ignorance of such things that I stopped talking about my lumbago (or rheumatics) and learned to toss off words like sacroiliac and slipped disk (even after an orthopedic surgeon asked me what I meant by it). It took some years for me to discover that the ordinary American, the layman, was no more knowledgeable than his British counterpart. He simply yielded to the national love of Latin and Greek (especially if he knew no Latin or Greek). Thus, I was enormously impressed when I heard somebody say, at a cocktail party, that he'd suffered a lesion of—or to—his clavicle. I tiptoed off to the dictionary to learn about this exotic affliction. What d'you think? He'd hurt his collarbone!

It used to be—and I'd like to think it's still so in some English-speaking countries—that when you had a pain and went to the doctor, a friend would say: "What did he do for you?" And you'd say: "He gave me a pill." No longer, not in this country. You are given "medication" and are not being treated: you are undergoing "therapy" (treatment in Greek). Chemotherapy, which means no more than treatment by a chemical, is now so exclusively applied to cancer that it seems cruel to remark that almost everything you put in your mouth, from an aspirin to a hamburger, is a chemical.

Another medical word that is very popular in America, and has been, I should guess, for a couple of decades, is the magic word: virus. All suffering people drop it to explain everything from a sniffle to a drowsiness. I used to drop it myself till a doctor present said thoughtfully, "I don't *think* it's a virus. I doubt it has protein coat." That's a stopper if ever I heard one. I looked that up too, and I'm ready anytime for any pedant who fixes me with his Ancient Mariner eye and says, "Do you know exactly what a virus *is*?" I reply at once, "Sure thing. Any of numerous kinds of very simple organisms smaller than bacteria, mainly of nucleic acid in protein coat, existing only in living cells and able to cause diseases." *That* shuts them up, even though I wouldn't know a nucleic acid if it were served to me chilled, with an olive, in a glass.

Some years ago, when I was traveling all over the country filming my television series *America*, one of the young women on the crew, a shrewd, modest English girl, who had not been here before, said, "They are a marvelous, warm people, and their slang is so racy. But why is it that in print, or in public, the rule seems to be: Never say in two syllables what you can say in five? Where did it all start?"

Well, there are two "its" here: the obsessive love of Latinism; and the disastrous decline in the teaching of elementary grammar and plain speaking. I suspect that the early warning signal of a coming influx of polysyllables was the decision (I think in Goethe's time) by the University of Göttingen to begin and maintain a close relation with Harvard. It was enough, after the liberal revolution of 1848, and more than enough in the later trek of German exiles, to guarantee invading hordes of sociologists and psychiatrists. It has become a badge, almost a sworn oath, of their trade that it is better to be overwrought than oversimple; that Anglo-Saxon English is a naive tool for examining human behavior either in the individual or in the mass; that the love of a man for a maid is not to be undertaken lightly, but gravely, writhingly, humorlessly, pedantically, as a perilous adventure in "interpersonal relationships."

As for the decline in teaching grammar, in some schools the deliberate abandoning of it, I believe it started when John Dewey conceived the beguiling theory that all knowledge can be "fun," if not orgasmic. The application of this theory far and wide by slap-happy people who thought of themselves as "progressives" led in the fullness of time to a masterpiece of wishful thinking that I saw enshrined in a newspaper ad at the end of last March. It said: "You Can Learn French by the fifteenth of May—*with no effort on your part!*" I thought of Charles Darwin, going down to various seashores on and off for over forty years with a broken teacup (he had no grant from a national science foundation) and scooping up sand and algae and brooding over them. At the end of which time, after considerable effort on his part, he published *The Origin of Species*. But then, Darwin was a Victorian, and he held to the Victorian prejudice that any knowledge that goes much below the surface takes time and tedium to acquire—however "bright" the student.

Some years ago, I was saying much of this—as it applied to the jargon of medicine—to the assembled staff of the Mayo Clinic. I mused that perhaps, after all, an appetite for jargon might be imbibed with the mother's milk: a matter of genes. I was rash enough to conclude, "Maybe you can no more cure a naturally pompous person than you can reflower a virgin." My lecture was reprinted in the *Mayo Clinic Bulletin*, which goes to the far corners of the earth. One of the first letters I received was from the University of Tokyo's department of gynecology. It said: "But, Mr. Cooke, we do it!"

If they can do it, maybe our high school teachers can make it unnecessary, by encouraging and training the child's instinct for directness and simplicity before the hymen, so to speak, of its innocence is broken. At any rate, I'm convinced that it is in the high schools at the latest that the old custom should be revived: the teaching, first, of grammar and idiom; and then, of cautionary courses in current jargon. The time to rinse the mind free of verbal cant cannot begin too early.

I trust that "the development of this basic linguistic concept mandates no further elaboration at this point in time." Or, as Chaucer more aptly put it, "There is no more to saye." Except, thank you and—"Have a nice day in the San Francisco area." ■

Presidential Aide Jack Valenti Recalls the Lessons Learned at the Center of Power

"I learned never to humiliate an antagonist and never desert a friend. . . . I learned that . . . the politician who persistently lifts his wet finger to test the political polls before he acts usually leaves office with a wet finger."

A WORLD WAR II combat hero from Texas, Jack Valenti founded an advertising agency in Houston in 1952 and became associated with the political campaigns of Lyndon Baines Johnson. Valenti was in charge of the press during the visit to Texas of President Kennedy and Vice-President Johnson on November 22, 1963; when the president was assassinated in the Dallas motorcade, Valenti accompanied the new president to Washington in Air Force One, the first special assistant named by President Johnson.

In later years, as Johnson was vilified by the Left for the war in Vietnam and by the Right for his Great Society, Valenti remained outspokenly loyal to his old chief, often the only voice that could be found for a spirited defense of LBJ's record and reputation. An articulate and forceful speaker, the diminutive Democrat—who left the White House to become president and CEO of the Motion Picture Association of America—wrote the best book about speechmaking, *Speak Up with Confidence.* He is a founder-member of the Judson Welliver Society, the association of White House speechwriters.

In this speech to the Federal Communications Bar Association, made in Washington on January 31, 1996, thirty years after becoming the movie industry's voice, Valenti reflected on the lessons learned in a career in or near the center of power.

The talk opens with the briefest of references to the dramatic moment he came to Washington, which was just enough; it moves to a series of paragraphs beginning "I learned that," giving the address a disciplined structure; and it concludes with a dramatic anecdote illustrating his major "lesson." Needless to say, the well-crafted speech by the Harvard-educated political pro was flawlessly delivered in a modified Texas accent.

□   □   □

. . . I would like to talk tonight about what I have learned since I arrived in the Federal City aboard Air Force One on November 22, 1963. . . .

I learned that in the White House there is one enduring standard by which every assistant to the president, every presidential adviser, every presidential consultant, must inevitably be measured. Not whether you went to Harvard or Yale, or whether you scored sixteen hundred on your SATs, or whether you are endlessly charming and charismatically enabled, or whether you made millions in what we sardonically call "the private sector." These are all attractive credentials, which one may wear modestly or otherwise. But when the decision crunch is on in the Oval Office they are all merely tracings on dry leaves in the wind. What does count, the ultimate and only gauge, is whether you have "good Judgment."

I learned that no presidential decision is ever made where the president had all the information he needed to make the decision. There is never enough facts. Very quickly, the decision corridor grows dark, the mapping indistinct, the exit inaccessible. What is not useful are precedents or learned disquisitions by op-ed page pundits, some of whom would be better suited to raising pigeons. . . .

It is well to remember, as Oscar Wilde once said, that from time to time nothing that is worth knowing can be taught. Judgment is something that springs from some little elf who inhabits an area between your belly and your brain, and who, from time to time, tugs at your nerve edges, and says, "No, not that way, the other way." . . .

I learned that the one political component above all else which can ensure electoral victory or crushing defeat is timing. A whack to your political solar plexus six to eight months before an election is survivable. Two weeks before the election, and you're dead. Ask Jimmy Carter. In politics, twenty hours is a millennium.

I learned that economic forecasts beyond about two weeks have the same odds of accuracy as guessing the winning numbers in the D.C. lottery. . . .

Economic forecasts are usually unwarranted assumptions leaping to a preconceived conclusion. Just remember, whenever an economist can't remember his phone number, he will give you an estimate.

I learned that when there is no unamiable issue like war, or prospect of war, or recession, or economic disaster, most people vote for a president viscerally, not intellectually. Most people choose a president romantically, a choice made in unfathomable ways, which is how romance is formed. Like John Kennedy and Ronald Reagan.

I learned never to humiliate an antagonist and never desert a friend. In a political struggle, never get personal else the dagger digs too deep. Your enemy today may need to be your ally tomorrow.

I learned that nothing lasts. What is up will inevitably go down and sooner or later in reverse. It took forty years, but the House changed masters. Victory is often the prelude to defeat. President Bush can rise to testify about that. Failure is often the precursor of triumph. Ask Bill Clinton. Richard Nixon tasted both ends of those beguiling equations. The breeding ground of politics is irrigated and nourished by change. As one who has fallen from political power, I can instruct George Stephanopoulos in how quickly you lose your charm and your enticements when you no longer sit at the right hand of the Sun King.

I learned that a political poll is Janus in disguise. The life of a poll is about ten nanoseconds. It is already in decay when it is published. A political poll, like the picture of Dorian Gray, is the face of entropy. The veteran professionals know that. The old pols use polls to raise money. When polls are up, go for the fat wallets. But the politician who persistently lifts his wet finger to test the political polls before he acts usually leaves office with a wet finger. . . .

But the greatest lesson I have learned, the most important of my education, is really the essential imperative of this century. It is called leadership. We brandish the word. We admire its light. But we seldom define it. Outside Caen in the Normandy countryside of France is a little cemetery. Atop one of the graves is a cross on which is etched these words: "Leadership is wisdom and courage and a great carelessness of self." Which means, of course, that leaders must from time to time put to hazard their own political future in order to do what is right in the long-term interests of those they have by solemn oath sworn to serve. Easy to say. Tough to do.

I remember when I first bore personal witness to its doing. It was in December 1963. Lyndon Johnson had been president but a few short weeks. At that time I was actually living on the third floor of the White House until my family arrived. The president said to me on a Sunday morning, "Call Dick Russell and ask him if he would come by for coffee with you and me."

Senator Richard Brevard Russell of Georgia was the single most influential and honored figure in the Senate. His prestige towered over all others in those years before the dialogue turned sour and mean. When in 1952, the Senate Democratic leader's post fell open, the other senators turned immediately to Russell, imploring him to take the job. "No," said Russell, "let's make Lyndon Johnson our leader, he'll do just fine." So at the age of forty-four, just four years in his first Senate term, LBJ became the youngest ever Democratic leader and in a short time the greatest parliamentary commander in Senate history.

When Russell arrived, the president greeted him warmly with a strong embrace, the six-foot-four LBJ and the smallish, compact Russell, with his gleaming bald head and penetrating eyes. The president steered him to the couch overlooking the Rose Garden in the West Hall on the second floor of the mansion. I sat next to Russell. The president was in his wing chair, his knees almost touching Russell's, so close did they sit.

The president drew even closer, and said in an even voice, "Dick, I love you and I owe you. If it had not been for you I would not have been leader, or vice-president, or now president. But I wanted to tell you face to face, please don't get in my way on this civil rights bill, which has been locked up in the Senate too damn long. I intend to pass this bill, Dick. I will not cavil. I will not hesitate. And if you get in my way, I'll run you down."

Russell sat mutely for a moment, impassive, his face a mask. Then he spoke, in the rolling accents of his Georgia countryside. "Well, Mr. President, you may just do that. But I pledge you that if you do, it will not only cost you the election, it will cost you the South forever."

President Johnson in all the later years in which I knew him so intimately never made me prouder than he did that Sunday morning so long, long ago. He touched Russell lightly on the shoulder, an affectionate gesture of one loving friend to another. He spoke softly, almost tenderly: "Dick, my old friend, if that's the price I have to pay, then I will gladly pay it."

Of all the lessons I have learned in my political life, that real-life instruction in leadership on a Sunday morning in the White House was the most elemental, and the most valuable. It illuminated in a blinding blaze the highest point to which the political spirit can soar. I have never forgotten it. I never will. ■

After *Bush v. Gore*, Justice Ruth Bader Ginsburg Speaks Out for Judicial Independence

"EACH side warned that the other risked casting a cloud of illegitimacy over the election."

IN THE PRESIDENTIAL ELECTION OF 2000—only the second in U.S. history in which the winner in the Electoral College lost the popular vote—the U.S. Supreme Court decided 5–4 that it was best able to resolve the controversy over election results in Florida. The intensely controversial case, *Bush v. Gore*, transfixed a nation that had never before placed the responsibility for making the call that would decide who would be the next president on any court. The famous saying of Finley Peter Dunne's fictional Mr. Dooley—that "the supreme coort follows th' iliction returns"—was turned on its head, as the election returns were ultimately decided by the Supreme Court.

Democratic voters were understandably angered at the high court's intervention that led to the election of Republican George W. Bush. Republicans—who usually called for judicial restraint and inveighed against judicial activism—were delighted with the decision of the Court, most of whose members were appointed by Republican presidents, to step into the political process. This led to questions about the Court's independence and charges of politicization.

Ruth Bader Ginsburg, the Brooklyn-born attorney known for her advocacy of women's rights and everyone's civil liberties, had been appointed to the Supreme Court by President Bill Clinton in 1993. She voted with the minority in *Bush v. Gore* and joined the vigorous dissent.

Speaking to the University of Melbourne Law School on February 1, 2001—little more than a week after the inauguration of President George W. Bush—Justice Ginsburg put the case in the context of other famous controversies decided by the Court. She concluded that "whatever final judgment awaits *Bush v. Gore* in the annals of history," public confidence in the whole federal judiciary (not just the Supreme Court) would be sustained "at a level never beyond repair"—a judicious way of saying that, in time, the drop in confidence could be fixed.

In this excerpt, I have deleted her published speech's footnotes, one of which states: "Justice Ginsburg acknowledges with appreciation the grand assistance of her 2000 Term law clerk, Goodwin Liu, in composing these remarks." Not many speakers do that.

□   □   □

. . . **O**f all the words recently spoken and written about judicial independence in the United States—and whatever one makes of the U.S. Supreme Court's part in calling the excruciatingly close November 2000 election for President Bush—a 1980 comment by the U.S. Chief Justice remains, in my view, right on target. On the obligation of a good judge, Chief Justice Rehnquist then said: He or she must strive constantly to do what is legally right, all the more so when the result is not the one the Congress, the president, or "the home crowd" wants. My aim in this lecture is to offer some thoughts, from the vantage point of a U.S. federal judge, on just how important—and difficult—it is for judges to do what is legally right, no matter what "the home crowd" wants.

If it is true, as Henry Fielding wrote, that examples work more forcibly on the mind than precepts, then allow me to begin with a few trying cases, situations in which the U.S. Supreme Court intervened to resolve controversies some thought best left to political decision makers—to the executive or the Congress. My first two illustrations today generate no sparks in the United States. The third awaits history's judgment.

I will recall first a 1974 case titled *United States v. Nixon*, which yielded a unanimous opinion written by Chief Justice Rehnquist's predecessor, Warren Burger. On Chief Justice Burger's death, a *New York Times* obituary praised the opinion as "the pinnacle of [Burger's] career and one of the [U.S.] judiciary's finest achievements." The case concerned a subpoena issued by U.S. District Judge John Sirica at the height of the Watergate scandal. Judge Sirica's subpoena directed the president to produce, for use in a criminal proceeding, tape recordings and documents capturing Oval Office conversations between Nixon and his closest advisers.

In his campaigns for the presidency, Nixon had repeatedly called for the restoration of "law and order." He promised to appoint judges equal to the task, people who would not be "soft on crime." A United States Supreme Court that included four Nixon appointees, including Chief Justice Burger and now Chief Justice Rehnquist, declared the law and affirmed Judge Sirica's order. The president obeyed, then promptly resigned from office.

Earlier in time, my second illustration is popularly known as the "steel seizure case," *Youngstown Sheet & Tube Co. v. Sawyer*. In the spring of 1952, the United States was heavily engaged in the Korean War. At home, inflation was rising, and labor unrest was widespread. For several months, the United Steel Workers of America had been seeking a substantial wage increase, which the steel companies had repeatedly refused. With negotiations at an impasse, the steel workers voted to strike beginning on April 9. On the evening of April 8, to keep the mills in operation, President Truman issued an executive order directing the secretary of commerce to take possession of eighty-five steel companies. The order declared that "a work stoppage would immediately jeopardize and imperil our national defense . . . and would add to the continuing danger of our soldiers, sailors, and airmen engaged in combat in the field."

The steel companies argued that the order was an unconstitutional encroachment on congressional authority. In response, the government urged that a strike would so endanger the well-being and safety of the nation that the president must be held to possess "inherent power" to seize the steel mills. The United States District Court in Washington, D. C., rejected the government's plea and enjoined enforcement of the president's order. But the full Court of Appeals immediately voted 5–4 to stay the district court injunction, with the eight judges appointed by Truman evenly divided on the issue. One month later, a 6–3 majority of the United States Supreme Court declared the president's order invalid; the authority to seize property, the Court held, is a lawmaking power which the Constitution vests in Congress alone "in both good and bad times."

While four of the justices in the majority were appointed by Truman's predecessor, Franklin Roosevelt, the fifth and sixth votes came from Justices Burton and Clark, both Truman appointees. In a concurring opinion, Justice Clark explained (borrowing words written by Justice Story more than a century earlier) that, although the Court gives "the most entire respect" to the executive branch, "[i]t is our duty to expound the laws as we find them in the records of state; and we cannot, when called upon by the citizens of the country, refuse our opinion, however it may differ from that of very great authorities." President Truman immediately complied with the Court's judgment. "[L]ess than thirty minutes after the justices finished reading their opinions," he dispatched a letter ordering the secretary of commerce to return the confiscated mills to their owners.

More than 150 years ago, a young French observer of democracy in America, Alexis de Tocqueville, made this prescient comment: "Scarcely any political question arises in the United States that is not resolved, sooner or later, into a judicial one." Were the Watergate and steel seizure cases not enough to illustrate Tocqueville's insight, my third example, *Bush v. Gore*, surely provides graphic confirmation of its truth. The Court's decision in that case ended thirty-six days of controversy over the 2000 presidential election.

The petition for review in *Bush v. Gore* was filed in the United States Supreme Court on the evening of December 8, 2000, hours after the Florida Supreme Court had ordered statewide manual recounts of certain disputed ballots. Whether the recounting was permissible under state and federal law raised questions whose stakes could not have been higher. On December 8, George W. Bush led Al Gore in the Florida vote tally by some hundreds of votes—a razor-thin margin in an election with over 6 million votes cast statewide. At the national level, Gore had won the popular vote, and with 267 all-important electoral votes compared to Bush's 246, Gore was only three electoral votes shy of victory under the presidential electoral system decreed by the U.S. Constitution. The winner of Florida's popular election would capture all of the state's twenty-five decisive electoral votes and, in turn, the presidency.

One would expect that the first instinct of any judge, faced with such a case, would be restraint. The Supreme Court's initial encounter with the controversy might fit that description. Just five days before it agreed to hear *Bush v. Gore*, the Supreme Court issued a unanimous decision declining to intervene at an earlier point in the unfolding drama, when the Florida Supreme Court had interpreted Florida election laws to allow manual recounts to go forward in certain counties. The U.S. Supreme Court found the underpinnings of the Florida Supreme Court's initial decision unclear, and therefore remanded the case for clarification whether federal law had been duly considered. In that measured response, the U.S. Supreme Court referred to precedent counseling restraint when "there is considerable uncertainty as to the precise grounds of [a state court] decision."

In the ensuing irresolution, pressure on the political and legal system continued to mount. Not since 1876 had a presidential contest been so close, and not since then had the nation waited so long for a definitive resolution. On December 9, one day after the Florida Supreme Court's decision ordering statewide manual recounts, the pressure pushed the unanimity of the United States Supreme Court past its breaking point, as a 5–4 majority voted to stay the recounts pending review and disposition of *Bush v. Gore*.

Ordinarily, interim stay orders of the Court, like grants of review, issue without explanation. But this was no ordinary case. Justice Stevens took the unusual step of issuing a written dissent, which Justice Souter, Justice Breyer, and I joined, stating reasons for concluding that the stay was unjustified. In the dissenters' view, the Court should have stayed out of the fray entirely, leaving its ultimate resolution to Congress. Justice Scalia took the even more unusual step of explaining why he voted in favor of a stay securing Court adjudication of the controversy. Each side warned that the other risked casting a cloud of illegitimacy over the election.

On December 12, three days after granting review, and one day after oral argument, the U.S. Supreme Court released its decision. Unaccompanied by the usual syllabus, and including six separate writings, the release first confused instant reporters. The outcome, however, is by now clear to all. In an unsigned opinion, five justices agreed that under the Equal Protection Clause of the U.S. Constitution, the Florida Election Code's "intent of the voter" standard provided insufficient guidance for manually recounting disputed ballots. The five justices further agreed that there was no time left to conduct recounts under constitutionally acceptable standards. That was so, the per curiam opinion explained, because the Florida Supreme Court had interpreted Florida election law to require completion of all vote counts by December 12, the date by which, under federal law, Florida had to certify its election results in order to gain for the state's electoral votes "conclusive" effect in Congress's tally of all electoral votes.

Four justices dissented. Two said that the "intent of the voter" standard presented equal protection concerns, but also said that those concerns might be met on remand. Two determined that the standard raised no equal protection problem, particularly in view of the range of local voting systems and ballot designs traditionally tolerated. (I was one of those two.) All four dissenting justices agreed that the December 12 deadline was illusory under both Florida law and federal law. Justice Breyer explained that neither the Florida Supreme Court nor the Florida Legislature adopted December 12 as the drop-dead date for counting votes, and that several provisions of federal law obligated Congress to count a state's electoral votes based on election results determined after December 12. Justice Souter wrote: "There is no justification for denying the state the opportunity to try to count all disputed ballots now." (I note that the Court's vote did not divide strictly on party lines. While Justice Breyer and I were appointed by President Clinton, a Democrat, our colleagues in dissent were appointed by Republican presidents: Justice Stevens by President Ford, Justice Souter by President Bush, the elder.)

Less than two months into the aftermath, I will not venture any dire or definitive declarations about the implications of *Bush v. Gore* for judicial independence. The wisdom of the Court's decision to intervene, and the wisdom of its ultimate determination, as I said earlier, await history's judgment. The initial commentary has been mixed. *Washington Post* columnist Robert Novak, fearing a tumultuous political climax in the United States Congress had the recounts gone forward, praised "the bare majority of the high court" for sav[ing] "the country from th[e] potential constitutional crisis resulting from Gore's doggedness." Columnist Charles Krauthammer agreed: "Political tension would only have grown—this would not have been resolved until January!—and created a train wreck. The majority of the court wisely declined this reckless invitation to a true constitutional crisis."

On the other side, author and columnist E. J. Dionne wrote: "The most troublesome aspect here is *not* that the five most conservative appointees on the court ruled in favor of the Republican presidential candidate. It is that the same five chose to intrude in Florida's election process having always claimed to be champions of the rights of states and foes of 'judicial activism' and 'judicial overreach.'" Five hundred fifty-four law professors signed on to a full-page newspaper ad declaiming in boldface: "It Is Not the Job of a Federal Court to Stop Votes from Being Counted." And the *New York Times* reporter whose beat is the U.S. Supreme Court, Linda Greenhouse, observed: "[T]hese are justices who are accustomed to both bitter division—often by the same 5-to-4 alignment—and to moving on to the next case. But there is something different about *Bush v. Gore* that raises the question about whether moving on will be quite so easy. This was something more than a dispute rooted in judicial philosophy. . . . [H]ad members of the majority been true to their judicial philosophy, the opinion would have come out differently."

Additional analysis, commentary, even counting are in the works, and I shall leave the flowing streams of words saved on PCs to the books and articles certain to appear. It may be fitting, however, to close my account of *Bush v. Gore* with this parting observation. In the weeks before the Court decided to hear the case, the editorial pages of major newspapers (though far from unanimous) contained abundant commentary urging the Court to end the election controversy with a swift and final resolution. A national crisis was looming, this commentary maintained, and only the Supreme Court could avert it. The popular conservative columnist William Safire, an unlikely proponent of judicial intervention, wrote: "The Supreme Court (whose unanimous ruling against Nixon on the tapes led to his resignation) [can] put its imprimatur on the best way to decide who shall occupy the presidency. And the vast majority of Americans would readily accept the decision." Less acceptable, perhaps, was the judicial solution proposed in a cartoon handed to me at a reception. It said: "I think they should let Ruth Bader Ginsburg flip a coin."

Coin flipping aside, these sentiments reflect, it seems to me, long and widely held trust in the fairness and reasoned decision making of the U.S. federal judiciary. That trust is attributable not only to the fact that the United States Constitution, for well over two hundred years, has been understood to arm federal courts with authority definitively to declare the law, even in turbulent controversies involving the nation's fundamental law. It is also a product of decision-making mores to which legions of federal judges adhere: restraint, economy, prudence, respect for other agencies of decision (an element elaborated on by Professor Dyzenhaus in his lecture), reasoned judgment, and, above all, fidelity to law. Whatever final judgment awaits *Bush v. Gore* in the annals of history, I am certain that the good work and good faith of the U.S. federal judiciary as a whole will continue to sustain public confidence at a level never beyond repair. ■

Bioethicist Leon Kass Warns against the "Brave New World" of Cloning

"In this age in which everything is held to be permissible so long as it is freely done, repugnance may be the only voice left that speaks up to defend the central core of our humanity. Shallow are the souls that have forgotten how to shudder."

A PHYSICIAN AND MOLECULAR BIOCHEMIST who studied and later taught at the University of Chicago, Dr. Kass turned from the practice of scientific research to the study of the ethics of the potential product of that research. In the early 1970s, as one of the founders of the Hastings Center in New York, he became a leader in the newly named field of bioethics, and the scholarly scientist and classicist stepped into the center of the most profound controversies. Though many scientists strongly believe his questioning of ends stands in the way of pursuing worthy means like the cure of diseases, other scientists and philosophers share his concerns about eugenics and the manipulation of moods and minds.

In 2001, the culturally conservative Kass was appointed by George W. Bush to head the President's Council on Bioethics, a diverse group that helped find a compromise about one of those controversies: the use of embryonic stem cells in research. In subsequent reports, the Bioethics Council went "beyond therapy" to examine the moral implications of progress toward age retardation and the artificial enhancement of the human body and brain.

One field that troubles most scientists is the cloning of human beings— to produce a genetically identical duplicate. On May 17, 2001, at a meeting about the legal, social, and ethical implications of human genetics at the University of Chicago, Dr. Kass took on this subject.

The address presented the problem with a stark medical metaphor: "Human nature itself lies on the operating table. . . ." In a staccato paragraph using sentence fragments, Kass lists some the "transforming powers" already upon us. This leads to his evocation of the 1932 novel by

Aldous Huxley, *Brave New World* (the title from Shakespeare's *The Tempest*: "O brave new world, that has such people in't!"). More directly than *1984*, the 1949 work of fiction by George Orwell, Huxley's sociopolitical novel deals with the dehumanizing danger of the chemical and biological manipulation of the human species.

In sounding the tocsin about this threat of a "posthuman world," Kass disarms his audience with lines like "I exaggerate somewhat, but in the direction of the truth" and "This afternoon I want to begin to persuade you. . . ." Self-questioning keeps the flow going: "What to think about this prospect? Nothing good." He then lists four objections to human cloning and examines them seriatim, a device that helps the listener follow his points (Four is about the limit—ten points is a nice round number for religious commandments and bills of rights, but in rhetorical arguments, more than four signals to the audience an interminable speech ahead.) By concluding with a specific legislative remedy and a call for "shifting the paradigm around," the ethicist places the burden of justifying exciting scientific gains on those unwilling to recognize the danger of a loss in being human.

□   □   □

The urgency of the great political struggles of the twentieth century, successfully waged against totalitarianisms first right and then left, seems to have blinded many people to a deeper truth about the present age: All contemporary societies are traveling briskly in the same utopian direction. All march eagerly to the drums of technological progress and fly proudly the banner of modern science; all sing loudly the Baconian anthem, "Conquer nature, relieve man's estate." Leading the triumphal procession is modern medicine, becoming daily ever more powerful in its battle against disease, decay, and death, thanks especially to the astonishing achievements in biomedical science and technology—achievements for which we must surely be grateful.

Yet contemplating present and projected advances in genetic and reproductive technologies, in neuroscience and psychopharmacology, and in the development of artificial organs and computer-chip implants for human brains, we now clearly recognize new uses for biotechnical power that soar beyond the traditional medical goals of healing disease and relieving suffering. Human nature itself lies on the operating table, ready for alteration, eugenic and psychic "enhancement," and wholesale redesign.

Some transforming powers are already here. The pill. In vitro fertilization. Bottled embryos. Surrogate wombs. Cloning. Genetic screening. Genetic manipulation. Organ harvests. Mechanical spare parts. Chimeras. Brain implants. Ritalin for the young, Viagra for the old, and Prozac for everyone.

Years ago Aldous Huxley saw it coming. In his charming but disturbing novel, *Brave New World*, he made its meaning strikingly visible for all to see. Huxley paints human life seven centuries hence, living under the gentle hand of a humanitarianism that has been rendered fully competent by genetic manipulation, psychopharmacology, hypnopaedia, and high-tech amusements. At long last, mankind has succeeded in eliminating disease, aggression, war, anxiety, suffering, guilt, envy, and grief. But this victory comes at the heavy price of homogenization, mediocrity, pacification, trivial pursuits, shallow attachments, debasement of tastes, spurious contentment, and souls without loves or longings. The Brave New World has achieved health, prosperity, community, stability, and nigh-universal contentment, only to be peopled by creatures of human shape but of stunted humanity. They consume, fornicate, take "soma," enjoy "centrifugal bumble-puppy," and operate the machinery that makes it all possible. They do not read, write, think, love, or govern themselves. Art and science, virtue and religion, family and friendship are all passé. What matters most is bodily health and immediate gratification. Babies and blessings both come out of bottles. Brave new man is so dehumanized that he does not even recognize what has been lost.

Huxley's novel is, of course, science fiction. Prozac is not yet Huxley's soma; cloning by nuclear transfer or splitting embryos is not exactly bokanovskification; MTV and virtual-reality parlors are not quite the "feelies"; and our current safe-and-consequenceless sexual practices are not universally as loveless or as empty as in the novel. But the kinships are disquieting. Indeed, the cultural changes technology has already wrought among us should make us even more worried than Huxley would have us be.

In Huxley's novel, everything proceeds under the direction of an omnipotent—albeit benevolent—world state. But the dehumanization he portrays does not really require despotism. To the contrary, precisely because the society of the future will deliver exactly what we most want—health, safety, comfort, plenty, pleasure, peace of mind, and length of days—mankind can reach the same humanly debased condition solely on the basis of free human choice. No need for World Controllers. Just give us the technological imperative, liberal democratic society, compassionate humanitarianism, moral pluralism, and free markets, and we can take ourselves to Brave New World all by ourselves—

and, what is most distressing, without even deliberately deciding to go. In case you hadn't noticed, the train has left the station and is gathering speed, but no one seems to be in charge.

Not the least of our difficulties in trying to exercise control over where biology is taking us is the fact that we do not get to decide, once and for all, for or against the destination of a posthuman world. The scientific discoveries and technical powers that will take us there come to us piecemeal, one at a time and seemingly independent from one another, each often attractively introduced as a measure that will "help us not to be sick." But sometimes we come to a clear fork in the road where decision is possible and where we know that the decision we make will make a world of difference, indeed, will make a permanently different world.

We stand now at the point of such a momentous decision. Events have conspired to provide us with a perfect opportunity to seize the initiative and to gain some control of the biotechnical project. I refer to the prospect of human cloning, a practice absolutely central to Huxley's fictional world. Indeed, creating and manipulating life in the laboratory is the gateway to the Brave New World, not only in fiction but also in fact.

"To clone or not to clone a human being" is no longer a fanciful question. Success in cloning first sheep, then also cows, mice, pigs, and goats, make it perfectly clear that a fateful decision is now at hand: whether we should welcome or even tolerate the cloning of human beings.

Human cloning, though partly continuous with previous reproductive technologies, is also something radically new, both in itself and in its easily foreseeable consequences—especially when coupled to powers for genetic "enhancement" and germ-line genetic modification visible on the horizon. I exaggerate somewhat, but in the direction of the truth: we are compelled to decide nothing less than whether human procreation is going to remain human, whether children are going to be *made-to-order* rather than begotten, and whether we wish to say yes in principle to the road that leads to the dehumanized hell of Brave New World.

This afternoon I want to begin to persuade you, first, that cloning is a serious evil, both in itself and in what it leads to; and second, that we ought to try to stop it by legislative prohibition. My motives are twofold. First, I am quite serious about trying to do something to prevent human cloning itself. Second, I care about getting our hands on the wheel of the runaway train now headed for a posthuman world, and I doubt that we will ever get a better chance.

What is cloning? Cloning, or asexual reproduction, is the production of individuals who are genetically identical to an already existing individual. Here's how it's done: Take a mature but unfertilized egg; remove its nucleus; replace it with a nucleus obtained from a specialized cell of an adult organism; after a few cell divisions, transfer the cloned embryo to a prepared uterus for pregnancy and delivery. Since almost all the hereditary material of a cell is contained within its nucleus, the renucleated egg and the individual into which it develops are genetically identical to the organism that was the source of the transferred nucleus. An unlimited number of genetically identical individuals—a clone—could be produced by nuclear transfer. Any person, male or female, newborn or adult, could be cloned, and in any quantity. Because stored cells can outlive their sources, one may even clone the dead.

Some possible misconceptions need to be avoided. First, cloning is not xeroxing: the clone of Bill Clinton, though his genetic double, would enter the world hairless, toothless, and peeing in his diapers, like any other human infant. But neither is cloning just like natural twinning: the cloned twin will be identical to an older, existing adult; it will arise not by chance but by deliberate design; and the entire genetic makeup will be preselected by the parents and/or scientists. Further, the success rate, at least at first, will probably not be very high. For this reason among others, it is unlikely that, at least for now, the practice would be very popular, and there is no immediate worry of mass-scale production of multicopies. Still, for the tens of thousands of people who sustain over three hundred assisted-reproduction clinics in the United States and already avail themselves of in vitro fertilization and other techniques, cloning would be an option with virtually no added fuss. Should commercial interests develop in "nucleus banking," as they have in sperm banking and egg harvesting; should famous athletes or other celebrities decide to market their DNA the way they now market their autographs and nearly everything else; should techniques of embryo and germ-line genetic testing and manipulation arrive as anticipated, increasing the use of laboratory assistance in order to obtain "better" babies—then cloning, if permitted, could become more than a marginal practice simply on the basis of free reproductive choice.

What to think about this prospect? Nothing good. Indeed, most people are repelled by nearly all aspects of human cloning: the possibility of mass production of human beings, with large clones of look-alikes, compromised in their individuality; the idea of father-son or mother-daughter twins; the bizarre prospect of a woman bearing and rearing a genetic copy of herself, her spouse, or even her deceased father or mother; the grotesqueness of conceiving a child as an exact replacement for another who has died; the utilitarian creation of embryonic duplicates of oneself, to be frozen away or created when needed to provide homologous tissues or organs for transplantation; the narcissism of those who would clone themselves and the arrogance of others who think they know who deserves to be cloned; the Frankensteinian hubris to create human life and increasingly to control its destiny; men playing at being God. Almost no one finds any of the suggested reasons for human cloning compelling; almost everyone anticipates its possible misuses and abuses. Moreover, the belief that human cloning cannot be prevented makes the prospect all the more revolting.

Revulsion is not an argument; and some of yesterday's repugnances are today calmly accepted—though, one must add, not always for the better. In crucial cases, however, repugnance is the emotional expression of deep wisdom, beyond reason's power fully to articulate it. Can anyone really give an argument fully adequate to the horror which is father-daughter incest (even with consent), or having sex with animals, or mutilating a corpse, or eating human flesh, or raping or murdering another human being?

Let me suggest that our repugnance at human cloning belongs in that category. We are repelled by the prospect of cloning human beings not because of the strangeness or novelty of the undertaking, but because we intuit and feel, immediately and without argument, the violation of things that we rightfully hold dear. We sense that cloning represents a profound defilement of our given nature as procreating beings and of the social relations built on this natural ground. In addition, we sense that cloning is a radical form of child abuse. In this age in which everything is held to be permissible so long as it is freely done, repugnance may be the only voice left that speaks up to defend the central core of our humanity. Shallow are the souls that have forgotten how to shudder.

Yet repugnance need not stand naked before the bar of reason. The wisdom of our horror at human cloning *can* be partially articulated. I offer four objections to human cloning: (1) it involves unethical experimentation; (2) it threatens identity and individuality; (3) it turns procreation into manufacture; and (4) it means despotism over children and perversion of parenthood.

First, any attempt to clone a human being would constitute an unethical experiment upon the resulting child-to-be. In all the animal experiments, fewer than 2–3 percent of cloning attempts succeed. Not only are there fetal deaths and stillborn infants, but there is also a high incidence of late-appearing disabilities and deformities in cloned animals that attain live birth. Nearly all scientists agree that attempts to clone a human being carry grave risks of producing unhealthy and disabled children. Considered opinion (even among scientists) is virtually unanimous:

attempts at human cloning are irresponsible and unethical. We cannot ethically even get to know whether or not human cloning is feasible.

Second, cloning, if successful, would create serious issues of identity and individuality. The clone may experience concerns about his distinctive identity not only because he will be in genotype and appearance identical to another human being, but, in this case, because he may also be twin to the person who is his "father" or "mother"—if one can still call them that. What would be the psychic burdens of being the "child" or "parent" of your twin? In the mistakenly-regarded-as-innocent case of intrafamilial cloning, what will happen when the adolescent clone of Mommy becomes the spitting image of the woman Daddy once fell in love with? In case of divorce, will Mommy still love the clone of Daddy, even though she can no longer stand the sight of Daddy himself? In addition, unlike "normal" identical twins, a cloned individual will be saddled with a genotype that has already lived. He will not be fully a surprise to the world: people are likely always to compare his performances in life with that of his alter ego, especially if he is a clone of someone gifted or famous. True, his nurture and circumstance will be different; genotype is not exactly destiny. But one must also expect parental efforts to shape this new life after the original— or at least to view the child with the original version always firmly in mind. For why else did they clone from the star basketball player, mathematician, and beauty queen—or even dear old Dad—in the first place?

Third, human cloning would represent a giant step toward turning begetting into making, procreation into manufacture (literally, something "handmade"), a process already begun with in vitro fertilization and genetic testing of embryos. With cloning, not only is the process in hand, but the total genetic blueprint of the cloned individual is selected and determined by the human artisans. To be sure, subsequent development is still according to natural processes; and the resulting children will be recognizably human. But we here would be taking a major step into making man himself simply another one of the man-made things.

How does begetting differ from making? In natural procreation, human beings come together, complementarily male and female, to give existence to another being who is formed, exactly as we were, by what we are—living, hence perishable, hence aspiringly erotic, hence procreative human beings. But in clonal reproduction, and in the more advanced forms of manufacture to which it will lead, we give existence to a being not by what we are but by *what we intend and design*. As with any product of our making, no matter how excellent, the artificer stands above it, not as an equal but as a superior, transcending it by his will and creative prowess. In human cloning, scientists and prospective "parents" adopt a technocratic attitude toward human children: human children become their artifacts. Such an arrangement is profoundly dehumanizing, no matter how good the product.

Finally, the practice of human cloning by nuclear transfer—like other anticipated forms of genetically engineering the next generation—would enshrine and aggravate a profound and mischief-making misunderstanding of the meaning of having children and of the parent-child relationship. When a couple normally chooses to procreate, the partners are saying yes to the emergence of new life in its novelty, are saying yes not only to having a child but also to having *whatever child this child* turns out to be. In accepting our finitude and opening ourselves to our replacement, we tacitly confess the limits of our control. Embracing the future by procreating means precisely that we are relinquishing our grip, in the very activity of taking up our own share in what we hope will be the immortality of human life and the human species. Thus, our children are not *our* children: They are not our property, they are not our possessions. Neither are they supposed to live our lives for us, nor anyone else's life but their own. Their genetic distinctiveness and independence are the natural foreshadowing of the deep truth that they have their own and never-before-enacted life to live. Though sprung from a past, they take an uncharted course into the future.

Much mischief is already done by parents who try to live vicariously through their children. Children are sometimes compelled to fulfill the broken dreams of unhappy parents. But whereas most parents normally have hopes for their children, cloning parents will have *expectations*. In cloning, such overbearing parents will have taken at the start a decisive step that contradicts the entire meaning of the open and forward-looking nature of parent-child relations. The child is given a genotype that has already lived, with full expectation that this blueprint of a past life ought to be controlling of the life that is to come. A wanted child now means a child who exists precisely to fulfill parental wants. Like all the more precise eugenic manipulations that will follow in its wake, cloning is thus inherently despotic, for it seeks to make one's children after one's own image (or an image of one's choosing) and their future according to one's will. . . .

Whether or not they share my reasons, most people share my conclusion: Human cloning is unethical in itself and dangerous in its likely consequences, including the precedent it will establish for designing our children. For us the real questions are: What should we do about it? How best to succeed? What we should do is to work to prevent human cloning by making it illegal. We should aim for an international legal ban if possible and for a unilateral national ban at a minimum—and soon, before the fact is upon us. To be sure, renegade scientists may secretly undertake to violate such a law, but we can deter them by criminal sanctions and monetary penalties, as well as by removing any incentives to proudly claim credit for their technological bravado and success. Such a ban on clonal baby making, moreover, will not harm the progress of basic genetic science and technology. On the contrary, it will reassure the public that scientists are happy to proceed without violating the deep ethical norms of the human community. And it will protect worthy science against a public backlash triggered by the brazen misconduct of the rogues.

I appreciate that a federal legislative ban is without American precedent, at least in matters technological (though the British and many other European nations have banned cloning of human beings, and we ourselves ban incest, polygamy, and other forms of "reproductive freedom"). Perhaps such a ban will prove ineffective; perhaps it will eventually be shown to have been a mistake. But—and this is maybe the most important result—it would at least place the burden of practical proof where it belongs, requiring proponents to show very clearly what great social or medical good can be had only by the cloning of human beings. Only for such a compelling case, yet to be made or even imagined, should we wish to risk this major departure in human procreation.

We Americans have lived by and prospered under a rosy optimism about scientific and technological progress. The technological imperative has, on balance, probably served us well, though we should admit that there is no accurate method for weighing benefits and harms. But there is very good reason for shifting the paradigm around, at least regarding those technological interventions into the human body and mind that will surely effect fundamental (and likely irreversible) changes in human nature, basic human relationships, and what it means to be a human being. Here we surely should not be willing to risk everything in the naïve hope that, should things go wrong, we can later set them right again.

The present danger posed by human cloning is, paradoxically, also a golden opportunity. In a truly unprecedented way, we can strike a blow for the human control of the technological project, for wisdom, prudence, and human dignity. The prospect of human cloning, so repulsive to contemplate, is the occasion for deciding whether we shall be slaves of unregulated innovation, and ultimately its artifacts, or whether we shall remain free human beings who guide our technique toward the enhancement of human dignity. The humanity of the human future is in our hands.

■ ■ ■

X

SPEECHES OF SOCIAL RESPONSIBILITY

British Statesman William Pitt the Younger Urges Abolition of the Slave Trade

"How shall we hope to obtain . . . forgiveness from heaven for those enormous evils we have committed . . . ?"

HE WAS KNOWN AS PITT THE YOUNGER for good reason: the second son of William Pitt was made prime minister of England at the age of twenty-three by George III in 1783, and he held that position until his resignation in 1801.

Pitt the Younger—then middle-aged—was recalled as prime minister three years later, when Napoleon loomed as a serious threat to England. After Nelson's victory at Trafalgar, Pitt was toasted on November 9, 1805, as "the savior of Europe," and his three-line reply ranks among the best examples of the modest response: "I return you many thanks for the honor you have done me. But Europe is not to be saved by any single man. England has saved herself by her exertions, and will, as I trust, save Europe by her example." A month later, Napoleon achieved his major victory at Austerlitz against England's allies, and the shock of that news caused Pitt's rapid decline; he died in early 1806, at the age of forty-six.

At the height of his rhetorical power, however, Pitt addressed the House of Commons at a late hour on April 2, 1792, on a controversial resolution: "That it is the opinion of this committee that the trade carried on by British subjects, for the purpose of obtaining slaves on the coast of Africa, ought to be abolished."

Pitt's speech in favor of the resolution relies on arguments of morality and British history. Through a series of rhetorical questions and parallel structures ("If then we feel . . . if we view . . . if we shudder"), Pitt argues "the most pressing and indispensable duty." The amended motion on abolishing slavery was carried, 230 to 85.

□   □   □

At this hour of the morning I am afraid, sir, I am too much exhausted to enter so fully into the subject before the committee as I could wish; but if my bodily strength is in any degree equal to the task, I feel so strongly the magnitude of this question that I am extremely earnest to deliver my sentiments, which I rise to do with the more satisfaction; because I now look forward to the issue of this business with considerable hopes of success.

The debate has this day taken a turn, which, though it has produced a variety of new suggestions, has, upon the whole, contracted this question into a much narrower point than it was ever brought into before.

I cannot say that I quite agree with the right honorable gentleman over the way; I am far from deploring all that has been said by my two honorable friends. I rather rejoice that they have now brought this subject to a fair issue, that something, at least, is already gained, and that the question has taken altogether a new course this night. It is true, a difference of opinion has been stated and has been urged with all the force of argument that could be given to it.

But give me leave to say that this difference has been urged upon principles very far removed from those which were maintained by the opponents of my honorable friend when he first brought forward his motion. There are very few of those who have spoken this night who have not thought it their duty to declare their full and entire concurrence with my honorable friend in promoting the abolition of the slave trade, as their ultimate object. However we may differ as to the time and manner of it, we are agreed in the abolition itself; and my honorable friends have expressed their agreement in this sentiment with that sensibility upon the subject which humanity does most undoubtedly require. I do not, however, think they yet perceive what are the necessary consequences of their own concession, or follow up their own principles to their just conclusion.

The point now in dispute between us is a difference merely as to the period of time at which the abolition of the slave trade ought to take place. I therefore congratulate this House, the country, and the world that this great point is gained; that we may now consider this trade as having received its condemnation; that its sentence is sealed; that this curse of mankind is seen by the House in its true light; and that the greatest stigma on our national character which ever yet existed is about to be removed! And, sir, (which is still more important) that mankind, I trust, in general, are now likely to be delivered from the greatest practical evil that ever has afflicted the human race—from the severest and most extensive calamity recorded in the history of the world!

In proceeding to give my reasons for concurring with my honorable friend in his motion, I shall necessarily advert to those topics which my honorable friends near me have touched upon, and which they stated to be their motives for preferring a gradual and, in some degree, a distant abolition of the slave trade to the more immediate and direct measure now proposed to you. Beginning, as I do, with declaring that in this respect I differ completely from my right honorable friends near me, I do not, however, mean to say that I differ as to one observation which has been pressed rather strongly by them. If they can show that their proposition of a gradual abolition is more likely than ours to secure the object which we have in view—that by proceeding gradually we shall arrive more speedily at our end, and attain it with more certainty, than by a direct vote immediately to abolish—if they can show to the satisfaction both of myself and the committee that our proposition has more the appearance of a speedy abolition than the reality of it, undoubtedly they will in this case make a convert of me and my honorable friend who moved the question; they will make a convert of every man among us who looks to this, which I trust we all do, as a question not to be determined by theoretical principles or enthusiastic feelings, but considers the practicability of the measure—aiming simply to effect his object in the shortest time, and in the surest possible manner.

If, however, I shall be able to show that our measure proceeds more directly to its object, and secures it with more certainty and within a less distant period, and that the slave trade will on our plan be abolished sooner than on his, may I not then hope that my right honorable friends will be as ready to adopt our proposition as we should in the other case be willing to accede to theirs?

One of my right honorable friends has stated that an act passed here for the abolition of the slave trade would not secure its abolition. Now, sir, I should be glad to know why an act of the British legislature, enforced by all those sanctions which we have undoubtedly the power and the right to apply, is not to be effectual: at least, as to every material purpose? Will not the executive power have the same appointment of the officers and the courts of judicature, by which all the causes relating to this subject must be tried, that it has in other cases? Will there not be the same system of law by which we now maintain a monopoly of commerce? If the same law, sir, be applied to the prohibition of the slave trade, which is applied in the case of other contraband commerce, with all the same means of the country to back it, I am at a loss to know why the actual and total abolition is not likely to be effected in this way, as by any plan or project of my honorable friends for bringing about a gradual termination of it. But my observation is extremely fortified by what fell from my honorable friend who spoke last: he has told you, sir, that if you will have patience with it for a few years, the slave trade must drop of itself, from the increasing dearness of the commodity imported, and the increasing progress, on the other hand, of internal population. Is it true, then, that the importations are so expensive and disadvantageous already that the internal population is even now becoming a cheaper resource? I ask, then, if you leave to the importer no means of importation but by smuggling, and if, besides all the present disadvantages, you load him with all the charges and hazards of the smuggler, by taking care that the laws against smuggling are in this case watchfully and rigorously enforced, is there any danger of any considerable supply of fresh slaves being poured into the islands through this channel? And is there any real ground of fear, because a few slaves may have been smuggled in or out of the islands, that a bill will be useless and ineffectual on any such ground? The question under these circumstances will not bear a dispute.

Perhaps, however, my honorable friends may take up another ground and say, "It is true your measure would shut out further importations more immediately; but we do not mean to shut them out immediately. We think it right, on grounds of general expediency, that they should not be immediately shut out." Let us therefore now come to this question of the expediency of making the abolition distant and gradual, rather than immediate.

The argument of expediency, in my opinion, like every other argument in this disquisition, will not justify the continuance of the slave trade for one unnecessary hour. Supposing it to be in our power (which I have shown it is) to enforce the prohibition from this present time, the expediency of doing it is to me so clear that if I went on this principle alone, I should not feel a moment's hesitation. . . .

Having now done with this question of expediency as affecting the islands, I come next to a proposition advanced by my right honorable friend which appeared to intimate that, on account of some patrimonial rights of the West Indians, the prohibition of the slave trade might be considered as an invasion on their legal inheritance.

Now, in answer to this proposition, I must make two or three remarks, which I think my right honorable friend will find some considerable difficulty in answering. First, I observe that his argument, if it be worth anything, applies just as much to gradual as immediate abolition. I have no doubt, that at whatever period he should be disposed to say the abolition should actually take place, this defense will equally be set up; for it certainly is just as good an argument against an abolition seven or seventy years hence as against an abolition at this moment. It supposes we have no right whatever to stop the importations; and even though the disadvantage to our plantations, which some gentlemen suppose to attend the measure of immediate abolition, should be admitted gradually to lessen by the lapse of a few years, yet in point of principle the absence of all right of interference would remain the same. My right honorable friend, therefore, I am sure will not press an argument not less hostile to his proposition than to ours. But let us investigate the foundation of this objection, and I will commence what I have to say, by putting a question to my right honorable friend. It is chiefly on the presumed ground of our being bound by a parliamentary sanction heretofore given to the African slave trade that this argument against the abolition is rested.

Does, then, my right honorable friend, or does any man in this House, think that the slave trade has received any such parliamentary sanction as must place it more out of the jurisdiction of the legislature forever after than the other branches of our national commerce? I ask, is there any one regulation of any part of our commerce which, if this argument be valid, may not equally be objected to, on the ground of its affecting some man's patrimony, some man's property, or some man's expectations? Let it never be forgotten that the argument I am canvassing would be just as strong if the possession affected were small and the possessors humble; for on every principle of justice, the property of any single individual, or small number of individuals, is as sacred as that of the great body of West Indians.

Justice ought to extend her protection with rigid impartiality to the rich and to the poor, to the powerful and to the humble. If this be the case, in what a situation does my right honorable friend's argument place the legislature of Britain? What room is left for their interference in the regulation of any part of our commerce? It is scarcely possible to lay a duty on any one article, which may not, when first imposed, be said in some way to affect the property of individuals, and even of some entire classes of the community. If the laws respecting the slave trade imply a contract for its perpetual continuance, I will venture to say, there does not pass a year without some act, equally pledging the faith of Parliament to the perpetuating of some other branch of commerce. In short, I repeat my observation that no new tax can be imposed, much less can any prohibitory duty be ever laid on any branch of trade that has before been regulated by Parliament, if this principle be once admitted. . . .

But, sir, let us see what was the motive for carrying on the trade at all? The preamble of the act states it—"Whereas the trade to and from Africa is very advantageous to Great Britain, and necessary for the supplying the plantations and colonies thereunto belonging with a sufficient number of Negroes at reasonable rates, and for that purpose the said trade should be carried on," etc. Here, then, we see what the Parliament had in view when it passed this act; and I have clearly shown that not one of the occasions on which it grounded its proceedings now exists. I may then plead, I think, the very act itself as an argument for the abolition. If it is shown that, instead of being "very advantageous" to Great Britain, this trade is the most destructive that can well be imagined to her interest; that it is the ruin of our seamen; that it stops the extension of our manufacturers; if it is proved in the second place that it is not now necessary for the "supplying our plantations with Negroes"; if it is further established that this traffic was from the very beginning contrary to the first principles of justice, and consequently that a pledge for its continuance, had one been attempted to have been given, must have been completely and absolutely void; where, then, in this act of Parliament is the contract to be found by which Britain is bound, as she is said to be, never to listen to her own true interests, and to the cries of the natives of Africa? Is it not clear that all argument, founded on the supposed pledged faith of Parliament, makes against those who employ it? I refer you to the principles which obtain in other cases. Every trade act shows undoubtedly that the legislature is used to pay a tender regard to all classes of the community. But if for the sake of moral duty, or national honor, or even of great political advantage, it is thought right, by authority of Parliament, to alter any long-established system, Parliament is competent to do it. The legislature will undoubtedly be careful to subject individuals to as little inconvenience as possible; and if any peculiar hardship should arise that can be distinctly stated, and fairly pleaded, there will ever, I am sure, be a liberal feeling towards them in the legislature of this country, which is the guardian of all who live under its protection. On the present occasion, the most powerful considerations call upon us to abolish the slave trade; and if we refuse to attend to them on the alleged ground of pledged faith and contract, we shall depart as widely from the practice of Parliament as from the path of moral duty. If indeed there is any case of hardship which comes within the proper cognizance of Parliament, and calls for the exercise of its liberality—well! But such a case must be reserved for calm consideration, as a matter distinct from the present question.

I beg pardon for dwelling so long on the argument of expediency, and on the manner in which it affects the West Indies. I have been carried away by my own feelings on some of these points into a greater length than I intended, especially considering how fully the subject has been already argued. The result of all I have said is that there exists no impediment, no obstacle, no shadow of reasonable objection on the ground of pledged faith, or even on that of national expediency, to the abolition of this trade. On the contrary, all the arguments drawn from those sources pleaded for it; and they plead much more loudly, and much more strongly in every part of the question, for an immediate than for a gradual abolition.

But now, sir, I come to Africa. That is the ground on which I rest, and here it is that I say my right honorable friends do not carry their principles to their full extent. Why ought the slave trade to be abolished? Because it is incurable injustice. How much stronger, then, is the argument for immediate than gradual abolition? By allowing it to continue even for one hour, do not my right honorable friends weaken—do not they desert—their own argument of its injustice? If on the ground of injustice it ought to be abolished at last, why ought it not now? Why is injustice to be suffered to remain for a single hour? From what I hear without doors, it is evident that there is a general conviction entertained of its being far from just; and from that very conviction of its injustice, some men have been led, I fear, to the supposition that the slave trade never could have been permitted to begin but from some strong and irresistible necessity—a necessity, however, which, if it was fancied to exist at first, I have shown cannot be thought by any man whatever to exist now. This plea of necessity, thus presumed, and presumed, as I suspect, from the circumstance of injustice itself, has caused a sort of acquiescence in the continuance of this evil. Men have been led to place it among the rank of those necessary evils which were supposed to be the lot of human creatures, and to be permitted to fall upon some countries or individuals, rather than upon others, by that being whose ways are inscrutable to us, and whose dispensations, it is conceived, we ought not to look into.

The origin of evil is indeed a subject beyond the reach of human understandings; and the permission of it by the Supreme Being is a subject into which it belongs not to us to enquire. But where the evil in question is a moral evil which a man can scrutinize, and where that moral evil has its origin with ourselves, let us not imagine that we can clear our consciences by this general, not to say irreligious and impious, way of laying aside the question. If we reflect at all on this subject, we must see that every necessary evil supposes that some other and greater evil would be incurred were it removed; I therefore desire to ask, what can be that greater evil, which can be stated to overbalance the one in question?—I know of no evil that ever has existed, nor can imagine any evil to exist, worse than the tearing of seventy or eighty thousand persons annually from their native land, by a combination of the most civilized nations, inhabiting the most enlightened part of the globe, but more especially under the sanction of the laws of that nation which calls herself the most free and the most happy of them all. Even if these miserable beings were proved guilty of every crime before you take them off (of which however not a single proof is adduced), ought we to take upon ourselves the office of executioners? And even if we condescend so far, still can we be justified in taking them, unless we have clear proof that they are criminals?

But if we go much farther—if we ourselves tempt them to sell their fellow creatures to us, we may rest assured that they will take care to provide by every method, by kidnapping, by village breaking, by unjust wars, by iniquitous condemnations, by rendering Africa a scene of bloodshed and misery, a supply of victims increasing in proportion to our demand. Can we then hesitate in deciding whether the wars in Africa are their wars or ours? It was our arms in the river Cameroon put into the hands of the trader that furnished him with the means of pushing his trade; and I have no more doubt that they are British arms, put into the hands of Africans, which promote universal war and desolation, than I can doubt their having done so in that individual instance.

I have shown how great is the enormity of this evil, even on the supposition that we take only convicts and prisoners of war. But take the subject in the other way; take it on the grounds stated by the right honorable gentlemen over the way; and how does it stand? Think of *eighty thousand* persons carried away out of their country by we know not what means! for crimes imputed! for light or inconsiderable faults! for debt perhaps! for the crime of witchcraft! or a thousand other weak and scandalous pretexts! besides all the fraud and kidnapping, the villainies and perfidy, by which the slave trade is supplied. Reflect on these eighty thousand persons thus annually taken off! There is something in the horror of it that surpasses all the bounds of imagination. Admitting that there exists in Africa something like to courts of justice; yet what an office of humiliation and meanness is it in us to take upon ourselves to carry into execution the partial, the cruel, iniquitous sentences of such courts, as if we also were strangers to all religion, and to the first principles of justice! But that country, it is said, has been in some degree civilized, and civilized by us. It is said they have gained some knowledge of the principles of justice. What, sir, have they gained principles of justice from us? Their civilization brought about by us!

Yes, we give them enough of our intercourse to convey to them the means, and to initiate them in the study of mutual destruction. We give them just enough of the forms of justice to enable them to add the pretext of legal trials to their other modes of perpetrating the most atrocious iniquity. We give them just enough of European improvements to enable them the more effectually to turn Africa into a ravaged wilderness. Some evidences say that the Africans are addicted to the practice of gambling, that they even sell their wives and children, and ultimately themselves. Are these then the legitimate sources of slavery? Shall we pretend that we can thus acquire an honest right to exact the labor of these people? Can we pretend that we have a right to carry away to distant regions men of whom we know nothing by authentic enquiry, and of whom there is every reasonable presumption to think that those who sell them to us have no right to do so? But the evil does not stop here. I feel that there is not time for me to make all the remarks which the subject deserves, and I refrain from attempting to enumerate half the dreadful consequences of this system. Do you think nothing of the ruin and the miseries in which so many other individuals, still remaining in Africa, are involved in consequence of carrying off so many myriads of people? Do you think nothing of their families which are left behind? Of the connections which are broken? Of the friendships, attachments, and relationships that are burst asunder? Do you think nothing of the miseries in consequence that are felt from generation to generation? Of the privation of that happiness which might be communicated to them by the introduction of civilization, and of mental and moral improvement? A happiness which you withhold from them so long as you permit the slave trade to continue. What do you yet know of the internal state of Africa? You have carried on a trade to that quarter of the globe from this civilized and enlightened country; but such a trade that, instead of diffusing either knowledge or wealth, it has been the check to every laudable pursuit. Instead of any fair interchange of commodities; instead of conveying to them, from this highly favored land, any means of improvement, you carry with you that noxious plant by which everything is withered and blasted, under whose shade nothing that is useful or profitable to Africa will ever flourish or take root. Long as that continent has been known to navigators, the extreme line and boundaries of its coasts is all with which Europe is yet become acquainted; while other countries in the same parallel of latitude, through a happier system of intercourse, have reaped the blessings of a mutually beneficial commerce. But as to the whole interior of that continent you are, by your own principles of commerce, as yet entirely shut out: Africa is known to you only in its skirts. Yet even there you are able to infuse a poison that spreads its contagious effects from one end of it to the other, which penetrates to its very center, corrupting every part to which it reaches. You there subvert the whole order of nature; you aggravate every natural barbarity, and furnish to every man living on that continent motives for committing, under the name and pretext of commerce, acts of perpetual violence and perfidy against his neighbor.

Thus, sir, has the perversion of British commerce carried misery instead of happiness to one whole quarter of the globe. False to the very principles of trade, misguided in our policy, and unmindful of our duty, what astonishing—I had almost said, what *irreparable*—mischief have we brought upon that continent? I would apply this thought to the present question. How shall we ever repair this mischief? How shall we hope to obtain, if it be possible, forgiveness from heaven for those enormous evils we have committed, if we refuse to make use of those means which the mercy of Providence hath still reserved to us for wiping away the guilt and shame with which we are now covered? If we refuse even this degree of compensation, if, knowing the miseries we have caused, we refuse even now to put a stop to them, how greatly aggravated will be the guilt of Great Britain! and what a blot will the history of these trans-actions for ever be in the history of this country! Shall we, then, *delay* to repair these injuries, and to begin rendering this justice to Africa? Shall we not count the days and hours that are suffered to intervene and to delay the accomplishment of such a work? Reflect what an immense object is before you—what an object for a nation to have in view, and to have a prospect, under the favor of Providence, of being now permitted to attain! I think the House will agree with me in cherishing the ardent wish to enter without delay upon the measures necessary for these great ends: and I am sure that the immediate abolition of the slave trade is the first, the principal, the most indispensable act of policy, of duty, and of justice that the legislature of this country has to take, if it is indeed their wish to secure those important objects to which I have alluded, and which we are bound to pursue by the most solemn obligations.

There is, however, one argument set up as an universal answer to everything that can be urged on our side, whether we address ourselves to gentlemen's understandings or to their hearts and consciences. It is necessary I should remove this formidable objection; for though not often stated in distinct terms, I fear it is one which has a very wide influ-ence. The slave trade system, it is supposed, has taken so deep root in Africa, that it is absurd to think of its being eradicated; and the abolition of that share of trade carried on by Great Britain (and especially if her example is not followed by other powers) is likely to be of very little service. Give me leave to say, in answer to so dangerous an argument, that we ought to be extremely sure indeed of the assumption on which it rests, before we venture to rely on its validity; before we decide that an evil which we ourselves contribute to inflict is incurable, and on that very plea refuse to desist from bearing our part in the system which produces it. You are not sure, it is said, that other nations will give up the trade, if you should renounce it. I answer, if this trade is as criminal as it is asserted to be, or if it has in it a thousandth part of the criminality which I and others, after thorough investigation of the subject, charge upon it, God forbid that we should hesitate in determining to relinquish so iniquitous a traffic, even though it should be retained by other countries! God forbid, however, that we should fail to do our utmost towards inducing other countries to abandon a bloody commerce which they have probably been in great measure led by our example to pursue! God forbid that we should be capable of wishing to arrogate to ourselves the glory of being singular in renouncing it!

I tremble at the thought of gentlemen's indulging themselves in this argument (an argument as pernicious as it is futile), which I am combating. "We are friends," say they, "to humanity. We are second to none of you in our zeal for the good of Africa—but the French will not abolish— the Dutch will not abolish. We wait, therefore, on prudential principles, till they join us or set us an example."

How, sir, is this enormous evil ever to be eradicated, if every nation is thus prudentially to wait till the concurrence of all the world shall have been obtained? Let me remark, too, that there is no nation in Europe that has, on the one hand, plunged so deeply into this guilt as Britain, or that is so likely, on the other, to be looked up to as an example, if she should have the manliness to be the first in decidedly renouncing it. But, sir, does not this argument apply a thousand times more strongly in a contrary way? How much more justly may *other* nations point to *us*, and say, "Why should we abolish the slave trade when Great Britain has not abolished? Britain, free as she is, just and honorable as she is, and deeply also involved as she is in this commerce above all nations, not only has not abolished but has refused to abolish. She has investigated it well; she has gained the completest insight into its nature and effects; she has collected volumes of evidence on every branch of the subject. Her senate has deliberated—has deliberated again and again—and what is the result? She has gravely and solemnly determined to sanction the slave trade. She sanctions it at least for a while—her legislature, therefore, it is plain, sees no guilt in it, and has thus furnished us with the strongest evidence that she can furnish—of the justice unquestionably—and of the policy also, in a certain measure and in certain cases at least, of permitting this traffic to continue."

This, sir, is the argument with which we furnish the other nations of Europe, if we again refuse to put an end to the slave trade. Instead, therefore, of imagining that by choosing to presume on their continuing it, we shall have exempted ourselves from guilt, and have transferred the whole criminality to them, let us rather reflect that on the very principle urged against us, we shall henceforth have to answer for their crimes, as well as our own. We have strong reasons to believe that it depends upon us whether other countries will persist in this bloody trade or not. Already we have suffered one year to pass away, and now that the question is renewed, a proposition is made for gradual, with the view of preventing immediate, abolition. I know the difficulty that exists in attempting to reform long-established abuses; and I know the danger arising from the argument in favor of delay, in the case of evils which nevertheless are thought too enormous to be borne, when considered as perpetual. But by proposing some other period than the present, by prescribing some condition, by waiting for some contingency, or by refusing to proceed till a thousand favorable circumstances unite together—perhaps until we obtain the general concurrence of Europe (a concurrence which I believe never yet took place at the commencement of any one improvement in policy or in morals)—year after year escapes, and the most enormous evils go unredressed. We see this abundantly exemplified not only in public but in private life. Similar observations have been applied to the case of personal reformation. If you go into the streets, it is a chance but the first person who crosses you is one, *Vivendi recte qui prorogat horam.* We may wait; we may delay to cross the stream before us, till it has run down; but we shall wait forever, for the river will still flow on, without being exhausted. We shall be no nearer the object which we profess to have in view, so long as the step which alone can bring us to it is not taken. Until the actual, the only, remedy is applied, we ought neither to flatter ourselves that we have as yet thoroughly laid to heart the evil we affect to deplore nor that there is as yet any reasonable assurance of its being brought to an actual termination. . . .

There was a time, sir, which it may be fit sometimes to revive in the remembrance of our countrymen, when even human sacrifices are said to have been offered in this island. But I would peculiarly observe on this day, for it is a case precisely in point, that the very practice of the slave trade once prevailed among us. Slaves, as we may read in Henry's history of Great Britain, were formerly an established article of our exports. "Great numbers," he says, "were exported like cattle, from the British coast, and were to be seen exposed for sale in the Roman market." It does not distinctly appear by what means they were procured; but there was unquestionably no small resemblance, in the particular point, between the case of our ancestors and that of the present wretched natives of Africa—for the historian tells you that "adultery, witchcraft, and debt were probably some of the chief sources of supplying the Roman market with British slaves—that prisoners taken in war were added to the number—and that there might be among them some unfortunate gamesters who, after having lost all their goods, at length staked themselves, their wives, and their children." Every one of these sources of slavery has been stated, and almost precisely in the same terms, to be at this hour a source of slavery in Africa. And these circumstances, sir, with a solitary instance or two of human sacrifices, furnish the alleged proofs that Africa labors under a natural incapacity for civilization; that it is enthusiasm and fanaticism to think that she can ever enjoy the knowledge and the morals of Europe; that Providence never intended her to rise above a state of barbarism; that Providence has irrevocably doomed her to be only a nursery for slaves for us free and civilized Europeans. Allow of this principle, as applied to Africa, and I should be glad to know why it might not also have been applied to ancient and uncivilized Britain. Why might not some Roman senator, reasoning on the principles of some honorable gentlemen, and pointing to *British barbarians*, have predicted with equal boldness, "*There* is a people that will never rise to civilization—*there* is a people destined never to be free—a people without the understanding necessary for the attainment of useful arts; depressed by the hand of nature below the level of the human species; and created to form a supply of slaves for the rest of the world." Might not this have been said, according to the principles which we now hear stated, in all respects as fairly and as truly of Britain herself, at that period of her history, as it can now be said by us of the inhabitants of Africa?

We, sir, have long since emerged from barbarism—we have almost forgotten that we were once barbarians—we are now raised to a situation which exhibits a striking contrast to every circumstance, by which a Roman might have characterized us, and by which we now characterize Africa. There is indeed one thing wanting to complete the contrast, and to clear us altogether from the imputation of acting even to this hour as barbarians; for we continue to this hour a barbarous traffic in slaves; we continue it even yet in spite of all our great and undeniable pretensions to civilization. We were once as obscure among the nations of the earth, as savage in our manners, as debased in our morals, as degraded in our understandings, as these unhappy Africans are at present. But in the lapse of a long series of years, by a progression slow and, for a time, almost imperceptible, we have become rich in a variety of acquirements, favored above measure in the gifts of Providence, unrivaled in commerce, preeminent in arts, foremost in the pursuits of philosophy and science, and established in all the blessings of civil society; we are in the possession of peace, of happiness, and of liberty; we are under the guidance of a mild and beneficent religion; and we are protected by impartial laws, and the purest administration of justice: we are living under a system of government which our own happy experience leads us to pronounce the best and wisest which has ever yet been framed—a system which has become the admiration of the world. From all these blessings, we must forever have been shut out, had there been any truth in those principles which some gentlemen have not hesitated to lay down as applicable to the case of Africa. Had those principles been true, we ourselves had languished to this hour in that miserable state of ignorance, brutality, and degradation in which history proves our ancestors to have been immersed. Had other nations adopted these principles in their conduct towards us; had other nations applied to Great Britain the reasoning which some of the senators of this very island now apply to Africa, ages might have passed without our emerging from barbarism; and we, who are enjoying the blessings of British civilization, of British laws, and British liberty, might at this hour have been little superior either in morals, in knowledge, or refinement to the rude inhabitants of the coast of Guinea.

If, then, we feel that this perpetual confinement in the fetters of brutal ignorance would have been the greatest calamity which could have befallen us; if we view with gratitude and exultation the contrast between the peculiar blessings we enjoy and the wretchedness of the ancient inhabitants of Britain; if we shudder to think of the misery which would still have overwhelmed us, had Great Britain continued to the present times to be the mart for slaves to the more civilized nations of the world, through some cruel policy of theirs, God forbid that we should any longer subject Africa to the same dreadful scourge, and preclude the light of knowledge, which has reached every other quarter of the globe, from having access to her coasts!

I trust we shall no longer continue this commerce, to the destruction of every improvement on that wide continent, and shall not consider ourselves as conferring too great a boon, in restoring its inhabitants to the rank of human beings. I trust we shall not think ourselves too liberal if, by abolishing the slave trade, we give them the same common chance of civilization with other parts of the world, and that we shall not allow to Africa the opportunity—the hope—the prospect of attaining to the same blessings which we ourselves, through the favorable dispensations of divine Providence, have been permitted, at a much more early period, to enjoy. If we listen to the voice of reason and duty, and pursue this night the line of conduct which they prescribe, some of us may live to see a reverse of that picture from which we now turn our eyes with shame and regret. We may live to behold the natives of Africa engaged in the calm occupations of industry, in the pursuit of a just and legitimate commerce. We may behold the beams of science and philosophy breaking in upon their land, which, at some happy period in still later times, may blaze with full luster; and joining their influence to that of pure religion, may illuminate and invigorate the most distant extremities of that immense continent. Then may we hope that even Africa, though last of all the quarters of the globe, shall enjoy at length, in the evening of her days, those blessings which have descended so plentifully upon us in a much earlier period of the world. Then also will Europe, participating in her improvement and prosperity, receive an ample recompense for the tardy kindness (if kindness it can be called) of no longer hindering that continent from extricating herself out of the darkness which, in other more fortunate regions, has been so much more speedily dispelled. . . .

I shall vote, sir, against the adjournment; and I shall also oppose to the utmost every proposition which in any way may tend either to prevent or even to postpone for an hour the total abolition of the slave trade: a measure which, on all the various grounds which I have stated, we are bound, by the most pressing and indispensable duty, to adopt. ∎

Lord Byron Puts Poetic Passion into His Defense of Labor's Rights

"Is there not blood enough upon your penal code! . . . Can you commit a whole country to their own prisons?"

THE FIGUREHEAD OF ROMANTIC POETRY in the early nineteenth century, George Gordon Noel Byron is remembered primarily for such works as *Don Juan* and *Childe Harold's Pilgrimage*. Before he came of age, he was exhibiting his political and cultural defiance: "I'll publish right or wrong: Fools are my theme, let satire be my song." Romance was an important part of his life, and his affairs with noblewomen in England and Italy, and possibly with his half sister, added the piquancy of scandal to his reputation and fuel to his poetic fire. The highborn poet, however, also took his seat in the House of Lords at an early age, and when he turned twenty-four, he gave his maiden speech to that assembly.

For that speech on February 27, 1812, Lord Byron chose a controversial stand on a serious wartime issue. The Industrial Revolution in England had helped impoverish the working class. Handloom weavers were hit especially hard by the introduction of larger, more efficient frames for weaving; the loss of income led the unemployed to desperate and violent measures, including widespread destruction of the new frames. In response to this violence, Parliament considered a bill that called for the death penalty for those who broke the frames.

Lord Byron opposed the draconian measures of the Frame-Breaking Bill in his slashing speech to the House of Lords. Questioning the wisdom of this hasty legislation, Byron at a pivotal point in the speech raises a succession of eleven questions, trying to force the legislators into rethinking their position. In the final line, he refers to George Jeffreys, a seventeenth-century jurist known for brutality and injustice.

Byron's plea for labor's rights failed to sway the House of Lords, however, and the Frame-Breaking Bill was enacted (although most of the death sentences for frame breakers were eventually commuted to deportation). Byron's success with *Childe Harold* soon followed, and by 1816 he had left England for travels abroad, never to return. He was an idealistic aristocrat, hating oppression but not liking the oppressed; he died in Greece, at age thirty-six, while lending his eloquence and support to the cause of Greek freedom.

□   □   □

The subject now submitted to your lordships, for the first time, though new to the House, is by no means new to the country. I believe it had occupied the serious thoughts of all descriptions of persons long before its introduction to the notice of that legislature whose interference alone could be of real service. As a person in some degree connected with the suffering county, though a stranger not only to this House in general but to almost every individual whose attention I presume to solicit, I must claim some portion of your lordships' indulgence, whilst I offer a few observations on a question in which I confess myself deeply interested.

To enter into any detail of these riots would be superfluous; the House is already aware that every outrage short of actual bloodshed has been perpetrated, and that the proprietors of the frames obnoxious to the rioters, and all persons supposed to be connected with them, have been liable to insult and violence. During the short time I recently passed in Notts, not twelve hours elapsed without some fresh act of violence; and on the day I left the county, I was informed that forty frames had been broken the preceding evening as usual, without resistance and without detection. Such was then the state of that county, and such I have reason to believe it to be at this moment.

But whilst these outrages must be admitted to exist to an alarming extent, it cannot be denied that they have arisen from circumstances of the most unparalleled distress. The perseverance of these miserable men in their proceedings tends to prove that nothing but absolute want could have driven a large and once honest and industrious body of the people into the commission of excesses so hazardous to themselves, their families, and the community. At the time to which I allude, the town and county were burdened with large detachments of the military; the police was in motion, the magistrates assembled, yet all these movements, civil and military, had led to—nothing. Not a single instance had occurred of the apprehension of any real delinquent actually taken in the act, against whom there existed legal evidence sufficient for conviction. But the police, however useless, were by no means idle: several notorious delinquents had been detected; men liable to conviction, on the clearest evidence, of the capital crime of poverty; men who had been nefariously guilty of lawfully begetting several children, whom, thanks to the times, they were unable to maintain.

Considerable injury has been done to the proprietors of the improved frames. These machines were to them an advantage, inasmuch as they superseded the necessity of employing a number of workmen, who were left in consequence to starve. By the adoption of one species of frame in particular, one man performed the work of many, and the superfluous laborers were thrown out of employment. Yet it is to be observed that the work thus executed was inferior in quality, not marketable at home, and merely hurried over with a view to exportation. It was called, in the cant of the trade, by the name of spider work.

The rejected workmen, in the blindness of their ignorance, instead of rejoicing at these improvements in arts so beneficial to mankind, conceived themselves to be sacrificed to improvements in mechanism. In the foolishness of their hearts, they imagined that the maintenance and well-doing of the industrious poor were objects of greater consequence than the enrichment of a few individuals by any improvement in the implements of trade which threw the workmen out of employment, and rendered the laborer unworthy of his hire. And it must be confessed that although the adoption of the enlarged machinery, in that state of our commerce which the country once boasted, might have been beneficial to the master without being detrimental to the servant, yet, in the present situation of our manufactures, rotting in warehouses without a prospect of exportation, which the demand for work and workmen equally diminished, frames of this construction tend materially to aggravate the distresses and discontents of the disappointed sufferers.

But the real cause of these distresses, and consequent disturbances, lies deeper. When we are told that these men are leagued together, not only for the destruction of their own comfort, but of their very means of subsistence, can we forget that it is the bitter policy, the destructive warfare, of the last eighteen years which has destroyed their comfort, your comfort, all men's comfort—that policy which, originating with "great statesmen now no more," has survived the dead to become a curse on the living unto the third and fourth generation! These men never destroyed their looms till they were become useless, worse than useless; till they were become actual impediments to their exertions in obtaining their daily bread.

Can you then wonder that in times like these, when bankruptcy, convicted fraud, and imputed felony are found in a station not far beneath that of your lordships, the lowest, though once most useful portion of the people, should forget their duty in their distresses, and become only less guilty, than one of their representatives? But while the exalted offender can find means to baffle the law, new capital punishments must be devised, new snares of death must be spread, for the wretched mechanic who is famished into guilt. These men were willing to dig, but the spade was in other hands; they were not ashamed to beg, but there was none to relieve them. Their own means of subsistence were cut off; all other employments preoccupied; and their excesses, however to be deplored and condemned, can hardly be the subject of surprise.

It has been stated that the persons in the temporary possession of frames connive at their destruction; if this be proved upon inquiry, it were necessary that such material accessories to the crime should be principals in the punishment. But I did hope that any measure proposed by His Majesty's government for your lordships' decision would have had conciliation for its basis; or, if that were hopeless, that some previous inquiry, some deliberation, would have been deemed requisite; not that we should have been called at once, without examination and without cause, to pass sentences by wholesale and sign death warrants blindfold. . . .

In what state of apathy have we been plunged so long that now, for the first time, the House has been officially apprised of these disturbances? All this has been transacting within one hundred and thirty miles of London, and yet we, "good easy men! have deemed full sure our greatness was a ripening," and have sat down to enjoy our foreign triumphs in the midst of domestic calamity. But all the cities you have taken, all the armies which have retreated before your leaders, are but paltry subjects of self-congratulation, if your land divides against itself, and your dragoons and executioners must be let loose against your fellow citizens. You call these men a mob, desperate, dangerous, and ignorant; and seem to think that the only way to quiet the *bellua multorum capitum* is to lop off a few of its superfluous heads. But even a mob may be better reduced to reason by a mixture of conciliation and firmness than by additional irritation and redoubled penalties. Are we aware of our obligations to a *mob?* It is the mob that labor in your fields, and serve in your houses—that man your navy, and recruit your army—that have enabled you to defy all the world—and can also defy you, when neglect and calamity have driven them to despair. You may call the people a mob, but do not forget that a mob too often speaks the sentiments of the people. And here I must remark with what alacrity you are accustomed to fly to the succor of your distressed allies, leaving the distressed of your own country to the care of Providence or—the parish. When the Portuguese suffered under the retreat of the French, every arm was stretched out, every hand was opened—from the rich man's largess to the widow's mite, all was bestowed to enable them to rebuild their villages and replenish their granaries. And at this moment, when thousands of misguided but most unfortunate fellow countrymen are struggling with the extremes of hardship and hunger, as your charity began abroad, it should end at home. A much less sum, a tithe of the bounty bestowed on Portugal, even if these men (which I cannot admit without inquiry) could not have been restored to their employments, would have rendered unnecessary the tender mercies of the bayonet and the gibbet. But doubtless our funds have too many foreign claims to admit a prospect of domestic relief—though never did such objects demand it.

I have traversed the seat of war in the Peninsula; I have been in some of the most oppressed provinces of Turkey; but never, under the most despotic of infidel governments, did I behold such squalid wretchedness as I have seen, since my return, in the very heart of a Christian country. And what are your remedies? After months of inaction, and months of action worse than inactivity, at length comes forth the grand specific, the never-failing nostrum of all state physicians from the days of Draco to the present time. After feeling the pulse and shaking the head over the patient, prescribing the usual course of warm water and bleeding—the warm water of your mawkish police, and the lancets of your military—these convulsions must terminate, in death, the sure consummation of the prescriptions of all political Sangrados. Setting aside the palpable injustice and the certain inefficiency of the bill, are there not capital punishments sufficient on your statutes? Is there not blood enough upon your penal code! that more must be poured forth to ascend to heaven and testify against you? How will you carry this bill into effect? Can you commit a whole country to their own prisons? Will you erect a gibbet in every field, and hang up men like scarecrows? Or will you proceed (as you must to bring this measure into effect) by decimation; place the country under martial law; depopulate and lay waste all around you; and restore Sherwood Forest as an acceptable gift to the crown in its former condition of a royal chase, and an asylum for outlaws? Are these the remedies for a starving and desperate populace? Will the famished wretch who has braved your bayonets be appalled by your gibbets? When death is a relief, and the only relief it appears that you will afford him, will he be dragooned into tranquillity? Will that which could not be effected by your grenadiers be accomplished by your executioners? If you proceed by the forms of law, where is your evidence? Those who have refused to impeach their accomplices when transportation only was the punishment will hardly be tempted to witness against them when death is the penalty.

With all due deference to the noble lords opposite, I think a little investigation, some previous inquiry, would induce even them to change their purpose. That most favorite state measure, so marvelously efficacious in many and recent instances, *temporizing*, would not be without its advantage in this. When a proposal is made to emancipate or relieve, you hesitate, you deliberate for years, you temporize and tamper with the minds of men; but a death bill must be passed offhand, without a thought of the consequences. Sure I am, from what I have heard and from what I have seen, that to pass the bill under all the existing circumstances, without inquiry, without deliberation, would only be to add injustice to irritation and barbarity to neglect. The framers of such a bill must be content to inherit the honors of that Athenian lawgiver whose edicts were said to be written, not in ink, but in blood. But suppose it passed—suppose one of these men, as I have seen them meager with famine, sullen with despair, careless of a life which your lordships are perhaps about to value at something less than the price of a stocking frame; suppose this man surrounded by those children for whom he is unable to procure bread at the hazard of his existence, about to be torn forever from a family which he lately supported in peaceful industry, and which it is not his fault that he can no longer so support; suppose this man—and there are ten thousand such from whom you may select your victims—dragged into court to be tried for this new offense, by this new law—still there are two things wanting to convict and condemn him, and these are, in my opinion, twelve butchers for a jury and a Jeffreys for a judge! ■

Social Reformer
Maria Stewart Advocates
Education for Black Women

"LET every female heart become united. . . ."

MARIA STEWART rose in Boston's Franklin Hall on September 21, 1832, and delivered the first public lecture ever given by an American woman, following by four years the first such address by the British-born Frances Wright. Mrs. Stewart's speech was directed to her fellow black women of the Afric-American Female Intelligence Society with a clear message: "Daughters of Africa, awake! arise! distinguish yourselves."

Born Maria Miller in Connecticut in 1803 and orphaned at an early age, Maria Stewart became a servant to a clergyman's family. She was married in 1826 in Boston and widowed three years later. A conversion to Christianity and the desire for education led to her "calling" as a writer and teacher and to her moving from Boston to New York and eventually to Washington. Before she left Boston, however, the abolitionist editor William Lloyd Garrison encouraged her work by publishing some of her essays.

Addressing her audience with a series of questions, Maria Stewart sought equality for blacks through increased education. Her secular sermonizing drew heavily on biblical imagery ("hanging our heads like bulrushes") and parallel structure ("Look at our young men. . . . Look at our middle-aged men. . . . Look at our aged sires . . .").

In 1832, however, a hostile audience—male and female—was not ready for such messages, particularly from a woman on a public platform. After a year of increasingly angry reactions from the public, Maria Stewart decided to leave Boston, and despite a distinguished career as an educator and hospital administrator, she chose never to give another public speech.

□   □   □

Oh, do not say you cannot make anything of your children; but say, with the help and assistance of God, we will try. Perhaps you will say that you cannot send them to high schools and academies. You can have them taught in the first rudiments of useful knowledge, and then you can have private teachers, who will instruct them in the higher branches.

It is of no use for us to sit with our hands folded, hanging our heads like bulrushes, lamenting our wretched condition; but let us make a mighty effort, and arise. Let every female heart become united, and let us raise a fund ourselves; and at the end of one year and a half, we might be able to lay the cornerstone for the building of a high school, that the higher branches of knowledge might be enjoyed by us.

Do you ask, what can we do? Unite and build a store of your own. Fill one side with dry goods and the other with groceries. Do you ask, where is the money? We have spent more than enough for nonsense to do what building we should want. We have never had an opportunity of displaying our talents; therefore the world thinks we know nothing. . . .

Few white persons of either sex are willing to spend their lives and bury their talents in performing mean, servile labor. And such is the horrible idea that I entertain respecting a life of servitude, that if I conceived of there being no possibility of my rising above the condition of servant, I would gladly hail death as a welcome messenger. Oh, horrible idea, indeed, to possess noble souls, aspiring after high and honorable acquirements, yet confined by the chains of ignorance and poverty to lives of continual drudgery and toil.

Neither do I know of any who have enriched themselves by spending their lives as house domestics, washing windows, shaking carpets, brushing boots, or tending upon gentlemen's tables. I have learned, by bitter experience, that continued hard labor deadens the energies of the soul and benumbs the faculties of the mind; the ideas become confined, the mind barren. Continual hard labor irritates our tempers and sours our dispositions; the whole system becomes worn out with toil and fatigue, and we care but little whether we live or die.

I do not consider it derogatory, my friends, for persons to live out to service. There are many whose inclination leads them to aspire no higher: and I would highly commend the performance of almost anything for an honest livelihood; but where constitutional strength is wanting, labor of this kind, in its mildest form is painful: and, doubtless, many are the prayers that have ascended to heaven from Afric's daughters for strength to perform their work. Most of our color have dragged out a miserable existence of servitude from the cradle to the grave. And what literary acquirements can be made, or useful knowledge derived, from either maps, books or charts, by those who continually drudge from Monday morning until Sunday noon? . . .

O ye fairer sisters, whose hands are never soiled, whose nerves and muscles are never strained, go learn by experience! Had we had the opportunity that you have had to improve our moral and mental faculties, what would have hindered our intellects from being as bright, and our manners from being as dignified, as yours? Had it been our lot to have been nursed in the lap of affluence and ease, and to have basked beneath the smiles and sunshine of fortune, should we not have naturally supposed that we were never made to toil? And why are not our forms as delicate and our constitutions as slender as yours? Is not the workmanship as curious and complete? . . .

Look at our young men—smart, active, and energetic, with souls filled with ambitious fire; if they look forward, alas! What are their prospects? They can be nothing but the humblest laborer, on account of their dark complexion; hence many of them lose their ambition and become worthless.

Look at our middle-aged men, clad in their rusty plaids and coats. In winter, every cent they earn goes to buy their wood and pay their rent; their poor wives also toil beyond their strength, to help support their families.

Look at our aged sires, whose heads are whitened with the frosts of seventy winters, with their old wood saws on their backs. Alas, what keeps us so? Prejudice, ignorance and poverty.

But ah! Did the pilgrims, when they first landed on these shores, quietly compose themselves, and say, "The Britons have all the money and all the power, and we must continue their servants forever?" Did they sluggishly sigh and say, "Our lot is hard; the Indians own the soil, and we cannot cultivate it?" No, they first made powerful efforts to raise themselves. And, my brethren have you made a powerful effort? Have you prayed the legislature for mercy's sake to grant you all the rights and privileges of free citizens, that your daughters may rise to that degree of respectability which true merit deserves, and your sons above the servile situations which most of them fill? ■

Suffragist Elizabeth Cady Stanton Pleads for Women's Rights

"WHATEVER is done to lift woman to her true position will help to usher in a new day of peace and perfection for the race."

"WE ASK WOMAN'S ENFRANCHISEMENT," said Elizabeth Cady Stanton in her 1868 address at the Woman Suffrage Convention in Washington.

With Susan B. Anthony, Elizabeth Cady Stanton was at the forefront of the nineteenth-century American movement for women's rights. Married to the journalist and abolitionist Henry Brewster Stanton in a ceremony that left out the word "obey," she proved a powerful orator and took an active part in the first American convention for women's rights, held at Seneca Falls, New York, in 1848. There she drew up a declaration of sentiments, patterned on the Declaration of Independence, that many consider the first persuasive document of the American women's rights movement; it began, "We hold these truths to be self-evident, that all men and women are created equal." With her associate Susan B. Anthony, she espoused the right of a wife to divorce a drunken or brutal husband, a position at that time considered the height of uppityness. Until her death in 1902, she used her skills as writer and speaker to urge economic and legal rights as well as political equality for women.

When Mrs. Stanton addressed the Washington convention, her speech began with a litany of vices, carefully catalogued as "the masculine element" in a male-dominated world. To a modern audience, her closing analogy of nature and human behavior suggests the pathetic fallacy (John Ruskin's term for ascribing human traits or sympathies to nature), but her arguments against acquisition and materialism still hold force.

□ □ □

I urge a sixteenth amendment, because "manhood suffrage," or a man's government, is civil, religious, and social disorganization. The male element is a destructive force, stern, selfish, aggrandizing, loving war, violence, conquest, acquisition, breeding in the material and moral world alike discord, disorder, disease, and death. See what a record of blood and cruelty the pages of history reveal! Through what slavery, slaughter, and sacrifice, through what inquisitions and imprisonments, pains and persecutions, black codes and gloomy creeds, the soul of humanity has struggled for the centuries, while mercy has veiled her face and all hearts have been dead alike to love and hope!

The male element has held high carnival thus far; it has fairly run riot from the beginning, overpowering the feminine element everywhere, crushing out all the diviner qualities in human nature, until we know but little of true manhood and womanhood, of the latter comparatively nothing, for it has scarce been recognized as a power until within the last century. Society is but the reflection of man himself, untempered by woman's thought; the hard iron rule we feel alike in the church, the state, and the home. No one need wonder at the disorganization, at the fragmentary condition of everything, when we remember that man, who represents but half a complete being, with but half an idea on every subject, has undertaken the absolute control of all sublunary matters.

People object to the demands of those whom they choose to call the strong-minded, because they say "the right of suffrage will make the women masculine." That is just the difficulty in which we are involved today. Though disfranchised, we have few women in the best sense; we have simply so many reflections, varieties, and dilutions of the masculine gender. The strong, natural characteristics of womanhood are repressed and ignored in dependence, for so long as man feeds woman she will try to please the giver and adapt herself to his condition. To keep a foothold in society, woman must be as near like man as possible, reflect his ideas, opinions, virtues, motives, prejudices, and vices. She must respect his statutes, though they strip her of every inalienable right, and conflict with that higher law written by the finger of God on her own soul. She must look at everything from its dollar-and-cent point of view, or she is a mere romancer. She must accept things as they are and make the best of them. To mourn over the miseries of others, the poverty of the poor, their hardships in jails, prisons, asylums, the horrors of war, cruelty, and brutality in every form, all this would be mere sentimentalizing. To protest against the intrigue, bribery, and corruption of public life, to desire that her sons might follow some business that did not involve lying, cheating, and a hard, grinding selfishness, would be arrant nonsense.

In this way man has been molding woman to his ideas by direct and positive influences, while she, if not a negation, has used indirect means to control him, and in most cases developed the very characteristics both in him and herself that needed repression. And now man himself stands appalled at the results of his own excesses, and mourns in bitterness that falsehood, selfishness, and violence are the law of life. The need of this hour is not territory, gold mines, railroads, or specie payments but a new evangel of womanhood, to exalt purity, virtue, morality, true religion, to lift man up into the higher realms of thought and action.

We ask woman's enfranchisement, as the first step toward the recognition of that essential element in government that can only secure the health, strength, and prosperity of the nation. Whatever is done to lift woman to her true position will help to usher in a new day of peace and perfection for the race.

In speaking of the masculine element, I do not wish to be understood to say that all men are hard, selfish, and brutal, for many of the most beautiful spirits the world has known have been clothed with manhood; but I refer to those characteristics, though often marked in woman, that distinguish what is called the stronger sex. For example, the love of acquisition and conquest, the very pioneers of civilization, when expended on the earth, the sea, the elements, the riches and forces of nature, are powers of destruction when used to subjugate one man to another or to sacrifice nations to ambition.

Here that great conservator of woman's love, if permitted to assert itself, as it naturally would in freedom against oppression, violence, and war, would hold all these destructive forces in check, for woman knows the cost of life better than man does, and not with her consent would one drop of blood ever be shed, one life sacrificed in vain.

With violence and disturbance in the natural world, we see a constant effort to maintain an equilibrium of forces. Nature, like a loving mother, is ever trying to keep land and sea, mountain and valley, each in its place, to hush the angry winds and waves, balance the extremes of heat and cold, of rain and drought, that peace, harmony, and beauty may reign supreme. There is a striking analogy between matter and mind, and the present disorganization of society warns us that in the dethronement of woman we have let loose the elements of violence and ruin that she only has the power to curb. If the civilization of the age calls for an extension of the suffrage, surely a government of the most virtuous educated men and women would better represent the whole and protect the interests of all than could the representation of either sex alone. ■

Evangelist
Sojourner Truth Speaks
for Women's Rights

"AND ain't I a woman? Look at me!"

BORN A SLAVE NAMED ISABELLA, this American abolitionist received her freedom when New York State emancipated slaves in 1827. She moved to New York City, heard what she believed to be heavenly voices, and took the name Sojourner Truth in 1843, when she quit being a maidservant to become an evangelist. Her opening line was a stunner: "Children, I talk to God and God talks to me!"

Sojourner Truth traveled throughout the North (a "sojourner" stays only temporarily in one place) to spread a message that combined religious and abolitionist ideas. After a despondent speech by Frederick Douglass in 1850, she asked her frequent platform mate a question that still reverberates in theological circles: "Frederick, is God dead?" Although illiterate, this mother of five powerfully conveyed her equal-rights message in dialect, with plain words and commonsense reasoning, drawing on her own experiences to persuade listeners of her sincerity. During the Civil War, President Lincoln appointed her counselor to the freedmen of the capital.

Blacks and women were in competition for suffrage, and few black women attended early women's rights meetings. Sojourner Truth was an exception; at the 1851 Ohio Women's Rights Convention, in Akron, she spoke of feminism with the same fervor that marked her preaching on abolitionism and religion. Through a conversational form of direct address ("Well, children") and the use of repetition (the question "And ain't I a woman?" is raised four times), Sojourner Truth moved listeners in the early days of the fight for women's rights. She said she wanted her language reported in standard English, "not as if I was saying tickety-ump-ump-nicky-nacky," and in some quotation books her "ain'ts" are changed to "aren'ts," but I think such editorial prettification loses the flavor and force of the eloquence.

□   □   □

Well, children, where there is so much racket there must be something out of kilter. I think that 'twixt the Negroes of the South and the women at the North, all talking about rights, the white men will be in a fix pretty soon. But what's all this here talking about?

That man over there says that women need to be helped into carriages, and lifted over ditches, and to have the best place everywhere. Nobody ever helps me into carriages, or over mud puddles, or gives me any best place! And ain't I a woman? Look at me! Look at my arm. I have plowed and planted, and gathered into barns, and no man could head me! And ain't I a woman? I could work as much and eat as much as a man—when I could get it—and bear the lash as well! And ain't I a woman? I have borne thirteen children, and seen them most all sold off to slavery, and when I cried out with my mother's grief, none but Jesus heard me! And ain't I a woman?

Then they talk about this thing in the head; what's this they call it? [Intellect, someone whispers.] That's it, honey. What's that got to do with women's rights or Negro's rights? If my cup won't hold but a pint, and yours holds a quart, wouldn't you be mean not to let me have my little half-measure full?

Then that little man in black there, he says women can't have as much rights as men, 'cause Christ wasn't a woman! Where did your Christ come from? Where did your Christ come from? From God and a woman! Man had nothing to do with him.

If the first woman God ever made was strong enough to turn the world upside down all alone, these women together ought to be able to turn it back, and get it right side up again! And now they is asking to do it, the men better let them.

Obliged to you for hearing me, and now old Sojourner ain't got nothing more to say. ■

Abolitionist William Lloyd Garrison Admits of No Compromise with the Evil of Slavery

"My singularity is that when I say that freedom is of God and slavery is of the devil, I mean just what I say. My fanaticism is that I insist on the American people abolishing slavery or ceasing to prate of the rights of man."

ON THE FIRST DAY OF 1831, after seven weeks in a Baltimore jail following a libel conviction, editor William Lloyd Garrison returned to his native Massachusetts to found the *Liberator*.

"I will be as harsh as truth and as uncompromising as justice," he wrote in his first issue. "I am in earnest—I will not equivocate—I will not excuse—I will not retreat a single inch; and I will be heard!" He did not, and he was; Garrison continued the *Liberator* for thirty-five years, until the Thirteenth Amendment was passed; though its circulation never exceeded three thousand, its editor's rousing, intemperate tone helped fan the passion of abolition; the newspaper also provided an outlet for ideas on women's suffrage and prohibition of the sale of liquor.

Garrison was a secessionist himself; in 1843, he advocated northern secession from the Union because, in his fierce words, "the compact which exists between the North and the South is a covenant with death and an agreement with hell," permitting human slavery in the colonies. This extremism did not endear the editor to others working for emancipation without war, trying vainly to effect change without the bloodshed and hatred of regional conquest. Garrison even opposed the Civil War as a fraud until Lincoln issued the Proclamation of Freedom in late 1862.

The following speech, delivered in 1854, is typical of his absolutism. Its style rejects platitudes and embraces certitudes; it hammers home declarative sentences; it parades "if . . . then" consequential reasoning; and it will be heard.

□   □   □

. . . Let me define my positions, and at the same time challenge anyone to show wherein they are untenable.

I am a believer in that portion of the Declaration of American Independence in which it is set forth, as among self-evident truths, "that all men are created equal; that they are endowed by their Creator with certain inalienable rights; that among these are life, liberty, and the pursuit of happiness." Hence, I am an abolitionist. Hence, I cannot but regard oppression in every form—and most of all, that which turns a man into a thing—with indignation and abhorrence. Not to cherish these feelings would be recreancy to principle. They who desire me to be dumb on the subject of slavery, unless I will open my mouth in its defense, ask me to give the lie to my professions, to degrade my manhood, and to stain my soul. I will not be a liar, a poltroon, or a hypocrite, to accommodate any party, to gratify any sect, to escape any odium or peril, to save any interest, to preserve any institution, or to promote any object. Convince me that one man may rightfully make another man his slave, and I will no longer subscribe to the Declaration of Independence. Convince me that liberty is not the inalienable birthright of every human being, of whatever complexion or clime, and I will give that instrument to the consuming fire. I do not know how to espouse freedom and slavery together. I do not know how to worship God and Mammon at the same time. If other men choose to go upon all fours, I choose to stand erect, as God designed every man to stand. If, practically falsifying its heaven-attested principles, this nation denounces me for refusing to imitate its example, then, adhering all the more tenaciously to those principles, I will not cease to rebuke it for its guilty inconsistency. Numerically, the contest may be an unequal one, for the time being; but the author of liberty and the source of justice, the adorable God, is more than multitudinous, and he will defend the right. My crime is that I will not go with the multitude to do evil. My singularity is that when I say that freedom is of God and slavery is of the devil, I mean just what I say. My fanaticism is that I insist on the American people abolishing slavery or ceasing to prate of the rights of man. . . .

The abolitionism which I advocate is as absolute as the law of God, and as unyielding as his throne. It admits of no compromise. Every slave is a stolen man; every slaveholder is a man stealer. By no precedent, no example, no law, no compact, no purchase, no bequest, no inheritance, no combination of circumstances, is slaveholding right or justifiable. While a slave remains in his fetters, the land must have no rest. Whatever sanctions his doom must be pronounced accursed. The law that makes him a chattel is to be trampled underfoot; the compact that is formed at his expense, and cemented with his blood, is null and void; the church that consents to his enslavement is horribly atheistical; the religion that receives to its communion the enslaver is the embodiment of all criminality. Such, at least, is the verdict of my own soul, on the supposition that I am to be the slave; that my wife is to be sold from me for the vilest purposes; that my children are to be torn from my arms, and disposed of to the highest bidder, like sheep in the market. And who am I but a man? What right have I to be free, that another man cannot prove himself to possess by nature? Who or what are my wife and children, that they should not be herded with four-footed beasts, as well as others thus sacredly related? . . .

If the slaves are not men; if they do not possess human instincts, passions, faculties, and powers; if they are below accountability, and devoid of reason; if for them there is no hope of immortality, no God, no heaven, no hell; if, in short, they are what the slave code declares them to be, rightly "deemed, sold, taken, reputed and adjudged in law to be chattels personal in the hands of their owners and possessors, and their executors, administrators and assigns, to all intents, constructions, and purposes whatsoever"; then, undeniably, I am mad, and can no longer discriminate between a man and a beast. But, in that case, away with the horrible incongruity of giving them oral instruction, of teaching them the catechism, of recognizing them as suitably qualified to be members of Christian churches, of extending to them the ordinance of baptism, and admitting them to the communion table, and enumerating many of them as belonging to the household of faith! Let them be no more included in our religious sympathies or denominational statistics than are the dogs in our streets, the swine in our pens, or the utensils in our dwellings. It is right to own, to buy, to sell, to inherit, to breed, and to control them, in the most absolute sense. All constitutions and laws which forbid their possession ought to be so far modified or repealed as to concede the right.

But, if they are men; if they are to run the same career of immortality with ourselves; if the same law of God is over them as over all others; if they have souls to be saved or lost; if Jesus included them among those for whom he laid down his life; if Christ is within many of them "the hope of glory"; then, when I claim for them all that we claim for ourselves, because we are created in the image of God, I am guilty of no extravagance, but am bound, by every principle of honor, by all the claims of human nature, by obedience to Almighty God, to "remember them that are in bonds as bound with them," and to demand their immediate and unconditional emancipation. . . .

These are solemn times. It is not a struggle for national salvation; for the nation, as such, seems doomed beyond recovery. The reason why the South rules, and the North falls prostrate in servile terror, is simply this: with the South, the preservation of slavery is paramount to all other considerations—above party success, denominational unity, pecuniary interest, legal integrity, and constitutional obligation. With the North, the preservation of the Union is placed above all other things—above honor, justice, freedom, integrity of soul, the Decalogue and the Golden Rule—the infinite God himself. All these she is ready to discard for the Union. Her devotion to it is the latest and the most terrible form of idolatry. She has given to the slave power a carte blanche, to be filled as it may dictate—and if, at any time, she grows restive under the yoke, and shrinks back aghast at the new atrocity contemplated, it is only necessary for that power to crack the whip of disunion over her head, as it has done again and again, and she will cower and obey like a plantation slave—for has she not sworn that she will sacrifice everything in heaven and on earth, rather than the Union?

What then is to be done? Friends of the slave, the question is not whether by our efforts we can abolish slavery, speedily or remotely—for duty is ours, the result is with God; but whether we will go with the multitude to do evil, sell our birthright for a mess of pottage, cease to cry aloud and spare not, and remain in Babylon when the command of God is "Come out of her, my people, that ye be not partakers of her sins, and that ye receive not of her plagues." Let us stand in our lot, "and having done all, to stand." At least, a remnant shall be saved. Living or dying, defeated or victorious, be it ours to exclaim, "No compromise with slavery! Liberty for each, for all, forever! Man above all institutions! The supremacy of God over the whole earth!" ■

Chief Seattle Cautions Americans to Deal Justly with His People

"THE white man will never be alone. Let him be just and deal kindly with my people, for the dead are not altogether powerless."

THE EPONYM OF THE LARGEST CITY in Washington, Chief Seattle led the Duwamish and Suquamish tribes of the Pacific Northwest in the mid-nineteenth century. Controversy still surrounds the words of Chief Seattle more than a century after his death in 1866. Conservationists have long offered apocryphal and manufactured words from this chief, but the best evidence suggests that the following speech is a fair account of his words.

Believed to have been delivered on January 12, 1854, this speech to the white man was translated from the chief's native tongue into Chinook jargon and then into English. It was transcribed by Dr. Henry Smith, a pioneer who heard the speech but who waited until 1887, more than thirty years later, to publish it in the *Seattle Sunday Star*.

As Chief Seattle recounts the disappearance of his people from the land, he enforces his call for justice with powerful imagery and striking simile ("as . . . the wounded doe that hears the approaching footsteps of the hunter"). Throughout his speech, cautionary notes linking the fates of the native and the intruder are sounded, and the ominous tone conveyed in parallel structure ("A few more moons, a few more winters") leads Chief Seattle to contemplate our "common destiny" with a skeptic's idealism: "We *may* be brothers after all. We shall see."

□   □   □

Yonder sky, which has wept tears of compassion on our fathers for centuries untold, and which to us looks eternal, may change. Today it is fair; tomorrow it may be overcast with clouds. My words are like the stars that never set. What Seattle says, the great chief Washington can rely upon, with as much certainty as our paleface brothers can rely upon the return of the seasons. The son of the white chief says his father sends us greetings of friendship and good will. This is kind, for we know he has little need of our friendship in return, because his people are many. They are like the grass that covers the vast prairies, while my people are few, and resemble the scattering trees of a windswept plain.

The great, and I presume also good, white chief sends us word that he wants to buy our lands but is willing to allow us to reserve enough to live on comfortably. This indeed appears generous, for the red man no longer has rights that he need respect, and the offer may be wise, also, for we are no longer in need of a great country. There was a time when our people covered the whole land as the waves of a wind-ruffled sea cover its shell floor. But that time has long since passed away with the greatness of tribes almost forgotten. I will not mourn over our untimely decay, nor reproach my paleface brothers with hastening it, for we, too, may have been somewhat to blame.

When our young men grow angry at some real or imaginary wrong and disfigure their faces with black paint, their hearts, also, are disfigured and turn black, and then their cruelty is relentless and knows no bounds, and our old men are not able to restrain them.

But let us hope that hostilities between the red man and his paleface brothers may never return. We would have everything to lose and nothing to gain.

True it is that revenge, with our young braves, is considered gain, even at the cost of their own lives, but old men who stay at home in times of war, and old women who have sons to lose, know better.

Our great father Washington . . . sends us word by his son, who no doubt is a great chief among his people, that if we do as he desires, he will protect us. His brave armies will be to us a bristling wall of strength, and his great ships of war will fill our harbors so that our ancient enemies far to the northward, the Simsians and Hydas, will no longer frighten our women and old men. Then he will be our father, and we will be his children.

But can this ever be? Your God loves your people and hates mine; he folds his strong arms lovingly around the white man and leads him as a father leads his infant son, but he has forsaken his red children; he makes your people wax strong every day, and soon they will fill the land; while our people are ebbing away like a fast receding tide that will never flow again. The white man's God cannot love his red children, or he would protect them. They seem to be orphans and can look nowhere for help. How, then, can we become brothers? How can your father become our father and bring us prosperity and awaken in us dreams of returning greatness?

Your God seems to be partial. He came to the white man. We never saw him; never even heard his voice; he gave the white man laws, but he had no word for his red children, whose teeming millions filled this vast continent as the stars fill the firmament. No, we are two distinct races and must ever remain so. There is little in common between us. The ashes of our ancestors are sacred, and their final resting place is hallowed ground, while you wander away from the tombs of your fathers seemingly without regret.

Your religion was written on tables of stone by the iron finger of an angry God, lest you might forget it. The red man could never remember nor comprehend it.

Our religion is the traditions of our ancestors, the dreams of our old men, given them by the great Spirit, and the visions of our sachems, and is written in the hearts of our people.

Your dead cease to love you and the homes of their nativity as soon as they pass the portals of the tomb. They wander far off beyond the stars, are soon forgotten, and never return. Our dead never forget the beautiful world that gave them being. They still love its winding rivers, its great mountains and sequestered vales, and they ever yearn in tenderest affection over the lonely-hearted living and often return to visit and comfort them.

Day and night cannot dwell together. The red man has ever fled the approach of the white man, as the changing mists on the mountain side flee before the blazing morning sun.

However, your proposition seems a just one, and I think my folks will accept it and will retire to the reservation you offer them, and we will dwell apart and in peace, for the words of the great white chief seem to be the voice of nature speaking to my people out of the thick darkness that is fast gathering around them like a dense fog floating inward from a midnight sea.

It matters but little where we pass the remainder of our days. They are not many. The Indian's night promises to be dark. No bright star hovers about the horizon. Sad-voiced winds moan in the distance. Some grim Nemesis of our race is on the red man's trail, and wherever he goes he will still hear the sure approaching footsteps of the fell destroyer and prepare to meet his doom, as does the wounded doe that hears the approaching footsteps of the hunter. A few more moons, a few more winters, and not one of all the mighty hosts that once filled this broad land or that now roam in fragmentary bands through these vast solitudes will remain to weep over the tombs of a people once as powerful and hopeful as your own.

But why should we repine? Why should I murmur at the fate of my people? Tribes are made up of individuals and are no better than they. Men come and go like the waves of the sea. A tear, a tamanamus, a dirge, and they are gone from our longing eyes forever. Even the white man, whose God walked and talked with him, as friend to friend, is not exempt from the common destiny. We *may* be brothers after all. We shall see.

We will ponder your proposition, and when we have decided we will tell you. But should we accept it, I here and now make this the first condition: that we will not be denied the privilege, without molestation, of visiting at the graves of our ancestors and friends. Every part of this country is sacred to my people. Every hillside, every valley, every plain and grove, has been hallowed by some fond memory or some sad experience of my tribe. Even the rocks that seem to lie dumb as they swelter in the sun along the silent seashore in solemn grandeur thrill with memories of past events connected with the fate of my people, and the very dust under your feet responds more lovingly to our footsteps than to yours, because it is the ashes of our ancestors, and our bare feet are conscious of the sympathetic touch, for the soil is rich with the life of our kindred.

The sable braves, and fond mothers, and glad-hearted maidens, and the little children who lived and rejoiced here, and whose very names are now forgotten, still love these solitudes, and their deep fastnesses at eventide grow shadowy with the presence of dusky spirits. And when the last red man shall have perished from the earth and his memory among the white men shall have become a myth, these shores shall swarm with the invisible dead of my tribe, and when your children's children shall think themselves alone in the field, the shop, upon the highway, or in the silence of the woods, they will not be alone.

In all the earth there is no place dedicated to solitude. At night, when the streets of your cities and villages shall be silent, and you think them deserted, they will throng with the returning hosts that once filled and still love this beautiful land. The white man will never be alone. Let him be just and deal kindly with my people, for the dead are not altogether powerless. ■

Susan B. Anthony Argues for Women's Rights

"It was we, the people; not we, the white male citizens. . . ."

WHEN SUSAN BROWNELL ANTHONY championed the cause of women's suffrage in the nineteenth century, ridicule and taunting were common reactions to her fiery words. The daughter of a Quaker abolitionist, she fought from an early age to gain equal pay and education for women. With Elizabeth Cady Stanton, she organized the National Woman Suffrage Association and helped establish the first laws in New York State to recognize a woman's rights to own property and have control of her children.

In 1872, Susan B. Anthony's efforts to obtain the right to vote gained notoriety when she led a group of women to the polls in the presidential election. This march set the pattern for the use of civil disobedience and subsequent court action to attract attention and adherents. Her indictment and conviction for what she called the "alleged crime" of voting (with a $100 fine that she refused to pay) helped publicize her cause.

In the speech that follows, she defends her actions by asserting her equal rights as a citizen. Her pioneering stance is expressed by rhetorical questioning ("Are women persons?") and reference to Noah Webster and his fellow lexicographers on the defining of "citizen." Most forceful is her use of a repeated word in parallel structure to bolster the constitutional argument: "It was we, the people; not we, the white male citizens; nor yet we, the male citizens; but we, the whole people. . . ."

□   □   □

Friends and fellow citizens, I stand before you tonight under indictment for the alleged crime of having voted at the last presidential election, without having a lawful right to vote. It shall be my work this evening to prove to you that in thus voting, I not only committed no crime but, instead, simply exercised my citizen's rights, guaranteed to me and all United States citizens by the National Constitution, beyond the power of any state to deny.

The preamble of the federal Constitution says:

"We, the people of the United States, in order to form a more perfect union, establish justice, insure domestic tranquillity, provide for the common defense, promote the general welfare, and secure the blessings of liberty to ourselves and our posterity, do ordain and establish this Constitution for the United States of America."

It was we, the people; not we, the white male citizens; nor yet we, the male citizens; but we, the whole people, who formed the Union. And we formed it, not to give the blessings of liberty, but to secure them; not to the half of ourselves and the half of our posterity, but to the whole people—women as well as men. And it is a downright mockery to talk to women of their enjoyment of the blessings of liberty while they are denied the use of the only means of securing them provided by this democratic-republican government—the ballot.

For any state to make sex a qualification that must ever result in the disfranchisement of one entire half of the people is to pass a bill of attainder, or an ex post facto law, and is therefore a violation of the supreme law of the land. By it the blessings of liberty are forever withheld from women and their female posterity. To them this government has no just powers derived from the consent of the governed. To them this government is not a democracy. It is not a republic. It is an odious aristocracy; a hateful oligarchy of sex; the most hateful aristocracy ever established on the face of the globe; an oligarchy of wealth, where the rich govern the poor. An oligarchy of learning, where the educated govern the ignorant, or even an oligarchy of race, where the Saxon rules the African, might be endured; but this oligarchy of sex, which makes father, brothers, husband, sons, the oligarchs over the mother and sisters, the wife and daughters, of every household—which ordains all men sovereigns, all women subjects, carries dissension, discord, and rebellion into every home of the nation.

Webster, Worcester, and Bouvier all define a citizen to be a person in the United States, entitled to vote and hold office.

The only question left to be settled now is: Are women persons? And I hardly believe any of our opponents will have the hardihood to say they are not. Being persons, then, women are citizens; and no state has a right to make any law, or to enforce any old law, that shall abridge their privileges or immunities. Hence, every discrimination against women in the constitutions and laws of the several states is today null and void, precisely as is every one against Negroes. ■

Governor Huey Long of Louisiana Proposes to End the Depression by Redistributing Wealth

"'EVERY Man a King.' Every man to eat when there is something to eat; all to wear something when there is something to wear. That makes us all a sovereign."

TWO GREAT AMERICAN NOVELS—Adria Locke Langley's *A Lion Is in the Streets* and Robert Penn Warren's *All the King's Men*—were written about Huey Long, who was elected governor of Louisiana in 1928 and U.S. senator two years later and who was a rising star on the national political scene until felled by an assassin in 1935. That fascination with Long's character was because he was part idealist, part demagogue; part visionary able to bring schools and new hope to people ground into poverty, part power-hungry politician who set up a near-dictatorship in his state.

The New Deal despite its stirring first hundred days, had not rescued the nation from the grip of the Great Depression. Huey Long's "Share Our Wealth" program appealed to the resentment of the legions of unemployed against what he called the super-rich. By mingling economic statistics with lessons of economic morality "in effect" from the Almighty, Long employed the new medium of radio to build a national following. According to FDR speechwriter Samuel I. Rosenman, Roosevelt feared a challenge from the Democratic populist-progressive Long more than from any Republican.

This is excerpted from a thirty-minute radio speech delivered in January 1935.

□   □   □

. . . I contend, my friends, that we have no difficult problem to solve in America, and that is the view of nearly everyone with whom I have discussed the matter here in Washington and elsewhere throughout the United States—that we have no very difficult problem to solve.

It is not the difficulty of the problem which we have; it is the fact that the rich people of this country—and by rich people I mean the super-rich—will not allow us to solve the problems, or rather the one little problem that is afflicting this country, because in order to cure all of our woes it is necessary to scale down the big fortunes, that we may scatter the wealth to be shared by all of the people. . . .

I believe that was the judgment and the view and the law of the Lord, that we would have to distribute wealth every so often, in order that there could not be people starving to death in a land of plenty, as there is in America today.

We have in America today more wealth, more goods, more food, more clothing, more houses than we have ever had. We have everything in abundance here.

We have the farm problem, my friends, because we have too much cotton, because we have too much wheat, and have too much corn, and too much potatoes.

We have a home-loan problem, because we have too many houses, and yet nobody can buy them and live in them.

We have trouble, my friends, in the country, because we have too much money owing, the greatest indebtedness that has ever been given to civilization, where it has been shown that we are incapable of distributing the actual things that are here, because the people have not money enough to supply themselves with them, and because the greed of a few men is such that they think it is necessary that they own everything, and their pleasure consists in the starvation of the masses, and in their possessing things they cannot use, and their children cannot use, but who bask in the splendor of sunlight and wealth, casting darkness and despair and impressing it on everyone else.

"So, therefore," said the Lord in effect, "if you see these things that now have occurred and exist in this and other countries, there must be a constant scattering of wealth in any country if this country is to survive." . . .

Now, my friends, if you were off on an island where there were a hundred lunches, you could not let one man eat up the hundred lunches, or take the hundred lunches and not let anybody else eat any of them. If you did, there would not be anything else for the balance of the people to consume.

So, we have in America today, my friends, a condition by which about ten men dominate the means of activity in at least 85 percent of the activities that you own. They either own directly everything or they have got some kind of mortgage on it, with a very small percentage to be excepted. They own the banks, they own the steel mills, they own the railroads, they own the bonds, they own the mortgages, they own the stores, and they have chained the country from one end to the other until there is not any kind of business that a small, independent man could go into today and make a living, and there is not any kind of business that an independent man can go into and make any money to buy an automobile with; and they have finally and gradually and steadily eliminated everybody from the fields in which there is a living to be made, and still they have got little enough sense to think they ought to be able to get more business out of it anyway.

If you reduce a man to the point where he is starving to death and bleeding and dying, how do you expect that man to get hold of any money to spend with you? It is not possible.

Then, ladies and gentlemen, how do you expect people to live, when the wherewith cannot be had by the people? . . .

Now, we have organized a society, and we call it Share Our Wealth Society, a society with the motto "Every Man a King."

Every man a king, so there would be no such thing as a man or woman who did not have the necessities of life, who would not be dependent upon the whims and caprices and *ipse dixit* of the financial barons for a living. What do we propose by this society? We propose to limit the wealth of big men in the country. There is an average of $15,000 in wealth to every family in America. That is right here today.

We do not propose to divide it up equally. We do not propose a division of wealth, but we propose to limit poverty that we will allow to be inflicted upon any man's family. We will not say we are going to try to guarantee any equality, or $15,000 to a family. No; but we do say that one-third of the average is low enough for any one family to hold, that there should be a guarantee of a family wealth of around $5,000; enough for a home, an automobile, a radio, and the ordinary conveniences, and the opportunity to educate their children; a fair share of the income of this land thereafter to that family so there will be no such thing as merely the select to have those things, and so there will be no such thing as a family living in poverty and distress.

We have to limit fortunes. Our present plan is that we will allow no one man to own more than $50 million. We think that with that limit we will be able to carry out the balance of the program. It may be necessary that we limit it to less than $50 million. It may be necessary, in working out of the plans that no man's fortune would be more than $10 million or $15 million. But be that as it may, it will still be more than any one man, or any one man and his children and their children, will be able to spend in their lifetimes; and it is not necessary or reasonable to have wealth piled up beyond that point where we cannot prevent poverty among the masses.

Another thing we propose is old-age pension of $30 a month for everyone that is sixty years old. Now, we do not give this pension to a man making $1,000 a year, and we do not give it to him if he has $10,000 in property, but outside of that we do.

We will limit hours of work. There is not any necessity of having over-production. I think all you have got to do, ladies and gentlemen, is just limit the hours of work to such an extent as people will work only so long as it is necessary to produce enough for all of the people to have what they need. Why, ladies and gentlemen, let us say that all of these labor-saving devices reduce hours down to where you do not have to work but four hours a day; that is enough for these people, and then praise be the name of the Lord, if it gets that good. Let it be good and not a curse, and then we will have five hours a day and five days a week, or even less than that, and we might give a man a whole month off during a year, or give him two months; and we might do what other countries have seen fit to do, and what I did in Louisiana, by having schools by which adults could go back and learn the things that have been discovered since they went to school.

We will not have any trouble taking care of the agricultural situation. All you have to do is balance your production with your consumption. You simply have to abandon a particular crop that you have too much of, and all you have to do is store the surplus for the next year, and the government will take it over. . . .

Those are the things we propose to do. "Every Man a King." Every man to eat when there is something to eat; all to wear something when there is something to wear. That makes us all a sovereign. . . .

And we ought to take care of the veterans of the wars in this program. That is a small matter. Suppose it does cost a billion dollars a year—that means that the money will be scattered throughout this country. We ought to pay them a bonus. We can do it. . . .

Now, my friends, we have got to hit the root with the ax. Centralized power in the hands of a few, with centralized credit in the hands of a few, is the trouble.

Get together in your community tonight or tomorrow and organize one of our Share Our Wealth Societies. If you do not understand it, write me and let me send you the platform; let me give you the proof of it.

This is Huey P. Long talking, United States senator, Washington, D.C. Write me and let me send you the data on this proposition. Enroll with us. Let us make known to the people what we are going to do. I will send you a button, if I have got enough of them left. We have got a little button that some of our friends designed, with our message around the rim of the button, and in the center "Every Man a King." . . .

Now that I have but a minute left, I want to say that I suppose my family is listening in on the radio in New Orleans, and I will say to my wife and three children that I am entirely well and hope to be home before many more days, and I hope they have listened to my speech tonight, and I wish them and all of their neighbors and friends everything good that may be had.

I thank you, my friends, for your kind attention, and I hope you will enroll with us, take care of your own work in the work of this government, and share or help in our Share Our Wealth Societies. ■

Labor's John L. Lewis Defends His Union's Right to Strike

"LABOR, like Israel, has many sorrows."

"I HAVE PLEADED YOUR CASE," the president of the United Mine Workers told his rank and file, "not in the tones of a feeble mendicant asking alms but in the thundering voice of the captain of a mighty host, demanding the rights to which free men are entitled."

This son of a Welsh immigrant miner steeped his oratory in biblical cadences and metaphors; his sonorous voice was especially effective on radio. John L. Lewis formed the Committee for Industrial Organization in 1935 (renamed Congress of Industrial Organizations in 1938) because he believed that the American Federation of Labor was failing the industrial workers, and he was not afraid to ignite the public wrath with strikes.

In this speech, delivered September 3, 1937, he responded to a flip "a plague on both your houses" comment by Franklin Roosevelt with his allusion to "one who has been sheltered in labor's house," a nice juxtaposition of tropes. The speech had force in the writing—"No tin hat brigade of goose-stepping vigilantes or bibble-babbling mob of blackguarding and corporation-paid scoundrels will prevent the onward march of labor" has a ring to it. But the address gained in the delivery; Lane Kirkland, when he was president of the AFL-CIO, upon hearing the cue "many sorrows" at a dinner, would adopt a deep voice and deliver the penultimate paragraph of John L. Lewis's most memorable speech.

□   □   □

The United States Chamber of Commerce, the National Association of Manufacturers, and similar groups representing industry and financial interests are rendering a disservice to the American people in their attempts to frustrate the organization of labor and in their refusal to accept collective bargaining as one of our economic institutions.

These groups are encouraging a systematic organization under the sham pretext of local interests. They equip these vigilantes with tin hats, wooden clubs, gas masks, and lethal weapons and train them in the arts of brutality and oppression.

No tin hat brigade of goose-stepping vigilantes or bibble-babbling mob of blackguarding and corporation-paid scoundrels will prevent the onward march of labor, or divert its purpose to play its natural and rational part in the development of the economic, political, and social life of our nation.

Unionization, as opposed to communism, presupposes the relation of employment; it is based upon the wage system, and it recognizes fully and unreservedly the institution of private property and the right to investment profits. It is upon the fuller development of collective bargaining, the wider expansion of the labor movement, the increased influence of labor in our national councils, that the perpetuity of our democratic institutions must largely depend.

The organized workers of America, free in their industrial life, conscious partners of production, secure in their homes, and enjoying a decent standard of living, will prove the finest bulwark against the intrusion of alien doctrines of government.

Do those who hatched this foolish cry of communism in the CIO fear the increased influence of labor in our democracy? Do they fear its influence will be cast on the side of shorter hours, a better system of distributed employment, better homes for the underprivileged, Social Security for the aged, a fairer distribution of our national income? Certainly the workers that are being organized want a voice in the determination of these objectives of social justice.

Certainly labor wants a fairer share of the national income. Assuredly labor wants a larger participation in increased productive efficiency. Obviously the population is entitled to participate in the fruits of the genius of our men of achievement in the field of material sciences.

Labor has suffered just as our farm population has suffered from a viciously unequal distribution of the national income. In the exploitation of both classes of workers has been the source of panic and depression, and upon the economic welfare of both rests the best assurance of a sound and permanent prosperity.

Under the banner of the Committee for Industrial Organization, American labor is on the march. Its objectives today are those it had in the beginning: to strive for the unionization of our unorganized millions of workers and for the acceptance of collective bargaining as a recognized American institution.

It seeks peace with the industrial world. It seeks cooperation and mutuality of effort with the agricultural population. It would avoid strikes. It would have its rights determined under the law by the peaceful negotiations and contract relationships that are supposed to characterize American commercial life.

Until an aroused public opinion demands that employers accept that rule, labor has no recourse but to surrender its rights or struggle for their realization with its own economic power.

Labor, like Israel, has many sorrows. Its women weep for their fallen, and they lament for the future of the children of the race. It ill behooves one who has supped at labor's table and who has been sheltered in labor's house to curse with equal fervor and fine impartiality both labor and its adversaries when they become locked in deadly embrace.

I repeat that labor seeks peace and guarantees its own loyalty, but the voice of labor, insistent upon its rights, should not be annoying to the ears of justice nor offensive to the conscience of the American people. ■

FDR Reminds the Daughters of the American Revolution about Their Lineage

"REMEMBER always that all of us . . . are descended from immigrants and revolutionists."

THIS TALK IS REMEMBERED AS the "My fellow immigrants" speech, as if President Roosevelt had startled his audience with the salutation "My fellow immigrants"—which he did not. Yet the theme of the brief remarks was tastefully shocking: that the conservative, wellborn audience, which considered him "a traitor to his class" for his social legislation, should not forget its immigrant heritage. He was conducting a modern revolution in the New Deal, and he forced the listeners to recall the word "revolution" in their organization's title.

The day before, on April 20, 1938, the DAR had adopted resolutions contrary to his leftist programs, but had applauded his plans to expand the navy. He seized on this approval to end his carefully considered "unprepared" remarks in an upbeat way, lest his gentle chastisement appear to be what it was.

□   □   □

I couldn't let a fifth year go by without coming to see you. I must ask you to take me just as I am, in a business suit—and I see you are still in favor of national defense—take me as I am, with no prepared remarks. You know, as a matter of fact, I would have been here to one of your conventions in prior years—one or more—but it is not the time that it takes to come before you and speak for half an hour, it is the preparation for that half hour. And I suppose that for every half-hour speech that I make before a convention or over the radio, I put in ten hours preparing it.

So I have to ask you to bear with me, to let me just come here without preparation to tell you how glad I am to avail myself of this opportunity, to tell you how proud I am, as a revolutionary descendant, to greet you.

I thought of preaching on a text, but I shall not. I shall only give you the text, and I shall not preach on it. I think I can afford to give you the text because it so happens, through no fault of my own, that I am descended from a number of people who came over in the *Mayflower*. More than that, every one of my ancestors on both sides—and when you go back four generations or five generations it means thirty-two or sixty-four of them—every single one of them, without exception, was in this land in 1776. And there was only one Tory among them.

The text is this: remember, remember always that all of us, and you and I especially, are descended from immigrants and revolutionists.

I am particularly glad to know that today you are making this fine appeal to the youth of America. To these rising generations, to our sons and grandsons and great-grandsons, we cannot overestimate the importance of what we are doing in this year, in our own generation, to keep alive the spirit of American democracy. The spirit of opportunity is the kind of spirit that has led us as a nation—not as a small group but as a nation—to meet the very great problems of the past.

We look for a younger generation that is going to be more American than we are. We are doing the best that we can, and yet we can do better than that, we can do more than that, by inculcating in the boys and girls of this country today some of the underlying fundamentals, the reasons that brought our immigrant ancestors to this country, the reasons that impelled our revolutionary ancestors to throw off a fascist yoke.

We have a great many things to do. Among other things in this world is the need of being very, very certain, no matter what happens, that the sovereignty of the United States will never be impaired.

There have been former occasions, conventions of the Daughters of the American Revolution, when voices were raised, needed to be raised, for better national defense. This year, you are raising those same voices and I am glad of it. But I am glad also that the government of the United States can assure you today that it is taking definite, practical steps for the defense of the nation. ■

Walter Lippmann Scores His Generational Cohort for Having Taken "the Easy Way"

"'FOR every good that you wish to preserve, you will have to sacrifice your comfort and your ease. There is nothing for nothing any longer.'"

WALTER LIPPMANN helped found the progressive magazine the *New Republic;* he became the most influential "serious" newspaper columnist from 1931 to his retirement in 1967, and was the man to whom the epithet "pundit"—in Hindi, "learned man"; in American English, "sage commentator"—was most often applied. In his book *The Good Society,* he set forth a political philosophy based on a moral order; his intellectualism, internationalist bent, and aristocratic nature earned the respect of the nation's leaders, whose confidences he tended to keep in return for an opportunity to advise in private.

In the summer of 1940, world war was on the horizon. Lippmann, who himself had underestimated the threat of Hitler, recognized the danger that his generation of leaders had failed to counter. He spoke to the Harvard class of 1910's thirtieth reunion to brace them and himself for the storm to come. This text is from the Lippmann papers at the Yale library, which includes the speaker's editing. A despairing line, "I do not know whether we shall see again in our lives a peace that we shall believe can last," is crossed out.

□   □   □

I think I am speaking for all of you when I say that we have come here in order that we may pause for a moment in which to fortify our faith and to renew our courage and to make strong our spirit.

We have come back to Harvard and when we go away, we shall have realized what ordinary words can scarcely make real to us: we shall realize what it is that is threatened with destruction, what it is that we are called upon to defend. We walk again through the Yard and we shall think of the three centuries during which on this ground men have believed in the dignity of the human soul, and how, believing this, they have cherished, and labored patiently in, the great central tradition of the Western world. This memory will fortify our faith, and we shall say to ourselves that this glory, which is ours, this glory which we have known since our youth, this glory which has given to each of us whatever there is in him that matters at all, we shall say that this glory shall not perish from the earth.

We have come back here, along with those we love, to see one another again. And by being together we shall remember that we are part of a great company, we shall remember that we are not mere individuals isolated in a tempest, but that we are members of a community—that what we have to do, we shall do together, with friends beside us. And their friendliness will quiet our anxieties, and ours will quiet theirs. And as they live up to what we expect of them, we shall find the resolution to live up to what they expect of us. And so we shall renew our courage, and we shall find the strength that we shall need.

I am speaking solemnly because this is a solemn hour in the history of the modern world. No one here today will imagine he can divert himself by forgetting it. But though the world roars and rages about us, we must secure our peace of mind, a quiet place of tranquillity and of order and of purpose within our own selves. For it is doubt and uncertainty of purpose and confusion of values which unnerves men. Peace of mind comes to men only when, having faced all the issues clearly and without flinching, they have made their decision and are resolved.

For myself I like to think these days of the words of Washington which Gouverneur Morris reported, words spoken when the Constitutional Convention in Philadelphia seemed about to fail: Washington, said Morris, "was collected within himself. His countenance had more than usual solemnity, His eye was fixed, and seemed to look into futurity." "It is," said he, "too probable that no plan we propose will be adopted. Perhaps another dreadful conflict is to be sustained. If to please the people, we offer what we ourselves disapprove, how can we afterwards defend our work? Let us raise a standard to which the wise and honest can repair. The event is in the hands of God."

Upon the standard to which the wise and honest generation must now repair, it is written, "You have lived the easy way; henceforth, you will live the hard way." It is written, "You came into a great heritage made by the insight and the sweat and the blood of inspired and devoted and courageous men; thoughtlessly and in utmost self-indulgence you have all but squandered this inheritance. Now only by the heroic virtues which made this inheritance can you restore it again." It is written, "You took the good things for granted. Now you must earn them again." It is written, "For every right that you cherish, you have a duty which you must fulfill. For every hope that you entertain, you have a task that you must perform. For every good that you wish to preserve, you will have to sacrifice your comfort and your ease. There is nothing for nothing any longer."

For twenty years the free peoples of the Western world took the easy way, ourselves more lightheartedly than any others. That is why we were stricken. That is why the defenses of Western civilization crumbled. That is why we find ourselves today knowing that we here in America may soon be the last stronghold of our civilization—the citadel of law and of liberty, of mercy and of charity, of justice among men and of love and of good will.

We are defending that citadel; we have made it the center of the ultimate resistance to the evil which is devastating the world. But more than that, more than the center of resistance, we mean to make it the center of the resurrection, the source of the energies by which the men who believe as we do may be liberated, and the lands that are subjugated redeemed, and the world we live in purified and pacified once more. This is the American destiny, and unless we fulfill that destiny we shall have betrayed our own past and we shall make our own future meaningless, chaotic, and low.

But we shall not resist the evil that has come into the world, nor prepare the resurrection in which we believe, if we continue to take, as we have taken so persistently, the easy way in all things. Let us remind ourselves how in these twenty years we have at the critical junctures taken always the road of the least effort and the method of the cheapest solution and of greatest self-indulgence.

In 1917–1918, we participated in a war which ended in the victory of the free peoples. It was hard to make a good and magnanimous peace. It was easier to make a bad and unworkable peace. We took the easiest way.

Having sacrificed blood and treasure to win the war, having failed to establish quickly and at the first stroke a good and lasting peace, it was too hard, it was too much trouble to keep on trying. We gave up. We took the easy way, the way that required us to do nothing, and we passed resolutions and made pious declarations saying that there was not going to be any more war, that war was henceforth outlawed.

Thus we entered the postwar twenties, refusing to organize the peace of the world because that was too much trouble, believing—because that was no trouble at all—that peace would last by declaring that it ought to last. So enchanted were we with our own noble but inexpensive sentiments that, though the world was disorganized and in anarchy, we decided to disarm ourselves and the other democracies. That was also the easy way. It saved money. It saved effort.

In this mood we faced the problems of reconstruction from the other war. It was too much trouble to make a workable settlement of reparations and of the war debts. It was easier to let them break down and wreck the finances of the world. We took the easier way. It was too much trouble to work out arrangements for the resumption of trade because it was too much trouble to deal with the vested interests and the lobbyists and the politicians. It was easier to let the trade of the world be strangled by tariffs, quotas, and exchange controls. And we took the easy way. It was easier to finance an inflationary boom by cheap money than it was to reestablish trade based upon the exchange of goods. We indulged ourselves in the inflationary boom and let it run (because it was too much trouble to check it) into a crash that threw about twenty-five millions, here and abroad, out of work, and destroyed the savings of a large part of the people of all countries.

Having got to that, it was too hard to liquidate the inflation. It was easier to cover up the inflation and pretend that it did not exist. So we took the easier way—we maintained the tariffs, we maintained the wage costs and the overhead expenditures of the boom, and thus made it impossible to recover from the crash.

The failure of the recovery produced at the foundations of Western civilization a revolutionary discontent. It was easy to be frightened by the discontent. So we were properly frightened. But it was hard to make the effort and the sacrifice to remedy the discontent. And because it was hard, we did not do it. All that we did was to accuse one another of being economic royalists on the one hand, economic lunatics on the other. It was easier to call names than it was to do anything else, and so we called names.

Then out of this discontent there was bred in the heart of Europe and on the edge of Asia an organized rebellion against the whole heritage of Western civilization. It was easy to disapprove, and we disapproved. But it was hard to organize and prepare the resistance: that would have required money and effort and sacrifice and discipline and courage. We watched the rebellion grow. We heard it threaten the things we believe in. We saw it commit, year after year, savage crimes. We disliked it all. But we liked better our easygoing ways, our jobs, our profits, and our pleasures, and so we said, It is bad, but it won't last; it is dangerous, but it can't cross the ocean; it is evil, but if we arm ourselves, and discipline ourselves, and act with other free peoples to contain it and hold it back, we shall be giving up our ease and our comfort, we shall be taking risks, and that is more trouble than we care to take.

So we are where we are today. We are where we are because whenever we had a choice to make, we have chosen the alternative that required the least effort at the moment. There is organized mechanized evil loose in the world. But what has made possible its victories is the lazy, self-indulgent materialism, the amiable, lackadaisical, footless, confused complacency of the free nations of the world. They have dissipated, like wastrels and drunkards, the inheritance of freedom and order that came to them from hardworking, thrifty, faithful, believing, and brave men. The disaster in the midst of which we are living is a disaster in the character of men. It is a catastrophe of the soul of a whole generation which had forgotten, had lost, and had renounced the imperative and indispensable virtues of laborious, heroic, and honorable men.

To these virtues we shall return in the ordeal through which we are now passing, or all that still remains will be lost and all that we attempt, in order to defend it, will be in vain. We shall turn from the soft vices in which a civilization decays, we shall return to the stern virtues by which a civilization is made, we shall do this because, at long last, we know that we must, because finally we begin to see that the hard way is the only enduring way.

You had perhaps hoped, as I did when we came together for our twenty-fifth reunion, that tonight we should have reached a point in our lives when we could look forward in a few more years to retiring from active responsibility in the heat of the day, and could look forward to withdrawing into the calm of a cooler evening. You know that that is not to be. We have not yet earned our right to rest at ease. When we think of the desperate misery and the awful suffering that has befallen the people of France and of Great Britain and of Austria and Czechoslovakia and Poland and Denmark and Norway and the Netherlands and Belgium, we shall not, I hope, complain or feel sorry for ourselves.

I like to think—in fact, I intend to go away from here thinking—that having remembered the past we shall not falter, having seen one another again, we shall not flinch. ■

Elder Statesman
Bernard Baruch Offers
America's First Plan to
Control Nuclear Weapons

"WE are here to make a choice between the quick and the dead."

THE SELF-MADE MILLIONAIRE FINANCIER was chosen by President Wilson to head the War Industries Board during World War I; for the rest of his long life (he died in 1965, at ninety-four), Bernard Baruch preferred the role of unofficial, behind-the-scenes presidential adviser. In Lafayette Park, across Pennsylvania Avenue from the White House, can be found the "Bernard M. Baruch Bench of Inspiration"; with ostentatious humility, he frequently held court there.

Appointed in 1946 by President Truman to present the U.S. plan for control of atomic energy to the UN, Baruch turned to Herbert Bayard Swope, three-time Pulitzer Prize–winning reporter and editor who was his lifelong friend and publicist, to draft a speech. Swope (who pointed out to me in 1952 that Baruch credited him with the coinage of the phrase "cold war") put the story in the lead by posing a life-and-death choice: "the quick [living] and the dead" is a biblical phrase that occurs in Acts 10:42 and 1 Peter 4:5. It was picked up by Shakespeare in *Hamlet*, to be said by Laertes as he leaps into the grave of his sister, Ophelia: "Now pile your dust upon the quick and dead. . . ."

The speech was delivered to a UN meeting in New York's Hunter College gymnasium on June 14, 1946. The plan it introduced was vetoed by the Soviet Union, which soon developed its own nuclear weapons; at that point, U.S. disarmament policy could no longer be so forthright. However, the Swope-turned phrases are timeless—"better pain as the price of peace than death as the price of war"—and the world came to realize that "we are now facing a problem more of ethics than of physics."

☐   ☐   ☐

We are here to make a choice between the quick and the dead. That is our business.

Behind the black portent of the new atomic age lies a hope which, seized upon with faith, can work our salvation. If we fail, then we have damned every man to be the slave of fear. Let us not deceive ourselves: we must elect world peace or world destruction.

Science has torn from nature a secret so vast in its potentialities that our minds cower from the terror it creates. Yet terror is not enough to inhibit the use of the atomic bomb. The terror created by weapons has never stopped man from employing them. For each new weapon a defense has been produced, in time. But now we face a condition in which adequate defense does not exist.

Science, which gave us this dread power, shows that it can be made a giant help to humanity, but science does not show us how to prevent its baleful use. So we have been appointed to obviate that peril by finding a meeting of the minds and the hearts of our peoples. Only in the will of mankind lies the answer.

In this crisis we represent not only our governments but, in a larger way, we represent the peoples of the world. We must remember that the peoples do not belong to the governments, but that the governments belong to the peoples. We must answer their demands; we must answer the world's longing for peace and security.

In that desire the United States shares ardently and hopefully. The search of science for the absolute weapon has reached fruition in this country. But she stands ready to proscribe and destroy this instrument—to lift its use from death to life—if the world will join in a pact to that end.

In our success lies the promise of a new life, freed from the heart-stopping fears that now beset the world. The beginning of victory for the great ideals for which millions have bled and died lies in building a workable plan. Now we approach the fulfillment of the aspirations of mankind. At the end of the road lies the fairer, better, surer life we crave and mean to have.

Only by a lasting peace are liberties and democracies strengthened and deepened. War is their enemy. And it will not do to believe that any of us can escape war's devastation. Victor, vanquished, and neutrals alike are affected physically, economically, and morally.

Against the degradation of war we can erect a safeguard. That is the guerdon for which we reach. Within the scope of the formula we outline here, there will be found, to those who seek it, the essential elements of our purpose. Others will see only emptiness. Each of us carries his own mirror in which is reflected hope—or determined desperation—courage or cowardice.

There is famine throughout the world today. It starves men's bodies. But there is a greater famine—the hunger of men's spirit. That starvation can be cured by the conquest of fear, and the substitution of hope, from which springs faith—faith in each other; faith that we want to work together toward salvation; and determination that those who threaten the peace and safety shall be punished.

The peoples of these democracies gathered here have a particular concern with our answer, for their peoples hate war. They will have a heavy exaction to make of those who fail to provide an escape. They are not afraid of an internationalism that protects; they are unwilling to be fobbled off by mouthings about narrow sovereignty, which is today's phrase for yesterday's isolationism.

The basis of a sound foreign policy, in this new age, for all the nations here gathered, is that: anything that happens, no matter where or how, which menaces the peace of the world, or the economic stability, concerns each and all of us.

That, roughly, may be said to be the central theme of the United Nations. It is with that thought we gain consideration of the most important subject that can engage mankind—life itself.

Now, if ever, is the time to act for the common good. Public opinion supports a world movement toward security. If I read the signs aright, the peoples want a program, not composed merely of pious thoughts, but of enforceable sanctions—an international law with teeth in it.

We of this nation, desirous of helping to bring peace to the world and realizing the heavy obligations upon us, arising from our possession of the means for producing the bomb and from the fact that it is part of our armament, are prepared to make our full contribution toward effective control of atomic energy.

But before a country is ready to relinquish any winning weapons, it must have more than words to reassure it. It must have a guarantee of safety, not only against the offenders in the atomic area, but against the illegal users of other weapons—bacteriological, biological, gas—perhaps—why not?—against war itself.

In the elimination of war lies our solution, for only then will nations cease to compete with one another in the production and use of dread "secret" weapons which are evaluated solely by their capacity to kill. This devilish program takes us back not merely to the Dark Ages but from cosmos to chaos. If we succeed in finding a suitable way to control atomic weapons, it is reasonable to hope that we may also preclude the use of other weapons adaptable to mass destruction. When a man learns to say "A" he can, if he chooses, learn the rest of the alphabet, too.

Let this be anchored in our minds:

Peace is never long preserved by weight of metal or by an armament race. Peace can be made tranquil and secure only by understanding and agreement fortified by sanctions. We must embrace international cooperation or international disintegration.

Science has taught us how to put the atom to work. But to make it work for good instead of for evil lies in the domain dealing with the principles of human duty. We are now facing a problem more of ethics than of physics.

The solution will require apparent sacrifice in pride and in position, but better pain as the price of peace than death as the price of war. ■

Senator Robert Taft Opposes War Crimes Trials as Ex Post Facto Law

"THE trial of the vanquished by the victors cannot be impartial, no matter how it is hedged about with the forms of justice."

ROBERT A. TAFT, son of President William Howard Taft ("Mere size is no sin"), dominated the U.S. Senate in the decade after World War II. He led the fight to break down wartime restrictions such as price controls, lest they become permanent in peacetime, and urged the rollback of other reaches for more central power that marked the New Deal crisis era. Brilliant and abrasive, personally stiff and remote, he became known as Mr. Republican; "To err is Truman" was the famous crack of his wife,

Martha; he is remembered for his bill restraining the power of organized labor. Though the exponent of a principled policy to limit the concentration of executive power, his most lasting contribution to the nation's economy was housing legislation revered by liberals.

One reason he lost the Republican nomination to Eisenhower in 1952 was his willingness to support unpopular causes in the name of political principle. As World War II ended, and the enormity of Nazi atrocities came to light, the Allied nations moved toward trying Hitler's aides for the new crime of genocide. Taft reminded Americans that trying anyone for acts later designated as crimes was against all Anglo-American legal principles; pundit David Lawrence, his conservative supporter, called this "a technical quibble," and Ohio's *Toledo Blade* summed up the opinion of the majority in saying Taft's speech to Kenyon College on October 5, 1946, demonstrated that he "had a wonderful mind which knows practically everything and understands practically nothing."

On later review, however, at least another passage of his "equal justice under law" speech—about our failure to protest Stalin's takeover of the Baltic states—seems prescient in its evocation of human rights as a greater determinant of foreign policy than is the use of force.

The tone of this Taft speech is formal and dispassionate, the reasoning logical, the style legalistic and bloodless, but in all carrying the weight of principle.

□   □   □

. . . I desire today to speak particularly of equal justice, because it is an essential of individual liberty. Unless there is law, and unless there is an impartial tribunal to administer that law, no man can be really free. Without them only force can determine controversy, as in the international field today, and those who have not sufficient force cannot remain free. Without law and an appeal to a just and independent court to interpret that law, every man must be subject to the arbitrary discretion of his ruler or of some subordinate government official.

Over the portal of the great Supreme Court building in Washington are written the words "Equal Justice under Law." The Declaration of Independence, the Constitution of the United States and every pronouncement of the founders of the government stated the same principle in one form or another. Thomas Jefferson in his first inaugural emphasized above everything the necessity for "equal and exact justice to all men of whatever state or persuasion, religious or political."

In England the progress towards a definite law, administered by efficient and impartial courts or tribunals, was slow and uncertain. The common law developed slowly and only became clear and definite after many centuries. For a long time the courts were anything but impartial, and the actual application of the law was often unfair and unjust. But reverence for the principle must have existed, or it would not have been transported so early to the shores of America to become the dominant theory of government in the colonies. . . .

Unfortunately, the philosophy of equal justice under law, and acceptance of decisions made in accordance with respected institutions, has steadily lost strength during recent years. It is utterly denied in totalitarian states. There the law and the courts are instruments of state policy. It is inconceivable to the people of such a state that a court would concern itself to be fair to those individuals who appear before it when the state has an adverse interest. Nor do they feel any need of being fair between one man and another. Therefore they see no reason for presenting logical argument to justify a position. Nothing is more typical of the Communist or the Fascist than to assert and reassert an argument which has been completely answered and disproved, in order to create public opinion by propaganda to the ignorant.

The totalitarian idea has spread throughout many nations where in the nineteenth century, the ideals of liberty and justice were accepted. Even in this country, the theory that the state is finally responsible for every condition, and that every problem must be cured by giving the government arbitrary power to act, has been increasingly the philosophy of the twentieth century. It infects men who still profess complete adherence to individual liberty and individual justice, so that we find them willing to sacrifice both to accomplish some economic or social purpose. There is none of the burning devotion to liberty which characterized Patrick Henry and even the conservative leaders of the American Revolution.

We see the ignoring of justice internationally when a powerful nation takes the position that its demands must be complied with, "or else," and refuses to argue or discuss the question. We see it within this country in some labor groups and in some business groups who present ultimatums backed by economic force, and refuse to submit even to partial arbitration. It is present in the world so long as any nation refuses to submit its disputes to argument or adjudication. . . .

Even more discouraging is the attitude of the people and the press. Government action which twenty-five years ago would have excited a sense of outrage in thousands is reported in a few lines and, if disapproved at all, is disapproved with a shrug of the shoulders and a hopeless feeling that nothing can be done about it.

To a large extent this feeling has been promoted by the attack on the

Supreme Court, and the effort to make the courts instruments of executive policy. The old Court may have been too conservative, but the judges believed they were interpreting the laws and Constitution as they were written, and most of the country believed that they were honestly impartial. Today the Court regards itself as the maker of policy—no maker of policy can command respect for impartial dispensation of justice.

I believe more strongly than I can say that if we would maintain progress and liberty in America, it is our responsibility to see not only that laws be rewritten to substitute law for arbitrary discretion but that the whole attitude of the people be educated to a deep devotion to law, impartiality, and equal justice. It is even more important to the entire world that these principles be established as the guide for international action. In my opinion they afford the only hope of future peace. Not only must there be a more definite law to govern the relations between nations, not only must there be tribunals to decide controversies under that law, but the peoples of the world must be so imbued with respect for law and the tribunals established that they will accept their decisions without an appeal to force.

Whether we have a league of sovereign nations like the United Nations, or a world state, there cannot be an end of war if any important people refuse to accept freely the principle of abiding by law, or if truly impartial tribunals are not established.

Unfortunately, I believe we Americans have also in recent foreign policy been affected by principles of expediency and supposed necessity, and abandoned largely the principle of justice. We have drifted into the acceptance of the idea that the world is to be ruled by the power and policy of the great nations and a police force established by them rather than by international law. . . .

During the war, and since, I have felt that there has been little justice in our treatment of the neutral countries. We took the position, in effect, that no nation had the right to remain neutral, and bullied these countries to an extreme restrained only by consideration of policy, but not of justice.

The treatment of enemy countries has seldom been just after any war, but only now are we beginning to get some justice into our treatment of Germany. Our treatment has been harsh in the American Zone as a deliberate matter of government policy, and has offended Americans who saw it, and felt that it was completely at variance with American instincts. We gave countenance to the revengeful and impracticable Morgenthau plan, which would have reduced the Germans to economic poverty. We have fooled ourselves in the belief that we could teach another nation democratic principles by force. Why, we can't even teach our own people sound principles of government. We cannot teach liberty and justice in Germany by suppressing liberty and justice.

I believe that most Americans view with discomfort the war trials which have just been concluded in Germany and are proceeding in Japan. They violate that fundamental principle of American law that a man cannot be tried under an ex post facto statute.

The trial of the vanquished by the victors cannot be impartial, no matter how it is hedged about with the forms of justice. I question whether the hanging of those who, however despicable, were the leaders of the German people will ever discourage the making of aggressive war, for no one makes aggressive war unless he expects to win. About this whole judgment there is the spirit of vengeance, and vengeance is seldom justice. The hanging of the eleven men convicted will be a blot on the American record which we shall long regret.

In these trials we have accepted the Russian idea of the purpose of trials—government policy and not justice—with little relation to Anglo-Saxon heritage. By clothing policy in the forms of legal procedure, we may discredit the whole idea of justice in Europe for years to come. In the last analysis, even at the end of a frightful war, we should view the future with more hope if even our enemies believed that we had treated them justly in our English-speaking concept of law, in the provision of relief and in the final disposal of territory. I pray that we do not repeat this procedure in Japan, where the justification on grounds of vengeance is much less than in Germany.

Our whole attitude in the world, for a year after V-E Day, including the use of the atomic bomb at Hiroshima and Nagasaki, seems to me a departure from the principles of fair and equal treatment, which has made America respected throughout the world before this Second World War. Today we are cordially hated in many countries. I am delighted that Secretary [of State James F.] Byrnes and Senator [Arthur H.] Vandenburg have reversed our policy in many of the respects I have referred to. But abroad as at home we have a long way to go to restore again to the American people our full heritage of an ingrained belief in fairness, impartiality, and justice.

Peace in the world can only come if a law is agreed to relating to international relations, if there is a tribunal which can interpret that law and decide disputes between nations, and if the nations are willing to submit their disputes to impartial decision regardless of the outcome. There can be no peace until the public opinion of the world accepts, as a matter of course, the decisions of an international tribunal.

War has always set back temporarily the ideals of the world. This time, because of the tremendous scope of the war, the increased barbarism of its methods and the general prevalence of the doctrine of force and expediency even before the war, the effect today is even worse and the duration of the postwar period of disillusionment may be longer.

As I see it, the English-speaking peoples have one great responsibility. That is to restore to the minds of men a devotion to equal justice under law. ■

Governor Kissin' Jim Folsom of Alabama Startles the South with a Concern for the Negro

"OUR Negroes, who constitute 35 percent of our population in Alabama—are they getting 35 percent of the fair share of living?"

IN 1949, SOUTHERN POLITICIANS cared little about civil rights; on the contrary, the votes were to be had by exploiting what later came to be known as racism. James Folsom, at the end of the third year of his first term as Alabama's governor, was known as Big Jim for his size and as Kissin' Jim for his habit of enthusiastically bussing women (the sobriquet buttressed by a much-publicized paternity suit against him); he was a populist in the Huey Long tradition, with no intellectual pretensions. Thus, his seriously Christian Christmas message, broadcast on December

25, 1949, came as something of a surprise to constituents, and years later southern scholars saw in it political-social thinking that was considerably ahead of its time.

□ □ □

I am happy to have this opportunity to talk to the people of Alabama on Christmas Day. This is the greatest day, the most revered day, of our entire calendar. It is the birthday of Christ, who was the greatest humanitarian the world has ever known.

This is a day to talk about loving our neighbors, lending help to the less fortunate, and bringing joy to others by good work.

We set aside Thanksgiving Day to honor the Almighty's bountifulness to us; we celebrate the Fourth of July, which marks the freedom of our country; but on Christmas Day we pay tribute for the freedom of our souls.

It is great to live in America, with all of its plenty and bounty—yet it behooves us not to forget that we are the most blessed people on earth. And to remember that with that greatness goes a like share of responsibility.

The world looks to America today for leadership, for physical relief, for spiritual uplifting. These things we must provide if we are to retain our position of greatness. Because, like the foolish and the wise virgins, those who have and use not, from them their possessions shall be taken away. They will wither away because they are not used.

This nation has prospered in many and magnificent ways, and it has done so under the freedom of a democratic government, a government in which the people retain the final source of power through their exercise of the ballot.

The very foundation of democracy itself rests upon Christianity, upon the principles set forth by Christ himself. And I believe that it is no mere speculation to say that, without a government which guaranteed the freedom of religious worship, this nation would never have become the great America which it is today.

So often in our democracy we have failed to make the most of the very weapons itself—that is, providing a human, decent way of life for all of our people.

Under the extensive freedom of a democratic country, there emerges a pattern of life which creates economic barriers among the people. And as a democracy grows in years and expansiveness, there comes about a controlling minority group. That group controls because through advantages and opportunities it obtains great portions of wealth. Wealth means power and power influence. And so often that influence becomes an evil thing, in that it is used for a few, and not for the good of all. It is for that reason that we must have laws to establish control over power and authority, control over forces which are based on self-gain and exploitation. And it is necessary that we have laws to establish a measure of assistance and help for those who are not able to grub out a meager, respectable living.

And so we founded in this country great and far-reaching welfare programs. These programs were not created, nor are they operated, as a great leveler, but rather as an obligation of a democracy to its people, in order that the unfortunate may feast on more than crumbs and clothe themselves with more than rags.

What has gone before us in the way of welfare work exemplifies rich rewards of human endeavor. But we are actually just becoming of age, just beginning to scratch the surface in fulfilling the needs which are so widespread. So long as we have a person hungry, ill clothed, or without medical aid, we can take no pride in what has been done.

It is good at Christmas for us to turn our thoughts to the neglected, because Christmas is a time to think of others and not of ourselves. It is a time for us to ask questions of our inner self.

It is indeed a proud thing to know that the people of this state are concerned enough about these questions to vote a giant hospital-building program which will extend into every county in Alabama. This program is one of the greatest things that has ever happened in Alabama, and its effect will be such as to make for a far healthier and happier people.

Our Negroes, who constitute 35 percent of our population in Alabama—are they getting 35 percent of the fair share of living? Are they getting adequate medical care to rid them of hookworms, rickets, and social diseases? Are they provided with sufficient professional training which will produce their own doctors, professors, lawyers, clergymen, scientists—men and women who can pave the way for better health, greater earning powers, and a higher standard of living for all of their people? Are the Negroes being given their share of democracy, the same opportunity of having a voice in the government under which they live?

As long as the Negroes are held down by deprivation and lack of opportunity, the other poor people will be held down alongside them.

There are others, too, who should share in our thoughts of the neglected—wounded veterans, the blind, the shut-ins, the crippled, and on and on.

The job for us here in Alabama is a *positive* one. It is time for us to adopt a *positive* attitude toward our fellowman.

Let's start talking fellowship and brotherly love and doing-unto-others, and let's do more than talk about it—let's start living it.

In the past few years there has been too much negative living, too much stirring up of old hatreds, and prejudices, and false alarms. And the best way in the world to break this down is to lend our ears to the teachings of Christianity and the ways of democracy.

We must all constantly strive to put our democracy to fuller service for our people in order that all may be more richly rewarded with the fullness of the earth.

And certainly that is in keeping with the spirit of Christ, who said, "Do unto others as you would have them do unto you."

I hope the time will soon come when nations are brought together by the spirit of Christmas in much the same manner in which families join in reunion during the Holy Week.

People feel better when they gather together for the sake of love and fellowship. Their hearts are cleansed and kindled by the warm fire of eternal goodness. Nothing but good comes out of people at Christmastime—and that is how it should be at all times.

The great carpenter of Bethlehem showed us the way more than two thousand years ago, and yet we have learned so little from his teachings.

Before lasting peace will ever prevail in this world, nations have got to respect the laws of human decency which Christ preached in his teachings. Nations have got to become as families. They have got to gather around the Cross of Christianity if good is ever to triumph over evil. And before nations can do that, the leaders of nations must be fired with the challenge to see that equal justice, equal opportunity, and equal freedom become a reality for every man, woman, and child.

I believe that the people of all nations, the people of Alabama, the people of China, Africa, Russia, and tiny Luxembourg—I believe that all of them want to see lasting peace and goodness on this earth. And it is that great desire in the hearts of the people that gives me hope for a brighter future, a world without constant warfare, suffering, and distress.

I believe that such a goal is within our grasp—that it can become a force real and wonderful for all people, if we will set our hearts and our minds to that end.

It has been a humble privilege for me to talk with you today. I appreciate the opportunity from the bottom of my heart.

And now, this is your governor, wishing for each and every one of you a goodly share of Christmas spirit, a table filled with the fruits of the earth, and a heart filled with love of the little babe of Bethlehem. ■

Senator Margaret Chase Smith Issues a "Declaration of Conscience" against Senator Joseph McCarthy

"I do not want to see the Republican party ride to political victory on the Four Horsemen of Calumny—fear, ignorance, bigotry, and smear."

"TWENTY YEARS OF TREASON" and "soft on communism" were the phrases that Republican senator Joseph McCarthy threw against entrenched Democrats in 1950. "Tail Gunner Joe" exploited a suspicion—justified in the case of Alger Hiss and a few others—that the Communist conspiracy reached high into the U.S. government.

The Democratic counterattack was against "McCarthyism," a derogation of the Wisconsin senator's blunderbuss methods. On June 1, 1950, the only woman in the Senate—Margaret Chase Smith, of Maine—led seven Republican senators in a "Declaration of Conscience" dissociating themselves from the intimidating McCarthy crusade and joining the attack on McCarthyism.

Mrs. Smith organized the declaration tightly, speaking "as a Republican . . . as a woman . . . as a United States senator . . . as an American" and constructing her speech to make each "as" a point of departure. The declaration was hailed by liberals and moderates of both parties, but not until 1954 was Senator McCarthy censured by the Senate for his excess of zeal in denouncing Communists.

□   □   □

Mr. President, I would like to speak briefly and simply about a serious national condition. It is a national feeling of fear and frustration that could result in national suicide and the end of everything that we Americans hold dear. It is a condition that comes from the lack of effective leadership either in the legislative branch or the executive branch of our government. That leadership is so lacking that serious and responsible proposals are being made that national advisory commissions be appointed to provide such critically needed leadership.

I speak as briefly as possible because too much harm has already been done with irresponsible words of bitterness and selfish political opportunism. I speak as simply as possible because the issue is too great to be obscured by eloquence. I speak simply and briefly in the hope that my words will be taken to heart.

Mr. President, I speak as a Republican. I speak as a woman. I speak as a United States senator. I speak as an American.

The United States Senate has long enjoyed worldwide respect as the greatest deliberative body in the world. But recently that deliberative character has too often been debased to the level of a forum of hate and character assassination sheltered by the shield of congressional immunity.

It is ironical that we senators can in debate in the Senate, directly or indirectly, by any form of words, impute to any American who is not a senator any conduct or motive unworthy or unbecoming an American— and without that nonsenator American having any legal redress against us—yet if we say the same thing in the Senate about our colleagues we can be stopped on the grounds of being out of order.

It is strange that we can verbally attack anyone else without restraint and with full protection, and yet we hold ourselves above the same type of criticism here on the Senate floor. Surely the United States Senate is big enough to take self-criticism and self-appraisal. Surely we should be able to take the same kind of character attacks that we "dish out" to outsiders.

I think that it is high time for the United States Senate and its members to do some real soul-searching and to weigh our consciences as to the manner in which we are performing our duty to the people of America and the manner in which we are using or abusing our individual powers and privileges.

I think it is high time that we remembered that we have sworn to uphold and defend the Constitution. I think it is high time that we remembered that the Constitution, as amended, speaks not only of the freedom of speech but also of trial by jury instead of trial by accusation.

Whether it be a criminal prosecution in court or a character prosecution in the Senate, there is little practical distinction when the life of a person has been ruined.

Those of us who shout the loudest about Americanism in making character assassinations are all too frequently those who, by our own words and acts, ignore some of the basic principles of Americanism—the right to criticize; the right to hold unpopular beliefs; the right to protest; the right of independent thought.

The exercise of these rights should not cost one single American citizen his reputation or his right to a livelihood, nor should he be in danger of losing his reputation or livelihood merely because he happens to know someone who holds unpopular beliefs. Who of us does not? Otherwise none of us could call our souls our own. Otherwise thought control would have set in.

The American people are sick and tired of being afraid to speak their minds lest they be politically smeared as Communists or Fascists by their opponents. Freedom of speech is not what it used to be in America. It has been so abused by some that it is not exercised by others.

The American people are sick and tired of seeing innocent people smeared and guilty people whitewashed. But there have been enough proved cases, such as the Amerasia case, the Hiss case, the Coplon case, the Gold case, to cause nationwide distrust and strong suspicion that there may be something to the unproved, sensational accusations.

As a Republican, I say to my colleagues on this side of the aisle that the Republican party faces a challenge today that is not unlike the challenge which it faced back in Lincoln's day. The Republican party so successfully met that challenge that it emerged from the Civil War as the champion of a united nation—in addition to being a party which unrelentingly fought loose spending and loose programs.

Today our country is being psychologically divided by the confusion and the suspicions that are bred in the United States Senate to spread like cancerous tentacles of "know nothing, suspect everything" attitudes. Today we have a Democratic administration which has developed a mania for loose spending and loose programs. History is repeating itself— and the Republican party again has the opportunity to emerge as the champion of unity and prudence.

The record of the present Democratic administration has provided us with sufficient campaign issues without the necessity of resorting to political smears. America is rapidly losing its position as leader of the world simply because the Democratic administration has pitifully failed to provide effective leadership.

The Democratic administration has completely confused the American people by its daily contradictory grave warnings and optimistic assurances, which show the people that our Democratic administration has no idea of where it is going.

The Democratic administration has greatly lost the confidence of the American people by its complacency to the threat of communism here at home and the leak of vital secrets to Russia through key officials of the Democratic administration. There are enough proved cases to make this point without diluting our criticism with unproved charges.

Surely these are sufficient reasons to make it clear to the American people that it is time for a change and that a Republican victory is necessary to the security of the country. Surely it is clear that this nation will continue to suffer so long as it is governed by the present ineffective Democratic administration.

Yet to displace it with a Republican regime embracing a philosophy that lacks political integrity or intellectual honesty would prove equally disastrous to the nation. The nation sorely needs a Republican victory. But I do not want to see the Republican party ride to political victory on the Four Horsemen of Calumny—fear, ignorance, bigotry, and smear.

I doubt if the Republican party could do so, simply because I do not believe the American people will uphold any political party that puts political exploitation above national interest. Surely we Republicans are not so desperate for victory.

I do not want to see the Republican party win that way. While it might be a fleeting victory for the Republican party, it would be a more lasting defeat for the American people. Surely it would ultimately be suicide for the Republican party and the two-party system that has protected our American liberties from the dictatorship of a one-party system.

As members of the minority party, we do not have the primary authority to formulate the policy of our government. But we do have the responsibility of rendering constructive criticism, of clarifying issues, of allaying fears by acting as responsible citizens.

As a woman, I wonder how the mothers, wives, sisters, and daughters feel about the way in which members of their families have been politically mangled in Senate debate—and I use the word "debate" advisedly.

As a United States senator, I am not proud of the way in which the Senate has been made a publicity platform for irresponsible sensationalism. I am not proud of the reckless abandon in which unproved charges have been hurled from this side of the aisle. I am not proud of the obviously staged, undignified countercharges, which have been attempted in retaliation from the other side of the aisle.

I do not like the way the Senate has been made a rendezvous for vilification, for selfish political gain at the sacrifice of individual reputations and national unity. I am not proud of the way we smear outsiders from the floor of the Senate and hide behind the cloak of congressional immunity and still place ourselves beyond criticism on the floor of the Senate.

As an American, I am shocked at the way Republicans and Democrats alike are playing directly into the Communist design of "confuse, divide, and conquer." As an American, I do not want a Democratic administration whitewash or cover-up any more than I want a Republican smear or witch-hunt.

As an American, I condemn a Republican Fascist just as much as I condemn a Democrat Communist. I condemn a Democrat Fascist just as much as I condemn a Republican Communist. They are equally dangerous to you and me and to our country. As an American, I want to see our nation recapture the strength and unity it once had when we fought the enemy instead of ourselves. . . . ■

Malcolm X Exhorts Afro-Americans to Confront White Oppression

"I have never advocated any violence. . . . But I think the black man in this country . . . will be more justified when he stands up and starts to protect himself, no matter how many necks he has to break and heads he has to crack."

BORN IN NEBRASKA AS MALCOLM LITTLE, he went to jail at the age of twenty-one for six years after conviction for drug pushing and burglary, emerging as Malcolm X, the name symbolizing what he said he had been and had become: "Ex-smoker. Ex-drinker. Ex-Christian. Ex-slave."

He was the most articulate Black Muslim, preaching black nationalism in the explosive era of the early sixties. "There is a time to be cool and a time to be hot," he said, and he openly despised the more moderate and nonviolent leaders then called Negro. He scorned the preachment of love and morality as answers to the repression of his people, urging "vigorous action in self-defense" with slashing figures of speech: "You don't stick a knife in a man's back nine inches and then pull it out six inches and say you're making progress." He saw America as irredeemably racist, and blacks as victims of a historic wrong that could not be erased by what he derided as tokenist measures accepted as progress by most of his integrationist peers. Determined to shock his way into the public consciousness, he mocked Reverend Martin Luther King, Jr., whose nonviolence he saw as paralyzing, and the media-sensitive activist outraged establishment commentators by welcoming all news of misfortunes or disasters that befell whites, from tornadoes and plane crashes to the assassination of John F. Kennedy. "When I'm talking," he explained, "I use everything that's around." But this last shocker caused his discipline by Elijah Muhammad, leader of the Nation of Islam, and Malcolm X's subsequent breaking away from that group.

His speaking style was disciplined, intimate, not strident, filled with metaphor and ear-catching internal dialogue. The passage in the speech made in Detroit on February 14, 1965, on African self-hatred is low-keyed eloquence not often heard in modern political discourse. He made this speech the evening after his house had been bombed by Black Muslims enraged by his apostasy. One week later, beginning another speech in New York, he was shot to death.

□   □   □

Attorney Milton Henry, distinguished guests, brothers and sisters, ladies and gentlemen, friends and enemies: I want to point out first that I am very happy to be here this evening, and I am thankful to the Afro-American Broadcasting Company for the invitation to come here this evening. As Attorney Milton Henry has stated—I should say Brother Milton Henry because that's what he is, our brother—I was in a house last night that was bombed, my own. It didn't destroy all my clothes, but you know what fire and smoke do to things. The only thing I could get my hands on before leaving was what I have on now.

It isn't something that made me lose confidence in what I am doing, because my wife understands and I have children from this size on down, and even in their young age they understand. I think they would rather have a father or brother or whatever the situation may be who will take a stand in the face of reaction from any narrow-minded people rather than to compromise and later on have to grow up in shame and disgrace.

So I ask you to excuse my appearance. I don't normally come out in front of people without a shirt and tie. I guess that's somewhat a holdover from the Black Muslim movement, which I was in. That's one of the good aspects of that movement. It teaches you to be very careful and conscious of how you look, which is a positive contribution on their part. But that positive contribution on their part is greatly offset by too many liabilities. . . .

I hope you will forgive me for speaking so informally tonight, but I frankly think it is always better to be informal. As far as I am concerned, I can speak to people better in an informal way than I can with all of this stiff formality that ends up meaning nothing. Plus, when people are informal, they are relaxed. When they are relaxed, their mind is more open, and they can weigh things more objectively. Whenever you and I are discussing our problems, we need to be very objective, very cool, calm, and collected. That doesn't mean we should always be. There is a time to be cool and a time to be hot. See—you got messed up into thinking that there is only one time for everything. There is a time to love and a time to hate. Even Solomon said that, and he was in that book too. You're just taking something out of the book that fits your cowardly nature when you don't want to fight, and you say, "Well, Jesus said don't fight." But I don't even believe Jesus said that. . . .

Look right now what's going on in and around Saigon and Hanoi and in the Congo and elsewhere. They are violent when their interests are at stake. But for all that violence they display at the international level, when you and I want just a little bit of freedom, we're supposed to be nonviolent. They're violent in Korea, they're violent in Germany, they're violent in the South Pacific, they're violent in Cuba, they're violent wherever they go. But when it comes time for you and me to protect ourselves against lynchings, they tell us to be nonviolent.

That's a shame. Because we get tricked into being nonviolent, and when somebody stands up and talks like I just did, they say, "Why, he's advocating violence." Isn't that what they say? Every time you pick up your newspaper, you see where one of these things has written into it that I am advocating violence. I have never advocated any violence. I have only said that black people who are the victims of organized violence perpetrated upon us by the Klan, the Citizens Councils, and many other forms should defend ourselves. And when I say we should defend ourselves against the violence of others, they use their press skillfully to make the world think that I am calling for violence, period. I wouldn't call on anybody to be violent without a cause. But I think the black man in this country, above and beyond people all over the world, will be more justified when he stands up and starts to protect himself, no matter how many necks he has to break and heads he has to crack. . . .

The Klan is a cowardly outfit. They have perfected the art of making Negroes be afraid. As long as the Negro is afraid, the Klan is safe. But the Klan itself is cowardly. One of them never come after one of you. They all come together. They're scared of you. And you sit there when they're putting the rope around your neck saying, "Forgive them, Lord, they know not what they do." As long as they've been doing it, they're experts at it, they know what they're doing. No, since the federal government has shown that it isn't going to do anything about it but *talk,* then it is a duty, it's your and my duty as men, as human beings, it is our duty to our people, to organize ourselves and let the government know that if they don't stop that Klan, we'll stop it ourselves. *Then* you'll see the government start doing something about it. But don't ever think that they're going to do it just on some kind of morality basis. No. So I don't believe in violence—that's why I want to stop it. And you can't stop it with love, not love of those things down there. No! So, we only mean vigorous action in self-defense, and that vigorous action we feel we're justified in initiating by any means necessary.

Now, for saying something like that, the press calls us racist and people who are "violent in reverse." This is how they psycho you. They make you think that if you try to stop the Klan from lynching you, you're practicing violence in reverse. Pick up on this, I hear a lot of you parrot what the man says. You say, "I don't want to be a Ku Klux Klan in reverse." Well, if a criminal comes around your house with his gun, brother, just because he's got a gun and he's robbing your house, and he's a robber, it doesn't make you a robber because you grab your gun and run him out. No, the man is using some tricky logic on you. I say it is time for black people to put together the type of action, the unity, that is necessary to pull the sheet off of them so they won't be frightening black people any longer. That's all. And when we say this, the press calls us "racist in reverse." "Don't struggle except within the ground rules that the people you're struggling against have laid down." Why, this is insane, but it shows how they can do it. With skillful manipulating of the press they're able to make the victim look like the criminal and the criminal look like the victim. . . .

When you start thinking for yourselves, you frighten them, and they try and block your getting to the public, for the fear that if the public listens to you then the public won't listen to them anymore. And they've got certain Negroes whom they have to keep blowing up in the papers to make them look like leaders. So that the people will keep on following them, no matter how many knocks they get on their heads following them. This is how the man does it, and if you don't wake up and find out how he does it, I tell you, they'll be building gas chambers and gas ovens pretty soon—I don't mean those kind you've got at home in your kitchen—[and] . . . you'll be in one of them, just like the Jews ended up in gas ovens over there in Germany. You're in a society that's just as capable of building gas ovens for black people as Hitler's society was. . . .

Now, what effect does [the struggle over Africa] have on us? Why should the black man in America concern himself since he's been away from the African continent for three or four hundred years? Why should we concern ourselves? What impact does what happens to them have upon us? Number one, you have to realize that up until 1959 Africa was dominated by the colonial powers. Having complete control over Africa, the colonial powers of Europe projected the image of Africa negatively. They always project Africa in a negative light: jungle savages, cannibals, nothing civilized. Why then, naturally it was so negative that it was negative to you and me, and you and I began to hate it. We didn't want anybody telling us anything about Africa, much less calling us Africans. In hating Africa and in hating the Africans, we ended up hating ourselves, without even realizing it. Because you can't hate the roots of a tree, and not hate the tree. You can't hate your origin and not end up hating yourself. You can't hate Africa and not hate yourself.

You show me one of these people over here who has been thoroughly brainwashed and has a negative attitude toward Africa, and I'll show you one who has a negative attitude toward himself. You can't have a positive attitude toward yourself and a negative attitude toward Africa at the same time. To the same degree that your understanding of and attitude toward Africa become positive, you'll find that your understanding of and your attitude toward yourself will also become positive. And this is what the white man knows. So they very skillfully make you and me hate our African identity, our African characteristics.

You know yourself that we have been a people who hated our African characteristics. We hated our heads, we hated the shape of our nose, we wanted one of those long doglike noses, you know; we hated the color of our skin, hated the blood of Africa that was in our veins. And in hating our features and our skin and our blood, why, we had to end up hating ourselves. And we hated ourselves. Our color became to us a chain—we felt that it was holding us back; our color became to us like a prison which we felt was keeping us confined, not letting us go this way or that way. We felt that all of these restrictions were based solely upon our color, and the psychological reaction to that would have to be that as long as we felt imprisoned or chained or trapped by black skin, black features, and black blood, that skin and those features and that blood holding us back automatically had to become hateful to us. And it became hateful to us.

It made us feel inferior; it made us feel inadequate, made us feel helpless. And when we fell victims to this feeling of inadequacy or inferiority or helplessness, we turned to somebody else to show us the way. We didn't have confidence in another black man to show us the way, or black people to show us the way. In those days we didn't. We didn't think a black man could do anything except play some horns—you know, make some sound and make you happy with some songs and in that way. But in serious things, where our food, clothing, shelter, and education were concerned, we turned to the man. We never thought in terms of bringing these things into existence for ourselves, we never thought in terms of doing things for ourselves. Because we felt helpless. What made us feel helpless was our hatred for ourselves. And our hatred for ourselves stemmed from our hatred for things African. . . .

After 1959 the spirit of African nationalism was fanned to a high flame, and we then began to witness the complete collapse of colonialism. France began to get out of French West Africa, Belgium began to make moves to get out of the Congo, Britain began to make moves to get out of Kenya, Tanganyika, Uganda, Nigeria, and some of these other places. And although it looked like they were getting out, they pulled a trick that was colossal.

When you're playing ball and they've got you trapped, you don't throw the ball away—you throw it to one of your teammates who's in the clear. And this is what the European powers did. They were trapped on the African continent, they couldn't stay there—they were looked upon as colonial and imperialist. They had to pass the ball to someone whose image was different, and they passed the ball to Uncle Sam. And he picked it up and has been running it for a touchdown ever since. He was in the clear, he was not looked upon as one who had colonized the African continent. At that time, the Africans couldn't see that though the United States hadn't colonized the African continent, it had colonized twenty-two million blacks here on this continent. Because we're just as thoroughly colonized as anybody else.

When the ball was passed to the United States, it was passed at the time when John Kennedy came into power. He picked it up and helped to run it. He was one of the shrewdest backfield runners that history has ever recorded. He surrounded himself with intellectuals—highly educated, learned, and well-informed people. And their analysis told him that the government of America was confronted with a new problem. And this new problem stemmed from the fact that Africans were now awakened, they were enlightened, they were fearless, they would fight. This meant that the Western powers couldn't stay there by force. Since their own economy, the European economy and the American economy, was based upon their continued influence over the African continent, they had to find some means of staying there. So they used the friendly approach.

They switched from the old, openly colonial imperialistic approach to the benevolent approach. They came up with some benevolent colonialism, philanthropic colonialism, humanitarianism, or dollarism. Immediately everything was Peace Corps, Operation Crossroads, "We've got to help our African brothers." Pick up on that: Can't help us in Mississippi. Can't help us in Alabama, or Detroit, or out here in Dearborn, where some real Ku Klux Klan lives. They're going to send all the way to Africa to help. . . .

One of the things that made the Black Muslim movement grow was its emphasis upon things African. This was the secret to the growth of the Black Muslim movement. African blood, African origin, African culture, African ties. And you'd be surprised—we discovered that deep within the subconscious of the black man in this country, he is still more African than he is American. He *thinks* that he's more American than African, because the man is jiving him, the man is brainwashing him every day. He's telling him, "You're an American, you're an American." Man, how could you think you're an American when you haven't ever had any kind of an American treat over here? You have never, never. Ten men can be sitting at a table eating, you know, dining, and I can come and sit down where they're dining. They're dining; I've got a plate in front of me, but nothing is on it. Because all of us are sitting at the same table, are all of us diners? I'm not a diner until you let me dine. Just being at the table with others who are dining doesn't make me a diner, and this is what you've got to get in your head here in this country.

Just because you're in this country doesn't make you an American. No, you've got to go farther than that before you can become an American. You've got to enjoy the fruits of Americanism. You haven't enjoyed those fruits. You've enjoyed the thorns. You've enjoyed the thistles. But you have not enjoyed the fruits, no sir. You have fought harder for the fruits than the white man has, you have worked harder for the fruits than the white man has, but you've enjoyed less. When the man put the uniform on you and sent you abroad, you fought harder than they did. Yes, I know you—when you're fighting for them, you can fight.

The Black Muslim movement did make that contribution. They made the whole civil rights movement become more militant, and more acceptable to the white power structure. He would rather have them than us. In fact, I think we forced many of the civil rights leaders to be even more militant than they intended. I know some of them who get out there and "boom, boom, boom" and don't mean it. Because they're right on back in their corner as soon as the action comes. . . .

The worst thing the white man can do to himself is to take one of these kinds of Negroes and ask him, "How do your people feel, boy?" He's going to tell that man that we are satisfied. That's what they do, brothers and sisters. They get behind the door and tell the white man we're satisfied. "Just keep on keeping me up here in front of them, boss, and I'll keep them behind you." That's what they talk when they're behind closed doors. Because, you see, the white man doesn't go along with anybody who's not for him. He doesn't care are you for right or wrong; he wants to know are you for him. And if you're for him, he doesn't care what else you're for. As long as you're for him, then he puts you up over the Negro community. You become a spokesman. . . .

Brothers and sisters, let me tell you, I spend my time out there in the streets with people, all kinds of people, listening to what they have to say. And they're dissatisfied, they're disillusioned, they're fed up, they're getting to the point of frustration where they begin to feel, "What do we have to lose?" When you get to that point, you're the type of person who can create a very dangerously explosive atmosphere. This is what's happening in our neighborhoods, to our people.

I read in a poll taken by *Newsweek* magazine this week, saying that Negroes are satisfied. Oh, yes, *Newsweek*, you know, supposed to be a top magazine with a top pollster, talking about how satisfied Negroes are. Maybe I haven't met the Negroes he met. Because I know he hasn't met the ones that I've met. And this is dangerous. This is where the white man does himself the most harm. He invents statistics to create an image, thinking that that image is going to hold things in check. You know why they always say Negroes are lazy? Because they want Negroes to be lazy. They always say Negroes can't unite, because they don't want Negroes to unite. And once they put this thing in the Negro's mind, they feel that he tries to fulfill their image. If they say you can't unite black people, and then you come to them to unite them, they won't unite, because it's been said that they're not supposed to unite. It's a psycho that they work, and it's the same way with these statistics.

When they think that an explosive era is coming up, then they grab their press again and begin to shower the Negro public, to make it appear that all Negroes are satisfied. Because if you know you're dissatisfied all by yourself and ten others aren't, you play it cool; but if you know that all ten of you are dissatisfied, you get with it. This is what the man knows. The man knows that if these Negroes find out how dissatisfied they really are—even Uncle Tom is dissatisfied, he's just playing his part for now—this is what makes the man frightened. It frightens them in France and frightens them in England, and it frightens them in the United States.

And it is for this reason that it is so important for you and me to start organizing among ourselves, intelligently, and try to find out: "What are we going to do if this happens, that happens or the next thing happens?" Don't think that you're going to run to the man and say, "Look, boss, this is me." Why, when the deal goes down, you'll look just like me in his eyesight; I'll make it tough for you. Yes, when the deal goes down, he doesn't look at you in any better light than he looks at me. . . .

I say again that I'm not a racist, I don't believe in any form of segregation or anything like that. I'm for brotherhood for everybody, but I don't believe in forcing brotherhood upon people who don't want it. Let us practice brotherhood among ourselves, and then if others want to practice brotherhood with us, we're for practicing it with them also. But I don't think that we should run around trying to love somebody who doesn't love us. ■

Holocaust Witness Elie Wiesel Asks President Reagan to Reconsider a Visit to a German Cemetery

"THAT place, Mr. President, is not your place. Your place is with the victims of the SS."

ELIE WIESEL, who lost his family to Nazi genocide, came to the United States from his native Romania in 1956 to "bear witness" to the Holocaust, or Shoah. In novels and nonfiction writings in France and the United States, and in talks before audiences around the world, the quiet-voiced Wiesel reminds listeners and readers of unspeakable crimes and inexplicable silence.

In 1985, President Ronald Reagan planned a state visit to West Germany, its purpose to acknowledge the importance of that country's membership in the alliance of free nations and to help Germans bury their own guilty past. Among the ceremonies planned by Chancellor Helmut Kohl and the White House staff was a visit to a cemetery in Bitburg, near a U.S. military installation. After the schedule was announced, it was discovered that among the graves were several of members of Hitler's Waffen SS, notorious for their anti-Semitism. Mr. Kohl let it be known that he and most Germans would be offended at a cancellation; many Jews in the United States took offense at the insensitive scheduling.

Mr. Reagan decided to go ahead with the visit to Bitburg—there to pointedly turn his back at the Nazi graves—but first he gave Elie Wiesel, then chairman of the U.S. Holocaust Memorial Council, the opportunity to present his objection publicly to the president at a White House ceremony presenting him with a medal of achievement. Gently, and with appropriate respect, the Jewish leader showed why the decision to visit Bitburg had been a mistake.

□   □   □

Mr. President, . . . I am grateful to you for the medal. But this medal is not mine alone. It belongs to all those who remember what SS killers have done to their victims.

It was given to me by the American people for my writings, teaching, and for my testimony. When I write, I feel my invisible teachers standing over my shoulders, reading my words and judging their veracity. And while I feel responsible for the living, I feel equally responsible to the dead. Their memory dwells in my memory.

Forty years ago, a young man awoke, and he found himself an orphan in an orphaned world. What have I learned in the last forty years? Small things. I learned the perils of language and those of silence. I learned that in extreme situations when human lives and dignity are at stake, neutrality is a sin. It helps the killers, not the victims. I learned the meaning of solitude, Mr. President. We were alone, desperately alone.

Today is April 19, and April 19, 1943, the Warsaw Ghetto rose in arms against the onslaught of the Nazis. They were so few and so young and so helpless. And nobody came to their help. And they had to fight what was then the mightiest legion in Europe. Every underground received help except the Jewish underground. And yet they managed to fight and resist and push back those Nazis and their accomplices for six weeks. And yet the leaders of the free world, Mr. President, knew everything and did so little, or nothing, or at least nothing specifically to save Jewish children from death. You spoke of Jewish children, Mr. President. One million Jewish children perished. If I spent my entire life reciting their names, I would die before finishing the task.

Mr. President, I have seen children, I have seen them being thrown in the flames alive. Words, they die on my lips. So I have learned, I have learned, I have learned the fragility of the human condition.

And I am reminded of a great moral essayist. The gentle and forceful Abe Rosenthal, having visited Auschwitz, once wrote an extraordinary reportage about the persecution of Jews, and he called it "Forgive them not, Father, for they knew what they did."

I have learned that the Holocaust was a unique and uniquely Jewish event, albeit with universal implications. Not all victims were Jews. But all Jews were victims. I have learned the danger of indifference, the crime of indifference. For the opposite of love, I have learned, is not hate, but indifference. Jews were killed by the enemy but betrayed by their so-called allies, who found political reasons to justify their indifference or passivity.

But I have also learned that suffering confers no privileges. It all depends what one does with it. And this is why survivors, of whom you spoke, Mr.

President, have tried to teach their contemporaries how to build on ruins, how to invent hope in a world that offers none, how to proclaim faith to a generation that has seen it shamed and mutilated. And I believe, we believe, that memory is the answer, perhaps the only answer.

A few days ago, on the anniversary of the liberation of Buchenwald, all of us, Americans, watched with dismay and anger as the Soviet Union and East Germany distorted both past and present history.

Mr. President, I was there. I was there when American liberators arrived. And they gave us back our lives. And what I felt for them then nourishes me to the end of my days and will do so. If you only knew what we tried to do with them then. We who were so weak that we couldn't carry our own lives, we tried to carry them in triumph.

Mr. President, we are grateful to the American army for liberating us. We are grateful to this country, the greatest democracy in the world, the freest nation in the world, the moral nation, the authority in the world. And we are grateful, especially, to this country for having offered us haven and refuge, and grateful to its leadership for being so friendly to Israel.

And, Mr. President, do you know that the ambassador of Israel, who sits next to you, who is my friend, and has been for so many years, is himself a survivor? And if you knew all the causes we fought together for the last thirty years, you should be prouder of him. And we are proud of him.

And we are grateful, of course, to Israel. We are eternally grateful to Israel for existing. We needed Israel in 1948 as we need it now. And we are grateful to Congress for its continuous philosophy of humanism and compassion for the underprivileged.

And as for yourself, Mr. President, we are so grateful to you for being a friend of the Jewish people, for trying to help the oppressed Jews in the Soviet Union. And to do whatever we can to save Shcharansky and Abe Stolar and Iosif Begun and Sakharov and all the dissidents who need freedom. And of course, we thank you for your support of the Jewish state of Israel.

But, Mr. President, I wouldn't be the person I am, and you wouldn't respect me for what I am, if I were not to tell you also of the sadness that is in my heart for what happened during the last week. And I am sure that you, too, are sad for the same reasons.

What can I do? I belong to a traumatized generation. And to us, as to you, symbols are important. And furthermore, following our ancient tradition, and we are speaking about Jewish heritage, our tradition commands us "to speak truth to power."

So may I speak to you, Mr. President, with respect and admiration, of the events that happened?

We have met four or five times. And each time I came away enriched, for I know of your commitment to humanity.

And therefore I am convinced, as you have told us earlier when we spoke, that you were not aware of the presence of SS graves in the Bitburg cemetery. Of course you didn't know. But now we all are aware.

May I, Mr. President, if it's possible at all, implore you to do something else, to find a way, to find another way, another site? That place, Mr. President, is not your place. Your place is with the victims of the SS.

Oh, we know there are political and strategic reasons, but this issue, as all issues related to that awesome event, transcends politics and diplomacy.

The issue here is not politics, but good and evil. And we must never confuse them.

For I have seen the SS at work. And I have seen their victims. They were my friends. They were my parents.

Mr. President, there was a degree of suffering and loneliness in the concentration camps that defies imagination. Cut off from the world with no refuge anywhere, sons watched helplessly their fathers being beaten to death. Mothers watched their children die of hunger. And then there was Mengele and his selections. Terror, fear, isolation, torture, gas chambers, flames, flames rising to the heavens.

But, Mr. President, I know and I understand, we all do, that you seek reconciliation. And so do I, so do we. And I too wish to attain true reconciliation with the German people. I do not believe in collective guilt, nor in collective responsibility. Only the killers were guilty. Their sons and daughters are not.

And I believe, Mr. President, that we can and we must work together with them and with all people. And we must work to bring peace and understanding to a tormented world that, as you know, is still awaiting redemption.

I thank you, Mr. President. ■

Astronomer Carl Sagan Contemplates the Potential Self-Destruction of the Earth

"WE make mistakes. We kill our own."

CARL EDWARD SAGAN, professor of physical sciences and director of the Laboratory of Planetary Studies at Cornell University from 1968 until his death in 1996, was a familiar face in an unfamiliar field. His lecturing and his narrating of television programs about space made his face and voice familiar outside the scientific world; in 1978, Sagan won the Pulitzer Prize for *The Dragons of Eden.*

Every quarter century, the peace memorial at Gettysburg National Cemetery Park is rededicated; Presidents Wilson, Franklin Roosevelt, and Eisenhower have been the speakers. In 1988, on the 125th anniversary of the battle in which 51,000 were killed or wounded, the astronomer took the occasion to offer a message on the need for nuclear disarmament. The speech, jointly written with his wife, Ann Druyan, is a good example of how a solemn occasion can be an appropriate setting for a discussion of a controversial issue.

□   □   □

Fifty-one thousand human beings were killed or wounded here, ancestors of some of us, brothers of us all. This was the first full-fledged example of an industrialized war, with machine-made arms and railroad transport of men and matériel. This was the first hint of an age yet to come, our age; an intimation of what technology bent to the purposes of war might be capable. The new Spencer repeating rifle was used here. In May 1863, a reconnaissance balloon of the Army of the Potomac detected movement of Confederate troops across the Rappahannock River, the beginning of the campaign that led to the Battle of Gettysburg.

That balloon was a precursor of air forces and strategic bombing and reconnaissance satellites.

A few hundred artillery pieces were deployed in the three-day battle of Gettysburg. What could they do? What was war like then? . . . Ballistic projectiles, launched from the cannons that you can see all over this Gettysburg Memorial, had a range, at best, of a few miles. The amount of explosive in the most formidable of them was some twenty pounds, roughly one-hundredth of a ton of TNT. It was enough to kill a few people.

But the most powerful chemical explosives used eighty years later, in World War II, were the blockbusters, so-called because they could destroy a city block. Dropped from aircraft, after a journey of hundreds of miles, each carried about ten tons of TNT, a thousand times more than the most powerful weapon at the Battle of Gettysburg. A blockbuster could kill a few dozen people.

At the very end of World War II, the United States used the first atomic bombs to annihilate two Japanese cities. Each of those weapons had the equivalent power of about ten thousand tons of TNT, enough to kill a few hundred thousand people. One bomb.

A few years later the United States and the Soviet Union developed the first thermonuclear weapons, the first hydrogen bombs. Some of them had an explosive yield equivalent to ten million tons of TNT; enough to kill a few million people. One bomb. Strategic nuclear weapons can now be launched to any place on the planet. Everywhere on earth is a potential battlefield now.

Each of these technological triumphs advanced the art of mass murder by a factor of a thousand. From Gettysburg to the blockbuster, a thousand times more explosive energy; from the blockbuster to the atomic bomb, a thousand times more; and from the atomic bomb to the hydrogen bomb, a thousand times still more. A thousand times a thousand, times a thousand is a billion; in less than one century, our most fearful weapon has become a billion times more deadly. But we have not become a billion times wiser in the generations that stretch from Gettysburg to us.

The souls that perished here would find the carnage of which we are now capable unspeakable. Today, the United States and the Soviet Union have booby-trapped our planet with almost sixty thousand nuclear weapons. Sixty thousand nuclear weapons! Even a small fraction of the strategic arsenals could without question annihilate the two contending superpowers, probably destroy the global civilization, and possibly render the human species extinct. No nation, no man should have such power. We distribute these instruments of apocalypse all over our fragile world, and justify it on the grounds that it has made us safe. We have made a fool's bargain.

The 51,000 casualties here at Gettysburg represented one-third of the Confederate army and one-quarter of the Union army. All those who died, with one or two exceptions, were soldiers. The best-known exception was a civilian in her own house who thought to bake a loaf of bread and, through two closed doors, was shot to death; her name was Jennie Wade. But in a global thermonuclear war, almost all the casualties will be civilians, men, women, and children, including vast numbers of citizens of nations that had no part in the quarrel that led to the war, nations far removed from the northern mid-latitude "target zone." There will be billions of Jennie Wades. Everyone on earth is now at risk. . . .

Two months before Gettysburg, on May 3. 1863, there was a Confederate triumph, the Battle of Chancellorsville. On the moonlit evening following the victory, General Stonewall Jackson and his staff, returning to the Confederate lines, were mistaken for Union cavalry. Jackson was shot twice in error by his own men. He died of his wounds.

We make mistakes. We kill our own.

There are some who claim that since we have not yet had an accidental nuclear war, the precautions being taken to prevent one must be adequate. But not three years ago we witnessed the disasters of the *Challenger* space shuttle and the Chernobyl nuclear power plant, high-technology systems, one American, one Soviet, into which enormous quantities of national prestige had been invested. There were compelling reasons to prevent these disasters. In the preceding year, confident assertions were made by officials of both nations that no accidents of that sort could happen. We were not to worry. The experts would not permit an accident to happen. We have since learned that such assurances do not amount to much.

We make mistakes. We kill our own.

This is the century of Hitler and Stalin, evidence—if any were needed— that madmen can seize the reins of power of modern industrial states. If we are content in a world with nearly sixty thousand nuclear weapons, we are betting our lives on the proposition that no present or future leaders, military or civilian—of the United States, the Soviet Union, Britain, France, China, Israel, India, Pakistan, South Africa, and whatever other nuclear powers there will be—will ever stray from the strictest standards of prudence. We are gambling on their sanity and sobriety even in times of great personal and national crisis, all of them, for all times to come. I say this is asking too much of us. Because we make mistakes. We kill our own. . . .

We have made a fool's bargain. We have been locked in a deadly embrace with the Soviet Union, each side always propelled by the abundant malefactions of the other; almost always looking to the short term— to the next congressional or presidential election, to the next party congress— and almost never seeing the big picture.

Dwight Eisenhower, who was closely associated with this Gettysburg community, said, "The problem in defense spending is to figure out how far you should go without destroying from within what you are trying to defend from without." I say we have gone too far. . . .

The Civil War was mainly about union; union in the face of differences. A million years ago, there were no nations on the planet. There were no tribes. The humans who were here were divided into small family groups of a few dozen people each. They wandered. That was the horizon of our identification, an itinerant family group. Since then, the horizons have expanded. From a handful of hunter-gatherers, to a tribe, to a horde, to a small city-state, to a nation, and today to immense nation-states. The average person on the earth today owes his or her primary allegiance to a group of something like a hundred million people. It seems very clear that if we do not destroy ourselves first, the unit of primary identification of most human beings will before long be the planet Earth and the human species. To my mind, this raises the key question: whether the fundamental unit of identification will expand to embrace the planet and the species, or whether we will destroy ourselves first. I'm afraid it's going to be very close.

The identification horizons were broadened in this place 125 years ago, and at great cost to North and South, to blacks and whites. But we recognize that expansion of identification horizons as just. Today there is an urgent, practical necessity to work together on arms control, on the world economy, on the global environment. It is clear that the nations of the world now can only rise and fall together. It is not a question of one nation winning at the expense of another. We must all help one another or all perish together.

On occasions like this it is customary to quote homilies; phrases by great men and women that we've all heard before. We hear, but we tend not to focus. Let me mention one, a phrase that was uttered not far from this spot by Abraham Lincoln: "With malice toward none, with charity for all. . . ." *Think* of what that means. This is what is expected of us, not merely because our ethics command it, or because our religions preach it, but because it is necessary for human survival.

Here's another: "A house divided against itself cannot stand." Let me vary it a little: A species divided against itself cannot stand. A planet divided against itself cannot stand. And [to be] inscribed on this Eternal

Light Peace Memorial, which is about to be rekindled and rededicated, is a stirring phrase: "A World United in the Search for Peace."

The real triumph of Gettysburg was not, I think, in 1863 but in 1913, when the surviving veterans, the remnants of the adversary forces, the Blue and the Gray, met in celebration and solemn memorial. It had been the war that set brother against brother, and when the time came to remember, on the fiftieth anniversary of the battle, the survivors fell, sobbing, into one another's arms. They could not help themselves.

It is time now for us to emulate them, NATO and the Warsaw Pact, Israelis and Palestinians, whites and blacks, Americans and Iranians, the developed and the underdeveloped worlds.

We need more than anniversary sentimentalism and holiday piety and patriotism. Where necessary, we must confront and challenge the conventional wisdom. It is time to learn from those who fell here. Our challenge is to reconcile, not *after* the carnage and the mass murder, but *instead* of the carnage and the mass murder.

It is time to act. ■

Playwright-Dissident Václav Havel Assumes the Presidency of Czechoslovakia

"LET us teach ourselves and others that politics can be not only the art of the possible—especially if this means speculations, calculations, intrigues, secret deals, and pragmatic maneuvering—but also the art of the impossible, namely, the art of improving ourselves and the world."

THE FOREMOST CZECH PLAYWRIGHT spent three terms in jail for "subversion." During the longest, from 1979 to 1983, he wrote a classic of dissenters' literature, *Letters to Olga,* in the form of letters to his wife. Told by the Communist leaders that he would be released if he requested a pardon, Václav Havel refused to legitimate his conviction, grimly choosing to serve his full term—indicative of his philosophy of "responsibility as destiny."

In the United States during World War II, playwright Robert E. Sherwood wrote speeches for FDR; in Czechoslovakia in the last throes of the Cold War, playwright Václav Havel wrote and delivered his own speeches, but he did not fool himself about the ability of the writer to mislead as well as lead. "The power of words is neither unambiguous nor clear-cut," this intellectual turned politician told a group of Germans in 1989. "It is not merely the liberating power of [Lech] Walesa's words or the alarm-raising power of [Andrey] Sakharov's. . . . Words that electrify society with their freedom and truthfulness are matched by words that mesmerize, deceive, inflame, madden; words that are harmful, even lethal. The word as arrow. . . . The selfsame word can at one time be the cornerstone of peace, while at another, machine-gun fire resounds in its every syllable."

This is his address on assuming office on New Year's Day, 1990. As his symbol of uncaring, removed-from-the-people government, he uses "political leaders [who] did not look or did not want to look out the windows of their airplanes," returning to that image repeatedly in the best-written speech during the demise of the Communist empire.

□   □   □

My dear fellow citizens, for forty years on this day you heard from my predecessors the same thing in a number of variations: how our country is flourishing, how many millions of tons of steel we produce, how happy we all are, how we trust our government, and what bright prospects lie ahead of us.

I assume you did not propose me for this office so that I, too, should lie to you.

Our country is not flourishing. The enormous creative and spiritual potential of our nations is being wasted. Entire branches of industry produce goods that are of no interest to anyone, while we lack the things we need. The state, which calls itself a workers' state, humiliates and exploits workers. Our outmoded economy wastes what little energy we have. A country that once could be proud of the educational level of its citizens now spends so little on education that it ranks seventy-second in the world. We have polluted our land, rivers, and forests, bequeathed to us by our ancestors; we now have the most contaminated environment in all of Europe. People in our country die sooner than in the majority of European countries.

Allow me a small personal observation: when I recently flew to Bratislava, I found some time during various discussions to look out of the window of the plane. I saw the industrial complex of the Slovnaft chemical plant and the giant Petržalka housing project right behind it. The view was enough for me to understand that for decades our statesmen and political leaders did not look or did not want to look out the windows of their airplanes. No study of statistics available would have enabled me faster and better to understand the situation we have gotten ourselves into.

But all this is not even the main problem. The worst thing is that we live in a contaminated moral environment. We have fallen morally ill because we became used to saying one thing and thinking another. We have learned not to believe in anything, to ignore each other, to care only about ourselves. Notions such as love, friendship, compassion, humility, or forgiveness have lost their depth and dimensions; for many of us, they represent nothing more than psychological idiosyncracies, or appear to be some kind of relic from times past, rather comical in the era of computers and spaceships. Only a few of us managed to cry out loud that the powers that be should not be all-powerful; that special farms producing uncontaminated, top-quality food just for the powerful should send their produce to schools, children's homes, and hospitals. The previous regime, armed with its arrogant and intolerant ideology, reduced man to a means of production and nature to a tool of production. Thus it attacked both their very essence and their mutual relationship. It reduced gifted and autonomous people to nuts and bolts in some monstrously huge, noisy, and stinking machine, whose real purpose is not clear to anyone. Such a machine can do nothing but slowly and inexorably wear itself out along with all its nuts and bolts.

When I talk about the contaminated moral atmosphere, I am not talking only about the gentlemen who eat organic vegetables and do not look out the windows of their planes. I mean all of us. We have all become used to the totalitarian system and accepted it as an immutable fact, thus helping to perpetuate it. In other words, we are all—though naturally to various degrees—responsible for the creation of the totalitarian machinery. None of us is just its victim; we are all also responsible for it.

Why do I say this? It would be very unwise to think of the sad legacy of the last forty years as something alien or something inherited from a distant relative. On the contrary, we have to accept this legacy as something we have inflicted on ourselves. If we accept it as such, we will understand that it is up to all of us, and only us, to do something about it. We cannot blame the previous rulers for everything—not only because it would be untrue but also because it could weaken our sense of duty, our obligation to act independently, freely, sensibly, and quickly. Let us not be mistaken: even the best government in the world, the best parliament, and the best president cannot do much on their own. And in any case, it would be wrong to expect a cure-all from them alone. Freedom and democracy, after all, require everyone to participate and thus to share responsibility.

If we realize this, then all the horrors that the new Czechoslovak democracy has inherited will cease to appear so horrific. If we realize this, hope will return to our hearts.

In the effort to rectify matters of common concern, we have something to build on. The recent past—and in particular, the last six weeks of our peaceful revolution—has shown the enormous human, moral, and spiritual potential: the civic culture that has slumbered in our society beneath the mask of apathy. Whenever someone categorically claimed that we were this or that, I always objected that society is a very mysterious creature and that it is not wise to trust the face it chooses to show you. I am happy I was not mistaken. People all around the world wondered how those meek, humiliated, cynical citizens of Czechoslovakia, who seemed to believe in nothing, found the strength to cast off the totalitarian system in several weeks, and do it in a decent and peaceful manner. And let us ask, Where did young people who never knew another system get their longing for truth, their love of free thought, their political imagination, their civic courage, and their civic prudence? How did their parents—precisely the generation thought to be lost—join them? How is it possible that so many people immediately grasped what had to be done, without needing anyone else's advice or instructions?

I think there are two main reasons. First of all, people are never merely a product of the external world—they are always able to respond to something superior, however systematically the external world tries to snuff out that ability. Second, humanistic and democratic traditions, about which there had been so much idle talk, did after all slumber in the subconscious of our nations and national minorities. These traditions were inconspicuously passed from one generation to another, so that each of us could discover them at the right time and transform them into deeds.

Of course, we had to pay for our present freedom. Many citizens died in prison in the 1950s. Many were executed. Thousands of human lives were destroyed. Hundreds of thousands of talented people were forced to leave the country. Those who defended the honor of our nations during World War II, those who rebelled against totalitarian rule, those who simply managed to remain themselves and think freely—all were persecuted. We should not forget any of those who paid for our present freedom in one way or another. Independent courts should consider the possible guilt of those who were responsible for the persecutions, so that the whole truth about our recent past is fully revealed.

We must also bear in mind that other nations have paid even more dearly for their present freedom, and that indirectly they have also paid for ours. The rivers of blood that flowed in Hungary, Poland, Germany, and not long ago in such a horrific manner in Romania, and the sea of blood shed by the nations of the Soviet Union, must not be forgotten, because all human suffering concerns every human being. But the sacrifices of these peoples must not be forgotten also because their suffering forms the tragic background to our own newfound freedom and to the gradual emancipation of the nations of the Soviet bloc. Without the changes in the Soviet Union, Poland, Hungary, and East Germany, what happened here could scarcely have taken place, and certainly not in such a calm and peaceful manner.

The fact that we enjoyed optimal international conditions does not mean that someone has directly supported us during the recent weeks. In fact, after hundreds of years, both our nations have raised their heads high without relying on the help of stronger countries. It seems to me that this constitutes the great moral asset of the present moment. This moment holds within itself the hope that in the future we will no longer suffer from the complexes of those indebted to someone else. Now it is solely up to us whether the promise of this moment will be fulfilled, and whether our civic, national, and political self-respect will be revived.

Self-respect is not pride.

Quite the contrary: only a person or a nation with self-respect, in the best sense of the word, is capable of listening to others while accepting them as equals, of forgiving enemies while expiating their own sins. Let us try to infuse our communities with this kind of self-respect; let our country's behavior on the international stage be marked by this kind of self-respect. Only then will we restore our self-confidence, our respect for one another, and our respect for other nations.

Our state should never again be an appendage or a poor relative of any other state. While it is true that we must accept and learn many things from other countries, we must do so as an equal partner who has something to offer.

Our first president, T. G. Masaryk, wrote: Jesus, not Caesar. Thus he followed our philosophers Chelčický and Comenius. I dare to say that we may even have an opportunity to spread this idea abroad, to introduce a new element into European and global politics. Our country, if that is what we want, can now permanently radiate love, understanding, and the power of the spirit and of ideas. It is precisely this glow that we can offer as our contribution to international politics.

Masaryk rooted his politics in morality. Let us try—in a new era and in a new way—to restore this conception of politics. Let us teach ourselves and others that politics should be animated by the desire to contribute to the community, rather than by the need to cheat or rape the community. Let us teach ourselves and others that politics can be not only the art of the possible—especially if this means speculations, calculations, intrigues, secret deals, and pragmatic maneuvering—but also the art of the impossible, namely, the art of improving ourselves and the world.

We are a small country, yet at one time we were the spiritual crossroads of Europe. Is there any reason why we could not regain that distinction? Would it not be a way to repay those whose help we are going to need?

Our home-grown mafia—those who do not look out of the windows of their planes and eat specially fed pigs—may still linger in our midst, muddying the waters from time to time. But it is no longer our main enemy. The international mafia of which it is a part is even less our enemy. Our main enemy today is our own bad habits: indifference to the common good, vanity, personal ambition, selfishness, and envy. The main struggle will have to be fought against these foes.

Free elections and an election campaign lie ahead of us. Let us not allow this struggle to dirty the clean face of our gentle revolution. Let us not allow the world's sympathy, which we won so quickly, to be lost with equal speed in the coming skirmishes for power. Let us not allow selfish desires to bloom once again under the noble veil of the desire to serve the common good. It is not really important which party, club, or group will prevail in the elections. The important thing is that the winners will be the best of us—in the moral civic, political and professional sense—regardless of the winner's political affiliations. The future policies and prestige of our state will depend on the personalities that we shall select and later elect to our representative bodies.

My dear fellow citizens!

Three days ago the deputies of the Federal Assembly, expressing your will, elected me president of the republic. You therefore rightly expect that I should mention the tasks that I as president see before me.

The first of these is to use all my powers and influence to ensure that we shall soon step up to ballot boxes in free elections, and that our path toward this historic event will be dignified and peaceful.

My second task is to guarantee that we approach these elections as two genuinely self-governing nations, which mutually respect their interests, national identity, religious traditions, and symbols. As a Czech who swore his presidential oath to an eminent and personally close Slovak, I feel a special obligation, knowing the various bitter experiences that Slovaks have gone through in the past, to see to it that the interests of the Slovak nation are respected, and that the way to any state office, including the highest one, will never be closed to Slovaks in the future.

My third task is to do everything in my power to improve the lot of children, old people, women, the sick, national minorities, and all citizens who for any reason are worse off than others. The best food or hospitals must no longer be prerogatives of the powers that be: they must first be offered to those who need them most.

As the supreme commander of the armed forces, I want to ensure that the defense capability of our country will no longer serve as a pretext for anyone to thwart peace initiatives, including the reduction of military service, the establishment of alternative military service, and the general humanization of military life.

In our country, there are many prisoners who were convicted of serious crimes and are being punished for them. However, they had to undergo—in spite of the good will of some investigators, judges, and, above all, defense lawyers—a debased judiciary process that curtailed their rights. Now they live in prisons that, rather than attempting to awake the better qualities that inhere in every human being, humiliate people and destroy them physically and mentally. In view of this fact, I have decided to declare a relatively extensive amnesty. I ask the prisoners to understand that the damage caused by forty years of unjust interrogations, trials, and imprisonments cannot be repaired overnight, and that all the changes that are being speedily prepared will nonetheless still require a certain amount of time. By rebelling, the prisoners will neither help society nor themselves. I also call upon the public not to fear the prisoners after they are released, not to make their lives difficult, and to help them in a Christian spirit to seek within themselves that which the prisons did not help them to find: the ability to repent and the desire to live an upright life.

My honorable task is to strengthen the authority of our country in the world. I would be glad if other countries respected us for showing understanding, tolerance, and love of peace. I would be happy if Pope John Paul II and the Dalai Lama of Tibet could visit our country before the elections, if only for one day. I would be happy if our friendly relations with all nations were strengthened. I would be happy if we succeeded before the elections in establishing diplomatic relations with the Vatican and Israel. I would also like to contribute to peace by my brief visit tomorrow to our close neighbors, namely, the German Democratic Republic and the Federal Republic of Germany. Nor shall I forget our other neighbors—Poland, Hungary, and Austria.

In conclusion, I would like to say that I want to be a president who will speak less and work more. To be a president who will not only look out the windows of his airplane, but who will always be among his fellow citizens and listen to them attentively.

You may ask what kind of republic I dream of. Let me reply: I dream of a republic that is independent, free, and democratic; a republic with economic prosperity, yet social justice; a humane republic that serves the individual and therefore hopes that the individual will serve it in turn; a republic of well-rounded people, because without such people, it is impossible to solve any of our problems, whether they be human, economic, ecological, social, or political.

The most distinguished of my predecessors opened his first speech with a quote from Comenius [the great Czech educator of the seventeenth century]. Allow me to end my first speech with my own paraphrase of the same statement: My people, your government has returned to you! ■

Vice-President Albert Gore Slams the Cynics and Asserts His Credo

"THE root of the word 'cynic' is the same as the Greek word for 'dog,' and some scholars say the Cynics got their name because they barked at society. Sounds almost like some of our talk-radio shows."

SON OF A LIBERAL SENATOR from Tennessee, Al Gore graduated from Harvard and served in Vietnam, returned to become a reporter and editorial writer for the *Nashville Tennessean*, served in the House and Senate from that state, and was chosen to be Bill Clinton's running mate in 1992 and 1996.

In his vice-presidency, his speeches—delivered with a strong voice and in a slow, clear cadence—tended to be programmatic and to point with pride at administration accomplishments, which vice-presidential rhetoric traditionally does. However, in debate, the experienced legislator knows how to score points, savaging his opponent while maintaining his Boy Scout look: the televised debate with H. Ross Perot diminished that skilled TV performer and established Gore as a powerful advocate for Clinton's causes.

He has shown a willingness to use the most emotional personal experiences to rivet a national TV audience. In his first acceptance speech, Gore went into detail about the injury to his young son; in his second acceptance in 1996 his late sister Nancy's death from cancer was the setting for his condemnation of tobacco use. Democrats were moved; Republicans thought he exploited personal tragedy; an objective speech analyst would have to say his long "stories" were effective, if overdone.

They did run counter to his reputation for wooden delivery. Gore tends to stand stiffly and orate as if he were explaining to a three-year-old. The comedian Mark Russell called Gore's 1996 debate with GOP vice-presidential nominee Jack Kemp "a huddle between a quarterback and the goalpost." However plodding and syrupy his delivery, Gore was well prepared and resolutely "on message," and was seen to have won the debate.

At the Harvard commencement on June 9, 1994, Gore made the most profound speech of his vice-presidency, examining the loss of trust in government that has afflicted his generation. The young man who left in 1969 returned with a different, and less disillusioned, view of the world.

□   □   □

Harvard commencement is a special occasion. How could anyone not have been thrilled by this morning's assembly—twenty-five thousand people packed into Harvard Yard to celebrate one of the great occasions of life. I loved it all. And I have especially enjoyed my twenty-fifth reunion. . . .

I remember the twenty-fifth reunion class when they came in 1969 walking around the Yard with their children. That was the class of 1944. They were part of the generation President Clinton commemorated this week in Normandy, the group that went from Harvard to boot camp and basic training and from there were transfused into the weary divisions battling across Europe. Only eleven members of the class were present at graduation; all the rest had by then already left to enlist. Some did not come back to their reunion. Their names are carved in stone in Memorial Church just behind me. Many did come back and some of them are here again today for their fiftieth reunion. We salute you.

Back in 1969 our graduating class was in no mood to salute or to celebrate your sacrifice or your achievement. But we understood then and understand now ever more clearly that without any question, because of your service, the world changed in 1944. Indeed, our world a half-century later is still shaped by the events of that tumultuous and triumphant year.

I want to describe today the reasons why I believe the world also changed in important and enduring ways because of the events of 1969, a year of contradiction and contrasts, of glory and bitterness.

In July 1969 one quarter of the population of the world watched on live television while Neil Armstrong brought his space module *Eagle* down to the Sea of Tranquillity, slowly climbed down a ladder and pressed his left boot into the untrod surface of the moon.

But 1969 was also the year Charles Manson and his followers made the innocent words "Helter Skelter" symbols of a bloodbath. It was the year of music in the rain at Woodstock and the year of the My Lai massacre in Vietnam.

While we went to class and heard lectures and wrote papers and listened to music and talked and played sports and fell in love, the war in Vietnam was blasting that small country apart physically and ripping

America apart emotionally. A dark mood of uncertainty from that tragic conflict clouded every single day we were here.

The year 1969 began with the inauguration of Richard Nixon, a ceremony that seemed to confirm for many of us the finality of a change in our national mood and ratify the results of a downward spiral that had begun with the assassination of President Kennedy five years, two months, and two days earlier. . . .

After all, the war raged on for five more years and the downward spiral in our national mood reached a new low when the Watergate scandal led to the growing belief that our government was telling lies to our people.

The resignation of President Nixon, his subsequent pardon, the oil shocks, 21 percent interest rates, hostages held seemingly interminably and then swapped in return for weapons provided to terrorists who called us "the Great Satan," a quadrupling of our national debt in only a dozen years, a growing gap between rich and poor, and steadily declining real incomes—all of these continued an avalanche of negative self-images which have profoundly changed the way Americans view their government.

A recent analysis of public opinion polling data covering the years since my class came to Harvard demonstrates the cumulative change in our national mood. When my class entered as freshmen in the fall of 1965, the percentage of people who believed that government generally tries to do the right thing was over 60 percent. Today it is only 10 percent. The percentage believing that government favors the rich and the powerful was then 29 percent. Today it is 80 percent. And it is important to note that these trends hold true for Democrats and Republicans, conservatives and liberals.

In fact, this may be an apocryphal story, but someone actually claimed the other day the situation has gotten so bad that when they conducted a new poll and asked people about their current level of cynicism, 18 percent said they were more cynical than five years ago, 9 percent thought they were less cynical, and 72 percent suspected the question was some kind of government ploy, and refused to answer.

Democracy stands or falls on a mutual trust—government's trust of the people and the people's trust of the governments they elect. And yet at the same time democratic culture and politics have always existed in a strange blend of credulity and skepticism. Indeed, a certain degree of enduring skepticism about human nature lies at the foundation of our representative democracy. James Madison argued successfully in the *Federalist Papers* that the United States Constitution should create a protective balance of power among the factions that were bound to rise in any society.

Democracy did not mean unity in the body politic. People do have reasonable differences. Human ignorance, pride, and selfishness would always be with us, prompting inevitable divisions and conflicting ambitions.

Yet, freedom and order could be protected with safeguards ensuring that no one branch of government and no one group or faction would be able to dictate to all the rest. We were the first large republic to build a nation on the revolutionary premise that the people are sovereign and that the freedom to dispute, debate, disagree, and quarrel with each other created a fervent love of country that could hold us together against the world. It is still a revolutionary premise. And it is still built on a skeptical view of human nature that refuses to believe in perfection in intellect, logic, knowledge, or morals in any human being.

And so the ceaseless American yearning for the ideal life has always stumbled uneasily over a persistent American skepticism about the parties and leaders who claim to have the wisdom and ability to guide us to our destiny. We revere our institutions, and at the same time we watch our leaders as though we were hawks circling overhead, eager to dive with claws extended onto any flaw or failure that we see.

Even our most beloved president, George Washington, wrote in his last letter to Thomas Jefferson, on July 6, 1796: "I had no conception . . . that every act of my administration would be tortured . . . in such exaggerated form and indecent terms as could scarcely be applied to a Nero, a notorious defaulter or even a common pickpocket." . . .

The last time public cynicism sank to its present depth may have been exactly one hundred years ago, when Mark Twain said, "There is no distinctly native American criminal class except Congress." That was a time when Americans felt the earth moving under their feet. Debt and depression forced farmers off the land and into cities that they found cold and strange and into factories where human beings became scarcely more than the extensions of machines. Cynicism was soon abroad in the land.

We are now in the midst of another historic and unsettling economic transformation. Now the information revolution is leading to a loss of jobs in many factories, as computers and automation replace human labor.

After World War II, 35 percent of America's employment was on the factory floor. Today fewer than 17 percent of our labor force works in manufacturing. Just as most of those who lost their jobs on the farm a hundred years ago eventually found new work in factories, so today new jobs are opening up in new occupations created by the information revolution—but this time the transition is taking place more swiftly and the economic adjustment is, for many, more difficult and disorienting.

In this respect we are actually doing better than most other nations.

Every industrial society in the world is having enormous difficulty in creating a sufficient number of new jobs—even when their economies heat up. So, not surprisingly, public cynicism about leadership has soared in almost every industrial country in the world.

History is a precarious source of lessons. Nevertheless, I am reminded that similar serious economic problems prevailed in Athens in the fourth century B.C., when the philosophical school we now know as Cynicism was born. The Cynics were fed up with their society and its social conventions and wanted everybody to know it. The root of the word" cynic" is the same as the Greek word for "dog," and some scholars say the Cynics got their name because they barked at society. Sounds almost like some of our talk-radio shows. . . .

Cynicism is deadly. It bites everything it can reach—like a dog with a foot caught in a trap. And then it devours itself. It drains us of the will to improve; it diminishes our public spirit; it saps our inventiveness; it withers our souls. Cynics often see themselves as merely being world-weary. There is no new thing under the sun, the cynics say. They have not only seen everything, they have seen *through* everything. They claim that their weariness is wisdom. But it is usually merely posturing. Their weariness seems to be most effective when they consider the aspirations of those beneath them, who have neither power nor influence nor wealth. For these unfortunates, nothing can be done, the cynics declare.

Hope for society as a whole is considered an affront to rationality; the notion that the individual has a responsibility for the community is considered a dangerous radicalism. And those who toil in quiet places and for little reward to lift up the fallen, to comfort the afflicted, and to protect the weak are regarded as fools.

Ultimately, however, the life of a cynic is lonely and self-destructive. It is our human nature to make connections with other human beings. The gift of sympathy for one another is one of the most powerful sentiments we ever feel. If we do not have it, we are not human. Indeed it is so powerful that the cynic who denies it goes to war with himself. . . .

As the public's willingness to believe the worst increases—that is to say, as cynicism increases—the only political messages that seem to affect the outcome of elections are those that seek to paint the opposition as a gang of bandits and fools who couldn't be trusted to pour water out of a boot if the directions were written on the heel.

This fixation on character assassination rather than on defining issues feeds the voracious appetite of tabloid journalism for scandal. And now whets the growing appetite of other journalistic organizations for the same sort of fare. . . .

Where, then, do we search for healing? What is our strategy for reconciliation with our future and where is our vision for sustainable hope?

I have come to believe that our healing can be found in our relationships to one another and in a shared commitment to higher purposes in the face of adversity.

At the 1992 Democratic convention, I talked about a personal event that fundamentally changed the way I viewed the world: an accident that almost killed our son. I will not repeat the story here today except to say that the most important lesson for me was that people I didn't even know reached out to me and to my family to lift us up in their hearts and in their prayers with compassion of such intensity that I felt it as a palpable force, a healing reaching out of those multitudes of caring souls and falling on us like a mantle of divine grace.

Since then I have dwelled on our connections to one another and on the fact that as human beings, we are astonishingly similar in the most important parts of our existence.

I don't know what barriers in my soul had prevented me from understanding emotionally that basic connection to others until after they reached out to me in the dark of my family's sorrow. But I suppose it was a form of cynicism on my part. If cynicism is based on alienation and fragmentation, I believe that the brokenness that separates the cynic from others is the outward sign of an inner division between the head and the heart. There is something icily and unnaturally intellectual about the cynic. This isolation of intellect from feelings and emotions is the essence of his condition. For the cynic, feelings are as easily separated from the reality others see as ethics are separated from behavior, and as life is cut off from any higher purpose.

Having felt their power in my own life, I believe that sympathy and compassion are revolutionary forces in the world at large and that they are working now.

A year after the accident, when our family's healing process was far advanced, I awoke early one Sunday morning in 1990, turned on the television set, and watched in amazement as another healing process began, when Nelson Mandela was released from prison. Last month, I attended his inauguration when he was sworn as president of the new South Africa in what was a stupendous defeat for cynicism in our time. Many were moved to tears as he introduced three men who had come as his personal guests—three of his former jailers—and described how they had reached across the chasm that had separated them as human beings and had become personal friends. . . .

For my part, in the twenty-five years since my Harvard graduation, I have come to believe in hope over despair, striving over resignation, faith over cynicism.

I believe in the power of knowledge to make the world a better place. Cynics may say: Human beings have never learned anything from history. All that is truly useful about knowledge is that it can provide you with advantages over the pack. But the cynics are wrong: We have the capacity to learn from our mistakes and transcend our past. Indeed. in this very place we have been taught that truth—*veritas*—can set us free.

I believe in finding fulfillment in family, for the family is the true center of a meaningful life. Cynics may say: All families are confining and ultimately dysfunctional. The very idea of family is outdated and unworkable. But the cynics are wrong: It is in our families that we learn to love.

I believe in serving God and trying to understand and obey God's will for our lives. Cynics may wave the idea away, saying God is a myth, useful in providing comfort to the ignorant and in keeping them obedient. I know in my heart—beyond all arguing and beyond any doubt—that the cynics are wrong.

I believe in working to achieve social justice and freedom for all. Cynics may scorn this notion as naive, claiming that all our efforts for equal opportunity, for justice, for freedom, have created only a wasteland of failed hopes. But the cynics are wrong: Freedom is our destiny; justice is our guide; we shall overcome.

I believe in protecting the earth's environment against an unprecedented onslaught. Cynics may laugh out loud and say there is no utility in a stand of thousand-year-old trees, a fresh breeze, or a mountain stream. But the cynics are wrong: We are part of God's earth, not separate from it.

I believe in you. Each of you individually. And all of you here as a group. The cynics say you are motivated principally by greed and that ultimately you will care for nothing other than yourselves. But the cynics are wrong. You care about each other, you cherish freedom, you treasure justice, you seek truth.

And finally, I believe in America. Cynics will say we have lost our way, that the American century is at its end. But the cynics are wrong. America is still the model to which the world aspires. Almost everywhere in the world the values that the United States has proclaimed, defended, and tried to live are now rising.

In the end, we face a fundamental choice: cynicism or faith. Each equally capable of taking root in our souls and shaping our lives as self-fulfilling prophecies. We must open our hearts to one another and build on all the vast and creative possibilities of America. This is a task for a confident people, which is what we have been throughout our history and what we still are now in our deepest character.

I believe in our future. ■

Prime Minister Benazir Bhutto of Pakistan Argues That Male Domination of Women Offends Her Islamic Religion

"To those who claim to speak for Islam but who would deny to women our place in society, I say: The ethos of Islam is equality, equality between the sexes. . . . Islam forbids injustice; injustice against people, against nations, against women."

"I HAVE ENDURED a great deal in my forty years on this planet," Benazir Bhutto told an Atlanta audience in 1993. "The members of my party have been victimized, tortured, kidnapped, sometimes raped, and even killed. My brave husband . . . was imprisoned for over two painful years, held hostage against my political career for no other crime than being married to me. Every possible method of coercion was applied to me to abandon my struggle, my party, my people, and to give in to forces of tyranny pressuring me to quit politics."

Adjusting her Muslim head scarf—a gesture from this handsome woman that punctuates and adds dramatic emphasis to oratorical pauses— she recalled a line of the poet Tennyson quoted to her by her father, the former Prime Minister Zulfiqar Ali Bhutto, writing from his cell before he was hanged by the dictator who had seized power: "Ah, what shall I be at fifty . . . If I find the world so bitter at twenty-five."

Within a few months, her Pakistani countrymen and women entrusted her with the prime ministership for the second time; in 1996, a military-backed leader, charging corruption, ousted her again.

Born to the aristocracy, educated by Catholic nuns at a convent school, and later at Harvard and Oxford, favorite child of Pakistan's leader, Ms. Bhutto learned the dark side of life in solitary confinement after her father's downfall. She spoke out to defend his reputation when such talk was costly, which had an effect on her speaking style: well-modulated but forthright, well-mannered with a touch of defiance.

When Sarajevo was under siege, she joined Tansu Ciller, prime minister of Turkey, in a visit to embattled Muslims in the Bosnian capital, helping to focus world attention on their suffering. The picture of two Muslim women, both leaders of their nations, asserting solidarity with their coreligionists under fire, also reminded Westerners that not all Islam was male-dominated. In Beijing on September 4, 1995, she spoke to a world conference of women and drove that point home with an eloquence derived from a tempestuous life in politics.

□   □   □

As the first woman ever elected to head an Islamic nation, I feel a special responsibility about issues that relate to women.

In addressing the new exigencies of the new century, we must translate dynamic religion into a living reality. We must live by the true spirit of Islam, not only by its rituals. And for those of you who may be ignorant of Islam, cast aside your preconceptions about the role of women in our religion.

Contrary to what many of you may have come to believe, Islam embraces a rich variety of political, social, and cultural traditions. The fundamental ethos of Islam is tolerance, dialogue, and democracy.

Just as in Christianity and Judaism, we must always be on guard for those who will exploit and manipulate the Holy Book for their own narrow political ends, who will distort the essence of pluralism and tolerance for their own extremist agendas.

To those who claim to speak for Islam but who would deny to women our place in society, I say:

The ethos of Islam is equality, equality between the sexes. There is no religion on earth that, in its writing and teachings, is more respectful of the role of women in society than Islam.

My presence here, as the elected woman prime minister of a great Muslim country, is testament to the commitment of Islam to the role of women in society.

It is this tradition of Islam that has empowered me, has strengthened me, has emboldened me.

It was this heritage that sustained me during the most difficult points in my life, for Islam forbids injustice; injustice against people, against nations, against women.

It denounces inequality as the gravest form of injustice.

It enjoins its followers to combat oppression and tyranny.

It enshrines piety as the sole criteria for judging humankind.

It shuns race, color, and gender as a basis of distinction amongst fellow men.

When the human spirit was immersed in the darkness of the Middle Ages, Islam proclaimed equality between men and women. When women were viewed as inferior members of the human family, Islam gave them respect and dignity.

When women were treated as chattels, the Prophet of Islam *(Peace Be Upon Him)* accepted them as equal partners.

Islam codified the rights of women. *The Koran* elevated their status to that of men. It guaranteed their civic, economic, and political rights. It recognized their participative role in nation building.

Sadly, the Islamic tenets regarding women were soon discarded. In Islamic society, as in other parts of the world, their rights were denied. Women were maltreated, discriminated against, and subjected to violence and oppression, their dignity injured and their role denied.

Women became the victims of a culture of exclusion and male dominance. Today more women than men suffer from poverty, deprivation, and discrimination. Half a billion women are illiterate. Seventy percent of the children who are denied elementary education are girls.

The plight of women in the developing countries is unspeakable. Hunger, disease, and unremitting toil is their fate. Weak economic growth and inadequate social support systems affect them most seriously and directly.

They are the primary victims of structural adjustment processes, which necessitate reduced state funding for health, education, medical care, and nutrition. Curtailed resource flows to these vital areas impact most severely on the vulnerable groups, particularly women and children.

This, Madam Chairperson, is not acceptable. It offends my religion. It offends my sense of justice and equity. Above all, it offends *common* sense.

That is why Pakistan, the women of Pakistan, and I personally have been fully engaged in recent international efforts to uphold women's rights. *The Universal Declaration of Human Rights* enjoins the elimination of discrimination against women.

The *Nairobi Forward Looking Strategies* provide a solid framework for advancing women's rights around the world. But the goal of equality, development, and peace still eludes us.

Sporadic efforts in this direction have failed. We are satisfied that the *Beijing Platform of Action* encompasses a comprehensive approach toward the empowerment of women. This is the right approach and should be fully supported.

Women cannot be expected to struggle alone against the forces of discrimination and exploitation. I recall the words of Dante, who reminded us that "The hottest place in Hell is reserved for those who remain neutral in times of moral crisis."

Today in this world, in the fight for the liberation of women, there can be no neutrality.

My spirit carries many a scar of a long and lonely battle against dictatorship and tyranny. I witnessed, at a young age, the overthrow of democracy, the assassination of an elected prime minister, and a systematic assault against the very foundations of a free society.

But our faith in democracy was not broken. The great Pakistani poet and philosopher Dr. Allama Iqbal says, "Tyranny cannot endure forever." It did not. The will of our people prevailed against the forces of dictatorship.

But, my dear sisters, we have learned that democracy alone is not enough.

Freedom of choice alone does not guarantee justice.

Equal rights are not defined only by political values.

Social justice is a triad of freedom, an equation of liberty:

> Justice is political liberty.
> Justice is economic independence.
> Justice is social equality.

Delegates, sisters, the child who is starving has no human rights.

The girl who is illiterate has no future.

The woman who cannot plan her life, plan her family, plan a career, is fundamentally not free. . . .

I am determined to change the plight of women in my country. More than sixty million of our women are largely sidelined.

It is a personal tragedy for them. It is a national catastrophe for my nation. I am determined to harness their potential to the gigantic task of nation building. . . .

I dream of a Pakistan in which women contribute to their full potential. I am conscious of the struggle that lies ahead. But, with your help, we shall persevere. Allah willing, we shall succeed.

■   ■   ■

XI

MEDIA
SPEECHES

Thomas Jefferson Returns Fire of "the Artillery of the Press"

"DURING this course of administration, and in order to disturb it, the artillery of the press has been leveled against us, charged with whatsoever its licentiousness could devise or dare. These abuses of an institution so important to freedom and science are deeply to be regretted, inasmuch as they tend to lessen its usefulness and to sap its safety."

THE TONE OF President Jefferson's second inaugural address was less lofty than his first. He had been through the political wars; he had taken heat from critics on his extraconstitutional Louisiana Purchase; and he had won reelection decisively despite having been subjected to the harassment of the calumniators of the press.

One journalist in particular got under his skin: J. T. Callender of the *Richmond Recorder*. Jefferson's anti-Federalist allies had once used Callender as a conduit for a story of adultery that damaged Alexander Hamilton; when the writer later sought favors from Jefferson and was rebuffed, he turned on the president with a story about a pre-Revolutionary affair the young Jefferson had had with a neighbor's wife. The charge was especially annoying to the president because it was true.

The style of the speech remains gracefully formal, but a certain testiness, even petulance, can be felt, along with the satisfaction of a public figure who has triumphed over his tormentors. Jefferson notes that laws are available to stop "falsehood and defamation," but claims to be too busy with the public's business to deal with his detractors: "the offenders have therefore been left to find their punishment in the public indignation." He sternly reminds the press of "the salutary coercions of the law," then draws back to allow the miscreants practicing "demoralizing licentiousness" to suffer only "the censorship of public opinion."

This is not the Jefferson most frequently quoted by civil libertarians. His second inaugural address, delivered in the Capitol in Washington on March 4, 1805, is an example of a speech by a political figure angry at having been embarrassed but determined, as a statesman, not to let it get the better of him.

□   □   □

. . . **O**n taking this station on a former occasion I declared the principles on which I believed it my duty to administer the affairs of our Commonwealth. My conscience tells me I have on every occasion acted up to that declaration according to its obvious import and to the understanding of every candid mind.

In the transaction of your foreign affairs we have endeavored to cultivate the friendship of all nations, and especially of those with which we have the most important relations. We have done them justice on all occasions, favored where favor was lawful, and cherished mutual interests and intercourse on fair and equal terms. We are firmly convinced, and we act on that conviction, that with nations as with individuals our interests soundly calculated will ever be found inseparable from our moral duties, and history bears witness to the fact that a just nation is trusted on its word when recourse is had to armaments and wars to bridle others.

At home, fellow-citizens, you best know whether we have done well or ill. The suppression of unnecessary offices, of useless establishments and expenses, enabled us to discontinue our internal taxes. These, covering our land with officers and opening our doors to their intrusions, had already begun that process of domiciliary vexation which once entered is scarcely to be restrained from reaching successively every article of property and produce. If among these taxes some minor ones fell which had not been inconvenient, it was because their amount would not have paid the officers who collected them, and because, if they had any merit, the State authorities might adopt them instead of others less approved.

The remaining revenue on the consumption of foreign articles is paid chiefly by those who can afford to add foreign luxuries to domestic comforts, being collected on our seaboard and frontiers only, and, incorporated with the transactions of our mercantile citizens, it may be the pleasure and the pride of an American to ask, What farmer, what mechanic, what laborer, ever sees a tax-gatherer of the United States? These contributions enable us to support the current expenses of the government, to fulfill contracts with foreign nations, to extinguish the native right of soil within our limits, to extend those limits, and to apply such a surplus to our public debts as places at a short day their final redemption, and that redemption once effected the revenue thereby liberated may, by a just repartition of it among the states and a corresponding amendment of the Constitution, be applied *in time of peace* to rivers, canals, roads, arts, manufactures, education, and other great objects within each state. *In time of war,* if justice by ourselves or others must sometimes produce war, increased as the same revenue will be by increased population and consumption, and aided by other resources reserved for that crisis, it may meet within the year all the expenses of the year without encroaching on the rights of future generations by burthening them with the debts of the past. War will then be but a suspension of useful works, and a return to a state of peace, a return to the progress of improvement.

I have said, fellow-citizens, that the income reserved had enabled us to extend our limits, but that extension may possibly pay for itself before we are called on, and in the meantime may keep down the accruing interest; in all events, it will replace the advances we shall have made. I know that the acquisition of Louisiana has been disapproved by some from a candid apprehension that the enlargement of our territory would endanger its union. But who can limit the extent to which the federative principle may operate effectively? The larger our association the less will it be shaken by local passions; and in any view is it not better that the opposite bank of the Mississippi should be settled by our own brethren and children than by strangers of another family? With which should we be most likely to live in harmony and friendly intercourse?

In matters of religion I have considered that its free exercise is placed by the Constitution independent of the powers of the general government. I have therefore undertaken on no occasion to prescribe the religious exercises suited to it, but have left them, as the Constitution found them, under the direction and discipline of the church or state authorities acknowledged by the several religious societies.

The aboriginal inhabitants of these countries I have regarded with the commiseration their history inspires. Endowed with the faculties and the rights of men, breathing an ardent love of liberty and independence, and occupying a country which left them no desire but to be undisturbed, the stream of overflowing population from other regions directed itself on these shores; without power to divert or habits to contend against it, they have been overwhelmed by the current or driven before it; now reduced within limits too narrow for the hunter's state, humanity enjoins us to teach them agriculture and the domestic arts; to encourage them to that industry which alone can enable them to maintain their place in existence and to prepare them in time for that state of society which to bodily comforts adds the improvement of the mind and morals. We have therefore liberally furnished them with the implements of husbandry and household use; we have placed among them instructors in the arts of first necessity, and they are covered with the aegis of the law against aggressors from among ourselves.

But the endeavors to enlighten them on the fate which awaits their present course of life, to induce them to exercise their reason, follow its dictates, and change their pursuits with the change of circumstances have powerful obstacles to encounter; they are combated by the habits of their bodies, prejudices of their minds, ignorance, pride, and the influence of interested and crafty individuals among them who feel themselves something in the present order of things and fear to become nothing in any other. These persons inculcate a sanctimonious reverence for the customs of their ancestors; that whatsoever they did must be done through all time; that reason is a false guide, and to advance under its counsel in their physical, moral, or political condition is perilous innovation; that their duty is to remain as their Creator made them, ignorance being safety and knowledge full of danger; in short, my friends, among them also is seen the action and counteraction of good sense and of bigotry; they too have their antiphilosophists who find an interest in keeping things in their present state, who dread reformation, and exert all their faculties to maintain the ascendency of habit over the duty of improving our reason and obeying its mandates.

In giving these outlines I do not mean, fellow-citizens, to arrogate to myself the merit of the measures. That is due, in the first place, to the reflecting character of our citizens at large, who, by the weight of public opinion, influence and strengthen the public measures. It is due to the sound discretion with which they select from among themselves those to whom they confide the legislative duties. It is due to the zeal and wisdom of the characters thus selected, who lay the foundations of public happiness in wholesome laws, the execution of which alone remains for others, and it is due to the able and faithful auxiliaries, whose patriotism has associated them with me in the executive functions.

During this course of administration, and in order to disturb it, the artillery of the press has been leveled against us, charged with whatsoever its licentiousness could devise or dare. These abuses of an institution so important to freedom and science are deeply to be regretted, inasmuch as they tend to lessen its usefulness and to sap its safety. They might, indeed, have been corrected by the wholesome punishments reserved to and provided by the laws of the several states against falsehood and defamation, but public duties more urgent press on the time of public servants, and the offenders have therefore been left to find their punishment in the public indignation.

Nor was it uninteresting to the world that an experiment should be fairly and fully made, whether freedom of discussion, unaided by power, is not sufficient for the propagation and protection of truth—whether a government conducting itself in the true spirit of its constitution, with zeal and purity, and doing no act which it would be unwilling the whole world should witness, can be written down by falsehood and defamation. The experiment has been tried; you have witnessed the scene; our fellow-citizens looked on, cool and collected; they saw the latent source from which these outrages proceeded; they gathered around their public functionaries, and when the Constitution called them to the decision by suffrage, they pronounced their verdict, honorable to those who had served them and consolatory to the friend of man who believes that he may be trusted with the control of his own affairs.

No inference is here intended that the laws provided by the states against false and defamatory publications should not be enforced; he who has time renders a service to public morals and public tranquillity in reforming these abuses by the salutary coercions of the law; but the experiment is noted to prove that, since truth and reason have maintained their ground against false opinions in league with false facts, the press, confined to truth, needs no other legal restraint; the public judgment will correct false reasonings and opinions on a full hearing of all parties; and no other definite line can be drawn between the inestimable liberty of the press and its demoralizing licentiousness. If there be still improprieties which this rule would not restrain, its supplement must be sought in the censorship of public opinion.

Contemplating the union of sentiment now manifested so generally as auguring harmony and happiness to our future course, I offer to our country sincere congratulations. With those, too, not yet rallied to the same point the disposition to do so is gaining strength; facts are piercing through the veil drawn over them, and our doubting brethren will at length see that the mass of their fellow-citizens with whom they cannot yet resolve to act as to principles and measures, think as they think and desire what they desire; that our wish as well as theirs is that the public efforts may be directed honestly to the public good, that peace be cultivated, civil and religious liberty unassailed, law and order preserved, equality of rights maintained, and that state of property, equal or unequal, which results to every man from his own industry or that of his father's. When satisfied of these views it is not in human nature that they should not approve and support them. In the meantime let us cherish them with patient affection, let us do them justice, and more than justice, in all competitions of interest, and we need not doubt that truth, reason, and their own interests will at length prevail, will gather them into the fold of their country, and will complete that entire union of opinion which gives to a nation the blessing of harmony and the benefit of all its strength.

I shall now enter on the duties to which my fellow-citizens have again called me, and shall proceed in the spirit of those principles which they have approved. I fear not that any motives of interest may lead me astray; I am sensible of no passion which could seduce me knowingly from the path of justice, but the weaknesses of human nature and the limits of my own understanding will produce errors of judgment sometimes injurious to your interests. I shall need, therefore, all the indulgence which I have heretofore experienced from my constituents; the want of it will certainly not lessen with increasing years. I shall need, too, the favor of that Being in whose hands we are, who led our fathers, as Israel of old, from their native land and planted them in a country flowing with all the necessaries and comforts of life; who has covered our infancy with His providence and our riper years with His wisdom and power, and to whose goodness I ask you to join in supplications with me that He will so enlighten the minds of your servants, guide their councils, and prosper their measures that whatsoever they do shall result in your good, and shall secure to you the peace, friendship, and approbation of all nations. ■

Broadcaster
Edward R. Murrow
Despairs of the Future
of TV Journalism

"THIS instrument can teach, it can illuminate; yes, and it can even inspire. But it can do so only to the extent that humans are determined to use it to those ends. Otherwise it is merely wires and lights in a box."

"THIS [DRAMATIC PAUSE] IS LONDON." CBS correspondent Ed Murrow's distinctive voice brought the blitz home to Americans early in World War II. After the war, he returned to the United States and led the way to what his colleague Eric Sevareid called "electronic journalism." Departing from the strict-objectivity policy laid down to individual broadcasters by Board Chairman William Paley, Murrow in 1954 attacked Senator Joseph McCarthy in a stunning documentary. That earned the respected Murrow Paley's enmity, and on the next Election night he was replaced as commentator by Sevareid and relegated to a minor role.

When asked to speak to the Radio and Television News Directors Association, Murrow replied, "Somebody ought to make a speech on one of those occasions which would outrage all of our employers." According to Sig Mickelson, a former president of CBS News, Murrow "was rebelling at what he regarded as petty restrictions that had been imposed on him." Most other newsmen found a higher motive in Murrow's biting of the hand that fed him.

The October 15, 1958, speech was delivered neither angrily nor spiritedly; one of those present at the Chicago convention described Murrow's delivery as in "the accents of despair." Afterward, Murrow told an interviewer: "I've always been on the side of the heretics against those who burned them, because the heretics so often are proved right in the long run. Dead—but right!"

The opening sentence of the speech was doubly prophetic. "This just might do nobody any good" acknowledged that his heresy would harm him at CBS, and expressed his pessimism at stopping the commercialization of broadcast news. But the opening teaser of "heretical and even dangerous thoughts" made his listeners aware that the speaker was shortening his CBS career with his speech.

□   □   □

This just might do nobody any good. At the end of this discourse a few people may accuse this reporter of fouling his own comfortable nest, and your organization may be accused of having given hospitality to heretical and even dangerous thoughts. But the elaborate structure of networks, advertising agencies, and sponsors will not be shaken or altered. It is my desire, if not my duty, to try to talk to you journeymen with some candor about what is happening to radio and television. . . .

You should also know at the outset that, in the manner of witnesses before congressional committees, I appear here voluntarily—by invitation—that I am an employee of the Columbia Broadcasting System, that I am neither an officer nor a director of that corporation, and that these remarks are of a "do-it-yourself" nature. If what I have to say is responsible, then I alone am responsible for the saying of it. . . . I have no feud, either with my employers, any sponsors, or with the professional critics of radio and television. But I am seized with an abiding fear regarding what these two instruments are doing to our society, our culture, and our heritage. . . .

Recently, network spokesmen have been disposed to complain that the professional critics of television have been "rather beastly." There have been hints that somehow competition for the advertising dollar has caused the critics of print to gang up on television and radio. This reporter has no desire to defend the critics. They have space in which to do that on their own behalf. But it remains a fact that the newspapers and magazines are the only instruments of mass communication which remain free from sustained and regular critical comment. If the network spokesmen are so anguished about what appears in print, let them come forth and engage in a little sustained and regular comment regarding newspapers and magazines. It is an ancient and sad fact that most people in network television, and radio, have an exaggerated regard for what appears in print. And there have been cases where executives have refused to make even private comment on a program for which they were responsible until they had read the reviews in print. This is hardly an exhibition of confidence.

The oldest excuse of the networks for their timidity is their youth. Their spokesmen say, "We are young; we have not developed the traditions nor acquired the experience of the older media." If they but knew it, they are building those traditions, creating those precedents, every day. Each time they yield to a voice from Washington or any political pressure, each time they eliminate something that might offend some section of the community, they are creating their own body of precedent and tradition. They are, in fact, not content to be "half safe."

Nowhere is this better illustrated than by the fact that the chairman of the Federal Communications Commission publicly prods broadcasters to engage in their legal right to editorialize. Of course, to undertake an editorial policy, overt and clearly labeled, and obviously unsponsored, requires a station or a network to be responsible. Most stations today probably do not have the manpower to assume this responsibility, but the manpower could be recruited. Editorials would not be profitable; if they had a cutting edge, they might even offend. It is much easier, much less troublesome, to use the money-making machine of television and radio merely as a conduit through which to channel anything that is not libelous, obscene, or defamatory. In that way one has the illusion of power without responsibility. . . .

My memory also goes back to the time when the fear of a slight reduction in business did not result in an immediate cutback in bodies in the news and public affairs department, at a time when network profits had just reached an all-time high. We would all agree, I think, that whether on a station or a network, the stapling machine is a poor substitute for a newsroom typewriter.

One of the minor tragedies of television news and information is that the networks will not even defend their vital interests. When my employer, CBS, through a combination of enterprise and good luck, did an interview with Nikita Khrushchev, the president uttered a few ill-chosen, uninformed words on the subject, and the network practically apologized. This produced a rarity. Many newspapers defended the CBS right to produce the program and commended it for initiative. But the other networks remained silent.

Likewise, when John Foster Dulles, by personal decree, banned American journalists from going to Communist China, and subsequently offered contradictory explanations, for his fiat the networks entered only a mild protest. Then they apparently forgot the unpleasantness. Can it be that this national industry is content to serve the public interest only with the trickle of news that comes out of Hong Kong, to leave its viewers in ignorance of the cataclysmic changes that are occurring in a nation of six hundred million people? I have no illusions about the difficulties of reporting from a dictatorship, but our British and French allies have been better served—in their public interest—with some very useful information from their reporters in Communist China. . . .

Sometimes there is a clash between the public interest and the corporate interest. A telephone call or a letter from the proper quarter in Washington is treated rather more seriously than a communication from an irate but not politically potent viewer. It is tempting enough to give away a little airtime for frequently irresponsible and unwarranted utterances in an effort to temper the wind of criticism.

Upon occasion, economics and editorial judgment are in conflict. And there is no law which says that dollars will be defeated by duty. Not so long ago the president of the United States delivered a television address to the nation. He was discoursing on the possibility or probability of war between this nation and the Soviet Union and Communist China—a reasonably compelling subject. Two networks, CBS and NBC, delayed that broadcast for an hour and fifteen minutes. If this decision was dictated by anything other than financial reasons, the networks didn't deign to explain those reasons. That hour-and-fifteen-minute delay, by the way, is about twice the time required for an ICBM to travel from the Soviet Union to major targets in the United States. It is difficult to believe that this decision was made by men who love, respect, and understand news.

So far, I have been dealing largely with the deficit side of the ledger, and the items could be expanded. But I have said, and I believe, that potentially we have in this country a free enterprise system of radio and television which is superior to any other. But to achieve its promise, it must be both free and enterprising.

There is no suggestion here that networks or individual stations should operate as philanthropies. But I can find nothing in the Bill of Rights or the Communications Act which says that they must increase their net profits each year, lest the Republic collapse. I do not suggest that news and information should be subsidized by foundations or private subscriptions. I am aware that the networks have expended, and are expending, very considerable sums of money on public affairs programs from which they cannot hope to receive any financial reward. I have had the privilege at CBS of presiding over a considerable number of such programs. I testify, and am able to stand here and say, that I have never had a program turned down by my superiors because of the money it would cost.

But we all know that you cannot reach the potential maximum audience in marginal time with a sustaining program. This is so because so many stations on the network—any network—will decline to carry it. Every licensee who applies for a grant to operate in the public interest, convenience and necessity makes certain promises as to what he will do in terms of program content. Many recipients of licenses have, in blunt language, welshed on those promises. The money-making machine somehow blunts their memories. The only remedy for this is closer inspection and punitive action by the FCC. But in the view of many this would come perilously close to supervision of program content by a federal agency.

So it seems that we cannot rely on philanthropic support or foundation subsidies; we cannot follow the "sustaining route"—the networks cannot pay all the freight—and the FCC cannot or will not discipline those who abuse the facilities that belong to the public. What, then, is the answer? Do we merely stay in our comfortable nests, concluding that the obligation of these instruments has been discharged when we work at the job of informing the public for a minimum of time? Or do we believe that the preservation of the Republic is a seven-day-a-week job, demanding more awareness, better skills, and more perseverance than we have yet contemplated.

I am frightened by the imbalance, the constant striving to reach the largest possible audience for everything; by the absence of a sustained study of the state of the nation. Heywood Broun once said, "No body politic is healthy until it begins to itch." I would like television to produce some itching pills, rather than this endless outpouring of tranquilizers. It can be done. Maybe it won't be, but it could. Let us not shoot the wrong piano player. Do not be deluded into believing that the titular heads of the networks control what appears on their networks. They all have better taste. All are responsible to stockholders, and in my experience all are honorable men. But they must schedule what they can sell in the public market.

And this brings us to the nub of the question. In one sense it rather revolves around the phrase heard frequently along Madison Avenue: The Corporate Image. I am not precisely sure what this phrase means, but I would imagine that it reflects a desire on the part of the corporations who pay the advertising bills to have the public image, or believe, that they are not merely bodies with no souls, panting in pursuit of elusive dollars. They would like us to believe that they can distinguish between the public good and the private or corporate gain. So the question is this: Are the big corporations who pay the freight for radio and television programs wise to use that time exclusively for the sale of goods and services? Is it in their own interest and that of the stockholders so to do? The sponsor of an hour's television program is not buying merely the six minutes devoted to commercial message. He is determining, within broad limits, the sum total of the impact of the entire hour. If he always, invariably, reaches for the largest possible audience, then this process of insulation, of escape from reality, will continue to be massively financed, and its apologists will continue to make winsome speeches about giving the public what it wants, or "letting the public decide."

I refuse to believe that the presidents and chairmen of the boards of these big corporations want their corporate image to consist exclusively of a solemn voice in an echo chamber, or a pretty girl opening the door of a refrigerator, or a horse that talks. They want something better, and on occasion some of them have demonstrated it. But most of the men whose legal and moral responsibility it is to spend the stockholders' money for advertising are removed from the realities of the mass media by five, six, or a dozen contraceptive layers of vice-presidents, public relations counsel, and advertising agencies. Their business is to sell goods, and the competition is pretty tough.

But this nation is now in competition with malignant forces of evil who are using every instrument at their command to empty the minds of their subjects and fill those minds with slogans, determination, and faith in the future. If we go on as we are, we are protecting the mind of the American public from any real contact with the menacing world that squeezes in upon us. We are engaged in a great experiment to discover whether a free public opinion can devise and direct methods of managing the affairs of the nation. We may fail. But we are handicapping ourselves needlessly.

Let us have a little competition. Not only in selling soap, cigarettes, and automobiles, but in informing a troubled, apprehensive, but receptive public. Why should not each of the twenty or thirty big corporations which dominate radio and television decide that they will give up one or two of their regularly scheduled programs each year, turn the time over to the networks, and say in effect; "This is a tiny tithe, just a little bit of our profits. On this particular night we aren't going to try to sell cigarettes or automobiles; this is merely a gesture to indicate our belief in the importance of ideas." The networks should, and I think would, pay for the cost of producing the program. The advertiser, the sponsor, would get name credit but would have nothing to do with the content of the program. Would this blemish the corporate image? Would the stockholders object? I think not. For if the premise upon which our pluralistic society rests, which as I understand it is that if the people are given sufficient undiluted information, they will then somehow, even after long, sober second thoughts, reach the right decision—if that premise is wrong, then not only the corporate image but the corporations are done for.

There used to be an old phrase in this country, employed when someone talked too much. It was: "Go hire a hall." Under this proposal the sponsor would have hired the hall; he has bought the time; the local station operator, no matter how indifferent, is going to carry the program—he has to. Then it's up to the networks to fill the hall. I am not here talking about editorializing but about straightaway exposition as direct, unadorned, and impartial as fallible human beings can make it. Just once in a while let us exalt the importance of ideas and information. Let us dream to the extent of saying that on a given Sunday night the time normally occupied by Ed Sullivan is given over to a clinical survey of the state of American education, and a week or two later the time normally used by Steve Allen is devoted to a thoroughgoing study of American policy in the Middle East. Would the corporate image of their respective sponsors be damaged? Would the stockholders rise up in their wrath and complain? Would anything happen other than that a few million people would have received a little illumination on subjects that may well determine the future of this country, and therefore the future of the corporations? . . .

It may be that the present system, with no modifications and no experiments, can survive. Perhaps the money-making machine has some kind of built-in perpetual motion, but I do not think so. To a very considerable extent the media of mass communications in a given country reflect the political, economic, and social climate in which they flourish. That is the reason ours differ from the British and French, or the Russian and Chinese. We are currently wealthy, fat, comfortable, and complacent. We have currently a built-in allergy to unpleasant or disturbing information. Our mass media reflect this. But unless we get up off our fat surpluses and recognize that television in the main is being used to distract, delude, amuse, and insulate us, then television and those who finance it, those who look at it, and those who work at it, may see a totally different picture too late.

I do not advocate that we turn television into a twenty-seven-inch wailing wall, where longhairs constantly moan about the state of our culture and our defense. But I would just like to see it reflect occasionally the hard, unyielding realities of the world in which we live. I would like to see it done inside the existing framework, and I would like to see the doing of it redound to the credit of those who finance and program it. Measure the results by Nielsen, Trendex, or Silex—it doesn't matter. The main thing is to try. The responsibility can be easily placed, in spite of all the mouthings about giving the public what it wants. It rests on big business, and on big television, and it rests at the top. Responsibility is not something that can be assigned or delegated. And it promises its own reward: good business and good television.

Perhaps no one will do anything about it. I have ventured to outline it against a background of criticism that may have been too harsh only because I could think of nothing better. Someone once said—I think it was Max Eastman—that "that publisher serves his advertiser best who best serves his readers." I cannot believe that radio and television, or the corporations that finance the programs, are serving well or truly their viewers or listeners, or themselves.

I began by saying that our history will be what we make it. If we go on as we are, then history will take its revenge, and retribution will not limp in catching up with us.

We are to a large extent an imitative society. If one or two or three corporations would undertake to devote just a small fraction of their advertising appropriation along the lines that I have suggested, the procedure would grow by contagion; the economic burden would be bearable, and there might ensue a most exciting adventure—exposure to ideas and the bringing of reality into the homes of the nation.

To those who say people wouldn't look; they wouldn't be interested; they're too complacent, indifferent, and insulated, I can only reply: There is, in one reporter's opinion, considerable evidence against that contention. But even if they are right, what have they got to lose? Because if they are right, and this instrument is good for nothing but to entertain, amuse, and insulate, then the tube is flickering now and we will soon see that the whole struggle is lost.

This instrument can teach, it can illuminate; yes, and it can even inspire. But it can do so only to the extent that humans are determined to use it to those ends. Otherwise it is merely wires and lights in a box. There is a great and perhaps decisive battle to be fought against ignorance, intolerance, and indifference. This weapon of television could be useful.

Stonewall Jackson, who knew something about the use of weapons, is reported to have said, "When war comes, you must draw the sword and throw away the scabbard." The trouble with television is that it is rusting in the scabbard during a battle for survival. ■

Playwright-Journalist-Diplomat Clare Boothe Luce Criticizes the American Press

"A large, unmeasurable percentage of the total editorial space in American newspapers is concerned not with public affairs or matters of stately importance. It is devoted instead to entertainment, titillation, amusement, voyeurism, and tripe."

SHE ENJOYED BOTH SIDES OF THE PUBLIC EYE: journalist and diplomat, playwright and politician. Clare Boothe Luce began her varied career as a magazine editor, working for *Vogue* and *Vanity Fair* in the early thirties. In 1935, she married Henry Robinson Luce, the publisher who cofounded *Time* magazine and later started *Fortune* and *Life*. As a writer, she gained fame for work that ranged from Broadway plays to wartime reporting from Indochina. As a politician, she served as a Republican congresswoman in the forties, and she was appointed ambassador to Italy a decade later.

She was a popular speaker and dinner companion because she laced her conversation with anecdotes about her friends, most of whom were world famous; her imitation of Winston Churchill was hilarious. Converted to Catholicism by Bishop Fulton Sheen, she became a force in conservative politics, ridiculing Henry Wallace's foreign policy in 1943 as "globaloney." Mrs. Luce made use of her wide-ranging interests and background in addressing other journalists: "What's Wrong with the American Press?" was her speech to the Women's National Press Club on April 21, 1960.

In this speech, even as she commends daily American newspapers as "the best press in the world," Mrs. Luce lectures journalists on the failures of journalism to meet its "commercial challenge." She offers examples of "the debasement of popular taste" and forcefully uses rhetorical questions in persistent parallel to argue against that pressure ("Should the American press bow to it? Accept it? Cater to it? Foster it?"). Although feminists would quarrel with the notions of "masculine superiority" in the peroration, the speech primarily emphasizes balance, particularly in the closing duality of "the promise of success and the promise of enlightenment."

□   □   □

I am happy and flattered to be a guest of honor on this always exciting and challenging occasion. But looking over this audience tonight, I am less happy than you might think and more challenged than you could know. I stand here at this rostrum invited to throw rocks at you. You have asked *me* to tell *you* what's wrong with *you*—the American press. The subject not only is of great national significance but also has, one should say, infinite possibilities—and infinite perils to the rock thrower.

For the banquet speaker who criticizes the weaknesses and pretensions, or exposes the follies and sins, of his listeners—even at their invitation—does not generally evoke an enthusiastic—no less a friendly—response. The delicate art of giving an audience hell is always one best left to the Billy Grahams and the Bishop Sheens.

But you are an audience of journalists. There is no audience anywhere who should be more bored—indeed, more revolted—by a speaker who tried to fawn on it, butter it up, exaggerate its virtues, play down its faults, and who would more quickly see through any attempt to do so. I ask you only to remember that I am not a volunteer for this subject tonight. You asked for it!

For what is good journalism all about? On a working, finite level it is the effort to achieve illuminating candor in print and to strip away cant. It is the effort to do this not only in matters of state, diplomacy, and politics but also in every smaller aspect of life that touches the public interest or engages proper public curiosity. It is the effort to explain everything from a summit conference to why the moon looks larger coming over the horizon than it does when it has fully risen in the heavens. It is the effort, too, to describe the lives of men—and women—big and small, close at hand or thousands of miles away, familiar in their behavior or unfamiliar in their idiosyncrasies. It is—to use the big word—the pursuit of and the effort to state the truth.

No audience knows better than an audience of journalists that the pursuit of the truth, and the articulation of it, is the most delicate, hazardous, exacting, and *inexact* of tasks. Consequently, no audience is more forgiving (I hope) to the speaker who fails or stumbles in his own pursuit of it. The only failure this audience could never excuse in any speaker would be the failure to try to tell the truth, as he sees it, about his subject.

In my perilous but earnest effort to do so here tonight, I must begin by saying that if there is much that is wrong with the American press, there is also much that is right with it.

I know, then, that you will bear with me, much as it may go against your professional grain, if I ask you to accept some of the good with the bad—even though it may not make such good copy for your newspapers.

For the plain fact is that the U.S. daily press today is not inspiringly good; it is just far and away the best press in the world.

To begin with, its news-gathering, news-printing, news-dissemination techniques and capacities are without rivals on the globe.

The deserving American journalist himself enjoys a far more elevated status than his foreign counterpart anywhere. And this, not only because Americans passionately believe that a free press is vital to the preservation of our form of democracy, but because the average American journalist has, on the record, shown himself to be less venal, less corrupt, and more responsible than the average journalist of many foreign lands.

No capital under the sun has a press corps that is better equipped, and more eager to get the news, the news behind the news, and the news ahead of the news, the inside—outside—topside—bottomside news, than the Washington press corps.

I must add only half-jokingly that if the nation's dailies are overwhelmingly pro-Republican in their editorial policy, then the Washington press corps is a large corrective for this political imbalance. Not because Washington reporters are *all* Democrats. Rather because they place on the administration in power their white-hot spotlight of curiosity and exposure. So that no one—Republican or Democrat—can sit complacently in office in this capital unobserved by the men and women of the press who provide the news and information that can make or break an elected or appointed officeholder.

Certainly no press corps contains more journalists of competence and distinction, zeal and dedication. What minds regularly tap more "reliable sources" in government, politics, diplomacy? What breasts guard and unguard more "high level" confidences more jealously? What hearts struggle more conscientiously and painfully to determine to what extent truth telling, or shall we say "leaking," will serve or unserve the public interest? What typewriters send out more facts, figures, statistics, views, and opinions about great public questions and great public figures?

And in what other country of the world are there so many great newspapers? Who could seriously challenge the preeminence among the big-city quality press of the *New York Times*? Where in the world is there a "provincial" newspaper (I use the term only in its technical sense) greater than, to take only one outstanding example, the *Milwaukee Journal*? Even the biggest and splashiest of the foreign English-language press, the *London Daily Mirror,* cannot touch in popular journalism the *New York Daily News.* (And since we are talking in superlatives—good and bad—is there a worse paper in England, Japan, France, or India than the *New York Sunday Enquirer?)*

While the range between the best and the worst is very wide, America's some eighteen hundred newspapers nevertheless average out a higher quality, variety, and volume of information than any other press in the world.

Certainly no other press has greater freedom, more freely granted by the people, to find the news and to print it as it finds it. The American press need not be caught in the subtle toils of subsidies by groups or interests. It does not have to fight government newsprint allocations—that overt or covert censorship exercised in many so-called free countries. Except as the American press is guided by the profit motive, which is in turn guided by the public demand for its papers, it is an unguided press.

All this is what is right with the American press. And the result of this situation is that our people have more ways to be well informed about issues and events near and far than any people in the world. And they are, by and large, better informed.

But now let us come to the question of the evening: "What is wrong with the American press?" We cannot answer this question unless we will voluntarily abandon our relative measurement of it against the press of other countries. We must measure it, in absolute terms, against its own highest ideal of freedom, responsibility, and—let us not forget—success.

It is easy to point to many instances in which the American press—especially its individual members—tend to abuse their freedom and shirk their responsibility.

For example, one could note that nowadays the banner of press freedom is more often raised in matters of printing crime, sex, and scandal stories than it is in matters of printing the truth about great national figures, policies, and issues. Or that too many members of the working press uncritically pass on—even if they do not personally swallow—too much high-level government and political cant, tripe, and public relations; or that there are too many journalists who seem willing to sell their birthright of candor and truth in order to become White House pets, party pets, corporation pets, Pentagon or State Department or trade union or governor's mansion pets; who wistfully yearn after gray eminency, or blatantly strive for publicity for themselves, on lecture platforms or political rostrums.

While agreeing with most journalists that people are not as much interested in the issues as they should be, one could at the same time note that neither are many journalists. One could mention that such journalists seem to have forgotten that *men, not names* alone, make news, and that men are made by the clarity with which they state issues, and the resolution with which they face them. One could express the hope that more journalists would encourage rather than avoid controversy and argument, remembering that controversy and argument are not the enemies of democracy but its friends. One could wish for fewer journalist prodigies of the well-written factual story, and more gifted talents for drawing explanations from the facts, or that working pressmen would be more creative in reporting the news, or that they would reflect less in themselves of what in this decade they have so roundly condemned in American leadership: apathy, cynicism, lukewarmness, and acceptance of the status quo about everything, from juvenile delinquency to nuclear destruction. One could pray, above all, for journalists who cared less about ideologies and more about ideas.

But such criticisms and complaints—important as they may be—cover only one area of the American press. It is, alas, a relatively small area. A large, unmeasurable percentage of the total editorial space in American newspapers is concerned not with public affairs or matters of stately importance. It is devoted instead to entertainment, titillation, amusement, voyeurism, and tripe.

The average American newspaper reader wants news, but he wants lots of things from his newspaper besides news: he wants the sports page, the comics, fashion, homemaking, advice-to-the-lovelorn, do-it-yourself psychiatry, gossip columns, medical, cooking, and decorating features, TV, movie, and theater coverage, Hollywood personality stories, Broadway and society prattle, church columns, comics, bridge columns, crossword puzzles, big-money contests. Above all, he wants news that concerns not a bit the public weal but that people just find "interesting" reading.

I confess to enjoying much of this myself. And I do not mean to suggest that every newspaper must read like the London *Times*. But the plain fact is that we are witnessing in America what Professor William Ernest Hocking and others have called the debasement of popular taste.

Is it necessary? An editor of my acquaintance was asked recently whether the new circulation rise of his increasingly wild-eyed newspaper was being achieved at the expense of good journalism. He replied, "But you don't understand; our first journalistic need is to survive." I submit that a survival achieved by horribly debasing the journalistic coin is short-lived. The newspaper that engages in mindless, untalented sensationalism gets caught up in the headlong momentum it creates in its readers' appetites. It cannot continue satisfying the voracious appetites it is building. Such journalism may suddenly burn brightly with success; but it will surely burn briefly.

We have the familiar example of television closely at hand. The American press has rightly deplored the drivel, duplicity, and demeaning programming that has marked much of television's commercial trust. A critic, of course, need not necessarily always have clean hands. The press is right to flail what is wrong in television, just as it is obliged to recognize the great service television has provided in areas where its public affairs, news, and good programs have succeeded in adding something new and enriching to American life.

But if the press criticizes what is wrong in television without recognizing the moral for itself, it will have missed a valuable and highly visible opportunity for self-improvement.

The double charge against the American press may thus be stated: its failure to inform the public better than it does is the evasion of its responsibility; its failure to educate and elevate the public taste rather than following that taste like a blind, wallowing dinosaur is an abuse of its freedom.

In view of the river of information which flows daily from the typewriters of American correspondents at home and abroad, why are the American people not better informed? Whose fault is it? At first glance it would seem to be the fault of the publishers, and especially editors. But the publisher or editor who does not give his readers plenty of what they want is going to lose circulation to a competitor who does. Or if he has a news monopoly in his city, and feels too free to shortchange them on these things, he is going to lose circulation as his reader slack is taken up by the radio, the TV, and the magazines.

Add that even the news the reader wants in most cities, especially the smaller cities throughout the United States, is primarily local news. He remains, even as you and I, more interested in the news of his neighbors, his community, and his city than he is in the news out of Washington, Paris, or Rome.

Can we quarrel with this? We cannot. The Declaration of Independence itself set the pattern of the American way, and with it American reading habits. Life, liberty, and the pursuit of happiness were to be man's prime and legitimate goals.

Perhaps the history of our country would have been better—and happier—if "the pursuit of truth, information, and enlightenment" had been his third great goal. But that was not the way our founding fathers saw things. And that is not the way the American public sees them now.

The fact is that while "man" is a rational animal, *all* men and *all* women are not preeminently rational, logical, and thoughtful in their approach to life. They do not thirst, above all, for knowledge and information about the great domestic and international issues, even though these issues may profoundly affect not only their pocketbooks but their very lives.

Today, as yesterday, people are primarily moved in their choice of reading by their daily emotions, their personal, immediate, existential prejudices, biases, ambitions, desires, and—as we know too well in the Freudian age—by many subconscious yearnings and desires, and irrational hates and fears.

Very well then: let us accept the fact.

Should the American press bow to it? Accept it? Cater to it? Foster it?

What else (the cynical and sophisticated will ask) is there to do?

The American press, no less than the TV and radio, is big business. It is now, as never before, a mass medium. As big business, it faces daily vast problems of costliness and competition. As a mass medium, it cannot handle these problems without seeking to satisfy the public's feelings, desires, and wants. It publishes in the noisiest and most distracted age in our history. It seems doomed to satisfy endlessly the tastes of the nation— pluralistic, pragmatic, emotional, sensuous, and predominantly irrational. By its big-business mass media nature it seems compelled to seek ever more and more to saturate the mass markets, to soak the common-denominator reader-sponge with what it wants.

Certainly we must face this fact: if the American press, as a mass medium, has formed the minds of America, the mass has also formed the medium. There is action, reaction, and interaction going on ceaselessly between the newspaper-buying public and the editors. What is wrong with the American press is what is in part wrong with American society.

Is this, then, to exonerate the American press for its failures to give the American people more tasteful and more illuminating reading matter? Can the American press seek to be excused from responsibility for public lack of information as TV and radio often do, on the grounds that, after all, "we have to give the people what they want or we will go out of business"?

No. Not without abdicating its own American birthright, it cannot. The responsibility *is* fixed on the American press. Falling directly and clearly on publisher and editor, this responsibility is inbuilt into the freedom of the press itself. The freedom guaranteed by the Constitution under the First Amendment carries this responsibility with it.

"Freedom," as Clemenceau said, "is nothing in the world but the opportunity for self-discipline"—that is to say, voluntarily to assume responsibility.

There are many valiant publishers, editors, and journalists in America who have made and are making courageous attempts to give readers a little more of what they should have, and a little less of what they want—or, as is more often true, what they only think they want, because they have no real knowledge of what is available to them. America owes these publishers and editors and journalists an incomparable debt of gratitude.

What is really wrong with the American press is that there are not enough such publishers and editors. There is hardly an editor in this room who could not—if he passionately would—give every day, every year, a little more honest, creative effort to his readers on the great issues which face us—the issues which, in the years to come, must spell peace or disaster for our democracy. A beginning would be to try courageously, which is to say consistently, to keep such news (however brief) on the front page, playing it in some proportion to its real importance. For a newspaper, which relegates to the back pages news which is vital to the citizenry as a whole, in favor of sensational, "circulation building" headlines about ephemeral stories of crime, lust, sex, and scandal, is actively participating in the debasement of public taste and intelligence. Such a newspaper, more especially its editor, is not only breaking faith with the highest of democratic journalism, he is betraying his nation. And, you may be surprised to hear me say, he may even be courting commercial failure.

For there is enough in American life in these exciting sixties to keep interested and absorbed many of the readers who have been written off as impossible to reach except through cheap sensationalism. The commercial challenge is not to achieve success by reaching backward into cliché-ridden ideas, stories, and situations. It is rather to recognize that uniquely now in this country there is natural and self-propelled drive toward a better life, more sustaining and relevant interests. There is, in sum, an infinity of new subjects that make exciting, inviting, and important exploration for the American press.

There can be no doubt that honorable and patriotic publishers and devoted and dedicated editors can increase little by little, in season and out, the public's appetite for better information. There can also be no doubt that they can also decrease, little by little, in the rest of their papers the type of stories which appeals to the worst in human nature by catering to the lowest-common-denominator taste in morals and ethics.

Teddy Roosevelt once said that a good journalist should be part Saint Paul and part Saint Vitus.

A good editor today must be part Santa Claus, part Saint Valentine, part Saint Thomas (the doubter), part Saint Paul, and certainly he must be part Saint Jude. Saint Jude, as you know, is the patron saint of those who ask for the impossible.

It is not impossible to ask that the American press begin to reverse its present trend, which Dean Ed Barrett of the Columbia School of Journalism calls "giving the public too much froth because too few want substance." If this trend is not reversed (which it can be only by your determined effort), the American press will increasingly become the creature, rather than the creator, of man's tastes. It will become a passive, yielding, and, curiously, an effeminate press. And twixt the ads for the newest gas range, and the firmest girdle, the cheapest vacuum cleaner, and the best buy in Easter bonnets; twixt the sports page, the fashion page, the teenage columns, the children's comics; twixt the goo, glop, and glamour handouts on Elvis Presley and Elizabeth Taylor, and above all twixt the headlines on the sexiest murders, and the type of political editorializing which sees the great presidential issues of the day as being between the case of the "boyish forelock" versus the "tricky ski-jump nose," the press will lose its masculine prerogative, which is to educate, inform, engage the interest of, and guide the minds of free men and women in a great democracy.

As I know that the American Society of Newspaper Editors holds hard to the belief in masculine superiority in the realm of the intellect, and could only view with horror the picture of the fourth estate as the "kept man" of the emotional masses, I—for one—am certain this will not happen.

Let us watch then, with hope, for the signs of a new, vigorous, masculine leadership in the American press. For if you fail, must not America also fail in its great and unique mission, which is also yours: to lead the world towards life, liberty, and the pursuit of enlightenment—so that it may achieve happiness? It is that goal which the American press must seize afresh—creatively, purposefully, energetically, and with a zeal that holds a double promise: the promise of success and the promise of enlightenment. ■

FCC's Newton Minow Excoriates Broadcasters for Failing to Serve the Public Interest

"SIT down in front of your television set when your station goes on the air . . . and keep your eyes glued to that set until the station signs off. I can assure you that you will observe a vast wasteland."

ON MAY 9, 1961, soon after President John F. Kennedy appointed Adlai Stevenson's law partner, Newton Minow, to be chairman of the Federal Communications Commission, the Chicago lawyer stunned the National Association of Broadcasters meeting in Washington with a denunciation of its stewardship of the public's airwaves. When he was finished, a broadcaster told him, "That was the worst speech I ever heard in my whole life." Trying to be kind, the head of the NAB, LeRoy Collins, assured the speaker, "That man has no mind of his own. He just repeats everything he hears."

The phrase that helped make the speech memorable borrowed the title of a well-known poem by T. S. Eliot, "The Waste Land," punched up with a short adjective that added to the picture of desolation. Thirty years afterward, Minow told a media group, "The 1961 speech is remembered for two words—but not the two I intended to be remembered. The words we tried to advance were 'public interest.'" In that Kennedy-era slap in the industry's face, Minow had asked, "What do we mean by 'the public interest'? Some say the public interest is merely what interests the public. I disagree." Three decades later, Minow clung to his Kennedy cadences and added, "To me the public interest meant, and still means, that we should constantly ask, 'What can television do for our country?'"

□　□　□

. . . It may also come as a surprise to some of you, but I want you to know that you have my admiration and respect. Yours is a most honorable profession. Anyone who is in the broadcasting business has a tough row to hoe. You earn your bread by using public property. When you work in broadcasting, you volunteer for public service, public pressure, and public regulation. You must compete with other attractions and other investments, and the only way you can do it is to prove to us every three years that you should have been in business in the first place.

I can think of easier ways to make a living.

But I cannot think of more satisfying ways.

I admire your courage—but that doesn't mean I would make life any easier for you. Your license lets you use the public's airwaves as trustees for 180 million Americans. The public is your beneficiary. If you want to stay on as trustees, you must deliver a decent return to the public—not only to your stockholders. So, as a representative of the public, your health and your product are among my chief concerns. . . .

I have confidence in your health. But not in your product.

It is with this and much more in mind that I come before you today.

One editorialist in the trade press wrote that "the FCC of the New Frontier is going to be one of the toughest FCCs in the history of broadcast regulation." If he meant that we intend to enforce the law in the public interest, let me make it perfectly clear that he is right—we do.

If he meant that we intend to muzzle or censor broadcasting, he is dead wrong.

It would not surprise me if some of you had expected me to come here today and say in effect, "Clean up your own house, or the government will do it for you."

Well, in a limited sense, you would be right—I've just said it.

But I want to say to you earnestly that it is not in that spirit that I come before you today, nor is it in that spirit that I intend to serve the FCC.

I am in Washington to help broadcasting, not to harm it; to strengthen it, not to weaken it; to reward it, not to punish it; to encourage it, not threaten it; to stimulate it, not censor it.

Above all, I am here to uphold and protect the public interest.

What do we mean by "the public interest"? Some say the public interest is merely what interests the public.

I disagree.

So does your distinguished president, Governor Collins. In a recent speech he said, "Broadcasting, to serve the public interest, must have a soul and a conscience, a burning desire to excel, as well as to sell; the urge to build the character, citizenship, and intellectual stature of people, as well as to expand the gross national product. . . . By no means do I imply that broadcasters disregard the public interest. . . . But a much better job can be done, and should be done."

I could not agree more.

And I would add that in today's world, with chaos in Laos and the Congo aflame, with Communist tyranny on our Caribbean doorstep and relentless pressure on our Atlantic alliance, with social and economic problems at home of the gravest nature, yes, and with technological knowledge that makes it possible, as our president has said, not only to destroy our world but to destroy poverty around the world—in a time of peril and opportunity, the old complacent, unbalanced fare of action-adventure and situation comedies is simply not good enough.

Your industry possesses the most powerful voice in America. It has an inescapable duty to make that voice ring with intelligence and with leadership. In a few years this exciting industry has grown from a novelty to an instrument of overwhelming impact on the American people. It should be making ready for the kind of leadership that newspapers and magazines assumed years ago, to make our people aware of their world.

Ours has been called the jet age, the atomic age, the space age. It is also, I submit, the television age. And just as history will decide whether the leaders of today's world employed the atom to destroy the world or rebuild it for mankind's benefit, so will history decide whether today's broadcasters employed their powerful voice to enrich the people or debase them. . . .

Like everybody, I wear more than one hat. I am the chairman of the FCC. I am also a television viewer and the husband and father of other television viewers. I have seen a great many television programs that seemed to me eminently worthwhile, and I am not talking about the much-bemoaned good old days of "Playhouse 90" and "Studio One."

I am talking about this past season. Some were wonderfully entertaining, such as "The Fabulous Fifties," the "Fred Astaire Show," and the "Bing Crosby Special"; some were dramatic and moving, such as Conrad's "Victory" and "Twilight Zone"; some were marvelously informative, such as "The Nation's Future," "CBS Reports," and "The Valiant Years." I could list many more—programs that I am sure everyone here felt enriched his own life and that of his family. When television is good, nothing—not the theater, not the magazines or newspapers—nothing is better.

But when television is bad, nothing is worse. I invite you to sit down in front of your television set when your station goes on the air and stay there without a book, magazine, newspaper, profit-and-loss sheet, or rating book to distract you—and keep your eyes glued to that set until the station signs off. I can assure you that you will observe a vast wasteland.

You will see a procession of game shows, violence, audience participation shows, formula comedies about totally unbelievable families, blood and thunder, mayhem, violence, sadism, murder, western badmen, western good men, private eyes, gangsters, more violence, and cartoons. And, endlessly, commercials—many screaming, cajoling, and offending. And most of all, boredom. True, you will see a few things you will enjoy. But they will be very, very few. And if you think I exaggerate, try it.

Is there one person in this room who claims that broadcasting can't do better?

Well, a glance at next season's proposed programming can give us little heart. Of seventy-three and a half hours of prime evening time, the networks have tentatively scheduled fifty-nine hours to categories of "action-adventure," situation comedy, variety, quiz, and movies.

Is there one network president in this room who claims he can't do better?

Well, is there at least one network president who believes that the other networks can't do better?

Gentlemen, your trust accounting with your beneficiaries is overdue.

Never have so few owed so much to so many.

Why is so much of television so bad? I have heard many answers: demands of your advertisers; competition for ever higher ratings; the need always to attract a mass audience; the high cost of television programs; the insatiable appetite for programming material—these are some of them. Unquestionably these are tough problems not susceptible to easy answers.

But I am not convinced that you have tried hard enough to solve them.

I do not accept the idea that the present overall programming is aimed accurately at the public taste. The ratings tell us only that some people have their television sets turned on, and of that number, so many are tuned to one channel and so many to another. They don't tell us what the public might watch if they were offered half a dozen additional choices. A rating, at best, is an indication of how many people saw what you gave them. Unfortunately it does not reveal the depth of the penetration, or the intensity of reaction, and it never reveals what the acceptance would have been if what you gave them had been better—if all the forces of art and creativity and daring and imagination had been unleashed. I believe in the people's good sense and good taste, and I am not convinced that the people's taste is as low as some of you assume.

My concern with the rating services is not with their accuracy. Perhaps they are accurate. I really don't know. What, then, is wrong with the ratings? It's not been their accuracy—it's been their use.

Certainly I hope you will agree that ratings should have little influence where children are concerned. The best estimates indicate that during the hours of 5 to 6 P.M., 60 percent of your audience is composed of children under twelve. And most young children today, believe it or not, spend as much time watching television as they do in the schoolroom. I repeat—let that sink in—most young children today spend as much time watching television as they do in the schoolroom. It used to be said that there were three great influences on a child: home, school, and church. Today there is a fourth great influence, and you ladies and gentlemen control it.

If parents, teachers, and ministers conducted their responsibilities by following the ratings, children would have a steady diet of ice cream, school holidays, and no Sunday school. What about your responsibilities? Is there no room on television to teach, to inform, to uplift, to stretch, to enlarge the capacities of our children? Is there no room for programs deepening their understanding of children in other lands? Is there no room for a children's news show explaining something about the world to them at their level of understanding? Is there no room for reading the great literature of the past, teaching them the great traditions of freedom? There are some fine children's shows, but they are drowned out in the massive doses of cartoons, violence, and more violence. Must these be your trademarks? Search your consciences and see if you cannot offer more to your young beneficiaries, whose future you guide so many hours each and every day.

What about adult programming and ratings? You know, newspaper publishers take popularity ratings too. The answers are pretty clear; it is almost always the comics, followed by the advice-to-the-lovelorn columns. But, ladies and gentlemen, the news is still on the front page of all newspapers, the editorials are not replaced by more comics, the newspapers have not become one long collection of advice to the lovelorn. Yet newspapers do not need a license from the government to be in business—they do not use public property. But in television—where your responsibilities as public trustees are so plain—the moment that the ratings indicate that westerns are popular, there are new imitations of westerns on the air faster than the old coaxial cable could take us from Hollywood to New York. Broadcasting cannot continue to live by the numbers. Ratings ought to be the slave of the broadcaster, not his master. And you and I both know that the rating services themselves would agree.

Let me make clear that what I am talking about is balance. I believe that the public interest is made up of many interests. There are many people in this great country, and you must serve all of us. You will get no argument from me if you say that, given a choice between a western and a symphony, more people will watch the western. I like westerns and private eyes too—but a steady diet for the whole country is obviously not in the public interest. We all know that people would more often prefer to be entertained than stimulated or informed. But your obligations are not satisfied if you look only to popularity as a test of what to broadcast. You are not only in show business; you are free to communicate ideas as well as relaxation. You must provide a wider range of choices, more diversity, more alternatives. It is not enough to cater to the nation's whims—you must also serve the nation's needs.

And I would add this—that if some of you persist in a relentless search for the highest rating and the lowest common denominator, you may very well lose your audience. Because, to paraphrase a great American who was recently my law partner, the people are wise, wiser than some of the broadcasters—and politicians—think.

As you may have gathered, I would like to see television improved. But how is this to be brought about? By voluntary action by the broadcasters themselves? By direct government intervention? Or how?

Let me address myself now to my role, not as a viewer, but as chairman of the FCC. I could not if I would chart for you this afternoon in detail all of the actions I contemplate. Instead, I want to make clear some of the fundamental principles which guide me.

First: the people own the air. They own it as much in prime evening time as they do at six o'clock Sunday morning. For every hour that the people give you, you owe them something. I intend to see that your debt is paid with service.

Second: I think it would be foolish and wasteful for us to continue any worn-out wrangle over the problems of payola, rigged quiz shows, and other mistakes of the past. There are laws on the books which we will enforce. But there is no chip on my shoulder. We live together in perilous, uncertain times; we face together staggering problems; and we must not waste much time now by rehashing the clichés of past controversy. To quarrel over the past is to lose the future.

Third: I believe in the free-enterprise system. I want to see broadcasting improved, and I want you to do the job. I am proud to champion your cause. It is not rare for American businessmen to serve a public trust. Yours is a special trust because it is imposed by law.

Fourth: I will do all I can to help educational television. There are still not enough educational stations, and major centers of the country still lack usable educational channels. If there were a limited number of printing presses in this country, you may be sure that a fair proportion of them would be put to educational use. Educational television has an enormous contribution to make to the future, and I intend to give it a hand along the way. If there is not a nationwide educational television system in this country, it will not be the fault of the FCC.

Fifth: I am unalterably opposed to governmental censorship. There will be no suppression of programming which does not meet with bureaucratic tastes. Censorship strikes at the taproot of our free society.

Sixth: I did not come to Washington to idly observe the squandering of the public's airwaves. The squandering of our airwaves is no less important than the lavish waste of any precious natural resource. I intend to take the job of chairman of the FCC very seriously. I believe in the gravity of my own particular sector of the New Frontier. There will be times perhaps when you will consider that I take myself or my job *too* seriously. Frankly, I don't care if you do. For I am convinced that either one takes this job seriously—or one can be seriously taken.

Now, how will these principles be applied? Clearly, at the heart of the FCC's authority lies its power to license, to renew or fail to renew, or to revoke a license. As you know, when your license comes up for renewal, your performance is compared with your promises. I understand that many people feel that in the past licenses were often renewed pro forma. I say to you now, Renewal will not be pro forma in the future. There is nothing permanent or sacred about a broadcast license.

But simply matching promises and performance is not enough. I intend to do more. I intend to find out whether the people care. I intend to find out whether the community which each broadcaster serves believes he has been serving the public interest. When a renewal is set down for hearing, I intend—wherever possible—to hold a well-advertised public hearing, right in the community you have promised to serve. I want the people who own the air and the homes that television enters to tell you and the FCC what's been going on. I want the people—if they are truly interested in the service you give them—to make notes, document cases, tell us the facts. For those few of you who really believe that the public interest is merely what interests the public—I hope that these hearings will arouse no little interest.

The FCC has a fine reserve of monitors—almost 180 million Americans gathered around 56 million sets. If you want those monitors to be your friends at court—it's up to you.

Some of you may say, "Yes, but I still do not know where the line is between a grant of a renewal and the hearing you just spoke of." My answer is, Why should you want to know how close you can come to the edge of the cliff? What the commission asks of you is to make a conscientious good-faith effort to serve the public interest. Every one of you serves a community in which the people would benefit by educational, religious, instructive, or other public service programming. Every one of you serves an area, which has local needs—as to local elections, controversial issues, local news, local talent. Make a serious, genuine effort to put on that programming. When you do, you will not be playing brinkmanship with the public interest. . . .

Another, and perhaps the most important, frontier: television will rapidly join the parade into space. International television will be with us soon. No one knows how long it will be until a broadcast from a studio in New York will be viewed in India as well as in Indiana, will be seen in the Congo as it is seen in Chicago. But as surely as we are meeting here today, that day will come—and once again our world will shrink.

What will the people of other countries think of us when they see our western badmen and good men punching each other in the jaw in between the shooting? What will the Latin American or African child learn of America from our great communications industry? We cannot permit television in its present form to be our voice overseas.

There is your challenge to leadership. You must reexamine some fundamentals of your industry. You must open your minds and open your hearts to the limitless horizons of tomorrow.

I can suggest some words that should serve to guide you:

> Television and all who participate in it are jointly accountable to the American public for respect for the special needs of children, for community responsibility, for the advancement of education and culture, for the acceptability of the program materials chosen, for decency and decorum in production, and for propriety in advertising. This responsibility cannot be discharged by any given group of programs, but can be discharged only through the highest standards of respect for the American home, applied to every moment of every program presented by television.
>
> Program materials should enlarge the horizons of the viewer, provide him with wholesome entertainment, afford helpful stimulation, and remind him of the responsibilities which the citizen has toward his society.

These words are not mine. They are yours. They are taken literally from your own Television Code. They reflect the leadership and aspirations of your own great industry. I urge you to respect them as I do. And I urge you to respect the intelligent and farsighted leadership of Governor LeRoy Collins and to make this meeting a creative act. I urge you at this meeting and, after you leave, back home, at your stations and your networks, to strive ceaselessly to improve your product and to better serve your viewers, the American people.

I hope that we at the FCC will not allow ourselves to become so bogged down in the mountain of papers, hearings, memoranda, orders, and the daily routine that we close our eyes to the wider view of the public interest. And I hope that you broadcasters will not permit yourselves to become so absorbed in the chase for ratings, sales, and profits that you lose this wider view. Now more than ever before in broadcasting's history, the times demand the best of all of us.

We need imagination in programming, not sterility; creativity, not imitation; experimentation, not conformity; excellence, not mediocrity. Television is filled with creative, imaginative people. You must strive to set them free.

Television in its young life has had many hours of greatness—its "Victory at Sea," its Army-McCarthy hearings, its "Peter Pan," its "Kraft Theater," its "See It Now," its "Project 20," the World Series, its political conventions and campaigns, the Great Debates—and it has had its endless hours of mediocrity and its moments of public disgrace. There are estimates that today the average viewer spends about two hundred minutes daily with television, while the average reader spends thirty-eight minutes with magazines and forty minutes with newspapers. Television has grown faster than a teenager, and now it is time to grow up.

What you gentlemen broadcast through the people's air affects the people's taste, their knowledge, their opinions, their understanding of themselves and of their world. And their future.

The power of instantaneous sight and sound is without precedent in mankind's history. This is an awesome power. It has limitless capabilities for good—and for evil. And it carries with it awesome responsibilities—responsibilities which you and I cannot escape.

In his stirring inaugural address, our president said, "And so, my fellow Americans: ask not what your country can do for you—ask what you can do for your country."

Ladies and gentlemen:

Ask not what broadcasting can do for you—ask what you can do for broadcasting.

I urge you to put the people's airwaves to the service of the people and the cause of freedom. You must help prepare a generation for great decisions. You must help a great nation fulfill its future.

Do this, and I pledge you our help. ■

Historian Daniel J. Boorstin Examines the Coverage of Dissent

"DISSENT is the great problem of America today. It overshadows all others."

A SCHOLAR AND HISTORIAN, Daniel J. Boorstin became our librarian of Congress in 1975. Before coming to Washington to head the Smithsonian's Museum of Science and Technology in 1969, during a time of Vietnam War tumult on American campuses, he had taught American history for a quarter of a century at the University of Chicago. In 1974, he was awarded the Pulitzer Prize for *The Americans: The Democratic Experience,* treating American history as a coming together of cultures in a quest for the unknown. His 1984 *The Discoverers,* in the research for which he was aided by his wife, Ruth Boorstin, was one of the most successful nonfiction works of the late twentieth century.

He had an original mind: no other historian had seriously considered the impact on American cities of the invention of the elevator or the effect on work and living habits of the development of air-conditioning. As an authority on America's culture and history, and as the originator of the term "pseudo-event" to describe the misplaced celebration of celebrity, Professor Boorstin was in 1967 invited to give a talk to the managing editors of the Associated Press. His speech on dissension and the news was delivered on October 13, 1967, in Chicago. He died in Washington, D.C., in 2004.

Boorstin shapes his argument by delineating the difference between "dissent," engendering a feeling of apartness, and "disagreement," fostering debate without attempting to secede from society. With repeated transitions ("Moreover") and a series of pointed questions ("What is really news?"), he ties together his discussion of the media and the "law of the conspicuousness of dissent." The peroration, in fact, directly questions the press about finding ways to report news that will not "create and nourish new dissent."

☐ ☐ ☐

Gentlemen, it's a great pleasure and privilege to be allowed to take part in your meeting. It is especially a pleasure to come and have such a flattering introduction, the most flattering part of which was to be called a person who wrote like a newspaperman.

The historians, you know, sometimes try to return that compliment by saying that the best newspapermen write like historians but I'm not sure how many of the people present would consider that a compliment.

This afternoon I would like to talk briefly about the problems we share, we historians and newspapermen, and that we all share as Americans.

About sixty years ago Mark Twain, who was an expert on such matters, said there are only two forces that carry light to all corners of the globe, the sun in the heaven and the Associated Press. This is, of course, not the only view of your role. Another newspaperman once said it's the duty of a newspaper to comfort the afflicted and afflict the comfortable.

If there ever was a time when the light and the comfort which you can give us was needed, it's today. And I would like to focus on one problem.

It seems to me that dissent is the great problem of America today. It overshadows all others. It's a symptom, an expression, a consequence, and a cause of all others.

I say dissent and not disagreement. And it is the distinction between dissent and disagreement which I really want to make. Disagreement produces debate, but dissent produces dissension. "Dissent," which comes from the Latin, means originally to feel apart from others.

People who disagree have an argument, but people who dissent have a quarrel. People may disagree but may both count themselves in the majority, but a person who dissents is by definition in a minority. A liberal society thrives on disagreement but is killed by dissension. Disagreement is the lifeblood of democracy; dissension is its cancer.

A debate is an orderly exploration of a common problem that presupposes that the debaters are worried by the same question. It brings to life new facts and new arguments which make possible a better solution. But dissension means discord. As the dictionary tells us, dissension is marked by a break in friendly relations. It is an expression not of a common concern but of hostile feelings. And this distinction is crucial.

Disagreement is specific and programmatic; dissent is formless and unfocused. Disagreement is concerned with policy; dissenters are concerned with identity, which usually means themselves. Disagreers ask, What about the war in Vietnam? Dissenters ask. What about me? Disagreers seek solutions to common problems; dissenters seek power for themselves.

The spirit of dissent stalks our land. It seeks the dignity and privilege of disagreement, but it is entitled to neither. All over the country on more and more subjects, we hear more and more people quarreling and fewer and fewer people debating. How has this happened? What can and should we do about it?

This is my question this afternoon. In the first place I would like to remind you of one feature of the situation which suggests it may not be as desperate as it seems. This is what I would call the law of the conspicuousness of dissent, which is another way of saying there never is quite as much dissent as there seems.

I will start from an oddity of the historical record which other American historians can confirm for you.

When we try to learn, for example, about the history of religion in the United States we find that what is generally described as that subject is a history of religious controversies. It's very easy to learn about the Halfway Covenant problem, the Great Awakening, the Unitarian controversies, the Americanist controversies, and so on. But if we want to learn about the current of daily belief of Americans in the past it's very difficult.

And this is the parable of the problem of history. If we want to learn about the history of divorce, there are many excellent histories of divorce; but if we want to learn about the history of marriage, we'll find there are practically none.

Similarly if we want to learn about eating and drinking habits, there are some excellent histories of vegetarianism and food fads, some first-rate histories of prohibition, but almost no good histories of eating and drinking.

Why is this the case?

It is simply because of what I would call the law of the conspicuousness of dissent. Controversies, quarrels, disagreements leave a historical debris of printed matter, not to mention broken heads and broken reputations. Carry Nation smashing up a bar makes much more interesting reading and is more likely to enter the record than the peaceable activity of the bartender mixing drinks. But this may lead us to a perverse emphasis. How have people lived and thought and felt and eaten and drunk and married in the past? Interests are focused on the cataracts, the eddies, the waterfalls, and whirlpools. But what of the stream?

This is a natural bias of the record, and it equally affects the reporting of news. It is obvious that a sermon is less newsworthy than a debate and a debate still less newsworthy than a riot. This is all obvious, but it has serious consequences for the condition of our country today. The natural bias of the record tends to lead us to emphasize and inevitably overemphasize the extent of dissent.

Secondly, the rise and multiplication of media. The profession which you gentlemen represent together with the American standard of living leads us also towards the exaggeration of the importance of dissent in our society. Since dissent is more dramatic and more newsworthy than agreement, media inevitably multiply and emphasize dissent. It is an easier job to make a news story of men who are fighting with one another than it is to describe their peaceful living together.

All this has been reinforced by certain obvious developments in the history of the newspaper and the other media within the last half century or so—the increasingly frequent and repetitious news reporting. The movement from the weekly newspaper to the daily newspaper to several editions a day, the rise of radio reporting of news every hour on the hour with news breaks in between, all require that there be changes to report. There are increasingly voluminous spaces both of time and of print which have to be filled.

And all these reports become more and more inescapable from the attention of the average citizen. In the bar, on the beach, in the automobile, the transistor radio reminds us of the headaches of our society. Moreover, the increasing vividness of reports also tempts us to depict objects and people in motion, changing, disputing. The opportunity to show people in motion and to show them vividly had its beginning, of course, in the rise of photography and Mathew Brady's pioneer work in the Civil War and then more recently with the growth of the motion picture and television. All this tempts us to get a dramatic shot of a policeman striking a rioter or vice versa. We now have tape recorders on the scene in which people can express their complaints about anything.

Moreover, the rise of opinion is a new category. The growth of opinion polling has led to the very concept of "opinion" as something people can learn about. There was a time when information about the world was divided into the category of fact or the category of ideas. But more recently, especially with the growth of market research in this century, people now must have opinions. They are led to believe by the publication of opinion polls that their opinion—whether it be on the subject of miniskirts or marijuana or foreign policy—is something that separates them from others. Moreover, if they have no opinion, even that now puts them in a dissenting category.

Then there is the rise of what I call secondary news. News about the news. With an increasingly sophisticated readership and more and more media, we have such questions as whether a news conference will be canceled; will someone refuse to make a statement; is the fact that Jackie Kennedy denied there was a supposed engagement between her and Lord Harlech itself a kind of admission. What is really news?

Moreover, the very character of American history has accentuated our tendency to dissent. We are an immigrant society. We are made up of many different groups who came here and who felt separate from one another, who were separated not so much by doctrine or belief as by the minutiae of daily life. By language, religious practices, cuisine, and even manners. Until the 1930s and 1940s, the predominant aim of those who were most concerned in this country with the problem of immigration was to restrict immigration or to assimilate those immigrants who were admitted. To "Americanize the immigrant"—this was the motto of those who were most concerned with this question.

But in the last few decades we have had a movement from "assimilation" to "integration." And this is an important distinction. In about the 1930's Louis Adamic began writing, and, in his book *A Nation of Nations* in 1945, he began an emphasis which has been often repeated. It was no longer the right of the immigrant to be Americanized, to be assimilated; it was now the right of the immigrant to remain different. The ideal ceased to be that of fitting into the total society and instead became the right to retain your differences. Symptoms of this were such phenomena in politics as the rise of the balanced ticket, a ticket which consists of outspoken and obvious representatives of different minorities. It brought with it the assumption that the only 100 percent American is the person who is only partly American. It led General Eisenhower to make something of his German name and his German background which had not occurred to very many of us before. It encouraged John F. Kennedy to exploit his Irish background, the notion being that one was more fully American by being partly something else.

This sense of separateness and the power of minorities developed alongside two great movements. One, in the social sciences—the growth of literature, much of which stems from universities in this area, and especially from the University of Chicago—a literature of the social sciences which came to show minorities who they were, where they were, and what their power might be.

Gunnar Myrdal's book *American Dilemma*, which was quoted by the Supreme Court integration decision of 1954, was a very good illustration of this. The rise of opinion polling also led into this. People in small groups were reminded that they had a power and a locale which they had not known before. Stokely Carmichael himself has referred to this on several occasions—that he may represent a group which is not very numerous but he knows where they are. They're in crucial places where they can exercise power.

Alongside this change in our thinking and this extension of our knowledge came a change in technology which I would call the rise of "flow technology." Minimum speed forty miles an hour. This means that while formerly, in order to do damage to other people, it was necessary for you to set things in motion—to wave your arms or wield a club—now when the economy and the technology are in motion, if you want to cause damage you need only stop and the other people do the damage. This is a parable which was illustrated in the blackout in New York, the stall-ins and sit-ins. At a time when certain students seized the administration building at a neighboring university last year, all they had to do was to hold that one building. All the salary checks flowed through the IBM machines in that building, and they were able to throw a monkey wrench into the machinery.

This has the effect of developing what I would call a minority veto psychology. Small groups have more power than ever before. In small numbers there is strength. This results in the quest for minority identity. Whereas formerly people used to change their names to sound more American, to try to fit into the background, now the contrary seems to be occurring.

And we find symptoms of this in the intellectual world. Perhaps that is a misnomer—I should say rather in the world of those who consider themselves or call themselves intellectuals. I find in this world today, in this country, a growing belief in the intrinsic virtue of dissent. It's worth noting that some of the greatest American champions of the right to disagree and to express disagreement—Thomas Jefferson, Oliver Wendell Holmes, Jr., William James, John Dewey, and others—were also great believers in the duty of the community to be peacefully governed by the will of the majority. But more recently dissent itself has been made into a virtue. Dissent for dissent's sake. We have a whole group of magazines these days dedicated not to this or that particular program or social reform nor this or that social philosophy but simply to dissent.

Professional dissenters do not and cannot seek to assimilate their program or ideals into American culture. Their main object is to preserve their separate identity as a dissenting minority. They're not interested in the freedom of anybody else. The motto of this group might be an emendation of the old maxim of Voltaire which I'm sure you've all heard. But nowadays people would say, "I do not agree with a word you say. And I will defend to the death *my* right to say so."

Once upon a time our intellectuals competed for their claim to be spokesmen of the community. Now the time has almost arrived when the easiest way to insult an intellectual is to tell him that you or most other people *agree* with him. The way to menace him is to put him in the majority, for the majority must run things and must have a program, and dissent needs no program.

Dissent, then, has tended to become the conformity of our most educated classes. In many circles to be an outspoken conformist, that is, to say that the prevailing ways of the community are *not* "evil," requires more courage than to run with the dissenting pack.

The conformity of nonconformity, the conformity of dissent produces little that is fruitful in its conclusions and very little effective discussion or internal debate. For the simple reason that it does not involve anybody in attacking or defending any program. Programs, after all, are the signs of "the establishment."

The situation that I have described leads to certain temptations which afflict the historian as well as the newsman, and among these temptations I would like to include the tendency to stimulate and accentuate dissent rather than disagreement. To push disagreement toward dissent so that we can have a more dramatic or reportable event. To push the statement of a program toward the expression of a feeling of separateness or isolation.

There is an increasing tendency also to confuse disagreement with dissent. For example, the homosexuals in our society who are a group who feel separate (and are from one point of view a classic example of what we mean by the dissenter) now articulate their views in declarations and statements. Nowadays they become disagreers; they have formed Mattachine societies; they issue programs and declarations. This, I would say, is good.

But on the other hand we find disagreers who are increasingly tempted to use the techniques of dissent. Students who disagree about the war in Vietnam use the techniques of dissent, of affirming their secession from society, and this is bad.

The expressions of disagreement may lead to better policy, but dissent cannot.

The affirmations of differentness and feeling apart cannot hold a society together. In fact, these tend to destroy the institutions which make fertile disagreement possible, and fertile institutions decent. A sniper's bullet is an eloquent expression of dissent, of feeling apart. It doesn't express disagreement. It is formless, inarticulate, unproductive. A society of disagreers is a free and fertile and productive society. A society of dissenters is a chaos leading only to dissension.

Now I would like in conclusion to suggest that we are led to a paradox.

A paradox which must be solved. A free and literate society with a high standard of living and increasingly varied media, one that reaches more and more people more and more of the time—such a society finds it always easier to dramatize its dissent rather than disagreement. It finds it harder and harder to discover, much less to dramatize, its agreement on anything. This ends then in some questions which I will pose to you gentlemen to which I hope you may have answers. At least they seem to me to be crucial ones.

First, is it possible to produce interesting newspapers that will sell but which do not dramatize or capitalize on or catalyze dissent and dissension, the feeling of apartness in the community? Is it possible to produce interesting newspapers that will sell but which do not yield to the temptation to create and nourish new dissent by stirring people to feel apart in new ways?

Second, is it possible at the same time to find new ways of interesting people in disagreement in specific items and problems and programs and specific evils?

Finally, is it possible for our newspapers—without becoming Pollyannas or chauvinists or superpatriots or Good Humor salesmen—to find new ways of expressing and affirming, dramatizing, and illuminating what people agree upon?

This is your challenge. The future of American society in no small measure depends on whether and how you answer it. ■

Vice-President
Spiro Agnew
Castigates the Media

"THE views of this fraternity do not represent the views of America."

WHEN THE REPUBLICAN PRESIDENTIAL NOMINEE Richard M. Nixon chose Governor Spiro T. Agnew of Maryland, a moderate Republican, to be his running mate in 1968, he had in mind a steady politician who could deliver a fair speech and not cause too much controversy. That was not how it worked out.

During the campaign, "Spiro Who?" was laughed at by reporters for his gaffes ("You've seen one slum and you've seen 'em all") and reviled for ethnic insensitivity ("How's the 'Fat Jap'?"), causing him to counter with "I'm a Greek—excuse me, I'm Grecian." The vice-presidential nominee developed a burning dislike for most members of what he called "the elite press."

So did Patrick J. Buchanan, a young Nixon speechwriter who supervised the daily news summary and bridled at the barbs aimed at the administration. He was especially angered at the "instant analysis" after the president's November 3, 1969, "silent majority" speech, and drafted a speech for delivery by the vice-president at a Republican gathering in Des Moines, Iowa. When Mr. Nixon reviewed the draft, he made a couple of minor emendations and said to Buchanan, "This really flicks the scab off, doesn't it?"

It really did. The political target became the huntsman; Mr. Agnew read the speech—all the more biting because of its reasoned tone—with relish. Suddenly speechmaking became an event again; network news executives, to show fairness, felt constrained to cover Mr. Agnew's criticism of themselves, and the Buchanan-Agnew antimedia message—soon followed up with a blast at "an effete corps of impudent snobs" at our nation's most prestigious schools—struck a chord of resentment in much of the public.

The following year, Ted Agnew became the Nixon "point man" in the midterm political campaign, flaying "radic-libs" (a not too subtle play on "comsymps") across the country. Most 1970 Republican candidates welcomed the "red meat" in the Agnew speeches, which were written by Buchanan, Bryce Harlow, and me; one who did not was George Bush, running for the Senate in Texas as a moderate. He spurned the Agnew right-wing rhetoric and lost to Lloyd Bentsen.

I contributed the "nattering nabobs of negativism" alliteration to an Agnew speech in San Diego, a dig at pessimists that was inspired by Adlai Stevenson's "prophets of gloom and doom." But none of the carefully crafted, sociopolitical speeches of Agnew matched the impact of the Des Moines speech; for at least a generation, he killed "instant analysis."

In 1973, with the presidency all but in his grasp as the Watergate scandal began to unfold, Agnew pleaded no contest to corruption charges and copped a plea by resigning his vice-presidency. His disgrace as a pol on the take cast a cloud over his message for years, but some of the themes in his speeches (anti-drug culture, anti-elitism, resentment toward Washington establishments, all clothed in unabashed or strident patriotism) were later taken up by political speakers in both parties.

□ □ □

Tonight I want to discuss the importance of the television news medium to the American people. No nation depends more on the intelligent judgment of its citizens. No medium has a more profound influence over public opinion. Nowhere in our system are there fewer checks on vast power. So nowhere should there be more conscientious responsibility exercised than by the news media. The question is, Are we demanding enough of our television news presentations? And, are the men of this medium demanding enough of themselves?

Monday night, a week ago, President Nixon delivered the most important address of his administration, one of the most important of our decade. His subject was Vietnam. His hope was to rally the American people to see the conflict through to a lasting and just peace in the Pacific. For thirty-two minutes, he reasoned with a nation that has suffered almost a third of a million casualties in the longest war in its history.

When the president completed his address—an address that he spent weeks in preparing—his words and policies were subjected to instant analysis and querulous criticism. The audience of seventy million Americans—gathered to hear the president of the United States—was inherited by a small band of network commentators and self-appointed analysts, the *majority* of whom expressed, in one way or another, their hostility to what he had to say.

It was obvious that their minds were made up in advance. Those who recall the fumbling and groping that followed President Johnson's dramatic disclosure of his intention not to seek reelection have seen these men in a genuine state of nonpreparedness. This was not it.

One commentator twice contradicted the president's statement about the exchange of correspondence with Ho Chi Minh. Another challenged the president's abilities as a politician. A third asserted that the president was now "following the Pentagon line." Others, by the expressions on their faces, the tone of their questions. and the sarcasm of their responses, made clear their sharp disapproval. . . .

Every American has a right to disagree with the president of the United States, and to express publicly that disagreement.

But the president of the United States has a right to communicate directly with the people who elected him, and the people of this country have the right to make up their own minds and form their own opinions about a presidential address without having the president's words and thoughts characterized through the prejudices of hostile critics before they can even be digested. When Winston Churchill rallied public opinion to stay the course against Hitler's Germany, he did not have to contend with a gaggle of commentators raising doubts about whether he was reading public opinion right, or whether Britain had the stamina to see the war through. When President Kennedy rallied the nation in the Cuban missile crisis, his address to the people was not chewed over by a roundtable of critics who disparaged the course of action he had asked America to follow.

The purpose of my remarks tonight is to focus your attention on this little group of men who not only enjoy a right of instant rebuttal to every presidential address but, more importantly, wield a free hand in selecting, presenting, and interpreting the great issues of our nation.

First, let us define that power. At least forty million Americans each night, it is estimated, watch the network news. Seven million of them view ABC; the remainder being divided between NBC and CBS. According to Harris polls and other studies, for millions of Americans the networks are the sole source of national and world news.

In Will Rogers's observation, what you knew was what you read in the newspaper. Today, for growing millions of Americans, it is what they see and hear on their television sets.

How is this network news determined? A small group of men, numbering perhaps no more than a dozen "anchormen," commentators, and executive producers, settle upon the 20 minutes or so of film and commentary that is to reach the public. This selection is made from the 90 to

180 minutes that may be available. Their powers of choice are broad. They decide what forty to fifty million Americans will learn of the day's events in the nation and the world.

We cannot measure this power and influence by traditional democratic standards, for these men can create national issues overnight. They can make or break—by their coverage and commentary—a moratorium on the war. They can elevate men from local obscurity to national prominence within a week. They can reward some politicians with national exposure and ignore others. For millions of Americans, the network reporter who covers a continuing issue, like ABM or civil rights, becomes, in effect, the presiding judge in a national trial by jury.

It must be recognized that the networks have made important contributions to the national knowledge. Through news, documentaries, and specials, they have often used their power constructively and creatively to awaken the public conscience to critical problems.

The networks made "hunger" and "black lung" disease national issues overnight. The TV networks have done what no other medium could have done in terms of dramatizing the horrors of war. The networks have tackled our most difficult social problems with a directness and immediacy that is the gift of their medium. They have focused the nation's attention on its environmental abuses, on pollution in the Great Lakes and the threatened ecology of the Everglades.

But it was also the networks that elevated Stokely Carmichael and George Lincoln Rockwell from obscurity to national prominence. Nor is their power confined to the substantive.

A raised eyebrow, an inflection of the voice, a caustic remark dropped in the middle of a broadcast can raise doubts in a million minds about the veracity of a public official or the wisdom of a government policy.

One federal communications commissioner considers the power of the networks to equal that of local, state, and federal governments combined. Certainly, it represents a concentration of power over American public opinion unknown in history.

What do Americans know of the men who wield this power? Of the men who produce and direct the network news, the nation knows practically nothing. Of the commentators, most Americans know little, other than that they reflect an urbane and assured presence, seemingly well informed on every important matter.

We do know that, to a man, these commentators and producers live and work in the geographical and intellectual confines of Washington, D.C., or New York City—the latter of which James Reston terms the "most unrepresentative community in the entire United States." Both communities bask in their own provincialism, their own parochialism. We can deduce that these men thus read the same newspapers, and draw their political and social views from the same sources. Worse, they talk constantly to one another, thereby providing artificial reinforcement to their shared viewpoints. . . .

The views of this fraternity do *not* represent the views of America. That is why such a great gulf existed between how the nation received the president's address—and how the networks reviewed it.

As with other American institutions, perhaps it is time that the networks were made more responsive to the views of the nation and more responsible to the people they serve.

I am not asking for government censorship or any other kind of censorship. I am asking whether a form of censorship already exists when the news that forty million Americans receive each night is determined by a handful of men responsible only to their corporate employers and filtered through a handful of commentators who admit to their own set of biases.

The questions I am raising here tonight should have been raised by others long ago. They should have been raised by those Americans who have traditionally considered the preservation of freedom of speech and freedom of the press their special provinces of responsibility and concern. They should have been raised by those Americans who share the view of the late Justice Learned Hand that "right conclusions are more likely to be gathered out of a multitude of tongues than through any kind of authoritative selection."

Advocates for the networks have claimed a First Amendment right to the same unlimited freedoms held by the great newspapers of America.

The situations are not identical. Where the *New York Times* reaches 800,000 people, NBC reaches twenty times that number with its evening news. Nor can the tremendous impact of seeing television film and hearing commentary be compared with reading the printed page. And in the networks' endless pursuit of controversy, we should ask, What is the end value—to enlighten or to profit? What is the end result—to inform or to confuse? How does the ongoing exploration for more action, more excitement, more drama, serve our national search for internal peace and stability?

Gresham's law seems to be operating in the network news.

Bad news drives out good news. The irrational is more controversial than the rational. Concurrence can no longer compete with dissent. One minute of Eldridge Cleaver is worth ten minutes of Roy Wilkins. The labor crisis settled at the negotiating table is nothing compared to the confrontation that results in a strike—or, better yet, violence along the picket line. Normality has become the nemesis of the evening news.

The upshot of all this controversy is that a narrow and distorted picture of America often emerges from the televised news. A single dramatic piece of the mosaic becomes, in the minds of millions, the whole picture. The American who relies upon television for his news might conclude that the majority of American students are embittered radicals, that the majority of black Americans feel no regard for their country, that violence and lawlessness are the rule, rather than the exception, on the American campus. None of these conclusions is true.

Television may have destroyed the old stereotypes—but has it not created new ones in their place?

What has this passionate pursuit of "controversy" done to the politics of progress through logical compromise, essential to the functioning of a democratic society?

The members of Congress or the Senate who follow their principles and philosophy quietly in a spirit of compromise are unknown to many Americans—while the loudest and most extreme dissenters on every issue are known to every man in the street.

How many marches and demonstrations would we have if the marchers did not know that the ever-faithful TV cameras would be there to record their antics for the next news show.

We have heard demands that senators and congressmen and judges make known all their financial connections—so that the public will know who and what influences their decisions or votes. Strong arguments can be made for that view. But when a single commentator or producer, night after night, determines for millions of people how much of each side of a great issue they are going to see and hear, should he not first disclose his personal views on the issue as well?

In this search for excitement and controversy, has more than equal time gone to that minority of Americans who specialize in attacking the United States, its institutions, and its citizens?

Tonight, I have raised questions. I have made no attempt to suggest answers. These answers must come from the media men. They are challenged to turn their critical powers on themselves. They are challenged to direct their energy, talent, and conviction toward improving the quality and objectivity of news presentation. They are challenged to structure their own civic ethics to relate their great freedom with their great responsibility.

And the people of America are challenged too, challenged to press for responsible news presentations. The people can let the networks know that they want their news straight and objective. The people can register their complaints on bias through mail to the networks and phone calls to local stations. This is one case where the people must defend themselves, where the citizen—not government—must be the reformer, where the consumer can be the most effective crusader.

By way of conclusion, let me say that every elected leader in the United States depends on these men of the media. Whether what I have said to you tonight will be heard and seen at all by the nation is not *my* decision; it is not *your* decision; it is *their* decision.

In tomorrow's edition of the *Des Moines Register* you will be able to read a news story detailing what I said tonight; editorial comment will be reserved for the editorial page, where it belongs. Should not the same wall of separation exist between news and comment on the nation's networks.

We would never trust such power over public opinion in the hands of an elected government—it is time we questioned it in the hands of a small and unelected elite. The great networks have dominated America's airwaves for decades; the people are entitled to a full accounting of their stewardship. ■

Arthur Ochs Sulzberger of the *New York Times* Discusses Business and the Press

"FIFTY years ago, an American president could say, with much justification, that 'the business of America is business.' We've gone beyond that. The business of America is freedom."

PUNCH SULZBERGER—so nicknamed by his grandfather Adolph Ochs, first successful publisher of the *New York Times,* as counterpoint to his sister, Judy—was president and publisher of the newspaper and its related publications and broadcasting stations from 1963 to 1992, when he retired as publisher, continuing as chairman and chief executive officer. A former marine, he made the decision to publish the Pentagon Papers in 1971; in the firestorm that followed, he said, "We gave away no national secrets. We didn't jeopardize any American soldiers or marines overseas. These papers are a part of history."

In his lifetime at the *Times,* he was more businessman than reporter; on March 14, 1977, he spoke to the Detroit Economic Club at a time when many corporate executives were persuading themselves that journalism was printing more bad news about business than good. His theme was "Is the press antibusiness?" and, remembering his reporting days, he put the story in the lead.

□   □   □

It's good to be here in Detroit, the home of the "Big Two"—the *Detroit News* and the *Detroit Free Press.* About a year ago, I was looking through a newspaper, and I came across a story that gave me my topic for today: Is the press antibusiness?

The story that triggered that question in my mind was a report of the dreary 1975 earnings of the New York Times Company.

Happily, I can address that question today in a more objective frame of mind. The 1976 figures, as reported in the paper, show circulation, advertising, and earnings on a satisfying march upward. The article about it looked decidedly probusiness. In fact, I cannot recall a morning on which I read the *Wall Street Journal* with greater pleasure.

Is the press antibusiness? That question breeds another: How can the press be antibusiness when the press is business, and often big business at that? After all, like many of you in the room today, we, too, face boards of directors, union leaders, the EEOC, the SEC, and stockholders. It's hard to remember a *Times* annual meeting which Evelyn Y. Davis missed.

But the fact that the press is often big business itself does not really enable us to duck the question: Are we antibusiness? A great many businessmen suggest that a new tone is creeping into journalism. They find that the big corporation *too* is often portrayed as the villain and the consumer movement the hero; that bad news is reported with glee, and good corporate news is relayed grudgingly; that the profit motive is *derogated* by writers who seem to prefer more government control and, at best, have little or no training in the world of finance. Too often they feel the deadline conflicts with accuracy, and the deadline too often wins. It is argued that a general public distrust of institutions is being *focused* by the media into a lack of confidence in all American business enterprise.

Let me pass along a tip on how to detect bias in any speaker on this subject. If he talks about "the media," he's against us; if he talks about "the press," he's for us. I speak to you today as a member of the press.

Let me grant this at the outset: press coverage of business has changed and is still changing. A more analytical—a more skeptical, sometimes more critical—approach is being taken. And this is not only true with business reporting; government, education, the courts, and the press itself are subject to this new scrutiny.

The printing of handouts—or "editing with a shovel"—is on the decline, and that's good.

But why, journalists are asked, don't we play up the good news? Why does the corporate bribe or the drop in earnings get the big headline—while the advance in technology or the rise in earnings gets buried?

One answer, of course, is in the nature of news: we give more space to a plane crash than to a report on the thousands of safe landings made every day. I would never suggest that "good news is no news," but I would suggest that bad news is often big news.

Another answer is in the changing nature of the news business. In every field, editors are emphasizing two basic questions. One is *How?* How will this affect the reader's life? And newspapers respond with more service columns, more pieces on personal investing, and more columns on the significance of business news on readers' lives. The other is *Why?*

Why did they abandon the merger? Why did they fire the boss? Readers, investors, and creditors all want these answers. And as business becomes more complex, more international, answers to these questions become increasingly important.

On this point, I should add that not all reporting of good news is necessarily welcome to businessmen. For example, when the Bell Telephone System became the first corporation in history to earn one billion dollars in a single quarter, we thought the achievement ought to be recognized, and displayed the story on the front page. But a New Jersey public-service commissioner saw it there, and rejected a rate increase on the ground that profits were too high. Bell System executives might well think it would be wiser in the future to hide their light under a bushel. So, I don't think "Why don't you play up the good news?" is a valid question. That's not our function. Our job is to give the reader accurate information he can use about what is important and what interests him. That is also an important goal of business.

Let's get to basics. Fifty years ago, an American president could say, with much justification, that "the business of America is business." We've gone beyond that. The business of America is freedom.

For the journalist, that means the freedom to get to the root of the truth, the freedom to criticize, the freedom to goad and stimulate every institution in our society, including our own.

For businessmen, that means the freedom to compete fairly, on the basis of value and service. And it means the freedom to defend themselves against unfair charges by pressure groups, to assert the principle of the profit motive, and to fight off excessive or stultifying government regulation.

For the consumer of your product and mine, it means the freedom to hold our claims to account, the freedom to complain like hell and get attention paid to those complaints, and the freedom to choose a competitor if we fail them.

Let me, then, practice what I preach about the new coverage of business news. Here are a few ideas we can use in our business lives.

First, *get out front*. Teamwork may be great, and the organization spirit is commendable, but business news is made by people. Individuals. Human beings. Business leadership ought to include some public leadership—but the trouble is, the public perception of business leaders is all too often that of the *bland* leading the *bland*. Oh, there are some exceptions, and Detroit is home to some of them. Yet, in a recent poll, 93 percent of the people interviewed could identify Walter Cronkite; 79 percent, Henry Kissinger; 66 percent, George Meany; but when they were asked about Thomas Murphy and John de Butts, they wondered if the pollsters were putting them on. Less than 3 percent could identify the heads of General Motors and AT&T.

Why are there so few business heroes? Is the press trying to hide the identity of businessmen, or are businessmen worried about becoming celebrities? It is true that with public renown comes vulnerability, both personal and corporate; many businessmen choose, out of modesty or caution, to stay out of the limelight. A faceless official spokesman often becomes the voice of the company.

Even publishers should show their faces now and then. I think it's a fine thing when somebody comes up to me after a speech and says, "You're doing a great job with your newspaper, Mr. Chandler."

Next, *stop talking the inside lingo of business*. Whenever businessmen get together, they bemoan the fact that business is "failing to communicate," whatever that means. One reason may be that they're talking a specialized language that the public is not about to take the time to learn.

That language barrier concerns us at the *Times*. Occasionally, we hear the charge that newspaper and television reporters are poorly prepared to talk to business people about financial subjects. And it is true that the subject matter is becoming more complex, involving nuclear safety, or tanker technology, changes in accounting rules, and the like. From our side, we're hiring more reporters with formal educations in business subjects—*not* so much to talk the language of businessmen, but to interpret these complex subjects for the lay reader.

Third, *go looking for complaints*. That sounds strange, I know—most of us have all the complaints we can handle. But I was reading a *U.S. News and World Report* survey of some five thousand heads of households. The biggest problem business had was credibility: most people say they do not believe what business claims about its products. That's troublesome, but the same survey turned up this hopeful note: of the one-fourth of the people who had made a complaint to a manufacturer about a product in the past year, nearly half of them said they were satisfied in the way those complaints were handled.

Think about that: one of the biggest pluses American business has going for it is the satisfaction of the customer who complains, and whose complaints are heard. And it's better that *they* complain to the businessman than to write to their congressman.

We deal with gripes in the newspaper business all the time. One of the best-read sections of every paper is the "Letters to the Editor," and the best letters are the ones that slam us all over the page. The *Times* also has a "corrections" corner, originally because we thought that was the responsible thing to do, but now it is turning into a well-read feature. Why? Because nobody's perfect—customers and readers understand that, and react well to efforts to improve.

And, finally, *do some complaining yourself.* Fight for your rights—everyone else is, and business has just as much a right to be heard as any other force in our society.

Just about every survey about public perceptions of business shows that the strongest antibusiness feeling is on the college campus. That's a big challenge, and it invites a kind of sensitive confrontation. Businessmen, especially young businessmen, should assume that burden; it cannot be solved only by taking an ad in the college newspaper. To combat antibusiness feeling at its source, businessmen have to arrange to tie into college activities, participate in seminars, and have honest answers to student questions about environmental and human concerns. Nor is there any need to be on the defensive; we know that the market system outperforms any other, and it includes the irreplaceable element of personal freedom. That's not something to apologize for; that's something to proudly assert.

I think you'll find more places in which to make that kind of affirmation. Many newspapers are adopting op-ed pages, seeking expressions of outside opinion.

On the *Times,* one of our most popular Sunday features is a page of outside opinion labeled "Point of View," where businessmen and academics and government officials blaze away on everything from energy policy to capital shortages.

More than ever, across the spectrum of our lives, that element of controversy is a vital part of the news. News is not only what happens but what people think has happened, and what values they attach to what *has,* or *has not,* taken place. Business is a prime part of that creative controversy; so is journalism. Sometimes it hurts; most of the time it's fairly exciting and quite constructive.

My point is this: it is not so much a matter of the *press* being antibusiness, which I have to admit it *sometimes* is. Nor is it a matter of *business* being antipress, which you will have to admit it *usually* is. That tension between press and business—in a relationship not quite so adversary as that which exists between press and government—is the healthy tension in a land of separated and balancing centers of power.

Is the press antibusiness? The answer is no. Is the press antidullness, antistuffiness, anticorporate secrecy? The answer is yes.

Is a probing, skeptical, searching press coverage good for business? I think so. You may not agree completely. You might look at modern business news coverage the way John Wanamaker looked at advertising: half of it is wasted, he felt, but he never knew which half.

Business and journalism share certain great values: we are both pro-opportunity; we are both proconsumer; we are both proprofit; and we are both profreedom.

We are looking at each other now with new eyes, in a kind of institutional midlife crisis. And I think we're both going to come through it stronger than ever. ∎

A. M. Rosenthal of the *New York Times* Defines Freedom of the Press

---

"*JUDGE Medina . . . laid it pretty heavily on reporters and editors and publishers who were too quick to compromise . . . : 'Fight like hell every inch of the way.'*"

AS EXECUTIVE EDITOR OF THE *NEW YORK TIMES* from 1977 to 1986, Abe Rosenthal thought his mission in life was "to keep the paper straight"—that is, to resist in the news pages not only government's influence, as in the case of the Pentagon Papers, but also the subtler nudges of cultural and ideological bias. In the early stage of his half century at the *Times*, he won a Pulitzer Prize for international reporting from Poland; the Communist regime also honored him by expelling him. On reaching retirement age, the crusading editor stepped up to the post of op-ed columnist, where he won human rights awards for his espousal of the cause of individual dissidents oppressed by tyranny.

On November 18, 1981, he spoke at Colby College in Waterville, Maine, at a convocation honoring the memory of Elijah Parish Lovejoy, a Colby graduate of 1826, who died defending his printing press against a mob violently opposed to his stand on the abolition of slavery.

Rosenthal's speech begins with a surefire attention getter: "Let me tell you a little true story. . . ." (Audiences love to listen to stories, especially when they know a point will follow.) The speaker sets up his key message with a colorful quotation midway in the speech, which he reprises in a ringing conclusion.

□   □   □

Let me tell you a little true story about how a reporter I knew operated. Every day he would go out and cover his beat the best way he knew and the *only* way he knew: by talking to people in the town about what concerned them, about the cost of living, about the feel of life, about what they thought about their leaders, about politics.

Every night that reporter went home, wrote a story, and then carefully burned his notes or flushed them down the toilet. It was a pity, because he knew he might forget what he couldn't write that day if he burned his notes. But he also knew the police had permission to search his files anytime.

A lot of people did not want to talk to the reporter, because they felt he might reveal their names on purpose or through a slip of the typewriter. They were defenseless people, and they were afraid.

The reporter never urged them to talk, because he understood their fear. Others, however, did talk to the reporter, precisely because they felt powerless and wanted somebody to tell the truths they knew. They accepted his word that he would suffer imprisonment before telling their names.

The government became very annoyed at this reporter. They questioned him directly about his sources, and, of course, he did not respond.

They bugged his home and followed him wherever he went, and they searched his office and tracked his phone calls. Finally, the government got really angry and said, You can't write about us any more, you can't have access, go away. But some of the people about whom he had written and whose names he had never revealed kissed him when he went away, and gave him roses, and everybody said he was a hero, and later he was loaded with honors.

I was the reporter, and the beat I covered was Communist Poland. That was the first time I had to operate worrying about the police and courts and the first time I had to burn notes and think about going to jail. I thought it would be the last, because I resolved never again to work in a totalitarian society.

Now it is twenty years later, and I am the editor of the same newspaper for which I was a reporter in Poland. I spend my time dealing with news and with staff matters, but there is one subject that now takes up a considerable amount of my time and thoughts and that has to do with whether reporters should burn their notes, whether they are going to go to jail, what are the possibilities of a sudden police search, whether people who once talked to us will talk any more, whether other papers can be fined out of existence, whether the police will secretly commandeer our phone records to find our sources of information, whether we will be allowed to cover the administration of justice, how to get the police to reveal necessary information.

New York, not Warsaw.

I do not tell you all this to imply that we have gone totalitarian or that the Republic will fall. But I do tell you that the *process* essential to a free press—one of the institutions that will help guarantee that we do *not* go totalitarian, that the Republic will *not* fall—is under attack, and not from our enemies or the enemies of freedom. That we could handle. No, it is under attack from some of the very people whose professions have helped create and strengthen a free press, some of the lawyers and judges of our country, honorable men and women who traditionally have been the philosophic allies of the free press. And it is under attack from federal legislators and politicians who certainly do not see themselves as enemies of a free press. They just think the American press is a little too free for their tastes.

They want to prevent the press from printing certain kinds of information. They say that obviously this does not affect such respected newspapers as the *Times* or the *Washington Post* or the *Boston Globe*. All they're aiming at, they say, is certain nasty fringe publications. Now, I happen to agree that some of their targets are indeed nasty and fringe, but it is precisely the fringes, not just the center, that the First Amendment was designed to protect.

Simply see what has happened in the past few years. A dozen or so reporters and editors have been sent to jail for no other crime than trying to protect their sources, exactly what I did in Poland every day and for which Americans praised me. Others are now under orders to reveal sources or face jail. The courts have permitted newsrooms to be searched. Thousands of memoranda and files have been subpoenaed in different actions around the country. One large newspaper, our own, has been fined hundreds of thousands of dollars. Now every small newspaper lives under the threat of being fined into bankruptcy at the decision of a judge. Laws erected by state governments to protect the reporter's right to work freely have been destroyed by some courts.

Many judges have decided that reporters can be barred from essential parts of the court process, pretrial hearings, which constitute so important a part of the administration of justice. Other courts have placed severe restraints on participants in the judicial process, preventing press and public from finding out what is going on. A wall of judicial protection has been built around information held by the police behind which they can operate in relative secrecy.

In more and more cases, courts have upheld the principle of prior restraint—that is, preventing the press from publishing what it feels *should* be published. Until a few years ago this was unthinkable.

And in case after case, by demanding notes and files and sending reporters to jail for not revealing sources, courts in effect have ruled that they have the power to enforce publication of what reporters and editors feel should *not* be published, because the information is either confidential or simply inaccurate, untrustworthy, or damaging to innocent people, just raw material.

In totality, courts now have ruled themselves overseers of essential decision-making processes of the free press that the First Amendment was designed to safeguard from government encroachment—what to publish, when to publish, how to operate, what to think. . . .

I do not think there is a plot against the press on the part of the courts. I *do* think that there is a resentment against the press that comes from many things. I do feel that most of that resentment comes from the virtues rather than the failures of the press, the unpleasant virtues of telling the people the truth about Vietnam, Watergate, corruption in government or in business, the aggressiveness and cantankerousness which are part of our makeup and function.

We annoy the hell out of people. And we have our faults, by God, we have our faults. There are scores of publications I wouldn't read, let alone work for. And there are a few for which I have loathing and contempt.

But there is a difference between resenting the press or even loathing it and trying to control it.

The First Amendment was written not to protect the press from the admiration of government but from the loathing of government, all branches of government.

Courts and the press are involved, it seems to me, in two philosophic differences. One is that some judges feel that it is incumbent upon them to protect what the government says for the national security of the United States. National security usually turns out to be a matter of political or diplomatic interest or plain embarrassment. The price of prior restraint, a fancy way of saying judicial censorship, strikes me as a very expensive price indeed to pay to save government face.

Remember what the government said would happen if we published the Pentagon Papers? National calamity, revelation of state secrets, disaster upon disaster. The government position was a fraud, and the government, I believe, knew it. . . .

As Judge Harold Medina once put it, any judge who knows his business and who has a stiff backbone can afford a fair trial without any invasion of the freedom of the press.

In that speech of his, Judge Medina laid it pretty heavily on judges who he thought violated the First Amendment. He also laid it pretty heavily on reporters and editors and publishers who were too quick to compromise. He gave them a piece of advice: "Fight like hell every inch of the way."

Well, we are fighting, and it seems that almost every time we turn around there is a new battle to be fought.

One had to do with the seizure of the telephone records of our Atlanta bureau by the Department of Justice. They were not investigating us; they were investigating the Ku Klux Klan, which we also had been investigating, without informing us or giving us a chance to fight. Southern Bell bowed to a subpoena of the Department of Justice and turned over all the records from our Atlanta bureau and from the home of our bureau chief. The purpose of the subpoena was to find out who our reporters were talking to.

This clandestine investigation of a reporter's work is a clear violation of the spirit of the First Amendment. I'm happy to say that that particular threat has been considerably eased. Because of complaints from the press and the bar, the Justice Department issued new guidelines that made unnotified seizure much less likely. . . .

The press is not asking for privilege. That word implies some special gift to be bestowed upon the press or withheld from the press at somebody's discretion, a judge's or a legislator's or a policeman's. No, we are not talking about the privilege of the press, but the right and ability and duty of the press to function in any meaningful sense.

Yes, this all concerns editors, reporters, and publishers, but I beseech you to consider that this concerns each of you as citizens of a country based on freedom of thought and expression.

Every individual American has to ask herself or himself some questions:

- □ Do you want a society in which newspapers have to operate under the fear of being fined to death?
- □ Do you want a society in which newspaper offices can be searched without advance hearings?
- □ Do you want a society in which the public does not know what is taking place in vital parts of the court processes?
- □ Do you want a society in which the police process is made virtually secret?
- □ Do you want a society that is the totality of all these things?

Please think about it. If your answer is "No, I don't want that kind of society," then fight like hell every inch of the way. ■

Radio and Television Journalist Daniel Schorr, at Seventy-five, Makes a Few "Confessions"

"THE older I get, the more I begin to realize that life isn't that simplicity of the young reporter saying, 'Out of my way, Bud, I want that story, and if I get that story, there it goes.' I have a greater and greater sense of complications."

DAN SCHORR became famous as a CBS television correspondent, a member of the team Edward R. Murrow assembled, which is remembered by broadcast journalists with the awe that Yankee fans show in recalling their "Murderers' Row." Schorr was never a go-along, get-along type, even within his company: his uncompromising integrity led to clashes with CBS boss William Paley and later with CNN boss Ted Turner. What he called his "inescapable decision of journalistic conscience" led him to broadcast and publish a report by the House Intelligence Committee that the House had voted to suppress; in a dramatic confrontation that affected press freedom in Washington, he faced down the irate committee, which decided not to pursue him for contempt of Congress.

On October 3, 1991, in celebration of his seventy-fifth birthday a month before, National Public Radio—proud to have him as its senior commentator—gave a party at the Smithsonian Institution's "castle." To an audience of politicians, friends, and fellow journalists, Schorr proceeded to reminisce, as if off the cuff; as the structure of the speech shows, however, the extemporaneous remarks were thought through in advance. The combination of a startling fact about his early career and a surprising ambivalence about what seemed to be such clear-cut judgments in his later career gripped the audience; it was one of those speeches, excerpted here from a transcript of the tape, that offer food for thought to both sources and broadcasters long after it is delivered.

□   □   □

... Let me make to you a couple of confessions, and maybe you'll learn a little bit about how I view a profession that is very, very dear to me, but part of an industry about which I've learned to have a great many reservations.

First confession: I actually never really intended to go into broadcasting at all. All my young life what I wanted was to be a newspaper reporter, especially a foreign correspondent, and most especially, a correspondent for the *New York Times*. Back in the very early 1950s, I was a stringer for the *New York Times,* in Holland, writing assiduously. Finally, I went to New York and said, "You know, I really want to be a staff correspondent for the *New York Times."* The managing editor asked me to go through a trial period in New York to see whether I could cover local news as well as foreign news, and I did. Finally he said, "Go back to Holland. I think we're going to do it. It'll take a few weeks, maybe a couple of months, and then we'll appoint you to our staff."

Time passed, and I wasn't appointed to the staff. In the midst of my waiting, there came this cable from this man, Edward R. Murrow, of CBS, for which I had done a few broadcasts. A cable I can remember as though it were yesterday. It said, "Would you at all consider joining the staff of CBS News with an initial assignment in Washington?"

Flattered though I was to be asked, I thought, well, this is radio, television. This is entertainment stuff. This isn't really for me. So I sent a cable to the *Times*, to Turner Catledge, the managing editor, and said I was wondering when this appointment was going to take place, because I'd had another offer, which I might have difficulty refusing unless we could sort of settle a date. And, to my surprise, a cable came back saying, "We suggest you take this other offer."

So I said okay. And I joined the staff of CBS. A year or so later, visiting New York, I was invited to dinner by two editors of the *New York Times*: Emanuel Friedman, the foreign editor, and Ted Bernstein. assistant managing editor. They said they had a confession to make to me. "You probably wonder why you didn't get the job on the *Times* that was promised to you." And I said yes, in fact, I did wonder what had happened there. "Well, it's been weighing heavily on our consciences, and we've decided to tell you. What happened was that, just about the time you were to be appointed, the *Times* decided to freeze the hiring of Jews because, in case it became necessary to cover a Middle Eastern war, they had too many Jewish correspondents. That freeze lasted about six months, and during that time, your appointment came up. That is why you were not appointed to the *New York Times."*

And so that was how my career was shaped. . . .

That leads to my second confession. Having looked with the disdain that real newspaper people had for this entertainment thing called radio and television, I began to enjoy it in part. And that bothered me. I recall asking a CBS producer for advice. I said, "Tell me, I can write a story, all right, but what is the secret of success for a journalist in television? I mean, how do you do it on television to make it work?" And he said, "The secret of success in television is sincerity. If you can fake that, you've got it made." . . .

But I haven't told you my gravest confession of all. You will understand that I have the reporter's ethic—perhaps mystique—that I cannot stand in the way of information getting to the public. People can keep secrets, and, certainly, governments. But once I know, it's not a secret any more. And then I cannot be the arbiter of what the public is allowed to know. In principle, I do not suppress news.

On one occasion, during Watergate, when I was getting a lot of exposure on CBS, a taxi driver taking me to the airport in New York turned around to me and said, "Mr. Schorr, I've seen you on television. Why don't you tell us what's going on in Washington, what's really going on?" I said, "How do you mean? I really do my best." And he said, "Nah, but you people know things, you know all these big shots, and you're all in bed together, and there are things you don't tell us." I said, "Believe me, I'm not an insider, some people call me a quintessential outsider." (You might not think that looking at this audience tonight.) But it always has been important to me that I don't decide what the public should know. If I know, then the public should know.

I acted on that premise in 1976, when I had a copy of a report that the House Intelligence Committee had drafted, but which the House of Representatives, in its wisdom, decided to suppress. It developed that I now had the only copy of this report in the "free world." I not only divulged its contents in stories on CBS but then felt it was my duty to see that the whole report was published. I got into a lot of trouble—and at one point faced the threat of being cited for contempt of Congress—because of my principle that I don't suppress news.

Yet, a couple of times in my life I did. I'm not sure yet that I did right, but I did it. I'll tell you one of those episodes.

In 1957, I was in Poland working on a documentary for the CBS "See It Now" program. In the course of wandering around Poland for a couple of months, I came to a place in eastern Poland, a small town, where I saw an amazing sight. A bunch of people with horse-drawn carts on which their possessions were piled, like a scene from *Fiddler on the Roof*. I went up to them, and soon realized that they were Jews. I didn't speak Polish, so I spoke to them in Yiddish, and they addressed me in Yiddish, and they explained to me that they were going to Israel. That was quite remarkable, because in 1957, Jews were not being allowed to leave Soviet bloc countries to go to Israel. So I did interviews with them on film in Yiddish—nice little vignettes to go in this documentary of Poland today after Stalin. But I needed to know how this had been arranged.

Returning to Warsaw, I asked the Israeli minister how Jews were getting out of Poland to go to Israel. He asked, "How do know about that?" I said, "Well, I met some. I interviewed them.""Where?" he said. And I said, "Well in this town. In eastern Poland." He said, "Well, if you know that much, I'll tell you more, and then you can decide what you will do."

You see, the Soviet Union, at the end of the war, had occupied a part of Poland containing many Jews. They didn't want to stay there. And an arrangement was worked out among Israel, Poland, and the Soviet Union. Jews there could be "repatriated" to Poland, with the understanding that they would almost immediately leave for Israel, because Poland didn't want them. The Soviets, worried about reactions among their Arab friends, had stipulated that if the arrangement became known, it would stop immediately. "So," said my Israeli minister friend, "that's the story. If you want to go ahead, go ahead. But if you do, that's the end of Jews getting out of the Soviet Union." I said well, I'd have to see what I'd do about that.

This was all on 16-mm film, and we were shipping rolls of film every day to New York as part of this program that we would structure later. And I kept this roll of film there on my desk. I thought to call Murrow and see what he thought—couldn't call on an open telephone. And so the film remained with me in Poland. I didn't ship it. We finished the program; it went on the air. I came back to New York and saw Murrow, and said to him, "I think I've got to tell you something." And I told him that story. And he said, "I understand." Not quite approving. Not quite disapproving. Just saying, "I understand."

This episode has worried me over these years. How could I justify this suppression to myself? Oddly enough, I never really found a rationale for that until recently.

Washington Post reporter Milton Coleman once quoted Jesse Jackson using words like "Hymies" and "Hymie-town," which created a political sensation. But it developed, from Coleman's later account, that Jackson had preceded his anti-Semitic remarks by asking, "Can we talk 'black talk' for a minute?" And Coleman had let Jackson go on talking "black talk." I don't think Coleman should have reported what followed, because a reporter is not just a reporter. There are other circles of which one is a member. And isn't asking to talk "black talk" like saying, "It's off the record"?

The Jackson-Coleman incident, some thirty years later, may have illuminated for me—maybe I'm rationalizing—why I could not expose the emigration of Jews from Poland. If I hadn't spoken Yiddish, I wouldn't have had the interview. Maybe this was like "black talk." It summoned you to membership in some other group beyond being just a reporter. And the older I get, the more I begin to realize that life isn't that simplicity of the young reporter saying, "Out of my way, Bud, I want that story, and if I get that story, there it goes." I have a greater and greater sense of complications.

Well, at seventy-five, I end up not having many problems like that, thanks to NPR and its wonderful way of dealing with me. I don't have the tyranny of bright lights and sound bites. Radio analysis is a simple matter of sitting down and writing it, and, if it seems to be in reasonable English, and if it's not too long, it goes on the air and maybe makes a small contribution to understanding. I'm still in a profession I love, always have loved, always will love. My profession may have become a tail on a big kite—the media industry. But at seventy-five I still see journalism as a noble and ennobling profession. ■

Author Salman Rushdie Cries Out from a Life "Trapped inside a Metaphor"

"'FREE speech is a nonstarter,' says one of my Islamic extremist opponents. No, sir, it is not. Free speech is the whole thing, the whole ball game. Free speech is life itself."

COLUMBIA UNIVERSITY'S GRADUATE SCHOOL OF JOURNALISM held a dinner on December 11, 1991, honoring the two-hundredth anniversary of the First Amendment and one of its foremost modern defenders, retired Supreme Court justice William Brennan. My role in the proceedings was to read from the historic Brennan decision in *New York Times v. Sullivan,* emphasizing the line about "the principle that debate on public issues should be uninhibited, robust and wide-open, and that it may well include vehement, caustic, and sometimes unpleasantly sharp attacks on government and public officials."

The assembled media bigwigs wondered why trucks and dogs of the New York City Police Department's bomb squad were outside, and why we were all frisked before entry into the hall. The reason became clear when Salman Rushdie, author of *The Satanic Verses,* who was condemned to death by Islam's ayatollah Khomeini for blasphemy, suddenly appeared at the rostrum. Brennan's ringing words had never been more dramatically illustrated; here was a man under threat of terrorist execution for what was taken to be too sharp an attack on a religion. To an audience stunned by his appearance, Rushdie spoke quietly but challengingly, wrapping his plea for political action to end his hostage status inside a metaphor of "a thousand days in a balloon." As the audience rose to applaud, three plainclothesmen escorted the condemned author out a rear exit and back into hiding.

□   □   □

A hot-air balloon drifts slowly over a bottomless chasm, carrying several passengers. A leak develops; the balloon starts losing height. The pit, a dark yawn, comes closer. Good grief! The wounded balloon can bear just one passenger to safety; the many must be sacrificed to save the one! But who should live, who should die? And who could make such a choice?

In point of fact, debating societies everywhere regularly make such choices without qualms, for of course what I've described is the given situation of that evergreen favorite the balloon debate, in which, as the speakers argue over the relative merits and demerits of the well-known figures they have placed in disaster's mouth, the assembled company blithely accepts the faintly unpleasant idea that a human being's right to life is increased or diminished by his or her virtues or vices—that we may be born equal but thereafter our lives weigh differently in the scales.

It's only make-believe, after all. And while it may not be very nice, it does reflect how people actually think.

I have now spent over a thousand days in just such a balloon; but, alas, this isn't a game. For most of these thousand days, my fellow travelers included the Western hostages in the Lebanon and the British businessmen imprisoned in Iran and Iraq, Roger Cooper and Ian Richter. And I had to accept, and did accept, that for most of my countrymen and countrywomen, my plight counted for less than the others'. In any choice between us, I'd have been the first to be pitched out of the basket and into the abyss. "Our lives teach us who we are," I wrote at the end of my essay "In Good Faith." Some of the lessons have been harsh, and difficult to learn.

Trapped inside a metaphor, I've often felt the need to redescribe it, to change the terms. This isn't so much a balloon, I've wanted to say, as a bubble, within which I'm simultaneously exposed and sealed off. The bubble floats above and through the world, depriving me of reality, reducing me to an abstraction. For many people, I've ceased to be a human being. I've become an issue, a bother, an "affair." Bulletproof bubbles, like this one, are reality proof, too. Those who travel in them, like those who wear Tolkien's rings of invisibility, become wraith-like if they're not careful. They get lost. In this phantom space a man may become the bubble that encases him, and then one day—pop!—he's gone forever.

It's ridiculous—isn't it?—to have to say, "But I *am* a human being, unjustly accused, unjustly embubbled." Or is it I who am being ridiculous, as I call out from my bubble, "I'm still trapped in here, folks; somebody, please, get me out"?

Out there where you are, in the rich and powerful and lucky West, has it really been so long since religions persecuted people, burning them as heretics, drowning them as witches, that you can't recognize religious persecution when you see it? . . . The original metaphor has reasserted itself. I'm back in the balloon, asking for the right to live.

What is my single life worth? Despair whispers in my ear, "Not a lot." But I refuse to give in to despair.

I refuse to give in to despair, because I've been shown love as well as hatred. I know that many people do care, and are appalled by the crazy, upside-down logic of the post-*fatwa* world, in which a single novelist can be accused of having savaged or "mugged" a whole community, becoming its tormentor (instead of its tarred-and-feathered victim) and the scapegoat for all its discontents. Many people do ask, for example, "When a white pop star turned Islamic fanatic speaks approvingly about killing an Indian immigrant, how does the Indian immigrant end up being called the racist?"

Or, again, "What minority is smaller and weaker than a minority of one?"

I refuse to give in to despair even though, for a thousand days and more, I've been put through a degree course in worthlessness, my own personal and specific worthlessness. My first teachers were the mobs marching down distant boulevards, baying for my blood and finding, soon enough, their echoes on English streets. I could not understand the force that makes parents hang murderous slogans around their children's necks. I have learned to understand it. It burns books and effigies and thinks itself holy. But at first, as I watched the marchers, I felt them trampling on my heart.

Once again, however, I have been saved by instances of fair-mindedness, of goodness. Every time I learn that a reader somewhere has been touched by *The Satanic Verses,* moved and entertained and stimulated by it, it arouses deep feelings in me. And there are more and more such readers nowadays, my postbag tells me, readers (including Muslims) who are willing to give my burned, spurned child a fair hearing at long last. Milan Kundera writes to say that he finds great tenderness towards Muslim culture in the book, and I'm stupidly grateful. A Muslim writes to say that in spite of the book's "shock tactics" its ideas about the birth of Islam are very positive; at once. I find myself wishing upon a star that her coreligionists may somehow, impossibly, come to agree with her.

Sometimes I think that, one day, Muslims will be ashamed of what Muslims did in these times, will find the "Rushdie affair" as improbable as the West now finds martyr burning. One day they may agree that—as the

European Enlightenment demonstrated—freedom of thought is precisely freedom from religious control, freedom from accusations of blasphemy. Maybe they'll agree, too, that the row over *The Satanic Verses* was at bottom an argument about who should have power over the grand narrative, the story of Islam, and that that power must belong equally to everyone. That even if my novel were incompetent, its attempt to retell the story would still be important. That if I've failed, others must succeed, because those who do not have power over the story that dominates their lives, power to retell it, rethink it, deconstruct it, joke about it, and change it as times change, truly are powerless, because they cannot think new thoughts.

One day. Maybe. But not today.

Today, my education in worthlessness continues, and what Saul Bellow would call my "reality instructors" include the media pundit who suggests that a manly death would be better for me than hiding like a rat; the letter writer who points out that of course the trouble is that I *look* like the devil, and wonders if I have hairy shanks and cloven hooves; the "moderate" Muslim who writes to say that Muslims find it "revolting" when I speak about the Iranian death threats (it's not the *fatwa* that's revolting, you understand, but my mention of it); the rather more immoderate Muslim who tells me to "shut up," explaining that if a fly is caught in a spider's web, it should not attract the attention of the spider. I ask the reader to imagine how it might feel to be intellectually and emotionally bludgeoned, from a thousand different directions, every day for a thousand days and more.

Back in the balloon, something longed-for and heartening has happened. On this occasion, mirabile dictu, the many have not been sacrificed but saved. That is to say, my companions, the Western hostages and the jailed businessmen, have by good fortune and the efforts of others managed to descend safely to earth and have been reunited with their families and friends, with their own, free lives. I rejoice for them and admire their courage, their resilience. And now I'm alone in the balloon.

Surely I'll be safe now? Surely now the balloon will drop safely towards some nearby haven, and I, too, will be reunited with my life? Surely it's my turn now?

But the balloon is over the chasm again; and it's still sinking. I realize that it's carrying a great deal of valuable freight. Trading relations, armaments deals, the balance of power in the Gulf—these and other matters of great moment are weighing down the balloon. I hear voices suggesting that if I stay aboard, this precious cargo will be endangered. The national interest is being redefined; am I being redefined out of it? Am I to be jettisoned, after all?

When Britain renewed relations with Iran at the United Nations in 1990, the senior British official in charge of the negotiations assured me in unambiguous language that something very substantial had been achieved on my behalf. The Iranians, laughing merrily, had secretly agreed to forget the *fatwa*. (The diplomat telling me the story put great stress on this cheery Iranian laughter.) They would "neither encourage nor allow" their citizens, surrogates, or proxies to act against me. Oh, how I wanted to believe that! But in the year and a bit that followed, we saw the *fatwa* restated in Iran, the bounty money doubled, the book's Italian translator severely wounded, its Japanese translator stabbed to death; there was news of an attempt to find and kill me by contract killers working directly for the Iranian government through its European embassies. Another such contract was successfully carried out in Paris, the victim being the harmless and aged ex–prime minister of Iran, Shapour Bakhtiar.

It seems reasonable to deduce that the secret deal made at the United Nations hasn't worked. Dismayingly, however, the talk as I write is all of improving relations with Iran still further, while the "Rushdie case" is described as a side issue.

Is this a balloon I'm in, or the dustbin of history?

Let me be clear: *there is nothing I can do to break this impasse*. The *fatwa* was politically motivated to begin with, it remains a breach of international law, and it can only be solved at the political level. To effect the release of the Western hostages in the Lebanon, great levers were moved; great forces were brought into play; for Mr. Richter, seventy million pounds in frozen Iraqi assets were "thawed." What, then, is a novelist under terrorist attack worth?

Despair murmurs, once again, "Not a plugged nickel."

But I refuse to give in to despair.

You may ask why I'm so sure there's nothing I can do to help myself out of this jam.

At the end of 1990, dispirited and demoralized, feeling abandoned, even then, in consequence of the British government's decision to patch things up with Iran, and with my marriage at an end, I faced my deepest grief, my unquenchable sorrow at having been torn away from, cast out of, the cultures and societies from which I'd always drawn my strength and inspiration—that is, the broad community of British Asians, and the broader community of Indian Muslims. I determined to make my peace with Islam, even at the cost of my pride. Those who were surprised and displeased by what I did perhaps failed to see that I was not some deracinated Uncle Tom Wog. To these people it was apparently incomprehensible that I should seek to make peace between the warring halves of the world, which were also the warring halves of my soul—and that I should seek to do so in a spirit of humility, instead of the arrogance so often attributed to me.

In "In Good Faith" I wrote, "Perhaps a way forward might be found through the mutual recognition of [our] mutual pain," but even moderate Muslims had trouble with this notion: what pain, they asked, could I possibly have suffered? *What was I talking about?* As a result, the really important conversations I had in this period were with myself.

I said, "Salman, you must send a message loud enough to be heard all over the world. You must make ordinary Muslims see that you aren't their enemy, and make the West understand a little more of the complexity of Muslim culture." It was my hope that Westerners might say, "Well, if he's the one in danger, and yet he's willing to acknowledge the importance of his Muslim roots, then perhaps we ought to start thinking a little less stereotypically ourselves." (No such luck, though. The message you send isn't always the one that's received.)

And I said to myself, "Admit it, Salman, the story of Islam has a deeper meaning for you than any of the other grand narratives. Of course, you're no mystic, mister, and when you wrote, 'I am not a Muslim,' that's what you meant. No supernaturalism, no literalist orthodoxies, no formal rules for you. But Islam doesn't have to mean blind faith. It can mean what it always meant in your family, a culture, a civilization, as open-minded as your grandfather was, as delightedly disputatious as your father was, as intellectual and philosophical as you like. Don't let the zealots make Muslim a terrifying word," I urged myself; "remember when it meant 'family' and 'light.' "

I reminded myself that I had always argued that it was necessary to develop the nascent concept of the secular Muslim, who, like the secular Jews, affirmed his membership of the culture while being separate from the theology. I had recently read the contemporary Muslim philosopher Fouad Zakariya's *Laïcité au Islamisme,* and been encouraged by Zakariya's attempt to modernize Islamic thought. "But, Salman," I told myself, "you can't argue from outside the debating chamber. You've got to cross the threshold, go inside the room, and *then* fight for your humanized, historicized, secularized way of being a Muslim." I recalled my near-namesake, the twelfth-century philosopher ibn-Rushd (Averroës), who argued that (to quote the great Arab historian Albert Hourani), "not all the words of the Qu'ran should be taken literally. When the literal meaning of Qu'ranic verses appeared to contradict the truths to which philosophers arrived by the exercise of reason, those verses needed to be interpreted metaphorically." But ibn-Rushd was a snob. Having propounded an idea far in advance of its time, he qualified it by saying that such sophistication was only suitable for the elite; literalism would do for the masses. "Salman," I asked myself. "is it time to pick up ibn-Rushd's banner and carry it forward—to say, nowadays such ideas are fit for everybody, for the beggar as well as the prince?"

It was with such things in mind—and with my thoughts in a state of some confusion and torment—that I spoke the Muslim creed before witnesses. But my fantasy of joining the fight for the modernization of Muslim thought, for freedom from the shackles of the Thought Police, was stillborn. It never really had a chance. Too many people had spent too long demonizing or totemizing me to listen seriously to what I had to say. In the West, some "friends" turned against me, calling me by yet another set of insulting names. Now I was spineless, pathetic, debased; I had betrayed myself, my cause; above all, I had betrayed *them.*

I also found myself up against the granite, heartless certainties of Actually Existing Islam, by which I mean the political and priestly power structure that presently dominates and stifles Muslim societies. Actually Existing Islam has failed to create a free society anywhere on earth, and it wasn't about to let me, of all people, argue in favor of one. Suddenly I was (metaphorically) among people whose social attitudes I'd fought all my life—for example, their attitudes about women (one Islamicist boasted to me that his wife would cut his toenails while he made telephone calls, and suggested I find such a spouse) or about gays (one of the imams I met in December 1990 was on TV soon afterwards, denouncing Muslim gays as sick creatures who brought shame on their families and who ought to seek medical and psychiatric help). Had I truly fallen in among such people? *That was not what I meant at all.*

Facing the utter intransigence, the philistine scorn of so much of Actually Existing Islam, I reluctantly concluded that there was no way for me to help bring into being the Muslim culture I'd dreamed of, the progressive, irreverent, skeptical, argumentative, playful, and *unafraid* culture which is what I've always understood as *freedom.* Not me, not in this lifetime, no chance. Actually Existing Islam, which has all but deified its Prophet, a man who always fought passionately against such deification, which has supplanted a priest-free religion by a priest-ridden one, which makes literalism a weapon and redescriptions a crime, will never let the likes of me in.

Ibn-Rushd's ideas were silenced in their time. And throughout the Muslim world today, progressive ideas are in retreat. Actually Existing Islam reigns supreme, and just as the recently destroyed "Actually

Existing Socialism" of the Soviet terror state was horrifically unlike the utopia of peace and equality of which democratic socialists have dreamed, so also is Actually Existing Islam a force to which I have never given in, to which I cannot submit.

There is a point beyond which conciliation looks like capitulation. I do not believe I passed that point, but others have thought otherwise.

I have never disowned my book, nor regretted writing it. I said I was sorry to have offended people, because I had not set out to do so, and so I am. I explained that writers do not agree with every word spoken by every character they create—a truism in the world of books, but a continuing mystery to *The Satanic Verses*'s opponents. I have always said that this novel has been traduced. Indeed, the chief benefit of my meeting with the six Islamic scholars on Christmas Eve, 1990, was that they agreed that the novel had no insulting motives. "In Islam, it is a man's intention that counts," I was told. "Now we will launch a worldwide campaign on your behalf to explain that there has been a great mistake." All this with much smiling and friendliness and handshaking. It was in this context that I agreed to suspend—not cancel—a paperback edition, to create what I called a space for reconciliation.

Alas, I overestimated these men. Within days, all but one of them had broken their promises and recommenced to vilify me and my work as if we had not shaken hands. I felt (most probably I had been) a great fool. The suspension of the paperback began at once to look like a surrender. In the aftermath of the attacks on my translators, it looks even more craven. It has now been more than three years since *The Satanic Verses* was published; that's a long, long "space for reconciliation." Long enough. I accept that I was wrong to have given way on this point. *The Satanic Verses* must be freely available and easily affordable, if only because if it is not read and studied, then these years will have no meaning. Those who forget the past are condemned to repeat it.

"Our lives teach us who we are." I have learned the hard way that when you permit anyone else's description of reality to supplant your own—and such descriptions have been raining down on me, from security advisers, governments, journalists, archbishops, friends, enemies, mullahs—then you might as well be dead. Obviously, a rigid, blinkered, absolutist worldview is the easiest to keep hold of; whereas the fluid, uncertain, metamorphic picture I've always carried about is rather more vulnerable. Yet I must cling with all my might to that chameleon, that chimera, that shapeshifter, my own soul; must hold on to its mischievous, iconoclastic, out-of-step clown instincts, no matter how great the storm. And if that plunges me into contradiction and paradox, so be it;

I've lived in that messy ocean all my life. I've fished in it for my art. This turbulent sea was the sea outside my bedroom window in Bombay. It is the sea by which I was born, and which I carry within me wherever I go.

"Free speech is a nonstarter," says one of my Islamic extremist opponents. No, sir, it is not. Free speech is the whole thing, the whole ball game. Free speech is life itself. That's the end of my speech from this ailing balloon. Now it's time to answer the question, What is my single life worth?

Is it worth more or less than the fat contracts and political treaties that are in here with me? Is it worth more or less than good relations with a country which, in April 1991, gave eight hundred women seventy-four lashes each for not wearing a veil; in which the eighty-year-old writer Mariam Firouz is still in jail, and has been tortured; and whose foreign minister says, in response to criticism of his country's lamentable human rights record, "International monitoring of the human rights situation in Iran should not continue indefinitely. . . . Iran could not tolerate such monitoring for long"?

You must decide what you think a friend is worth to his friends, what you think a son is worth to his mother, or a father to his son. You must decide what a man's conscience and heart and soul are worth. You must decide what you think a writer is worth, what value you place on a maker of stories, and an arguer with the world.

Ladies and gentlemen, the balloon is sinking into the abyss. ■

Columnist William F. Buckley, Jr., Finds the Coming Senate Acquittal of President Clinton to Be "Forgiving the Unforgivable"

"AMERICA is correctly proud of its capacity to forgive, but also we are aware that forgiveness is a joint exercise. Forgiveness presupposes contrition."

NO OTHER NEWSPAPER COLUMNIST, magazine founder, or television commentator can claim to be father of a major modern political movement. By dint of personality as much as force of intellect, William F. Buckley was the polemical journalist who made modern conservatism respectable in the United States. His espousal of what had long been a minority view led to the presidential candidacy of Senator Barry Goldwater (defeated overwhelmingly in 1964) and to the victories of Ronald Reagan in the 1980s.

Buckley's speaking style is charmingly confrontational. His elitist manner is unabashed, his choice of words on the podium a challenge to most audiences: an example is "rodomontade," a rolling, mouth-filling word for "arrogance." Yet the controversialist appeals to audiences filled with liberals by presenting his ideas in a thoughtful, unexcited tone that induces rather than commands respect.

"I have seen Hubert Humphrey, and indeed Bill Clinton, draw blood from a stone in public speeches," he wrote, "attacking the skeptics in the manner of Jimmy Durante, who would, if necessary to entertain his audience, take an axe to the piano." Buckley chooses a different style: "The other way is to strive to communicate to your audience that if they exhibit the curiosity and attentiveness to hear you out, their favors in attending will match yours in appearing, and both parties will leave the hall with a sense that neither wasted its time."

Speaking on January 27, 1999, to a dinner of "The Moles," a society of underground and underwater engineers, Buckley addressed the raging issues raised by the House of Representatives' impeachment of President Clinton, at a time when the public was transfixed by the sudden fame of Paula Jones and Monica Lewinsky.

The speech is constructed on a half-dozen "propositions," which in logic means an affirmation of an arguable position but has a second sense, probably not intended, of a proposed private encounter. When Buckley introduces a literary allusion—"La Rochefoucauld is endlessly relevant"—and quotes it as "hypocrisy is the tribute that vice pays to virtue," he then brings it up to date with a reference to a heated denial of stealing from the collection plate being evidence of belief that such an act is wrong. When he uses the German word "Schadenfreude," he defines it as "the pleasure that people can get from the miseries of others." When he uses "solipsism," unfamiliar to most, he defines it as if in passing as "the theory that the self is the only thing that can be measured, that, indeed, matters." When an extensive vocabulary is used in this explanatory way, the audience members think, "Sure—I knew that."

□   □   □

We face, tonight and seemingly every night, the problem faced in 1945 by General Anthony McAuliffe. He was the hero of the Battle of the Bulge, fought out bitterly fifty-four years ago, in the closing yet desperate months of the world war. In Belgium in December 1944 the American fighting divisions were encircled. The Nazis sent their ultimatum to the commanding American general. It seemed that all of America was transported to his celebrated reply to this demand for surrender. His answer was, "Nuts."

Very nice; but a month or two after General McAuliffe had returned to Washington, he had got as tired of hearing the word "Nuts" as Rachmaninoff had become of hearing the C-sharp minor prelude, which he had composed at age nineteen and was required to perform as an encore every time his fingers touched the keyboard.

So what happened was one more party given in the general's honor, by a celebrated Washington hostess. She was delicately approached the night before by the general's aide and told, "Please, Mrs. Witherspoon, do not mention the Nuts business; it drives the general crazy."

She promised, and the party went swimmingly, and as the general prepared to depart he gave his thanks to the hostess, who smiled graciously and said, "I was delighted to meet you, General McNuts."

So it is. Here I am—substituting for Senator Bradley, who is in New Hampshire showing young voters how to use snowballs as basketballs—addressing representatives of the construction and engineering industry on what subject?

Nuts.

There is no way to avoid the subject. Even then one runs the risk. I am writing these words on Tuesday night. I postponed their composition as long as I could. But who knows what is happening this very evening, disorienting these thoughts? How will the Senate vote on two critical motions? Though, come to think of it, whatever contributions I have to make on the subject can't really be disoriented. They are a part of the story, moral and historical.

The Lewinsky matter and its implications are overwhelming in their demand for attention. At the most dramatic political level it is asked, Should the United States Senate convict the president of the United States on charges brought by formal impeachment proceedings by the House of Representatives, removing him from office? At the most dramatic public level, we ask, What in the way of behavior does the American public, in the year of Our Lord 1999, expect of its president? Or, perhaps more accurately, What in 1999 will the American public settle for in the behavior of its president?

I have endeavored to formulate a few propositions, the first being that *The Paula Jones case should have been aborted for reasons not always put forward.*

Nine members of the Supreme Court ruled almost two years ago that the suit brought against the president by Mrs. Jones should stay on the trial court's calendar. The offenses complained of—sexual harassment and intimidation—had been committed before the defendant became president of the United States. No special immunity, therefore, attached to him. Moreover, there was no reason to assume—the Court implicitly argued—that Mr. Clinton could not simultaneously defend himself at trial and conduct the nation's business. It was suggested in effect that if it happened that the trial were to fall on the very same day as a projected bombing of Iraq, the trial judge could reasonably be expected to put off the proceedings for a week or two.

There is a sense in which this lawsuit crept up on the American public substantially unnoticed, rather like the lazily apprehended knowledge that the way things were arranged, computers were destined to crash at midnight at the end of the day that brings on the next millennium. On the computer front, we simply have assumed, or at least I have, that the wizards of Silicon Valley will find the right plug to pull at some point before midnight, and the cyberworld will continue to hum. Though I do recall an Austrian intellectual who years ago pointed out the difference between builders and theorists. "The engineers," he said, "build the Brooklyn Bridge. The scientists buy it." In the same way, something—it was generally thought, until the appearance of Miss Lewinsky—would happen and Paula Jones would go away and Mr. Clinton would continue on through his term.

I proposed, three years ago in my newspaper column, that Republican and Democratic leaders agree for the sake of the public tranquillity to view Paula Jones's challenge as a bipartisan problem. Back then, Mrs. Jones was asking for damages of $700,000 and for an apology from the president.

If she had persisted in demanding an apology, we'd have needed to see a display of diplomatic statesmanship in Mr. Clinton. Even if entirely innocent, he might have been counseled to go ahead and authorize an apology written as if he might only conjecturally have been guilty. Every day people in commerce sign consent decrees in which they acknowledge the hypothetical possibility of guilt even when absolutely convinced of their innocence. Mr. Clinton could have reasoned that his concern for presidential decorum outweighed any appearance he might permit of hypothetical guilt. He could have said, "Whatever I did that gave offense to Mrs. Jones, I regret."

That and $700,000 could have rescued us all from a long life in the trough ahead.

And of course the question is left with us now, Was the failure to settle, back then, an early warning sign of defective presidential leadership? Our Chief Executive is also our First Politician. Expert politicians are expected to avoid unnecessary crises. Mr. Clinton is every day proving—most notably a week ago with his State of the Union address—that he is a politician who can survive crisis, but that's different. The best governors are those who don't permit crises to generate, hugely easing the problem of surviving them.

My next proposition is that *Many Americans seemed to be saying that public servants can be expected to be—casual—in the matter of conjugal morality.*

The editorial writer of the *Orlando Sentinel* expressed his views on the subject: "In our hearts, most of us know that few (if any) among us could pass such scrutiny. . . . But the success of our system is based on its ability to recruit normal people for extraordinary service. If we exclude the normal, we invite the extreme."

The paper went on to urge, beginning with the next presidential inauguration, the following reform, patterned on the marriage ceremony. At weddings, the editor reminds us, words such as the following are spoken: "Let all those who oppose this union speak now or forever hold their peace." The editor proposes a law that would grant "blanket immunity" from criminal or civil prosecution to the president and to every officeholder who is in the line of succession to the president under the Constitution.

Very interesting. What is a normal person? It isn't safe to assume that the Orlando editor thinks entirely "normal" a man who has dropped his pants—literally—in front of a subordinate, as an invitation to dalliance. A distinction appears to be asserting itself on the matter of sexual promiscuity, the shorthand of which would read: If it's about sex, it's okay.

The May issue of *Playboy* magazine carried an editorial by founder-philosopher-rake Hugh Hefner, who joyfully welcomed Bill Clinton into the fraternity of the enlightened. "President Clinton," Hef wrote, "has become a sort of sexual Rorschach test. I," he observed proudly, "have been in a similar position for more than forty years." The founder of the Playboy Philosophy was willing to share his crown. "The sexually charged atmosphere of the White House," he wrote, "has lit a thousand points of lust—around watercoolers, on the Internet, in bedrooms, on telephones—and a thousand points of tolerance." These points of tolerance are now telling us in effect that illegal behavior is a tolerable thing, if its purpose is merely to pull down the shade on what was going on.

My next proposition is that, *Granted what actually did happen, Mr. Clinton's administration during those long months made the public learning process difficult.*

It finally required a DNA test done on the stain on a woman's dress to catalyze Mr. Clinton's repentance of August 17. That reluctance to speak candidly is a difficulty which his closest associate, Vice-President Gore, also seems to suffer from. Your friendly family lawyer will advise you that what Mr. Gore did a year earlier, when accosted with his fund-raising meeting at the Buddhist temple in California, was "to plead in the alternative." Here is how pleading in the alternative goes: (1) My client didn't do it. (2) If my client did it, it was legal. (3) Even though it wasn't legal, it should have been. And (4) my client won't do it again.

But then suddenly, in February, Mr. Clinton, speaking through his wife, Hillary, explained that the entire business was the working of a "vast right-wing conspiracy."

Well of course it's true that there are extremists on the Right as on the Left. The kooks go on. There are the wild militiamen of the Right in Idaho, and, from the Left, every now and again we hear such things as that Wall Street is planning another depression, the Pentagon another war, or that AIDS was an invention of the CIA to arrest the growth of the black population. But it was never plain that the extremists were in charge of the investigation, at the judicial or legislative level.

Motives are always mixed. It is wrong to deny that certain satisfactions are taken from adversities that affect certain others. Our disagreeable neighbor, our unspeakable cousin, Notre Dame if you're rooting for Army, Army if you're rooting for Notre Dame.

Sometimes this human weakness goes as far as Schadenfreude, the pleasure that people can get from the miseries of others. This is human nature. Suppose that a fairy with the proverbial magic wand had volunteered early in June 1972 to waft down upon the Oval Office just when President Nixon was about to give orders to call off the FBI on the grounds that Watergate was a CIA-related affair. Pffft!! The smoking gun would have been undischarged!! Richard Nixon would never have uttered his fateful, mortal words, words which his tape machine would spit out in July 1974, ejecting him from the White House.

Would the American Left have been pleased that this subversive latency in American history had been aborted? Let's face it, no. What the Left most wanted was to discredit Nixon and get rid of him. If the same magic lady were to appear tomorrow and offer to restore Miss Lewinsky's virginity, do we suppose that the right wing would be happy about it? One more virgin, in exchange for the exposure of a defective Democratic president?

So grant that some of the ill will is entrenched and opportunistic. Does it all reduce to mere political factionalism?

My next proposition is that *Whatever the concerns for morality and integrity, the political consideration inevitably figures.*

What would happen if Clinton were removed? Al Gore would become president. Gore's agenda is to the left of Clinton's. If Mr. Clinton were gone, President Gore would be there to pursue his own visions. He'd be unencumbered by the bedraggled Clinton, who no matter what the Senate does in the days ahead will not be able to sneeze during the balance of his term without the body-language people wondering what his real motives are. Why should a Republican Congress, looking out for itself, prefer President Gore to President Clinton?

Another thing: If Clinton were removed, Gore would run for election in the year 2000 with the bouncy launch of a sitting president. Why should Republicans prefer an opponent who would be running with all the advantages of the White House working for him?

If I were a consultant to the GOP, instead of spending my life as an expert on engineering and construction, and if I were concerned exclusively with the fruits of power, I would beg the leadership to just drop the whole thing, kick in a little censure motion for appearances' sake, and go on to things like Iraq and Social Security. Let Clinton stay where he is, I'd advise. Let his presence in the White House fray the Democratic rhetoric about integrity and family values.

My next proposition is that *The heat of the rhetoric of this period is itself informative*.

Even as Senator McCarthy aroused huge and hysterical fears fifty years ago about subversion of government by Communists, we hear now, at about the same pitch, suspicion of subversion of government by conservatives. There was, for instance, that meeting last week. There was Harvard law professor Alan Dershowitz, who protests everything on earth except the guilt of most of his clients, advising everyone that a vote for impeachment was a vote for bigotry, for fundamentalism, against environmentalism, and against choice by incipient mothers. Nobel Prize–winning author Toni Morrison saw Dershowitz and raised him one: The Hyde people in Congress, she said, are "an arrogant theocracy genuflected at the knees of a minority." Author Blanche Cook dismissed the congressional majority as "filthy mean-minded swiny people." Elizabeth Holtzman, the former congresswoman, gave a judicious explanation: "What is at stake is the right of the American people, by majority vote, to elect a president of the United States and not have it undone by moralizing, sanctimonious—" but the reporter notes that the roar of approbation from the crowd drowned out her last words, leaving us to wonder that Ms. Holtzman is so enthusiastic about the strategic wisdom of the same American voters who chased her out of office.

There is the other position, namely, that Republican legislators who voted to impeach, and senators who incline to convict, are upholding their oaths to act according to their understanding of the Constitution. Will the voters, in protest, commit a Republican genocide in November of 2000?

How will the Republicans, on the defensive, protect themselves? What will they say it was that motivated their pursuit of Mr. Clinton?

Well, they might begin by quoting Mr. Clinton's most eloquent defender, former senator Dale Bumpers, who brought the whole country to a standstill last week in admiration of his speech pleading with the Senate not to convict his old friend. How did he characterize what Mr. Clinton actually did? The words used by Senator Bumpers were that President Clinton's conduct was "indefensible, outrageous, unforgivable, and shameless."

Before he was through, it became clear that Senator Bumpers means by indefensible, something which you can defend—after all, Clinton was only trying to cover up a sex thing. And Bumpers means by "unforgivable" something you can forgive. After all, Clinton was only, well, only trying to cover up a sex thing. That leaves us with only "outrageous" and "shameless." And what do you do about conduct that is outrageous and shameless? Why, you . . . transcend it.

Time magazine asks its readers a question in the current issue: "All things considered, twenty-five years from now do you think Bill Clinton will be remembered for: (1) His accomplishments as president?"—that got 18 percent. "Or (2) Controversies over his personal life and financial dealings?"—that got 72 percent.

Twenty-five years from now people will remember his presidency not for what he accomplished as president, but for his personal conduct. If that is so, are Republicans really expected to worry in November, twenty-two months from now, about the time they have given to reflection on his conduct?

Here is a measure of the frustration felt by those who do really believe that what Mr. Clinton did was indefensible and outrageous. It is that in our culture it is not possible to give a president authority simply to proceed as a detached political technician. It is a part of human nature to admire and even to love people who exercise great power. Ivan the Terrible was cheered by the crowds and beseeched not to give up his crown. Stalin and Hitler and Perón and Huey Long received thunderous public approval. One day after Mr. Clinton's State of the Union address, one week after twenty hours' enumeration of the deeds and words that caused Senator Bumpers to assert the need to forgive the unforgivable, Clinton was in Buffalo, speaking at a great rally. The minister who gave the invocation called him "the greatest president for our people of all time." Yesterday he was exchanging ruminations on virtue with the pope.

Will the Republicans who believe they are standing by the moral and constitutional imperatives be assaulted, in November 2000, for having kept open the question of Mr. Clinton's removal? But what will the opponents of the GOP incumbents say? "There were those," Whittaker Chambers once wrote me, "who, at the great nightfall, took loving thought to preserve the tokens of hope and truth."

My final proposition is that *America is correctly proud of its capacity to forgive, but also we are aware that forgiveness is a joint exercise.*

Forgiveness presupposes contrition.

There is something continuingly provocative in Mr. Clinton's personal appearance. He doesn't—ever—look guilty. When he gave his State of the Union speech last week his expressions recalled the face of Winston Churchill on V-E Day. His manner was as triumphant as if he had single-handedly accomplished the rape of all the Sabine women. Good old Tricky Dick Nixon never let the public down in these matters. He *always* looked guilty, never more so than when he was facing the public and averring his innocence. His face was a polygraph. Clinton's face is that of the freshly minted altar boy. He is Oscar Wilde's Dorian Gray. We have looked at that face through the corrosive mists of Gennifer Flowers, draft evasion, platonic experiences with marijuana, through Vincent Foster, Webster Hubbell, the Lincoln Bedroom, through Huang, FBI files, Mrs. Willey on *60 Minutes*, and what we see is something in the nature of incredulity. For that reason, a convincing apology from him is as inconceivable as a sex change. Bill Clinton couldn't bring it off. The Church made Henry II march over to Canterbury and get himself flogged publicly to atone for the assassination of Becket. Clinton has no comparable recourse, besides which we have the separation of church and state, and he would veto the proposal.

But the public does not seem to be determined to exact convincing contrition. We might ask: What is the matter with the public? Why does it not understand the gravity of what is happening? Can it be that there is something missing at the other end of the democratic scale, as between the governor and the governed? W. B. Yeats wrote a letter, back in the 1930s, to a Dublin daily newspaper which had published serial criticisms of the Lord Mayor, the most recent of which had asked, "What has the Lord Mayor of Dublin done lately to commend himself to the people of Dublin?" Yeats's letter read, "What have the people of Dublin done lately to commend themselves to the Lord Mayor?"

From time to time it is, perhaps you will agree with me—some of you, anyway—appropriate to wonder about the judgment of the majority. Whatever happens in the days ahead, the questions touched upon in the last year will be pondered for many years, by historians of course, but also by moralists. There will be those who applaud the presidential denials. La Rochefoucauld is endlessly relevant. Remember, he wrote that hypocrisy is the tribute that vice pays to virtue. If you heatedly deny having stolen from the collection plate, we can at least take satisfaction from your implicit position, which is that it is wrong to steal from the collection plate.

Mr. Clinton can, in the sense we speak of, be set down as in favor of virtue, even if he didn't inhale it. What the moral tribunals will say of America's behavior during the long year since last January is again difficult to predict. Perhaps they will say that America showed a great sophistication in separating private conduct from public conduct. Or they might say that the United States was so waterlogged with good times and good interest rates and no wars to fight that we lost our capacity for moral refinement.

Or they might say this—the question that most interests me—they might say that for most Americans, conduct, unless it directly affects them, is no longer evaluated by what were once publicly acknowledged as public standards. That would be the triumph of what some would call personal detachment. Ayn Rand's followers would call it the triumph of self-concern. Others would wonder about solipsism, the theory that the self is the only thing that can be measured, that, indeed, matters.

That would be bad news, and I reject it. The task ahead is to reconstruct our basic allegiance to what is right. Come to think of it, where best to launch that movement than at a conference of engineers and constructors? I wish you Godspeed. Keep America intact, and keep your eyes on the infrastructures we all rely on. Good night. ■

Editor John S. Carroll Finds a Unity in the Pulitzer Prizes

"What they all share, all twenty-one of them, is this: a moral vision. Each of these works is animated by an ardently held view of what constitutes right in the world, and what is wrong. That moral vision, and the skills one needs to give it voice, are what we celebrate today."

JOHN CARROLL, editor of the *Los Angeles Times* and before that of the *Baltimore Sun*, served on the Pulitzer Prize Board for nine years, the last—2003—as chairman. As one who served eight of those years and followed him as chairman (the tradition is up and out), I can report that Carroll is not only a remarkable judge of journalism but also a worthy ally or adversary in the illuminating and lively discussions of books, plays, and compositions that take place in that most leakproof of sanctums.

When the award certificates are handed out at a luncheon in the Low Library of Columbia University in New York, the outgoing chairman usually makes a brief speech of welcome to the assembled editors, reporters, artists, poets, dramatists, composers, authors, and photographers, along with their proud publishers, agents, and families. On May 30, 2002, in the aftermath of the year that saw journalists cover the September 11 attacks, Carroll decided to open a permissible window on the board's secret deliberations, thereby to examine the impact of the awards on recipients and to gently remind the much-feted winners that "we sever our roots at our peril."

□   □   □

On behalf of the Pulitzer Prize Board, a warm welcome to all. To the winners, I offer the board's congratulations and thanks. Thank you for your illuminating work. And thanks, especially, for affirming, in a year disfigured by terrorism, the vitality—indeed, the necessity—of journalism, arts, and letters.

This is, despite it all, a happy day, and we should have no reservations about celebrating it robustly. Dreadful as September 11 and its aftermath have been, we are not defeated, or cowed, or reduced to a state of permanent mourning. It has been said before, and on this occasion it bears repeating: We defy our attackers by living life to the fullest.

I feel particularly heartened by this year's accomplishments in journalism. In recent decades, and especially in the nineties, we in journalism have seen a contagion of dubious practices: Sensationalism. Obsession with celebrity. The favoring of splashy design and bright color over meaningful content. The routine trumping of journalistic values by business decisions. The neglect of such traditional topics as government and foreign affairs, which are—or were, before September 11—disparaged in some newspaper-owning corporations as boring and old-fashioned.

This was a year when the sky twice went dark, first with smoke from the World Trade Center, and then with journalistic chickens coming home to roost. What a welcome sight, those chickens! What vindication! Newspapers that had stayed the course, never wavering in their mission of giving citizens the information they need to govern themselves, were richly rewarded. They were rewarded not merely with Pulitzer Prizes but, more importantly, with the respect and heartfelt gratitude of their communities.

This is especially true of the *New York Times*, which distinguished itself this year with seven awards. And it is also true of other newspapers, large and not-so-large, which did so much to untangle and explain the shocking and confusing events of September. Some journalists risked their lives, and thousands, in newsrooms across the country, worked long hours, long weeks, long months, investing their talents and their skills and their hearts in the pages of their newspapers. Today, in those newsrooms, there is pride. It is a well-earned pride, and it deserves to be celebrated.

In literature, music, and drama, with their longer periods of gestation, we have yet to feel the full effect of September 11. The terror and its aftermath will no doubt ripple through our books, poems, plays, and music for many years to come, just as the ripples of earlier American traumas pervade the work we celebrate today.

We have, for example, a book that takes us back to Birmingham, Alabama, recounting another terror in America, the oppression and bombings of the civil rights period. Going back still further, we relive the birth-trauma of our nation as it played out in the memorable life of John Adams. In the future, we will rely on you, our writers and playwrights and poets and composers, to help us grasp the full meaning of September 11.

At first glance, one might wonder what else these diverse works of journalism, letters, and the arts might have in common. Is this just a grab bag of awards we present every year? Or is there a unity in the Pulitzer Prizes?

What they all share, all twenty-one of them, is this: a moral vision. Each of these works is animated by an ardently held view of what constitutes right in this world, and what is wrong. That moral vision, and the skills one needs to give it voice, are what we celebrate today.

Some of our winners might be wondering how it came to pass that they, of all people, are being recognized with Pulitzer Prizes. Others, of course, may be wondering what on earth took us so long. Either way, here's how it happened.

In each of the twenty-one categories, there is a jury. The jurors range in number from three to five, depending on the volume of submissions. Each jury picks three finalists. Then the Pulitzer Board convenes to select the winners.

As a member for eight years, I can tell you that the heavy lifting for the board begins in December. And I choose the phrase "heavy lifting" deliberately.

Shortly before I joined the board, one of the finalists was a book called *The Ants*, which was, as you might imagine, a book about ants. A board member from Iowa dutifully went to his local bookstore, not optimistic about finding a copy of *The Ants* in Des Moines. But there it was, deep in the back of the store, a huge tome, a true doorstop of a book. He lugged it up to the cash register, paid for it, and as he was leaving he heard the clerk holler to a colleague, "Hey, somebody bought one!"

The Ants, incidentally, was a winner in 1991.

Thus, with the purchase of the books in mid-December, does the board set off on its annual marathon, reading fifteen books and thirty-three journalistic finalists (some of which are as long as books), seeing or reading three plays, listening to three music CDs, and viewing three finalists in editorial cartooning and six in photography.

In early April we gather in the World Room of the Columbia journalism school for two days of discussion and decision making. The debate is robust, characterized by passionately held views and, on occasion, good-natured ridicule. Such open expression is made possible by the understanding that whatever is said in the World Room will never be repeated outside.

What result does all this produce?

In my opinion, the board's judgment in the journalism categories tends to be very good, though of course not infallible. In the letters, the Pulitzer Prize is not an award for scholarship or original research. Although the board does include scholars with the best of credentials, it consists mostly of newspaper editors, who tend to know a little bit about a lot of things but are manifestly not experts. I think of it as a book club, a group of intelligent laymen who make recommendations on books that other intelligent laymen might benefit from reading.

Each year's decisions tend to prompt protests on behalf of those who didn't win, or against those who did. Sometimes the critics have a point. Yes, the board is human. But, lest I proceed too far down this path of self-criticism, I want to proclaim my confidence that this year the board got it entirely right, every single person we are about to honor is truly worthy.

What does it mean to you, to have won a Pulitzer Prize?

The Pulitzer Prizes reward past work, but their hope is to foster even better work in the future—better work by those who aspire to win, and also by those who have already won. That hope of the founder, Joseph Pulitzer, is amply fulfilled by two of today's recipients. Tom Friedman of the *New York Times* is collecting his third Pulitzer, a rare achievement, and David McCullough, is receiving his second. In conferring the prize, I'm not overly concerned that either of these two writers will spend much time resting on his growing heap of laurels.

Others, particularly those who receive the Pulitzer at an early age, have been known to make the age-old mistake of believing their own press notices. The result can be harmful. I can describe the symptoms, as they appear among newspaper journalists: Lots of speaking engagements. Very few published stories. A disdain of the mundane tasks that often, for better or worse, constitute daily journalism—tasks like writing an obituary, tracking down an elusive middle initial, or standing in the rain waiting for someone who probably won't talk to you anyway.

The first Pulitzer winner I knew well was Acel Moore, who in 1977 won for investigative reporting at the *Philadelphia Inquirer.* Acel had earned it. He had no college degree, and only after a long apprenticeship as a clerk was he promoted to reporter. He was, in short, a man who had written his share of obits, which, often as not in Philadelphia, were phoned in by a large funeral home called Levine's.

When word reached the newsroom that Acel had won a Pulitzer, we all cheered and clapped him on the back and drank champagne, and then his phone began to ring with calls from well-wishers.

One reporter, a charming rascal named John Corr, slipped to the back of the newsroom and dialed Acel's extension.

Acel picked up the phone, thinking it was yet another well-wisher. Instead, the voice on the phone said, "Hey Acel, this is Bernie at Levine's. I got one for you."

Acel paused, no doubt pondering whether his post-Pulitzer life would include taking obits, from Levine's. Then, with resignation in his voice, he responded: "Okay, lay it on me."

That, I submit, was the correct answer. Few of us are brilliant enough to transcend the drudgery of our chosen craft. If we shun the mundane, if we partake only in the glamour of the job, we risk forfeiting all those skills and attitudes and connections that got us here in the first place.

We sever our roots at our peril. . . .

I would like to conclude my remarks by expressing two hopes for our winners. My first hope is that this award will inspire you to achieve still more, and to derive even greater satisfaction from it. May this day prove to be a beginning, not an end.

And second, my hope is that this day—the thirtieth of May, 2002—will prove to be the happiest of days for you, unclouded by worry. People who achieve much tend to be their own cruelest bosses. Give yourself the day off. Don't worry about that next book, or that next story, or that next poem. Make it a day of sheer joy. Truly, you have earned it.

■　　■　　■

XII

POLITICAL SPEECHES

Demosthenes Attacks
His Accuser

"WHAT greater crime can an orator be charged with than that his opinions and his language are not the same?"

HERE IS DEMOSTHENES' "ON THE CROWN"—reputedly the greatest oration by the greatest orator of the ancient world. Judged by modern standards, it is not such a great speech—too obviously self-serving, replete with obscure references, and too long even in this edited form. But this classic of rhetoric must be judged, and remembered, in the context of its time—delivered in Greece in 330 B.C.—when few men could assemble their thoughts, devise an argumentation strategy, and speak out to persuade their audience as this man did.

Demosthenes of Greece, an agitator and statesman, pitted his lifetime's oratory and ideas of freedom against Philip of Macedon, a general with a lust for world conquest. As Macedonia encroached on Greece, Demosthenes loosed a series of denunciations at Philip (from whose name we get the noun "philippic"), defining the difference between civilization and barbarism, but the word could not stop the advance of the sword. "We shall go to war, I am told, when it is necessary," said the orator, who perfected the interrogative technique. "If the necessity has not come yet, when will it come?" It came and went; Philip was victorious, and Demosthenes lived his final years in a repressed nation-state.

Friends of the orator wanted to present him with a golden crown as a loser's reward, but the Macedonian party, led by Aeschines, charged that it was an unlawful act to so compensate any official who had not reported fully on his conduct and, worse, that it was an attempt to place a lie in the Athenian archives. After seven years, a trial was held; Aeschines laid out the case against the entire public life of Demosthenes, with an argument that was seen to be a refutation of the honor of Athens and a condemnation of his courageous philippics. Called upon to defend himself and his award of the honorary crown, Demosthenes took his freedom and perhaps his life in his hands to answer the charges.

The technique he chose was to attack his accuser. The device was not new; in the biblical Book of Job, written a couple of centuries earlier, the first words of the accused and angry God were directed at his human challenger: "Who is this that darkens counsel with words devoid of knowledge?" Demosthenes refused to be compared with other Greek patriots; instead, he compared his own career with that of Aeschines, whom he addressed at the start as an "accursed scribbler" and then proceeded to derogate further.

The speech was successful; the one who brought the charges against Demosthenes and his supporters was exiled, and the accused was awarded a crown.

☐   ☐   ☐

Accursed scribbler! you, to deprive me of the approbation and affection of my countrymen, speak of trophies and battles and ancient deeds, with none of which had this present trial the least concern; but I— O you third-rate actor!—I that rose to counsel the state how to maintain her preeminence! in what spirit was I to mount the hustings? In the spirit of one having unworthy counsel to offer?—I should have deserved to perish! . . .

Of what a statesman may be responsible for, I allow the utmost scrutiny; I deprecate it not. What are his functions? To observe things in the beginning, to foresee and foretell them to others—this I have done: again, wherever he finds delays, backwardness, ignorance, jealousies, vices inherent and unavoidable in all communities, to contract them into the narrowest compass, and on the other hand, to promote unanimity and friendship and zeal in the discharge of duty. All this, too, I have performed; and no one can discover the least neglect on my part. Ask any man, by what means Philip achieved most of his successes, and you will be told, by his army, and by his bribing and corrupting men in power. Well, your forces were not under my command or control, so that I cannot be questioned for anything done in that department. But by refusing the price of corruption I have overcome Philip; for as the offer of a bribe, if it be accepted, as vanquished the taker, so the person who refuses it and is not corrupted has vanquished the person offering. Therefore is the commonwealth undefeated as far as I am concerned.

For my part, I regard anyone who reproaches his fellowman with fortune as devoid of sense. He that is best satisfied with his condition, he that deems his fortune excellent, cannot be sure that it will remain so until the evening: how then can it be right to bring it forward, or upbraid another man with it? As Aeschines, however, has on this subject (besides many others) expressed himself with insolence, look, men of Athens, and observe how much more truth and humanity there shall be in my discourse upon fortune than in his.

I hold the fortune of our commonwealth to be good, and so I find the oracles of Dodonaean Jupiter and Pythian Apollo declaring to us. The fortune of all mankind, which now prevails, I consider cruel and dreadful: for what Greek, what barbarian, has not in these times experienced a multitude of evils? That Athens chose the noblest policy, that she fares better than those very Greeks who thought, if they abandoned us, they should abide in prosperity, I reckon as part of her good fortune; if she suffered reverses, if all happened not to us as we desired, I conceive she has had that share of the general fortune which fell to our lot. As to my fortune (personally speaking) or that of any individual among us, it should, as I conceive, be judged of in connection with personal matters. Such is my opinion upon the subject of fortune, a right and just one, as it appears to me, and I think you will agree with it. Aeschines says that my individual fortune is paramount to that of the commonwealth, the small and mean to the good and great. How can this possibly be?

However, if you are determined, Aeschines, to scrutinize my fortune, compare it with your own, and, if you find my fortune better than yours, cease to revile it. Look, then, from the very beginning. And I pray and entreat that I may not be condemned for bad taste. I don't think any person wise, who insults poverty or who prides himself on having been bred in affluence: but by the slander and malice of this cruel man I am forced into such a discussion, which I will conduct with all the moderation which circumstances allow.

I had the advantage, Aeschines, in my boyhood of going to proper schools, and having such allowance as a boy should have who is to do nothing mean from indigence. Arrived at man's estate, I lived suitably to my breeding; was choirmaster, ship commander, ratepayer; backward in no acts of liberality public or private, but making myself useful to the commonwealth and to my friends. When I entered upon state affairs, I chose such a line of politics that both by my country and by many people of Greece I have been crowned many times, and not even you, my enemies, venture to say that the line I chose was not honorable. Such, then, has been the fortune of my life: I could enlarge upon it, but I forbear, lest what I pride myself in should give offense.

But you, the man of dignity, who spit upon others, look what sort of fortune is yours compared with mine. As a boy you were reared in abject poverty, waiting with your father in his school, grinding the ink, sponging the benches, sweeping the room, doing the duty of a menial rather than a freeborn man. After you were grown up, you attended your mother in the initiations, reading her books and helping in all the ceremonies, at night wrapping the noviciates in fawn skin, swilling, purifying, and scouring them with clay and bran. . . .

But passing over what may be imputed to poverty, I will come to the direct charges against your character. You espoused such a line of politics (when at last you thought of taking to them) that, if your country prospered, you lived the life of a hare, fearing and trembling and ever expecting to be scourged for the crimes of which your conscience accused you, though all have seen how bold you were during the misfortunes of the rest. A man who took courage at the death of a thousand citizens—what does he deserve at the hands of the living? A great deal more than I could say about him I shall omit; for it is not all I can tell of his turpitude and infamy, which I ought to let slip from my tongue, but only what is not disgraceful to myself to mention.

Contrast now the circumstances of your life and mine, gently and with temper, Aeschines; and then ask these people whose fortune they would each of them prefer. You taught reading, I went to school; you performed initiations, I received them; you danced in the chorus, I furnished it; you were assembly clerk, I was a speaker; you acted third parts, I heard you; you broke down, and I hissed; you have worked as a statesman for the enemy, I for my country. I pass by the rest; but this very day I am on my probation for a crown, and am acknowledged to be innocent of all offense; while you are already judged to be a pettifogger, and the question is whether you shall continue that trade or at once be silenced by not getting a fifth part of the votes. A happy fortune, do you see, you have enjoyed, that you should denounce mine as miserable! . . .

You undertook this cause to exhibit your eloquence and strength of lungs, not to obtain satisfaction for any wrong. But it is not the language of an orator, Aeschines, that has any value, nor yet the tone of his voice, but his adopting the same views with the people, and his hating and loving the same persons that his country does. He that is thus minded will say everything with loyal intention; he that courts persons from whom the commonwealth apprehends danger to herself rides not on the same anchorage with the people and, therefore, has not the same expectation of safety. But—do you see?—I have; for my objects are the same with those of my countrymen; I have no interest separate or distinct. Is that so with you? How can it be—when immediately after the battle you went as ambassador to Philip, who was at that period the author of your country's calamities, notwithstanding that you had before persisted in refusing that office, as all men know?

And who is it that deceives the state? Surely the man who speaks not what he thinks. On whom does the crier pronounce a curse? Surely on such a man. What greater crime can an orator be charged with than that his opinions and his language are not the same? Such is found to be your character. And yet you open your mouth and dare to look these men in the faces! Do you think they don't know you?—or are sunk in such slumber and oblivion as not to remember the speeches which you delivered in the assembly, cursing and swearing that you had nothing to do with Philip, and that I brought that charge against you out of personal enmity without foundation? No sooner came the news of the battle than you forgot all that; you acknowledge and avowed that between Philip and yourself there subsisted a relation of hospitality and friendship—new names these for your contract of hire. For upon what plea of equality or justice could Aeschines, son of Glaucothea, the timbrel player, be the friend or acquaintance of Philip? I cannot see. No! You were hired to ruin the interests of your countrymen; and yet, though you have been caught yourself in open treason, and informed against yourself after the fact, you revile and reproach me for things which you will find any man is chargeable with sooner than I.

Many great and glorious enterprises has the commonwealth, Aeschines, undertaken and succeeded in through me; and she did not forget them. Here is the proof. On the election of a person to speak the funeral oration immediately after the event, you were proposed, but the people would not have you, notwithstanding your fine voice, nor Demades, though he had just made the peace, nor Hegemon, nor any other of your party—but me. And when you and Pythocles came forward in a brutal and shameful manner (O merciful heaven!) and urged the same accusations against me which you now do, and abused me, they elected me all the more. The reason—you are not ignorant of it—yet I will tell you.

The Athenians knew as well the loyalty and zeal with which I conducted their affairs, as the dishonesty of you and your party; for what you denied upon oath in our prosperity, you confessed in the misfortunes of the republic. They considered, therefore, that men who got security for their politics by the public disasters had been their enemies long before, and were then avowedly such. They thought it right also, that the person who was to speak in honor of the fallen and celebrate their valor should not have sat under the same roof or at the same table with their antagonists; that he should not revel there and sing a paean over the calamities of Greece in company with their murderers, and then come here and receive distinction; that he should not with his voice act the mourner of their fate, but that he should lament over them with his heart. This they perceived in themselves and in me, but not in any of you; therefore, they elected me and not you. . . .

There is indeed a retirement just and beneficial to the state, such as you, the bulk of my countrymen, innocently enjoy; that however is not the retirement of Aeschines; far from it. Withdrawing himself from public life when he pleases (and that is often), he watches for the moment when you are tired of a constant speaker, or when some reverse of fortune has befallen you, or anything untoward has happened (and many are the casualties of human life); at such a crisis he springs up an orator, rising from his retreat like a wind; in full voice, with words and phrases collected, he rolls them out audibly and breathlessly, to no advantage or good purpose whatsoever, but to the detriment of some or other of his fellow citizens and to the general disgrace.

Yet from this labor and diligence, Aeschines, if it proceeded from an honest heart, solicitous for your country's welfare, the fruits should have been rich and noble and profitable to all—alliances of states, supplies of money, conveniences of commerce, enactment of useful laws, opposition to our declared enemies. All such things were looked for in former times; and many opportunities did the past afford for a good man and true to show himself; during which time you are nowhere to be found, neither first, second, third, fourth, fifth, nor sixth—not in any rank at all—certainly on no service by which your country was exalted. For what alliance has come to the state by your procurement? What succors, what acquisition of good will or credit? What embassy or agency is there of yours, by which the reputation of the country has been increased? What concern domestic, Hellenic, or foreign, of which you have had the management, has improved under it? What galleys? What ammunition? What arsenals? What repair of walls? What cavalry? What in the world are you good for? What assistance in money have you ever given, either to the rich or the poor, out of public spirit or liberality? None. . . .

My politics and principles, if considered fairly, will be found to resemble those of the illustrious ancients, and to have had the same objects in view, while yours resemble those of their calumniators; for it is certain there were persons in those times, who ran down the living, and praised people dead and gone, with a malignant purpose like yourself. . . .

Two things, men of Athens, are characteristic of a well-disposed citizen—so may I speak of myself and give the least offense: In authority, his constant aim should be the dignity and preeminence of the commonwealth; in all times and circumstances his spirit should be loyal. This depends upon nature; power and might, upon other things. Such a spirit, you will find, I have ever sincerely cherished. Only see. When my person was demanded—when they brought Amphictyonic suits against me—when they menaced—when they promised—when they set these miscreants like wild beasts upon me—never in any way have I abandoned my affection for you. From the very beginning I chose an honest and straightforward course in politics, to support the honor, the power, the glory of my fatherland, these to exalt, in these to have been my being. I do not walk about the marketplace gay and cheerful because the stranger has prospered, holding out my right hand and congratulating those who I think will report it yonder, and on any news of our own success shudder and groan and stoop to the earth, like these impious men, who rail at Athens, as if in so doing they did not rail at themselves; who look abroad, and if the foreigner thrives by the distresses of Greece, are thankful for it, and say we should keep him so thriving to all time.

Never, O ye gods, may those wishes be confirmed by you! If possible, inspire even in these men a better sense and feeling! But if they are indeed incurable, destroy them by themselves; exterminate them on land and sea; and for the rest of us, grant that we may speedily be released from our present fears, and enjoy a lasting deliverance! ∎

John Winthrop Defines the Mission of Government Officials

"LIBERTY is the proper end and object of authority. . . ."

IN 1630, in a sermon aboard the *Arbella* sailing for the New World, Puritan lawyer John Winthrop took a text from Matthew 5:14—"A city that is set on a hill cannot be hid"—and delivered a message to his fellow emigrants that is chiseled in stone on the Boston Common: "For we must consider that we shall be a city upon a hill. The eyes of all people are upon us, so that if we shall deal falsely with our God in this work we have undertaken, and so cause him to withdraw his present help from us, we shall be made a story and a byword through the world." The "city on a hill" metaphor was picked up by John F. Kennedy and used frequently by Ronald Reagan.

Winthrop, elected annually to the governorship twelve times, established what amounted to a conservative, aristocratic theocracy in Massachusetts, but he also began to articulate the need of individual liberty for civil order, a concept that helped form the basis of the early American legal system. He made this speech on behalf of the authority of magistrates at the conclusion of a lawsuit brought against him as governor in 1645 in Plymouth Colony.

□   □   □

. . . We account him a good servant who breaks not his covenant. The covenant between you and us is the oath you have taken of us, which is to this purpose, that we shall govern you and judge your causes by the rules of God's laws and our own, according to our best skill. When you agree with a workman to build you a ship or house, etc., he undertakes as well for his skill as for his faithfulness, for it is his profession, and you pay him for both. But when you call one to be a magistrate, he doth not profess nor undertake to have sufficient skill for that office, nor can you furnish him with gifts, etc.; therefore you must run the hazard of his skill and ability. But if he fails in faithfulness, which by his oath he is bound unto, that he must answer for. . . .

There is a twofold liberty—natural (I mean as our nature is now corrupt) and civil or federal. The first is common to man with beasts and other creatures. By this, man, as he stands in relation to man simply, hath liberty to do what he lists; it is a liberty to evil as well as to good. This liberty is incompatible and inconsistent with authority, and cannot endure the least restraint of the most just authority. The exercise and maintaining of this liberty makes men grow more evil, and in time to be worse than brute beasts: *omnes sumus licentia deteriores.* This is that great enemy of truth and peace, that wild beast, which all the ordinances of God are bent against, to restrain and subdue it.

The other kind of liberty I call civil or federal; it may also be termed moral, in reference to the covenant between God and man, in the moral law, and the politic covenants and constitutions, amongst men themselves. This liberty is the proper end and object of authority, and cannot subsist without it; and it is a liberty to that only which is good, just, and honest. This liberty you are to stand for, with the hazard (not only of your good, but) of your lives, if need be. Whatsoever crosseth this is not authority but a distemper thereof. This liberty is maintained and exercised in a way of subjection to authority; it is of the same kind of liberty wherewith Christ hath made us free. The woman's own choice makes such a man her husband; yet, being so chosen, he is her lord, and she is to be subject to him, yet in a way of liberty, not of bondage; and a true wife accounts her subjection her honor and freedom, and would not think her condition safe and free but in her subjection to her husband's authority. Such is the liberty of the church under the authority of Christ, her king and husband; his yoke is so easy and sweet to her as a bride's ornaments; and if through forwardness or wantonness, etc., she shake it off, at any time, she is at no rest in her spirit until she take it up again; and whether her lord smiles upon her, and embraceth her in his arms, or whether he frowns, or rebukes, or smites her, she apprehends the sweetness of his love in all, and is refreshed, supported, and instructed by every such dispensation of his authority over her.

On the other side, ye know who they are that complain of this yoke and say, let us break their bands, etc. We will not have this man to rule over us. Even so, brethren, it will be between you and your magistrates. If you stand for your natural corrupt liberties, and will do what is good in your own eyes, you will not endure the least weight of authority but will murmur, and oppose, and be always striving to shake off that yoke; but if you will be satisfied to enjoy such civil and lawful liberties, such as Christ allows you, then will you quietly and cheerfully submit unto that authority which is set over you, in all the administrations of it, for your good. Wherein, if we fail at any time, we hope we shall be willing (by God's assistance) to hearken to good advice from any of you, or in any other way of God; so shall your liberties be preserved, in upholding the honor and power of authority amongst you. ■

Edmund Burke Makes a Case for Conciliation with America

"THE use of force alone is but temporary. . . . A nation is not governed which is perpetually to be conquered."

"YOU COULD NOT STAND FIVE MINUTES with that man beneath a shed while it rained," wrote Dr. Samuel Johnson of Edmund Burke, "but you must be convinced you had been standing with the greatest man you had ever seen." The Dublin-born politician apparently carried with him an air of independence and integrity, which gave his well-reasoned speeches and epigrammatic phrases added authority.

In an age of revolution, Burke opposed radical practices but not revolutionary political theory; he favored the abolition of slavery, attacked the exploitation of India in the trial of Warren Hastings, and was the foremost defender of the American colonists' rights. Burke is seen today as a conservative, a political appellation coined after his time, partly because he put individual decision making based on moral or philosophical standards ahead of following the opinion of the majority.

That antidemagogic if not antidemocratic idea was best represented in his speech to the electors of Bristol, then the second-largest city in England, soon after his election in 1774: "Certainly, gentlemen, it ought to be the happiness and glory of a representative to live in the strictest union, the closest correspondence, and the most unreserved communication with his constituents. Their wishes ought to have great weight with him; their opinion high respect; their business unremitted attention. It is his duty to sacrifice his repose, his pleasures, his satisfactions, to theirs; and, above all, ever, and in all cases, to prefer their interest to his own. But his unbiased opinion, his mature judgment, his enlightened conscience, he ought not to sacrifice to you, to any man, or to any set of men living. These he does not derive from your pleasure—no, nor from the law and the Constitution. They are a trust from Providence, for the abuse of which he is deeply answerable. Your representative owes you, not his industry only, but his judgment; and he betrays, instead of serving you, if he sacrifices it to your opinion." Noble thought, puissantly put; politicians today remember that he kept his promise of intellectual independence and lost the next election.

Burke's speech on conciliation with America, made in the House of Commons on March 22, 1775, is notable rhetorically for (a) its shapeliness, the easy-to-follow enumeration, and the march of argument; (b) its internal dialogue, as the speaker asks and at first logically and then passionately answers ("No! surely no!") his own questions; (c) its cascading verbs ("pervades, feeds, unites, invigorates, vivifies"); and (d) its juxtaposition of current events with eternal principles ("Abstract liberty, like other mere abstractions, is not to be found").

□   □   □

. . . **A**merica, gentlemen say, is a noble object. It is an object well worth fighting for. Certainly it is, if fighting a people be the best way of gaining them. Gentlemen in this respect will be led to their choice of means by their complexions and their habits. Those who understand the military art will, of course, have some predilection for it. Those who wield the thunder of the state may have more confidence in the efficacy of arms. But I confess, possibly for want of this knowledge, my opinion is much more in favor of prudent management than of force—considering force not as an odious but a feeble instrument for preserving a people so numerous, so active, so growing, so spirited as this, in a profitable and subordinate connection with us.

First, sir, permit me to observe that the use of force alone is but temporary. It may subdue for a moment, but it does not remove the necessity of subduing again; and a nation is not governed which is perpetually to be conquered.

My next objection is its uncertainty. Terror is not always the effect of force; and an armament is not a victory. If you do not succeed, you are without resource; for, conciliation failing, force remains; but, force failing, no further hope of reconciliation is left. Power and authority are sometimes bought by kindness, but they can never be begged as alms by an impoverished and defeated violence.

A further objection to force is that you impair the object by your very endeavors to preserve it. The thing you fought for is not the thing which you recover, but depreciated, sunk, wasted, and consumed in the contest. Nothing less will content me than *whole* America. I do not choose to consume its strength along with our own, because in all parts it is the British strength that I consume. I do not choose to be caught by a foreign enemy at the end of this exhausting conflict, and still less in the midst of it. I may escape; but I can make no insurance against such an event. Let me add, that I do not choose wholly to break the American spirit, because it is the spirit that has made the country.

Lastly, we have no sort of experience in favor of force as an instrument in the rule of our colonies. Their growth and their utility have been owing to methods altogether different. Our ancient indulgence has been said to be pursued to a fault. It may be so; but we know, if feeling is evidence, that our fault was more tolerable than our attempt to mend it and our sin far more salutary than our penitence.

These, sir, are my reasons for not entertaining that high opinion of untried force by which many gentlemen, for whose sentiments in other particulars I have great respect, seem to be so greatly captivated.

But there is still behind a third consideration concerning this object, which serves to determine my opinion on the sort of policy which ought to be pursued in the management of America, even more than its population and its commerce—I mean its temper and character. In this character of the Americans a love of freedom is the predominating feature which marks and distinguishes the whole; and, as an ardent is always a jealous affection, your colonies become suspicious, restive, and untractable, whenever they see the least attempt to wrest from them by force, or shuffle from them by chicane, what they think the only advantage worth living for. This fierce spirit of liberty is stronger in the English colonies, probably, than in any other people of the earth, and this from a variety of powerful causes, which, to understand the true temper of their minds, and the direction which this spirit takes, it will not be amiss to lay open somewhat more largely.

The people of the colonies are descendants of Englishmen. England, sir, is a nation which still, I hope, respects, and formerly adored, her freedom. The colonists emigrated from you when this part of your character was most predominant; and they took this bias and direction the moment they parted from your hands. They are, therefore, not only devoted to liberty but to liberty according to English ideas and on English principles. Abstract liberty, like other mere abstractions, is not to be found. Liberty inheres in some sensible object; and every nation has formed to itself some favorite point which, by way of eminence, becomes the criterion of their happiness. . . .

Perhaps a more smooth and accommodating spirit of freedom in them would be more acceptable to us. Perhaps ideas of liberty might be desired, more reconcilable with an arbitrary and boundless authority. Perhaps we might wish the colonists to be persuaded that their liberty is more secure when held in trust for them by us, as guardians during a perpetual minority, than with any part of it in their own hands. But the question is not whether their spirit deserves praise or blame. What, in the name of God, shall we do with it? You have before you the object, such as it is, with all its glories, with all its imperfections on its head. You see the magnitude, the importance, the temper, the habits, the disorders. By all these considerations we are strongly urged to determine something concerning it. We are called upon to fix some rule and line for our future conduct which may give a little stability to our politics, and prevent the return of such unhappy deliberations as the present. Every such return will bring the matter before us in a still more untractable form. For, what astonishing and incredible things have we not seen already? What monsters have not been generated from this unnatural contention? . . .

We are indeed, in all disputes with the colonies, by the necessity of things, the judge. It is true, sir; but I confess that the character of judge in my own cause is a thing that frightens me. Instead of filling me with pride, I am exceedingly humbled by it. I cannot proceed with a stem, assured, judicial confidence, until I find myself in something more like a judicial character. . . . Sir, these considerations have great weight with me, when I find things so circumstanced that I see the same party at once a civil litigant against me in point of right and a culprit before me; while I sit as criminal judge on acts of his whose moral quality is to be decided on upon the merits of that very litigation. Men are every now and then put, by the complexity of human affairs, into strange situations; but justice is the same, let the judge be in what situation he will. . . .

In this situation, let us seriously and coolly ponder, what is it we have got by all our menaces, which have been many and ferocious? What advantage have we derived from the penal laws we have passed, and which, for the time, have been severe and numerous? What advances have we made toward our object by the sending of a force which, by land and sea, is no contemptible strength? Has the disorder abated? Nothing less. When I see things in this situation, after such confident hopes, bold promises, and active exertions, I cannot, for my life, avoid a suspicion that the plan itself is not correctly right.

If, then, the removal of the causes of this spirit of American liberty be, for the greater part, or rather entirely, impracticable; if the ideas of criminal process be inapplicable or, if applicable, are in the highest degree inexpedient, what way yet remains? No way is open but the third and last—to comply with the American spirit as necessary or, if you please, to submit to it as a necessary evil.

If we adopt this mode, if we mean to conciliate and concede, let us see of what nature the concessions ought to be. To ascertain the nature of our concessions, we must look at their complaint. The colonies complain that they have not the characteristic mark and seal of British freedom. They complain that they are taxed in Parliament in which they are not represented. If you mean to satisfy them at all, you must satisfy them with regard to this complaint. If you mean to please any people, you must give them the boon which they ask—not what you may think better for them, but of a kind totally different. . . .

Such is steadfastly my opinion of the absolute necessity of keeping up the concord of this empire by a unity of spirit, though in a diversity of operations, that, if I were sure the colonists had, at their leaving this country, sealed a regular compact of servitude; that they had solemnly abjured all the rights of citizens; that they had made a vow to renounce all ideas of liberty for them and their posterity to all generations, yet I should hold myself obliged to conform to the temper I found universally prevalent in my own day, and to govern two millions of men, impatient of servitude, on the principles of freedom. I am not determining a point of law. I am restoring tranquillity, and the general character and situation of a people must determine what sort of government is fitted for them. That point nothing else can or ought to determine.

My idea, therefore, without considering whether we yield as matter of right, or grant as matter of favor, is *to admit the people of our colonies into an interest in the Constitution,* and, by recording that admission in the journals of Parliament, to give them as strong an assurance as the nature of the thing will admit, that we mean forever to adhere to that solemn declaration of systematic indulgence. . . .

The Americans will have no interest contrary to the grandeur and glory of England, when they are not oppressed by the weight of it; and they will rather be inclined to respect the acts of a superintending legislature, when they see them the acts of that power which is itself the security, not the rival, of their secondary importance. In this assurance my mind most perfectly acquiesces, and I confess I feel not the least alarm from the discontents which are to arise from putting people at their ease; nor do I apprehend the destruction of this empire from giving, by an act of free grace and indulgence, to two millions of my fellow citizens, some share of those rights upon which I have always been taught to value myself. . . .

A revenue from America transmitted hither—do not delude yourselves—you never can receive it—no, not a shilling. We have experienced that from remote countries it is not to be expected. If, when you attempted to extract revenue from Bengal, you were obliged to return in loan what you had taken in imposition, what can you expect from North America? For certainly, if ever there was a country qualified to produce wealth, it is India; or an institution fit for the transmission, it is the East India Company. America has none of these aptitudes. If America gives you taxable objects on which you lay your duties here, and gives you, at the same time, a surplus by a foreign sale of her commodities to pay the duties on these objects which you tax at home, she has performed her part to the British revenue. But with regard to her own internal establishments, she may, I doubt not she will, contribute in moderation; I say in moderation, for she ought not to be permitted to exhaust herself. She ought to be reserved to a war, the weight of which, with the enemies that we are most likely to have, must be considerable in her quarter of the globe. There she may serve you, and serve you essentially.

For that service, for all service, whether of revenue, trade, or empire, my trust is in her interest in the British Constitution. My hold of the colonies is in the close affection which grows from common names, from kindred blood, from similar privileges, and equal protection. These are ties which, though light as air, are as strong as links of iron. Let the colonies always keep the idea of their civil rights associated with your government; they will cling and grapple to you, and no force under heaven will be of power to tear them from their allegiance. But let it be once understood that your government may be one thing, and their privileges another;

that these two things may exist without any mutual relation; the cement is gone; the cohesion is loosened; and everything hastens to decay and dissolution. As long as you have the wisdom to keep the sovereign authority of this country as the sanctuary of liberty, the sacred temple consecrated to our common faith, wherever the chosen race and sons of England worship freedom, they will turn their faces toward you. The more they multiply, the more friends you will have. The more ardently they love liberty, the more perfect will be their obedience. Slavery they can have anywhere. It is a weed that grows in every soil. They may have it from Spain; they may have it from Prussia; but, until you become lost to all feeling of your true interest and your natural dignity, freedom they can have from none but you. This is the commodity of price, of which you have the monopoly. This is the true Act of Navigation, which binds to you the commerce of the colonies, and through them secures to you the wealth of the world. Deny them this participation of freedom, and you break that sole bond which originally made, and must still preserve, the unity of the empire. Do not entertain so weak an imagination as that your registers and your bonds, your affidavits and your sufferances, your cockets and your clearances, are what form the great securities of your commerce. Do not dream that your letters of office, and your instructions, and your suspending clauses are the things that hold together the great contexture of this mysterious whole. These things do not make your government. Dead instruments, passive tools as they are, it is the spirit of the English communion that gives all their life and efficacy to them. It is the spirit of the English Constitution which, infused through the mighty mass, pervades, feeds, unites, invigorates, vivifies every part of the empire, even down to the minutest member.

Is it not the same virtue which does everything for us here in England?

Do you imagine, then, that it is the land tax which raises your revenue, that it is the annual vote in the committee of supply which gives you your army? Or that it is the mutiny bill which inspires it with bravery and discipline? No! surely no! It is the love of the people; it is their attachment to their government, from the sense of the deep stake they have in such a glorious institution, which gives you your army and your navy, and infuses into both that liberal obedience without which your army would be a base rabble and your navy nothing but rotten timber.

All this, I know well enough, will sound wild and chimerical to the profane herd of those vulgar and mechanical politicians, who have no place among us—a sort of people who think that nothing exists but what is gross and material and who, therefore, far from being qualified to be directors of the great movement of empire, are not fit to turn a wheel in the machine. But to men truly initiated and rightly taught, these ruling and master principles, which, in the opinion of such men as I have mentioned, have no substantial existence, are in truth everything and all in all. Magnanimity in politics is not seldom the truest wisdom; and a great empire and little minds go ill together. If we are conscious of our situation, and glow with zeal to fill our place as becomes our station and ourselves, we ought to auspicate all our public proceeding on America with the old warning of the church *Sursum corda!* We ought to elevate our minds to the greatness of that trust to which the order of Providence has called us. By adverting to the dignity of this high calling, our ancestors have turned a savage wilderness into a glorious empire, and have made the most extensive and the only honorable conquests, not by destroying, but by promoting, the wealth, the number, the happiness of the human race. Let us get an American revenue as we have got an American empire. English privileges have made it all that it is; English privileges alone will make it all it can be.

In full confidence of this unalterable truth, I now, *quod felix faustumque sit,* lay the first stone in the temple of peace; and I move you, "That the colonies and plantations of Great Britain in North America, consisting of fourteen separate governments, and containing two millions and upwards of free inhabitants, have not had the liberty and privilege of electing and sending any knights and burgesses, or others, to represent them in the high court of Parliament." ■

Benjamin Franklin Addresses the Federal Convention

"I consent, sir, to this Constitution because I expect no better, and because I am not sure that it is not the best."

THE CONSTITUTIONAL CONVENTION was made up of young men, half under forty; Benjamin Franklin of Pennsylvania was eighty-two, twenty years older than anybody else there, and the most adept conciliator. Although his ideas for a plural executive and unsalaried officials were rejected, his was the compromise that made an amalgamation of large and small states possible: the states would be represented equally in the Senate and the people equally in the House.

Franklin was too infirm to deliver the speeches he wrote. On September 17, 1787, as the wrangled-over Constitution was set to be signed—despite the misgivings of many of those present—lawyer James Wilson read Franklin's words in Independence Hall. The proceedings were secret, but within ten weeks copies were available in Boston. One of the leakers was Franklin himself, who sent "a Copy of that little Speech" to a printer friend there; it was reprinted widely, contributing—despite its doubtful tone—to the pressure toward ratification by the states.

The document produced by the delegates in Philadelphia has acquired the status of American scripture, its original copies viewed reverently and the intent of the founders in some passages hotly debated. A certain irony exists in the way the Constitution was introduced by Franklin: not great, but nothing better could be expected. In not overselling it, he helped sell it to his fellow doubters.

□   □   □

Mr. President, I confess that I do not entirely approve of this Constitution at present, but, sir, I am not sure I shall never approve it: for, having lived long, I have experienced many instances of being obliged, by better information or fuller consideration, to change opinions even on important subjects, which I once thought right, but found to be otherwise. It is therefore that the older I grow, the more apt I am to doubt my own judgment, and to pay more respect to the judgment of others. Most men, indeed, as well as most sects in religion, think themselves in possession of all truth, and that wherever others differ from them it is so far error. Steele, a Protestant, in a dedication tells the pope that the only difference between our two churches, in their opinions of the certainty of their doctrine, is, the Romish church is infallible and the Church of England is never in the wrong. But though many private persons think almost as highly of their own infallibility as of that of their sect, few express it so naturally as a certain French lady, who in a little dispute with her sister, said, I don't know how it happens, Sister, but I meet with nobody but myself that's *always* in the right. *Il n'y a que moi qui a toujours raison.*

In these sentiments, sir, I agree to this Constitution, with all its faults, if they are such; because I think a general government necessary for us, and there is no *form* of government but what may be a blessing to the people if well administered; and I believe farther that this is likely to be well administered for a course of years, and can only end in despotism as other forms have done before it, when the people shall become so corrupted as to need despotic government, being incapable of any other. I doubt, too, whether any other convention we can obtain may be able to make a better constitution: for when you assemble a number of men to have the advantage of their joint wisdom, you inevitably assemble with those men all their prejudices, their passions, their errors of opinion, their local interests, and their selfish views. From such an assembly can a perfect production be expected? It therefore astonishes me, sir, to find this system approaching so near to perfection as it does; and I think it will astonish our enemies, who are waiting with confidence to hear that our councils are confounded, like those of the builders of Babel, and that our states are on the point of separation, only to meet hereafter for the purpose of cutting one another's throats. Thus I consent, sir, to this Constitution because I expect no better, and because I am not sure that it is not the best. The opinions I have had of its errors, I sacrifice to the public good. I have never whispered a syllable of them abroad. Within these walls they were born, and here they shall die. If every one of us in returning to our constituents were to report the objections he has had to it, and use his influence to gain partisans in support of them, we might prevent its being generally received, and thereby lose all the salutary effects and great advantages resulting naturally in our favor among foreign nations, as well as among ourselves, from our real or apparent unanimity. Much of the strength and efficiency of any government, in procuring and securing happiness to the people depends on opinion, on the general opinion of the goodness of that government as well as of the wisdom and integrity of its governors. I hope therefore that for our own sakes, as a part of the people, and for the sake of our posterity, we shall act heartily and unanimously in recommending this constitution, wherever our influence may extend, and turn our future thoughts and endeavors to the means of having it well administered.

On the whole, sir, I cannot help expressing a wish that every member of the convention who may still have objections to it would with me on this occasion doubt a little of his own infallibility, and, to make *manifest* our *unanimity*, put his name to this instrument. ■

Thomas Jefferson Appeals for Unity at His Inauguration

"SOMETIMES it is said that man cannot be trusted with the government of himself. Can he, then, be trusted with the government of others?"

"A LITTLE REBELLION now and then is a good thing," Thomas Jefferson wrote to James Madison in 1787 from his post in Paris; other founders in the United States, facing local rebellions that imperiled the new nation, could not afford such detached idealism.

A leader of the American Revolution and a man of far-ranging interests, Thomas Jefferson served in various positions after the Revolution, including those of governor of Virginia and secretary of state. Before his death in

1826, he chose this epitaph for his gravesite: "Here was buried Thomas Jefferson, author of the Declaration of American Independence, of the statute of Virginia for religious freedom, and father of the University of Virginia." No mention is made there of his presidency, but in 1800 Jefferson was elected to the first of his two terms; speechwriters on the subject of education have cited that order of his priorities ever since.

Jefferson's first inaugural address, delivered when he became the third U.S. president, was the first to be delivered in Washington, D.C. A proponent of agrarian democracy and states' rights, he listed in his speech the concerns of his administration, beginning with "equal and exact justice to all men." Although more powerful as a writer than as a speaker, and despite his having led the Anti-Federalists' partisan challenge to Hamiltonian centralism, he sought to unite warring parties with his stirring contention "We are all Republicans; we are all Federalists," aiming to "pursue our own federal and republican principles." With the repeated use of "Let us" as a uniting imperative, he established the priorities of government and drew from some ancient imagery to support his position; borrowing a "ship of state" metaphor that predates Sophocles, Jefferson asked "for that guidance and support which may enable us to steer with safety the vessel in which we are all embarked."

□   □   □

Friends and fellow citizens, called upon to undertake the duties of the first executive office of our country, I avail myself of the presence of that portion of my fellow citizens which is here assembled, to express my grateful thanks for the favor with which they have been pleased to look toward me, to declare a sincere consciousness, that the task is above my talents, and that I approach it with those anxious and awful presentiments which the greatness of the charge, and the weakness of my powers, so justly inspire. A rising nation, spread over a wide and fruitful land, traversing all the seas with the rich productions of their industry, engaged in commerce with nations who feel power and forget right, advancing rapidly to destinies beyond the reach of mortal eye—when I contemplate these transcendent objects, and see the honor, the happiness, and the hopes of this beloved country committed to the issue and the auspices of this day, I shrink from the contemplation, and humble myself before the magnitude of the undertaking. Utterly, indeed, should I despair, did not the presence of many whom I see here remind me that, in the other high authorities provided by our constitution, I shall find resources of wisdom, of virtue, and of zeal, on which to rely under all difficulties. To you, then, gentlemen, who are charged with the sovereign functions of legislation, and to those associated with you, I look with encouragement for that guidance and support which may enable us to steer with safety the vessel in which we are all embarked, amidst the conflicting elements of a troubled world.

During the contest of opinion through which we have passed, the animation of discussions and of exertions has sometimes worn an aspect which might impose on strangers unused to think freely, and to speak and to write what they think; but this being now decided by the voice of the nation, announced according to the rules of the Constitution, all will, of course, arrange themselves under the will of the law and unite in common efforts for the common good. All, too, will bear in mind this sacred principle, that though the will of the majority is in all cases to prevail, that will, to be rightful, must be reasonable; that the minority possess their equal rights, which equal laws must protect, and to violate which would be oppression.

Let us then, fellow citizens, unite with one heart and one mind; let us restore to social intercourse that harmony and affection without which liberty and even life itself are but dreary things. And let us reflect that, having banished from our land that religious intolerance under which mankind so long bled and suffered, we have yet gained little, if we countenance a political intolerance, as despotic, as wicked, and as capable of as bitter and bloody persecutions. During the throes and convulsions of the ancient world, during the agonizing spasms of infuriated man, seeking through blood and slaughter his long-lost liberty, it was not wonderful that the agitation of the billows should reach even this distant and peaceful shore; that this should be more felt and feared by some, and less by others, and should divide opinions as to measures of safety; but every difference of opinion is not a difference of principle. We have called by different names brethren of the same principle. We are all Republicans; we are all Federalists. If there be any among us who wish to dissolve this Union, or to change its republican form, let them stand undisturbed as monuments of the safety with which error of opinion may be tolerated, where reason is left free to combat it. I know, indeed, that some honest men fear that a republican government cannot be strong, that this government is not strong enough. But would the honest patriot, in the full tide of successful experiment, abandon a government which has so far kept us free and firm, on the theoretic and visionary fear, that this government, the world's best hope, may, by possibility, want energy to preserve itself? I trust not. I believe this, on the contrary, the strongest government on earth. I believe it the only one where every man, at the call of the law, would fly to the standard of the law, and would meet invasions of the public order as his own personal concern. Sometimes it is said that man cannot be trusted with the government of himself. Can he, then, be trusted with the government of others? Or have we found angels, in the form of kings, to govern him? Let history answer this question.

Let us, then, with courage and confidence, pursue our own federal and republican principles, our attachment to union and representative government. Kindly separated by nature and a wide ocean from the exterminating havoc of one quarter of the globe; too high-minded to endure the degradation of the others, possessing a chosen country, with room enough for our descendants to the thousandth and thousandth generation, entertaining a due sense of our equal right to the use of our own faculties, to the acquisition of our own industry, to honor and confidence from our fellow citizens, resulting not from birth but from our actions and their sense of them, enlightened by a benign religion, professed in deed and practiced in various forms, yet all of them inculcating honesty, truth, temperance, gratitude, and the love of man, acknowledging and adoring an overruling Providence, which, by all its dispensations, proves that it delights in the happiness of man here, and his greater happiness hereafter—with all these blessings, what more is necessary to make us a happy and prosperous people? Still one thing more, fellow citizens, a wise and frugal government, which shall restrain men from injuring one another, shall leave them otherwise free to regulate their own pursuits of industry and improvement, and shall not take from the mouth of labor the bread it has earned. This is the sum of good government; and this is necessary to close the circle of our felicities.

About to enter, fellow citizens, upon the exercise of duties which comprehend everything dear and valuable to you, it is proper you should understand what I deem the essential principles of our government and, consequently, those which ought to shape its administration. I will compress them within the narrowest compass they will bear, stating the general principle, but not all its limitations. Equal and exact justice to all men, of whatever state or persuasion, religious or political; peace, commerce, and honest friendship with all nations, entangling alliances with none; the support of the state governments in all their rights, as the most competent administrations for our domestic concerns, and the surest bulwarks against antirepublican tendencies; the preservation of the general government in its whole constitutional vigor, as the sheet anchor of our peace at home and safety abroad; a jealous care of the right of election by the people. a mild and safe corrective of abuses which are lopped by the sword of revolution where peaceable remedies are unprovided; absolute acquiescence in the decisions of the majority, the vital principle of republics, from which there is no appeal but to force, the vital principle and immediate parent of despotism; a well-disciplined militia, our best reliance in peace, and for the first moments of war, till regulars may relieve them; the supremacy of the civil over the military authority; economy in the public expense, that labor may be lightly burdened; the honest payment of our debts, and sacred preservation of the public faith; encouragement of agriculture, and of commerce as its handmaid; the dif-fusion of information, and arraignment of all abuses at the bar of the public reason; freedom of religion, freedom of the press, and freedom of person, under the protection of the habeas corpus, and trial by juries impartially selected. These principles form the bright constellation, which has gone before us, and guided our steps through an age of revolution and reformation. The wisdom of our sages, and blood of our heroes, have been devoted to their attainment; they should be the creed of our politi-cal faith, the text of civic instruction, the touchstone by which to try the services of those we trust; and should we wander from them in moments of error or of alarm, let us hasten to retrace our steps and to regain the road which alone leads to peace, liberty, and safety.

I repair, then, fellow citizens, to the post you have assigned me. With experience enough in subordinate offices to have seen the difficulties of this, the greatest of all, I have learned to expect that it will rarely fall to the lot of imperfect man, to retire from this station with the reputation and the favor which bring him into it. Without pretensions to that high confidence you reposed in our first and greatest revolutionary character, whose preeminent services had entitled him to the first place in his coun-try's love, and destined for him the fairest page of the volume of faithful history, I ask so much confidence only as may give firmness and effect to the legal administration of your affairs. I shall often go wrong through defect of judgment. When right, I shall often be thought wrong by those whose positions will not command a view of the whole ground. I ask your indulgence for my own errors, which will never be intentional; and your support against the errors of others, who may condemn what they would not, if seen in all its parts. The approbation implied by your suf-frage is a great consolation to me for the past; and my future solicitude will be to retain the good opinion of those who have bestowed it in advance, to conciliate that of others, by doing them all the good in my power, and to be instrumental to the happiness and freedom of all.

Relying, then, on the patronage of your good will, I advance with obedience to the work, ready to retire from it whenever you become sensible how much better choices it is in your power to make. And may that infinite power which rules the destinies of the universe lead our councils to what is best, and give them a favorable issue for your peace and prosperity. ∎

Historian-Legislator Thomas Macaulay Calls on Parliament to Lift the Political Restrictions on the Jews

"LET us do justice to them. Let us open to them the door of the House of Commons. Let us open to them every career in which ability and energy can be displayed. Till we have done this, let us not presume to say that there is no genius among the countrymen of Isaiah, no heroism among the descendants of the Maccabees."

THE NEED FOR "THE BEST GOVERNMENT" concerned Thomas Babington Macaulay, British author and historian born at the turn of the nineteenth century. At twenty-four, he wrote, "That is the best government which desires to make the people happy, and knows how to make them happy." Six years later, this Whig orator was elected to Parliament, where he advocated such radical causes as free trade, the abolition of slavery, and freedom of the press. As a historian, he had an uncommon grasp of metaphor, writing to a Jefferson biographer, "Your Constitution is all sail and no anchor." About Machiavelli, he turned this line: "Nothing is so useless as a general maxim." And his aphorisms were insightful: "Reform, that you may preserve" and "There is only one cure for the evils which newly acquired freedom produces, and that cure is freedom." This led William Lamb to conclude, "I wish I was as cocksure of anything as Tom Macaulay is of everything."

Nobody could construct a long sentence better, or one that could be read with more effectiveness, than this historian-legislator. In a speech to the House of Commons on October 10, 1831, urging that society must be governed by public opinion rather than the sword, there appears this passage:

"Sir, we read that, in old times, when the villeins were driven to revolt by oppression, when the castles of the nobility were burned to the ground, when the warehouses of London were pillaged, when a hundred thousand insurgents appeared in arms on Blackheath, when a foul murder perpetrated in their presence had raised their passions to madness, when they were looking round for some captain to succeed and avenge him whom they had lost—just then, before Hob Miller, or Tom Carter, or Jack Straw, could place himself at their head, the king rode up to them, and exclaimed, 'I will be your leader!'—and at once the infuriated multitude laid down their arms, submitted to his guidance, dispersed at his command."

That was followed by a paragraph of short, powerful sentences: "Herein let us imitate him. Let us say to the people, 'We are your leaders—we, your own House of Commons.' This tone it is our interest and our duty to take. The circumstances admit of no delay. Even while I speak, the moments are passing away—the irrevocable moments, pregnant with the destiny of a great people. The country is in danger; it may be saved: we can save it. This is the way—this is the time. In our hands are the issues of great good and great evil—the issues of the life and death of the state."

It was in his maiden speech to the House of Commons on April 17, 1833, that Macaulay startled his elders.

□   □   □

. . . **M**y honorable friend, the member for the University of Oxford, began his speech by declaring that he had no intention of calling in question the principles of religious liberty. He utterly disclaims persecution, that is to say, persecution as defined by himself. It would, in his opinion, be persecution to hang a Jew, or to flay him, or to draw his teeth, or to imprison him, or to fine him; for every man who conducts himself peaceably has a right to his life and his limbs, to his personal liberty and his property. But it is not persecution, says my honorable friend, to exclude any individual or any class from office; for nobody has a right to office: In every country official appointments must be subject to such regulations as the supreme authority may choose to make; nor can any such regulations be reasonably complained of by any member of the society as unjust. He who obtains an office obtains it, not as matter of right, but as matter of favor. He who does not obtain an office is not wronged; he is only in that situation in which the vast majority of every community must necessarily be. There are in the United Kingdom five-and-twenty million Christians without places; and, if they do not complain, why should five-and-twenty thousand Jews complain of being in the same case? . . .

Now, surely my honorable friend cannot have considered to what conclusions his reasoning leads. Those conclusions are so monstrous that he would, I am certain, shrink from them. Does he really mean that it would not be wrong in the legislature to enact that no man should be a judge unless he weighed twelve stone, or that no man should sit in Parliament unless he were six feet high? . . . And would he think himself sufficiently answered by being told, in his own words, that the appointment to office is a mere matter of favor, and that to exclude an individual or a class from office is no injury? . . .

My honorable friend has appealed to us as Christians. Let me, then, ask him how he understands that great commandment which comprises the law and the prophets. Can we be said to do unto others as we would that they should do unto us if we wantonly inflict on them even the smallest pain? As Christians, surely we are bound to consider first, whether, by excluding the Jews from all public trust, we give them pain; and, secondly, whether it be necessary to give them that pain in order to avert some greater evil. That by excluding them from public trust we inflict pain on them my honorable friend will not dispute. As a Christian, therefore, he is bound to relieve them from that pain unless he can show, what I am sure he has not yet shown, that it is necessary to the general good that they should continue to suffer.

But where, he says, are you to stop, if once you admit into the House of Commons people who deny the authority of the Gospels? Will you let in a Mussulman [Muslim]? Will you let in a Parsee? Will you let in a Hindoo, who worships a lump of stone with seven heads? I will answer my honorable friend's question by another. Where does he mean to stop? Is he ready to roast unbelievers at slow fires? If not, let him tell us why: and I will engage to prove that his reason is just as decisive against the intolerance which he thinks a duty as against the intolerance which he thinks a crime. Once admit that we are bound to inflict pain on a man because he is not of our religion, and where are you to stop?

Why stop at the point fixed by my honorable friend rather than at the point fixed by the honorable member for Oldham, who would make the Jews incapable of holding land? And why stop at the point fixed by the honorable member for Oldham rather than at the point which would have been fixed by a Spanish Inquisitor of the sixteenth century? When once you enter on a course of persecution, I defy you to find any reason for making a halt till you have reached the extreme point.

When my honorable friend tells us that he will allow the Jews to possess property to any amount, but that he will not allow them to possess the smallest political power, he holds contradictory language. Property is power. The honorable member for Oldham reasons better than my honorable friend. The honorable member for Oldham sees very clearly that it is impossible to deprive a man of political power if you suffer him to be the proprietor of half a county, and therefore very consistently proposes to confiscate the landed estates of the Jews. But even the honorable member for Oldham does not go far enough. He has not proposed to confiscate the personal property of the Jews. Yet it is perfectly certain that any Jew who has a million may easily make himself very important in the state. By such steps we pass from official power to landed property, and from landed property to personal property, and from property to liberty, and from liberty to life. . . .

My honorable friend should either persecute to some purpose, or not persecute at all. He dislikes the word persecution, I know. He will not admit that the Jews are persecuted. And yet I am confident that he would rather be sent to the King's Bench Prison for three months, or be fined a hundred pounds, than be subject to the disabilities under which the Jews lie. How can he, then, say that to impose such disabilities is not persecution, and that to fine and imprison is persecution? All his reasoning consists in drawing arbitrary lines. What he does not wish to inflict he calls persecution. What he does wish to inflict he will not call persecution. What he takes from the Jews he calls political power. What he is too good-natured to take from the Jews he will not call political power. The Jew must not sit in Parliament: but he may be the proprietor of all the ten-pound houses in a borough. He may have more fifty-pound tenants than any peer in the kingdom. He may give the voters treats to please their palates, and hire bands of gypsies to break their heads, as if he were a Christian and a marquess. All the rest of this system is of a piece. The Jew may be a juryman, but not a judge. He may decide issues of fact, but not issues of law. He may give a hundred thousand pounds damages; but he may not in the most trivial case grant a new trial. He may rule the money market: He may influence the exchanges: He may be summoned to congresses of emperors and kings. Great potentates, instead of negotiating a loan with him by tying him in a chair and pulling out his grinders, may treat with him as with a great potentate, and may postpone the declaring of war or the signing of a treaty till they have conferred with him. All this is as it should be: but he must not be a privy councillor. He must not be called Right Honorable, for that is political power.

And who is it that we are trying to cheat in this way? Even Omniscience. Yes, sir; we have been gravely told that the Jews are under the divine displeasure, and that if we give them political power God will visit us in judgment. Do we, then, think that God cannot distinguish between substance and form? Does not He know that, while we withhold from the Jews the semblance and name of political power, we suffer them to possess the substance? The plain truth is that my honorable friend is drawn in one direction by his opinions, and in a directly opposite direction by his excellent heart. He halts between two opinions. He tries to make a compromise between principles which admit of no compromise. He goes a certain way in intolerance. Then he stops, without being able to give a reason for stopping. But I know the reason. It is his humanity. Those who formerly dragged the Jew at a horse's tail, and singed his beard with blazing furze-bushes, were much worse men than my honorable friend; but they were more consistent than he. . . .

But, says my honorable friend, it has been prophesied that the Jews are to be wanderers on the face of the earth, and that they are not to mix on terms of equality with the people of the countries in which they sojourn. Now, sir, I am confident that I can demonstrate that this is not the sense of any prophecy which is part of Holy Writ. For it is an undoubted fact that, in the United States of America, Jewish citizens do possess all the privileges possessed by Christian citizens. Therefore, if the prophecies mean that the Jews never shall, during their wanderings, be admitted by other nations to equal participation of political rights, the prophecies are false. But the prophecies are certainly not false. Therefore, their meaning cannot be that which is attributed to them by my honorable friend.

Another objection which has been made to this motion is that the Jews look forward to the coming of a great deliverer, to their return to Palestine, to the rebuilding of their temple, to the revival of their ancient worship, and that therefore they will always consider England, not their country, but merely as their place of exile. But, surely, sir, it would be the grossest ignorance of human nature to imagine that the anticipation of an event which is to happen at some time altogether indefinite, of an event which has been vainly expected during many centuries, of an event which even those who confidently expect that it will happen do not confidently expect that they or their children or their grandchildren will see, can ever occupy the minds of men to such a degree as to make them regardless of what is near and present and certain. Indeed, Christians, as well as Jews, believe that the existing order of things will come to an end. Many Christians believe that Jesus will visibly reign on earth during a thousand years. Expositors of prophecy have gone so far as to fix the year when the millennial period is to commence. The prevailing opinion is, I think, in favor of the year 1866; but, according to some commentators, the time is close at hand. Are we to exclude all millenarians from Parliament and office on the ground that they are impatiently looking forward to the miraculous monarchy which is to supersede the present dynasty and the present Constitution of England, and that therefore they cannot be heartily loyal to King William?

In one important point, sir, my honorable friend, the member for the University of Oxford, must acknowledge that the Jewish religion is of all erroneous religions the least mischievous. There is not the slightest chance that the Jewish religion will spread. The Jew does not wish to make proselytes. He may be said to reject them. He thinks it almost culpable in one who does not belong to his race to presume to belong to his religion. It is therefore not strange that a conversion from Christianity to Judaism should be a rarer occurrence than a total eclipse of the sun. There was one distinguished convert in the last century, Lord George Gordon; and the history of his conversion deserves to be remembered. For if ever there was a proselyte of whom a proselytizing sect would have been proud, it was Lord George; not only because he was a man of high birth and rank; not only because he had been a member of the legislature; but also because he had been distinguished by the intolerance nay, the ferocity, of his zeal for his own form of Christianity. But was he allured into the synagogue? Was he even welcomed to it? No, sir; he was coldly and reluctantly permitted to share the reproach and suffering of the chosen people; but he was sternly shut out from their privileges. He underwent the painful rite which their law enjoins. But when, on his deathbed, he begged hard to be buried among them according to their ceremonial, he was told that his request could not be granted.

I understand that cry of "Hear." It reminds me that one of the arguments against this motion is that the Jews are an unsocial people, that they draw close to each other and stand aloof from strangers. Really, sir, it is amusing to compare the manner in which the question of Catholic emancipation was argued formerly by some gentlemen with the manner in which the question of Jew emancipation is argued by the same gentlemen now. When the question was about Catholic emancipation, the cry was, "See how restless, how versatile, how encroaching, how insinuating, is the spirit of the Church of Rome. See how her priests compass earth and sea to make one proselyte, how indefatigably they toil, how attentively they study the weak and strong parts of every character, how skilfully they employ literature, arts, sciences, as engines for the propagation of their faith. You find them in every region and under every disguise, collating manuscripts in the Bodleian, fixing telescopes in the Observatory of Peking, teaching the use of the plough and the spinning wheel to the savages of Paraguay. Will you give power to the members of a Church so busy, so aggressive, so insatiable?" Well, now the question is about people who never try to seduce any stranger to join them, and who do not wish anybody to be of their faith who is not also of their blood. And now you exclaim. "Will you give power to the members of a sect which remains sullenly apart from other sects, which does not invite, any, which hardly even admits, neophytes?" The truth is, that bigotry will never want a pretence. Whatever the sect be which it is proposed to tolerate, the peculiarities of that sect will, for the time, be pronounced by intolerant men to be the most odious and dangerous that can be conceived. . . .

Another charge has been brought against the Jews, not by my honorable friend the member for the University of Oxford—he has too much learning and too much good feeling to make such a charge—but by the honorable member for Oldham, who has, I am sorry to see, quitted his place. The honorable member for Oldham tells us that the Jews are naturally a mean race, a sordid race, a money-getting race; that they are averse to all honorable callings; that they neither sow nor reap; that they have neither flocks nor herds; that usury is the only pursuit for which they are fit; that they are destitute of all elevated and amiable sentiments. Such, sir, has in every age been the reasoning of bigots. They never fail to plead in justification of persecution the vices which persecution has engendered. England has been to the Jews less than half a country; and we revile them because they do not feel for England more than a half patriotism. We treat them as slaves, and wonder that they do not regard us as brethren. We drive them to mean occupations, and then reproach them for not embracing honorable professions. We long forbade them to possess land; and we complain that they chiefly occupy themselves in trade. We shut them out from all the paths of ambition; and then we despise them for taking refuge in avarice. During many ages we have, in all our dealings with them, abused our immense superiority of force; and then we are disgusted because they have recourse to that cunning which is the natural and universal defence of the weak against the violence of the strong. But were they always a mere money-changing, money-getting, money-hoarding race? Nobody knows better than my honorable friend the member for the University of Oxford that there is nothing in their national character which unfits them for the highest duties of citizens. He knows that, in the infancy of civilization, when our island was as savage as New Guinea, when letters and arts were still unknown to Athens, when scarcely a thatched hut stood on what was afterwards the site of Rome, this contemned people had their fenced cities and cedar palaces, their splendid Temple, their fleets of merchant ships, their schools of sacred learning, their great statesmen and soldiers, their natural philosophers, their historians and their poets. What nation ever contended more manfully against overwhelming odds for its independence and religion? What nation ever, in its last agonies, gave such signal proofs of what may be accomplished by a brave despair? And if, in the course of many centuries, the oppressed descendants of warriors and sages have degenerated from the qualities of their fathers, if, while excluded from the blessings of law, and bowed down under the yoke of slavery, they, have contracted some of the vices of outlaws and of slaves, shall we consider this as matter of reproach to them? Shall we not rather consider it as matter of shame and remorse to ourselves? Let us do justice to them. Let us open to them the door of the House of Commons. Let us open to them every career in which ability and energy can be displayed. Till we have done this, let us not presume to say that there is no genius among the countrymen of Isaiah, no heroism among the descendants of the Maccabees.

Sir, in supporting the motion of my honorable friend, I am, I firmly believe, supporting the honor and the interests of the Christian religion. I should think that I insulted that religion if I said that it cannot stand unaided by intolerant laws. Without such laws, it was established, and without such laws it may be maintained. It triumphed over the superstitions of the most refined and of the most savage nations, over the graceful mythology of Greece and the bloody idolatry of the northern forests. It prevailed over the power and policy of the Roman empire. It tamed the barbarians by whom that empire was overthrown. But all these victories were gained not by the help of intolerance, but in spite of the opposition of intolerance. The whole history of Christianity proves that she has little indeed to fear from persecution as a foe, but much to fear from persecution as an ally. May she long continue to bless our country with her benignant influence, strong in her sublime philosophy, strong in her spotless morality, strong in those internal and external evidences to which the most powerful and comprehensive of human intellects have yielded assent, the last solace of those who have outlived every earthly hope, the last restraint of those who are raised above every earthly fear! But let not us, mistaking her character and her interests, fight the battle of truth with the weapons of error, and endeavor to support by oppression that religion which first taught the human race the great lesson of universal charity. ■

William Cobbett Heaps Scorn on Opponents of His Bill to Reduce Child Labor

"THREE hundred thousand little girls, from whose labor, if we only deduct two hours a day, away goes the wealth, away goes the capital, away go the resources, the power, and the glory of England!"

COBBETT, WHO USED THE PSEUDONYM PETER PORCUPINE, was the first media giant. He attacked the army establishment in England and was driven to America to escape prosecution; in Philadelphia, he supported the despised King George III and was hit with the largest libel judgment yet levied in America; returning to England, he turned on the government there and was jailed for libel. Yet, wherever Cobbett wrote, his iconoclastic prose was widely read by commoners, and his vigorous diatribes and denunciations marshaled the force of public opinion as never before. Essayist William Hazlitt marveled at Cobbett's patriotism of contrariety and coined a phrase that has been applied to journalism ever since: "One has no notion of him as making use of a fine pen, but a great mutton-fist; his style stuns his readers. . . . He is a kind of *fourth estate* in the politics of the country."

The lifelong agitator was elected to Parliament in 1833, and he covered his own speeches in his *Political Register*. One bill he supported was to reduce the long hours of girls under eighteen working in factories; he recounted the triumph of the mill owners in his reform journal:

"The debate was closing at half-after twelve; and the main argument of the opponents was that if two hours' labor from these children, under eighteen years of age, were taken off, the consequences, on a *national scale,* might be 'truly dreadful'! It might, and would, destroy manufacturing capital; prevent us from carrying on competition with foreign manufacturers; reduce mills to a small part of their present value; and break up, as it were, the wealth and power of the country; render it comparatively feeble; and expose it to be an easy prey to foreign nations. What I said, was that which here follows, as near as I can recollect, word for word."

□   □   □

Sir, I will make but one single observation upon this subject; and that is this: that this *"reformed"* House has, this night, made a *discovery* greater than all the discoveries that all former Houses of Commons have ever made, even if all their discoveries could have been put into one. Heretofore, we have sometimes been told that our ships, our mercantile traffic with foreign nations by the means of those ships, together with our body of rich merchants; we have sometimes been told that these form the source of our wealth, power, and security, At other times, the land has stepped forward, and bid us look to it, and its yeomanry, as the sure and solid foundation of our greatness and our safety, At other times, the bank has pushed forward with her claims, and has told us that great as the others were, they were nothing without *"public credit,"* upon which not only the prosperity and happiness but the very independence of the country depended. But, sir, we have this night discovered that the shipping, the land, and the bank and its credit are all nothing worth compared with the labor of three hundred thousand little girls in Lancashire! Aye, when compared with only an eighth part of the labor of those three hundred thousand little girls, from whose labor, if we only deduct two hours a day, away goes the wealth, away goes the capital, away go the resources, the power, and the glory of England! With what pride and what pleasure, sir, will the right honorable gentleman opposite and the honorable member for Manchester behind me go northward with the news of this discovery, and communicate it to that large portion of the little girls whom they have the honor and the happiness to represent! ■

Senator Henry Clay Calls for the Great Compromise to Avert Civil War

"AND now let us discard . . . all hankerings after the gilded crumbs which fall from the table of power."

IN 1849, as the North demanded the exclusion of slavery from the new territories in the West, and as the South explored the notion of secession to protect its slavery-based cotton economy, a senator from Kentucky tried to work out "a measure of mutual sacrifice." Senator Henry Clay had earned the sobriquet of the Great Compromiser nearly thirty years before, with his Missouri Compromise, dividing new states and lands between slave and free. His last settlement included the admission of California as a free state, which the North wanted, and the rigorous application of a fugitive slave law, which southerners called for; with the support of Daniel Webster and Stephen Douglas, Henry Clay succeeded in delaying the onset of the Civil War for a decade.

Clay's oratory was closely studied by Lincoln, who saw how Dutch dialect words like "hankering" could be used in formal addresses. Clay also looked to America's moral leadership by example: "What will be the judgment of mankind?" was a theme picked up by a generation of politicians who followed him. In this selection from an 1850 speech introducing a Senate resolution, the Whig who could command national leadership—but never achieve the presidency—deals with the idea of compromise and the danger of its failure.

□ □ □

It has been objected against this measure that it is a compromise. It has been said that it is a compromise of principle, or of a principle. Mr. President, what is a compromise? It is a work of mutual concession—an agreement in which there are reciprocal stipulations—a work in which, for the sake of peace and concord, one party abates his extreme demands in consideration of an abatement of extreme demands by the other party: it is a measure of mutual concession—a measure of mutual sacrifice. Undoubtedly, Mr. President, in all such measures of compromise, one party would be very glad to get what he wants, and reject what he does not desire but which the other party wants. But when he comes to reflect that, from the nature of the government and its operations, and from those with whom he is dealing, it is necessary upon his part, in order to secure what he wants, to grant something to the other side, he should be reconciled to the concession which he has made in consequence of the concession which he is to receive, if there is no great principle involved, such as a violation of the Constitution of the United States. I admit that such a compromise as that ought never to be sanctioned or adopted. But I now call upon any senator in his place to point out from the beginning to the end, from California to New Mexico, a solitary provision in this bill which is violative of the Constitution of the United States.

The responsibility of this great measure passes from the hands of the committee, and from my hands. They know, and I know, that it is an awful and tremendous responsibility. I hope that you will meet it with a just conception and a true appreciation of its magnitude, and the magnitude of the consequences that may ensue from your decision one way or the other. The alternatives, I fear, which the measure presents are concord and increased discord—a servile civil war, originating in its causes on the lower Rio Grande and terminating possibly in its consequences on the upper Rio Grande in the Santa Fe country, or the restoration of harmony and fraternal kindness. I believe from the bottom of my soul that the measure is the reunion of this Union. I believe it is the dove of peace, which, taking its aerial flight from the dome of the Capitol, carries the glad tidings of assured peace and restored harmony to all the remotest extremities of this distracted land. I believe that it will be attended with all these beneficent effects. And now let us discard all resentment, all passions, all petty jealousies, all personal desires, all love of place, all hankerings after the gilded crumbs which fall from the table of power. Let us forget popular fears, from whatever quarter they may spring. Let us go to the limpid fountain of unadulterated patriotism and, performing a solemn lustration, return divested of all selfish, sinister, and sordid impurities, and think alone of our God, our country, our consciences, and our glorious Union— that Union without which we shall be torn into hostile fragments, and sooner or later become the victims of military despotism or foreign domination.

Mr. President, what is an individual man? An atom, almost invisible without a magnifying glass—a mere speck upon the surface of the immense universe; not a second in time, compared to immeasurable, never-beginning, and never-ending eternity; a drop of water in the great deep, which evaporates and is borne off by the winds; a grain of sand, which is soon gathered to the dust from which it sprung. Shall a being so small, so petty, so fleeting, so evanescent, oppose itself to the onward march of a great nation which is to subsist for ages and ages to come— oppose itself to that long line of posterity which, issuing from our loins, will endure during the existence of the world? Forbid it, God.

Let us look to our country and our cause, elevate ourselves to the dignity of pure and disinterested patriots, and save our country from all impending dangers. What if, in the march of this nation to greatness and power, we should be buried beneath the wheels that propel it onward! What are we—what is any man—worth who is not ready and willing to sacrifice himself for the benefit of his country when it is necessary?

I call upon all the South. Sir, we have had hard words, bitter words, bitter thoughts, unpleasant feelings toward each other in the progress of this great measure. Let us forget them. Let us sacrifice these feelings. Let us go to the altar of our country and swear, as the oath was taken of old, that we will stand by her; that we will support her; that we will uphold her Constitution; that we will preserve her Union; and that we will pass this great, comprehensive, and healing system of measures, which will hush all the jarring elements and bring peace and tranquillity to our homes.

Let me, Mr. President, in conclusion, say that the most disastrous consequences would occur, in my opinion, were we to go home, doing nothing to satisfy and tranquilize the country upon these great questions. What will be the judgment of mankind, what the judgment of that portion of mankind who are looking upon the progress of this scheme of self-government as being that which holds the highest hopes and expectations of ameliorating the condition of mankind—what will their judgment be? Will not all the monarchs of the Old World pronounce our glorious Republic a disgraceful failure? Will you go home and leave all in disorder and confusion—all unsettled—all open?

The contentions and agitations of the past will be increased and augmented by the agitations resulting from our neglect to decide them. Sir, we shall stand condemned by all human judgment below, and of that above it is not for me to speak. We shall stand condemned in our own consciences, by our own constituents, and by our own country. The measure may be defeated. I have been aware that its passage for many days was not absolutely certain. From the first to the last, I hoped and believed it would pass, because from the first to the last I believed it was founded on the principles of just and righteous concession, of mutual conciliation. I believe that it deals unjustly by no part of the Republic; that it saves their honor and, as far as it is dependent upon Congress, saves the interests of all quarters of the country. But, sir, I have known that the decision of its fate depended upon four or five votes in the Senate of the United States, whose ultimate judgment we could not count upon the one side or the other with absolute certainty. Its fate is now committed to the Senate, and to those five or six votes to which I have referred. It may be defeated. It is possible that, for the chastisement of our sins and transgressions, the rod of Providence may be still applied to us, may be still suspended over us. But, if defeated, it will be a triumph of ultraism and impracticability—a triumph of a most extraordinary conjunction of extremes; a victory won by abolitionism; a victory achieved by free-soilism; a victory of discord and agitation over peace and tranquility; and I pray to Almighty God that it may not, in consequence of the inauspicious result, lead to the most unhappy and disastrous consequences to our beloved country. ■

Karl Marx Calls for the Dictatorship of the Proletariat

"ALTHOUGH the atmosphere in which we live weighs upon everyone with a twenty-thousand-pound force, do you feel it?"

AS REVOLUTIONIST AND GERMAN SOCIAL PHILOSOPHER, Karl Heinrich Marx rejected idealism in favor of materialism, seeking to uplift the working class through demands for extreme social reform. His radical views caused him to spend much of his life in exile; he was living in Belgium in 1848 when he published *The Communist Manifesto*, written with Friedrich Engels, with its ominous opening, "A specter is haunting Europe—the specter of communism," and its ringing conclusion, "Workers of the world, unite! You have nothing to lose but your chains." By 1849, he had settled permanently in London. From there, during the American Civil War, he contributed a column to Horace Greeley's *New York Tribune*.

The essence of his original philosophic idea was that economics determined politics, that public rather than private ownership of the means of production was the best economics, and that "class struggle" was inevitable when the class in charge was no longer benefiting the mass of the people. Though his central prediction of the collapse of capitalism was mistaken, and tens of millions suffered and died as a result of the application of his philosophy, the idea of class struggle had validity: after the "new class" of Communist apparatchiks took control of the economy of the Soviet empire, the lower class felt the unrelenting pinch of permanent depression as well as political oppression and swept out its class enemy.

When the founding of the *People's Paper* was celebrated with a London banquet in 1856, Karl Marx was asked to speak. Invited to give the first toast, he knew that he was "to speak for the sovereignty of the proletariat in all countries."

Throughout this after-dinner speech, Marx sounds themes familiar to his social thought: the needed revolution of workingmen for "the emancipation of their own class," the universal domination of "capital rule and wages slavery," and the historical imperative for the inevitable success of the proletariat. That imperative is made most forceful in the parallel structure of the speech's closing sentence.

□   □   □

The so-called revolutions of 1848 were but poor incidents—small fractures and fissures in the dry crust of European society. However, they announced the abyss.

Beneath the apparently solid surface, they betrayed oceans of liquid matter, only needing expansion to rend into fragments continents of hard rock. Noisedly and confusedly they proclaimed the emancipation of the proletarian, i.e., the secret of the nineteenth century, and of the revolution of that century.

That social revolution, it is true, was no novelty invented in 1848. Steam, electricity, and the self-acting mule were revolutionists of a rather more dangerous character than even citizens Barbès, Raspail, and Blanqui. But, although the atmosphere in which we live weighs upon everyone with a twenty-thousand-pound force, do you feel it? No more than European society before 1848 felt the revolutionary atmosphere enveloping and pressing it from all sides.

There is one great fact, characteristic of this, our nineteenth century, a fact which no party dares deny. On the one hand, there have started into life industrial and scientific forces which no epoch of the former human history had ever suspected. On the other hand, there exist symptoms of decay far surpassing the horrors recorded of the latter times of the Roman Empire. In our days everything seems pregnant with its contrary; machinery gifted with the wonderful power of shortening and fructifying human labor, we behold starving and overworking it. The newfangled sources of wealth, by some strange, weird spell, are turned into sources of want. The victories of art seem bought by the loss of character.

At the same pace that mankind masters nature, man seems to become enslaved to other men or to his own infamy. Even the pure light of science seems unable to shine but on the dark background of ignorance. All our invention and progress seem to result in endowing material forces with intellectual life, and in stultifying human life into a material force.

This antagonism between modern industry and science on the one hand, modern misery and dissolution on the other hand; this antagonism between the productive powers and the social relations of our epoch is a fact, palpable, overwhelming, and not to be controverted. Some parties may wail over it; others may wish to get rid of modern arts in order to get rid of modern conflicts. Or they may imagine that so signal a progress in industry wants to be completed by as signal a regress in politics.

On our part, we do not mistake the shape of the shrewd spirit that continues to mark all these contradictions. We know that to work well the newfangled forces of society, they only want to be mastered by newfangled men—and such are the workingmen. They are as much the invention of modern time as machinery itself. In the signs that bewilder the middle class, the aristocracy, and the poor prophets of regression, we do recognize our brave friend Robin Goodfellow, the old mole, that can work in the earth so fast, that worthy pioneer—the revolution.

The English workingmen are the firstborn sons of modern industry. They will then, certainly, not be the last in aiding the social revolution produced by that industry, a revolution which means the emancipation of their own class all over the world, which is as universal as capital rule and wages slavery.

I know the heroic struggles the English working class have gone through since the middle of the last century—struggles less glorious because they are shrouded in obscurity and burked by the middle-class historians to revenge the misdeeds of the ruling class. There existed in the Middle Ages in Germany a secret tribunal called the *Vehmgericht*. If a red cross was seen marked on a house, people knew that its owner was doomed by the *Vehm*. All the houses of Europe are now marked with the mysterious red cross. History is the judge—its executioner, the proletarian. ■

Lincoln, in His First Inaugural, Asserts the Necessity of Majority Rule

"A majority held in restraint by constitutional checks and limitations . . . is the only true sovereign of a free people. Whoever rejects it does of necessity fly to anarchy or to despotism."

ELECTED, FROM A FIELD OF FOUR, by less than 40 percent of the popular vote; faced with the secession of seven states in the weeks before his inauguration as the sixteenth president; burdened by a weak and divided army unready to take the field—Abraham Lincoln made the theme of his first speech as chief magistrate (as the job was then called) that he was prepared to fight a war to maintain the Union.

The address on March 4, 1861, is a lawyerly and logical explication of the need for the acceptance of majority rule in the business of democracy: "If the minority will not acquiesce, the majority must, or the government must cease. . . . If a minority in such case will secede rather than acquiesce, they make a precedent which in turn will divide and ruin them, for a minority of their own will secede. . . ."

The southern states were hoping to leave in peace, preserving their "peculiar institution" of slavery—specifically condoned by the nation's founders—from feared abolition by the North. Lincoln, who opposed the extension of slavery into western territories but did not favor abolition in those states where it already existed, felt called upon to make absolutely clear that there could be no peaceful secession, no easy way out. "Plainly the central idea of secession is the essence of anarchy," he insisted; the American experiment in democracy permitted no minority to refuse acquiescence to majority rule.

At the same time, Lincoln wanted the onus for warmaking to fall upon the seceders: "In *your* hands, my dissatisfied fellow countrymen, and not in *mine*, is the momentous issue of civil war. . . . *You* have no oath registered in heaven to destroy the government, while *I* shall have the most solemn one to 'preserve, protect, and defend it.'" Here was the legal mind at work: the Constitution contained no prohibition of secession, or enforcement language to preserve the Union, except perhaps in the specified oath of office, and that was "to preserve, protect, and defend the Constitution"—not, as Lincoln implied, to preserve the government, or a union consisting of all states that had adopted that document.

In his penetrating, high-pitched voice, Lincoln claimed further that he had no choice but to resist secession, because the president "derives all his authority from the people"—a concept rooted primarily in the radical Declaration of Independence, which had also proclaimed all men to be created equal—and not from the ratifying states, as southerners and others held who relied more on the conservative Constitution. In Lincoln's interpretation of sovereign power, the people had not vested the president with the authority to fix the terms of separation. Thus, he made war the inevitable consequence of secession and declared himself constitutionally unable to stop it.

Rather than close on that inflexible and almost truculent note, Lincoln accepted a suggested peroration from the New York governor whom he had defeated for the Republican nomination and had chosen to be secretary of state. William Seward's draft closing, using the metaphor of the celestial harp and playing on the meaning of the homophones "chord" and "cord," has been preserved: "I close. We are not, and must not be, aliens or enemies, but fellow countrymen and brethren. Although passion has strained our bonds of affection too hardly, they must not, I am sure they will not, be broken. The mystic chords which, proceeding from so many battlefields and so many patriot graves, pass through all the hearts and all hearths in this broad continent of ours, will yet again harmonize in their ancient music when breathed upon by the guardian angel of the nation."

For a vivid example of Lincoln's ability to transform fine oratory into great oratory, compare Seward's suggested language with the Lincoln revision at the close.

□   □   □

. . . Apprehension seems to exist among the people of the southern states that by the accession of a Republican administration their property and their peace and personal security are to be endangered. There has never been any reasonable cause for such apprehension. Indeed, the most ample evidence to the contrary has all the while existed and been open to their inspection. It is found in nearly all the published speeches of him who now addresses you. I do but quote from one of those speeches when I declare that I have no purpose, directly or indirectly, to interfere with the institution of slavery in the states where it exists. I believe I have no lawful right to do so, and I have no inclination to do so. . . .

It is seventy-two years since the first inauguration of a president under our national Constitution. During that period fifteen different and greatly distinguished citizens have in succession administered the executive branch of the government. They have conducted it through many perils, and generally with great success. Yet, with all this scope of precedent, I now enter upon the same task for the brief constitutional term of four years under great and peculiar difficulty. A disruption of the federal Union, heretofore only menaced, is now formidably attempted.

I hold that in contemplation of universal law and of the Constitution the Union of these states is perpetual. Perpetuity is implied, if not expressed, in the fundamental law of all national governments. It is safe to assert that no government proper ever had a provision in its organic law for its own termination. Continue to execute all the express provisions of our national Constitution, and the Union will endure forever, it being impossible to destroy it except by some action not provided for in the instrument itself.

Again: If the United States be not a government proper, but an association of states in the nature of contract merely, can it, as a contract, be peaceably unmade by less than all the parties who made it? One party to a contract may violate it—break it, so to speak—but does it not require all to lawfully rescind it?

Descending from these general principles, we find the proposition that in legal contemplation the Union is perpetual confirmed by the history of the Union itself. The Union is much older than the Constitution. It was formed, in fact, by the Articles of Association in 1774. It was matured and continued by the Declaration of Independence in 1776. It was further matured, and the faith of all the then thirteen states expressly plighted and engaged that it should be perpetual, by the Articles of Confederation in 1778. And finally, in 1787, one of the declared objects for ordaining and establishing the Constitution was *"to form a more perfect Union."*

But if destruction of the Union by one or by a part only of the states be lawfully possible, the Union is *less* perfect than before the Constitution, having lost the vital element of perpetuity.

It follows from these views that no state upon its own mere motion can lawfully get out of the Union; that *resolves* and *ordinances* to that effect are legally void; and that acts of violence within any state or states against the authority of the United States are insurrectionary or revolutionary, according to circumstances.

I therefore consider that in view of the Constitution and the laws the Union is unbroken, and to the extent of my ability, I shall take care, as the Constitution itself expressly enjoins upon me, that the laws of the Union be faithfully executed in all the states. . . .

That there are persons in one section or another who seek to destroy the Union at all events and are glad of any pretext to do it I will neither affirm nor deny; but if there be such, I need address no word to them. To those, however, who really love the Union may I not speak?

Before entering upon so grave a matter as the destruction of our national fabric, with all its benefits, its memories, and its hopes, would it not be wise to ascertain precisely why we do it? Will you hazard so desperate a step while there is any possibility that any portion of the ills you fly from have no real existence? Will you, while the certain ills you fly to are greater than all the real ones you fly from; will you risk the commission of so fearful a mistake?

All profess to be content in the Union if all constitutional rights can be maintained. Is it true, then, that any right plainly written in the Constitution has been denied? I think not. Happily, the human mind is so constituted that no party can reach to the audacity of doing this. Think, if you can, of a single instance in which a plainly written provision of the Constitution has ever been denied. If by the mere force of numbers a majority should deprive a minority of any clearly written constitutional right, it might in a moral point of view justify revolution—certainly would if such right were a vital one. But such is not our case. All the vital rights of minorities and of individuals are so plainly assured to them by affirmations and negations, guaranties and prohibitions, in the Constitution that controversies never arise concerning them. But no organic law can ever be framed with a provision specifically applicable to every question, which may occur in practical administration. No foresight can anticipate nor any document of reasonable length contain express provisions for all possible questions. Shall fugitives from labor be surrendered by national or by state authority? The Constitution does not expressly say, *May* Congress prohibit slavery in the territories? The Constitution does not expressly say, *Must* Congress protect slavery in the territories? The Constitution does not expressly say.

From questions of this class spring all our constitutional controversies, and we divide upon them into majorities and minorities. If the minority will not acquiesce, the majority must, or the government must cease. There is no other alternative, for continuing the government is acquiescence on one side or the other. If a minority in such case will secede rather than acquiesce, they make a precedent which in turn will divide and ruin them, for a minority of their own will secede from them whenever a majority refuses to be controlled by such minority. For instance, why may not any portion of a new confederacy a year or two hence arbitrarily secede again, precisely as portions of the present Union now claim to secede from it? All who cherish disunion sentiments are now being educated to the exact temper of doing this.

Is there such perfect identity of interests among the states to compose a new union as to produce harmony only and prevent renewed secession?

Plainly the central idea of secession is the essence of anarchy. A majority held in restraint by constitutional checks and limitations, and always changing easily with deliberate changes of popular opinions and sentiments, is the only true sovereign of a free people. Whoever rejects it does of necessity fly to anarchy or to despotism. Unanimity is impossible. The rule of a minority, as a permanent arrangement, is wholly inadmissible; so that, rejecting the majority principle, anarchy or despotism in some form is all that is left.

I do not forget the position assumed by some that constitutional questions are to be decided by the Supreme Court, nor do I deny that such decisions must be binding in any case upon the parties to a suit as to the object of that suit, while they are also entitled to very high respect and consideration in all parallel cases by all other departments of the government. And while it is obviously possible that such decision may be erroneous in any given case, still the evil effect following it, being limited to that particular case, with the chance that it may be overruled and never become a precedent for other cases, can better be borne than could the evils of a different practice. At the same time, the candid citizen must confess that if the policy of the government upon vital questions affecting the whole people is to be irrevocably fixed by decisions of the Supreme Court, the instant they are made in ordinary litigation between parties in personal actions the people will have ceased to be their own rulers, having to that extent practically resigned their government into the hands of that eminent tribunal. Nor is there in this view any assault upon the court or the judges. It is a duty from which they may not shrink to decide cases properly brought before them, and it is no fault of theirs if others seek to turn their decisions to political purposes.

One section of our country believes slavery is *right* and ought to be extended, while the other believes it is *wrong* and ought not to be extended. This is the only substantial dispute. The fugitive slave clause of the Constitution and the law for the suppression of the foreign slave trade are each as well enforced, perhaps, as any law can ever be in a community where the moral sense of the people imperfectly supports the law itself. The great body of the people abide by the dry legal obligation in both cases, and a few break over in each. This, I think, cannot be perfectly cured, and it would be worse in both cases *after* the separation of the sections than before. The foreign slave trade, now imperfectly suppressed, would be ultimately revived without restriction in one section, while fugitive slaves, now only partially surrendered, would not be surrendered at all by the other.

Physically speaking, we cannot separate. We cannot remove our respective sections from each other nor build an impassable wall between them. A husband and wife may be divorced and go out of the presence and beyond the reach of each other, but the different parts of our country cannot do this. They cannot but remain face to face, and intercourse, either amicable or hostile, must continue between them. Is it possible, then, to make that intercourse more advantageous or more satisfactory *after* separation than *before*? Can aliens make treaties easier than friends can make laws? Can treaties be more faithfully enforced between aliens than laws can among friends? Suppose you go to war, you cannot fight always; and when, after much loss on both sides and no gain on either, you cease fighting, the identical old questions, as to terms of intercourse, are again upon you.

This country, with its institutions, belongs to the people who inhabit it. Whenever they shall grow weary of the existing government, they can exercise their *constitutional* right of amending it or their *revolutionary* right to dismember or overthrow it. . . .

The chief magistrate derives all his authority from the people, and they have conferred none upon him to fix terms for the separation of the states. The people themselves can do this if also they choose, but the executive as such has nothing to do with it. His duty is to administer the present government as it came to his hands and to transmit it unimpaired by him to his successor.

Why should there not be a patient confidence in the ultimate justice of the people? Is there any better or equal hope in the world? In our present differences, is either party without faith of being in the right? If the Almighty Ruler of nations, with his eternal truth and justice, be on your side of the North, or on yours of the South, that truth and that justice will surely prevail by the judgment of this great tribunal of the American people.

By the frame of the government under which we live this same people have wisely given their public servants but little power for mischief, and have with equal wisdom provided for the return of that little to their own hands at very short intervals. While the people retain their virtue and vigilance, no administration by any extreme of wickedness or folly can very seriously injure the government in the short space of four years.

My countrymen, one and all, think calmly and *well* upon this whole subject. Nothing valuable can be lost by taking time. If there be an object to *hurry* any of you in hot haste to a step which you would never take *deliberately,* that object will be frustrated by taking time; but no good object can be frustrated by it. Such of you as are now dissatisfied still have the old Constitution unimpaired and, on the sensitive point, the laws of your own framing under it; while the new administration will have no immediate power, if it would, to change either. If it were admitted that you who are dissatisfied hold the right side in the dispute, there still is no single good reason for precipitate action. Intelligence, patriotism, Christianity, and a firm reliance on him who has never yet forsaken this favored land are still competent to adjust in the best way all our present difficulty.

In *your* hands, my dissatisfied fellow countrymen, and not in *mine,* is the momentous issue of civil war. The government will not assail *you.* You can have no conflict without being yourselves the aggressors. *You* have no oath registered in heaven to destroy the government, while *I* shall have the most solemn one to "preserve, protect, and defend it."

I am loath to close. We are not enemies but friends. We must not be enemies. Though passion may have strained, it must not break our bonds of affection. The mystic chords of memory, stretching from every battle-field and patriot grave to every living heart and hearthstone all over this broad land, will yet swell the chorus of the Union, when again touched, as surely they will be, by the better angels of our nature. ■

Representative J. Proctor Knott Uses Satire to Sink a Land Grant Bill

"I think every gentleman on this floor is as well satisfied as I am that Duluth is destined to become the commercial metropolis of the universe. . . ."

CITIZENS OF DULUTH, MINNESOTA, have every right to take offense at this 1871 speech to the House of Representatives. Representative J. Proctor Knott of Kentucky stuck his tongue in his cheek and rose to his feet to discuss what seemed a straightforward land grant bill. The second half of the nineteenth century had seen many such land grants by Congress to the railroad companies, and this bill would have given away vast tracts in return for extending the railroad along the St. Croix River to Duluth, Minnesota.

A native of Kentucky, James Proctor Knott began his career as a Missouri lawyer and was serving as that state's attorney general when the Civil War started. He was imprisoned briefly for his southern sympathies, and returned to Kentucky upon his release. Known for his oratory, he was elected six times to the House of Representatives, and in his second of those terms, he delivered his views on the Duluth railroad bill in an address to the House on January 27, 1871.

Frequent laughter and cries of "Go on! Go on!" interrupted Knott's inspired discourse, and by the time that he was finished speaking, the House was ready to take a vote. The ridicule worked: the land grant bill was defeated.

□   □   □

Mr. Speaker, if I could be actuated by any conceivable inducement to betray the sacred trust reposed in me by those to whose generous confidence I am indebted for the honor of a seat on this floor; if I could be influenced by any possible consideration to become instrumental in giving away, in violation of their known wishes, any portion of their interest in the public domain for the mere promotion of any railroad enterprise whatever, I should certainly feel a strong inclination to give this measure my most earnest and hearty support; for I am assured that its success would materially enhance the pecuniary prosperity of some of the most valued friends I have on earth—friends for whose accommodation I would be willing to make almost any sacrifice not involving my personal honor, or my fidelity as the trustee of an express trust. And that fact of itself would be sufficient to countervail almost any objection I might entertain to the passage of this bill, not inspired by an imperative and inexorable sense of public duty.

But, independent of the seductive influences of private friendship, to which I admit I am, perhaps, as susceptible as any of the gentlemen I see around me, the intrinsic merits of the measure itself are of such an extraordinary character as to commend it most strongly to the favorable consideration of every member of this House—myself not expected—notwithstanding my constituents, in whose behalf alone I am acting here, would not be benefited by its passage one particle more than they would be by a project to cultivate an orange grove on the bleakest summit of Greenland's icy mountains.

Now, sir, as to those great trunk lines of railway, spanning the continent from ocean to ocean, I confess my mind has never been fully made up. It is true they may afford some trifling advantages to local traffic, and they may even in time become the channels of a more extended commerce. Yet I have never been thoroughly satisfied either of the necessity or expediency of projects promising such meager results to the great body of our people. But with regard to the transcendent merits of the gigantic enterprise contemplated in this bill, I never entertained the shadow of a doubt.

Years ago, when I first heard that there was somewhere in the vast terra incognita, somewhere in the bleak regions of the great Northwest, a stream of water known to the nomadic inhabitants of the neighborhood as the river St. Croix, I became satisfied that the construction of a railroad from that raging torrent to some point in the civilized world was essential to the happiness and prosperity of the American people, if not absolutely indispensable to the perpetuity of republican institutions on this continent. I felt instinctively that the boundless resources of that prolific region of sand and pine shrubbery would never be fully developed without a railroad constructed and equipped at the expense of the government—and perhaps not then. I had an abiding presentiment that some day or other the people of this whole country, irrespective of party affiliations, regardless of sectional prejudices, and "without distinction of race, color, or previous condition of servitude," would rise in their majesty and demand an outlet for the enormous agricultural productions of those vast and fertile pine barrens, drained in the rainy season by the surging waters of the turbid St. Croix. . . .

Now, sir, I repeat I have been satisfied for years that if there was any portion of the inhabited globe absolutely in a suffering condition for want of a railroad, it was these teeming pine barrens of the St. Croix. At what particular point on that noble stream such a road should be commenced, I knew was immaterial, and so it seems to have been considered by the draftsmen of this bill. It might be up at the spring, or down at the foot log, or the water gate, or the fish dam, or anywhere along the bank, no matter where. But in what direction it should run, or where it should terminate, were always to my mind questions of the most painful perplexity. I could conceive of no place on "God's green earth" in such straitened circumstances for railroad facilities as to be likely to desire or willing to accept such a connection. I knew that neither Bayfield nor Superior City would have it, for they both indignantly spurned the munificence of the government when coupled with such ignominious conditions, and let this very same land grant die on their hands years and years ago rather than submit to the degradation of a direct communication by railroad with the piny woods of the St. Croix; and I knew that what the enterprising inhabitants of those giant young cities would refuse to take would have few charms for others, whatever their necessities or cupidity might be.

Hence, as I have said, sir, I was utterly at a loss to determine where the terminus of this great and indispensable road should be, until I accidentally overheard some gentleman the other day mention the name of Duluth. Duluth! The word fell upon my ear with peculiar and indescribable charm, like the gentle murmur of a low fountain stealing forth in the midst of roses, or the soft, sweet accents of an angel's whisper in the bright, joyous dream of sleeping innocence. Duluth! 'Twas the name for which my soul had panted for years, as the hart panteth for the water brooks. But where was Duluth? Never, in all my limited reading, had my vision been gladdened by seeing the celestial word in print. And I felt a profounder humiliation in my ignorance that its dulcet syllables had never before ravished my delighted ear. I was certain the draftsmen of this bill had never heard of it, or it would have been designated as one of the termini of this road. I asked my friends about it, but they knew nothing of it. I rushed to the library and examined all the maps I could find. I discovered in one of them a delicate, hairlike line, diverging from the Mississippi near a place marked Prescott, which I suppose was intended to represent the river St. Croix, but I could nowhere find Duluth.

Nevertheless, I was confident it existed somewhere, and that its discovery would constitute the crowning glory of the present century, if not of all modern times. I knew it was bound to exist in the very nature of things; that the symmetry and perfection of our planetary system would be incomplete without it; that the elements of material nature would long since have resolved themselves back into original chaos if there had been such a hiatus in creation as would have resulted from leaving out Duluth. In fact, sir, I was overwhelmed with the conviction that Duluth not only existed somewhere but that, wherever it was, it was a great and glorious place. I was convinced that the greatest calamity that ever befell the benighted nations of the ancient world was in their having passed away without a knowledge of the actual existence of Duluth; that their fabled Atlantis, never seen save by the hallowed vision of inspired poesy, was, in fact, but another name for Duluth; that the golden orchard of the Hesperides was but a poetical synonym for the beer gardens in the vicinity of Duluth. I was certain that Herodotus had died a miserable death, because in all his travels and with all his geographical research he had never heard of Duluth. I knew that if the immortal spirit of Homer could look down from another heaven than that created by his own celestial genius upon the long lines of pilgrims from very nation of the earth to the gushing fountain of poesy opened by the touch of his magic wand, if he could be permitted to behold the vast assemblage of grand and glorious productions of the lyric art called into being by his own inspired strains, he would weep tears of bitter anguish that, instead of lavishing all the stores of his mighty genius upon the fall of Ilion, it had not been his more blessed lot to crystallize in deathless song the rising glories of Duluth. Yet, sir, had it not been for this map, kindly furnished me by the legislature of Minnesota, I might have gone down to my obscure and humble grave in an agony of despair, because I could nowhere find Duluth. Had such been my melancholy fate, I have no doubt that with the last feeble pulsation of my breaking heart, with the last faint exhalation of my fleeting breath, I should have whispered, "Where is Duluth?"

But thanks to the beneficence of that band of ministering angels who have their bright abodes in the far-off capital of Minnesota, just as the agony of my anxiety was about to culminate in the frenzy of despair, this blessed map was placed in my hands; and as I unfolded it a resplendent scene of ineffable glory opened before me, such as I imagine burst upon the enraptured vision of the wandering peri through the opening of Paradise. There, there for the first time, my enchanted eye rested upon the ravishing word "Duluth."

. . . This map, sir, is intended, as it appears from its title, to illustrate the position of Duluth in the United States; but if gentlemen will examine it,

I think they will concur with me in the opinion that it is far too modest in its pretensions. It not only illustrates the position of Duluth in the United States but exhibits its relations with all created things. It even goes further than this. It lifts the shadowy veil of futurity and affords us a view of the golden prospects of Duluth far along the dim vista of ages yet to come.

If gentlemen will examine it, they will find Duluth, not only in the center of the map, but represented in the center of a series of concentric circles one hundred miles apart, and some of them as much as four thousand miles in diameter, embracing alike, in their tremendous sweep, the fragrant savannas of the sunlit South and the eternal solitudes of snow that mantle the icebound North. How these circles were produced is, perhaps, one of the most primordial mysteries that the most skillful paleologist will never be able to explain. But the fact is, sir, Duluth is preeminently a central place, for I am told by gentlemen who have been so reckless of their own personal safety as to venture away into those awful regions where Duluth is supposed to be that it is so exactly in the center of the visible universe that the sky comes down at precisely the same distance all around it.

I find by reference to this map that Duluth is situated somewhere near the western end of Lake Superior; but as there is no dot or other mark indicating its exact location, I am unable to say whether it is actually confined to any particular spot or whether "it is just lying around there loose." I really cannot tell whether it is one of those ethereal creations of intellectual frostwork, more intangible than the rose-tinted clouds of a summer sunset; one of those airy exhalations of the speculator's brain, which I am told are ever flitting in the form of towns and cities along those lines of railroad, built with government subsidies, luring the unwary settler as the mirage of the desert lures the famishing traveler on, and ever on, until it fades away in the darkening horizon; or whether it is a real, bona fide, substantial city, all "staked off," with the lots marked with their owners' names, like that proud commercial metropolis recently discovered on the desirable shores of San Domingo. But, however that may be, I am satisfied Duluth is there, or thereabout, for I see it stated here on this map that it is exactly thirty-nine hundred and ninety miles from Liverpool, though I have no doubt, for the sake of convenience, it will be moved back ten miles, so as to make the distance an even four thousand.

Then, sir, there is the climate of Duluth, unquestionably the most salubrious and delightful to be found anywhere on the Lord's earth. Now, I have always been under the impression, as I presume other gentlemen have, that in the region around Lake Superior it was cold enough for at least nine months in the year to freeze the smokestack off a locomotive. But I see it represented on this map that Duluth is situated exactly halfway between the latitudes of Paris and Venice, so that gentlemen who have inhaled the exhilarating airs of the one, or basked in the golden sunlight of the other, may see at a glance that Duluth must be a place of untold delights, a terrestrial paradise, fanned by the balmy zephyrs of an eternal spring, clothed in the gorgeous sheen of ever-blooming flowers, and vocal with the silvery melody of nature's choicest songsters. In fact, sir, since I have seen this map, I have no doubt that Byron was vainly endeavoring to convey some faint conception of the delicious charms of Duluth when his poetic soul gushed forth in the rippling strains of that beautiful rhapsody:

> Know ye the land of the cedar and vine,
> Where the flowers ever blossom, the beams ever shine;
> Where the light wings of zephyr, oppressed with perfume,
> Wax faint o'er the gardens of Gul in her bloom;
> Where the citron and olive are fairest of fruit,
> And the voice of the nightingale never is mute;
> Where the tints of the earth and the lines of the sky,
> In color though varied, in beauty may vie?

As to the commercial resources of Duluth, sir, they are simply illimitable and inexhaustible, as is shown by this map. I see it stated here that there is a vast scope of territory, embracing an area of over two million square miles, rich in every element of material wealth and commercial prosperity, all tributary to Duluth. Look at it, sir! Here are inexhaustible mines of gold; immeasurable veins of silver; impenetrable depths of boundless forest; vast coal measures; wide, extended plains of richest pasturage—all, all embraced in this vast territory, which must, in the very nature of things, empty the untold treasures of its commerce into the lap of Duluth.

Look at it, sir! Do not you see from these broad, brown lines drawn around this immense territory that the enterprising inhabitants of Duluth intend someday to inclose it all in one vast corral, so that its commerce will be bound to go there whether it would or not? And here, sir I find within a convenient distance the Piegan Indians, which, of all the many accessories to the glory of Duluth, I consider by far the most inestimable. For, sir, I have been told that when the smallpox breaks out among the women and children of that famous tribe, as it sometimes does, they afford the finest subjects in the world for the strategic experiments of any enterprising military hero who desires to improve himself in the noble art of war, especially for any valiant lieutenant general whose—

> Trenchant blade, Toledo trusty,
> For want of fighting has gone rusty.
> And eats into itself for lack
> Of somebody to hew and hack.

Sir, the great conflict now raging in the Old World has presented a phenomenon in military science unprecedented in the annals of mankind—a phenomenon that has reversed all the traditions of the past as it has disappointed all the expectations of the present. A great and warlike people, renowned alike for their skill and valor, have been swept away before the triumphant advance of an inferior foe, like autumn stubble before a hurricane of fire. For aught I know, the next flash of electric fire that shimmers along the ocean cable may tell us that Paris, with every fiber quivering with the agony of impotent despair, writhes beneath the conquering heel of her loathed invader. Ere another moon shall wax and wane, the brightest star in the galaxy of nations may fall from the zenith of her glory, never to rise again. Ere the modest violets of early spring shall open their beauteous eyes, the genius of civilization may chant the wailing requiem of the proudest nationality the world has ever seen, as she scatters her withered and tear-moistened lilies o'er the bloody tomb of butchered France. But, sir, I wish to ask if you honestly and candidly believe that the Dutch would have ever overrun the French in that kind of style if General Sheridan had not gone over there and told King William and von Moltke how he had managed to whip the Piegan Indians!

And here, sir, recurring to this map, I find in the immediate vicinity of the Piegans "vast herds of buffalo" and "immense fields of rich wheat lands."

[Here the hammer fell. Many cries: "Go on! Go on!"

The Speaker: Is there objection to the gentleman of Kentucky continuing his remarks? The chair hears none, the gentleman will proceed.]

I was remarking, sir, upon these vast "wheat fields" represented on this map in the immediate neighborhood of the buffaloes and the Piegans, and was about to say that the idea of there being these immense wheat fields in the very heart of a wilderness, hundreds and hundreds of miles beyond the utmost verge of civilization, may appear to some gentlemen as rather incongruous, as rather too great a strain on the "blankets" of veracity. But to my mind there is no difficulty in the matter whatever. The phenomenon is very easily accounted for. It is evident, sir, that the Piegans sowed that wheat there and plowed it with buffalo bulls. Now, sir, this fortunate combination of buffaloes and Piegans, considering their relative positions to each other and to Duluth, as they are arranged on this map, satisfies me that Duluth is destined to be the beef market of the world.

Here, you will observe, are the buffaloes, directly between the Piegans and Duluth; and here, right on the road to Duluth, are the Creeks. Now, sir, when the buffaloes are sufficiently fat from grazing on these immense wheat fields, you see it will be the easiest thing in the world for the Piegans to drive them on down, stay all night with their friends the Creeks, and go into Duluth in the morning. I think I see them now, sir, a vast herd of buffaloes, with their heads down, their eyes glaring, their nostrils dilated, their tongues out, and their tails curled over their backs, tearing along toward Duluth, with about a thousand Piegans on their grass-bellied ponies, yelling at their heels! On they come! And as they sweep past the Creeks they join in the chase, and away they all go, yelling, bellowing, ripping, and tearing along, amid clouds of dust, until the last buffalo is safely penned in the stockyards of Duluth!

Sir, I might stand here for hours and hours, and expatiate with rapture upon the gorgeous prospects of Duluth, as depicted upon this map. But human life is too short and the time of this House far too valuable to allow me to linger longer upon the delightful theme. I think every gentleman on this floor is as well satisfied as I am that Duluth is destined to become the commercial metropolis of the universe, and that this road should be built at once. I am fully persuaded that no patriotic representative of the American people who has a proper appreciation of the associated glories of Duluth and the St. Croix will hesitate a moment to say that every able-bodied female in the land between the ages of eighteen and forty-five who is in favor of "women's rights" should be drafted and set to work upon this great work without delay. Nevertheless, sir, it grieves my very soul to be compelled to say that I cannot vote for the grant of lands provided for in this bill.

Ah, sir, you can have no conception of the poignancy of my anguish that I am deprived of that blessed privilege! There are two insuperable obstacles in the way. In the first place, my constituents, for whom I am acting here, have no more interest in this road than they have in the great question of culinary taste now perhaps agitating the public mind of Dominica, as to whether the illustrious commissioners who recently left this capital for that free and enlightened republic would be better fricasseed, boiled, or roasted, and in the second place these lands, which I am asked to give away, alas, are not mine to bestow! My relation to them is simply that of trustee to an express trust. And shall I ever betray that trust? Never, sir! Rather perish Duluth! Perish the paragon of cities! Rather let the freezing cyclones of the bleak Northwest bury it forever beneath the eddying sands of the raging St. Croix! ∎

British Conservative Benjamin Disraeli Speaks Up for Tory Principles

"I express here my confident conviction that there never was a moment in our history when the power of England was so great and her resources so vast and inexhaustible."

WHEN BENJAMIN DISRAELI first won a seat in Parliament, in 1837, the same year that Victoria ascended to the throne, his maiden speech was a personal and political disaster. His flowery language and affected style of dress caused him to be laughed off the floor of the House of Commons.

A dozen years later, however, Disraeli had become recognized as the leader of the House's Conservative party, and his skillful use of language allowed him to achieve success not only as a novelist but also as a persuasive statesman. With the rising fortunes of the Conservative party against Gladstone's liberalism, Disraeli eventually served as prime minister, securing the Suez Canal for England and adding "empress of India" to the titles of Queen Victoria, who made him earl of Beaconsfield.

On April 3, 1872, Disraeli—who had once said, "Damn principle! Stick to your party"—delivered his forceful speech outlining the principles of the Conservative party. That speech, in Manchester, pared here from its original length of more than three hours, aligns the Conservative party's cause with the English Constitution and attacks the Liberal party, if not Prime Minister Gladstone himself. In a striking metaphor, Disraeli describes the ministers on the treasury bench in the House of Commons as "a range of exhausted volcanoes. Not a flame flickers on a single pallid crest. But the situation is still dangerous." By 1874, Disraeli had again become prime minister.

□   □   □

. . .The Conservative party are accused of having no program of policy. If by a program is meant a plan to despoil churches and plunder landlords, I admit we have no program. If by a program is meant a policy which assails or menaces every institution and every interest, every class and every calling in the country, I admit we have no program. But if to have a policy with distinct ends, and these such as most deeply interest the great body of the nation, be a becoming program for a political party, then I contend we have an adequate program, and one which, here or elsewhere, I shall always be prepared to assert and to vindicate.

Gentlemen, the program of the Conservative party is to maintain the Constitution of the country. I have not come down to Manchester to deliver an essay on the English Constitution; but when the banner of republicanism is unfurled—when the fundamental principles of our institutions are controverted—I think, perhaps, it may not be inconvenient that I should make some few practical remarks upon the character of our Constitution—upon that monarchy limited by the coordinate authority of the estates of the realm, which, under the title of Queen, Lords, and Commons, has contributed so greatly to the prosperity of this country, and with the maintenance of which I believe that prosperity is bound up.

Gentlemen, since the settlement of that Constitution, now nearly two centuries ago, England has never experienced a revolution, though there is no country in which there has been so continuous and such considerable change. How is this? Because the wisdom of your forefathers placed the prize of supreme power without the sphere of human passions. Whatever the struggle of parties, whatever the strife of factions, whatever the excitement and exaltation of the public mind, there has always been something in this country round which all classes and parties could rally, representing the majesty of the law, the administration of justice, and involving, at the same time, the security for every man's rights and the fountain of honor. Now, gentlemen, it is well clearly to comprehend what is meant by a country not having a revolution for two centuries. It means, for that space, the unbroken exercise and enjoyment of the ingenuity of man. It means for that space the continuous application of the discoveries of science to his comfort and convenience. It means the accumulation of capital, the elevation of labor, the establishment of those admirable factories which cover your district; the unwearied improvement of the cultivation of the land, which has extracted from a somewhat churlish soil harvests more exuberant than those furnished by lands nearer to the sun. It means the continuous order which is the only parent of personal liberty and political right. And you owe all these, gentlemen, to the throne. . . .

The first consideration of a minister should be the health of the people. A land may be covered with historic trophies, with museums of science and galleries of art, with universities, and with libraries; the people may be civilized and ingenious; the country may be even famous in the annals and action of the world, but, gentlemen, if the population every ten years decreases, and the stature of the race every ten years diminishes, the history of that country will soon be the history of the past. . . .

I doubt not there is in this hall more than one publican who remembers that last year an act of Parliament was introduced to denounce him as a "sinner." I doubt not there are in this hall a widow and an orphan who remember the profligate proposition to plunder their lonely heritage. But, gentlemen, as time advanced it was not difficult to perceive that extravagance was being substituted for energy by the government. The unnatural stimulus was subsiding. Their paroxysms ended in prostration. Some took refuge in melancholy, and their eminent chief alternated between a menace and a sigh. As I sat opposite the treasury bench, the ministers reminded me of one of those marine landscapes not very unusual on the coast of South America. You behold a range of exhausted volcanoes. Not a flame flickers on a single pallid crest. But the situation is still dangerous. There are occasional earthquakes, and ever and anon the dark rumbling of the sea. . . .

Gentlemen, don't suppose, because I counsel firmness and decision at the right moment, that I am of that school of statesmen who are favorable to a turbulent and aggressive diplomacy. I have resisted it during a great part of my life. I am not unaware that the relations of England to Europe have undergone a vast change during the century that has just elapsed.

The relations of England to Europe are not the same as they were in the days of Lord Chatham or Frederick the Great. The queen of England has become the sovereign of the most powerful of Oriental states. On the other side of the globe there are now establishments belonging to her, teeming with wealth and population, which will, in due time, exercise their influence over the distribution of power. The old establishments of this country, now the United States of America, throw their lengthening shades over the Atlantic, which mix with European waters. These are vast and novel elements in the distribution of power. I acknowledge that the policy of England with respect to Europe should be a policy of reserve, but proud reserve; and in answer to those statesmen—those mistaken statesmen who have intimated the decay of the power of England and the decline of its resources—I express here my confident conviction that there never was a moment in our history when the power of England was so great and her resources so vast and inexhaustible.

And yet, gentlemen, it is not merely our fleets and armies, our powerful artillery, our accumulated capital, and our unlimited credit on which I so much depend, as upon that unbroken spirit of her people, which I believe was never prouder of the imperial country to which they belong. Gentlemen, it is to that spirit that I above all things trust. I look upon the people of Lancashire as fairly representative of the people of England. I think the manner in which they have invited me here, locally a stranger, to receive the expression of their cordial sympathy, and only because they recognize some effort on my part to maintain the greatness of their country, is evidence of the spirit of the land. I must express to you again my deep sense of the generous manner in which you have welcomed me, and in which you have permitted me to express to you my views upon public affairs. Proud of your confidence, and encouraged by your sympathy, I now deliver to you, as my last words, the cause of the Tory party, of the English Constitution, and of the British Empire. ■

Kalakaua, Last King of Hawaii, Assumes the Throne

"THEN let my motto be 'The man and woman who shall live correctly and bring forth children, they are my people.'"

WHEN THE PREVIOUS KING DIED without an heir to the throne of Hawaii, David Kalakaua, over the strong objection of a more popular candidate, Dowager Queen Emma, was chosen to succeed him; American and British warships put down the subsequent rioting. On April 13, 1874, he spoke at the capital city of Lahaina, and "His Majesty's Address to the People of Lahaina" served to announce the policies of this new king.

The Hawaiian Islands had both prospered and suffered during the first half of the nineteenth century. A financial boom of European and American trade followed Captain James Cook's 1778 discovery of the islands, but along with the trade came infectious diseases and the replacement of much native tradition by Western culture.

The king's address sought to unify his people through the common purposes of increasing commerce and repopulating the islands. His allusions to Hawaiian history point back to 1810, when Kamehameha I became the sole ruler of the islands and brought peace to the area. Kalakaua's analogy of restoring a dilapidated house leads into specific statements of his intended policy, particularly the critical need for strengthening the family unit and increasing the native population of Hawaii.

☐   ☐   ☐

People of Lahaina, before addressing to you the brief remarks which I propose to make on this occasion, I cannot omit referring to some memories of my late lamented predecessor, who made a short visit here last year, on the journey which he undertook for the benefit of his health. The late king was deeply solicitous for the welfare of his people, but the condition of his health was such that he was unable to carry out his plans for their good. I regarded the late king and his two immediate predecessors with strong affection, for on these sands and among these fields of Lahaina, they and I have played together as boys, in the family of our grandmother, Hoapili Wahine. The recollections of those days long past come before me vividly now.

And now I have come hither to see you, as my children, and that you may look upon me as your father. I thank you very much, people of the district of Lahaina, for the very warm and loyal reception which you have given us, one which neither myself, the queen, nor the members of the royal family can cease to remember with pleasure.

The principal object which I have had in view in making this journey among my people, is that we may all be incited to renewed exertions for the advancement and prosperity of our nation, the extinction of which has been prophesied.

Figures of the census have been published to show that we are a dying race. But shall we sit still, and indolently see the structure created by our fathers fall to pieces without lifting a hand to stay the work of destruction? If the house is dilapidated, let us repair it. Let us thoroughly renovate our own selves, to the end that, causes of decay being removed, the nation may grow again with new life and vigor, and our government may be firmly established—that structure which our fathers erected.

There are some of the old folks remaining and here present, the people of the time of Kamehameha I, who heard that celebrated saying "The old men, the old women, and the children may sleep by the wayside without fear." That motto remains good to this day. Kamehameha II broke the taboo on social intercourse—his word was *O ka ainoa*. Said Kamehameha III, "The righteous man is my man," and this sentiment prevails today among us, both foreigners and natives. I believe that if I shall make the main object of my reign the increase of the nation, there may be secured both the stability of the government and the national independence. Then let my motto be "The man and woman who shall live correctly and bring forth children, they are my people." And I charge you parents, take every care of your little ones. And to you children also I say, obey your parents.

The increase of the people, the advancement of agriculture and commerce—these are the objects which my government will mainly strive to accomplish. ■

Prime Minister Gladstone Argues for Toleration and the Rights of Freethinkers in the House of Commons

---

"THE *true and the wise course is not to deal out religious liberty by halves, by quarters, and by fractions but to deal it out entire. . . ."*

BRITISH STATESMAN WILLIAM EWART GLADSTONE—the GOM, or Grand Old Man—served as England's prime minister four times in the late nineteenth century. As the dominant voice of the liberal party, Gladstone opposed imperialism abroad and sought reforms at home, seeking to liberate Ireland from English rule and advocating the need for education and religious toleration.

A devout Christian, Gladstone nevertheless spoke out in 1883 for an "affirmation bill" that would allow freethinkers to affirm their allegiance without pretense of religion. Freethinker Charles Bradlaugh was seeking to enter the House of Commons without an oath of "So help me God," and on April 26, 1883, Gladstone lent his support to the affirmation bill.

The complete text of Gladstone's speech included references to classical and historical authorities in arguing for religious toleration of the irreligious and for "the interests of civil liberty." In its shortened form, the speech shows the oratorical power of Gladstone, particularly his use of balanced phrases ("a real test, a real safeguard") and parallelism ("not a wholesome, but an unwholesome, lesson" and "the most inexpressible calamity which can fall either upon a man or upon a nation"). Despite the forceful conclusion of his impassioned argument, Gladstone was unable to prevent the narrow defeat of the affirmation bill.

"You cannot fight against the future," Gladstone had warned in an 1866 speech on the Reform Bill. "Time is on our side." The same proved true of his words on admitting freethinkers; Charles Bradlaugh took the oath in the following Parliament, and within five years an affirmation bill had been passed.

In the U.S. Constitution, the presidential oath reads, "I do solemnly swear (or affirm). . . ." The chief justice, at the swearing-in, always asks the president-elect to choose (the only president to choose to "affirm" was Herbert Hoover, a Quaker, whose religion frowns on swearing in public).

□   □   □

. . .The right honorable gentleman who led the opposition to this bill said that this was not a question of difference of religion, but that it was a question between religion and irreligion—between religion and the absence of all religion—and clearly the basis of the right honorable gentleman's speech was not that we were to tolerate any belief but that we were not to tolerate no belief. I mean by tolerating to admit, to recognize, to legislate for the purpose of permitting entrance into the House of Commons.

My honorable friend the member for Finsbury, in an able speech, still more clearly expressed similar views. He referred to the ancient controversies as all very well; they touched, he said, excrescences and not the vital substance. Now, sir, I want to examine what is the vital substance, and what are the excrescences. He went further than this and used a most apt, appropriate, expressive, and still more significant phrase. He said, "Yes, it is true you admit religions some of which may go near the precipice; but now you ask us to go over it." Gentlemen opposite cheered loudly when that was said by the honorable gentleman behind me. They will not give me a single cheer now. They suspect I am quoting this with some evil intent. The question is, am I quoting them fairly? Or is it the fact that some gentlemen have not sufficiently and fairly considered their relation to the present bill, except that they mean to oppose whatever proceeds from the government?

But my honorable friend has considered very well what he said when he used the remarkable simile about the precipice. I wish to see what is the value of this main and principal contention—this doctrine of the precipice—this question between religion and irreligion, between some belief, which is to be tolerated, and no belief, which cannot be tolerated—that is to say, so far as it relates to admission into this House. The honorable and learned gentleman the member for Launceston held exactly the same language. He adopted a phrase which had fallen from the honorable member for Portsmouth which he thought had been unfairly applied; and he said he wished that there should be some form of belief and some recognition of belief—something of what is called in philosophical discussion the recognition of the supernatural. That, I believe, is a phrase which goes as near to what honorable gentlemen opposite mean as anything can. It is the recognition of the existence, at any rate, of the supernatural that is wanted. That is the main contention of the party opposite; and what I want to know is whether that contention—that proposition—offers us a good solid standing ground for legislation. Whatever test is applied—the test of the Constitution, the test of civil and political freedom, or, above all, the test of religion, and of reverence for religious conviction—I do not hesitate to say that, confidently as I support this bill, there is no ground upon which I support it with so much confidence as because of what I think is the utter hollowness and falseness of the argument that is expressed in the words I have just cited, and in the idea that is at the bottom of those words, and the danger of making them the basis of constitutional action.

Sir, what does this contention do? In the first place, it evidently violates civil freedom to this extent—that, in the words of Lord Lyndhurst, which are as wide as anything that any gentleman on this side could desire—there is to be a total divorce between the question of religious differences and the question of civil privilege and power; that there is to be no test whatever applied to a man with respect to the exercise of civil functions, except the test of civil capacity, and a fulfillment of civil conditions. Those were the words of Lord Lyndhurst—those are the words on which we stand. It is now proposed to depart from this position, and to say that a certain class of persons, perhaps a very narrow class—I do not argue that now—because it is said to have no religion is to be excepted, and alone excepted, from the operation of that great and broad principle. In my opinion, it is in the highest degree irrational to lay down a broad principle of that kind, and after granting $^{99}/_{100}$ of all, it means to stop short, in order to make an invidious exclusion of the exceedingly limited number of persons who may possibly be affected by, and concerned in, its application.

Honorable gentlemen will, perhaps, be startled when I make my next objection to the contention of the opponents of the bill. It is that it is highly disparaging to Christianity. They invite us to do that which, as a legislature, we ought never to do—namely, to travel over theological ground, and, having taken us upon that ground, what is it that they tell us? They tell us that you may go any length you please in the denial of religion, provided only you do not reject the name of the Deity. They tear religion—if I may say so—in shreds, and they set aside one particular shred of it, with which nothing will ever induce them to part. They divide religion into the dispensable and the indispensable—I am not speaking now of the cases of those who declare, or who are admitted under special laws, and I am not speaking of Jews or any of those who make declarations—I am speaking of those for whom no provision is made, except the provision of the oath, let that be clearly understood—they divide, I say, religion into what can be dispensed with and what cannot be dispensed with, and then they find that Christianity can be dispensed with. I am not willing, sir, that Christianity, if an appeal is made to us as a Christian legislature, should stand in any rank lower than that which is indispensable.

Let me illustrate what I mean. Supposing a commander has to dispatch a small body of men for the purpose of some difficult and important undertaking. They are to go without baggage and without appliances. Everything they take they must carry on their backs. They have to dispense with all luxuries and all comforts, and to take with them only that which is essential. That is precisely the same course which you ask us to take in drawing us upon theological ground. You require us to distinguish between superfluities and necessaries, and you say in regard to Christianity, "Oh, that is one of the superfluities—that is one of the excrescences, that has nothing to do with the vital substance—the great and solemn name of the Deity—which is indispensable." The adoption of such a proposition as that—and it is at the very root of your contention—seems to me to be in the highest degree disparaging to the Christian faith. . . .

I am convinced that upon every religious, as well as upon every political ground, the true and the wise course is not to deal out religious liberty by halves, by quarters, and by fractions but to deal it out entire, and to leave no distinction between man and man on the ground of religious differences from one end of the land to the other.

But, sir, I go a little further in endeavoring to test and to probe this great religious contention of the "precipice," which has been put forward, amidst fervent cheers from honorable gentlemen opposite, by my honorable friend behind me; and I want to know, is your religious distinction a real distinction at all? I will, for the sake of argument, and for no other purpose whatever, go with you on this dangerous ground of splitting religion into slices, and I ask you, "Where will you draw the line?" You draw it at the point where the abstract denial of God is severed from abstract admission of the Deity. My proposition is that your line is worthless. There is much on your side of the line which is just as objectionable as the atheism on the other side. If you call on us to draw these distinctions, let them be rational distinctions. I do not say let them be Christian distinctions; but let them be rational distinctions. . . .

You are working up the country to something like a crusade on this question, endeavoring to strengthen in the minds of the people the false notion that you have got a real test, a real safeguard—that Christianity is still generally safe, with certain unavoidable exceptions, under the protecting aegis of the oath within the walls of this chamber. And it is for that you are entering on a great religious war! I hold, then, that this contention of our opponents is disparaging to religion; it is idle; and it is also highly irrational. For if you are to have a religious test at all of the kind that you contemplate—the test of theism, which the honorable member of Portsmouth frankly said he wished to adopt—it ought to be a test of a well-ascertained theism; not a mere abstract idea dwelling in the air, and in the clouds, but a practical recognition of a divine governing power, which will some day call all of us to account for every thought we conceive, and for every word we utter.

I fear I have detained the House for a long time. But after all that has been said, and after the flood of accusations and invective that has been poured out, I have thought it right at great length and very seriously to show that, at all events, whether we be beaten or not, we do not decline the battle, and that we are not going to allow it to be said that the interests of religion are put in peril, and that they are to find their defenders only on the opposite side of the House. That sincere and conscientious defenders of those interests are to be found there I do not question at this moment; but I do contend with my whole heart and soul that the interests of religion, as well as the interests of civil liberty, are concerned in the passage of this measure.

My reasons, sir, for the passing of the bill may be summed up in a few words. If I were asked to put a construction on this oath as it stands, I probably should give it a higher meaning than most gentlemen opposite. It is my opinion, as far as I can presume to form one, that the oath has in it a very large flavor of Christianity. I am well aware that the doctrine of my honorable and learned friend the attorney general is that there are other forms of positive attestation, recognized by other systems of religion, which may enable the oath to be taken by the removal of the words "So help me God," and the substitution of some other words, or some symbolical act, involving the idea of Deity, and responsibility to the Deity. But I think we ought to estimate the real character of this oath according to the intention of the legislature. The oath does not consist of spoken words alone. The spoken words are accompanied by the corroborative act of kissing the book. What is the meaning of that? According to the intention of the legislature, I certainly should say that that act is an import of the acceptance of the divine revelation. There have been other forms in other countries. I believe in Scotland the form is still maintained of holding up the right hand instead of kissing the book. In Spain the form is, I believe, that of kissing the cross. In Italy, I think, at one time, the form was that of laying the hand on the gospel.

All these different forms meant, according to the original intention, an acceptance of Christianity. But you do not yourselves venture to say that the law could be applied in that sense. A law of this kind is like a coin spick-and-span, brand-new from the mint, carrying upon it its edges in all their sharpness and freshness; but it wears down in passing from hand to hand, and, though there is a residuum, yet the distinctive features disappear. Whatever my opinion may be as to the original vitality of the oath, I think there is very little difference of opinion as to what it has now become. It has become, as my honorable friend says, a theistic test. It is taken as no more than a theistic test. It does, as I think, involve a reference to Christianity. But while this is my personal opinion, it is not recognized by authority, and at any rate, does not prevail in practice; for some gentlemen in the other House of Parliament, if not in this also, have written works against the Christian religion, and yet have taken the oath. But, undoubtedly, it is not good for any of us to force this test so flavored, or even if not so flavored, upon men who cannot take it with a full and a cordial acceptance. It is bad—it is demoralizing to do so. It is all very well to say, "Oh, yes; but it is their responsibility." That is not, in my view, a satisfactory answer.

A seat in this House is to the ordinary Englishman in early life or, perhaps, in middle and mature life, when he has reached a position of distinction in his career, the highest prize of his ambition. But if you place between him and that prize not only the necessity of conforming to certain civil conditions but the adoption of certain religious words, and if these words are not justly measured to the condition of his conscience and of his convictions, you give him an inducement—nay, I do not go too far when I say you offer him a bribe to tamper with those convictions—to do violence to his conscience in order that he may not be stigmatized by being shout out from what is held to be the noblest privilege of the English citizen—that of representing his fellow citizens in Parliament. And, therefore, I say that, besides our duty to vindicate the principle of civil and religious liberty, which totally detaches religious controversy from the enjoyment of civil rights, it is most important that the House should consider the moral effect of this test. It is, as the honorable member for Portsmouth is neither more nor less than right in saying, a purely theistic test. Viewed as a theistic test, it embraces no acknowledgment of Providence, of divine government, of responsibility, or of retribution. It involves nothing but a bare and abstract admission—a form void of all practical meaning and concern.

This is not a wholesome, but an unwholesome, lesson. Yet more. I own that although I am now, perhaps, going to injure myself by bringing the name of Mr. Bradlaugh into this controversy, I am strongly of opinion that the present controversy should come to a close. I have no fear of atheism in this House. Truth is the expression of the divine mind; and however little our feeble vision may be able to discern the means by which God will provide for its preservation, we may leave the matter in his hands, and we may be quite sure that a firm and courageous application of every principle of justice and of equity is the best method we can adopt for the preservation and influence of truth. I must painfully record my opinion that grave injury has been done to religion in many minds— not in instructed minds, but in those which are ill instructed or partially instructed, which have a large claim on our consideration—in consequence of steps which have, unhappily, been taken.

Great mischief has been done in many minds through the resistance offered to the man elected by the constituency of Northampton, which a portion of the community believe to be unjust. When they see the profession of religion and the interests of religion ostensibly associated with what they are deeply convinced is injustice, they are led to questions about religion itself, which they see to be associated with injustice. Unbelief attracts a sympathy which it would not otherwise enjoy; and the upshot is to impair those convictions and that religious faith, the loss of which I believe to be the most inexpressible calamity which can fall either upon a man or upon a nation. ■

Democratic Candidate William Jennings Bryan Delivers His "Cross of Gold" Speech

"YOU shall not crucify mankind upon a cross of gold."

WILLIAM JENNINGS BRYAN, UNSWERVING ADVOCATE of the free coinage of silver, was three times an unsuccessful Democratic candidate for president. His first nomination, at the age of thirty-six, came at the Democratic National Convention in Chicago in 1896.

At that convention, Bryan delivered his "Cross of Gold" speech. Preferring free and unlimited silver coinage, Bryan eloquently opposed the financiers and "sound money" supporters of the gold standard and argued in favor of reflating the economy by increasing the supply of money to benefit the nation's farmers and laborers. In the 1896 election, however, Bryan—and this central idea of populism—was defeated by the Republican candidate, William McKinley, who argued for bimetallism of gold and silver only in conjunction with other world powers.

A fundamentalist in his religious convictions, Bryan concludes this powerful speech with Christian imagery ("crown of thorns" and the related words "crucify" and "cross") that impressed upon his audience the suffering inherent in maintaining the gold standard. Extensive use of rhetorical questions and parallel structure ("is as much a business man as," for example, links four successive clauses) helps reinforce Bryan's common-man appeal, nowhere more evident than in his vision of an idyllic West, with "the pioneers away out there . . . near to nature's heart, where they can mingle their voices with the voices of birds."

In the 1896 campaign, Bryan used the cross-of-gold theme in an astonishing total of six hundred speeches, causing Senator David Hill of New York, one of his Republican critics, to ask, "When does he think?"

□   □   □

Mr. Chairman and Gentlemen of the Convention:
I would be presumptuous, indeed, to present myself against the distinguished gentlemen to whom you have listened if this were a mere measuring of abilities; bu this is not a contest between persons. The humblest citizen in all the land, when clad in the armor of righteous cause, is stronger than all the hosts of error. I come to speak to you in defense of a cause as holy as the cause of liberty—the cause of humanity. . . .

When you [turning to the gold delegates] come before us and tell us that we are about to disturb your business interests, we reply that you have disturbed our business interests by your course.

We say to you that you have made the definition of a business man too limited in its application. The man who is employed for wages is as much a business man as his employer; the attorney in a country town is as much a business man as the corporation counsel in a great metropolis; the merchant at the crossroads store is as much a business man as the merchant of New York; the farmer who goes forth in the morning and toils all day, who begins in spring and toils all summer, and who by the application of brain and muscle to the natural resources of the country creates wealth is as much a business man as the man who goes to the board of trade and bets upon the price of grain; the miners who go down a thousand feet into the earth, or climb two thousand feet upon the cliffs, and bring forth from their hiding places the precious metals to be poured into the channels of trade are as much business men as the few financial magnates who, in a back room, corner the money of the world. We come to speak of this broader class of business men.

Ah, my friends, we say not one word against those who live upon the Atlantic Coast, but the hardy pioneers who have braved all the dangers of the wilderness, who have made the desert to blossom as the rose—the pioneers away out there [pointing to the West] who rear their children near to nature's heart, where they can mingle their voices with the voices of the birds—out there where they have erected schoolhouses for the education of their young, churches where they praise their Creator, and cemeteries where rest the ashes of their dead—these people, we say, are as deserving of the consideration of our party as any people in this country. It is for these that we speak. We do not come as aggressors. Our war is not a war of conquest; we are fighting in the defense of our homes, our families, and posterity. We have petitioned, and our petitions have been scorned; we have entreated, and our entreaties have been disregarded; we have begged, and they have mocked when our calamity came. We beg no longer; we entreat no more; we petition no more. We defy them! . . .

And now, my friends, let me come to the paramount issue. If they ask us why it is that we say more on the money question than we say upon the tariff question, I reply that, if protection has slain its thousands, the gold standard has slain its tens of thousands. If they ask us why we do not embody in our platform all the things that we believe in, we reply that when we have restored the money of the Constitution all other necessary reforms will be possible; but that until this is done there is no other reform that can be accomplished.

Why is it that within three months such a change has come over the country? Three months ago when it was confidently asserted that those who believe in the gold standard would frame our platform and nominate our candidates, even the advocates of the gold standard did not think that we could elect a president. And they had good reason for their doubt, because there is scarcely a state here today asking for the gold standard which is not in the absolute control of the Republican party. But note the change. Mr. McKinley was nominated at St. Louis upon a platform which declared for the maintenance of the gold standard until it can be changed into bimetallism by international agreement. Mr. McKinley was the most popular man among the Republicans, and three months ago everybody in the Republican party prophesied his election. How is it today? Why, the man who was once pleased to think that he looked like Napoleon—that man shudders today when he remembers that he was nominated on the anniversary of the Battle of Waterloo. Not only that, but as he listens he can hear with ever-increasing distinctness the sound of the waves as they beat upon the lonely shores of St. Helena.

Why this change? Ah, my friends, is not the reason for the change evident to anyone who will look at the matter? No private character, however pure, no personal popularity, however great, can protect from the avenging wrath of an indignant people a man who will declare that he is in favor of fastening the gold standard upon this country, or who is willing to surrender the right of self-government and place the legislative control of our affairs in the hands of foreign potentates and powers.

We go forth confident that we shall win. Why? Because upon the paramount issue of this campaign there is not a spot of ground upon which the enemy will dare to challenge battle. If they tell us that the gold standard is a good thing, we shall point to their platform and tell them that their platform pledges the party to get rid of the gold standard and substitute bimetallism. If the gold standard is a good thing, why try to get rid of it? I call your attention to the fact that some of the very people who are in this convention today and who tell us that we ought to declare in favor of international bimetallism—thereby declaring that the gold standard is wrong and that the principle of bimetallism is better—these very people four months ago were open and avowed advocates of the gold standard, and were then telling us that we could not legislate two metals together, even with the aid of all the world. If the gold standard is a good thing, we ought to declare in favor of its retention and not in favor of abandoning it; and if the gold standard is a bad thing, why should we wait until other nations are willing to help us to let go? Here is the line of battle, and we care not upon which issue they force the fight; we are prepared to meet them on either issue or on both. If they tell us that the gold standard is the standard of civilization, we reply to them that this, the most enlightened of all the nations of the earth has never declared for a gold standard and that both the great parties this year are declaring against it. If the gold standard is the standard of civilization, why, my friends, should we not have it? If they come to meet us on that issue we can present the history of our nation. More than that; we can tell them that they will search the pages of history in vain to find a single instance where the common people of any land have ever declared themselves in favor of the gold standard. They can find where the holders of fixed investments have declared for a gold standard, but not where the masses have.

Mr. Carlisle said in 1878 that this was a struggle between "the idle holders of idle capital" and "the struggling masses, who produce the wealth and pay the taxes of the country"; and, my friends, the question we are to decide is, Upon which side will the Democratic party fight—upon the side of "the idle holders of idle capital" or upon the side of "the struggling masses"? That is the question which the party must answer first, and then it must be answered by each individual hereafter. The sympathies of the Democratic party, as shown by the platform, are on the side of the struggling masses who have ever been the foundation of the Democratic party. There are two ideas of government. There are those who believe that, if you will only legislate to make the well-to-do prosperous, their prosperity will leak through on those below. The Democratic idea, however, has been that if you legislate to make the masses prosperous, their prosperity will find its way up through every class which rests upon them.

You come to us and tell us that the great cities are in favor of the gold standard; we reply that the great cities rest upon our broad and fertile prairies. Burn down your cities and leave our farms, and your cities will spring up again as if by magic; but destroy our farms, and the grass will grow in the streets of every city in the country.

My friends, we declare that this nation is able to legislate for its own people on every question, without waiting for the aid or consent of any other nation on earth; and upon that issue we expect to carry every state in the Union. I shall not slander the inhabitants of the fair state of Massachusetts nor the inhabitants of the state of New York by saying that, when they are confronted with the proposition, they will declare that this nation is not able to attend to its own business. It is the issue of 1776 over again. Our ancestors, when but three millions in number, had the courage to declare their political independence of every other nation; shall we, their descendants, when we have grown to seventy millions, declare that we are less independent than our forefathers? No, my friends, that will never be the verdict of our people. Therefore, we care not upon what lines the battle is fought. If they say bimetallism is good, but that we cannot have it until other nations help us, we reply that, instead of having a gold standard because England has, we will restore bimetallism, and then let England have bimetallism because the United States has it. If they dare to come out in the open field and defend the gold standard as a good thing, we will fight them to the uttermost. Having behind us the producing masses of this nation and the world, supported by the commercial interests, the laboring interests, and the toilers everywhere, we will answer their demand for a gold standard by saying to them, You shall not press down upon the brow of labor this crown of thorns; you shall not crucify mankind upon a cross of gold. ■

"Bull Moose" Candidate Theodore Roosevelt Gives the "Speech That Saved His Life"

"I have just been shot; but it takes more than that to kill a Bull Moose. But fortunately I had my manuscript . . . this is where the bullet went through—and it probably saved me from it going into my heart. The bullet is in me now, so that I cannot make a very long speech, but I will try my best."

IN A REMARK REPORTED BY JAMES BOSWELL but no longer often quoted in full, Samuel Johnson said, "Sir, a woman preaching is like a dog's walking on his hinder legs. It is not done well; but you are surprised to find it done at all."

This address by Theodore Roosevelt, campaigning on the independent "Bull Moose" ticket to return to the presidency, was too long, rambling, and melodramatic to be rated a "great" speech. But the wonder of it is that it was delivered at all.

As noted by the national archivist Roger Bruns, because of his poor eyesight Teddy Roosevelt "often prepared his speeches on small pieces of paper with large words and spaces between the lines to help him see the material during delivery. Thus, the manuscripts of his speeches were often quite thick."

On the evening of October 14, 1912, getting into a car on his way to a campaign speech in Milwaukee, a man named John Shrank, who had been stalking the former president for days, shot him in the chest. Wrestled to the ground, the would-be assassin was reported to have said, "Any man looking for a third term ought to be shot." Shrank spent the rest of his life in a mental institution.

The .32 caliber bullet was slowed by the thick sheaf of paper that Roosevelt had stuffed in his breast pocket. The speech had literally saved his life. With bloodstains seeping through his shirt, the former pugilist, big-game hunter, and advocate of "the strenuous life" insisted on being taken to the auditorium rather than a hospital. With a sure sense of the dramatic, the gutsy—some would say foolhardy—TR was determined to deliver his speech or die trying.

He ad-libbed around the text, of course, taking full advantage of the drama in front of the horrified audience. He brandished his text with the hole in it, opened his jacket to reveal his bloodstained shirt, and waved away medical help: "I know these doctors, when they get hold of me, will never let me go back, and there are just a few more things I want to say to you."

The "few more things" stretched into a talk variously estimated at fifty to ninety minutes, and he was helped from the platform wanting to continue. The following excerpts are from both the prepared text in his papers and reports of the speech as delivered. Roosevelt ultimately ran ahead of the incumbent Republican president, William Howard Taft, and the Socialist Eugene Debs, but the divided GOP vote enabled the Democratic candidate, New Jersey governor Woodrow Wilson, to be elected.

□   □   □

Friends, I shall ask you to be as quiet as possible. I don't know whether you fully understand that I have just been shot; but it takes more than that to kill a Bull Moose.

But fortunately I had my manuscript, so you see I was going to make a long speech, and there is a bullet—there is where the bullet went through—and it probably saved me from it going into my heart. The bullet is in me now, so that I cannot make a very long speech, but I will try my best.

And now, friends, I want to take advantage of this incident to say a word of solemn warning to my fellow countrymen. First of all, I want to say this about myself: I have altogether too important things to think of to feel any concern over my own death; and now I cannot speak to you insincerely within five minutes of being shot.

I am telling you the literal truth when I say that my concern is for many other things. It is not in the least for my own life. I want you to understand that I am ahead of the game, anyway. No man has had a happier life than I have led; a happier life in every way. I have been able to do certain things that I greatly wished to do, and I am interested in doing other things. I can tell you with absolute truthfulness that I am very much uninterested in whether I am shot or not. It was just as when I was colonel of my regiment. I always felt that a private was to be excused for feeling at times some pangs of anxiety about his personal safety, but I cannot understand a man fit to be a colonel who can pay any heed to his personal safety when he is occupied as he ought to be with the absorbing desire to do his duty.

I am in this cause with my whole heart and soul. I believe that the Progressive movement is making life a little easier for all our people; a movement to try to take the burdens off the men and especially the women and children of this country. I am absorbed in the success of that movement. . . .

I say this by way of introduction, because I want to say something very serious to our people and especially to the newspapers. I don't know anything about who the man was who shot me tonight. . . . He shot to kill. He shot—the shot, the bullet went in here—I will show you. [Opens jacket, shows bloodstained shirt.]

I am going to ask you to be as quiet as possible for I am not able to give the challenge of the bull moose quite as loudly. Now, I do not know who he was or what he represented. He was a coward. He stood in the darkness in the crowd around the automobile and when they cheered me, and I got up to bow, he stepped forward and shot me in the darkness.

Now, friends, of course, I do not know, as I say, anything about him; but it is a very natural thing that weak and vicious minds should be inflamed to acts of violence by the kind of awful mendacity and abuse that have been heaped upon me for the last three months by the papers in the interest of not only Mr. Debs but of Mr. Wilson and Mr. Taft.

Friends, I will disown and repudiate any man of my party who attacks with such foul slander and abuse any opponent of any other party; and now I wish to say seriously to all the daily newspapers, to the Republicans, the Democrat, and Socialist parties, that they cannot, month-in month-out and year-in and year-out, make the kind of untruthful, of bitter assault that they have made and not expect that brutal, violent natures, or brutal and violent characters, especially when the brutality is accompanied by a not very strong mind—they cannot expect that such natures will be unaffected by it.

Now, friends, I am not speaking for myself at all, I give you my word, I do not care a rap about being shot; not a rap. I have had a good many experiences in my time and this is one of them. What I care for is my country.

I wish I were able to impress upon my people—our people, the duty to feel strongly but to speak the truth of their opponents. I say now, I have never said one word on the stump against any opponent that I cannot defend. I have said nothing that I could not substantiate and nothing that I ought not to have said—nothing that I—nothing that, looking back at, I would not say again.

[Waves off doctor approaching him onstage.] I am not sick at all. I am all right.

Now, friends, it ought not to be too much to ask that our opponents . . . make up their minds to speak only the truth, and not use that kind of slander and mendacity which if taken seriously must incite weak and violent natures to crimes of violence. Don't you make any mistake. Don't you pity me. I am all right. I am all right and you cannot escape listening to the speech either . . .

This effort to assassinate me emphasizes to a peculiar degree the need for the Progressive movement. Friends, every good citizen ought to do everything in his or her power to prevent the coming of the day when we shall see in this country two recognized creeds fighting one another; when we shall see the creed of the "Have-nots" arraigned against the creed of the "Haves." When that day comes then such incidents as this tonight will be commonplace in our history. When . . . you permit the conditions to grow such that the poor man as such will be swayed by his sense of injury against the men who try to hold what they improperly have won, when that day comes, the most awful passions will be let loose and it will be an ill day for our country.

Now, friends, what we who are in this movement are endeavoring to do is forestall any such movement for justice now—a movement in which we ask all just men of generous hearts to join with the men who feel in their souls that lift upward which bids them refuse to be satisfied themselves while their countrymen and countrywomen suffer from avoidable misery. Now, friends, what we Progressives are trying to do is to enroll rich or poor, whatever their social or industrial position, to stand together for those elementary rights which are the foundation of good citizenship in this great Republic of ours. [A renewed effort was made to persuade Mr. Roosevelt to conclude his speech.] My friends are a little more nervous than I am. Don't you waste any sympathy on me. I have had an A-1 time in life and I am having it now.

I never in my life was in any movement in which I was able to serve with such wholehearted devotion as in this; in which I was able to feel as I do in this that common weal. I have fought for the good of our common country.

And now, friends, I shall have to cut short much of that speech that I meant to give you, but I want to touch on just two or three points. . . . I know these doctors, when they get hold of me, will never let me go back, and there are just a few more things that I want to say to you.

I have got to make one comparison between Mr. Wilson and myself, simply because he has invited it and I cannot shrink from it. Mr. Wilson has seen fit to attack me, to say that I did not do much against the trusts when I was president. I have got two answers to make to that. In the first place what I did, and then I want to compare what I did when I was president with what Mr. Wilson did not do when he was governor.

When I took the office the antitrust law was practically a dead letter and the interstate commerce law in as poor a condition. I had to revive both laws. I did. I enforced both. It will be easy enough to do now what I did then, but the reason that it is easy now is because I did it when it was hard. . . .

Mr. Wilson has said that the states are the proper authorities to deal with the trusts. Well, about 80 percent of the trusts are organized in New Jersey. The Standard Oil, the Tobacco, the Sugar, the Beef, all those trusts are organized in the state of New Jersey and the laws of New Jersey say that their charters can at any time be amended or repealed if they misbehave themselves and give the government ample power to act about those laws, and Mr. Wilson has been governor a year and nine months and he has not opened his lips. The chapter describing what Mr. Wilson has done about trusts in New Jersey would read precisely like a chapter describing snakes in Ireland, which ran: "There are no snakes in Ireland." Mr. Wilson has done precisely and exactly nothing about the trusts. . . .

When the Republican party—not the Republican party—when the bosses in control of the Republican party, the Barneses and Penroses, last June stole the nomination and wrecked the Republican party for good and all—I want to point out to you that nominally they stole that nomination from me, but it was really from you. They did not like me, and the longer they live the less cause they will have to like me. But while they don't like me, they dread you. You are the people that they dread. They dread the people themselves, and those bosses and the big special interests behind them made up their mind that they would rather see the Republican party wrecked than see it come under the control of the people themselves. So I am not dealing with the Republican party.

There are only two ways you can vote this year. You can be progressive or reactionary. Whether you vote Republican or Democratic it does not make a difference, you are voting reactionary.

Now, the Democratic party in its platform and through the utterances of Mr. Wilson has distinctly committed itself to the old flintlock, muzzle-loaded doctrine of states' rights, and I have said distinctly we are for people's rights. . . . I ask you to look at our declaration and hear and read our platform about social and industrial justice and then, friends, vote for the Progressive ticket without regard to me, without regard to my personality—for only by voting for that platform can you be true to the cause of progress throughout this Union. [Helped off platform.] ■

Claude Bowers Conjures the Ghosts of Democrats Past to Keynote a Convention

"A clear call comes to us today to fight anew under the Jeffersonian banner, with the Jacksonian sword, and in the Wilsonian spirit, and, crashing the gates of privilege, make Jeffersonian democracy a living force again in the lives and homes of men."

A GOOD KEYNOTE ADDRESS is at once a leisurely evocation of the glory of a partisan past and a brief promise of a glorious future. In the television age, it is also a showcase for a promising young politician, and a party's presentation of what it considers the best image of the party to the public. A keynoter is usually not assigned to deal with the central issue of the time, its key note; rather, it is the orator's job at the start of a gathering of partisans to uplift, exhort, and galvanize the troops.

An example of this kind of keynote address is that of Claude Bowers at the 1928 Democratic National Convention in Houston. That convention nominated Al Smith to face Herbert Hoover, just nominated by the Republicans in Kansas City to succeed Calvin Coolidge. Bowers (1878–1958) was a political columnist for the *New York Journal* and a popular historian, whose best-known works were *The Party Battles of the Jackson Era* and *Jefferson and Hamilton* (he revered Jefferson and despised Hamilton). He later served as FDR's ambassador to Spain during its civil war and to Chile in the 1940s.

The orator associates the Republicans with Hamilton and dissociates them from their Lincoln; he foresees a "plunderbund," or association of predators, if the opposition stays in power; and he makes the coming political contest an Armageddon between the forces of good and evil: "They are led by money-mad cynics and scoffers—and we go forth to battle for the cause of man." It made everybody in the hall feel good.

□   □   □

L adies and Gentlemen of the Convention:
The American Democracy has mobilized today to wage a war of extermination against privilege and pillage. We prime our guns against autocracy and bureaucracy. We march against that centralization which threatens the liberties of the people. We fight for the republic of the fathers, and for the recovery of the covenant from the keeping of a caste and class. We battle for the honor of the nation, besmirched and bedraggled by the most brazen and shameless carnival of corruption that ever blackened the reputation of a decent and self-respecting people.

We stand for the spirit of the preamble of the Declaration that is made a mockery; for the Bill of Rights that is ignored; for the social and economic justice which is refused; for the sovereign right of states that are denied; and for a return to the old-fashioned civic integrity of a Jackson, a Tilden, a Cleveland, and a Wilson. We stand for the restoration of the government to the people who built it by their bravery and cemented it with their blood. . . .

The issues are as fundamental as they were when Jefferson and Hamilton crossed swords more than a century ago. To understand the conflicting views of these two men on the functions of government is to grasp the deep significance of this campaign.

Now, Hamilton believed in the rule of an aristocracy of money, and Jefferson in a democracy of men.

Hamilton believed that governments are created for the domination of the masses, and Jefferson that they are created for the service of the people.

Hamilton wrote to Morris that governments are strong in proportion as they are made profitable to the powerful; and Jefferson knew that no government is fit to live that does not conserve the interest of the average man.

Hamilton proposed a scheme for binding the wealthy to the government by making government a source of revenue to the wealthy; and Jefferson unfurled his banner of equal rights.

Hamilton would have concentrated authority remote from the people, and Jefferson would have diffused it among them.

Hamilton would have injected governmental activities into all the affairs of men; and Jefferson laid it down as an axiom of freedom that "that government is best which governs least."

Just put a pin in this: there is not a major evil of which the American people are complaining now that is not due to the triumph of the Hamiltonian conception of the state. And the tribute to Hamilton at Kansas City was an expression of fealty to him who thought that governments are strong in proportion as they are made profitable to the powerful; who proposed the plan for binding the wealthy; who devised the scheme to tax the farm to pay the factory; and whose purpose was to make democracy in America a mockery and a sham.

Thus we are challenged once more to a conflict on the fundamentals; and a clear call comes to us today to fight anew under the Jeffersonian banner, with the Jacksonian sword, and in the Wilsonian spirit, and, crashing the gates of privilege, make Jeffersonian democracy a living force again in the lives and homes of men. . . .

You cannot believe with Lincoln in a government "of the people, by the people, and for the people," and with Hamilton in a government of the wealthy, by the influential, and for the powerful.

There are Lincoln Republicans and Hamilton Republicans, but never the twain shall meet. . . .

What a majestic figure was he who led us in those fruitful years! The cold, even light of his superb intellect played upon the most intricate problems of the times, and they seemed to solve themselves. He lifted the people to such heights of moral grandeur as they had never known before; and his name and purpose made hearts beat faster in lowly places where his praise was sung in every language in the world. And when at length, his body broken, but his spirit soaring still, he fell stricken, while still battling for his faith, there passed to time and to eternity and to all mankind the everlasting keeping of the immortal memory of Woodrow Wilson.

We submit that a party that stands for that democracy which is inseparable from the liberties of men, and has given a Jefferson, a Jackson, and a Wilson to the service of mankind, has earned the right, in times like these, to the cooperation of independents and progressives in the struggle for the preservation of popular government, and the purging of the nation of that corruption which has made America a byword and a hissing in the very alleys of the world. . . .

Never in a century has there been such a call to us to battle for the faith of our fathers as there is today; and never has the control of government been so completely concentrated in the hands of a willing caste as now. The dreams of the Hamiltonians have literally come true while the people slept. They wanted organized wealth in possession of the government—and we have it. They wanted the sovereign rights of states denied—and we have it. They wanted bureaucratic agents swarming over the land like the locusts of Egypt—and we have it. They wanted government made profitable to the powerful—and we have it. They wanted, through administration, to make a mockery of democracy—and we have it. The Hamiltonian state is necessarily a temple of gold resting on the bowed back of peasants in other people's fields—and we almost have that now. They would deify dollars and minimize men, limit self-government and centralize power, cripple democracy, empower bureaucracy, welcome plutocracy—and we will soon have that, too.

Give the plunderbund but eight years more of such governmental cooperation, and a combination of power companies will put a few men in control of the public utilities of a mighty empire. Make no mistake about it—that is the great Jacksonian struggle of tomorrow. And with that sinister possibility upon us, the people must determine whether they will entrust their interest to those who believe that governments are strong in proportion as they are made profitable to the powerful or to the Jeffersonians, who believe that governments are created for the service of mankind. Once in possession and entrenched, the plunderbund of the power monopoly cannot be dislodged by the fighting force of a dozen Andrew Jacksons. . . .

We are mobilized to lead the people back to the old paths of constitutional liberty and to the good way. We are going back—back to the old landmarks of liberty and equality when ordinary men had rights that even power respected; when justice, not privilege, was the watchword of the state; when the preamble of the declaration and the bill of rights had meaning; when the nation embraced every section and every class. . . .

Our principles have been written in the triumphs of the people and baptized in the blood of our bravest and our best. Jefferson phrased them, Jackson vitalized them, Wilson applied them, and we go forth to battle for them now.

We face a foe grown arrogant with success. It were infamy to permit the enemy to divide us, or divert us, on the eve of such a battle. Issues are involved that go to the determination of the future of our institutions and our children. The call that comes to us is as sacred as the cause of humanity itself. From the grave at the Hermitage comes the solemn warning that no party ever won or deserved to win that did not organize and fight unitedly for victory—and we shall thus organize and fight. This is a unique campaign. . . .

And we shall win because our cause is just. The predatory forces before us seek a triumph for the sake of the sacking. Their shock troops are the Black Horse Cavalry whose hoofbeats have made hideous music on Pennsylvania Avenue during the last eight years. They are led by money-mad cynics and scoffers—and we go forth to battle for the cause of man. In the presence of such a foe "he who dallies is a dastard and he who doubts is damned." In this convention we close debate and grasp the sword. The time has come. The battle hour has struck. "Then to your tents, O Israel!" ■

President Franklin D. Roosevelt's First Inaugural Instills Confidence in a Depression-Racked Nation

"THIS great nation will endure as it has endured, will revive and will prosper. So, first of all, let me assert my firm belief that the only thing we have to fear is fear itself—nameless, unreasoning, unjustified terror which paralyzes needed efforts to convert retreat into advance."

TWO EMOTIONS—despair and panic—gripped the nation in the depression winter of 1932–33. One out of four workers could not find a job; world grain prices were at a 300-year low; governors of thirty-eight states had closed the banks. In the preceding summer, the Democratic candidate, in his acceptance speech, had promised "a new deal for the American people" and had won the election in a popular landslide, but in the long interregnum between November and March he had not worked with the defeated President Hoover to help revive the economy or refortify spirits. In Europe, fascism was on the rise, and in the United States, the desire for a "man on horseback" to take charge of a moribund America was a threat—indeed, the strongest applause in the new president's speech came after the line warning he might call for "broad executive power to wage a war against the emergency."

Franklin D. Roosevelt, who moved from the New York governorship to the presidency at age fifty-one, had no dictatorship in mind; instead, he saw the need for a dramatic infusion of confidence with a ringing speech, followed by a great show of government activity, to shake the nation out of its mental as well as economic depression. He had in mind some banking regulation and a mild stimulus, with cuts in federal payrolls offset by increases in relief payments—relatively conservative steps in retrospect, considering the scope of the crisis, but seen as daring at the time.

Working from a draft prepared by Columbia University professor Raymond Moley, one of his "brain trusters," he wrote out a speech designed to lift spirits. The public had derided his predecessor's efforts on that score as "Prosperity is just around the corner"; FDR added his scorn to the failed exhortations, but was not afraid to offer "Plenty is at our doorstep." The most famous line, about "fear itself," is sometimes attributed to FDR's reading of Henry David Thoreau's "Nothing is so much to be feared as fear," and a nearly identical line can be found in Sir Francis Bacon's works, but Professor Moley told the anthologist in 1966 that the line was submitted by Louis Howe, the gnomic Roosevelt adviser, who saw the phrase in a newspaper ad a few weeks before the inaugural.

The speech opens with an attack on "the money changers" who had been driven from the temple—a biblical allusion to an act by Jesus—which made the bankers and the moneyed class in general the already routed villain, An "action program" is promised, but not specified; a moral lesson is drawn, frowning at the previous decade's "mad chase of evanescent profits"; a martial call for discipline and sacrifice is made, the metaphor extended with "I assume unhesitatingly the leadership of this great army of our people dedicated to a disciplined attack. . . ." Then comes the warning that if this plan doesn't work, he will ask Congress for greater power to bring "discipline and direction under leadership," because the people have made him "the present instrument of their wishes."

The general promise to do something—to stop the drift and reverse direction—coupled with the steel in the speech of the imposition of "discipline" into the chaos, and the vigor of the voice heard on radio, had an electric effect on popular opinion. The bold tone and buoyant delivery encouraged people parched for hope.

□   □   □

This is a day of national consecration.
I am certain that my fellow Americans expect that on my induction into the presidency I will address them with a candor and a decision which the present situation of our nation impels. This is preeminently the time to speak the truth, the whole truth, frankly and boldly. Nor need we shrink from honestly facing conditions in our country today. This great nation will endure as it has endured, will revive and will prosper. So, first of all, let me assert my firm belief that the only thing we have to fear is fear itself—nameless, unreasoning, unjustified terror which paralyzes needed efforts to convert retreat into advance. In every dark hour of our national life a leadership of frankness and vigor has met with that understanding and support of the people themselves which is essential to victory. I am convinced that you will again give that support to leadership in these critical days.

In such a spirit on my part and on yours we face our common difficulties. They concern, thank God, only material things. Values have shrunken to fantastic levels; taxes have risen; our ability to pay has fallen; government of all kinds is faced by serious curtailment of income; the means of exchange are frozen in the currents of trade; the withered leaves of industrial enterprise lie on every side; farmers find no markets for their produce; the savings of many years in thousands of families are gone.

More important, a host of unemployed citizens face the grim problem of existence, and an equally great number toil with little return. Only a foolish optimist can deny the dark realities of the moment.

Yet our distress comes from no failure of substance. We are stricken by no plague of locusts. Compared with the perils which our forefathers conquered because they believed and were not afraid, we have still much to be thankful for. Nature still offers her bounty, and human efforts have multiplied it. Plenty is at our doorstep, but a generous use of it languishes in the very sight of the supply. Primarily this is because rulers of the exchange of mankind's goods have failed through their own stubbornness and their own incompetence, have admitted their failure, and have abdicated. Practices of the unscrupulous money changers stand indicted in the court of public opinion, rejected by the hearts and minds of men.

True, they have tried, but their efforts have been cast in the pattern of an outworn tradition. Faced by failure of credit, they have proposed only the lending of more money. Stripped of the lure of profit by which to induce our people to follow their false leadership, they have resorted to exhortations, pleading tearfully for restored confidence. They know only the rules of a generation of self-seekers. They have no vision, and when there is no vision the people perish.

The money changers have fled from their high seats in the temple of our civilization. We may now restore that temple to the ancient truths. The measure of the restoration lies in the extent to which we apply social values more noble than mere monetary profit.

Happiness lies not in the mere possession of money; it lies in the joy of achievement, in the thrill of creative effort. The joy and moral stimulation of work no longer must be forgotten in the mad chase of evanescent profits. These dark days will be worth all they cost us if they teach us that our true destiny is not to be ministered unto but to minister to ourselves and to our fellowmen.

Recognition of the falsity of material wealth as the standard of success goes hand in hand with the abandonment of the false belief that public office and high political position are to be valued only by the standards of pride of place and personal profit; and there must be an end to a conduct in banking and in business which too often has given to a sacred trust the likeness of callous and selfish wrongdoing. Small wonder that confidence languishes, for it thrives only on honesty, on honor, on the sacredness of obligations, on faithful protection, on unselfish performance; without them it cannot live.

Restoration calls, however, not for changes in ethics alone. This nation asks for action, and action now.

Our greatest primary task is to put people to work. This is no unsolvable problem if we face it wisely and courageously. It can be accomplished in part by direct recruiting by the government itself, treating the task as we would treat the emergency of a war, but at the same time, through this employment, accomplishing greatly needed projects to stimulate and reorganize the use of our natural resources.

Hand in hand with this we must frankly recognize the overbalance of population in our industrial centers and, by engaging on a national scale in a redistribution, endeavor to provide a better use of the land for those best fitted for the land. The task can be helped by definite efforts to raise the values of agricultural products and with this the power to purchase the output of our cities. It can be helped by preventing realistically the tragedy of the growing loss through foreclosure of our small homes and our farms. It can be helped by insistence that the federal, state, and local governments act forthwith on the demand that their cost be drastically reduced. It can be helped by the unifying of relief activities, which today are often scattered, uneconomical, and unequal. It can be helped by national planning for and supervision of all forms of transportation and of communications and other utilities which have a definitely public character. There are many ways in which it can be helped, but it can never be helped merely by talking about it. We must act and act quickly.

Finally, in our progress toward a resumption of work we require two safeguards against a return of the evils of the old order: there must be a strict supervision of all banking and credits and investments, so that there will be an end to speculation with other people's money; and there must be provision for an adequate but sound currency.

These are the lines of attack. I shall presently urge upon a new Congress, in special session, detailed measures for their fulfillment, and I shall seek the immediate assistance of the several states.

Through this program of action we address ourselves to putting our own national house in order and making income balance outgo. Our international trade relations, though vastly important, are in point of time and necessity secondary to the establishment of a sound national economy. I favor as a practical policy the putting of first things first. I shall spare no effort to restore world trade by international economic readjustment, but the emergency at home cannot wait on that accomplishment.

The basic thought that guides these specific means of national recovery is not narrowly nationalistic. It is the insistence, as a first consideration, upon the interdependence of the various elements in and parts of the United States—a recognition of the old and permanently important manifestation of the American spirit of the pioneer. It is the way to recovery. It is the immediate way. It is the strongest assurance that the recovery will endure.

In the field of world policy I would dedicate this nation to the policy of the good neighbor—the neighbor who resolutely respects himself and, because he does so, respects the rights of others—the neighbor who respects his obligations and respects the sanctity of his agreements in and with a world of neighbors.

If I read the temper of our people correctly, we now realize as we have never realized before our interdependence on each other; that we cannot merely take but we must give as well; that if we are to go forward, we must move as a trained and loyal army willing to sacrifice for the good of a common discipline, because without such discipline no progress is made, no leadership becomes effective. We are, I know, ready and willing to submit our lives and property to such discipline, because it makes possible a leadership which aims at a larger good. This I propose to offer, pledging that the larger purposes will bind upon us all as a sacred obligation with a unity of duty hitherto evoked only in time of armed strife.

With this pledge taken, I assume unhesitatingly the leadership of this great army of our people dedicated to a disciplined attack upon our common problems.

Action in this image and to this end is feasible under the form of government which we have inherited from our ancestors. Our Constitution is so simple and practical that it is possible always to meet extraordinary needs by changes in emphasis and arrangement without loss of essential form. That is why our constitutional system has proved itself the most superbly enduring political mechanism the modern world has produced. It has met every stress of vast expansion of territory, of foreign wars, of bitter internal strife, of world relations.

It is to be hoped that the normal balance of executive and legislative authority may be wholly adequate to meet the unprecedented task before us. But it may be that an unprecedented demand and need for undelayed action may call for temporary departure from that normal balance of public procedure.

I am prepared under my constitutional duty to recommend the measures that a stricken nation in the midst of a stricken world may require. These measures, or such other measures as the Congress may build out of its experience and wisdom, I shall seek, within my constitutional authority, to bring to speedy adoption.

But in the event that the Congress shall fail to take one of these two courses, and in the event that the national emergency is still critical. I shall not evade the clear course of duty that will then confront me. I shall ask the Congress for the one remaining instrument to meet the crisis— broad executive power to wage a war against the emergency, as great as the power that would be given to me if we were in fact invaded by a foreign foe.

For the trust reposed in me I will return the courage and the devotion that befit the time. I can do no less.

We face the arduous days that lie before us in the warm courage of national unity; with the clear consciousness of seeking old and precious moral values; with the clean satisfaction that comes from the stern performance of duty by old and young alike. We aim at the assurance of a rounded and permanent national life.

We do not distrust the future of essential democracy. The people of the United States have not failed. In their need they have registered a mandate that they want direct, vigorous action. They have asked for discipline and direction under leadership. They have made me the present instrument of their wishes. In the spirit of the gift I take it.

In this dedication of a nation we humbly ask the blessing of God. May he protect each and every one of us. May he guide me in the days to come. ■

Winston Churchill Warns the West of the Soviet "Iron Curtain"

"FROM Stettin in the Baltic to Trieste in the Adriatic, an iron curtain has descended across the Continent."

THE WARTIME LEADER OF BRITAIN, turned out of office by a populace that preferred an experiment with socialism, came to the United States to alert the Western world to the danger of an expansionist Soviet Union. At the suggestion of President Harry Truman, a Missourian, he chose the small Westminster College, in Fulton, Missouri, as his forum—not a prestigious setting, but he was accompanied on the train from Washington by the president, who played a gentle game of poker on the way.

This is a Beethoven symphony of a speech, delivered March 5, 1946. Too often, anthologists cut it to a third of its length, and historians cite it for the "iron curtain" coinage. About that phrase: Churchill titled his speech "The Sinews of Peace," using a muscular metaphor to send the message that peace required strength. The phrase "iron curtain" had been used since the eighteenth century as the name for the fireproof curtain in theaters. As a metaphor, it was used by the earl of Munster in 1819, by H. G. Wells in 1904, and frequently by the German general staff. In May of 1945, Churchill cabled Truman about the Russians: "An iron curtain is drawn down their frontier. We do not know what is going on behind." Ten months later, he used the phrase twice in his Fulton speech, and it provided the label needed to describe the Soviet conquest of Eastern Europe.

It begins with the sounds of an orchestra tuning up: an amusing play on the name Westminster, as the speaker gets in tune with his audience. Then the duh-duh-duh-dum of a beginning: "The United States stands at this time at the pinnacle of world power. It is a solemn moment. . . ." The first movement is about the "overall strategic concept" of providing safety from war and tyranny: Churchill proposes a police force for the United Nations around the world, and acknowledges the Soviet domination of Eastern Europe but calls for the West "to proclaim in fearless tones the great principles of freedom and the rights of man."

The second movement's point is helped by introducing it as "the crux" of what the speaker has "traveled here to say": that is, a "special relationship" must be encouraged between the British Commonwealth and the United States, which might lead one day to a common citizenship, but is surely needed now to preserve peace with freedom in the face of the new Soviet threat.

The third movement is a dark delineation of that threat: "A shadow has fallen upon the scenes so lately lighted [he first said 'lightened'] by the Allied victory." But—and then came the iron curtain line. He lists the fallen countries—"somber facts to have to recite on the morrow of a victory"—and hints at his concern about the agreement at Yalta (where Roosevelt trusted Stalin against Churchill's better judgment).

Finally, in the speech's fourth movement, he reprises the crux of what he came to say: that the answer to the threat is the special relationship of the English-speaking peoples, in fraternal association on the "high roads of the future." For whom and for how long? "Not only for us but for all, not only for our time for a century to come."

In substance, the "Iron Curtain" speech reads well five decades later, after the collapse of the Soviet empire, and after the Americans and British led the world into stopping the threat in the Persian Gulf in the early nineties. Though its use of a catchphrase overshadowed its own substance, and though it was not delivered by a prime minister speaking in defiance of bombers overhead, this is the most Churchillian of Churchill's speeches.

□   □   □

I am very glad, indeed, to come to Westminister College this afternoon, and I am complimented that you should give me a degree from an institution whose reputation has been so solidly accepted. It is the name Westminister, somehow or other, which seems familiar to me. I feel as if I'd heard of it before. Indeed, now that I come to think of it, it was at Westminster that I received a very large part of my education in politics, dialectics, rhetoric, and one or two other things. In fact, we have both been educated at the same, or similar, or at any rate kindred, establishments.

It is also an honor, ladies and gentlemen, perhaps almost unique, for a private visitor to be introduced to an academic audience by the president of the United States. Amid his heavy burdens, duties, and responsibilities—

unsought but not recoiled from—the president has traveled a thousand miles to dignify and magnify our meeting here today and to give me an opportunity of addressing this kindred nation, as well as my own country-men across the ocean and perhaps some other countries too.

The president has told you that it is his wish, as I am sure it is yours, that I should have full liberty to give my true and faithful counsel in these anxious and baffling times. I shall certainly avail myself of this free-dom and feel the more right to do so because any private ambitions I may have cherished in my younger days have been satisfied beyond my wildest dreams.

Let me, however, make it clear that I have no official mission or status of any kind and that I speak only for myself. There is nothing here but what you see. I can, therefore, allow my mind, with the experience of a lifetime, to play over the problems which beset us on the morrow of our absolute victory in arms, and to try to make sure, with what strength I have, that what has been gained with so much sacrifice and suffering shall be preserved for the future glory and safety of mankind.

Ladies and gentlemen, the United States stands at this time at the pin-nacle of world power. It is a solemn moment for the American democ-racy. For with this primacy in power is also joined an awe-inspiring accountability to the future. As you look around you, you must feel not only the sense of duty done, but also you must feel anxiety lest you fall below the level of achievement. Opportunity is here now, clear and shin-ing, for both our countries. To reject it or ignore it or fritter it away will bring upon us all the long reproaches of the aftertime.

It is necessary that constancy of mind, persistency of purpose, and the grand simplicity of decision shall rule and guide the conduct of the English-speaking peoples in peace as they did in war. We must—and I believe we shall—prove ourselves equal to this severe requirement.

President McCluer, when American military men approach some seri-ous situation, they are wont to write at the head of their directive the words "Overall Strategic Concept." There is wisdom in this, as it leads to clarity of thought. What, then, is the overall strategic concept which we should inscribe today? It is nothing less than the safety and welfare, the freedom and progress, of all the homes and families of all the men and women in all the lands. And here I speak particularly of the myriad cot-tage or apartment homes where the wage earner strives, amid the acci-dents and difficulties of life, to guard his wife and children from privation and bring the family up in the fear of the Lord or upon ethical concep-tions which often play their potent part.

To give security to these countless homes they must be shielded from the two gaunt marauders—war and tyranny. We all know the frightful disturbance in which the ordinary family is plunged when the curse of war swoops down upon the breadwinner and those for whom he works and contrives.

The awful ruin of Europe, with all its vanished glories, and of large parts of Asia, glares us in the eyes.

When the designs of wicked men or the aggressive urge of mighty states dissolve, over large areas, the frame of civilized society, humble folk are confronted with difficulties with which they cannot cope. For them all is distorted, all is broken or is even ground to pulp.

When I stand here this quiet afternoon, I shudder to visualize what is actually happening to millions now and what is going to happen in this period when famine stalks the earth. None can compute what has been called "the unestimated sum of human pain." Our supreme task and duty is to guard the homes of the common people from the horrors and miseries of another war. We are all agreed on that.

Our American military colleagues, after having proclaimed their "over-all strategic concept" and computed available resources, always proceed to the next stop—namely, the method. Here again there is widespread agreement.

A world organization has already been erected for the prime purpose of preventing war. UNO, the successor of the League of Nations, with the decisive addition of the United States and all that that means, is already at work.

We must make sure that its work is fruitful, that it is a reality and not a sham, that it is a force for action and not merely a frothing of words, that it is a true temple of peace, in which the shields of many nations can someday be hung up, and not merely a cockpit in a tower of Babel.

Before we cast away the solid assurances of national armaments for self-preservation, we must be certain that our temple is built not upon shifting sands or quagmires but upon the rock. Anyone can see, with his eyes open, that our path will be difficult and also long, but if we persevere together as we did in the two world wars—though not, alas, in the interval between them—I cannot doubt that we shall achieve our common purpose in the end.

I have, however, a definite and practical proposal to make for action. Courts and magistrates may be set up, but they cannot function without sheriffs and constables. The United Nations Organization must immediately begin to be equipped with an international armed force. In such a matter we can only go step by step; but we must begin now.

I propose that each of the powers and states should be invited to dedicate a certain number of air squadrons to the service of the world organization. These squadrons would be trained and prepared in their own countries but would move around in rotation from one country to another. They would wear the uniform of their own countries with different badges. They would not be required to act against their own nation but in other respects they would be directed by the world organization.

This might be started on a modest scale, and it would grow as confidence grew.

I wished to see this done after the First World War, and I devoutly trust that it may be done forthwith.

It would, nevertheless, ladies and gentlemen, be wrong and imprudent to entrust the secret knowledge or experience of the atomic bomb, which the United States, Great Britain, and Canada now share, to the world organization while it is still in its infancy. It would be criminal madness to cast it adrift in this still agitated and un-united world.

No one in any country has slept less well in their beds because this knowledge and the method and the raw materials to apply it are at present largely retained in American hands.

I do not believe we should all have slept so soundly had the positions been reversed and some Communist or neo-Fascist state monopolized, for the time being, these dread agents. The fear of them alone might easily have been used to enforce totalitarian systems upon the free democratic world, with consequences appalling to human imagination.

God has willed that this shall not be, and we have at least a breathing space to set our house in order, before this peril has to be encountered, and even then, if no effort is spared, we should still possess so formidable a superiority as to impose effective deterrents upon its employment or threat of employment by others.

Ultimately, when the essential brotherhood of man is truly embodied and expressed in a world organization, with all the necessary practical safeguards to make it effective, these powers would naturally be confided to that organization.

Now I come to the second of the two marauders, to the second danger which threatens the cottage home and ordinary people—namely, tyranny. We cannot be blind to the fact that the liberties enjoyed by individual citizens throughout the United States and throughout the British Empire are not valid in a considerable number of countries, some of which are very powerful.

In these states, control is enforced upon the common people by various kinds of all-embracing police governments, to a degree which is overwhelming and contrary to every principle of democracy. The power of the state is exercised without restraint, either by dictators or by compact oligarchies operating through a privileged party and a political police.

It is not our duty at this time, when difficulties are so numerous, to interfere forcibly in the internal affairs of countries which we have not conquered in war, but we must never cease to proclaim in fearless tones the great principles of freedom and the rights of man, which are the joint inheritance of the English-speaking world and which, through Magna Carta, the Bill of Rights, the habeas corpus, trial by jury, and the English common law, find their most famous expression in the American Declaration of Independence.

All this means that the people of any country have the right and should have the power by constitutional action, by free, unfettered elections, with secret ballot, to choose or change the character or form of government under which they dwell, that freedom of speech and thought should reign, that courts of justice independent of the executive, unbiased by any party, should administer laws which have received the broad assent of large majorities or are consecrated by time and custom. Here are the title deeds of freedom, which should lie in every cottage home. Here is the message of the British and American peoples to mankind. Let us preach what we practice; let us practice what we preach.

I have not stated the two great dangers which menace the homes of the people: war and tyranny. I have not yet spoken of poverty and privation, which are in many cases the prevailing anxiety. But if the dangers of war and tyranny are removed, there is no doubt that science and cooperation can bring in the next few years, certainly in the next few decades, to the world, newly taught in the sharpening school of war, an expansion of material well-being beyond anything that has yet occurred in human experience.

Now, at this sad and breathless moment, we are plunged in the hunger and distress which are the aftermath of our stupendous struggle; but this will pass and may pass quickly, and there is no reason except human folly or subhuman crime which should deny to all the nations the inauguration and enjoyment of an age of plenty.

I have often used words which I learned fifty years ago from a great Irish-American orator, a friend of mine, Mr. Bourke Cochran, "There is enough for all. The earth is a generous mother; she will provide in plentiful abundance food for all her children if they will but cultivate her soil in justice and in peace." So far I feel that we are in full agreement.

Now, while still pursuing the method of realizing our overall strategic concept, I come to the crux of what I have traveled here to say.

Neither the sure prevention of war nor the continuous rise of world organization will be gained without what I have called the fraternal association of the English-speaking peoples. This means a special relationship between the British Commonwealth and Empire and the United States of America.

Ladies and gentlemen, this is no time for generalities, and I will venture to be precise.

Fraternal association requires not only the growing friendship and mutual understanding between our two vast but kindred systems of society but the continuance of the intimate relationships between our military advisers, leading to common study of potential dangers, the similarity of weapons and manuals of instruction, and the interchange of officers and cadets at technical colleges.

It should carry with it the continuance of the present facilities for mutual security by the joint use of all naval and air force bases in the possession of either country all over the world.

This would perhaps double the mobility of the American navy and air force. It would greatly expand that of the British Empire forces, and it might well lead, if and as the world calms down, to important financial savings.

Already we use together a large number of islands; more may well be entrusted to our joint care in the near future. The United States has already a permanent defense agreement with the Dominion of Canada, which is so devotedly attached to the British Commonwealth and Empire. This agreement is more effective than many of those which have often been made under formal alliances. This principle should be extended to all the British Commonwealths with full reciprocity.

Thus, whatever happens, and thus only, shall we be secure ourselves and able to work together for the high and simple causes that are dear to us and bode no ill to any. Eventually there may come, I feel eventually there will come, the principle of common citizenship, but that we may be content to leave to destiny, whose outstretched arm so many of us can already clearly see.

There is, however, an important question we must ask ourselves. Would a special relationship between the United States and the British Commonwealth be inconsistent with our overriding loyalties to the world organization? I reply that, on the contrary, it is probably the only means by which that organization will achieve its full stature and strength. There are already the special United States relations with Canada, which I just mentioned, and there are the relations between the United States and the South American republics.

We British have also our twenty years' treaty of collaboration and mutual assistance with Soviet Russia. I agree with Mr. Bevin, the foreign secretary of Great Britain, that it might well be a fifty years' treaty so far as we are concerned. We aim at nothing but mutual assistance and collaboration with Russia. We have an alliance, the British, with Portugal, unbroken since the year 1384 and which produced fruitful results at a critical moment in the recent war. None of these clash with the general interest of a world agreement or a world organization. On the contrary, they help it.

"In my father's house are many mansions." Special associations between members of the United Nations which have no aggressive point against any other country, which harbor no design incompatible with the Charter of the United Nations, far from being harmful, are beneficial, and, as I believe, indispensable.

I spoke earlier, ladies and gentlemen, of the temple of peace. Workmen from all countries must build that temple. If two of the workmen know each other particularly well and are old friends, if their families are intermingled and if they have faith in each other's purpose, hope in each other's future, and charity toward each other's shortcomings, to quote some good words I read here the other day, why cannot they work together at the common task as friends and partners?

Why can they not share their tools and thus increase each other's working powers? Indeed they must do so, or else the temple may not be built, or, being built, it may collapse, and we shall all be proved again unteachable and have to go and try to learn again for a third time, in a school of war, incomparably more rigorous than that from which we have just been released.

The Dark Ages may return, the Stone Age may return on the gleaming wings of science, and what might now shower, shower immeasurable material blessings upon mankind, may even bring about its total destruction. Beware, I say; time is plenty short. Do not let us take the course of allowing events to drift along until it is too late.

If there is to be a fraternal association of the kind I have described, with all the extra strength and security which both our countries can derive from it, let us make sure that that great fact is known to the world, and that it plays its part in steadying and stabilizing the foundations of peace. There is the path of wisdom. Prevention is better than cure.

A shadow has fallen upon the scenes so lately lightened, lighted by the Allied victory. Nobody knows what Soviet Russia and its Communist international organization intends to do in the immediate future, or what are the limits, if any, to their expansive and proselytizing tendencies.

I have a strong admiration and regard for the valiant Russian people and for my wartime comrade Marshal Stalin. There is deep sympathy and good will in Britain—and I doubt not here also—toward the peoples of all the Russias and a resolve to persevere through many differences and rebuffs in establishing lasting friendships.

We understand the Russian need to be secure on her western frontiers from the removal, by the removal of all possibility of German aggression. We welcome Russia to her rightful place among the leading nations of the world. We welcome her flag upon the seas. Above all we welcome or should welcome constant, frequent, and growing contacts between the Russian people and our own peoples on both sides of the Atlantic.

It is my duty, however—and I am sure you would not wish me not to state the facts as I see them to you—it is my duty to place before you certain facts about the present position in Europe.

From Stettin in the Baltic to Trieste in the Adriatic, an iron curtain has descended across the Continent. Behind that line lie all the capitals of the ancient states of Central and Eastern Europe. Warsaw, Berlin, Prague, Vienna, Budapest, Belgrade, Bucharest, and Sofia; all these famous cities and the populations around them lie in what I might call the Soviet sphere, and all are subject, in one form or another, not only to Soviet influence but to a very high and in some cases increasing measure of control from Moscow.

Police governments are pervading from Moscow. But Athens alone, with its immortal glories, is free to decide its future at an election under British, American, and French observation.

The Russian-dominated Polish government has been encouraged to make enormous and wrongful inroads upon Germany, and mass expulsions of millions of Germans on a scale grievous and undreamed-of are now taking place.

The Communist parties, which were very small in all these eastern states of Europe, have been raised to preeminence and power far beyond their numbers and are seeking everywhere to obtain totalitarian control.

Police governments are prevailing in nearly every case, and so far, except in Czechoslovakia, there is no true democracy. Turkey and Persia are both profoundly alarmed and disturbed at the claims which are being made upon them and at the pressure being exerted by the Moscow government.

An attempt is being made by the Russians, in Berlin, to build up a quasi-Communist party in their zone of occupied Germany by showing special favors to groups of left-wing German leaders. At the end of the fighting last June, the American and British armies withdrew westward, in accordance with an earlier agreement, to a depth at some points of 150 miles upon a front of nearly 400 miles, in order to allow our Russian allies to occupy this vast expanse of territory which the Western democracies had conquered.

If now the Soviet government tries, by separate action, to build up a pro-Communist Germany in their areas, this will cause new serious difficulties in the American and British zones, and will give the defeated Germans the power of putting themselves up to auction between the Soviets and the Western democracies. Whatever conclusions may be drawn from these facts—and facts they are—this is certainly not the liberated Europe we fought to build up. Nor is it one which contains the essentials of permanent peace.

The safety of the world, ladies and gentlemen, requires a unity in Europe from which no nation should be permanently outcast. It is from the strong parent races in Europe that the world wars we have witnessed, or which occurred in former times, have sprung.

Twice in our own lifetime we have—the United States against her wishes and her traditions, against arguments the force of which it is impossible not to comprehend—twice we have seen them drawn by irresistible forces into these wars in time to secure the victory of the good cause, but only after frightful slaughter and devastation have occurred.

Twice the United States has had to send several millions of its young men across the Atlantic to fight the wars. But now we all can find any nation, wherever it may dwell, between dusk and dawn. Surely we should work with conscious purpose for a grand pacification of Europe within the structure of the United Nations and in accordance with our Charter.

That, I feel, opens a course of policy of very great importance.

In front of the iron curtain which lies across Europe are other causes for anxiety. In Italy the Communist party is seriously hampered by having to support the Communist-trained Marshal Tito's claims to former Italian territory at the head of the Adriatic. Nevertheless, the future of Italy hangs in the balance.

Again one cannot imagine a regenerated Europe without a strong France. All my public life I have worked for a strong France, and I have never lost faith in her destiny, even in the darkest hours. I will not lose faith now.

However, in a great number of countries, far from the Russian frontiers and throughout the world, Communist fifth columns are established and work in complete unity and absolute obedience to directions they receive from the Communist center. Except in the British Commonwealth and in the United States, where communism is in its infancy, the Communist parties or fifth columns constitute a growing challenge and peril to Christian civilization. These are somber facts for anyone to have to recite on the morrow of a victory gained by so much splendid comradeship in arms and in the cause of freedom and democracy, but we should be most unwise not to face them squarely while time remains.

The outlook is also anxious in the Far East and especially in Manchuria. The agreement which was made at Yalta, to which I was party, was extremely favorable to Soviet Russia, but it was made at a time when no one could say that the German war might not extend all through the summer and autumn of 1945 and when the Japanese war was expected by the best judges to last for a further eighteen months from the end of the German war. In this country you are so well informed about the Far East, and such devoted friends of China, that I do not need to expatiate on the situation there.

I had, however, felt bound to portray the shadow which, alike in the West and in the East, falls upon the world. I was a minister at the time of the Versailles treaty and a close friend of Mr. Lloyd George, who was the head of the British delegation at that time, I did not myself agree with many things that were done, but I have a very vague impression in my mind of that situation, and I find it painful to contrast it with that which prevails now. In those days there were high hopes and unbounded confidence that the wars were over, and that the League of Nations would become all-powerful. I do not see or feel that same confidence or even the same hopes in the haggard world at the present time.

On the other hand, ladies and gentlemen, I repulse the idea that a new war is inevitable—still more that it is imminent. It is because I am sure that our fortunes are still in our hands, in our own hands, and that we hold the power to save the future, that I feel the duty to speak out now that I have the occasion and opportunity to do so.

I do not believe that Soviet Russia desires war. What they desire is the fruits of war and the indefinite expansion of their power and doctrines.

But what we have to consider here today while time remains, is the permanent prevention of war and the establishment of conditions of freedom and democracy as rapidly as possible in all countries. Our difficulties and dangers will not be removed by closing our eyes to them. They will not be removed by mere waiting to see what happens; nor will they be removed by a policy of appeasement.

What is needed is a settlement, and the longer this is delayed, the more difficult it will be and the greater our dangers will become.

From what I have seen of our Russian friends and allies during the war, I am convinced that there is nothing they admire so much as strength, and there is nothing for which they have less respect than for weakness, especially military weakness.

For that, for that reason, the old doctrine of a balance of power is unsound. We cannot afford, if we can help it, to work on narrow margins, offering temptations to a trial of strength.

If the Western democracies stand together in strict adherence to the principles of the United Nations Charter, their influence for furthering those principles will be immense and no one is likely to molest them. If, however, they become divided or falter in their duty, and if these all-important years are allowed to slip away, then indeed catastrophe may overwhelm us all.

Last time I saw it all coming and cried aloud to my own fellow countrymen and to the world, but no one paid any attention. Up till the year 1933 or even 1935, Germany might have been saved from the awful fate which has overtaken her, and we might all have been spared the miseries Hitler let loose upon mankind.

There never was a war in history easier to prevent by timely action than the one which has just desolated such great areas of the globe. It could have been prevented, in my belief, without the firing of a single shot, and Germany might be powerful, prosperous, and honored today; but no one would listen and one by one we were all sucked into the awful whirlpool.

We surely, ladies and gentlemen, I put it to you, but surely we must not let that happen again. This can only be achieved by reaching now, in 1946, this year 1946, by reaching a good understanding on all points with Russia under the general authority of the United Nations Organization and by the maintenance of that good understanding through many peaceful years, by the world instrument, supported by the whole strength of the English-speaking world and all its connections.

There is the solution which I respectfully offer to you in this address to which I have given the title "The Sinews of Peace."

Let no man underrate the abiding power of the British Empire and Commonwealth. Because you see, because you see the forty-six millions in our island harassed about their food supply, of which they only grow one-half, even in wartime, or because we have difficulty in restarting our industries and export trade after six years of passionate war effort, do not suppose that we shall not come through these dark years of privation as we have come through the glorious years of agony, or that half a century from now, you will not see seventy or eighty millions of Britons spread about the world and united in defense of our traditions, and our way of life, and of the world causes which you and we espouse.

If the population of the English-speaking Commonwealth be added to that of the United States, with all such cooperation implies in the air, on the sea, all over the globe, and in science and in industry, and in moral force, there will be no quivering, precarious balance of power to offer its temptation to ambition or adventure. On the contrary, there will be an overwhelming assurance of security.

If we adhere faithfully to the Charter of the United Nations and walk forward in sedate and sober strength, seeking no one's land or treasure, seeking to lay no arbitrary control upon the thoughts of men, if all British moral and material forces and convictions are joined with your own in fraternal association, the high roads of the future will be clear, not only for us but for all, not only for our time but for a century to come. ■

Judge Noah Sweat of Mississippi Shows How to Straddle a Fence with Satiric Flair

"IF when you say 'whisky' you mean the devil's brew, . . . then certainly I am against it. But, if when you say 'whisky' you mean the oil of conversation. . . ."

PROHIBITION OF ALCOHOLIC BEVERAGES was still a hot issue in Mississippi in 1948, long after most of the rest of the nation had retired the controversy with repeal of the Eighteenth Amendment. Noah S. ("Soggy") Sweat (the nickname was short for "Sorghum Top," after the tassel atop sugarcane) was running for state representative in Alcorn County, and came up with an ingenious way of evading the issue: he made fun of the way it made other politicians squirm. He won, serving later as prosecutor and finally as judge of the First Judicial District in the 1970s.

He copyrighted his "if by whisky" speech in 1952 because so many other political figures were using it without attribution. It was written to satirize the fine art of fence straddling, and should be delivered with a straight face above a firm jaw.

□   □   □

My friends, I had not intended to discuss this controversial subject at this particular time. However, I want you to know that I do not shun controversy. On the contrary, I will take a stand on any issue at any time, regardless of how fraught with controversy it might be. You have asked me how I feel about whisky. All right, here is how I feel about whisky.

If when you say "whisky" you mean the devil's brew, the poison scourge, the bloody monster that defiles innocence, dethrones reason, destroys the home, creates misery and poverty, yea, literally takes the bread from the mouths of little children; if you mean the evil drink that topples the Christian man and woman from the pinnacle of righteous, gracious living into the bottomless pit of degradation, and despair, and shame, and helplessness, and hopelessness—then certainly I am against it.

But, if when you say "whisky" you mean the oil of conversation, the philosophic wine, the ale that is consumed when good fellows get together, that puts a song in their hearts and laughter on their lips, and the warm glow of contentment in their eyes; if you mean Christmas cheer; if you mean the stimulating drink that puts the spring into the old gentleman's step on a frosty, crispy morning; if you mean the drink that enables a man to magnify his joy, and his happiness, and to forget, if only for a little while, life's great tragedies, and heartaches, and sorrows; if you mean that drink the sale of which pours into our treasuries untold millions of dollars, which are used to provide tender care for our little crippled children, our blind, our deaf, our dumb, our pitiful aged and infirm; to build highways and hospitals and schools—then certainly I am for it.

This is my stand. I will not retreat from it. I will not compromise. ■

Hubert H. Humphrey
Divides the Democratic
Party on the Urgent
Issue of Civil Rights

"THERE are those who say—this issue of civil rights is an infringement on states' rights. The time has arrived for the Democratic party to get out of the shadow of states' rights and walk forthrightly into the bright sunshine of human rights."

IN THEIR 1948 NATIONAL CONVENTION in Philadelphia, the Democrats under President Harry Truman were in particular disarray: Henry Wallace had taken the extreme left wing with him to form the Progressive party, and Strom Thurmond threatened to take the old "solid South" into a Dixiecrat offshoot if a civil rights plank appeared in the platform. As a result, Republican Thomas E. Dewey was considered a shoo-in.

Hubert Horatio Humphrey, mayor of Minneapolis and candidate for the U.S. Senate, in what later came to be known as a defining moment in his career, called for confrontation rather than compromise on the issue of civil rights. His opening profession that the plank had no region or racial group in mind was disingenuous—the controversy was about abuse of black people's rights in the southern states, and everyone in the convention hall knew it—but the sincerity of his passionate appeal was undeniable: "There are those who say to you—we are rushing this issue of civil rights. I say we are 172 years late."

Humphrey carried the day; the liberals' plank was adopted, the Dixiecrats bolted, and Truman went on to win in a startling upset. The exuberant Humphrey served sixteen years in the Senate and an uncomfortable term as Lyndon Johnson's vice-president; he returned to the Senate after losing a close presidential race to Richard Nixon in 1968.

His speaking style was unmistakable: it bubbled and crackled with enthusiasm. Where other speakers would dutifully say, "It's a pleasure to be here today," he would pop up with "Golly, I'm just as pleased as Punch to be here," and go on and on with verve and good feeling—in FDR's Wordsworth-based characterization of Al Smith, a "happy warrior" in the liberal cause.

He used the phrases "human rights" and "civil rights" in this speech. In 1948, the 200-year-old French phrase, translated as "the rights of man," had been changed by Eleanor Roosevelt at the United Nations because some delegates made the point that the rights did not apply to women. She insisted on her title as chairman of the United Nations Commission on Human Rights. Thus, the phrase "human rights" was in the air at the time of the Democratic convention, and Humphrey appropriated it to take some of the sting out of "civil rights" by broadening the appeal. In time, "human rights" came to mean the rights of dissidents of any color or sex under oppressive rule, and "civil rights" the rights of blacks to enjoy the full advantages of the Bill of Rights.

□ □ □

. . . I realize that I am dealing with a charged issue—with an issue which has been confused by emotionalism on all sides. I realize that there are those here—friends and colleagues of mine, many of them—who feel as deeply as I do about this issue and who are yet in complete disagreement with me.

My respect and admiration for these men and their views was great when I came here.

It is now far greater because of the sincerity, the courtesy, and the forthrightness with which they have argued in our discussions.

Because of this very respect—because of my profound belief that we have a challenging task to do here—because good conscience demands it—I feel I must rise at this time to support this report—a report that spells out our democracy, a report that the people will understand and enthusiastically acclaim.

Let me say at the outset that this proposal is made with no single region, no single class, no single racial or religious group in mind.

All regions and all states have shared in the precious heritage of American freedom. All states and all regions have at least some infringements of that freedom—all people, all groups have been the victims of discrimination.

The masterly statement of our keynote speaker, the distinguished United States senator from Kentucky, Alben Barkley, made that point with great force. Speaking of the founder of our party, Thomas Jefferson, he said:

> He did not proclaim that all white, or black, or red, or yellow men are equal; that all Christian or Jewish men are equal; Protestant and

Catholic men are equal; that all rich or poor men are equal; that all good or bad men are equal.

What he declared was that all men are equal; and the equality which he proclaimed was equality in the right to enjoy the blessings of free government in which they may participate and to which they have given their consent.

We are here as Democrats. But more important, as Americans—and I firmly believe that as men concerned with our country's future, we must specify in our platform the guarantees which I have mentioned.

Yes, this is far more than a party matter. Every citizen has a stake in the emergence of the United States as the leader of the free world. That world is being challenged by the world of slavery. For us to play our part effectively, we must be in a morally sound position.

We cannot use a double standard for measuring our own and other people's policies. Our demands for democratic practices in other lands will be no more effective than the guarantees of those practiced in our own country.

We are God-fearing men and women. We place our faith in the brotherhood of man under the fatherhood of God.

I do not believe that there can be any compromise of the guarantees of civil rights which I have mentioned.

In spite of my desire for unanimous agreement on the platform, there are some matters which I think must be stated without qualification. There can be no hedging—no watering down.

There are those who say to you—we are rushing this issue of civil rights. I say we are 172 years late.

There are those who say—this issue of civil rights is an infringement on states' rights. The time has arrived for the Democratic party to get out of the shadow of states' rights and walk forthrightly into the bright sunshine of human rights.

People—human beings—this is the issue of the twentieth century. People—all kinds and all sorts of people—look to America for leadership, for help, for guidance.

My friends—my fellow Democrats— I ask you for a calm consideration of our historic opportunity. Let us forget the evil passions, the blindness of the past. In these times of world economic, political, and spiritual— above all, spiritual—crisis, we cannot—we must not—turn from the path so plainly before us.

That path has already led us through many valleys of the shadow of death. Now is the time to recall those who were left on that path of American freedom.

For all of us here, for the millions who have sent us, for the whole two billion members of the human family—our land is now, more than ever, the last best hope on earth. I know that we can—I know that we shall—begin here the fuller and richer realization of that hope—that promise of a land where all men are free and equal, and each man uses his freedom and equality wisely and well. ■

President Harry Truman Whistle-Stops the Nation, Blasting the "Do-Nothing" Congress

"THE Democratic party stands for the people. The Republican party stands, and always has stood, for special interests."

"YOU HAVE A STAKE in this election," the underdog to Thomas E. Dewey said to the individuals who made up a small crowd in Massachusetts in 1948. "It will affect your job, your chance to get a raise, your chance to get a better home. . . . It will mean the difference between moving ahead and going backward." Simple, direct, unaffected, personal—that was the Truman style, in contrast to the formal presentations of his opponent. The "accidental president," who stepped into FDR's shoes with "Who, me?" as his reported comment, had the ability to identify with the man in the street and the woman in the grocery store.

Harry Truman's White House addresses, from the announcement of the destruction of Hiroshima to the Truman Doctrine and the Fair Deal, were prepared by writers including George Elsey, Clark Clifford, and William Hillman. They were solid and workmanlike speeches, fact-filled and frank, delivered in a stilted, hurried way that made it seem as if the speaker wanted it over with.

All that changed when he went on the stump. "My first formal experience at extemporaneous speaking," he wrote later, "had come just a few weeks before I opened the whistle-stop tour in June. After reading an address to the American Society of Newspaper Editors in April, I decided to talk 'off the cuff' on American relations with Russia. When I finished my remarks about thirty minutes later, I was surprised to get the most enthusiastic reaction." Instead of reading on the stump, he spoke up and out; instead of reacting to charges that he had caused the high cost of living, he went on the offensive. Like Demosthenes, he focused on a villain, but in this case a collective villain: the "do-nothing" Eightieth Congress (which he may have picked up from FDR's "do-nothing policy of Hoover"). Between Labor Day and election day, Truman perfected the whistle-stop campaign, giving 275 short speeches. Here is a typical one, delivered in Elizabeth, New Jersey, on October 7, 1948:

□   □   □

. . . **Y**ou are here because you are interested in the issues of this campaign. You know, as all the citizens of this great country know, that the election is not all over but the shouting. That is what they would like to have you believe, but it isn't so—it isn't so at all. The Republicans are trying to hide the truth from you in a great many ways. They don't want you to know the truth about the issues in this campaign. The big fundamental issue in this campaign is the people against the special interests. The Democratic party stands for the people. The Republican party stands, and always has stood, for special interests. They have proved that conclusively in the record that they made in this "do-nothing" Congress.

The Republican party candidates are going around talking to you in high-sounding platitudes trying to make you believe that they themselves are the best people to run the government. Well now, you have had experience with them running the government. In 1920 to 1932, they had complete control of the government. Look what they did to it! . . .

This country is enjoying the greatest prosperity it has ever known because we have been following for sixteen years the policies inaugurated by Franklin D. Roosevelt. Everybody benefited from these policies—labor, the farmer, businessmen, and white-collar workers.

We want to keep that prosperity. We cannot keep that if we don't lick the biggest problem facing us today, and that is high prices.

I have been trying to get the Republicans to do something about high prices and housing ever since they came to Washington. They are responsible for that situation, because they killed price control and they killed the housing bill. That Republican Eightieth "do-nothing" Congress absolutely refused to give any relief whatever in either one of those categories.

What do you suppose the Republicans think you ought to do about high prices?

Senator Taft, one of the leaders in the Republican Congress, said, "If consumers think the price is too high today, they will wait until the price is lower. I feel that in time the law of supply and demand will bring prices into line."

There is the Republican answer to the high cost of living.

If it costs too much, just wait.

If you think fifteen cents is too much for a loaf of bread, just do without it and wait until you can afford to pay fifteen cents for it.

If you don't want to pay sixty cents a pound for hamburger, just wait.

That is what the Republican Congress thought you ought to do, and that is the same Congress that the Republican candidate for president said did a good job.

Some people say I ought not to talk so much about the Republican Eightieth "do-nothing" Congress in this campaign. I will tell you why I will talk about it. If two-thirds of the people stay at home again on election day as they did in 1946, and if we get another Republican Congress like the Eightieth Congress, it will be controlled by the same men who controlled that Eightieth Congress—the Tabers and the Tafts, the Martins and the Hallecks, would be the bosses. The same men would be the bosses the same as those who passed the Taft-Hartley Act, and passed the rich man's tax bill, and took Social Security away from a million workers.

Do you want that kind of administration? I don't believe you do—I don't believe you do.

I don't believe you would be out here interested in listening to my outline of what the Republicans are trying to do to you if you intended to put them back in there.

When a bunch of Republican reactionaries are in control of the Congress, then the people get reactionary laws. The only way you can get the kind of government you need is by going to the polls and voting the straight Democratic ticket on November 2. Then you will get a Democratic Congress, and I will get a Congress that will work with me. Then we will get good housing at prices we can afford to pay; and repeal of that vicious Taft-Hartley Act; and more Social Security coverage; and prices that will be fair to everybody; and we can go on and keep sixty-one million people at work; we can have an income of more than $217 billion, and that income will be distributed so that the farmer, the workingman, the white-collar worker, and the businessman get their fair share of that income.

That is what I stand for.

That is what the Democratic party stands for.

Vote for that, and you will be safe! ■

Adlai Stevenson Makes the Model of a Concession Speech

"LINCOLN . . . said he felt like a little boy who had stubbed his toe in the dark. He said that he was too old to cry, but it hurt too much to laugh."

A CONCESSION SPEECH must be graceful, brave, proud, and rueful; it must not be humble, envious, or vengeful, be filled with "if only"s, or reflect any of the qualities of the sore loser that lie within almost every loser. ("Show me a man who loses gracefully," said an anonymous football coach, "and I'll show you a loser.") Churchill had said, "In defeat, defiance," but he meant national defeat; in political defeat, defiance is bad form.

Here is the speech conceding victory to his opponent by Adlai Stevenson on November 5, 1952, in the ballroom of the Leland Hotel in Springfield, Illinois.

□   □   □

Ihave a statement that I should like to make. If I may, I shall read it to
you.

My fellow citizens have made their choice and have selected General
Eisenhower and the Republican party as the instruments of their will for
the next four years.

The people have rendered their verdict, and I gladly accept it.

General Eisenhower has been a great leader in war. He has been a vigorous and valiant opponent in the campaign. These qualities will now be
dedicated to leading us all through the next four years.

It is traditionally American to fight hard before an election. It is equally
traditional to close ranks as soon as the people have spoken.

From the depths of my heart I thank all of my party and all of those
independents and Republicans who supported Senator Sparkman and me.

That which unites us as American citizens is far greater than that
which divides us as political parties.

I urge you all to give General Eisenhower the support he will need to
carry out the great tasks that lie before him.

I pledge him mine.

We vote as many, but we pray as one. With a united people, with faith
in democracy, with common concern for others less fortunate around the
globe, we shall move forward with God's guidance toward the time when
his children shall grow in freedom and dignity in a world at peace.

I have sent the following telegram to General Eisenhower at the
Commodore Hotel in New York: "The people have made their choice and
I congratulate you. That you may be the servant and guardian of peace
and make the vale of trouble a door of hope is my earnest prayer. Best
wishes. Adlai E. Stevenson."

Someone asked me, as I came in, down on the street, how I felt, and I
was reminded of a story that a fellow townsman of ours used to tell—
Abraham Lincoln. They asked him how he felt once after an unsuccessful
election. He said he felt like a little boy who had stubbed his toe in the
dark. He said that he was too old to cry, but it hurt too much to laugh. ■

Premier Nikita Khrushchev, in a "Secret Speech," Tears Down Stalin's Reputation

"COMRADES, the cult of the individual acquired such monstrous size chiefly because Stalin himself, using all conceivable methods, supported the glorification of his own person."

MERCURIAL, SHREWD, ENERGETIC, EARTHY, unpredictable, bullying—these were the adjectives used in the West about Nikita Khrushchev when he ran the Soviet Union from 1955 to 1964. In retrospect, he is seen as having been a liberalizing force, a Gorbachev precursor, though his administrative reforms did not liberate most of those in what Aleksandr Solzhenitzyn called the gulag, or system of prison camps, and his attempt to put missiles into Cuba brought the world to the brink of war.

In February of 1956, he laid out the case against Joseph Stalin to the Twentieth Party Congress in Moscow. Its proceedings were secret, but the CIA obtained a transcript of Khrushchev's "secret speech"—perhaps from a KGB source acting with tacit Kremlin approval—and leaked it to Western media. The accusation that Sergey Kirov of Leningrad had been murdered, placed within the context of Stalin's other depredations, was a bombshell; the reference to the "doctors' plot" to kill Stalin was another, because it exposed the dictator's anti-Semitism.

Although Khrushchev blames Stalin for the phrase "enemy of the people," that was the title of an Ibsen play; however, "cult of the individual" was popularized in the highly publicized "secret speech."

□ □ □

Comrades! In the report of the Central Committee of the party at the twentieth congress, in a number of speeches by delegates to the Congress, as also formerly during the plenary CC/CPSU [Central Committee of the Communist Party of the Soviet Union] sessions, quite a lot has been said about the cult of the individual and about its harmful consequences.

After Stalin's death the Central Committee of the party began to implement a policy of explaining concisely and consistently that it is impermissible and foreign to the spirit of Marxism-Leninism to elevate one person, to transform him into a superman possessing supernatural characteristics akin to those of a god. Such a man supposedly knows everything, sees everything, thinks for everyone, can do anything, is infallible in his behavior.

Such a belief about a man, and specifically about Stalin, was cultivated among us for many years.

At the present we are concerned with a question which has immense importance for the party now and for the future—[we are concerned] with how the cult of the person of Stalin has been gradually growing, the cult which became at a certain specific stage the source of a whole series of exceedingly serious and grave perversions of party principles, of party democracy, of revolutionary legality. . . .

Because of the fact that not all as yet realize fully the practical consequences resulting from the cult of the individual, the great harm caused by the violation of the principle of collective direction of the party, and because of the accumulation of immense and limitless power in the hands of one person, the Central Committee of the party considers it absolutely necessary to make the material pertaining to this matter available to the Twentieth Congress of the Communist Party of the Soviet Union.

In December 1922, in a letter to the party congress, Vladimir Ilyich [Lenin] wrote, "After taking over the position of secretary general, Comrade Stalin accumulated in his hands immeasurable power, and I am not certain whether he will be always able to use this power with the required care."

This letter, a political document of tremendous importance, known in the party history as Lenin's "testament," was distributed among the delegates to the Twentieth Party Congress.

It was precisely during this period (1935–1937–1938) that the practice of mass repression through the government apparatus was born, first against the enemies of Leninism—Trotskyites, Zinovievites, Bukharinites, long since politically defeated by the party, and subsequently also against many honest Communists, against those party cadres who had borne the heavy load of the civil war, and the first and most difficult years of industrialization and collectivization, who actively fought against the Trotskyites and the rightists for the Leninist party line.

Stalin organized the concept "enemy of the people." This term automatically rendered it unnecessary that the ideological errors of a man or men engaged in a controversy be proven; this term made possible the use of the most cruel repression, violating all norms of revolutionary legality, against anyone who in any way disagreed with Stalin, against those who were only suspected of hostile intent, against those who had bad reputations in the main, and in actuality, the only proof of guilt used, against all norms of current legal science, was the "confession" of the accused himself; and, as subsequent probing proved, "confessions" were acquired through physical pressures against the accused.

It was determined that of the 139 members and candidates of the party's Central Committee who were elected at the seventeenth congress, 98 persons, that is, 70 percent, were arrested and shot (mostly in 1937–38).

The same fate met not only the Central Committee members but also the majority of the delegates to the Seventeenth Party Congress. Of 1,966 delegates with either voting or advisory rights, 1,108 persons were arrested on charges of antirevolutionary crimes, that is, decidedly more than a majority. This very fact shows how absurd, wild, and contrary to common sense were the charges of counterrevolutionary crimes made, as we now see, against a majority of participants at the seventeenth party congress.

After the criminal murder of Sergey M. Kirov, mass repressions and brutal acts of violation of Socialist legality began. . . .

Now, when the cases of some of these so-called "spies" and "saboteurs" were examined, it was found that all their cases were fabricated. Confessions of guilt of many arrested and charged with enemy activity were gained with the help of cruel and inhuman tortures.

Comrade Eikhe was arrested April 29, 1938, on the basis of slanderous materials, without the sanction of the prosecutor of the USSR, which was finally received fifteen months after the arrest.

Eikhe was forced under torture to sign ahead of time a protocol of his confession prepared by the investigative judges in which he and several other eminent party workers were accused of anti-Soviet activity.

On October 1, 1939, Eikhe sent his declaration to Stalin in which he categorically denied his guilt and asked for an examination of his case. In the declaration he wrote, "There is no more bitter misery than to sit in the jail of a government for which I have always fought."

On February 4 Eikhe was shot. It has been definitely established now that Eikhe's case was fabricated; he has been posthumously rehabilitated. . . .

The power accumulated in the hands of one person, Stalin, led to serious consequences during the great patriotic war.

A cable from our London embassy dated June 18, 1941, stated, "As of now Cripps is deeply convinced of the inevitability of armed conflict between Germany and the USSR which will begin not later than the

middle of June. According to Cripps, the Germans have presently concentrated 147 divisions (including air force and service units) along the
Soviet borders."

Despite these particularly grave warnings, the necessary steps were not
taken to prepare the country properly for defense and to prevent it from
being caught unawares.

When the Fascist armies had actually invaded Soviet territory and military operations began, Moscow issued the order that Stalin, despite evident facts, thought that the war had not yet started, that this was only a
provocative action on the part of several undisciplined sections of the
German army, and that our reaction might serve as a reason for the
Germans to begin the war.

Stalin was very much interested in the assessment of Comrade Zhukov
as a military leader. He asked me often for my opinion of Zhukov. I told
him then, "I have known Zhukov for a long time; he is a good general
and a good military leader."

After the war Stalin began to tell all kinds of nonsense about Zhukov,
among others the following: "You praised Zhukov, but he does not deserve
it. It is said that before each operation at the front Zhukov used to behave
as follows: he used to take a handful of earth, smell it, and say. 'We can
begin the attack,' or the opposite, 'The planned operation cannot be carried out.'" I stated at that time, "Comrade Stalin, I do not know who
invented this, but it is not true."

It is possible that Stalin himself invented these things for the purpose
of minimizing the role and military talents of Marshal Zhukov.

All the more monstrous are the acts whose initiator was Stalin and
which are rude violations of the basic Leninist principles of the nationality policy of the Soviet state. We refer to the mass deportations from their
native places of whole nations, together with all Communists and
Komsomols without any exception; this deportation action was not dictated by any military considerations.

The Ukrainians avoided meeting this fate only because there were too
many of them and there was no place to which to deport them.
Otherwise, he would have deported them also.

Let us also recall the "Affair of the Doctor Plotters." Actually there was
no "affair" outside of the declaration of the woman doctor Timashuk,
who was probably influenced or ordered by someone (after all, she was
an unofficial collaborator of the organs of state security) to write Stalin a
letter in which she declared that doctors were applying supposedly
improper methods of medical treatment.

Such a letter was sufficient for Stalin to reach an immediate conclusion that there are doctor plotters in the Soviet Union. He issued orders to arrest a group of eminent Soviet medical specialists. He personally issued advice on the conduct of the investigation and the method of interrogation of the arrested persons.

Stalin personally called the investigative judge, gave him instructions, advised him on which investigative methods should be used; these methods were simple—beat, beat, and, once again, beat.

Comrades, the cult of the individual acquired such monstrous size chiefly because Stalin himself, using all conceivable methods, supported the glorification of his own person. This is supported by numerous facts. One of the most characteristic examples of Stalin's self-glorification and of his lack of even elementary modesty is the edition of his "Short Biography," which was published in 1948.

"Stalin is the worthy continuer of Lenin's work, or, as it is said in our party, Stalin is the Lenin of today." You see how well it is said; not by the nation but by Stalin himself.

Comrades, we must abolish the cult of the individual decisively, once and for all. . . .

We are absolutely certain that our party, armed with the historical resolutions of the twentieth congress, will lead the Soviet people along the Leninist path to new successes, to new victories.

Long live the victorious banner of our party—Leninism! ■

President John F. Kennedy, in His Inaugural, Takes Up the Torch for a New Generation

"AND SO, my fellow Americans, ask not what your country can do for you—ask what you can do for your country."

"IN YOUR HANDS, my dissatisfied fellow countrymen," said Lincoln in his first inaugural "and not in mine, is the momentous issue of civil war." John F. Kennedy adopted the cadences of Lincoln (and corrected Lincoln's redundant "fellow countrymen") with "In your hands, my fellow citizens, more than mine, will rest the final success or failure of our course." He also followed Lincoln in the use of quotation from both the Old and the New Testament, quoting from Isaiah and the Epistle of Saint Paul to the Romans. The most Lincolnesque of all was the use of the oratorical "let"; Kennedy began eight sentences with it, moving from "Let the word go forth . . . that the torch has been passed" (stressing the point that he was the first president born in the twentieth century) to "So let us begin anew" and "But let us begin" (which Lyndon Johnson later used as the basis of his "Let us continue") to a paragraph that was later cited by Vietnam hawks as evidence of a determined Cold War mind-set: "Let every nation know . . . that we shall pay any price, bear any burden, meet any hardship, support any friend, oppose any foe to assure the survival and the success of liberty."

The use of antithesis ("Let us never negotiate out of fear. But let us never fear to negotiate") and parallelism ("United, there is little we cannot do. . . . Divided, there is little we can do") made many passages memorable, culminating in the "ask not" line, which dramatized an idealism and selflessness in calling for sacrifice, though not specifying a particular sacrifice. But rhetorical devices aside, this speech—patterned on the Lincoln style, though not seeking to match the Lincoln legal substance or philosophical profundity—set the standard by which presidential inaugurals have been judged in the modern era. Such skilled political writers as

Adlai Stevenson, John Kenneth Galbraith, Arthur M. Schlesinger, Jr., and Walter Lippmann were consulted by Kennedy alter ego Ted Sorensen, but the result was not a committee product; rather, the excitingly delivered outdoor speech exuded youth and idealism, a sense of history, and a feeling for language that reflected the taste and cool passion of the speaker himself. In the light of Kennedy's subsequent assassination, the association with Lincoln's cadences makes a rereading especially poignant.

☐   ☐   ☐

We observe today not a victory of a party but a celebration of freedom—symbolizing an end as well as a beginning—signifying renewal as well as change. For I have sworn before you and Almighty God the same solemn oath our forebears prescribed nearly a century and three quarters ago.

The world is very different now. For man holds in his mortal hands the power to abolish all forms of human poverty and all forms of human life. And yet the same revolutionary beliefs for which our forebears fought are still at issue around the globe—the belief that the rights of man come not from the generosity of the state but from the hand of God.

We dare not forget today that we are the heirs of that first revolution. Let the word go forth from this time and place, to friend and foe alike, that the torch has been passed to a new generation of Americans—born in this century, tempered by war, disciplined by a hard and bitter peace, proud of our ancient heritage—and unwilling to witness or permit the slow undoing of those human rights to which this nation has always been committed, and to which we are committed today at home and around the world.

Let every nation know, whether it wishes us well or ill, that we shall pay any price, bear any burden, meet any hardship, support any friend, oppose any foe to assure the survival and success of liberty.

This much we pledge—and more. To those old allies whose cultural and spiritual origins we share, we pledge the loyalty of faithful friends. United, there is little we cannot do in a host of cooperative ventures. Divided, there is little we can do—for we dare not meet a powerful challenge at odds and split asunder.

To those new states whom we welcome to the ranks of the free, we pledge our word that one form of colonial control shall not have passed away merely to be replaced by a far more iron tyranny. We shall not always expect to find them supporting our view. But we shall always hope to find them strongly supporting their own freedom—and to remember that, in the past, those who foolishly sought power by riding the back of the tiger ended up inside.

To those peoples in the huts and villages of half the globe struggling to break the bonds of mass misery, we pledge our best efforts to help them help themselves, for whatever period is required—not because the Communists may be doing it, not because we seek their votes, but because it is right. If a free society cannot help the many who are poor, it cannot save the few who are rich.

To our sister republics south of our border, we offer a special pledge— to convert our good words into good deeds—in a new alliance for progress—to assist free men and free governments in casting off the chains of poverty. But this peaceful revolution of hope cannot become the prey of hostile powers. Let all our neighbors know that we shall join with them to oppose aggression or subversion anywhere in the Americas. And let every other power know that this hemisphere intends to remain the master of its own house.

To that world assembly of sovereign states, the United Nations, our last best hope in an age where the instruments of war have far out-paced the instruments of peace, we renew our pledge of support—to prevent it from becoming merely a forum for invective—to strengthen its shield of the new and the weak—and to enlarge the area in which its writ may run.

Finally, to those nations who would make themselves our adversary, we offer not a pledge but a request: that both sides begin anew the quest for peace, before the dark powers of destruction unleashed by science engulf all humanity in planned or accidental self-destruction.

We dare not tempt them with weakness. For only when our arms are sufficient beyond doubt can we be certain beyond doubt that they will never be employed.

But neither can two great and powerful groups of nations take comfort from our present course—both sides overburdened by the cost of modern weapons, both rightly alarmed by the steady spread of the deadly atom, yet both racing to alter that uncertain balance of terror that stays the hand of mankind's final war.

So let us begin anew—remembering on both sides that civility is not a sign of weakness, and sincerity is always subject to proof. Let us never negotiate out of fear. But let us never fear to negotiate.

Let both sides explore what problems unite us instead of belaboring those problems which divide us. Let both sides, for the first time, formulate serious and precise proposals for the inspection and control of arms—and bring the absolute power to destroy other nations under the absolute control of all nations.

Let both sides seek to invoke the wonders of science instead of its terrors. Together let us explore the stars, conquer the deserts, eradicate disease, tap the ocean depths, and encourage the arts and commerce.

Let both sides unite to heed in all corners of the earth the command of Isaiah—to "undo the heavy burdens and to let the oppressed go free."

And if a beachhead of cooperation may push back the jungle of suspicion, let both sides join in a new endeavor—not a new balance of power, but a new world of law, where the strong are just and the weak secure and the peace preserved.

All this will not be finished in the first one hundred days. Nor will it be finished in the first one thousand days, nor in the life of this administration, nor even perhaps in our lifetime on this planet. But let us begin.

In your hands, my fellow citizens, more than mine, will rest the final success or failure of our course. Since this country was founded, each generation of Americans has been summoned to give testimony to its national loyalty. The graves of young Americans who answered the call to service surround the globe.

Now the trumpet summons us again—not as a call to bear arms, though arms we need—not as a call to battle, though embattled we are—but a call to bear the burden of a long twilight struggle, year in and year out, "rejoicing in hope, patient in tribulation"—a struggle against the common enemies of man: tyranny, poverty, disease, and war itself.

Can we forge against these enemies a grand and global alliance, North and South, East and West, that can assure a more fruitful life for all mankind? Will you join in that historic effort?

In the long history of the world, only a few generations have been granted the role of defending freedom in its hour of maximum danger. I do not shrink from this responsibility—I welcome it. I do not believe that any of us would exchange places with any other people or any other generation. The energy, the faith, the devotion which we bring to this endeavor will light our country and all who serve it—and the glow from that fire can truly light the world.

And so, my fellow Americans, ask not what your country can do for you—ask what you can do for your country.

My fellow citizens of the world, ask not what America will do for you, but what together we can do for the freedom of man.

Finally, whether you are citizens of America or citizens of the world, ask of us here the same high standards of strength and sacrifice which we ask of you. With a good conscience our only sure reward, with history the final judge of our deeds, let us go forth to lead the land we love, asking his blessing and his help, but knowing that here on earth God's work must truly be our own. ∎

President Charles de Gaulle Offers Self-Determination to the Algerian People

"What had to be done was done."

"Je suis la France" ("I am France"), spoken by a defiant de Gaulle after his country's surrender to the Nazis in 1940, was typical of the innocent arrogance of a leader who thought he embodied the spirit of his nation—and, on occasion, did. His stiff-neckedness in the face of weakness caused Winston Churchill to say, "The heaviest cross I bear is the Cross of Lorraine."

Throughout the fifties, France was torn apart by the "Algerian question": the desire of many in the colony to break free and the fear of many others, especially in the army, that the French in Algeria would be driven out. Only Charles de Gaulle—head of the Free French in exile during World War II, in retirement after an electoral setback in 1953—had the prestige and the will to use authority to end the rebellion. Only he could tell the angry French generals, "You are not the army's army; you are France's army."

The exponent of grandeur—"France cannot be France without greatness"—was given power to rule by decree in 1958; when an opponent compared him to Robespierre, he mockingly delivered this riposte: "I always thought I was Jeanne d'Arc and Bonaparte. How little one knows oneself." He understood the importance of speaking and of keeping silent: "There can be no power without mystery," he wrote in *The Edge of the Sword*. "There must always be a 'something' which others cannot altogether fathom, which puzzles them, stirs them, and rivets their attention. . . . Nothing more enhances authority than silence. It is the crowning virtue of the strong, the refuge of the weak, the modesty of the proud, the pride of the humble, the prudence of the wise, and the sense of fools. . . ." He exuded certitude; when a Nixon speechwriter asked him about separatism in Canada's Quebec in 1969, de Gaulle answered with absolute assurance, "One day Quebec will be free."

Charles de Gaulle served as president of the Fifth Republic from 1958 to 1969. On June 8, 1962, he gave the following address over radio and television, preparing his people for the independence of Algeria.

□   □   □

In twenty-three days, the Algerian problem in its substance will be resolved for France. Algeria will determine its own future. Algeria and France will be able to cooperate organically and regularly with each other. The Algerians of European stock will have the necessary guarantees to participate, in full freedom, in full equality, and in full brotherhood, in the life of the new Algeria. This is what France will have wanted and obtained.

Yes, in twenty-three days, the Algerian people, through the self-determination referendum, are going to ratify the Evian agreements, institute independence, and sanction cooperation, just as the French people, through the referendum of last April 8, subscribed to it for their part. Thus, over and above all the crises and all the passions, it is through the free decision and reasoned agreement of two peoples that a new phase in their relationships and a new chapter of their history are about to open.

This being so, what role can and must the Frenchmen of Algeria—who have settled there, who love Algeria, who have done so much there already, and of whom Algeria has so great a need—what role can and must these French people play in the Algeria of tomorrow? Once again I should like to express the hope that they will play their part fully, as soon as the last bloody mists with which some criminal madmen are still trying to blind them are dispelled. What role also can and must the leaders of the Moslem community play, for the good of their country—whether it be the leaders that are in office or the leaders that are about to take office, and who are certain before long to assume the capital responsibilities in the Algerian republic? What role, finally, must and can France play in the development of a nation to which she is attached by so many ties and which, everything commands her to help become free and prosperous? After 132 years of the existence of the problem, which had tragic consequences on several occasions, and after seven years of senseless and grievous fighting, this result will bear the imprint of justice and reason. However, in order to attain this, France has had to overcome severe obstacles.

When, in 1958, we came to grips with the affair, we found—who has been able to forget it?—the powers of the republic drowned in impotence, a plot of usurpation being formed in Algiers and drawn toward France by the collapse of the state, the nation suddenly finding itself on the brink of civil war. At the same time, the Moslem rebellion, having reached its climax and banking on our domestic crises, declared itself determined to triumph by arms, claimed to be sure of obtaining world support and offered the French community a single choice for its future: "the suitcase or the coffin." But, once the state was on its feet again and the catastrophe avoided—a recovery soon confirmed by the country's adoption of the necessary institutions by an 80 percent majority of the voters—it was possible, step by step, to bring the affair to its end.

It was necessary that, in Algeria, our army have control of the battlefield and the frontiers so that no failure could in any way jeopardize the will of France. It was necessary for us to squarely adopt self-determination and cooperation as political goals, while the implementation of the Constantine Plan was making all Algeria realize how essential France's aid was for its life. Thus the rebellion, renouncing its excesses and responding to the wish of the masses, came, little by little, to take the road to peace, to establish contact with us, and, finally, to conclude agreements permitting Algeria to express its will with full knowledge of the facts. It was necessary that the international attempts at interference and pressure, which were multiplying endlessly, have no hold over our policy. It was necessary that the successive plots be shattered: the affair of the barricades, the insurrection of April 1961, and, since then, the desperate acts of terrorist subversion, carried out, alas, by Frenchmen who resort to assassination, theft, and blackmail—all uprisings aimed at forcing the hand of the government, at shaking its foundations, toppling it, and hurling France into the abyss.

What had to be done was done. But—as everyone saw—it is because the new institutions enable the state to act—whereas the old ones only hindered it—that the government can make decisions instead of constantly equivocating and that it stands fast instead of forever tottering and stumbling. Above all, women and men of France, everyone has seen that the loyal confidence which you as a body have bestowed upon me has spurred and sustained me day after day and that this direct agreement between the people and the one who has the responsibility of leading it has become, in modern times, essential to the republic.

To maintain, in this domain, what has just been tested—such must be our conclusion, once the Algerian question has been settled. In these times that are difficult and dangerous, but filled with hope, how many things, indeed, have to be done that govern our destiny. To pursue our development—in the fields of economy, welfare, population, education, science, technology; to practice cooperation with those states of the world—above all, those of Africa—with which we are linked by virtue of ideals, language, culture, economy, and security; to contribute to the advancement of the two billion men who populate the underdeveloped countries; to equip ourselves with defense forces of such a kind that, for anyone, attacking France would mean certain death; to ensure together with our allies the integrity of the free world in the face of the Soviet threat; to help Western Europe build its unity, its prosperity, its strength, and its independence; to hasten the day when, perhaps—the totalitarian regime having lost its virulence and lowered its barriers—all the peoples of our continent will meet in an atmosphere of equilibrium, common sense, and friendship; in short, to accomplish the mission of France, we must, yes we must, be and freely remain a great and united people.

For the past four years, despite all the storms, this is fundamentally what we have been, as we then decided to be, overwhelmingly and solemnly, by means of universal suffrage. Justice and efficiency have thereby received their due. Women and men of France, we shall, by the same means, at the proper time, have to make sure that, in the future and above and beyond men who pass, the republic may remain strong, well ordered, and continuous.

Vive la République! Vive la France! ∎

Barry Goldwater Ignites
the Conservative Movement

"I would remind you that extremism in the defense of liberty is no vice! And let me remind you also that moderation in the pursuit of justice is no virtue!"

THE YEAR **1964** marked a great division in Republican ranks. Conservatives, denied the opportunity to lead the party when Thomas Dewey and, later, Dwight Eisenhower defeated Robert Taft, moved to gain control after the defeat of Richard Nixon in 1960. Their targets were Governor Nelson Rockefeller of New York and Governor William Scranton of Pennsylvania, representatives of the "eastern establishment" in conservative eyes.

After routing the "moderates" in primaries and state conventions, the militant rightists took command of the Republican National Convention, at the Cow Palace, in San Francisco. Barry Goldwater, Arizona senator and author of *The Conscience of a Conservative*, was their standard-bearer, and he was tired of being excoriated as an "extremist" by liberal Republicans. In a speech written by Karl Hess based on a strategy devised by F. Clifton White, Goldwater scorned the usual unity speech and took a forthright stand for individualism and anticommunism; he all but invited the liberal wing to take a walk with his rousing, well-balanced lines that did not find vice in all "extremism" and did not accept Rockefeller's "moderation" as virtuous.

I was in the hall that July 16, 1964, holding one end of a Scranton banner that said, "Stay in the Mainstream," and looked toward the Nixon box when the conventioneers went wild at the stick-it-to-Rocky lines. The once and future candidate, stony-faced, sat on his hands.

Though buried under the Lyndon Johnson landslide, and contained during the Nixon years, the conservative movement blossomed under Ronald Reagan, who got his national political start as a Goldwater speechmaker in the 1964 campaign.

□   □   □

. . . From this moment, united and determined, we will go forward together, dedicated to the ultimate and undeniable greatness of the whole man. Together we will win.

I accept your nomination with a deep sense of humility. I accept, too, the responsibility that goes with it, and I seek your continued help and your continued guidance. My fellow Republicans, our cause is too great for any man to feel worthy of it. Our task would be too great for any man, did he not have with him the heart and the hands of this great Republican party. And I promise you tonight that every fiber of my being is consecrated to our cause, that nothing shall be lacking from the struggle that can be brought to it by enthusiasm, by devotion, and plain hard work.

In this world no person, no party can guarantee anything, but what we can do and what we shall do is to deserve victory, and victory will be ours. The good Lord raised this mighty Republic to be a home for the brave and to flourish as the land of the free—not to stagnate in the swampland of collectivism, not to cringe before the bully of communism.

Now, my fellow Americans, the tide has been running against freedom. Our people have followed false prophets. We must, and we shall, return to proven ways—not because they are old, but because they are true.

We must, and we shall, set the tide running again in the cause of freedom. And this party, with its every action, every word, every breath, and every heartbeat, has but a single resolve, and that is freedom.

Freedom made orderly for this nation by our constitutional government. Freedom under a government limited by laws of nature and of nature's God. Freedom balanced so that liberty lacking order will not become the slavery of the prison cell; balanced so that liberty lacking order will not become the license of the mob and of the jungle.

Now, we Americans understand freedom; we have earned it, we have lived for it, and we have died for it. This nation and its people are freedom's models in a searching world. We can be freedom's missionaries in a doubting world.

But, ladies and gentlemen, first we must renew freedom's mission in our own hearts and in our own homes.

During four, futile years the administration which we shall replace has distorted and lost that faith. It has talked and talked and talked and talked the words of freedom, but it has failed and failed and failed in the works of freedom.

Now failure cements the wall of shame in Berlin; failures blot the sands of shame at the Bay of Pigs; failures marked the slow death of freedom in Laos; failures infest the jungles of Vietnam; and failures haunt the houses of our once great alliances and undermine the greatest bulwark ever erected by free nations, the NATO community.

Failures proclaim lost leadership, obscure purpose, weakening wills, and the risk of inciting our sworn enemies to new aggressions and to new excesses.

And because of this administration we are tonight a world divided. We are a nation becalmed. We have lost the brisk pace of diversity and the genius of individual creativity. We are plodding at a pace set by centralized planning, red tape, rules without responsibility, and regimentation without recourse.

Rather than useful jobs in our country, people have been offered bureaucratic make-work; rather than moral leadership, they have been given bread and circuses; they have been given spectacles, and, yes, they've even been given scandals.

Tonight there is violence in our streets, corruption in our highest offices, aimlessness among our youth, anxiety among our elderly; and there's a virtual despair among the many who look beyond material success toward the inner meaning of their lives. And where examples of morality should be set, the opposite is seen. Small men seeking great wealth or power have too often and too long turned even the highest levels of public service into mere personal opportunity.

Now, certainly simple honesty is not too much to demand of men in government. We find it in most. Republicans demand it from everyone. They demand it from everyone no matter how exalted or protected his position might be.

The growing menace in our country tonight, to personal safety, to life, to limb and property, in homes, in churches, on the playgrounds and places of business, particularly in our great cities, is the mounting concern—or should be—of every thoughtful citizen in the United States. Security from domestic violence, no less than from foreign aggression, is the most elementary and fundamental purpose of any government, and a government that cannot fulfill this purpose is one that cannot long command the loyalty of its citizens.

History shows us, demonstrates that nothing, nothing prepares the way for tyranny more than the failure of public officials to keep the streets safe from bullies and marauders.

Now, we Republicans see all this as more—much more—than the result of mere political differences or mere political mistakes. We see this as the result of a fundamentally and absolutely wrong view of man, his nature, and his destiny.

Those who seek to live your lives for you, to take your liberty in return for relieving you of yours, those who elevate the state and downgrade the citizen, must see ultimately a world in which earthly power can be substituted for divine will. And this nation was founded upon the rejection of that notion and upon the acceptance of God as the author of freedom.

Now, those who seek absolute power, even though they seek it to do what they regard as good, are simply demanding the right to enforce their own version of heaven on earth, and let me remind you they are the very ones who always create the most hellish tyranny.

Absolute power does corrupt, and those who seek it must be suspect and must be opposed. Their mistaken course stems from false notions, ladies and gentlemen, of equality. Equality, rightly understood as our founding fathers understood it, leads to liberty and to the emancipation of creative differences; wrongly understood, as it has been so tragically in our time, it leads first to conformity and then to despotism.

Fellow Republicans, it is the cause of Republicanism to resist concentrations of power, private or public, which enforce such conformity and inflict such despotism.

It is the cause of Republicanism to ensure that power remains in the hands of the people—and, so help us God, that is exactly what a Republican president will do with the help of a Republican Congress.

It is further the cause of Republicanism to restore a clear understanding of the tyranny of man over man in the world at large. It is our cause to dispel the foggy thinking which avoids hard decisions in the delusion that a world of conflict will somehow resolve itself into a world of harmony, if we just don't rock the boat or irritate the forces of aggression—and this is hogwash.

It is further the cause of Republicanism to remind ourselves, and the world, that only the strong can remain free: that only the strong can keep the peace.

Now, I needn't remind you, or my fellow Americans regardless of party, that Republicans have shouldered this hard responsibility and marched in this cause before. It was Republican leadership under Dwight Eisenhower that kept the peace, and passed along to this administration the mightiest arsenal for defense the world has ever known.

And I needn't remind you that it was the strength and the unbelievable will of the Eisenhower years that kept the peace by using our strength, by using it in the Formosa Strait, and in Lebanon, and by showing it courageously at all times.

It was during those Republican years that the thrust of Communist imperialism was blunted. It was during those years of Republican leadership that this world moved closer not to war but closer to peace than at any other time in the last three decades.

And I needn't remind you—but I will—that it's been during Democratic years that our strength to deter war has been stilled and even gone into a planned decline. It has been during Democratic years that we have weakly stumbled into conflicts, timidly refusing to draw our own lines against aggression, deceitfully refusing to tell even our people of our full participation and tragically letting our finest men die on battlefields unmarked by purpose, unmarked by pride or the prospect of victory.

Yesterday it was Korea; tonight it is Vietnam. Make no bones of this. Don't try to sweep this under the rug. We are at war in Vietnam. And yet the president, who is the commander in chief of our forces, refuses to say—refuses to say, mind you—whether or not the objective over there is victory, and his secretary of defense continues to mislead and misinform the American people, and enough of it has gone by.

And I needn't remind you—but I will—it has been during Democratic years that a billion persons were cast into Communist captivity and their fate cynically sealed.

Today, today in our beloved country, we have an administration which seems eager to deal with communism in every coin known—from gold to wheat, from consulates to confidence, and even human freedom itself.

Now, the Republican cause demands that we brand communism as the principal disturber of peace in the world today. Indeed, we should brand it as the only significant disturber of the peace. And we must make clear that until its goals of conquest are absolutely renounced and its rejections with all nations tempered, communism and the governments it now controls are enemies of every man on earth who is or wants to be free.

Now, we here in America can keep the peace only if we remain strong. Only if we keep our eyes open and keep our guard up can we prevent war.

And I want to make this abundantly clear—I don't intend to let peace or freedom be torn from our grasp because of lack of strength, or lack of will—and that I promise you Americans.

I believe that we must look beyond the defense of freedom today to its extension tomorrow. I believe that the communism which boasts it will bury us will instead give way to the forces of freedom. And I can see in the distant and yet recognizable future the outlines of a world worthy of our dedication, our every risk, our every effort, our every sacrifice along the way. Yes, a world that will redeem the suffering of those will be liberated from tyranny.

I can see, and I suggest that all thoughtful men must contemplate, the flowering of an Atlantic civilization, the whole world of Europe reunified and free, trading openly across its borders, communicating openly across the world.

It is a goal far, far more meaningful than a moon shot. It's a truly inspiring goal for all free men to set for themselves during the latter half of the twentieth century. I can also see, and all free men must thrill to, the events of this Atlantic civilization joined by a straight ocean highway to the United States. What a destiny! What a destiny can be ours to stand as a great central pillar linking Europe, the Americas, and the venerable and vital peoples and cultures of the Pacific!

I can see a day when all the Americas, North and South, will be linked in a mighty system—a system in which the errors and misunderstandings of the past will be submerged one by one in a rising tide of prosperity and interdependence.

We know that the misunderstandings of centuries are not to be wiped away in a day or wiped away in an hour. But we pledge, we pledge, that human sympathy—what our neighbors to the south call an attitude of simpatico—no less than enlightened self-interest will be our guide.

And I can see this Atlantic civilization galvanizing and guiding emergent nations everywhere. Now, I know this freedom is not the fruit of every soil. I know that our own freedom was achieved through centuries by unremitting efforts by brave and wise men. And I know that the road to freedom is a long and a challenging road, and I know also that some men may walk away from it, that some men resist challenge, accepting the false security of governmental paternalism.

And I pledge that the America I envision in the years ahead will extend its hand in help in teaching and in cultivation so that all new nations will be at least encouraged to go our way, so that they will not wander down the dark alleys of tyranny or to the dead-end streets of collectivism.

My fellow Republicans, we do no man a service by hiding freedom's light under a bushel of mistaken humility. I seek an American proud of its past, proud of its ways, proud of its dreams, and determined actively to proclaim them. But our examples to the world must, like charity, begin at home.

In our vision of a good and decent future, free and peaceful, there must be room, room for the liberation of the energy and the talent of the individual, otherwise our vision is blind at the outset.

We must assure a society here which, while never abandoning the needy or forsaking the helpless, nurtures incentives and opportunity for the creative and the productive.

We must know the whole good is the product of many single contributions. And I cherish the day when our children once again will restore as heroes the sort of men and women who, unafraid and undaunted, pursue the truth, strive to cure disease, subdue and make fruitful our natural environment, and produce the inventive engines of production—science and technology.

This nation, whose creative people have enhanced this entire span of history, should again thrive upon the greatness of all those things which we—we as individual citizens—can and should do.

During Republican years, this again will be a nation of men and women, of families proud of their role, jealous of their responsibilities, unlimited in their aspiration—a nation where all who can will be self-reliant.

We Republicans see in our constitutional form of government the great framework which assures the orderly but dynamic fulfillment of the whole man as the great reason for instituting orderly government in the first place.

We see in private property and in economy based upon and fostering private property the one way to make government a durable ally of the whole man rather than his determined enemy. We see in the sanctity of private property the only durable foundation for constitutional government in a free society.

And beyond all that, we see and cherish diversity of ways, diversity of thoughts, of motives, and accomplishments. We don't seek to live anyone's life for him. We only seek to secure his rights, guarantee him opportunity, guarantee him opportunity to strive, with government performing only those needed and constitutionally sanctioned tasks which cannot otherwise be performed.

We Republicans seek a government that attends to its inherent responsibilities of maintaining a stable monetary and fiscal climate, encouraging a free and a competitive economy, and enforcing law and order.

Thus do we seek inventiveness, diversity, and creative difference within a stable order, for we Republicans define government's role where needed at many, many levels—preferably, though, the one closest to the people involved: our towns and our cities, then our counties, then our states, then our regional contacts, and only then the national government.

That, let me remind you, is the land of liberty built by decentralized power. On it also we must have balance between the branches of government at every level.

Balance, diversity, creative difference—these are the elements of Republican equation. Republicans agree, Republicans agree heartily to disagree on many, many of their applications. But we have never disagreed on the basic fundamental issues of why you and I are Republicans.

This is a party—this Republican party is a party for free men. Not for blind followers and not for conformists.

Back in 1858 Abraham Lincoln said this of the Republican party—and I quote him because he probably could have said it during the last week or so—It was composed of strained, discordant, and even hostile elements. End of the quote, in 1958 [*sic*].

Yet all of these elements agreed on paramount objective: to arrest the progress of slavery, and place it in the course of ultimate extinction.

Today, as then, but more urgently and more broadly than then, the task of preserving and enlarging freedom at home and safeguarding it from the forces of tyranny abroad is great enough to challenge all our resources and to require all our strength.

Anyone who joins us in all sincerity, we welcome. Those, those who do not care for our cause, we don't expect to enter our ranks, in any case. And let our Republicanism so focused and so dedicated not be made fuzzy and futile by unthinking and stupid labels.

I would remind you that extremism in the defense of liberty is no vice!

And let me remind you also that moderation in the pursuit of justice is no virtue!

The beauty of the very system we Republicans are pledged to restore and revitalize, the beauty of this federal system of ours, is in its reconciliation of diversity with unity. We must not see malice in honest differences of opinion, and no matter how great, so long as they are not inconsistent with the pledges we have given to each other in and through our Constitution.

Our Republican cause is not to level out the world or make its people conform in computer-regimented sameness. Our Republican cause is to free our people and light the way for liberty throughout the world. Ours is a very human cause for very humane goals. This party, its good people, and its unquestionable devotion to freedom will not fulfill the purposes of this campaign which we launch here now until our cause has won the day, inspired the world, and shown the way to a tomorrow worthy of all our yesteryears.

I repeat, I accept your nomination with humbleness, with pride, and you and I are going to fight for the goodness of our land. Thank you. ■

President Richard M. Nixon Rallies "the Silent Majority" to Support the War in Vietnam

"AND so tonight—to you, the great silent majority of my fellow Americans—I ask for your support."

"THERE IS NOTHING the president has reflected on with greater anguish," Henry Kissinger told the Nixon senior staff in the Roosevelt Room of the White House a few hours before the president was to address the nation, "than what he is about to say tonight. Night after night, he has worked until two or three in the morning, producing draft after draft. . . . The president told me, 'I don't know if the country can be led here—but we must try.'"

The antiwar movement was gathering momentum in the first year of the Nixon presidency; on October 15, 1969, a well-organized moratorium, a nationwide day of protest including a march on Washington, increased the pressure of public opinion to speed the war's end. Columnist David Broder warned of "the breaking of the presidency," much as Lyndon Johnson's ability to govern had been shattered. In a radio campaign address three years later, Nixon reviewed the circumstances of his "Silent Majority" speech:

"In every presidency there are moments when success or failure seems to hang in the balance. . . . One of those moments came toward the end of my first year in office. . . . On November 3, 1969, I came before my fellow Americans on radio and television to review our responsibilities and to summon up the strength of our national character.

"The great silent majority of Americans—good people with good judgment who stand ready to do what they believe to be right—immediately responded. The response was powerful, nonpartisan, and unmistakable. The majority gave its consent, and the expressed will of the people made it possible for the government to govern successfully. I have seen the will of the majority in action. . . . That is why I cannot ally myself with those who habitually scorn the will of the majority."

In 1969, while much of the media focused on antiwar protest, the majority was afflicted with what sociologists call "pluralistic ignorance," an unawareness of being in the majority. Nixon, in this speech—which offered a rationale rather than new concessions—characterized his opposition as "a vocal minority," took some of the steam out of the doves' campaign by reminding his supporters they were the majority, and effectively bought nearly half a year of time with which to negotiate.

The anthologist was shown a copy of the speech half an hour before delivery and noticed a historical error in the peroration: Woodrow Wilson, who was associated with the phrase "war to end wars," never used it in his writings; the coiner was historian H. G. Wells. A few moments before airtime, I made this nitpicking point to the president, who rolled his eyes and said the hell with it, but in delivery changed "wrote" to "spoke," which may well be true and, in any case, cannot be disproven. I did not catch another error: we all thought he was speaking from the actual desk used by President Wilson; however, it turned out that the "Wilson desk" belonged to Henry Wilson, vice-president in the Grant administration; this mistake is corrected in a footnote in the collected presidential works.

The speech was effective because it was tightly organized, appealed to reason, and utilized such presentation devices as (a) the interior dialogue answering questions ("Well, now, who is at fault?"), (b) the enumeration of points to come ("Two other significant developments"), and (c) the presentation of alternatives in such a way as to lead to an inescapable conclusion ("I can order an immediate, precipitate withdrawal. . . . Or we can persist in our search for a just peace"). Some in the audience winced at banalities— "this would have been a popular and easy course. . . . It is not the easy way"—but soon recognized the evocative power of "the silent majority."

That phrase had been used a few months before by Vice-President Agnew, and nobody picked it up; it had been used often in history, usually in reference to the dead. Nixon had spoken of "the silent center" in his 1968 campaign, and had no idea his "silent majority" would be seized upon to encapsulate the "us" against the minority "them." He was sensitive to memorable phrases; a policy enunciated on the island of Guam was being called "the Guam Doctrine," but nobody elected Guam, and in this speech he straightened that out with "what has been described as the Nixon Doctrine." When I asked him afterward whether he knew he was launching a big phrase with "the silent majority," he said, "If I thought it would be picked up, I would have capitalized it in the text."

□   □   □

Good evening, my fellow Americans:
  Tonight I want to talk to you on a subject of deep concern to all Americans and to many people in all parts of the world—the war in Vietnam.

I believe that one of the reasons for the deep division about Vietnam is that many Americans have lost confidence in what their government has told them about our policy. The American people cannot and should not be asked to support a policy which involves the overriding issues of war and peace unless they know the truth about that policy.

Tonight, therefore, I would like to answer some of the questions that I know are on the minds of many of you listening to me.

How and why did America get involved in Vietnam in the first place?

How has this administration changed the policy of the previous administration?

What has really happened in the negotiations in Paris and on the battlefront in Vietnam?

What choices do we have if we are to end the war?

What are the prospects for peace?

Now, let me begin by describing the situation I found when I was inaugurated on January 20.

□ The war had been going on for four years.
□ 31,000 Americans had been killed in action.
□ The training program for the South Vietnamese was behind schedule.
□ 540,000 Americans were in Vietnam with no plans to reduce the number.
□ No progress had been made at the negotiations in Paris, and the United States had not put forth a comprehensive peace proposal.
□ The war was causing deep division at home and criticism from many of our friends as well as our enemies abroad.

In view of these circumstances, there were some who urged that I end the war at once by ordering the immediate withdrawal of all American forces.

From a political standpoint this would have been a popular and easy course to follow. After all, we became involved in the war while my predecessor was in office. I could blame the defeat which would be the result of my action on him and come out as the peacemaker. Some put it to me quite bluntly: this was the only way to avoid allowing Johnson's war to become Nixon's war.

But I had a greater obligation than to think only of the years of my administration and of the next election. I had to think of the effect of my decision on the next generation and on the future of peace and freedom in America and in the world.

Let us all understand that the question before us is not whether some Americans are for peace and some Americans are against peace. The question at issue is not whether Johnson's war becomes Nixon's war.

The great question is, How can we win America's peace?

Well, let us turn now to the fundamental issue. Why and how did the United States become involved in Vietnam in the first place?

Fifteen years ago, North Vietnam, with the logistical support of Communist China and the Soviet Union, launched a campaign to impose a Communist government on South Vietnam by instigating and supporting a revolution.

In response to the request of the government of South Vietnam, President Eisenhower sent economic aid and military equipment to assist the people of South Vietnam in their efforts to prevent a Communist takeover. Seven years ago, President Kennedy sent sixteen thousand military personnel to Vietnam as combat advisers. Four years ago, President Johnson sent American combat forces to South Vietnam.

Now, many believe that President Johnson's decision to send American combat forces to South Vietnam was wrong. And many others—I among them—have been strongly critical of the way the war has been conducted.

But the question facing us today is, Now that we are in the war, what is the best way to end it?

In January, I could only conclude that the precipitate withdrawal of American forces from Vietnam would be a disaster not only for South Vietnam but for the United States and for the cause of peace.

For the South Vietnamese, our precipitate withdrawal would inevitably allow the Communists to repeat the massacres which followed their takeover in the North fifteen years before.

□ They then murdered more than fifty thousand people and hundreds of thousands more died in slave labor camps.

□ We saw a prelude of what would happen in South Vietnam when the Communists entered the city of Hue last year. During their brief rule there, there was a bloody reign of terror in which three thousand civilians were clubbed, shot to death, and buried in mass graves.

□ With the sudden collapse of our support, these atrocities of Hue would become the nightmare of the entire nation—and particularly for the million and a half Catholic refugees who fled to South Vietnam when the Communists took over in the North.

For the United States, this first defeat in our nation's history would result in a collapse of confidence in American leadership, not only in Asia but throughout the world.

Three American presidents have recognized the great stakes involved in Vietnam and understood what had to be done.

In 1963, President Kennedy, with his characteristic eloquence and clarity, said, "We want to see a stable government there, carrying on a struggle to maintain its national independence. We believe strongly in that. We are not going to withdraw from that effort. In my opinion, for us to withdraw from that effort would mean a collapse not only of South Vietnam but Southeast Asia. So we are going to stay there."

President Eisenhower and President Johnson expressed the same conclusion during their terms of office.

For the future of peace, precipitate withdrawal would thus be a disaster of immense magnitude.

- □ A nation cannot remain great if it betrays its allies and lets down its friends.
- □ Our defeat and humiliation in South Vietnam without question would promote recklessness in the councils of those great powers who have not yet abandoned their goals of world conquest.
- □ This would spark violence wherever our commitments help maintain the peace—in the Middle East, in Berlin, eventually even in the Western Hemisphere.

Ultimately, this would cost more lives. It would not bring peace; it would bring more war.

For these reasons, I rejected the recommendation that I should end the war by immediately withdrawing all of our forces. I chose instead to change American policy on both the negotiating front and battlefront.

In order to end a war fought on many fronts, I initiated a pursuit for peace on many fronts.

In a television speech on May 14, in a speech before the United Nations, and on a number of other occasions I set forth our peace proposals in great detail.

- □ We have offered the complete withdrawal of all outside forces within 1 year.

- □ We have proposed a cease-fire under international supervision.
- □ We have offered free elections under international supervision with the Communists participating in the organization and conduct of the elections as an organized political force. And the Saigon government has pledged to accept the result of the elections.

We have not put forth our proposals on a take-it-or-leave-it basis. We have indicated that we are willing to discuss the proposals that have been put forth by the other side. We have declared that anything is negotiable except the right of the people of South Vietnam to determine their own future. At the Paris peace conference, Ambassador Lodge has demonstrated our flexibility and good faith in forty public meetings.

Hanoi has refused even to discuss our proposals. They demand our unconditional acceptance of their terms, which are that we withdraw all American forces immediately and unconditionally and that we overthrow the government of South Vietnam as we leave.

We have not limited our peace initiatives to public forums and public statements. I recognized, in January, that a long and bitter war like this usually cannot be settled in a public forum. That is why in addition to the public statements and negotiations I have explored every possible private avenue that might lead to a settlement.

Tonight I am taking the unprecedented step of disclosing to you some of our other initiatives for peace—initiatives we undertook privately and secretly because we thought we thereby might open a door, which publicly would be closed.

I did not wait for my inauguration to begin my quest for peace.

- □ Soon after my election, through an individual who is directly in contact on a personal basis with the leaders of North Vietnam, I made two private offers for a rapid, comprehensive settlement. Hanoi's replies called in effect for our surrender before negotiations.
- □ Since the Soviet Union furnishes most of the military equipment for North Vietnam, Secretary of State Rogers, my assistant for national security affairs, Dr. Kissinger, Ambassador Lodge, and I, personally, have met on a number of occasions with representatives of the Soviet government to enlist their assistance in getting meaningful negotiations started. In addition, we have had extended discussions directed toward that same end with representatives of other governments which have diplomatic relations with North Vietnam. None of these initiatives have to date produced results.

□ In mid-July, I became convinced that it was necessary to make a major move to break the deadlock in the Paris talks. I spoke directly in this office, where I am now sitting, with an individual who had known Ho Chi Minh [president, Democratic Republic of Vietnam] on a personal basis for twenty-five years. Through him, I sent a letter to Ho Chi Minh.

I did this outside of the usual diplomatic channels with the hope that with the necessity of making statements for propaganda removed, there might be constructive progress toward bringing the war to an end. Let me read from that letter to you now.

Dear Mr. President:

I realize that it is difficult to communicate meaningfully across the gulf of four years of war. But precisely because of this gulf, I wanted to take this opportunity to reaffirm in all solemnity my desire to work for a just peace. I deeply believe that the war in Vietnam has gone on too long and delay in bringing it to an end can benefit no one—least of all the people of Vietnam. . . .

The time has come to move forward at the conference table toward an early resolution of this tragic war. You will find us forthcoming and open-minded in a common effort to bring the blessings of peace to the brave people of Vietnam. Let history record that at this critical juncture, both sides turned their face toward peace rather than toward conflict and war.

I received Ho Chi Minh's reply on August 30, three days before his death. It simply reiterated the public position North Vietnam had taken at Paris and flatly rejected my initiative.

The full text of both letters is being released to the press.

□ In addition to the public meetings that I have referred to, Ambassador Lodge has met with Vietnam's chief negotiator in Paris in eleven private sessions.

□ We have taken other significant initiatives which must remain secret to keep open some channels of communication which may still prove to be productive.

But the effect of all the public, private, and secret negotiations which have been undertaken since the bombing halt a year ago and since this administration came into office on January 20, can be summed up in one sentence: no progress whatever has been made except agreement on the shape of the bargaining table.

Well now, who is at fault?

It has become clear that the obstacle in negotiating an end to the war is not the president of the United States. It is not the South Vietnamese government.

The obstacle is the other side's absolute refusal to show the least willingness to join us in seeking a just peace. And it will not do so while it is convinced that all it has to do is to wait for our next concession, and our next concession after that one, until it gets everything it wants.

There can now be no longer any question that progress in negotiation depends only on Hanoi's deciding to negotiate, to negotiate seriously.

I realize that this report on our efforts on the diplomatic front is discouraging to the American people, but the American people are entitled to know the truth—the bad news as well as the good news—where the lives of our young men are involved.

Now let me turn, however, to a more encouraging report on another front.

At the time we launched our search for peace, I recognized we might not succeed in bringing an end to the war through negotiation. I therefore put into effect another plan to bring peace—a plan which will bring the war to an end regardless of what happens on the negotiating front.

It is in line with a major shift in U.S. foreign policy which I described in my press conference at Guam on July 25. Let me briefly explain what has been described as the Nixon Doctrine—a policy which not only will help end the war in Vietnam but which is an essential element of our program to prevent future Vietnams.

We Americans are a do-it-yourself people. We are an impatient people. Instead of teaching someone else to do a job, we like to do it ourselves. And this trait has been carried over into our foreign policy.

In Korea and again in Vietnam, the United States furnished most of the money, most of the arms, and most of the men to help the people of those countries defend their freedom against Communist aggression.

Before any American troops were committed to Vietnam, a leader of another Asian country expressed this opinion to me when I was traveling in Asia as a private citizen. He said, "When you are trying to assist another nation defend its freedom, U.S. policy should be to help them fight the war but not to fight the war for them."

Well, in accordance with this wise counsel, I laid down in Guam three principles as guidelines for future American policy toward Asia:

□ First, the United States will keep all of its treaty commitments.
□ Second, we shall provide a shield if a nuclear power threatens the

freedom of a nation allied with us or of a nation whose survival we consider vital to our security.

□ Third, in cases involving other types of aggression, we shall furnish military and economic assistance when requested in accordance with our treaty commitments. But we shall look to the nation directly threatened to assume the primary responsibility of providing the manpower for its defense.

After I announced this policy, I found that the leaders of the Philippines, Thailand, Vietnam, South Korea, and other nations which might be threatened by Communist aggression welcomes this new direction in American foreign policy.

The defense of freedom is everybody's business—not just America's business. And it is particularly the responsibility of the people whose freedom is threatened. In the previous administration, we Americanized the war in Vietnam. In this administration, we are Vietnamizing the search for peace.

The policy of the previous administration not only resulted in our assuming the primary responsibility for fighting the war but, even more significantly, did not adequately stress the goal of strengthening the South Vietnamese so that they could defend themselves when we left.

The Vietnamization plan was launched following Secretary Laird's visit to Vietnam in March. Under the plan, I ordered first a substantial increase in the training and equipment of South Vietnamese forces.

In July, on my visit to Vietnam, I changed General Abrams's orders so that they were consistent with the objectives of our new policies. Under the new orders, the primary mission of our troops is to enable the South Vietnamese forces to assume the full responsibility for the security of South Vietnam.

Our air operations have been reduced by over 20 percent.

And now we have begun to see the results of this long overdue change in American policy in Vietnam.

□ After five years of Americans going into Vietnam, we are finally bringing American men home. By December 15, over sixty thousand men will have been withdrawn from SouthVietnam—including 20 percent of all of our combat forces.

□ The South Vietnamese have continued to gain in strength. As a result they have been able to take over combat responsibilities from our American troops.

Two other significant developments have occurred since this administration took office.

□ Enemy infiltration, infiltration which is essential if they are to launch a major attack, over the last three months is less than 20 percent of what it was over the same period last year.

□ Most important, United States casualties have declined during the last two months to the lowest point in three years.

Let me now turn to our program for the future.

We have adopted a plan which we have worked out in cooperation with the South Vietnamese for the complete withdrawal of all U.S. combat ground forces, and their replacement by South Vietnamese forces on an orderly scheduled timetable. This withdrawal will be made from strength and not from weakness. As South Vietnamese forces become stronger, the rate of American withdrawal can become greater.

I have not and do not intend to announce the timetable for our program. And there are obvious reasons for this decision which I am sure you will understand. As I have indicated on several occasions, the rate of withdrawal will depend on developments on three fronts.

One of these is the progress which can be or might be made in the Paris talks. An announcement of a fixed timetable for our withdrawal would completely remove any incentive for the enemy to negotiate an agreement. They would simply wait until our forces had withdrawn and then move in.

The other two factors on which we will base our withdrawal decisions are the level of enemy activity and the progress of the training programs of the South Vietnamese forces. And I am glad to be able to report tonight progress on both of these fronts has been greater than we anticipated when we started the program in June for withdrawal. As a result, our timetable for withdrawal is more optimistic now than when we made our first estimates in June. Now, this clearly demonstrates why it is not wise to be frozen in on a fixed timetable.

We must retain the flexibility to base each withdrawal decision on the situation as it is at that time rather than on estimates that are no longer valid.

Along with this optimistic estimate, I must—in all candor—leave one note of caution.

If the level of enemy activity significantly increases, we might have to adjust our timetable accordingly.

However, I want the record to be completely clear on one point.

At the time of the bombing halt just a year ago, there was some confusion as to whether there was an understanding on the part of the enemy that if we stopped the bombing of North Vietnam they would stop the shelling of cities in South Vietnam. I want to be sure that there is no misunderstanding on the part of the enemy with regard to our withdrawal program.

We have noted the reduced level of infiltration, the reduction of our casualties, and are basing our withdrawal decisions partially on those factors.

If the level of infiltration or our casualties increase while we are trying to scale down the fighting, it will be the result of a conscious decision by the enemy.

Hanoi could make no greater mistake than to assume that an increase in violence will be to its advantage. If I conclude that increased enemy action jeopardizes our remaining forces in Vietnam, I shall not hesitate to take strong and effective measures to deal with that situation.

This is not a threat. This is a statement of policy, which as commander in chief of our armed forces, I am making in meeting my responsibility for the protection of American fighting men wherever they may be.

My fellow Americans, I am sure you can recognize from what I have said that we really only have two choices open to us if we want to end this war.

□ I can order an immediate, precipitate withdrawal of all Americans from Vietnam without regard to the effects of that action.

□ Or we can persist in our search for a just peace through a negotiated settlement if possible, or through continued implementation of our plan for Vietnamization if necessary—a plan in which we will withdraw all of our forces from Vietnam on a schedule in accordance with our program, as the South Vietnamese become strong enough to defend their own freedom.

I have chosen this second course. It is not the easy way. It is the right way. It is a plan which will end the war and serve the cause of peace—not just in Vietnam but in the Pacific and in the world.

In speaking of the consequences of a precipitate withdrawal, I mentioned that our allies would lose confidence in America.

Far more dangerous, we would lose confidence in ourselves. Oh, the immediate reaction would be a sense of relief that our men were coming home. But as we saw the consequences of what we had done, inevitable remorse and divisive recrimination would scar our spirit as a people.

We have faced other crises in our history and have become stronger by rejecting the easy way out and taking the right way in meeting our challenges. Our greatness as a nation has been our capacity to do what had to be done when we knew our course was right.

I recognize that some of my fellow citizens disagree with the plan for peace I have chosen. Honest and patriotic Americans have reached different conclusions as to how peace should be achieved.

In San Francisco a few weeks ago, I saw demonstrators carrying signs reading. "Lose in Vietnam, bring the boys home."

Well, one of the strengths of our free society is that any American has a right to reach that conclusion and to advocate that point of view. But as president of the United States, I would be untrue to my oath of office if I allowed the policy of this nation to be dictated by the minority who hold that point of view and who try to impose it on the nation by mounting demonstrations in the street.

For almost two hundred years, the policy of this nation has been made under our Constitution by those leaders in the Congress and the White House elected by all of the people. If a vocal minority, however fervent its cause, prevails over reason and the will of the majority, this nation has no future as a free society.

And now I would like to address a word, if I may, to the young people of this nation who are particularly concerned, and I understand why they are concerned, about this war. I respect your idealism. I share your concern for peace. I want peace as much as you do.

There are powerful personal reasons I want to end this war. This week I will have to sign eighty-three letters to mothers, fathers, wives, and loved ones of men who have given their lives for America in Vietnam. It is very little satisfaction to me that this is only one-third as many letters as I signed the first week in office. There is nothing I want more than to see the day come when I do not have to write any of those letters.

- □ I want to end the war to save the lives of those brave young men in Vietnam.
- □ But I want to end it in a way which will increase the chance that their younger brothers and their sons will not have to fight in some future Vietnam someplace in the world.
- □ And I want to end the war for another reason. I want to end it so that the energy and dedication of you, our young people, now too often directed into bitter hatred against those responsible for the war, can be turned to the great challenges of peace, a better life for all Americans, a better life for all people on this earth.

I have chosen a plan for peace. I believe it will succeed.

If it does succeed, what the critics say now won't matter. If it does not succeed, anything I say then won't matter.

I know it may not be fashionable to speak of patriotism or national destiny these days. But I feel it is appropriate to do so on this occasion.

Two hundred years ago this nation was weak and poor. But even then, America was the hope of millions in the world. Today we have become the strongest and richest nation in the world. And the wheel of destiny has turned so that any hope the world has for the survival of peace and freedom will be determined by whether the American people have the moral stamina and the courage to meet the challenge of free world leadership.

Let historians not record that when America was the most powerful nation in the world we passed on the other side of the road and allowed the last hopes for peace and freedom of millions of people to be suffocated by the forces of totalitarianism.

And so tonight—to you, the great silent majority of my fellow Americans—I ask for your support.

I pledged in my campaign for the presidency to end the war in a way that we could win the peace. I have initiated a plan of action which will enable me to keep that pledge.

The more support I can have from the American people, the sooner that pledge can be redeemed; for the more divided we are at home, the less likely the enemy is to negotiate at Paris.

Let us be united for peace. Let us also be united against defeat. Because let us understand: North Vietnam cannot defeat or humiliate the United States. Only Americans can do that.

Fifty years ago, in this room and at this very desk, President Woodrow Wilson spoke words which caught the imagination of a war-weary world. He said, "This is the war to end war." His dream for peace after World War I was shattered on the hard realities of great power politics, and Woodrow Wilson died a broken man.

Tonight I do not tell you that the war in Vietnam is the war to end wars. But I do say this: I have initiated a plan which will end this war in a way that will bring us closer to that great goal to which Woodrow Wilson and every American president in our history has been dedicated—the goal of a just and lasting peace.

As president I hold the responsibility for choosing the best path to that goal and then leading the nation along it.

I pledge to you tonight that I shall meet this responsibility with all of the strength and wisdom I can command in accordance with your hopes, mindful of your concerns, sustained by your prayers.

Thank you, and good night. ■

Representative Barbara Jordan Makes the Constitutional Case for the Impeachment of Nixon

"I am not going to sit here and be an idle spectator to the diminution, the subversion, the destruction of the Constitution."

BARBARA JORDAN, a lawyer, the first black woman elected to the Texas state senate, was a member of the House Judiciary Committee that contemplated the impeachment of President Nixon for "high crimes and misdemeanors." As the hearings began, Republican Representative Latta of New Jersey, a Nixon defender, invited "those who propose impeachment to martial the hard facts in support of their position."

Representative Jordan of Texas opened with an attention-grabbing line thanking Chairman Peter Rodino for "the glorious opportunity of sharing the pain of this inquiry." Her presentation juxtaposed quotations from early constitutional ratification debates on the matter of impeachment with certain actions of Mr. Nixon's aides. Delivered in her deep, ringing voice, with her oratorical technique of exaggerated enunciation of long words, her opening statement gripped the audience in the room and watching on television. It earned her the role of keynoter at the 1976 Democratic National Convention.

□   □   □

Mr. Chairman, I join my colleague Mr. Rangel in thanking you for giving the junior members of this committee the glorious opportunity of sharing the pain of this inquiry. Mr. Chairman, you are a strong man, and it has not been easy but we have tried as best we can to give you as much assistance as possible.

Earlier today we heard the beginning of the Preamble to the Constitution of the United States, "We, the people." It is a very eloquent beginning. But when that document was completed, on the seventeenth of September in 1787, I was not included in that "We, the people." I felt somehow for many years that George Washington and Alexander Hamilton just left me out by mistake. But through the process of amendment, interpretation, and court decision I have finally been included in "We, the people."

Today, I am an inquisitor. I believe hyperbole would not be fictional and would not overstate the solemness that I feel right now. My faith in the Constitution is whole, it is complete, it is total. I am not going to sit here and be an idle spectator to the diminution, the subversion, the destruction of the Constitution.

"Who can so properly be the inquisitors for the nation as the representatives of the nation themselves?" *(Federalist,* no. 65.) The subject of its jurisdiction are those offenses which proceed from the misconduct of public men. That is what we are talking about. In other words, the jurisdiction comes from the abuse of violation of some public trust. It is wrong, I suggest, it is a misreading of the Constitution for any member here to assert that for a member to vote for an article of impeachment means that that member must be convinced that the president should be removed from office. The Constitution doesn't say that. The powers relating to impeachment are an essential check in the hands of this body, the legislature, against and upon the encroachment of the executive. In establishing the division between the two branches of the legislature, the House and the Senate, assigning to the one the right to accuse and to the other the right to judge, the framers of this Constitution were very astute. They did not make the accusers and the judges the same person.

We know the nature of impeachment. We have been talking about it awhile now. "It is chiefly designed for the president and his high ministers" to somehow be called into account. It is designed to "bridle" the executive if he engages in excesses. "It is designed as a method of national inquest into the conduct of public men." (Hamilton, *Federalist,* no. 65.) The framers confined in the Congress the power if need be, to remove the president in order to strike a delicate balance between a president swollen with power and grown tyrannical, and preservation of the independence of the executive. The nature of impeachment is a narrowly channeled exception to the separation-of-powers maxim; the federal convention of 1787 said that. It limited impeachment to high crimes and misdemeanors and discounted and opposed the term "maladministration." "It is to be used only for great misdemeanors," so it was said in the North Carolina ratification convention. And in the Virginia ratification convention: "We do not trust our liberty to a particular branch. We need one branch to check the others."

The North Carolina ratification convention: "No one need be afraid that officers who commit oppression will pass with immunity."

"Prosecutions of impeachments will seldom fail to agitate the passions of the whole community," said Hamilton in the *Federalist Papers,* no. 65. "And to divide it into parties more or less friendly or inimical to the accused." I do not mean political parties in that sense.

The drawing of political lines goes to the motivation behind impeachment; but impeachment must proceed within the confines of the constitutional term "high crimes and misdemeanors."

Of the impeachment process, it was Woodrow Wilson who said that "nothing short of the grossest offenses against the plain law of the land will suffice to give them speed and effectiveness. Indignation so great as to overgrow party interest may secure a conviction; but nothing else can."

Common sense would be revolted if we engaged upon this process for petty reasons. Congress has a lot to do. Appropriations, tax reform, health insurance, campaign finance reform, housing, environmental protection, energy sufficiency, mass transportation. Pettiness cannot be allowed to stand in the face of such overwhelming problems. So today we are not being petty. We are trying to be big because the task we have before us is a big one.

This morning, in a discussion of the evidence, we were told that the evidence which purports to support the allegations of misuse of the CIA by the president is thin. We are told that that evidence is insufficient. What that recital of the evidence this morning did not include is what the president did know on June 23, 1972. The president did know that it was Republican money, that it was money from the Committee for the Re-Election of the President, which was found in the possession of one of the burglars arrested on June 17.

What the president did know on June 23 was the prior activities of E. Howard Hunt, which included his participation in the break-in of Daniel Ellsberg's psychiatrist, which included Howard Hunt's participation in the Dita Beard ITT affair, which included Howard Hunt's fabrication of cables designed to discredit the Kennedy administration.

We were further cautioned today that perhaps these proceedings ought to be delayed because certainly there would be new evidence forthcoming from the president of the United States. There has not even been an obfuscated indication that this committee would receive any additional materials from the president. The committee subpoena is outstanding, and if the president wants to supply that material, the committee sits here.

The fact is that yesterday, the American people waited with great anxiety for eight hours, not knowing whether their president would obey an order of the Supreme Court of the United States.

At this point I would like to juxtapose a few of the impeachment criteria with some of the president's actions.

Impeachment criteria: James Madison, from the Virginia ratification convention. "If the president be connected in any suspicious manner with any person and there be grounds to believe that he will shelter him, he may be impeached."

We have heard time and time again that the evidence reflects payment to the defendants of money. The president had knowledge that these funds were being paid and that these were funds collected for the 1972 presidential campaign.

We know that the president met with Mr. Henry Petersen twenty-seven times to discuss matters related to Watergate and immediately thereafter met with the very persons who were implicated in the information Mr. Petersen was receiving and transmitting to the president. The words are "if the president be connected in any suspicious manner with any person and there be grounds to believe that he will shelter that person, he may be impeached."

Justice Story: "Impeachment is intended for occasional and extraordinary cases where a superior power acting for the whole people is put into operation to protect their rights and rescue their liberties from violations."

We know about the Huston plan. We know about the break-in of the psychiatrist's office. We know that there was absolute complete direction in August 1971 when the president instructed Ehrlichman to "do whatever is necessary." This instruction led to a surreptitious entry into Dr. Fielding's office.

"Protect their rights." "Rescue their liberties from violation."

The South Carolina ratification convention impeachment criteria: those are impeachable "who behave amiss or betray their public trust."

Beginning shortly after the Watergate break-in and continuing to the present time, the president has engaged in a series of public statements and actions designed to thwart the lawful investigation by government prosecutors. Moreover, the president has made public announcements and assertions bearing on the Watergate case which the evidence will show he knew to be false.

These assertions, false assertions, impeachable, those who misbehave. Those who "behave amiss or betray their public trust."

James Madison again at the Constitutional Convention: "A president is impeachable if he attempts to subvert the Constitution."

The Constitution charges the president with the task of taking care that the laws be faithfully executed, and yet the president has counseled his aides to commit perjury, willfully disregarded the secrecy of grand jury proceedings, concealed surreptitious entry, attempted to compromise a federal judge while publicly displaying his cooperation with the processes of criminal justice.

"A president is impeachable if he attempts to subvert the Constitution." If the impeachment provision in the Constitution of the United States will not reach the offenses charged here, then perhaps that eighteenth-century Constitution should be abandoned to a twentieth-century paper shredder. Has the president committed offenses and planned and directed and acquiesced in a course of conduct which the Constitution will not tolerate? That is the question. We know that. We know the question. We should now forthwith proceed to answer the question. It is reason, and not passion, which must guide our deliberations, guide our debate, and guide our decision. ■

President Gerald Ford Takes Office after Nixon's Resignation

"My fellow Americans, our long national nightmare is over."

MICHIGAN'S GERALD FORD, Republican House minority leader and a lifelong man of the Congress, was appointed by Richard Nixon to replace Spiro Agnew after that vice-president stepped down to avoid prosecution. When Nixon was also forced to resign, Ford became the nation's first appointed president.

After the trauma of Watergate, the country needed reassurance. Ford was determinedly plain—"a Ford, not a Lincoln"—and his first address to his fellow citizens as president was both solemn and simple. The speech, drafted by his veteran aide Robert Hartmann, made use of balanced phrases ("troubles our minds and hurts our hearts"; "not elected me as your president by your ballots, and so I ask you to confirm me as your president with your prayers") and concluded with the Lincolnesque "as God gives me to see the right" and the Wilsonian "God helping me."

This was a highly effective short speech, and the words "our long national nightmare is over" touched a chord. Mr. Ford never again reached these oratorical heights.

□   □   □

The oath that I have taken is the same oath that was taken by George Washington and by every president under the Constitution. But I assume the presidency under extraordinary circumstances never before experienced by Americans. This is an hour of history that troubles our minds and hurts our hearts.

Therefore, I feel it is my first duty to make an unprecedented compact with my countrymen. Not an inaugural address, not a fireside chat, not a campaign speech—just a little straight talk among friends. And I intend it to be the first of many.

I am acutely aware that you have not elected me as your president by your ballots, and so I ask you to confirm me as your president with your prayers. And I hope that such prayers will also be the first of many.

If you have not chosen me by secret ballot, neither have I gained office by any secret promises. I have not campaigned either for the presidency or the vice-presidency. I have not subscribed to any partisan platform. I am indebted to no man, and only to one woman—my dear wife—as I begin this very difficult job.

I have not sought this enormous responsibility, but I will not shirk it. Those who nominated and confirmed me as vice-president were my friends and are my friends. They were of both parties, elected by all the people and acting under the Constitution in their name. It is only fitting then that I should pledge to them and to you that I will be the president of all the people.

Thomas Jefferson said the people are the only sure reliance for the preservation of our liberty. And down the years, Abraham Lincoln renewed this American article of faith asking, "Is there any better way or equal hope in the world?"

I intend, on Monday next, to request of the speaker of the House of

Representatives and the president pro tempore of the Senate the privilege of appearing before the Congress to share with my former colleagues and with you, the American people, my views on the priority business of the nation and to solicit your views and their views. And may I say to the Speaker and the others, if I could meet with you right after these remarks, I would appreciate it.

Even though this is late in an election year, there is no way we can go forward except together and no way anybody can win except by serving the people's urgent needs. We cannot stand still or slip backwards. We must go forward now together.

To the peoples and the governments of all friendly nations, and I hope that could encompass the whole world, I pledge an uninterrupted and sincere search for peace. America will remain strong and united, but its strength will remain dedicated to the safety and sanity of the entire family of man, as well as to our own precious freedom.

I believe that truth is the glue that holds government together, not only our government but civilization itself. That bond, though strained, is unbroken at home and abroad.

In all my public and private acts as your president, I expect to follow my instincts of openness and candor with full confidence that honesty is always the best policy in the end.

My fellow Americans, our long national nightmare is over.

Our Constitution works; our great Republic is a government of laws and not of men. Here the people rule. But there is a higher power, by whatever name we honor him, who ordains not only righteousness but love, not only justice but mercy.

As we bind up the internal wounds of Watergate, more painful and more poisonous than those of foreign wars, let us restore the golden rule to our political process, and let brotherly love purge our hearts of suspicion and of hate.

In the beginning, I asked you to pray for me. Before closing, I ask again your prayers, for Richard Nixon and for his family. May our former president, who brought peace to millions, find it for himself. May God bless and comfort his wonderful wife and daughters, whose love and loyalty will forever be a shining legacy to all who bear the lonely burdens of the White House.

I can only guess at those burdens, although I have witnessed at close hand the tragedies that befell three presidents and the lesser trials of others.

With all the strength and all the good sense I have gained from life, with all the confidence my family, my friends, and my dedicated staff impart to me, and with the good will of countless Americans I have encountered in recent visits to forty states, I now solemnly reaffirm my promise I made to you last December 6: to uphold the Constitution, to do what is right as God gives me to see the right, and to do the very best I can for America.

God helping me, I will not let you down.

Thank you. ∎

Egypt's President Anwar el-Sadat Travels to Jerusalem to Address Israel's Knesset

"TODAY I tell you, and I declare it to the whole world, that we accept to live with you in permanent peace based on justice."

"DON'T ASK ME to make diplomatic relations with them," said Anwar el-Sadat in 1970, a few months before Israel's longtime foe became president of Egypt. "Never. Never. Leave it to the coming generations to decide that, not me." Yet it was Sadat's willingness to go to Jerusalem, in effect recognizing the state of Israel, that broke the logjam that had existed between Arab and Jew since the foundation of the Jewish state after World War II.

Prime Minister Menachem Begin, his Israeli interlocutor, matched the Arab leader's daring by ceding to Egypt "every inch" of Sinai territory that Egypt lost in its attacks on Israel in return for formal, peaceful relations and security arrangements. At the Camp David meetings later presided over by President Jimmy Carter, agreement was reached, and Sadat could proudly allude to the words of the Old Testament prophet Isaiah: "Let us work together until the day comes when they beat their swords into plowshares and their spears into pruning hooks." Fundamentalists answered this plea with assassination in 1981.

Sadat's speech in Arabic to the Knesset came only ten days after he told a reporter he would "go to the ends of the earth" to pursue peace, a statement that was promptly followed by Israel's expected invitation. Although the speech broke little negotiating ground on prickly questions like the status of Jerusalem, the fact of his presence—and the personal danger he was willing to assume—charged his words with emotion. The concluding blessing, *Salam Aleikum,* is close to the Hebrew phrase *Sholom Aleichem,* meaning "Peace be with you"—and the overlapping of the languages accentuated the common desire of speaker and spoken to.

□   □   □

. . . I come to you today on solid ground to shape a new life and to establish peace. We all love this land, the land of God; we all, Moslems, Christians, and Jews, all worship God.

Under God. God's teachings and commandments are love, sincerity, security, and peace.

I do not blame all those who received my decision when I announced it to the entire world before the Egyptian People's Assembly. I do not blame all those who received my decision with surprise and even with amazement—some gripped even by violent surprise. Still others interpreted it as political, to camouflage my intentions of launching a new war.

I would go so far as to tell you that one of my aides at the presidential office contacted me at a late hour following my return home from the People's Assembly and sounded worried as he asked me, "Mr. President, what would be our reaction if Israel actually extended an invitation to you?"

I replied calmly, "I would accept it immediately. I have declared that I would go to the ends of the earth. I would go to Israel, for I want to put before the people of Israel all the facts."

I can see the faces of all those who were astounded by my decision and had doubts as to the sincerity of the intentions behind the declaration of my decision. No one could ever conceive that the president of the biggest Arab state, which bears the heaviest burden and the main responsibility pertaining to the cause of war and peace in the Middle East, should declare his readiness to go to the land of the adversary while we were still in a state of war. . . .

Here I would go back to the big question: How can we achieve a durable peace based on justice? In my opinion, and I declare it to the whole world, from this forum, the answer is neither difficult nor is it impossible despite long years of feuds, blood, faction, strife, hatreds, and deep-rooted animosity.

The answer is not difficult, nor is it impossible, if we sincerely and faithfully follow a straight line.

You want to live with us, part of the world.

In all sincerity I tell you we welcome you among us with full security and safety. This in itself is a tremendous turning point, one of the landmarks of a decisive historical change. We used to reject you. We had our reasons and our fears, yes.

We refused to meet with you, anywhere, yes.

We were together in international conferences and organizations, and our representatives did not, and still do not, exchange greetings with you. Yes. This has happened and is still happening.

It is also true that we used to set as a precondition for any negotiations with you a mediator who would meet separately with each party.

Yes. Through this procedure, the talks of the first and second disengagement agreements took place.

Our delegates met in the first Geneva conference without exchanging direct word. Yes, this has happened.

Yet today I tell you, and I declare it to the whole world, that we accept to live with you in permanent peace based on justice. We do not want to encircle you or be encircled ourselves by destructive missiles ready for launching, nor by the shells of grudges and hatreds. . . .

I hail the Israeli voices that call for the recognition of the Palestinian people's right to achieve and safeguard peace.

Here I tell you, ladies and gentlemen, that it is no use to refrain from recognizing the Palestinian people and their right to statehood as their right of return. We, the Arabs, have faced this experience before, with you. And with the reality of the Israeli existence, the struggle which took us from war to war, from victims to more victims, until you and we have today reached the edge of a horrible abyss and a terrifying disaster unless, together, we seize this opportunity today of a durable peace based on justice.

You have to face reality bravely, as I have done. There can never be a solution to a problem by evading it or turning a deaf ear to it. Peace cannot last if attempts are made to impose fantasy concepts on which the world has turned its back and announced its unanimous call for the respect of rights and facts.

There is no need to enter a vicious circle as to Palestinian rights. It is useless to create obstacles; otherwise, the march of peace will be impeded or peace will be blown up. As I have told you, there is no happiness based on the detriment of others.

Direct confrontation and straightforwardness are the shortcuts and the most successful way to reach a clear objective. Direct confrontation concerning the Palestinian problem and tackling it in one single language with a view to achieving a durable and just peace lie in the establishment of that peace. With all the guarantees you demand, there should be no fear of a newly born state that needs the assistance of all countries of the world.

When the bells of peace ring, there will be no hands to beat the drums of war. Even if they existed, they would be stilled. . . .

Ladies and gentlemen, peace is not a mere endorsement of written lines. Rather, it is a rewriting of history. Peace is not a game of calling for peace to defend certain whims or hide certain admissions. Peace in its essence is a dire struggle against all and every ambition and whim.

Perhaps the example taken and experienced, taken from ancient and modern history, teaches that missiles, warships, and nuclear weapons cannot establish security. Instead, they destroy what peace and security build.

For the sake of our peoples and for the sake of the civilization made by man, we have to defend man everywhere against rule by the force of arms so that we may endow the full of humanity with all the power of the values and principles that further the sublime position of mankind.

Allow me to address my call from this rostrum to the people of Israel. I tell them, from the Egyptian people, who bless this sacred mission of peace, I convey to you the message of peace of the Egyptian people, who do not harbor fanaticism and whose sons—Moslems, Christians and Jews—live together in a state of cordiality, love, and tolerance.

This is Egypt, whose people have entrusted me with their sacred message. A message of security, safety, and peace to every man, woman, and child in Israel. Let all endeavors be channeled toward building a huge stronghold for peace instead of building destructive rockets.

Introduce to the entire world the image of the new man in this area so that he might set an example to the man of our age, the man of peace everywhere. Ring the bells for your sons. Tell them that those wars were the last of wars and the end of sorrows. Tell them that we are entering upon a new beginning, a new life, a life of love, prosperity, freedom, and peace.

You, sorrowing mother, you, widowed wife, you, the son who lost a brother or a father, all the victims of wars, fill the air and space with recitals of peace, fill bosoms and hearts with the aspirations of peace. Make a reality that blossoms and lives. Make hope a code of conduct and endeavor.

The will of peoples is part of the will of God. Ladies and gentlemen, before I came to this place, with every beat of my heart and with every sentiment, I prayed to God Almighty. While performing the prayers at the Al Aksa mosque and while visiting the Holy Sepulcher I asked the Almighty to give me strength and to confirm my belief that this visit may achieve the objective I look forward to for a happy present and a happier future.

I have chosen to set aside all precedents and traditions known by warring countries. In spite of the fact that occupation of Arab territories is still there, the declaration of my readiness to proceed to Israel came as a great surprise that stirred many feelings and confounded many minds. Some of them even doubted its intent.

Despite all that, the decision was inspired by all the clarity and purity of belief and with all the true passions of my people's will and intentions, and I have chosen this road considered by many to be the most difficult road.

I have chosen to come to you with an open heart and an open mind. I have chosen to give this great impetus to all international efforts exerted for peace. I have chosen to present to you, in your own home, the realities, devoid of any scheme or whim. Not to maneuver, or win a round, but for us to win together the most dangerous of rounds embattled in modern history, the battle of permanent peace based on justice.

It is not my battle alone. Nor is it the battle of the leadership in Israel alone. It is the battle of all and every citizen in our territories, whose right it is to live in peace. It is the commitment of conscience and responsibility in the hearts of millions.

When I put forward this initiative, many asked what is it that I conceived as possible to achieve during this visit and what my expectations were. And as I answer the questions, I announce before you that I have not thought of carrying out this initiative from the precepts of what could be achieved during this visit. And I have come here to deliver a message. I have delivered the message, and may God be my witness.

I repeat with Zachariah: Love, right, and justice. From the holy Koran I quote the following verses: We believe in God and in what has been revealed to us and what was revealed to Abraham, Ishmael, Isaac, Jacob, and the thirteen Jewish tribes. And in the books given to Moses and Jesus and the prophets from their Lord, who made no distinction between them. So we agree. *Salam Aleikum*—Peace be upon you. ■

Senator Edward M. Kennedy Exhorts Fellow Democrats to Hold Fast to Liberalism

"SOMEDAY, long after this convention, long after the signs come down, and the crowds stop cheering, and the bands stop playing, may it be said of our campaign that we kept the faith."

THE YOUNGEST OF THE KENNEDY BROTHERS, although the worst extemporaneous speaker of the three, turned out to be far better than Robert and the rival of Jack in reading speeches before large audiences.

In 1980, Senator Edward Kennedy had challenged a sitting Democratic president for his party's nomination; had effectively divided the party and carried the state of New York in the primaries; and had, after a stumbling interview with correspondent Roger Mudd and the national recollection of the 1969 death of the senator's companion at Chappaquiddick, been defeated by President Carter.

At the Democratic National Convention in New York, a month after the Republicans had selected conservative Ronald Reagan to be the GOP standard-bearer, Ted Kennedy sounded a certain trumpet for a liberalism that was being derogated by many in his own party as "throwing money at problems." In a speech written by Robert Shrum, he did not defend Lyndon Johnson's Great Society—indeed, he pointedly overlooked his brother's successor in identifying Democrats as "the party of the New Freedom [Wilson], the New Deal [FDR], and the New Frontier [Kennedy]." His purpose was to identify his own reach for power as the espousal of the embattled liberal cause; though the cause seemed to be going out of fashion, he was determined to hold high the sputtering torch that had been passed to his generation.

This speech contains the themes and cadences we have come to call Kennedyesque. It begins with a self-deprecating line to take some of the tension out of the air, and then quickly assumes a classic oratorical tone: "not to argue for a candidacy but to affirm a cause" is on the order of the Shakespearean "hear me for my cause." After blazing away at the

Republicans, Kennedy turns to his theme: "The poor may be out of political fashion, but they are not without human needs. The middle class may be angry, but they have not lost the dream. . . ."

From Martin Luther King's dream, he recalls FDR's "this generation of Americans has a rendezvous with destiny"—in Kennedy's paraphrase, "each generation of Americans has a rendezvous with a different reality." When he comes to the environment, without overtly referring to his brother Robert's 1968 campaign theme song, "This Land Is Your Land," he uses its lyrics: "To all those who inhabit our land, from California to the New York island, from the Redwood Forest to the Gulf Stream waters. . . ."

Kennedy uses some straw men: "Some say . . . I reply" and "Let us reject the counsel of retreat and the call to reaction." And his reference to President Carter, the party's nominee, is ungracious in its brevity. But the double evocation of poetry works effectively, and the final lines build to a powerful conclusion mixing sentiment and defiance.

□   □   □

Well, things worked out a little different than I thought, but let me tell you, I still love New York.

My fellow Democrats and my fellow Americans, I have come here tonight not to argue for a candidacy but to affirm a cause.

I am asking you to renew the commitment of the Democratic party to economic justice. I am asking you to renew our commitment to a fair and lasting prosperity that can put America back to work.

This is the cause that brought me into the campaign and that sustained me for nine months, across a hundred thousand miles, in forty different states. We had our losses; but the pain of our defeats is far, far less than the pain of the people I have met. We have learned that it is important to take issues seriously, but never to take ourselves too seriously.

The serious issue before us tonight is the cause for which the Democratic party has stood in its finest hours—the cause that keeps our party young— and makes it, in the second century of its age, the largest political party in this Republic and the longest-lasting political party on this planet.

Our cause has been, since the days of Thomas Jefferson, the cause of the common man—and the common woman. Our commitment has been, since the days of Andrew Jackson, to all those he called "the humble members of society—the farmers, mechanics, and laborers." On this foundation, we have defined our values, refined our policies, and refreshed our faith.

Now I take the unusual step of carrying the cause and the commitment of my campaign personally to our national convention. I speak out of a deep sense of urgency about the anguish and anxiety I have seen across America. I speak out of a deep belief in the ideals of the Democratic party, and in the potential of that party and of a president to make a difference. I speak out of a deep trust in our capacity to proceed with boldness and a common vision that will feel and heal the suffer—the division of our party.

The economic plank of this platform on its face concerns only material things; but is also a moral issue that I raise tonight. It has taken many forms over many years. In this campaign, and in this country that we seek to lead, the challenge in 1980 is to give our voice and our vote for these fundamental Democratic principles:

Let us pledge that we will never misuse unemployment, high interest rates, and human misery as false weapons against inflation.

Let us pledge that employment will be the first priority of our economic policy.

Let us pledge that there will be security for all who are now at work.

Let us pledge that there will be jobs for all who are out of work—and we will not compromise on the issue of jobs.

These are not simplistic pledges. Simply put, they are the heart of our tradition; they have been the soul of our party across the generations. It is the glory and the greatness of our tradition to speak for those who have no voice, to remember those who are forgotten, to respond to the frustrations and fulfill the aspirations of all Americans seeking a better life in a better land.

We dare not forsake that tradition. We cannot let the great purposes of the Democratic party become the bygone passages of history. We must not permit the Republicans to seize and run on the slogans of prosperity.

We heard the orators at their convention all trying to talk like Democrats. They proved that even Republican nominees can quote Franklin Roosevelt to their own purpose. The grand old party thinks it has found a great new trick. But forty years ago, an earlier generation of Republicans attempted that same trick. And Franklin Roosevelt himself replied, "Most Republican leaders . . . have bitterly fought and blocked the forward surge of average men and women in their pursuit of happiness. Let us not be deluded that overnight those leaders have suddenly become the friends of average men and women. . . . You know, very few of us are that gullible."

And four years later, when the Republicans tried that trick again, Franklin Roosevelt asked, "Can the Old Guard pass itself off as the New

Deal? I think not. We have all seen many marvelous stunts in the circus—but no performing elephant could turn a handspring without falling flat on its back."

The 1980 Republican convention was awash with crocodile tears for our economic distress, but it is by their long record and not their recent words that you shall know them.

The same Republicans who are talking about the crisis of unemployment have nominated a man who once said—and I quote—"Unemployment insurance is a prepaid vacation plan for freeloaders." And that nominee is no friend of labor.

The same Republicans who are talking about the problems of the inner cities have nominated a man who said—and I quote—"I have included in my morning and evening prayers every day the prayer that the federal government not bail out New York." And that nominee is no friend of this city and of our great urban centers.

The same Republicans who are talking about security for the elderly have nominated a man who said just four years ago that participation in Social Security "should be made voluntary." And that nominee is no friend of the senior citizen.

The same Republicans who are talking about preserving the environment have nominated a man who last year made the preposterous statement—and I quote—"Eighty percent of air pollution comes from plants and trees." And that nominee is no friend of the environment.

And the same Republicans who are invoking Franklin Roosevelt have nominated a man who said in 1976—and these are his exact words—"Fascism was really the basis of the New Deal." And that nominee, whose name is Ronald Reagan, has no right to quote Franklin Delano Roosevelt.

The great adventure which our opponents offer is a voyage into the past. Progress is our heritage, not theirs. What is right for us as Democrats is also the right way for Democrats to win.

The commitment I seek is not to outworn views but to old values that will never wear out. Programs may sometimes become obsolete, but the ideal of fairness always endures. Circumstances may change, but the work of compassion must continue. It is surely correct that we cannot solve problems by throwing money at them; but it is also correct that we dare not throw our national problems onto a scrap heap of inattention and indifference. The poor may be out of political fashion, but they are not without human needs. The middle class may be angry, but they have not lost the dream that all Americans can advance together.

The demand of our people in 1980 is not for smaller government or bigger government but for better government. Some say that government is always bad, and that spending for basic social programs is the root of our economic evils. But we reply, the present inflation and recession cost our economy $200 billion a year. We reply, inflation and unemployment are the biggest spenders of all.

The task of leadership in 1980 is not to parade scapegoats or to seek refuge in reaction but to match our power to the possibilities of progress.

While others talked of free enterprise, it was the Democratic party that acted—and we ended excessive regulation in the airline and trucking industry. We restored competition to the marketplace. And I take some satisfaction that this deregulation was legislation that I sponsored and passed in the Congress of the United States.

As Democrats, we recognize that each generation of Americans has a rendezvous with a different reality. The answers of one generation become the questions of the next generation. But there is a guiding star in the American firmament. It is as old as the revolutionary belief that all people are created equal—and as clear as the contemporary condition of Liberty City and the South Bronx. Again and again, Democratic leaders have followed that star—and they have given new meaning to the old values of liberty and justice for all.

We are the party of the New Freedom, the New Deal, and the New Frontier. We have always been the party of hope. So this year, let us offer new hope—new hope to an America uncertain about the present but unsurpassed in its potential for the future.

To all those who are idle in the cities and industries of America, let us provide new hope for the dignity of useful work. Democrats have always believed that a basic civil right of all Americans is the right to earn their own way. The party of the people must always be the party of full employment.

To all those who doubt the future of our economy, let us provide new hope for the reindustrialization of America. Let our vision reach beyond the next election or the next year to a new generation of prosperity. If we could rebuild Germany and Japan after World War II, then surely we can reindustrialize our own nation and revive our inner cities in the 1980s.

To all those who work hard for a living wage, let us provide new hope that the price of their employment shall not be an unsafe workplace and death at an earlier age.

To all those who inhabit our land, from California to the New York island, from the Redwood Forest to the Gulf Stream waters, let us provide new hope that prosperity shall not be purchased by poisoning the air, the rivers, and the natural resources that are the greatest gift of this continent. We must insist that our children and grandchildren shall inherit a land which they can truly call America the beautiful.

To all those who see the worth of their work and their savings taken by inflation, let us offer new hope for a stable economy. We must meet the pressures of the present by invoking the full power of government to master increasing prices. In candor, we must say that the federal budget can be balanced only by policies that bring us to a balanced prosperity of full employment and price restraint.

And to all those overburdened by an unfair tax structure, let us provide new hope for real tax reform. Instead of shutting down classrooms, let us shut off tax shelters.

Instead of cutting out school lunches, let us cut off tax subsidies for expensive business lunches that are nothing more than food stamps for the rich.

The tax cut of our Republican opponents takes the name of tax reform in vain. It is a wonderfully Republican idea that would redistribute income in the wrong direction. It is good news for any of you with incomes over $200,000 a year. For the few of you, it offers a pot of gold worth $14,000. But the Republican tax cut is bad news for middle-income families. For the many of you, they plan a pittance of $200 a year. And that is not what the Democratic party means when we say tax reform.

The vast majority of Americans cannot afford this panacea from a Republican nominee who has denounced the progressive income tax as the invention of Karl Marx. I am afraid he has confused Karl Marx with Theodore Roosevelt, that obscure Republican president who sought and fought for a tax system based on ability to pay. Theodore Roosevelt was not Karl Marx—and the Republican tax scheme is not tax reform.

Finally, we cannot have a fair prosperity in isolation from a fair society. So I will continue to stand for national health insurance. We must not surrender to the relentless medical inflation that can bankrupt almost anyone—and that may soon break the budgets of government at every level.

Let us insist on real controls over what doctors and hospitals can charge. Let us resolve that the state of a family's health shall never depend on the size of a family's wealth.

The president, the vice-president, and the members of Congress have a medical plan that meets their needs in full. Whenever senators and representatives catch a little cold, the Capitol physician will see them immediately, treat them promptly, and fill a prescription on the spot. We do not get a bill even if we ask for it. And when do you think was the last time a member of Congress asked for a bill from the federal government?

I say again, as I have said before, if health insurance is good enough for the president, the vice-president, and the Congress of the United States, then it is good enough for all of you and for every family in America.

There were some who said we should be silent about our differences on issues during this convention. But the heritage of the Democratic party has been a history of democracy. We fight hard because we care deeply about our principles and purposes. We did not flee this struggle. And we welcome this contrast with the empty and expedient spectacle last month in Detroit, where no nomination was contested, no question was debated, and no one dared to raise any doubt or dissent.

Democrats can be proud that we chose a different course—and a different platform.

We can be proud that our party stands for investment in safe energy instead of a nuclear future that may threaten the future itself. We must not permit the neighborhoods of America to be permanently shadowed by the fear of another Three Mile Island.

We can be proud that our party stands for a fair housing law to unlock the doors of discrimination once and for all. The American house will be divided against itself so long as there is prejudice against any American family buying or renting a home.

And we can be proud that our party stands plainly, publicly, and persistently for the ratification of the Equal Rights Amendment. Women hold their rightful place at our convention; and women must have their rightful place in the Constitution of the United States. On this issue, we will not yield, we will not equivocate, we will not rationalize, explain, or excuse. We will stand for ERA and for the recognition at long last that our nation had not only founding fathers but founding mothers as well.

A fair prosperity and a just society are within our vision and our grasp. We do not have every answer. There are questions not yet asked, waiting for us in the recesses of the future.

But of this much we can be certain, because it is the lesson of all our history:

Together, a president and the people can make a difference. I have found that faith still alive wherever I have traveled across the land. So let us reject the counsel of retreat and the call to reaction. Let us go forward in the knowledge that history only helps those who help themselves.

There will be setbacks and sacrifices in the years ahead. But I am convinced that we as a people are ready to give something back to our country in return for all it has given us. Let this be our commitment: whatever sacrifices must be made will be shared—and shared fairly. And let this be our confidence at the end of our journey and always before us shines that ideal of liberty and justice for all.

In closing, let me say a few words to all those I have met and all those who have supported me at this convention and across the country.

There were hard hours on our journey. Often we sailed against the wind, but always we kept our rudder true. There were so many of you who stayed the course and shared our hope. You gave your help; but even more, you gave your hearts. Because of you, this has been a happy campaign. You welcomed Joan and me and our family into your homes and neighborhoods, your churches, your campuses, and your union halls. When I think back on all the miles and all the months and all the memories, I think of you. I recall the poet's words, and I say, "What golden friends I had."

Among you, my golden friends across this land, I have listened and learned.

I have listened to Kenny Dubois, a glassblower in Charleston, West Virginia, who has ten children to support, but has lost his job after thirty-five years, just three years short of qualifying for his pension.

I have listened to the Trachta family, who farm in Iowa and who wonder whether they can pass the good life and the good earth on to their children.

I have listened to a grandmother in East Oakland, who no longer has a phone to call her grandchildren, because she gave it up to pay the rent on her small apartment.

I have listened to young workers out of work, to students without the tuition for college, and to families without the chance to own a home. I have seen the closed factories and the stalled assembly lines of Anderson, Indiana, and South Gate, California. I have seen too many—far too many—idle men and women desperate to work. I have seen too many— far too many—working families desperate to protect the value of their wages from the ravages of inflation.

Yet I have also sensed a yearning for new hope among the people in every state where I have been. I felt it in their handshakes; I saw it in their faces. I shall never forget the mothers who carried children to our rallies. I shall always remember the elderly who have lived in an America of high purpose and who believe it can all happen again.

Tonight, in their name, I have come here to speak for them. For their sake, I ask you to stand with them. On their behalf, I ask you to restate and reaffirm the timeless truth of our party.

I congratulate President Carter on his victory here. I am confident that the Democratic party will reunite on the basis of Democratic principles— and that together we will march toward a Democratic victory in 1980.

And someday, long after this convention, long after the signs come down and the crowds stop cheering, and the bands stop playing, may it be said of our campaign that we kept the faith. May it be said of our party in 1980 that we found our faith again.

May it be said of us, both in dark passages and in bright days, in the words of Tennyson that my brothers quoted and loved—and that have special meaning for me now:

> I am a part of all that I have met. . . .
> Though much is taken, much abides. . . .
> That which we are, we are—
> One equal temper of heroic hearts,
>   . . . strong in will
> To strive, to seek, to find, and not to yield.

For me, a few hours ago, this campaign came to an end. For all those whose cares have been our concern, the work goes on, the cause endures, the hope still lives, and the dream shall never die. ■

President Ronald Reagan Foresees the Crisis of Communism

"IN an ironic sense Karl Marx was right. We are witnessing today a great revolutionary crisis, a crisis where the demands of the economic order are conflicting directly with those of the political order. . . . It is the Soviet Union that runs against the tide of history by denying human freedom and human dignity to its citizens."

RONALD REAGAN, who came on the political scene in a television speech supporting Barry Goldwater in 1964, remained an unabashed ideologue even after his own election in 1980. But in a thoughtful ideological address to both Houses of Parliament at the Palace of Westminster in London two years later, President Reagan exposed the weakness corroding the Communist economy. Following passages that were not taken seriously by most commentators until Mikhail Gorbachev revealed the extent of Soviet decline in the late eighties, the resolutely optimistic Mr. Reagan challenged the Communist world to a peaceful competition of ideas: "Let us be shy no longer. Let us go to our strength. Let us offer hope. Let us tell the world that a new age is not only possible but probable."

When read in the context of what was not widely known to be going on in the Soviet Union at the time, including the circumstances that brought about *perestroika* and *glasnost* that Mr. Reagan was later to embrace at a Moscow summit, this June 8, 1982, speech to Parliament was presidential oratory with prophetic power.

□   □   □

. . . We're approaching the end of a bloody century plagued by a terrible political invention—totalitarianism. Optimism comes less easily today, not because democracy is less vigorous, but because democracy's enemies have refined their instruments of repression. Yet optimism is in order because day by day democracy is proving itself to be a not at all fragile flower. From Stettin on the Baltic to Varna on the Black Sea, the regimes planted by totalitarianism have had more than thirty years to establish their legitimacy. But none—not one regime—has yet been able to risk free elections. Regimes planted by bayonets do not take root.

The strength of the Solidarity movement in Poland demonstrates the truth told in an underground joke in the Soviet Union. It is that the Soviet Union would remain a one-party nation even if an opposition party were permitted because everyone would join the opposition party. . . .

Historians looking back at our time will note the consistent restraint and peaceful intentions of the West. They will note that it was the democracies who refused to use the threat of their nuclear monopoly in the forties and early fifties for territorial or imperial gain. Had that nuclear monopoly been in the hands of the Communist world, the map of Europe—indeed, the world—would look very different today. And certainly they will note it was not the democracies that invaded Afghanistan or suppressed Polish Solidarity or used chemical and toxin warfare in Afghanistan and Southeast Asia.

If history teaches anything, it teaches self-delusion in the face of unpleasant facts is folly. We see around us today the marks of our terrible dilemma—predictions of doomsday, antinuclear demonstrations, an arms race in which the West must, for its own protection, be an unwilling participant. At the same time we see totalitarian forces in the world who seek subversion and conflict around the globe to further their barbarous assault on the human spirit. What, then, is our course? Must civilization perish in a hail of fiery atoms? Must freedom wither in a quiet, deadening accommodation with totalitarian evil?

Sir Winston Churchill refused to accept the inevitability of war or even that it was imminent. He said, "I do not believe that Soviet Russia desires war. What they desire is the fruits of war and the indefinite expansion of their power and doctrines. But what we have to consider here today while time remains is the permanent prevention of war and the establishment of conditions of freedom and democracy as rapidly as possible in all countries."

Well, this is precisely our mission today: to preserve freedom as well as peace. It may not be easy to see; but I believe we live now at a turning point.

In an ironic sense Karl Marx was right. We are witnessing today a great revolutionary crisis, a crisis where the demands of the economic order are conflicting directly with those of the political order. But the crisis is happening not in the free, non-Marxist West but in the home of Marxism-Leninism, the Soviet Union. It is the Soviet Union that runs against the tide of history by denying human freedom and human dignity to its citizens. It also is in deep economic difficulty. The rate of growth in the national product has been steadily declining since the fifties and is less than half of what it was then.

The dimensions of this failure are astounding: a country which employs one-fifth of its population in agriculture is unable to feed its own people. Were it not for the private sector, the tiny private sector tolerated in Soviet agriculture, the country might be on the brink of famine. These private plots occupy a bare 3 percent of the arable land but account for nearly one-quarter of Soviet farm output and nearly one-third of meat products and vegetables. Overcentralized, with little or no incentives, year after year the Soviet system pours its best resources into the making of instruments of destruction. The constant shrinkage of economic growth combined with the growth of military production is putting a heavy strain on the Soviet people. What we see here is a political structure that no longer corresponds to its economic base, a society where productive forces are hampered by political ones.

The decay of the Soviet experiment should come as no surprise to us. Wherever the comparisons have been made between free and closed societies—West Germany and East Germany, Austria and Czechoslovakia, Malaysia and Vietnam—it is the democratic countries that are prosperous and responsive to the needs of their people. And one of the simple but overwhelming facts of our time is this: of all the millions of refugees we've seen in the modern world, their flight is always away from, not toward the Communist world. Today on the NATO line, our military forces face east to prevent a possible invasion. On the other side of the line, the Soviet forces also face east to prevent their people from leaving.

The hard evidence of totalitarian rule has caused in mankind an uprising of the intellect and will. Whether it is the growth of the new schools of economics in America or England or the appearance of the so-called new philosophers in France, there is one unifying thread running through the intellectual work of these groups—rejection of the arbitrary power of the state, the refusal to subordinate the rights of the individual to the superstate, the realization that collectivism stifles all the best human impulses. . . .

Chairman Brezhnev repeatedly has stressed that the competition of ideas and systems must continue and that this is entirely consistent with relaxation of tensions and peace.

Well, we ask only that these systems begin by living up to their own constitutions, abiding by their own laws, and complying with the international obligations they have undertaken. We ask only for a process, a direction, a basic code of decency, not for an instant transformation.

We cannot ignore the fact that even without our encouragement there has been and will continue to be repeated explosions against repression and dictatorships. The Soviet Union itself is not immune to this reality. Any system is inherently unstable that has no peaceful means to legitimize its leaders. In such cases, the very repressiveness of the state ultimately drives people to resist it, if necessary, by force.

While we must be cautious about forcing the pace of change, we must not hesitate to declare our ultimate objectives and to take concrete actions to move toward them. We must be staunch in our conviction that freedom is not the sole prerogative of a lucky few but the inalienable and universal right of all human beings. So states the United Nations Universal Declaration of Human Rights, which, among other things, guarantees free elections.

The objective I propose is quite simple to state: to foster the infrastructure of democracy, the system of a free press, unions, political parties, universities, which allows a people to choose their own way to develop their own culture, to reconcile their own differences through peaceful means.

This is not cultural imperialism; it is providing the means for genuine self-determination and protection for diversity. Democracy already flourishes in countries with very different cultures and historical experiences. It would be cultural condescension, or worse, to say that any people prefer dictatorship to democracy. Who would voluntarily choose not to have the right to vote, decide to purchase government propaganda handouts instead of independent newspapers, prefer government to worker-controlled unions, opt for land to be owned by the state instead of those who till it, want government repression of religious liberty, a single political party instead of a free choice, a rigid cultural orthodoxy instead of democratic tolerance and diversity.

Since 1917 the Soviet Union has given covert political training and assistance to Marxist-Leninists in many countries. Of course, it also has promoted the use of violence and subversion by these same forces. Over the past several decades, West European and other social democrats, Christian democrats, and leaders have offered open assistance to fraternal, political, and social institutions to bring about peaceful and democratic progress. Appropriately, for a vigorous new democracy, the Federal Republic of Germany's political foundations have become a major force in this effort.

We in America now intend to take additional steps, as many of our allies have already done, toward realizing this same goal. The chairmen and other leaders of the national Republican and Democratic party organizations are initiating a study with the bipartisan American Political

Foundation to determine how the United States can best contribute as a nation to the global campaign for democracy now gathering force. They will have the cooperation of congressional leaders of both parties, along with representatives of business, labor, and other major institutions in our society. I look forward to receiving their recommendations and to working with these institutions and the Congress in the common task of strengthening democracy throughout the world.

It is time that we committed ourselves as a nation—in both the public and private sectors—to assisting democratic development. . . .

What I am describing now is a plan and a hope for the long term—the march of freedom and democracy which will leave Marxism-Leninism on the ash heap of history as it has left other tyrannies which stifle the freedom and muzzle the self-expression of the people. And that's why we must continue our efforts to strengthen NATO even as we move forward with our zero-option initiative in the negotiations on intermediate-range forces and our proposal for a one-third reduction in strategic ballistic missile warheads.

Our military strength is a prerequisite to peace, but let it be clear we maintain this strength in the hope it will never be used, for the ultimate determinant in the struggle that's now going on in the world will not be bombs and rockets but a test of wills and ideas, a trial of spiritual resolve, the values we hold, the beliefs we cherish, the ideals to which we are dedicated.

The British people know that, given strong leadership, time, and a little bit of hope, the forces of good ultimately rally and triumph over evil. Here among you is the cradle of self-government, the Mother of Parliaments. Here is the enduring greatness of the British contribution to mankind, the great civilized ideas: individual liberty, representative government, and the rule of law under God.

I've often wondered about the shyness of some of us in the West about standing for these ideals that have done so much to ease the plight of man and the hardships of our imperfect world. This reluctance to use those vast resources at our command reminds me of the elderly lady whose home was bombed in the blitz. As the rescuers moved about, they found a bottle of brandy she'd stored behind the staircase, which was all that was left standing. And since she was barely conscious, one of the workers pulled the cork to give her a taste of it. She came around immediately and said, "Here now—there now, put it back. That's for emergencies."

Well, the emergency is upon us. Let us be shy no longer. Let us go to our strength. Let us offer hope. Let us tell the world that a new age is not only possible but probable.

During the dark days of the Second World War, when this island was incandescent with courage, Winston Churchill exclaimed about Britain's adversaries, "What kind of people do they think we are?" Well, Britain's adversaries found out what extraordinary people the British are. But all the democracies paid a terrible price for allowing the dictators to under-estimate us. We dare not make that mistake again. So, let us ask our-selves, "What kind of people do we think we are?" And let us answer, "Free people, worthy of freedom and determined not only to remain so but to help others gain their freedom as well."

Sir Winston led his people to great victory in war and then lost an elec-tion just as the fruits of victory were about to be enjoyed. But he left office honorably and, as it turned out, temporarily, knowing that the lib-erty of his people was more important than the fate of any single leader. History recalls his greatness in ways no dictator will ever know. And he left us a message of hope for the future, as timely now as when he first uttered it, as opposition leader in the Commons nearly twenty-seven years ago, when he said, "When we look back on all the perils through which we have passed and at the mighty foes that we have laid low and all the dark and deadly designs that we have frustrated, why should we fear for our future? We have," he said, "come safely through the worst."

Well, the task I've set forth will long outlive our own generation. But together, we too have come through the worst. Let us now begin a major effort to secure the best—a crusade for freedom that will engage the faith and fortitude of the next generation. For the sake of peace and justice, let us move toward a world in which all people are at last free to determine their own destiny. ■

Ambassador Jeane Kirkpatrick Blasts the "San Francisco Democrats"

"WHEN the Soviet Union walked out of arms control negotiations . . . the San Francisco Democrats did not blame Soviet intransigence. They blamed the United States. But then, they always blame America first."

A GEORGETOWN UNIVERSITY political science professor wrote an article in *Commentary* magazine titled "Dictatorships and Double Standards," an unapologetic assertion of American foreign policy values that brought her to the attention of Ronald Reagan. From 1981 to 1985, as U.S. ambassador to the United Nations, Jeane Kirkpatrick spoke out dramatically, usually didactically, and not always diplomatically against Soviet expansionism; she became known as one of the hawks among the Reagan advisers.

At the Republican National Convention in Dallas on August 20, 1984, she went on the attack against her fellow Democrats, in support of Reagan's reelection. An accomplished writer and lecturer, accustomed to intellectual combat, she knew that a convention hall political speech required a more striking and polemical style, and she received help in framing this speech from conservative columnist William F. Buckley, Jr.

The purpose was to attract Democrats away from their party, as Mrs. Kirkpatrick had been drawn, by pointing to a dismaying self-flagellation practiced by some Democratic doves. Her point was that the best way to peace was through strength, an argument that she emphasized twice with "and we are at peace"; her reinforcing theme was pride in American accomplishments. She selected a villain (as Demosthenes showed, a speech does well with a villain) who was not the Democratic candidate, undislikable Walter Mondale, but the activists who dominated the television screens at the recent Democratic convention in San Francisco. These "San Francisco Democrats"—supposedly far from the mainstream Democrats who watched at home—were those who "blamed America first." The use of that phrase was skillful, recalling the isolationist America-firsters who did not see the danger in Hitler.

The speech stung Democrats who did not want to be seen as the party of minorities and complainers; that was its goal. Ambassador Kirkpatrick was not chosen to be secretary of state, however, and left the UN post to resume her teaching and writing in her more accustomed analytical style.

□   □   □

This is the first Republican convention I have ever attended. I am grateful that you should invite me, a lifelong Democrat; on the other hand, I realize you are today inviting many lifelong Democrats to join our common cause. . . .

I shall speak tonight of foreign affairs, even though the other party's convention barely touched the subject. When the San Francisco Democrats treat foreign affairs as an afterthought, as they did, they behaved less like a dove or a hawk than like an ostrich—convinced it could shut out the world by hiding its head in the sand.

Today, foreign policy is central to the security, to the freedom, to the prosperity, even to the survival of the United States. And *our* strength, for which we make many sacrifices, is essential to the independence and freedom of our allies and of our friends.

Ask yourself, What would become of Europe if the United States withdrew? What would become of Africa if Europe fell under Soviet domination? What would become of Europe if the Middle East came under Soviet control? What would become of Israel, if surrounded by Soviet client states? What would become of Asia if the Philippines or Japan fell under Soviet domination? What would become of Mexico if Central America became a Soviet satellite? What then could the United States do?

These are questions the San Francisco Democrats have not answered. These are questions they have not even *asked*.

The United States cannot remain an open, democratic society if we are left alone—a garrison state in a hostile world. We need independent nations with which to trade, to consult, and cooperate. We need friends and allies with whom to share the pleasures and protection of our civilization. We cannot, therefore, be indifferent to the subversion of others' independence or to the development of new weapons by our adversaries or of new vulnerabilities by our friends.

The last Democratic administration did not seem to notice much, care much, or do much about these matters. And at home and abroad, our country slid into deep trouble. North and South, East and West, our relations deteriorated.

The Carter administration's motives were good, but their policies were inadequate, uninformed, and mistaken. They made things worse, not better. Those who had least, suffered most. Poor countries grew poorer. Rich countries grew poorer, too. The United States grew weaker.

Meanwhile, the Soviet Union grew stronger. The Carter administration's unilateral "restraint" in developing and deploying new weapon systems was accompanied by an unprecedented Soviet buildup, military and political.

The Soviets, working on the margins and through the loopholes of SALT I, developed missiles of stunning speed and accuracy and targeted the cities of our friends in Europe. They produced weapons capable of wiping out our land-based missiles. And then, feeling strong, Soviet leaders moved with boldness and skill to exploit their new advantages. Facilities were completed in Cuba during those years that permit Soviet nuclear submarines to roam our coasts, that permit Soviet planes to fly reconnaissance missions over the eastern United States, and permit Soviet electronic surveillance to monitor our telephone calls and telegrams.

Those were the years the Ayatollah Khomeini came to power in Iran, while in Nicaragua the Sandinistas developed a one-party dictatorship based on the Cuban model.

From the fall of Saigon in 1975 until January 1981, Soviet influence expanded dramatically—into Laos, Cambodia, Afghanistan, Angola, Ethiopia, Mozambique, South Yemen, Libya, Syria, Aden, Congo, Madagascar, Seychelles, and Grenada. Soviet bloc forces sought to guarantee what they call the "irreversibility" of their newfound influence and to stimulate insurgencies in a dozen other places. During this period, the Soviet Union invaded Afghanistan, murdered its president, and began a ghastly war against the Afghan people.

The American people were shocked by these events. We were greatly surprised to learn of our diminished economic and military strength; we were demoralized by the treatment of our hostages in Iran, and we were outraged by harsh attacks on the United States in the United Nations. As a result, we lost confidence in ourselves and in our government.

Jimmy Carter looked for an explanation for all these problems and thought he found it in the American people. But the people knew better. It was not malaise we suffered from, it was Jimmy Carter—and Walter Mondale.

And so in 1980 the American people elected a very different president. The election of Ronald Reagan marked an end to the dismal period of retreat and decline. His inauguration, blessed by the simultaneous release of our hostages, signaled an end to the most humiliating episode in our national history.

The inauguration of President Reagan signaled a reaffirmation of historic American ideals. Ronald Reagan brought to the presidency confidence in the American experience; confidence in the legitimacy and success of American institutions; confidence in the decency of the American people, and confidence in the relevance of our experience to the rest of the world.

That confidence has proved contagious. Our nation's subsequent recovery in domestic and foreign affairs, the restoration of our economic and military strength, has silenced talk of inevitable American decline and reminded the world of the advantages of freedom.

President Reagan faced a stunning challenge, and he met it. In the three and one-half years since his inauguration, the United States has grown stronger, safer, more confident, *and we are at peace.* . . .

And at each step of the way, the same people who were responsible for America's decline have insisted that the president's policies would fail.

They said we could never deploy missiles to protect Europe's cities. But today Europe's cities enjoy that protection.

They said it would never be possible to hold elections in El Salvador, because the people were too frightened and the country too disorganized. But the people of El Salvador proved them wrong, and today President Napoléon Duarte has impressed the democratic world with his skillful, principled leadership.

They said we could not use America's strength to help others—Sudan, Chad, Central America, the Gulf states, the Caribbean nations—without being drawn into war. But we have helped others resist Soviet, Libyan, and Cuban subversion, *and we are at peace.*

They said that saving Grenada from totalitarianism and terror was the wrong thing to do—they didn't blame Cuba or the Communists for threatening American students and murdering Grenadans—they blamed the United States instead. But then, somehow, they always blame America first.

When our marines, sent to Lebanon on a multinational peacekeeping mission with the consent of the United States Congress, were murdered in their sleep, the "blame America first crowd" did not blame the terrorists who murdered the marines, they blamed the United States. But then, they always blame America first.

When the Soviet Union walked out of arms control negotiations, and refused even to discuss the issues, the San Francisco Democrats did not blame Soviet intransigence. They blamed the United States. But then, they always blame America first.

When Marxists dictators shoot their way to power in Central America, the San Francisco Democrats do not blame the guerrillas and their Soviet allies, they blame United States policies of one hundred years ago. But then, they always blame America first.

The American people know better. They know that Ronald Reagan and the United States did not cause the Marxist dictatorship in Nicaragua, or the repression of Poland, or the brutal new offensives in Afghanistan, or the destruction of the Korean airliner, or new attacks on religious and ethnic groups in the Soviet Union, or the jamming of Western broadcasts, or the denial of Jewish emigration, or the brutal imprisonment of Anatoly Shcharansky and Ida Nudel, or the obscene treatment of Andrey Sakharov and Elena Bonner, or the re-Stalinization of the Soviet Union.

The American people also know that it is dangerous to blame ourselves for terrible problems we did not cause. They understand just as the distinguished French writer Jean-François Revel understands the danger of endless self-criticism and self-denigration. He wrote, "Clearly, a civilization that feels guilty for everything it is and does will lack the energy and conviction to defend itself."

With the election of Ronald Reagan, the American people declared to the world that we *have* the necessary energy and conviction to defend ourselves as well as a deep commitment to peace.

And now, the American people, proud of our country, proud of our freedom, proud of ourselves, will reject the San Francisco Democrats and send Ronald Reagan back to the White House. ■

Labour's Neil Kinnock Excoriates Mrs. Thatcher's Toryism

"WHY am I the first Kinnock in a thousand generations to be able to get to university? . . . It was because there was no platform upon which they could stand. . . ."

NELL KINNOCK, the youngest leader in the history of the British Labour party, brought his socialists back from the brink of leftist, unilateralist politics in the late eighties but could not topple the Tories' Margaret Thatcher. His oratorical style came to the attention of Americans when a candidate for the Democratic nomination in 1988, Senator Joe Biden, was accused of having plagiarized a Kinnock speech—which, it turned out, he had. The American's candidacy might have been saved by a simple willingness to attribute; nobody minds what speechwriters call "heavy lifting" as long as the source is acknowledged.

Kinnock's appeal to the heart and conscience of the voter was worth stealing: universal in its theme, personal in its presentation. In his stump speech, delivered without notes at the Wales Labour party conference in Llandudno on May 15, 1987, the Labour leader ripped into Thatcherism as a heartless philosophy that was more concerned with the stock market than with the whole economy, cared not for the worker's needs, and brought back the law of the jungle. His passionate speech, with minor changes, could be delivered with great effect by a liberal against a conservative anywhere in the world.

□   □   □

Thank you very much for that warm welcome. I couldn't wish for a welcome other than one that came from a man of Aberdare, Roger Vallis, a good comrade and friend for over twenty years, a man who I admire for every reason, as does the whole Labour movement in Wales.

I am happy to report that we are definitely in the last month of Thatcherism. We are in the last few weeks of that job-destroying, justice-trampling, oil-wasting, truth-twisting, service-smashing, nation-splitting, bunch-of-twisters-under-one-person government. The last few weeks.

But apart from that they've got a great record. Well, they must be a great record! Mrs. Thatcher's told them to fight on that record; to fight with pride, she said. She's been telling her party, "Fight with pride on our record." I hope they do. Oh, I hope they take some notice of her there. I hope they do fight on their record—I hope they do fight with pride. "Pride goeth before destruction, and a haughty spirit before a fall." And so, surely, fall they will on June the eleventh. They certainly deserve to. After eight years in government, a three million unemployment figure is not seen as the badge of shame; it's not seen as a cause of disappointment. A three million unemployment figure to them is a source of "celebration." Lord Young leads the cheering; Norman Tebbit does the lap of honor; Nigel Lawson, who couldn't do a lap of anything, he's just poppin' the corks, celebrating the fact that there are only three million unemployed; and the prime minister has decided to mark the event by becoming immortal!

On Tuesday, I read it in the papers: "Fourth-term target for Thatcher— on to the twenty-first century." Well, I suppose that fits. She's been lecturing us about the nineteenth century; now she's talking about the twenty-first century—all she's missed out is this century, the one that we're living in! That's all she's missed out!

But I've been watching her on TV this week. Apparently that's all I'm going to be able to do, 'cause she won't debate with me face-to-face on the issues. I've been watching her. I saw her on Wednesday night, and I realized that in addition to all the great reasons and great causes for getting rid of the Thatcher government, of displacing Mrs. Thatcher from Downing Street, there was another reason—one of humanity, one of compassion, one of consideration—we have to do it for Denis [Thatcher] as well!

But it was Monday night's performance that I found most interesting. She said she was full of ideas for continuing in the direction that they've been going. Full of ideas for continuing in the direction they've been going—well, we know what she means. New ideas like privatizing schools! New ideas like decontrolling rents! New ideas like paying for health care! What wonderful "fresh," "new" ideas! What a great way to greet the dawn of the twenty-first century, with these wonderful "new" ideas. But anybody attracted by those "ideas"—the privatization ideas, the decontrolling ideas; the flog-off, the sell-off ideas—had better ask themselves one question. They'd better ask themselves why every single one of those "new" ideas was abandoned fifty and more years ago. If, if the payment for schooling was such a wonderful idea, why was it abolitioned, treated as a great leap forward for the people of this country? If uncontrolled rents did so much for housing, so much for families, why were they ever controlled? What malicious government ever decided that the landlords couldn't be left to deal with these things in their mercy? And when it came to paying for health care, if that was such a blessing, why was the ending of that system hailed as the greatest step forward in civilization, in postwar history? Believe me, the reason is simple, very simple. The system that existed before those changes, the very system that Margaret Thatcher wants to reintroduce in this country was wrong, and it was wretched, and it was squalid and brutal; it was rotten with injustice, and with misery, and with derision. That's why they got rid of it! That's why it was discarded—by popular demand! And that is why it must never be restored by prime ministerial demand.

That's why this election has come just in time! Just in time for those whose lives and skills are being wasted by unemployment. Just in time for the children in a school system that is deprived and derided by a secretary of state for education who won't send his own child to local schools. The election comes just in time for the old, who are being cheated out of pensions, and housing benefits, and much else. It's come just in time for our health service, with its three-quarters of a million people in pain on the waiting list. And it's come just in time, too, for all those who are not poor. Those who do not have children going through the schooling system. Those who are not old and anxious, not young and unemployed, not badly housed, not waiting for an operation—it's come in time for those people, too. All the people who are not badly off, but who know that Tory Britain is a more divided, deprived, and dangerous place now than it has been for decades past! All those people—the election has come just in time for them. Because they know, as you know, that when Britain has a prime minister that has allowed unemployment and poverty and waiting lists and closures and crime to go up, and up, and up, that is a prime minister who must not be allowed to go on, and on, and on.

Listen, comrades. Our country has taken a beating in the last eight years, from a government with an "on your bike" employment policy, a "stay in bed to keep warm" retirement policy, a "flag day" health service policy, and a "jumble sale" education system policy.

People all over this country know that Britain couldn't take thirteen years of that. Britain can't take thirteen years of Thatcherism. Britain can't serve such a life sentence without it becoming a death sentence for even more industries, and communities, and hopes—yes, and people, too! Because unemployment and poverty are not just "ailments," not just misfortunes! They are mortal afflictions, as every experience and figure shows. Not that it bothers the prime minister. It doesn't seem to influence her at all. She will have us think that we are in the middle of a great "recovery." Difficult to see the evidence, unless of course you wait until the end of the news. *There* you can see the recovery! The stock market is up! There's the evidence for recovery! Unemployed? Don't worry, stay at home and watch the stock market going up on the television! Worried about redundancy? Don't worry, you can pass your time by looking at the Financial Times Share Index!

It strikes me very often, you know, that the reason that they put the stock market reports on the back end of the news alongside all those thrilling items about gerbils having triplets is because it's got just about as much relevance to real life, as the gerbil incident. But there's, there's the evidence for the great recovery!

"Recovery" is an awful funny word to use about eight years in which manufacturing production hasn't got back to the 1979 levels. "Recovery" is a very strange term to describe an economy that hasn't had an *increase* of two million unemployed since 1979. "Recovery" is a very peculiar label for a situation in which manufacturing investment is 20 percent *lower* than it was in 1979. "Recovery"—it's hardly the word to describe a country that in 1979 had a three-billion-pound *surplus* in manufacturing goods, and in 1987 has got an eight-billion-pound *deficit* in manufacturing goods! Buying more finished goods from the rest of the world than we're selling to the rest of the world for the first time in all our history—and that is a "recovery"? Is it a recovery when one in five of sixteen- to twenty-five-year-olds haven't got a job? Is it a recovery when you can hardly buy anything with a "Made in Britain" label in any shop, in any high street in this land? Is it a recovery when scientists are leaving in droves? Does that all become a recovery? I don't think it's much of a recovery.

Of course, there's been a little recent "speeding-up"; a slight "late thaw." It isn't recovery; it's a small remission in the condition of the economy that has gone through eight years of uninterrupted decline. And how has this little boomlet come about? How has it been ushered in this spring? Is it because the Tory policies are working? Is it because, for instance, at last they've achieved success with their strict monetary control? No, it can't be that, because we've got absolutely *record* credit and debt. There is no monetary control. So has the improvement come about because another policy's worked? Is it because they've cut taxation? Well, it can't be that, because the tax burden on the national economy is 18 percent higher than it was in 1979, and the tax burden on the average family is 10 percent higher than it was in 1979. So it can't be the great tax cuts. Is it because of strict controls on public expenditure? Has Willy Whitelaw's "Star Chamber" won at last? It can't be that either, because last autumn after years of talk about "strict limits" on public expenditure there was an *overun* on public spending by 2.5 billion pounds. But, all of a sudden, it didn't matter any more. It was a sign of strength, instead of being an offense, directly, against the most cherished "nostrums" of Tory economic policy. Can this little boomlet be coming because the policy of letting the exchange rate find its own level, subject to market influences, eventually work? No. Because since last summer they've been spending *billions* on trying to control the exchange rate. So why has there been a slowdown in the rate of decline? Is it because their policies have worked? No. It's the opposite. It isn't because they've been *applying* their policies; it's because in the last six months they've been *abandoning* their policies! That's why we've got a slight recovery in the British economy at the present time.

They haven't taken what they call "the next step forward"; they've stood on their heads. That's what they've been doing. They've done it in a few other areas too. Remember, it's only a few months ago when they couldn't afford to spend on roads. They couldn't afford to spend on nurses. They couldn't afford to spend on the Air Bus. They couldn't afford to spend on cancer screening or on hospital waiting lists. They couldn't afford to keep small schools open. They couldn't afford to make heating allowances for the old. But, all of a sudden, in the last couple of months, *everything* is possible! It's not big. The Air Bus gets *half* of what it needs; the twenty-five million to cut the waiting lists—twelve and a half million of that will have to go on five thousand hip-replacement operations. So what are they going to get? A cut in the waiting lists of ninety-five thousand for twelve and a half million quid? They must be joking! I mean, small schools being kept open! It's a lovely idea. I'm expecting the parents from Havergrenist Primary School in my area to come to me and say, "Mr. Kinnock, do you think you could drop a line to Kenneth Baker or Nicholas Edwards if you can find him, and say, Could we have our school back?" It's rubbish! It's not going to happen. They're not going to keep those schools open; they have just given the impression that, suddenly, there is a great deal . . . of opportunity.

They haven't been making this recovery because of the successes of Tory policy. They haven't been operating Tory policy at all as the election approached. What they've done is to drop those policies, jettison them, put them into cold storage, stick them in the box. And they've done it because the Tories knew they couldn't face the country, in an election, on Tory policies. They couldn't face the country with their own policies. They knew that, faced with the oncoming election, and against the background of what they'd done in the previous years, they have to stimulate, and soften, and sweeten. They have to show some concern. They knew they had to turn the stick into a carrot as the general election came along. That's the total sum of the recovery. . . .

We don't think it's a soft sentiment. We don't think it's "wet," as Mrs. Thatcher calls it. We care all the time. We don't think it's a weak idea. We care all the time because we think that *care* is not weakness. Care to us is the very essence, the greatest demonstration of strength. That's what makes us democratic socialists. That's what makes us so categorically different from them. We believe that strength without care is savage, and brutal, and selfish. It's the strength of the jungle. We believe that strength, with care, is compassion; the practical action that is needed to help people *lift themselves*, lift themselves to their full stature, their full potential. The strength to care. Not the strength of the jungle but the strength of humanity. That's real care! It's not soft, it's not weak, it's strong and tough, and efficient. And where do we get the strength to provide that care? Do we wait around hoping for some stroke of good fortune? Waiting for some benign giant to turn up to deliver the people? Do we look for some socially conscious Samson to provide the care? We are rationalists. We're socialists. We're realists. We know that if we are going to *get* and going to *give* the standard of care that humanity requires we've got to get on with doing it, together. So we cooperate. We collect together. We coordinate so that everyone can contribute and everyone can benefit; everyone has responsibilities, like everyone enjoys rights. That's how we put care into action. That's how we make the weak strong. That's how we lift the needy. That's how we make the sick whole. That's how we give the talent the chance to flourish. That's how we turn the unemployed claimant into the employed contributor—by that collective action. By all being contributers, and all being beneficiaries. That's the sensible way to ensure that strength is translated into care. We do it together. We call it collective strength, collective care. And it's whole purpose is individual freedom. There's no paradox there.

When we speak of collective strength and collective freedom, collectively achieved, we are not fulfilling that nightmare that Mrs. Thatcher tries to paint, and all her predecessors have tried to saddle us with. We're not talking about uniformity; we're not talking about regimentation; we're not talking about *conformity*— that's their creed. The uniformity of the dole queue; the regimentation of the unemployed young and their compulsory work schemes. The *conformity* of people who will work in conditions, and take orders, and accept pay *because* of mass unemployment that they would laugh at in a free society with full employment.

That kind of freedom for the individual, that kind of liberty, can't be secured by most of the people for most of the time if they're just left to themselves, isolated, stranded, with their whole life chances dependent upon luck! Why am I the first Kinnock in a thousand generations to be able to get to university? Why is Glenys the first woman in her family in a thousand generations to be able to get to university? Was it because *all* our predecessors were "thick"? Did they lack talent—those people who could sing, and play, and recite and write poetry; those people who could make wonderful, beautiful things, with their hands; those people who could dream dreams, see visions; those people who had such a sense of perception as to know in times so brutal, so oppressive, that they could win their way out of that by coming together? Were those people not university material? Couldn't they have knocked off all their "A" Levels in an afternoon? But why didn't they get it? Was it because they were weak—those people who could work eight hours underground and then come up and play football? Weak? Those women who could survive eleven childbearings, were they weak? Those people who could stand with their backs and their legs straight and face the great—the people who had control over their lives, the ones that owned their workplaces and tried to own them—and tell them, "No, I won't take your orders." Were they weak? Does anybody really think that they didn't get what we had because they didn't have the talent, or the strength, or the endurance, or the commitment? Of course not. It was because there was no platform upon which they could stand, no arrangement for their neighbors to subscribe to their welfare, no method by which the communities could translate its desires for those individuals into provision for those individuals. And now, Mrs. Thatcher, by dint of privatization, and means test, and deprivation, and division, wants to nudge us back into the situation where everybody can either stand on their own feet or live on their knees.

That's what this election is about as she parades her visions and values, and we choose to contest them as people with root in this country, with a future only in this country, with pride in this country. People who know that if we are to have and sustain real individual liberty in this country, it requires the collective effort of the whole community.

Of course, you'll hear the Tories talking a lot about freedom. You're going to hear a lot of that over the next month; a lot of talk of freedom from people who have spent much of the last eight years crushing individual freedoms under the weight of unemployment and poverty. Squeezing individual rights with cuts, and with means tests, and with charges. I think of the youngsters I meet. Three, four, five years out of school. Never had a job. And they say to me, "Do you think we'll ever get a job?" These are young men and women living in a free country, but they don't feel free.

I think of the fifty-five-year-old woman I meet, waiting months to go into hospital for an operation, her whole existence clouded by pain. She is a citizen of a free country, but she doesn't feel free.

I think of the young couple, two years married, living in their mam and dad's front room 'cause they can't get a home. Seeing their family relationship deteriorate from what was the greatest friendship, and kinship, in their family on their wedding day, to the most bitter contradictions and conflicts within that household. Those young people, they live in a free country, but they don't feel free.

I think of the old couple. We all know them. The old people, going for months through the winter afraid to turn the heat up. Staying at home, afraid to go out after dark. Old people for whom the need to buy a new pair of shoes is an economic crisis! They live in a free country—indeed they're of the generation that *fought* for a free country—but they don't feel free.

How can—how can they, and millions like them, have their individual freedom if there is not collective provision? How can they have *strength* if they haven't that, just that little bit of support—of care? That helping hand. They can't have either. They can't have either strength or care now, because they are locked out of being able to discharge their responsibilities, just as surely as they are locked out of their ability to enjoy rights. And they are fellow citizens. They want to be able to use both rights and responsibilities. They don't want featherbedding. They want a foothold. They don't want cosseting, or cotton-wooling, they want a chance to *contribute*. The greatest privilege is to be able to bear responsibility, not discharge rights. Rights are great. They can be plastered on walls, written in bills; but it's responsibilities that you *can* discharge—that's when you feel strong, because you've got the means, you've got the strength, you've got the rights. They can't discharge responsibilities or rights, and they want the freedom to do so. That's the freedom we want them, as democratic socialists, to have. That's a freedom that we seek power to get and to spread in our country.

Freedom, with fairness. That's our aim. And the means that we choose for pursuing that aim, achieving that aim, is investment. Investment in people. Investing in people to cut unemployment by one million in the first two years of the Labour government. Investing in people to build and to repair the homes and the schools and the hospitals and the roads that this country needs. Investing in people to gain new jobs, and new strength in industry; investing in people to provide the teaching, and the healing, and the caring services. Investing in people to pull them out of poverty in our country by paying higher pensions. By freeing them from pain by making extra commitment to the health service. By giving them the means to flourish by investing in education.

Of course, they're big bills! Nobody's offering miracles; that was the preserve of the monetarists. But what we do say is, With the chance, with the tools for the job, with that bit of backing, with that investment, then we can secure the objectives of building strength for the individual and for the whole country. That's why we say invest in people—and the resources are there. Oh, it isn't that the resources are not there; the resources are there in Nigel Lawson's 2p tax cut! The tuppenny tories! They've shown us that the resources are there. Spent the way that Nigel Lawson wants to spend it, it'll cost 2.5 billion pounds, and it will create in this country about eighty thousand jobs. It'll create a lot more jobs elsewhere, 'cause most of the cash will be spent on imports. If that same 2.5 billion pounds was *targeted* on construction, on manufacturing, on caring, it would produce three hundred thousand jobs. That's the bargain for Britain! . . .

There's certainly a lot to do, 'cause Mrs. Thatcher's greatest demonstration of patriotism was to remove capital controls and to allow, in the eight years that she's been prime minister, a net outflow of sixty thousand million pounds in investment from our country that wouldn't have otherwise gone. Going to finance the technological revolutions of our competitors; going to strengthen *their* industry when our country has been run down and a quarter of our manufacturing industry lost: two million manufacturing jobs lost as a result of policies of a prime minister that is shoveling support to those who are in contention with us in the markets of the world. . . .

They've been shutting down, selling off, selling out this country. And everyone in this country, whoever they are, whatever they do, wherever they live, whatever their politics, is going to ask a question in this election that is absolutely central: How do we pay our way if that is the future? How do we pay our way with a future empty of any industrial policy or strategy? How do we pay our way in the world; how do we pay for the necessities; how do we help the needy of the world; how do we influence others in this world if we can't pay our way? How, too, do we pay our way at home if we've not got the source of wealth generation— the way to make a national living? How do we generate the wealth necessary to give employment, to provide education, to finance health care, to pay for decent pensions? Can we do any of that?

The answer is, at home and abroad, if we don't make the goods, and market the goods, then we don't pay our way! That's the future I'm not prepared to accept. It's a future that I'm not prepared to offer to my children, or offer to my contemporaries. I want to be able, in twenty years' time, because we've made our commitment to building industrial strength and generating jobs, in twenty years' time I want to be able to go down any street in Britain and meet a thirty-six-year-old who is sixteen at the moment, or meet a fifty-year-old who is thirty at the moment, and be able to look them in the eye and say, Yes, it was the case, that in the late 1980s 'cause we could see what was happening in the future, and we knew what the needs of our economy were, we were prepared to commit the resources and give us a *strength* of industrial development that Torism could never provide. I want to be one of those people. And this whole generation of the Labour movement wants it, to be able to stand alongside those people of the 1940s who never had to blush when they met us in the 1960s 'cause *they* could say to us, Yes, we built. Yes, we provided. Yes, we tried to make a future. That—that's the constructive way. That's the way to make a future for all the people who contribute to doing it—no free rides, no easy options, no miracles, no cheap routes. Planning, and providing, to make that future. Oh, we can do it! This country has the skills and the abilities, knowledge and wisdom, and the commitment to do it. We can do it.

But we can't do it with the Tories, for they only offer a future of failure, a future of rundown. A future of great prosperity for the few and great insecurity and decline for the many. That's where we've been heading through industrial contraction, and trade loss, and unemployment, ever since Margaret Thatcher went into 10 Downing Street eight years ago.

It is because of that record that we have some of the greatest reasons for seeing that she is put out of 10 Downing Street in a month's time. And in a few weeks' time that is what we, and the British people, will do. ■

Henry Kissinger Warns against the Reemergence of Isolationism

"IF Europe permits itself to be tempted by disguised neutralism and America revels in disguised isolationism, all that has been celebrated in this hall for a generation will be in jeopardy."

AS NATIONAL SECURITY ADVISER AND SECRETARY OF STATE in the Nixon and Ford administrations, Henry Kissinger brought an intellectual heft and historical sweep to his writings and speeches on foreign policy. His memoirs are the most meatily readable of any in his generation; his lectures, often laced with a wry humor playing off his own persona, commanded attention long after he left the official corridors of power.

Because he deals with weighty subjects and his delivery is more a university lecturer's than an orator's, his speeches require work by both the speaker and the listener. Kissinger uses two tried-and-true techniques of organization to keep audiences following his points. These are (1) numbering the principles or proposals he is making and (2) preceding the sections of a speech with the questions he proposes to answer. Does this system succeed? Is it more effective than the old "Tell 'em what you're going to tell 'em; tell 'em; tell 'em what you told 'em" device used by so many other speakers?

In the following speech about the future of two continents, topical references to arms control have been deleted. Dr. Kissinger was accepting the Karlspreis award in Aachen, West Germany, on May 28, 1987, a decade after he left public office. He begins by acknowledging his sense of place and concludes with a not overly familiar quotation from Bismarck to make the point of the "spiritual unity" of Europe and America.

□   □   □

To be honored in this country and in this city has a special meaning for me. I grew up in Germany in painful circumstances. Yet, despite the trauma of those years, I have always retained a deep attachment to the land of my youth. As a very young man serving in the armed forces of the country which had given my family refuge, I saw the ultimate consequences of the hatreds of that period in the ruins of this city. In that desolate physical and moral landscape, it would have seemed inconceivable that a thriving new town could emerge from the rubble. Or that it would find a respected place in a Europe which for the first time in centuries has returned to its original vocation as the repository of the common values and purposes of Western civilization. . . .

All great achievements in our common history were dreams before they became realities—from the cathedrals raised towards the heavens by peasant societies over decades; to the voyages across uncharted oceans by men moved by both faith and greed; to the development, unique in world history, of a concept of natural law which recognized the inherent worth and rights of all human beings.

The conviction that there were transcendent values beyond the power of the state to grant or to modify is the most singular accomplishment of Western history. It was often violated, but it always recurred and in the end triumphed. Four principles characterize this common heritage.

1. The state is not the personal possession of the ruler but reflects a community of citizens—*cives, citoyen, Mitbürger.* All citizens, recognizing that in the classical period there was the blight of slavery, possessed equal rights and were involved in shaping the destiny of their community. Even at the height of the Roman Empire, it saw itself as a city-state governed by free citizens. These rights were in time extended to the entire empire—the first such gesture in history.

2. Even the most powerful rulers are subject to law—written or customary. Ever since the majestic structure of Roman law, Western societies have insisted that their governments were based on law, not on personal will. This concept was amplified during the Christian era to include the idea that a divine law administered by a separate hierarchy was beyond the control of temporal authority. No other civilization has developed such absolute concepts of justice and such an insistence on the limits of temporal power.

3. In Western societies officials must justify themselves by service—the very word "minister" derives from that concept.

4. To be a Roman citizen was to be free above all; citizenship indeed was called *libertas Romana.* Indeed, the history of the West can be interpreted as a never-ending struggle for freedom in ever new forms; in the freedom for citizens inside the thousands of towns formed all over Europe in the tenth and eleventh centuries; in the religious liberty expressed in Luther's idea of the "freedom of a Christian"; in the Dutch struggle for national freedom against Spain; in the limitations of royal

power first by the aristocracy and then by the people culminating in the American and French revolutions with their affirmation of the rights of men.

The battles for freedom may have had local origins, but the underlying concept was in each case universal. This ancient city, built on the ruins of a Roman spa, participated in that epic theme of Western history since before Europe forgot that it was European.

The united Europe of Charlemagne disappeared in the centuries there-after amidst the selfishness, the wars, and the suffering that accompanied the fragmentation of Europe. But the ideal remained even when the rise of the nation-state seemed to doom Europe to permanent fragmentation.

In the fullness of time these values spread across the Atlantic into my adopted country, where, unconstrained by national rivalries and unen-crusted by tradition, they acquired a drive, even an innocence that his-tory's legacy did not allow on the old continent. In that philosophical sense the frontier of Europe rests on the Pacific coast of North America.

In terms of that tradition, European unity and Atlantic partnership are not antithetical but complementary; they are not simply practical necessi-ties—though that undoubtedly plays an important part. They are, above all, an expression of basic and ancient values which have been reborn in the anguish of the Western civil wars of the first half of the twentieth cen-tury. They have taught us that no goal is worthy of unconditional commit-ment—not even peace—unless it is founded on justice and liberty.

We can take pride in what has been achieved in some forty years of common efforts. We need only compare the speeches of prizewinners in the early fifties with what has been said in the eighties to measure how far Europe has come in forging its unity and gaining self-confidence.

We need only compare the sense of imminent danger of that earlier period with the current debate over the modalities of arms control to realize to what extent security has come to be taken for granted on both sides of the Atlantic.

But history knows no resting places; what does not advance must sooner or later decline.

European unity was forged in the crucible of the suffering by two world wars—so unexpected a shock after the complacent faith of the nineteenth century in uninterrupted progress—and the economic chaos that followed. Atlantic partnership was spawned by the fear of aggression by a totalitar-ian Soviet state. But what is Europe's role now that internecine conflicts have been largely put aside and prosperity has been achieved? What is the goal of the Atlantic enterprise in an era of negotiation?

In short, what do we now understand by peace? What do we under-stand by security? What do we understand by progress?

This is not the occasion to attempt detailed answers. But let me state a few general principles.

When the Atlantic Alliance was formed, it was assumed that the threat to peace was similar to recently familiar totalitarian phenomena: a large-scale invasion across sovereign borders with the avowed aim of domina-tion of the world by military means. Since then, it has become clear that the Soviet challenge is both more complex and more subtle. It rests on what Marxist-Leninists consider the correlation of forces, but that corre-lation can be shifted gradually and patiently by pressure, by ambiguity, and occasionally by exploiting the West's desire for peace and its diversity of views on how to achieve that end.

Western leaders have been responding to their publics' desire for peace by constantly expressing their readiness for negotiation; they have not always been equally clear about the program for these negotiations. Sensitivity to public pressures is so great that militant minorities have occasionally achieved a disproportionate influence. Gradually the belief has gained ground that internal Soviet transformations will solve the problem of peace and the West's own lack of clarity as to objectives.

That a more flexible leadership has come to power in the Kremlin is beyond doubt. In foreign policy it has—so far, at least—been able to obscure the increasingly evident structural dilemmas of a centrally planned society by great skill in public relations. It has been more suc-cessful than it should be in promoting divisions in Europe and weaken-ing the cohesion of the Atlantic Alliance. This is because the West has not answered for itself this fundamental question: Are concessions justified by Soviet internal developments, or should they be analyzed primarily in terms of Soviet foreign policy conduct?

Some argue that Gorbachev needs a success to sustain himself. The danger is that success so defined is likely to be inimical to the West. Perhaps Soviet domestic reform will lead automatically to a more concil-iatory Soviet policy. It is equally possible that Gorbachev seeks to achieve maneuvering room for domestic reform by demonstrating to foreign pol-icy hard-liners that flexible tactics are more effective than crude threats in tilting the correlations of forces against the West.

I do not choose among these possibilities except to point out that to gear foreign policy to a psychological assessment of Soviet leaders leaves the West vulnerable to sudden changes in Soviet leadership and the Soviets unconstrained in the political competition, in time perhaps even in the military field. Exclusive preoccupation with arms control involves the risk that arms control becomes a safety valve for political pressure rather than a means for easing tensions. Paradoxically such attitudes may keep the West from establishing whether Gorbachev, in the end, is willing to be as imaginative in foreign as in domestic policy.

Peace requires, above all, a vision of its content. The West must, to be sure, take into account Soviet concerns—since no agreement that fails to take the mutual interest into account can last—but the ultimate justification is the compatibility of any peace program with our values and our security. . . .

I would be less than honest if I did not emphasize that I have never been more worried about trends which, just as in the days after Charlemagne, appear at what should be the moment of our greatest success. If Europe permits itself to be tempted by disguised neutralism and America revels in disguised isolationism, all that has been celebrated in this hall for a generation will be in jeopardy.

Neither Europe nor America can evade any longer a fundamental review of their security policy and ultimately of their foreign policy. Recent events, precisely because they are irreversible, have accelerated what technology would have imposed in any event—a reconsideration of the comfortable assumptions that destructiveness can be equated with security but also of the shallow counterargument that one can escape the nuclear age by returning to a technology that produced unceasing warfare for centuries. Western leaders must stop pretending that nuclear weapons can be abolished; too many exist in too many countries; too much knowledge will remain in the minds of scientists for this to be feasible. But equally they should not rely on nuclear weapons to solve all their problems.

In walking this fine line, America has had the principal responsibility of leadership. But in the period ahead the contribution of a united Europe is essential. A one-sided relationship will lead to the demoralization of both sides of the Atlantic. Europe must build a structure for the consideration of strategic issues either by building on the WEU or by some other mechanism, and America must support this. A useful symbolic step in this direction would be to make the next NATO commander a European.

And beyond strategy there is lacking an adequate mechanism within the Atlantic Alliance to discuss conflicts outside NATO. This prevents either a common position or even a procedure to define permissible disagreement.

The West is now suffering from the consequences of past successes. A generation of peace has produced on the European side of the Atlantic the temptations of emancipation from superpower relationships; on the American side there are signs of the reemergence of historic isolationism—especially as the country's center of gravity shifts westward. But America, the daughter of Europe, can no more turn its back on its heritage than Europe can seek salvation in an illusory equidistance from the so-called superpowers, of which in fact Europe should be one. The West, whose historic tragedy it has been to sacrifice its spiritual unity on the altar of shortsighted self-interest, must not repeat what this prize celebrates having transcended.

Much has been built in the generation since this prize was first given. The building must not stop, especially as the challenges ahead of us are far less daunting than the road already traversed. No one any longer believes that our adversaries represent the wave of the future. No generation has had a better prospect for building a better and more secure world.

But we risk wasting our opportunity by an obsession with the tactical and the short-term, by domestic politics and by confusing the plausible with the true.

The great German statesman Bismarck said, "World history with its great transformations does not come upon us with the even speed of a railway train. No, it moves forward in spurts but then with irresistible force. One must take care whether one can discern the Lord's march through history, seek to grasp the hem of his cloak and let oneself be swept along the greatest distance possible."

Modern politics too often produces an orgy of self-righteousness amidst a cacophony of sounds. Is it too much to ask for a moment of silent reflection to permit us to listen for God's footsteps so that we can grasp the hem of his cloak?

No generation can do more.

But also it dare not do less. ■

George H. W. Bush
Accepts the
Republican Nomination

"This is America: . . . a brilliant diversity spread like stars, like a thousand points of light in a broad and peaceful sky."

RONALD REAGAN'S VICE-PRESIDENT, derided as a "wimp" and a "preppie," trailed the Democratic nominee, Michael Dukakis, by 17 points in opinion polls when he entered the New Orleans Convention Hall on August 18, 1988.

George H. W. Bush (with the aid of Reagan speechwriter Peggy Noonan) defined himself and his philosophy with his acceptance speech, which helped change the poll ratings dramatically. The speech clarified the differences between himself and his opponent on criminal punishment, the perception of patriotism (some civil libertarians had objected to the recitation of the Pledge of Allegiance in classrooms), and taxation: a key line was "Read my lips, no new taxes." ("Read my lips" was a vogue emphasizer, showing the speaker to be familiar with youthful lingo. A similar device, "Go ahead, make my day"—a movie tough-guy challenge parodied by President Reagan—was used subtly to kid about his dissimilarity with his old boss: "Go ahead, make my twenty-four-hour time period." Subtleties rarely get across in convention hall speeches.)

The "mission" theme, providing a bridge between his combat service and goals for the nation, was a subtlety that worked; the pledge at the conclusion was a sledgehammer blow to widen the difference on the Pledge of Allegiance "issue."

□   □   □

I accept your nomination for president. I mean to run hard, to fight hard, to stand on the issues—and I mean to win.

There are a lot of great stories in politics about the underdog winning, and this is going to be one of them.

And we're going to win with the help of Senator Dan Quayle of

Indiana, a young leader who has become a forceful voice in preparing America's workers for the labor force of the future, what a superb job he did here tonight. Born in the middle of the century, in the middle of America, and holding the promise of the future—I'm proud to have Dan Quayle at my side.

Many of you have asked, "When will this campaign really begin?" Well, I've come to this hall to tell you, and to tell America: tonight is the night.

For seven and a half years, I have helped the president conduct the most difficult job on earth. Ronald Reagan asked for, and received, my candor. He never asked for, but he did receive, my loyalty. And those of you who saw the president's speech this week, and listened to the simple truth of his words, will understand my loyalty all these years.

But now you must see me for what I am: the Republican candidate for president of the United States. And now I turn to the American people to share my hopes and intentions, and why and where I wish to lead.

And so tonight is for big things. But I'll try to be fair to the other side. I'll try to hold my charisma in check. And I reject the temptation to engage in personal references. My approach this evening is, as Sergeant Joe Friday used to say, "Just the facts, ma'am."

And after all, after all, the facts are on our side.

I seek the presidency for a single purpose, a purpose that has motivated millions of Americans across the years and the ocean voyages. I seek the presidency to build a better America. It's that simple, and that big.

I'm a man who sees life in terms of missions—missions defined and missions completed. And when I was a torpedo bomber pilot they defined the mission for us. And before we took off we all understood that no matter what, you try to reach the target. And there've been other missions for me—Congress and China, the CIA. But I am here tonight, and I am your candidate, because the most important work of my life is to complete the mission that we started in 1980. How, and how do we complete it? We build on it.

The stakes are high this year and the choice is crucial, for the differences between the two candidates are as deep and wide as they have ever been in our long history.

Not only two very different men, but two very different ideas of the future will be voted on this election day.

And what it all comes down to is this: my opponent's view of the world sees a long, slow decline for our country, an inevitable fall mandated by impersonal historical forces.

But America is not in decline. America is a rising nation.

He sees America as another pleasant country on the UN roll call, some-where between Albania and Zimbabwe. And I see America as the leader, a unique nation with a special role in the world.

And this has been called the American century, because in it we were the dominant force for good in the world. We saved Europe, cured polio, went to the moon, and lit the world with our culture. And now we're on the verge of a new century, and what country's name will it bear? I say it will be another American century.

Our work is not done; our force is not spent.

There are those who say there isn't much of a difference this year. But, America, don't let 'em fool ya.

Two parties this year ask for your support. Both will speak of growth and peace. But only one has proved it can deliver. Two parties this year ask for your trust, but only one has earned it.

Eight years ago I stood here with Ronald Reagan, and we promised, together, to break with the past and return America to her greatness. Eight years later look at what the American people have produced: the highest level of economic growth in our entire history, and the lowest level of world tensions in more than fifty years.

Some say this isn't an election about ideology, that it's an election about competence. Well, it's nice of them to want to play on our field. But this election isn't only about competence, for competence is a nar-row ideal. Competence makes the trains run on time but doesn't know where they're going. Competence is the creed of the technocrat who makes sure the gears mesh but doesn't for a second understand the magic of the machine.

The truth is, this election is about the beliefs we share, the values that we honor, and the principles that we hold dear.

But, since someone brought up competence—consider the size of our triumph: a record number of Americans at work, a record high percent-age of our people with jobs, a record high of new businesses, high rate of new businesses, a record high rate of real personal income.

These are facts. And one way you know our opponents know the facts is that to attack our record they have to misrepresent it. They call it a "Swiss cheese economy." Well, that's the way it may look to the three blind mice. But when they were in charge it was all holes and no cheese.

You know the litany. Inflation was 13 percent when we came in. We got it down to 4. Interest rates, interest rates were more than 21. And we cut them in half. Unemployment, unemployment was up and climbing, and now it's the lowest in fourteen years.

My friends, eight years ago this economy was flat on its back—intensive care. And we came in and gave it emergency treatment—got the temperature down by lowering regulation, and got the blood pressure down when we lowered taxes. And pretty soon the patient was up, back on his feet and stronger than ever.

And now who do we hear knocking on the door but the same doctors who made him sick. And they're telling us to put them in charge of the case again. My friends, they're lucky we don't hit them with a malpractice suit!

We've created seventeen million new jobs the past five years, more than twice as many as Europe and Japan combined. And they're good jobs. The majority of them created in the past six years paid an average of more than $22,000 a year. And someone better take "a message to Michael": tell him that we have been creating good jobs at good wages. The fact is, they talk and we deliver. They promise and we perform.

And there are millions of young Americans in their twenties who barely remember the days of gas lines and unemployment lines. And now they're marrying and starting careers. And to those young people I say, "You have the opportunity you deserve, and I'm not going to let them take it away from you."

The leaders of this expansion have been the women of America, who helped create the new jobs and filled two out of every three of them. And to the women of America I say, "You know better than anyone that equality begins with economic empowerment. You're gaining economic power, and I'm not going to let them take it away from you."

There are millions of Americans who were brutalized by inflation. We arrested it, and we're not going to let it out on furlough. And we're going to keep that Social Security trust fund sound and out of reach of the big spenders. To America's elderly I say, "Once again you have the security that is your right, and I'm not going to let them take it away from you."

I know the liberal Democrats are worried about the economy. They're worried it's going to remain strong. And they're right, it is, with the right leadership it will remain strong.

But let's be frank. Things aren't perfect in this country. There are people who haven't tasted the fruits of the expansion. I've talked to farmers about the bills they can't pay. And I've been to the factories that feel the strain of change. And I've seen the urban children who play amid the shattered glass and the shattered lives. And there are the homeless. And you know, it doesn't do any good to debate endlessly which policy mistake of the seventies is responsible. They're there. And we have to help them.

But what we must remember if we're to be responsible, and compassionate, is that economic growth is the key to our endeavors.

I want growth that stays, that broadens, that touches, finally, all Americans, from the hollows of Kentucky to the sunlit streets of Denver, from the suburbs of Chicago to the broad avenues of New York, and from the oil fields of Oklahoma to the farms of the Great Plains.

And can we do it? Of course we can. We know how. We've done it. And if we continue to grow at our current rate, we will be able to produce thirty million jobs in the next eight years. And we will do it—by maintaining our commitment to free and fair trade, by keeping government spending down, and by keeping taxes down.

Our economic life is not the only test of our success. One issue overwhelms all the others, and that's the issue of peace.

And look at the world on this bright August night. The spirit of democracy is sweeping the Pacific rim. China feels the winds of change. New democracies assert themselves in South America. And one by one the unfree places fall, not to the force of arms but to the force of an idea: freedom works.

And we have a new relationship with the Soviet Union—the INF treaty, the beginning of the Soviet withdrawal from Afghanistan, the beginning of the end of the Soviet proxy war in Angola, and with it the independence of Namibia. Iran and Iraq move toward peace.

It's a watershed. It is no accident.

It happened when we acted on the ancient knowledge that strength and clarity lead to peace; weakness and ambivalence lead to war. You see, weakness tempts aggressors. Strength stops them. I will not allow this country to be made weak again. Never.

The tremors in the Soviet world continue. The hard earth there has not yet settled. Perhaps what is happening will change our world forever. And perhaps not. A prudent skepticism is in order. And so is hope. But either way, we're in an unprecedented position to change the nature of our relationship. Not by preemptive concession, but by keeping our strength. Not by yielding up defense systems with nothing won in return, but by hard, cool engagement in the tug and pull of diplomacy.

My life has been lived in the shadow of war; I almost lost my life in one.

And I hate war. Love peace. And we have peace. And I am not going to let anyone take it away from us.

Our economy is strong but not invulnerable, and the peace is broad but can be broken. And now we must decide. We will surely have change this year, but will it be change that moves us forward, or change that risks retreat?

In 1940, when I was barely more than a boy, Franklin Roosevelt said we shouldn't change horses in midstream. My friends, these days the world moves even more quickly, and now, after two great terms, a switch will be made. But when you have to change horses in midstream, doesn't it make sense to switch to one who's going the same way?

An election that's about ideas and values is also about philosophy. And I have one.

At the bright center is the individual. And radiating out from him or her is the family, the essential unit of closeness and of love. For it's the family that communicates to our children—to the twenty-first century—our culture, our religious faith, our traditions and history.

From the individual to the family to the community, and then on out to the town, to the church and the school, and, still echoing out, to the country, the state, and the nation—each doing only what it does well, and no more. And I believe that power must always be kept close to the individual, close to the hands that raise the family and run the home.

I am guided by certain traditions. One is that there's a God and he is good, and his love, while free, has a self-imposed cost; we must be good to one another.

I believe in another tradition that is, by now, imbedded in the national soul. It's that learning is good in and of itself. You know, the mothers of the Jewish ghettos of the East would pour honey on a book so the children would know that learning is sweet. And the parents who settled hungry Kansas would take their children in from the fields when a teacher came. That is our history.

And there is another tradition. And that's the idea of community—a beautiful word with a big meaning, though liberal Democrats have an odd view of it. They see "community" as a limited cluster of interest groups, locked in odd conformity. And in this view, the country waits passive while Washington sets the rules.

But that's not what community means, not to me. For we are a nation of communities, of thousands and tens of thousands of ethnic, religious, social, business, labor union, neighborhood, regional, and other organizations, all of them varied, voluntary, and unique.

This is America: the Knights of Columbus, the Grange, Hadassah, the Disabled American Veterans, the Order of Ahepa, the Business and Professional Women of America, the union hall, the Bible study group, LULAC, Holy Name—a brilliant diversity spread like stars, like a thousand points of light in a broad and peaceful sky.

Does government have a place? Yes. Government is part of the nation of communities—not the whole, just a part.

And I don't hate government. A government that remembers that the people are its master is a good and needed thing.

And I respect old-fashioned common sense, and I have no great love for the imaginings of the social planners. You see, I like what's been tested and found to be true. For instance:

Should public school teachers be required to lead our children in the Pledge of Allegiance? My opponent says no—and I say yes.

Should society be allowed to impose the death penalty on those who commit crimes of extraordinary cruelty and violence? My opponent says no—but I say yes.

And should our children have the right to say a voluntary prayer, or even observe a moment of silence in the schools? My opponent says no—but I say yes.

And should free men and women have the right to own a gun to protect their home? My opponent says no—but I say yes.

And is it right to believe in the sanctity of life and protect the lives of innocent children? My opponent says no—but I say yes. You see we must change—we've got to change from abortion to adoption. And let me tell you this—Barbara and I have an adopted granddaughter. On the day of her christening we wept with joy. I thank God that her parents chose life.

I'm the one who believes it is a scandal to give a weekend furlough to a hardened first-degree killer who hasn't even served enough time to be eligible for parole.

I'm the one who says a drug dealer who is responsible for the death of a policeman should be subject to capital punishment.

And I'm the one who will not raise taxes. My opponent now says he'll raise them as a last resort, or a third resort. But when a politician talks like that, you know that's one resort he'll be checking into. And I—my opponent won't rule out raising taxes. But I will, and the Congress will push me to raise taxes, and I'll say no, and they'll push, and I'll say no, and they'll push again. And I'll say to them, Read my lips, no new taxes.

Let me tell you more about the mission on jobs. My mission is: thirty in eight—thirty million jobs in the next eight years.

Every one of our children deserves a first-rate school. The liberal Democrats want power in the hands of the federal government, and I want power in the hands of the parents. And I will encourage merit schools. I will give more kids a Head Start. And I'll make it easier to save for college.

I want a drug-free America, and this will not be easy to achieve. But I want to enlist the help of some people who are rarely included. Tonight I challenge the young people of our country to shut down the drug dealers around the world. Unite with us, work with us.

Zero tolerance isn't just a policy; it's an attitude. Tell them what you think of people who underwrite the dealers who put poison in our society. And while you're doing that, my administration will be telling the dealers, "Whatever we have to do we'll do, but your day is over, you are history."

I'm going to do whatever it takes to make sure the disabled are included in the mainstream. For too long they've been left out. But they're not going to be left out any more.

And I am going to stop ocean dumping. Our beaches should not be garbage dumps, and our harbors should not be cesspools. And I'm going to have the FBI trace the medical wastes, and we're going to punish the people who dump those infected needles into our oceans, lakes, and rivers.

Let's clean the air. We must reduce the harm done by acid rain.

And I'll put incentives back into the domestic energy industry, for I know from personal experience there is no security for the United States in further dependence on foreign oil.

In foreign affairs, I'll continue our policy of peace through strength. I'll move toward further cuts in strategic and conventional arsenals of both the United States and the Soviet Union and the Eastern bloc and NATO. I'll modernize and preserve our technological edge, and that includes strategic defense. And a priority, ban chemical and biological weapons from the face of the earth. That will be a priority with me. And I intend to speak for freedom, stand for freedom, be a patient friend to anyone, East or West, who will fight for freedom.

It seems to me the presidency provides an incomparable opportunity for "gentle persuasion."

And I hope to stand for a new harmony, a greater tolerance. We've come far, but I think we need a new harmony among the races in our country. And we're on a journey into a new century, and we've got to leave that tired old baggage of bigotry behind.

Some people who are enjoying our prosperity are forgetting—forgotten what it's for. But they diminish our triumph when they act as if wealth is an end in itself.

And there are those who've dropped their standards along the ways, as if ethics were too heavy and slowed their rise to the top. There's graft in city hall and there's greed on Wall Street and there's influence peddling in Washington, and the small corruptions of everyday ambition.

But, you see, I believe public service is honorable. And every time I hear that someone has breached the public trust, it breaks my heart.

And I wonder sometimes if we've forgotten who we are. But we're the people who sundered a nation rather than allow a sin called slavery— and we're the people who rose from the ghettos and the deserts.

And we weren't saints, but we lived by standards. We celebrated the individual, but we weren't self-centered. We were practical, but we didn't live only for material things. We believed in getting ahead, but blind ambition wasn't our way.

The fact is, prosperity has a purpose. It's to allow us to pursue "the better angels," to give us time to think and grow. Prosperity with a purpose means taking your idealism and making it concrete by certain acts of goodness. It means helping a child from an unhappy home learn how to read—and I thank my wife, Barbara, for all her work in helping people to read and all her work for literacy in this country. It means teaching troubled children through your presence that there is such a thing as reliable love. Some would say it's soft and insufficiently tough to care about these things. But where is it written that we must act as if we do not care, as if we're not moved? Well, I am moved. I want a kinder, and gentler nation.

Two men this year ask for your support. And you must know us.

As for me, I've held high office and done the work of democracy day by day. Yes, my parents were prosperous; and their children sure were lucky. But there were lessons we had to learn about life. John Kennedy discovered poverty when he campaigned in West Virginia; there were children who had no milk. And young Teddy Roosevelt met the new America when he roamed the immigrant streets of New York. And I learned a few things about life in a place called Texas. And when I was working on this part of the speech, Barbara came in and asked what I was doing, and I looked up and I said I'm working hard. And she said, "Oh, dear, don't worry. Relax. Sit back. Take off your shoes and put up your silver foot."

Now, we moved to west Texas forty years ago, forty years ago this year. And the war was over, and we wanted to get out and make it on our own. And those were exciting days. We lived in a little shotgun house, one room for the three of us. Worked in the oil business and then started my own.

And in time we had six children. Moved from the shotgun to a duplex apartment to a house. And lived the dream—high school football on Friday nights, Little League, neighborhood barbecue.

People don't see their own experience as symbolic of an era, but of course we were. And so was everyone else who was taking a chance and pushing into unknown territory with kids and a dog and a car. But the big thing I learned is the satisfaction of creating jobs, which meant creating opportunity, which meant happy families, who in turn could do more to help others and enhance their own lives. I learned that a good done by a single good job could be felt in ways you can't imagine.

It's been said that I'm not the most compelling speaker, and there are actually those who claim that I don't always communicate in the clearest, most concise way. But I dare them to keep it up. Go ahead, make my twenty-four-hour time period. Now, I may not be the most eloquent, but I learned that early on that eloquence won't draw oil from the ground. And I may sometimes be a little awkward, but there's nothing self-conscious in my love of country. And I'm a quiet man, but I hear the quiet people others don't—the ones who raise the family, pay the taxes, meet the mortgage. And I hear them and I am moved, and their concerns are mine.

A president must be many things. He must be a shrewd protector of America's interests, and he must be an idealist who leads those who move for a freer and more democratic planet.

And he must see to it that government intrudes as little as possible in the lives of the people; and yet remember that it is right and proper that a nation's leader take an interest in the nation's character. And he must be able to define—and lead—a mission.

For seven and a half years I've worked with a president—I've seen what crosses that big desk. I've seen the unexpected crisis that arrives in a cable in a young aide's hand. And I've seen the problems that simmer on for decades and suddenly demand resolution. And I've seen modest decisions made with anguish, and crucial decisions made with dispatch.

And so I know that what it all comes down to, this election—what it all comes down to, after all the shouting and the cheers—is the man at the desk. And who should sit at that desk.

My friends, I am that man.

I say it—I say it without boast or bravado. I've fought for my country, I've served, I've built—and I'll go from the hills to the hollows, from the cities to the suburbs to the loneliest town on the quietest street, to take our message of hope and growth for every American to every American.

I will keep America moving forward, always forward—for a better America, for an endless, enduring dream and a thousand points of light.

This is my mission. And I will complete it.

Thank you. You know, it is customary to end an address with a pledge, or saying, that holds a special meaning. And I've chosen one that we all know by heart, one that we all learned in school. And I ask everyone in this great hall to stand and join me in this. We all know it.

"I pledge allegiance to the flag of the United States of America and to the Republic for which it stands, one nation, under God, indivisible, with liberty and justice for all."

Thank you. God bless you. ■

President Mikhail Gorbachev
of the Soviet Union
Acknowledges His Fault

"WE are all one, side by side, and we shouldn't spit on each other."

AFTER SIX YEARS OF *PERESTROIKA*, with the Soviet Union's economy crumbling and its constituent republics demanding more power, a
group of Communist hard-liners and KGB generals staged a coup to
return to autocratic central rule. The military forces would not fire on the
people, however; the coup failed, its leaders were arrested, and a chastened and subdued Mikhail Gorbachev returned to Moscow to negotiate
a loose confederation of republics.

On September 3, 1991, during a session of the Congress of People's
Deputies, the leader who had been criticized for taking half-measures
and for trusting villainous aides—who had, after all, set in train the
events he could not control—made a brief defense of himself before calling for a new constitutional framework. A feisty and charismatic presence at the rostrum, enjoying the sound of his own extemporaneous
words, Mr. Gorbachev has rarely made a memorable speech, because he
does not take the time to prepare a coherent address. When he does read
a speech on a formal occasion, as at the UN, his presentation turns as
leaden as his bureaucratic prose. In this passage spoken at a critical
moment in his nation's history, he refers to himself in the third person,
which is a good technique in critical self-appraisal. His use of the stark
verb "spit" at the end to admonish those who had shown their contempt
for him, is especially vivid.

□   □   □

Distinguished members of the Congress, in the past week the people
have decided on their fate, not only in the parliaments, not only in
public conflicts and clashes of views and in the meetings, but also on the
barricades.

We have seen a tragedy. We've seen bloodletting.

My evaluation of this is known to all of you. I had in mind to present them to you in fuller form if I was going to speak as a person presenting a report. But here I will limit myself to saying that everything that has occurred has been a very hard lesson for me to learn.

But at the same time it confirms that despite the high drama of these events, as a result of this coup d'état against the constitution, despite the fact that it made everything in our country even more tense than it was on the day before the signature of the new union treaty on a union of sovereign states, which is designed to strengthen our cooperation, and despite the fact that we have lost time for solving economic problems and despite the fact that the social situation in the country is on the verge of catastrophe—despite all of this, I say that this coup d' état did confirm that what we have been doing since 1985 made it possible to create new realities and a new basis for our country so that from the very beginning, and this was stated on the eighteenth when this mission came to the Crimea, that it was condemned to failure.

The people did not accept it. The army stayed side by side with the people. For the first time, we saw a new generation that has come into existence in these last several years and that was willing to give up its lives for these new realities.

We've seen that we did not work in vain, you and I in our new thinking, in forming new relations between the government and the people who, at that difficult moment, decided with the democrats and against the putschists. We thus have accomplished something.

And of course we made many mistakes at the same time in this connection, as concerns our direction and these revolutionary transformations which we are undertaking, and this includes Gorbachev, too.

Gorbachev has changed to the extent that he has remained devoted to the choice he made in 1985. If there have been mistakes, if there have been miscalculations in tactics and in measures—but he also did not notice that it was necessary to move more rapidly along the path of liberating ourselves from those totalitarian structures.

What is more, he was not able—I know that not only at public meetings but even in the Congress, people say anything they want about the president, but while I am president, I think there should be some understanding of my position.

Today you have a president. Tomorrow you may have another president. In any case, we are all one, side by side, and we shouldn't spit on each other. This is just my reaction to all of these doubts that have been cast on my conduct. ∎

Commentator Patrick J. Buchanan Brings a Note of Populism to the GOP

"WE'RE going to bring the jobs home and we're going to keep America's jobs here, and when I walk into the Oval Office, we start looking out for America first."

IN 1965, a young polemicist, a Goldwater "true believer" fresh from writing editorials for the conservative *St. Louis Globe-Democrat*, was hired by Richard Nixon to work at his New York law firm on political articles and speeches. Pat Buchanan treated his typewriter like an anvil, pounding furiously, in bursts, fingers unable to keep up with his thoughts. He had his own style—gutsy, brawling, declarative, unequivocal—that his older and politically more sophisticated colleagues had to soften.

After four years in the Nixon White House as one of the three senior speechwriters, including a stint writing "red meat" speeches for Vice-President Spiro Agnew (see p. 805), Buchanan began a career in and out of the opinion media, returning for a time to serve as President Reagan's communications director. Privately amiable and polite, publicly combative, he took the plunge into his own presidential candidacy in 1992, surprising President Bush in New Hampshire with a 38 percent protest vote. Three years later, on March 20, 1995, he returned to Manchester, New Hampshire, to launch his second campaign for the Republican presidential nomination. This time, his message of social conservatism, nativism, and foreign-policy anti-internationalism had a new and resonant wrinkle: economic populism.

At first scorned by party elders steeped in free-market, laissez-faire economic philosophy, Buchanan touched a nerve among workers concerned about loss of jobs to foreign producers. His positions, hammered home on the stump, in small gatherings and on talk radio, had an impact; he stunned Senator Bob Dole, long considered the front-runner for the Republican 1996 nomination, with a victory in the New Hampshire primary before running out of gas in South Carolina.

In this passage from his announcement speech, note the way he tells a story. That was advice taken from Nixon, who told his speechwriters, "Whenever you get a chance in a speech, tell the people a story. They'll tune out a speech, but they'll listen to a story." He also uses traditional "pointer phrases," like "I say to you," setting up the point to follow. An effective technique is the juxtaposition of short, declarative sentences: "This campaign is about you. We are on your side." Buchanan also likes to use "America first," aware of its 1930s isolationist connotation, taking a delight in rubbing it into his internationalist detractors.

□   □   □

. . . Three years ago when I came to New Hampshire, I went up to the North Country on one of my first visits. I went up to the James River paper mill. It was a bad day, just before Christmas, and many of the workers at the plant had just been laid off. They were sullen and they were angry and they didn't want to talk to anyone.

So as I walked down that line of workers, I will never forget: Men shook my hand and looked away. Then one of them, with his head down, finally looked up, and with tears in his eyes said, "Save our jobs." As I rode back down to Manchester, I wondered what it was I could do for that factory worker.

When I got back to Manchester that night, I read a story in the *Union Leader* about the United States Export-Import Bank funding a new paper mill in Mexico.

What are we doing to our own people? What is an economy for if not so that workers and their families can enjoy the good life their parents knew, so that incomes rise with every year of hard work, and so that Americans once again enjoy the highest standard of living in the world? Isn't that what an economy is for?

Our American workers are the most productive in the world; our technology is the finest. Yet, the real incomes of American workers have fallen 20 percent in twenty years.

Why are our people not realizing the fruits of their labor?

I will tell you. Because we have a government that is frozen in the ice of its own indifference, a government that does not listen anymore to the forgotten men and women who work in the forges and factories and plants and businesses of this country.

We have, instead, a government that is too busy taking the phone calls from lobbyists for foreign countries and the corporate contributors of the Fortune 500.

Well, I have not forgotten that man at James River, and I have come back to give him my answer here in New Hampshire.

When I am elected president of the United States, there will be no more NAFTA sellouts of American workers. There will be no more GATT deals done for the benefit of Wall Street bankers. And there will be no more fifty-billion-dollar bailouts of Third World socialists, whether in Moscow or Mexico City.

In a Buchanan White House, foreign lobbyists and corporate contributors will not sit at the head of the table. I will.

We're going to bring the jobs home and we're going to keep America's jobs here, and when I walk into the Oval Office, we start looking out for America first.

So, to those factory workers in the North Country and to the small businessmen and businesswomen, I say to you: This campaign is about you. We are on your side.

Whatever happened to the idea of Americans as one nation, one people? Whatever happened to the good, old idea that all Americans, of all races, colors, and creeds, were men and women to whom we owed loyalty, allegiance, and love? What happened to the idea that America was a family going forward together?

When I was writing my column a couple of months ago, I read a story from New York about fifty-eight new partners made at Goldman Sachs, each of whom had gotten a bonus of at least five million dollars that year. Fine. One month later, the story ran that because profits were down at Goldman Sachs, one thousand clerical workers were being laid off—one thousand men and women at the lowest levels at Goldman Sachs. That was a shameful act of corporate greed.

But let me tell you about another story. Down in LaGrange, Georgia, I visited one of the most modern textile plants in America—only this textile plant had been burned to the ground. All the employees were saved, but the factory was a total ruin. And, after the fire, when the factory workers were called into the assembly hall of the administration building, they thought they were going to be told what so many others have been told before: Now that the plant has burned, we'll be moving to Mexico or Taiwan.

But the managers of the Milliken plant came down from Spartanburg and they said to these six hundred workers: You are our family. We have suffered a loss together. We are going to look for a new job for every single worker in this plant, and beyond that, we're going to build a brand new Milliken plant, the most modern in the world, right here on this site in LaGrange, Georgia. We want our workers to join together and help us build it.

And in August, it will rise again. And every one of those workers will be kept on and brought back to his old job.

Isn't that the idea of free enterprise we Republicans and conservatives believe in? Isn't that the idea and the spirit of one people working together that we must recapture? So I say to the workers and managers at that textile plant down in LaGrange, Georgia, and to all the other plants and businesses and small businesses around America: This campaign is about you. This fight is your fight.

And we Americans must also start recapturing our lost national sovereignty.

The men who stood at Lexington and at Concord Bridge, at Bunker Hill and Saratoga, they gave all they had, that the land they loved might be a free, independent, sovereign nation.

Yet, today, our birthright of sovereignty, purchased with the blood of patriots, is being traded away for foreign money, handed over to faceless foreign bureaucrats at places like the IMF, the World Bank, the World Trade Organization, and the UN.

Look how far we have gone:

A year ago, two United States helicopters flying surveillance over northern Iraq were shot down by American fighter planes in a terrible incident of friendly fire. Captain Patrick McKenna of the Citadel, where I just visited, commanded one of those helicopters. Every American on board was killed. And when the story hit the news, the vice-president, then visiting in Marrakesh at the World Trade Organization meeting, issued a statement that said the parents of these young men and women can be proud their sons and daughters died in the service of the United Nations.

But those young men and women didn't take an oath to the United Nations. They took an oath to defend the Constitution and the country we love. And let me say to you, when Pat Buchanan gets into that Oval Office as commander in chief, no young men and women will ever be sent into battle except under American officers and to fight under the American flag.

So let me say to those brave young patriots who have volunteered to serve in the armed forces of the United States to defend us, our peace and our security: This campaign is about you.

Look how far we have gone:

Rogue nations that despise America, right now, are plotting to build weapons of mass destruction and to buy or to build the missiles to deliver them to our country. Yet the United States of America remains naked to a

missile attack. We have no defense. Why? Because a twenty-year-old compact with a cheating Soviet regime, that has been dead half a decade, prevents us from building our missile defense.

Well, that dereliction of duty ends the day I take the oath.

I will maintain a military for the United States that is first on the land,
first on the seas, first in the air, first in space—and I will not ask any nation's
permission before I build a missile defense for the United States of America.

To those Americans who have served this country in her wars from
Europe to the Pacific, from Korea to Vietnam: This campaign is about
you. It is about never letting America's guard down again.

What is the matter with our leaders?

Every year millions of undocumented aliens break our laws, cross our
borders, and demand social benefits paid for with the tax dollars of
American citizens. California is being bankrupted. Texas, Florida, and
Arizona are begging Washington to do its duty and defend the states, as
the Constitution requires.

When I was in California in 1992, I spoke on this issue in San Diego. A
woman came, uninvited, to the sheriff's office where I was holding a press
conference, and asked if she could join me at that press conference. I said,
"Why?" She said, "I had a boy, a teenage boy, who was killed in an automobile accident by drunken drivers who were on a spree, who had walked
into this country, had no driver's license, and did not belong here."

Three months ago I talked, in the same city of San Diego, to a young
Border Patrol agent. He had been decorated as a hero. He showed me the
back of his head. There was a scar all over it. Illegal aliens had crossed the
border, he went to apprehend them, and they waited to trap him. When
he walked into their trap, they smashed his head with a rock and came to
kill him. Only when he took out his gun and fired in self-defense did his
friends come and save his life.

Yet our leaders, timid and fearful of being called names, do nothing.
Well, they have not invented the name I have not been called. So, the
Custodians of Political Correctness do not frighten me. And I will do
what is necessary to defend the borders of my country even if it means
putting the National Guard all along our southern frontier.

So, to the people of California, Florida, Texas, and Arizona being bankrupted paying the cost of Washington's dereliction of duty, to that brave
Border Patrol agent and the men and women who serve with him, and
to that woman who lost her boy became her government would not do
its duty: This campaign is about you.

And as we defend our country from threats from abroad, we shall fight
and win the cultural war for the soul of America. Because that struggle is

about who we are, what we believe, and the kind of people we shall become. And that struggle is being waged every day in every town and schoolroom of America.

When many of us were young, public schools and Catholic schools, Christian schools and Jewish schools, instructed children in their religious heritage and Judeo-Christian values, in what was right and what was wrong. We were taught about the greatness and goodness of this land we call God's country, in which we are all so fortunate to live.

When I was a little boy, three years old, three and a half years old, my mother's four brothers, one by one, came down to our house, and said good-bye, and we took them to the bus station or the train station to send them off to Europe. Then we got reports from places like Anzio and Sicily, and, in the end, they all came home. But in our school days, when I was five years old or six years old, in first grade, occasionally we would go out in the playground and there would be a short ceremony for some fellow who did not come back from the Ardennes or Anzio or the Bulge.

And that's what we were taught, and that's what we loved.

But today, in too many of our schools our children are being robbed of their innocence. Their minds are being poisoned against their Judeo-Christian heritage, against America's heroes, and against American history, against the values of faith and family and country.

Eternal truths that do not change from the Old and New Testament have been expelled from our public schools, and our children are being indoctrinated in moral relativism, and the propaganda of an anti-Western ideology.

Parents everywhere are fighting for their children. And to the mothers and fathers waging those battles, let me say: This campaign is your campaign. Your fight is our fight. You have my solemn word: I will shut down the U.S. Department of Education, and parental right will prevail in our public schools again.

"What does it profit a man if he gain the whole world and suffer the loss of his immortal soul?" That is true also of nations. No matter how rich and prosperous we may become in material things, we cannot lose this battle for the heart and soul of America.

For as de Tocqueville said long ago, America is a great country because she is a good country, and if she ceased to be good, she will cease to be great.

Yet, today, America's culture—movies, television, magazines, music—is polluted with lewdness and violence. Museums and art galleries welcome exhibits that mock our patriotism and our faith. Old institutions and symbols of an heroic, if tragic, past—from Columbus Day to the Citadel at South Carolina, which graduated Captain McKenna, from

Christmas carols in public schools to southern war memorials—they are all under assault. This campaign to malign America's heroes and defile America's past has as its end: to turn America's children against what their parents believe and what they love.

But because our children are our future, we can't let that happen. We can't walk away from this battle. I pledge to you: I will use the bully pulpit of the presidency of the United States to the full extent of my power and ability, to defend American traditions and the values of faith, family, and country, from any and all directions. And, together, we will chase the purveyors of sex and violence back beneath the rocks whence they came.

So, to those who want to make our country America the beautiful again, and I mean beautiful in every way: This campaign is about you.

In the history of nations, we Americans are the freedom party. We are the first people, the only nation dedicated to the proposition that all men and women are created equal, that they are endowed by their creator with the inalienable right to life, liberty, and the pursuit of happiness. And nothing can stop us from going forward to a new era of greatness, in a new century about to begin, if we only go forward together, as one people, one nation, under God.

So to these ends, and for these purposes, I humbly, but proudly, declare my candidacy for the presidency of the United States. ■

British Prime Minister Tony Blair Exhorts His Party to Fight Terrorism

"THE kaleidoscope has been shaken. The pieces are in flux. Soon they will settle again. Before they do, let us reorder this world around us."

THE "SPECIAL RELATIONSHIP," in Churchill's phrase, between Britain and America was strengthened by the ability of Britain's prime minister, Tony Blair, to work closely with U.S. presidents as different in personality and policy as Bill Clinton and George W. Bush.

Blair's speaking style, both in extemporaneous debate and in formal addresses, combines passion with calculation. His sentences are short and declarative. He modulates his voice to make his points clearly, showing him in command of his text. Though he uses words that sometimes are unfamiliar to American ears—"perforce" is a favorite, meaning "by force of circumstance"—his use of internal dialogue helps simplify complex ideas. His obvious enjoyment of his oratory communicates itself to his audiences.

He knows how to shake hands with his audience. When speaking to a joint meeting of the U.S. Congress in 2003—only the fourth British prime minister to do so—he opened with, "On our way down here, Senator Frist was kind enough to show me the fireplace where, in 1814, the British had burnt the Congress Library. I know this is kind of late, but—sorry!"

The speech excerpted here, with the domestic policy proposals edited out, was to his Labour party conference in Brighton on October 2, 2001, three weeks after the shock of September 11. The joint U.S.-British military response—first in Afghanistan, later in Iraq—was yet to come, but was presaged in this annual address to fellow party members, many of whom were to turn against him in his close alliance with the United States in pursuing the war on terror.

In terms of rhetorical technique, note Blair's quick summarization of the points made by advocates of delay, setting up his tough-minded response. Note, too, his four sentences beginning with "Today," the last the longest, building a rhythm. He also involves the listener with "People ask me . . . My answer is." In a device made famous by Franklin Roosevelt in his "I see an America where" speech, Blair begins six consecutive sentences with "I think of." On a deeper level, he picks up the theme in the U.S. Pledge of Allegiance—"with liberty and justice for all"—and concludes with an appeal for a combination of freedom and justice.

To focus on the need to act decisively during a tumultuous time, the prime minister concludes with an original and memorable image. A kaleidoscope is a tube-shaped optical instrument that delights youngsters as a toy, but is symbolic of colorful and rapid change as it breaks up and rearranges pieces of colored glass. "Soon they will settle again. Before they do, let us reorder the world around us."

□   □   □

In retrospect the millennium marked only a moment in time. It was the events of 11 September that marked a turning point in history, where we confront the dangers of the future and assess the choices facing humankind.

It was a tragedy. An act of evil. From this nation, goes our deepest sympathy and prayers for the victims and our profound solidarity with the American people.

We were with you at the first. We will stay with you to the last. . . .

Be in no doubt: bin Laden and his people organized this atrocity. The Taliban aid and abet him. He will not desist from further acts of terror. They will not stop helping him.

Whatever the dangers of the action we take, the dangers of inaction are far, far greater.

Look for a moment at the Taliban regime. It is undemocratic. That goes without saying.

There is no sport allowed, or television or photography. No art or culture is permitted. All other faiths, all other interpretations of Islam are ruthlessly suppressed. Those who practice their faith are imprisoned. Women are treated in a way almost too revolting to be credible. First driven out of university; girls not allowed to go to school; no legal rights; unable to go out of doors without a man. Those that disobey are stoned.

There is now no contact permitted with western agencies, even those delivering food. The people live in abject poverty. It is a regime founded on fear and funded on the drugs trade. The biggest drugs hoard in the world is in Afghanistan, controlled by the Taliban. Ninety percent of the heroin on British streets originates in Afghanistan.

The arms the Taliban are buying today are paid for with the lives of young British people buying their drugs on British streets.

That is another part of their regime that we should seek to destroy.

So what do we do?

"Don't overreact," some say. We aren't.

We haven't lashed out. No missiles on the first night just for effect.

"Don't kill innocent people." We are not the ones who waged war on the innocent. We seek the guilty.

"Look for a diplomatic solution." There is no diplomacy with bin Laden or the Taliban regime.

"State an ultimatum and get their response." We stated the ultimatum; they haven't responded.

"Understand the causes of terror." Yes, we should try, but let there be no moral ambiguity about this: nothing could ever justify the events of 11 September, and it is to turn justice on its head to pretend it could.

The action we take will be proportionate; targeted; we will do all we humanly can to avoid civilian casualties. But understand what we are dealing with. Listen to the calls of those passengers on the planes. Think of the children on them, told they were going to die. . . .

There is no compromise possible with such people, no meeting of minds, no point of understanding with such terror.

Just a choice: Defeat it or be defeated by it. And defeat it we must.

Any action taken will be against the terrorist network of bin Laden.

As for the Taliban, they can surrender the terrorists; or face the consequences and again in any action the aim will be to eliminate their military hardware, cut off their finances, disrupt their supplies, target their troops, not civilians. We will put a trap around the regime.

I say to the Taliban: Surrender the terrorists; or surrender power. It's your choice. . . .

Round the world, 11 September is bringing governments and people to reflect, consider, and change. And in this process, amidst all the talk of war and action, there is another dimension appearing.

There is a coming together. The power of community is asserting itself. We are realizing how fragile are our frontiers in the face of the world's new challenges.

Today conflicts rarely stay within national boundaries.

Today a tremor in one financial market is repeated in the markets of the world.

Today confidence is global; either its presence or its absence.

Today the threat is chaos; because for people with work to do, family life to balance, mortgages to pay, careers to further, pensions to provide, the yearning is for order and stability and if it doesn't exist elsewhere, it is unlikely to exist here.

I have long believed this interdependence defines the new world we live in.

People say: We are only acting because it's the USA that was attacked. Double standards, they say. But when Milosevic embarked on the ethnic cleansing of Muslims in Kosovo, we acted.

The skeptics said it was pointless, we'd make matters worse, we'd make Milosevic stronger, and look what happened: We won, the refugees went home, the policies of ethnic cleansing were reversed and one of the great dictators of the last century, will see justice in this century. . . .

We know this also. The values we believe in should shine through what we do in Afghanistan.

To the Afghan people we make this commitment. The conflict will not be the end. We will not walk away, as the outside world has done so many times before.

If the Taliban regime changes, we will work with you to make sure its successor is one that is broad-based, that unites all ethnic groups, and that offers some way out of the miserable poverty that is your present existence.

And, more than ever now, with every bit as much thought and planning, we will assemble a humanitarian coalition alongside the military coalition so that inside and outside Afghanistan, the refugees, $4\frac{1}{2}$ million on the move even before 11 September, are given shelter, food, and help during the winter months.

The world community must show as much its capacity for compassion as for force.

The critics will say: But how can the world be a community? Nations act in their own self-interest. Of course they do. But what is the lesson of the financial markets, climate change, international terrorism, nuclear proliferation, or world trade? It is that our self-interest and our mutual interests are today inextricably woven together.

This is the politics of globalization.

I realize why people protest against globalization.

We watch aspects of it with trepidation. We feel powerless, as if we were now pushed to and fro by forces far beyond our control.

But there's a risk that political leaders, faced with street demonstrations, pander to the argument rather than answer it. The demonstrators are right to say there's injustice, poverty, environmental degradation.

But globalization is a fact and, by and large, it is driven by people.

Not just in finance, but in communication, in technology, increasingly in culture, in recreation. In the world of the internet, information technology, and TV, there will be globalization. And in trade, the problem is not there's too much of it; on the contrary, there's too little of it.

The issue is not how to stop globalization.

The issue is how we use the power of community to combine it with justice. If globalization works only for the benefit of the few, then it will fail and will deserve to fail. But if we follow the principles that have served us so well at home—that power, wealth, and opportunity must be in the hands of the many, not the few—if we make that our guiding light for the global economy, then it will be a force for good and an international movement that we should take pride in leading.

Because the alternative to globalization is isolation.

Confronted by this reality, round the world, nations are instinctively drawing together. In Quebec, all the countries of North and South America deciding to make one huge free trade area, rivaling Europe. In Asia, ASEAN. In Europe, the most integrated grouping of all, we are now fifteen nations. Another twelve countries negotiating to join, and more beyond that.

A new relationship between Russia and Europe is beginning.

And will not India and China, each with three times as many citizens as the whole of the EU put together, once their economies have developed sufficiently as they will do, not reconfigure entirely the geopolitics of the world and in our lifetime?

That is why, with 60 percent of our trade dependent on Europe, 3 million jobs tied up with Europe, much of our political weight engaged in Europe, it would be a fundamental denial of our true national interest to turn our backs on Europe.

We will never let that happen.

For fifty years, Britain has, uncharacteristically, followed, not led, in Europe.

At each and every step. There are debates central to our future coming up: how we reform European economic policy; how we take forward European defense; how we fight organized crime and terrorism.

Britain needs its voice strong in Europe, and, bluntly, Europe needs a strong Britain, rock-solid in our alliance with the USA, yet determined to play its full part in shaping Europe's destiny.

We should only be part of the single currency if the economic conditions are met. They are not window dressing for a political decision. They are fundamental. But if they are met, we should join, and if met in this Parliament, we should have the courage of our argument, to ask the British people for their consent in this Parliament.

Europe is not a threat to Britain. Europe is an opportunity.

It is in taking the best of the Anglo-Saxon and European models of development that Britain's hope of a prosperous future lies. The American spirit of enterprise; the European spirit of solidarity. We have, here also, an opportunity. Not just to build bridges politically, but economically.

What is the answer to the current crisis? Not isolationism but the world coming together with America as a community.

What is the answer to Britain's relations with Europe? Not opting out, but being leading members of a community in which, in alliance with others, we gain strength.

What is the answer to Britain's future? Not each person for themselves, but working together as a community to ensure that everyone, not just the privileged few, get the chance to succeed.

This is an extraordinary moment for progressive politics.

Our values are the right ones for this age: the power of community, solidarity, the collective ability to further the individual's interests.

People ask me if I think ideology is dead. My answer is:

In the sense of rigid forms of economic and social theory, yes.

The twentieth century killed those ideologies, and their passing causes little regret. But, in the sense of a governing idea in politics, based on values, no. The governing idea of modern social democracy is community. Founded on the principles of social justice. That people should rise according to merit not birth; that the test of any decent society is not the contentment of the wealthy and strong but the commitment to the poor and weak.

But values aren't enough. The mantle of leadership comes at a price: the courage to learn and change; to show how values that stand for all ages can be applied in a way relevant to each age.

Our politics only succeed when the realism is as clear as the idealism.

This party's strength today comes from the journey of change and learning we have made.

We learnt that however much we strive for peace, we need strong defense capability where a peaceful approach fails.

We learnt that equality is about equal worth, not equal outcomes.

Today our idea of society is shaped around mutual responsibility; a deal, an agreement between citizens, not a one-way gift, from the well-off to the dependent.

Our economic and social policy today owes as much to the liberal social democratic tradition of Lloyd George, Keynes, and Beveridge as to the socialist principles of the 1945 government.

Just over a decade ago, people asked if Labour could ever win again. Today they ask the same question of the opposition. Painful though that journey of change has been, it has been worth it, every stage of the way.

On this journey, the values have never changed. The aims haven't. Our aims would be instantly recognizable to every Labour leader from Keir Hardie onwards. But the means do change.

The journey hasn't ended. It never ends. The next stage for New Labour is not backwards; it is renewing ourselves again. Just after the election, an old colleague of mine said: "Come on, Tony, now we've won again, can't we drop all this New Labour and do what we believe in?"

I said: "It's worse than you think. I really do believe in it."

We didn't revolutionize British economic policy—Bank of England independence, tough spending rules—for some managerial reason or as a clever wheeze to steal Tory clothes.

We did it because the victims of economic incompetence—15 percent interest rates, 3 million unemployed—are hardworking families. They are the ones—and even more so, now—with tough times ahead—that the economy should be run for, not speculators, or currency dealers or senior executives whose pay packets don't seem to bear any resemblance to the performance of their companies.

Economic competence is the precondition of social justice. . . .

In all of this, at home and abroad, the same beliefs throughout: that we are a community of people, whose self-interest and mutual interest at crucial points merge, and that it is through a sense of justice that community is born and nurtured.

And what does this concept of justice consist of?

Fairness, people all of equal worth, of course. But also reason and tolerance. Justice has no favorites; not amongst nations, peoples, or faiths.

When we act to bring to account those that committed the atrocity of 11 September, we do so not out of bloodlust.

We do so because it is just. We do not act against Islam. The true followers of Islam are our brothers and sisters in this struggle. Bin Laden is no more obedient to the proper teaching of the Koran than those Crusaders of the twelfth century who pillaged and murdered represented the teaching of the Gospel.

It is time the West confronted its ignorance of Islam. Jews, Muslims, and Christians are all children of Abraham.

This is the moment to bring the faiths closer together in understanding of our common values and heritage, a source of unity and strength.

It is time also for parts of Islam to confront prejudice against America and not only Islam but parts of Western societies too.

America has its faults as a society, as we have ours.

But I think of the Union of America born out of the defeat of slavery.

I think of its Constitution, with its inalienable rights granted to every citizen, still a model for the world.

I think of a black man, born in poverty, who became chief of their armed forces and is now Secretary of State Colin Powell, and I wonder frankly whether such a thing could have happened here.

I think of the Statue of Liberty and how many refugees, migrants, and the impoverished passed its light and felt that if not for them, for their children, a new world could indeed be theirs.

I think of a country where people who do well don't have questions asked about their accent, their class, their beginnings but have admiration for what they have done and the success they've achieved.

I think of those New Yorkers I met, still in shock, but resolute; the fire-fighters and police, mourning their comrades but still head held high.

I think of all this and I reflect: Yes, America has its faults, but it is a free country, a democracy, it is our ally, and some of the reaction to 11 September betrays a hatred of America that shames those that feel it.

So I believe this is a fight for freedom. And I want to make it a fight for justice too.

Justice not only to punish the guilty.

But justice to bring those same values of democracy and freedom to people round the world.

And I mean: freedom, not only in the narrow sense of personal liberty but in the broader sense of each individual having the economic and social freedom to develop their potential to the full. That is what community means, founded on the equal worth of all.

The starving, the wretched, the dispossessed, the ignorant, those living in want and squalor from the deserts of Northern Africa to the slums of Gaza, to the mountain ranges of Afghanistan: they too are our cause.

This is a moment to seize.

The kaleidoscope has been shaken. The pieces are in flux. Soon they will settle again.

Before they do, let us reorder this world around us.

■   ■   ■

XIII

COMMENCEMENT
SPEECHES

President Woodrow Wilson Calls the Midshipmen to Their Duty

"YOU cannot forget your duty for a moment, because there might come a time when that weak spot in you should affect you. . . , and then the whole history of the world might be changed by what you did not do or did wrong."

WHEN OUR TWENTY-SEVENTH PRESIDENT attended the 1916 graduation ceremony at the United States Naval Academy, at Annapolis, he had no prepared comments. Few speakers are so confident of their ability to deliver appropriate remarks on such a formal occasion. The short speech that follows is impromptu, off the cuff, ad lib—but Woodrow Wilson must have given the matter some thought while being introduced.

President Wilson's subsequently printed address, "Responding to the New Call of Duty," took its title from his praise of the graduating class in the second sentence of the speech. (Wilson liked the word "new"; a collection of his campaign speeches in 1912 was called *The New Freedom*, designed to top Theodore Roosevelt's *The New Nationalism*.) Delivered three years after his inauguration, Wilson's talk offered four paragraphs in alluding not only to his college background but also to the gravity of the world situation in June 1916, as he was preparing to campaign for reelection with the slogan "He Kept Us Out of War."

The presidential remarks stress the "special obligation" for the graduates through direct address and parallel structure ("not of private duty merely, but of public duty also"). With parallelism even in his advice ("you get your zest by doing a thing that is difficult, not a thing that is easy"), Wilson conveyed a sense of the trouble ahead.

Ten months after President Wilson's remarks to the class of 1916, the United States declared war on Germany.

□　□　□

Mr. Superintendent, young gentlemen, ladies and gentlemen: It had not been my purpose when I came here to say anything today, but as I sit here and look at you youngsters, I find that my feeling is a very personal feeling indeed. I know some of the things that you have been through, and I admire the way in which you have responded to the new call of duty. I would feel that I had not done either you or myself justice if I did not tell you so.

I have thought that there was one interesting bond that united us. You were at Washington three years ago and saw me get into trouble, and now I am here to see the beginning of your trouble. Your trouble will last longer than mine, but I doubt if it will be any more interesting. I have had a liberal education in the last three years, with which nothing that I underwent before bears the slightest comparison. But what I want to say to you young gentlemen is this: I can illustrate it in this way. Once and again when youngsters here or at West Point have forgotten themselves and done something that they ought not to do and were about to be disciplined, perhaps severely, for it, I have been appealed to by their friends to excuse them from the penalty. Knowing that I have spent most of my life at a college, they commonly say to me, "You know college boys. You know what they are. They are heedless youngsters very often, and they ought not to be held up to the same standards of responsibility that older men must submit to." And I have always replied, "Yes; I know college boys. But while these youngsters are college boys, they are something more. They are officers of the United States. They are not merely college boys. If they were, I would look at derelictions of duty on their part in another spirit; but any dereliction of duty on the party of a naval officer of the United States may involve the fortunes of a nation and cannot be overlooked." Do you not see the difference? You cannot indulge yourselves in weaknesses, gentlemen. You cannot forget your duty for a moment, because there might come a time when that weak spot in you should affect you in the midst of a great engagement, and then the whole history of the world might be changed by what you did not do or did wrong.

So that the personal feeling I have for you is this: we are all bound together, I for the time being and you permanently, under a special obligation, the most solemn that the mind can conceive. The fortunes of a nation are confided to us. Now, that ought not to depress a man. Sometimes I think that nothing is worthwhile that is not hard. You do not improve your muscle by doing the easy thing; you improve it by doing the hard thing, and you get your zest by doing a thing that is difficult, not a thing that is easy. I would a great deal rather, so far as my sense of enjoyment is concerned, have something strenuous to do than have something that can be done leisurely and without a stimulation of the faculties.

Therefore, I congratulate you that you are going to live your lives under the most stimulating compulsion that any man can feel, the sense, not of private duty merely, but of public duty also. And then if you perform that duty, there is a reward awaiting you which is superior to any other reward in the world. That is the affectionate remembrance of your fellow men—their honor, their affection. No man could wish for more than that or find anything higher than that to strive for. And, therefore, I want you to know, gentlemen, if it is any satisfaction to you, that I shall personally follow your careers in the days that are ahead of you with real personal interest. I wish you Godspeed, and remind you that yours is the honor of the United States. ■

Editor William Allen White Calls the Prewar Generation to Its Duty

"LIBERTY, *if it shall cement man into political unity, must be something more than a man's conception of his rights, much more than his desire to fight for his own rights. True liberty is founded upon a lively sense of the rights of others and a fighting conviction that the rights of others must be maintained.*"

IN 1896, the new editor of the *Emporia* (Kansas) *Gazette*—a Republican and a liberal—wrote a ringing editorial titled "What's the Matter with Kansas?" This blast at the Populist party helped elect William McKinley and called national attention to a small-town newspaperman who could express the values of tens of millions of upright, tolerant people. He coined the phrase "tinhorn politician" and styled himself as an authentic voice of the grass roots. He was editor of the *Gazette* for forty-nine years; though its circulation never rose to more than eight thousand, it became his platform for commentary that gained and held international recognition.

In June of 1936, he gave a commencement address to the graduating class of Northwestern University, in Illinois. These graduates were the young men and women who in five years would be bearing the brunt of the American participation in World War II. He revealed "the screw loose in [his] mental processes," warning, "You have this dementia in your blood," and identifying its manifestation: "Your fathers, mothers, and remote ancestors for several thousand years believed in the reality of duty. Upon that madness they built the world."

He presents long thoughts in short sentences. He anticipates by a generation the longing for a "new frontier," and packs much food for thought in such passages as "You may love for the moment the indolent sense of futility that comes with the grand cynicism of youth. But life, experience, the hazards of your day, and time will bring out of you the courage bred into you."

□   □   □

About all that a commencement orator can do for his auditors is to turn their faces around. He looks back upon the world as he thinks it was. Then he considers the world as he thinks it is. Finally in his receding perspective he discloses the pictured phantasm which he hopes will be the future. Thereupon his young listeners may see mirrored in the gloss of his picture the world which they think they will make. It is a pleasant exercise. This commencement oratory which floods our land every June may be an effective anesthetic which youth may take at its second birth, out of the solid, unyielding, factual environment of childhood and of books, out of the substantial fabric of the curriculum with its sure reward of grade, class standing, and satisfying compensation into the bewildering, hazy, and altogether ironic mockeries that we call, in humorous euphony, real life. I stand here tiptoeing near the end of my three score years and ten. There you sit across an abysm scarcely fifty feet wide but deeper than the distance to the moon. I come out of one dream world that is memory. You go into a visionary world that is hope. I tell you of the things that I imagine are true in my world. You hold in your hearts the picture of your world that shall be. We dwell on these two different planets. How can I hope to get across the chasm of time and space any hint, even a flickering shadow of my truth that will reach your hearts? For my world seemed to be a static world when I stood fifty years ago where you stand now. My forebears since Caesar's day had not greatly changed the tools with which they made their clothes, got their food, built their houses; nor had they changed greatly in those twenty centuries the philosophy upon which they erected their future. Today you look back upon a world that has moved so far in one hundred years that nothing you see and feel, touch and taste, hope, believe, and love is as it was when your grandfathers learned from their grandfathers how to live in another day. So what I shall say here you may well discount. It is only the truth as I see it. Yet it may have some bearing, though heaven only knows what, upon your lives. Perhaps I can tell you something, and being called here, I shall try. . . .

We know we have not done God's work perfectly. The world we have made out of the inheritance of our grandfathers is a pretty sad botch. It is full of gross injustices. Obviously a couple of centuries of hard work needs to be done on it, before America is turned out, finished in its millennial beauty. But with all these inequities, the old thing does hold together. We turn our country over to you in one piece—which is something. Even if it isn't a pretty piece, it is yours, with its spiritual hereditaments. And may I be pardoned the vanity of one who worked on the job if I try to give you some idea of what has held this nation in unity during a century and a half when in many other parts of the globe races and tongues and economic units have been breaking into small states, magnifying nationalism into a vice.

Today, as never before, nationalism in small geographical areas is pulling men into bitter disunion and controversy. Some flame of envy and rancor is abroad in the world. We see it moving across the face of Europe in various tyrannies, each exalting its own nationalism, each challenging liberty in its own way—Italy under fascism, Germany under the Nazis, Russia under communism, Spain boiling with confusion, while the two principles of dictatorship, that of the plutocracy and that of the proletariat, struggle for possession of that brave land. These isms are types of one pestilence which is threatening civilization. That this spiritual pestilence will attack America, no one can doubt.

How can we Americans immunize ourselves? The class of '37 must find out why small geographical, social, racial units are erupting into a virulent nationalism that threatens Western civilization. It's your problem, esteemed descendants, but here's a hint that might help you to solve it.

I am satisfied that the disease has its root in a lack of social faith. The thing that has bound America into one nation is tolerance—tolerance and patience; indeed, tolerance and patience upheld by a sense of duty.

At this point, dearly beloved members of the class of '37, I propose to reveal the screw loose in my mental processes, also to show you something of the aberration of your forebears. You have this dementia in your blood, and you might as well know it. Your fathers, mothers, and remote ancestors for several thousand years believed in the reality of duty. Upon that madness they built the world. Not that I wish to brag about it—this sense of duty—but I still hug the delirium of my generation to my heart and believe there is something in those old-fashioned eccentricities known as the Christian virtues. Don't get excited. I am not preaching piety. I have no plan of salvation to offer you, no theology to defend. But I feel, and my generation has believed in a general way, that democracy with its freedom, with its patience, with its tolerance, with its altruism, is a sort of rough attempt to institutionalize the Christian philosophy. And when I say rough, I mean rough, something like a 20 percent realization of a noble ideal. Our American Constitution, for instance, is a national compact of our individual and of our social duties. It has worked in this country after a fashion. Yet the same Constitution, or nearly the same, has been adopted in a dozen other lands and has failed. Why has it held us to an essential unity? I am satisfied that our Constitution has stood up because Americans actually have established here a sort of code of duties. That has been the crystallizing principle that has held us together—duty of man to man, of region to region, of class to class, of race to race, of faith to faith. That duty has bred something more than neighborly tolerance. It has engendered a profound desire in every American's heart to make life as pleasant as it may be made—not merely for himself, indeed not chiefly for himself, but for others. Thus we have found and cherished true liberty.

Liberty, if it shall cement man into political unity, must be something more than a man's conception of his rights, much more than his desire to fight for his own rights. True liberty is founded upon a lively sense of the rights of others and a fighting conviction that the rights of others must be maintained. Only when a people have this love of liberty, this militant belief in the sacredness of another man's self-respect, do races and nations possess the catalyzer in their political and social organism which produces the chemical miracle of crystallized national unity and strength. We Americans have had it for three hundred years on this continent. It was in the blood of our fathers. It was the basis of our faith in humanity when we wrote our Constitution. It has been with us a long time on this continent—this capacity for compromise, this practical passion for social justice and for altruistic equity in settling the genuine differences of men. This high quality of mutual respect is no slight gift. It is a heroic spiritual endowment, this knack of getting along together on a continental scale.

We have set as a national custom the habit of majority rule. This custom is maintained not by arms but by a saving sense in the heart of every minority that any majority will not be puffed up, will not infringe upon the rights of the minority. Matching this duty of the majority to be fair, we have set up the component duty of the minority to be patient, but to agitate until the justice of a losing cause has convinced the winning majority. This American tradition of political adjustment cuts through every line of cleavage and all differences in our social organization—regions, classes, races, creeds. Here is the way it has worked. As our country has expanded geographically, this political genius for unity has tapped our store of certain basic virtues: neighborly forbearance, meekness, unselfishness, and that belief in the essential decency of one's neighbors which for want of a better word we have called love. Now, in our land abideth these three—faith in our fellows, hope in the triumph of reason, and love for humanity. With all the grievous faults and glaring weaknesses of our federal union, these things are the centripetal spiritual forces which have solidified America.

These commonsense qualities which have grown out of the Beatitudes have helped to preserve the American Union for the last century and a half. Now, what are you going to do about it, you who stand here at the threshold of the reality of your past, looking into the evanescent horizon of your future? We who shall soon be petrified into pedestaled ghosts as your ancestors have a notion that you, our descendants, don't have much use for duty, for patience, and for tolerance. We get the general idea that you have no sort of faith in the strength of the humble. Yet it is out of this lack of faith that a new challenge has appeared in the world, a challenge aimed at democracy, a challenge which scorns these lowly neighborly virtues that have held our world together. This challenge is finding its way into our American life. We are being told that the majority sometimes has emergency mandates to ignore the rights of the minorities. We have set up rulers all over the earth who preach against the virtue of patience. It is a new thing in our America to hear men defending the tyrannies of Europe—communism, fascism, and the Nazis—declaring that the minority may oppress the majority if the minority happens to be convinced that it is right. It is even a stranger doctrine in America, which holds that a passing majority, by reason of its being a ballot box majority at one or two elections, has an inherent right immediately to suppress and ruthlessly destroy an honest minority.

Now, as an ancestor, let me caution you, my heirs and assigns, that these new political attitudes are symptoms of greed for power. They will fool you if you channel your thinking into narrow dialectics. Don't take your logical premise from your class self-interest. Don't build your logic upon a purely selfish structure. Don't think as plutocrats. Don't reason as members of the middle class or as proletarians. Such thinking is too sure of its own syllogisms ever to be just. Such thinking rejects the possibility that there is truth and that there may be reason in the contention of another class of society. This same discord that has torn asunder so many peoples in Europe, where fifty years ago democracy seemed to be taking root, today is seeding in our land. Capitalists are scorning labor leaders. Labor leaders are preaching distrust and hatred for capitalists. The revelations of the La Follette committee in the United States Senate now investigating the infringement of civil liberties certainly lay bare the cancer of hatred in our economic body that is poisoning our national blood. The class-conscious arrogance of wealth is creating its own class morals. Proletarian logic is justifying the use of force in class conflict and condoning cunning. The industrial enterpriser shuts his eyes to the tragedy of the farmer's economic plight. Then the farmer envies the financier.

But I feel sure the tide will turn. You who stand here, chisel in hand, about to hew out the future, have something in you; humanity's most precious mental gift—the eternal resilience, the everlasting bounce in man. You may love for the moment the indolent sense of futility that comes with the grand cynicism of youth. But life, experience, the hazards of your day, and time will bring out of you the courage bred into you. You will find that you have the urge that we had. You will want to believe in something in spite of yourselves. You will want to construct something. For you are the sons and daughters of a creative people, inventive, resourceful, daring. And above all, in spite of the many unpleasant things you have learned in this cloister, in spite of the hard realities that have molded your youth, you are mystics, you are crusaders, you are incorrigible visionaries in the noblest sense of these words. The eternal verities of your inheritance, the organizing brains, the industry, the noble purpose that during the nineteenth century made America a kindlier and more beautiful land than ever before was brought forth on this planet, will be beckoning you, urging you, indeed, sternly commanding you to follow whatever is fine and just in the achievement of your country. . . .

The residuum of what I am trying to say is this: you must reorganize life in your America and point your achievement toward a fairer distributive system. Abundance is here for the taking. Don't bemoan your lost frontier. It is even now flashing on your horizon. A gorgeous land lies before you fair and more beautiful than man before has ever known. Out of the laboratories will come new processes to multiply material things for your America, to multiply them almost infinitely; but only if you will hold open the channels of free science, unfettered thought, and the right of a man to use his talents to the utmost provided he gives honest social returns for the rewards he takes. Don't delude yourselves about your new frontier. For on that frontier which will rise over the laboratories you will find the same struggle, the same hardships, the same inequities that your forefathers have found on every frontier since the beginning of time. You will find rapacious men trying to grab more than their share of the common bounties of the new frontier. You will find human greeds and human perfidies there as we found them fifty years ago and as our fathers found them generations upon generations before. Energetic buccaneers always thrive wherever men are pioneering. In every one of the ten long generations during which your ancestors have been conquering this continent and building a proud civilization here, they have struggled as you will struggle against the injustices of life which are bred out of the lust for power in unsocial men. But don't let that discourage you. . . .

And now, in closing, on behalf of your fathers who are bequeathing to you their choicest gifts, let me say that your heritage is not in these great lovely cities, not this wide and fertile land, not the mountains full of undreamed-of riches. These you may find in other continents. What we leave you that is precious are the few simple virtues which have stood us in good stead in the struggle of our generation. We will and bequeath to you our enthusiasm, our diligence, our zeal for a better world, that were the lode stars of our fathers. As our legatees we assign you our tolerance, our patience, our kindness, our faith, hope, and love, which make for the self-respect of man. These qualities of heart and mind grow out of a conviction that the democratic philosophy as mode of thinking will lead mankind into a nobler way of life. . . . ■

Economist Arthur Burns Shares Three Discoveries with Young Israelis

"I do not hold with those who say that power corrupts men. Rather, it is the other way around; men without morality corrupt power."

DR. ARTHUR BURNS, an immigrant to the United States from Austria at the age of eight, founded the Bureau of Economic Research, became chairman of the Council of Economic Advisers under Dwight Eisenhower, and served as Richard Nixon's domestic policy counselor before being appointed chairman of the Federal Reserve Board. He finished his career, coming full circle, as ambassador to West Germany.

His speaking style was precise; his official writing was afflicted with too many facts and figures. But because he had an organized mind and liked to make a clear point, his extemporaneous speaking and rare informal addresses were models of clarity.

The following commencement address, made at Hebrew University, in Jerusalem, on July 6, 1970, is uneditable—that is, it cannot be cut without the cut showing. That demonstrates a tight construction in speech-writing, with points logically marching to a satisfying conclusion. It begins with a couple of anecdotes, drawing the audience in with easy-to-follow stories about people. Then Dr. Burns previews, or billboards, the three elements to come in his speech: discoveries in economics (where he's the expert), power management (always of interest), and the achievement of ideals (which should be on the minds of young people).

He then delivers as advertised, each discovery helpfully labeled and briefly expounded. At the end, like a good college lecturer to students taking notes, he summarizes his trinity of points. Then he poses three questions, designed to give his listeners something to puzzle out in each of the three areas as they live their lives. Not an exciting speech, but reflective of the speaker: helpful; structured; wise.

□   □   □

This is my third visit to Israel. I remember, just before my first visit here, in 1958, being admonished not to come by several United States ambassadors.

The reason for the warning was plain. Israel was then in the midst of the Lebanon crisis. With tension mounting by the hour, even a professor ought to have enough sense to stay away from a country about to become involved in war. The men who told me this were seasoned diplomats; they were gravely alarmed by the state of affairs.

But when I came here, I was struck by just the opposite—not by the tension, not by the alarm, but by the coolness of the Israeli people in the midst of international anxiety.

There is an ironic saying we have in America, paraphrasing a line in a Kipling poem: "If you can keep your head while all about you are losing theirs, perhaps you do not understand the gravity of the situation."

But the fact was that the Israelis I met here—some of whom had been my students at Columbia University in years past—fully understood the gravity of the international situation. They kept the calm that is found in the eye of a hurricane.

I was struck then, as I am struck now, by what Ernest Hemingway defined as the essence of courage—"grace under pressure."

That quality of calm courage is found only in a people with a clear sense of purpose and a firm sense of duty. This simple fact must weigh heavily in every assessment by outsiders of the future of Israel.

On another visit, I asked David Ben-Gurion how the Israelis were able to achieve so rapidly their advances in industry and commerce. As you know, many economists associate economic growth with a nation's endowment of natural resources. England's early progress was attributed to her coal; America's to her abundant minerals and vast agricultural resources. But Israel was not blessed with large mineral deposits, much of its land was barren, and even water was in short supply.

How, I therefore asked the prime minister, was Israel able to build such a strong economy in such a short time? He answered, "We did it first by dreaming, then by doing what the economists said was impossible."

Keeping in mind that gentle reminder of fallibility, I would like to speak to you today about three discoveries in seemingly different fields—in the management of economic affairs, in the management of power, and in the achievement of ideals.

You are a part of those discoveries, and the way the young people of Israel govern their lives will have an important impact on the use of those discoveries in the years ahead.

The first discovery, in the field of economic management, is this: the human element is basic in the creation of an economy that combines full employment with high productivity and relative price stability.

The great debate you read about in economics today is between those who feel that fiscal policy is all-important and those who believe that monetary policy is all-important. The two schools joust in learned debate, but both are also beginning to take account of the human element in economic affairs—that is, the dreams, fears, and hopes that so often upset the most expert calculations.

And so we are gradually discovering—or perhaps I should say rediscovering—that there is more to economic policy than the established principles of economics. When the older writers on economics entitled their treatises "political arithmetic" or "political economy," they were telling us something we have forgotten: that man's hope is a crucial element in man's fate.

What is your role in this discovery? Right now, right here in Israel, you are proving that hope is perhaps the most powerful of all economic forces. You are proving that a spirit of purpose can give meaning to human energy and overcome a lack of material resources. In this, you are not breaking any rules of economics; but you are developing new rules of political economy.

A generation ago, the only thing we had to fear was fear itself; today, the only thing we should despair of is despair. In nations all around the world, on both sides of the Iron Curtain, an enervating mood of despair is becoming fashionable, especially on the part of some young people. The cultivation of despair can do as much to undermine the strength of some economies as the cultivation of hope can do to overcome the apparent weaknesses of other economies.

This brings me to a second discovery that is being made, in a related but different field—in the exercise of power in the world.

Power traditionally has been thought of in military terms. And, of course, as you know better than most, the survival of freedom in the world as it is today would be impossible without military power.

But I do not hold with those who say that power corrupts men. Rather, it is the other way around; men without morality corrupt power. And the world is making a remarkable discovery about the exercise of power: with nations, as with individual men, the most effective application of power is the power of moral example.

This, I submit, is what has made and continues to make America great. We have a dream of freedom, of equal opportunity, and of human dignity. It is true, of course, that our reach exceeds our grasp, but by striving to make our way of life better and to help other nations enrich their freedom, we set a moral example that is one of the greatest sources of our power. We are criticized so much around the world because people expect so much of America; I would never trade away those high expectations for mere approval.

And this, too, is what makes Israel a "great power" in her own right. The power of her example in dignifying life, in conquering disease, and in extending technical assistance to other poor nations, can never be underestimated. I know that President Nixon feels this deeply. Not long ago, in discussing why America supports Israel, he put it this way: "Americans admire a people who can scratch a desert and produce a garden. The Israelis have shown qualities that Americans identify with: guts, patriotism, idealism, a passion for freedom. I have seen it. I know."

The young people of Israel born to this noble example, have a special responsibility both to their own nation and to the world to preserve and enhance those qualities. You must continue to show the world that you know the difference between bravery and bravado. You must continue to show the world how dearly you hold the moral precepts of brotherhood. You must continue to show the world your readiness to seek peace and progress for yourselves and for your neighbors.

The example of Israel is nowhere more vivid than in the field of education. You have the privilege of being graduated today from one of the great universities of the world. But what impresses the world is not so much your fine educational facilities or the magnificence of Mount Scopus, where you began to build this university, but the fact that education in Israel permeates the very existence of her people.

You do not "go to school" in Israel; in a sense, this whole land—every home, factory, kibbutz, or even army camp—is a school. Education is an exciting part of life. The mistake that others sometimes make, and that I trust you will never make, is to treat education as a chore instead of a joy; to treat graduation as an end of education rather than as a beginning.

You consider yourselves pioneers in many things, and rightly so, but I suggest that there is a discovery you are making that you may not be aware of: that a passion for learning diffused throughout a society is the surest road to the achievement of its ideals.

The president of the United States likes to say, "When you're through learning, you're through." And he's right—the strength of a nation, like the strength of an individual, depends on its ability to learn how to change and to grow.

Perhaps the greatest thing that can be said about the people of Israel is that in fighting for the life of your nation, you have stimulated the life of the mind.

Today I have been speaking of three discoveries that are being made in the world, and of your part in them in the years ahead.

In creating a lasting prosperity, the human element is at last being recognized as of fundamental importance.

In exercising power in the world, the power of moral example can be far greater than material riches or equipment.

In achieving ideals, a reverence for learning and education is indispensable.

As you take leave of the university, as you graduate into a new life of the mind, may each of you ask yourself this: What am I doing to increase the sum of hope in this world? What am I doing to nourish the sense of purpose that founded this nation and made it strong? What am I doing to teach someone else what I have learned?

In asking questions like these, you will come to new discoveries, you will rise to new challenges, and you will justify the faith of your fathers and the admiration of millions of free men all around the world.

I am deeply honored to join the fellowship of this graduating class and I salute you: *Shalom.* ■

Humorist Art Buchwald
Speaks To
Law Graduates

"No matter what you read in the newspapers or see on television, I assure you that we're all going to make it."

A KEENING OBSERVER OF WASHINGTON POLITICS, Art Buchwald knows how to ask the tough questions, like "Have you ever seen a candidate talking to a rich person on television?"

The winner of the 1982 Pulitzer Prize for distinguished commentary, Buchwald as political humorist reaches an international audience through the worldwide syndication of his column to more than 550 newspapers. He outlectures Mark Twain. Among his recent books are *I Think I Don't Remember* (1987) and *Whose Rose Garden Is It Anyway?* (1989).

On May 7, 1977, Buchwald delivered the commencement day address at Catholic University's Columbus School of Law, in Washington, D.C.

The commencement address is vintage Buchwald, from the presidential salutation ("My fellow Americans") to the common-man close ("Now, I could have said something very profound today, but you would have forgotten it in ten minutes"). With chapter and verse of biblical and court-case allusions, Buchwald prepares the law graduates for trying careers.

□　□　□

My fellow Americans, or as we're going to be saying for the next four years—How y'all? It is a great honor for me to address the graduating class of Catholic Law School of 130 men and 85 persons. You couldn't have selected a better person to be your commencement speaker today.

I am no stranger to the bar. I first became interested in the law when I was working in Paris for the *Herald Tribune*, and I covered a trial which had to do with a couple caught in a very compromising situation in a Volkswagen. Now, everyone in France was interested in the case because it had to do with such a small car. The defense lawyer argued it was impossible to do what the couple had been accused of doing in a Volkswagen. The judge said he didn't know if this was true or not, so he appointed a commission to study it. It took them six months to render their verdict, and they said "it was possible but very difficult."

What does a speaker say to a fresh-faced, well-scrubbed graduating class of neophyte lawyers? Your studies are over, and now you will leave these hallowed halls, this ivy-covered campus, to go out and practice the second-oldest profession in the world.

It is an honorable calling that you have chosen. Some of you will soon be defending poor, helpless insurance companies who are constantly being sued by greedy widows and orphans trying to collect on their policies. Others will work tirelessly to protect frightened, beleaguered oil companies who are being attacked by wicked and depraved antitrust officials. A few of you will devote your lives to suing doctors, while many of you will choose to sue the patients. As lawyers you will see to it that whether you represent General Motors, Coca-Cola, or the telephone company, the little fellow will get his day in court.

There are some of you who have chosen to go into criminal law— which I must admit is getting harder and harder to distinguish from civil law. To you I say, this, too, is an honorable undertaking—only if you keep one thing in mind, and that is to always get your fee in advance. No matter how hard you defended him, a convicted criminal is the most reluctant of all clients to pay the lawyer after the jury has returned a verdict of guilty.

This great government of ours has made the law profession the growth industry of America. Every time a new regulation is issued, a new law is passed, and an old law is repealed, fifty thousand lawyers are needed to explain it. Just one amendment to the IRS code will give every lawyer in this country enough work to last him thirteen years. One memorandum from the Food and Drug Administration will provide enough litigation to feed your families for the rest of your lives. Our country looks kindly on lawyers. Our government hires them to make the rules. Then the private sector is forced to hire lawyers to find ways of breaking them.

The beauty of the law is that the more complicated lawmakers make it, the more work it generates for other lawyers. Had the Ten Commandments been written by a government lawyer, Moses could never have carried them on a stone tablet. He would have had to haul them down from Mount Sinai on the Rock of Gibraltar. And if you ever get discouraged, remember this: even if the meek do inherit the earth, some lawyer will have to probate the will.

I am not trying to give you the impression that your life will be all milk and Gulf Oil. The fact of the matter is that the legal profession faces many problems these days. According to a recent survey, lawyers rated lower than garbage collectors in the public's esteem. Now, I think this is an unfair image. I know many lawyers who would make good garbage collectors—but I don't know one garbage collector who would make a good lawyer.

Another problem you face is that you will soon be forced to advertise. This is an anathema to most lawyers, but it's coming and there is no sense fighting it. I think if you have to advertise you should put most of your money into television. I have been working on some TV commercials which might be appropriate. One, which I already have in script form, would show a nattily dressed man standing in front of the Atlanta Federal Prison. He would say, "Hi, I used to be a vice-president of Lockheed Aircraft. I'd be inside these gates now if it hadn't been for Covington & Burling. If you have committed a white-collar crime—or are thinking of committing one, call this toll-free number: 800-367-2345. We have a special sale this week on income tax fraud and SEC violations. Don't delay. Had the men inside this prison called Covington & Burling, they would be standing out here with me today." . . .

The tendency today in this country is to wring our hands and say everything is rotten, but I don't feel that way. I am basically an optimist—otherwise I would never fly Allegheny Airlines. I don't know if this is the best of times or the worst of times, but I can assure you of this: this is the only time you've got—and you can either sit on your *expletive deleted* or go out and pick a daisy.

Now we seem to be going through a period of nostalgia, and everyone seems to think yesterday was better than today. I personally don't think it was, and I would advise you not to wait ten years from now before admitting today was great. If you're hung up on nostalgia, pretend today is yesterday, and just go out and have one hell of a time.

You know, if you were looking for a name for this country right now, you'd have to call it the uptight society. Everyone seems uptight about something. The white students want out of our system; the black students want in; the people are mad at the cops; and the priests aren't talking to the cardinals. And doing the column the way I do, I discovered that for every uptight person in this country, there's an uptight organization to back him up. And I discovered that the most uptight organization in this country right now is the National Rifle Association. Now, before you get to like me, I am for gun registration, and it's very personal with me. My neighbor has a gun, and he can't even water his lawn straight. But every time I do an article for gun registration, I get hundreds of letters, all neatly typewritten, telling me I'm trying to destroy the Constitution. And I discovered that everybody in this country who owns a gun also owns a typewriter. So my solution to the gun registration problem is to make everybody register his typewriter. People are very uptight about pornography and what it is doing to all our lives. Now, I'll be very honest with you. I have always wanted to write a pornographic book. But I get so excited doing the research that I can never get around to the book. . . .

My final message to you today is that no matter what you read in the newspapers or see on television, I assure you that we're all going to make it. For two hundred years this country has muddled through one crisis after another, and we have done it without changing our form of government. And it seems like centuries, but it was only three years ago that a president of the United States was forced to resign from office under the darkness of clouds, and he was asked to leave the office because he lied to the American people. I was at the White House that night to hear his resignation speech. What impressed me more than anything else was that while one leader of our country was resigning and another was taking his place, I did not see one tank or one helmeted soldier in the street, and the only uniforms I saw that night were on two motorcycle policemen who were directing traffic on Pennsylvania Avenue. Two hundred million people were able to change presidents overnight without one bayonet being unsheathed. And I believe that any country in the world that can still do that can't be all bad.

Now, I could have said something very profound today, but you would have forgotten it in ten minutes; so I chose to give this kind of speech instead so that in twenty years from now when your children ask you what you did on graduation day, you can proudly say, "I laughed."

Thank you, and God bless you. ∎

Language Maven
William Safire Denounces
the Telephone as the
Subverter of Good English

"It is harder to put your foot in your mouth when you have your pen in your hand."

LOOK, THIS DOESN'T COMPARE with Pericles and Patrick Henry, but every anthologist is entitled to the inclusion of one of his own. It was delivered at my alma mater, Syracuse University, on May 13, 1978, and the graduates lapped it up.

□   □   □

Classmates:

I entered Syracuse University with the class of '51, dropped out after two years, and am finally receiving my degree with the class of '78. There is hope for slow learners.

My subject today is "The Decline of the Written Word." If the speech I have written is disjointed and confusing, you will get my point the hard way.

We have not heard a really eloquent speech out of the White House in a long time. Why? When you ask the speechwriters of Mr. Ford and Mr. Carter, they give you this explanation: they say that "high-flown rhetoric" is not their man's style.

But that is not responsive. A flowery speech is a bad speech. Simple, straight English prose can be used to build a great speech. There has to be a more profound reason for the reluctance of the presidents of the seventies to write out their thoughts plainly and deliver them in words we can all understand.

If you press the president's aides—and that's my job, to press them hard—they'll admit that their man much prefers to "ad-lib" answers to questions. He's not good at what they call a "set" speech.

What do they really mean by that? They mean a speech—a written speech, developing an idea—is not what people want to hear. People prefer short takes, Q. and A.; the attention span of most Americans on serious matters is about twenty seconds, the length of a television clip.

In the same way, people do not want to read articles as they once did; today, if you cannot get your message in a paragraph, forget it.

As a result, we're becoming a short-take society. Our presidency, which Theodore Roosevelt called a "bully pulpit," has become a forum for twenty-second spots. Our food for thought is junk food.

What has brought this about? I don't blame President Carter for this—he reflects the trend; he did not start it. I don't flail out at the usual whipping boy, television.

The reason for the decline of the written word—speeches, written articles—is that we, as a people, are writing less and talking more. Because it takes longer to prepare our thoughts on paper that means we are ad-libbing more, and it also means we are thinking more superficially. An ad-lib has its place, but not ad nauseam.

That's one of those sweeping statements that pundits are permitted to make. But let me turn reporter for a minute and prove to you that we're talking more and writing less.

Most people are not writing personal letters any more. Oh, the volume of first-class mail has doubled since 1950, but here's the way the mail breaks down. Over 80 percent is business related; over 10 percent is greeting card and Christmas card; and only 3 percent is from one person to another to chew the fat.

More and more, we're relying on commercial poets and cartoonists to express our thoughts for us. Tomorrow is Mother's Day; how many of us are relying on canned sentiments? I remember my brother once laboriously handmade a card for my mother: on the front was "I'll never forget you, Mother," and inside it said, "You gave away my dog." Okay, he was sore, but at least he was original.

The greatest cultural villain of our times has a motherly image: Ma Bell. The telephone company. Instead of writing, people are calling; instead of communicating, they're "staying in touch."

There you are, all about to be holders of college degrees. When was the last time you wrote, or received, a long, thoughtful letter? When was the last time you wrote a passionate love letter? No, that takes time, effort, thought—there's a much easier way, the telephone. The worst insult is when kids call home, collect, for money; when my kids go to college, the only way they'll get a nickel out of me is to write for it.

As the percentage of personal mail has dwindled, the number of telephone installations since 1950 has quadrupled. The average person's need to write has been undermined by simple economics: as the cost of a letter has gone up, the cost of a call has gone down.

During World War I, a first-class letter cost two cents an ounce; in a few weeks, it will be fifteen cents an ounce. In that same sixty years, a New York–to-San Francisco call has gone from twenty dollars for three minutes down to fifty-three cents today, if you're willing to call at night or on a weekend. The penny postcard is a dime. Letters up almost 800 percent; phone calls down to one-fortieth of the cost to grandpa. No wonder the market share of communication has dropped for letter writers. In the year I was a freshman here, the Postal Service had over a third of the communication business; today, it is one-sixth, and falling.

And it's going to get worse: phonevision is on the way. We have seen what happened to the interpersonal correspondence of love in the past generation. The purple passages of prose, and tear-stained pages of the love letter—that's gone now. It has become the heavy breathing, grunts, and "like, I mean, y'know, wow" of the love call. The next stage, with the visual dimension, will not even require a loud sigh: we can just wave at each other to say hello; wiggle our fingers to express affection; raise our eyebrows to ask, "What's new?," get a shrug in reply, and sign off with a smile and a wink.

We need not degenerate further from written English to verbal grunts, and then to sign language. We need to become modern reactionaries; I consider myself a neo-Neanderthal and my happiest moment of the year comes as daylight savings ends in October, when I can turn back the clock.

How do we save ourselves from the tyranny of the telephone? How do we liberate our language from the addiction to the ad-lib?

If this were an off-the-cuff presentation, I would drift off into a fuzzy evasion like "There are no easy answers." But one thing I have learned in preparing my first commencement address, and the main advice I shall burden you with today is this: there are plenty of easy answers. The big trick is to think about them and write them down.

There are four steps to the salvation of the English language, and thus to the rejuvenation of clear thinking in your working lives.

First, remember that first drafts are usually stupid. If you shoot off your mouth with your first draft—that is, if you say what you think before you've had a chance to think—your stupidity shines forth for all to hear. But, if you write your first draft—of a letter, a memo, a description of some transcendental experience that comes to you while jogging—then you fall on your face in absolute privacy. You get the chance to change it all around. It is harder to put your foot in your mouth when you have your pen in your hand.

Second, reject the notion that honesty and candor demand that you "let it all hang out." That's not honesty; that's intellectual laziness. Tuck some of it in; edit some of it out. Talking on your feet, spinning thoughts off the top of your head, and just rapping along in a laid-back way have been glorified as "expressing your natural self." But you did not get an education to become natural; you got an education to become civilized. Composition is a discipline; it forces us to think. If you want to "get in touch with your feelings," fine—talk to yourself; we all do. But, if you want to communicate with another thinking human being, get in touch with your thoughts. Put them in order; give them a purpose; use them to persuade, to instruct, to discover, to seduce. The secret way to do this is to write it down and then cut out the confusing parts.

Third, never forget that you own the telephone; the telephone does not own you. Most people cannot bear to listen to a phone ring without answering it. It's easy to not answer a letter, but it's hard to not answer a phone. Let me pass along a solution that has changed my life. When I was in the Nixon administration, my telephone was tapped—I had been associating with known journalists. So I took an interest in the instrument itself. Turn it upside down; you will notice a lever that says "louder." Turn it away from the direction of louder. That is the direction of emancipation. If somebody needs to see you, he'll come over. If others need to tell you what they think, or even express how they feel, they can write. There are those who will call you a recluse—but it is better to listen to your own different drummer than to go through life with a ringing in your ears.

My fourth point will impress upon you the significance of the written word. Those of you who have been secretly taking notes, out of a four-year habit, will recall that I spoke of "four steps" to the salvation of the English language. Here it is: there is no fourth step. I had the fourth step in mind when I began, but I forgot it.

Now, if I were ad-libbing, I would remember I had promised four points, and I would do what so many stump speakers do—toss in the all-purpose last point, which usually begins, "There are no easy answers." But, in writing down what you think, you can go back and fix it—instead of having to phumph around with a phony fourth point, you can change your introduction to "there are three steps." Perhaps you wonder why I did not do so. Not out of any excess of honesty, or unwillingness to make a simple fix—I just wanted you to see the fourth step take shape before your very eyes.

Is the decline of the written word inevitable? Will the historians of the future deal merely in oral history? I hope not. I hope that oral history will limit itself to the discovery of toothpaste and the invention of mouthwash. I don't want to witness the decomposing of the art of composition, or be present when we get in touch with our feelings and lose contact with our minds.

I'm a conservative in politics, which means I believe that we as a people have to lead our leaders, to show them how we want to be led.

Accordingly, I think we have to send a message to the podium from the audience: we're ready for more than Q. and A. We're ready for five or ten minutes of sustained explication. A "fireside chat" will not turn out our fires. On the contrary—if a speaker will take the time to prepare, we are prepared to pay in the coin of our attention.

That, of course, is contrary to the trend, against the grain. It can come only from people who care enough to compose, who get in the habit of reading rather than listening, of being in communication instead of only in contact.

When Great Britain was fighting World War II alone, an American president did something that would be considered cornball today: FDR sent Churchill a poem, along with a letter, that read:

> Sail on, O Ship of State!
> Sail on, O Union, strong and great!
> Humanity with all its fears,
> With all the hopes of future years,
> Is hanging breathless on thy fate!

Churchill took the message—delivered to him by Wendell Willkie, who had just been defeated by FDR—and selected a poem in answer. At that moment, looking east, England faced invasion; looking to the west across the Atlantic, Churchill saw potential help. The poem he sent concluded with the words:

> And not by eastern windows only,
> When daylight comes, comes in the light;
> In front, the sun climbs slow, how slowly,
> But westward, look, the land is bright.

High-flown rhetoric? Perhaps. And perhaps poetry, which had an honorable place in a 1961 inauguration, is too rich for some tastes today.

And now I remember the fourth step. I like to think we can demand some sense of an occasion, some uplift, some inspiration from our leaders. Not empty words and phony promises—but words full of meaning, binding thoughts together with purpose, holding promise of understand-able progress. If we ask for it, we'll get it—if we fail to ask, we'll get more Q. and A.

I believe we can arrest the decline of the written word, thereby achiev-ing a renaissance of clarity. And not by eastern establishment windows only. The hope is on this side of the Potomac, the Charles, and the Hudson rivers—westward, look, the land is bright. ■

Financier Felix G. Rohatyn Examines a Fragile Economy

"WHEN a democratic society does not meet the test of fairness . . . freedom is in jeopardy. Whether the attack comes from the left or from the right is irrelevant; both extremes are equally lethal."

WHEN FELIX G. ROHATYN rose to address the graduating class of his alma mater, Middlebury College, in Vermont, his speech in May 1982 drew heavily on his own experience as a leader in business and public affairs. Rohatyn, born in Austria in 1928, came to the United States dur-ing World War II and was naturalized in 1950. An investment banker and chairman of the Municipal Assistance Corporation (New York City's fiscal watchdog agency), Rohatyn was largely responsible for helping New York City survive its financial crisis of the midseventies.

These experiences led into Rohatyn's discussion of the economy in 1982, as it began pulling out of severe recession. Called "The Fragile

System," Democrat Rohatyn's speech focused on the challenges facing our nation's economy in the boom times of the Reagan era.

With the anaphora of "There is no reason" to enumerate seven needed changes in policy, Rohatyn posits a reformation of the American economy. A listing of the nation's worries, combined with his recollections of the handling of New York City's fiscal crisis, underscores his direct address to the class of 1982, particularly in his perorational avoidance of sentiment in a nice "I do not envy you, but I do not feel sorry for you."

□   □   □

It has been more than thirty years since I graduated, without the slightest distinction, from a small, idyllic, some might say ivory tower college in Vermont called Middlebury. I had come to the United States in 1942, a refugee from Nazi-occupied France. America meant freedom and opportunity for me; Franklin Roosevelt was America; Middlebury was part of a heady postwar period, of belonging somewhere, of becoming a U.S. citizen, of having a future. A small, bouncy, bald professor named Benjamin Wissler taught me the difference between a fact and an assumption, between reasoning and guessing. Even though, soon after graduation, I was drafted for the Korean War and graduated from that experience as a sergeant of infantry, also without distinction, nothing during that period dimmed my conviction that in the U.S. tomorrow would be better than today, as would every tomorrow thereafter. Insofar as I am concerned, America has far exceeded my personal expectations. No European country would have given a Jewish refugee, of Polish extraction, the opportunities in business and in public affairs that this country has given me.

And yet it would be disingenuous and unrealistic not to recognize that the world as a whole and the U.S. in particular, are profoundly changed from my graduating year of 1949.

A friend of mine, one of the more civilized corporate chairmen, said to me recently, "I no longer give commencement addresses; the graduates are entitled to an upbeat speech, and I am no longer capable of delivering it." It gave me pause because I certainly do not have an upbeat speech; however, a realistic assessment of where we are cannot be equated with hopelessness. We saved New York City from bankruptcy against much greater odds than those facing this country today. But we did it by being ruthlessly realistic about the mess we were dealing with and by assuming, quite correctly, that when things look very bad, they usually turn out to be worse than they look. . . .

The United States is more than a nation; it is a continent. Within this continent lie our greatest challenges and the most serious threat to our democratic form of government: income and class disparities on the one hand, regional disparities on the other. The Reagan administration's approach to these issues was to state that tax policy should not be used to effect social change and that citizens should vote with their feet. As a result, a completely laudable attempt to improve American productivity by stimulating investment has resulted in an economic program incoherent in its application.

Budget cuts have been largely concentrated on lower-income programs such as food stamps and welfare and have not, so far, touched the large, middle-income support programs, indexed to the cost of living, such as Social Security and pensions. Massive tax cuts, coupled with enormous and apparently indiscriminate increases in military spending, have created the perspective of enormous federal deficits for years to come. The growth in the economy which was expected to pay for these programs is, time and again, choked off by high interest rates.

At the same time, a strong regional tide is running away from this part of the country. Unless vigorous actions are taken soon, older America, the Northeast and Midwest—tied to traditional industries like autos, steel, glass and rubber, seriously wounded by Japanese competition—will not provide the jobs, the schools, the taxbase to maintain the physical plant of its cities, and the minimum requirements of its citizens. Half this country will be basking in the sun, swimming in oil and defense contracts, while the other half will sink further and further into physical decay, social stress, and despair.

The basic test of a functioning democracy is its ability to create new wealth and see to its fair distribution. When a democratic society does not meet the test of fairness, when, as in the present state, no attempt seems to be made at fairness, freedom is in jeopardy. Whether the attack comes from the left or from the right is irrelevant; both extremes are equally lethal. . . .

Maybe for the first time in its history, the United States is faced with doubts about its destiny. In less than twenty-five years we have gone from the American century to the American crisis.

The United States today is a country in transition. It is in transition from being the world's dominant military power to sharing that role with the Soviet Union; it is in transition from an industrial to a service society; from being a predominantly white, northern European society based in the Northeast and Midwest to being a multiracial society with its center of gravity in the Sunbelt. A society in transition cannot be governed by rigid dogma; on the contrary, it requires a government which is flexible, pragmatic, even sometimes deliberately ambiguous. Shared values must be clear, but the means to the end cannot be rigid. From fascism to communism, from monarchy to anarchy, the ends of government are purportedly the same. Justice with opportunity, higher standards of living, peace in our time. The means to the end are very different, however, and the means are what determine whether we live in a free society.

The critical issues we face today are not the levels of interest rates or what kind of package finally comes out of budget negotiations. These things are important, but our fascination with numbers must not obscure the real issues. These are, in no particular order:

□ The rapid growth of a permanent underclass in America: the residents of inner-city ghettos, black and Hispanic, undereducated, underskilled, without real hope of participating in the future of the country;

□ The regional split between Sunbelt and Frostbelt, which is accelerating and which will leave the northern half of the United States in serious difficulty;

□ The decline of our traditional manufacturing sectors, the decay of our older cities and the decline in the quality of urban life;

□ Illegal immigration in great numbers, especially from Mexico, which will create additional social tensions unless we produce enough jobs to absorb our own unemployed along with new arrivals;

□ Nuclear proliferation and the need to control and reduce the level of nuclear weapons while being realistic about Soviet power.

To be fair and evenhanded, I should probably attempt to sketch the many reasons today to be optimistic about the future. The new technologies and inventions, the exploration of space and the oceans, communications and education, advances in medicine and knowledge of the human body, plus the myriad new developments we cannot even conceive of today. We must also be realistic in recognizing that we are today the strongest economic power in the world and that we are facing a Soviet system which is spiritually and financially bankrupt.

If I seem to dwell on the problems, it is probably for two reasons. First, because I have been trained, professionally, to look after the bad news first and let the good news take care of itself. Second, because I believe that in our problems lie the most serious challenges to our system and in their resolution lie some of the greatest opportunities for tomorrow.

And yet the list of problems that I reviewed is by no means a complete list, and their diversity and complexity indicate the futility of trying to deal with them by across-the-board economic theories and "hands-off" government. The role of government, in the last decades of this century, will be *the* paramount question to be decided.

Today, we are witnessing a paradox: a government which abdicates to a theoretical marketplace most of its responsibilities for the welfare of the people, while wishing to intrude on people's most private decisions. How does one equate the conservative passion to intrude on such issues as abortion, school prayer, and the death penalty with its equally fervent passion for the free market as the fount of all benefits? Today's conservative experiment will fail because it has no relevance to the world we live in, just as yesterday's liberalism failed for exactly the same reason. We are soon, however, going to run out of time for experiments.

Benny Wissler once snappily explained to me that there was no such thing as *the wrong answer;* there was only *a wrong answer.* It was only recently, however, that I concluded that, especially in government and public life, there may not be any such thing as *the right answer.* There may, at best, exist a process whereby trends can be affected and the direction of social and economic behavior temporarily influenced. This is the antithesis of the planned, central domination of government, but it means government committed to oppose destabilizing trends before they become flood tides. It is a permanent but ever-changing process.

A Rabelaisian friend of mine once compared saving New York City to making love to a gorilla. "You don't stop when you're tired," he said to me; "you stop when he's tired." The gorilla never tires, and government can never abdicate its responsibilities. . . .

There is no reason why a hardheaded liberalism cannot live with the reality that we cannot spend ourselves into bankruptcy.

There is no reason why social programs, impeccable in their objectives, have to be grossly abused, or expanded to include those who really don't need them.

There is no reason why an economy, geared mostly to private-sector growth, cannot at the same time permit limited government intervention where needed. A modern version of the Reconstruction Finance Corporation of the 1930s could help rebuild our cities and restructure our basic industries without threatening our basic free-enterprise system.

There is no reason why limited and temporary protection for our hard-hit industries cannot be conditioned on restrained wage and price behavior by labor and management; this might become the model for an incomes policy where wage and price behavior could be linked to productivity.

There is no reason why large savings cannot be effected in defense, and particularly in reducing nuclear delivery systems, if we are willing to pay the price of larger standing conventional forces.

There is no reason to abandon human rights abroad and deal with murderers from the right because they happen to be anti-Communist. Nor is there reason to tolerate murderers from the left on the romantic notion that they are agrarian reformers.

However, although there is no reason why these results cannot be achieved, we must be realistic about the political difficulty of bringing this about. Without the active support of the American people and the active cooperation of business, labor, and government, it cannot happen.

In times of upheaval, the passions must be for moderation and not for extremes. As Anwar Sadat well knew, the passion for moderation may be one of the most dangerous passions today, and yet it is especially vital to our future. Sadat took the risks and paid the price. Even though today's technology provides us with mountains of instant data, it is useless without judgment. And if judgments are to have value, policy decisions have to be made early. When the crisis is clear, it is often too late to act. That is the dilemma of statesmanship and the possibly fatal flaw in a political system which only seems to act when it is too late.

France has given the world a lot; not least is the skepticism of Montaigne and of Voltaire. Skepticism is what is needed today—skepticism of easy solutions, of cant, of ideology of the left or right. Skepticism does not equate with cynicism; it is not inconsistent with the fiercest patriotism or the firmest belief in basic values. But it can be the anchor to windward when our basic institutions seem to be adrift with the tides.

Yesterday, your president spoke to you of the American dream; today, I speak to you of the American reality. They are not inconsistent with each other, but unless you face the latter, you will never achieve the former. Ladies and gentlemen of the class of 1982, I do not envy you, but I do not feel sorry for you. You will have an exciting time, and it is likely to be hard going. The United States is in need of change, and your challenge will be to provide it as well as to adjust to it. As the rate of change accelerates, as the problems become greater and the solutions more elusive, get involved in public affairs. It is a great adventure.

Politics is not the only way to become involved in public life. There will be many structures such as Municipal Assistance Corporation, where private citizens can play important roles. I had the privilege of participating in a great adventure, the rescue of New York City. It was an experience both terrifying and exhilarating, which I would not have missed for anything. It taught me what you will find out. To be skeptical and always look over your shoulder, but to get involved deeply and to shoot for the moon. To beware of lawyers and consultants and people who do not take risks and who do not get their hands dirty. There are even more experts today than there are problems, but there is no greater strength than an open mind combined with a willingness to take risks. Middlebury opened my mind, as I am sure it did yours. In order to take risks, however, you have to go in harm's way. What happens then and how you perform, will depend on the fates as well as on your character. ■

Governor Mario Cuomo Speaks over the Heads of the Graduates to the Parents

"WE have for a full lifetime taught our children to be go-getters. Can we now say to them that if they want to be happy they must be go-givers?"

THE GOVERNOR OF NEW YORK is often a political leader with the potential for national stature, and Mario Cuomo made the most of a keynote address at the 1984 Democratic National Convention to establish himself as a party leader; his emotional evocation of "family values," combined with a view of the nation as an extended family, marked him as a politician to watch.

In that same summer, on June 3, 1984, he delivered a commencement address to Iona College, in New Rochelle, New York. As he wrote to the anthologist, "This is certainly not a great speech, but it is my favorite. Others have received more attention; this one says best what is most important to me."

Cuomo is a politician, like Adlai Stevenson, who pays close attention to words and writes many of his own speeches. When a columnist chided him for convoluted "Jesuitical reasoning," the governor quickly countered with "That's how little you know—it's Vincentian reasoning."

□   □   □

. . . It was an Irishman who gave me the best advice I've ever been given about the art of delivering a commencement speech.

Father Flynn was the president of my alma mater, St. John's, and the first time I was ever asked to speak at a graduation, I asked him how I should approach it.

"Commencement speakers," said Father Flynn, "should think of themselves as the body at an old-fashioned Irish wake. They need you in order to have the party, but nobody expects you to say very much."

That's advice I intend to remember today. . . .

I know that you are thinking—good parents and grandparents, loved ones of the graduates—what I'm thinking. "We've been through it all, at least most of it, or a lot of it. There's so much ahead that they ought to know about. So many temptations they should ignore. So much we can tell them about how to begin answering these hard questions."

We have the *obligation* to tell them, to reduce as much as possible the pain of their learning only from their own blunders.

We have the obligation. But do we have the right?

Can we, who found the ultimate truth so elusive for so long, tell them with confidence now of the futility of gathering up riches and the things of the world?

It's clear to us that all the newly won power over space and time, the conquest of the forces of nature, the fulfilling of age-old challenges, have not made us any happier or surer of ourselves.

We have built rockets and spaceships and shuttles; we have harnessed the atom; we have dazzled a generation with a display of our technological skills. But we still spend millions of dollars on aspirin and psychiatrists and tissues to wipe away the tears of anguish and uncertainty that result from our confusion and our emptiness.

Most of us have achieved levels of affluence and comfort unthought of two generations ago.

We've never had it so good, most of us.

Nor have we ever complained so bitterly about our problems.

The closed circle of pure materialism is clear to us now—aspirations become wants, wants become needs, and self-gratification becomes a bottomless pit.

All around us we have seen success in this world's terms become ultimate and desperate failure. Teenagers and college students, raised in affluent surroundings and given all the material comforts our society can offer, commit suicide.

Entertainers and sports figures achieve fame and wealth but find the world empty and dull without the solace or stimulation of drugs.

Men and women rise to the top of their professions after years of struggling. But despite their apparent success, they are driven nearly mad by a frantic search for diversions, new mates, games, new experiences—anything to fill the diminishing interval between their existence and eternity.

We know because we've been there. But do we have the right to tell these graduates that the most important thing in their lives will be their ability to believe in believing? And that without that ability, sooner or later they will be doomed to despair?

Do you think they would believe us if we told them today, what we *know* to be true: That after the pride of obtaining a degree and maybe later another degree and after their first few love affairs, that after earning their first big title, their first shiny new car and traveling around the world for the first time and having had it *all*—they will discover that none of it counts unless they have something real and permanent to believe in?

Tell me, ladies and gentlemen, are we the ones to tell them what their instructors have tried to teach them for years?

That the philosophers were right. That Saint Francis, Buddha, Muhammad, Maimonides—all spoke the truth when they said the way to serve yourself is to serve others; and that Aristotle was right, before them, when he said the only way to assure yourself happiness is to learn to give happiness.

Don't you remember that we were told all this when we were younger? But nevertheless, we got caught up in the struggle and the sweat and the frustration and the joy of small victories, and forgot it all. Until recently when we began to look back.

How simple it seems now. We thought the Sermon on the Mount was a nice allegory and nothing more. What we didn't understand until we got to be a little older was that it was the whole answer, the whole truth. That the way—the *only* way—to succeed and to be happy is to learn those rules so basic that a shepherd's son could teach them to an ignorant flock without notes or formulae.

We carried Saint Francis's prayer in our wallets for years and never learned to live the message.

Do we have the right now to tell them that when Saint Francis begged the Lord to teach him to want to console instead of seeking to be consoled—to teach him to want to love instead of desiring to be loved—that he was really being intensely selfish? Because he knew the only way to be fulfilled and pleased and happy was to *give* instead of trying to get.

We have for a full lifetime taught our children to be go-getters. Can we now say to them that if they want to be happy they must be go-*givers*?

I wonder if we can, in good conscience, say these things to them today when we ourselves failed so often to practice what we would preach.

I wonder if we—who have fought, argued, and bickered and so often done the wrong thing to one another—are the ones to teach them love.

How do we tell them that one ought not to be discouraged by imperfection in the world and the inevitability of death and diminishment? How do we tell them when they lose a child, or are crippled, or know that they will themselves die too soon—that God permits pain and sickness and unfairness and evil to exist, *only* in order to permit us to test our mettle and to earn a fulfillment that would otherwise not be possible?

How can we tell our children *that*—when we have ourselves so often cried out in bitter despair at what we regarded to be the injustice of life—and when we have so often surrendered?

How can we tell them that it is their *duty* to use all that they have been given to make a better world, not only for themselves and their families, but for all who live in this world, when it was our generation that permitted two great wars and a number of smaller ones, our generation that made the world a place where the great powers are so alienated from one another that they can't even play together in an Olympics?

Do we have the right to tell them, as our teachers told us, that they have an obligation in justice to participate in politics and government? Can we without shame say to them that our system of democracy works well only when there is involvement by all? That in our democracy the policies that become law, the rules of justice, the treatment of individuals are the responsibility of *each* citizen? That you get what you deserve out of our system, and that indifference deserves nothing good?

When we ourselves have chosen to sit at home on so many election days muttering grim remarks about the politicians who appear on the television set, instead of doing what we could to change things, for the better?

Will they believe us if we said these things?

Would we be able to explain the embarrassment of our own failures?

Do you blame me, ladies and gentlemen, for being reluctant to deliver to them the message that is traditional on commencement day?

But maybe, ladies and gentlemen, this problem is not as great as I've made it out to be.

I've been taking a closer look at these graduates. They are actually taller, stronger, smarter than we were, smart enough maybe to take our mistakes as their messages, to make our weaknesses their lessons, and to make our example—good and not so good—part of their education.

I think I see in their eyes a depth of perception that perhaps we didn't have. A sense of truth, deeper and less fragile than ours.

As you talk to them, you get the feeling that they are certainly mature enough to see the real problems of our society: the need for peace, the need to keep pure the environment God offered us, the need to provide people the dignity of earning their own way.

Indeed, as I think about it, I have to conclude that these young people before me today are the best reason for hope that this world knows.

I see them as believers and doers who will take what we will pass on to them so clumsily, and make it something better than we have ever known. Honoring us by their works, but wanting to be better than we have been.

I tell you, ladies and gentlemen, looking at them now, closer and harder than I have before, I have a feeling about these people that makes me want to live long enough to see and be part of the world they will create.

Now, ladies and gentlemen, parents and grandparents, I would like to tell them, the graduates, all of this, and I know that if we thought they wouldn't be embarrassed by hearing it, we would all be telling them about how proud we are of them and how much we believe in them and their future. But again maybe we don't have to tell them; maybe they know. Maybe they can tell just by seeing the love in our eyes today.

Congratulations, ladies and gentlemen, on the good children you have cared for and raised. ■

Labor's Lane Kirkland Rejects the Labels "Liberal" and "Conservative"

"As for those terms 'liberal' and 'conservative,' as one who has been afflicted by both labels, . . . I doubt their utility in this day and age for anyone except slapdash journalists."

LANE KIRKLAND was revered by speechwriters as one of their own who made it to the top of his profession. He began as a merchant seaman during World War II and later drafted nautical charts to pay for his college degree at Georgetown's School of Foreign Service, but he veered from diplomacy to the labor movement in 1948 as a researcher. The AFL-CIO lent him to the Truman and later the Stevenson campaigns as a speechwriter; in 1961, he became an assistant to George Meany, writing that redoubtable labor leader's speeches, and in 1979 succeeded Meany as president of the AFL-CIO. He died in 1999.

In speeches, as in his career, he was an organizer; his speeches march to a point. He returned to his native state of South Carolina (where his great-great-grandfather signed the Declaration of Secession) in 1985 to deliver the commencement address to the University of South Carolina. The opening makes the proper obeisance to the lessons of life required of commencement speakers, but with a twist: his quotation is taken from a recent western movie. (A mark of originality in a speech is a fresh source to cite, especially one unlikely to yield wisdom; by reading universal meaning into a colorful statement, the speaker shows both his common touch and his philosophical depth.) Its message about the relevance of history is reprised, extended, and deepened at the end in an unfamiliar quotation from Sidney Hook and a famous line from George Santayana.

The second section centers on the social changes of the past two generations. Short paragraphs begin with "I remember" (sometimes with a poetic evocation, as "I remember a South Carolina that was too poor to paint and too proud to whitewash") and are followed by "When I note" or "When I see" lines that chide today's healthy patients for throwing their old crutches at the doctor.

With a transition line, "I did not come here today to organize but to philosophize," he then applies the lesson of those hard-fought-for social changes to current political labeling. The students, and a broader public beyond, needed this clarification of labels: the labor movement under his leadership was liberal in economic affairs and conservative or hawkish in foreign affairs; its staunch espousal of the rights of Poland's Solidarity movement worried many U.S. doves who usually associate with domestic liberals—a situation that confused those who like their categories tidy. Kirkland delivers the message at the end that "there really are things one ought to be conservative about and things one ought to be liberal about, and they do change." Unlike most commencement addresses, which tend to meander self-indulgently, this is an easy-to-hear speech with a shape and a purpose.

□   □   □

I understand that commencement audiences are tolerant, to a degree, of speakers who reminisce and wax philosophical about what lessons they have picked up along the way about life and all that.

As to the lessons of life, I can't improve on some lines from a western movie called *Missouri Breaks.*

Two cutthroats with murderous designs on each other are sharing a campfire. One is strumming a guitar and singing an old gospel song called "Life Is like a Mountain Railroad."

He stops and asks the other fellow in a taunting manner, "Is life really like a mountain railroad?" "Naw," the other replies. "Then what is life like?" asks the first character. "Mister," came the reply, "life ain't like nothing I ever heard of before."

That takes care of what life is all about, and I can vouch for it. I can assure the graduates here that life ain't going to be like anything you ever heard of before.

Nevertheless, nothing in my experience has contradicted what I absorbed in my youth in South Carolina, and I remember it well.

I remember the names of the six Confederate generals from Camden, enshrined in the Pantheon, where I played as a kid: Cantey, Chesnut, Deas, Kennedy, Kershaw, and Villepigue.

There still echoes in my mind the sound of the hours struck by the old bell in the clock tower of the Opera House in Newberry, where for a dime on Saturdays I could join my peers in tribute to Ken Maynard and Hoot Gibson and even witness the last death throes of live vaudeville in America.

I remember it well.

I remember some other things whenever I return to a thriving and beautified South Carolina.

I remember a South Carolina that was too poor to paint and too proud to whitewash.

And the more fiercely the current national debate rages about the appropriate role of the federal government and its various programs, the more clearly I remember a South Carolina before there was such a role, when states' rights ruled and enterprise was free to do as it pleased.

I remember when the destitute aged were sheltered not in the bosom of a warm and loving family but in county poor farms. Then Social Security came and tore those poor houses down, freeing young and old alike of that specter.

When I note the now flourishing institutions of higher learning spread across this state, I remember when some fine little colleges were one jump ahead of the sheriff, were hard-pressed to put meals on their student tables, and couldn't meet their payrolls. They were rescued and made solvent by the National Youth Administration, wartime training programs, and the GI Bill of Rights.

When I see now the clear waters of our rivers, I remember when the Broad, the Wateree, the Bush, and the Saluda ran brick-red from the erosion of farms and deforested uplands. The Soil Conservation Service and the millions of trees planted by the thirty or so CCC camps that were placed in South Carolina had something to do with the improvement. Free enterprises such as the paper and forest products industries shared abundantly in the benefits of those government initiatives.

I remember when kerosene lit the farms of this land until the REA electrified and humanized them, bridging the cultural gap between town and country—and incidentally creating new markets for the appliance industry.

When I hear complaints about affirmative action, I remember some mean things that used to happen in this land, in the treatment of people by people. While we still have a way to go, does anyone really think we would have approached our present level of equity and civility without the intervention of the federal government? I have met no South Carolinian who has expressed to me any desire to return to the old days of racial cruelty and exclusion.

I did not come here today to organize but to philosophize. Yet, when I hear it said that southern working people have some cultural aversion to the exercise of the right of freedom of association, I cannot help but remember the old days when cotton mills sometimes bristled with

National Guard bayonets and machine guns to enforce that alleged aversion. Still today the question returns to my mind: if southern workers don't want their own unions, why have states and corporations found it so expedient to collaborate in forging measures to thwart the effective pursuit of that aspiration?

Lest it be thought that these reflections are just another expression of outmoded "liberal" balderdash, let me point out that such stout conservatives as James Byrnes, Olin Johnston, and Burnet Maybank were among the authors of the larger federal role that helped bring this state into the modern age.

I do not counsel worship at the altar of government for its own sake, for I share fully the wholesome antipathy to government—federal, state, or local—unrestrained by strong free and private institutions, for one of which I speak.

I do suggest that the citizens of a modern republic should not go too far in support of those who would dismantle or ruin the benign capacity of their government, for they may need it badly some day. When it happens to you, you'll know it's true.

As for those terms "liberal" and "conservative," as one who has been afflicted by both labels, depending on the stance of the afflictor and the foreign or domestic nature of the issue, I doubt their utility in this day and age for anyone except slapdash journalists.

Real meaning has surely been drained from a term when the clammy hand of fashion appears in the form of a hyphen preceded by "neo," as in "neo-conservative" and "neo-liberal." In all areas of human discourse, "neo hyphen" is a sure sign of something that is not long for this world.

If, as has been said, a modern "liberal" is someone who believes that his country's adversaries are probably right, I strongly reject that label.

And what is the objective meaning of the word "conservative," when its leadership has brought us a $200 billion annual deficit, put forward a measure that will mindlessly gut our defense forces year after year, and now, in the wake of Geneva, escorts clamoring hordes of businessmen east in pursuit of Moscow gold, exposing to that "evil empire" the soft underbelly of freedom, the stateless avarice of capital?

Hear now the words of Shakespeare, in *Henry IV*, on this matter: "From the Orient to the drooping West . . . stuffing the ears of men with false reports. I speak of peace, while covert enmity, under the smile of safety, wounds the world."

Today's graduates ought not waste too much time worrying about which category they ought to fit. There may be a few pure liberals and pure conservatives about who march in lockstep, but I don't really know any, present parties included.

The great rank and file of the American people are liberal about some things and conservative about others, and the shifting distribution of such impulses depends largely upon circumstances and interest.

That is the way it should be, because there really are things one ought to be conservative about and things one ought to be liberal about, and they do change.

I owe to Sidney Hook a thought that I offer as my final conclusion from all this. From him I learned the difference between a truth and a deep truth. A deep truth is a truth the converse of which is equally true.

For example, it is true, as Santayana said, that those who cannot remember the past are doomed to repeat it.

Yet it is equally true that those who do remember the past may not know when it is over.

That is a deep truth.

Thank you, and good luck to you all. ■

Professor Jacob Neusner Defines the Social Contract between Teacher and Student

"OUR theory of teaching is to tell students, 'Don't ask, discover!' . . . Learning takes place . . . when you find out for yourself."

JACOB NEUSNER is the most provocative and prolific scholar in the world of Judaic studies. While a professor at Brown University, a fellow of the Institute for Advanced Studies at Princeton, and a research professor at the University of South Florida in Tampa, he has written 240 learned books, including *Canon and Connection: Intertextuality in Judaism,* a popular work, *How to Grade Your Professors,* and one best-seller with Reverend Andrew Greeley, *The Bible and Us: A Priest and a Rabbi Read Scripture Together.*

Few scholars relish controversy; however, Neusner's views on the Talmud, on government support of the arts and humanities, and on the dynamics of academic life keep him in hot water, which he never avoids. The following speech, delivered at Elizabethtown College, in Pennsylvania, on September 25, 1991, is not a commencement speech but a convocation—an address to incoming rather than departing students. It uses internal interrogation ("What should you ask of your professors? . . . What should your professors ask of you?") to hold interest, and he gives specific advice to teachers and students about the real purpose of education: teaching people to teach themselves.

□   □   □

The beginning of the school year challenges us to ask tough questions: What do I expect in the next ten months or so? For you don't have to be here, and it's costing plenty of money for you to stay here. Not only so, but a college like Elizabethtown takes teaching seriously and is not an expensive baby-sitting operation. Your families have sent you here, and your college and its professors have received you here, because they, and you, must agree it is the most important thing you can do with your life this year. You should therefore ask why. Given all of the many things you can do with your time and money, why should you turn your back on everything else in the world and spend the next ten months here, in these classrooms and laboratories and library, and with these professors? Only if the answer is, because there is nothing more important, should you stay here. And why should that be so? Because you're going to learn things here that matter and that you cannot learn in any other place or circumstance. What that means has nothing to do with acquiring information; you can learn more from an encyclopedia than you can from me or any other professor. What it means is that you're going to learn in a way in which you can only learn here and nowhere else: that is the social contract of the college classroom; it is what we promise you, and what you must demand of us.

Since everybody knows we learn all the time and everywhere, that is a considerable claim in behalf of Elizabethtown College, or University of South Florida, where I teach, or any of the other thousands of colleges and universities in this country, public and private, religious and secular, famous and homely, where, this morning, a year of studies starts. Why do I think you've made the right decision to come here: why is this the most important thing you can do with your life this year, this month, this minute? The answer is, because here, if your teachers teach and if you learn, you will learn a new way of learning, one that will guide you for all time to come. That's the one point I want to leave with you: demand of your teachers and yourself not merely information but a way of learning that you can use every day for the rest of your life. It is what we professors promise, and sometimes even deliver: the secret of how to learn by discovering things on your own—learn not by asking but by finding out on your own.

It is the particularly American way of learning, which is, by discovering things for yourself. We American professors at our best aim at teaching by helping students learn on their own. Our theory of teaching is to tell students, "Don't ask, discover!" The more we tell you, the less you learn. The more you learn, the more we teach. And learning takes place, in a country as practical and as rich in innovation as this country, when you find out for yourself. Professors are there to guide, to help, to goad, to irritate, to stimulate. Students are there to explore, to inquire, to ask questions, to experiment, to negotiate knowledge. The ideal teachers for our students therefore are people like Socrates, Jesus, and Hillel, and what you have to ask of your professors here at Elizabethtown is that they measure themselves by the model of Socrates, Jesus, and Hillel. . . .

Great teachers don't teach. They help students learn. Students teach themselves. Three of the all-time greats—Socrates, Jesus, and his Jewish contemporary the sage Hillel—share a dislike of heavyweight speeches. They spoke briefly, painting pictures and telling tales ("parables"), and always raised more questions than they settled.

Socrates was the greatest philosopher of all time, and all he did was walk around the streets and ask people irritating questions. Jesus was certainly the most influential teacher in history, and his longest "lecture"—for instance, the Sermon on the Mount—cannot have filled up an hour of classroom time or a page in a notebook. And Hillel's greatest lesson, in answer to someone who told him to teach the entire Torah while standing on one foot—"What is hateful to yourself, don't do to someone else. That's the whole Torah, all the rest is commentary. Now go study"—directed people to go off and learn on their own.

The great teacher makes a few simple points. The powerful teacher leaves one or two fundamental truths. And the memorable teacher makes the point not by telling but by helping the students discover on their own. Learning takes place through discovery, not when you're told something but when you figure it out for yourself. All a really fine teacher does is make suggestions, point out problems, above all, ask questions, and more questions, and more questions. . . .

Our teaching encourages not only discovery but initiative. Good teaching in our schools leads to risk-taking; good teaching in theirs [the Germans'], to note-taking. Successful professors in our system present learning as answers to important questions; successful professors in their system go over familiar facts and pass their opinion on this and that. They tell people things. We want people to make their own discoveries. . . .

All Socrates did was ask questions; he never really gave any answers, nothing you could memorize and say back on an exam. And, with all due respect, Jesus did not dictate long lectures, so the students could carry home thick notebooks. And Hillel would have lasted about a minute and a half—"Now, go study"—indeed! Our kids would have given Socrates a good time, and I think they would have patience for a teacher who just told them stories, like Jesus, or who advised them that everything he could teach he could tell them by standing on one foot, like Hillel. Now, there's real teaching: taking the risk of telling people what you really think, and why you think it, and what difference it makes.

In this country, with its tradition of pragmatism and experiment, we aim at helping students teach themselves, asking them questions to stimulate their own inquiry. We do not indoctrinate; we stimulate. We do not just tell people things; we try to make knowledge important because knowing helps answer urgent questions. The best classes state the problem, for students to find the answer.

It's no accident that in America, many of us teachers demand of our students, "Don't ask, discover!" We have an educational tradition that serves the needs of a society in process, a nation never fully finished, a country in quest, a people of peoples in perpetual search. That is why entire fields of learning are founded here—social science as we know it now, for instance. That explains why new ideas, new sciences, find in this country a ready hearing, a warm welcome.

True, we pay a price for this intellectual restlessness of ours: our kids are better at process than at proposition. They seem to know less; when they need to know, they go and learn. So they spend more time in the laboratory, work harder at writing their own thoughts, do research on their own. But then they spend less time learning what we know, work less hard at fully understanding other people's thoughts, sometimes do research aimed at reinventing the wheel. We've made our choices. For an open society, an always changing economy, a responsible politics of participation and endless negotiation, we need an alert, inventive citizen.

What should you ask of your professors? (1) Don't tell me things; let me find out for myself. (2) But when I need help, give it to me. (3) And when my work is poor, don't tell me it's good. Many professors would rather be liked than be understood; not a few find it easier to indulge the students than teach them. Don't accept from professors compliments when they owe you criticism. And love them when they're tough. Proverbs says, "Rebuke a wise person, and you'll be loved, rebuke a fool and you'll be hated." Show yourselves wise, and you'll get professors who care about what you know.

What should your professors ask of you? (1) Don't ask me to sell you my subject; let me explain it to you. Once you're in the classroom, relevance is a settled question: this is what you want to know; now let me teach it. (2) Don't stop work in the middle of the semester. It's *easy* to start with enthusiasm, and it's *easy* to end with commitment. But in the middle of a course, it's hard to sustain your work; the beginning is out of sight, the end and goal and purpose of the course not yet on the horizon. Do your best when the weather looks bleak. (3) Don't sit back and wait to be told things; *stay* with me and allow the logic of the course to guide us both; join me, think with me. The most remarkable student I've ever taught was a late-middle-aged woman who audited a course of mine at University of South Florida in Sarasota; after five minutes in each class session of three hours, she would say, "Oh, is this what you mean?" And she would proceed to lay out for me the entire argument that I was beginning to develop. Yes, a remarkable student, but I never walked into class without fearing that I would run out of things to tell people in the first ten minutes. You owe your teachers that moment of trepidation: make them afraid they'll run out of things to tell you. They won't, of course, but you'll make them work and give them life. The challenge is not in disagreeing or agreeing but in understanding: uncovering the logic and accepting its dictates. That you owe your teachers.

Your imagination is our richest national resource; an open and active mind, our most precious intangible treasure. That's what we try to do at our universities and colleges in this country: teach people to teach themselves, which is what life is all about—during the coming year, and during all the years of your lives and mine. ■

General Colin Powell Urges African-American Students to Reject Racial Hatred

"AFRICAN-AMERICANS *have come too far and we have too far yet to go to take a detour into the swamp of hatred. We, as a people who have suffered so much from the hatred of others, must not now show tolerance for any movement or philosophy that has at its core the hatred of Jews or anyone else.*"

COLIN POWELL' S SPEAKING was done mainly in the spacious rooms along the corridors of Pentagon power. As aide to Reagan Secretary of Defense Caspar Weinberger, and later as National Security Advisor to President George H. W. Bush, the softspoken Powell—son of a Harlem merchant who ultimately rose to the highest rank ever held by an African-

American in the United States armed forces—was a superb military briefer: succinct, confident, prepared to be interrupted with penetrating questions.

That experience served him well in a more public role as chairman of the Joint Chiefs of Staff during the Persian Gulf War. His appearances before the press played to his rhetorical strength: factual, decisive, confident, but good-humored and never overbearing, in contrast to the bombastic, domineering briefings of General Norman Schwarzkopf.

For a whirlwind few months in the fall of 1995, Powell—who had turned down an offer from President Clinton to become secretary of state—became the media favorite for the Republican nomination for president. His television interviews, culminating with his surprise declination at a world-watched press conference, showed a fine combination of pride and humility as he fielded questions with agility and a command presence.

His "set" speech—essentially autobiographical, anecdotal, patriotic, and noncontroversial, in the Eisenhower tradition—drew high lecture fees and leaned heavily on platitudes. But before he hit the lecture trail, in this short commencement speech made on May 14, 1994, to the mostly black student body at Howard University in Washington, D. C., Powell stepped into a tense situation: Three weeks before, anti-Semitism had appeared on the campus of the 126-year-old institution in the person of Khalid Abdul Muhammed, a former top aide to Minister Louis Farrakhan. A rally audience of fifteen hundred, including few Howard students, cheered the attack on the sins of whites, particularly Jews; this subsequently roiled the academic atmosphere with controversy about who should be allowed to speak about what. The university president resigned in the wake of the furor.

In his commencement address, the calming Powell juxtaposed the recent examples of peacemaking by Nelson Mandela and Yitzhak Rabin, a black and a Jew. As the most successful American black, Powell's unequivocal words—from "We must find nothing to stand up and cheer about or applaud in a message of racial or ethnic hatred" to the evocation of Lincoln in "the last best hope of Earth"—carried great weight with the graduates. Though Powell supported the use of campus facilities for what was essentially "hate speech," his disapproval of its content positioned him apart from the separatist message gaining strength in the black community of Minister Farrakhan, culminating the following year in his "Million Man March." General Powell found reason not to attend.

□ □ □

The real challenge in being a commencement speaker is figuring out how long to speak.

The graduating students want a short speech, five to six minutes and let's get it over. They are not going to remember who their commencement speaker was anyway. P-O-W-E-L-L.

Parents are another matter. Arrayed in all their finery they have waited a long time for this day, some not sure it would ever come, and they want it to last. So go on and talk for two or three hours. We brought our lunch and want our money's worth.

The faculty member who suggested the speaker hopes the speech will be long enough to be respectable, but not so long that he has to take leave for a few weeks beginning Monday.

So the poor speaker is left figuring out what to do. My simple rule is to respond to audience reaction. If you are appreciative and applaud a lot early on, you get a nice, short speech. If you make me work for it, we're liable to be here a long time.

You know, the controversy over Howard's speaking policy has its positive side. It has caused the university to go through a process of self-examination, which is always a healthy thing to do.

Since many people have been giving advice about how to handle this matter, I thought I might as well too.

First, I believe with all my heart that Howard must continue to serve as an institute of learning excellence where freedom of speech is strongly encouraged and rigorously protected.

That is at the very essence of a great university and Howard is a great university.

And freedom of speech means permitting the widest range of views to be present for debate, however controversial those views may be.

The First Amendment right of free speech is intended to protect the controversial and even outrageous word, and not just comforting platitudes, too mundane to need protection.

Some say that by hosting controversial speakers who shock our sensibilities, Howard is in some way promoting or endorsing their message. Not at all. Howard has helped put their message in perspective while protecting their right to be heard. So that the message can be exposed to the full light of day.

I have every confidence in the ability of the administration, the faculty and the students of Howard to determine who should speak on this campus. No outside help needed, thank you.

I also have complete confidence in the students of Howard to make informed, educated judgments about what they hear.

But for this freedom to hear all views, you bear a burden to sort out wisdom from foolishness.

There is great wisdom in the message of self-reliance, of education, of hard work, and of the need to raise strong families.

There is utter foolishness, evil, and danger in the message of hatred, or of condoning violence, however cleverly the message is packaged or entertainingly it is presented.

We must find nothing to stand up and cheer about or applaud in a message of racial or ethnic hatred.

I was at the inauguration of President Mandela in South Africa earlier this week. You were there too by television and watched that remarkable event.

Together, we saw what can happen when people stop hating and begin reconciling.

DeKlerk the jailer became DeKlerk the liberator, and Mandela the prisoner became Mandela the president.

Twenty-seven years of imprisonment did not embitter Nelson Mandela. He invited his three jail keepers to the ceremony.

He used his liberation to work his former tormentors to create a new South Africa and to eliminate the curse of apartheid from the face of the earth. What a glorious example! What a glorious day it was!

Last week you also saw Prime Minister Rabin and PLO Chairman Arafat sign another agreement on their still difficult, long road to peace, trying to end hundreds of years of hatred and two generations of violence. Palestinian authorities have now begun entering Gaza and Jericho.

In these two historic events, intractable enemies of the past have shown how you can join hands to create a force of moral authority more powerful than any army and which can change the world.

Although there are still places of darkness in the world where the light of reconciliation has not penetrated, these two beacons of hope show what can be done when men and women of goodwill work together for peace and for progress.

There is a message in these two historic events for us assembled here today. As the world goes forward, we cannot start going backward.

African-Americans have come too far and we have too far yet to go to take a detour into the swamp of hatred.

We, as a people who have suffered so much from the hatred of others, must not now show tolerance for any movement or philosophy that has at its core the hatred of Jews or anyone else.

Our future lies in the philosophy of love and understanding and caring and building. Not of hatred and tearing down.

We know that. We must stand up for it and speak up for it!

We must not be silent if we would live up to the legacy of those who have gone before us from this campus.

I have no doubt that this controversy will pass and Howard University will emerge even stronger, even more than ever a symbol of hope, of promise, and of excellence.

That is Howard's destiny!

Ambassador Annenberg, one of your honorees today, is a dear friend of mine and is one of America's leading businessmen and greatest philanthropists.

You have heard of his recent contribution to American education and his generous gift to Howard.

A few years ago I told Mr. Annenberg about a project I was involved in to build a memorial to the Buffalo Soldiers, those brave black cavalrymen of the West whose valor had long gone unrecognized.

Ambassador Annenberg responded immediately, and with his help the memorial now stands proudly at Fort Leavenworth, Kansas.

The Buffalo Soldiers were formed in 1867, at the same time as Howard University. It is even said that your mascot, the bison, came from the bison, or buffalo, soldiers.

Both Howard and the Buffalo Soldiers owe their early success to the dedication and faith of white military officers who served in the Civil War.

In Howard's case, of course, it was your namesake, Major General Oliver Howard.

For the 10th Cavalry Buffalo Soldiers, it was Colonel Benjamin Grierson who formed and commanded that regiment for almost twenty-five years. And he fought that entire time to achieve equal status for his black comrades.

Together, Howard University and the Buffalo Soldiers showed what black Americans were capable of when given the education and opportunity; and when shown respect and when accorded dignity.

I am a direct descendant of those Buffalo Soldiers, of the Tuskegee Airmen, and of the navy's Golden Thirteen, and Montfort Point Marines, and all the black men and women who served this nation in uniform for over three hundred years.

All of whom served in their time and in their way and with whatever opportunity existed then to break down the walls of discrimination and racism to make the path easier for those of us who came after them.

I climbed on their backs and stood on their shoulders to reach the top of my chosen profession to become chairman of the American Joint Chiefs of Staff.

I will never forget my debt to them and to the many white "Colonel Griersons" and "General Howards" who helped me over the thirty-five years of my life as a soldier.

They would say to me now, "Well done. And now let others climb up on your shoulders."

Howard's Buffalo Soldiers did the same thing, and on their shoulders now stand governors and mayors and congressmen and generals and doctors and artists and writers and teachers and leaders in every segment of American society.

And they did it for the class of 1994. So that you can now continue climbing to reach the top of the mountain, while reaching down and back to help those less fortunate.

You face "Great Expectations." Much has been given to you and much is expected from you.

You have been given a quality education, presented by a distinguished faculty who sit here today in pride of you.

You have inquiring minds and strong bodies given to you by God and by your parents, who sit behind you and pass on to you today their still unrealized dreams and ambitions.

You have been given citizenship in a country like none other on earth, with opportunities available to you like nowhere else on earth, beyond anything available to me when I sat in a place similar to this thirty-six years ago.

What will be asked of you is hard work. Nothing will be handed to you. You are entering a life of continuous study and struggle to achieve your goals.

A life of searching to find that which you do well and love doing. Never stop seeking.

I want you to have faith in yourselves. I want you to believe to the depth of your soul that you can accomplish any task that you set your mind and energy to.

I want you to be proud of your heritage. Study your origins. Teach your children racial pride and draw strength and inspiration from the cultures of our forebears.

Not as a way of drawing back from American society and its European roots.

But as a way of showing that there are other roots as well. African and Caribbean roots that are also a source of nourishment for the American family tree.

To show that African-Americans are more than a product of our slave experience.

To show that our varied backgrounds are as rich as that of any other American not better or greater, but every bit as equal.

Our black heritage must be a foundation stone we can build on, not a place to withdraw into.

I want you to fight racism. But remember, as Dr. King and Dr. Mandela have taught us, racism is a disease of the racist. Never let it become yours. White South Africans were cured of the outward symptoms of the disease by President Mandela's inauguration, just as surely as black South Africans were liberated from apartheid.

Racism is a disease you can help cure by standing up for your rights and by your commitment to excellence and to performance.

By being ready to take advantage of your rights and the opportunities that will come from those rights.

Never let the dying hand of racism rest on your shoulder, weighing you down. Let racism always be someone else's burden to carry.

As you seek your way in the world, never fail to find a way to serve your community. Use your education and your success in life to help those still trapped in cycles of poverty and violence.

Above all, never lose faith in America. Its faults are yours to fix, not to curse.

America is a family. There may be differences and disputes in the family, but we must not allow the family to be broken into warring factions.

From the diversity of our people, let us draw strength and not cause weakness.

Believe in America with all your heart and soul and mind. It remains the "last best hope of Earth."

You are its inheritors and its future is today placed in your hands.

Go forth from this place today inspired by those who went before you. Go forth with the love of your families and the blessings of your teachers.

Go forth to make this a better country and society. Prosper, raise strong families, remembering that all you will leave behind is your good works and your children.

Go forth with my humble congratulations.

And let your dreams be your only limitations. Now and forever.

Thank you and God bless you.

Have a great life! ■

Brain-Science Philanthropist David J. Mahoney Envisions Active Lives Lived to One Hundred Years

"MEDICAL science will give most of you the body to blow out a hundred candles on your birthday cake, and the brain scientists will give you the life of your mind. . . . Unlike most of today's centenarians, you will be able to remember and use what you've learned in your century. . . . It's up to you to make sure you have a varied life that's worth remembering."

AFTER A BUSINESS CAREER that took him from the mailroom of an ad agency to the head of a billion-dollar corporation (Canada Dry, Hunt Foods, McCall's), Bronx-born David J. Mahoney took on a greater challenge as a philanthropist: making the public aware of the potential of neuroscience, and marshaling public and private research support for breakthroughs in the treatment of brain diseases and the improvement of processes like memory.

As head of the Charles A. Dana Foundation, Mahoney organized many of the world's leading brain scientists into an alliance that set specific goals for the developments of new drugs and genetic discoveries for Alzheimer's, Parkinson's, Huntington's and Lou Gehrig's diseases; to new treatments for the management of pain, manic depression, and rehabilitation after stroke; to ways to preserve memory in the aging brain.

In a speech to the graduating class at New Jersey's Rutgers University on May 16, 1996, the philanthropist that Nobel Prize–winner James Watson called "the Mary Lord of our generation" brought the esoteric down to earth: How should people in their early twenties deal with a life that could well be one-fourth longer than that of their parents?

He put forward a "centenarian strategy." The speech is organized into two parts: First, here's a "problem" you didn't realize you have, and then, here are five specific ways to deal with it. The style is crisp and businesslike, but the theme is stunningly visionary: "the challenge of a life with an active fourth quarter."

David Mahoney died in 2000 at the age of 76, as did his son at the age of 40. His grandson, now a teenager, has, in Mahoney's optimistic projection, "more than a good chance to break a hundred."

□   □   □

This speech is going to make you roll your eyes and smile. You're going to wonder—what kind of super-optimist did they get to make this year's commencement address? Okay, here comes a challenge you didn't know you had: Each one of you is going to have to start planning now to live to be one hundred.

No, I'm not planning to live to a hundred myself. Nor is my son, David Jr.—he'll consider himself lucky to get to ninety. But his son, now age six, at the tag end of your generation, has more than a good chance to break a hundred. And so do all of you in the class of '96.

I'm not alone in making this prediction. A strange thing happened on Air Force One recently: The president of the United States sat on the floor of the aircraft, up against a bulkhead, and spoke to the traveling press pool for three hours. Not a word was on the record. The rules were "psychological background"—that meant the press could report what President Clinton was thinking, but could not say he was the one who told them. They could attribute his ruminations only to a mysterious source called "the highest authority."

Some of us read that pool report with care because we like to know what's going on in the head of the man who runs the country. And sure enough, there was a line in it that was, to me, a stunner. Quote: "He feels biology will be to the twenty-first century what physics was to the twentieth century. He believes people might routinely live beyond one hundred years."

That comes to us from "the highest authority"—not God, but from the CEO of the world's only superpower, who has access to the best scientific minds in the country. And he was not talking about one person in a thousand living to be a hundred, as happens today; he believes that people will "routinely" make it all the way to triple digits. Of course, the reporters were more interested in politics and scandal, and nobody followed up on the most intriguing notion of the day: an extra-long generation tacked on to the average human's life.

Of course, the actuaries at the insurance companies look back, not forward, to report past life expectancy. Based on past history, the tables say all of you here can expect to live to only seventy-seven years and nine months. Don't knock it—that's a 10 percent longer life than Americans born fifty years ago, and it beats the biblical "three score and ten." But the actuaries are careful to say they're only historians, and they're not making forecasts.

So don't be fooled by an "expectancy" age that presumes we won't get a cure for cancer—which we will. Don't accept a presumption that organ transplants won't become everyday operations, which they will. And then factor in the medical breakthroughs stemming from the Human Genome Project, which is going to use genetics to cure hereditary diseases and bring down the death rate. And if we were able, in these past fifty years, to triumph over the microbe with antibiotics, isn't it logical to assume that in the coming generations we will be able to conquer viruses? Taken together, the medical advances in your lifetime are near certain to add a generation to your life. You will play in a whole new fourth quarter.

Let me tell you what opened my mind to these possibilities. I am chairman of the Charles A. Dana Foundation, which supports research in brain science. Five years ago, I put a challenge to a group of the brainiest neuroscientists in the world, many of them Nobel laureates, including James Watson, the codiscoverer of DNA. I said: "Name ten brain problems you can solve in the coming decade if you get the proper support." At first they were reluctant to go out on a limb, but they realized how important it was to offer realistic hope in order to get research support. They signed on to ten challenges—just ten—that together can beat dozens of neurological diseases in this decade.

We're halfway through this decade—how are we doing? Well, the latest Dana Alliance progress report shows that we have found the gene for Lou Gehrig's disease and the first drug for it is coming out this year. We've got not one but four genes involved in Alzheimer's disease and twenty-two new drugs for it are in trials. We have the first really good medication for schizophrenia and more in the pipeline, and just this year the FDA approved the first emergency drug that can protect against disability if someone having a stroke receives it quickly.

Next on the list: treatments that will block the action of cocaine. Brain tissue transplants—and not with human fetuses, either—that will cure Parkinson's disease. At least one and probably more genes that cause manic-depressive illness. And the first drugs that can induce injured spinal cord cells to reconnect—so that people will have a better shot at recovering movement. These aren't my predictions; they are the estimates of the best minds in the field, who have a track record of delivering the cures they talk about.

That's why I agree with "the highest authority" in Air Force One about your generation living to a hundred. Get your minds around that: Most of you, now in your early twenties, might well have the chance to be centenarians. What does that mean to you right now?

You think of centenarians as toothless old geezers doddering around if they're lucky, confined to wheelchairs if they're not. You think of the line of George Burns when he reached one hundred: "At my age, you don't buy green bananas." Or you're thinking of the gag about Senator Strom Thurmond—that when he willed his body parts to a hospital, the doctors saw a list of parts that they weren't even using anymore.

You think of extreme old age—if you think of it at all—as a time of being a liability to society and a burden to the family. Of falling apart physically and losing your marbles mentally. Of making no contribution. And—worst of all—of having no fun. As Ira Gershwin wrote in *Porgy and Bess:* "Methusaleh lived nine hundred years. But who calls that livin', when no gal will give in, to no one who's nine hundred years."

But what if brain scientists are able to keep pace with the scientists of the body? Let's assume that immunologists will be able to prevent or cure everything from cancer to AIDS, and organ transplants and blood-work and genetic engineering will cope with most other ailments and diseases. Without an active brain—without a working memory and the ability to learn—"who calls *that* livin'"?

I'm here to tell you that neuroscience is keeping pace with, even setting the pace for, all other medical disciplines. This year, as you can learn from our heavily hit Web site on the Internet, we're expanding the Dana Alliance for Brain Initiatives on a global scale. Here's our guarantee: as body scientists keep you alive to a hundred, brain scientists will keep your life worth living.

What do you do with this information? I submit that you throw out all previous notions of one career followed by a lazy retirement. That was the strategy of your grandfathers and it's strictly wheelchair thinking. You need a new strategy for a lifetime of alertness that lasts a whole century.

The Centenarian Strategy delivers a swift kick in the head to the current idea of hitting the ground running, working your youth into a frazzle, taking every better offer as it comes, making a pile as early as you can and then coasting on that momentum until your last downsizing company forces you into retirement.

The Centenarian Strategy also runs counter to the planning of idealistic young people who look to a life of public service, of social work or environmental action, setting aside money for psychic income and expecting the government to care for them in old age.

Keeping that active fourth quarter in view—remembering that brain scientists have already found that you are much less likely to vegetate if you stay active and keep exercising your mind as well as your body—then here are the five fundamentals of the Centenarian Strategy:

1. Diversify your career from the very beginning.

Stop thinking of jobs in series, one after the other; instead, think of careers in parallel. That means planning your vocation along with your avocation, and keep them as separate as possible. If you want to go into business, plan an avocation of music or art; if you are inclined toward the law or the media, diversify into education or landscaping. If you want to be a poet, think about politics on the side, and study it seriously.

Don't confuse an avocation with recreation. Watching basketball on television, or surfing the Internet for the latest interactive game, can be a lively part of life, but it's not a creative avocation. And don't confuse a serious avocation with a hobby; do-it-yourselfing is fun, and so are clay modeling, and gardening and fiddling with old cars. Hobbies are ways to relax and to make friends, and everybody should have some; but a real avocation is a subtext to a career, and a part of your working week to pursue with a certain dedication. Why? Not only because it gives balance to your second quarter, but because it positions you for the time that will come, in the third or fourth quarter, to switch gears. And then switch them again—you'll have the time, and public policy will change to give you incentives to keep working or avocating.

The point is to not be singleminded about career. Be double-minded, or triple-minded; keep a pot or two on your back burners.

2. Take advantage of your opportunity to wind up a millionaire.

Financial independence will take a lot of pressure off that fourth quarter and make it something to look forward to. The Age of Entitlement is coming to an end. The baby boomers who count only on Social Security and Medicare will be disappointed. You in the post-boomer generation should not rely on society's safety net and think more about your own personal nest egg.

The trick is to use the new tools the government is giving you to save, to avoid taxes in your IRAs and 401(k) accounts, and to invest in broad index funds that are sure to grow. To the centenarian, credit-card living is out, leveraged saving is in. Use your tax leverage to make your savings grow exponentially. In this savings race, the tortoise beats the hare; by taking full advantage of the plans out there now, and more sure to come in the next decade, you need not be a rocket scientist to become a millionaire—in real terms—by your fourth quarter. Especially if you're part of a two-income family. About that family—

3. *Invest in your family dimension.*

As life gets longer, young people are getting married later. Fine; that deliberation about a big choice should ultimately reverse the divorce rate. But make a commitment early in your second quarter; the smartest thing you can do in diversifying your life is to stop playing the field.

The wave of the future, in the Centenarian Strategy, is to frame your life in traditional family settings. Do your market research in singlehood, choose for the long term and then commit to marriage; have kids; avoid divorce; raise your likelihood of having grandchildren. Following this course, you can expect at least a couple of great-grandchildren to enjoy, to work with, and to help as you approach the century mark. If you plan properly now to protect your wallet and your intellect, you can be a family asset, not a liability, later; and your family, with all the headaches, will enrich your life.

4. *Pace yourself; it's a small world and a long life.*

The centenarian thinks about success differently, with a longer view. He or she measures success in getting to personal satisfaction, which does not always mean getting to the top of the heap. Making money is important, never derogate building an estate that you and your progeny can use. But developing long-term loyalties in all the strands of your career and avocation and hobbies and recreation pays off in that satisfaction. Those loyalties also make life easier later; you can get things done across the different strands, helping someone in your avocation who has helped you in your career.

Ask yourself along the way: Whose approval is important to you? Whose is not? The centenarians do not stop to smell the flowers; they carry the flowers along.

5. *Plan for at least one thoroughgoing discombobulation in your life.*

This can be a good shock, like meeting someone amazing, or developing a talent you never knew you had, or finding an opportunity that takes your career or avocation in a wholly new direction. Or you can find yourself, after years of success and loyal service, out on your ear in a merger or a downsizing or a hostile takeover.

It happened to me. I was running a multibillion-dollar conglomerate, doing just fine, but when I tried to take it private, somebody beat me to the punch. I wound up with a big bunch of money, which meant I got no sympathy from my friends, but I was out of a job. No airplane, no executive support system, no daily calendar full of appointments with big shots—no place to go in the morning.

Did I let it bother me? You bet I did. I plunged into the deepest blue funk imaginable. But luckily—and this was not part of any life strategy—

I had an avocation to turn to. It was a philanthropy, the Dana Foundation, and it had long been leading me into supporting the field of brain science. So I threw myself into that, applying what I had learned in marketing and finance to a field that needed an outsider with those credentials. And for the past ten years, I've gotten more sheer satisfaction out of marshaling the force of public opinion behind research into imaging, memory and conquering depression than anything I ever did as a boy wonder or a boardroom biggie.

But it would not have happened if I did not have that anchor to windward—the other, wholly unrelated activity to turn to. Success, or a resounding setback, in one career can lead to success, of another kind, in the parallel career.

That, in a nutshell, is how to cope with a challenge no graduating class has ever had—the challenge of a life with an active fourth quarter. Medical science will give most of you the body to blow out a hundred candles on your birthday cake, and the brain scientists will give you the life of your mind. That active memory will be their gift to you.

Unlike most of today's centenarians, you will be able to remember and use what you've learned in your century. You will be able, in the poet's words, to enjoy "the last of life, for which the first was made." It's up to you to make sure you have a varied life that's worth remembering.

Good luck. Happy commencement. And a happy hundredth birthday.

■ ■ ■

XIV

UNDELIVERED SPEECHES

President John F. Kennedy's Prepared Remarks at Dallas on November 22, 1963

"WE in this country, in this generation, are—by destiny rather than choice—the watchmen on the walls of world freedom."

KENNEDY'S VISIT TO DALLAS—a Texas city whose vote he lost in his 1960 election victory—was in the nature of a precampaign swing designed to mend fences. He planned, after his Dallas motorcade, to deliver a speech at the Trade Mart in which he would begin to sketch part of his vision for a second term.

The planned address was vintage Kennedy: high-minded, eloquent, but not without a jab at his presumed opponent in 1964, Senator Barry Goldwater. Without naming the Arizona senator, and using the alliteration of "words"/"weapons," "vituperation"/"victory," Kennedy's prepared address derided "voices preaching doctrines wholly unrelated to reality . . . which apparently assume that words will suffice without weapons, that vituperation is as good as victory. . . ." After recalling the slogan of Democratic candidate Adlai Stevenson in 1952—"talk sense to the American people"—Kennedy, praised as a master of the use of words himself, seemed to remember that the victor in that election was the less eloquent Dwight Eisenhower, and proceeded to play down the power of political rhetoric. "Words alone are not enough. . . . If we are strong, our strength will speak for itself. If we are weak, words will be of no help."

The young president's speech went on to specify how speeches themselves were not the cause of the turning points in world affairs. "It was not the Monroe Doctrine that kept all Europe away from this hemisphere—it was the strength of the British fleet and the width of the Atlantic Ocean. It was not General Marshall's speech at Harvard"—where the Marshall Plan was first articulated—"which kept communism out of Western Europe—it was the strength and stability made possible by our military and economic assistance." He drove the point home by recalling his own action in the Cuban missile crisis, where "our successful defense of freedom was due not to the words we used, but to the strength we stood ready to use on behalf of the principles we stand ready to defend."

Paradoxically, in derogating the power of oratory he did not fail to choose his words with skill: note his balance of "use" and used," which overlapped "stood ready" and "stand ready" in that sentence. In the same way, he had just used "strength" twice as the fundaments of his bridge between the two sentences about Monroe and Marshall.

In his conclusion, after quoting Luke 2:14, "peace on earth, good will toward men," so often evoked on Christmas cards, he wanted to end on a much less familiar, right-makes-might note—that undergirding the need for strength that he had been stressing, as war in Vietnam loomed, must be the righteousness of America's cause. To do this, his script turned to a more admonitory verse in the book of Psalms, 127:1, "Except the Lord keep the city, the watchman waketh but in vain."

Kennedy did not leave the city of Dallas alive. His fine words about how fine words were not enough were never delivered.

□   □   □

I am honored to have this invitation to address the annual meeting of the Dallas Citizens Council, joined by the members of the Dallas Assembly—and pleased to have this opportunity to salute the Graduate Research Center of the Southwest. . . .

In a world of complex and continuing problems, in a world full of frustrations and irritations, America's leadership must be guided by the lights of learning and reason, or else those who confuse rhetoric with reality and the plausible with the possible will gain the popular ascendancy with their seemingly swift and simple solutions to every world problem.

There will always be dissident voices heard in the land, expressing opposition without alternatives, finding fault but never favor, perceiving gloom on every side and seeking influence without responsibility. Those voices are inevitable.

But today other voices are heard in the land—voices preaching doctrines wholly unrelated to reality, wholly unsuited to the sixties, doctrines which apparently assume that words will suffice without weapons, that vituperation is as good as victory and that peace is a sign of weakness. At a time when the national debt is steadily being reduced in terms of its burden on our economy, they see that debt as the greatest single threat to our security. At a time when we are steadily reducing the number of federal employees serving every thousand citizens, they fear those supposed hordes of civil servants far more than the actual hordes of opposing armies.

We cannot expect that everyone, to use the phrase of a decade ago, will "talk sense to the American people." But we can hope that fewer people will listen to nonsense. And the notion that this nation is headed for defeat through deficit, or that strength is but a matter of slogans, is nothing but just plain nonsense.

I want to discuss with you today the status of our strength and our security because this question clearly calls for the most responsible qualities of leadership and the most enlightened products of scholarship. For this nation's strength and security are not easily or cheaply obtained, nor are they quickly and simply explained. There are many kinds of strength and no one kind will suffice. Overwhelming nuclear strength cannot stop a guerrilla war. Formal pacts of alliance cannot stop internal subversion. Displays of material wealth cannot stop the disillusionment of diplomats subjected to discrimination.

Above all, words alone are not enough. The United States is a peaceful nation. And where our strength and determination are clear, our words need merely to convey conviction, not belligerence. If we are strong, our strength will speak for itself. If we are weak, words will be of no help.

I realize that this nation often tends to identify turning points in world affairs with the major addresses which preceded them. But it was not the Monroe Doctrine that kept all Europe away from this hemisphere—it was the strength of the British fleet and the width of the Atlantic Ocean. It was not General Marshall's speech at Harvard which kept communism out of Western Europe—it was the strength and stability made possible by our military and economic assistance.

In this administration also it has been necessary at times to issue specific warnings—warnings that we could not stand by and watch the Communists conquer Laos by force, or intervene in the Congo, or swallow West Berlin, or maintain offensive missiles on Cuba. But while our goals were at least temporarily obtained in these and other instances, our successful defense of freedom was due not to the words we used, but to the strength we stood ready to use on behalf of the principles we stand ready to defend. . . .

It should be clear by now that a nation can be no stronger abroad than she is at home. Only an America which practices what it preaches about equal rights and social justice will be respected by those whose choice affects our future. Only an America which has fully educated its citizens is fully capable of tackling the complex problems and perceiving the hidden dangers of the world in which we live. And only an America which is growing and prospering economically can sustain the worldwide defenses of freedom, while demonstrating to all concerned the opportunities of our system and society.

It is clear, therefore, that we are strengthening our security as well as our economy by our recent record increases in national income and output—by surging ahead of most of Western Europe in the rate of business expansion and the margin of corporate profits, by maintaining a more stable level of prices than almost any of our overseas competitors, and by cutting personal and corporate income taxes by some $11 billion, as I have proposed, to assure this nation of the longest and strongest expansion in our peacetime economic history.

This nation's total output—which three years ago was at the $500 billion mark—will soon pass $600 billion, for a record rise of over $100 billion in 3 years. For the first time in history we have 70 million men and women at work. For the first time in history average factory earnings have exceeded $100 a week. For the first time in history corporation profits after taxes—which have risen 43 percent in less than three years—have an annual level of $27.4 billion.

My friends and fellow citizens: I cite these facts and figures to make it clear that America today is stronger than ever before. Our adversaries have not abandoned their ambitions, our dangers have not diminished, our vigilance cannot be relaxed. But now we have the military, the scientific, and the economic strength to do whatever must be done for the preservation and promotion of freedom.

That strength will never be used in pursuit of aggressive ambitions—it will always be used in pursuit of peace. It will never be used to promote provocations—it will always be used to promote the peaceful settlement of disputes.

We in this country, in this generation, are—by destiny rather than choice—the watchmen on the walls of world freedom. We ask, therefore, that we may be worthy of our power and responsibility, that we may exercise our strength with wisdom and restraint, and that we may achieve in our time and for all time the ancient vision of "peace on earth, good will toward men." That must always be our goal, and the righteousness of our cause must always underlie our strength. For as was written long ago: "Except the Lord keep the city, the watchman waketh but in vain." ■

President Clinton Rejects a Contrite Speech Draft and Elects to "Move On"

DRAFT *speech submitted with apologetic tone: "What I did was wrong—and there is no excuse for it."*

SPEECH *as delivered with defiant tone: "It's nobody's business but ours. Even presidents have private lives."*

RARELY DO WE HAVE THE OPPORTUNITY to consider the choice of speeches before a president at a critical moment in his life.

On August 17, 1998, President Bill Clinton, under threat of subpoena, appeared before a federal grand jury impaneled by Independent Counsel Ken Starr to answer questions about whether he lied under oath during a deposition in a civil suit brought by Paula Corbin Jones charging sexual harassment. Though denying that he committed perjury, Clinton admitted having had an "inappropriate sexual relationship" with Monica Lewinsky, a White House intern.

Assuming that intense media interest would crack through grand jury secrecy, the president decided to make the admission himself directly to the U.S. public. Most political observers friendly to the president and some White House aides expected that short, nationally televised speech to be contrite; by frankly apologizing, they felt that he could rely on the forgiveness in the American psyche (and in enough members of the House of Representatives) to be able to leave the subject behind. A speech draft was submitted to pursue that ameliorating course.

But the president was profoundly angered by the unrelenting nature of the questioning before the grand jury. He did not merely edit the "soft" alternative; rather, on short notice, Mr. Clinton with some help from aides wrote an entirely different speech. Gone was the word "remorse." Though he did not flinch from characterizing his conduct as "wrong," he charged that the original Jones lawsuit was politically motivated and noted that the independent counsel's investigation was itself under investigation. Rather than demean himself by asking forgiveness, the president asked his viewers to "turn away from the spectacle of the past seven months." The undelivered contrite draft concluded with "God bless you, and good night"; the speech as given ended more formally: "Thank you for watching, and good night."

As some on his staff anticipated, the defiant speech was not well received. But the Clinton counterpunch had the advantage of coming straight from the shoulder; though it contributed to the House impeachment, it did not lead to a Senate conviction. From the speechwriting point of view, both addresses were crafted excellently, providing us with an example of different ways to deal with the same crisis.

□   □   □

Draft Speech (Undelivered)

My fellow Americans:
No one who is not in my position can understand the remorse I feel today. Since I was very young, I have had a profound reverence for this office I hold. I've been honored that you, the people, have entrusted it to me. I am proud of what we have accomplished together.

But in this case, I have fallen short of what you should expect from a president. I have failed my own religious faith and values. I have let too many people down. I take full responsibility for my actions—for hurting my wife and daughter, for hurting Monica Lewinsky and her family, for hurting friends and staff, and for hurting the country I love. None of this ever should have happened.

I never should have had any sexual contact with Monica Lewinsky, but I did. I should have acknowledged that I was wrong months ago, but I didn't. I thought I was shielding my family, but I know in the end, for Hillary and Chelsea, delay has only brought more pain. Their forgiveness and love, expressed so often as we sat alone together this weekend, means more than I can ever say.

What I did was wrong—and there is no excuse for it. I do want to assure you, as I told the grand jury under oath, that I did nothing to obstruct this investigation.

Finally, I also want to apologize to all of you, my fellow citizens. I hope you can find it in your heart to accept that apology. I pledge to you that I will make every effort of mind and spirit to earn your confidence again, to be worthy of this office, and to finish the work on which we have made such remarkable progress in the past six years.

God bless you, and good night.

August 17, 1998, speech as delivered

G ood evening.
This afternoon in this room, from this chair, I testified before the Office of Independent Counsel and the grand jury. I answered their questions truthfully, including questions about my private life—questions no American citizen would ever want to answer. Still, I must take complete responsibility for all my actions, both public and private. And that is why I am speaking to you tonight.

As you know, in a deposition in January, I was asked questions about my relationship with Monica Lewinsky. While my answers were legally accurate, I did not volunteer information. Indeed, I did have a relationship with Ms. Lewinsky that was not appropriate. In fact, it was wrong. It constituted a critical lapse in judgment and a personal failure on my part for which I am solely and completely responsible. But I told the grand jury today—and I say to you now—that at no time did I ask anyone to lie, to hide or destroy evidence, or to take any other unlawful action.

I know that my public comments and my silence about this matter gave a false impression. I misled people, including even my wife. I deeply regret that. I can only tell you I was motivated by many factors. First, by a desire to protect myself from the embarrassment of my own conduct.

I was also very concerned about protecting my family. The fact that these questions were being asked in a politically inspired lawsuit, which has since been dismissed, was a consideration, too.

In addition, I had real and serious concerns about an independent counsel investigation that began with private business dealings twenty years ago—dealings, I might add, about which an independent federal agency found no evidence of any wrongdoing by me or my wife over two years ago. The independent counsel investigation moved on to my staff and friends, then into my private life. And now the investigation itself is under investigation.

This has gone on too long, cost too much, and hurt too many innocent people. Now, this matter is between me, the two people I love most—my wife and our daughter—and our God.

I must put it right, and I am prepared to do whatever it takes to do so. Nothing is more important to me personally. But it is private, and I intend to reclaim my family life for my family. It's nobody's business but ours. Even presidents have private lives. It is time to stop the pursuit of personal destruction and the prying into private lives and get on with our national life.

Our country has been distracted by this matter for too long, and I take my responsibility for my part in all of this. That is all I can do. Now it is time—in fact, it is past time—to move on. We have important work to do, real opportunities to seize, real problems to solve, real security matters to face.

And so tonight, I ask you to turn away from the spectacle of the past seven months, to repair the fabric of our national discourse, and to return our attention to all the challenges and all the promise of the next American century.

Thank you for watching, and good night. ∎

President Nixon's Prepared Text in case the *Apollo XI* Moon Landing Ended in Tragedy

"FATE has ordained that the men who went to the moon to explore in peace will stay to rest in peace."

AS JULY 20, 1969, APPROACHED—the day that astronauts aboard *Apollo XI* were scheduled to set foot on the moon—White House speechwriters excitedly submitted drafts of a triumphant statement and "talking points" for the president of the United States to use in communicating live with the first earthlings on another celestial body.

The euphoria was suspended by a telephone call from Frank Borman, the veteran astronaut selected by the National Aeronautics and Space

Administration to be liaison with the White House. "You want to be thinking of some alternative posture for the president," he said solemnly, "in the event of mishaps on *Apollo XI*." When I failed to react promptly, he dispensed with NASA's euphemistic language and put the problem starkly: "Like what to do for the widows."

He explained that the time of greatest danger would not be landing the lunar vehicle, with Neil Armstrong and "Buzz" Aldrin inside, on the moon. NASA scientists and engineers were most concerned about the ability of the astronauts to get the vehicle off the moon into lunar orbit, where it could join the circling command module, captained by Michael Collins, for its return to Earth. What if the planned liftoff failed and the men were marooned on the moon? "We would have to close down communication." It would not do for the world watching on television to see the men slowly starve to death or commit suicide.

All euphoria gone, I sent a memo to H. R. Haldeman, the White House chief of staff, suggesting that if such a terrible moment came, "the president should telephone each of the widows-to-be" to offer the nation's condolences. "After the president's statement, at the point when NASA ends communication with the men: a clergyman should adopt the same procedure as a burial at sea, commending their souls to 'the deepest of the deep,' concluding with the Lord's Prayer." But I wondered if submitting a draft of that sorrowful presidential statement would be in order, or would be taken as an ill augury—considered bad luck to be too prepared for the worst.

The thought occurred to me that General Eisenhower had faced that question on the eve of D-Day, and had scribbled down a brief message in the event of disaster. He threw it away the next day, after the Allied forces secured a landing in Europe, but an aide retrieved it. (I had occasion to read the original copy recently: "Our landings in the Cherbourg-Havre have failed to gain a satisfactory foothold and I have withdrawn the troops. My decision to attack at this time and place was based upon the best information available. The troops, the air and the Navy did all that bravery and devotion to duty could do. If any blame or fault attaches to the attempt it is mine alone.")

With that as precedent, I asked for a copy of a famous poem, "The Soldier" by Rupert Brooke, a sailor in the Royal Navy who was killed in World War I. He had written, "If I should die, think only this of me:/ That there's some corner of a foreign field/ That is forever England." (At historic moments, speechwriters turn to poets. In 1986, the world watched in horror as the space shuttle *Challenger* exploded on takeoff, killing all seven aboard. Peggy Noonan, a writer for President Ronald Reagan, paraphrased lines from "High Flight," a poem by John Gillespie Magee, Jr., an American killed flying for the RCAF in World War II: "they prepared for the journey and waved good-bye and 'slipped the surly bonds of earth' to 'touch the face of God.'")

But in 1969, the moon-shot euphoria was justified as the moon landing was celebrated as a triumph. Haldeman, who had never handed the draft remarks to Nixon, tossed the memo in a file that went back to NASA. I kept no copy and forgot about it completely. Decades later, the *Los Angeles Times* columnist Jim Mann unearthed the two-page typescript while doing research in the National Archives and did a column about it pegged to the thirtieth anniversary of the moon landing. On that occasion, NBC's Tim Russert had Armstrong, Aldrin, and Collins on *Meet the Press* and slowly read the tribute to them as the camera panned their faces. Alive to hear their would-be eulogy, the former astronauts were visibly moved.

The National Archives put on a major exhibition in its rotunda in 2001, showing great and small artifacts of American history ranging from George Washington's account book to the Emancipation Proclamation in Lincoln's handwriting, from John Wayne's application to become a spy with the OSS to the scrap of paper on which Eisenhower had taken responsibility for failure on June 5, 1945. (Apparently nervous that night, Ike had misdated it July 5.)

There in the blazon of history's majesties and oddities, in a glass case right next to Lincoln's proclamation, was my little speech. Frankly, its presence there knocked me out. Evaluating it now more coolly, and recognizing that the repeated use of "men" and "mankind" would today be found jarring, I decided it worthy of inclusion in this anthology. Though it is hardly a "great" speech, and one happily never delivered, the short address shows how the context of a dreaded dramatic occasion can make memorable words written to be spoken aloud.

□   □   □

Fate has ordained that the men who went to the moon to explore in peace will stay on the moon to rest in peace.

These brave men, Neil Armstrong and Edwin Aldrin, know that there is no hope for their recovery. But they also know that there is hope for mankind in their sacrifice.

These two men are laying down their lives in mankind's most noble goal: the search for truth and understanding. They will be mourned by their families and friends; they will be mourned by their nation; they will be mourned by the people of the world; they will be mourned by a Mother Earth that dared send two of her sons into the unknown.

In their exploration, they stirred the people of the world to feel as one; in their sacrifice, they bind more tightly the brotherhood of man.

In ancient days, men looked at stars and saw their heroes in the constellations. In modern times, we do much the same, but our heroes are epic men of flesh and blood.

Others will follow, and surely find their way home. Man's search will not be denied. But these men were the first, and they will remain the foremost in our hearts.

For every human being who looks up at the moon in the nights to come will know that there is some corner of another world that is forever mankind.

■ ■ ■

PERMISSIONS

Adlai E. Stevenson. From *Major Campaign Speeches of Adlai E. Stevenson*. Both speeches reprinted by permission of the estate of Adlai E. Stevenson.

Eugene J. McCarthy. From *Year of the People* by Eugene J. McCarthy. Copyright ©1969 by Eugene J. McCarthy. Used by permission of Doubleday, a division of Random House, Inc.

Margaret Thatcher. Reprinted by permission.

Will Rogers. Reprinted by permission of the Will Rogers Memorial Commission.

Eric Sevareid. Reprinted by permission of Don Congdon Associates, Inc. Copyright © 1977 by Eric Sevareid.

Boris Yeltsin. Reprinted by permission of the Associated Press.

Orson Welles. Used by permission of the Estate of Orson Welles.

Job. From *The New English Bible*. © Oxford University Press and Cambridge University Press 1961, 1970. Reprinted by permission of Cambridge University Press.

Natan Sharansky. From *Fear No Evil;* Random House, New York. Copyright © 1988 by Natan Sharansky. Reprinted by permission of the author.

Bishop Fulton Sheen. Reprinted by permission of The Society for the Propagation of the Faith.

Karl Barth. From *Deliverance to the Captives* by Karl Barth. Copyright © 1961 by SCM Press Ltd. Reprinted by permission of HarperCollins Publishers, Inc.

Rabbi Louis Finkelstein. Reprinted by permission of Rabbi Ezra M. Finkelstein for the estate of Rabbi Louis Finkelstein, former Chancellor of the Jewish Theological Seminary of America.

Billy Graham. From *Billy Graham in the Soviet Union,* by Billy Graham, © 1985 by Billy Graham Evangelistic Association, Minneapolis, Minnesota; used by permission; all rights reserved.

Branch Rickey. Reprinted by permission of Stephen S. Adams, Jr., for the estate of Branch Rickey.

Dr. Martin Luther King, Jr. Reprinted by arrangement with the Estate of Martin Luther King, Jr., c/o Writers House as agents for the proprietor in New York, NY. Copyright © 1963 by Martin Luther King, Jr., copyright renewed 1991 by Coretta Scott King.

Alistair Cooke. Christmas "Letter from America" reprinted by permission of the author.

Frank Lloyd Wright. Reprinted by permission, courtesy of the Frank Lloyd Wright Archives.

Alistair Cooke. From *The Patient Has the Floor* by Alistair Cooke. Copyright © 1986 by Alistair Cooke. Reprinted by permission of Alfred A. Knopf, a division of Random House, Inc.

Jack Valenti. Reprinted by permission of Jack Valenti.

Ruth Bader Ginsburg. Reprinted by permission of Ruth Bader Ginsburg.

Leon R. Kass. Reprinted by permission of Leon R. Kass.

Walter Lippmann. From the Walter Lippmann Papers, Manuscripts and Archives, Yale University Library. Reprinted by permission of the Yale University Library, New Haven, CT.

Malcolm X. Excerpts from *Malcolm X Speaks,* copyright © 1965 & 1989 by Betty Shabazz and Pathfinder Press. Reprinted by permission of Pathfinder Press.

Index